Marcel Proust

VIKING

75 years

Marcel Proust

JEAN-YVES TADIÉ

Translated by Euan Cameron

VIKING

VIKING
Published by the Penguin Group
Penguin Putnam Inc., 375 Hudson Street,
New York, New York 10014, U.S.A.
Penguin Books Ltd, 27 Wrights Lane, London W8 5TZ, England
Penguin Books Australia Ltd, Ringwood, Victoria, Australia
Penguin Books Canada Ltd, 10 Alcorn Avenue,
Toronto, Ontario, Canada M4V 3B2
Penguin Books (N.Z.) Ltd, 182–190 Wairau Road,
Auckland 10, New Zealand

Penguin Books Ltd, Registered Offices:
Harmondsworth, Middlesex, England

First American edition
Published in 2000 by Viking Penguin,
a member of Penguin Putnam Inc.

1 3 5 7 9 10 8 6 4 2

The author would like to thank Oxford University Press for allowing him to reprint extracts
from his inaugural lecture given at the University of Oxford in 1990, published under the title
Portrait of the Artist, and the Houghton Library, Harvard University, for permission to quote
from letters by Reynaldo Hahn.

LIBRARY OF CONGRESS CATALOGING IN PUBLICATION DATA
Tadié, Jean-Yves, 1936–
[Marcel Proust, English]
Marcel Proust / Jean-Yves Tadié ; translated by Euan Cameron.
p. cm.
Includes bibliographical references and index.
ISBN 0-670-87655-0
1. Proust, Marcel, 1871–1922. 2. Novelists, French—20th century—Biography. I. Title.
PQ2631.R63 Z925213 2000
843'.912—dc21   00-020565

This book is printed on acid-free paper.

Printed in the United States of America
Set in MT Garamond

For Arlette, and for Alexis, Benoît and Jérôme

Contents

Translator's Note

Page references to Proust's work refer to the French editions of his books, and in particular to the four-volume Pléiade edition of *À la recherche du temps perdu*, published by Gallimard (1987–9) under the general editorship of Jean-Yves Tadié. English translations of passages from the novel are my own, but I have frequently referred to the C. K. Scott-Moncrieff translation, which was revised by Terence Kilmartin in 1981 and published in three volumes (Chatto & Windus/Penguin), and revised further by D. J. Enright, in the light of the Pléiade definitive text, in six volumes (Chatto & Windus/Vintage) in 1992.

Proust's great novel is referred to throughout by its French title, as are the individual volumes: *Du côté de chez Swann** *(Swann's Way), À l'ombre des jeunes filles en fleurs (Within a Budding Grove), Le Côté de Guermantes (The Guermantes Way), Sodome et Gomorrhe (Sodom and Gomorrah), La Prisonnière (The Captive), Albertine disparue (The Fugitive), Le Temps retrouvé (Time Regained).*

Comparatively few of the twenty-one volumes of Proust's letters have been translated into English. I have generally translated the letters quoted myself, though in some instances I have referred to the three volumes of *Marcel Proust: Selected Letters* (Collins, 1983, 1989, 1992), edited by Philip Kolb and translated by Ralph Manheim (vol. I) and Terence Kilmartin (vols. II and III). A fourth volume, containing a selection of letters from 1918 to Proust's death in 1922, translated by Joanna Kilmartin, was published in January 2000. Any errors in translation from Proust's correspondence, and in the quotations from *Les Plaisirs et les Jours, Jean Santeuil* and *Contre Sainte-Beuve*, must be my own responsibility.

In the French edition of this book, the wealth of material contained in the notes appeared as footnotes on the page. For this edition, I have

---

* This includes 'Combray', 'Un Amour de Swann' ('Swann in Love'), and 'Noms de pays: le nom' ('Place-names: The Name')

incorporated those that directly concern Proust's life and *À la recherche du temps perdu*, or that are helpful in understanding the text, as footnotes, but have transferred the remainder to the Notes section at the back of the book.

I should like to thank Jean-Yves Tadié for his valuable advice, his encouragement and his hospitality in Dinard, as well as the following who offered suggestions or came to my rescue in one way or another: Malcolm Bowie, Isabelle Daudy, Sophie Dunoyer de Segonzac, D. J. Enright, Éric Green, Nelly and Tobie Munthe; and, at Penguin, Peter Carson and Andrew Kidd. I am especially grateful to Daphne Tagg for her astute comments and her sensitive and sympathetic editing of my text.

Euan Cameron
September 1999

Preface

Why a new biography of Proust? As well ask an artist the reason for yet another still life, or another portrait. The moment comes when it seems justifiable to synthesize the existing works, rejecting whatever does not appear to be verifiable, considering any recent discoveries, and, above all, taking into account those things that only the work of an editor permits him to know – the history of the manuscripts and of the work as it goes through the process of being written; the true biography of a writer or an artist is that of his work. It is also the only story that does not end with death. Proust said of Ruskin: 'The events of his life are intellectual ones and the important dates are those in which he perceives a new art form.'

Another aspect of this work is that it attempts to justify all its assertions, hence the abundant notes and footnotes – which there is no obligation to read – that supply evidence for them. Unresolved questions remain, as a result of the temporary or permanent disappearance of vital documents: Proust's correspondence with Agostinelli, the majority of his letters to his father and several of those to his mother, Reynaldo Hahn's diary, which survives but which no one is allowed to examine. Letters sent to the writer have seldom been kept; his books have mostly been dispersed. While the task of the critic is to encompass an entire library in a single book, that of the biographer is to embrace the man (or woman) himself. Frequently, when the conjuror opens his magic box, the subject, or the work in question, has disappeared. Just as the novelist can never fully fathom the recesses of the characters he creates, neither can the biographer; we must simply accept.

I shall endeavour to depict the individual in so far as he is a type: the child of a middle-class family, a pupil at the Lycée Condorcet, a student at the École des Sciences Politiques, an asthmatic, a 'young poet' who wrote more letters than he received, a person who took the waters at seaside resorts. What was it like to be a writer in 1890, to be homosexual, to be an invalid, or a doctor? By dipping into the history or culture of the time at regular intervals, I hope to escape the tedium of anecdotes that are too specific. There then comes the moment when the great artist ceases to be merely a type and, now irretrievably different, breaks loose from the bonds of history and from structures.

Precisely because it is harder to interpret than it is to relate, and because we must rely to a degree on hypothesis, this book is also a theorem. Ever since 1959, when I began publishing books about Proust, I and my team have been the instigators of other works; in one sense I am now reaping my harvest. This is especially true of our edition of *À la recherche du temps perdu* in the 1987 Bibliothèque de la Pléiade edition, and of its Introduction, elements of which, recounting the history of the work, will be found in these pages. I have simply remained true to myself. Having studied the writer's art in *Proust et le roman*, sketched a critical panorama in *Lectures de Proust*, and published, with a team of scholars, the principal early drafts of *À la recherche*, as well as an abundant selection of their variants, it only remained for me to tackle this irritating problem: is it possible to recount the story of Proust's life, and if so, how and why? People readily criticize long, erudite 'American-style' biographies and the academics who write them. Yet nowhere in this lengthy book will you come across a single insignificant fact, and very few that do not relate to Proust's great work: thus it is that, as often as possible, I have dated the introduction of a theme, an image or a character from the novel that was gestating, for we are dealing with one single novel. Proust made use of everything he experienced or thought about during his lifetime. And I too, though frequently surpassed by the surprises of his art, believed that I understood what he knew, or thought, or felt, and it is my wish to convey this to the reader, to those countless readers throughout the world, from America to China and Japan, who love this man and his work. A few undiscovered facts, and an interpretation: a life is like a musical score; there are many ways of performing it, neither overdoing the *rubato*, nor playing, as the grandmother of Proust's hero would say, 'too drily'. A biographer's tone of voice can be heard and show its age. One may plead too much; another may produce hagiography; another may be melodramatic. A life can be interpreted like a sonata or a play: so it is better to imitate la Berma and choose a transparent, invisible approach. Which is not to say that the writing of it will suffer: style is made up of sacrifices.

All that we can know about Proust, everything that it is useful to know in order to understand him and his work. No detail that is not relevant.

Yet what is most important for me, is not what George Painter, and after him Ghislain de Diesbach, demonstrated so ably: the nature of the salons and the social life of the period. Painter read everything that could be read of what was written at the time, the life, the period, the salons, the memories. Not one anecdote is missing: the offensive can begin; not one of those anecdotes which can be found in book after book, and which no longer produce a smile. His successors have quoted them in their turn, without asking themselves whether they were not a little faded, or too well known. Painter had of course read everything: but he had not met any of the witnesses, who were still alive at the time he wrote, and he relied purely on written memories. Yet there were some people who did not write anything, and others who did not write down all they knew. All that is irretrievably lost. It was a world that André Maurois knew well. His well-balanced biography has been forgotten, because he did not pride himself on a cheap knowledge of Freud, because he did not know of the existence of *Jean Santeuil* and of *Contre Sainte-Beuve*, and had not, in the light of their revelations, revised his book. In certain pages of his *À la recherche de Marcel Proust*, those dealing with delicate subjects, such as Jeanne Proust's Jewish background, with her son's poor health and his inversion, not a word need be altered. Other writers, conversely, express themselves on such matters with brutality, a lack of subtlety, and a surprising amount of unsubstantiated opinion. I do not deny the importance of the amatory, or purely sexual life; it has been restored to its essential place, to the few bouts of unhappiness that gave rise to *Sodome et Gomorrhe*.

Since the life has become the novel, and the novel the entire life, it should be no surprise to find an essay in literary criticism in this book. It describes Proust's intellectual universe and how it was constituted, as well as the books, paintings and pieces of music that influenced him. The derivation of ideas matters more than the ancestry of a family. We are reading the history of a mind: the growth of a culture in the process of creation. It was at this time that, in a broader sense, the world of his dreams and desires was being formed, his favourite trees and landscapes, the friendships, the men and women. And then there was the suffering and distress, the jealousies, the illnesses. The loneliness of the artist who for so long was misjudged and unacknowledged, of the homosexual who was the grandson of Jewish bankers and village grocers, of the asthmatic lost in the fumes. Finally, the courage and expectations of the man whose favourite maxim, taken from a Gospel in which he did not believe, was: 'Work while you have light.' This is the story of that work, and that light.

Yet even if we knew all the facts about Proust's life, and had heard all the testimonies, we would still have to interpret them. It is here that a biographer's task resembles that of the novelist, because it is a matter of delving beneath appearances, of providing a sense and meaning, of choosing between several hypotheses. But whereas the novelist can allow himself the luxury of five possible explanations at one and the same time, and Proust frequently produced many a firework in this way, the biographer can only resort to such measures in desperation: he must make a choice, and he sometimes does so with a strange sense of gratuitousness, of too great a freedom, which stems from nothing other than ignorance of the truth. 'The art of the biographer lies precisely in making a choice. He need not concern himself with being truthful; he must create from among a chaos of human traits ... Long-suffering demiurges have assembled ideas, facial movements, events for the biographer. The fruits of their labours can be found in chronicles, memoirs, correspondences and scholarly footnotes. From the midst of this unwieldy jumble, the biographer marshals the means to compose a form which is quite unlike any other.'[1]

The inner life may be revealed in a person's correspondence – but not in Proust's, for he never divulged anything, or stopped doing so once he had left the lycée. Not a single love letter has yet been unearthed. We shall never know whether the letters which he wrote to Agostinelli were of a passionate nature: with the exception of one letter, which was returned to the sender, they were all burned. Deeply moving though that letter is, it speaks only of friendship, not passion. Those to Lucien Daudet have not all been released: they will be one day. Those to Reynaldo Hahn occasionally display jealousy; several years of correspondence are missing, and the composer's diary will not be available to us for another forty years. A few traces of an obsessive friendship remain: what lies behind this curiosity? And behind our own? It's a question of method: the biographer depends on memoirs and memories of the period. But tracing the inner life? Others might consult the letters one by one, and there are twenty-one volumes of them. But to relate their contents, with all their omissions, their deceptions and misunderstood jokes, is not to recount the story of a life. Hence the temptation to which Painter succumbed without any qualms: to draw from the novel in order to explain, or understand, the life. The feelings of the Narrator become those of Marcel Proust, and Albertine actually existed. Furthermore, Painter knew who the models for her were, and it is reassuring also to know that they were women. Thus we read a biography that is transfused by the novel, in which entire pages of Proust's work are spilled out, but without his style. Painter's success, as Barthes has shown, lies mainly in this impression it gives of reading a novel, one that is both about a life and a work, avoiding the immense effort required to read *À la recherche du temps perdu*. Unfortunately, the novel is to biography what the historical novel is to history. What malign spirit, for instance, could have possessed Painter to write that Proust had composed a lost novel between 1905 and 1908? This chronological gap should have been plugged at any price.

Those who have restricted themselves to the social and worldly figure, to the 'creation of other people's thoughts', have had less to worry about. All that has to be done with other people's thoughts is reassemble them; sadly, they remain superficial, they are still the thoughts of others, who are unable to understand the heart and spirit of the author. All that can be grasped is snobbery or worldly success, a sick man's eccentricities, a recluse's seclusion. What is lacking is the biography of the artist and his work: 'We are not concerned here with chronicling the slow elaboration of *À la recherche du temps perdu* and its numerous mutations.'[2] It may not be the most fascinating account to write, yet it is the most important aspect to know. The biography of a great writer is not that of a man of the world, or a pervert, or an invalid: it is that of a man who draws his stature from what he writes, because he has sacrificed everything to it, including his lesser qualities. These aspects matter, of course, but they are there to be overcome. In a notebook which he did not publish himself, the writer Marcel Jouhandeau mentioned stories about a boy at the public baths; he would have done better to reflect on the story of *Sodome et Gomorrhe*, or to have explained by what metamorphosis Proust moved from the gossip-mongers to the main work. So what are the incidents that make up a life such as this? A life cannot be told without relating it to the incidents that comprise it; this is the double meaning of the word 'relationship'. And yet life is lived from day to day in confusion and uncertainty: for a long time Proust himself was afraid that he would not be able to realize his vocation – up until 1908, when he was thirty-seven. Nevertheless, he wrote: 'Everything in an artist's life is connected according to the implacable logic of inner evolutions.'[3] And again: 'For me circumstances count. But a circumstance is one-tenth chance and nine-tenths my own disposition.'[4] Biography reveals 'an inner disposition that was stronger than chance, and an inner evolution that developed according to an implacable logic'; the incidents, the meetings, even the love affairs themselves matter no more than they did in the life of one of Proust's masters: Jean Racine. If the history of the work itself is not related, the story of the author in the process of writing it, how many hours, days and years in the life of the artist are overlooked? Had he not used this time to write, perhaps he would have led a more interesting life, or one that is easier to describe. Perhaps he would not have shut himself away in a room (odd, isn't it? But then one has to write somewhere); perhaps he would not have died at the age of fifty-one, like Balzac.

One objection that has to be confronted when beginning a biography of Proust is his own violent criticism of this literary genre in *Contre Sainte-Beuve*, in his Foreword to Jacques-Émile Blanche's book *Propos de peintre, De David à Degas*, or when creating the character of Mme de Villeparisis. But life must always go on: Proust never stopped anybody. In fact, he himself was constantly curious about the lives of the writers and artists he loved, forever asking questions about those who were alive, such as Hardy, or reading biographies, or letters, including those of Balzac and Ruskin, Musset and Sainte-Beuve. In his 1921 article on Baudelaire, he sketched a biography of the poet. He observed in passing that Victor Hugo 'objectifies himself in Booz' and invigorates the poem with his personality: 'He tries to convince the women that if they have any taste, they would prefer the old bard to the young whippersnapper.' Vigny objectifies himself in Samson and is jealous of Marie Dorval's female friendships. And why is it that Baudelaire is interested in lesbians? 'Would it not have been interesting to know why Baudelaire chose this role of intermediary in love affairs, and how he set about playing it?' Here Proust explains one of the functions of biography: to say 'why?', 'how?', and not merely 'what?' It is no longer a question of description, but of internal experiences, which would be transformed into literature and into the characters of the novel. Biography does not tell us about 'some vague wholly prefabricated novel',[5] but about the source of the novel and what made it possible. It lends shape to what is shapeless, unity to diversity, meaning to appearance. It enables us to hear once more the voice which has been stilled, and it restores life to that vanished genre, the dialogue of the dead – which is a dialogue with the living.

Acknowledgements

I should like to thank the following for the information, advice and documentation which they have provided:

A. Beretta Anguissola, Marie-Christine Besson, Thierry Bodin, Anne Borel, Christian Bouwens van der Boijen, Florence Callu, Bill Carter, Pietro Citati, Catherine Fotiadi, Éric Green, the Houghton Library (Harvard University), the children of Pierre Lavallée, Marie-Claude Mauriac, Nathalie Mauriac, Richard Parish, J.-B. Pontalis, Hugues Pradier, the Proust-Kolb Archive, Pierre Robert, Baron and Baronne Élie de Rothschild, Nadia Saleh, Marc Tadié, Frédéric Vitoux.

To Antoine Gallimard, who was kind enough to encourage this project and give it his constant support; to Jean-Loup Champion, for his friendship throughout the editorial process, to Thierry Laget, who reread the manuscript, all my gratitude.

CHAPTER I

Roots

AUTEUIL

To begin with, two villages. One on the father's side, the other, on the mother's. The first of them, Illiers, belongs to the timeless French countryside; the second, Auteuil, is a town set in the country, or *rus in urbe*. Here are to be found not the peasant ancestors, but the liberal-minded financiers of the urban bourgeoisie, and literary memories of Boileau, Racine and La Fontaine. In the one, Marcel Proust spent his holidays as a child, immortalized in 'Combray'; the other was where he was born – something that was not recognized for a long time – and where he no doubt experienced the bedtime scene himself. The two villages came to be juxtaposed in *Jean Santeuil*, then reunited in *Du côté de chez Swann*. Proust did not return to either of them in adult life; Illiers would have affected his asthma; the house in Auteuil no longer existed except in his heart.

In order to imagine the Auteuil that Marcel Proust knew, it is still possible to walk around the hamlets of Boileau and Boulainvilliers, the Villa Montmorency and the rue de l'Yvette. The gardens, the houses set apart and the private mansions give an even keener effect of being in the country, precisely because they are in the town and combine rusticity and comfort with solitude and its remedies. Everything is false, and yet everything is real: the Bois de Boulogne is an artificial forest and yet the woods of the Bois are real, as are its lake, its island, and its 'chalet' which the Narrator* visits with Albertine, as he dreams of Brittany and Mme de Stermaria.

It was in the village of Auteuil that Louis Weil, Marcel Proust's great-uncle, acquired 96 rue La Fontaine, a property of 1,500 square metres. He had bought it from the actress Eugénie Doche, who had created the role

---

* I shall refer to the protagonist of *À la recherche du temps perdu*, who writes as 'I', in this way.

of *La Dame aux Camélias*:[1] it was therefore a house that already had a feeling of antiquity about it and was impregnated with an atmosphere of the other-worldly, of actresses and 'ladies in pink', so dear to Uncle Louis. The main gate had two small buildings on either side. The garden boasted a fountain and an orangery; the three-storey house, with a floor area of 110 square metres, was built, according to the land registry, in stone. The Proust family lived in one of the two gate-houses (four rooms and an attic). In 1919, when Proust wrote the Foreword to *Propos de peintre* by his neighbour in Auteuil, Jacques-Émile Blanche, he showed little regard for this house, which he described as being 'as devoid of good taste as possible'.[2] One must, of course, recognize the part played if not by modesty, then at least by that aristocratic politeness which always led Proust to disparage whatever surrounded him, and yet praise excessively anything that belonged to others. For he nevertheless conveyed the immense pleasure he derived from his bedroom, with its big blue satin curtains, its wash-stand and its wardrobe with a mirror, and from the ground floor of the main building, with its little drawing-room 'hermetically sealed against the heat'; the pantry, where the cider, that rustic beverage, was cooling; and the dining-room, where, in the dusk, the crystal knife-rests gleamed.[3] The furniture was described by a cousin: 'sinister, tasteless, massive, cluttered, gloomy'[4] – it consisted of the mahogany and dark wooden furniture that was fashionable in the time of Louis-Philippe and Napoleon III, and which Louis Weil had acquired from Eugénie Doche. This Auteuil of his childhood and youth, Proust reflected in 1919, 'had migrated into invisibility', 'shaded by arbours which no longer existed'. And yet, since Auteuil still exists, what has been 'transformed into memory' is the house itself at 96 rue La Fontaine, sold in 1897, after the deaths of Louis Weil and his father, by their heirs, Jeanne Proust and Georges Weil, and then razed to make way for blocks of flats, which in turn were demolished during the construction of the avenue Mozart. On the site where this house once stood there is now a bank, almost as if Proust's shade should for ever be pursued by banks: he was obliged to move from his apartment at 102 Boulevard Haussmann (roughly at the time that he wrote about Auteuil in his Foreword) when the building was sold to the Varin-Bernier bank.

The gardens of Auteuil, Proust tells us, only succeeded in giving him 'hay fever'.[5] At his uncle's there was a fountain, into which, it was said, Marcel fell, just as Paul Valéry once did in a public park, and the fountain is depicted in *Jean Santeuil* as surrounded by hawthorn trees,[6] just like those he had seen at Auteuil, before the bushes at Illiers.* The disturbing beauty of hawthorns is associated with springtime illness, and recuperation: 'Springtime makes me ill,' says the child to the hawthorns, in a draft of the book, and the bushes reply: 'Really? Very well, we shall look after you. You remember when we came into your bedroom.' 'Of course! It was from that day on that I most loved you.'† These tears touched the young man 'in the deepest recesses of his past', that of Auteuil buried beneath Illiers.[7]

Beyond, were the chestnut trees, recalled in *Jean Santeuil*: 'Further away, are the huge chestnuts whose branches hang low like small trees, a youthful breed of giants which, with their immense leaves, wear their high blossom like massive, delicate towers.'[8] Beneath their shade, the family sat in front of the house, around a 'cast-iron table'. Proust evoked this other childhood tree in *Les Plaisirs et les Jours*,[9] and again in *Du côté de chez Swann*, on the boulevards, in a Paris square, in the Bois de Boulogne, as evidence of spring when its leaves are green, of autumn when tinted orange; trees in summer did not interest Proust: this was why he connected chestnut trees with lilac, whose invisible, enduring fragrance pursued him, and why he went to Versailles to see the lilac trees again.

The Count of Monte-Cristo left his residence on the Avenue des Champs-Élysées one evening for a 'little journey' *extra muros*, which took him, twenty minutes later, to Auteuil, 28 rue La Fontaine, where he had bought a country house, 'on the outskirts of the village'.[10] The village of Auteuil, to the west of Paris, did not become a part of the city until 1859, and the Proust family continued to differentiate between the two: Marcel addressed his letters from Auteuil, or he set off for Paris by omnibus, by train (from Auteuil station), horse-drawn carriage, or by river steamer (when the weather was too hot to take the train). An 1855 guidebook describes it as follows: 'A village out of a comic opera. The houses are square-shaped, with two storeys and green painted shutters . . . For six months of the year, Auteuil is a veritable reproduction of Pompeii or Herculaneum; the streets are deserted, the doors are shut, the blinds strictly lowered, the houses silent and uninhabited. The citizens of Auteuil

---

* *RTP*, vol. I, draft LXII, p. 857: 'I don't know whether it was on the pathway . . . that I saw the hawthorn for the first time.' The Combray-Illiers pathway is a memory-screen which conceals Auteuil. In the garden, Marcel sat in a wickerwork chair (ibid., draft III, p. 651).

† Ibid, p. 863. Cf. p. 858. The hawthorn blossom is similar to apple blossom: 'The sight of the apple trees filled me with wild delight and made me cry out with such joy that Doctor Piperaud, whom we met one day, said: "this little boy needs a good telling-off " ' (p. 820).

are spending the winter in Paris during this time. They may be retired notaries or former lawyers and bankers who are no longer in business. As soon as the fine weather comes, everyone reappears with their obligatory retinue of cooks, stable boys, coachmen and servants.'[11] This was very much the social group to which Marcel's great-uncle and grandfather belonged. They spent the summer there, although the grandfather, having dined there every evening, returned each night to Paris, which he never left for a single day throughout the eighty-five years he lived in the city.[12] Professor and Mme Proust lived there 'in springtime and in early summer'.[13] This short journey was enough to provide a change of scenery, rest and memories. The proximity of the station, of the train, which served only the Paris terminus of Saint-Lazare, and of the viaduct, gave Proust his taste for railway timetables, for trips that he dreamed about in bed, for the 'great unfulfilled departures' which Fauré celebrated in *L'Horizon chimérique*.

Its etymology suggests that Auteuil signifies 'a small height' (*altum* + diminutive), forty-one metres at its highest point (as against the hill at Chaillot which is seventy metres high). It was there, close to where the present Mirabeau bridge stands, that in 52 BC, Julius Caesar's lieutenant, Labienus, crossed the Seine to attack Lutetia's Gaulish troops, commanded by Camulogenus, on the plains of Grenelle. A forest covered this region in Gallo-Roman times (the Bois de Boulogne is one among several traces of it; Jacques Hillairet, the historian of Paris, mentions that remnants of a Druid altar were found on the site of the hamlet of Boileau; we know that Proust alludes to Druids in connection with the Bois). Auteuil was placed under the patronage of the Norman abbey of Bec-Hellouin, which in 1109 was amalgamated with the Abbey of Sainte-Geneviève in Paris. The abbeys retained their power until the Revolution. Auteuil was separated from Passy by the rue de Seine (rue Berton), and bordered the southern tip of the village of 'Boullongne'. The monks used Auteuil as a country retreat, which was confiscated at the time of the Revolution. The artist Gérard lived on the site of their former house, as did Fernand Gregh, Proust's friend and the future academician (on the corner of the rue François-Gérard and rue Rémusat).

Auteuil was raised to the status of a parish by Bishop Maurice de Sully (who began the building of Notre-Dame). It was a small hamlet built between the fourteenth and seventeenth centuries, grouped around its church and its castle, comprising four streets (the avenue de Versailles, the rue d'Auteuil, the rue Boileau and the rue La Fontaine). During the last third of Louis XV's reign the village became fashionable: Molière,

Racine, Boileau, whose property later belonged to Hubert Robert, and Champmeslé, Aguesseau's chancellor, all had their country houses here. So too, in the eighteenth century, did the Mlles Verrières and La Tour, and Mme Helvétius. In the nineteenth came Ampère, Cabanis, M.-J. Chénier, Volney, Chateaubriand, Mme Récamier, Guizot, J. Janin, Carpeaux, Gavarni, Hugo and the Goncourts. In 1800 there were a dozen streets. It was then that the construction of country houses began, and Parisians came to spend the summer here (there were 1,000 inhabitants in 1810; 4,185 in 1851). The fortified walls erected by Thiers girdled Auteuil in 1844.

As from 1 January 1860, the borough of Auteuil was annexed to Paris by the Law of 16 June 1859. By 1895, its population had grown to 22,500 inhabitants. The price of flats was approximately the same as in Paris. There was no industry, just a few quarries and some mineral water, the 'springs of Auteuil'. One of the springs, in the rue de la Cure, disappeared at about the time of the First World War, the one in the rue Poussin in about 1900. The railway line (from Saint-Lazare to Auteuil) dates from 1853, the station from 1854. Along the site of the former railway tracks, Haussmann constructed the boulevards Montmorency and Exelmans, and he began the avenue Mozart (completed in 1897). The hamlet of Boileau (1840) was built over the former home of the poet; the Villa Montmorency, built by Pereire, over that of the Duchesse de Montmorency (1854); and the viaduct-bridge of Auteuil was erected in 1866. The original church of Auteuil (1319) was on the site of the present one. Two chapels were added to its nave (1320) in the seventeenth century. Dilapidated and too small, and damaged by bombing at the time of the Commune, it was replaced (1877–92) by the present-day Romano-Byzantine church.

The Goncourts' town house can still be seen on the Boulevard de Montmorency. Edmond de Goncourt described it in detail in *La Maison d'un artiste*, which Proust wrote a pastiche of in *Le Temps retrouvé*. In his journal, Goncourt describes the siege of Paris (the period when Mme Proust was pregnant) and the suffering during the Franco-Prussian war of 1870: 'Cursed Auteuil! This suburb may have been deprived of communication with the rest of Paris, devastated by mobilization, starved, bombarded, and it still has the misfortune to be occupied by the Prussians.'[14] During the Commune, Auteuil was again shelled by the government troops installed at Versailles, and not by the Communards: 'The ruins start at the Boulevard de Montmorency,' wrote Edmond de Goncourt on 24 May 1871, 'houses in which only four blackened walls remain; houses that have collapsed and crumbled to the ground. Mine is still standing, with a huge hole in the second floor. Yet how many shell bursts has it withstood!'[15] On 25 May he walked among the 'ruins of Auteuil, where the damage and destruction is such that it might have been caused by a whirlwind'. The entrance to the rue d'Auteuil was nothing but 'smoking debris'; seen from the hill of Mortemart, the whole of Paris seemed to be on fire. It was after these two cataclysms, and amidst the wreckage, that Marcel Proust was born.

In his memories of the village, the writer would retain the rue des Perchamps, the rue de la Source, and the viaduct (it was destroyed after the Second World War) over which the local train ran, which are to be found in the early drafts of 'Combray': 'Sometimes we would go as far as the viaduct, with its striding stone arches that began at the station and which represented in my mind the very image of the anxiety that lay beyond the civilized world, for every year, on the way from Paris, we were advised not to miss the station, to pay careful attention as to whether it was Combray, and to be ready beforehand since the train would depart in five minutes' time, and would start negotiating the viaduct. In one of my worst dreams, I imagined that I had not heard anyone call out Combray, that the train had left and that I was travelling at top speed over the viaduct, into a country beyond the Christian lands of which Combray marked the outer limit.'* In *Jean Santeuil*, Proust also preserved 'the ferruginous water' at the Villa Montmorency, which the child, accompanied by the maid, used to go to drink using a metal cup which was attached by a chain. The notice with the words 'ferruginous water' hardly seems a detail of much interest. And yet the child must have been struck by it, for this unusual and sonorous word was transferred intact, along with the icy water, to become associated with the tinkle of the bell ringing at Combray, as well as with Swann, in the first and last pages of the book; with Swann, and therefore with the whole drama of the bedtime scene, which certainly took place at Auteuil: 'Its ferruginous, interminable, frozen sound', 'the recurring ringing sound, ferruginous, interminable, piercing and cool', that came from the fountain of Auteuil, opening and closing the work and giving it an additional structural cohesion, a new circular movement, as endless and infinite as the spring.[16]

---

* *RTP*, vol. I, draft LXIV, p. 871, and 'Combray', p. 113. It is true that there is also a viaduct at Illiers and that the two walks may have been confused. On the viaduct at Illiers, see P.-L. Larcher, 'La Ferme des Aigneaux', *BAMP*, no. 16, 1966, p. 407.

ILLIERS

'Villages like Illiers and Brou, frontier posts between the Beauce and the first intimations of the Perche, already have a hybrid character. The beams and the wood used in the construction of the houses, the orchards which surround them, such as the apple trees which multiply in the fields, make us aware in a thousand details of the changing character of the Beauce. Already, the River Loir and its rising tributaries reveal their slow, deep and grassy paths.'[17] These words, written not by Proust but by a foremost geographer, reveal our novelist's delicate geographical sensibility. Many an observation about the physical structure of Combray and its surroundings confirm this perception, which had its roots in Illiers. To deepen the reader's sense of time and space in a way that was both artistic and scientifically accurate, Proust buried a thousand years of history at Illiers-Combray, only to dig them up again with mock surprise: this is the case, for example, with the Merovingian crypt of the church.[18] Reading Augustin Thierry had nurtured both his knowledge and his imagination. Thierry's *Récits des temps mérovingiens* are embedded in the foundations of the church at Combray. As for the name of the town, it takes its origin from the castle of Combray, seven kilometres to the north of Lisieux, on the road to Pont-l'Évêque. This provenance is much more likely than the suggestion that it derives from Combourg, from Cambrai,[19] or even Combres, near Illiers. Many Proustian place-names have their roots in this part of Lower Normandy, where the author spent his holidays from 1907 onwards, that is to say during the writing of *Du côté de chez Swann* and *À l'ombre des jeunes filles en fleurs*.[20]

Illiers,[21] an important township in the department of the Eure-et-Loir, twenty-five kilometres from Chartres and 114 from Paris, a market town on the borders of the rich cereal country of the Beauce and the livestock region of the Perche, is one of those communities on the fringes of the Île-de-France* (a region in which the majority of French writers have

---

* Proust's love for the Île-de-France is attested by Jacques Truelle's belated account (after the publication of *Du côté de chez Swann*): ' "However [Proust told him], the more I travel, the more I love the countryside and eventually I come to love nothing else. Who knows whether one day I shall not go to the country of Gilberte for good and then it really will be 'Time regained' ". . . In preference he would go back to the plains of Beauce or to a spot in the Île-de-France. His predilection for these was obvious in everything he said. Discussing certain people, he said: "What I like about them is that they are so very much 'Île-de-France' ", and he remarked that: "No book has ever moved me as much as *Sylvie* by Gérard de Nerval" ' (*Hommage à M. Proust*).

been born) which sustains the Parisian bourgeoisie: sooner or later, a man like Proust would have to leave it for the capital. The birthplace of his father's family, for fifteen years it was a haven for him, during part of the Easter holidays (and the summer ones too). Thus it was here that Marcel acquired, subconsciously to begin with, his knowledge of the structure of life in a village or small town, and of the neighbouring countryside – a knowledge that was acquired as a native, not as a tourist. Illiers, with its town, its local villages, communities and hamlets, as well as its surrounding countryside, is, as much as Paris, one of the 'deep seams in his mental landscape'. In one of his father's last speeches, at a prize-giving ceremony at Illiers in 1903, Professor Proust described these flat plains that had become fashionable again: 'Today, it is among these wide spaces whose power lies in their monotony that the landscape painter will most willingly go in search of his innermost, but also his deepest, feelings, among these interminable wheat fields which, like the sea, alter according to the whims of sunbeams and shadows, the breeze and the swell.'[22]

Everything took place around the church: Proust illustrated this discovery in every description he gave of Illiers, and later of Combray. In *Jean Santeuil*, in which Illiers appears mostly under its real name, we read: 'It was actually a town which was dominated by its church, criss-crossed by processions, decked out with moveable altars, in which the priest lived here, the sacristan there, the nuns there, filled with the sound of the church bells which, on the days of the high mass, aroused the stream of people on their way to mass, and with the smell of the cakes prepared for the lunch that followed.'[23] The church, which dates from the fourteenth century, is called Saint-Jacques; a second church, Saint-Hilaire (like the church in Combray), was destroyed during the Revolution; the name has the same etymology as the church in Illiers.[24] In the earliest 1908 drafts of *À la recherche*, 'Combray' is no more than 'a church, symbolizing the town, representing it, speaking of it and for it far and wide'.[25] When Proust published 'L'Église de village', a text that is similar in style to *Du côté de chez Swann*, in *Le Figaro* of 3 September 1912,[26] he did not indicate whether the church in question was that of the actual village or the fictional one, thus lending an autobiographical tone to this narrative.

The church at Illiers has the same structure and serves the same purpose as that at Combray; but the latter is supplemented with numerous borrowings from other churches and from works of literature.

My intention is not to search for the biographical sources of *À la recherche du temps perdu*, to translate 'Combray' into Illiers, or to enable one to understand the definitive text directly, nor is it to write the 'novel of a child'. It is to portray Illiers *before* Swann. As for the church, its fascination has surely been reinforced by the shadow of a much more famous building. To reach Illiers, the Proust family had to change trains at Chartres, where they stopped sometimes to admire the spires.[27] On the one hand, the sumptuous cathedral; on the other, its modest contemporary, the village church. In between the two, numerous other churches – those visited, seen in photographs, or described by Ruskin or Émile Mâle – were destined to sustain Proust's youthful fascination. Furthermore, the church at Combray was enlivened by ceremonies that, in 1904, he feared might be suppressed under the government's new anti-clerical laws, and had been one of the joys of his childhood: 'The memories I have of the Corpus Christi processions are the most wonderful of my childhood.'*

The rue du Saint-Esprit leads out of the church square, and at number 5 Proust placed the Santeuils' house,[28] and later that of Aunt Léonie, because that was where his aunt Élisabeth Amiot, the sister of Professor Proust, lived. The road continued into the rue de l'Oiseau (later the rue du Docteur-Galopin). To the west ran the rue Saint-Hilaire. From the station, the railway track certainly led to a viaduct. The promenade and the ruined castle would be retained by the novelist, as would the River Loir, which would become the Vivonne, but the maps of the two towns are not identical.[29] On the Place du Marché, opposite the church, was the Proust-Torcheux grocery shop, run by Marcel's paternal grandmother, and not far from this there was the draper's shop that belonged to his uncle Jules Amiot, Élisabeth Proust's husband.

Some, but not all, of the place-names in the vicinity of Illiers would be used at Combray. Méréglise, a village four kilometres to the west of Illiers, appears under this name in Proust's introduction to his translation of Ruskin's *Sesame and Lilies*, it lies towards the 'hilly Perche'. To the south are Tansonville and its manor house (to which he adds Uncle Amiot's garden, the 'Pré-Catelan',[30] which borders the 'steep hawthorn path'). In the same direction, two kilometres away, there is the Montjouvain mill, and at a distance of five kilometres, Vieuvicq. To the north-west is the hamlet of Mirougrain. Marinville is a hamlet without a church tower, but there is a Martinville in the Calvados, and Proust's description of the

---

* *Corr.*, vol. V, p. 27, 6 January 1905; also these lines which anticipate *Du côté de chez Swann*: 'Soon I will probably no longer be able to hear the sound of bells either, except in this inner atmosphere where the sounds that once moved us but no longer exist still reverberate.'

church tower which bears this name may have been inspired by those at Caen.[31] Other place-names from the country around Illiers would be transposed to other parts of France: La Rachepelière[32] became La Raspeli-ère, Marcouville can be found on the railway route to Balbec, as can Ermenonville. The novelist blends truth, half-truth and the false in a game which must have provided him with much amusement as far as it remained in the preserve of the imagination. Proust knew enough about provincial and rural life to be able to re-create it. The landscapes of childhood are those of the geographer as much as they are those of its creator. As for the biographer, he must describe that which fires the memory and the circumstances that create it. The most French of French villages, in historical as much as biographical terms, has become the most literary of literary villages.

In *Jean Santeuil*, when Proust portrays the house of his uncle and aunt, the Amiots, he only describes the rooms that a solitary child, who was fond of his food, liked best: the bedroom, the dining-room, the kitchen. The child's bedroom with its floral wallpaper, its wooden bed and mahog-any desk, the water jug in a basin, and the adjoining lavatory. The magic lantern that projected its images on the bare walls. One door led into his mother's bedroom.[33] The dining-room with the round mahogany table and the chairs, and, whenever the table was laid, the napkins that were folded like 'white headdresses', the wine in a carafe, the walls that were 'studded with old plates', with 'maxims' and a calendar,[34] the fireplace that heated the room, and the clock.[35] The kitchen is the domain of Ernestine Gallou, the earliest of the models for Françoise, who is obliging and efficient, but cruel to the serving girls and to animals.[36] She has her own room next to the kitchen. There is also a gardener on the staff.

As well as the little garden that belonged to the house, with its single pathway and the flowerbeds of pansies lined with bricks and tiles,[37] Uncle Amiot owned the Pré-Catelan, 'an immense garden, which starts as a terreplein on the banks of the Loir, and rises gradually, over sloping ground or stone steps leading to an artificial grotto, until it reaches the elevated plains where the Beauce begins, that could be seen through a lattice gate'.[38] At the top of the garden were an arbour that was conducive to reading, an asparagus bed, a small pond, and a sort of mechanical device turned by a horse that enabled water to be brought up from the canal. Walking, boating, fishing, reading – these seem to have been the principal distractions engaged in by the little boy and the adolescent who preferred the company of adults to playing with his three Amiot cousins, whom, in fact, he avoided. It is worth stressing that unlike many children who spend time in the country on their own (or even with their younger brothers), Marcel never, either in his letters or in his books, suggested that he suffered from loneliness at Illiers. The only causes for sadness were those occasions when he was parted from his mother, the separation symbolized by the spires of Chartres, where he accompanied her to see her off. It was because every moment of country life, every minute spent at Illiers, filled him with radiant happiness that Proust wrote the poetical pages he devoted to it in *Jean Santeuil*, and later in 'Combray'. Everything to do with it fascinated him, from the topographical details to the botany, the culinary rites, and the unending walks. Everything to do with this life was not merely observed but absorbed, as if by a sponge, and kept in reserve for the day when the adult would provide himself with the literary means to describe what the child saw and felt, that 'sequence of desires and pleasures laden with curiosity, affection and humanity',[39] – what he referred to, in an expression that combined history with geography, as 'the happy days at Illiers'.[40] They coalesce with Auteuil in their immersion in the house, the garden, family life, and in the protection that his uncle, aunt, grandparents, father and, above all, his mother afforded, all of whom dreamt of 'a wonderful life together'.[41] If in Paris life was more luxurious, in the country it was poetry every single day: 'Out of aesthetic necessity,' Proust wrote to the Princesse de Caraman-Chimay in 1905, 'I have demoted my childhood a peg, not that there was anything elegant about it . . .'[42] Auteuil belonged to his maternal lineage, Illiers was his paternal heritage. They would both be fused, through memory, into a blessed unity which makes it impossible to distinguish any longer between two branches of the same tree.

But not without the help of books. In order to evoke Illiers, in order to create Combray, Proust turned to *Illiers*,[43] a work written by Fr J. Marquis, parish priest of Illiers and an honorary canon. Mme de Cambremer alludes to this in *Sodome et Gomorrhe*: 'When he was our neighbour, he would enjoy himself consulting all the old charts, and he compiled a rather curious little booklet about the local place-names. That must have given him a taste for it too, for it appears he is spending his latter years writing an important book about Combray and its surroundings . . . It requires the labour of a Benedictine monk.'[44] In *À la recherche* Proust did not flatter priests,[45] but by including Marquis in the novel, he pays tribute to a man who had 'taught him Latin and the names of the flowers in his garden', and from whose monograph he had, furthermore, learnt the names of

people and places, as well as their etymology. He made use of *Illiers* for
'Combray' and for Balbec: 'The other day,' wrote Marcel when he had
just completed *Du côté de chez Swann*, 'leafing through a book about the
little town we come from and where one road is named after Papa and
another after my uncle, and where the little park is my uncle's garden,
etc., I read the names of these former Marcel Prousts with their modest
occupations, clerks or priests or bailiffs from the fourteenth to the seventeenth centuries; I thought of those distant relatives not without a certain
affection . . .'* When Professor Proust, in one of his last official functions,
gave the prize-giving speech (probably written by Marcel)[46] on 27 July
1903, his son was upset that, because of the Ferry laws,† the priest, who
was as much a symbol of his village as the church steeple, had not been
invited: 'And I who remember that little village straggled over the miserly
earth, the mother of avarice, where the only striving upwards towards the
sky of the Beauce, dappled with clouds, but often of a divine blue, too,
and which, each evening was transfigured at sunset, where the only striving
upwards remains that of the pretty church steeple . . . it seems to me
improper that the old priest should not be invited to the prize-giving as
a representative in the village of something that is harder to define than
the social standing symbolized by the chemist, the retired tobacconist,
and the optician, but who is all the same sufficiently respectable, if only
on account of the spiritual dimension of the pretty church steeple which
faces the west and merges with the pink clouds with so much love and
which nevertheless, in the eyes of a stranger setting foot in the village for
the first time, has more of an air, a greater nobility, more indifference,
more intelligence and, that which we all need, more love about it than
other buildings, whatever the effects of the most recent decrees.'[47] Illiers
is at once a church, and a man, the bringer of a spiritual sense and the
possessor of a long history, the meanings of names, and the origins of
the language.

---

* *Corr.*, vol. XII, 1913, p. 209. This is why, in reply to M. Daireaux's question at Cabourg: 'What
province are you from?', Marcel replies: 'From the Eure-et-Loir.' 'My only excuse was that this little
town is perhaps the only one in France to have, simultaneously, one part that belongs to the Beauce
and another to the Perche.' Odette replies similarly to a question about which province the
Guermantes come from: 'the Aisne' (*RTP*, vol. I, p. 510 and n. 2).

† The statesman Jules Ferry (1832–93) was anticlerical, and his government passed decrees
secularizing schools and dissolving those religious orders that were not authorized to teach. *Tr.*

THE WEIL FAMILY

The Weil family illustrated the upward social mobility of the Jews, just as Marcel's father, Adrien Proust, represented the rise of the Catholic, provincial petite bourgeoisie. A grocer's wife and a well-known doctor. A porcelain manufacturer, some financiers or magistrates, a wife, without a profession, of course, but highly cultivated. Two distinctive families, but which exemplify two historical destinies.

On 28 September 1791, the Assemblée Nationale voted in a decree, ratified on 13 November by Louis XVI and thus becoming law, which gave full citizenship to all French Jews.[48] Persecutions took place during the Terror, however. One of the effects of the revolutionary wars was that the Jews from Germany emigrated to France, from Frankfurt (the Rothschilds), from Trier, from Mainz and Worms. They made up 58 per cent of the Jewish population of Paris in 1810.[49] When Napoleon's armies evacuated the German territories, the Jews discovered the same desperate situation that they had known before the Revolution.

The Weils originally came from Württemberg, where they were ceramic manufacturers. Baruch Weil, Marcel's maternal great-grandfather, worked in the porcelain factory at Niederwiller that belonged to the Comte de Custine and was later declared the property of the nation. He left Alsace for Paris; at the beginning of the Empire era he owned a porcelain factory in the tenth *arrondissement*, where he manufactured Paris ware. He married Sarah Nathan, who died on 19 April 1814, giving birth to her second son, Nathé Weil. Baruch remarried, his first wife's sister, and from this second marriage there were two children, Lazard, known as Louis (Marcel's favourite great-uncle), and Adèle. The family belonged to the Republican tradition. Adolphe Crémieux, Baruch's brother-in-law and Mme Proust's great-uncle, who was Minister for Justice in 1848, did away with the death penalty for political crimes and abolished slavery in the colonies. In 1870, he was once again appointed Minister for Justice. On 16 May 1877 he signed the manifesto against President MacMahon. Strangely enough, he is not mentioned in *À la recherche du temps perdu*.

In 1872 there were only 86,000 Jews among a population of 39 million (there were 180,000 in England, 600,000 in Germany, 2 million in Austria-Hungary, 5 million in Russia, 100,000 in the Low Countries). It was thus a very small community in which the children of merchants, businessmen and artisans quickly took up intellectual occupations and integrated with the middle classes. Proust's schoolfriends at the Lycée Condorcet, Léon and René Blum, were the sons of a ribbon salesman at 243 rue Saint-Denis, and a haberdasher's daughter from the Place Dauphine. In addition to Henri Bergson, who would marry one of Marcel's cousins, ten other members of Proust's family published books.

The Jewish community in Paris during the Second Empire (1852–70) consisted of a population of about 25,000, fewer and fewer of whom attended the synagogue except for marriages that were not to gentiles; burials still took place at the Jewish cemetery.[50] The Weils certainly belonged to this category, though not the musician Fromental Halévy, author of *La Juive* and a member of the central consistory. Adolphe Crémieux resigned from the presidency of the consistory because his children were baptized without his knowledge. Among Jews, Baruch Weil, who was an industrialist, and his sons Nathé and Louis, who were businessmen, belonged to a privileged minority: the percentage of Jews who were workers, artisans and members of the liberal professions 'would never attain the French national average, while the proportion of Jews among small shopkeepers would always remain higher'.[51] Nevertheless 10 per cent of the Jewish population of France consisted of landlords and people of private means; 15 per cent were members of the liberal professions. On the other hand, very few were land-owners (the Weils did own a country house, but it was at Auteuil). A great many Jews were involved in the law, as was Georges Weil, Jeanne Proust's brother, and Gustave Bédarrides, Adolphe Crémieux's cousin and president of the chamber at the Court of Cassation in 1877. In the army, the proportion of Jewish officers was average. One notable doctor was Michel Lévy, a GP and author of a well-considered *Traité d'hygiène*. This dealt with personal hygiene ('the pathogenic causes of the physical and moral personality') – he even covers the subject of 'nostalgia' (among the French expeditionary force in Greece, in 1831), which, 'once diagnosed, can only be cured by repatriation', the role of meteorology, food, clothing, sleep, and gymnastics – but public hygiene is also addressed: population, fertility, 'atmosphere', urban hygiene, sexual life, crime, in short the preservation of the community. We can detect the influence of this *Traité* on Professor Proust, and through him, perhaps, on his son: like Balzac, Michel Lévy saw Paris as 'a city of hardship and degradation, hidden beneath a city of gold and marble'.[52]

Mixed marriages were unusual during the Second Empire (6 per cent, between Jews and Catholics, in Bordeaux), but they were much more common among the more comfortably off Jewish middle class to which the Weils belonged.[53] The fact that they no longer practised their religion, and that their daughter wanted to escape the narrow world of finance for the liberal professions, must have enabled them to accept the marriage of Nathé's daughter Jeanne to a Catholic more easily. The question of the mixed marriage was resolved by Mlle Weil's undertaking to have her children baptized; she nevertheless refused to become a convert.[54] Among the witnesses to the marriage, which took place on 3 September 1870, the certificate mentions the name of Adolphe Crémieux, 'great-uncle of the bride'.* Here we come across one of the most renowned characters in French Judaism, a man who was a minister in the provisional governments of both the Second and the Third Republics. His opposition to the Empire did not prevent him from intervening successfully with Napoleon III on behalf of the Romanian Jews. President of the Alliance Israélite Universelle from 1863, he was also Grand Master of the Supreme Council of the Scottish Rite;[55] during the Third Republic, he was made a senator for life (1875) and was given a state funeral (1880). His wife, Amélie, held a liberal salon at which writers such as Lamartine, Hugo, Musset, Mérimée and Alexandre Dumas would gather, as well as politicians, and musicians such as Rossini, Meyerbeer, Auber and Halévy. It was at her aunt's salon that Proust's grandmother, Adèle Weil, acquired the romantic, liberal and social culture that she passed on to her daughter. Certain of the guests of the young Mme de Villeparisis, in *À la recherche*, had been those of Amélie Crémieux.

Nathé Weil

Proust's maternal grandfather, Nathé, born in 1814, was the son of Baruch Weil, the porcelain manufacturer. His Paris ware acquired a fine reputation and was compared to that of Sèvres. In a paper written in 1827, in which the influence of Saint-Simon's ideas can be detected, Baruch Weil called for an exhibition hall to be 'devoted especially to general exhibitions of Industry'.[56] At once an artist and a businessman, he exemplified the two tendencies which would be developed by his descendants. He died in 1828.[57] Nathé's career is somewhat obscure. A sleeping partner in the foreign-exchange dealers Ramel, later Blin, at 18 Boulevard Montmartre,

---

* His wife, Amélie Sylvy, was the sister of Rose Sylvy, wife of Nathanaël Berncastel and mother of Adèle (1824–80), who married Nathé Weil (1814–96) and was the mother of Jeanne Proust. Amélie was therefore great-aunt of the bride.

from 1865 to 1890,[58] he had, on their behalf, certainly had dealings on the stock market,[59] that is to say he was an unofficial stockbroker, acting as a foreign-exchange dealer on the open market. Ever since his marriage to Adèle Berncastel at the age of thirty-one, he was officially described as that quintessential nineteenth-century character, a *'rentier'*, or person of private means. Nathé Weil's proclivity for stock-exchange speculations would be passed on in an unexpected way to his grandson Marcel, who, incidentally, confided his most secret adventures to his grandfather. The Weils lived at 40 *bis* rue du Faubourg-Poissonnière, a district popular with stockbrokers and businessmen that was also close to the theatre and opera so beloved by the family. It was a six-room apartment in an attractive building, at the rear of the courtyard and on the second floor above the mezzanine level. In *À la recherche*, the '40 *bis*' becomes the address of Great-Uncle Adolphe on the Boulevard Malesherbes. The Weils always spoke French; they would interject a few Yiddish expressions, for amusement, or so as not to be understood by the staff – words such as *mechore*, a servant. They adored the theatre and the opera; as to religious ceremonies, not being regular attenders, they only observed the important feasts, particularly where dietary laws or the sabbath were concerned.[60]

It was to his grandfather that Marcel appealed whenever he needed a present, a subscription to *La Revue bleue* (in September 1886), or money to pay a prostitute. Once he was an adolescent, he adopted a joking tone and manner with him, but also one of affection: 'My dear little grandfather', 'My dearest', and even of vulgarity: 'Only once in a lifetime can one be so upset that one's unable to fuck.'[61] And it was to him that he solemnly announced the results of the first part of the *baccalauréat* (3 August 1887): 'I can inform you that I have gained a second-class distinction and that the chancellor said to me: Monsieur Proust, we are happy to come to you. Your examination result will remain a happy memory for myself and my colleagues. We congratulate you warmly.' And since, where Marcel was concerned, affection was intertwined with financial matters, Nathé Weil performed the role of banker for him, providing him with an allowance and loans.[62] There were also letters containing political observations (on the September 1889 elections), in which both of them hoped for a 'Republican majority' (and not a Boulangiste one).[63]

Louis Weil

Louis Weil, Nathé's brother, was a businessman.[64] A button and haberdashery manufacturer, in 1843 he worked for the house of Weil, Trélon and Langlois-Sauer, 29 rue Greneta, and later for Trélon, Weidon and Weil at 11 rue Bercy-Saint-Antoine: 'Manufacturers of novelty buttons, uniforms, silk of every kind, porcelain known as agate and used instead of mother of pearl; religious medals for export; retailers of buttons, gloves and English soft furnishings; sole retailers in France for genuine B. Sanders & Sons buttons; sole retailers of genuine B. Huntsmann English steel goods'. Is it not like reading a novel by Balzac, or the wedding announcement chapter in *Albertine disparue*? In 1851 this respectable manufacturer lived at 35 rue d'Hauteville. His wealth was accrued through his marriage, on 29 June 1844, to Émilie Oppenheim, a banker's daughter. Left a childless widower (hence the legend of the bachelor uncle) in 1870, his home was at 29 rue Bleue (very close to his brother), and he also owned 102 Boulevard Haussmann and 96 rue La Fontaine.[65] On Marcel Proust's birth certificate, Louis Weil is described as 'person of private means'. He dedicated his spare time to his family or to beautiful actresses or singers such as Marie Van Zandt,[66] or to demi-mondaines (like Laure Hayman) whose photographs he collected. The photographs of singers have been preserved; those such as Juliette Bilbault-Vauchelet, of the Opéra-Comique ('To M. Weil, a souvenir of my sincere friendship', 1879) or Marie Heilbron, who starred in *La Traviata* ('A souvenir of great friendship offered to the kindest of men, to my dear friend M. Weil'); those of actresses such as Jeanne Granier, and Louise Théo, who also inscribed one to 'M. Marcel Proust, nephew of my dear friend M. L. Weil, with my sincere friendship, November 1888'.[67]

One can imagine the glamour such an uncle had in the eyes of his nephews! Marcel, too, was a *rentier*, who collected photographs and, later, paid in order to be loved. The theme of the uncle and the nephew can be found in Uncle Adolphe and the Narrator, in Charlus and Saint-Loup. It raises some curious reflections: 'One does not always get away with being someone's nephew with impunity. Very often a hereditary trait is sooner or later transmitted by that route. An entire portrait gallery, bearing the title of the German play *Uncle or Nephew?* could be created.'[68] In 'Combray', Uncle Adolphe is 'a former soldier, who had retired from the army with the rank of major':[69] this is a discreet tribute to another Weil brother, Abraham Alphonse (1822–86). When Louis died, in 1896, the funeral announcement mentioned that he had been a manufacturer, a member of the Commission des Valeurs de Douane, and of the Comptoir National D'escompte, a chevalier of the Légion d'honneur, and an officer of the Académie.[70] Proust retained the wealthy man for *À la recherche*, and he kept for himself a share of the riches and a flat, a liking for gambling, the model of the 'lady in pink' – and the memory of a tomb: 'There is no longer anyone, not even me since I am unable to get up, to go and visit the little Jewish cemetery that runs the length of the rue du Repos, where my grandfather, following a ritual that he never understood, would go every year to place a pebble on his parents' tomb.' Marcel himself, let it be stressed, did not consider himself a Jew.[71]

Among his many dazzling affairs, Louis Weil had been the lover and protector of Laure Hayman, the celebrated courtesan, who was born on a hacienda in the foothills of the Andes, the daughter of an English engineer with Creole blood.[72] Very beautiful, and a favourite of the Duc d'Orléans and the King of Greece, she was the inspiration of painters (Madrazo, Tissot, Stewart, Drian) and of writers such as Lavedan and Bourget, who made her the model for his 'Gladys Harvey' (reprinted in *Pastels* in 1888). One day, in about 1899, Marcel Proust asked his childhood friend Maurice Duplay whether he had read *Pastels*, and told him that the original story took place at a private dining-room *chez* Laurent, on the Champs-Élysées, and had as its heroine 'a famous tart', Laure Hayman, who had been 'extremely close' to his uncle Louis Weil: 'I have a peculiar desire, a whim ... One afternoon when I'm feeling in reasonably good shape, at a time when it's not too busy, I should like to go to Laurent's. Laure Hayman certainly used to go there. She would have dined in the private dining-room, at least once, with my uncle. I should like to know that room, shut myself inside and spend some time there dreaming.' Marcel then showered the staff with tips, plagued them with questions and eventually persuaded the manager to show him a private dining-room: 'I think he lied in order to get rid of us,' said Marcel.[73] In this visit, in which the nephew attempts to revive the memory of his uncle, it is as if the writer were imagining a scene in which Uncle Adolphe would meet the lady in pink.

Strangest of all was the fact that, after Adrien Proust's death, it was discovered that he too had been on friendly terms with Laure Hayman. This may be why in the novel, after Doctor Cottard's death, it came to be realized that he had been Odette's lover.[74] Adrien Proust referred to Laure Hayman whenever he wished to give an example of elegance, youth and beauty, and also of intelligence, taste, goodness, tact, refinement and kind-heartedness. When Marcel went to call on Laure Hayman, she used to inform his father, who kept saying to him, 'You were seen' and 'it appears . . .'. 'And I guessed immediately that you had been to see him that day,' Marcel wrote to Laure. 'For some years now it has no longer been possible. But he still spoke about you just as much.'[75] 'We've been torn apart', Marcel informed Laure, as if to pave the way for the young Narrator being forbidden to see the lady in pink again. Then in 1906, Laure Hayman, who was a sculptress herself, suggested to Marcel that she should carve a bust of his father for his tomb at Père-Lachaise, an 'image', he says, 'based purely on the living memory of a long friendship'.[76]

To return to Uncle Louis, he used to like discussing art at table, and teasing Mme Proust's cousin because she did not care for Ingres (generously, however, he provided her with a pension and a dowry for her daughter);[77] in general, he displayed that ironic wit which was common to the whole Weil family. Proust used his memories of him not just in the creation of the character of Uncle Adolphe, the lover of Odette, but also in the way he described the great-aunts' habit of thanking people by making allusions: 'For a week he had been making announcements at table about Dupont that were destined for Octave's ears: "It's the foremost house in Paris, isn't it Nathé?"'[78] Nathé himself appears in *Jean Santeuil* under the guise of M. Sandre, a 'sweet and violent' character, whose only concern is for his daughter's happiness, his son-in-law's career and his grandson's health: 'Old people do not love each other, they love their children.'[79] This is also the main characteristic that Jeanne Proust retains of her mother when she cites their common admiration for Mme de Sévigné: '"I know of another mother who does not consider herself at all, who is *given over* entirely to her children." Doesn't that apply very much to your grandmother?'[80] Nathé Weil had abandoned the running of the house to his wife, Adèle Berncastel, as well as the education of the children, Georges and Jeanne. They had received a modern education, one that provided them with some culture, a taste for travel and reading new books, and which was without religious prejudice: the family did not practise, even if Nathé observed the important feasts and went to the temple on the day of Yom Kippur. Their staff were Catholics, and consisted of a cook, a manservant and a maid.[81] This family, from the middle-class bourgeoisie, never tried to break into the Jewish upper classes – the Pereires, the Foulds or the Rothschilds, whose daughters married into the upper ranks of French aristocracy. There was the same distance between them and the Rothschilds as between Bloch and Sir Rufus Israel in *À la recherche*. Marcel Proust was the first offspring of the Weil family to mingle with the Rothschilds, with Henri and Robert, and with the Foulds – with Mme Léon Fould and her son Eugène – but that was probably because he did not consider himself a Jew, and because he wanted to know all strata of high society.

Georges Weil

One of the earliest letters that has been preserved from Marcel to his mother documents his meetings with his Uncle Georges (who was two years older than his sister Jeanne and died, of the same illness, a few months after her, just as Nathé died after Louis)) in the Allées des Acacias in the Bois de Boulogne; the boy experienced such pleasure talking to him that he caused his uncle, who was a magistrate and was on his way to the law courts, to miss his bus. Thus we see that the unity of this family was enshrined not merely in the life they led together at Auteuil, but in conversation, in what Mlle de Montpensier described as 'the principal pleasure of existence'. Much later, in 1903, Marcel divulged to Fernand Gregh: 'I have an uncle who has been very ill with a stomach complaint for many years, who is extremely neurasthenic.'[82] Doctor Dubois, who had a clinic in Berne, told Georges Weil: 'There is nothing I can do for you, there is nothing wrong with you'; this convinced him, and his condition improved. This is how Du Boulbon behaves towards the Narrator's grandmother in *Le Côté de Guermantes*.[83] Like the grandmother, Georges Weil died of uraemia. Here we have corroboration of what those anthropologists of primitive societies refer to as the role of the maternal uncle.

Adèle Berncastel

Marcel's maternal grandmother, Adèle Berncastel, was born in Paris on 5 February 1824. She married Nathé Weil on 6 December 1845. She was cultivated, an excellent pianist, and an admirer of Mme de Sévigné, and it is clear from a few of the letters her grandson wrote that she was not dissimilar to the grandmother in 'Combray'. On her birthday, for instance, the little boy wishes for her, 'no more of Mamma's teasing, and no more of Grandfather's impatience and no more culinary discussions with my uncle or medical (hygienic) ones with Papa'.[84] Adèle was always the family's scapegoat on account of her kindness and subtle nature; her grandson was her champion and the only person who would always understand her. It would therefore be incorrect to see only Jeanne Proust in the grandmother of *À la recherche*; in 'Combray', it is her mother whom her husband upsets by drinking brandy; it is she who, through the courageous example she sets of public-spiritedness, makes the child realize that 'indifference to the sufferings we cause is the most terrible and lasting form of cruelty in this life'. Marcel's tone is gentler when he reproached his grandmother (he was fifteen) for not liking Gautier's *Le Capitaine Fracasse*: 'How can you as a subscriber to *La Revue des deux mondes*, as a relentless consumer of apricots and cooked cherries, how . . . did you not feel the excitement in your stomach at that wonderful phrase . . . " 'All I have is cod, ham and some soup.' 'Give us soup, some ham and some cod,' cried the half-starved crew in unison." ' Then he is swept away with tenderness, by the indirect use of a literary quotation, by a piece of German syntax in French, by Molière: 'Fair lady', 'To die for your eyes, fair marquise of love'.[85]

At the same time, the child always remembered the relationship between his grandmother and his mother; he makes it one of the chief themes of 'Combray', *À l'ombre des jeunes filles en fleurs*, of *Le Côté de Guermantes*. The grandmother, the isolated old sovereign, a Queen Lear in her country garden, and yet beloved by her only daughter, who is without envy or jealousy, who is without any unconscious or sexual impulses, whose life has outlived her sorrows.

JEANNE PROUST

What do we know of Marcel Proust's mother? Over the years an image of her, intangible and static, has taken root. A woman who is discreet, a devoted wife, a wonderful mother, and yet over-possessive. The stereotype of a woman of the nineteenth-century bourgeoisie, who has also acquired, quite unusually, a great deal of culture. We can only discover more about her by referring to her papers – not, unfortunately, her private diaries, which have not survived, though Marcel mentioned one that she kept at the time of Mme Weil's death – but her letters; we shall look at her translations when we examine Proust's own work as a translator.

What strikes the reader of Jeanne Proust's letters initially is her sense of comedy and humour. It is clear that this humour must have infused the conversations around the family table, and those between the mother and her two sons, as well as with her parents and her brother Georges.[86]

Humour is an attribute that is acquired through one's family or social background: which is why, rightly or wrongly, such importance is attached to it, be it at the École Normale Supérieure or in Great Britain. Here is Mme Proust, for example, describing the inmates at her hotel, at Salies-de-Béarn, in 1889: 'We have come across (one always comes across them!) the decadent Belgian from last year, who is grown still more decadent and whose only enthusiasm is for Joséphin Péladan. There is also a Brazilian who pounds the piano from eight o'clock in the morning until midnight and only stops to give way to a girl from Libourne who performs a few singing exercises. With all the energy left in her throat the poor little creature launches into: "Yes-sssssss/ sorrow-ow-ow-ow/ will cut sho-ort-ort-ort my life!" Her mother accompanies her with her lorgnette – then her chin drops to her chest so jolting is the beat of the rhythm she is trying to obtain. The poor girl's twenty-four mawkish double-crochets have to keep to the tempo. Afterwards, the mother gets to her feet, barely suppressing her triumph, and arranges the music etc.'[87] She is especially inspired by connoisseurs of art, such as the English at the Louvre ('We don't have to go to Paris to see English beings here').[88] Are we not already observing the guests at the hotel in Balbec, or at the Verdurin salon? The same talent for observation and for creating comical situations, or for making ordinary reality appear funny. At any rate, they certainly loved music at the Weils' house; in 1918 Marcel remembered having heard his cousin Louise Crémieux singing Mozart,[89] during certain children's evenings 'at home'.

Again, we come across the mother playing tricks on her son Robert, who was nicknamed Ferdinand le Noceur[90] [the reveller] or Proustovich ('nice – when he wasn't grumpy'), by allowing him to confuse work by Casimir Delavigne with that of Lamartine (just as the pianist at the Verdurins' salon mistakes Meyerbeer for Debussy), which made him laugh and which struck him as 'most unusual': Robert does not seem to have had his brother's sense of humour, and, at the age of seventeen, he was even 'unbearable'. She made fun equally of Marcel 'the trooper' – 'Your "lay down arms" has not the pace of a chorus in *Faust*'[91] – and of the conversation of her father Nathé and her Uncle Louis, who extolled the merits of the jeweller from whom he bought a chain: 'We shall no doubt be hearing shortly "that it was he who gave Marie-Antoinette the stolen 'Queen's necklace'"'.[92] She does not even shrink from the old French scatology, which would be dear to Marcel (as the Albarets, his servants in later years, have testified): 'Keep a close watch on Monsieur's bowels that we don't have the 90,000th copy of *La Débâcle*!',* or again, at Évian in 1900, 'Your father devoted his entire attention to examining the light and dark shades of his urine.'[93] When Mme Alphonse Daudet, whose maiden name was Julia Allard, went to Lourdes, she dubbed her 'Julia de Sacré-Cœur': 'After the pilgrimage we'll all have to wear hair-shirts and go on perpetual retreat.'[94] Marcel, and, no doubt, Professor Proust, displayed the same lack of belief. Her fondness for humorous adaptations of literary quotations was shared by her son: 'Don't you think that Robert was trying to make me pose [in a photograph] like Goethe, who said as he looked up at the fourth floor: "I like what is above me"; he made me pose with my head in the air – and I look inspired.'[95]

Quotations were part of the culture that was acquired and transmitted within the family: Jeanne Weil, in common with other young women at the time, was not allowed to take her *baccalauréat*; she may not have received any education except at home. She spoke and read German and English, and could translate from the latter; she played the piano,[96] and she was a voracious reader of whatever books she could find on the family bookshelves, or those which, like her mother, she borrowed from a reading room (one of those reading rooms which Proust was asked about towards the end of his life). Her letters are scattered with references to books, much as Marcel might have made. Mother and son are steeped in a world of literary allusions, shared reading, pleasure in words, and having the correct accent.[97] After the death of Mme Nathé Weil, she wrote, 'Sometimes I also find thoughts and words in Madame de Sévigné that give me pleasure. She says . . . "I know of another mother who does not consider herself at all, who is *given over* entirely to her children." Doesn't that apply exactly to your grandmother? . . . Then, again, there is the following, on the subject of worries she dare not voice: "Another great friendship, my dear child, could be based upon all the feelings that I hide from you."'[98] The grandmother in *À la recherche* also has this same liking for Mme de Sévigné, as well as for the memoirs of Mme de Beauséant; Mme Proust read Mme de Rémusat and Mme du Deffand. Like the Narrator, she could quote from Racine[99] as well as from Balzac and the writers whom Marcel first admired: 'Loti, Sévigné and Musset . . . After Loti would come *Mauprat*.'[100] She read the feuilletons by Faguet, France and Desjardins in

---

* *Corr.*, vol. I, p. 181, 17 August 1892; a reference to the success of Zola's novel, which the family were reading. [The pun is on the word *débâcle*, which suggests diarrhoea, as well as military defeat. *Tr.*]

the newspapers; her brother lent her Gautier's *Voyage en Russie*; among Marcel's books, besides *Splendeurs et misères des courtisanes*, there was Goethe's *Wilhelm Meister*,[101] which he wrote about. History was no stranger to her, for she read Lavisse on Frederick the Great, and later Michelet[102] (of whom Marcel wrote a pastiche in 1908). When she lost her mother, reading Loti, on Marcel's advice, brought her some comfort: 'I can't stop,' she wrote on 23 April 1890, 're-reading these lines: "And I should like, on the first appearance of this blessed person in this book of memoirs, to salute her with special words, if that were possible, with words that do not exist and which are made for her, words which, of their own accord, would enable beneficent tears to flow, which would bring a measure of sweet consolation."'[103] Life was like this, criss-crossed with literature, even in dreams: 'Looking somewhat sad, you appeared to me in my sleep.'[104] Life, and also death: 'She died reciting a passage by Molière and one by the playwright Labiche. She said to me, of the nurse who had gone out and left us alone for a moment: "*His departure could not be more appropriate*," "That little one should not be afraid. His Mother will not leave him. *He'd better not see that I am at Étampes and my spelling at Arpajon . . .*" and then she was no longer able to speak. Only once did she see that I was holding back my tears and she frowned, screwed up her face and smiled, and I could just make out, amidst her already confused mumbling: "*If you are not a Roman, be worthy of one.*"'* A lifetime spent in literature uttered its last in a final breath, just as if it were books that interpret existence and death.

The converse of this life was practical organization: with an absent husband, one son busy studying, the other disliking housework, she had to do everything herself. While maintaining the standard of living appropriate to a professor at the faculty of medicine and employing numerous servants, in ever larger and more sumptuous apartments, from the rue Roy to 45 rue de Courcelles, at the same time Mme Proust always displayed the ability to economize: 'I left the gas burning all night,' she wrote from the Hotel Métropole at Dieppe; 'you see, the lighting is included.'[105] When she was away from Paris, she sent Marcel his cheque on the first of the month,[106] and she kept an eye on his expenditure, which she often judged to be excessive. Generally speaking, she attempted to pass on some of her own qualities to him: 'So do try, my dearest, to be *just a little* tidier and avoid these torments you create for yourself. Tidiness

---

* *Corr.*, vol. III, p. 302. This text was not used in the account of the grandmother's death in *Le Côté de Guermantes*.

will be more valuable to you than anything else because you will be spared so much exhaustion! . . . regulate your body and your stomach according to the important principles.'[107] She took trouble over any carelessness in her son's appearance, something that many biographers would comment upon, as if in this as in other spheres she wanted to prepare him for living alone (which would not have been abnormal, when one considers that Marcel was still residing with his mother at the age of thirty-four): 'My dearest, will you please reply to my domestic questions: Are all your belongings excluding your head and including your feet in perfect order? The things that have to be washed – cleaned – inspected – re-soled – marked – darned – lined – collars changed – button-holes etc . . . try to ensure that everything is kept tidy (I know that without practising what one preaches you are very capable of managing).'[108] In 1902–3, there were some lively quarrels between mother and son; he complained that the heating had been cut off, and that his friends were obliged to keep their overcoats on when they visited him. All Mme Proust's efforts to change the way her son spent his time had the very opposite effect.

The same attention to tidiness, discipline and to being methodical prompted Mme Proust (and probably her husband) to impose proper health checks on their son, and not to neglect the slightest detail, almost as if everybody in this family, when not actually ill, behaved like a doctor. These checks provided information and remedies, but above all they comforted and distracted the patient, who, even if he was aware of his symptoms, left the bad news on paper, in the hands of his mother, who did her best to prevent him 'resorting to medicaments again'.[109] She did not have the same conception of hygiene as Marcel: her letters record her fondness not merely for 'regulatory walks' from Auteuil to Passy with Doctor Proust, but also for the rain, for the biting wind on one's face, and for the 'brisk weather' that suited her.[110] The grandmother at Combray shares these attitudes. A woman for whom orderliness, hygiene and good health were all-important, Mme Proust tended to worry as much as her husband did about the life her son led, and about his relationships. The letters in which she questioned him about these matters have not survived, but certain of those written in reply are clear enough: 'I will not disguise the fact that Doctor Cottet seemed to me to be very worked up as far as I was concerned. *Does he live in Paris during the winter?* Of course (and I am only adding this foolish remark because of my mother's imagination) I mean worked up in the best sense so don't start imagining that it's to do with a bad relationship, good god!!!!!!'[111] So it was as if it were a work of charity, in order to ask her for money, that Marcel raised the subject of his relationship with a young roof-mender by the name of Pierre Poupetière.[112] Whatever Mme Proust may have known, or suspected, she did not stop supervising, restraining or reproaching him. Marcel was therefore constrained, not to put it more strongly, into half-confessions and to curious denunciations: 'You will certainly remember that I mentioned the name Weisweiller as someone of bad company. I could not know this beforehand because it only became evident later on. I only told you what Loche had said to me . . . It would have been pure *folly* to attach any significance to this.'[113] Both Swann and the Narrator would inherit this obsession with interrogations, as would Odette and Albertine the evasive or untruthful replies. It was something that was present from the beginning in Marcel's conversations with his mother. His mother's questioning constantly weighed upon her son, who, in turn, cross-questioned his friends, and it ended with him forming strange pacts with men such as Reynaldo Hahn or Antoine Bibesco, whereby everyone had to confess everything to one another.

We have not described Jeanne Weil's appearance; let us not try to compete with Balzac, nor with the photographs (or paintings). But the resemblance of Marcel to his mother is striking (particularly in the little-known photograph of Jeanne as a child):[114] the eyes, nose and mouth, the oval face, the chin, the smile; how often must this likeness have been pointed out to Marcel! Hence the care that he took in searching among his relations for similar likenesses between mother and son, in order to project it on to his characters, such as Mme de Surgis, or, reversing the roles, M. Vinteuil and their children. When his mother died, his sole preoccupation was to ensure the survival of her features. But it was not a happy transition: inversion, the apparent reversal of sexes, and tendencies reproved by society broke the charm of heredity. 'Even though they were not inverts and sought the company of women, the sons did not always look like their father, and in their faces they consummate the profanation of their mother.'*

We possess little documentary evidence of Mme Proust's relationship with her son Robert. The same feelings of affection permeate her letters to both her sons: this was how she wrote to Robert on his thirtieth birthday: 'Today, my little one, my wishes for your second batch of fifteen

---

* *RTP*, vol. III, p. 300 and n. 1, p. 1514, Proust adds: 'But let us leave to one side a subject which would be worth a chapter to itself: mothers who have been vilified.'

years are bestowed with equal affection on both of you.* And as your uncle would say: "Give a hug to the two children!" '[115] Robert, too, was: 'my dearest big boy', and he was sent 'a thousand tender kisses'. There is nothing to prove that he was less favoured, nor even less loved. The family tradition, which Jeanne Weil had observed in her own parents, was to share everything, books as well as feelings, a common fusion of minds and hearts. There was nothing in her behaviour that could have given rise to one son's jealousy of the other. There is nothing, where they are concerned, to corroborate this jealousy, which exists only in the minds of biographers and Proust's posthumous psychoanalysts (they are not necessarily psychoanalysts by profession) who believe they can trace in Marcel the same hostility that Freud maintained Goethe felt towards his brother. Furthermore, Mme Proust's affection is so fulsome that it extends to Marcel's friends: 'I love people who love my own poor little one.'[116]

ADRIEN PROUST

A brilliant doctor, one who qualified before he was even forty, now makes his appearance, someone who came from a very different social milieu, but whose intelligence paid no heed to social origins. A face with powerful features, with fine, large eyes (blue in his case), a beard (then in fashion) that was cut square, and a physique that was less stocky than in later portraits;[117] he is not a dandy, no Montesquiou or Sagan; he is a handsome man. He displays all the dignity that Proust would depict in every one of his famous doctors and senior executives, from Dieulafoy to Norpois, and which can be seen in nineteenth-century portraits of noteworthy men. This former pupil of a small seminary, this deserving scholar from the Collège de Chartres (he still recalled at the end of his life that his name was listed on the roll of honour), this Republican of whom, according to a police report, no mention was made during the siege and 'insurrection',[118] has been presented to us by biographers as a Catholic: wrongly so. He no more remained Christian in his faith than his wife practised as a religious Jew. A curious episode demonstrates this: in 1882 Doctor Proust complained about giving witness at a trial, on account of the presence of a crucifix in the room.[119] Was this so as to display his Republican, pro-government loyalties? Because he was a Freemason?[120] So as to be true to the positivist tradition of doctors of that period, typified by Cottard?

---

* She is referring to Marthe, Robert's wife.

Under the Second Empire, the Faculty of Medicine, where Clemenceau studied, was both Republican and atheist.

How did he meet his future wife? How did the improbable conjunction of these two families come about? Doctor Robert Soupault, a friend of Proust, has given the most likely clue, when he disclosed that the husband's witnesses were the brothers Gustave and Charles Cambanellas, who lived at 5 rue Mogador: Adrien Proust lived nearby at the time, at 35 rue Joubert. Gustave Cambanellas was a doctor of medicine, Charles a partner in a foreign-exchange dealers. Thus were the worlds of medicine and finance conjoined.[121]

An unlikely encounter of humble, petit bourgeois, provincial, almost rural, society with good Parisian Jewish stock? We must step backwards in time a little. Ever since the sixteenth century, the Proust family had figured among the prominent townspeople of Illiers: in 1621, Gilles Proust was bailiff; in 1633, Robert Proust was the collector for the seigneurie; Michel Proust was bailiff of Illiers in 1673. Marcel's grandfather, Louis François Valentin (1801–53), married Virginie Torcheux (born 1808) in 1827, and ran the grocery opposite the church.[122] Virginie was left a widow at the age of forty-five, and she died aged eighty-one in 1889 (Marcel was then eighteen, but he did not mention this either in his letters or in his books). Her eldest daughter Élisabeth (born in 1828), who was married to Jules Amiot, lived not far away from her. Mme Proust did not attend her son's wedding: this was not out of hostility, since the Proust family subsequently came to spend their holidays each year at Illiers. It must have been the prospect of travelling to Paris that alarmed her – no one would dare suggest that the family would have been ashamed of a woman whose photograph did not exactly exude elegance, nor that Virginie Proust should have been opposed to marriage with a Jewess, or to a civil marriage.

Adrien was born on 18 March 1834. After attending the primary school at Illiers, he continued his studies as a scholarship boy at the Collège de Chartres. Having passed his examinations in literature and science, he left for Paris to study medicine, an example of the type often described by Balzac and Zola: the young man from the provinces (such as Desplein or Horace Bianchon, up from Sancerre and living in some wretched Quartier Latin boarding-house), initially without great resources, who conquers Paris. A medical career, even more than an academic one, has always been a means to social improvement. The careers of Adrien's friends, Professor Laboulbène or Samuel Pozzi, are further illustrations of this: 'Medicine has a democratic grain; without a name, without family, without financial help, virtually without any money, but with courage, one can ascend every pinnacle; titles of nobility and aristocratic appendages are few, they risk little and they succeed unremarkably ... After all, this faculty, like the Faculty of Law, is an observatory which keeps an eye on the social evolution and politics of the nation.'[123] A living can be made from giving medical treatment, locum duties, taking small classes, until the first clients provide an income.

From one competitive exam to another, Adrien Proust's career was exemplary and it led him in record time to the most important and most senior hospital, academic and administrative posts.[124] He was carried along on that scientific, and later scientistic, tide that surged through France, and whose ideological framework was defined by men such as Renan, Littré and Claude Bernard. In the medical field, although they were not yet able to prescribe treatments, as Pinel demonstrated, they were beginning to describe and classify illnesses in rigorous detail; Bichat invented histology; Bretonneau defined diphtheria and typhoid; Cruveilhier's treatise on pathological anatomy appeared in 1849.[125] Adrien Proust attended the latter's courses, as well as those given by Trousseau, Velpeau and Nélaton. Charcot and Potain were among those who passed their *agrégation* at this time. Qualifying as a doctor of medicine in 1862, with a thesis entitled 'On the ideopathic pneumothorax without perforation', Adrien Proust was appointed head of clinic in 1863, and he passed his *agrégation* in 1867, at the age of thirty-three, after submitting a paper on 'the different forms of brain softening', in which he relied mainly on the research done by his friend Cotard,[126] a name which would not go unnoticed (with a difference of one letter); in August 1870, he was made a chevalier of the Légion d'honneur. Throughout the Commune, he was head of department at La Charité hospital. It was not until 1873 that he began to turn his attention to hygiene, the subject to which he would devote the rest of his career; he published an *Essay on international hygiene, and its application in the treatment of plague, yellow fever and Asian cholera*. It was at this time that he travelled to Persia to study the growth of cholera; he believed the disease originated in India. It became necessary to persuade the British to impose sanitary controls in the sub-continent and to look upon 'Egypt as Europe's barrier against cholera'[127] (*Defending Europe against Cholera*, 1893): in fact, the route to India was the route followed by this disease, but it moved in the opposite direction. Eight international conferences were needed to impose genuine sanitary controls on the British and the Turks; at the last of these, in 1905, the president of the French delegation was the ambassador

Camille Barrère, a friend of Adrien Proust and the model for Norpois. The professor had in this way acquired wide experience, and he had made political and diplomatic friendships, which would be to the benefit of the Narrator's father in *À l'ombre des jeunes filles en fleurs*. Head of department at the Lariboisière hospital from 1877, he held the same position at the Hôtel-Dieu until 1900.

In 1879, he was elected to the Academy of Medicine; in 1884, he was appointed Inspector-General of Health Services; in 1885, he attained the summit of his career, at the age of fifty-one, when he was offered the chair of hygiene at the Faculty of Medicine in Paris. Doctor Le Masle, Robert Proust's biographer, saw him as 'the geographer of infectious diseases which he had put on the map', the guardian of our 'maritime hygiene', but also a teacher whose courses and clinical examinations were well attended, and who had numerous patients[128] – thus assuring him considerable personal wealth, as his way of life testified: a large apartment, plenty of servants, holidays in luxury hotels. In *Le Côté de Guermantes* Proust described the portrait of him painted by Lecomte de Nouy: 'A professor, in his scarlet satin gown, trimmed with ermine like that of a doge (that is to say a duke) of Venice shut up in his ducal palace.'[129] He takes the opportunity to generalize and define the characteristics of this constituent body: the stringency of those biased in its favour is the ransom of integrity and the highest standards of morality, 'which are bent in more tolerant and freer circles that soon become dissolute'. A professor, therefore, who, 'was just as virtuous, just as much attached to noble principles, but equally pitiless towards any foreign element as that other duke, excellent but terrible, who was M. de Saint-Simon'.[130]

Among the numerous writings which mark out Adrien Proust's career – twenty or so books, and many more articles, which are void of literary qualities – it is worth drawing attention to his *Traité d'hygiène* (third edition, 1902), his works on neurology (*De la paralysie labio-glosso-pharyngée; De l'aphasie*),[131] in the 'Bibliothèque d'hygiène thérapeutique', which he edited, published by Masson, and *L'Hygiène du neurasthénique* (in collaboration with Gilbert Ballet).[132] Furthermore, he was a contributor to *La Revue des deux mondes* ('Les nouvelles routes des grandes épidémies', 1893; 'Le pèlerinage de La Mecque', 1895). In what has become, due to his sudden death, a testament, the prize-giving speech he gave at Illiers on 27 July, Adrien Proust defined his concept of hygiene. Standing facing the old town, he declared that hygiene should transform towns today, under pain of death, at the cost of aesthetic charm, and the beauty of streets and

houses. Adrien's house was the opposite of Marcel's: 'New houses . . .
are flooded with light and air which are the two most powerful tonics and
antiseptics we know.' Thus, on the banks of the Loir, 'one of the prettiest
French rivers', whose marshy course the hygienist deplores, he finds no
consolation in the water lilies so dear to Marcel: 'What a wonderful natural
tapestry will be destroyed when they come to purify our lovely river.'
Hygiene represents a set of rules, precious precepts, and it constitutes one
of the most important branches of education. It advocates cleanliness,
the fight against alcohol and 'the dangers of dust, when it transmits the
germs of contagious illness'. Since at this period, which was also that of
Zola, people believed in heredity (which Marcel himself would analyse),
education and hygiene were thought to reduce or prevent its effects.
Nowadays, the humblest artisan is assured of greater comfort than 'the
great king himself with his wig and his knee-breeches full of infectious
dust, living in his gilded halls which had no protection from mephitic
fumes'.[133]

Not only had Marcel read these works, but the presence at home of a
father who wrote and published prompted him to transpose him, as a
model – and sometimes to collaborate with him: in June 1903, for a speech
at Chartres, in which the cathedral is partially described: 'At the front
porch of Chartres, you can see a character by the name of Magus, the
magician who symbolizes alchemy and Hermetic studies, the conqueror
of evil which lurks at his feet';[134] on 27 July 1903, for the prize-giving at
the upper primary school at Illiers: 'There is one subject to which young
people's minds are closed, or which they can only approach with a sort
of foreboding, and that is poetry, it is the melancholia of memory.'[135]
Marcel has internalized this father who wrote, and who, in the year of his
death, remembered; where the one longed to belong to the Académie des
Sciences Morales et Politiques (like the Narrator's father or the Prince de
Faffenheim in the novel), the other aimed for the Académie française
('Marcel will be a member of the Académie française,' his father would
say). None of Doctor Proust's letters survive;[136] Marcel, for his part,
wrote constantly about medical consultations, complete with realistic
prescriptions. His father's friends had increased his knowledge: Doctor
Laboulbène; Professor Guyon, a specialist in wordplay, who was a urologist
and Robert Proust's teacher; Professor Dieulafoy, his father's colleague
at the Hôtel-Dieu (1839–1913), who came to attend the grandmother on
her death-bed in Le Côté de Guermantes; Professor Duplay,[137] and Pozzi no
doubt, to whose house Adrien Proust took his thirteen- and fifteen-year-

old sons for a meal. Doctor Brouardel, a hygienist himself and dean of the Faculty of Medicine, attended the conferences at Venice and Dresden with Adrien, and his wife painted Doctor Proust's portrait.[138] Entertaining was, in fact, one of the duties of a great doctor: 'Doctors and surgeons are very much admired by the mistress of the house in this latter part of the century in which their skills are in the spotlight. [To have] a professor is extremely fashionable. Being entertained by one too.'[139] Less worldly than Pozzi or Robin (the lover of Liane de Pougy, and the possible inspiration for the scene at Montjouvain), Adrien Proust nevertheless had to submit to some form of social life, and particularly to the dinners which Marcel organized at home.

What is more, his private life was not without incident. As doctor to the Opéra-Comique, he received from the singer Marie Van Zandt, who was also the friend of Louis Weil, a photograph of her dressed as a man, with an inscription dated 23 October 1881.[140] Marcel, who inherited this photograph, may have used it as his inspiration for Odette in the role of Miss Sacripant painted by Elstir.[141] Did he not succumb to the temptations offered by his beautiful clients? In the model couple depicted by Le Masle, Adrien Proust's official biographer, who took his cue from Robert Proust (who himself . . .), one spouse was rather more 'model' than the other. Here, Robert Soupault displays the indulgence of a colleague, with some slightly contradictory remarks: 'The gossip was that he flitted around with ladies of easy virtue, and that one day, joking with one of his colleagues, he protested: "They're getting dreadful. Soon, we'll be expected to pay them." He was also supposed to have had some success with society ladies. This did not go far. There is no report of any conjugal incident. Mme Proust, a very sensible wife, did not notice, or did not wish to notice anything. Much later, Marcel said privately: "Maman never knew anything." But he was very much aware.'[142]

More surprising still, when Robert Proust, having reached the age of thirty, evinced a desire to marry, his father, with no regard for Mme Proust, made him wed the daughter of one of his lady friends. (Robert, imitating his father, kept an accredited mistress, Mme Fournier, for whom, it is said, he provided accommodation not far from where he worked, using Marcel, especially during the war years, as a messenger.) A scrap of paper, intended for Le Temps retrouvé, also describes Cottard's infidelity, which was discovered, after his death, by his wife; some letters revealed that her husband had always maintained a relationship at regular intervals with Odette (as did Adrien Proust with Laure Hayman); the Narrator thinks about consoling her: 'Since he cheated you, and since he went to so much trouble to hide it from you, it was because he was frightened of upsetting you, it was because he respected you and preferred you . . . In heaven, there is no one else but you whom he would wish to see again.'[143]

Professor Proust did not strike everyone in the same seductive light, however. André Germain, the son of the manager of the Crédit Lyonnais (and who was briefly married to Alphonse Daudet's daughter), was an unfair and unkind, but occasionally amusing observer, who recalled, in a text that is little known, the relationship of father and son: 'His father, so different to him – a decent, very common man, who, had he been more snobbish would have made him blush – was certainly loved by him.' At dinner at the Germains', 'he seemed really dull and insignificant'. One evening, after Robert had recovered unharmed from an accident, Adrien declared: 'Whereas my other son, my poor Marcel, is nearly always in a wretched state.' 'In the way in which the father had said "my poor Marcel", there was infinite pity and hopelessness.'[144] Adrien could be touching and attentive in his behaviour towards his son, as when he brought him his post in the mornings and announced triumphantly that there was a letter from Mme de Noailles.[145] He declared proudly to Montesquiou, 'Marcel is working at his cathedrals,' who in turn remarked to Marcel: 'In his eyes, the Middle Ages . . . only endured for your sake.'[146] This tender-hearted father did his best to contend with his son's 'bad habits' by sending him off to brothels, and he was not averse to discussing medical matters with him: in the case of a complaint that displayed physical symptoms, but whose origins were psychological, a visit to a quack doctor, recommended by Marcel, would cure the pain in twenty minutes, whereas his father's more classical and practical remedy would take two months.[147] Here, the son is closer to Du Boulbon, and the father to Cottard – for whom he is, among others, a model – in his scientistic realism and in his belief in the objective character of symptoms, illnesses and their treatments. Cottard treats the grandmother as Adrien Proust would have treated her; this is also why – though who, even today, can cure asthma? – he is unable to cure his son.[148]

Marcel's feelings for his father were thus complex[149] and fluctuating, and he could not release himself from his image except by enshrining him in his novels. In *Jean Santeuil*, M. Santeuil is an executive at the Ministry for Foreign Affairs. He feels obliged to display 'a peasant-like violence which a long life, heaped with honours, had not managed to eradicate'.[150] In his youth, 'the honours, those who were arrogant and biased, a pragmatism that was haughty and irrational [had been] the proud and harsh illusions of his life';[151] the quest for honours and his professional career took up his entire life, but, as he grew older, he discovered the gentleness and 'the melancholy idealism caused by the disillusions of reality among those souls who are too pragmatic'.[152] Did he find love? *Jean Santeuil* confirms that in this society (although this has been a constant from Marguerite of Navarre to Honoré de Balzac), 'a marriage of love, that is to say one brought about by love, would be considered a proof of vice'. 'I cannot leave this couple, whose union was not a matter of free choice, but the result of middle-class proprieties and middle-class notions of respectability, but who, none the less, will remain united until death.'[153] And, if Mme Santeuil is much more intelligent than her husband, if she has the cultured background, tact and sensitivity that is so absent in him, she is none the less 'convinced that all these virtues mattered little, since a man of her husband's superiority lacked nothing'.[154]

In *À la recherche du temps perdu*, the picture of the father is far less negative than in *Jean Santeuil*. An executive at the ministry (no doubt of Foreign Affairs; but no longer a lawyer), he was extremely well regarded in the higher spheres of government, yet though he led an honourable and detached life, he was unable to gain election to the Académie des Sciences Morales et Politiques.[155] From him, the Narrator inherits an apparent calmness and a sense of irony, which conceal the 'endless secret fury' and 'arbitrary impulses', and even his liking for meteorology.[156] It was during one of these sudden reversals that the hero's father permitted the mother to go to him in his room: 'And since then not an evening has passed without my confiding to him in my prayers the gratitude that I was unable to convey that evening.'[157] The Narrator nevertheless experiences the same paranoiac feelings towards his parents – 'that old longing to oppose an imaginary plot being hatched against me by my parents who assumed that I would be obliged to obey'.[158] It is not a matter of delving into the novels in order to recount an actual life, but of uncovering the novelist's attitude towards the person of his father. If, in *À la recherche du temps perdu*, the father is absolved from M. Santeuil's defects, it is because another hero-figure takes on certain of Doctor Proust's characteristics: Doctor Cottard. Not in his jokes, nor in the high society he keeps, but in his unfaithfulness to his wife, his death through overwork (which also resembles Bergotte's death, and, in the place in which it occurs, the grandmother's sudden attack in the public convenience), and particularly in his concept of medicine,[159] which differs from the psychosomatic notions of Du Boulbon: in his case the reliability of clinical diagnosis is combined with a disdain for psychological theories; for the latter, everything has to do with the nerves; for Cottard, nothing does. These two approaches persist still in modern medicine. There are further allusions, here and there, which remind one of Adrien Proust, such as this guarded reference (which also applies to Marcel's mother), to what Doctor Proust knew about his son's habits: 'There is probably no one, however virtuous he may be, who, through the complexity of circumstances, may not one day find himself liable to be living at close quarters with the very vice he has condemned so categorically.'* Marcel's father is therefore present throughout his work, almost as if the writer had, up until his death, carried on a conversation, consciously and unconsciously, with his parents. Marcel, too, was unwaveringly steadfast in his work, and lived only for himself; even in the amorous escapades, the publications (twenty-one volumes signed by Adrien Proust), the journeys (achieved by the one, dreamed of by the other), there is nothing in which one cannot trace the influence of the father. Finally, the subject of medicine is not present solely in the characters, or in the illnesses that feature in *À la recherche* – Proust's view of the world, of life and its passions, was also medical: everything is a matter of pathology, of symptoms, and every description becomes a diagnosis; nowhere more so than where love is concerned.

The father's research was useful to the son: they each studied a different complaint; for the latter, passion was an illness. Adrien Proust was a specialist in cholera and plague. This may be the reason why, when Marcel looks upon love as a disease, the causes of which are infinitesimal, he compares it with this other disease caused by the Virgule bacillus. Similarly, the doctor maintained that plague was spread by rats (Camus was influenced by Adrien Proust's book, *La Défense de l'Europe contre la peste*,[160] when he wrote *The Plague*: the novel, as we know, describes an invasion by rats), so it seems likely that this animal was mentioned at home, in his conversation, and even at table, in front of the little boy: the doctor's cultural background was such that he would not often have talked of much else apart from his work. A journalist who interviewed Adrien Proust bore witness to this preoccupation: 'The fear of rats, catching rats, is, as I always say, the first principle of anti-plague prophylaxis . . . Speaking

---

* *RTP*, vol. I, p. 146 (referring to M. Vinteuil and to his daughter). Cf. *JS*, p. 872: 'We cannot go anywhere near the most perverted beings without recognizing them as humans. And our sympathy for their humanity encourages our tolerance for their perversity.'

of which, would you like to see my lodgers? And there, in a row of jars, were an entire family of white mice, with pink noses.'[161] We shall come across rats and mice in Marcel's life as well as in his work.[162] The child focused and projected on to these paternal animals his anxieties, his obsessions and his lust for rebellion and destruction. Like all parents, his own inspired in him love as well as hatred, imitation and opposition, inspiration and the will to destroy. *Jean Santeuil* testifies to this unvoiced hostility, which, in *À la recherche du temps perdu*, was transformed into a feeling of guilt. Ever since Laius, all parents have given birth to children who feel guilty, but are innocent.

Roger Duchêne has published Adrien Proust's will,[163] in which he bequeathed 1,650,000 gold francs,[164] which represents approximately 27 million francs by 1990 standards.* His wealth was therefore considerable. It is accounted for by the fact that Professor Proust was at the height of his profession, and therefore had private patients. Among Parisian doctors it is estimated that in 1898 five to six of them earned between 200,000 to 300,000 francs a year, ten to fifteen earned from 100,000 to 150,000, and a hundred earned from 40,000 to 50,000 francs. Another survey, in 1901, reveals that forty doctors in Paris earned from 200,000 to 300,000; fifty earned 100,000 to 200,000 francs a year.[165] It is necessary to multiply these figures by 18.7 to calculate the equivalent in 1999 and one must remember that there was no tax on income or on capital. The deceased's last will and testament is given in two paragraphs: 'I appoint as my sole legatee, in fee simple, without any exception, my wife, Mme Jeanne Weil. The present legacy will be subject to the requirements of the law, but it will include the widest disposable portion permitted by the law whether in ownership or usufruct.' Given that the major share of the legacy was bequeathed to Mme Proust, Marcel (and his brother) immediately inherited a capital sum of 250,000 francs, the equivalent of 4,250,000 francs in 1990 terms.† His mother would not permit him to dispose of this capital, however, and would only allow him, as he wrote to a friend, 'a small pension'.

---

* This is according to the conversion table published by the Banque Transatlantique (April 1991). [Equivalent to approximately £2,725,000 in 1999. *Tr.*]

† Equivalent to about £420,750 in 1999. *Tr.*

CHAPTER II

Childhood

Once we have made use of *Jean Santeuil* and *Du côté de chez Swann*, and later, *À l'ombre des jeunes filles en fleurs*, there is very little else that is known about Marcel Proust's childhood. In fact, we have at our disposal neither autobiography, such as those books which Proust loved, like *Le Livre de mon ami*, *Le Roman d'un enfant*, and *Le Petit Chose* (in which one should not underestimate the part played by fiction), nor family documents. Whole years passed before correspondence was to fill the void. We know that Marcel was born on 10 July 1871 at Auteuil. He was baptized on 5 August of the same year; his godfather was Eugène Mutiaux, of 66 rue d'Hautcville, his godmother, Marie-Hélène Houette, of 39 Boulevard Malesherbes. One lonely evening in July 1916, while Proust was rummaging through drawers in a little drawing-room he hardly ever used, he found, hidden among old visiting cards, his father's decorations and a list of names of those who had sent flowers for his burial, his own certificates of baptism and of his first communion at Saint-Louis-d'Antin.[1]

One event did occur, when Marcel was two years old, whose repercussions cannot be underestimated, and which have, in fact, been assessed very differently: the birth of his brother Robert (Robert Sigismond Léon), on 24 May at Auteuil.

Others, by supposition and without any evidence, have maintained that Robert's birth affected his brother traumatically and that his jealousy was aroused, and all the more dangerously so because he was unaware of it (had he been aware, in fact, we would have had proofs of it).[2] The two brothers were actually brought up in the same way and were attired similarly, as we can see from the succession of family photographs, in accordance with the fashions of the day, in dresses (1876) and in kilts, in leggings and a large bow, or, with their mother sitting between them, in frock coats (about 1896). The resemblance is all the more striking the younger they are: the same fine eyes, the same forehead and nose (later

Marcel's would show where it was broken). Robert's face is very slightly heavier and wider. From adolescence onwards, the differences are more marked, one being more vigorous, sportsmanlike and thick-set, the other frailer and almost evanescent. Marcel Proust twice reminisced about his brother, once in an article about a concert ('Un dimanche') and also, in 1908, in the fictional essay which precedes *Contre Sainte-Beuve*, the manuscript of which is now lost: 'His hair had been curled just like that of the concierge's children when they are about to be photographed, his full face was framed by a helmet of full, black hair decorated with large bows like the butterflies in one of Velázquez's infantas; I looked at him with the smile of an older child for a brother he loves, a smile in which one does not really know whether there is more admiration, ironic superiority or affection.'[3] Robert, still wearing a dress, must have been less than seven years old, he was 'five and a half';[4] he evinced the same sensitivity as did Marcel when confronted with separation (in this case it was his baby goat that he was leaving behind), but, more outwardly violent, he veers from affection to anger or to the sort of jealousy that every child experiences: 'Marcel's had more chocolate cream than me.'[5] We should remember that Marcel, however much he may have looked upon his brother with the superiority of someone who was older, showed him both admiration and affection. As children, both brothers read the same books.[6] As an adolescent, Robert read Marcel's letters home, just as his mother did,[7] and she would write back to him, while he was doing his military service, providing him with the fullest details of everything his brother said and did, and all his scholastic activities.[8]

So it was that one Sunday in summer, at Auteuil, when the Prousts had invited their friends the Duplays to dinner, Robert, who had gone boating on the Grenouillière, was late, much to his mother's consternation; she was extremely displeased with this bad behaviour. At table, Professor Proust, ever the optimist, was smiling. Marcel, on the other hand, was upset because of his brother's absence and his mother's anxiety. When Robert appeared at the end of dinner, his mother refused to kiss him. Marcel pretended he was not feeling well and indicated to his brother to follow him out of the room. Mme Proust went to see what was the matter, and, ten minutes later, returned to the table with Robert; a reconciliation had taken place, thanks to the elder son cleverly engineering a temporary indisposition.[9] This incident reveals Marcel's affectionate nature and shows how, far from exploiting his brother's misdemeanour, he could not bear any lack of harmony within the family.[10]

Furthermore, in 1887, their grandmother testified to their 'perfect understanding'. The elder boy praised his younger brother to their mother: 'Dick really is a treasure, both morally as well as intellectually and physically.'[11] We can see why Marcel, quoting Corneille, should have dedicated *Les Plaisirs et les Jours* to Robert: 'O brother more dear than daylight.'[12] Robert's engrossing studies, the fact that he succeeded brilliantly in his medical examinations, together with his sports (cycling, boating, motoring) and his sentimental activities (his mother reproached him for not visiting Rheims cathedral when he was doing his military service there)[13] meant that he lived a very different life to Marcel. But this did not lead to tension, a lessening in their affection for one another, or quarrels. Both brothers shared the same opinions about Dreyfus's innocence and demonstrated the same patriotism during the First World War, and it was to Robert that Marcel appealed for help in obtaining the Légion d'Honneur, he whom he asked to pin the cross of the Légion on him in 1921, and who was with him on the day of his death. We can therefore appreciate the truth of the lines written by Robert Proust in *Hommage à Marcel Proust* published by the Nouvelle Revue Française in 1925: 'As far back in my recollections of childhood at that period, when one's earliest memories begin to crystalize, I constantly have before me the image of my brother watching over me with a sweetness that is infinite, enveloping and, so to speak, maternal . . . For me he always had the fraternal and watchful attitude of an older person, but additionally I sensed in him traces of our dear departed ones and up until the last he always remained for me much more than the guardian of these mental relics; he was my entire past; my whole youth was locked away inside his unique personality.'[14] There is no sense of aggression, no regret, no revenge in these comments of a sibling who loved his own brother so tenderly. Just as in their photographs, which juxtapose them at different ages during their lives, Marcel and Robert Proust stood side by side, in heart and mind. After Marcel's death, Robert supervised the publication of his work, and corrected certain documents, notably *Albertine disparue*,[15] as if he were the author.

We may pay too much heed to the unconscious; but what is the unconscious if it does not reveal itself? We are reduced to the reasoning of probability: 'he could not have had . . .' Some have gone so far as to attribute Marcel's first asthma attack, at the age of nine, to the fact that his brother was no longer being dressed in child's clothing, thus passing from the stage of 'little girl' to that of a boy, 'a redoubtable rival in the conquest of maternal affection'.[16] These children's clothes, quite customary dress at the period, no more suggested that their wearer was a girl than a Scotsman's kilt means that he is a woman.

Another argument is more serious: if Proust bore no resentment for his brother, he would have excluded him from his work. One might reply that the brother of the Narrator is the only character not needed in *À la recherche du temps perdu*. The Narrator's parents, already removed from 'Autour de Madame Swann' onwards, and so much in the way in *La Prisonnière* that they are packed off on a journey, are anterior to the action of the book, which is the discovery of a literary vocation. A brother, who is a contemporary, but neither an artist nor someone in society, would not have had any role to play in this scenario. We can see already, in *Jean Santeuil*, how the pages devoted to the staff-room at the Pitié appear as an hors-d'œuvre.[17] The experience would have been enough for Proust, who was unable to finish *Jean Santeuil* precisely because he was bogged down in autobiographical detail that was too disparate. Finally, had Robert Proust been introduced into the work, he would have been a key, or '*clé*' that would have been difficult to hide. And if he disappeared from the drafts of 'Combray', it was in order to render the evening solitude still more dramatic.

THE CURLS

Another episode must rank among Proust's first – perhaps his earliest – memories: it concerns the little Marcel of those early years, all adorned in curls. Until now, this has gone unnoticed, only mentioned, as if in passing, in a few lines in 'Combray'.[18] It is the 'dread' of being pulled by his curls, that Proust described in several successive rough drafts of 'Combray', his very persistence providing proof of the terrifying nature of the fantasy: 'Our priest crept up stealthily behind me to pull me by my curls, something which had been the terror and torture of my childhood.' The priest is substituted here by an uncle, there by a great-uncle. The sensation remained, only disappearing, wrote Proust, using a revealing term because it was inappropriate, once 'the organ which had been the seat of the pain' had been removed.[19] Quite clearly, there was something appalling about this torment, which is referred to again and again, with further details being added, and which was of greater importance than many of the biographical events that are known: 'I could feel in my curls, which brushed my ears, the dread of their being pulled, I wanted to escape, I couldn't, and there he was, pulling at them, it was less unbearable than I had imagined, but it was still very painful and it was going to start again.' It was not fear of pain in this case, but the loss of an organ, and peace could only be restored once it had gone for good; yet the curls being shorn did not prevent the agony recurring. What is this agony, a transference of Samson's[20] hair, if not the fear of castration? The source of so many other agonies, it is the world of 'the old law': 'In actual fact, it may have been replaced by other sufferings and other fears, but the axis of the world had been shifted.'[21] Replaced? No, since it could be recalled by sleep and because narrating it meant recounting it, terror was always lurking, in a nightmare, in a memory, in a sentence.

Was not the little boy's sensitivity, his fragility, his affection even for his parents and grandparents, put sternly to the test by a nineteenth-century education? A letter from Marcel, written to his grandfather on 2 April 1879, testifies to this: 'My dear grandfather, Forgive me for my sin for I've eaten less than I normally do I cried for a quarter of an hour and after that I was sobbing. I ask your Forgiveness. Forgive me father who should be honoured and respected by everyone.'* It is likely that Nathé Weil and his brother would have exercised the authority of a father who was frequently absent, thus reinforcing a tendency for feelings of guilt in their young relative.

THE EVENING KISS

No letter or external document exists that describes the bedtime scene in *Du coté de chez Swann*, to which so much importance is attached that both the surrender of the parents and the Narrator's lack of willpower are attributed to it. The drafts, however, demand that we refer to the frequently auto biographical document that is *Jean Santeuil*. This does not mean that we should fill the lacunae in our documentation by borrowing from fiction, nor relate again a celebrated scene which Proust describes so much better. Starting with clues, rather than certainties, the fact that there are so many thematic repetitions provides proof of a mental structure that we cannot ignore.

Jean Santeuil is seven when the scene takes place.[22] But does it take place only once? The novelist must have had to draw together and dramatize in one unique scene a moment which was often repeated, perhaps at Illiers, definitely at Auteuil[23] (according to the description in *Jean Santeuil* and the reference to 'Combray' as the house which no longer

---

* *Corr.* vol. XXI, p. 539. (Marcel was seven and a half years old at this time and his French has all the charm of a child's spelling. *Tr.*)

existed). 'For Jean, going to bed each day constituted a truly tragic moment that was all the more cruel for the vague sense of horror it inspired.' Jean experienced this agony every evening, 'the horrible, indefinable pain which would gradually grow into something immense like solitude, silence and the night'. His mother soothed his suffering with her kiss 'which immediately vanquished all anxiety as well as his insomnia'. The drama occurred when his mother, who was entertaining not Swann, but Doctor Surlande, did not come upstairs to kiss her son. The child, after a vain attempt to persuade the servant Augustin (as later Françoise) to fetch his mother, calls her from the window. She comes up, and the child loses control of himself, torn between feelings of guilt and longing, 'now making use of the violence that remorse was turning against himself'. For the mother, it is a 'step back-wards' to the tension of earlier years (which proves that this must have occurred frequently). Against all expectations, it is not the doctor, but Jean who takes these torments seriously, and his mother's words ('He suffers from his nerves') have a profound influence on his life: it is because his suffering was attributed, in the course of rational conversation, not to a weakness of will, but to 'an involuntary nervous condition', not to a fault to be overcome, but to an illness, not to willpower, but to the unconscious. The imagery of *Jean Santeuil* certainly suggests that ageless monster, that ubiquitous receptacle that is the unconscious: 'His childhood moved rest-lessly in the depths of a well of sadness from which nothing could yet help him to escape and which no notion of the cause of his gloom could illuminate. Furthermore, it was only much later that he knew the causes, and then only the secondary ones, for the basic cause always seemed to him so inseparable from himself that he could only get rid of his sadness by renouncing his own personality.'[24] The child, therefore, experienced 'nervous' illness at the age of seven (though he was ill before), before suffering from asthma, and had always been haunted by a terror, or neurosis, of being abandoned. He fought against it all his life, helped by the presence of his family, his servants, his friends or secretaries, and by his housekeepers: Marcel was a recluse who was unable to live alone. The crucial scene of *À la recherche* stemmed from something which, far from being unique, as in a work of art, happened repeatedly with all the dreary banality of life.

This is confirmed by a letter that Marcel wrote to Maurice Barrès in January 1906, after Mme Proust's death: 'Our entire life has been but a preparation, hers to teach me how to manage without her when the time came for her to leave me, and so it has been ever since childhood, when she refused to come back over and over again to say goodnight to me before going out for the evening, when she left me in the country and I watched the train carry her away, and, later on, at Fontainebleau,[25] and even this summer when she went to Saint-Cloud, I would find any excuse to telephone her – at all hours of the day. These worries which might be defused by a few words spoken over the telephone, or by her visit to Paris, or a kiss, how powerfully they afflict me now when I know that nothing can ever allay them.'[26] This letter confirms that the scene was repeated in several places: a departure, a return home that has been declined or accepted, a kiss or 'a few words'. It is a pity that this heartrending admission should have been made to an author who behaved with so little friendship and so little kindness towards Proust. In contrast, the scenes of the night-time reading definitely took place at Auteuil: in 1901, when he was paying his condolences to the Princesse de Polignac, Marcel wrote: 'She made me think back to how weary you were, my dearest little Maman, when you sat close to me at night at Auteuil, when she told me about the nights she had spent with her husband and how they chatted about Mark Twain at three o'clock in the morning.'[27]

AT THE CHAMPS-ÉLYSÉES

Families that lived in the eighth *arrondissement* of Paris used to send their children – and still do – to play in the Parc Monceau or in the Champs-Élysées, accompanied, at that time, by their nannies. Marcel Proust was taken to the Champs-Élysées; it was there, on 1 May 1880, that he fell down and broke his nose; 'He despaired elegantly,' wrote Fernand Gregh, 'of a slight lump on the bridge of his nose'[28] (it is possible that this fall may have caused breathing difficulties and induced the asthma which occurred at about this time). There are few traces of this accident in the photographs, and none in his writings. Near the Théâtre des Ambassadeurs and L'Alcazar,* by a fountain with bronze nymphs there was a large lawn with carousels; in summer Marcel came here every day to play, or to talk to those children who were prepared to listen to him, for he was already 'reciting poems to everyone'.[29] A little boy who used to play with him has told us that he was gripped with fear when he felt

---

* Les Ambassadeurs and L'Alcazar were two *café-concerts* at this period, from which snatches of music could be heard: 'Marcel told me that he had constructed in his imagination idealized *café-concert* shows, with all those tunes and those fleeting visions' (M. Duplay, *Mon ami Marcel Proust*, Gallimard, 1972, p. 8). Marcel's love of music-hall may date from this time.

Marcel take him by the hand and tell him all about his needs 'in an all-enveloping and tyrannical way'.[30] Later, we shall come across these intransigent pacts of friendship, with Reynaldo Hahn and with Antoine Bibesco. At this time he was still interested in little girls, he thought he could fall in love, even if it meant talking only about literature to them. Although he was unable to recognize Gilberte Swann among them, Robert Dreyfus remembered 'two sisters, tall, elegant and beautiful, the eldest of whom, in particular, of foreign origin and very much from high society, prompted a passionate predilection in the tender Marcel'. This is identical to the scene in *Jean Santeuil*: 'A young Russian girl with a mass of black hair, bright teasing eyes and rosy cheeks, and who glowed with that health, that life, that joyfulness that were so lacking in Jean', used to come every day with her governess and her sister.[31] In the early novel, the two sisters retain their home in the rue de Chaillot, and their actual first names, Marie and Nelly. The name Kossichef disguises that of Benardaky. Their father, Nicolas de Benardaky, was born in St Petersburg in 1838; a former master of ceremonies at the Russian court, he had two daughters from his marriage to Marie de Lebrock: the first, Marie, would marry Prince Michel Radziwill, the second, Nelly, the Vicomte de Contades. Benardaky lived at 65 rue de Chaillot and he was to write humorous books illustrated by Caran d'Ache (*À la découverte de la Russie*, 1895; *Le Prince de Kozamakoff*, 1896; *Théâtre de famille*, 1898). He was a collector of Chinese, Sèvres and Saxe porcelain, of silverware and antique furniture, tapestries, snuff-boxes and miniatures; one could probably find the same *objets d'art* at his home as could be found at Swann's. He did not belong to the Jockey Club, but he was a member of the Automobile-Club and the Polo.[32] Mme Nicolas de Benardaky, whose 'immense wealth and life of pleasure' Proust described, and who was the sister-in-law of both the Comtesse Vera de Talleyrand and Ambassador Nisard, aroused much admiration in society gatherings. She created a particular stir at a fancy-dress ball held at the Cernuschi's *hôtel particulier*, where she appeared at midnight, disguised as a Valkyrie; Paul Nadar photographed her in this costume.[33]

In a letter to Antoinette Faure, Proust described Marie de Benardaky in the Champs-Élysées at the age of sixteen, as 'very pretty and more and more exuberant',* which goes to show that one reached puberty later

---

* Corr., vol. I, p. 99, 15 July 1887. Cf., however, *Chroniques*, p. 100, article from *Le Figaro* (1912): 'When I was twelve, I played in the Champs-Élysées with a girl whom I loved, whom I have never seen again, who is married, who is the mother of a family and whose name I saw the other day

than one does today. The following year, he would have other affections, but he would write that Marie was 'the exhilaration and despair of [his] childhood'.[34] Marie's and Marcel's parents were to put an end to this sentimental intrigue; in his case, at least, they would live to regret it. Antoinette Faure and her sister Lucie, daughters of Félix Faure, the future President of the Republic, were part of the group of girls with whom Marcel mixed in the Champs-Élysées, where he went 'almost every day'.[35] Lucie became a writer (*Newman*, 1900; *Les Femmes dans l'œuvre de Dante*, 1902) and married the historian Georges Goyau, later to be a member of the Académie française. Also to be seen there were Gabrielle Schwartz and Jeanne Pouquet, the future wife of Gaston de Caillavet.

We can still glimpse Marcel as he was, in the Champs-Élysées, in the years that marked the end of childhood and of adolescence, thanks to the testimony of Robert Dreyfus: 'An exceptional person, a child of eccentric and giddy precocity, he delighted his often much rougher little friends, and he rather amazed them. But the ones he astonished even more were those of a more respectable age: they were unanimous in marvelling at his sophisticated manners, his graceful gentleness, his complexity and kindness. Yes, I can see him now, handsome and very timid, swathed in woollen clothing, rushing up to ladies old or young, bowing as they passed, and always finding the words to touch their heart.'[36] Marcel did his best to introduce Dreyfus to Racine, Hugo, Musset, Lamartine, Baudelaire and Leconte de Lisle, as well as to the art of Mounet-Sully or Sarah Bernhardt. In this Champs-Élysées group, which comprised future scholars, industrialists, doctors, engineers or diplomats, and which was thus very representative of the upper echelons of the bourgeoisie at the time of the Third Republic, there were already the makings of a veritable little literary gathering. Just as at the Lycée Condorcet, it was those destined for literary careers who were the most numerous: Jean de Tinan, who died at the age of eighty, Louis de La Salle, who would remain Proust's friend and would be killed in the war, and Dreyfus himself. For the time being, they gossiped. Marcel displayed such a precocious conversational facility that one day, on the top deck of a bus, Mme Catusse, a close friend of his mother's, berated him: 'Are you going to speak like that all the time?' Thirty years later, he would still remember this.[37]

Marcel Proust declared his adolescent tastes in the answers he gave to

---

among the subscribers to *Le Figaro*.' Cf. *Corr.*, vol. XVIII, p. 288, dedication of *À l'ombre des jeunes filles en fleurs* to R. Dreyfus.

a questionnaire in Antoinette Faure's album or keepsake book. These written questionnaires were very much in vogue at the time; one asked one's friends to complete them:[38] those that have been recovered provide valuable information as to the sensibilities of an age, a milieu or an individual. The first questionnaire Proust filled in must have been between the ages of thirteen, as has frequently been stated, and fifteen: it was actually during the autumn of 1886 that Marcel read Augustin Thierry,[39] who is quoted twice. Antoinette Faure's album is entitled *Confessions* and has the sub-title [in English] '*An album to record thoughts, feelings etc.*'. The aim of most of the questions is to elicit a self-portrait without the person who replies to them being aware of this. That is why they are concerned with virtues and faults, tastes, occupations, the passions, relationships with men and with women, and finally, the meaning of life. Marcel's responses are as significant for what they say as for what they omit. Thus for moral qualities (energy, virtuousness, working hard) he substitutes intellectual virtues (intelligence) and psychological attitudes (gentleness, idealism). The adolescent boy's favourite occupations are: 'reading, day-dreaming, poetry, history, theatre'. The young Marcel had already developed a taste for theatre as he stood dreaming in front of the *Morris column**** on the Boulevard Malesherbes which advertised *Le Demi-monde* (1882) by Dumas *fils*, for example, or *Phèdre*† and *Les Caprices de Marianne* at the Comédie-Française.[40] His notion of unhappiness betrayed a secret torment, a permanent fixation and a perpetual child-like aspect, in what was both a sort of cry, and a confession: 'To be separated from Mother.' The need to be included in the family circle or among a community of friends is revealed in his idea of happiness: 'To live close to all those I love, to be among the delights of the countryside, with lots of books and music scores, and not far from the Théâtre-Français.' It is the world of Illiers, Auteuil and the eighth *arrondissement*, which we encounter in *Jean Santeuil* and in 'Combray'. Curiously, nowhere did Proust mention the hawthorn as his favourite flower. His literary tastes mirrored those of his grandmother: George Sand, Augustin Thierry (whom he read with fervour, and quoted in 'Combray'), or the sentimental love of his adolescence: Musset. He would come to enjoy more demanding or more important

---

* The name for the pillars used in Paris streets to advertise forthcoming attractions. *Tr.*

† The performances of *Phèdre* by Sarah Bernhardt, which inspired those given by Berma, were the gala at the Opéra on 19 May 1892 and, in particular, the series of performances at the Théâtre de la Renaissance, from 19 November 1893 (*RTP*, vol. I, p. 992, n. 1, and p. 1320).

authors, but he had direct experience of the ones he mentioned and he did not wish to appear better read than he was. What he had to say about women revealed an idealization which would prove to be dangerous: as his favourite type of heroine, he desired 'a woman of genius who lived the life of an ordinary woman'; either he was thinking of his mother, or else he could not think of any name to put down. The same went for fiction: 'Those who manage to be more than women but still retain their own sex.' As for femininity, it was 'all that is tender, poetical, pure and beautiful in every species'. Here Proust was preparing the way for what was to be a lifelong admiration for women – Mme Straus, the Comtesse Greffulhe, the Comtesse de Chevigné, the Princesse Soutzo – without ever touching them, and for his quest for femininity among young men. On the other hand, one might wonder why he should 'have very much liked to be Pliny the Younger':* Was it because the author was on the curriculum for fourth- (or second-) year studies? Because he was a tireless letter writer, like all the Weil-Proust family? Was it to do with the cult of virile friendships, for Trajan, Tacitus and others, which probably aroused a yearning in the polymorphous adolescent? Or because he was the perfect nephew, protected by a shadowy uncle? His celebrated response to the question 'For what fault have you most toleration?': 'For the private life of geniuses', contains the whole of *Contre Sainte-Beuve* in six words. It is a premonition, a confession, a manifesto, an aesthetic.

ONANISM

Another adolescent attraction is revealed in rough drafts and in certain pages of *Jean Santeuil* in a way that is at once discreet and haunting, as transgressions in the private life of the future 'genius': 'Sometimes a schoolboy could be seen with a girl in a boat that had been moored. He had just discovered within himself the wondrous essence of a pleasure that was as new, as delightful, and so entirely unlike any ordinary earthly pleasure, as was the lilac or the dark orris-root, a pleasure that the warm sun seemed to stimulate still more, and which also seemed to bestow life with something eternally sweet which had not been there before.'[41] Here we can see that if the girl is the cause of the pleasure, she is not its

---

* The Latin author would only be mentioned once in *À la recherche du temps perdu*, juxtaposed humorously with the name of Mme de Simiane, in reference to the letters written by the Guermantes ladies, based on those of the Gramonts or the Greffulhes (*RTP*, vol. II, p. 737).

instrument; that the boy does not experience any feelings of guilt, and finally that the solitary pleasure is associated with the scent of lilac and orris-root, as it would be in 'Combray'. In *À la recherche*, these flowers always exude a special charm, which comes from their early association with the awakening of adolescent sexuality. This 'first pleasure', 'for at the age when love is not yet known one is only concerned with oneself', took place according to Proust in 'the fifteenth year', and he saw it initially as being detached from the idea of a woman; it is afterwards that one associates it with her, and that one imagines her to be the cause: 'You want to believe that you are not alone, that you are in her arms, for one does not seek this solitary pleasure for oneself.'[42] In a further draft, this innocence is lost: in a room in which there are strings of orris-seed, with shoots of young lilac growing through the window, the hero, who is twelve years old, is examining himself, 'in search of a pleasure'[43] that is unknown. But he feels so upset and frightened that it is as if he is performing a surgical operation on himself: 'I felt as if I was going to die at any moment.' At the same time, heightened by pleasure, his thoughts are 'more vast, more powerful' than the universe: 'At last an opal stream spurted out, in successive bursts, like the moment the [Hubert Robert] fountain at Saint-Cloud gushes forth.' The silvery stream represents at once the opposite of 'natural life' and the devil.[44] What we find here, therefore, is a strong sense of guilt that is associated with pleasure and in which there is no female image.

There are various indications and testimonies that lead us to believe that masturbation remained Proust's principal sexual pastime until the end of his life. The notion that sexuality is equated with loss had been turned into a collective fantasy by Doctor Tissot in his treatise *L'Onanisme. Dissertations produites par la masturbation* (1760): 'Frequent emissions of semen can have a loosening, withering, weakening and enervating effect, and produce all sorts of harm.'[45] Nineteenth-century medical literature, which associated it with neurasthenia, not to say homosexuality, and indeed as a dangerous habit, added weight to the adolescent boy's sense of 'fear', which he described, just as the religious writers, for whom it was a mortal sin, had increased his feeling of guilt – from which Gide also suffered, and which he described in his *Journal*. When he revised 'Combray', Proust amended his text and left 'in the little room that smelt of orris-root' no more than a scant mention of 'sensual pleasure'.[46] The lilac-blossom, that is always 'lingering and invisible' in the memory, and which is a witness to his masturbation (which may occur more frequently in springtime), is associated with his asthma attacks: despite the cauterizations of his nose, Marcel is taken back to Paris, 'with the appearance of the first lilac', with 'his hands and feet the colour of violet, like a drowned man'.[47]

Professor Proust sought to dissuade his son from such habits by sending him to houses of ill-repute. That was why, one day in 1888, Marcel urgently begged thirteen francs from his grandfather: 'This is the reason. I needed to see a woman so badly in order to cure my bad habit of masturbation that papa gave me 10 francs to go to the brothel, but 1st in my turmoil I broke a chamber pot, 3 francs, 2nd in all this same turmoil I was unable to fuck. So there I was just as I was before needing 10 francs more to release myself and these further 3 francs for the pot. But I dare not ask papa for money so soon and I was hoping that you would come to my aid in circumstances which as you know are not only exceptional but still more *unique*.'[48] So the cure proved to be fruitless, but on several occasions Marcel resorted to blackmail over masturbation: another time, his father begged him 'to stop masturbating for at least four days'[49] at the very moment that his mother had forbidden him to see Jacques Bizet. Daniel Halévy remarked: 'Poor Proust. Gifted as nobody else: there he was overtaxing himself. Weak, young, he indulged in coitus, masturbation, perhaps pederasty!' Since it is the only sexual act that the Narrator is made to perform in any precise way, one may wonder if it was not the only one that Proust, too, enclosed within his solitude, ever experienced. His visits to houses of ill-repute scarcely brought him much satisfaction.

THE UNDERWORLD OF THE SWIMMING POOL

The act of writing preserves, it imprisons, it releases. A childhood is only ever relived in flashes, all the more painful particularly because they are rare. Among those moments that Proust entrusted to the pages of *Jean Santeuil*, and to *Albertine disparue* twenty years later, are his visits to the Deligny baths. There, the real world tipped over into unreality. A fantastical place, where the dark, sunless water appeared to be communicating 'with invisible depths covered with human bodies in trunks',[50] it seemed to him like the entry to the underworld and to the glacial seas. That is why it provoked a 'mixture of fear and disgust' in him. In *Jean Santeuil* (but not in *Albertine disparue* for, in the meantime, Mme Proust had died), this terrifying image is redeemed by the appearance of the mother in her swimming costume, as if by the birth of Venus: a person could thus return from the deep waters, and this person was his mother: 'Seeing his mother playing and laughing there [Jean thinks], blowing him kisses and coming back looking beautiful in her shiny, little rubber cap, it would not have surprised him to be told that he was the son of a goddess.'[51] However, once his mother had died, Marcel was left alone with the memory of the infernal swimming pool, which became the basin of the Arsenal, in the Venice of *Albertine disparue*, that is deserted by the mother. Yet is there not something else behind this image of Mme Santeuil emerging from the waves like Venus and playing there like a siren, that Proust should censor her and eliminate her from his revised version? The biography of a book goes deeper than that of a life. A passage from *Albertine disparue* tells us that Venus is in fact nothing more than 'Jupiter's desire'.[52] The mother-Aphrodite, who is seen almost naked, through a kind of trans-gression similar to that of the 'primitive scene', but on her own, without any partner other than the young spectator, offers herself to his desires. The infernal sea, which has brought about this impulse one moment, quickly engulfs it the next; all that remains of the memory of the swimming pool is the terrifying entrance to the subterranean world, to the 'river of the six-fold recesses', the exploration of which involves his dreams, a return to Book XI of *The Odyssey*, Book VI of *The Aeneid*, and Book IV of *The Georgics*. And the water from the swimming pool, in which the novelist, who was so unathletic, never swam, returned to haunt him, like a sign of guilt; this too was merely his desire, which remained forever guilty, which was always punished, always resurgent. It is significant that in the one and only line describing the very different swimming pool in which the father swims, it does not arouse any such reverie.[53]

THE FIRST ATTACK OF ASTHMA

If he played in the Champs-Élysées, the child could not have been very ill. Yet, from the age of nine, Marcel suffered from an illness that was both well known and mysterious, and which would accelerate, if not cause, his premature death: asthma. One day in 1881, probably in the springtime (Marcel would be ten in July), after a long walk in the Bois de Boulogne with his parents and Professor Duplay (a professor of medicine) and his family (his son Maurice remained a friend of Proust's), 'Marcel,' Robert related, 'was struck by a frightening spasm of suffocation which, with my terrified father watching, almost proved to be fatal.'[54] Marcel appears to have suffered from a severe attack of hay fever, or a sudden cold, and had developed an allergy to pollen and spring flowers, and eventually to the countryside (to which he returned, however, one last time as an adolescent in 1886, when his parents went to settle Aunt Amiot's inheritance), if not to Auteuil. It was the attacks, not the patient, that were temperamental: the same causes did not always produce the same effects.

This disease, which is characterized by suffocated breathing, is caused in part by a deficiency in the immune system. Interpretations differ on this point. It has always been fashionable to attribute psychological causes (in Marcel's case, his jealousy of his brother, the longing to be loved by his mother and to have her near him). In our own time, with the development of research into allergies, the causes are thought to be organic, and are ascribed to congenital deficiencies. Patients are no longer treated by psychoanalysis, but with cortisone. From an objective, physiological view-point, the patient, who may be deeply worried by the illness and suffers from the attacks (which may even kill him), can develop psychological symptoms: anxiety, need for affection, fear of being alone, nervous tension. In the event of setbacks or sometimes through emotional blackmail, the patient can even provoke the attacks himself; but the development is secondary, it is not the prime cause. Marcel did not wish to be an invalid; he was obliged to accept his illness. Only someone who has never had asthma could think that the advantages outweigh the inconveniences. Proust only once described one of his attacks in his literary output, and that was in 'L'Indifférent', a story which he preferred to consign to a magazine and not to republish in *Les Plaisirs et les Jours*: 'A child who from birth has been able to breathe without thinking about it does not know how essential to life is the air, which he is not even aware of, that fills his breast so sweetly. Has he, in a bout of fever, or a convulsion, just been suffocating? In the desperate efforts he makes, he is struggling, with his entire being, for his life, for his lost tranquillity, which can only be restored to him with the air from which he never knew he could be separated.'[55] In 1921, Marcel would describe how, as a sufferer from 'hay asthma', he had undergone 110 nasal cauterizations to destroy the nose's erectile tissue and counteract pollen.[56]

From *cinquième** onwards, Marcel was absent more often in the third term than during any other: it was the period of springtime allergies. In *première*,† and in the philosophy class, no mention is made of this: he and his family must have hoped that the disease would disappear, as is often

* Second form, or seventh grade. *Tr.*
† Lower sixth, or eleventh grade. *Tr.*

the case, at puberty. Between 1886 and 1895, the patient had a remission. This was fortunate, for from what he could read about it in his father's library (Jaccoud's forty-volume dictionary, with an article on asthma by Germain See[57]), Marcel was given little hope of any efficacious remedy. A specialist, Professor Brissaud (who was the main acknowledged model for Du Boulbon), whom Marcel consulted, wrote: 'The patient, in many respects, knows what is good and what is bad for him. His experience is at least as good as our own, and we would be wise to acknowledge this.'[58] This was why, having consulted all the top specialists and having undergone all existing treatments, Marcel eventually relied on his own remedies: this was the reason that he lived in a closeted room so as to protect himself from allergies, pollen and dust, why it was forbidden to shake the rugs, and why he preferred spending time at the seaside. When he went to stay with the Daudets, at Amboise, it was for one night; with the Clermont-Tonnerres, at Glisolles, it was also at night-time, so that he could see the roses in Agostinelli's headlights. When he went to see the Bois de Boulogne again, so as to complete the walk which now ends *Du côté de chez Swann*, it was in a closed car. When he visited Laurent's, on the Champs-Élysées, on the tracks of Laure Hayman and his uncle Louis Weil, it was with a silk scarf over his nose.[59]

CHILDHOOD READING

Biographers often forget that in a writer's life the books that he or she has read may be more important than the people they have met; they may tell us everything there is to know about some chance hostess, yet nothing about Racine or Balzac. It is true that Proust's references to his childhood reading were extremely rare and tucked away in the fold of a letter or in a page of a novel. Thus, on the subject of Mme Swann's winter garden, the Narrator recalls 'the New Year present of books by P.-J. Stahl'[60] (the pseudonym of the publisher Hetzel) and Mlle Lili, the heroine of certain of his works. She is given a miniature greenhouse, the sight of which delights the reader as much as if it were his own. Now that he is old, he wonders whether 'in those blessed years winter was not the most beautiful of seasons'.[61] In the Champs-Élysées, Mlle Lili, like Gilberte, plays tag and shares her sweets with her friends. No mention is made of the Comtesse de Ségur. *Sodome et Gomorrhe* describes 'the rapt and excited air of a child reading a novel by Jules Verne' (as Aimé waits for a tip).[62] Marcel may have read *Voyages extraordinaires*, for he and his brother had read an imitation of it entitled *Les Voyages imaginaires*, and he derived his 'greatest delight' from *Tour du monde, Nouveau Journal des voyages* (1860–94).[63] Concerning one of Jules Verne's masters, Edgar Allan Poe, he wrote: 'Even his straightforward adventure books such as Arthur Gordon Pym remain, in the desolation of my life, one of the blessings of memory.'[64]

Proust was eight years old when he read a book that he would never forget, Alfred de Musset's *Histoire d'un merle blanc*: 'Alfred de Musset's *Merle blanc* was my favourite reading as a child and those words about the rose and the scarab were the daily litanies, misunderstood but adored, of my eighth year.'[65] What must have so moved the child was the anguish of being abandoned that pervades the story. The subject is the unhappy fate of an unusual blackbird who is mistreated by his father and flies away; he writes his memoirs, then abandons literature in order to take refuge in the countryside.

In his article 'On reading' (*La Renaissance latine*, 1905), Proust recalled Théophile Gautier's *Le Capitaine Fracasse*. In his unpublished novel, *Jean Santeuil*, he had already, ten years earlier, described how much he owed to it,[66] and what he later disliked about it. Our feelings for books follow on from one to another, as do our love affairs, expressing the same desire. One observes, with some surprise, that what the child liked in Gautier were not the adventures, but his sentences which, as with those of Anatole France's later on, were among the most beautiful he knew: 'Perhaps those phrases would sound extremely mediocre in his ears now', but at that time, the adolescent boy discovered a feeling of beauty in them that corresponded to the feelings in his own heart. To judge from the amount of thought he lavished on it, the book was also an 'oracle which one would like to consult about everything'. The emotions we experience at an early age are more powerful than those we experience later, and are not dependent on a general understanding of the plot, the characters or the action, about which we can easily be mistaken. Whether it be short or long, the sentence or phrase is always the minimum measure of our aesthetic enjoyment.

At about this period of his adolescence, at the same time as he was reading Déroulède's poetry, Proust enjoyed a novel that is completely forgotten today, *Picciola* by Xavier Saintine (1836)[67] – which he liked just as much as he did Gautier, the hawthorn bushes and Déroulède's poems. He appreciated the 'vague poetry of its images', even more than in Mérimée's *Colomba*, in which the irony spoiled the charm of the moonlight for him.[68] The novel tells of a prisoner's love for a flower, and later for a girl, 'Picciola as a plant and Picciola as a girl', and this theme appealed to the man in Proust in love with hawthorns and with budding maidenhood.

Proust's love for *The Arabian Nights* also dates from his adolescence. He read it in Galland's translation[69] and gazed at scenes from it on Creil porcelain plates; later, he would recall this 'character who enchanted [his] adolescence and who changed the old lamps into new ones'.[70] In *À la recherche* we come across Aladdin, Ali Baba, Sindbad, the 'sleeper awoken', the 'beauteous Zobéide'. And above all, in *Le Temps retrouvé*, the wish to write the 'Arabian Nights' of another age.

CHAPTER III

The Schoolboy

AN UNASSUMING PUPIL

After joining the Pape-Carpentier class, which Jacques Bizet, the son of the composer and of Geneviève Halévy also attended, Marcel Proust entered the Lycèe Condorcet,[1] class of *cinquième*, division D, on 2 October 1882. He was eleven years old. He was probably given earlier coaching at home; as was the custom among wealthy families at the period, he would have been given lessons by his grandmother and his mother, but also by governesses and tutors. At the age of nine, he knew a little Latin and German (taught, no doubt, by Mme Nathé Weil, for he wrote a few lines in German to her in February 1881).[2] His early letters reveal his love of reading; at the age of nine, for example, he wrote to his cousin, Pauline Neuburger, on 5 September 1880: 'I leave tomorrow for Dieppe, and I am delighted that I am able to spend my time reading.'[3] For the young Marcel, the beach would always be the place where one read, probably in the shade of the beach huts, and he would later come to describe his trips down to the sea, his pockets stuffed with books by Stevenson.[4]

Robert Dreyfus has depicted the charm of Condorcet in the 1880s: 'The Lycée Condorcet was never a prison. In those days, it was like a sort of inner circle, whose appeal was so subtle that certain pupils – Marcel Proust, for instance, and my other friends – often did their best to arrive before the time we were officially meant to be there: so impatient were we to see one another again and chat beneath the sparse shade of the trees that adorned the Havre courtyard, while we awaited the rolling of the drum, which advised us, rather than commanded us, that we should make our way to the classrooms. The discipline was not harsh, it even struck our families as being a little too relaxed.'[5] The climate was therefore rather more liberal than in the scholarly lycées of the Quartier Latin. Yet Jacques-Émile Blanche, who was ten years older than Proust, remembered his *cinquième* class as being of a level that would be unimaginable today.[6] His tutor was already making him read Zola's *L'Assommoir* in a review, *La République des lettres*, which also published Maupassant and Mallarmé (who taught at the same lycée). The boy used to say he was force-fed on politics and modern history. All the pupils were interested in literature, even if it was of poor quality: 'Many of my "serious" friends were afflicted with priggishness and an appalling taste in literature';[7] they were made to learn monologues from Henri de Bornier's *La Fille de Roland*, which was a huge success at the Comédie-Française. The children used to go to the classical matinées which were accompanied by lectures, put on by the theatre. As far as the social milieu of the pupils was concerned, it 'represented Parisian society on a smaller scale'[8] or, more precisely, the future governing class, which was concentrated on the eighth *arrondissement* and the Monceau district. The children received a high level of education, but one that was essentially literary, that was based on the humanities and on philosophy, and that did not disregard contemporary literary life. They were versed in exercises that led to them writing, being published and speaking in public: in the top classes these schoolchildren edited magazines and worked on newspapers, as did their teachers. And their names contributed to the philosophy, history, political science, literature and to the banking world of the future. Whence, perhaps, its reputation as a 'college of dilettantes',[9] a term that would cause so much harm to Proust, particularly in the eyes of Barrès and, when he had to read *Du côté de chez Swann* for *La Nouvelle Revue Française*, in those of Gide, a pupil from a staunch left-bank school.

Marcel Proust would never be a student who would struggle, but neither would he come top of the class. When he went to the lycée, his results, except in specific science subjects, were adequate. But he did not attend very often; his reading, the family conversations and his private lessons meant that he could maintain the required level without too much effort. All in all, the lycée broke in only occasionally on a private life that had otherwise been organized quite happily. This is very much what is mirrored in *Du côté de chez Swann* and *À l'ombre des jeunes filles en fleurs*. It does not even occur to us to be surprised not to find school life mentioned, particularly since the young Marcel, like any sickly child, such as Gide or Sartre, must have been the butt of the crudest jokes from his schoolmates: he himself has described those made by removing a consonant from his name.* One curiously little-known account describes the child constantly

---

* The word '*prout*' means a fart! *Tr.*

going to the lavatory:[10] this may be not so much to do with the habits we have already mentioned as with his nervousness and the need for a hiding-place.

In *cinquième*, Proust obtained fifth place in the certificate of merit for French, fourth place for Greek translation and second prize in biology.[11] In *quatrième* (1883–84), at the age of twelve, after frequent absences, he only achieved third place in biology. His teacher was Colomb, the immortal author, under the name of Christophe, of *La Famille Fenouillard, Sapeur Camember* and *L'Idée fixe du savant Cosinus*. The latter's own teacher, Gaston Bonnier (author of a famous *Flora*, and whose work Proust also read), whose assistant he would be at the Sorbonne, complained that on botanical expeditions 'his constant joking' distracted pupils from 'descriptive botany'.[12] This tone of 'constant joking' would be adopted by Proust, just as it was by his teacher. Furthermore, at the lycée he never stopped passing notes to his classmates. As to the rewards of natural science, they are evident in the future writer's precocious inclination for a field (transposed in *Picciola*, the novel he so loved, in which the heroine is a flower), which would provide him with his most powerful images, from the hawthorns to the girls in their budding grove, from the Guermantes-birds to the fertilization of the orchid, the image of Sodom.

In *quatrième*, Marcel was given favourable assessments in Latin, Greek and history. It was in German (he would never be any good at living languages!), in geography and in mathematics that his teachers were stricter and described his work as 'mediocre' or 'average'. In his second term, it was observed that he was 'absent for three weeks', and in the summer term that he had been 'absent since May'. One of his first stories, of a type that is in keeping with the level of *quatrième*[13] and *troisième* alike, was published; no correction marks have been made. This short, realistic tale, in the style of Maupassant, about a builder who sacrifices himself to save a friend, is not merely a sentimental story. The narrator intervenes in an ironical way; he draws attention to the clichés in his own description and he throws in a number of quotations from classical writers, from Corneille to Tacitus. It opens with the lilac and the hawthorn, which the author of 'Combray' so loved. Finally, the conclusion is twofold: after the act of heroism, Marcel stressed that the hero met with nothing but ingratitude: 'It is sad, but true.' The psychological coup-de-théâtre is seen here for the first time from the pen of a very young writer, as is the portrayal of a sentiment that we will encounter again in Gilberte and Mlle Vinteuil. Another essay dealt with 'The Trial of Piso before the Roman Senate'.[14]

Piso is accused of having caused the death of Germanicus, by his widow, the great Agrippina. Through a series of dramatic twists, we learn of the death of Piso, of his guilt and that of Tiberius, as well as the death of Piso's son. It is an exercise in imitation, very similar to Tacitus (who is mentioned in the previous essay); the elegance and assurance of style are those of Burnouf's translation and they already display Proust's gift for pastiche: reproduce before producing, re-create before creating – this was just as much the aim of classical education as it was the doctrine of the 'ancients'; in these same years, these Graeco-Latin exercises had their literary extension in *Salammbô*, *Thaïs* or *Aphrodite*. An essay he wrote in *troisième*, dated 1 December 1884, had as its subject 'the dying gladiator';[15] this was a very messy draft, full of crossings out, the finished copy of which was delivered to his teacher, M. Guillemot. Having composed a framework (a method he would always retain), Marcel developed it by setting the cruelty of the perverted people against the dying man's dream, one that is imbued with nostalgia and the desire to obtain his family's forgiveness: 'For him these memories are a harsh punishment.' At the same time, the gladiator pronounces a cruel curse, which will be that used – though to his own detriment – by the Narrator of *Le Temps retrouvé*: 'May all these men die unhappy, far from their wives and children, full of remorse, insulted at their last gasps.' After this pitiless vow, there follows a conventional pardon: the fact remains that profound themes are being aroused in this scholarly composition: that of perversion (the word is used), the sense of guilt, the desire for self-punishment. A few stylistic mannerisms reveal the influence of Flaubert and Anatole France ('a sweet and cruel image of his past life'). At a very young age, Marcel thus devoted himself to describing death, something he would do only twice in *À la recherche du temps perdu*, in the case of the grandmother, and later Bergotte; the deaths of other characters are only mentioned by allusion.

Another essay on ancient themes described the sack of Carthage by the Romans, based on an outline by Sainte-Beuve in the style of Plutarch. The Romans ask the Greek children to write their names on a tablet. 'A handsome young boy who must have been about thirteen years old,* with a perfect face, a fine figure and a proud and courageous expression' responds with two heroic verses from Homer. In his conclusion, which was not dictated by the outline, Marcel addressed the relationships between life, death and literature: 'The study of literature enables us to scorn death,

---

* In other words, a boy of Marcel's age and with his looks.

it raises us above earthly concerns by speaking to us of the things of the spirit; it refines all our feelings; and that reasoned, almost philosophical courage is much finer than physical courage or the boldness of the senses, for it is in reality the courage of the spirit.'[16] Marcel's credo was formed from the age of thirteen, and it never wavered: poetry stood 'above life and its wretchedness', and it contained its own rewards. A handsome adolescent boy bears witness to this; the idea springs from a deep and affective source – but it no longer leads to God.

Marcel's school papers, which are preserved in the Department of Manuscripts at the Bibliothèque Nationale,[17] and which were donated by Mme Mante-Proust, include still more Roman essays. 'Scipio Æmilianus at Carthage' is purely conventional. But 'The Death of Caius Taranius' discusses the relationship between parents and children and the father's disappointed expectations in his love for his son; Caius Taranius is a Roman Vinteuil: 'Taranius had a son whom he loved tenderly. He was the focus of all his feelings, all his fears, all his hopes. What did his own life matter beside that of this beloved son.' This son went and betrayed his father's hiding-place to the triumvirate, he was 'a cowardly man who never bore you the slightest affection . . . But you, poor father, were totally unaware of this.' When he does discover it, he gives himself up to be beaten. In the same way, a composer dies of the sorrow his daughter brings him: a writer's themes are supplied from adolescence onwards. Similarly, in a sketch for a piece of homework about Chateaubriand's and Lamartine's love of their native land, Marcel revealed how 'the association of ideas and feelings' can conjure up precious memories.

A letter from Cicero to Atticus features the proconsul restoring the tomb of Archimedes. As a result of slavery, the Greeks, 'degraded beings who no longer care about the religion that is the most sacred of all, the religion of patriotism', have allowed the monument to fall into ruin. The meditation on death and history shows that 'it is by examining more deeply the laws that govern human nature that we find our consolation for life, its bitterness and its failings'. Proust's Latin homework also displayed his knowledge of Tacitus: 'Tiberius was afflicted by a violent neurosis which was manifest in a character that was strange, unstable, sombre, hypocritical, superstitious, suspicious and cruel.'[18] Charlus belonged to the same breed of men.

It is not surprising that Marcel should have obtained 'very good' and 'good' mentions in French while in *troisième*. The comments he received for literature were comparable, though those for Greek were not as good.

But the appraisals drew attention to his absences, which were frequent in the Easter term and continuous in the summer term: this was due to the spring and its effect on his asthma. There were no rewards at the end of the year; one of his teachers noted: 'Success will return with his health.' Marcel obtained his best reports in history ('very good' in the first two terms). His teacher was M. Jallifier (who appears in *Jean Santeuil* under the name of Jaconnier),[19] to whom Marcel went for private lessons, and who was probably a guest at his parents' home.[20] The long discussions that he had with this man developed and sustained his love of history, which is apparent from *Jean Santeuil* onwards and which, in a subtle but profound way, pervades *À la recherche*.* If one does not have a feeling for this subject as a child, it cannot be acquired, it never comes back as naturally again. 'I remember,' Dreyfus, himself a historian, remarked, 'the first emotions we experienced in any historical context were when, one day in the Champs-Élysées, the Duc d'Aumale, who was passing by, was pointed out to us . . . then, on another occasion, we saw Marshal MacMahon, who was taking a walk with his wife.'[21]

Proust spent two years in *seconde*. In the year 1885–6, he was almost constantly away ('always absent', noted his history teacher). In March 1886, he composed an essay on Christopher Columbus entitled 'L'Éclipse',[22] in which, in a style inspired by Chateaubriand, he confronted the 'savages' and civilization, in a setting that was 'splendid and symbolic'. The descriptive skill of the landscape artist, inspired by Baudelaire, is seen in another essay from the same year, 'Les Nuages'. Here we encounter the dialogue with Nature, which will culminate in the hawthorns of 'Combray': 'How many times, in a rapture of delight, did I tell my troubles to the leaves and the birds, in the belief that I was opening my heart to living creatures who understood me, yet at the same time that I was doing so to superior and divine beings who would provide me with poetic consolation.'[23] Sorrows, melancholy, exile, the recurrence of 'consolation' are features both of the age of puberty, an age that is easily saddened, as well as of the survival, in 1885, among the young Symbolist generation, of romantic motifs: anguish, dreams, pantheism.

In the autumn, before the start of the year that he repeated, Marcel

---

* *RTP*, vol. IV, p. 254: 'The muse that has gathered up all that the most exalted Muses of philosophy and art have rejected, everything that is not founded upon truth, everything that is merely contingent, but that reveals other laws as well: that muse is History!' Cf. *Études proustiennes*, vol. I, pp. 306–8.

travelled to Illiers; his parents were going there following the death of Doctor Proust's elder sister, Aunt Amiot. There he was thrilled to discover not the landscape of his childhood, nor the memory of the person who is thought to have inspired Aunt Léonie, but Augustin Thierry's *Histoire de la conquête de l'Angleterre*. Such was his joyful state of mind that, two years later, he would describe this period as 'the year of Augustin Thierry'.[24] The youthful reader of these unexpected books tried to rediscover in their pages the elusive images of his magic lantern, the strange, barbaric names of the monarchs of the Early Middle Ages and the statues from the cathedrals. From *Récits des temps merovingiens*,[25] he would use a quotation, as well as some of the themes, in 'Combray'. Furthermore, Marcel's ever alert sensibility must have been enthralled by this long dirge on the vanquished of history, its crushed minorities, the murdered pretenders, and even by the scenes of torture which would inhabit the medieval imagination of the shackled Baron de Charlus. The reading of old books may, in fact, stimulate the urge to seek for fantasies and may resurface belatedly to inspire literary creativity. It was Augustin Thierry who provided Marcel with Charlus's feudal hell.

While he was repeating his year, his mathematics teacher, M. Brichet, marked him more and more strictly as the months went by: 'weak', 'does not work'. It was true that Marcel did spend his time writing literary notes to Daniel Halévy, 'while a problem was being solved'.[26] In physics, M. Seignette (the names of Brichet and Seignette, in one of those private jokes Proust was so fond of, were forerunners of Brichot and Saniette) was more indulgent: 'Application and progress good'. His history master, M. Gazeau, who was kind, intelligent, much loved by his pupils, solemn, brilliant and 'very up-to-date with the latest publications', according to an inspection report, awarded him second prize in history and entered him for the *concours général*.*

In that same year, Marcel met Marie de Benardaky in the Champs-Élysées; he took the exams for the *concours général*'[27] in history on 13 July and in Greek translation on 22 July; he was also a replacement candidate in French, but did not take part in the competition. The Condorcet prizes were awarded on 2 August. Marcel, who did not succeed in the *concours général*, obtained second prize in history and geography at the lycée, and was given honourable mentions of excellence in Latin and in French. The academic year ended much later than it does in our own time and it

---

* An annual competition open to top senior pupils at French lycées. *Tr.*

recommenced at the beginning of October, the summer holidays lasting for two months. During that same summer, on 14 July, Marcel saw General Boulanger* pass through the streets of Auteuil, which 'had never been so lively'. This man played a part in the adolescent's muddled political sympathies. While Jeanne Proust's political sympathies were 'Orléaniste-Republican' (that is to say, though she was a Republican, she disapproved of the fact that Boulanger, the Minister for War, should have expelled the princes from the army and rejected the claims of the Orléans family in May 1887),† Marcel was initially rather attracted by the general and the enthusiasm he aroused, 'so unexpected, so *romantic*, in the dreary, humdrum life', which 'stirs all one's most primitive, wildest and bellicose instincts'. Faced with these primitive passions, which are those of any 'call to arms', Proust nevertheless admitted to the daughter of the future President of the Republic, Félix Faure, that Boulanger was 'very common and a vulgar bass drummer'.[28] Never again would Marcel be drawn to him; neither would he be attracted by nationalism or the blind popular fervour that sustains every dictatorship. At the time of the elections, in February 1884, he questioned his grandfather: 'Was a Republican majority, of the size they expected, actually feasible?'[29] When he recalled the political crises he had lived through, Boulangisme would not be mentioned again. His political opinions would remain moderate, except during the Dreyfus affair and the First World War.

Curiously enough, apart from the time spent at Auteuil, we know very little about Marcel's childhood holidays from the time he went to Illiers until the end of his schooldays. In 1880, he was taken to Dieppe; in September 1888, he recalled the visits long ago to Tréport, where he 'had enjoyed breathing the fresh air, the smells and stretching [his] limbs',[30] and, in 1891, 'those years at the seaside', at Cabourg no doubt – 'where my grandmother and I would chat as we walked head-on against the wind'.[31] Because of their proximity to Paris and London, these watering-places were among the oldest of their kind in France. They were gradually being ousted, among smart society in any case, by Trouville, and later by Cabourg

---

* Boulanger's name does not occur either in *Jean Santeuil* or in *À la recherche*, whereas Barrès dedicated *L'Appel du soldat* to him.

† General Georges Boulanger (1837–91) was a reactionary political adventurer who played an important part in the suppression of the Commune (1871). Championed by Clemenceau and the Radicals, he was appointed Minister of War. Immensely popular at one time, he became the leader of a nationalist right-wing movement, supported by many Royalists and Republicans for their own ends, known as Boulangisme. *Tr.*

(redeveloped) and Deauville. The Comtesse Greffulhe, however, had entertained her father-in-law in 1887 at the sumptuous La Case villa in Dieppe.[32] Jacques-Émile Blanche described a day spent in the town: 'The ladies sit on the terrace of the Casino, around the bandstand . . . Chatting, doing their tapestry . . . "frivolity". They scour the *Gazette rose* for the list of foreigners and the week's theatre programmes. We consume waffles or hot *"mirlitons"* from Lafosse, the famous pastrycook. Our womenfolk go to benediction. I am sent to bed. The grown-ups go down to dinner.' The children paddled on the beach or fished for shrimps or crabs in front of the tents or bathing-huts.[33] Lord Salisbury, who owned a villa there, was welcomed by the town; in 1867, the Prince of Wales stayed at Dieppe, in the company of the Marquise de Galliffet.[34] Pieces by Offenbach and Hervé were played: music lovers never tired of them.

In a photograph taken in the summer of 1887, in which everyone is wearing elegant town clothes, we can see the Prince de Polignac, the Prince de Sagan, Vicomtesse Greffulhe, Robert de Montesquiou, Gabriel Fauré, Vicomte Greffulhe and Jacques-Émile Blanche.[35] Another generation, another social milieu: yet in a very short time, they would all meet again, they or their compositions, in *Jean Santeuil* or in *À la recherche du temps perdu*.

In 1886, Marcel went with his mother, who was taking the waters at Salies-de-Béarn, to stay at the Hôtel de la Paix. The adolescent boy did not have much fun there. Salies offered only sorrow and boredom 'to those without sufficient "double muscles" as Tartarin puts it, to go and seek in the cool of the neighbouring countryside that grain of poetry that is essential to our existence, and which, alas, is totally lacking on the terrace, full of cackling and tobacco smoke, where we pass the time of day'.[36] He did, however, play croquet with some friends. Mme Proust visited this small spa town, some fifty kilometres from Pau and Bayonne, on several occasions to take the waters; in 1888, the year in which the thermal baths were destroyed by fire, she took Robert (but not Marcel, who would have been bored).[37] Marcel's stay there provided him with the opportunity to compose a portrait of a woman who was to play an important role in his life, Mme Catusse, a close friend of his mother's, to whom he, who was so moved by singing, was initially attracted by her 'delightfully pure and marvellously dramatic voice': she sang songs by Massenet and Gounod, composers who were frequently mentioned by Proust in his letters. 'A most beautiful head, two bright and gentle eyes, a skin that is delicate and white, a face worthy of the dreams of a painter in love with beauty, framed by a head of fine dark hair.' The portrait artist quotes Leconte de Lisle and Musset, the poets he liked in those years: this is not *À la recherche*; it is already the art of *Les Plaisirs et les Jours*. To his grandmother, he expressed his admiration for *Le Capitaine Fracasse*, and, having a colossal appetite, declared that he had read *Eugénie Grandet* ('very beautiful, very sad'), sixty-six pages of Hugo, 250 verses of the *Aeneid* (which he had translated) and some Greek.[38]

RHÉTORIQUE

An enormous change took place when Marcel, at the age of sixteen, moved up to *rhétorique* [the lower sixth form] in the autumn of 1887. Not only was he taught by a teacher who was passionate about literature, but he discovered a group of young friends with whom he would set up several literary magazines. From 1887 to 1888, the adolescent boy who played with Marie de Benardaky in the Champs-Élysées and found solace from the violence of the playground became a young man who was attracted by his own kind, by other boys. During that academic year, his literary vocation and his sexual sensibilities were formed simultaneously. The lycée would become a paradise (as the barracks at Orléans would do, two years later) which introduced him to good books and to handsome young men.

Proust's Latin master, M. Cucheval, makes an appearance in his description of 'the salon de la Princesse de Polignac' (1903): at a reception the butler asks the master of the house, 'This gentleman says his name is M. Cucheval,* should he be announced all the same?'[39] It is hardly surprising that the unfortunate Latin teacher should have considered his disciple 'erratic and whimsical', and deplored the 'homework that was often not handed in'. Marcel reckoned him 'passionately and abundantly vulgar. A cruel *schoolmaster*, coarse and uncouth . . . he behaves idiotically and the savage is totally unaffected by delightful combinations of syllables and forms'.[40] More significant was Maxime Gaucher, 'an immensely open-minded and delightful spirit'[41] and a man of letters, who contributed to *La Revue littéraire* and *La Revue bleue*. His superiors commented: 'Very literary mind. A writer who is much esteemed and well-liked.' Eugène Manuel, the general inspector of schools, noted 'the doctrinal freedom, which sometimes skims any literary scepticism and encourages the prema-

---

* M. Cucheval's unfortunate name suggests a horse's buttocks! *Tr.*

ture intellectual emancipation of the students'.[42] For all that, Gaucher was sufficiently open-minded to put up with Marcel's 'apostolate':[43] probably on account of his chosen poet of the moment: Leconte de Lisle. In his article on Baudelaire written towards the end of his life, Proust could still recall the glittering radiance and the disillusioned tone of de Lisle's ringing verse; he uses it to define Bergotte's style; Bloch's words are permeated with it. Within himself, the writer would always continue to make use of the people, the books, the places that no longer meant anything to him.

André Ferré has published some of the notes and outlines for homework that Marcel wrote as a *rhétoricien*:[44] in addition, in the midst of a course on 'the secondary comic authors in the eighteenth century', there is a reference to Favart's *La Chercheuse d'esprit*, which is repeated in *Sodome et Gomorrhe*,[45] and a sketch of the male and female roles in Racine's tragedies. Here Proust observed 'the simmering sensitivity which made him the maddest of lovers in his dealings with women', while his 'woman's sensitivity on the other hand rather harmed his portrayal of masculine vigour'. This is the first trace of Proust's fondness for Racine, whom he considered a brother and someone very much like himself; it was a feeling that was also evident in his sketch for an essay (not published by Ferré) on the ritual subject: 'Corneille portrays men . . .' in which Marcel noted 'the influence of Racine on modern literature', who 'affirms the power of love'.[46]

Racine's name and his work suffuse the characters of *À la recherche du temps perdu* – Bergotte, Berma, Albertine and the Balbec girls, for example – and they can be found in Proust's critical work, from his translations of Ruskin to his article on Baudelaire. Another outline, based on an idea of Diderot's, already specifies one of the principles of Proustian aesthetics: 'Pure sensitivity, in which the intelligence has not been brought into play, may excite our emotions, but never our admiration, nor those heightened pleasures of the intelligence that a true work of art affords us because it allows us to see that sense of order and meaning, that harmonious logic, which is usually hidden from us by life.' One final piece of work on Corneille and Racine, and his love for them, which has become well known ever since André Maurois published it,[47] revealed extraordinary gifts of analysis and critical imagination in his search for 'the axis of genius' and 'the rules of its development'. The stylistic quality can be seen in the precision of the adjectives used, the maturity of his enumerations, its intelligence and its clarity: 'To love Racine passionately is simply to love the most profound, the most gentle, the most sorrowful, the most sincere intuitive instinct among so many charming, martyred lives.'[48] With Proust, unlike those writers who have drafted novels from childhood, such as Flaubert, Aragon and Sartre, before the creation and fabrication of fiction it is the aesthetic that takes shape, not so much in what is said as the way in which it is said. We can speculate on what must have happened, and how Marcel informed Robert Dreyfus, who was about to enter *rhétorique*: 'For several months, I read out all my French homework in class, and I was hissed and cheered. If Gaucher had not been there, I would have been torn to bits.'[49] By the time two months had elapsed, Marcel had a dozen disciples, he 'was causing class warfare', and passed for certain among them 'as a poseur'.

Unfortunately, Gaucher, who was dying, was replaced by M. Dupré: 'He's boring. It's true he knows Dierx and Leconte de Lisle (his books)', but that is not enough: 'He displays too many reservations.'[50] This resulted in less appreciative reports compared to those of his predecessor: 'Erratic, but some ability.' Proust, however, treated his teachers as equals, he commended Dreyfus to M. Dupré, he discussed Daniel Halévy for one hour with M. Jallifier, and he looked upon the general teaching establishment with rather more delicacy than he did the tutors and general inspectors.[51] The schoolboy now seemed to have an inspiration and a sense of vocation: 'I know perfectly well that one should not write at a gallop. But I have so much I want to say. It's as if the waves were hurrying me along.'[52] This is what separates the future writer from those who will never achieve their aim, the young man who has 'so much to say' from those for whom language is not the main purpose of existence. At the end of the year, Marcel was awarded first prize for 'novices' in French composition,[53] and obtained a good pass in the first part of the *baccalauréat*.[54]

What is more, he did not devote the year solely to academic work, and agreed to write for student magazines. Robert Dreyfus mentions several: *Lundi*, 'a review of letters and the arts', bearing an epigraph by Verlaine, 'the triumphant eclecticism of the Beautiful'.[55] A 'Revue de seconde', which lasted for thirteen issues and incorporated its predecessor (some issues carried the title 'Le Lundi', others did not), was published by fourth- and fifth-form pupils, as well as those from *rhétorique*, between 21 November 1887 and 1 March 1888, under the editorship of Daniel Halévy. At the age of sixteen, Proust contributed a column of literary criticism written in the style of Sainte-Beuve and Jules Lemaître (whose literary column appeared in *La Revue bleue* and whose theatre criticism was published on Mondays in *Le Journal des débats*). In his '*causerie* on drama' in issue no. 2, Proust reviewed a performance of *Horace*: having been impressed by the local colour of the play's Roman setting, he identifies the spirit of Corneille, 'at once subtle and sublime, composed with reason and heroism, the spirit of the patriotic soldier and the patient lawyer'.[56] It is worth noting that even though Proust disapproved of searching for the explanation for a work in the biography of its author, he never denied that the creative personality of the author could be found in the work. The second *causerie* concerned Brunetière's view of Gautier and it praised *Le Capitaine Fracasse*, a book that was dear to Proust,[57] for the way it evoked the past and for its painterly skills. Contrary to Brunetière, who, following Faguet, deplored Gautier's lack of ideas, he detected a portent of modern decadence, in common with Anatole France:[58] 'Were I ever to found a republic like Plato, I would found it on total decadence; ideas would be banished there, its citizens would look up at the sky and they would contemplate.'[59] Marcel, who, in accordance with the latest fashion, looked upon himself as a 'decadent', would soon change his mind about this affiliation.

These young people had also envisaged a *Revue verte* and a *Revue lilas*,* which would be published in part at the beginning of the new term in 1888, when Marcel moved up to *philosophie*, and his friends Daniel Halévy, Robert Dreyfus and Jacques Bizet joined *rhétorique*. But we should first introduce this group of friends. Daniel Halévy, born in 1872, was almost fifteen and about to begin *troisième* when Proust met him in the courtyard of the Lycée Condorcet. Like Marcel, he had a Jewish forebear who had come from Germany.[60] A product of the liberal Parisian bourgeoisie and the son of a writer, Ludovic Halévy,[61] who had been a member of the Académie française since 1884, and of a mother who was just as cultivated as Jeanne Proust, he was a generous-minded, intelligent and extremely good-looking boy† (a fact that Marcel was not unaware of), who was to be in the mainstream of new thinking in the first half of the twentieth century. His essays on Péguy, Michelet and Nietzsche would play a formative role. His Cahiers Verts series for Grasset would publish all the important writers of the inter-war years, from Malraux to Mauriac (though not Proust, who at that time was tied to Gallimard). In his ideas he grew

---

* At this period magazines drew their titles from the colour of their front cover: *La Revue bleue*, and later *La Revue blanche*.

† See his photograph in *Écrits de jeunesse* (as well as those of R. Dreyfus and J. Bizet).

apart from Marcel, and they would disagree about everything, from a liking for Péguy to post-1918 nationalism; however, it was their 'consanguinity of minds' which drew them together, not the content of their ideas.

Robert Dreyfus wrote to Marcel Proust during the summer of 1888 to obtain information about his future sixth-form teachers. His friendship with Marcel dated from the time they played together in the Champs-Élysées; one boy was seventeen years old, the other fifteen. Dreyfus was later to become an essayist and historian, the author, notably, of the first important essay on Gobineau (which he dedicated to Proust); he published his *Souvenirs sur Marcel Proust* in 1926, in the Cahiers Verts series, an intelligent and sensitive study which provided first-hand information about Proust's adolescence. He had been Marcel's confidant in his fruitless approaches to Daniel Halévy and Jacques Bizet.

Marcel had known the latter ever since they were pupils in the Pape-Carpentier class. Born on 10 July 1872, Bizet was exactly one year younger than him. The son of Georges Bizet and Geneviève Halévy,[62] and therefore a cousin of Daniel's, his father was caring and affectionate, while his mother, to whom we shall return later, was an intelligent woman who was also a depressive. The household was often torn apart; Georges died of a heart attack on 2 June 1875, three months after the failure of *Carmen*. His son was three years old. Geneviève Bizet looked after her son and she began to receive visitors once more, at the rue de Douai, from 1880 onwards.[63] Some of Jacques' letters, from which it is obvious that he was just as passionately in love with his mother as Marcel was, have been preserved.[64] This brilliantly gifted, sensitive and wealthy boy would, within a few years, become a drug-addict. He committed suicide on 7 November 1922, twelve days before Marcel's death. Maurice Sachs, the grandson of Alice Sachs, who was married to Jacques Bizet for a time, developed a touching affection for the latter, which he described in his posthumously published novel *Le Sabbat*. Of course, there was nothing about the handsome young man, who looked so like the author of *Carmen*, that gave any hint of the tragic fate that lay in store, apart, perhaps, from the history of depression on his mother's side of the family and the lack of a father.[65] For a brief period, Marcel would identify some of these same symptoms in himself.

In the spring of 1888,* Marcel, who only the previous year had seemed to be attracted by girls, fell in love with Jacques Bizet. This brief rapture

* As far as we can be sure from the dates of letters.

is summed up in three letters. In the first, Marcel complained about his parents, who were threatening to send him to a boarding-school in the country. The threat may have been invented by Marcel, or else his parents were dissatisfied with his poor academic results, and, like all parents, had threatened him with boarding-school; or perhaps they were endeavouring to put a stop to his 'bad habits'. In his despondent state, which he described in *Jean Santeuil*,[66] he declared: 'My only consolation when I am truly sad lies in loving someone and in being loved. And you're the one to whom this really applies, you who had so many problems at the beginning of winter, you who wrote me a delightful letter the other day.'[67]

On 14 June 1888, Daniel Halévy, having observed that 'Poor Proust is totally crazy', copied out in his diary a second letter, possibly dating from the previous month, to Jacques Bizet ('the letter I found the hardest to write in my entire life'), whom Proust addresses as *'chéri'*. Mme Proust had forbidden this young man access to her house and did not allow Marcel to go to his home; Daniel listed the reasons: 'a fondness that was a little excessive, was it not? And which might degenerate . . . into *sensual* affection'; too great a similarity, where failings were concerned: 'independent spirit, nervousness, disorganized mind; perhaps even masturbation'. The letter does not allow us to suppose, contrary to what has been said, that the two boys might have been discovered together, but only that Mme Proust may have heard their close relatives (Robert Proust, or their friend Jacques Baignères, or an uncle of Bizet's) speak ill of Jacques, or disapproved of Marcel's excessive affection. Following this ban, there was a 'furious scene, gradual desperation, threats, illness . . . nothing could be done', and, confronted by his father, there was even the blackmail of masturbation. Marcel then decided to prove that Jacques was a 'delightful creature', to have him allowed back into the house, or, if not, to meet him out of town, adding rather naïvely and touchingly: 'I shall make a café our home together.' Marcel, however, seems to have been more deeply committed than Jacques, for he continued: 'But forgive me, I am talking to you as if you were a great friend when I hardly know you and you must find me rather clinging.'[68] Jacques Bizet rejected these advances. Marcel then wrote to him:[69] 'I admire your good sense, even though I regret it', while at the same time reaffirming the 'reasons of the body' as well as the heart's reasons. 'Perhaps you are right. And yet I still find it sad not to be able to pick the lovely flower, which we shall soon no longer be able to pluck. For by then it will be a fruit . . . a forbidden one.' Proust seemed to want to suggest that a passing 'encounter' would not signify conclusive pederasty, and that there was an age at which these relationships were still permitted without becoming compromised. As if in affirmation of his long and affectionate friendship, Marcel did not abandon Jacques, and his feelings for him would not cool for another year.[70]

In that decidedly torrid month of May, he explained to Halévy the meaning he attached to pederasty: 'I know . . . that there are some young men (and if you are interested . . . I shall give you some very important items of interest about this, that belong to me and which were sent to me), some young men . . . who love other boys, who constantly long to see them (as I do Bizet) and weep and suffer when they are apart, and wish for only one thing, to hug them and kneel before them, who love them because of their *flesh*, who covet them with their eyes, who call them darling and my angel, in all seriousness, who write passionate letters to them yet who would not commit pederasty for all the world. And yet, generally, love overwhelms them and they masturbate one another*. . . They are, in short, lovers. And I don't know why their love should be any more unsavoury than the usual kind of love.' It is probably on account of these letters that Halévy and Bizet stopped talking to Proust for a month; he then apologized to Daniel for his letter: 'When I noticed you weren't speaking the other day, I thought that my letter must have annoyed you. It was extremely tactless of me to write as I did, and very tactless of you to be angry and especially to look angry . . . If I have incurred your displeasure I do beg your forgiveness for I had no intention of doing so.'

Halévy's reaction is all the more understandable, given that at the same time as Marcel was pursuing Jacques Bizet, he had not ignored his cousin. We shall come across this process – which consists of loving two people at the same time and making one believe that he loves the other, while simultaneously confiding in him – later in Proust's life, and even in his work: between the Narrator, Albertine and Andrée, between Odette, Swann and Charlus. The trio became a quartet when Marcel, at the end of August 1888, confessed to Dreyfus: 'Why, when he[†] has behaved very pleasantly towards me, after all, does he drop me *completely*, and making it all too obvious, and then after a month come to say hello, after he had stopped speaking to me entirely? And his cousin Bizet? Why does he tell

---

* These final words appear to define Proustian sexuality, which seems to exclude the sexual act. Hence the affirmation that they 'would not commit pederasty for all the world'.
   † Daniel Halévy.

me he wants to be friends with me, and then drop me even more painfully? What do they want of me? To be rid of me, annoy me, mystify me, or what? I used to think they were so nice!'[71] One can imagine the drama that had been taking place. Marcel, in the throes of adolescence, felt misunderstood both at home and at the lycée. Solitary, and yet longing hopelessly for affection, he was searching for friends to whom he could give himself totally; they, however, soon considered him to be too 'clinging': 'Oh! Clinging, that has always been my nightmare.'[72] He was soon accused of having pederastic tendencies, which he sometimes confessed to without spelling them out and sometimes challenged because he refused to be nailed down, to be rooted to a single image. When Dreyfus replied to the questions that Marcel put to him, Marcel asserted: 'I don't think that a type is a character. I *believe* that what we think we can tell about a character is nothing more than the effect of an association of ideas. I express myself entirely personally, while at the same time admitting that I may be incorrect.'[73] Thus lived experience, together with his reading of Anatole France, enabled Marcel to construct a psychology which would vary very little: everyone is made up of 'different gentlemen'; we would be mistaken to base a character upon one single trait.

In addition to these friends, we should mention Abel Desjardins,[74] a fellow student and future colleague of Robert Proust's. Marcel still remembered him in 1919, when he received a letter from Abel congratulating him on his latest work: 'I loved you too much, love you too much, to pay attention to the compliments you pay me. My feelings are stirred by the friendship you are kind enough to show me once more. How unfortunate that we should not be able to exercise it, in an almost daily intimacy.'[75] And he remembered that, when almost a child, 'Years of sadness were illuminated by a moment of delight: it was Abel Desjardins' gift of a photograph, on the back of which he had inscribed these words: "To my best friend".' At the time that Proust was leaving Boulevard Haussmann, and burning his manuscripts and photographs, he suddenly pulled up 'in front of a small boy with a thin nose, a mocking expression, wearing a cocked hat and [he] exclaimed . . . : "Ah! Not that one!" . . . I could not have burnt that one, for it was still alive.'[76]

Marcel spent his holidays at Auteuil (apart from an interlude, in September, at the home of his schoolfriend Joyant, at L'Isle-Adam, and a visit to Chantilly),[77] where his mother left him to go and take the waters at Salies-de-Béarn. It is startling to see the same boy, so brilliant in class, so ready to write for literary magazines, so enterprising among his friends, behaving like a small child again, upset at being abandoned by his mother, and being lectured to by his great-uncle Louis Weil: 'Grandfather . . . just said that I was foolish . . . and grandmother nodded and laughed, saying that it did not in the least show that I loved "my mother".'[78] At table, his eyes were red, and he rubbed them. Reading *Le Mariage de Loti*,* however, delighted him: he rediscovered the pleasure he derived from reading in the old days, at Illiers, which he recalled in his preface to *Sésame et les lys*. His taste for Loti must have dulled by 1893, when he published 'Mondanité de Bouvard et Pécuchet' in *La Revue blanche*: he 'always produced the same sound' and 'his novels are all written with a single note, for his lyre has only one chord'.[79] What appealed to Marcel about *Le Mariage de Loti*? The unfamiliar setting? The autobiographical fiction? The poetic narrative? The fact that here was a new writer, who was original and avant-garde, in whose work he found some of the exotic poetry of Leconte de Lisle, another of those he admired at that time? And why should he have stopped liking him? In the pages he devoted to Nerval in 1907–8, Proust juxtaposed the poetic impressions that are based on very precise reality in *Sylvie* with the 'much too subjective Pierre Loti'.[80] He thus rejected a part of himself, which he attempted to display in every book, as well as the 'monotony' of a style whose variety is not its main strength. On the other hand, it is clear that in 1888 Marcel was only too easily inclined to unburdening himself.

Which is what he did to Robert Dreyfus, the third member of the 'little group of four friends',[81] in an extraordinary portrait in which he depicted himself with his 'perpetual great yearnings', his 'great passions' and his 'adjectives'. He was a 'man for making declarations'; 'under the pretext of loving a friend like a father, he loves him like a woman', he sought out casual conversations, then meeting places, he wrote 'feverish letters'; he would let it be known that 'your eyes are divine and that your lips tempt him', all with the greatest fickleness. 'Is he on the game,† is he a lunatic, is he a malingerer, is he an imbecile?' 'He does have the key to many a short novel.'[82] None of his friends has described Marcel at the age of seventeen as well, or as cruelly: lucid, ironic, masochistic, aware of a tendency within himself which he reveals with an insolence that is short-lived, denouncing – in a declaration – his mania for making declarations, muddling truth with lies, but who, after all, in 'many a short novel', was

---

* He would come across this work again in *L'Île du rêve*, by his friend Reynaldo Hahn.

† Proust actually wrote: '*Est-ce un p . . .*', literally, is he a whore? *Tr.*

already a novelist. Dreyfus was angry about this account, and Marcel replied immediately, as he did to Halévy: 'There's been a misunderstanding, and I was very upset by the angry tone you adopted.'[83]

Marcel then referred to his 'platonic passion for a famous courtesan',[84] in which he sketched a picture of the 'flower of Parisian beauty in 1888' in the Avenue des Acacias. This portrait of Laure Hayman, Uncle Louis's friend, is the first sketch of Odette in the Bois de Boulogne; Proust does not fail to make the comparison with Botticelli (here a Virgin), or to observe the modern, Baudelairean beauty of 'the cunningly contrived ripples of her purple dress'.[85] He admires her too much as a work of art for his 'passion' to be other than platonic. When he moved into society, beginning with the mothers of his friends, Mme Laure Baignères and Mme Straus, Marcel entertained similar feelings for the latter. Mme Laure Baignères (Laure Boillay) held a salon at which, just as at Mme Verdurin's, music was performed. Her sister-in-law, Mme Arthur Baignères (Charlotte de Formeville), and her husband were close friends of Alphonse Daudet, whom Marcel would meet at their home. Their son Paul sketched and painted, and he owned a copy of a Vermeer.

MADAME STRAUS

A family, intelligence, poor health, a witty tongue, a salon, a villa, two husbands, illustrious suitors – all these Geneviève Halévy, later Mme Georges Bizet and Mme Émile Straus,[86] possessed – yet she left behind no account of her life. We do not know when Marcel met her for the first time: probably outside the Pape-Carpentier class, and later in *rhétorique* at the Lycée Condorcet, when he first became enamoured of her son; he gradually transferred his affections to the mother, just as the Narrator transfers his from Gilberte to Odette Swann.* Adolescents sometimes discover in their friends' mothers a more glittering image of their own, and one that involves neither risk nor fear.

Geneviève was the daughter of Fromental Halévy, whose opera *La Juive* (1835), was still at the height of its fame, as Proust well knew, and of Léonie Rodrigues, whose father was a banker. Several members of both families had been patients at the Doctor Blanche clinic for nervous

---

* The opposite of the hero of Thomas Hardy's novel *The Well-Beloved*, which Proust admired, who loves grandmother, mother and daughter in succession. It was their resemblance which was so captivating as much as the fact that they were related, and his affection grew rather than diminished.

ailments. The future Mme Straus had had a miserable childhood. Her father died when she was thirteen years old, and she lost her elder sister, who was engaged to Ludovic Halévy, when she was fifteen; her mother was committed to an asylum. When she was nineteen, in 1868, she observed in her diary: 'The passing years do nothing to lessen the awful memory of the cruel moments that have separated me from everything I loved.'[87] She nevertheless became engaged to Georges Bizet, who was eleven years older (he was born in 1838) and her father's favourite pupil.[88] She married him in 1869. The young couple moved into the building at 22 rue de Douai where the entire Halévy family lived. The household, beset as it was by a possessive mother-in-law, Geneviève's nervous depression and Georges' work, was, despite the birth of Jacques in 1872, scarcely ever a happy place. The failure of *Carmen* in 1875, in which the part of the heroine was sung by Galli-Marié (who, it was rumoured, was extremely close to the composer) and inspired by Geneviève,[89] was a disaster for the couple. Georges Bizet died from a heart attack at the age of thirty-seven. In 1876, the painter Delaunay immortalized the young widow, who would never look as beautiful in any photographs.[90] With her black dress, her large, captivating eyes and her sensual mouth in the shape of a kiss 'that would never be vouchsafed upon any lips', she was the goddess of neurasthenia. When, in spite of her widowhood, she began to receive guests once more, Geneviève was surrounded by admirers: Meilhac, her cousin Ludovic Halévy, Porto-Riche, Maupassant, Bourget, Hervieu and Joseph Reinach. To the surprise of many, however, it was the lawyer Émile Straus whom she married in 1886: 'It was the only way to be rid of him,' she was to say.[91] A man of influence, and possibly a half-brother of the Rothschilds, who adored Geneviève, he was not very popular, except with Proust, who would address some important letters to him. Others joked about the husband in their correspondence with his wife.[92] Edmond de Goncourt made observations about the couple in his *Journal*, from 1886 to 1895. He considered Émile 'intelligent; shrewdly observant and kindly', as voluble as a lawyer, and a man with a 'damnedly Mephistophelian air'.[93] His piercing gaze recast the members of the household into characters from Racine – or from Proust – through the reversal of roles, and it cast a new light on the interest the latter derived from his visits there: 'Apparently, Mme Bizet was Strauss' [*sic*] mistress before they were married, but possessing her was not enough for him. In this liaison, it was the woman who had the male temperament and did not wish to be tied, and it was the man who had the female disposition and who required his beloved to be entirely his, for ever and always.'[94] At the young woman's home, Goncourt described 'the alloying of the madness of the Halévys with the madness of family X, to which her mother belonged',[95] which he had observed in 'the feverish expression in her dark, gentle, velvet eyes' and in the flirtatiousness of her 'obsessive posing'.[96] Her concept of love, as revealed to Edmond de Goncourt, displayed a pessimism worthy of the author of *Du côte de chez Swann*[97] and revealed one of the themes of her future conversations with Proust. Furthermore, it was the author of the *Journal* who saw Mme Straus as the model for the heroine of Maupassant's *Notre cœur*, 'a portrait of the worldly Parisienne', 'a flirt who is without heart, without affection, without sense',[98] and who never ceased playing this role at the centre of her circle of friends. For her part, Geneviève seemed to have been happy to be portrayed in this book, as she was later in *Le Côté de Guermantes*. Goncourt was the first to notice that she was 'a real artist in caricature' and that she had 'a journalist's way with words',[99] as instanced by her reply to Gounod, who considered part of *Manon* to be 'octagonal': 'I was just about to say so.'[100]

It is hardly surprising that Mme Straus, so like a character out of a novel, who attracted so many artists and writers and who, in the case of the least refined among them, was the inspiration for his finest novel, appears in *Les Plaisirs et les Jours*, in *Pastiches et mélanges*, and in *Le Côté de Guermantes*. The Duchesse, reduced to a form of words, was based upon Mme Straus: '*Everything* that is spiritual in it comes from you,' Proust wrote to her;[101] the wordplay and the conversation were already literary. It is clear that the Meilhac and Halévy wit, which the Guermantes and Swann share, stems not only from Ludovic, Offenbach's and Bizet's librettist (and a novelist too), but also from Geneviève: it was the Halévy wit which Marcel had heard ever since he was an adolescent. Other characteristics of Oriane also derive from Mme Straus: her melancholy, her world-weariness, her impetuousness, her excessive and short-lived affection ('My little Charles'), her love of the 'salon', the husband who is proud of his wife's repartee (though, unlike the Duc and despite passing moments of crisis, M. Straus worshipped his wife).

Daniel Halévy, who wrote two fine portraits of his aunt, described Mme Straus' salon better than anyone: the first was held at 22 rue de Douai, where the guests included the Baronne Alphonse de Rothschild, Comtesse Potocka (another model for *Notre cœur*), the Duchesse de Richelieu and the Comtesse de Chevigné; the second was at 134 Boulevard Haussmann: 'There were the surviving relatives from the period of the

Second Empire, my father, Meilhac, Degas, and Cavé, and the two Ganderax. There were the talented newcomers: not Anatole France (whom Mme Arman kept locked up), but, very frequently, Jules Lemaître. There were Bourget, Hervieu and Forain; the actors Lucien Guitry, Réjane and Emma Calvé; I saw that haughty relic, the Princesse Mathilde; and the foreigners Lady de Grey, Lord Lytton, George Moore, whom Jacques Blanche had brought along, and the unforgettable ephebe, Marcel Proust.'[102] Apart from the last, there is not a single great writer among these famous names: neither Verlaine nor Zola, neither Mallarmé nor Bloy. It is true that no one invited them; such was the empty self-satisfaction of the salons of the Belle Époque, biased as they were towards the Académie.

At an early stage Proust invited Mme Straus and her son to the theatre, sent her flowers[103] and paid her compliments. Throughout his life, he pretended to be in love with her. This was both because she expected this behaviour from all her admirers and because she epitomized everything he was able to love in a woman – wit, charm, elegance, affection, motherliness – yet he did not have to desire her, for it was entirely excusable not to desire the mother of one's friends. Similar tendencies to those of Proust have often resulted in the most tender friendships with older women (Geneviève was twenty-two years older than Proust). Finally, just as Proust was charmed by seascapes before he described them, so there was the initially subconscious attraction of the future artist for his model. The autobiographer relates what he has lived through; the novelist lives in order to relate.

Such was the 'child of 1888', whom nobody has described better than Paul Desjardins: 'This young Persian prince with his huge gazelle eyes and languorous eyelids; an expression that was at once respectful, undulating, caressing and anxious; a collector of pleasures, for whom nothing was dull; irritated by the obstacles with which nature thwarted man's efforts – especially so fragile a man as he; endeavouring to make something active out of the passivity that seemed to be his lot; who strove for the *most*, for what was *too much*, even in his delightful kindness: this romantic child, I would draw him readily, from memory.'[104]

PHILOSOPHIE

The *philosophie* class, which Marcel entered on 1 October 1888, was renowned for having a great teacher, Alphonse Darlu. Born in 1849, he had passed first in the *agrégation de philosophie* in 1871, he had taught at the Lycée Condorcet since 1885; he finished his career as an inspector-general for the Instruction Publique (1900), retired in 1919, and died in 1921. In 1893 he founded the *Revue de métaphysique et de morale*,[105] in which he very occasionally published his lectures[106] and reading notes[107] under the title 'A Philosopher's Reflections on Questions of the Day'. The position of philosophy teacher was a recent appointment in the schools of the newly formed Republic; it was filled by a long line of men, including Lachelier, Lagneau, Émile Chartier and, later, Michel Alexandre, who were less concerned with publishing books than with shaping minds, and doing so at the lycée rather than at university: their life's work was their class; Darlu's classes at Condorcet[108] were spoken of in the same breath as Alain's at the Lycée Henri IV. Lachelier was not mistaken when, after paying a visit to the school in February 1889, he observed: 'I was often struck by the passionate interest shown by the pupils, by their knowledge, their perception and their philosophical turn of mind. M. Darlu is a teacher who thinks and can make others think, who loves philosophy and can make others love it. To succeed, he needed the highly intelligent atmosphere of Condorcet . . .'[109]

The *philosophie* class was described by Barrès in *Les Déracinés* (1897); it was based upon M. Bouteillier's class at the lycée in Nancy (1879–80), which the author had known under the direction of Burdeau, and later of Lagneau. In it, he demonstrated how 'the University is a powerful instrument of the State in the shaping of minds . . . They are Republicans in the lycées.' M. Bouteillier would 'lift these impressionable children above their native passions, towards reason, towards humanity'. Vast horizons were opened up to them, out of the class phrases would flow 'with the force of a musical theme which made them responsive to the natural law'. Like Darlu and all this generation, Bouteillier was a Kantian in both the cognitive and the moral disciplines: 'The world is merely wax upon which our mind, like a seal, imposes its imprint';[110] the conduct of each one of us ought to be able to be presented as a universal maxim. This teaching was criticized by Barrès, who accused it of imposing the power of the Republic over people's minds without regard for the individual and his 'roots'. In this he followed in the steps of Bourget:

Le Disciple (1889) already displayed the harmful influences of Adrien Sixte's positivist teaching. When Proust depicted M. Beulier's class in *Jean Santeuil*, he was using the same descriptive analysis, but he had the opposite ideological intentions. Far less reactionary, and much more Republican than his predecessors, he praised the teaching which they criticized, and he described the professor humorously, but without Barrès' scathing irony. M. Beulier resembles Darlu: the same Bordeaux accent, the same 'energetic and ruddy' demeanour. His discourse comprises truth, goodness, certainty and science. Among his pupils, he seeks out an artistic and decadent style.[111] As a result he provoked a sense of disappointed expectation in Jean, who had imagined that, with the help of quotations from Renan and Barrès, Beulier would be full of a 'disillusioned gentleness', and that his ideas would be dilettante and sceptical, like those of Leconte de Lisle – in other words, he shared the same experiences the Narrator had with Bergotte. With deftness and humour, Proust embodied in his characterization the attitudes of those pupils who have a talent for literature and who as a result imagine philosophy to be some melodious and graceful discourse, and who are therefore shocked at the philosopher's abstract reasoning, which is generally stripped of any style. And yet, gradually, the philosopher became one of those intermediaries whom Marcel had long had need of: 'Where his professor had sown a single word, Jean, who cultivated it lovingly, would after a little while discover an idea germinating.'[112]

There is a trace of these germinating ideas in a homework essay[113] which reflects the ideas of Lachelier as well as of Darlu and Marcel. We encounter the topics that have been broached, the relationships that have been outlined, the resolute affirmation and reasoning, in the philosophical pages of *À la recherche*. The title of the essay, 'La Spiritualité de l'âme', is indicative of the spiritual, though not religious, mind of the professor of philosophy at a time when philosophical, as well as political, thinking had broken with Catholicism, without relinquishing the soul, nor, on occasion, a vaguely divine principle: Ernest Renan was one of the great figures of the burgeoning Republic, and he dined with the Prousts.[114] In Marcel's essay, his initial thoughts are concerned with the soul and the body: 'a lesion in the brain breaks the balance of the mind for good'; this fear is present right up to the last pages of *Le Temps retrouvé*. The way we grasp phenomena raises problems of time and the unity of the self: 'We no more have an intuition of a one, identical self than we do an intuition of a material substance. What we do grasp is precisely that which is within the grasp of our knowledge, that is to say whatever exists in time, that is transient and specific.' Thought unites the self; it is the universal that is realized in the individual: 'How? That, doubtless, is the deep mystery of the moral being which philosophy will never entirely explain.' Nevertheless, it does enable us, as we can see in Kant's *Critique of Pure Reason*, to 'regulate our most private actions according to universal ends'. Darlu, as we know, was a Kantian moralist (who did not disregard the French moralists; M. Beulier taught Jean Santeuil 'the meaning, the spirit, the moral succour' of Joubert's works, and also that there was no need to possess a book materially, since its spiritual content, which was to do with its essence, was enough;[115] unlike many asthmatics, Marcel would never be a biblio-phile, nor a book collector). Proust would never lose that sense of the universal, nor that moral sense with which not only the most virtuous characters in his novel are blessed, such as the grandmother, but also the most perverse, such as Mlle Vinteuil and her friend. Darlu's system of morals was not Christian; it was closer to Tolstoy.[116] He had no faith beyond the cult of the truth.[117] Nevertheless, in an age when the positivism and scientism that were inherited from Taine were still highly influential, here was a French philosophy that was derived from Aristotle and, in particular, from Kant, along with Ravaisson, Renouvier, Fouillée and Boutroux (Proust's teacher at the Sorbonne), which defended the causes of metaphysics, idealism and spiritualism. In an age when sensitivity and intelligence were especially receptive and fascinated by ideas and faith, it was this philosophical approach which, through Darlu, Proust adopted. He would not forget it, even when he was to write: 'No man has ever had any influence on me (except Darlu and I recognized that it was bad).'[118] He was all the more influenced by it when he had private lessons, or when he accompanied his teacher after the lessons, detaining him with questions right up to his doorstep; in this way he became something of a joke and a legendary figure in the Darlu family.[119]

The day after the beginning of term (2 October 1888), Marcel wrote an astonishing letter to his new teacher, in which he unburdened himself to a stranger in a manner that, as he himself was aware, was exceptionally intimate, and in which he cast light on his inner life from 'the age of fourteen or fifteen'.[120] At this period, in fact, he was beginning to withdraw into himself and to examine his inner life. At about the age of sixteen, this analysis became a torment and an intolerable physical obsession. Marcel took advantage of the improvement in his health to 'respond to the exhaustion and despair that this constant self-examination caused'.

His suffering was then 'intellectualized', which had an effect upon what was 'his greatest joy', his literary existence: 'When I read a poem by Leconte de Lisle, for instance, all the time that I am enjoying the infinite sensual delights as I did in the past, the other *I* is watching me, enjoying observing the causes of my pleasure, seeing a certain connection in them between myself and the work, and thus destroying the certainty of the work's *own* beauty, above all it immediately starts imagining different prerequisites for beauty, and finally kills virtually all my enjoyment.' The pain that gnaws away at the young Proust, as it did at Valéry, is self-consciousness, 'that gaze that is constantly focused upon [his] inner life'. It developed abnormally, and initially almost pathologically, but would later return as his creative conscience. The whole of *À la recherche* is structured around the division between the 'I' of the Narrator who reflects on his life and the empirical self who lives its life, in the same way that Valéry's *Jeune Parque* does between herself and her 'secret sister'. The cure therefore lay not, as Marcel first thought on 2 October 1888, during a crisis that was similar to Valéry's night in Genoa, in the destruction of the inner life, which he considered 'appalling', but in literary creation, in the man who writes and who analyses the self who has lived and is alive – just like the one who reads. The relationship between the creator and the work will be symmetrical with the relationship between the work and the reader.

Marcel would write yet more shameless confessions throughout his year in *philosophie*. Later, he would learn to be more reserved, though without abandoning his outbursts. They would be addressed to women – to Laure Hayman, Mme Straus, Louisa de Mornand, Mme de Chevigné, Princesse Soutzo – as if to assuage a deep need without incurring any danger, since prudence forbade him to yield directly. The year 1888–9 was the last in which Marcel spoke freely about himself, about his mind, his love, his body and his yearnings, and he did so with a fierceness which flew in the face of the languid young man portrayed in his photographs.

Ever since the preceding year, Daniel Halévy had been Marcel's confidant. In the autumn he had sent Halévy his sonnet 'Pederasty': 'I want to sleep with, love or live for ever/ With a warm child, Jacques, Pierre or Firmin.'[121] Halévy then criticized his friend for being 'a dandy' and 'world-weary'; wrongly, responded Marcel, who hurled himself ferociously into a veritable declaration: 'If I consider you to be lovely, if I find that your beautiful shining eyes reflect the delicate grace of your mind so perfectly that it seems to me that I am unable to love your mind completely unless I kiss your eyes, if your body and your eyes seem to me as slender and supple as your thoughts so that I feel that I could mingle more closely with your thoughts by sitting on your knee,* if, finally, it seems to me that the charm of your being you, your you in which I am unable to distinguish your lively mind from your delicate body, would refine and increase the "sweet joy of love" for me, there is nothing there that makes me deserve the scornful remarks which would be more fittingly addressed to a blasé womanizer seeking new pleasures in homosexuality.'[122] Proust then employed some specious arguments: after having had fun with a friend at the beginning of their youth, others had reverted to women; Socrates and Montaigne 'thought that these friendships that were both sensual and intellectual were worth more when one was young than relationships with foolish and corrupt women';† finally, where morals were concerned, Marcel tried to 'remain pure' and asked his friend not to treat him as a 'pederast'.

As we have seen, Proust would not give up Jacques Bizet completely until the end of the year. In October 1888 he dedicated a passage, 'Pour la revue Lilas', in which the same obsession returned: 'Oh! My little friend, why am I not sitting on your knee, my head on your breast, why don't you love me?'[123] According to Robert Dreyfus, Bizet was in fact only attracted to women. In February 1889 Jacques Bizet inscribed a photograph of himself (with prudent reticence) 'To my dearest friend (along with Daniel Halévy)'.[124] At the same period Marcel unburdened himself, curiously, to another schoolfriend, Raoul Versini. He struck up a friendship with him, wrote to him frequently and sometimes went to spend the night at his home when M. and Mme Proust were away on their travels; Raoul attempted to dissuade him from his tendencies. It was probably after one of these lectures that Marcel confided certain things to him, the truthfulness of which may be open to doubt.[125] He said he had been caught by surprise and, in 'a moment of madness', agreed to 'something very filthy', which a boy begged him to do; his partner was stronger than he and he had been unable to stop him: 'I agreed beforehand, that's all there was.' Marcel also confessed himself, 'one hour later', to their friend Abel Desjardins, and then to his father, who, aware of his proclivities, did not condemn him and only considered 'his error as nothing more than a surprise'.

---

* The Narrator would also take Albertine upon his lap – without anything further occurring, possibly.

† In *Sodome et Gomorrhe*, Proust would refute the 'Socratic' justification for homosexuality and would no longer invoke Montaigne. Even if he added, 'I think these old masters were mistaken, I'll tell you why.'

Marcel therefore related his 'error' to at least three people, one of whom was his father (which answers definitively the question: did his parents know?). Did he go further than 'anodyne simulations', as Gide puts it in *Paludes*, just this once? Did he, suffering from the shock and the traumatic effect of semi-rape, seek comfort for his moral misery and his feelings of guilt by confessing, not to a priest, since he was not a believer, but to certain of his friends (albeit not the usual ones: not Bizet, Halévy or Dreyfus)? He would, in short, feel himself obliged, out of some sort of compulsion, to relate everything that happened to him. He would be like Rousseau in this irrepressible need to confess, something for which the stories in *Les Plaisirs et les Jours* would soon provide an outlet and a camouflage. Between pleasure and regret, between ostentation and humiliation, the definitive and the temporary, this masochistic statement reveals for an instant the contradictions of the adolescent boy, who exhibits himself in order to be seduced, while at the same time knowing that his advances are rejected. He confesses so as to soothe himself, in order to be forgiven, perhaps so as to continue to be loved.*

Laure Hayman inspired both a strange passion in Marcel and some curious declarations.[126] At every period or stage of his life, he would combine a platonic emotional liaison with a woman – generally somebody well-known (if not 'famous', as he described this 'courtesan' in a letter to Dreyfus in September 1888) – with his involvements with young men. Mme Straus, Mme de Chevigné, Louisa de Mornand, Comtesse Greffulhe, Princesse Soutzo on the one hand; Reynaldo Hahn, Lucien Daudet, Fénelon, Morand, Agostinelli on the other. Thus we see the first intimations of the situation which he would describe and summarize to Gide in 1921: 'He said he never loved women except in a spiritual sense and that he had only known love with men.'[127] What was important was the coexistence of both spiritual and carnal love (as in the case of Gide, whose spiritual

---

* Note that in the early versions of 'La Confession d'une jeune fille' (*P et J*, p. 90, n. 5, pp. 948–9) there is a story that is very similar to Versini's letter: 'some young men came to see me. One of them induced me to do wrong almost by surprise. When the desire again became too strong, I did not have the will to resist. The habit of not resisting to the temptation of pleasure came to her quite naturally. There was no shortage of obscene boys. At first, I had appalling remorse, and I made vows which were misunderstood.' And between the lines: 'One day he took advantage of the feelings I had for him and which my mother knew about and induced me to do wrong almost by surprise . . . Only one of them was a scoundrel. He behaved in a way that was both gentle and bold. He was the one I fell in love with. My parents knew and were not at all sharp with me.' Self-abuse, remorse, the vows, the parents who knew: it is all there. Cf. 'Avant la nuit', *JS*, pp. 167–71.

love for his wife was combined with a desire for boys and his passionate feelings for Marc Allegret). Laure Hayman was a courtesan, but in addition her way of life, her style of dress, her beauty, her social graces, her admirers – who came from a variety of royal families, the nobility and from artistic and literary circles – made her a work of art. It was as a work of art that Marcel admired her and pretended to love her, endeavouring to cast himself as her possession, her 'little porcelain psychologist', as she called him. Laure collected Saxe porcelain, and Paul Bourget, one of her admirers, who, as we have seen, had portrayed the young woman (before Proust made her the model for Odette) in the guise of Gladys Harvey,[128] wrote to her: 'Little Marcel, your porcelain psychologist, as you call him, is quite simply delightful.' Using Laure as his intermediary, Marcel let Bourget know of his admiration for him, and the latter replied that he would be very pleased to meet the young man, just as the Narrator comes to meet Bergotte thanks to Odette. His classmates at the Lycée Condorcet, however, considered the situation ridiculous; they had discovered that Laure Hayman was wild about the young man (who thus replaced the great-uncle with his great-nephew), 'dragged him about everywhere', and that he visited her home, where he made the acquaintance of 'dukes, men of letters and future academicians'.[129] There was twenty years difference between them: it was like the Countess and Cherubino. She gave him a copy of *Gladys Harvey* as a present, bound in silk from one of her petticoats, which was inscribed: 'To Marcel Proust. You mustn't love someone like Gladys Harvey'[130] – in other words, she took his love for her more seriously than he deserved. He sent her flowers, and, later on, pieces of Saxe porcelain as well as poems. There was no lack of lilac, of 'hair like the sun', of discreetly sensuous descriptions ('a neck as slender as a Moorish column/ Pale breasts graced by a rose'), nor of the unconscious admission that woman may be a goddess, but she can also be a killer: 'My glorious spirit shall not see the dawn/ a god has sent you; killer of men, I adore you.'[131]

MAGAZINES

The indefatigable Marcel, whose ill-health, as he wrote to Darlu, was definitely giving him some respite, was also busy, like many a schoolboy before and since, setting up magazines or literary reviews. These consisted of short, edited pieces, with a limited circulation and they were often printed in manuscript form and discussed at the lycée; until his death, Marcel remained loyal to this type of publication. The first of them, in

October 1888, was *La Revue verte* (so called because of the colour of the paper that a teacher from *seconde* insisted upon so as to protect his eyes), only one copy of which was produced, to be circulated among subscribers: it is hardly surprising that it has disappeared; all that survives is a reply from the 'secretary', Marcel Proust, to a request from Daniel Halévy that he keep the magazine in his personal archives. Marcel emphasized that the purpose of the magazine was 'simple enjoyment' and that 'the articles were merely the playful and ephemeral reflections of the mobility of imaginations at play'.[132] A story by Jacques Bizet, entitled 'Georges Royer', also survives, about which Marcel commented as follows: 'The story of a failure is one of the most melancholy motifs that exist. Yet it is also one of the most profoundly human, one of the hardest to understand, one of the most mysteriously impenetrable.' Bizet was too young to have thought 'philosophically' about this, but the 'mysterious helplessness' of the character has an explanation that 'confronts us with laws that are extremely vexing, but inviolable'.[133] It is as if Marcel had foreseen, a very long time ago, that the story of a failure – or of two failures, Swann, and then the Narrator – would become his subject – and this is without taking into account *Jean Santeuil*, which was still not written, not to mention Jacques Bizet himself. The subject provoked a profound impact on him; he also believed that the mystery was explicable, and that psychology followed certain laws – something we shall come across in *Le Temps retrouvé*.

This hapax legomenon was followed by *La Revue lilas* in November 1888, so called 'because its cover was the same pale mauve as the slim exercise books we bought for two or three sous at the little stationer's shop in the Passage du Havre'.[134] Three contributions by Proust were preserved by Robert Dreyfus.[135] The first was a portrait in the Antique style – that style which inspired Flaubert, France and Louÿs, and which Proust would hardly ever succumb to again – of 'the charming Glaukos', 'alone, almost naked'. The young man is sorting through the 'letters of friendship' that he has received: 'They all begin: My dear little Glaukos, or my dearest Glaukos, or oh you my best of friends, or my soft little creature, or my little darling.' 'All these desperate dreams that he might be loved passionately in the way he wanted to be, by this person or that'*

---

* This continues: 'They were almost all realized. Yet a fulfilled friendship was not forthcoming.' This business of fickleness is a confession. *Écrits de jeunesse*, p. 120, dated by Dreyfus, 'before 15 October 1888', which slightly contradicts the November date, which he gives elsewhere, for the magazine.

were very much Marcel's dreams. What follows reveals more wish than fulfilment: 'Today his emotions have cooled. But he has many friends and he is deeply loved by some of them . . . Often seated on one of their trembling laps, cheek to cheek, one body tucked up against the other, they discuss Aristotle's philosophy together, or the poems of Euripides, each kissing and caressing the other as they make wise and elegant remarks.' In the history of Proustian sexuality, this is a moment for homosexual and Socratic fantasy, for Grecian nudity, for caresses (nothing more) and intelligence: Glaukos is Marcel as he longs to be. The narrator of the following passage, 'for the revue Lilas/ subject to it being destroyed at a later date/ to my dear friend Jacques Bizet', is alone in bed at night, while on a small table lie 'some delicately bound little books, some letters of friendship or love'. He then writes: 'Being unable to suppress them, I have consecrated everyday things, like the countryside. I have clothed them in myself and with private and splendid images . . . I am at the centre of everything':[136] it is the man who sleeps, from the very beginning of 'Combray', who holds these worlds transfixed. Finally, the 'Theatrical notes'[137] recall the figure of Jules Lemaître, whose theatre reviews Marcel read in *Le Journal des débats*, and various actors: Mounet-Sully, the 'divine', the 'execrable' Albert Lambert, the 'astonishing' Mlle Weber, and a considerable number of plays: *Athalie*, the review *Les Joyeusetés de l'année* (at the Palais-Royal), *Mignon, Cendrillon* (a *féerie*, or spectacular, at the Châtelet), *Le Pied de mouton*, a spectacular at the Porte-Saint-Martin, and *Mimi*, a vaudeville show at the Nouveautés. If Marcel really had seen all these shows in October 1888, he shared with the Narrator of *Du côté de chez Swann* and *À l'ombre des jeunes filles en fleurs* his enthusiasm for the theatre. And yet, unlike the great French nineteenth-century novelists, from Balzac and Zola to the Goncourts, Proust never wrote a play; actors, a love of the stage and quotations from Racine; all have their place in his books, but he is far too concerned with looking for what underlies dialogue to be satisfied with stage conversation.

These critical initiations are followed by the strict lessons on style that he gave to his unfortunate friend Daniel Halévy. In the margins of the poem 'Amour' (in two versions), which the latter wrote, Marcel noted: 'Foolish thinking, language and versifying', 'irritating cliché', 'childish', 'nothing but parasitic words', 'grotesque', 'not French'. His overall reproof is that Halévy did not express his thought sincerely, in its integrity. Marcel already knew – and it was one of the reasons for his confessions – that he must be absolutely and entirely truthful in what he wrote. Similarly, he condemns 'inapposite imagery', whatever may be 'naturalist *ergo* foolish', and anything that was 'decadent', that derived from those decadents whom Daniel Halévy admired and imitated, but whom Marcel, after being briefly drawn to them while in *rhétorique*, dismissed – something that would always protect him from writing in an artistic, modish or avant-garde style. The advice that he offered to his friend says much for his broad culture and his classical tastes: 'Read Homer, Plato, Lucretius, Virgil, Tacitus, Shakespeare, Shelley, Emerson, Goethe, La Fontaine, Racine, Villon, Théophile,* Bossuet, La Bruyère, Descartes, Montesquieu, Rousseau, Diderot, Flaubert, Sainte-Beuve, Baudelaire, Renan, France.'† The only living authors were the last two.

The year he spent in *philosophie* – at the end of which he was awarded first-prize honours in French essay writing as well as passing the *baccalauréat* – would help equip Marcel with an ideological, idealistic and rationalist, philosophical system. He would always retain his belief in ideas, in laws and in the Kantian conventions of perception. His early essays display great critical assurance. His interest in magazines portends a literary vocation. Finally, since he appeared to be attracted by young men, his sexuality inclined him towards his own kind, something he scarcely tried to conceal: he only denied it once he had admitted it. At the time that he left the lycée, many of the features of his personality were already formed, many of the themes of his work had, without his being aware of it, already taken shape, ready to be resuscitated in due course.

In his books, however, his schoolfriends hardly seem to have left him with very happy memories. They are recalled in a few pages of *Jean Santeuil*, in which, moreover, daily life at school is not mentioned, but they do not figure at all in *À la recherche*. Classes, friends and teachers have vanished: not a ghost of Robert de Billy, Dreyfus, Halévy or La Salle. The young man wrote *Les Plaisirs et les Jours* and forgot entirely about his studies. Of those years there remained the literary and philosophical culture which Proust frequently made use of, as well as his knowledge of the classics, of Latin phrases and the basic principles of metaphysics; there remained his first experiences of love, the discovery of his homosexuality and the promises, difficulties and rebuffs this would entail. Finally, the literary

---

* Théophile de Viau (1590–1626), classical poet and dramatist, always referred to by his first name. *Tr.*

† 'And, *super omnes*, Ludovic Halévy', concludes Marcel by way of homage to his friend's uncle (*Écrits de jeunesse*, pp. 157–67).

magazines that he and his friends founded gave us the first passages from *Les Plaisirs et les Jours*, or their early drafts; everything else consisted of the absences from school of a young invalid, whose pleasures were to be found at home. His adequate, uneven but scarcely brilliant academic results are proof that successful academic and literary careers do not necessarily go together: it is not those who come top of the class who write the most beautiful verse, nor the authors of *Le Petit Chose*, or *Le Livre de mon ami*, or *Le Roman d'un enfant*, but rather the eccentrics. For them, school was soon forgotten.

CHAPTER IV

Summer Holidays
(1889–91)

One can be several ages simultaneously. After passing his *baccalauréat* and obtaining his prizes at the end of July 1889, Marcel, like the small child he never ceased to be, sank into depression. His mother had left with Robert to take the waters at Salies-de-Béarn and was not at first aware of her elder son's 'moral isolation'; she was upset to see him '*sens dessus dessous*' (however, since there was still room for humour, she added: 'and also that you write it without underwear',* etc). Both his pulse and his style 'were beating too loudly'.[1] This was still very much the boy for whom the greatest misery was 'to be separated from maman'.

OSTENDE, THE FINALYS

Marcel was not alone, however. He was staying at Ostende with the Finalys, at one of Europe's most elegant resorts; every year the King of the Belgians launched the season there, and several concerts were given each day at the Casino, which had its own orchestra of 150 musicians. There was a fine sandy beach, some superb parks and festivities to keep the swimmers amused.[2] Horace Finaly was in the same form as Marcel at the Lycée Condorcet. Fernand Gregh has described the family, whom he considered 'Shakespearean'. Horace, 'who was to preside over the Banque de Paris et des Pays-Bas and, at one period, over the French Treasury, was at this time a fairly short, powerfully built boy, who was both a metaphysician and a melancholic, and who in his unwillingness to take up his fencing sword bore a great resemblance to Hamlet'.[3] He would serve as a model not just for Proust's Bloch, but for Giraudoux's Moses in *Bella*.[4] Hugo Finaly, the father, 'a little, short-legged, plump man, with

---

* Marcel had made a mistake: instead of writing *sens dessus*, he wrote *sans dessous*, which alters the meaning and occasioned Mme Proust's pun. *Tr.*

sideburns in the Austrian style, who might well have played the part of Polonius',[5] enshrined, in his position as head of the Banque de Paris et des Pays-Bas, that world of high finance with which Marcel had more to do than one might think, from Robert de Billy's father-in-law to the Foulds and the Rothschilds; Hugo Finaly appeared in his novel in the guise of Sir Rufus Israel or even Nissim Bernard. Mme Finaly, 'a superb woman', who would maintain connections with Marcel (when he was looking for a villa near Florence, for example), held a literary salon, which was attended by Porto-Riche. She also had a daughter, Marie, who had a pale face and sea-green eyes. 'What delightful and kind people these Finalys are,' wrote Marcel to Robert de Billy in 1893. 'How good-looking and intelligent they are! Mademoiselle Marie looks as if she had been painted by Dante Rossetti who had just met Shakespeare, the indisputable creator of Horatio, in the rue Pierre-Charron.'[6] Horatio, who was absorbed by classical civilization, was said to be able to read Homer in the original. Certain of his mannerisms are to be found in the character of Bloch, others in Octave, and the entire family may have been the inspiration for the Bloch family.[7] Mme Hugo Finaly's uncle, Horace de Landau, 'the ancestor, the great man',[8] lived in Florence; he was nicknamed '*roi Lire*' by Fernand Gregh, for he had made his fortune in Italy, where he had represented the Rothschilds. He was famous for his cultivated knowledge, his witty sayings and his library. He would give the Villa des Frémonts, at Trouville, to his niece just so as to 'tease' her. Arthur Baignères, who sold him the villa, exclaimed: 'He's Taquin the Proud';* Proust would put these words into the mouth of Oriane de Guermantes, talking about Charlus, when she gives a country house to her sister, Mme de Marsantes.[9] Marcel, writing to M. de Landau, hoped to 'immerse himself a little in the reddish-grey waves of his beard once more, the bright blue of [his] eyes and the pale blue of [his] tie'.[10] Getting to know this family was therefore to be extremely useful to the future writer.

We come across Ostende in *Jean Santeuil*, in the characteristic form of memory, since Proust lived events twice (at least): his actual, day-to-day existence, and his resurrection through memory. It was not when he was on this Belgian beach but ten years later that he thought and wrote, 'And very close by, was Ostende where he had been as a child . . . He was aware of a curious sensation as he thought of such a different past linking him with the present, and that by following the grey shore of this immense

---

* Another pun: the French for 'to tease' is *taquiner*. Tr.

grey sea . . . he would reach Ostende . . . which for him was a beach that was cut off from the rest of the world.'[11] And so it was that as he recalled 'the North Sea, the Baltic and Dieppe', Jean observed that only Nature 'by making us feel what we once felt before, can lead us to some point in the fabulous world of our memories which has become the world of truth'.[12]

During his stay there, Marcel provided proof of his delicate sensibility, in that he was upset because Mme Finaly was worried about her own mother's health. 'I can understand,' Mme Proust wrote to him, not without a touch of irony, 'how upset you must be by poor Mme Finaly's sadness but how old is her mother in fact?'[13] Furthermore, he seemed to be leading a trying, restless life: 'I advise absolute calm, a diet, hours of solitude and refusing to go on outings,' his mother wrote to him again. The stimulus of the North Sea stirred the young man, drawn by the waves, the wind and the storms.[14] This stimulus, which was 'too strong' according to Mme Proust, was not merely something physical and nervous; it was also artistic, and it enabled Marcel to recognize one of his great themes, one that he would take up several times in *Les Plaisirs et les Jours*: 'The sea will always fascinate those to whom world-weariness and the lure of mystery have already brought early sadness, like a premonition of the inadequacy of reality to satisfy them. Those who need rest even before they have experienced any fatigue will be consoled and mildly stimulated by the sea.'[15] This Baudelairean theme was complemented by another, which recalled nocturnal anxiety, the absence of the mother: 'The sea has the charm of those things that do not fall silent at night, which, in our restless lives, grant us leave to sleep, a promise that all will not vanish, like a nightlight for small children who feel less lonely when it glows.'[16] So it is that we see very old thoughts and anxieties finding their way into the most recent phrases, and Ostende as a precursor of Trouville.

MADAME ARMAN DE CAILLAVET

That summer Marcel was introduced into one of the principal literary salons in Paris. Mme Arman de Caillavet,[17] as far as Marcel Proust and his friend Fernand Gregh were concerned, represented great wealth, a salon and a passion. Léontine Lippman was born, like Anatole France, in 1844; her father was a banker of German extraction. Cultivated, intelligent, interested in the arts, and able to converse in four languages, she was still beautiful, with light blue eyes, dark hair and a lively and mocking smile, and she was steadfast in her friendships; as was frequently the case at the time, her feeling for literature was destined to find its expression in a literary salon. At first she had attended Mme Aubernon's, at which she must have met Anatole France in 1883. Married to Albert Arman (whose mother was a Caillavet), the compound name, together with the particle '*de*', had given her, like many another, an assumed nobility. The couple were hardly ever faithful to one another, but they did not divorce. An *hôtel particulier*, at 12 avenue Hoche, allowed her to entertain: in the salon, Mme Arman sat in a wing chair, to the right of the fireplace; Anatole France stood in front of it.[18] M. Arman kept making ironic remarks about the writer, and his wife would say: 'Be quiet, Albert, you're just talking nonsense.' M. de Caillavet's contribution to literature, apart from his matrimonial indulgence, consisted in writing a yachting column for *Le Figaro*, under the byline Jip Topsail. France helped him with one of his articles, but his elucidations were rejected by the newspaper: 'Ha! Ha! The great writer, the great academician! They thought all our embellishments were pointless!' France merely commented: 'M. Arman, who knows all about the art of writing . . .'[19]

This salon was attended each week by writers, members of parliament, lawyers, actors and artists, but not by musicians – neither France nor Mme Arman liked music; guests included Poincaré, Barthou, Jaurès, Clemenceau, Comte Primoli, the friend of Proust and Lucien Daudet, the painter Munkaczy (whom Proust would mention), Marcel Schwob, Barrès, before he was elected to the Académie française, and Maurras. Apart from these Sunday receptions, at which there might be more than a hundred guests, there were the Wednesday dinners, with their 'guided' conversations, reminiscent of Mme Verdurin,[20] attended by Dumas *fils*; the Hellenist Brochard, who was a professor at the Sorbonne (the model for Brichot), author of *Sceptiques grecs*, and Mme Arman's lover before Anatole France; Doctor Pozzi, a famous doctor, but also a very social one, who was eventually murdered by one of his former patients; Leconte de Lisle; Heredia and Renan. And France . . . In 1888 Mme Arman and he were lovers, impassioned, torn apart and burnt up with jealousy, a jealousy worthy of Swann or the Princesse de Guermantes. If Proust was able to identify the models behind the characters, France's *Le Lys rouge* may have revealed something of this passionate affair. If he merely judged it on appearances, which was enough for him to imagine Bergotte's private life, after Mme de Caillavet's death he came to know the drama that was being enacted so close at hand, through the revelations of Robert de Flers, a friend of the Armans' son, Gaston. Bergotte's private life would make him reprehensible and cause him to be disapproved of. But he had no muse or woman to inspire him, whereas Mme de Caillavet is said to have had a great influence on France's intellectual and literary development. After her death, he produced his masterpiece, *Les Dieux ont soif*, *La Révolte des anges*, and, the final return to his cherished childhood, *Le Petit Pierre* (1919) and *La Vie en fleur* (1922). A survivor from another age, France outlived Proust, but in his work he, too, endures, whether in or out of fashion, whether triumphantly acclaimed or outmoded.

PROUST AND FRANCE

Anatole France began writing for *Le Temps* on 21 March 1886. It was from this date that Proust, aged fifteen, first read him: 'Saturday is like a feast day for me, when *Le Temps* brings me the very purest of pleasures. For four years, I have read and re-read your divine books until I knew them by heart. And for four years I have enjoyed you so much that I believe I understand you a little.' He also read out these letters to his schoolfriends and his teachers (whom he 'catechized') at Condorcet: Darlu, 'a great thinker', had 'an extremely intelligent love' for these books. In *La Vie littéraire*, on several occasions, France mentioned his own conversations with Darlu, who was philosophical, idealistic, but not sceptical. France's role as far as Proust was concerned would be as a mediator; according to what was later to become the aesthetics of *Le Temps retrouvé*, the artist finds in books, ideas and in his fellow man 'a beauty that formerly [he] did not know how to make use of'. Only the 'physical person' of the writer was hard for the young man to imagine.[21] This person, as he appeared to him, can be seen in Bergotte, but also, with greater precision, in Fernand Gregh's memoirs.

Gregh was introduced by Marcel Proust at the home of Mme Arman de Caillavet and was one of the first subscribers to the literary magazine *Le Banquet*; he drew a picture of France as the two young men had seen him: a countenance conspicuous for its high intelligence, rippling with ideas, bowed down with courtesies, someone initially straightforward and good-natured. It was Mme de Caillavet 'who gave him his self-belief and the just ambition to write masterpieces'.[22] In her salon France was all smiles ('at times, however, from a certain period onwards, his face would be fraught with passion whenever he discussed politics'); he talked endlessly, but in bursts; he was less concerned with stories than with ideas, to which his anecdotes, spoken with hesitations and mumbling, merely lent force. With his hair cropped very short, his pointed beard and his curled moustache, he resembled 'a Bonapartist cavalry officer'. This martial aspect was balanced by his smile. Later on, he allowed his white beard to grow: 'In short, the magnificent old man, whose effigy Bourdelle sculpted, in which the smile of the sceptical philosopher is hidden beneath the somewhat sad gravity of someone who contemplates.' Those wonderful eyes, dark and 'moist with light', which saw everything without appearing to be looking.

His conversation allowed his immense culture to filter out. 'How do you manage, Monsieur France, to know so much?' Proust once asked him. 'It's very simple, my dear Marcel; when I was your age, I was not handsome like you, I was not particularly well liked, I did not go out in society and stayed at home reading, reading continuously.'[23] France, as he spoke, 'charmed one with a mixture of irony and kindness, wit and grace, simplicity and erudition, imagination and common sense';[24] he had the same manner that one comes across in the series he wrote for *Le Temps*, reprinted in *La Vie littéraire*, where there is the occasional trace of a wounded soul in the lightness of tone.

It was in October or November 1889 that Proust was introduced to Mme Arman de Caillavet and to Anatole France, and that he met Gaston de Caillavet. In 1922, he wrote to the latter's widow: 'No, I did not know Gaston at school. He may have been a pupil at the same lycée as me (Condorcet), but I never knew him there. I can't remember who it was who first took me to Gaston's mother's home, I know that I was about to go off to do military service, which I did when I was very young because it was the last year of what was termed voluntary service ... He was about to finish just as I started and it was during the very short "leaves" that I caught a glimpse of him at his mother's house. But he was so delightful to me when I was there that our friendship began immediately.'[25]

MILITARY SERVICE

On 11 November 1889 Marcel enlisted for his national service, on the one-year volunteer scheme. Thanks to the *loi organique* of 27 July 1872, he avoided serving his country for a further two years.* Changes had just

---

* This law, the fruit of a compromise between Thiers, who was in favour of a professional army drawn by lots, and the Assemblée, which wanted a national army recruited by a short, obligatory period of national service, along German lines, provided that every Frenchman between the ages of twenty to forty could be called up. The length of active service was five years. Half the contingent, drawn by lots, served throughout this period; the other half for one year. If you had a certain

been introduced as a result of the law of 18 July 1889, which did away with drawing lots and the volunteer scheme (retained during 1889) and introduced a three-year period of military service.* At the time, military life was beginning to attract criticism in intellectual circles. Abel Hermant's novel, *Le Cavalier Miserey* (1887), which had been denounced as 'anti-patriotic' by Anatole France, was burned by officers in the courtyard of a barracks and defended by Lyautey, himself an author, in 1891, in an unconventional article on 'The social role of the officer in general military service'. Lucien Descaves published *Sous-offs* in 1889, was prosecuted in court, but was acquitted. There were numerous anti-military writings from the pens of Darien, Zo d'Axa,[26] Gourmont, Péladan and Paul Adam. Equally Zola's *La Débâcle* (1892) depicted the army in an unfavourable light. Paul Valéry, who did his military service at the same time as Proust, exclaimed: 'Now I've already served a month of slavery, a month of painful sacrifice to the motherland! A month that has been enough for me to appreciate the harsh reality of Descaves' book . . . It's easy to speak of self-sacrifice with your feet up by the fire and a glass in hand. It's easy for those who have nothing to think about to spit forth words about the *Décadent* soldiers, that is to say about those who are nevertheless prepared to think, even though they are being strangled by their cartridge belts! For my part, the motherland is not to be found beneath the folds of a flag nor in a land constricted by frontiers.'[27]

Yet, in the opinion of the majority, the army enjoyed great prestige, up until the Dreyfus affair, under the leadership of General Saussier, Supreme Commander designate in the event of war, and the Chief of Staff, General de Miribel.[28] Like most young Frenchmen at the time, Marcel submitted unhesitatingly to the demands of military life, without a thought of asking to be discharged on grounds of health (whereas he would do so in the First World War). On 15 November 1889 he arrived at Orléans, where he enlisted in the seventy-sixth Infantry Regiment as a soldier (second-class).[29] Then began the 'military act' that Marcel 'admired the most', as he would write in response to a questionnaire.[30] There are few accounts of him: we

---

education and equipped yourself at your own cost, you could enlist before your class's call-up and contract for a 'conditional commitment' of one year; you had to pass an examination to attain the rank of non-commissioned officer in the reserves, then a second examination in order to become an officer in the reserves. (See J. Chastenet, *Histoire de la Troisième République*, vol. 1, Hachette, 1955, p. 133.)

*Except for a number of graduates, ministers of religion, and those with dependent families, who would serve for one year (Chastenet, *Histoire*, vol. II, p. 248).

know of only one letter that dates from his time as a volunteer. We are obliged to try to imagine him in the light of a few outside testimonies, some fictional accounts and retrospective allusions.

The young man began to learn fencing, gymnastics and how to train foot soldiers. His commanding officer asked him to sleep in town because his asthma attacks bothered his colleagues.[31] And so he lodged with Mme Renvoyzé, at 92 rue du Faubourg-Bannier in Orléans.[32] Gymnastics can scarcely have appealed to him: the Narrator of *Le Côté de Guermantes* recalls his regiment and the 'exercise called cross-beam', in which, hardly had he returned to the centre than he fell down.[33] Military dress, 'a long greatcoat and a heavy shako',[34] made him look like a character from a burlesque film. Robert de Billy, who met him in February 1890, at a dinner at the home of M. Boegner, the *Préfet* of the Loiret, remembered, many years later, 'his greatcoat that was too big for him. His gait and the way in which he spoke did not conform to the military ideal.'[35] Certainly after the first month, Proust the infantryman was not quite so happy as he would later say he was, for his mother's letters are full of all the customary consolations: 'Well, my darling, a month has gone by, and you only have to eat another eleven slices of the cake, of which one or two will be consumed on leave.' She even added another piece of gastronomic advice, of touching childishness: 'I have thought of a way of shortening the time for you. Take eleven bars of some chocolate that you like very much, tell yourself that you only want to eat a bar on the last day of every month – you will be amazed to see them disappear – and your exile along with them.'[36] Boredom and exile have to be endured 'cheerfully, that is to say courageously',[37] wrote Marcel to one of his friends who was undergoing the same fate. If we consider that Proust rarely described this period in his life, and only did so much later, when the moments of melancholy, idleness and fear had been forgotten and only happy memories remained, we must view Marcel Proust's 'military paradise'[38] with a few qualifications. He himself wrote to his father about 'this general melancholy'; the year away far from his parents, was, 'if not the cause, at least the pretext – consequently the excuse'. He also wrote of 'an extreme difficulty in concentrating, in reading, learning by heart and retaining anything' – signs of slight depression.[39]

Daily life must have been tempered by a number of exemptions, and yet Marcel seems, at times, to have led much the same existence as his colleagues. In one of his first draft notebooks for 'Combray', he recounts how 'Daylight is breaking over the barracks, and you have to hurry along to the canteen to drink the boiling hot milky coffee, before setting off on a march, in the early dawn, following the music through the sleeping town.'[40] He even had to fire a rifle, and he would not forget its recoil, which caused a pain 'in the shoulder-blade'.[41]

Can a life, therefore, that does not contain much happiness or great unhappiness provide pleasant memories? This is the subject of a page in *Les Plaisirs et les Jours* entitled 'Tableaux de genre du souvenir', in which the garrison town is cast, as it is in *Jean Santeuil* and *Le Côté de Guermantes*, as a series of Dutch 'genre paintings': 'My regimental life was full of scenes of this kind which I lived quite naturally, without feeling either overjoyed or particularly miserable, and which I recall with great sweetness. The rustic surroundings, the simplicity of certain of my colleagues who came from peasant backgrounds, whose bodies had remained better looking and more agile, whose minds were more unusual, whose hearts were more spontaneous and characters more natural than those of the young men with whom I had associated hitherto and with whom I would mix afterwards, the calmness of a life in which the things one does are more regulated and the imagination less enslaved than in any other.'[42] This passage, whose autobiographical nature Proust admitted to, clearly indicates what it was that sweetened his exile. Surrounded by his friends, Marcel must have encountered the same temptations, pleasures and happiness that he did at school. The mingling of social classes introduced a sense of disorientation in his desires; this he would remember later. Furthermore, a young, middle-class man was less isolated than he would be in our own time, when the exemptions, the 'shirkers' and '*coopération*'* have led to there being two types of national service and a social division. Neither, apparently, was he the object of any bullying on the part of his less privileged companions. Finally, Proust's family connections meant he was invited out by his officers (something scarcely likely today). In *La Jeunesse d'un clerc*, Julien Benda has given an account of the same privileged existence at this period: a barrack room full of peasants or labourers, mess companions 'who in no way disliked [him] for being richer than they', and even provided him with 'consideration' on account of his 'superior education', 'a certain understanding about [his] ineptitude for manual work . . . along with an undeniable pity for [his] lack of ability in such matters'. In addition to this there was a respect for discipline, the hierarchy, the

---

* In present-day France, national service may sometimes be spent working abroad, on an aid project, for example. *Tr.*

officers and an aptitude for 'laying aside intellectual life, and accepting a much more brutish existence, not to say finding pleasure in it . . . Perhaps beneath every intellectual there is a beast sleeping.'[43] The similarities between the two young men are striking. There can be little doubt that Marcel would have experienced the same inner calm instilled by discipline, a fixed timetable and the healthy regime so dear to Doctor Proust.[44] Regimental life replaced a family love that was sometimes harmful with an undeniable, incontestable paternalistic structure. There was no longer any need to wish for anything, since everything was decided for one; Marcel was often criticized by his parents for his lack of willpower. Fresh air and sleep were assured at regular hours. Furthermore, the young man's very sociable nature, the easy way in which he mixed with everybody, without distinction of colour or class, must surely have led to him being very quickly accepted by his fellow soldiers as well as by his superiors. A letter to the former lieutenant Pierre d'Orléans ('An appalling officer in every respect "and" of questionable morality', according to a military report) gives evidence of this: 'You ask me whether I have forgotten that I had as commanding officers a Walewski and a Neuville. I certainly do not forget. I preserve the most grateful and respectful memories of them. And they are not the only ones for whom I retain respect. I frequently think of Colonel Arvers, of Major Appert. The affection which I have for individual officers who were so good to me, I also feel in a more abstract way for the army in general. The development of my ideas has gradually led me to consider it as the way of life with which I sympathize most.'[45]

Among the officers were Medical Officer Kopff, who kept an eye on Marcel's health and was invited to the Prousts' home (in 1894 Marcel wrote that he 'was missing him very much' and 'adored him'),[46] Lieutenant de Cholet and Captain Walewski. Armand-Pierre, the Comte de Cholet, a member of the Jockey Club, of the Cercle de la rue Royale* and the Société Hippique, inscribed a photograph of himself to Marcel: 'To the conditional volunteer Marcel Proust/ one of his torturers, Orléans 1890.'

In *Jean Santeuil* Lieutenant de Cholet appears under the name Guy de Brucourt, 'who was considered by the regiment to be an outstanding officer'.[47] For Jean, he had 'all the glamour that his stripes, his exceptional rank, his beauty when he gave orders, and his perfect kindness commanded'. In his first novel, Proust gives him the scene in which the lieutenant responds to the hero's wave with a military salute, as if he had

---

* One of the smartest clubs in Paris. *Tr.*

been a soldier whom he did not know, a 'salute that had looked as if it had not noticed how keen he was to stop him'. This is the way in which Robert de Saint-Loup behaves towards the Narrator in *Le Côté de Guermantes*. Proust the novelist never forgot any of the injuries, however small they may have been, inflicted on Marcel the man. In an attempt to maintain friendly relations after national service, he would devote an article in 1892 to the Comte de Cholet's travel book, *Choses d'Orient*. Their relationship did not last very long.[48]

Marcel also made the acquaintance of the *noblesse d'Empire*, before he came to know Princesse Mathilde, and Louis d'Albufera, in the guise of Captain Walewski, who appears under the same name of Borodino* in both *Jean Santeuil* and *Le Côté de Guermantes*. Charles Walewski (1848–1914) was the son of Alexandre, Comte Walewski (1810–68), the natural son of Napoleon I and Marie Walewska, who became Minister for Foreign Affairs, and later Minister of State and of the Arts, under Napoleon III.[49] There was a rumour that his wife, Anne, known as Marianne, de Ricci, had been the emperor's mistress, which explains the sentence in *Le Côté de Guermantes*: 'It was with the brusqueness of the first Emperor in his voice that he addressed a reprimand to a brigadier, with the reflective melancholy of the second that he exhaled a puff of smoke from his cigarette.'[50] What fascinated Proust was heredity, because it was the living presence of the past, of history, of *la gloire*. Unlike the more ancient nobility, the *noblesse d'Empire* was much closer to the period he had been describing, that of the battlefields of Napoleon. Borodino, that is to say, Walewski, had the good fortune – something that was also fortunate for the novelist – to be directly descended not just from one but from two emperors. The actual character was transferred just as he was into the novel – into the two novels – because he was a secondary figure. There is always more than one key to the protagonists. In any case, Cholet and Borodino in *Jean Santeuil*, and Saint-Loup and Borodino in *À la recherche du temps perdu*, enshrine the two divisions of French nobility in the small town of Doncières (drawn, as *Jean Santeuil* clearly indicates, from Orléans, Provins and Fontainebleau).

Another aspect of the portrayal of military life should be noted, because it reflects Marcel's character and way of thinking – his method of questioning

---

* The other name for the Battle of the Moskowa, mentioned in *War and Peace*, for example, a book that was dear to Proust. The title of Prince of the Moskowa was bestowed by Napoleon I, not on Walewski, but on Maréchal Ney.

people. Unlike other writers, such as Mallarmé, Valéry and Malraux, who specialized in monologues, he never ceased asking questions: 'Very curious about all those things to do with the army, in which he was becoming interested . . . Jean, keen to have a clearer understanding of what military intelligence was, constantly questioned these officers, asking them who in [their] opinion was the most exceptional leader in this regiment, and in the army.'[51] In this way, a real fund of knowledge, a genuine military culture, was amassed that would be used again in *Les Plaisirs et les Jours*, in *Jean Santeuil* and in *Le Côté de Guermantes*. Such are the questions a prospective writer asks himself: what is it that will be useful? What is there to write about? The replies are paid into a savings account upon which it will always be possible to draw.

GASTON AND JEANNE

The monotony of life at Orléans was relieved by fencing, swimming, riding (which Marcel never mastered), and especially by the periods of leave,[52] which were probably weekly, that he spent in Paris, at his parents' home, but also at Mme de Caillavet's salon at 12 avenue Hoche. As we have seen, Marcel had made the acquaintance of Mme Arman's son, Gaston Arman* de Caillavet, who was born in 1869, while the latter was doing his voluntary service in Versailles. The literary reasons for his deep friendship for this chubby-faced, intelligent, witty and cheerful young man, who would become a talented writer himself, only became clear retrospectively; the inspiration for Gilberte Swann and Robert de Saint-Loup was based upon the equally fragile and divided marriage of Jeanne Pouquet and Gaston Arman; when they had a daughter, Simone, Proust would have the good fortune to know three generations: Mme Arman, her son and daughter-in-law, and her granddaughter (like Odette, Gilberte and Mlle de Saint-Loup). Like Gaston, Saint-Loup died prematurely. While he awaited this grim, and later tragic, conclusion, Marcel pretended to be attracted to the fiancée (the engagement was secret, since M. Pouquet had not been told) of his new friend. She was fifteen years old, with a long pigtail, which would be the inspiration for Gilberte's, and beautiful eyes. Marcel thought he had known her in the Champs-Élysées at the same time that he had met Marie de Benardaky; although she was pretty, she

---

* It is under this name that he is referred to in the correspondence. As we know, the 'de' was assumed.

did not have a pleasant character, and her letters to her fiancé, published by Michelle Maurois,[53] Simone de Caillavet's daughter-in-law, show that she soon became ironical, and later downright rude, towards Marcel. In 1926, when she published *Le Salon de Mme de Caillavet*, she would give an idealized and quite misleading picture of her relationship with him, an image that conformed to the golden legend. This sequence of conflicting snapshots gives an impression of a very different young man – the person who had admitted to a friend his fear of appearing 'clinging'; obsequious, importunate, excessively flattering, forever losing himself in polite phrases, he joined in all the couple's entertainments. He took the part of the prompter in a review written by Gaston and performed by Jeanne. So taken with the play was he, it was said that 'he forgot to prompt, he was laughing and applauding so much, to the indignation of the cast'.[54] At the tennis club on the Boulevard Bineau,[55] tea was brought by Marcel, who was not playing, who watched Jeanne's 'blonde plaits' streaming in the breeze. When he went to call on Jeanne and on her mother in the rue de Miromesnil, and they had gone out, he sat down in the linen room to gossip, as the Narrator does at the Swanns'. He once even rented a mansion near Orléans,[56] so that he could invite them, and no doubt Gaston, to stay; he entertained them, in any case, in the town in which he was garrisoned. Everything was ruined when he tried, as he would often do with men and women who were dear to him, to obtain a photograph of Jeanne; Gaston walked in in a furious rage;[57] his friend would always remember this mishap, as is clear from a letter to Simone de Caillavet: 'When I was in love with your maman, I went to amazing lengths to possess a photograph of her. But it was to no avail. I still receive New Year cards from people in the Périgord with whom I had become friendly simply so that I could try to get this photograph.'[58] Marcel, who was more generous, inscribed his photograph to Gaston: 'To the one Gaston, his own/ Marcel.'

Very soon, the captivated suitor becomes 'that lunatic Proust', 'that little nitwit Proust',[59] who is made use of so as to divert Jeanne's father's attentions. In Orléans, he appeared 'languorously' to the girl and her mother, 'in order to pay his respectful homage and his mawkish winks … After a few more moments of rambling, he took his leave with some exquisite observations in which, if I understood correctly, he was prostrating himself at Maman's feet and squirming at those of her daughter. He is an agreeable nutcase.'[60] In a flight of perceptiveness, she nevertheless understood that Marcel was observing and forming judgements about this couple, who treated him as a gooseberry, and was privy to their secret intimacy and their clandestine engagement: 'He's definitely a strange boy,' she wrote to Gaston, 'who often frightens me with his reflections about us. If he believes everything that he has said to me, we won't have much more left to tell him in two years' time! I do hope that all the things he tells me are merely simple suppositions which he reels off in a normal tone of voice just so as to see what my reactions will be! . . . At one point on Monday, your name was mentioned, whereupon he turned imperceptibly towards me and looked at me fixedly and with such a funny expression that I had to look away because I felt very uncomfortable . . . He regards you so much as my future husband that he said to me as he left: "I'm afraid I've stayed too long . . . Don't tell Gaston." '[61] There can be no doubt that Marcel would have known that true love united Gaston and Jeanne, and not Jeanne and Marcel. So why did he pretend to be in love? Was it to mislead people by allowing himself to be seen with a girl?* Or to draw himself closer to Gaston by sharing Jeanne's feelings for him? In becoming closer to Jeanne, he was also getting to know those mysterious creatures, women, about whom all novelists have a duty to be able to speak with some experience. Was not the best way of acquiring this knowledge, given that he was not affected by such feelings, to pretend to them? And he did so with some success, for Jeanne Pouquet would confess to her daughter in 1947: 'If one was to substitute "The tennis club on the Boulevard Bineau" for "Champs-Élysées" in the account of Marcel's love for Gilberte, I can trace almost word for word the evocations of his love for me, whose memory he endlessly exaggerated in the letters which I so absurdly destroyed.'[62]

Marcel's experiences with Jeanne and Gaston were the prototype for this triangular relationship. He would repeat it several times during his life, with Louisa de Mornand and Louis d'Albufera, with Antoine Bibesco and Bertrand de Fénelon, with the Princesse Soutzo and Paul Morand. In this perverse comedy, as in a play by Musset, the lover passes himself off as a confidant and the beloved is not the one whom one believes it to be. The problem is resolved: how can one love a man while appearing to

* As when he pretended to have had 'an absorbing affair' with a pretty Viennese girl, whom he met at the Perrin dancing class in the rue de la Victoire (*Corr.* vol. I, p. 53), or when he took flowers to Mme Chirade, a beautiful dairymaid from the rue Fontaine, acompanied by Daniel Halévy, who had extolled her to him: 'How beautiful she is! . . . As beautiful as Salammbô . . . Do you think it's possible to sleep with her?' Marcel and his unnecessary flowers were sent packing by the dairymaid (D. Halévy, *Pays parisiens*, Grasset, 1932, and *Corr. avec D. Halévy*, pp. 170–1).

love a woman? By competing for the woman with the man you love. Gaston, in any case, misunderstood this – as, perhaps, Paul Morand may have done in 1917 – for he was angry with Marcel, to the extent that their relationship, while not ceasing entirely, would never be the same again. Once Caillavet was dead, however, Proust would remain close to Jeanne both in person and in memory, just as the Narrator is to Gilberte de Saint-Loup,* as a token of the friendship which had made its mark on the widowhood they both shared.

THE DEATH OF THE GRANDMOTHER

The monotony of military life was shattered, however, by an event that was very different in its import to these spurious amatory deceptions: Mme Nathé Weil, at the age of sixty-eight, died of uraemia on 3 January 1890 – she had been unwell since 14 December, suffering from the same illness from which her daughter Jeanne and her son Georges would die – and was buried on 5 January. Although the death of Virginie Proust on 19 March 1889 had passed unnoticed, since Marcel had only a distant relationship with his paternal grandmother and never mentioned her, this latest bereavement must have affected him deeply. With her kindness, her originality, her cultured mind and her close understanding of the little boy, Adèle Weil enshrined all the qualities one expects of a grandparent. Marcel's grief was increased by the sight of his mother's, and he tried to comfort her, as intellectuals do, with books: Pierre Loti's *Le Roman d'un enfant* was published in *La Nouvelle Revue* between 15 January and 1 April. Mme Proust could not stop herself rereading it. 'You've done me good, my darling, by finding this book for me.'[63] In Loti, who had been one of his favourite writers as an adolescent, ever since he had come across *Le Mariage de Loti* in Auteuil, Marcel identified with the presence of a beloved maternal figure, an over-sentimental sensibility, a brotherly but unorthodox temperament, which would drive Loti to flee the world upon the high

* And as Proust also was to Gaston when Mme Arman de Caillavet died in 1910: 'My dear little Gaston, in a rush of tears I felt the whole of our past, the early days of our great friendship, when you were a soldier, and later when I was one, come flooding back to me' (*Corr.* vol. X, p. 24). In another letter he also recalled the time when Gaston accompanied him every Sunday evening to catch the Orléans train. According to Jeanne Pouquet, Gaston tore Marcel away from 'interminable farewells, from dissertations about [Anatole] France and small cakes', piled into a cab with him, watched every clock in anguish, and ran with him as far as the platform, pursued by the irate cab driver.

seas, and, in the case of Proust, to escape from it in his room; which would impel the former to seek out sailors, and the latter, hotel page-boys. The strength of the insubstantial *Roman d'un enfant* is to allow everybody, and thus Jeanne Proust, to recognize their own mother. She does not fail to do so, and she rereads Mme de Sévigné, an author whom, as we have seen, Mme Weil read. After the death of his own mother, Marcel would discover a notebook in which she had confided her grief over Mme Weil's death, and he would be overwhelmed by reading it, while at the same time recognizing his own sentiments. In 1890 it was as if Marcel had experienced a premonition of what he would refer to as 'the heart's intermissions' when describing the delayed grief that affected the Narrator after the death of his grandmother. In fact, it was in June that Mme Proust wrote to her son: 'Why didn't you write "because you spent your time crying and I'm feeling rather sad myself"? I would not have been more sad at that moment, my dearest, because you would have written to me. Your letter would have been a reflection of what you were feeling and for that reason alone would have given me pleasure. And anyway, I never feel sad knowing that you are thinking of your grandmother; on the contrary, it is extremely comforting to me.'[64] So it was very much Marcel's grandmother who, in the famous chapter in *Sodome et Gomorrhe*, became the Narrator's grand-mother, and not his mother: when Proust lost his mother, his own grief was immense and immediate.

THE END OF NATIONAL SERVICE

In August 1890 Marcel spent his leave at Cabourg, possibly at the home of the Derbanne family. In Notebook 31 of his drafts, he would describe Mme Derbanne as a prototype for Mme Verdurin (along with others: Lemaire, Thompson, Ménard-Dorian), and in a letter to Robert de Billy in 1908, he would recall her son Jacques.[65] Marcel's uniform brought him great success with women: 'Imagine,' he wrote to his father, 'to the Derbannes' great indignation, the maids of Cabourg, on noticing a tra-ditional *pioupiou* [soldier], blew me kisses. It is the maids of Orléans — whom I have neglected — taking their revenge.'[66] Just as the military institution took its revenge: at the end of August, the '*pioupiou*' finished sixty-third out of sixty-four in his examinations. He sought nothing less, he asserted later, perhaps with some exaggeration — since in his case a momentary thought or wish could be expanded by a memory which, if not mythomaniac, was at least imaginative and humorous — than to prolong his period with the regiment. He had created a very cosy home for himself there, a protective nest which allowed him to delay his choice of which subjects to study and of a career. As sociable as ever, he had built up a network of companions, if not friendships (his correspondence contains few traces of military relationships). Above all, he had grown to love the urban landscape of Orléans. This quiet city of 60,000 inhabitants, just two hours away from Paris by train, its life centred around the military garrison, offered proximity and variety. The rue du Faubourg-Bannier and the rue des Bons-Enfants can be found in *Jean Santeuil*, and in *À la recherche* the Place de la République, where Walewski lodged, became the Mall in which Borodino lived at Doncières. The rue de Saintrailles and the rue de la Bretonnerie are to be found in Combray. The name of Saint-Euverte, one of the early bishops of Orléans and the builder of the cathedral, is given to a marquis in *Du côté de chez Swann*. A district of the town, on the borders of Saint-Jean-de-Braye, was called Saint-Loup. Charlus considered Orléans cathedral to be 'the ugliest in France', although he admired the Cabu house, which he called 'Diane de Poitiers' house'.[67] Actual names, steeped in history, would mingle with invented names, at the cost of some imaginative displacement which provided enormous pleasure. And yet, throughout this year of national service, there was not a single story, no poems, no diary. It was not that Marcel was busy so much as he was glad to have an alibi: writing would be postponed until later on.

Scarcely had he returned to Paris, however, than, following one of the customs of the day, to study two degree courses simultaneously, he enrolled at both the École Libre des Sciences Politiques and at the Faculty of Law, probably less readily at the latter, but doing so at his father's instigation. Three years of austere study awaited him: the degree in literature, or in philosophy, would be deferred, because in the family's view neither would lead to any serious profession. Certainly at this period, law was seen as a lightweight occupation, reserved for young men of means, inclined towards idleness, which was a solution for those who did not know what career to take up. It is surprising to see Paul Valéry, in much the same circumstances and without any greater desire to do so, embarking on the same route. Political science would mean more to Marcel. *À la recherche du temps perdu* is full of accounts of international affairs: ambassadors, statesmen and soldiers, from Norpois to Faffenheim, argue about peace and war in Europe, and the Narrator himself discusses the century's great affair, the relationship between 'those who were pro-Germany or pro-France'. How much did Proust owe to Vandal's, Sorel's and Leroy-Beaulieu's courses?

What did Marcel want to do at the end of his national service? He had either persuaded himself, or else his parents had convinced him of it, that he was afflicted with one of those 'diseases of the will' described by Théodule Ribot. There is an echo of this in a letter of 22 November, written to Mme Straus when he had just returned to Paris: 'When I am too weak-willed to be able to focus my thoughts of affection, I need to write or do something.'[68] *Jean Santeuil* provides some vital information about this period, beginning with a declaration that retains all the irony of the situation in which Marcel found himself:[69] ' "If he has an inclination towards literature, then let him read law," an eminent professor of jurisprudence had said to M. Santeuil, who had gone to ask advice on his son's behalf. But what had seemed to be an inclination towards literature must have been something else, since law bored Jean and he failed his first examination.'[70] The whole misunderstanding is encompassed there, between a young man whose only love is literature, a subject that he wishes to make his life, and parents anxious to ensure a good career through profitable studies: 'He no longer dared say that he loved literature, for he had already had quoted to him the names of a number of lawyers and doctors known for their "literary" tastes.'[71] But he was bored by law; he could not see how to make use of his artistic talents in that field. There were no lawyers among his friends. In *À la recherche* we meet the 'President of the Cherbourg Bar' at Balbec, Caen's premier judge, a well-known lawyer from Le Mans,* and a famous Paris barrister; there is no professor of jurisprudence. That is not very many, compared to the work of Balzac, who profited more from his studies; Proust, for his part, obliterated them from his memory and his imagination, as well as from his daily life: he never understood that he should not relinquish his share in the building at 102 boulevard Haussmann, and he failed to leave a will. He was not impervious to the laws that regulated society, but he preferred to deduce them for himself, in sociological terms (he was a disciple of Tarde, whose ideas he discussed with Robert de Billy at this time), rather than having

* *RTP*, vol. II, p. 35. Proust was in touch with what was happening in the magistrature, since he mentions that 'several times the first president of Caen had been offered a seat at the Court of Appeal'. A sketch (vol. II, p. 914) mentions Fabre, the president of the Bar: Jules Fabre, a barrister, had a country house at Tilly-sur-Seulles (Calvados), thus close to Cabourg (*Le Bottin mondain*, 1903); cf. vol. III, p. 201 and n.1: 'He was one of those men whose professional experience rather led one to look down on their profession and who say for example: "I know that I am good at pleading, therefore I don't much care to go on pleading." '

them imposed, in every detail, legally (a word that does not occur in *À la recherche*). Lawsuits are only mentioned in the work allusively (setting aside the Dreyfus affair), either because the Narrator reads an account of one, or because of the risk of introducing characters under their real names, or else because the relationship of the Narrator and Albertine is a form of lawsuit in itself in which he is the judge and she is the guilty party.[72] Jurisprudence is transformed into a metaphor,[73] and is not much more than 'family jurisprudence' applied in this way to the smallest social unit. Among the great classical works, Proust would never allude to Montesquieu's celebrated *L'Esprit des lois*.

L'ÉCOLE LIBRE DES SCIENCES POLITIQUES

Founded after the war of 1870 by Émile Boutmy, in accordance with the ideas of Taine, the École Libre des Sciences Politiques still only had a few students: about three hundred. Its objective was to mould the senior civil service and the French political and diplomatic structures. Defeat had actually meant that many people now thought that, in order to match Germany, it was necessary to improve the training of students. Even though the politicians of the Third Republic were not products of the school, it was certainly responsible for 'the regime's administrative élite. It was obvious that the Quai d'Orsay, the Audit Office, the Council of State and the Inland Revenue all owed the high quality of their staff to the School.'[74] It imbued a broad political culture, while at the same time being intended for future men of action. The professors were chosen accordingly. In the *hôtel* de Mortemart, at 27 rue Saint-Guillaume (which had belonged to a family whose spirit was immortalized by Saint-Simon and Proust), Marcel enrolled in the diplomatic section, presided over by Albert Sorel. In what was then a two-year course, he taught alternate years on foreign policy from 1815 to 1878* and on the diplomacy of the Revolution and Empire periods. Albert Sorel, who was born in 1842, had had an unusual career:[75] he was taught by Guizot, employed as an attaché at the Ministry of Foreign Affairs, became a novelist and a contributor to *La Revue des Deux Mondes*, and he accompanied the National Defence

---

* Some of Marcel Proust's class notes have been traced taken in Sorel's lectures (BN, n.a.fr. 16611, ff. 74–85: the wars of revolution; ff. 99–126: Europe in the twentieth century). See also ff. 129–30: the functions of an ambassador. Other notes refer to Albert Vandal's course on oriental matters (ff. 86–98), or allude to a course on constitutional law, most probably that given by Émile Boutmy (ff. 131–50).

government to Tours (where he met Taine) in 1870. In 1875 he published an *Histoire diplomatique de la guerre franco-allemande*, and in 1876 he quit the 'service' to devote himself to history. *La Question d'Orient au XVIII* siècle came out in 1878; however, in 1881 Gambetta offered him two jobs, the political management of the Quai d'Orsay or the post of Ambassador to Berlin, both of which he refused. His great work was the eight-volume *L'Europe et la Révolution* (1885–1904). First, he developed his courses at the school based upon his reading of the archives, then he produced articles, and finally published each volume in turn.

He was elected to the Académie des Sciences Morales et Politiques in 1889 (as was Ralph Savaie, in *Jean Santeuil*).[76] Like Montesquiou, on whom he would publish an essay, like Tocqueville, whom he admired, Sorel tried to discern the rules underlying anecdotal accounts. One essential thesis emerges from his work: foreign policy during the Revolution was identical to that pursued by the monarchy; there is a logic to history, there are collective and hereditary surges. This was perhaps where Marcel developed his taste for the philosophy of history, which is expressed mainly in *Le Côté de Guermantes* and *Le Temps retrouvé*; this was also where he first heard M. de Norpois – not just at home, through meeting friends of his father's such as Camille Barrère. André Siegfried (born in 1875), who was a pupil of Sorel's, makes this connection himself: 'Sorel's manner, on the rostrum, was one of tasteful familiarity with his select audience. It was also the extremely flattering, confidential manner of an old man communicating his experiences, in semi-privacy, to the young who would succeed him. Since it was not very long since the age of greatness, this familiarity did not preclude a certain solemnity. In his celebrated style of teaching, there was even some reflection of the manner made famous by M. de Norpois.'[77] The Comte de Saint-Aulaire, who was a pupil of Sorel's at the same period, has recounted some of the master's ideas: 'The highest principles and the most generous sentiments are only masks for the most selfish interests.' 'There is no isolated factor in problems of international affairs, each one must be looked at in relation to the whole.' 'In binding herself to the Tsar, the Republic, which is the heir to the most ancient royal race in the world, is marrying a parvenu. She treats him as if she were doing him a great honour in deigning to accept his millions.' Even the image of Xerxes lashing the Hellespont can be found in Proust.[78] If we are to look for a key to Norpois, it lies primarily here rather than with Barrère or Francis Charmes. But, more crucially, if we are trying to find out how Proust's mind, culture and method of reasoning were shaped, then we must acknowledge that Sorel's courses were important experiences for him. Even though the unfolding of literary creation may be unforeseeable, we come across his teacher, along with others, in *Jean Santeuil*: 'He was seen as a delightful man of genius, as an interesting hysteric, and one went home with a feeling of intense pleasure, not quite sure whether one was returning from the Sorbonne or the Salpetrière. On this occasion, he had suddenly embarked on the subject of an opera he had attended the previous evening: "It's well-made, I tell you, very well-made. The orchestration is cabinet-maker's stuff." '[79] These images were then taken up again later in the Verdurin salon in *Du côté de chez Swann*.[80]

Marcel also attended Albert Vandal's course on oriental matters.[81] Wearing pince-nez one day and a monocle the next, Vandal 'liked to spice the fearful complexity of oriental affairs with lively remarks no doubt intended to imprint on [their] minds, with a pithy word, the Treaty of Koutschouk-Kainardji or the Ypsilanti incident'.[82] He had just published a book on Elizabeth of Russia, the first volume of a study of Napoleon and Alexander,[83] and he gave lectures on classical style, inspired by La Bruyère. As for the course given by Anatole Leroy-Beaulieu – who had published his account of his travels in *La Revue des deux mondes* (whence the humorous references in *Jean Santeuil* to 'A Sense of Infinity by the shores of Lake Tchad' and 'The Impulse towards what is best in the Balkan Peninsula', and references in *À l'ombre des jeunes filles en fleurs* to articles about 'the sense of nature by the shores of Lake Victoria-Nyanza' and on 'the automatic rifle in the Bulgarian army')[84] – his subject was the great European powers during the past twenty years. Anatole Leroy-Beaulieu,[85] author of a magisterial *Empire des tsars*, was a liberal who took a stand against Abdul-Hamid at the time of the massacre of the Armenians, and who supported the Poles; after the Dreyfus affair, he was to denounce the three 'antis': anti-Semitism, anti-clericalism and anti-Protestantism. In 1905, at the time of the separation of Church and State, Proust still recalled his preference for the ideas of Boutmy's successor as the head of the École Libre des Sciences Politiques, or 'Sciences-Po'.[86]

Thus we observe the fascination the subjects of Eastern Europe and Russia held for the school. This can be traced in *À la recherche du temps perdu*. Before the First World War, Central Europe is portrayed in the novel in the figures of Ferdinand I, King of Bulgaria, Nicholas II, King Théodose II, an imaginary oriental sovereign (though based on precedent) who was on an official visit to Paris, Prince de Faffenheim, the German prime minister and the German ambassador (Prince von Radolin). In the novel political relations with Central Europe are expounded in such a way that they make the advent of the First World War appear to have been carefully prepared: during the war diplomacy was carried on through other means. In the fictional war of *Le Temps retrouvé*, it is M. de Norpois' diplomacy that is maintained, as are the conversations at Doncières or those at the Guermantes' salons. On the subject of America, or even of Britain, there is little said; it was the foreign policy of his youth, that Proust preferred. The former pupil of the diplomatic section* of 'Sciences-Po' never wanted to be a diplomat;† yet he wrote the novel about diplomacy that those novelists who were diplomats – Chateaubriand, Stendhal, Gobineau, Giraudoux and Morand – never wrote, and M. de Norpois became the phantom of the rue Saint-Guillaume.‡

During that year, Marcel wooed Mme Straus assiduously. Sometimes he sent her bouquets of sumptuous chrysanthemums, recently introduced into France. These 'melancholy' flowers were a substitute for one of his letters to her – which we do not possess. Marcel also sent them to Robert de Billy's parents, as well as to Laure Hayman, to whom he spoke of 'these flowers that are proud and sad like you'.[87] They were to become, along with cattleyas, Odette Swann's favourite flowers, because chrysanthemums 'had the great merit of not looking like flowers, but appeared to be made of silk, of satin'.[88] Sometimes he swore that he would stop visiting Mme Straus on Sundays, in order to avoid his friends' awful accusation that he was 'clinging', as if this adhesion – almost an adherence – of his whole being were not the secret of perceiving the world: where a woman fascinated him, he could not take his eyes off her until he had discovered her secret: 'La Verité de Mme Straus', which he wrote one day in March 1891, is the reaction of the jilted admirer and also the successful analyst who would never progress further in the affections of the character of the future Oriane de Guermantes. According to him, in fact, only one 'way of life' appealed to her, as can be seen by the way she dressed, her

---

* There were two sections: diplomatic and administrative.

† Though he took three oral exams in 1892: the first on Sorel's course, 'Diplomatic History from 1818 to 1875', marked 4.75/6, 'highly intelligent'; on Vandal's course, 'Oriental Affairs', 5/6, 'generally good answers'; and on A. Leroy-Beaulieu's course, 'A Tableau of Contemporary Europe', 4.15/6. Archives of the Institut d'Études politiques, and *Corr.*, vol. 1, p. 62 and 172.

‡ 'Sciences-Po' is situated in the rue Saint-Guillaume; Norpois is the ghost of the street because the school leads to a diplomatic career. *Tr.*

wit and her intelligence. Like many neurasthenics, Mme Straus loved no one apart from herself, and she was her own work of art. This did not prevent Marcel from accompanying her, Jacques Bizet and Jacques Baignères to the Odéon on 21 March, for the revival of *Germinie Lacerteux*. This play, which Edmond de Goncourt had adapted (in 1888) from the novel he and his brother had written, told the story of a servant's moral decline. We are closer here to a Flaubertian servant, the forerunner of those in the works of Zola and Mirbeau, rather than to Françoise, the Narrator's tutelary goddess in *À la recherche*, from 'Combray' to *Albertine disparue*.

Réjane was wonderful in the role: she held the play together. 'Oh! Réjane, she was marvellous, throughout! And she employed the very simplest dramatic art', exclaimed Edmond de Goncourt,[89] who, at the time of the 1891 revival, compared her acting to that of Rachel.* All his life, Proust remembered this performance: 'Once, seeing Réjane in the roles of Sapho and Germinie Lacerteux, a recurring sadness overcame me, which still afflicts me intermittently after so many years.'[90] And he wrote to Jacques Porel, Réjane's son: 'Madame Réjane's art filled my inner life. Germinie Lacerteux's sorrows were among the greatest of my life, I still suffer from them and I am often moved for hours by the memory of that heartrending voice.'[91] Everything that in the character of Berma relates drama to truth stemmed from her: on the affected, grandiloquent stage of the final years of the nineteenth century, her performance was, as Proust was to say, a 'revolution'[92] – one that drew tears from his eyes: 'How much Réjane had to do with it, I do not know; but I left with my eyes so red that some sensitive members of the audience came up to me thinking that I had been attacked.'[93]

Marcel was soon to meet Edmond de Goncourt at the homes of both Mme Alphonse Daudet and Princesse Mathilde, and he would recall the good looks of the 'haughty, shy old man' and the nobility of his features, which resembled those of Daudet: 'For me the age of giants ended with the sight of their astonishing faces.'[94] If, however, Edmond had made himself the 'servant of what is true', he had not applied this rubric in a sufficiently broad or profound sense. He was unable to create living people, because, instead of using a 'notebook of sketches of forgotten

---

* Élisa Rachel (1821–58) enjoyed immense success in Paris as a tragedienne in classical roles. She was acclaimed in Brussels, Berlin, St Petersburg and also in London, where Charlotte Brontë saw her on stage. *Tr.*

scenes', he preferred direct observation, taking notes and using a diary, 'which is not what a great artist or a creative person does'.[95] Proust appreciated him most as an art critic, as the 'true impressionistic novelist whom everyone knew' and the historian 'of the highest worth', not as a dramatist: Germinie was the creation of Réjane rather than of Goncourt (who fell under the spell of naturalism, just as he did of 'the literature of fifteen years ago', of 'pre-*fin-de-siècle* literature').[96] Besides, at this period, Marcel, as a passionate lover of the theatre, went to see whatever he could, even *L'Impératrice Faustine*, a play by Stanislas Rzewuski, with Jane Hading.[97]

LE MENSUEL

No sooner had he returned from his national service and enrolled at the École Libre des Sciences Politiques, than Proust was busy writing and publishing. An important discovery, which we owe to M. Troulay,[98] has shown that from November 1890 until September 1891 Marcel was actively involved in editing a printed magazine (those at the Lycée Condorcet were in manuscript) called *Le Mensuel*. This publication, the first issue of which appeared in October 1890, was edited by Otto Bouwens Van der Boijin; the manager was Jules Bardoux, who printed the magazine at Villefranche-de-Rouergue, while the editorial office was at 45 rue de Lisbonne, Paris VIII[e], which was Otto's home. He was the son of a well-known architect, who lived with his parents and must have met Marcel at Sciences-Po. The magazine mentions several students of the school: Grunebaum-Balin, Gabriel Trarieux, Raymond Koechlin,[99] the future historian of Islamic art (who is mentioned in the drafts of *Le Temps retrouvé*), were all contributors or dedicatees of articles, as was Albert Vandal. In addition, the magazine carried a political section: an analytical summary of the principal events in foreign and domestic policy during the previous month. This was followed by 'Social Life', the theatre column, a list of 'First Nights', and the month's literary and historical anniversaries. The magazine was sold in four bookshops in the Saint-Augustin district. The first issue opened with an unambitious declaration: 'Let us remind ourselves briefly of the declared aims of *Le Mensuel*, which is published for the first time today, and which begs the indulgence of its kind readers. Our journal, in short, is merely a straightforward résumé of the month, a résumé, naturally, that is very brief. We warmly thank our subscribers for having kindly interested themselves in our possibly reckless venture, and we ask them to persuade their friends to follow their example. The Editors.' This was a manifesto that was full of excuses and that had limited ambitions. The fact was that Otto Bouwens was only eighteen; he signed his articles just with his initials. The career of this boy, who flashed through Proust's life up till this point like an invisible meteor, remains obscure. After finishing his studies, he became an unpaid assistant at the library of the Arsenal (perhaps it was he who gave Marcel the idea of taking the competitive exam for this job), and wrote plays and composed music. At the beginning of the century he married and followed a second career as a composer. The 1914 edition of *Tout-Paris* describes him as 'Baron' Otto, 'honorary librarian at the library of the Arsenal, composer, President of the Sorbonne Concert Society'. His Christian name is mentioned just once in Proust's correspondence, in a letter to Reynaldo Hahn concerning the proofs of a book about music.[100] How strange is this disappearance of a character with whom Marcel must have quarrelled and whom he stopped seeing! It was Otto, nevertheless, who enabled him to publish his first articles and thus played an important role in his career.

We are only aware that Proust had contributed to *Le Mensuel* once we have finished reading the series: the initials 'M.P.' only appear in issue number 5; the full signature only in issue 12 (the last). Yet the 'Social Life' column, coupled with a fashion column from issue 2 onwards, is signed 'Shooting Star'. The attention given to certain details which are to be found in *Du côté de chez Swann* lead us to believe this is a pseudonym of Marcel's (who, following Stendhal's example, but also one of the customs of the day, used a number of them in his youthful writings). In the third issue, published in December, a review of the 'international exhibition of painting' at the Georges Petit gallery, signed 'De Brabant', was by him. Although Otto kept the theatre column for himself, the list of 'First Nights' made mention of *Ferdinand le Noceur*, a comedy in four acts by Gandillot, and *L'Obstacle*, a comedy by Alphonse Daudet, with music by Reynaldo Hahn (who thus knew Daudet before he knew Proust). In February 'Social Life' featured the marriage of Jeanne Hugo to Léon Daudet; and in March the review *Ce que ça dit*, by Gaston Arman de Caillavet and Paul Grunebaum (at the home of Mme Pouquet). In April it was surely Proust who signed a review of a collection of poems by his friend Gabriel Trarieux, 'Confiteor', with the initial 'Y'; in May, as 'Fusain', he wrote 'Impressions of the Salons', which contained comments on Puvis de Chavannes, Whistler and Gallé. On the other hand, in the June 1891 issue, the initials 'R. D.' at the end of an article about *Confession d'un amant*

— by Marcel Prévost — are those of Robert Dreyfus. A piece about the *café-concert*, in July, quotes amusingly and frequently 'our colleague M.P.': signed 'Bob', this is certainly by Marcel. In the last issue, in September, as well as 'Choses normandes', signed 'Marcel Proust', there is an important article entitled 'Souvenir', attributed to Pierre de Touche. The tone, which is very close to that of the future 'Avant la nuit' (published in *La Revue blanche*), is Proust's; the heroine is already called Odette. Furthermore, the 'Social Life' column, which refers with increasing regularity as the year wears on to members of the aristocracy, reveals Marcel's upward social mobility and his interest in the musical salons: one notes the costume ball at the Princesse de Sagan's on June 22, and the *matinée dansante* at the Chalet des Îles in the Bois de Boulogne, given by Madeleine Lemaire on June 25 (Mme Verdurin would also entertain here).

In this publication, which Proust and Otto Bouwens produced virtually on their own, our interest is drawn above all to the articles on the music-hall, art criticism and fashion, the Norman 'landscape', and 'Souvenir', which is the only fictional text. Marcel, who was barely twenty, tried his hand at everything. And particularly at literary criticism: he applied the same strict principles to his friend Trarieux as he did to his friends at the Lycée Condorcet, Bizet and Halévy. Thus we see him condemn poetry that was scholarly, artificial, redolent of 'Baudelairean hieratism', which was outdated in 1891, as well as the pastiches of 'dead poets' and pantheistic philosophy. What the young critic advocates is that Trarieux should translate 'the murmur of inner voices' and that he should find in his poems the psychology and disposition of Verlaine and Laforgue, 'who in turn are direct descendants of Racine and A. de Musset. Add to these, if one wishes, Amiel and Sully-Prudhomme.' Trarieux's best poems were tinged with melancholy: 'He must surely have reflected on the sorrows of the heart.' The expression of feeling, melancholy and sincerity: these were the values that the future author of *Les Plaisirs et les Jours* defended, while not failing to mention Slav 'pity'. He described the task of the writer-translator again in *Le Temps retrouvé*.

When it came to exhibitions of modern painting, Marcel described 'the cast of mind of a young man' visiting a gallery of modern art: 'What is the point, he will say, of classical education, a knowledge of composition, of all the long years of studying the masters? A little intuition, a touch of good taste (and who lacks this nowadays?), a few Japanese albums, a lot of snapshots, isn't that all that is needed for those sparkling sketches which attract the public and make reputations ... Yet in literature one can immediately detect someone with a limited classical knowledge, some-one who has in his youth neglected what our ancestors called the "humani-ties"; similarly, in art one can recognize those who, not having studied sufficiently, rely purely on their improvisation for their art. However much a particular master of the modern school may wish to forget them, his dexterity, his marvellously assured drawing and his infallible eye serve to remind us that he could have won the Prix de Rome.'[101] Proust never stopped demonstrating that for him the greatest innovations in style and thinking were based upon a deep classical culture; he himself had undergone those 'long years of studying' which he felt were so necessary.

At the salon of the Société Nationale des Beaux-Arts on the Champs-Élysées, in the spring of 1891, Marcel admired Puvis de Chavannes, his 'world of dream and profound peace', 'that veiled, but in no way heavy atmosphere inhabited by characters from an ethereal, though not unreal existence ... the delights of a beautiful summer afternoon'. Amidst portraits by Delaunay, Bonnat, Carolus-Duran, Chaplin, Boldini, Blanche and Stevens, was a portrait by Whistler, who also exhibited 'a really exquisite seascape'.[102] It was Marcel's first encounter with this model for Elstir. Finally, these 'personal impressions' described an artist whom Proust would mention in À l'ombre des jeunes filles en fleurs: 'Gallé, the artist in glass, is perhaps our most brilliant poet: an owl's wing, some birds in the snow, dragon-flies with dark or gleaming colours provide him with his theme and manage to make us shiver all over.' In short, it was a case of 'awakening' in readers 'a few tried and tested artistic sensations'. The young critic hid his timidity under the pseudonym of 'Fusain'.

One senses that Proust was on much firmer ground when it came to literary criticism or actual experience. 'Pendant le Carême'[103] gives an account of five lectures on Yvette Guilbert.* In it he reveals a taste for music-hall, something that he would always enjoy, and which would lead him to write 'Éloge de la mauvaise musique' (Les Plaisirs et les Jours) and to mention Mayol or Paulus in À la recherche. Before Sarah Bernhardt or Réjane, it was Yvette Guilbert who inspired Proust to pen a portrait, in which he maintained that there was nothing 'fin-de-siècle' about the artist: 'What connection is there between this woman, who is so funny, so

---

* Poitiers (that is to say Reynaldo Hahn) mimicked her in Jean Santeuil, p. 566; cf. pp. 504–5, in which the Duchesse de Réveillon rehearses her songs daily with the 'delightful little diva' and invites her to her château, and in which the singer gives her impressions of the duchess to Le Gaulois. In 1891, at the time of Le Mensuel, she sang the Chat Noir [Black cat] repertory at Le Divan japonais nightclub (Y. Guilbert, La Chanson de ma vie, Grasset, 1927, pp. 90–7).

invigorating, so healthy, whose manner of speaking, so lacking in colour and in naturalism,* is mingled with so much good intention, such good will, so much of the charm and the good grace of Mme Judic,[104] what connection is there between her and the "flowers of vice", the sensuous and sickly flowers which, with their scrawny elegance, adorn so bizarrely the fantasies of Chéret and of Willette? Dressed in a simple white dress which made her long black gloves stand out still more, with her white powdered face, in the midst of which her exaggeratedly red mouth bleeds like a cut, she looked rather more like those creatures, brutally drawn and with their own intense life, which are scattered through a work of Raffaelli. As such, in her physical appearance – as well as in her diction – she makes one think of naturalism, of a naturalism that is already outdated, and so very different in any case from the art of today.' Here, at the age of nineteen, Marcel competes with the art of painting; his sketch of the singer is a portrait that has the strength of a Toulouse-Lautrec and shows that his imagination was already working in images and in literary and pictorial allusions: if Yvette Guilbert is reminiscent of a Raffaelli, Odette would conjure up a Botticelli. This passage also shows what Marcel thought of contemporary literature: naturalism, which he never cared for, was already 'outdated' as far as he was concerned, even though Zola's twenty-volume novel, *Les Rougon-Macquart*, was still being published. Finally, the article expresses in a firm hand the rules regarding literary criticism and aesthetics. Jules Lemaître,[105] whose theatre reviews in *Le Journal des débats* (1885–96) fascinated Marcel, as we have seen, claimed that as far as a masterpiece was concerned, it was impossible to make a judgement. At the music-hall, on the other hand, Lemaître 'tries to apply the "saw" theory† and to create a scientific basis for the simple *café-concert* song'. Here we can see his love of rules emerging, which Marcel owed to his training in philosophy and which underlies all his work: 'The things that can be reduced to formulae, because they are governed by laws, which, in a word, are the subject of science, are precisely the most physical, the most material manifestations

---

* In her memoirs Yvette Guilbert confirms this interpretation when she describes an evening at the Charpentiers, when she sang for Zola, Mirbeau, Hervieu, Loti, Goncourt and Daudet: 'At first I had wanted to charm Zola; for me he was the instigator of realism in art, of *truthfulness* in expression, and my "no tricks" nature corresponded to "his style". I, too, was close to the earth' (ibid., p. 150). The writers present that evening jotted down their impressions in a notebook which Louis de Robert, a friend of the singer and later of Proust, would give her as a present (ibid., pp. 154–8).

† A popular song or refrain that is repeated ad nauseam. *Tr.*

of what we do, whereas art, in its highest creations, because of its quasi-divine essence, avoids scientific investigation entirely.' A Jules Lemaître was incapable of formulating rules concerning real art; they would be left to Proust; but Lemaître could explain why one laughed, and Marcel paid particular attention to the behaviour of critics, because his art had its beginnings in criticism. Before writing literature, we should learn how to speak about it – by way of Lemaître, before Sainte-Beuve.

In July 1891 Marcel, under the pseudonym of Bob, devoted his column to music-halls:[106] 'the Horloge, Alcazar, Ambassadeurs, Folies-Bergère, Nouveau Cirque, Hippodrome, Cirque d'Été, etc.' – which gives an indication of the extent and number of nights out, no trace of which remains in the correspondence. There is a description, for example, of M. Clovis in a monologue at the Alcazar, in which he performs the part of an actor who attributes a play by M. Loti, a lieutenant-commander, 'to M. Pierre Loto, *lieutenant de vessie*'* Proust also attacked another famous theatre critic, Francisque Sarcey, and he showed a preference for male artists, among them 'our hilarious and already so classical Paulus':[107] 'You buxom beauties of the *café-concerts*, vegetable creatures, more of whose clothing one wishes had been left in the cloakroom, you do not deserve to have your charms analysed any more than the men do.' It is thus perverse of Marcel to end his column by recalling those women to whom it was dedicated, 'Mesdemoiselles Rosa-Josepha', the Siamese twins 'with only one abdominal cavity'. These louche shows prepared the writer for his descriptions of popular songs, and even his reading: 'As soon as I read an artist's work, I was very soon able to make out the tune beneath the words of the song.'[108] He also appreciated melodrama, which, he would say, the crucial scene at Montjouvain rather resembled. As far as the enthusiast was concerned, it was all fertile and dangerous ground – the music-hall as well as the Comédie-Française, Yvette Guilbert or Paulus as much as Sarah Bernhardt or Mounet-Sully. Finally, the Alcazar and the Hippodrome, with their atmosphere of sensual promiscuity and cigar smoke, provided the hope of laughter, of a great belly laugh, very different to anything to be found in the salons described in the 'Social Life' columns of *Le Mensuel*.

Fashion appealed to Marcel, just as it had to Mallarmé, who published

---

* Such puns or wordplay make little sense when translated. A lieutenant-commander is a *lieutenant de vaisseau*, while the word '*vessie*' literally means a bladder; *Le Loto* is the state-run lottery. *Tr.*

an entire diary, *La Dernière Mode* (1874), on the subject. It was with Réjane's 'comb made of tortoiseshell' at the Variétés that 'Shooting Star' made his first appearance, in November 1890, in *Le Mensuel*: and, since Proust made use of everything, the Narrator gives Albertine a 'tortoiseshell comb' which she wears in her hair. In *À l'ombre des jeunes filles en fleurs*, we also find the condemnation of the 'appalling bustle'.[109] The fashion columnist carefully notes the nuances which the new year had brought to dresses and blouses, accessories and hats: 'a large fedora, with long plumes, which obstructs the horizon and is discourteous to one's neighbour at the theatre', or else, and the image with its humorous change of tone and style, is already Proustian: 'a simple little thing, of a delicate shade, preferably pale blue, tossed into that stern collection like a lively, much brighter thought in the middle of a solemn speech: so much for the hat'. In March 1891 'Shooting Star' commented on the Louis XV jacket, the Henri II pèlerine, the Médici collar. Ten lines were given over to a 'grey outfit in perfect taste'. And Marcel, who must have hated having to hand over drama to his friend Otto, ended his column with a quotation from *Supplice d'une femme* by Dumas *fils*: 'Perhaps', as if to make fun of a phrase that scarcely deserves to be quoted. Through these virtuoso exercises, the discriminating creator of Odette Swann's and the Duchesse de Guermantes' outfits practised and prepared his descriptions of their changing appearances. It was through fashion that the young man discovered the passage of time.

Rather more literary exercises also occupied Marcel's gifted pen. In February 1891 he published his first poem, under the byline 'M.P.', entitled 'Poésie'; it was dedicated to Gustave L. de Waru,[110] a friend from Sciences-Po and nephew of the Comtesse de Chevigné, who would be a model for Oriane. The tone of this love poem is Baudelairean. Yet this love is not addressed to a woman, if the eyes that are recalled are those of the dedicatee:

> *La nuit! La mer! Les deux seules choses magiques!*
> *Serré dans son manteau magnifique et soyeux,*
> *Je m'y perds en noyant mes regards dans ses yeux,*
> *Ses yeux indifférents, langoureux et mystiques.**

Marcel spent that summer on the Normandy coast, first at Cabourg in September, then, in October, at Trouville, at Les Frémonts, the splendid

---

* Night! Sea! The only two magical things!/ Huddled within his magnificent silky coat,/ I lose myself by sinking my gaze in his eyes,/ His indifferent eyes, languorous and mystical.

estate on the coast that belonged to the Baignères family. Trouville's monuments are its villas, as the guidebooks have proclaimed since 1860 (and especially the Joanne guide, *Trouville et les bains de mer du Calvados*, 1870, constantly reprinted and mentioned by Proust in his epigraph to 'Choses normandes'); among these residences, private mansions or small châteaux were the Comtesse de Montebello's villa, in Louis XIII style, the Persian Villa, built in 1859 by M. de Gastine and bought in 1876 by the Princesse de Sagan, the manor of La Cour-Brûlée, built in 1864 for Mme Aubernon, and the manor of Les Roches, belonging to the Marquise de Galliffet (Mme Baignères' first cousin).

The first villas were built at the time of the July Monarchy in a neo-Louis XIII style; under the Second Empire, the style was eclectic, a mixture of periods, but it gradually veered towards reproduction of Norman or Anglo-Norman designs.[111] This was precisely the case with Les Frémonts, built in 1869 by Arthur Baignères, on land acquired in 1861 by his father-in-law, who was an associate of de Lesseps.[112] The house was built in an L-shape. It was here that Marcel learned to know 'the unique view from La Raspelière, situated at the crest of the hill and from which, in a large drawing-room with two fireplaces, an entire row of windows over-looked the gardens and the trees, through which could be seen the sea as far as Balbec and beyond, while the other row of windows overlooked the valley'.[113] In the vast salon (or, later, in Mme Straus's salon at Clos de Mûriers), he admired 'some sheaves of grasses, poppies and flowers of the field picked that same day'.[114] A variety of 'vistas', designed to be seen through the trees, created the charm of the estate. The Verdurins rented La Raspelière from the Cambremers, just as the Finalys, before buying Les Frémonts, rented it from the Baignères in 1892.

The two articles published by Marcel in the last issue of *Le Mensuel* (October 1891) describe this visit. 'Choses normandes' is a landscape. Every artist in his youth discovers a favourite landscape to which his spirit always returns, and which, from one description to the next, he shapes and refines through language each time he comes across it again during his lifetime. The image Marcel perceived in Normandy, and which he constructed in *Le Mensuel* and later in *Les Plaisirs et les Jours*, he would also identify in Brittany, at Beg-Meil, and he would incorporate it in *Jean Santeuil*, together with that of Évian. *Contre Sainte-Beuve*, *À l'ombre des jeunes filles en fleurs* and *Sodome et Gomorrhe II* gave the picture its most accomplished form, its colours and its glamour, both in the text of the novel and in Elstir's canvases, creating a mirror image through fiction. The general theme is that of the countryside that overlooks the sea, 'above Trouville for example': 'From a terrace, on which golden tea steams from a table that has been laid, one often glimpses "the sun shining over the sea", the sailing boats approaching, "all the bustling motion of those who are leaving, of those who still have the strength to desire and to want".' The beauty of the lofty site is perceived here thanks to Baudelaire, whose 'Chant d'automne'[115] as well as 'Le port', an extract from *Spleen de Paris*, Marcel quoted. The peace of the countryside is linked to that of the sea, or is a contrast to its tempests. The sea in sunlight is followed by a seascape lit by the moon. Another mirror image: in the evening, the observer 'from his gardens ... can no longer distinguish the sea and sky which have merged'. The fields in moonlight appear 'to be a lake'. In the countryside, to begin with, there are the pleasures of childhood, primitive and oral; and at night, the mystery of the sea: 'And so this countryside, the richest in France, which, with its limitless abundance of farms, of cattle, cream, cider-apple trees and its thick lawns, summons us only to eat and to sleep, adorns itself, once night has fallen, with a certain mystery and vies in melancholy with the vast plain of the sea.'* Finally, the author of 'Choses normandes', in this passage in which the style of Chateaubriand merges with that of Anatole France, paid homage to the Norman houses, the models for La Raspelière, the property of the Verdurins: 'in reality half-Norman, half-English, where the number of spiked turrets on the rooftops increases the vantage points and complicates the outline, where the windows for all their width have such an air of gentleness and cosiness, and where, from the windowboxes built into the walls beneath each window, flowers stream down'.[116] Thus, the Baignères' villa, Les Frémonts, spanned Proust's work, from the earliest printed texts to *Sodome et Gomorrhe* in which it becomes La Raspelière, whose position dominates 'the valley on one side, the sea on the other'. Against this background the petty intrigues of *Les Plaisirs et les Jours*, the love affairs in *À l'ombre des jeunes filles en fleurs*, or those of the Narrator and Albertine, of Charlus and Morel, are enacted.

After *Le Mensuel*, Proust came to realize that a landscape had to be brought to life. And so, in the same issue in which he gave us 'Choses normandes', he published, under the pseudonym of Pierre de Touche (to

---

* In the port of Carquethuit, in *À l'ombre des jeunes filles en fleurs*, Elstir takes up this theme, extending the metaphor a little further until the earth and the sea are fused, and each achieves its metamorphosis in the other.

avoid giving the impression that he had written the entire issue himself), his first short story (only two pages long): 'Souvenir'. What is particularly important and moving about this unknown and forgotten story, discarded by its author and not signed under his real name, is that it presents for the first time a ritualized script of the kind that Marcel Proust confined himself to thereafter, a tale of fantasy that culminated with *La Prisonnière* and *Le Temps retrouvé* and which, in the course of the novel, also brought to mind Balzac's *La Fille aux yeux d'or*. A man, living in a house that overlooks the sea, has just seen a woman whom he once knew and loved. Her father, now old and bent, does not recognize him. Odette is condemned to spend her time bedridden on a chaise longue after 'a dreadful illness', reading, gazing out to sea and recalling her memories. No one wants to look after her; her mother is dead, her father too old, her brother 'had been caused great distress by a woman who had deceived him horribly' (a further schema, to be repeated in his novels, which would afflict every Proustian love affair). Her younger sister is too young (like Robert Proust: the sad thing about younger brothers is that they are always too young). The narrator finally takes his leave of Odette: 'I wished I could have hugged her: I wanted to tell her that I loved her ... I was choked with tears. I strode through the long entrance hall and across that delightful garden, where the gravel of its pathways would never again, alas! grate beneath my feet.'

What did they represent, this girl punished for ever by fate, her incurable illness, this distance between herself and the narrator, this sense of time that has destroyed virtually everything? Was Marcel planning an impossible love affair? If we compare this story with 'Avant la nuit', which he published in *La Revue blanche* in December 1893, we encounter the same setting, the same situation: a 'maiden's confession', which might almost be that of Odette's in *Le Mensuel*,[117] addressed to her 'best friend'. The illness conceals a secret; it has been caused by a bullet that could not be removed, following a suicide attempt. Françoise (just as in *Jean Santeuil*) admits that her homosexuality is at the root of it. Here, the heroine is responsible for her own death; in *Les Plaisirs et les Jours*, for her mother's; in *Du côté de chez Swann*, for the death of her father, M. Vinteuil. In *Albertine disparue* she is responsible for her own death once more; but, in *Le Temps retrouvé*, it is the Narrator who feels he is to blame for the deaths of his grandmother and Albertine. Thus a constellation is taking shape in the 1891 story 'Souvenir': the incurable illness, the sense of guilt, the impossibility of love between a man and a woman (because of inversion, something that is not mentioned here, but brought to light two years later in 'Avant la nuit'), the 'confession',[118] the metamorphosis of the author into a woman, while at the same time doubling as the narrator. Everything is explained in *La Prisonnière*, where the Tolstoyan pity of the 1890s is exchanged for Dostoevsky, his crimes and his punishments.[119] In the year of his death, Proust observed: 'All Dostoevsky's novels could be entitled *Crime and Punishment*. . . But it is likely that he split between two characters what in reality would have been the story of only one. There is certainly a crime in his life and a punishment (which may have nothing to do with this crime), but he preferred to split them in two, to blame his attitude towards punishment on himself if needs be (*The House of the Dead*) and the crime on others.'[120] Before he had read Dostoevsky, and even more so later, Proust devised the same structure: a crime (or a mistake), and a punishment. The poetic setting of the Normandy countryside beside the sea encompassed a tragedy, even before the great works that lay ahead and the love affairs of the mature years.

At Les Frémonts, on 1 October 1891, Jacques-Émile Blanche drew a pencil sketch of Marcel.[121] The young man had met the painter, who was ten years older than him, at either Mme Straus' home, or Mme Baignères' house in Paris, or else at Princesse Mathilde's,[122] at about the time of his national service – not at Auteuil, where they were in fact neighbours. Blanche remembered Marcel 'in an unbuttoned military cape, wearing a shako of the infantry of the line. What a curious effect the combination of his hair and the pure oval shape of his young Assyrian face* made with a military uniform which was not fancy dress'.[123] The drawing certainly shows this 'pure oval shape' and the hair, but also the large eyes with their fixed, absent expression, the thin moustache and the small mouth with its generous lower lip. The head is sunk into the shoulders, his clothes, in which he is dressed for dinner, are almost excessive. In the absence of his mother, Marcel still looked elegant, but neglected. Contrary to what has been claimed, this drawing was not a sketch for the famous portrait which we shall discuss later. A greater talent than Blanche's would have been needed to depict the brilliance of this fine face, which looks so much older than its actual twenty years. The photographs of the young Proust, most of which were taken by the photographer Otto, produce the same effect of timeless maturity, of an extended youthfulness which he would

---

* Here we can see the topos of the oriental and the gazelle, etc., which we read about in Desjardins' article.

retain until his death. Proust liked them so much that, even at the time of the Prix Goncourt, he would never give people any other photograph of himself.

CHAPTER V

From Le Banquet *to* La Revue blanche

Despite his apparent inactivity, by the age of twenty, Marcel Proust, like Chateaubriand, had four separate careers. The first was his university career, for he had enrolled in November 1891 at the Faculty of Law and also as a second-year student of Political Science. The second career was social, the third literary, while his fourth consisted of sentimental pursuits. Over the years, he abandoned the first, then the second; but never the other two.

The fate of Marcel in love was tragic. He was often attracted by young men who were not homosexual. When the friendship that he offered them – and which disguised a deeper, or different, desire – appeared too intrusive or too demanding, they backed away. We cannot always tell from his friendships why, or for whom, Marcel experienced these feelings of love: should we mention Otto Bouwens?[1] Jacques Baignères, with whom he spent his holidays? In November 1891 Marcel arranged for his friend Edward Cachard, the son of an American lawyer and a French mother, to be introduced in Mme Straus' salon. But Cachard very soon showed himself to be very 'cold-hearted'[2] and he avoided Marcel's friendship. Proust would have other relationships with people who spoke English, such as Willie Heath, Sydney Schiff and Walter Berry, but, in spite of the examples of Balzac and Bourget, and despite (or because of) the fashion of the time, he would not depict any of them in *À la recherche du temps perdu*, where only the shadow of the Prince of Wales, a friend of Charles Swann, hovers over the aristocratic salons.

WILDE

Other relationships, but not one with Oscar Wilde. On 19 December 1891 *L'Écho de Paris* declared that Wilde was the 'great event' of Parisian literary salons.³ Marcel Schwob was the Irish-born writer's guide around the city's literary milieux, where he met Jean Lorrain, Pierre Louÿs, Léon Daudet, Jules Renard, Remy de Goncourt, André Gide (who fell in love with him, claimed Jules Renard in his *Journal*), Verlaine, and also Mallarmé (trapped between those two sworn enemies, Whistler and Wilde). The poet, who had been sent a copy of *The Portrait of Dorian Gray* in March 1891, had written to him at the time: 'To make it poignant again, amid the outrageous refinements of intellect, and human as well, in so perverse an atmosphere of beauty, is a miracle that you accomplish through use of all the writer's arts!'⁴ Wilde returned to Paris in the autumn to compete with the author of *Hérodiade* by writing – in French – *Salomé*,* a play derived from two paintings by Gustave Moreau that are mentioned in Huysman's *À rebours*. In Paris Wilde performed a role of his own, anxious as he was to charm, astonish and shock. His ambiguous looks had grown plump, like those of Charlus. His stories and his witty remarks went the rounds of Paris. His French was superb, as a letter to Edmond de Goncourt testifies: 'French by sympathy, I am Irish by race, and the English have condemned me to speak the language of Shakespeare . . . The English public, as usual hypocritical, prudish and philistine, has not known how to find the art in the work of art: it has searched for the man in it. Since it always confuses man with his creations, it thinks that to create Hamlet you must be a little melancholy, to imagine Lear, completely mad.'⁵

Jacques-Émile Blanche had introduced Proust to Wilde at the home of Mme Arthur Baignères. Marcel must have invited him to dinner. In the drawing-room in the Boulevard Malesherbes, Oscar, in front of Marcel's parents, turned on his heel, saying: 'How ugly your house is.' This remark, which could as easily have been uttered by Montesquiou, is authenticated by its inclusion in *La Prisonnière*, where it is spoken by Charlus 'with a mixture of insolence, wit and world-weariness'.⁶ Proust may have been dissuaded, if the anecdote is accurate, from devoting greater space to

---

* It is amusing to note that the work that inspired Richard Strauss was completed thanks to the Gypsy orchestra of Janesi Rigó (who ran off with the Princesse de Chimay, something that Charlus alludes to) at the Grand Café on the rue Scribe. Proust mentions the opera, not the play.

Wilde. He features in his work on two occasions, however. In *Contre Sainte-Beuve*, we see him as the aesthete and Balzacien: 'Oscar Wilde, whom life would later teach alas that there are more poignant sorrows than those provided us in books, said in his early period (at the time that he remarked: "It is only since the school of the Lake Poets that there are fogs on the Thames"): "The greatest sorrow of my life? The death of Lucien de Rubempré in *Splendeurs et misères des courtisanes*"', without knowing that he would become Lucien de Rubempré himself.* The fate of the homosexual is recalled in *Sodome et Gomorrhe I*: 'Their position unstable, like that of the poet once fêted in all the drawing-rooms, and applauded in every theatre in London, and the next day driven out of every lodging house, unable to find a pillow on which to lay his head.'[7] Proust's lack of sympathy did not prevent him pondering on Wilde's example, his aesthetics, his destiny.

PRINCESSE MATHILDE

Among Marcel's new acquaintances, perched half-way between history, society and literature, was the Princesse Mathilde. He was introduced to her at the home of Mme Straus; the princess was actually a friend of Fromental Halévy and of Georges Bizet, and later of his wife Geneviève, with whom she had an important correspondence.[8] The daughter of Jérôme Bonaparte and a cousin of Napoleon III, she entertained at 20 rue de Berri or at the Château de Catinat, at Saint-Gratien. Princesse Mathilde was the inspiration for countless comments, generally niggardly, lacking in intelligence and unpleasant, made by Edmond de Goncourt, a regular guest, in his *Journal*, and for some ferocious passages by Léon Daudet that lapse into caricature ('the princess herself, whom everyone agreed – I don't know why – to treat with airs and graces, was a portly old lady, with a face that was imperious rather than imperial, who made the mistake of wearing a low neckline');[9] all Daudet encountered was 'boredom' and indifference in this 'diabolical house', which furthermore was 'infested with Jews and Jewesses'. Marcel Proust drew a very different

---

* *CSB*, p. 273. Mme Arman de Caillavet wrote to Jeanne Pouquet: 'A horrible scandal has occurred to me which is purely hypothetical but probable. For two years I often used to come across Marcel when I called on Prouté, my art dealer. He told me he was going to the Passage des Beaux-Arts where he was writing a novel at the home of an obscure friend who was the only person who knew how to make him comfortable. But it's the Passage des Beaux-Arts where Oscar Wilde died under an assumed name' (M. Maurois, *Les Cendres brûlantes*, Flammarion, 1986, p. 110). An unlikely interpretation, but it has a poetic charm . . .

picture, initially in an article, 'Un salon historique. Le salon de S.A.I. la princesse Mathilde', that appeared in *Le Figaro*,[10] and later in *À l'ombre des jeunes filles en fleurs*.[11] These passages capture Marcel's delight at meeting his first princess, a woman imbued not merely with France's most glorious period of history, but also with literature; a woman of sufficient nobility to behave with simplicity itself, and who basked in a profusion of anecdotes concerning her heroic deeds. Her private life, after a broken marriage with the violent Prince Demidoff, the nephew of Czar Nicholas I, had been a disappointment, since her devoted escort had been unfaithful to her with her lady-in-waiting. Nevertheless she had been the friend of Mérimée, of Sainte-Beuve, of Taine (with whom she broke off relations following an article the historian wrote about Napoleon I) and of Flaubert, who told her in 1867: '"Who ever thinks of me?" you write to me. All those who know you, Princesse, and they do more than think. Writers, people whose job it is to observe and to feel, are not stupid! I also observe that my close friends, the Goncourts, Théo, father Beuve and I are not the least devoted among your entourage.'[12] We shall never know whether the princess and Flaubert were in love with one another: Comte Primoli has described a conversation, at Saint-Gratien, in which the princess, upon seeing Flaubert come in, a burning expression on his face, said she was ready to listen to anything, but only replied to him with incoherent mumbling, before rushing away.[13] A remark of Proust's, which he must have written thinking of his own friends, suggests that, as far as Flaubert was concerned, Princesse Mathilde preferred the man to his work: 'How many great writers, unknown in their lifetime, have not enjoyed precious friendships because of their sensitivity and their social charm – friendships which, in retrospect, we attribute to their genius!'[14]

At the time that Marcel attended the princess's salon, the most illustrious of her writer-friends were dead – apart from Goncourt – but he mentioned Dumas *fils*, Heredia, Renan, Porto-Riche, historians (including Gustave Schlumberger), magazine editors, such as Charles Ephrussi, the editor of the *Gazette des Beaux-Arts* (and one of the models for Swann), Ganderax, the editor of *La Revue de Paris*, and Pichot, the editor of *La Revue britannique*. Among the diplomats were Comte Benedetti, who was France's ambassador to Berlin in 1870. Members of the *noblesse d'Empire*, naturally enough, attended rue de Berri, including Essling, Murat and Ney, but also the Duc and Duchesse de Gramont, the Pourtalès and Prince Borghese. The princess's reconciliation with the Duc d'Aumale allowed Proust, in 1903, to describe the occasion in terms which foreshadow *Le Temps retrouvé*:

'They had not seen one another for more than forty years. They were young and beautiful then. Now they were still good-looking, but they were no longer young. Overcome with a sort of emotional coquetry, at first they stayed apart from each other, in the shadows, neither daring to reveal to the other how much they had changed.'[15]

In *À l'ombre des jeunes filles en fleurs* Proust makes use of his article for *Le Figaro* by condensing it, half as literature, half as history: 'It's Princesse Mathilde, [Swann] told me, you know, the friend of Flaubert, Sainte-Beuve and Dumas. Imagine, she's the niece of Napoleon I! Both Napoleon III and the Emperor of Russia asked her hand in marriage.' The princess's Second Empire style of dress seemed to 'meet the requirements of those who expected her to evoke another age'.[16] The old lady whom Marcel, at the age of twenty, first met when she was seventy, would be the only real royal personage (apart from the Queen of Naples) to make an appearance in his novel: the shadow of Napoleon, whose presence he had noticed in Balzac's novel *Une ténébreuse affaire*, was thus cast over the Prince of Borodino, in reality Walewski, and over Princesse Mathilde. There was no snobbery in this: 'An artist should serve only the truth and he should have no respect for rank. He should only take account of it in his portraits, in so far as it is a principle of differentiation, in the same way as are nationality, race and environment, for example. Every social situation has its interest and it can be equally appealing to the artist to depict the behaviour of a queen, as it is the behaviour of a seamstress.'[17]

BERGSON

On 7 January 1892 Proust's path crossed that of a man with whom he would often be compared: Henri Bergson. Marcel had been page-boy at the wedding of his cousin Louise Neuburger to the philosopher. Born in Paris in 1839, the son of a Slav musician who came from Eastern Poland and a young Englishwoman,[18] a scholar at the Lycée Condorcet and a brilliant pupil, who was awarded first prize in philosophy, as well as mathematics, in the *concours général*, and who entered the École Normale Supérieure in 1878,* Bergson was less influenced by Boutroux and Lachelier than was Proust: neo-Kantism was not his field. As a graduate in philosophy, he was appointed to the lycée at Angers, where he taught

---

* Among his fellow students were Jaurès, Durkheim and Desjardins. Proust would mention the first and the third of these.

without notes[19] and made use of Boutroux's lectures; in 1885 he was transferred to the lycée at Clermont-Ferrand, where he spent five years. It was there that he occupied his time writing his *Essai sur les données immédiates de la conscience*: he wrote one page after another, swept along by his inspiration, not bothering initially to connect the passages, and he only arrived at his title after many a hesitation; it became his doctoral thesis (1889).[20] In Paris he was appointed to the Lycée Rollin, and later the Lycée Henri IV; in 1894 he would fail to be elected to the Sorbonne, before being elected to the Collège de France in 1900. The relationship between the two cousins would not bring them any closer. There is something extraordinary about trying to imagine the conversations about memory, time, instinct, laughter, sleep, dreams, morality, religion and the laws of psychology – that never took place.* What were the reasons for this lack of intimacy between two people, and two minds, whose family links, background and ancestry would seem to propel them towards one another? Firstly, their difference in age, an important factor, given that one was thirty-two and the other twenty years old; the fact that Marcel was not particularly interested in his cousins in general, and that he viewed his teachers somewhat ironically (with the exception of Darlu, and even he was never invited to dinner); as for the specialists, he consulted them, but did not make friends of them. But above all, it may have been their resemblance that drew them apart: 'Bergson did not like to be preceded by anyone or questioned, and he preferred to be left alone by friends and colleagues. Scarcely lavish in his use of footnotes in his books, he occasionally inserted them in order to indicate his independent position with regard to those doctrines that one might absent-mindedly compare to his.'[21] Similarly, Proust, when he read *Matière et Mémoire*, took note of their different approaches,[22] and, in an interview, refused to allow *Swann* to be labelled as a 'Bergsonian novel'.[23] Politics divided them: at the time of the Dreyfus affair, when Marcel was collecting signatures on behalf of Zola, or Picquart, he must have been refused by his cousin, whose name does not appear on any petition. Bergson would say to Gilbert Maire: 'For a long time to begin with, I believed that my co-religionist was guilty; the false Henry made me incline towards his innocence and, in any case, made me a supporter of the retrial. All the same, I have always blamed the turbulent conduct of those who set out to obtain it and who trans-

---

* With one exception, as we shall see, when they were on the jury of the Prix Blumenthal, after the First World War.

formed into a deplorable civil war a trial which, in my opinion, could
have remained a judicial matter. I never shared the enthusiasm of the
Dreyfusiens: I considered everybody to be wrong in the Dreyfus affair.
And as you can imagine, such an attitude exposed me to the hostility of
both camps.'[24] In appearance Bergson was cold, albeit sensitive; Proust,
on the other hand, was warm and sentimental. The former's extreme
modesty did not suit the latter's confessional nature. That is the way with
great minds who have a need for solitude, at least when they retire into
their innermost selves, where they cut themselves off in order to create,
and where they are not going to encounter any more colleagues or cousins.
Later on, when Bergson did recall Proust, it was to relate the following
anecdote: Bergson had complained about noise; Proust then sang the
praises of Quiès ear-plugs and brought him a box; Bergson did not use
them. For the philosopher, the author of *À la recherche* was merely the
person who had brought him some Quiès ear-plugs.[25]

So one can understand why Proust's translation of Ruskin should have
elicited no more than a short article from the philosopher, and the award
of the Prix Goncourt these meagre lines: 'You know what I thought about
your book *Du côté de chez Swann**; the latest, *À l'ombre des jeunes filles en fleurs*,
is a worthy continuation to it. Rarely has introspection been taken so far.
It is a direct and continuous vision of the inner reality.'[26] Three sentences
for the dangerous rival who had stated that the distinction between the
involuntary and the voluntary memory dominated all his work, whereas
this did not feature in Bergson's philosophy, and was even contradicted
by it.[27] Bergson without Proust is no more surprising than Proust without
Bergson.

LE BANQUET

At the beginning of 1892 a group of friends, mostly former pupils of the
Lycée Condorcet, founded *Le Banquet,* the name of the review being
derived from Plato.[28] Jacques Bizet brought along Marcel Proust to
the first meeting, where he met Fernand Gregh, Robert Dreyfus, Louis
de La Salle, Daniel Halévy, and Horace Finaly. Later, they would be
joined by Gabriel Trarieux (a former colleague from *Le Mensuel*), Robert
de Flers, Henri Rabaud, Gaston de Caillavet, Léon Blum and Henri
Barbusse. The founding members were obliged to pay a monthly contri-

* But we don't, alas!

bution of ten francs. A print-run of 400 copies[29] cost 100 francs. The price of an annual subscription was ten francs. *Le Banquet* was printed on the presses of *Le Temps*. The editors used to hold their meetings at Rouquette, a bookshop at 71 Passage Choiseul, which name was printed on the front cover. The first meeting did not run entirely smoothly: after hours of discussion, the only title the group of young friends had come up with was 'Le Chaos'; at their next meeting, there were about fifteen other ones. The fact is that the group was good-natured, jocose and rarely took itself seriously. A supervisory committee was formed, consisting of Messrs Daniel Halévy, Robert Dreyfus and Marcel Proust.[30] After the second issue, Fernand Gregh assumed the role of editor-in-chief.

An editorial addressed 'To the reader', which did not express any really firm policy, opened the first issue. If the editors asserted they were adopting 'the most subversive anarchical doctrines', this was for bravura and was meant as a joke. These 'very serious young men' knew what they rejected: symbolism and 'Tolstoyism'; what they upheld was eclecticism: they wrote in order to 'pour out their feelings', to make their prose better known – but also to draw attention in France to 'the most interesting productions and the most interesting art from abroad'. The first issue opened, in fact, with an act from Ibsen's *Emperor and Galilean*, translated by Daniel Halévy. When they wrote about anarchy or 'spiritual exercises', they were not far removed from Barrès. There followed a sequence of short stories, poems, book or theatre reviews, and, representing foreign literature, Nietzsche,[31] Tennyson, Rossetti and Swinburne. Fernand Gregh, who also wrote under three pseudonyms, asserted that his three colleagues and he were 'opposed to the fashion for hermetics which was beginning to be the rage'. Thus this little magazine was different to the famous *Mercure de France*, and to *La Revue blanche* (which it none the less mentioned frequently), and bravely attempted to remain outside fashion. It is true that to evade one influence is to embrace another: the poems were not unlike those of Hugo, Musset, Verlaine and Sully-Prudhomme. In its prose, one can detect *fin-de-siècle* themes in 'Pessimisme' (which Gregh signed F. Miser!), or in Léon Blum's 'Méditation sur le suicide d'un de mes amis'.[32] According to Robert Dreyfus, one of the founders, it also had a cultural tradition: '*Le Banquet*, founded in reaction to symbolism, aimed to revive the pure, rich French tradition, with an intelligent merging of classicism and romanticism.'[33] Yet when Dreyfus published 'La situation en littérature' in issue number 5 (July 1892), in which he praised Barrès and Nietzsche, while at the same time criticizing their schools,* and the atmosphere of 'literary Terror', concluding with a eulogy of Voltaire, Proust wrote him an ironical letter; in it he expressed his concept of literary schools, which would not alter right up to *Le Temps retrouvé*. To claim that they follow one another, like governments or society fashions, is to have a 'material' vision of literature; works of art do not replace one another, as objects do, or politicians: 'This eulogy of Voltaire appears to conform to the recipe: admiring what is outdated is even more elegant than being fashionable, and besides, things become fashionable very quickly. Thus, when people started admiring Wagner, the ex-Wagnerians preferred Beethoven, then Bach, then Handel.'[34]

Just as at the start of a horse race, when nothing enables one to pick out the future winner from among the horses, so the charm of a magazine lies in the way the great writer, for whose first stirrings of talent we are searching, blends in with the rest of the group. While Proust's literary criticism already displayed great assurance of thought, his 'studies' or 'sketches' had the same rather obsolete charm as the pieces that appeared on the adjacent pages and which were not signed Marcel Proust. The first four studies appeared in April 1892, in issue number 2, placed third, after 'Frederich Nietzsche', by Daniel Halévy and Fernand Gregh, and some extracts from *Beyond Good and Evil*, which they were the first to make available ('The Two Moralities' and 'The Social Role of Christianity'). 'Les maîtresses de Fabrice' ends with a reference to Mme Straus, intelligent, gracious, mysterious, with deep eyes, but who, unlike the first two 'mistresses', does not love the hero. 'Cydalise' was written after returning from the salon of Princesse Mathilde, which Mme de Reszké (then de Mailly-Nesle) had attended that evening, dressed in red and conversing with Porto-Riche.† Beyond the description of her expressions and clothing, Marcel here makes apparent his admiration for this type of distant and melancholy woman, similar to those in paintings by Moreau and the Pre-Raphaelites, to Hérodiade and to Maeterlinck's characters: 'a princess come from afar, who was bored, and who always had a gentle languor about her', who was exiled and came from a race that had been wiped

---

* 'Naturalism is bankrupted; symbolism is bankrupted; dilettantism is bankrupted.'

† *Corr.*, vol. VII, p. 239, 1 August 1907. Proust tells Hahn at length what the apparition of Mme de Reszké meant to him: the fairy Viviane, with the face of Burne-Jones, of Moreau, akin to Mme Greffulhe (and therefore the Duchesse and the Princesse de Guermantes), 'a dream-like creature ... true beauty of Cornwall'; 'that although her eyes, her face, have a mystery of which she is unaware, that mystery is nevertheless what a poet must try to grasp and express'.

out. The third portrait, 'Les amies de la Comtesse Myrto', imitated La Bruyère, but it set out to depict social relationships with a preciosity that borders on the incomprehensible. In the fourth portrait we meet the courtesan Heldémone, who may have been drawn from Laure Hayman.

In May 1892, in issue number 3, Proust published five pieces.[35] The first two examine female snobbery towards what was considered 'chic'. 'Esquisse d'après Madame *** '[36] is Marcel's first portrait of Mme de Chevigné, who would provide the inspiration for the Duchesse de Guermantes' face: 'the hooked nose of a bird, the piercing, soft eyes, the white-gloved arm leaning on a box at the theatre'. 'I was never able to meet her sons or her nephews, who like her all had a hooked nose, thin lips, piercing eyes and a skin that was too delicate, without feeling thrilled at recognizing a breed that must have derived from a goddess and a bird.' The image would not change right up to *Le Côté de Guermantes*. The fourth sketch[37] is so intimate that it can only be interpreted by thinking of Marcel himself: 'Life is curiously sweet and easy among certain people of great natural distinction, who are witty and affectionate, but who are capable of every vice, even though they do not practise any publicly and not a single one could be attributed to them. There is something secretive and docile about them. And then their perversity adds a piquancy to the most innocent occupations, such as going for a walk at night, in the parks.' Gentility combined with the possibilities of the obscene, the secretive, the perverse – this was a combination that attracted Marcel to Mlle Vinteuil because it was something he found within himself. In the fifth sketch Fabrice, the 'fickle one', loves someone for six months and tries to imagine friendship once love has passed; but he deceives himself, for he does not reckon with forgetting,* another great Proustian theme (as much as memory, forgetting is involuntary) from 'Un amour de Swann' to *Albertine disparue*.

The first of the three essays in issue number 5 (July 1892) illustrates the gulf between life and the dream world, and contains a remarkable punch line: 'And out of our marriage with death who knows whether our conscious immortality may arise?' The second is a piece in the style of early Bourget, about women who confound every plan: 'They savour a book or life itself as they would a beautiful day or an orange',[38] and, sceptical and dilettante, they have no moral sense. The third is a meditation on eyes and their expressions, as mirrors of the divine or of love, 'they

---

* 'The thought that one day he would live without seeing her was incompatible with a feeling that had the illusion of his eternity.'

can also sting by promising a love to which the heart will not be true'.[39] The look in the eyes of Mme Straus or the Comtesse de Chevigné had already taught Marcel that they promised what they would not fulfil. For Proust, the divine dwells in a person's eyes, from Gilberte to Charlus. Here we come across one of his great themes.

Issue number 6 (November 1892) offered two other studies, both of them still in third place in order of appearance, 'La mer' and 'Portrait de Madame *** ', which were both dedicated to Louis de La Salle.[40] In Baudelairean style, the first of these paints the marine landscape that was dear to the author of *À l'ombre des jeunes filles en fleurs*: the maternal water is defined by purity, virginity, the beginning of the world, and mystery. Above all, the essay establishes, as we have seen, an important connection: 'The sea has the charm of those things that are not silent at night, which, in our restless lives, allow us leave to sleep and offer a promise that not everything will vanish, rather as nightlights do for small children who feel less lonely when they twinkle.'[41] The fear of falling asleep is identified with the fear of death; like the sound of the *miséricorde* bell at Combray (at Auteuil), the noise of the sea in Normandy induced sleep. Proust actually established the same links as Baudelaire between the sea and music, 'which imitates the movements of our soul'. The 'Portrait de Madame *** ' is not that of Mme de Chevigné,[42] but of Mme Guillaume Beer, *née* Elena Goldschmidt-Franchetti.[43] Her maiden name explains the fact that she 'combined the mystery of women of the North with Italian charms'. She was the muse of Leconte de Lisle, who celebrated her in 'La Rose de Louveciennes' (where she owned a house which Proust had visited), and later a writer under the pseudonym of Jean Dornis, so it is hardly surprising that she should have aroused in Marcel an 'artistic pleasure'. The 'studies' in *Le Banquet* end with this 'portrait of a lady'. But it was also here that Proust published his first real short story, 'Violante ou la mondanité', which was dedicated to Anatole France. There are certain autobiographical aspects to the heroine:[44] the 'lack of will-power' which worries the mother; the death of Violante's parents which liberates her; and her initiation by a young man of sixteen into 'extremely inconvenient things that she had never suspected'. 'She experienced a very gentle pleasure, but which immediately made her feel ashamed.' The young man goes away to sea, she sets to work on her 'everlasting interior novel', and only experiences love through suffering, 'which is the only way anyone learns to know her' (a conviction which Proust would always hold). Violante becomes lost in society life (while resisting the advances of a woman who appears to be over-fond of women), and thus seems to prefigure the Swanns, the Guermantes and the Charluses, in whom the deep longing to be imaginative, to be creative, to live alone according to one's own philosophy, has been blunted and defeated – the last word in the story – by habit. The entire existence of the socialites in *À la recherche* was thus sketched here, as were the circles of hell that the Narrator goes through in *Le Côté de Guermantes*.

Another Proust, whose writing is steadier and more self-assured, is also revealed in *Le Banquet*: the critic. In the first issue he reviewed 'Un conte de Noël' written by Louis Ganderax, the future editor (1897) of *La Revue de Paris*. In it Marcel puts forward a conception of time, of expectation and the future, that would never change: 'The day comes when we understand that tomorrow can be no different to yesterday, since it is composed of it.'[45] Ganderax had imagined that the 'deserted woman' found her lover again, and here Proust discovered what was to be one of the great themes of the stories that comprise *Les Plaisirs et les Jours*, and which he also introduced in 'Combray' and *Du côté de chez Swann*, before portraying Swann, Charlus and the Narrator as 'deserted men'. From the very earliest stories, a neurosis about being deserted lies at the heart of his work; it stemmed from Balzac, but also from within himself. Furthermore, he points out that a character placed in his 'world' can reveal how the tastes of a period and a class reflect both a general sentimental reality, and a particular fiction. We then see the appearance of one of the writers who had the greatest influence upon Proust, one who is mentioned so frequently in *À la recherche*: 'Was it not to a certain degree for the sake of the female members of the audience at court, tortured so deliciously by passion, that Racine, when he chose to depict the realization of tragic destinies, in dramas that combined pleasure with crime, preferred to evoke the shades of princesses and kings?'[46]

At the same period, on *Le Banquet* headed notepaper, Proust wrote a passage on Beauty;[47] it is effectively a reflection on reading, which shunts us around from book to book in search of true Beauty. We believe we have discovered it in Flaubert, or in Leconte de Lisle, but a doubt sets in. Beauty cannot be external, material, or shut up inside other people's books; it is internal, it is enclosed in our thoughts, like a soul. This is why artists, at the risk of being mistaken for lunatics, set off on their 'journey' in search of Beauty.* Written around the same time, 'Un livre contre

---

* The phrase '*à la recherche*' will be used again . . . It is because Beauty is to be found within time regained.

l'élégance', in issue number 2 in April 1892, criticized an essay by Édouard Delessert. In it Proust displayed his knowledge of the history of fashion, taking it to the point of erudition, with his allusions to Theocritus or its quotations from *Lysistrata*, while at the same time defending women's clothing, which was threatened by the new Republic, and depicted as 'rather like a solemn matron, well enough dressed as long as she is warm and secure, who with a foolish ardour, smashes her bottles of scent and pots of make-up upon the altar of work and austerity'.[48] This very maternal Republic seemed to suggest that true elegance, such as that of the Guermantes, had an aristocratic origin.

Ever since *Le Mensuel*, Marcel had displayed a prodigious aptitude for being able to discuss anything: even today, researchers and commentators have not always been able to trace the sources of his erudition. It was acquired in his youth, as when writing about 'the irreligion of the State', in issue number 3 of *Le Banquet*, in May, in an article under the byline 'Laurence', but identified as Proust's by Robert Dreyfus.[49] Here the student of political science denounced 'atheistic' teaching, the substitution of a state religion by state irreligion, 'the same trail of fanaticism, intolerance and persecution' which religion itself had brought about. Radicalism in power had a materialist philosophy, whereas 'it was to those minds who were so to speak elevated above themselves by Christianity that France owed its purest masterpieces'; the young pamphleteer was on the side of 'the great idealistic philosophies', and would never alter his position. In the same way, in 1904, he would also defend the cathedrals threatened with deconsecration or transformation into museums.[50]

That same month, in *Littérature et Critique*, under the title 'Choses d'Orient', Marcel published a review of *Voyage en Turquie d'Asie* by the Comte de Cholet, his former lieutenant at Orléans when he was doing his military service. The article was dedicated to a new friend of Proust's, who had offered his assistance to *Le Banquet* and had arranged to have the magazine published by the Rouquette bookshop: Henri de Rothschild, a future doctor, a well-known traveller and a playwright under the name of André Pascal.[51] For us, the interest of this article lies less in the art of the Ottoman Empire – in which one can still discern the influence of Vandal's lectures on Middle Eastern questions (Turkey does not feature in *À la recherche* except in the comic character of the Ambassadress) – than in the philosophy of travel which it expresses. Long quotations from Baudelaire's 'Voyage' voiced the feelings of 'a generation above all aware of the useless splendour of things', which is, ultimately, decadent. A new generation had taken its place, 'anxious above all to restore a purpose and a meaning to life, to give man the sense that he had to a certain extent created his own destiny. The moral reality of travel had been restored to him.'[52] It is not pointless escapism, but the result of an effort of will, and it produces a 'moral improvement'. Here we find the source of the Proustian philosophy of travel: when we think about it, Marcel's own trips to Belgium, Holland and Italy, to Burgundy and Normandy, also necessitated an effort of will and had as their aim the enhancement of his knowledge of churches, paintings and old towns. Every time he set off, Marcel must have had to conquer the anguish of departure; and on every occasion, he made use of what he had seen and visited in his written work. Marcel argued against the decadent, Barrésien notion of travel by upholding that which testified to 'the highest intelligence and the most admirable energy'.[53] The inspiration for his ideas came from reading *Devoir présent* by Paul Desjardins (1892),[54] which renounced dilettantism and advocated duty, the moral law and action. As in his article on state irreligion, Proust showed that he was aware of that new consciousness of the responsibilities of the writer expressed by Bourget (that is why he mentions *Le Disciple*), Vogüé and in Guyau's philosophy.[55] In 1892 Desjardins founded the Union pour l'Action Morale, which published its own *Bulletin*. Proust, who read the articles on philosophy in *Le Temps*, took sides against Robert Dreyfus, and asserted that Desjardins' faith 'is a light of reason compared to the scepticism of Barrès'.[56]

Naively autobiographical aspects abound in the writings of youth. Thus Proust, in reviewing Henri de Régnier's *Tel qu'en songe*,[57] harked back to the effect of family pressure on his career: 'Lawyers, doctors, administrators and society people are not the only ones who are incompetent in matters of poetry.'[58] The article specified certain principles of the Proustian aesthetic that had been established once and for all: over and above intelligence, there is 'a superior reasoning that is both one and infinite like feeling, and which is both the object and the instrument' of philosophers' meditations. Poetry was the work of 'this mysterious and profound feeling about things'. Beyond his praise for Henri de Régnier, with whom Proust would communicate by letter until the end of his life, to whom he would devote a pastiche and would avow, in public at least, an admiration that was not reciprocated, what is already important in these articles is to see a doctrine being born and taking shape long before its realization. The insistence attached to certain themes enables us to sense their importance.

'La Conférence parlementaire de la rue Serpente'[59] concerned the practice common at Oxford and Cambridge imitated by students of law and political science in Paris, of whom Marcel was one: that of creating a Parliament in miniature and emulating the debates of the House of Commons, in order to gain experience of political life, even if this meant running the risk of it seeming like a game of shadows. Marcel devoted a humorous column[60] to this spectacle that did not fail to confer on his orator friends praise that was thought excessive by the editors of *Le Banquet*, who dissociated themselves from the article by publishing a rejoinder, as if to criticize him for paying compliments in order to gain friends. Too kind, too nice, too social, that was what his friends from the Lycée Condorcet and *Le Banquet* were whispering: in the eyes of all these authors who are now forgotten (sometimes unjustly), Marcel seemed less of a writer than they themselves. Proust did not contribute to the last issue; the coffers being empty, the magazine ceased publication; it had lasted for a year, and eight instalments. In its pages, he had attempted his first 'sketches', published his first story and thrown out a few ideas; his colleagues had made Nietzsche known to their readers, and found their way out of symbolism, away from decadence and the anarchy preached by Barrès. They would continue at *La Revue blanche*.

FRIENDSHIPS

In the spring of 1892 Marcel's friends were split between the group at *Le Banquet* and that at the École Libre des Sciences Politiques (Sciences-Po). Common to both of them was Gabriel Trarieux, who believed he was a poetic innovator, and whom Proust described agreeably enough; someone always ready to inflict a reading of his poems on him[61] and who played 'the pretty boy' at the salons,[62] he would take private lessons in law at the same time as Proust and Jean Boissonnas. To the latter, a future diplomat, who 'flirted',[63] Marcel addressed some poems: 'In your hair the autumn lives once more/ . . . But the mysterious spring/ . . . It comes to life again in your person as well/ It is the pale golden green of your eyes.'[64] With Robert de Billy Marcel used to visit the Louvre; he was not interested in Poussin, but tried hard to find the artists mentioned by Baudelaire in 'Les Phares'; 'the golden atmosphere of dusks that were more dazzling in Claude Lorrain, more intimate in Cuyp, held his attention. Standing in front of *L'Embarquement pour Cythère*, he spoke of *Fêtes galantes* and of Verlaine's agony which had begun and would endure for another five years . . . Then he stopped for a long time before Van Dyck's portrait of the Duke of Richmond,* and I told him that all that youthful beauty . . . had been struck down by Cromwell's Ironsides. We philosophized on the death of the "Cavaliers" and of their king Charles and the echo of our thoughts can be found in the charming verses for which Reynaldo Hahn wrote a musical accompaniment.'[65] What is remarkable about Marcel is his anxiety to establish a link between poetry and painting, between image and language: using the medium of conversation before that of literature, he talked about paintings. It was Billy who also introduced Proust to medieval art, at the Musée de Cluny.

It was he, too, who introduced Marcel to a young man from Geneva, Edgar Aubert, whom they took along with them to various Parisian salons. Through Aubert Marcel came to understand the structure of Genevan high society, just as he had been initiated into French Protestant society by Robert de Billy, which he characterized humorously as 'charity, nurtured by the Bank'. Geneva, Alsace and the Cévennes were the three centres of an identical and complex society. Edgar Aubert, whom Marcel, in August 1892, called 'his little one',[66] 'whom he had begun to love wholeheartedly',[67] with 'his charming sadness and his mistrusting and almost restless uncertainty about everything that he was going to do' (something he shared with Marcel), died from appendicitis on 18 September. Proust kept his photograph 'with some verses translated from the English on the back which [he] did not remember but which seemed [to him] to be rather sad'.[68] He joined the procession of dead friends whom Proust brought together in the image of Robert de Saint-Loup and, possibly, in that of Albertine. As for the Protestants, in *À la recherche* they are associated with Jews or homosexuals (Swann, for instance, has a Protestant grandmother who is married to a Jew),[69] and seen as a minority; but their presence is very discreet.

In the spring of 1892 Marcel became friends with Robert de Flers, who later wrote for *Le Banquet*.[70] He wrote to Robert de Billy, in January 1893: 'Nothing has changed very much in my sentimental life, apart from the fact that I have found a friend . . . This is the young and charming, and intelligent, and good, and affectionate Robert de Flers.'[71] This friendship, born in the springtime, then developed in the autumn. Robert Pellevé de la Motte-Ango, the future Marquis de Flers, ambassador, editor of *Le*

---

* In actual fact, as Proust would acknowledge later (*Corr.*, vol. V, p. 311, July 1905), the Louvre had incorrectly captioned *L'Homme au pourpoint*, *Portrait du duc de Richmond*; Van Dyck died in 1641, the future duke was born in 1672.

Figaro, and the author, jointly with Gaston de Caillavet (whom he met, thanks to Marcel, along with Jeanne Pouquet, whom he would also court), of some brilliant light comedies, had all the gifts,* all the qualities. Was it his Christian name (which was also that of Dreyfus and Billy) that Proust gave to Saint-Loup (a character who was also modelled on Gaston de Caillavet, resulting in a subtle and secret game between the different motivations)? Flers also appears in a photograph in which he and Lucien Daudet flank a seated and triumphant Proust, a photograph which would incur the wrath of Mme Proust. In 1892 this former pupil of the Lycée Condorcet was twenty years old: he enrolled at the faculty of law and read for an arts degree. Eventually, Marcel saw him every day on the Boulevard Malesherbes. In 1903, when Marcel went to see *Le Sire de Vergy*, by Flers and Caillavet, an opera buffa with music by Claude Terrasse, he applauded so loudly that on three occasions he almost slapped Paul Hervieu,[72] who was sitting next to him.

A PORTRAIT

That spring of 1892 a legacy began to take shape which would, for good or ill, bequeath Marcel's image to posterity. Jacques-Émile Blanche asked him to sit for a portrait. On Saturdays Marcel would go from the villa at Auteuil, where his parents lived, to the Blanches, whose house was 'spread out, in scattered order' among beautiful gardens at 19 rue des Fontis (now rue du Docteur-Blanche). Doctor Antoine Blanche (1828–93), like his father Esprit Blanche (1796–1852), who had treated Nerval, looked after patients with nervous illnesses, and especially artists and writers (it was at his home that Maupassant ended his days), in the nursing home at the Princesse de Lamballe's lovely mansion (now the Turkish Embassy on the Avenue d'Ankara). Proust gave a witty description, thirty years later, of the doctor who, 'out of professional habit would urge [him] towards calm and moderation'. 'If I put forward an opinion with which Jacques Blanche disagreed too forcibly, the doctor, who was wonderfully skilful and full of kindness, but used to dealing with lunatics, reprimanded his son sharply: "Now, Jacques, don't torment him, don't upset him – Pull

---

* The critic Réné Doumic said to him, when he received him into the Académie française in 1921: 'You came from a line that extended from Dumas *fils* to Tristan Bernard and from Banville to yourself. You had all the gifts and all the talents, the natural and the passionate, imagination and authority, all the strings, the whole lyre' (quoted by M. Maurois, *Les Cendres brûlantes*, Flammarion, 1986, p. 35).

yourself together, my child, try to remain calm, he does not mean a word of what he said; drink a little cold water, in small sips, counting up to one hundred."[73]

Jacques-Émile Blanche himself was a pupil of Gervex, but initially a disciple of Manet and of Degas (whose portrait he would paint), who quickly acquired a reputation as a society portrait painter, as well as among intellectual and artistic circles, in Paris and in London. He was a friend of Whistler, Beardsley, Sickert, Henry James and George Moore. He lived through the last great period of the 'lifelike' portrait, in the style of Sargent, or of Boldini or Laszlo, but which hardly survives at all today except in Great Britain. He had already done a portrait of Barrès.[74] He painted Mallarmé (1889) and Gide, and later Cocteau, Stravinsky, Joyce, Max Jacob, Bergson, Bourdelle, Giraudoux, Valéry and the Groupe des Six, and he also owned a remarkable collection of impressionists.[75]

In character he was acidic, prematurely embittered, malicious and gossip-loving, or so he is portrayed, somewhat spitefully, by Léon Daudet ('he belonged to the race of tragic gossips')[76] and, rather more indulgently, by Gide in his *Journal*. Marcel, who would stop seeing him for a period of twenty-one years, from 1893 to 1914, referred to his talent as a very stylish conversationalist, who 'was considered very spiteful',[77] and to the danger he ran of dissipating himself in social life; this spitefulness was merely a 'protective neurosis' invented by nature so that, alienated from people in society, he was obliged to remain in his studio. It is unlikely that Blanche would have appreciated the consolation! Likewise, if Proust praised Blanche for his sense of the future, it was because of his choice of sitters, not because of his art: 'Simply listing the portraits that Jacques Blanche was painting at this time (with the exception of mine) was enough to show that in literature, too, it was the future that he was discovering, that he was choosing' – he was the only person to celebrate the talents of men of letters who were still unknown.

This was the painter who worked on the one portrait in oils of Marcel Proust that can be reliably attributed,* and that has survived. And yet it very nearly didn't; by and large, the testimony of the artist, in the *Nouvelle Revue Française*'s *Hommage* of January 1923, has been overlooked: 'The abysmal portrait of him that I painted was very lifelike; I had torn up this canvas. Proust discovered the face, but not the hands nor the lower body, which would have interested so many people today. The destruction of

---

* We shall mention the attribution of a portrait of Proust to Lucien Daudet further on.

the painting was the occasion for solicitors' letters.'* Blanche remembered 'Marcel wearing tails, the starched front of his shirt creased, his hair a little awry, breathing badly, his magnificent shining eyes encircled by dark shadows due to insomnia';[78] he was not sure whether he had succeeded in capturing the brilliance of the eyes. Marcel's face, looking rigid and as if paralysed by the effort of posing, is strangely inexpressive. Not a single feature is missing, but the real life which one might have expected from a painter who, all things considered, was a scholarly man, was missing.

Marcel, however, had liked his portrait, which was exhibited at the same time as eleven others at the Champs-de-Mars in 1893, and displayed it not merely in his successive flats, but featured it in *Jean Santeuil*. In a game of transposition which would soon become quite customary with him, he attributed the portrait of Jean Santeuil to La Gandara, another brilliant society portrait artist (1862–1917), a pupil of Gérôme, but also influenced by Manet, who painted the Comtesse Greffulhe and Montes-quiou. Associated with Blanche, with Helleu, Montesquiou, Degas and Whistler, the group he formed was known as the 'Japanese', on account of their liking for the art of the Far East.[79] Proust then juxtaposed the physiognomy of Jean as a schoolboy – badly dressed, febrile or dejected, excited when alone, but shy in public, his eyes encompassed by dark circles, but 'thoughtful', with their light and their troubled expressions – with the 'radiant young man who looked as if he were posing in front of the whole of Paris, without timidity or bravado, gazing out from his fine, white elongated eyes that looked like fresh almonds, eyes that did not seem to express any thought, but which looked capable of containing it, like a deep but empty pool, and with full, pale pink cheeks just turning to red at the ears'. The 'face, as luminous and fresh as a spring morning' revealed a beauty that was not so much 'thoughtful' as 'pensive', a 'life that was delicate and happy'.[80] This passage reveals Proust's fondness for this painting. In its virginal purity, far removed from his illnesses and all his anxieties, even if they were in the mind, and from all his misdemeanours, it is the portrait of Dorian Gray. Time may go by, unhappiness may come, he may be ravaged by asthma, the opportunities to dress in tails with an orchid in his buttonhole become rarer, and the parents who criticized him for going out may pass away, but one look at Blanche's work, and Proust could recapture his youth.

In the final days of July, Marcel sent Blanche a present (possibly a

---

* Unless Blanche is making this up, for none is known to us.

decanter) and informed him that he was remaining in Paris, in order to take his law exams, until 5 August. He had just passed the political science exams at the end of June.[81] This 'imminent exam' was making him tremble all day long, he wrote to Gregh, and at night he did not go to bed 'because of horrible asthma attacks', so much so that by the evening he did not have the courage to do anything. His asthma prevented him rejoining his family at Auteuil. On 5 August he passed the first part of the exam 'with good marks'. This was not the case with the second part, however, as he wrote to Robert de Billy, with an indifference which is easily explained by the lack of importance Marcel attached to his studies: 'I failed the second part of law and my family is in the doldrums. I will probably leave for Trouville on Sunday.'[82] The family doldrums did not prevent the irresponsible offspring from setting off to enjoy himself, without regrets or his law books.

HOLIDAYS 1892

Marcel spent the summer at Les Frémonts, in Trouville. On his recommendation, the Finalys had rented the villa from the Baignères. Paul Baignères[83] has left us a scrapbook drawing of Marcel (dated 29 August): seated in a rocking-chair, his expression absent-minded, with a parting in the hair that he was so proud of, his hand supporting his chin, and his little finger bent over a book, in a customary pose; he is dressed in a broad-striped jacket (is it the green Cheviot tweed coat that he mentions in connection with the portrait of Jean Santeuil?), and he is wearing ankle boots and leggings. His hand prevents us seeing one of 'those liberty cravats that were so disconcerting in all their nuances', of which he had many.[84] He is a young dandy – or trying his best to be one, for people would always make fun of his wardrobe, and Mme Proust would question him anxiously about the state of his clothes, which he did not look after very carefully – at the seaside, at a period when those who lived in villas scarcely ever mixed with those who stayed at hotels, nor with those who frequented the beach, for the villas were always situated on the higher slopes, and one led the same type of life, among the same sort of people, as one would in the Monceau district, if not in the Faubourg Saint-Germain.*

---

* The majority of members of the aristocracy spent their holidays at their country mansions. At Trouville, nevertheless, one might encounter the Montebellos, the Marquise de Galliffet and the Princesse de Sagan, who had come from the Manoir des Roches or the Villa Persane to Les Frémonts, these latter two 'former Empire beauties, in their elegance that is almost indescribable today' (*CSB*, p. 572; *Corr.*, vol. XVIII, pp. 69–70). In 1919, Proust would remind Louise Baignères,

No one has captured the charms of that summer, when 'the little band' of friends were gathered together on the coast at Trouville, better than Fernand Gregh. Marcel was staying with Louis de La Salle at Les Frémonts, Robert de Billy visited there more briefly, and 'his nobility of heart' made a great impression;[85] Gregh and Jacques Bizet were staying with the Strauses, who had rented the manor house of La Cour-Brûlée from Mme Aubernon. Mme Straus entertained the Prince d'Arenberg and the Comte d'Haussonville, and she made her entry into the drawing-room 'her arms full of flowers, her beautiful Tzigane face, her eyes burning, shaking with nervous twitches which one grew used to, gentle and gay . . . wonderfully womanly',[86] bursting with wit, humour and imagination. She took Marcel to the races, where he gambled and lost. At the centre of the group was Marie Finaly, Horace's sister, who had green eyes, was delightful and, by turns, cheerful and serious. Did Marcel have her in mind when he hummed 'in a rather shrill tone', Fauré's melody, based on Baudelaire's poems, 'J'aime de vos longs yeux la lumière verdâtre'?[87] To jump from this to speaking of 'child love' between Marcel and Marie, or to see the girl as a model for Albertine,[88] is to take a step too far; it is more likely that the young man wished to put his male friends off the scent so as not to frighten them away. It was with them that he went for walks in the countryside overlooking Trouville, along sunken paths which divided the apple orchards, heavy with their red fruit, and surrounded by hedges through which there was the occasional view of the sea. The most beautiful walk in the area was along the road to Honfleur. The friends visited the church at Hennequeville, which was covered with ivy,[89] like the one at Criqueboeuf,[90] and the Villerville valley, where Porto-Riche lived.[91] They enjoyed the evening view over the bay of Le Havre, the paths that smelt of milk and sea salt, the pools of moonlight on the ground, which Proust would find a model for in Hubert Robert's painting, *Jet d'eau*. They would go for walks at Les Creuniers, which is mentioned in *À l'ombre des jeunes filles en fleurs*. Other writers lived on the Côte de Grâce, including Henri de Régnier and Lucie Delarue-Mardrus. Above Honfleur a long avenue, lined with pine trees, the Allées Marguerite, would inspire certain passages in *Les Plaisirs et les Jours*.[92] For *Le Banquet* Marcel wrote 'La Mer', 'Portrait

who was worried about seeing her parents' name in his preface to *De David à Degas*, that her father's 'writing was known to very few. His style of conversation and the depths of his conversation, if one can put it this way, were known by only a few people who will themselves disappear . . . The pleasure of having a salon frequented by the literary and social élite . . . was something your mother felt and admitted wholeheartedly, and she was quite right to do so.'

de Madame *** ', his review of Henri de Régnier's *Tel qu'en songe* and 'Violante ou la mondanité'; he was a tireless letter-writer, using a pink notepaper which Captain Walewski thought was 'gorgeous' and Robert de Billy frightful, which earned him the unexpected description of 'ghastly little rascal'.[93] Anxious to be, if not loved, at least surrounded by people, he pointed out to Billy that Pierre de Segonzac was always sending him ten-page letters. At last he had 'found the friend of [his] dreams, affectionate and epistolarian', even though he had to pay excess postage every time: 'But what would one not do when one is in love?'[94] Thus did Marcel, who played at being charming and who laughed indulgently when Gregh compared him to a 'Neapolitan prince in a novel by Bourget', create the epistolary equivalent of flirting. 'He derived pleasure from seeing his adolescent grace reflected in the eyes of passers-by, and there was about him a little juvenile smugness and a hint of that "awareness of evil" which he already possessed at the age of eighteen and which was his muse. He sometimes exaggerated this ever witty, affected charm, just as he occasionally overdid his friendliness with flattery that was always intelligent; and among ourselves we even invented the verb *proustifier* to denote an attitude that is a little too conscious of being nice and too full of sentimental sweet talk, "of airs and graces".'[95]

It was probably that summer, too, that Marcel wrote a brilliant essay, intended for *Le Banquet*, which remained unpublished until 1954, on the history of French satire.[96] However, he avoided alluding to his contemporaries, for reasons that are curious but important: they are too familiar to us, and 'one makes wrong and difficult choices during periods of decadence'. The literature of the day – of 1892 – had been *'byzantinisée'* or, as Jules Lemaître, who had influenced Marcel for some time, put it, written by 'precious barbarians'. Proust never stopped taking a stand 'against decadence'. It was not just its imperfections; on the contrary, once one got to the end of the story, 'the overall dexterity of craftsmanship was so common that one could delude oneself about the poet; and to tell the truth the humblest of Parnassiens or even the Symbolists can reel off a sonnet better than the great Corneille. Furthermore, the infinite number of ideas that are acquired, repeated or even plagiarized, the excessive amount of "learnt writing" makes a fair judgement almost impossible.' Our age is thus crushed by its heritage, and by its technical know-how. Proust characterized the man of letters in the Middle Ages in terms which herald *Le Côté de Guermantes*: 'Society interested him in the multiple aspects it took on for him on his poet's rounds. While he amused a titled gentleman by scoffing at peasants who did not know they were being watched, he observed the gentleman and his family with curiosity while, at the same time, laughing up his sleeve. Sooner or later . . . it would be the peasants who would laugh at the nobility.' Reverting to his own times, Proust pointed out that people were too detached to be able to tackle injustice and flaws: 'Almost as if one was drawing attention to something ridiculous.' The old French gaiety could be found in the popular theatre, in *La Vie parisienne* and in 'revolutionary pamphlets'. So we see that the man who would decry anti-Dreyfusism, nationalism, anti-Semitism and Sodom, would also inherit the old tradition of French satire, as well as its wit and its laughter.

That same September Fernand Gregh composed a portrait of Marcel, who appears in it under the name of Fabrice, which was intended for *Le Banquet*, but which remained unpublished. Ready to defy people's contempt, Fabrice stresses his need to be loved; he is handsome, especially when he speaks and when his eyes sparkle and his face lights up; he has an enveloping charm, passive in appearance and active in reality: 'He looks as if he gives, and he takes.' As for his friends, Gregh captures a characteristic which defines the way Proust always behaved: 'He had as his friends all those who knew him, one after the other. But since he cared less for his friends than he did for the image of himself reflected in them, he did not take long to drop them with as great a facility as the skill he deployed in drawing them to him.' Fabrice can wait for an hour in the rain for friends whom a fortnight later he would not see again, and whom he would have forgotten in a year's time. The seducer also had great wit and intelligence, 'which made him a thousand times more likeable than his most brilliant flattering remarks'.[97] Around the same time, and as if to confirm that he had won the friendship of senior figures, as is suggested by this portrait, Anatole France dedicated to Marcel his story 'Madame de Luzy', which was published in his collection *L'Étui de nacre*** on 28 September. The month of September and Marcel's visit to Les Frémonts came to an end with the sale of the property.[†] Horace de Landau acquired it from M. and Mme Arthur Baignères, for his nephew and niece, M. and Mme Hugo Finaly, for a price of 152,000 francs. With his customary

---

* Proust immediately dedicated 'Violante ou la mondanité' to France; it was published in *Le Banquet* in February 1893.

† The Baignères, as we know, had rented it to the Finalys, which must have inspired the Cambremers' renting of La Raspelière to the Verdurins.

desire to be of help and to involve himself as an outsider in affairs that did not concern him, whether amatory or financial, Marcel interfered so successfully that M. de Landau made him a present of a fine walking-stick.

RENAN

Ernest Renan, whom Marcel admired greatly, but from whom he was beginning to detach himself, died on 2 October 1892. As always, Marcel emphasized not so much what he owed to him as what he criticized in him,* but the pastiche he wrote in 1908 displayed an unusual knowledge of the slightest inflections of Renan's thought and language. For a young man born in 1871, Renan and Taine were two important figures, who filled the entire intellectual horizon of that period, in the same way as Sartre and Camus did for someone born in 1935, only possibly more so, because their public-spirited philosophy permeated all aspects of the secular republic. In Renan's *Les Origines du christianisme*, there were two features that particularly appealed to Marcel, history and philosophy, but they were shorn of all technicalities and written in the sensitive, almost sentimental style, melodious and lyrical, of a real, if not innovatory, writer. The rather blurred musicality of his phrasing reminds one more of Gounod than of Wagner; associated with Anatole France, it would become the music of Bergotte.[98] Brichot, a colleague of Renan and Maspero at the Académie, shared his taste for anachronism and the '*Belle Hélène* [side] of Christianity'. If Proust seldom mentions the author of *La Vie de Jésus* in *À la recherche*, this is not the case in his preceding or parallel works – his translations of Ruskin, *Contre Sainte-Beuve*, or the introduction on style in Paul Morand's *Tendres Stocks*. Above all, he would make Renan the subject of one of his longest pastiches. These remarks and imitations often have a humorous and critical character. They have to be turned back to front in order to understand Marcel's initial and real feelings for this master, and what remained of his youthful admiration and of his considerable reading of Renan's work, from his *Origines du christianisme* to the *Drames philosophiques* and *Souvenirs d'enfance et de jeunesse*. Quite apart from the actual content, his work had three essential, seminal qualities. The first was the musicality of his often lengthy[99] sentences and his appetite for imagery, particularly that associated with memory. The second was the critical

---

* Proust took issue with Renan's aestheticism, like that of France (*Thaïs*) and of Barrès (*Le Jardin de Bérénice*), as far as charity was concerned, and he quoted *Marc Aurèle* (1881).

approach of the philosopher, the philologist and the historian, who contested dogma, turned received certainties upside down and went further than he appeared to in search of rules and codes, and their deep and hidden origins. The third was his portrayal of the past: in the characters of the Guermantes or in Françoise, Proust enshrined a Middle Ages that is still alive with the same skill that prompted Renan to depict Jesus as a 'young Jewish democrat', 'a provincial'[100] and a nineteenth-century contemporary; and Combray, on the borders of the Perche, is Renan's Brittany.

PLATONIC LOVE

On his return to Paris, Marcel, who ought to have been busy studying law (in November he passed the examinations he had failed in August) or literature, was also cultivating that flower of the age (which was just as strange as the fifteen chrysanthemums with their 'excessively long' stems that he sent to Laure Hayman on 2 November, 'these flowers that are proud and sad like you – proud to be beautiful, sad that everything should be so foolish'); Marcel was studying the coterie of people who gather around a woman, rather as they do in Maupassant's *Notre cœur*, and whom he would portray gathered around Oriane de Guermantes. 'When a woman, like a work of art, reveals to us the most refined charm, the subtlest grace, the most divine beauty, the most voluptuous intelligence, a common admiration for her unites us, as a brotherhood. Laure Hayman makes co-religionists of us.'[101] In their turn, the 'faithful' love one another and share an understanding among initiates: the debased form of this aristocratic coterie would produce the 'little clan' of the Verdurins. It will be observed that Marcel became one of the worshippers because the woman was 'a work of art'. Here we have an explanation for his behaviour from which he benefited twofold: one does not sleep with a work of art, but it is ready and waiting to be transformed, in his pages, into a writer's portrait.

As for Mme Straus, at the end of the year Marcel reminded her of the numerous portraits of her that he had published in *Le Banquet*, without ever being certain that she recognized herself in them,[102] and in his letters he played the part of the jealous admirer. She could only be seen surrounded by twenty people, and 'the young man is the one who is furthest away'. When one did catch her on her own, she only had five minutes to spare, and she was thinking of something else. 'But that is not all. If one talks to you about books, you think it pedantic, if one talks to you about people, you find it indiscreet (if one recounts anything), and over curious (if one enquires), if one speaks to you about yourself, you find it ridiculous.' And then, all of a sudden, one is restored by 'a little favour'. Mme Straus' error is not to be sufficiently 'imbued with this truth ... *that a great deal should be conceded* to platonic love'. This was why Marcel begged her to have 'a little indulgence towards the ardent platonic love' borne her.[103] What were these feelings, this passion? Robert de Billy, who was privy to the feelings that Marcel said he held for Mme de Chevigné, compared them to the love that intellectuals in the Middle Ages bore for a woman who was both an individual and an abstraction, 'Logic or Theology, unless she was transformed at their bidding into some Beauteous Welcome or Flower of Youth'.[104]

Laure de Sade, the Comtesse de Chevigné, lived in a town house at the rear of the courtyard of 36 rue de Miromesnil.[105] Blonde, with a hooked nose, a high-pitched voice, slim, petite and delicate, neither very beautiful nor very rich, but exceptionally well placed in society, a friend of the Grand-Duke Vladimir, the Prince of Wales, the Marquis de Breteuil, the Murats, the Rothschilds and the Duchesse de La Trémoille, she walked every morning in the Champs-Élysées, wearing a hat bedecked with cornflowers.[106] Having been introduced to her at the home of Mme Straus, Marcel would go and wait for her to pass by on the Avenue de Marigny.[107] This proud lady with her look of 'smiling disdain'[108] eventually grew impatient with his daily and assiduous attention. For her, too, Marcel shared the feelings of Petrarch for 'Laura', an ancestor of the Comtesse, and those of Marguerite de Bourgogne for Philibert le Beau, both of whose initials were interwoven in the church at Brou.[109] The profile, the hat, the waiting for her, this platonic passion – these reappear in the Duchesse de Guermantes and the Narrator, having first been used in a portrait in *Le Banquet*,[110] in which Proust already mentioned the profile of a bird, the 'piercing and gentle eyes'.

In 1921 Proust told Gide that he 'had only ever loved women spiritually'.[111] Again, we need to take into account these disembodied, desexualized 'spiritual passions'. They enabled the writer to imagine and depict women, especially when they are inaccessible, like the Duchesse de Guermantes, or even Gilberte. When they are young, becoming engaged or some other reason can take them away; when they are older and become maternal images, they no longer arouse physical desire; at best, like Aurélia and Sylvie, they only arouse aesthetic desire. In Mme Straus, Laure Hayman and Laure de Chevigné, Marcel fell in love with an idea, a legend, a myth, a mirror image of the soul, with everything that could be translated not into action, but into words.

OTHER FRIENDS

In December 1892 Robert de Billy was seconded to the French Embassy in Berlin, where he was to spend a year before being appointed embassy attaché in the ministerial staff in December 1893. It was an occasion for epistolary effusions from Marcel, 'an impalpable uninvited guest at your possibly lonely dinner – an unreal stranger seated, however reluctant you may be, by your bed if you are reading this letter in bed', towards his 'dearest little one'.[112] To Billy he confesses that he is not doing anything: this inactivity would be attributed to Jean Santeuil and to the Narrator of À la recherche, as would the feelings of remorse it provoked, 'foul beasts', he wrote curiously, that threatened to devour his 'innocent little body'. In the course of a sentence emerge the shadows of narcissism and sadomasochism. Marcel was doing so little work that he asked Billy to remind him of the list of the four examinations he must sit and the books that he should read, because he had lost it![113] A present from Edgar Aubert reached him from beyond the grave, which reawakened memories of 'those journeys home with him when he was so charming, so witty, so good, making up for something he had just said that was a little sharp or ironic with the gentleness of his expression or the clasp of his handshake'.[114] During Marcel's lifetime, the dream of the perfect friend would often, as here, take the form of the memory of the perfect deceased friend; in his work, it appears as Robert de Saint-Loup. He did not live in total solitude, however: 'I often see Gregh, La Salle, Waru, Bizet, Paul Baignères, who is doing my portrait, Jacques Baignères, Carbonnel, Henri de Rothschild, Segonzac and J. de Traz, but nobody as much as Robert de Flers, who comes to see me almost every day.'[115] At a dinner party, Marcel came across a plenipotentiary minister, M. de Florian, who seems to have been a model for Norpois: 'What art there is in his greeting, his handshake, his walk, his expression in repose, his silence, his conversation, his politeness, and that superior politeness, his wit. He is the most accomplished diplomat I have ever met.*

---

* Corr., vol. I, p. 202. The Comte de Florian, born in 1850, was plenipotentiary minister in London from 1892; he belonged to several learned societies and to the Cercle de l'Union.

Proust did not mention another friend, whom he had known since *rhétorique*: Pierre Lavallée.* Between January and February, Marcel had begun to address him as '*tu*' instead of the formal '*vous*', and they attended private lessons in law at the home of Professor Monnot. A future librarian and curator of the museum of the École des Beaux-Arts, Lavallée was attracted by Marcel's wit, his charm and depths, and the originality of his ideas and their expression. He has described 'the naïve, almost childish simplicity of his behaviour, which one was astonished to find was combined with a precociously mature intelligence'. The two friends would go out together, to the Louvre, as Marcel had with Billy, at the time that he was researching his 'Portraits de peintres', where they would stop to admire *L'Embarquement pour Cythère*, *Le Duc de Richmond*, attributed to Van Dyck, or Cuyp's *Le Départ pour la promenade*.† Equally, they would find a welcome at the salons of Madeleine Lemaire or Mme Arman, or, after dinner in town, at Weber's, the café on the rue Royale. Lavallée wrote: 'We used to walk down the boulevard Malesherbes as far as no. 9, his family home. But he dreaded the long nights without sleep and could not make up his mind whether to return home. He caught sight of a bench, and sat down. At two o'clock in the morning, we were still chatting.' Marcel expounded his moral concepts to Lavallée: 'To be indulgent towards others and harsh on oneself, it's fairly commonplace advice: in life, it's the only rule to follow.' He also revealed his hatred of arrogance, and above all, of the 'vulgarity of the self-satisfied bourgeois mind', of what he termed the 'ruling-class' mentality. All this was expressed against a background of constant mirth: a love of laughter and of seeing the funny side to life was a feature of Marcel's behaviour. In Lavallée, Robert Proust tells us, Marcel discovered a way of thinking and feeling that was very similar to his own. We see this when Proust inscribed a copy of *Les Plaisirs et les Jours* to him: against the background of their old and enduring friendship, he evoked the closeness of dreams, 'the meaning that is hidden from others, whose depths are known only to them'.

In 1893, during Lent, Robert de Flers took Marcel, who was not the first young man to hide his desires behind spiritual leanings, to the lectures

---

* Lavallée recalls his memories in *Corr. gén.*, vol. IV, pp. 3–6. His mother advised him against being friendly with Proust, who was too social; she sent her son an article by Marcel which she considered very ordinary. As a married man, Lavallée lived at rue de Vézelay, and one night his housekeeper refused entry to Marcel at three o'clock in the morning. His children referred to him as 'the gentleman who comes at night'.

† We find these paintings in 'Portraits de peintres', reprinted in *P et J*.

given by Abbé Vignot at the École Fénelon.[116] Later on, Marcel would often meet the Abbé Vignot, as well as the Abbé Hébert, at Lavallée's home. There are very few priests in *À la recherche*, and they are always encountered in odd situations: are they a memory of those meetings? Or, on the contrary, do they confirm that it is pointless to expect the novel to contain life in its entirety: the laws of imagination require that certain events do not transfer from one to the other. It was not just religion that Lavallée shared with Marcel: he lent him books (including those by Anatole France) and musical scores, and even *The Imitation of Christ* from which the epigraphs in *Les Plaisirs et les Jours*[117] were taken. Among the composers they discussed were Augusta Holmès, Fauré, Gounod and Wagner. In fact, music was frequently the subject of their conversations: according to this friend, Marcel had a natural sensitivity to music.[118] Marcel saw less of him once he had met Reynaldo Hahn, but Pierre Lavallée belonged to that family of art lovers, of connoisseurs, art historians[119] and curators – such as the Henraux brothers, Émile Mâle, Louis Gautier-Vignal, Emmanuel Bibesco and Bertrand de Fénelon – who spent their time visiting galleries, attending lectures and sharing information. Proust, with his prodigiously enquiring mind, discovered, thanks to them, subjects that could assuage his aesthetic curiosity and which could compensate for the immobility brought about by illness: he also travelled in the footsteps of others, visited the museums that other people had seen and attended concerts through the ears of friends.

Since 1856 the Lavallée family had owned the Château de Segrez[120] at Saint-Sulpice-de-Favières. Marcel would pay a brief visit there, which was interrupted by an attack of asthma (as happened at the Daudets). Yet Proust would describe this ancient home of the Marquis d'Argenson, one of Louis XV's ministers, in his correspondence, in 'La promenade' in *Les Plaisirs et les Jours*, and in *Jean Santeuil*. He only spent a night there, but he remembered everything, the trees, the fountains, the farmyard, the peacocks. As so often with friends, Pierre Lavallée's marriage, in 1900, strained their friendship.

WILLIE HEATH

Proust loved to portray his friends. At the time that Robert de Billy, who throughout 1893 continued to be a precious confidant, left for Berlin, Marcel addressed a 'Song for Robert' to him, written in the style both of Verlaine and of the music-hall:[121]

Droit comme un piquet, sec comme un pierre,
  Où qu'est son charme?
On n'aura jamais, sous sa paupière,
  Même une larme . . .

Ô route ou caillou – qu'avez vous qui grise,
  Choses sans larmes?

Pourtant il est des pays
Uniformes, secs et gris
Que d'aucuns trouvent jolis

Ils croient que leur ciel fâché
Recèle un Dieu, une âme
Que ne trahit nulle flamme.

Vous recelez un Dieu, Robert, entendez-vous?*

Billy attributed this poem (never quoted), in which Marcel pokes fun at his Protestant rigidity, to the reproaches he had levelled against his friend on the subject of his social and sentimental life. This had been enriched by meeting a young Englishman, Willie Heath, who had converted to Catholicism at the age of twelve, and who was also an acquaintance of the Abbé Vignot.[122] Paul Nadar has left us a photograph of him,[123] in which he is dressed in tails, with a carnation in his buttonhole, a cane and a pair of gloves in his hand, with a top hat and some books lying on a table, as if the photographer were trying to compete with a portrait artist. Of Marcel's relationship with Heath, we only know what we are told in the dedication of *Les Plaisirs et les Jours*, 'to my friend Willie Heath'.[124] Just as Swann recognized Botticelli's 'Daughter of Jethro' in Odette, so Willie reminded Proust of a gentleman painted by Van Dyck. He recognized the elegance, less of dress than of the body, imparted to the body by the soul, and an air of melancholy cast by the shade of the foliage (that of the Bois de Boulogne where the two friends went for walks), and, above all, by the approach of death – that of the Duke of Richmond, as well as that of Charles I. Thus the paintings that Marcel had contemplated with Pierre

---

* 'Straight as a post, dry as a stone,/ Where does his charm come from?/ Beneath his eyelid you will never see,/ Even a single tear . . ./ O stony path – what is your fascination,/ Things without tears?/ And yet there are countries,/ Uniform, dry and grey,/ That no one finds attractive./ They believe that their angry sky/ Harbours a God, a soul/ Which no flame betrays./ You harbour a God, Robert, do you hear?' *Tr.*

Lavallée are enshrined one by one in a magic figuration. There was something of the idealization of grief, and possibly of passion, in Leonardo da Vinci's *Saint John the Baptist* that reminded him of Heath, because of 'the mysterious intensity of [his] spiritual life', but also because he appeared with 'finger raised, his eyes impenetrable and smiling in front of the enigma that silenced you'. Heath thus combined the earnestness and spirit of childhood with a 'candid and delightful' gaiety. The two friends formed 'a dream, almost a plan, to live more and more together, among a select circle of noble-hearted men and women, sufficiently removed from foolishness, vice and malice to be able to feel sheltered from their vulgar arrows'.[125] The flight from vulgarity, the hatred of stupidity, the dream of a chosen group – in these themes we find the *fin-de-siècle* love, which is Pre-Raphaelite and Wildean, that Charlus suggests to the Narrator at Balbec, and which Marcel aspired to on several occasions: after his friends from the Lycée Condorcet and Sciences-Po, there would be Fénelon and Bibesco. In the meantime, the friends met for a dinner in June:[126] an aristocratic circle of people gathered around the table which must have afforded Marcel much aesthetic, emotional and social satisfaction.

MADELEINE LEMAIRE

On 13 April 1893 an event took place that would profoundly affect literary life and its protagonists: the meeting between Marcel Proust and Robert de Montesquiou at the home of Madeleine Lemaire. Proust described the small town house at 3 rue de Monceau, near the rue de Courcelles, 'which comprises a two-storey building giving directly on to the street, and a large hall with stained-glass windows, set among arborescent lilac trees that are fragrant from April onwards'.[127] The hall was the studio 'of someone who was strangely powerful, as famous overseas as in Paris itself, whose signature beneath a watercolour, or printed on an invitation card, made the watercolour more sought after than that of any other painter and the invitation more precious than one from any other hostess': Madeleine Lemaire, of whom Dumas *fils* would say that no one apart from God had painted more roses. It would be wrong to consider her merely as a painter of flowers, of those enormous purple-blue roses that she painted in a series: 'Her work includes as many landscapes, portraits and paintings of churches, for her extraordinary talent covers all genres.'[128]

A pupil of her aunt, Mme Herbelin (1820–1904) – to whom Proust would devote an article on her death in 1904[129] – and of Chaplin, Madeleine

Lemaire had made her début at the Salon of 1864 with a portrait. Among her works, it is worth mentioning *Le Sacre de l'Église* (1872), *Mlle Angot* (1873), *Colombine* (1874), *Corinne* (1876), *Manon* (1877), *Ophélie* (1878), *Portrait de M. J. E. Saintin* (1878), *Le Sermon pendant la grand-messe* (1901), *Le Sommeil de Manon* (1906) and *Les Bains de Chloris* (1907). This forgotten figure in the history of art, a painter of minor importance, but whose talent was classical and varied, is not widely known except for the illustrations, not just of flowers, that she did for *Les Plaisirs et les Jours*. Proust used her as his model for Mme Verdurin; she was referred to as 'the Mistress' by her followers,* she dubbed those she disliked 'bores'. But her creativity was stolen from her, to be conferred on Elstir, an artist inspired by painters of a different scale. It is equally revealing of Proust's methods of invention that he should have reduced all the artists invited by Mme Lemaire to just one, M. Biche. Transferring and abstracting were a part of his art.

Proust, at about this time, dedicated these little-known lines to the painter of flowers:

> *Vous faites plus que Dieu: un éternel printemps,*
> *Et c'est auprès des lis et des rosiers grimpants*
> *Que vous allez chercher vos couleurs, Madeleine.*
> *Vous avez la beauté fragile de l'éphémère . . .*
> *Œillet ou lis qu'a peint Madeleine Lemaire.*
> *Mais vous, qui vous peindra, belle jardinière*
> *Par qui tous les printemps nous plaisent tant de fleurs?*†

The reply to the last lines could be found in *À la recherche*.

To begin with, Madeleine Lemaire, whom Marcel must have met at the home of Mme Straus or Mme Arman, had invited fellow artists, such as the painters Jean Béraud (a second to Proust's duel with Jean Lorrain), Puvis de Chavannes, Detaille, Bonnat and Clairin. Very soon, she counted among her visitors the Princess of Wales, the Empress of Germany, the King of Sweden, the Queen of the Belgians, and her friend Princesse Mathilde. She launched herself on to the social scene, and Proust described her ascent in terms which foreshadow that of Mme Verdurin (she is aristocracy, what is more): 'Gradually, we learnt that in the studio there

---

* As is evident in R. Hahn's letters.

† *BAMP*, no. 12, 1962, p. 481. 'You create more than God: an eternal spring,/ And it is from among lilies and climbing roses/ That you go in search of your colours, Madeleine./ You have the fragile beauty of the ephemeral . . ./ A carnation or lily painted by Madeleine Lemaire./ But you, who will paint you, beautiful gardener/ Through whom so many flowers grace us every spring?' *Tr.*

sometimes took place small reunions at which, without any preparation, and without pretensions to being a "soirée", and with each of the guests "practising his trade" and giving of his talent, the small and intimate party would include attractions that the most sparkling "galas" were unable to assemble.'[130] Réjane, Coquelin, Bartet performed sketches; Massenet and Saint-Saëns played the piano. Very soon, Mme Lemaire's Tuesdays in May were attracting anyone who was anyone in Paris. Among the guests Proust noted politicians such as Paul Deschanel or Léon Bourgeois, foreign ambassadors, aristocrats such as the Comtesse de Chevigné, the Grand-Duchess Vladimir, the Duc and Duchesse de Luynes, the Duc and Duchesse d'Uzès, the writers France, Lemaître, Lavedan, Flers and Caillavet. Although Marcel praised Mme Lemaire's beautiful eyes and fine smile, she was actually very ugly, as was her daughter Suzette, 'so exquisite a hostess, towards whom every eye was turned, in admiration of her charm'.[131]

Not everyone was so eulogistic. Edmond de Goncourt related that, according to Dumas *fils*, who had known her very well, malice had taken on the proportions of a disease where this woman was concerned.[132] Montesquiou has given us a portrait of the woman who entertained him so often that is hardly flattering. Léon Daudet exclaimed: 'My God, how boring were those evenings at that dear woman's home, which, generally speaking, were attended by actors, artists and grand-dukes, Nicolas, Constantine, I don't know who else ... As for this good Mme Lemaire's flower paintings, they were chocolate-box pictures, inferior to those on the sweet boxes from Boissier's.'* The artist Jean-Louis Forain praised his hostess for her work, but he did so with an irritated and mocking expression, that clearly signified: 'How second-rate!'[133] In 'Un amour de Swann', Mme Verdurin borrows Mme Lemaire's taste for receptions, for music and for artists; she was discreet about Swann's and Odette's love affair, just as Mme Lemaire was about that of Marcel and Reynaldo Hahn; on the other hand, there were no paintings, nor even a château: the one at Réveillon, which belonged to the artist, plays a part in *Les Plaisirs et les Jours*, and came close to being the title of the book, as well as in *Jean Santeuil*. Madeleine Lemaire's salon was not meant to represent 'society', despite the presence of members of the aristocracy;[134] in this respect, Proust in 'Un amour de Swann' portrayed her accurately, with her authoritarian manner, her laughter, her loathing of 'bores', of 'deserters', her enjoyment

---

* A well-known confectioner's. *Tr.*

of 'performances' and her determination to impose her own artistic and musical tastes. This faithfulness would alienate him from the woman whom he had portrayed only too successfully. He would write to her at the time, in a copy of the ninth edition of *À l'ombre des jeunes filles en fleurs*: 'Did you not know that I bear only affection and admiration for you, did not all the newspapers and my articles remind you of this, oh dear, oh great Madeleine Lemaire.'[135]

THE ENCOUNTER WITH ROBERT DE MONTESQUIOU

One always imagines Montesquiou as an elderly man and, if viewed in the guise of Baron de Charlus (whose appearance Proust borrowed from Baron Doäzan), as being somewhat stout. Marcel was twenty-seven years old at the time that he was introduced to the count,[136] and the latter was only thirty-seven. His reputation preceded him: the famous name, the portraits, and, for someone who was subsequently to write so much, a single poetic work, *Les Chauves-souris*, published in 1892. The entry he wrote for *Qui êtes-vous?* (1909) says much about his pretentions: 'Related to a large number of the European aristocracy. Ancestry: Marshals of France: Blaise de Montluc, Jean de Gassion, Pierre de Montesquiou, Anne-Pierre de Montesquiou, who conquered Savoy, d'Artagnan (hero of *The Three Musketeers*), the Reverend Father de Montesquiou, Louis XVIII's minister, General Count A. de Montesquiou, aide-de-camp to Napoleon.' Not a single woman among these heroic ancestors (the King of Rome's governess is not mentioned), perhaps because his father, Thierry de Montesquiou, Anatole's second son, married Pauline Duroux, a middle-class Protestant who was the daughter of a family of bankers. Not only was Robert the youngest son of a youngest son, but he was the fourth and last child of a marriage which he must have considered a mismatch, to the point that he believed a servant was his real mother.[137] Throughout his life the count would say that he did not care very much for his parents; his ancestors, on the other hand, 'that breed of relative that is stripped of the over-familiar hostility of blood-ties', he 'liked very much' and believed he owed his virtues to them.[138] Among the contradictory elements of Count Robert de Montesquiou's character, there was an aspect of him that was opposed to his own social milieu, that did not share its literary tastes and did not care for the works it produced. There was also his penchant for young people (he was not attracted by marriage), to whom he offered all his aristocratic, literary and worldly patronage: like Socrates, he loved to lead the ephebi towards the Beau Idéal.

Thus when Marcel Proust was introduced to Robert de Montesquiou a current of mutual sympathy passed between them. Marcel admired this monument to French history, this dandy with his perfect profile, his captivating gaze, this poet who was the friend of Verlaine and Mallarmé; he himself was the very model of the polite and tender-hearted young gentleman, with the handsome, smooth face, the deep, slightly moist eyes, that appealed to the count; he would find other examples of this physical type in Lucien Daudet, the pianist Léon Delafosse, and, in particular, his secretary Gabriel de Yturri.* In public the count put on an act,[139] traces of which can be seen in the caricatures of the cartoonist Sem: his speech was accompanied by the gesticulations of his gloved hands, with a drop of the wrists as he reached the summit of a crescendo. His voice rose too, until it became strident, or dropped into moans, all in the interests of ceaseless gossip, while his eyes pierced you with a sharp look: 'And then there are the endless monologues, the dazzling conversations, the splendid stories. Montesquiou unlocks his private coffers, reveals his secrets. He talks, he drones on, he produces anecdotes, pithy sayings, flashes of wit. He parades sumptuous cavalcades before Proust's eyes.'[140] Marcel became so immersed in Montesquiou that he was able to mimic him at will, to laugh or tap his foot just as he did: everything that the count failed to transfer from speech to the written word would be done by Marcel. Everything that for the one was merely conversational vanity would become, for the other, a literary work: the words, in fact, had to be not just reported but analysed, restored to their context, to reveal the reality that lies beneath appearance, the comic or tragic that underlies solemnity, in order to attain the dignity of literature, not merely 'universal reporting'. Conversation does not require transcription, but metamorphosis: so many memoirs – as well as *romans-à-clef* – have failed because their authors have not realized this.

Montesquiou had seduced other writers who were more prominent than the young collaborator of *Le Banquet*, notably Mallarmé. In *Les Pas effacés* the count describes how he invited Mallarmé to visit him in his apartment on the Quai d'Orsay in 1883: 'He left my home in a state of cold excitement, which was characteristic of him, though it was not often that the temperature rose so high. I do not doubt therefore that it was in

* Montesquiou bequeathed all his possessions to another secretary, Henri Pinard.

great appreciation, with the utmost sympathy and in very sincere good faith, that the account he gave to Huysmans was so indistinct and superficial that it resembled a few moments spent, at night, in Ali Baba's cave . . . The proof is that, shortly afterwards, he told me he had described his visit to the author whose name I have just mentioned, and that he was thinking of portraying me in one of his books, like some modern, superior Fantasio.'[141] Details such as the celebrated golden tortoise are found, as Montesquiou points out, in Huysmans: 'Everything else in the work is pure (or impure) imagination. I have never met the author . . .' Contemporaries and posterity have ignored this warning, which must have been mentioned verbally before it was ever written down, and continue to see in Des Esseintes, the hero of Huysmans' novel *À rebours*, a portrait of Montesquiou. Edmond de Goncourt, who was equally fascinated by him, was certainly aware of the distinction: 'If there is a touch of "dottiness" about him, he always gets away with it because of his refinement. As for the conversation, apart from a little mannerism in the expressions, it is full of delicate observations, original perceptions, good ideas, pretty phrases, and when he has finished what he is saying, he often ends with a smile in his eyes and nervous gestures with his long fingers.'[142] Huysmans, unlike the author of *Sodome et Gomorrhe*, did not know what it meant to be a lord. He nevertheless sketched a more faithful portrait of the count than did Henri de Régnier in *Le Mariage de minuit*, in the guise of M. de Serpigny. The latter, more of a trinket-merchant than an artist, impertinent and little concerned with love, spoke in a 'shrill falsetto' voice; an aristocrat to artists, an artist to aristocrats, he claimed to be a ceramicist, and he had his pots made by a young man; like Montesquiou, he loved giving parties.* One comes across Montesquiou yet again portrayed as the Comte de Muzarett in *Monsieur de Phocas* (1901)† by Jean Lorrain, the author of *Rats ailés*; and as the peacock in Edmond Rostand's *Chantecler*. Thus the literary portrait, as distinct from the painted portrait, tended towards the critical, towards caricature (as in those by Sem), the ferocious: artists, on the other hand, have not distorted Montesquiou.

Had Proust read *À rebours* (he mentions Des Esseintes once, in 1918)?[143] No doubt aware of the count's refutations of the link, it was not long

---

* In the same novel Mme de Bocquincourt tending her roses was inspired by Mme de Beaulaincourt (just like Mme de Villeparisis, in Proust).

† In this *roman-à-clef* we also come across Oscar Wilde, in the guise of Claudius Ethal. The protagonist of the novel, the Duke de Freineuse, derives directly from Des Esseintes.

before he wrote to him: 'For some time I have realized that you scarcely fitted the type of the exquisite decadent with whose features (never as perfect as yours, yet fairly common at that period) you have been portrayed.'[144] Marcel did not read *Les Chauves-souris* – published in 1892 in a limited, numbered edition, on quality paper, in a large format (which served as a rather unfortunate model for *Les Plaisirs et les Jours*) – until he had met the author. The style of these poems owed much to Hugo, to Gautier and to the Parnassians, a little to Verlaine, and nothing to Mallarmé. Among poems dedicated to alter egos and other mysterious beings, one encounters Louis II of Bavaria, 'a brilliant and incomparable example of the great human bats [*chauves-souris*]', Charles VI, and Louis XIII:

> *L'efféminé souvent dompte la femme et l'homme*
> *Sans être dominé . . .*
> *Voulez-vous bien me dire où gît le faible, en somme,*
> *Et la faiblesse, alors, de cet efféminé?*
>
> ('Treizième Nocturne)*

At the end of the collection, after the Empress Eugénie ('a pelerine by Worth with gold braiding') and the Countess de Castiglione, whom Marcel would meet thanks to Montesquiou, and who, like him, would be the inspiration for one of the characters in his work, we meet the Comtesse Greffulhe. These few passages help explain why Marcel, after being introduced to the count, should write to him: 'I am hanging from the wings of your *Chauves-souris*';[145] he recognized himself in these alter egos, these effeminates, which the most illustrious among them described in superbly neo-Romantic terms, and he would be their creator's witness.

Gradually, Montesquiou, who cast himself as 'professor of beauty', infected Marcel with his tastes and revealed to him the artists about whom, like his master, Proust would write: Gustave Moreau, Whistler, Gallé, Helleu, El Greco, Watteau. Marcel may have already discovered artists such as these on his own, but the count's patronage confirmed their importance to him. Through him, the future author of *Le Côté de Guermantes* learnt to appreciate interior decoration, furniture, the beauty of objects to which he personally would always remain indifferent, but with which his characters would be discreetly surrounded: Montesquiou had a passion,

---

* 'The effeminate man often tames both man and woman/ Without being dominated . . ./ Will you kindly explain therefore what it is that is weak, after all,/ And wherein lies the weakness of this effeminate creature?' *Tr.*

shared with Goncourt, for trinkets. At his home there were so many that his much admired private apartments gave an alarming impression of clutter (more usual at this period than in our own), rather like Goncourt's 'artist's home'. This clutter corresponded to Baudelairean rules, because it represented the states of the soul, and the complicated designs were symbols to which the owner alone held the key:[146] thus the 'polar' harmonies in white, employed by Huysmans for his Des Esseintes. Personal meanings merged with cultural references: 'The references to art, to literature, and the furnishings would sometimes be fused together in an overwhelming way. There was Michelet's bird-cage, a cast of la Castiglione's knees, a drawing by La Gandara of the Comtesse Greffulhe's chin . . . Yturri's legs, in cyclist's pose, painted by Boldini.'[147] Yturri, the secretary, made Montesquiou more selective in his choice of objects; after he died, the clutter reappeared.

Nothing is more astonishing than to reread the dedication which Barrès inserted in the opening pages of his *Greco ou le Secret de Tolède*: 'TO COUNT ROBERT DE MONTESQUIOU,/ To the Poet/ To the creator of so many rare objects and illustrations,/ To one of the first apologists of El Greco,/ and who himself/ will one day find his discoverer and apologist,/ in homage and friendship from his admirer and neighbour.' When Barrès read these lines to the count, the latter burst into tears; it was the first token of esteem and admiration that he had ever received, leaving aside social compliments.[148] Barrès, who would never care for Proust, more or less proclaimed Marcel's 'invention' of Montesquiou. Into the mouth of Charlus Proust put expressions that all his contemporaries would recognize, brilliant pastiches, replicas of the imitations he gave of the count in salons; but, without doing so openly, he also slipped in here and there the occasional phrase an art critic might use: 'Make all this more like Montesquiou in tone', he jotted in the margins of one of his *cahiers*. However, although Proust borrowed certain of the count's tastes, and utilized them to create a character (indeed several, for as the drafts of *Le Côté de Guermantes* show, he makes use of them for Swann, too, the aesthete and lover of clothes and art), he also employed him as a foil: aestheticism degenerates into 'idolatry' when the artist decides to make a work of art out of his life and his surroundings. For Proust, art and life were separate domains, and the refutation of this attitude was at the heart of his philosophy. He would have occasion to say so in his editions of Ruskin: Wilde, Montesquiou, Balzac, Ruskin all committed the same sin – and so too, of course, did Goncourt.

No sooner had Marcel met the count, at a soirée on 13 April 1893 – a party at Madeleine Lemaire's at which Mlle Bartet recited her poems, following an 'elegant dinner' (according to *Le Gaulois*) – than the young man was allowed to come and see him. The appointment was arranged promptly, and Proust was so delighted by his visit that he sent the poet flowers which alluded to his verses, 'blissful lilies', 'pale Florentine irises that must have been grafted on to a rose'.[149] By return he received a copy of the de-luxe edition of *Les Chauves-souris*, which he described as 'an imperishable bouquet, a veritable incense-burner, were it to be the last of [his] memories', as 'a glorious trophy', in a style which is already modelled on that of the recipient. So began a correspondence which would fill an entire volume and which, when it was published in 1930, would do considerable harm to the image of Proust, who was deemed needlessly toadying, and even hypocritical in his excessive compliments.* In addition to the flowers which Marcel sent to Montesquiou, and to which the latter responded with his poems, the young man despatched, by the earliest post, a letter about *Les Chauves-souris*: 'Never have mere garden flowers smelt so good. What they tell us so confusedly and we perceive so feebly, you express with a divine clarity, yet without in the least dispelling any of their delicious mystery.' These floral poetics, so redolent of the symbolist period, would remain dear to Proust, as would his fondness for clarity when, paradoxically, it retains an aura of mystery. His admiration for Verlaine can also be seen in a compliment which might more readily be addressed to a woman: 'Your soul is a rare and refined garden, like the one which you allowed me to walk in the other day . . . Your poems and your eyes reflect whole continents which we shall never see.'[150] So it was that Marcel, encouraged by the count, decided to spend the month of August at Saint-Moritz.

At the end of June, six months before their publication, Montesquiou acquainted Marcel with the poems which would make up his second collection, *Chef des odeurs suaves*. With a sure touch, and alert to this gesture of trust, the younger man quoted the best verses ('*Yeux crevés, paons privés de tous leurs luminaires*')† or those which recall Hugo or Verlaine ('*Pleurez*

---

* Robert Proust, in his Introduction to the volume (*Corr. gen.*, vol. I) does not see it in this way: 'Montesquiou was truly an incomparable art critic, and from the outset, Marcel was attracted by the intelligence and delicacy of his opinions. From this period onwards, Montesquiou often came to the house (. . .) and for many years Marcel and he would remain very attached to one another.'
† 'Blinded eyes, peacocks bereft of all their glitter'.

avec/Avec l'étoile d'or que sa douceur argente'),* and he was particularly drawn to whatever embodied 'what is wholly mysterious, like music or faith', or which recalled 'certain passages of Wagner', 'certain expressions of da Vinci': as ever, music and the eyes. He took the opportunity to ask the poet for a photograph, which he would receive a week later, adorned with the inscription: 'Je suis le souverain des choses transitoires. 1893'.† The count is seen holding his hand to his forehead.‡ The gift of a photograph was, in Marcel's emotional life, an obligatory milestone, which he achieved as easily with men as he did with women. We know that just as he would ask in vain for a photograph of the Comtesse Greffulhe, so in *Le Côté du Guermantes* the Narrator, through the intermediary of Saint-Loup, would beg to no avail for a photograph of the Duchesse de Guermantes. In this way Proust assembled a large collection of photographs: never landscapes, always human beings whom he had known, loved or simply admired. He often toyed with these photographs in order to resuscitate his memories or his dreams; those of women he found particularly helpful in sketching his female characters; to view these characters simply as transvestites would therefore be pointless and inaccurate. As for Montesquiou, a passionate Narcissus who was obsessive about photographs of himself, he posed about two hundred times for his portrait (whereas photos of Proust himself are very rare).

Marcel was even so bold as to ask Montesquiou 'to show him some pictures of the female friends (the Comtesse Greffulhe, the Princesse de Léon) with whom [the count] was most frequently photographed'.[151] He would not have done so had not Montesquiou, like Charlus later, offered to play the role of mentor, introducing Proust to books as much as to people.[152] In addition, as a proof of friendship, but also because Marcel was anxious to find a sponsor, he asked Montesquiou for permission to dedicate 'a series of small sketches' to him, which he sent to *La Revue blanche*: despite the fact that he took Anatole France as a model, none of these sketches bore the name of Robert.

---

* 'Weep with her/ With the golden star which her sweetness coats in silver'.

† 'I am the sovereign of transitory things'.

‡ G. Cattaui, *M. Proust. Documents iconographiques*, Geneva, P. Cailler, 1956, p. 145 and *Corr.*, vol. I, p. 219. It is a little-known fact that Proust described this photograph, in his article on 'The Unaffectedness of M. de Montesquiou': 'I have in front of me as I write, a photograph of M. de Montesquiou which retains his perfect beauty, the reflective nobility of his features. Above this head with its hair slightly curled like those Greek statues which have the same graceful, brilliant charm, should be the words "the divine laurel of souls in exile". Beneath it, the poet had written

It was on 1 July, at the home of the Princesse de Wagram, that Marcel first noticed the Comtesse Greffulhe: 'She wore', he wrote to Montesquiou to tell him of his excitement, 'a hairstyle as graceful as a Polynesian's, and with mauve orchids that slid down to the nape of her neck . . . She is hard to decipher . . . But the entire mystery of her beauty is in her sparkle, in the enigmatic quality of her eyes especially. I have never met such a beautiful woman.'[153] Marcel, who had not been introduced to the countess, hoped that the impression she made on him would be transmitted to her; it complemented that made by the Comtesse de Chevigné, and the expression of the Duchesse de Guermantes had a similar effect.

During this period of discovery, if not love at first sight, Marcel wrote to Montesquiou once or twice a week, constantly raising the tone of his admiration: 'In these thoughtless, graceless times, that is to say an age that is basically uninspiring, you excel in the dual power of your thought and your energy. And I doubt that there can ever have been such supreme sophistication combined with this energy, this creative force of olden times, and this seventeenth-century intellectuality.'[154] As with Baudelaire, Montesquiou had a liking for maxims, and a habit of thinking in verse. The 'most subtle of artists' had thus written 'the most powerfully conceived' poetry. Marcel could not yet know that the poet's future work would disappoint his expectations. The count, touched by this 'young Brutus', who was 'clever and sensitive, judicious and lucid', allowed his satisfaction to be known.[155] During this sort of platonic honeymoon, the older man hoped to have found the fervent Roman acolyte that he longed for; the younger man was seeking a master, a counsellor, a model for him to imitate and portray, but also someone who could introduce him into aristocratic circles. For a brief time, there was also a physical attraction that united the dominated with the dominator, the mutual sympathy of inverts; yet there was no carnal love: only very young men really appealed to Marcel, those younger than him. Was Montesquiou impotent? Or simply prudent? We know of only one relationship, with his secretary Gabriel de Yturri, so beloved and so lamented; even then we do not know how far it went. In any case, at the time Marcel's admiration for Montesquiou – the man, the gossip, the artist – was sincere; even if his admiration did not last very long, the friendship engendered by these initial feelings was undeniable: at the end of Proust's life, he would seek

---

this verse which is the first line of a poem in *Les Chauves-souris*: "I am the sovereign of transitory things"' (*CSB*, p. 409).

to bestow the title of critic on this old, forgotten poet,* and it is as an art critic, in fact, that Montesquiou gave of his best, rather like the Goncourts, who, moreover, had perceived these very qualities in him.[156]

MUSIC

That same spring term of 1893, Marcel made several acquaintances through his interest in music. One was with a young woman, Germaine Giraudeau (1871–1955), a relative of his friend Pierre Lavallée.[157] Marcel was received by her mother, who lent him a score by Augusta Holmès; her father was a close friend of the Empress Eugénie and was 'in mourning for the Empire'. The only trace of Germaine's relationship with Marcel is a portrait in a book of autographs: 'In her beauty, everything is contrasted. The white cheeks and the black eyes.' Melancholy can be read in her expression, one can sense 'the inner dialogue', the storm that shakes her soul, at the moment Marcel confesses his 'present terrible sorrow so full of tears and bitterness in the throat, a despair which the overwhelming monotony of the burning sky darkly soothes'.[158] Around this time he was perfecting his liking for the portrait, as can be seen in *Les Plaisirs et les Jours* (although this particular portrait is not included); fortunately he had obtained a photograph of the girl. 'This adorable photograph has more *distinction* and *character* than the one of the little girl with the white tie . . . It is therefore even more pleasant for me to possess than the one I actually wanted.'[159] 'Pleasant to possess' – a photograph, or the portrait that he would drew from it, would be all that Proust would ever possess of a woman. As with Jeanne Pouquet and Marie Finaly, he briefly pretended to flirt; that would reassure his friends, the Lavallées.

Augusta Holmès was not a composer Marcel rated very highly. Was he more interested in the music of the Comte de Saussine, who was a composer of sorts and a music critic, and in the count himself rather more than in his work? The count held his salon at 16 rue Saint-Guillaume; Proust described it in 'Éventail', which he dedicated to him in the July–August issue of *La Revue blanche*: both 'deferential dukes and unpretentious novelists' gathered there.[160] In the music library, he noted the operas of

---

* See also the qualified praise that Montesquiou allows Proust in *Les Pas effacés*, vol. III, pp. 288–94 (written in March 1920, although published in 1923); cf., p. 273 ('within a budding grove' was more successful than the grove of 'bloody heroes'): 'Marcel Proust, for long someone of great charm for me, inspires in me as much friendship as warm admiration for his talent.'

Wagner, the symphonies of Franck and of Indy, and works for the piano by Haydn, Handel or Palestrina. As for the women present, 'they exemplify beauty without understanding it'. It was at Saussine's that Proust made the acquaintance of the young pianist Delafosse, whose strange destiny would be amatory and literary, rather than musical. Saussine published a novel, *Le Nez de Cléopâtre*, which Marcel hastened to review for the *Gratis Journal*, a simple publicity sheet distributed by the publisher of this masterpiece, Ollendorff; his text, as would frequently be Proust's lot, seems to have been cut.[161] Yet this modest article, which nobody took any notice of, least of all its author, contained some invaluable aesthetic remarks. To begin with, Marcel attempted to define the 'new generation', which differed from the preceding one and surpassed it in 'the intensity of its intellect, its soaring vision', in the importance attached to thought, which had been banished from the world by the materialists and from art by the naturalists: which alone gave life a background, and destiny a meaning. But one should not fall into the opposite trap: one loses the gift of life when one depends too much on reason: 'the work that has been thought about too much is rarely alive, and colours lose their intensity the moment one is overly analytical. This, no doubt, accounts for the unfortunate fate of so many modern pieces, which are doomed to immediate death the moment they are born.'[162] The conflict between life and abstraction would be at the heart of all Proust's work, as would 'transferring the Wagnerian leitmotiv into writing'.[163] This particular allusion arose because Marcel, at the same time that he was preparing his law examinations, which he would fail at the end of July, went to see *Die Walküre* at the Opéra, something he mentioned in the first version of 'Mélancolique villégiature de Mme de Breyves'.[164]

It is at this juncture, as he prepared to depart for Saint-Moritz, that he opened a new stage in his literary career by offering, for the first time, some articles to the prestigious review *La Revue blanche*.

CHAPTER VI

The Genesis of
Les Plaisirs et les Jours

SAINT-MORITZ

Marcel, accompanied by Louis de La Salle, the future writer and his friend from the Lycée Condorcet and *Le Banquet*, arrived at Saint-Moritz hoping to find Montesquiou and to be introduced through him to the famous. Saint-Moritz, far from being a winter sports station, was a summer resort for members of European high society, who, after a short visit to Bayreuth, would go there for the pure mountain air and the palatial comfort of its villas;[1] it was, according to the guide-books, 'the most celebrated summer resort in Europe'. Marcel did not fail to appreciate its beauty, something he described both in 'Présence réelle', which he would submit to *La Revue blanche*, and in an epistolary novel which he wrote during his stay.

Here he revealed his awareness of the incomparable green of the lakes which bathe the pine forests, of the glaciers and mountain peaks that line the horizon, of the larch trees on the banks of Sils-Maria lake, of the butterflies dancing on the water (an image he would use in *Sodome et Gomorrhe*, at La Raspelière). The scenery struck him as 'astonishingly Wagnerian, with its lakes the green of precious stones, and above the mountains, the clouds, trailing their vast blue shadows as they do at sea . . . and all around are pine forests, ideal for a descent of the Valkyries or for encountering Lohengrin'. The heroine of the 'epistolary novel' who writes these lines says it took fourteen hours to travel by horse-drawn coach from Coire (which is in fact the railway station that serves Saint-Moritz).[2] 'Présence réelle' also describes a walk on the Alp Grüm;[3] the walk takes an hour and a quarter, from the Bernina hospice, twenty-two kilometres from Saint-Moritz. 'The landscape of our childhood imagination materialized before our eyes. Glaciers sparkled nearby. At our feet, mountain torrents criss-crossed the wild, dark-green Engadine countryside. Then we passed a rather mysterious hill; and later, mauve-coloured slopes half-revealed and concealed by turns a landscape that was truly blue, and a glittering avenue that led towards Italy. The names were no longer the same, and they harmonized with these new, softer shades.' At the end of the piece he evoked these 'names, both German and Italian, of a strange sweetness: Sils-Maria, Silva Plana, Crestalta, Samaden, Celerina, Juliers, Val de Viola'.[4] Here we see the first appearance of the reverie on place-names which will be a part-title of *À l'ombre des jeunes filles en fleurs* (just as 'Noms de pays: le nom' is the third part of *Du côté de chez Swann*), and of his liking for high places, overlooking sea or lakes.

At Saint-Moritz Marcel did not stay in a grand hotel, but in a modest establishment, the Pension Veraguth. He did not meet many people, apart from Montesquiou, the Ephrussis, and above all Mme Léon Fould and her daughter[*] (who would note in her diary that Marcel appeared every day in the same, strange, squirrel-coloured tweed suit).[†] He accompanied Mme Fould and Élisabeth on all their walks and delighted them with his conversation. His voice, silky and of great sweetness, had an 'ingratiating, penetrating strength'. Marcel spoke quietly, but people listened to him. He shared young Élisabeth Fould's admiration for *Le Roman d'un enfant*. He took part patiently in skimming pebbles on the lake, which the Foulds liked to do; Mme Fould was fond of him, found him extremely pleasant and would invite him frequently to Paris where she would introduce him to a number of her friends. On the other hand, Ignace, brother of Charles Ephrussi, nicknamed him 'the Proustaillon'.

Marcel also met Mrs Meredith Howland. This American woman, who was born Adelaide Torrance, held a salon at her town house at 24 *bis* rue

---

[*] Élisabeth Fould, in her unpublished memoirs, describes Marcel in the following terms: 'Immense, dark, silky eyes . . . dark hair too, shining, dense, and a thick lock that fell over his forehead, a pale, sickly skin . . . he was always in need of fresh air.' She also recalls Marcel's eccentric taste in clothing, coming across him in the Champs-Élysées wearing three overcoats one on top of the other, or at a soirée wearing a dress-shirt with buttons that did not match. His behaviour seemed 'strange'. As for his genius, no one would have guessed: 'Papa, genuinely interested and well informed about literary matters, said of him: "He's a failure!" Yet Marcel knew everything, even that the Prince de Beauvau had written the poem: "Life is an onion which one peels in tears."' He left parties so late that one evening Charles Ephrussi took him by the shoulder and said to him: 'These people want to go to bed.' However, Marcel would make friends with Eugène Fould, who shared his habits. ('Marcel in my youth', *Adam International Review* no. 310, 1966.)

[†] 'Someone even made the comment that if one only had one suit, it was best to choose something less ostentatious' (ibid., p. 51).

de Berri. In *Le Temps retrouvé* the Duchesse de Guermantes would say of her that 'she had all the men at her home'.[5] Marcel dedicated his 'Mélancolique villégiature de Mme de Breyves' (which appeared in the September 1893 issue of *La Revue blanche*) to Mrs Howland: 'In respectful memory of the lakes of Engadine and particularly of the lake of Silva Plana. Saint-Moritz, August 93.' This story, which opens with a quotation from Racine and ends on a phrase of Baudelaire's (the two would always be Proust's masters), takes up Balzac's *The Abandoned Woman* (whereas in *À la recherche*, from Swann to the Narrator, it is the men who are abandoned: 'The Abandoned Man' could have made a good title for the love story which Marcel never stopped rewriting; but, when he was composing *Les Plaisirs et les Jours*, he reversed the sexes). The heroine, Françoise (just as in 'L'indifférent' and in *Jean Santeuil*), falls in love with a man whom she has scarcely ever seen and whom she wishes to introduce, with the help of various intermediaries,[6] to the third parties who feature in every Proustian intrigue. The growth of a passion for a 'fugitive' and the sorrows that it brings, love-sickness, remorse for 'causing her mother sadness', the peace that is to be found only 'among her servants', the attempt to detach herself from her own feelings and to look at them as if they were something outside herself, the imbalance between the beloved and the suffering or joy that he provokes, the fact that he is associated with a musical phrase from *Die Meistersinger* – all this foreshadows 'Un amour de Swann': thus when the heroine hears again at Trouville the tune that is the leitmotiv of the man she loves, she dissolves into tears (like Swann when he hears the phrase from the Vinteuil sonata at Mme de Saint-Euverte's soirée). The paradox is that the heroine, besides being tortured by feelings of guilt ('her goodness and her kindheartedness which, if she gave of herself, would infect the joy of these guilty love affairs with shame and remorse'), does not succeed in gaining the man with whom she is in love.[7]

However, the principal literary undertaking of Proust's visit to Saint-Moritz was something different. It was a plan decided upon before his departure, and it consisted of writing an epistolary novel for four voices,[8] which would bring together Louis de La Salle, Fernand Gregh, Daniel Halévy and Marcel Proust, who had all been involved in the editorship of *Le Banquet*. The friends shared out the roles at the end of July: Marcel was to be a young woman, Pauline de Gouvres-Dives, who is in love with a sergeant,[9] a part played by Louis de La Salle; Daniel Halévy was a priest; Fernand Gregh, a musician by the name of Chalgrain. They took as their models an epistolary novel, *La Croix de Berny*, written in 1846 by Théophile

Gautier, Delphine de Girardin, Jules Sandeau and Joseph Méry, as well as, for its overall structure, *Peints par eux-mêmes* by Paul Hervieu.[10] Furthermore, the little group had been charmed by Gabriele D'Annunzio's *L'Intrus*, which had just appeared in translation, and they planned to incorporate this flamboyant 'cult of the self'. Proust, who was reading Barbey d'Aurevilly, would also make use of 'Une page d'histoire',[11] depicting the Ravalets' country house and its atmosphere of shame and remorse.[12] This author, whom Proust would allude to again in *La Prisonnière*, was also an influence on his 'Mélancolique villégiature de Mme de Breyves'.

In her first letter Pauline confides her melancholy secret to the priest, and recalls her childhood in terms that foreshadow the first part of *À l'ombre des jeunes filles en fleurs*: 'Every time it rains, I feel sad when I remember how, as a little girl, I would stand for hours at my window wondering whether it would be a fine day, and whether my nanny would take me to the Champs-Élysées, where I used to play with the little boy whom I loved more than I will love anyone in my entire life.'[13] This was not the only personal characteristic that Marcel interpolated into the character of Pauline. The heroine, who 'leaves Paris in order to at least feel protected from wild temptations', suffered from the homesickness she experienced 'in new surroundings, especially in a new flat, and still more cruelly in a new bed'. She, too, goes to Saint-Moritz, and when she dreams of the defunct lords in their ruined castle, and of the crimes and hereditary vices which would linger in this eagle's eyrie,[14] it brings to mind Charlus' dream of feudal cruelty in *Le Temps retrouvé*. The whole drama hidden in Proust's letters can be found in the tragic subject which the young woman dreams about: the expectation of letters which bring happiness is counterbalanced by 'all the bad news about those who are ill, a mother hearing about an accidental death, those letters from a son to a mother, from a husband to his wife, that are so heartless that they create something between them that is insurmountable, against which all feelings of tenderness will be crushed – all of that will be there'. Another subject that the heroine contemplates reveals the influence both of Balzac and of the psychological society novel in the style of Bourget and Hervieu: the ultimate fear of marriage – against the backdrop of a salon on the outskirts of town 'an irrevocable series of misfortunes' would unfold – 'lives embalmed in tears, husbands deserting their despairing wives and leaving with their mistresses, suicides, murders, etc.'[15] Finally, this novel did not fail to depict the snob who would fill the pages of *Les Plaisirs et les Jours*, those peacocks dear to Montesquiou (who was at Saint-Moritz at the same time as Marcel). Proust, who put all of himself into this female character, was already conscious of the permanence of his own physical and moral nature, for ever fixed, as in the photographs of him.[16]

In this unfinished novel, or what we have of it, Proust's character seems to be far more important, and more interesting, than those of his friends. It allowed him to collaborate with his holiday companion, Louis de La Salle, in the way that he dreamt of doing, much later, with Reynaldo Hahn (on *A Life of Chopin*), or with René Peter (on an article on sadism); these projects, which allowed Marcel to struggle against his supposed laziness and to prolong a friendship, would not come to very much: writing had to be done on one's own. This, moreover, was what he had done in the essays he published in the July–August issue of *La Revue blanche*: 'Contre la franchise', 'Scénario', 'Éventail' (dedicated to Saussine), 'Mondanité de Bouvard et Pécuchet' ('To my three dear little Roberts, Robert Proust, Robert de Flers and Robert de Billy, to amuse us'), a lead piece dedicated to 'Gladys Harvey' (the name, we have seen, that Paul Bourget gave to Laure Hayman, the friend of Proust's great-uncle Louis Weil, who would be a model for Odette Swann), 'Reliques' (to Paul Baignères, who painted Marcel's portrait), 'Sources des larmes qui sont dans les amours passées', 'Amitié', 'Ephémère efficacité du chagrin' – nine 'studies' in all.[17] As a whole, they raised themes which would always remain at the heart of Proust's philosophy. The first theme was the link between memory, the past and what is forgotten, a link that was particularly important in the case of love, 'this contrast between the immensity of our past love and the absoluteness of our present indifference'.[18] This moral truth, Proust observed, becomes a psychological reality 'when a writer introduces it at the beginning of the passionate affair which he is describing'. In fact, Proust's most important contribution to an understanding of passion was to chronicle not just its birth, but its death; memory is less important than what is forgotten, something he continued to emphasize, right up to *Albertine disparue*, which is its apotheosis. Marcel's entire conception of passionate love was formed at this period; it remained for him to develop it, not to alter it. Thus 'Scénario' affirmed that the lover should affect indifference, and that a kiss would cause the beloved to run away. This theme is scarcely counterbalanced by the elegy to 'friendship', in which we can discern a personal undertone: 'It is like an even better bed, one that is alive with divine scents. It is our sweet, our profound, our impenetrable friendship . . . our warm affection.' Certainly, this was the way Marcel would display his own feelings towards the young men to whom he was attracted: nothing but friendship, trust and a miraculous affection. A third theme is the fecund nature of sorrow, which enables us to contemplate 'life as a whole and in reality'; sad books 'do us good similarly'.[19] A group of essays, which Proust would include among the 'Fragments de comédie italienne' in *Les Plaisirs et les Jours* fell more into the genre of the social or society novel, in the style of La Bruyère ('Contre la franchise'), or of pastiche, like the brilliant and funny 'Mondanité et mélomanie de Bouvard et Pécuchet'. Flaubert's characters interpret society and its conversation, as if they were actually there, and parade the clichés of the day about the most fashionable writers ('Leconte de Lisle was too impassive, Verlaine too sensitive'; 'Mallarmé no longer has any talent, but he's a brilliant conversationalist'; 'as for Anatole France, he writes well, but thinks poorly, unlike Bourget, who has depth, but an appalling style'). They then concoct a manual of good manners, in which they confide their views on the nobility ('It is cleric-ridden, backward, never reads, does nothing'), on the world of finance (which arouses 'respect but also loathing'), Protestant society, which Marcel knew through Billy, the artistic world (artists 'sleep by day, go out at night, and work nobody knows when'), and finally the Jews. Here Marcel assembled all the anti-Semitic clichés prevalent before the Dreyfus affair: 'They all have hooked noses, exceptional intelligence, a heart that is base and only concerned with interest rates . . . But why are their riches always incalculable and hidden away? What is more, they form a sort of vast secret society, like the Jesuits and Freemasons.' In this pastiche Marcel reinvented Flaubert; certain clichés from the *Dictionnaire des idées reçues*, which would not be published until 1911, already appear in the text! The literary allusions, the critical analysis, the gift for mimicry which would later allow him to surpass those he imitated are, in these essays in *La Revue blanche*, as in *Le Mensuel*, superior to the young novelist's inventiveness.

As early as July 1893 Marcel wrote a short story, 'L'indifférent', which would appear in March 1896 in *La Vie contemporaine*. It is a tale about childhood and the story of a love affair which anticipates 'Un amour de Swann'. When he was writing the latter in 1910, Proust searched for a printed copy of his earlier story, the manuscript of which he had not preserved. The account of childhood is dominated by a first attack of asthma, which confirms the autobiographical nature of his writing at the time.[20] In her love affair, the heroine takes as a maxim the refrain of *Carmen*, but in reverse: 'If I do not love you, you love me', and, like Odette, she wears cattleyas.

After Saint-Moritz, Marcel spent a week at Évian. It is not known where he stayed: it could have been at the Villa Quatorze, in Montreux, with Mme Laure Baignères (and Fernand Gregh); at the Villa Bassaraba, in Amphion, with the Princesse de Brancovan, 'friend of Paderewski and a fine musician herself';[21] at Coppet, with the Comte d'Haussonville, a future relative of Proust. In any case, on notepaper from the Casino and the Thermal Baths at Évian he wrote an article on Montesquiou.* Returning to Paris for a few days, Marcel voted in the general election of 3 September for F. Passy,[22] and not for the Conservative candidate, Denys Cochin, so as to do what his father, who was away, would have done. The situation was alluded to in *Jean Santeuil*: 'I am his son before I am myself.' Never did voting give him so much enjoyment. In thus attributing greater importance to his father than to himself, 'he grew in stature in his own eyes. He no longer voted as an isolated individual, but as proxy for a family which he had the honour to represent.' This harmony between father and son was destroyed, however, by the onset of the new term: Marcel passed all his examinations,[23] but without having decided on a career. His father, however, insisted that he made up his mind. Marcel confided in his friend Billy, who was already in the diplomatic corps. If he were to choose the Foreign Office, it would be in order to remain in Paris! But in that case his career would be just as 'tedious' as it would be at the Cour des Comptes [the Audit Office], which was harder to enter, but the rest of the time 'he would go for walks'. Or would it be better to be a magistrate? Wasn't it 'too poorly regarded' (even at this stage!)? 'What is left for me, given that I am not going to be a lawyer, a doctor, a priest, or – ?'[24] Marcel exclaimed despairingly. And he wrote to his father, at the end of the month, to say that he would not last three days in a lawyer's practice,[25] and would a thousand times rather become a stockbroker. Even though he believed that anything that was not to do with literature or philosophy would be time wasted, he also suggested sitting the competitive exams for entry to the Foreign Office or the École des Chartes,† since his father wanted him to go in for a 'practical' career. The ideal, however, would be to continue the literary and philosophical studies for which he believed he was intended.[26] Following this exchange of letters, and

---

* This is not absolute proof that the article was written that week, as P. Kolb maintains (*Corr.* vol. I, p. 240, n. 2). It seems to me more likely that Proust had kept some of the notepaper, and that he wrote the article in October 1893, at the time he spoke of it to Montesquiou.

† The Paris *grande école* for archivists and librarians. *Tr.*

throughout the numerous discussions at home, Marcel, as we shall see, would select a mediator, and would enrol for a degree in literature (philosophy) at the Sorbonne.

In spite of these worries, he spent a few days in Paris attending to his true career – a literary one – before rejoining his mother at Trouville. On 4 September he met Thadée Natanson, the editor of *La Revue blanche*; what he hoped for, in fact, was to obtain proofs of 'Mélancolique villégiature de Mme de Breyves' which would appear on 15 September, and to suggest an article on *Le Chef des odeurs suaves*, by his 'friend' Montesquiou, a book that had not yet been published. The article must have been turned down, for it did not appear until after Proust's death, in 1954. From 6 to 28 September Marcel and his mother stayed at Trouville, at the Hôtel des Roches Noires. He recalled this establishment in 'Souvenir':[27] 'Last year I spent some time at the Grand Hôtel de T—, situated at the far end of the beach and overlooking the sea. The insipid stench of the kitchens and the dirty waters, the luxurious banality of the curtains, which were the only diversion from the grey bareness of the walls, and which completed the furnishing of this haunt of *exiles*, had driven me into a state of almost morbid depression . . .'[28] But he also enjoyed returning to 'the salt and the offshore winds in the narrow Normandy lanes',[29] to his friends on the coast and to Mme Straus.

THE NEW TERM, 1893

Back in Paris, Marcel continued his brilliant military career: he was due to sit an examination to become an officer, but he begged his father to intervene with Doctor Kopff, the medical officer.[30] Above all, anxious to please Montesquiou, he told him of his plan for an article, the first of a series that was to remain unpublished. It is important to note that Proust wished to publish newspaper or magazine articles 'so as to simplify a form that is needlessly complicated'. He had not chosen the ideal person to address such a confidence to, but, nevertheless, he wanted to entitle his article 'The Unaffectedness of M. de Montesquiou', emphasizing the seventeenth-century aspect of the man and the wealth of his 'intellectuality', so as to appeal not just to those who were 'oversensitive', but to intellectuals too.[31] The count seemed happy with the plan, and he responded with an invitation to lunch at the Pavillon Montesquiou, at Versailles. Marcel then composed this article, in which he affirmed some essential aesthetic principles; there was an important school of thought at the time that centred on the notion of 'decadence': in this piece, Proust proclaimed his break with a section of young and avant-garde writers of the day by rejecting decadence. The paradox was that he should do so while writing about a man who, particularly after *À rebours*, was considered 'a sort of Prince of Decadence, ruling like a capricious despot over all the corruptions of the mind and all the subtleties of the Imagination'.[32] To claim that Montesquiou was not decadent was to strike at the heart of the enemy. In the article Proust maintained that 'Satanism is fairly short-lived and dandyism too'. The decadents had taken as their manifesto the passage in Gautier's preface to *Les Fleurs du mal* on the theory of decadence, the expression of a life that was artificial and depraved, a proof of greatness of which animals were incapable. These theories, the young Proust stated, were harmful, in the first place, because they did not treat Baudelaire as 'the greatest poet of the nineteenth century', the 'one intellectual and classic author', but as 'a genuine Satanist and Decadent', and because they created around him an 'obscuring legend', of which Montesquiou in turn was a victim (as was Proust himself, if one dwells on the evil, blasphemy and perversion present in his work). The second effect of this was to infantilize the new generation, which Proust defined in a way that now has an historic value: the young people of today (of 1893) all have 'a disease of the will, which makes them unsure how to behave and unable to think'; Marcel himself occasionally thought that he was afflicted by this 'disease' (a theme which the philosopher Théodule Ribot deals with in one of his books).

Proust therefore sought to show that Montesquiou was a man of strong will; in his voice and in his conversation he came over as more 'conquistador' than 'neurotic'. If decadence was connected to 'morbid nuances of feeling' without the capacity for thought, Montesquiou was sustained by classical literature and was a poet who was a thinker, 'an intellectual first and foremost', a man who cared about 'eternal things', a disciple of the real Baudelaire. (In his article on Baudelaire, written after the First World War, Proust would hark back to certain poems and certain arguments, notably the comparison with Racine.) All in all, this article, which did not deal solely with Montesquiou, set Proust against the contemporary trend, just as 'Contre l'obscurité' would do later on. The rejection of 'decadence', of pure sensation, of 'corruptness', the proclamation of a new classicism embodied by a Baudelaire who was a disciple of Racine's, are courageous assertions; it is hardly surprising that his article was turned down by *La Revue blanche*,[33] which supported the cause of the decadents, and also by *La Revue de Paris*.

HOW NOT TO CHOOSE A CAREER

At the beginning of October 1893 Marcel learnt of the death of his friend Willie Heath, 'who after a life of outstanding nobility died with heroic resignation'.[34] He considered dedicating a 'little book' to him, 'a collection of bits and pieces', which were 'mediocre', he granted, and took a 'great liberty' in certain places,[35] but were illustrated by Madeleine Lemaire: 'Therefore it will be talked about among writers, artists and prominent people everywhere who would otherwise not have known about it and will only keep it for the illustrations.'[36] From the autumn of 1893, when Marcel had the notion of a collection and obtained the agreement of the illustrator,[37] it would be another three years before the project saw the light of day; this was to be the fate of all Proust's works: he would announce a book that was not yet finished, which the publishers would turn down, and which would be expanded and improved upon thanks to this delay. He was nevertheless so convinced that publication would be imminent that he thought of dedicating the book to two of his friends who were dead and whom 'he will always love'.

At the beginning of November, very much at the prompting of his parents, Marcel turned to Charles Grandjean to ask him for some guidance 'in deciding upon his career'.[38] This man, who was the librarian at the Senate and a friend of Princesse Mathilde (at whose house Edmond de Goncourt found him 'not particularly pleasant'), gave Marcel his advice over the course of a month, until 8 December, when the latter discontinued their talks. Firstly, he considered the career of museum curator: a degree, a doctorate, École de Louvre, École de Rome – 'I can see myself already as director of the Versailles Museum,' wrote Marcel, who was nevertheless anxious: 'You make the tedious, rotten careers on offer sound wonderful, and I feel I am in a cave full of enchantment and glamour.'[39] Then Grandjean recommended the Cour des Comptes, which Marcel reckoned would take a long time to get into, and, above all, would be 'gruesome'; he would prefer the École des Chartes, even if it meant asking to work in a museum (Saint-Germain, Cluny? Versailles?) as a volunteer, while he got on with his literature degree 'or simply with personal work'. Grandjean maintained the view that young Proust was not made for the École des Chartes. Might he become an editor at the Senate? Or an inspector of fine arts? Half-way through November, his parents left him free to make his own plans, but felt that they were 'hardly those of a career strategy' and they were doubtful about museums. Marcel was offered a position as archivist at the Ministry of Foreign Affairs at the end of the month; there would be no salary during the first two years, and 'would it be very absorbing?' the former future diplomat wondered earnestly.

This month of consultations came to naught: the young man was still keen on museums; furthermore, he did not rule out any other career . . . At the age of twenty-two, Proust wanted to continue the literary studies for which he was destined. They would have led – regardless of what he may have wished – to teaching at secondary or higher level, like his friend from the Lycée Condorcet, Léon Brunschvicg, or his cousin by marriage, Henri Bergson. The École des Chartes would lead him back to books, manuscripts, libraries, and so to the Mazarine library in June 1895. In his letters, one catches a glimpse of the despair of the young writer, unable to make his parents accept the notion that literature is a career – given that his financial means and social rank precluded taking modest employment, as Zola and Maupassant had done to begin with, this meant doing nothing other than writing, just like artists and musicians who (apart from teaching sometimes) had no alternative employment. For a middle-class family the career of a writer still conjured up the Bohemian existence of Henri Murger, the author of the popular *Scènes de la vie de bohème* (or of Puccini). Balzac's parents had only accepted it because it increased their social standing and might make them rich. Perhaps the reason why Adrien Proust was even more intransigent was due to the fact that, coming from a humble background, he was a self-made man, and he had also had to come to terms with his son's illness and his life-style. To be sickly and an invert was one thing, but to be idle! However, Professor Proust could not spend his entire time remonstrating, and he would eventually succumb to his son's patient ruses, to the force of inertia, his gentle stubbornness and unending arguments. *Les Plaisirs et les Jours* was published in time to justify the alternative career. Its title would echo provocatively in the consciousness of a man who, like the Greek poet Hesiod, would have preferred the title *Les Travaux et les Jours*. Did Marcel, however, have the support of his mother, who, by and large, preferred asking him questions about the literary aspects of his work?[40] There is no letter to suggest this, and *Jean Santeuil* portrays both parents united against their son. In contrast, around this time Robert was working towards a career that would 'open wide his father's heart'.[41] Far from arousing the anger of the father against his elder son, the success of his younger child may have helped soothe him: he had two heirs, but only one to succeed him; if it was not to be Marcel Proust, the lawyer, then it would be Robert Proust, doctor of medicine.[42]

FURTHER ESSAYS FOR *LA REVUE BLANCHE*

On 1 December *La Revue blanche* published six essays by Proust, just as he began studying for his literature degree. This journal,[43] to which Marcel contributed from 1893 to 1896, after the collapse of *Le Banquet*, was founded in Liège in 1889 (it was white – *blanche* – because there was already a *Revue bleue* and a *Revue rose*, and because it stood for 'the sum of all colours').[44] The journal's editorial policy was inspired by the 'Nouvelle École', which its writers considered to be true to life, and to reality, but they nevertheless declared themselves to be open to all manner of opinions. The Natanson brothers, wealthy Poles from Paris, took a prominent role; Lucien Mühlfeld, the journal's assistant editor, joined in October 1890 and stayed until 1895; his place was then taken by Félix Fénéon. In 1891 the print-run was 2,500 copies. In style the new magazine resembled the *Mercure de France* of the time (founded in January 1890 by Alfred Valette), with a similar propensity for individualism, which would later extend to anarchy (that of early Barrès). However, it was not really a symbolist magazine, despite the fact that Régnier, Gourmont, Kahn and Mallarmé were among its contributors; these also included Tristan Bernard, Jules Renard, and the writers for *Le Banquet*, Léon Blum, Fernand Gregh and Marcel Proust, who would not become Symbolists. Thadée Natanson attracted artists such as Bonnard, Vuillard and Toulouse-Lautrec to the magazine, who each provided a print for the frontispiece. Lucien Mühlfeld was responsible for the book section, Pierre Veber for the theatre column, Thadée Natanson reviewed the exhibitions, Tristan Bernard and Léon Blum provided the sporting coverage.

In its 25 May 1893 issue *La Revue blanche* announced: 'We are pleased to inform our readers of the merging of *La Revue blanche* with the journal *Le Banquet*.' But neither Gregh nor Proust would really be associates of the magazine's editorial team; Marcel gave in his copy, corresponded with Thadée Natanson or Lucien Mühlfeld, the assistant editor. There was no real discussion between them, as there had been during the period of *Le Banquet*. For Marcel, the hopes or pleasures he once had of editing a magazine were at an end. In 1893 he published three series of articles, an important critical essay, 'Contre l'obscurité', in 1896, and that would be all. In December 1893 he submitted the series of 'studies' which consisted of 'Contre une snob', 'À une snob', 'Rêve', 'Présence réelle', 'Avant la nuit', and 'Souvenir'.[45] The first two are social comedies reminiscent of La Bruyère; at the same time, they explore themes which point to *Le Côté de Guermantes*: 'The features of your new friends are linked in your imagination with a long array of portraits of ancestors . . . Your imagination merges the present with the past.' 'Rêve' is a strange story, in which the hero experiences immense sensual and passive pleasure with a woman, but does so in a dream; however, just as later in 'Un amour de Swann', this dream plays a part in the evolution of the feelings that are experienced, up until the time that all memory of it disappears. The first manuscript version anticipates the beginning of 'Combray': 'I cast a backward glance at the slumber from which I had just awoken, and I was grateful that it had been refreshing, without disturbances or dreams. I went back to bed, read a newspaper, then shortly afterwards I blew out my candle, reflected for a few more moments, and at last fell asleep.'[46] 'Avant la nuit' is the most important of these pieces. It takes up and develops 'Souvenir', which appeared in *Le Mensuel*, and foreshadows 'La Confession d'une jeune fille'. On a terrace from which one can glimpse the sea through the apple trees, a young woman, Françoise (a Christian name used frequently in Proust's early writings), divulges her homosexuality to a male friend, and justifies it: 'If fruitful love, which is intended to perpetuate the human race and which is exalted as a social, human and family duty, is superior to purely voluptuous love, then there is no hierarchy among forms of love that are unproductive, and it is no less moral – or, rather, no more immoral – that a woman should find pleasure with another woman instead of with someone of the opposite sex. The cause of this love lies in a nervous disorder which is too all-exclusive to admit a moral content.'[47] This woman, 'predisposed to this kind of love', had had her curiosity aroused by, for example, 'certain small figures by Rodin'.[48] In fact, the young woman has shot herself in the chest. After her confession, the two characters are both in tears, united by a Tolstoyan pity: at this period Marcel was beginning to be influenced by the author of *Anna Karenina*, long before he wrote about him.

A STORMY FRIENDSHIP

From December 1893 onwards, Marcel worked for his literature degree: in actual fact, it was a philosophy degree, for which he studied, it appears, less at the Sorbonne than at private lessons. He often used this as an excuse to his correspondents: 'In order to prepare for my degree, I am having a hodgepodge of lessons' . . . 'What is more, the lessons which I have now resumed are taking up my time.'[49] He was also taught Latin,[50] and, of course, philosophy; he took this opportunity to re-establish his friendship with Darlu, his old teacher from the Lycée Condorcet. Thanks to him, we possess Proust's remarks on happiness: 'I am made to write dissertations proving that happiness is *one* thing. Since I am a sensible student and a good son, I do them; since I am a poor philosopher, I do them badly. But, more especially, I don't believe in any of it.'[51] Marcel added, significantly: 'I believe that all of us have our own personal happiness – when we are happy.' This is a novelist's attitude rather than a philosopher's: the specific as against the general, this conflict will underpin the intellectual framework of his entire œuvre. Through reading Rabier's *Leçons de philosophie*,[52] he was able to be responsive to what was said about art and about time: 'Art is the master of time: for it brings together both time that is past as well as the future which has not yet arrived . . . Art can protect its creations from the laws of time, for it can perpetuate the moment in life it has chosen to represent . . . Nature, achieving here and there a more or less perfect beauty in its creations, teaches the artist what seem to be the first words of a divine language, one whose secret it knows, but which it does not utter. It is for the artist to master and compose (. . .) the poem of beauty.'[53] Rabier also devoted many pages to the subject of memory, laying stress on the association of ideas and feelings: 'Each state of consciousness revitalizes its immediate situation with an impression analogous to the original impression.'[54]

The fact that Proust hoped to publish his magazine articles in volume form, in spite of a certain number of rejections, as well as his article on Montesquiou, slowed down his editorial work. His relationship with the count, however, was going through a stormy and tempestuous period, interspersed by a few calm interludes. Marcel did everything he could to please the irascible count: he took part, for example, in the conference Montesquiou gave on Marceline Desbordes-Valmore on 17 January 1894,[55] attended by a glittering audience: the Comtesse Greffulhe, Leconte de Lisle, Edmond de Goncourt, Jules Lemaître, Régnier, Verlaine and Sarah Bernhardt, and he did not hesitate to tell the speaker that the 'all-powerful' harmonies of his tone of voice and his diction had a truly magical quality, and that his conversation was a masterpiece.[56]

LÉON DELAFOSSE

Proust now did something which would have unfortunate consequences for his relationship with Montesquiou and would considerably affect the writing of *À la recherche du temps perdu*. A young pianist, Léon Delafosse, born in 1874, of very humble origins but exceptional beauty, who had won first prize at the Paris Conservatoire at the age of thirteen,[57] was introduced to Marcel at the home of the Comte de Saussine, where Proust first heard him play. The pianist had composed songs based on the poems in *Les Chauves-souris* (which would be sung on 22 May 1894 at the home of Madeleine Lemaire), and he would be playing the piano part in a *Fantaisie* for four voices and a quartet by Henry de Saussine (performed at the Salle Érard on 5 May), so Marcel obtained Montesquiou's permission for Delafosse to publish his songs: 'In my humble opinion, they are exquisite.'[58] Delafosse dedicated another song based on a poem from *Les Chauves-souris*, 'Baisers', to Proust.[59] Marcel, who may have been trying to impress the count, or through ostentation, then made the mistake of introducing the pianist to him (so far Proust had invited Delafosse home, along with his friend Lavallée, for instance, who was also a musician); Delafosse soon earned the nickname 'the Angel'.* Marcel thus sacrificed on the altar of his friendship with the count his attraction for the young virtuoso. For three years Montesquiou would involve Delafosse in all the artistic events he organized (even having him give a recital at Saint-Moritz, in the summer of 1897); he also dedicated the poem 'Table d'Harmonie' from *Roseaux pensants* (1897) to him. Initially, Marcel tried to make the count understand that 'our little musician' was shared by them,[60] and he wrote enthusiastic reviews of his concerts. An account in *La Presse* (2 June 1894, following a festival at Versailles the previous evening) – not signed, but written by Proust – of the six songs based on poems from *Les Chauves-souris* that were composed and played by Delafosse, praised 'the music, unaffected and subtle like the poetry with which it is at one in substance and feeling', which 'with unique and manifold charms imitates its spontaneous surges and thoughtful reprises'.[61] Although Marcel did

---

* *Corr.*, vol. I, p. 282, 22 March 1894: 'Having only once delighted you by bringing "the Angel" to see you . . .' In *Sodome et Gomorrhe*, Charles calls Morel 'a musical young Angelico'. However, when Delafosse and Marcel called upon the count for the first time, they were taken to the fair at Viroflay to listen to a barrel-organ. Yturri, annoyed at this rudeness, then made sure that the count listened to the pianist. (R. de Montesquiou, *Les Pas effacés, Mémoires*, Émile-Paul, 1923, vol. II, pp. 286–7.)

not stop seeing the musician, it is likely that Montesquiou wanted to have him to himself. Fauré would play a mediating role in this affair, for which he would be criticized by Proust:[62] Fauré protected Delafosse, who performed his music, and hoped to please the count, who had given him some poems for the original version of *Pavane*. The young writer would have to step aside for the poet, while still continuing to see the musician, and, eventually, when the count fell out with the pianist, Marcel would take up his quarrel in his letters and, much later, would allude to the verses in 'Mensonges', which he wrote for a musician with whom he had quarrelled. In the poem Proust evoked the eternal deception of love (of this love?) which pines for what does not exist in this world: 'Your hazy eyes, your eager eyes/ Your profound eyes alas! are empty.'

Yet Delafosse provided the opportunity, the pretext for Marcel to get over losing an attachment, or an exclusive one, at least: in July 1894 Reynaldo Hahn attended a recital given by the pianist in London, and so Marcel suggested a meeting: 'Delafosse's last letter leads me to suppose that he will return any day and will thus remove the only excuse I have for asking for a rendez-vous. So if you are able to meet me one of these afternoons at the earliest opportunity, at my home or yours or at the terrace of the café by the lake at the Tuileries or wherever you wish (. . .).'[63] One musician pursues the other. The fact remains, however, that Marcel, in his friendship with the Narrator, just as in his relationship and his quarrel with M. de Charlus, was very much inspired by Delafosse and his ties with Montesquiou – at first jealous and then resigned, Marcel had lit the way for their relationship, and borne witness to it.* Jean Lorrain described the same relationship in *Monsieur de Phocas*, in which the Comte de Muzarett, author of *Rats ailés*, takes the musician Delabarre under his wing: 'Choosing to launch the composer was a way for the dear count to polish up his rhymes.' In his *Portraits d'hommes*, 1930, Rachilde also sang

---

* Delafosse's career thus began under Montesquiou's patronage, with concerts in the salons, or at the Salle Érard (20 April and 5 May 1894; 21 and 28 March 1896; Fauré festival, St James Hall, London, 10 December 1896; at the home of the Baronne de Rothschild, 5 June 1897). The quarrel took place in 1897: 'Try to ensure that my love for your art is greater than my loathing for you yourself' (Montesquiou *Les Pas effacés*, vol. II, p. 295). The young pianist then turned to other patrons: 'He threw himself, not into the arms, for I don't believe she had any, but at the feet, which were extremely large, of an elderly Swiss lady' (ibid., p. 255, and A. Bertrand, op. cit., p. 653). According to André David, Delafosse, who, at the age of twenty, had had his portrait painted by Sargent, boasted that he had been the model for the character of Morel. The Swiss lady only allowed him to play in Paris, Geneva and Monte Carlo; he only performed for duchesses and royalty (*Soixante-quinze années de jeunesse*, A. Bonne, 1974, pp. 17–18).

Delafosse's praises; he died, forgotten, in 1951, but he composed a number of piano pieces, among them a Ballade dedicated to Flavie de Casa-Fuerte, and a Romance for cello for her son.[64]

Throughout this term, Montesquiou had two reasons to be annoyed with Marcel: firstly, the promised article on 'La Simplicité de M. de Montesquiou' did not appear, in spite of the efforts of its author; secondly, the count was irritated that Marcel, having introduced the pianist, persisted in trying to exercise patronage over him. Indeed, it was very much Montesquiou's style to assuage his feelings with displays of wrath, simulated quarrels and unkind remarks; in this way he established the upper hand over his entourage, and he made up for the absence of carnal relationships with a sadism that was purely verbal. Marcel, thoroughly disheartened, managed to glimpse in this a truth that he would only understand much later, when writing *Sodome et Gomorrhe*; one day in March, he refused to explain himself: '. . . convinced that we are unable, at a certain level, to understand one another and furthermore not taking it all too tragically. The maxim "a word to the wise is enough" is too narrow-minded.'[65] Montesquiou had debased 'the most touching devotion and sincere affection', he had been responsible for 'an everlasting misunderstanding' between them.

Proust, however, had devoted a little-known prose poem to the count's psyche, written in the neo-symbolist style verging on parody that Montesquiou adopted. In this mirror, all that was reflected was 'the visionary sage', until the day when 'a distraught young woman rushed up to him. She wanted to know whether the red, white and blue ribbons that restrained her impure bosom "gave" (. . .) "shameful offence".'[66] This rare flash of misogyny must have drawn the two inverts closer to one another. To appease the count, Marcel made him gifts of a 'bluebird', a flowering cherry, probably a bonsai,[67] an eighteenth-century angel for a crib, a symbol of the 'angel' musician Delafosse.[68] A succession of quarrels and reconciliations followed; Marcel was unable to distance himself, either socially or emotionally, from the count, and the visits to his home in Versailles were the focus of everything he did. This culminated in the celebration held on 30 May, shortly after the soirée at Madeleine Lemaire's house on 22 May (when Marcel met Reynaldo Hahn for the first time).

The rather hazy picture we have of these musical evenings should not allow us to forget one which Marcel attended in Montesquiou's company: a performance on 14 January, at the Concerts Colonne, of the flower-girl scenes from *Parsifal*.[69] It is conceivable that the title of the novel that was to win the Prix Goncourt referred to this work, which Proust mentions on several occasions; in the drafts of *Sodome*, it is after the performance of this opera that the Narrator discovers that Charlus is homosexual, and, in those of *Le Temps retrouvé*, that he recognizes an involuntary memory. Finally, Charlus is depicted in *À l'ombre des jeunes filles en fleurs*: shades of Montesquiou are everywhere.

The party that Montesquiou threw at Versailles on 30 May 1894 gave Proust an opportunity for intense social and journalistic activity. In fact, he published two accounts of the occasion, the first of them in *Le Gaulois* of 31 May, under the byline 'Tout-Paris'; the other purported to be a 'gossip column', in *La Presse* of 2 June, in order to restore certain passages omitted from the earlier one. Marcel has himself described how he wrote the article: 'Throughout the day, I made notes of descriptions of dresses, all of which were revised and corrected by the most elegant women.' Unfortunately, the proofreaders at *Le Gaulois* distorted his text: 'Instead of a detailed description of Sarah Bernhardt's dress, there were vague banalities, Mlle Bartet's periwinkles were transformed into cornflowers through a metempsychosis that was as daring but less harmonious than that which earned Delafosse your Muse's kiss.'* Proust's article, 'Une fête littéraire à Versailles',[70] described the setting first: at the far end of the railings on the Avenue de Paris, a pavilion, a red carpet in front of the door, flowers strewn on the ground; from an orchestra in a copse there 'murmurs sweet music'. 'At the entrance, pleasant, smiling and kindly, the lord of this peaceful abode received the guests he had invited.' A theatre had been erected in the garden; it is '*éphémère*' (F. M. R., the reversed initials of Robert de Montesquiou-Fezensac), and decorated with colonnades. Then the public, the 'Tout-Paris': first Marcel described the Comtesse Greffulhe, faithful to the mauve beloved of her cousin ('the dress is made of pink lilac silk, trimmed with orchids, and covered with silk muslin of the same shade, the hat adorned with orchids and overlaid with lilac-coloured taffeta'). There followed a list of twenty-three guests, among whom were some of Proust's future relatives, friends or models:

* *Corr.*, vol. I, p. 300. An allusion to a poem by Musset, in which the Muse says to the poet: 'Take your lute and give me a kiss'; is a discreetly erotic game being played here? For his descriptions, Proust is said to have consulted Mme de Pourtalès, Mme d'Hervey, Mme Aiméry de La Rochefoucauld, Mme de Brissac, Mlle Lemaire, Mme de Fitz-James. We can see how, thanks to these grand social occasions, Marcel is already making himself known to notable members of the aristocracy.

the Comtesse de Chevigné, Mme de Chaponay,* the Prince de Sagan ('who arrived in a steam-driven car with the Comte de Dion'), the Marquis du Lau, Charles Ephrussi,† Madeleine Lemaire, Barrès and his wife, the Daudets, Régnier, Béraud, Boldini, Tissot, Professor Dieulafoy, the Princesse de Brancovan, the Princesse Bibesco. After this catalogue of names, Proust described the soirée, in which performances of works by Bach, Chopin, Rubinstein and Lizst played by Delafosse are interspersed with recitals of poems by Coppée, Verlaine, Desbordes-Valmore, Chénier ('Ode à Versailles'), Leconte de Lisle, Heredia, and, naturally, works by the master of the house. The poems were read by Sarah Bernhardt (who was once in love with the count; it is said that their night together ended extremely badly), and the actresses Mlles Bartet and Reichenberg. After the interval – an opportunity to describe 'the Japanese greenhouse, with its rare flowers and delicate birds' and the buffet (courtesy of Potel and Chabot) – Delafosse accompanied Bagès, who sang songs composed by the pianist, based on poems by Montesquiou: 'It is over, the dream is ended. We must return to Paris (. . .) With what exquisite memories and with what regret we leave Versailles, the royal city, where, for a few hours, we could believe we were living at the time of Louis le Grand!'

The progress made by Proust since writing his social columns for *Le Mensuel* was considerable. He could now portray his surroundings, describe what went on and all the finery, he could evoke an historical atmosphere, and he could swan about among his future models. The material necessary for the composition of *Le Côté de Guermantes* was beginning to settle in his memory and in his imagination. The sketches and the 'characters', the studies and portraits which he was working on for *Les Plaisirs et les Jours* completed this training, providing at the same time a little objective analysis; what was still missing was a perception of the essence beneath the appearance, of history underlying the present moment, and the integration of social life in a fictional world, thanks to a plot that describes a failed conquest. 'Noms de personnes' would be the title of the first part of *Le Côté de Guermantes*; the 124 names from 'Une fête littéraire à Versailles' would one day merge with those in Balzac and Saint-Simon to relate a grand dream amidst a little reality.

What is more, Marcel had not renounced poetry. Apart from the poem 'Mensonges', he wrote two quatrains in Alexandrine form, a portrait of

---

* One of the models for Mme de Villeparisis.

† Critic and art-lover who is said to be one of the models for Swann.

Antoine Watteau, in the style of 'La Fête chez Thérèse' or of Verlaine: 'The dust of kisses from worn lips . . ./ What is indistinct becomes affectionate, and what is close at hand, distant.' In this same month of May there followed a comic episode in Proust's military career: as 'assistant administrative officer second-class in the regular army reserves' he was ordered to carry out a four-week period of instruction at the military hospital of Saint-Martin. Marcel would never carry out any period of instruction, because on 20 May he had an attack of breathlessness that lasted twenty-four hours.[71] At the end of June, during his parents' absence, Proust planned to give a dinner at home, to which he invited Montesquiou, the count's secretary, Yturri, and Anatole France, no doubt in order to ask forgiveness for still not having been able to place his phantom article (in an image which would be used again at a crucial turning-point in *Le Temps retrouvé*, he compared it to all the doors at which one knocks remaining unopened).[72] Marcel thanked the count, hoping that he would continue for a long time to be good to him,[73] but it was a disappointed friend who discovered that Montesquiou had been ill and had not said anything: 'I should have taken infinite pleasure in keeping you company, in bringing you herbal teas, replying to those who asked for news of you, reading aloud to you, plumping your pillow or bringing you a blanket, observing the impressions that illness might have on you. I would have brought you flowers . . .'[74] Friendship hovers here between 'voluntary servitude', filial piety, and the need to attract and to be loved: Marcel could not cope without Montesquiou and he adopted Gabriel de Yturri as mediator. Yturri was a former vendor of ties and cravats who had been transformed by Montesquiou into his secretary, confidant and master of ceremonies. Totally devoted to his master, his death would leave him inconsolable. The poet would then dedicate his book *Le Chancelier de fleurs* to him. So here was Marcel, obliged to pay court, not just to the inflexible count, with his lightning flashes of temper and largesse,[75] but to Yturri as well: 'I cannot tell you how much I am touched by your friendship, which is precious to me. I hope you will never cease fulfilling – with so much grace, power and charm – this role of intermediary between M. de Montesquiou and myself.'[76] These thoughts kept returning to the poet, who had departed for Saint-Moritz, when, on 11 August, Proust went for a walk with Anatole France in Versailles – the Versailles that he would evoke in *Les Plaisirs et les Jours*.

AUTUMN AT VERSAILLES

Proust's Versailles was not that of Louis XIV, but that of Montesquiou, who lived in the town for a time, at the Pavillon des Muses, gave parties there and described it in his poems. We should therefore view the writing of 'Versailles', in which Marcel described an autumn walk, as homage to the poet of *Les Perles rouges*: 'How often did I go to drink to the dregs, ecstatically (one notes the rare intensity of feeling), the bitter, intoxicating sweetness of those sublime autumnal days.' The name Versailles, which he did not hesitate to utter in the wake of so many others – Barrès, Rénier, Montesquiou[77] – and which prompted a reverie to which Proust would often return, was 'rusty and sweet'.[78] In his posthumous writings, Marcel recalled this walk, or one like it, and peppered it with quotations from *Les Perles rouges*: 'On my way back I thought of the poet whose noble countenance (. . .) had led me on this walk.'[79] So began a series of evocations which run through *À la recherche* as well as through *Les Plaisirs et les Jours*: the Tuileries made Marcel think of Versailles, whether because the sky reminded him of that above the royal burgh depicted in a painting by Van der Meulen, or because Albertine went there for a walk, on her own or with the Narrator, or, again, because the Princesse de Guermantes had a town house there.[80] A place of poetry, the home of the red chestnut tree, a town that was dilapidated and cursed, Versailles passed into Proust's œuvre as a result of his visits to Montesquiou and, as we shall see, on account of a long stay at the Hôtel des Reservoirs. Reynaldo Hahn also fell in love with the town, which he evoked in *Notes*, and to which, under the title 'Versailles', he devoted four pages of *Le Rossignol éperdu*.[81]

In July 1894, in anticipation of his forthcoming book, for which he still had no publisher, Marcel wrote his long dedication, which was the length of an introduction, to his dead friend Willie Heath. Since he mentions the portrait of the Duke of Richmond attributed to Van Dyck, 'one of the works he most admires', it is likely that he wrote his poem about the painter at this time:[82]

> Tu triomphes, Van Dyck, prince des gestes calmes,
> Dans tous les êtres beaux qui vont bientôt mourir.*

These pages include valuable insights into the privileges of illness, which

---

* Your triumph, Van Dyck, prince of the quiet gesture,/ Is in all the handsome creatures who will soon die.

allow one to feel closer to one's true self: 'When I was very young, no character in scripture struck me as being quite so wretched as Noah, because of the flood which kept him shut up in the ark for forty days. Later, I was frequently ill, and for days on end I was also obliged to remain inside "the ark". It was then that I understood that nowhere could Noah have a better view of the world than from the ark, even though it was enclosed and night ruled over the earth.' His mother, who never left him during his illness, like the dove in the ark, then 'never came back', or rather, she switched from tenderness to strictness: 'It was necessary to start to live again, to turn away from oneself, to listen to words that were harsher than my mother's; worse still, her words used, always so gentle up till then, were no longer the same, but were marked with the severity of life and its duties which I was to learn from her.'[83] It is an astonishing confession, an astonishing public incrimination of Mme Proust, who asserts her invisible presence in the future collection of stories just as she does in 'Combray'. The dove from the ark, the image of the Holy Ghost – does it not reappear in the title 'The Cloven Doves',* which Marcel had briefly considered as a title for *À la recherche*, as well as in the threatened birds, those symbols of eternity, at St Mark's in Venice, in *Albertine disparue*? To be ill, in any case, is to be protected, consoled, loved. With good health, life's cruel obligations are restored: 'One makes so many commitments in life that the time comes when, disappointed at never being able to keep them all, one turns towards the grave, one summons death, death which comes to the aid of destinies that are having difficulty fulfilling themselves.'[84] This would occur in November 1922.

THE CHÂTEAU DE RÉVEILLON

During the month of August, Marcel read *Anna Karenina*: this is what gives a Tolstoyan inflection to certain passages in *Les Plaisirs et les Jours*, such as 'La Mort de Baldassare Silvande'. However, in the pamphlet *The Christian Spirit and Patriotism*, which had just been translated, Tolstoy denounced the Franco-Russian celebrations and tried to demolish the notion of patriotism, while at the same time maintaining that the people

---

* R. Hahn (*Notes*, p. 139) describes the 'cloven doves' seen at the Jardin d'Acclimatation and at the Tuileries (with Marcel?) which, 'with their red wound that seemed as if it was still warm, looked like nymphs who had committed suicide for the sake of love and which a god had turned into birds'.

were only interested in socialism; in response Proust wrote a note, which remained unpublished during his lifetime, asserting some of his own political and moral views: patriotism, on the contrary, was a source of disinterestedness, it subjugates selfish instincts in favour of altruism. War itself derived a moral quality from the aspect that astonished Tolstoy: the absence of hatred among people who are fighting 'because of duty' (we find this view espoused by Saint-Loup in *Le Temps retrouvé*). In a world of Justice and Love, one cannot, as the anarchists did, make Charity triumph through violence: 'All existing riches could equally well be shared out through force. Never would Justice be so far from reigning on earth. Anti-Semites, by being violent, spreading slander and behaving in an exclusive way, could convert the world through force to Catholicism. That day, the world would be dechristianized, for Christianity manifests the inner God, the truth that is desired by our heart, endorsed by our conscience.'[85] The student of philosophy here revealed the rigour of his thought, his moral and patriotic feelings, and, in politics, his liberal conservatism (which we shall see developed at the time of the Dreyfus affair).

On 18 August Marcel left for the Château de Réveillon,[86] where Madeleine Lemaire had invited him to stay for a month. There he encountered Reynaldo Hahn again; their friendship deepened. In *Jean Santeuil*, the Château de Réveillon features under its own name,[87] and Hahn is Henri de Réveillon (the initials are the same in reverse: HR, RH). Much later,[88] Hahn would relate how Marcel was brought up short in front of a rose bush: the same incident appears in *Jean Santeuil*, before the flowers were transformed into the hawthorn trees in 'Combray'. The roses from this bush exude the same perfume as do the vases in the drawing-room 'at Uncle Jean's house': 'The pleasure that Jean then experienced came as much from himself as from the rose bush. Henri was aware of it and moved away to leave him more at ease, more able to delve into himself to find all the things he was reminded of by this scent.' Marcel went for walks in the park, talked to Loute, the dog belonging to the mistress of the house,[89] and struck up a friendship with Suzette Lemaire who, like her mother, painted flowers; meanwhile Mme Lemaire was able to show Marcel the first illustrations for his book.[90] Suzette showed great kindness to Marcel during this visit, and in September, when she was feeling sad at finding herself alone at Trouville, he wrote a letter to her: 'I managed to sleep last night and that hasn't happened to me for a long time . . . whenever I awoke I felt your dear little hands, so cool and deft, pressed to my forehead and I can assure you it was not unpleasant . . . I restore them to you in the shape of permitted kisses in return for all the good they have done me.'* Once again, Marcel played at flirting with a young girl; it may have been a case of disguising his relationship with Reynaldo, perhaps, too, of treating Suzette as a confidante (as Andrée does with Albertine) while at the same time pleasing the mother; the expressions he used were characterized by what they omitted: 'My dear little Mademoiselle Suzette, kindest of women and the only intelligent girl, my good little Mademoiselle Suzette, my little mother, my darling little sister, don't be cross with me.'[91] If, for Marcel, every woman of Madeleine Lemaire's age represented his mother, Suzette became a sister, someone in whom he could confide, with whom he could give or receive signs of affection, but with 'no expectation of carnal pleasure' – without risk.

Reynaldo's company inspired Marcel to write 'Mélomanie de Bouvard et Pécuchet', the second part of his Flaubert pastiche, between nine o'clock and a quarter to ten one evening when he did not feel like going to bed.[92] This piece of bravura mainly demonstrates the breadth of the author's musical culture, which ranges from *Domino noir* (a symbol of vulgarity in *À la recherche*) to César Franck, from Gounod to Verdi, Beethoven to Satie, from Bach to Saint-Saëns, Massenet and Chausson. At the core of the pastiche is Wagner (as he is at the heart of *La Prisonnière*). Bouvard's comment may be trite, but is none the less true: 'The illusion of the stage is necessary, as is the burying of the orchestra, and the darkness in the auditorium.' Nevertheless, he regards the youthful operas, *Lohengrin* and *Tannhäuser*, with disdain and he salvages *Rienzi*, only because 'to denounce it has become banal'. And when he asserts that 'Saint-Saëns lacks substance and Massenet form' (while Pécuchet does the opposite), he makes an important point. The funniest part of the pastiche is the allusion to Reynaldo Hahn (already touched upon in the discussion about Wagner, whose work Reynaldo disliked, and about whom there must have been discussions at the château, as a letter to Suzette Lemaire demonstrates): Bouvard and Pécuchet criticize 'his intimacy with Massenet' (whose pupil he is), his admiration for Nerval, and his name: the Teutonic sonorities

---

* *Corr.*, vol. I, pp. 337–8, 25 or 26 September 1894. P. Kolb points out that in 'La Mort de Baldassare Silvande', which Proust had just written, this becomes: 'Supernatural as a madonna, gentle as a nurse, I adored you and you soothed me. I loved you with a tenderness in which no expectation of carnal pleasure would trouble our delicate sagacity. In exchange, did you not offer me an incomparable friendship, exquisite tea, conversation that was naturally refined, and so many bunches of freshly cut roses. Only you, with your expressive, maternal hands knew how to cool my burning, fevered brow' (*P et J*, p. 19; the last words are a quotation from Montesquiou).

of the name of Hahn and the southern resonances of Reynaldo lead them to condemn him 'as hating Wagner rather than absolving him in favour of Verdi'. Pécuchet then discusses *Die Walküre* in the tones of M. de Norpois: 'That *Die Walküre* is popular even in Germany, I very much doubt . . . But, to French ears, it will always be the most infernal of tortures – and the most cacophonic! . . . Furthermore, does this opera not combine all that is most appalling about dissonance with all that revolts us most about incest?' Other friends of Proust are victims of the pastiche: Montesquiou and Delafosse, for example. Does the latter 'not compose songs about bats, in which the composer's extravagance will compromise the long-standing reputation of the pianist? Why did he not choose a pleasant bird? . . . It happens too in M. de Montesquiou's poetry, the fantasies of a blasé nobleman, let us admit . . . but put to music! When shall we have a "Requiem for Kangaroos"?' Never had Marcel carried his taste for ironic imitation, for eccentric mockery, or even his declaration of serious aesthetic principles[93] beneath an appearance of burlesque, quite so far. A great comic writer was being born.

It was at this point that Reynaldo gave Marcel his photograph, taken at the piano, in his apartment on the rue du Cirque: on the back of it were inscribed the first notes of his song based on Verlaine's poems (*Green*): 'Here is some fruit, some flowers, some leaves and some branches,/And then here is my heart, which beats only for you.'[94] From Réveillon, Reynaldo Hahn wrote to his friend, the pianist Édouard Risler (whom Proust would later invite to give recitals at the Ritz), that he had made the acquaintance of Marcel Proust, 'a charming boy, a literary man who, astonished to find a musician able to talk about literature . . . developed a great affection for him'.[95] These same qualities enabled the musician to acquire the respect of Mallarmé. On 21 April Marguerite Moreno would read an 'introduction' written by the poet for a concert of his work: 'Reynaldo Hahn has the gift of putting what he sees, intuitively, into music: you can imagine him, just recently, looking at paintings, at those in the Louvre, with the eye of a connoisseur, paintings that he hangs tacitly in the memory with such authority; for painting restores to this visionary an intuitive sense of line, light, colours, the piece of orchestral music that, primarily, it is . . . Besides drawing out the poetry that lies in everything, here he is tackling – and with such audacity too – poems that exist in the strict or literary sense, and, what is more, doing so triumphantly; there is nothing else, he perceives the heavenly chorus that is inscribed in the stanzas, which he arranges and reveals . . . These discreet sounds, these fits of swooning, in which the soul is present, reveal our rapture in reading.'[96] No one could express better the fact that Reynaldo, a musician, painter and writer, was familiar with all the arts.

REYNALDO HAHN

When Marcel met Reynaldo Hahn[97] at Madeleine Lemaire's house, this eighteen-year-old boy (he was born on 9 August 1875) had already composed some important pieces of music. His background was unusual: his mother, Elena Maria Echeneguacia (1831–1912), was Venezuelan and a Catholic; his father, Carlos Hahn, born in Hamburg of a Jewish family, had settled in Caracas, where he made a fortune in business, introduced the railway, telegraph and gas lighting, and founded an opera house. The couple would have twelve children, of whom ten survived. One of Reynaldo's sisters, Maria, would marry the painter and well-known collector Raymond de Madrazo. The Hahn family emigrated to Europe in 1877 as a result of political upheavals. Reynaldo would never return to Venezuela. The family set up home in Paris at 6 rue du Cirque. After the death of his father in 1897, the young man lived at 9 rue Alfred-de-Vigny.[98] By the age of five, Reynaldo played the piano extremely well; at the age of eight, he was composing; almost every evening his father would take him to the Opéra-Comique. At six, he played and sang Offenbach songs at the home of the Princesse Mathilde. He entered the Conservatoire when he was ten; noteworthy among his teachers were Lavignac, who wrote the famous *Voyage à Bayreuth*, and in particular Massenet; among his friends, Cortot, Ravel and Risler.[99] He displayed exceptional gifts of improvisation; 'We took lessons from an adorable teacher with much enthusiasm,' he would say of Massenet, his Darlu, who taught him 'not merely music, which can scarcely ever be taught, but life, which cannot be taught'. Aged fifteen, Hahn wrote his celebrated song *Si mes vers avaient des ailes*. Between the ages of thirteen to eighteen, he wrote the songs for his first collection, those that are best known, which were published in 1891; it was these songs, as well as Fauré's, among them *Les Présents* (based on a poem by Villiers de L'Isle-Adam), which Reynaldo sang to Marcel.

With his fine brown hair, his velvety, sparkling eyes, his little moustache (in short, the sort of looks that always appealed to Marcel), and with his artistic and literary gifts, Reynaldo won over the young dancer Cléo de Mérode when he was sixteen, just as Proust did Laure Hayman. At the time he met Marcel, Reynaldo had also written some incidental music for

Alphonse Daudet, who came to be very fond of him ('Papa's little Reynaldo', Lucien Daudet would say), and a comic opera adapted from *Le Mariage de Loti*, entitled *L'Île du rêve*. Proust did his best to give him some advice on the finer details of this work.[100] It would be incorrect to claim, as does one of Proust's biographers,[101] that Hahn was Saint-Saëns' 'lover'; the manner in which he wrote about the composer in *Notes* at this period does not for a moment allow us to suppose this. A recent publication even shows Saint-Saëns encountering Reynaldo and Marcel on the terrace at Saint-Germain and mistaking the latter for the former, whom he knew only through his music[102]. . . Equally, a scene in which Saint-Saëns behaved rudely towards Reynaldo discredits this hypothesis: one day, at Madeleine Lemaire's salon, the maestro delivered an affront to Hahn for which he was never forgiven. Someone had asked Saint-Saëns whether Reynaldo could sing one of his songs; he replied: 'Let him sing his own music if he wishes, but leave mine alone.'[103] Furthermore, Reynaldo had a melancholy temperament; his letters show him to be unhappy about everything, sometimes neurotically so; the failure of some of his compositions, especially his operas, must, after his early successes, have reinforced these tendencies. They explain what has not been noticed until now: namely, that the comic, satirical, burlesque tone of the correspondence between Reynaldo and Marcel belonged to the latter, who wished to amuse his friend and make him relax.

Highly gifted as a composer of songs, in his early works Hahn displayed harmonic weaknesses that help explain his dislike of Wagner and Debussy. At its best, the piano 'creates an acoustic halo of rare accomplishment to surround the voice: he carries and envelops it . . .'[104] We can thus imagine the impassioned discussions between the two young men (which are reflected in 'Mélomanie de Bouvard et Pécuchet') beneath the shade of the trees on Madeleine Lemaire's estate. Hahn wrote of this visit in his letters: 'Réveillon, an interesting and artistic old house; delightful company; Mme Lemaire smiling, her daughter Suzette obliging . . . Delafosse lissom; Proust enraptured and absent-minded, a first-rate fellow, a musician who thrills like an Aeolian harp at all the scattered harmonies; myself laughing. Fine, succulent cooking. I work very little and dream a great deal – dreaming being life's only real pleasure.'[105] One clings to this image of an enraptured, absent-minded Proust, who is no doubt dreaming only of rose bushes, and who is as much a musician as the composer himself. As for Reynaldo's laughter, it disguised his melancholy mood, which was the abiding tone not only of his diary, but of his character too.

This, then, was the composer who performed at those matinées which Proust would return to, on Sundays, after the First World War, to listen to him sing and play the piano. A witness would observe Marcel there, stuffing himself with little cakes.[106] Reynaldo left behind an important literary output: a biography of Sarah Bernhardt, fragments of a private diary (*Notes*) and some books on music: *Du chant*, which he dedicated in February 1921 'To My Dear Marcel, to my little and big Marcel',[107] *Thèmes variés* and *L'Oreille au guet*, an anthology of some of his musical criticism. If Reynaldo inspired the great passion in Proust which we encounter in 'Un amour de Swann', he does not appear under his own name, and nor does his work, in *À la recherche du temps perdu* (except when Cottard, during the 1914–18 war, dresses in an admiral's uniform that might have come out of *L'Île du rêve*, which is paltry homage!): not one waltz, no song, no opera. A letter from Proust to a mutual friend, Suzette Lemaire, in 1895 shows what it was that divided them. And this discourse highlights two different philosophical views of music.

For Reynaldo Hahn, music was the expression, almost the imitation, of feeling. It was purely psychology. This was why, for him, the most important music was vocal music (*Du chant*, 1913). It was music that was modelled on the word, and what is more he wrote wonderfully for it (for the stage – *Mozart*, *Ciboulette*, *La Carmélite*, *Ô mon bel inconnu* – as well as in his songs); his greatest admiration was for Massenet (to whom Proust, moreover, had written) or Saint-Saëns. For Proust, from now on, 'the essential purpose of music is to awaken in us the mysterious depths of our soul (which cannot be expressed by literature, nor, more generally, by all those finite modes of expression that rely either on words and hence ideas, to define things, or on defined objects – painting and sculpture –) – depths that begin at the point where what is finite, and all art that has the finite as its objective, stop; the point at which science, too, stops, and which may thus be described as religious'.[108] For the one, music explained particular feelings and adhered to the words. For the other, it was what language could not express, a wordless communication with consciousness, a link with the absolute.

It is true that at the age of fifteen Marcel had singled out 'Mozart and Gounod' as his favourite composers, and had heard Mme Catusse sing 'the divine songs of Massenet and Gounod'.[109] But when he discovered Wagner, the irrational – which does not mean the inhuman – surged forth into his musical world, and Hahn could not accept this. They concurred, however, in their liking for 'bad music', for music-hall and the songs of

Mayol, Yvette Guilbert and Bruant, about whom Reynaldo would write better than anyone in his books. A same love of song made them appreciate Fauré. Marcel admitted to Pierre Lavallée, in September 1894, that he adored *La Bonne Chanson*, the score of which he had just read (the first performance would be given at Suzette Lemaire's home on 26 March 1895, after Bagès, who had lent Marcel some of Fauré's manuscripts, including this one, had sung from it at the home of the Comte and Comtesse de Saussine): 'Apparently, it is unnecessarily complicated, etc., and very inferior besides. Bréville and Debussy (who is said to be a far greater genius than Fauré) are of this opinion. This makes no difference to me, I adore this work and, in fact, the songs I do not like are the very ones they pretend to prefer.'[110] Later, in 1902, as a homage to Proust's literary tastes, Hahn would compose *Les Muses pleurant la mort de Ruskin*, which he would dedicate to his friend.[111]

TROUVILLE, MOONLIGHT AND 'BALDASSARE'

An accident momentarily drew a cloud of sadness over these holidays: Robert Proust fell off his bicycle – he was riding a tandem with a girlfriend – and a cart, filled with coal, ran over his thigh. Mme Proust travelled down to Rueil to see him; the room was filled with hospital interns and colleagues; her husband returned from Vichy where he was taking his annual cure. The patient also had at his bedside 'the little tart who was looking after him', wrote Marcel, in 1915;[112] Robert had a delightful time at Rueil, mixing in society, and he recovered miraculously, so well, in fact, that by the middle of September his mother and older brother were able to depart for the Hôtel des Roches Noires at Trouville. Marcel went on walks with the Straus family, dined with Porto-Riche, met Gustave Schlumberger, the great historian of Byzantium* (who is seen occasionally at the homes of Brichot and 'the historian of the Fronde'), the Princesse de Monaco (the model for the Princesse de Luxembourg), and the Marquise de Galliffet, Mme Arthur Baignères' first cousin. Fortunately, social life, which slowed down in September, did not satisfy Marcel; the weather was delightful and he wrote some 'moonlit' pieces, in the style of Reynaldo:[113]

---

* 'On a stool, at the feet of Mme Geneviève Straus, one saw constantly the strange figure of Marcel Proust, still an adolescent, who, since then, has written books that are admired by some, but which to others, myself among them, are incomprehensible' (G. Schlumberger, *Mes souvenirs, 1844–1928*, Plon, 1934, vol. I, p. 305, and *Corr.*, vol. I, p. 237).

'Sonate clair de lune' and 'Comme à la lumière de la lune'.[114] The sonata, a subtle homage to Beethoven and to Hahn, described a walk, a dream, a sentimental conversation. The homage to the moon follows on from Chateaubriand, Baudelaire, Musset and Verlaine. But its obsessions were very much Marcel's, and they betray a sense of persecution: 'I heard my father scolding me, Pia making fun of me, my enemies hatching plots and none of it seemed real.' Should we not recognize, beneath Assunta's foreign Christian name, another, masculine name? 'Assunta's company, her singing, her gentleness to one whom she knew so slightly, her pale, pink and brown beauty (. . .) had distracted me.' When night has fallen, Assunta places her coat over the narrator and puts her hand around his neck; filled with the moon's tears, the couple weep, too: 'My heart saw clearly into her heart.' The second story describes love rather more discreetly than in this lovers' jaunt, as if to exorcize it; it is a love that is extinguished by a frightening lapse of memory; the melancholy tone, in which past happiness is mingled with sorrow, is very much Reynaldo's: 'This dusk light, this golden, fading light of spring evenings, both saddens and delights me. Countless memories hover there. And then, this light is so *commemorative*.'[115] We shall come across the moonlit nights that the two friends spoke of, that Marcel endeavoured to portray as the essential motif for a painter, throughout *À la recherche du temps perdu*, from 'Combray' to *Le Temps retrouvé*.

An important short story, 'La Mort de Baldassare Silvande', which Proust placed at the beginning of *Les Plaisirs et les Jours*, dates from this period. When it appeared in magazine form, it was dedicated to 'Reynaldo Hahn, poet, singer and musician':* 'I am working on something big, which I think is quite good,' Marcel wrote from the Hôtel des Roches Noires to Reynaldo, 'and I shall take the opportunity to cut from my book the story about Lepré and the opera, etc., which you are having copied', that is to say 'L'Indifférent', which would be used twice. 'Baldassare' is the story of a 37-year-old aristocrat, a musician by vocation, who is dying of paralysis. Certain characteristics, on the surface anodyne enough, but which reappear in the course of Proust's life and his work, deserve to be noted: the viscount has eyes that are 'sad and which, even in moments of

---

* It appeared in *La Revue hebdomadaire* of 29 October 1895, and the author was paid 150 francs. The dedication to R. Hahn was suppressed in book form. Proust's original plan was to dedicate the 'Principal stories or poems' in *Les Plaisirs et les Jours* 'to masters whom [he] admires or to friends whom [he] loves' (*Corr.*, vol. I, p. 239, 18 September 1894). The epigraphs for 'Baldassare' will, however, be taken from Emerson, Mallarmé, Mme de Sévigné, Shakespeare (*Macbeth*, *Hamlet*): the observance of friendship made way to that of culture.

happiness, seem to implore consolation for the wrongs that do not appear to affect him'. The eyes of Marcel, of Reynaldo, of Swann . . . Baldassare has a young nephew, who loved sitting on 'his knee, a place of refuge and of profound and sweet pleasure when he was younger'; a mistress, split between her sense of purity and her liking for pleasure, like Mlle Vinteuil: 'With a supreme effort she raised her eyes that begged for mercy towards him, at the same time as her eager mouth, in a movement of unconscious convulsion, asked once more to be kissed', while the hero appears to be keen on sadomasochism: 'Above all he closed his eyes as tight as he could, like an executioner overcome with remorse and who feels that his arm will tremble at the very moment he strikes his victim, if instead of imagining her being aroused by his anger and forcing her to appease his desires, he could watch her face to face and experience her pain for a moment.' Once the young woman has fallen asleep, Baldassare spends part of the night watching her, just as the Narrator does with Albertine. The landscape is one that recurs constantly at this time, with the mauve sea being glimpsed through apple trees. We come across peacocks out of Montesquiou's poems, the châteaux of Violante and of Réveillon, the fleeting image, among these aristocratic love-affairs, 'of a handsome lad of about fifteen years old'. The crucial moment is when distant village church bells remind the dying hero of his childhood: 'Throughout his life, as soon as he heard the distant sound of bells, he could not help but recall their sweetness in the evening air, when, still a child, he returned, across the fields, to the big house (. . .) He saw once more his mother as she kissed him when he came home, then when she put him to bed in the evening and warmed his feet in her hands, staying beside him when he was unable to sleep (. . .) Now there was no longer any time left for him to realize with what ardour his mother and sister, whom he had so cruelly deceived, had waited . . .'[116] Just as the Narrator of 'Combray' hears the church bells pealing in the evening air, mingled with his childhood tears, so the protagonist of this story reveals his involuntary memories, jumbled up with the sense of guilt he feels towards his mother: Baldassare has betrayed the vocation that his parents hoped he would have, for a reprehensible life of sex and worldliness. He is punished by death.

It has been said that in this story Proust owed everything to Tolstoy's *The Death of Ivan Illich* (1886).[117] Certainly, both are stories to do with illness and agony, both are about men who are racked with guilt, whose lives are almost over, who cling to memories of childhood, and who die reconciled to themselves. But, quite apart from how accomplished they are – for one cannot compare the genius of a 56-year-old with a beginner of twenty-three, a man who has for long confronted his obsessive fear of death with one who writes without having experienced it – the differences are more important than the similarities. Baldassare Silvande's life is a series of disconnected moments, into which Marcel has slipped his own obsessions, including the rapture of his final memories; in the case of Tolstoy, the hero must renounce his entire life in order to achieve peace. There is none of this profound, cruel, deeply moving and unsettling probing of the aging Tolstoy in 'Baldassare', but we can hear his muffled hammer blows in the death of Bergotte, a literary kinsman of Ivan Illich. Then Proust was no longer imitating, he had perfectly assimilated and reformulated one of his favourite writers. This story entranced Hahn, who admired it sufficiently to consider putting it to music.[118]

No sooner had he arrived at Trouville* than Marcel resorted to a curious ruse: he wished to entice Reynaldo Hahn there, but only after Mme Proust's departure: 'Since Mother will be leaving shortly you could come and console me after she has left.'[119] Otherwise, Marcel threatened to go and live 'at Étretat, at a friend's house'.† On 23 September, the eve of his mother's departure, Marcel, 'a little sad', returned to the offensive, promising a room with a view of the sea, next to his, at the same time demanding a speedy reply: 'So as not to make my waiting too restless do not leave the letter which you will have the kindness to write to me lying around in your pocket all week. I have received some letters from you which, instead of taking twelve hours to send have taken four days.'[120] Proust then endured the drama which he had experienced so often, that of being abandoned: his mother left, and Reynaldo did not come to take her place; he spent a sleepless night, could neither work nor go for a walk, and all he had as a distraction, 'sad (. . .) but most dear', was just one letter from his friend; so he requested another one, for his 'second day of solitude',[121] while at the same time trying to lure him down by mingling with the Strauses. This little scene, anodyne on the surface, reveals more about Marcel's psychology than do important events: a confessional note breaks through his feigned indifference, the appeal for sympathy is mingled with snobbery; but throughout these secret storms his intelligence stands

* 'Proust left yesterday for Trouville,' wrote Reynaldo Hahn, 'having spent the day with me. We went to the Louvre to see the Cuyps and Potters so as to remind ourselves of the conversations we had there!' – that is to say, at Réveillon. Cuyp and Potter are two painters whose 'portraits' he is composing.

† Léon Yeatman, whom Proust had known since the spring.

firm, whether Proust is expressing, in opposition to Hahn, his admiration for *Lohengrin*,[122] or whether he is advising him, clearly motivated by self-interest and apologetics, to read Plato's *The Banquet*.[123] Hahn is addressed as 'My dear friend' on 22 September, 'Dear Maestro' on the 24th, 'My dear little one' on the 25th; whatever Hahn may have thought, Proust's letters were no doubt a reflection of his own, but they were also evidence of an affection, increased by absence, for this person who, over the past weeks, had become more and more of 'an angel'.* For his part, Reynaldo noted, one day in 1894: 'I spent yesterday evening with Marcel . . . I would so like to help him to be more stable, rid him of some of his negative influences, drag him away from the pointless sort of life he likes to fall back upon. I think I'll succeed, for he has great trust in me – more than I deserve, I who am constantly battling to make myself more self-possessed.' And again: 'a deep and sensitive intelligence, a childlike sensibility, and a sweet and loyal kindness', or 'Our little Proust is very sincere, read his "Schumann", it's a masterpiece.'

'LA CONFESSION D'UNE JEUNE FILLE'

Proust was still thinking about his book and he asked Montesquiou's permission to dedicate a short story to him; the latter accepted, hoping that it would be 'the most beautiful of all'.[124] It was 'La Confession d'une jeune fille', which Proust would send to the count on 3 January 1895, promising him that he would be in the company of such other illustrious dedicatees as France and Heredia. This dedication,[125] which appeared in the proofs, was cut in the printed version, as were all the other dedications (though not the epigraphs). So this story dates from this very fertile summer, at the latest (it would replace 'Avant la nuit', but unlike the latter, was not published in *La Revue blanche*). The heroine, like that of 'Avant la nuit' and 'Souvenir' (in *Le Mensuel*), has tried to commit suicide, and is dying (like Baldassare Silvande and Tolstoy's heroes). She then remembers Les Oublis (which strongly resembles the Pré-Catelan at Illiers), where her mother sometimes spent the evening: 'She would come to bid me goodnight when I was in bed, an old custom which she had stopped,

---

* *Corr.*, p. 336, 25 or 26 September 1894, to Suzette Lemaire; as well as expressing his desire that their friendship should not go too far, his letter to her contains a literary credo which would not change: 'I have never written *one line* in order to write, but to express something which I cherished or gripped my imagination (. . .) I don't have a shred of self-esteem (unfortunately), not even as a writer . . .'

because it afforded me so much pleasure and so much sorrow: I was unable to go to sleep because I kept calling her back to say goodnight to me again, and eventually not daring to do so, which only made me feel that desperate need all the more – I would constantly be inventing new pretexts: my burning hot pillow which needed to be turned over, my frozen feet which only she could warm in her hands.'[126] Her mother shares this sadness at being apart, but she controls it, and conceals her affection, as did Mme Proust, beneath her 'usual coldness', which was very painful for her. Illness enables the heroine to claim a little more of her mother, who then behaves with 'sweetness and affection which are poured out at length without constraint or dissembling'. To be cured is agonizingly sad, because her mother leaves and resumes her strict, just and unforgiving mask. The young girl, aged fourteen, behaves badly with a young, fifteen-year-old male cousin, who is 'very devious', and who teaches her 'things that will make [them] shudder . . . with guilt and sensual joy'. Soon afterwards, the heroine confesses everything to her mother, who 'listens to her divinely without understanding her', and experiences a Tolstoyan happiness, tinged with the scent – which will permeate 'Combray' – of lilac; it is either a coincidence, or else Proust's taste for evoking the 'invisible and lingering lilac' must have been linked to a moment of confession – or at least emotional outburst – with his mother.* The young girl suffers from the disease which afflicts all Proustian protagonists, and which the young Marcel blamed himself for: procrastination, 'lack of will', that 'will' which the mother, said Proust in a remark worthy of Freud (though here the super-ego does not embody the father), 'had conceived and nurtured'. When, at the age of sixteen, the heroine falls in love with a 'perverse and wicked' young man, she becomes initiated into evil: but what love can be so criminal that it gives rise to such 'appalling remorse' and leads to confessions that are not understood, and that are eventually concealed by lies? What, if not homosexuality? Social life then serves as an alibi, but it brings with it a loss of interest in music, and of those moments of ecstasy in the countryside. 'I used to mix in society in order to calm myself down after having done something wrong, and as soon as I was calm again I would go wrong again': it is a 'suicide of the mind' and also 'the greatest of crimes against [her] mother'. In an attempt to change things, the heroine becomes engaged in order to please her sick

---

* 'What property did that morning smell of lilac possess that it should stifle so many fetid odours without blending with them or losing its fragrance?' (*P et J*, p. 88).

mother, when the drama breaks out in the crucial scene: under the influence of champagne, the girl yields to Jacques,[127] the young man who was responsible for her ill-spent past, and is caught in the act by her mother, who is watching from the balcony and who then falls down dead. Sensual pleasure is portrayed as 'a voluptuous and culpable act', and the 'body which indulges' displays the same ferocity as torturers do, in that it is detached from the heart or its soul, which experiences a 'sadness and an infinite desolation'. Being caught, by her mother, adds the fatal element and leads to the suicide of the girl, who only has a week to live.

However, it would be wrong, in the light of these pages, to imagine the young Marcel as a sickly youth, bloodless and *fin-de-siècle* in the manner of Des Esseintes. The young girl in 'La Confession' wants to pour out the joy she feels at having within her 'all this life ready to burst forth, to stretch out to infinity, among perspectives more vast and more magical than the farthest horizons of the forests and the sky', which she wishes she could reach in one bound.[128] The desire for conquest, the need to feel passionately, waiting for the hereafter, exhausting energies that are constantly renewed, tyrannical sexuality – all these stirred Marcel beneath the surface of his social, family or artistic life, among friends or at university – for he led all these lives simultaneously.

THE NEW TERM, 1894

Back in Paris once more, Marcel abandoned the idea of sitting his degree in October,* but resumed his social life and, thanks to Reynaldo, made the acquaintance of a remarkable woman, Mme Louis Stern. Born Ernesta de Herschel and originally from Trieste, she wrote lightweight novels under the pen-name of Maria Star. Her salon, at 68 rue du Faubourg-Saint-Honoré, was one of the most glittering of the period; the décor consisted of Italian Renaissance furniture, Persian carpets, oriental pottery, medieval Madonnas, Chinese horses and Hindu divinities, and it matched the personality of the mistress of the house. At a period when society was still very much compartmentalized, she gathered around her people from

---

* He wrote on 23 October to Mme de Brantes: 'I have been writing so much that it did not even occur to me to sit for the philosophy degree in October. I will do it in April at the earliest. However, I still do not know when you will receive – in the most lavish edition, intended especially for you – my little book, or rather my large book, for I have added so many new pieces.' Mme Lemaire, he added, had already done lots of drawings and begun the watercolours: 'It may all take a long time to produce' (*Corr.*, vol. II, p. 491).

the most diverse backgrounds: heads of state, artists, priests or Freemasons, over whom she ruled like a sorceress.[129] At the time of the Dreyfus affair, the novelist Paul Bourget was the only one to desert her. She had married the banker Louis Stern, who was also of Austrian origin. The Stern bank had been involved in the payment of the indemnity imposed by Bismarck in 1871, and later in the development of Tunisia. This salon, frequented by Reynaldo and Marcel, may also have been the inspiration for Mme Verdurin's.*

Although he would dine with his friends Lavallée, Yeatman, Hahn, Billy and Finaly, Marcel continued to visit Madeleine Lemaire's home. Then the group of friends would often go on to the theatre, where they saw *The Sycamore*, a comedy of manners by the contemporary English playwright Thomas Moore, and *La Barynia* by Judith Gautier, who adapted Indian, Chinese or Japanese novels for the Russian stage.[130] These plays, long forgotten, are evidence of the appeal the theatre had had for Marcel ever since childhood, which he shares with the Narrator of *À la recherche*, as he stands dreaming in front of the theatre posters, or on his way to hear la Berma in *Phèdre*. Proust himself used to go to see extravaganzas such as *Cendrillon* at the Châtelet[131] or *Le Pied de mouton* at the Eden-Théâtre, as well as *Mimi* at the Vaudeville, Darzens' *L'Amante du Christ* at the Théâtre-Libre,[132] or *Mignon* at the Opéra-Comique. In later years, his health prevented him from going to the theatre regularly, but he did go to see the Ballets Russes, and *Le Martyre de saint-Sébastien*, after 1910. As we have seen, Marcel's tastes extended to music-hall and the coarsest of dramas; surprisingly, he went to see rather more light plays than avant-garde ones. However, he attended the première of Verdi's *Othello* (in French, since everything in Paris was sung in French). What use would he make of all this? Who could have foreseen that the now vanished type of entertainment known as the spectacular, which Proust was so fond of, would be invoked in one of the most beautiful metaphors of *À la recherche*, that of the kitchen-maid and the asparagus at the 'masked ball' in *Le Temps retrouvé*, where the theatrical spectacular was transformed into a verbal spectacular?

That same autumn, Marcel, who had now written almost all the pieces which would constitute *Les Plaisirs et les Jours*, applied himself to trying to get the book published by Calmann-Lévy, with the help of Anatole France

---

* It was at Mme Stern's home that Marcel panicked at not finding Reynaldo there, just as Swann does with Odette (*Corr.*, vol. I, p. 380, 26 April 1895). Her salon was one of their meeting-places (ibid., p. 346). The Pallas-Stern Bank closed, sadly, in 1995.

(who was published by them), and by approaching a member of the Orléans family (which irritated Madeleine Lemaire, who felt she was being bypassed or, since her illustrations were not yet ready, that she was being rushed). He tried to make allowances for Madeleine and Suzette Lemaire by counterattacking in a way that reveals his true character and his clear-sightedness about himself: 'Don't tell me I am touchy and susceptible. Don't tell me, not because it's untrue – it is true – but because I know it already. It is true that I only behave like this with the people I like. You will tell me that that's a fine present to give them and I would do better to be like that among people I dislike. But what makes you think that we like people in order to please them? We like people because we cannot do otherwise.'* Very often the things that Marcel said and did risked alienating him from his friends. For example, so as to be seen in a good light by Mme de Cavaillet, he decided to tell her that Fernand Gregh did not like Anatole France's novel *Le Lys rouge* (and, doubtless, that he thought it was scandalous too); he then asked her to excuse Gregh, when she did not understand what was going on, and, finally, he had to put up with Gregh going about saying that 'Marcel repeats everything', which was what people were also saying in Paris.† The rumours and the gossip, which Marcel loved, occasionally rebounded on him. In any event, he did not care to be cut short by Madeleine Lemaire. When Suzette had the feeling that Marcel was distancing himself from them, Reynaldo explained to her: 'His expansive nature leads him to be open-hearted and he then has to become more introverted so as to avoid the little things his delicate heart must dread.' Mme Lemaire snubbed him. When Marcel extolled Gustave Moreau's depth of intelligence and Mme Lemaire exclaimed, 'Now there's a real dullard!', he must have felt doubly hurt – both his pride and his intellect would have been offended.[133] We see here that Mme Lemaire and her dullards are the key to Mme Verdurin and to her 'bores'.

On 9 December Marcel and his brother went to the Conservatoire, where performances were so much more perfect than anywhere else, to listen to Beethoven's Fifth Symphony. In the review that he wrote for *Le Gaulois*, which appeared on 14 January 1895, Proust began by describing at length the audience – just as he would describe those at the musical

---

* *Corr.*, vol. I, p. 348, 1 November 1894; further on, he writes: 'I am still too young to know what it is that makes for happiness in life. But I already know that it is neither love nor friendship.'

† For example Mme Ganderax, who called him 'a traitor' (ibid., pp. 351–4).

recitals at the homes of Mme de Saint-Euverte or Mme Verdurin in *À la recherche*. The mood of the audience changed from 'languorous voluptuousness' to 'an almost warlike vivacity', from sadness to consolation: 'They all looked more beautiful than they had done earlier, stripped, as it were, of their particular surroundings, and sufficiently outside themselves to look as if they belonged to the distant past.' Music hypnotizes and transports these transformed individuals into another world. Marcel himself described the very physical manner in which he listened: 'The music, pounding like a substitute heart that had replaced my own, slowed or quickened the pulsating of the blood in my veins as it pleased – so much so that I sometimes felt as if I were about to faint and as if I were stagnating within myself.'[134] During a concert, one glimpsed both truth and beauty, even if it meant 'disowning one's soul' afterwards, whenever one had the habit or the desire. This exercise anticipated the structure that Proust would give to the concert that is his novel: the audience, the performers, the meaning of the work are unveiled gradually by the literary equivalent of the musical work suggested by the narrative, the invitation to another life, to another world, that is initially rejected.

THE PHILOSOPHY DEGREE

Philosophy had not been entirely forgotten. Marcel had private lessons with Darlu (it is pointless to deny this man's influence, when not only did he open his pupil's mind in his last year at the lycée, but continued to do so while he prepared for his degree), and, with Léon Yeatman, he attended Victor Egger's courses at the Sorbonne. One of Egger's notebooks, in which he jotted down his assessment of an essay Proust wrote on 'Socrates' philosophy', has been preserved: 'Difficult to read, "English" handwriting* and, especially, lack of paragraphs . . . Written in one entire block, with hardly a space to distinguish between two sections. Intelligent, though. Made use of Boutroux, but others too, and has understood everything.'[135] His mark was 11. In March 1895, in his final exam, the written subjects, which give some idea of the content of the courses, dealt with 'The Unity and Diversity of the Self' (Janet), 'Descartes' Opinion on some Ancients' (Boutroux); the marks Egger gave were 6, 12–10, 14 (possibly a double correction). Marcel passed, after taking the oral examination, coming

---

* Proust's handwriting was 'backhand' [Known as '*écriture anglaise*']: it sloped from left to right.

twenty-third with 118 points;[136] his friends Jean Bazaine and Yeatman failed.

In his lessons, as well as covering the course work, Darlu had impressed on Marcel the notions of faith in the human spirit, Kantian idealism, belief in a 'thing in itself', in a reality hidden behind appearances, and the rigours of analysis, which flew in the face of the misty imprecision dear to the Symbolists and sometimes to Bergson. This is what prevented Proust from being an inheritor of German Romanticism and the philosophy of Schelling and Schopenhauer. For him, as with Kant's French disciples, such as Darlu, Lachelier (*Le Fondement d'Induction*) or Boutroux, concepts were always lucid and defined, examples were precise, reasoning was flawless, the writing unostentatious since it was necessary to reject effects of style, obscure illusions and the alibi of imagery. From Darlu, Marcel inherited the spiritualism without God which was the creed of the Sorbonne at this period, as well as of *La Revue de métaphysique et de morale* and of the nascent Third Republic. Firstly, there was the conviction that ethics was at the heart of philosophy: Marcel had no religious faith, but he did hold moral convictions. *Les Plaisirs et les Jours* expresses the concepts of fault, of confession, of virtue and vice: 'The unity of human life', Darlu used to say, 'is achieved in actions. Therefore philosophy aspires necessarily to morality.'[137] It was probably through him that Proust discovered Carlyle and Emerson;[138] Darlu described *The Imitation of Christ* as 'the breviary of many contemporary thinkers', and in fact Proust borrowed the epigraphs for *Les Plaisirs et les Jours* from this book (following the example of his friend Lavallée). In the domain of politics, Darlu maintained that 'in order to love one's country properly, one must love something else as well'; equally, his pupil would not confuse patriotism with nationalism. The professor therefore imparted his moral, scientific and philosophical beliefs, but not his religious faith. In the stories written by Proust at this time, the subordination of love, which also derives from Darlu's thinking, implies a sentimental pessimism which in no way negates the optimism of knowledge. Reason was neither positivist nor mystical, asserted Darlu in his introduction-cum-manifesto for *La Revue de métaphysique et de morale*, which began to appear in January 1892; reason (and not intuition) rescues us from religiosity and scientism: Brunetière, for example, moved from the latter to the former. In March 1895 Darlu summarized in a few lines the teaching of the Sorbonne, where Proust had just been a student: 'For about twenty years now the professors of philosophy, with their differences of stress rather than of doctrine, have been demonstrating to the successive generations of distinguished young men they instruct the limits to the relativity of science, the independence of morality over science – and, in a sense, its superiority over it – the abstract and even symbolic significance of the material mechanism, the superior reality of moral freedom, and the unattractive and immoral character of material-ism.'[139] The individual and society are interdependent, but the latter cannot make the former think: 'No one hears the truth except within himself. No one can know it, if he does not discover it with a new face.'[140]

This philosophy complemented the teaching that Marcel had so loved when he read Paul Desjardins (*Le Devoir présent*, 1891): 'All those devoted servants of anything that existed outside of themselves, the city, religion, justice, truth or even beauty when conceived as an act of worship' were praised by this thinker (1859–1940). Desjardins had known Marcel in 1888, had made him study Heraclitus and Lucretius (he would compare Proust to both of them), and has left us, as we know, a picture of him at this time. When Marcel began lessons with Darlu, his memories of the philosophy class were rekindled. The novelist would draw on these two periods for the passages in *Jean Santeuil* about M. Beulier's class. In it he also related an astonishing little fable: for New Year's Day, M. Beulier says he has brought Jean a present, a work by Joubert (about whom Proust wrote a posthumous article), which he reads from for a couple of hours, and then takes the book away, instead of giving it to Jean: 'Having provided Jean with its meaning, the soul, the moral support, he had given him everything. Therein lay the priceless and pure gift.'[141] This may be the origin of Proust's disdain for the possession of books: when he needed a book, he borrowed it; or, if he bought it, he returned it soon afterwards to the bookshop: this was the case with *The Imitation of Christ*, as it was with Émile Mâle. He gives, but he never keeps.

This year of studying for his philosophy degree was just as vital for Proust's development as his emotional or social life. Unfortunately, the absence of precise documentation, other than the names of his teachers, some mention of the courses, the lectures, private lessons and examin-ations, has led to our underestimating this period. It was at this time, in response to a newly published quiz, that Marcel referred to 'his heroes in real life' as being 'M. Darlu, M. Boutroux'.[142] His favourite painters were Rembrandt and Leonardo, to whom Séailles, who taught aesthetics at the Sorbonne, devoted a work (*Léonard de Vinci*, 1892), based on his thesis, *Essai sur le génie de l'art* (1883). In a dissertation on 'the immortality of the soul', Marcel took his inspiration from the ideas of Ravaisson and Boutroux:[143] a letter of thanks from Bergson confirmed that Proust was already familiar with the work of Ravaisson,[144] and that he attended lectures given by Boutroux. When Marcel wrote that 'sensations are conscious facts. The laws that link them are laws of the spirit (. . .) it is the Spirit that structures matter. However far we may be from being able to transform the soul into material elements, we can reduce matter to psychological elements', he was concurring with the critics of empiricism and of Condillac, led by Ravaisson, Lachelier (for whom the outer world existed only in the conscience) and Boutroux: 'Consciousness is not a specialization, a development, or even a perfecting of our psychological functions. Nor is it an aspect or a product of them. It is a new element, a creation.'[145] Similarly, Marcel wrote in one of his essays: 'The spirit must be more than a phenomenological object. The idea of a phenomenon is itself something that is beyond the phenomenal. The whole does not lie in the phenomenon.' According to Boutroux, 'Multiplicity does not contain the reason for the whole.' Thought consists of thinking about things, of being aware of their unity and their identity: 'It is an action that consists of reducing the multiple to a whole, the successive to the identical.'[146] In trying to establish psychological laws, Proust was a disciple of French philosophy, and particularly of Boutroux, whose early work was all to do with the notion of natural or spiritual laws. Moreover our 'relatively free' individual thought is not 'an abstraction shared by all mankind', but rather, 'an activity which is peculiar to us' and which reconciles 'the multiplicity of phenomena in the unity of the spirit'. Marcel inherited this theme of freedom from Lachelier, via Darlu: it was, in fact, the intellectual sphere of *La Revue de métaphysique et de morale*.[147] But unlike Lachelier, Proust stressed the individual. He also believed, like Boutroux, that 'true knowledge would be that which encompasses the history of human beings, rather than their nature, which is only one stage in their historical development'. Also for Proust, knowledge would be historical in a double sense: the knowledge of history, and, subject to history, the shifting viewpoint on things and human beings which alter.

Marcel's timetable also included the lectures of Paul Janet (1823–99),[148] whose subject, 'The Unity and Identity of Self', would be one of the principal themes of Proustian philosophy. Séailles also gave lectures that year, but his influence on Proust, who only refers to him once (to quote his homage to Émile Mâle), has probably been exaggerated; he did, however, instil in his pupils the philosophy of art, and the author of 'Baldassare Silvande' knew Séailles' work on Leonardo. Something of this can be seen in Proust's article on 'Chardin et Rembrandt', written in 1895. Séailles held the view that in the depths of the spirit, 'the work of the unconscious continues the thought of the mind and is responsible for the sudden inspirations that overtake the consciousness of the artist', and that art is 'inspired contemplation'. In a work of art, Séailles saw the continuity of nature, which expressed itself through the individual; Proust soon declared that art was the result of an 'instinctive desire' which 'yearns to break free of man in the form of a work of art'.[149] The crucial moment, the vision, and contemplation would always matter more in the plot of *À la recherche*, in so far as it is the story of a vocation, than does technique: the doctrine of vitalism was penetrating French thought, from Séailles to Bergson (who quoted the former and admired his *Génie*).

ALPHONSE DAUDET

In December 1894 Marcel met Alphonse Daudet and his wife, possibly at the Baignères'; and at the end of the month Reynaldo took him to their home. As a result of this meeting the young man would develop a sincere affection for one of the great names of contemporary literature, the only writer he ever really knew who came close to being a realist; he also became friends with Daudet's two sons, Léon and Lucien. Something of this affection can be seen in the letter Marcel wrote to him in February 1895: 'I cannot tell you, Monsieur, how touched I am by your kindness. My fondest dreams as a child could not have held out a prospect as unlikely or quite so delightful as to be so graciously received one day by the Master who even then inspired in me passionate admiration and respect.'[150] The author of *Le Petit Chose* and *Jack* was first and foremost a novelist of childhood; his *Lettres de mon moulin* and *Tartarin de Tarascon* had enchanted Marcel's early youth. A few months later, however, Proust would admit that he did not share the same aesthetic viewpoint, and that he preferred the man to his work: 'Daudet is charming, the son of a Moorish king who might have married a princess from Avignon, but he's too simplistic in his intelligence. He believes that Mallarmé deliberately baffles people . . . Laziness or narrow-mindedness.' Marcel was invited by the Daudets to a dinner party in the company of Goncourt, Coppée and Hahn, and he was shocked by 'the appalling materialism, so extraordinary among intellectual people'. 'They consider that character and genius are attributable to physical habits or race*. . . Even more astonishing in

---

* This is very much what the Goncourts always did: *Manette Salomon* and the *Journal* are steeped in anti-Semitism.

Daudet, whose pure mind still shines through the mists and storms of his nerves, a small star upon the sea. It's all very unintelligent.'[151] Effectively, the realism of the writers present led them to explain the works of Musset, Baudelaire and Verlaine on the basis of their lives, and even 'the type of spirits they drank': Proust was already objecting to the explanation of a work by what was less important than it, in opposition to Goncourt and Daudet, before taking issue with Sainte-Beuve. Daudet may have only 'an acute power of observation and yet it smells musty, it is a little vulgar and too pretentious, in spite of his extreme subtlety'. Mme Daudet is charming, 'but how bourgeois': it was true that when Marcel thanked her when he was invited for the first time, she made the gaffe, for which he did not forgive her, of replying: 'M. Hahn asked me to do so.'[152]

Marcel was attracted to Daudet not merely because he wanted to add a famous man to his acquaintance, but because of an inkling of their common destinies, which he would describe two years later: 'He had scarcely taken to his bed than his pains became unbearable and, every evening, he [Daudet] swallowed a bottle of chloral in order to get to sleep. I could not understand, however, how he managed to continue to write. I particularly remembered how the pains I suffered, so slight compared to his that he would probably have looked upon them as a respite, had made me indifferent to other people, to life, to everything outside my own wretched body, upon which my mind remained obstinately fixed, just as a sick person in bed keeps his face turned against the wall.'[153] Proust, too, would learn how to conquer his pain so as to be able to write, and to welcome other people with the same kindness as Daudet.

Although Marcel was incapable of talking about Daudet's aesthetics, because nothing was more foreign to him than the naturalism of Zola, Daudet and the Goncourts, he formed a notion of him as a 'work of art', and thus, by a skilful manoeuvre, he could transfer to the man the qualities that he was unable to confer upon his books: Daudet was the antithesis of Bergotte, who did not possess the virtues of his books. Marcel deliberately practised his skill at drawing portraits, ranking himself with Félix Bracquemond or Whistler (the one representing Goncourt, the other Montesquiou); the model is actually based as much on the painter as on the critic: 'Their way of thinking delineating the character of their features no less than the character of their books.'[154] What made Daudet the man a work of art was the fact that the 'plastic purity of his features' was not affected by the intensity of his suffering, and hence nature 'intoxicates [us] with all the sense of sorrow, of beauty, of the all-powerful will and spirit'.[155]

Nevertheless, Proust read nearly all of Daudet's novels: as well as those we have mentioned, *Les Rois en exil, Numa Roumestan* and *Sapho*, and he referred to *L'Immortel* in *À la recherche*. In them he discovered the theme of unhappy love: '*L'Arlésienne*, a work which I have never got over. The mortal sorrow it instils is the cause of almost all the follies I have committed in life and of those which are still left to me. Instead of making the little boy in my book mesmerized by the example of Swann, it should have been the Arlésienne. *L'Arlésienne* and *Sapho*, do you know any other works that inflict such incurable wounds?'[156] In effect these two works recount the same tragedy, that of a man subjugated by a woman who is not worthy of him, who is not 'his type': at the time that Marcel wrote these lines, he was experiencing just such amorous adventures with young men who could neither satisfy him nor make him happy.

FAURÉ

As we have seen, Proust had already begun to read, enjoy and play Fauré's music before he met him. When he was introduced to the composer at the home of Mme Louis Stern in 1895, he chatted with him for a long time and found him 'really very pleasant'; one of their topics of conversation was Reynaldo, to whom Marcel wrote: 'We spoke about you for a very long time and I believe I did so intelligently. He told me that all his music must rather irritate you since the same lines of verse must have taken on a definitive expression for you, etc. And I said that quite the contrary, I had heard you singing songs he wrote more often than your own, and that you sang the *Chant d'automne* so well.'[157] Fauré and Hahn had, in fact, composed songs based on the same poems by Verlaine. Very often, when Proust mentions poems of secondary quality in *À la recherche*, such as 'Ici-bas' by Sully-Prudhomme, or poems by Leconte de Lisle or Armand Silvestre, it is because they have been set to music by Fauré. A little later, in 1897, the latter received a letter from Marcel: 'I do not merely like, admire and adore your music, I have been, and still am, in love with it; well before you knew me, you used to thank me with a smile at concerts or gatherings, the clamour of my enthusiasm having obliged you, despite your scornful indifference to success, to take a fifth bow. The other evening I was intoxicated for the first time by the *Parfum impérissable* and it is a dangerous intoxication . . . I told Reynaldo things about this *Parfum* which even from a musical standpoint he agreed with . . . I know your work sufficiently well to be able to write a 300-page book about it.'[158] The fact was that for Marcel, behind these tunes, 'infinity seems to unfold'.[159] He soon invited Fauré to dinner, with the Polignacs,[160] the Blanches, the Heredias, the Régniers and Montesquiou.[161] In 1901, Proust declared to the Comtesse de Noailles that for him Fauré was a passion (like herself, or Gustave Moreau).[162] The composer disappeared from Proust's mind while he was working on Ruskin and he became less interested in music than he was in architecture and sculpture. In 1907, when he was about to begin *Contre Sainte-Beuve*, he once more thought about inviting Fauré,[163] particularly so that he could play at the Ritz.[164] He read and responded to his music criticism. What is more surprising is that Marcel saw in *Romances sans paroles* the charming expression of 'a mixture of litanies and fucking', harking back, it is true, to a remark of Montesquiou's. 'I suppose that is what a pederast would sing who was violating a choir-boy':[165] Charlus, here, is speaking to Charlus. In 1915 Proust revealed to Antoine Bibesco that he used Fauré's *Ballade* as a model for the drawn-out movements of Vinteuil's sonata.[166] 'And suddenly the music, having reached a certain point, from which he was preparing to follow it, after a moment's pause, abruptly changed direction . . .' Furthermore, the sonata's theme is introduced three times, as it is in the *Ballade*. The *Cantique de Jean Racine* (1888) is invoked in a draft of *La Prisonnière*: 'Take care that it relates to this happiness indicated in the analysis of Fauré's canticle.'[167] The Quatuor Poulet was invited to play Fauré's Quartet for Proust in 1916, and he used it as a model for Vinteuil's Septet and its relationship to the sonata (like Franck's Quartet).[168] Proust then explained to Gaston Poulet that the depth of the composer's talent made him seem so at ease (like Anatole France) that he understood everything and one never felt embarrassed in front of him.[169] Even in 1916 Marcel took medicaments so as to be able to attend a Fauré festival at the Odéon. And then, once Vinteuil had been created, the composer disappeared from the life and correspondence of the person who had taken from him all that he needed for his work. This journey from youth (during which we should not disregard the part played by Marcel's discussions with Hahn, who, as his writings testify,[170] was also a great admirer of Fauré) to maturity is one of prescience to realization. In this, as in everything, when Proust felt passionate about somebody else's creation, it was a sign that he was foreseeing his own work.

LA VIE PARISIENNE

To return to 1895, when he met Fauré: Marcel was often spotted at concerts with Reynaldo, notably by Willy, who recognized them at the Concerts Lamoureux on 10 February and, on 25 February at Harcourt's concert, where he met 'Reynaldo Hahn and Marcel Proust, who wore a rose that was not as red as his own red lips'.[171] Colette has given us a portrait of Marcel that is all but forgotten, yet which is shocking in its disdain: 'At "mother Barmann's" [that is to say Mme Arman] I was hounded, politely, by a pretty, young literary-minded boy. The young fellow had fine eyes, with a hint of blepharism ... He compared me – my short hair again! – to Myrtocleia, to a young Hermes, to a love of Prud'hon's ... My little flatterer, thrilled by his own evocations, never left me ... He contemplated me with his caressing eyes, with their long eyelashes ...'[172] Colette met Marcel on a Wednesday at Mme Arman's and did not much care for 'his over-weaning politeness, the excessive attention he paid to those he was talking to'; she once again described 'the large, brownish, melancholy eyes, a skin that was sometimes pink and sometimes pale, an anxious look in the eyes, a mouth which, when it shut, was pursed tightly as if for a kiss'.[173] Since Marcel had become a well-known personality in Parisian life and in society, a sort of dandy figure out of Balzac, the newspaper columnists listed his name among those present at shows and evening performances, often in the company of Reynaldo. He was seen at Montesquiou's on 30 January, at the Comédie-Française (5 February), at the Heredias on the 9th, the Daudets on the 14th, at the Comédie-Française again on the 25th to see *Hernani*, at the Daudets once more on the 28th, and on 1 March at the banquet at which Raymond Poincaré conferred the rosette of the Légion d'Honneur on Edmond de Goncourt. On 3 March it was a musical evening at the Princesse de Polignac's, and on 8 March he was at Montesquiou's home, where Mlle Bartet recited the count's poems in honour of the Comtesse Greffulhe, the Comtesse de Guerne and the Comtesse Potocka (three ladies about whom Proust would write) as well as a poem by the future Comtesse de Noailles, Anna de Brancovan. That evening, the audience included other models for the novelist: France, Haas, Whistler and Doctor Dieulafoy. Two days later Marcel dined with the Princesse Mathilde, and on 20 March he went to the ball that Mme Cahen d'Anvers gave for King Alexander of Serbia. The next day Mme Lemaire arranged an Augusta Holmès evening. Marcel listened to a scene from *Tristan* at the home of the

Lamoureux on 12 April, and one from Rameau's *Dardanus* at the Princesse de Polignac's on 23 April. The fact that he obtained his degree in literature and philosophy could easily go unnoticed. This list of dates might seem too long, were it not for the fact that it reveals the frenetic rhythm of Marcel's social and night life.* The altercations with his parents and the remorse that such an existence engendered, since he was being disloyal to the vocation on whose behalf he had refused to embark upon a career, reappear in the character of Honoré in 'Un dîner en ville',[174] a story which may date from this period, for Marcel hoped that Mme Lemaire would publish it that May in *Le Gaulois*; he thought it was similar in genre to the pieces in this publication, only rather more literary.[175] The magazine would not publish it, but it would take 'Portraits de peintres'.

'PORTRAITS DE PEINTRES'

On 28 May 1895 there was a grand poetry and music evening at the home of Madeleine Lemaire. Marcel had invited Montesquiou, writing to him as follows: 'Tomorrow we shall hear a few of my worst poems (. . .)! If only among all the fine music that will be played tomorrow evening, you could derive some pleasure from noting that these young men's poems reveal not only admiration for your own verse, but imitation . . .'[176] A number of actors and musicians, even choirs, had gathered for the evening; there was a review in *Le Gaulois* the following day, which mentioned 'the beautiful pieces that M. Hahn had composed based on the finely wrought poems by M. Marcel Proust. Each of the portraits of painters is a small gem.' Risler, who had come from Chartres, where he was doing his national service, was at the piano.† In the audience were all Marcel's aristocratic connections. Reynaldo thought it was a 'novel idea' to 'create, musically, illustrations for a book . . . some simple vignettes' which evoked the text[177] (shortly afterwards, he considered illustrating *Le Jardin de Bérénice*, by Barrès, possibly in the form of a trio composed at Beg-Meil). So 'Portraits de peintres' was an illustration of an illustration, since Proust was trying to produce the verse equivalents of the paintings he had seen at the Louvre,

* Marcel could also be seen at Mme Legrand's (Mme Lenoir in *P et J*, Mme Leroi in *RTP*), at Mme Seminario's, and at Mme Howland's (at whose home Feuillet's *Le Voyageur* was performed).

† Édouard Risler (1873–1929), a friend of Hahn's and later of Proust's, the son of Auguste Risler, the painter of historical scenes, and a pupil of Diemer, had obtained first prize at the Conservatoire in 1896; a répétiteur at Bayreuth in 1896, he would later achieve glittering international fame, in particular for his interpretations of Liszt and Beethoven.

notably in 1891 with Robert de Billy.[178] This literary process, which was in fact used by Montesquiou in *Les Hortensias bleus*,* can be traced back to Baudelaire's 'Phares' and to Gautier's 'transpositions of art'. Fromentin, in *Les Maîtres d'autrefois*, had written about Cuyp and Potter, and must have influenced Proust. In these almost anodyne pieces we can see the origins of some well-known passages: the description of Elstir's paintings in *À l'ombre des jeunes filles en fleurs*. Note the evocation of the 'profound moments', the fondness for cavaliers with golden curls and the 'pink feather in the hat', the memory of Willie Heath induced by Van Dyck. Marcel wrote several versions of these poems.[179] From October 1894 onwards, he was informing Mme de Brantes 'that a composer of genius – and one who was twenty years old – had written music for the poetry section of the book and that Monsieur France had written a preface'.[180] He added that the composer was not Delafosse, the co-author of 'Mensonges', who would not feature in the book. The final version was published first in *Le Gaulois* of 21 June 1895, then, with the score, by Ménestrel,[181] and in *Les Plaisirs et les Jours*, in 1896. The influence of Hugo, Baudelaire, Heredia (who was in the audience), Montesquiou and Gautier smothers the originality of these delightful pieces, just as traces of Gounod, Massenet and Saint-Saëns can be seen in the music that accompanies them. It is therefore understandable that the perceptive young couple should not have repeated the experience, even for the 'Portraits de musiciens', which were probably composed shortly afterwards. For posterity, which was not supposed to know that in the posthumous *Jean Santeuil* Hahn was portrayed in the character of Réveillon, the absence of Proust in Reynaldo's music is matched only by the absence in *À la recherche* of Reynaldo, whom the quatrain cut from the portrait of Van Dyck alludes to as 'the enchanter/ Reynaldo, zither player, poet and singer'.[182]

Reynaldo was the inspiration for 'Critique de l'espérance à la lumière de l'amour', 'written in a quarter of an hour and never corrected'. 'Morally it is wrong,' Marcel declared. 'But since, just for a minute, I felt it to be true, it takes on a psychological truth . . .'[183] These pages are only comprehensible when seen in the context of Marcel being in love, since the theory of love which they contain is addressed to a specific reader,

* 'Mac Neilliana', on a drawing by Whistler; *De Verlana*, '*Verlaine*, landscape clouded with roses'; 'Temple', on Puvis de Chavannes; on composers, 'Pieces': 'It's Schumann, it's Chopin, less austere than Bach', in which Proust, who chose the same artists for his 'Portraits de musiciens', would recognize himself.

Reynaldo, even though Proust denied this later; in Marcel's letters, denial is often an affirmation. His letters rely on a theory of time that is clearly formulated and which he would never repudiate. The present contains an 'incurable imperfection': 'No sooner has a future moment become the present than it is stripped of its charms, to be found again, it is true . . . on the paths of memory.' Hope is given no basis in reality, because it stems only from our hearts. 'Thoughtful and sorrowful men' (of whom Marcel was one) know that happiness in love is itself the most melancholy of experiences: despite the kisses, 'you yourself are unattainable and, with you, happiness'. This melancholy vision of happiness was shared by both of them – as Reynaldo's diary shows. 'Since we have spoken out aloud about this secret that each of us had hidden from the other, there can be no more happiness for us.'[184] Only memory remains, 'the indulgent and powerful Memory that wishes us well'. There is no point in hoping for happiness, because it is nothing but a phenomenon of memory.

A PHANTOM LIBRARIAN

What prompted Proust, on 29 May, to apply for the post of 'unremunerated assistant' at the Bibliothèque Mazarine? (At that time many public service careers did start with unpaid jobs as assistants, for example in the Foreign Office.) Firstly, the advice of Charles Grandjean, the librarian at the Sénat; secondly, the example provided by those illustrious writers who had found a haven, an alibi and a subsistence among other people's books: Anatole France, Leconte de Lisle and, at the Mazarine, Sainte-Beuve, who was appointed curator there in 1841. On 8 June, ranked third but last in the competitive exam, Marcel was to be seconded to a department that did not strike him as very exciting, the *dépôt légal*, or legal copyright office,[185] which was situated in the rue de Grenelle and not on the Quai Conti; by asking the Ministry of Public Education to intervene, he did his best to have the candidate who came second appointed in his place, pleading, as he was to do regularly, grounds of ill health; he met with a rebuff from M. Alfred Franklin, the librarian, who declared: 'M. Proust seemed to me to enjoy very good health', and added that 'if he was concealing his infirmities, if he was so weak that he was unable to endure five hours of work every other day, he was wrong to apply for a job which he was in no state to fill; all he need do is resign'.[186] At the beginning of July, after he had received his official letter of appointment, Marcel politely threatened the librarian with the intervention of Gabriel Hanotaux, the historian, but who, more importantly, was Minister for Foreign Affairs and a friend of Adrien Proust, asking 'either for leave, or for permission to resign'.[187] As a result he obtained two months' leave, which he would then extend from 15 October to 15 November: 'In order to complete the cure,' he wrote to the librarian, 'of nerve-induced asthma, from which I have almost entirely recovered, thanks to the two-month leave which you have already been kind enough to grant me.'[188] At the end of the year, the unpaid assistant obtained one year's leave. This administrative comedy gradually moved towards its conclusion on 1 March 1900, when Proust was considered to have resigned. The most prominent personalities in the nation, Hanotaux and Poincaré, had intervened so that our former would-be clerk did not have to perform any function. It was typical of Marcel to deploy considerable energy and to use all his connections to pull out of a situation in which he had placed himself: just as he did following an attack of asthma, he felt so much better afterwards! By trying to find a job, he had proved his willingness to his father: since they did not wish to give him a suitable posting, there was nothing for it but to withdraw and devote himself to the only career from which one cannot be sacked, which was literature. So we see that Marcel, like many of those 'highly-strung people' whom he would describe, though kind and conciliatory in appearance, was in reality terribly stubborn and was forever achieving, through devious paths, his own ends.

CHAPTER VII

The Pleasures of Jean Santeuil

KREUZNACH

In *À l'ombre des jeunes filles en fleurs* the Narrator recalls 'the German countryside which [he had] visited one year with [his] grandmother to take the waters', and in *Le Côté de Guermantes* he locates it 'at the foot of a mountain honoured by the feet of Goethe, and set among vineyards from which, at the Kurhof, we drank illustrious growths whose composite, sonorous names were like the epithets given by Homer to his heroes'. Once the cure was over, he would go boating every evening on the river, passing through the clouds of mosquitoes; he walked in the forest or gazed at the bluish hills behind the Kurhaus, while he dreamed of Rhinegraves, burgraves and the Palatine princes of the Holy German Empire.[1] These lines refer to the visit that Marcel and his mother, who left for the resort in July 1895,[2] made to Bad Kreuznach, a Rhineland watering place on the River Nahe; they stayed at the Kurhaus Hotel. On the left bank of the river soars the Schlossberg, covered with vineyards on its southern slopes; you can travel by boat as far as Münster-am-Stein: in *Le Côté de Guermantes* Proust took the name of Prince Faffenheim-Munsterburg-Weiningen from these places so that, upon hearing his name, he would be able to conjure up a vision of some medieval, romantic Germany: 'I tried to imagine the names of these lands and those of the many other margraves and Teutonic squires for whom he was Rhinegrave, and yet I recognized them! It was the sweet name of the friendly river where I stretched out in the bottom of the boat, drifting to a halt among the reeds, it was also the familiar, much loved name of the village which was my destination when I hired the boat saying "as far as . . ." and whose name Maman uttered when I returned for dinner: "Did you have time to go as far as . . ." They were all names that were known and well-loved, full of memories, not the unknown, such sweet names, which, when placed end to end, as they often were when dining with Maman and talking about our day, made up the sonorous, foreign title – four lines in *Le Gotha* – of the Rhinegrave.'[3] Nevertheless, Marcel experienced that evening sadness, that nervous condition whose recurrence he would recall with dread.[4] Proust arranged his stay at Bad Kreuznach of his own accord, without his mother having asked him to come, so that she should not be left on her own (which annoyed Madeleine Lemaire, who would have liked him to go to Réveillon); while there he scarcely wrote to Reynaldo. This 'nonconformist', as his indulgent friend put it, just worked.

SAINT-GERMAIN-EN-LAYE

However, it was not long before we find Marcel, in mid-July, with Reynaldo's family at Saint-Germain-en-Laye. Mme Miguel Seminario, the composer's sister, greeted him. Reynaldo seemed depressed, and he told Risler that he had come there so as to 'drown his great moral problems in the pure, bracing air'. 'In everyday life all men are obliged to bear their share of sorrow ... In moments of despair one likes to escape from everyone, to hide one's troubles, to confide in oneself. So I have come here, to my sister Clarita, who has rented a house for the whole summer.' Marcel (who does not appear to have stayed continuously at Saint-Germain) paid him regular visits, and his 'sweetness' and his 'intelligence' were 'truly restorative': 'He is one of the élite, a superior being.'[5]

By now everybody seemed to be inviting the two young men together, as a couple. For instance, Montesquiou, whose 'test of the very greatest friendship',[6] Marcel would place in the mouth of Charlus, invited them to Versailles for the first time in order to meet the Comtesse de Noailles and Barrès: but they missed the train, and, besides, they did not have tails, which was unforgivable; the count invited them on two further occasions that month: 'Come with your brother Hahn,' he wrote (signing himself FMR) to Marcel, who, that evening, was due to dine with Mme Aubernon, at the Manoir du Cœur-Volant, at Louveciennes: these dinner parties and the train which took him to Versailles would come in useful when he came to write about Mme Verdurin. At the end of the month, and until the beginning of August, the two would meet frequently at Saint-Germain-en-Laye: 'Reynaldo was welcomed with shouts of joy by his nephews and nieces, who are very good-looking. Mme Seminario unfortunately had a migraine and I was unable to see her.'[7] Relations appear to have been more cordial with Maria, another sister (Marcel called her 'dear sister'), to whom the young man wrote these revealing lines, having first compared her to Diana, the huntress of the Saint-Germain forest: 'You inspire nothing but awe, which, for a well-educated imagination, is inseparable from the vision of beauty!'[8] For all that, was everything straightforward between the two friends? Marcel remembered 'a thousand really awful complications to do with life, health and national service' which prevented them from making any precise plans.[9]

DIEPPE

On 10 August, however, Proust was with Reynaldo, at Dieppe, staying with Madeleine Lemaire (until 30 August).* As usual, she was the obliging hostess, doing her best 'to make life comfortable and easy for them. The meals were excellent, and as for music, Reynaldo not having a piano, there is the sea and the wind' to provide it, and, 'papa being on holiday', the sea to look after Marcel's health: 'I feel very well thanks to this doctor who treats one like a painter of frescoes would.' The two friends seemed to be getting on harmoniously once more: 'Reynaldo is divine in his wit, his kindness and his charm.'† A trip to Petit-Abbeville, where Marcel admired the beech trees on the road to Rouen,[10] provided the opportunity for him to write 'Sous-bois'. This was a new exercise for his imagination, of the sort that the philosopher Gaston Bachelard would describe: 'Our spirit does not delight in stretching out over the world, as it does by the sea, on the plains or in the mountains, but is happy to be separated from it; and, hemmed in on all sides by the deep-rooted trunks, it soars upwards just as the trees do.' The two young men were 'lying on their backs, their heads tilted back on the dry leaves', observing, 'from the heart of a profound tranquillity the joyful agility of [their] spirit'.[11] The trees, so prevalent in *À la recherche*, and particularly in the episode of the three trees at Hudimesnil, are, so ancient and so young, 'the obscure and inexhaustible reserve' of our lives. And on the train Marcel happened to meet M. de Saint-Marceaux, a sculptor (1845–1915), who told him 'marvellous things,

* 'Before setting off for Brittany,' Hahn wrote to Risler . . . 'We took over a week hesitating about the definitive choice of our itinerary – indecisive as we both are, it was hard to reach a decision, and as usual, now that we have done so, we reckon – vaguely – that all the other ones were better' (*BAMP*, no. 43, 1993, pp. 45–6).

† *Corr.*, vol. I, p. 418. Here, the sea is a *father* substitute. The sea, music, his parents and the beloved are bound together here by Proust himself, and they will remain so: Albertine plays the pianola to the Narrator, just as Reynaldo does for Marcel.

delightful things too, on the subject of dance', while the young man claimed to be 'a little in love' with Cléo de Mérode, who lived at Dieppe, and had a small role at the Opéra.[12]

BEG-MEIL

The young men then finalized their trip to Brittany. '[Marcel] feels a bit oppressed,'* wrote Reynaldo to his sister Maria, 'it is possible that his father has advised him against Brittany. As for me, I am feeling marvellously well and I like Dieppe. We walk a lot. It is four o'clock in the morning . . . Everything is fast asleep: these ladies below, Marcel next to me, but ever so lightly, so much so that even the noise of my pen makes me feel terribly anxious. He has had a slight asthma attack. Let us hope that he is allowed to go on this trip to Brittany, which I have been looking forward to so much!'[13] Madeleine Lemaire did not see it like this; like Mme Verdurin, she did not want to be deserted by her faithful: 'Marcel is much better,' she wrote. 'Ah! If only they would give up their trip to Brittany! I insist on them eating at regular times, which they won't do in poor-quality hotels.' Leading a free and healthy life, the two young men succeeded in 'isolating themselves completely from everything and everybody'; but they met Saint-Saëns, who had come to see Madeleine Lemaire: the disciple made himself known to the master, who did not realize who he was when he met him.†

On 4 September Marcel and Reynaldo left for Belle-Île-en-Mer – a journey of fourteen hours by train as far as Quiberon, and then by boat – where Sarah Bernhardt had a house. Marcel recalled this 'pilgrimage to the places made illustrious by Sarah Bernhardt';[14] Reynaldo, 'the foul aridity of Belle-Île, the stifling heat of Quiberon'. Did they encounter the great actress? Curiously, it was Reynaldo, and not Proust, who mentioned that they paid a visit to Sarah Bernhardt.[15] From 6 September they were

---

* On 20 August Marcel wrote to Maria Hahn saying that he did not know whether he would be able to remain in Dieppe 'not being able to breathe very well there' (*Corr.*, vol. I., p. 417). Or again: 'I am feeling very agitated on account of insomnia, but I am enjoying this visit thanks to Reynaldo' (ibid., p. 419). The latter, on the other hand, who was 'more than melancholic' before going to Dieppe, was cured, and was reading *Anna Karenina* (which Marcel had read in August 1894) with enthusiasm.

† *BAMP*, no. 43, 1993, p. 49. Letter from R. Hahn to É. Risler, 31 August 1895. As we know, Saint-Saëns had thought that Marcel was the composer. 'Unto every one that hath shall be given'.

at Beg-Meil, at the little Hôtel Fermont, or at the Hôtel de la Plage;* they stayed in an annexe, a hundred metres away from the main building, where they took their meals; the room, Reynaldo wrote to his sister, only cost two francs; the hotel was full of 'fly shit', it was even on the writing paper. The hotel register reads 'Reynaldo Hahn, composer' and 'Marcel Proust, man of letters', arriving from Belle-Île. At this time Beg-Meil was nothing but an 'immense strand surrounded by cliffs covered with trees and thickets', with a 'salubrious and temperate climate',[16] which contrasted with 'the very overrated and very unhealthy Belle-Île' described by Marcel in a letter, in which he was still doing his best to find 'large apple trees, a smell of cider mixed with that of seaweed [that] provides the freshness of Normandy. To one side, there is the sea, very Breton and sad. To the other Concarneau Bay, which is blue, with a backdrop that is exactly like that of the Lake of Geneva.'[17] They reached Beg-Meil by taking the ferry from Concarneau. It was the Bénac family, friends of the Prousts, who had recommended this resort. From the Bénacs' house, which still stands, Marcel would contemplate the view of the sea, sheltered from the sun by an umbrella held by Reynaldo.[18]

In all his letters, Proust used the same imagery to extol the 'delightful places where the Normandy apples ripen at the edge of the rocks, mingling the smell of cider with the scent of seaweed, beside a fabulous Lake of Geneva'.† With his taste for scatalogical jokes inherited from his family, a habit he would never relinquish, which, after all, can be traced back to Molière or Rabelais, Marcel pointed out that the farm-guesthouse at which they were staying had no lavatories: 'And indeed, this would be just the place one might disseminate Vigny's line: *Ne me laisse jamais seul avec la nature* [Never leave me alone with nature]. For it is to nature that we are obliged to consign everything,' and he remembered the sting of the nettles.[19] Reynaldo, as usual, was less happy, and he poured out his complaints to his friends and to his sisters: 'The sun burns me, the mosquitoes bite me, the filth of the inns makes me ill. In this respect,

---

* This hotel still existed in 1994, although it was threatened with demolition. It comprised twenty bedrooms and a dining-room (*Ouest-France*, Quimper edition, 18 August 1944: 'When Marcel Proust came to Beg-Meil').

† We come across the Lake of Geneva in *Jean Santeuil*; Jean, glimpsing it, in a flash of involuntary memory sees the sea again (*JS*, pp. 398–9): 'It was the smell of a certain house we lived in by the sea, an irritating wooden villa . . . where I had felt so sad, and where everything seemed to me so lacking in beauty.' We see how Proust reversed the timing of events in his life: at Beg-Meil, it was anticipation; in the novel, a memory.

what a hell Brittany is! . . . To have to travel two leagues on foot in order to see an apple tree that is identical to every other one, and, perspiring, have to drink something resembling vinegar in dirty glasses given us by a peasant . . . no thank you!'[20] Even though he declared himself not sufficiently foolish – 'neither is Marcel' – to be unable to understand the 'feel of Brittany and what one ought to experience', he did not care for this land, on which he heaped sarcasm, while at the same time listing the places they visited: Auray, Concarneau, Douarnenez, Audierne, Quimper, the Pointe du Raz. The lack of comfort at their inn seems to have been very irksome: 'We are both too sensitive to be satisfied with the unbelievable discomfort of this wild country. It is hard to get used, from one day to the next, to the absence of washbasins and lavatories, to food that is *indescribable*. . . and to windows without curtains, etc.'[21] At the end of September, however, Hahn relented, and found nature miraculous: 'I have never seen anything quite like it. The sunsets are amazing. By turns, we saw the sea turn blood-red, violet, pearly, silvery, golden, white and emerald green, and yesterday, thanks to the beneficent sun, we saw the sea turn completely pink, covered with blue sails.' The two young men read Mme de Sévigné, and *Splendeurs et misères des courtisanes*, 'in which there are things that one would find absurd in anyone other than Balzac'.[22]

At Beg-Meil Proust rediscovered the type of scenery that had appealed to him in Normandy: the apple trees descending to the sea. He described it in numerous passages of *Jean Santeuil*.[23] It was there, in fact, that he began the novel, almost as if the place, the romantic bliss that allowed him to have his beloved entirely to himself, the completion of *Plaisirs et les Jours*, to which he only added a few pages more, and his stimulating reading, had triggered his inspiration. In the meantime, and thanks to Reynaldo's presence, Marcel had written the 'Portraits de musiciens' which follow the 'Portraits de peintres' in *Les Plaisirs et les Jours*: 'Chopin' (initially dedicated to Édouard Risler), 'Gluck', 'Mozart', 'Schumann' – eighty lines of verse in honour of the favourite composers of his youth. He devoted one of the most beautiful passages of *À la recherche* to a phrase of Chopin's, played by Mme de Cambremer; Schumann's *Carnival in Vienna* is one of the models for Vinteuil's Sonata.* Just as Mozart's friendship for a young Englishman would later serve as an example, or an alibi, to Marcel, so

---

* Proust describes Gluck's *Iphigénie* and the Clarinet Quintet, as well as a concert by Mozart, in *À la recherche*. Mme Verdurin calls Morel her 'little Mozart' (as, no doubt, did Mme Lemaire Reynaldo, who dedicated the 'Portraits de peintres' to her). See also *CSB*, pp. 192–3, and p. 281.

would 'Cherubino and Don Juan'![24] These poems would be turned down by Juliette Adam's *La Nouvelle Revue* in October and by *La Revue hebdomadaire* in November.[25] They testify less to a great knowledge of the music than to a poetic talent that is closer to Montesquiou and his poem-portraits. The lines on Gluck allude to five of his operas (*Alceste, Armide*, mentioned in *À la recherche*, both his *Iphigénie*s and *Orphée et Eurydice*). The poem devoted to Schumann makes play with the titles of his thirteen lieder and of the *Carnival* op. 9, as well as the *Kinderscenen*. In 'Mozart', we find *The Marriage of Figaro, Don Giovanni* and *The Magic Flute*. The art of pastiche, of quotation, of constructing in mosaic, was emerging here, as it does in 'Mondanité et mélomanie de Bouvard et Pécuchet'. It will be found again in *À la recherche*, in which is buried an entire thesaurus.

HARRISON

The first lines of *Jean Santeuil* describe the farm belonging to the Bénacs, the friends of Proust, who had suggested the trip: 'I had gone to spend the month of September with a friend at Kerengrimen,[26] which at that time [in 1895] was nothing more than a farm, cut off from any village, and tucked away among the apple orchards by Concarneau Bay'.[27] Artists used to frequent this farm: in fact, Marcel and Reynaldo met the American painter, Alexander Harrison, who had rented a studio there. Born in Philadelphia in 1853, a pupil of Gérome and Bastien-Lepage, and an acquaintance of Monet and Rodin, at that time he had taken a liking to Brittany, where he was now staying. He had been awarded a gold medal as well as the Légion d'honneur at the Exposition Universelle of 1889. His paintings, which depict seascapes and beaches, enjoyed great success in France.[28] *Jean Santeuil* describes 'a beautiful effect of sunlight[29] painted by Harrison – a canvas that he had given to his host . . . in which, through the power that affection and talent possess, the artist was able to portray this landscape for someone who did not yet know it complete with everything that would only be revealed in due course by a continuous attachment'.[30]

It was Harrison who advised the young men to go to the Pointe de Penmarch, 'a kind of mixture of Holland, the West Indies and Florida (Harrison dixit) from which a storm is the most sublime sight imaginable'.[31] Elstir would say the same about Carquetuit: 'It rather reminds me of certain aspects of Florida',[32] using, in order to compare this place to the Pointe du Raz, the same words that Proust had addressed to a friend:

'You mustn't fail to go to the Pointe du Raz, historically and geographically you know that it is literally Finisterre ... the giant granite cliff around which the wild sea constantly rages, overlooking the Baie des Trépassés, opposite the Île de Sein. These are gloomy places and the famous curse that hangs over them has to be experienced. But I admit that I infinitely prefer Penmarch.'[33] Harrison, who had stayed in Florida for several years, had thus played the role of 'stimulating guide': 'I only tolerate the others', wrote Proust in *Le Carnet de 1908*, 'as stimulating guides (Harrison Florida).' A prototype of Elstir, as far as the encounter and the seascapes are concerned, Harrison was also the model for the writer C. in *Jean Santeuil*, whose working methods were more like those of a painter than a novelist ('He closely followed the flight of the birds that flew over the sea, listening to the wind and looking at the sky'),[34] and who also gave advice on sightseeing. Thus a real painter was metamorphosed into a novelist in Proust's first novel, and his opinions were borrowed by Marcel when he described Finistère to his friends, before he becomes once more the model for Elstir as he is first depicted, in *À l'ombre des jeunes filles en fleurs*.

LANDSCAPES

Like his writer C., at Beg-Meil Proust spent his time portraying landscapes, as well as a few characters. Among the latter, the Sauvalgues were inspired by the Bénacs; they were among M. and Mme Proust's oldest friends; the husband had been the manager of the Banque de Paris et des Pays-Bas and secretary to the board of directors of the State Railways (1886–95); they had spoken of Beg-Meil, where they owned a property, to Marcel; 'The Sauvalgues said that it was an enchanting place, that they had more or less discovered it themselves and they advised everybody to go there. They had bought a small property ... Their life's happiness was there.'[35]

The first piece of scenery described is the peninsula of Beg-Meil, its lighthouse, its heather and thistles, and its two marine landscapes. At the time, it was rare to see a farm where the orchards ran down to the sea. It was at one of these farms, transformed into a modest hotel, that Proust and Hahn stayed. Peasants still slept in their old box beds. Did the two friends share such a bed? A few sentences seem to suggest as much: 'Then it would be time to go to sleep in the box beds, the dark night filled with strange dreams that are interrupted when the noise of the storm rattles the windowpanes and awakens the sleepers, with their soft, drowsy kisses, their arms wrapped round their necks and their legs entwined, their kisses that deepen the silence, as the wind hurls itself against the casements, seizes the roof and sets the chimney damper sighing, when the head raises itself from the pillow, without disturbing the other's encircling arms, to listen to the noise . . . then plunges down again and shelters beneath the sheets for warmth and affection within, while outside, all is cold and hostile.'[36] Above the farm was the 'sombre and vast' church, with its rustic elegance, the first of those country or village churches which Proust would always be fond of:[37] 'L'Église de village' was the title of a pre-publication extract that appeared in *Le Figaro* in 1912; Balbec, too, is rich in descriptions of church towers. Further away was the church at Decazeville, which contained a *Descente de Croix* by Gustave Moreau.[38] The Pointe de Penmarch was the focus of their visit: the storm scene, which would be no more than a dream in *À la recherche*, is described in *Jean Santeuil* in a manner that is typical of Proust:[39] he transforms into reverie, into an image of desire, that which he actually experienced, and even wrote about in early versions of the definitive text. Jean goes to watch the storm, accompanied by a sailor who guides and protects him, and who crawls on his hands and knees in order that he should not be blown away by the wind.

In October Jean Santeuil – like Marcel, no doubt – 'covered with a rug, read or wrote in the apple orchard in front of the inn', placing an ink-bottle on top of his papers so that they were not blown away by the wind, and there was nothing that could threaten his sense of well-being. In the afternoon or the evening, he would go to the sea to fish, taking his ink-bottle with him, in case he wanted to write, or else he would enjoy watching the boats returning home: 'He had given his heart to something that was more profound than trivialities, that was more enduring than love.'[40] Marcel did not return to Brittany, any more than Jean Santeuil did: 'Gradually, his affections were diverted to new friends, to new places, for the very same reason that they had once been drawn to the little Bay of Concarneau, to these fishermen who brought him a part of their catch each morning, to the lad who took him in his boat at sunset, who understood his fear of jellyfish . . . , his love of the open sea . . . of church bells.'[41] Proust would again describe the sadness of going away from the sea in the autumn in *À l'ombre des jeunes filles en fleurs*; he once happened to be the last resident at the Grand Hôtel at Cabourg, a strange bird, left isolated on the sea wall at the end of the season. In 1904 he was still extolling the virtues of Beg-Meil to Léon Yeatman: 'It's not a place to go and see, but it's a delightful place in which to live. And if you go by boat

from Beg-Meil to Concarneau one evening, your oars will scatter all the
colours of the setting sun over the dazzling, sleepy waters.' Describing
Penmarch, he added: 'With a storm there, you will be mad with joy. And
you will see gentle and scarred beaches clinging to the cliffs like so many
Andromedas.'[42] Finally, Beg-Meil provided Proust with many of the
place-names to be found in *Jean Santeuil.*

RÉVEILLON

It was not until 27 October, after having extended his leave from the
Mazarine library until 15 November, that Marcel returned to Paris.[43] Three
days before their departure from Beg-Meil, he and Reynaldo had visited
Douarnenez and the Pointe du Raz, in a tropical heatwave. Proust had
planned to set off again, without Reynaldo, for the Château de Segrez, in
order to work in the company of his friend Pierre Lavallée: but the
arrangements, which had been going on for two months, came to nothing.
Instead, he returned to Madeleine Lemaire's house at Réveillon, where he
remained until November.

It was here that Marcel wrote 'Vent de mer à la campagne': 'This
pell-mell of wind and light makes this corner of Champagne look like
coastal scenery.'[44] The countryside was only bearable if one could catch
a glimpse, either in dreams, or by some trick of memory or Baudelairean
correspondence, the sea in between the trees. This prose-poem was also
an invocation to the loved one: 'Keep this cluster of fresh roses on your
knee and let my heart weep between your clasped hands.' The piece was
preceded by an epigraph from Theocritus, which also refers to the gift of
a flower, 'a young poppy', which in Proust's poem 'sheds its petals in the
buttonhole' of the lover. During this time, in fact, Marcel was translating
poems by the author of the *Idylls*, with the intention of placing them at
the top of certain pages of his future book. Thus, he borrowed from
Cyclops a quotation intended for the fifth part of 'Mélancolique villégiature
de Mme de Breyves', having first translated *Cyclops*, altering the gender
of the character by making it female:[45] 'She pined from dawn by the
seaweed-covered shore'; thus, Polyphemus became Mme de Breyves; the
printed text, however, harks back to Leconte de Lisle's translation. At
Réveillon Marcel must have rediscovered the bucolic delights of the *Idylls*,
which he then partially translated and used the quotations in his letters,
as he would in his work; it is worth noting that Leconte de Lisle combined
his translation of Theocritus and of Hesiod, who would provide Proust

with the title for his first book, in a single volume. It was while thinking of the summers in Champagne that Marcel must have translated these lines from Theocritus' *Thalysia*: 'Everything breathed the fullness of the long summer, everything breathed the dawn of autumn' and 'Oh! If once again I were able to wave the great winnowing fan over the sacred stacks of cereal, and see the smiling Goddess with her sheaves and poppies held in her two hands.' Thus does the sunlight of Theocritus discreetly illuminate the Proustian countryside, from *Plaisirs* to 'Combray'. *La Prisonnière* recalls 'Theocritus' shepherd who sighed for a young boy', which, put like this, was merely reflecting 'the fashion of the time'.[46] Again, in 1896, Marcel concealed his feelings beneath the Greek illusion, which was dear, too, to the author of *Corydon*;* he would renounce it, in order to assert that the only true homosexuality was not that of 'custom', as in Virgil, Plato or Theocritus, but that of modern times, 'the involuntary, excitable kind, that one concealed from others and disguised to oneself'.[47]

In 'Les marronniers', which he himself dated, 'Réveillon, October 1895', Marcel painted another picture of the grounds of the château, evoking the chestnut trees that were so dear to him, whether at Versailles, at the Tuileries, in the Bois de Boulogne,[48] at Combray or in the paintings of Helleu. He described the great avenue that led up to the château:[49] 'Above all, I loved to stop beneath the vast chestnut trees[50] when they were turning an autumnal yellow. How many hours did I spend in those mysterious, verdant grottoes, gazing at the murmuring cascades of pale gold above my head that poured down their coolness and their darkness.'[51] The vast Louis XIII Château de Réveillon, constructed over the remains of a castle, had been rebuilt in the eighteenth century, and in 1719 had belonged to René-Louis d'Argenson, Garde des Sceaux, before being restored by Jules Robert de Cotte, with the assistance of Oudry and Claude Audran; here Marcel could admire the beautiful rococo furnishings, Oudry's *Fables*† (which he would describe in *À la recherche*), a *Pietà* by Lebrun and a number of large tapestries of various royal palaces.

At Réveillon Proust continued writing a long section of *Jean Santeuil*[52] in which Reynaldo Hahn is Henri de Réveillon.‡ Not all these pages date from this visit (some of them allude to the Dreyfus affair), but they were

---

* The somewhat scandalous novel by André Gide, published in 1924, containing Socratic dialogues in which the author proclaimed his homosexuality. *Tr.*

† Oudry was the eighteenth-century painter who drew illustrations for La Fontaine's fables. *Tr.*

‡ E.g. p. 457: 'Henri sat at the piano', sang a song for him, and 'Jean, who was enchanted, listened to him standing by the fire in his night-shirt'.

all inspired by it. Thus, he describes the château's long marble galleries, the painted wood-panelling, the vases of flowers that Suzette Lemaire had arranged,[53] the many walks that Henri and Jean took together; the great courtyard behind the house, the caretaker's house, on the roof of which a peacock displayed his full array of sparkling colours, as in one of Montesquiou's poems. Here he saw a lonely foxglove in a valley, 'so isolated, a mere perishable flower, but so important as an enduring concept of nature, as one of life's immense range of species. "And I too," he said to himself, "have very often felt isolated from the rest of the world like this poor foxglove." '[54] The image of the solitary flower would be developed in *Sodome et Gomorrhe I*, in which one flower has difficulty fertilizing another.[55] It is at Réveillon that Jean takes Henri's arm affectionately and tells him: 'My dearest Henri, I am very happy to have you on this earth.' The chapter concludes with a number of endings – Proust did not choose between them – all of which have to do with the delights of autumn or of winter, as in the room at Doncières or Orléans. Winter is the season in which the asthmatic, allergic to flowers and trees alike, finds a little respite, one in which the creator shuts himself away in his bedroom, far from the abandoned statues in the grounds, almost as if the breath of the wind has become the breath of inspiration as well as respiration. It is understandable that the bedroom at the Château de Réveillon and the delights of the walks there should feature in the early drafts of *Du côté de chez Swann*.[56] Madeleine Lemaire protected the curious couple: 'How indulgent you are towards us, we who are such lunatics and so badly brought up . . . What other woman or great artist would put up, as you do, with the quirks and the company of two old-fashioned young men?'[57]

CHARDIN AND REMBRANDT

Back in Paris, Marcel dined at the Daudets; the glittering company, as we have seen, inspired only a ferocious portrait, in which he distanced himself from naturalism, although it was tempered by Alphonse's sentimental charm. Edmond de Goncourt, who was present, failed as usual to mention Marcel's name: this little fellow (he refers to 'little Hahn') did not interest him. Yet we cannot simply dismiss Proust for not playing a prominent role in Goncourt's work: from this stems the spurious Goncourt *Journal* in *Le Temps retrouvé*. Those critics who maintain that Marcel was never admitted into high society could say the same about the literary world.

This was what he would discover in the context of two articles, one of which was a piece of art criticism.

'I have just written a short essay on the philosophy of art, if that term is not too pretentious, in which I attempt to show how the great artists initiate us into a knowledge and love of the exterior world, how they are the ones "through whom our eyes are prised open" – opened on the world. In the essay I use Chardin's work as an example, and I try to show his influence on our life and the charm and wisdom which it instils into our most ordinary days by initiating us into the world of still life.'58 That November, as he often did, Marcel visited the Louvre with Reynaldo: 'The portrait of Chardin with a scarf ', wrote Reynaldo, 'is staggering; that right eye, tired and swollen, that eye that has seen everything, which knows how to see everything; the shade of the scarf; the exquisite delicacy.'59 Encouraged by this enthusiasm, Marcel devoted eight long pages to Chardin, his first important piece of art criticism. First of all, he imagines a short novel about a young man who is bored by his daily life, and whom Marcel (always ready to instruct youth) would take to the Louvre to see 'this generous painting of what he considers to be mediocrity': he then explains *La Mère laborieuse, La Pourvoyeuse, Fruits et animaux, Ustensiles variés* and *La Raie* to him. Chardin had found all these things beautiful to look at, and then beautiful to paint: 'The pleasure you derive from his painting of a room in which someone is sewing, of an office, a kitchen or a dresser, is captured in passing, radiating the joy, both deepened and perpetuated, that the sight of a dresser, a kitchen, an office had given him . . .'60 Our 'inert conscience' needs Chardin to awaken in us the subconscious pleasure that 'the spectacle of humble existence and still life' can give us. In this way still life will become living nature 'and through understanding the life of his painting you will have captured the beauty of life'. Proust then took great pleasure in describing these still lives, which foreshadow those that he would depict in 'Combray' or which he would attribute to Elstir.61 One important aspect of the Proustian aesthetic has been revealed: for the true artist, there is no subject that is without interest and there is no such thing as a lesser genre; an old man can become an object of beauty; like Hahn, Proust described Chardin's self-portrait: 'The worn eyes are revived, looking as though they have seen much, jested much, loved much.' The friends exchanged their impressions, but those of Marcel are more profound; he then goes on to meditate on the old man whom the young cannot understand, as he does on his grandfather who is soon to die. Returning to physical things, he describes the room in which people and objects are gathered; the room itself is the soul's confidant, the sanctuary of the past, 'more so than an object and perhaps more than a person too'; we can already foresee what a brilliant creator of interiors Proust will be: 'How many private friendships do we come to learn about in an apparently dull room!' There is a friendship, a rapport, 'between beings and objects, between life and the past'.[62] The important lesson about this aesthetic, which will become that of Elstir, is 'the divine equality of everything in the mind of the onlooker, in the light which embellishes them'. As for Rembrandt, he surpassed reality.[63] Beauty is no longer in things, which are nothing in themselves; it is light which renders things beautiful: beauty lies entirely in the eye of the artist, for whom light, in the painting, is its incarnation. For Proust therefore, art criticism consisted not so much in being able to describe a painting, which was something that a novelist or poet could do very well, as in revealing that the work means what it does to us because of what it means to the artist – whether he be conscious of it or not. A work of art brings together, beneath appearances, the essence of man and of things.

A DINNER PARTY AT BOULEVARD MALESHERBES

Half-way through December, Marcel, on behalf of his parents, invited a number of personalities from the literary world to dinner: Montesquiou, José María de Heredia, Henri de Régnier and his celebrated wife Marie, together with childhood friends such as Robert de Billy,[64] the daughters of Félix Faure, the President of the Republic, and those of Gabriel Hanotaux, who had recently held the post of Minister of Foreign Affairs and would do so again very shortly.[65] Marie de Heredia, a beautiful young woman of scintillating intelligence, had gathered around her a circle of admirers who had proclaimed her 'queen of the Canaques';* Marcel was one of them;† she would always remember this and, after the war, she would count on his support in her hopes, which were unfulfilled, of being

---

* Les Canaques were a group of friends who took their name from the inhabitants of South Sea islands such as the former colony of Nouvelle Calédonie. *Tr.*

† 'I was very worried about you, dear Canaque, you didn't come to our last Saturday,' wrote Marie to Marcel before the summer of 1895, addressing him as 'first Canaque of France' (*Corr.*, vol. I, p. 405). See, too, Marcel's letters expressing admiration for Marie's poetry, light-hearted banter about the Canaque, and his congratulations on her marriage to Régnier, 'a noble union of two of the most brilliant poetic temperaments of our day' (ibid., vol. XX, pp. 605–11). Other Canaques included Léon Blum, Philippe Berthelot and Pierre Louÿs.

elected to the Académie française. Madly in love with Pierre Louÿs,[66] who corrupted her a little, she was forced to marry Henri de Régnier, who offered to restore the Heredias' finances, which had been jeopardized by the gambling indulged in by the author of *Trophées*. She would never forgive Régnier for the deal he made, and she became the mistress of literary Paris, from Bernstein to Vaudoyer, Jaloux and Henriot (all friends of Proust). Proust, on the other hand, was interested in Régnier's work, and had already devoted an article to him (he would write his pastiche in 1908). He would praise *La Canne de jaspe* in 1897, for 'no one could write better',[67] and *La Double Maîtresse*, 'the admirable and delightful companion of [his] days'.[68] Having moved on from the rather facile symbolism of his early poetry to novels that he wrote not so much from choice as to earn a living, Régnier interested Proust because of the neo-classical elegance of his style – that of a lukewarm Anatole France with a touch of irony added – and because of his studied syntax, his sense of the *mot juste*, as well as certain common themes, such as the past, Versailles and Venice. To Heredia, whose poetry he had liked at the time he admired Leconte de Lisle, and some traces of whose poems are reproduced in his own poetry, Marcel had wanted to dedicate his 'Portraits de peintres et de musiciens'.[69] He was hoping that Régnier would help with its magazine publication, so the dinner invitation was not entirely free of ulterior motives. Régnier was not much interested in Marcel and wrote of him in his diary with the scorn of a gentleman and a famous writer for a man who was '*à côté*' [a failure]. As for Hanoteaux, we have seen that he assisted Marcel in his efforts not to turn up at the library. Finally, a teenager crept in at the end of the evening: Lucien Daudet.

SAINT-SAËNS

Music also played an important part that month. On 8 December Marcel attended a concert at the Conservatoire at which Saint-Saëns played 'Mozart's concerto',* and he noted his impressions the following day. How can one define beauty, since it does not correspond exactly to what a romantic imagination expects? The pianist's playing can only be described

---

* Possibly the C Major Concerto. On the subject of Mozart, Saint-Saëns wrote: 'I gave concerts deliberately so that his concertos could be heard; I played them in the main concert halls of Paris, London and Brussels, something that generally they do not dare to do' (letter of 3 January 1901, Chassaing-Rivet-Fournier Catalogue, Drouot, 22 May 1995, no. 213).

negatively, and in these negations we encounter all Proust's humour: 'In Saint-Saëns' playing there was no *pianissimo*, where one feels one may be about to faint if they continue any longer and which a consoling *forte* interrupts just in time, none of those harmonies which, when repeated several times, cause your nerve ends to tremble all over, none of those *fortissimi* which break over your arms and legs like tidal waves . . .' The playing of a great performer is bright, naked, clear and transparent: it is la Berma in *Phèdre*. The art of the music critic goes further: in the pianist's performance he can identify the art of the composer 'of the most beautiful symphony since Beethoven' and of so many operas: 'None of the beautiful, inspired music of the *C-minor Symphony*, none of the sad flavour of *Henri VIII*, the beautiful choruses in *Samson et Dalila* – none was missing.'[70]

On the occasion of the dress rehearsal of *Frédégonde*, an opera by Guiraud completed by Saint-Saëns, *Le Gaulois* of 14 December carried an article by Proust: 'Figures parisiennes; Camille Saint Saëns'. 'A genius inspired by music, endowed with a deep sensibility', he hides his true self like Flaubert or France beneath his skill as a 'great composer'.* He is neo-classical, in that he draws on Bach and Beethoven, thus conferring 'through archaism his noble credentials to modernity', bestowing on a commonplace the value of a general idea or, at least, a flash of wit (as in the *Suite algérienne*): he then manages to summarize 'the essence of a race' in *Samson et Dalila*, the spirit of a civilization in *Henri VIII*, and to transpose the style of the Renaissance goldsmith in his opera *Ascanio*. He is able to 'make a religion be understood', 'to pity a woman, to see Eros'. The composer, a musical humanist, 'at every moment instils bursts of inventiveness and genius into what seemed to be a field bound by tradition, imitation and knowledge'.[71] Beneath the praise, ones senses some reservation: Saint-Saëns, a marvellous craftsman, a highly cultivated man, is no more original than Anatole France. The similarity between the two artists had also struck Reynaldo Hahn: 'Important links between Anatole France and Saint-Saëns; the same stylist's approach, the same lightly worn knowledge, the same adept and joyful application of established principles, the same taste, the discreet charm, the same belief in themselves and in their pens, the same facility that is based on a complete and one might say innate mastery of technique.'[72]

---

* Here Proust quoted a perception of Buffon, the writer and naturalist, from which he would later draw inspiration in his article on Flaubert as well as in *Le Temps retrouvé*: 'All the intellectual beauty to be found in a fine style, all the aspects with which it is composed are as many truths . . . more precious perhaps than those which may make up the core of a conversation.'

This first night of *Frédégonde*, which prompted the article, reappears in *Jean Santeuil*.[73] In the characters of M. and Mme Marmet Proust was also taking his revenge on M. and Mme Straus, with whom he had fallen out temporarily:* the gloomy story concerns a theatre box to which Jean was invited, only to have the invitation withdrawn, rather than the music. But Saint-Saëns plays a much more important role in this novel thanks to the 'little phrase', that is to say the initial theme of his First Sonata for Piano and Violin. Françoise, Jean's mistress, who here represents Reynaldo, sits at the piano: 'He had recognized that little phrase in Saint-Saëns' sonata which he used to ask her to play almost every evening in the heyday of their love and which she used to play endlessly, ten or twenty times over.'[74] These very fine passages, proof that the artist who wrote *Jean Santeuil* was not, whatever may be said, always inferior to the author of *À la recherche*, will be repeated in 'Un amour de Swann', the early drafts of which do not mention the name of Vinteuil, but rather that of Saint-Saëns.[75] In Proust's first novel, the 'little phrase' is described as 'desolate'; its pure and rapid motion signifies that all things pass, except the phrase itself, which survives love, lovers and mankind, as if it contained a 'peaceful, disenchanted, mysterious and smiling spirit, which outlived our sorrows and seemed superior to them'.[76] Ten years later, the little phrase reminds Jean of his love for Françoise. It was the little phrase from the First Sonata, 'the violin hovering on the same note', that spoke directly to Jean, 'telling him everything that it had to say'.[77] But Proust was still not capable of defining what it was 'it had to say'.

A PUBLICATION CONSTANTLY DEFERRED

Towards the end of 1895, with his book completed (apart from a story with which he intended to end the book, as well as an episode from his own life), Marcel was talking anxiously to J. Hubert, the production director at Calmann-Lévy. On various occasions, he asked the latter to intervene with Madeleine Lemaire; in November, Marcel was still hoping that the book would be able to be published before the end of the year.[78] At Christmas, he wanted it to appear in February: 'But if you say February to Mme Lemaire, she will say to herself "March will be early enough".'[79]

---

* One can see the reproaches M. Straus may have levelled at Marcel: 'On Monday, do you intend to arrive at eight o'clock and leave at midnight, as you did on the other occasions? You are tactless enough to do that.'

He added that Mme Lemaire had delayed the book for four years (in actual fact, since 1893, and Proust had taken the opportunity to add new material) and he suggested that the fifty little drawings for the chapter heads, which the publisher already had, should be distributed more or less evenly, 'because, not having specific subjects, they could go here or there just as well'; as to colour, it could be limited to the de-luxe editions.[80] Unfortunately, Hubert actually encouraged the lady to produce new drawings. Proust then regretted that 'The insignificant little pieces assembled together under the title *Comédie italienne*, having more drawings than the important stories, are seen in greater relief, and since that is what is least good in my book, it annoys me that the reader should have his eye drawn to them.'[81] In January Marcel was urging Hubert to ask the illustrator for two illustrations for 'Baldassare' and for two others for 'La fin de la jalousie' (which was therefore completed by this date, a fact that is not without consequence in our understanding of the evolution of Marcel's love life). Hubert was the first of those publishers who would endure Marcel's numerous grievances, that were always concealed beneath flowers. But Calmann-Lévy were in no hurry, particularly since Hubert had a number of reservations about the book: the dedication was too long, certain pieces were confused and uninteresting; there were examples of ingenuousness on every line, a rather awkward sentence structure, and a 'profusion of slightly contradictory epithets'.

AN END TO JEALOUSY

This short story, which was probably the last that Marcel wrote for his collection, and the one which he placed at the end of the book, was his favourite: in August 1913 he explained that *Du côté de chez Swann* 'may resemble "La Fin de la jalousie" a little'.[82] It does contain many autobiographical aspects. Asthma, the use of sleeping pills, the fear of the mother leaving, the sentimental names at the beginning ('My little donkey',* 'those words to which they had so quickly given their own meanings, those little words which could seem so empty and which they filled with infinite meaning. Trusting unconsciously in the inventive and fecund spirit of their love, they gradually found themselves acquiring a language of their own'), the kisses on the neck,[83] the distinction between the purely physical love affairs, which were of no consequence, and spiritual love: throughout

---

* Reynaldo called Marcel 'the pony'.

the collection, as in this story, Honoré is the incarnation of Marcel,[84] just as Françoise, here and in *Jean Santeuil*, is that of Reynaldo. As in every love story written by Proust, the hero has a premonition that this passion will not last long, according to 'the psychological law of his own fickleness', about which he makes a veiled confession here. The hero then promises to conceal his new love from Françoise and to allow her 'gradually to concentrate her life elsewhere'. Learning, however, as does the protagonist of Bourget's *Mensonges*, that Françoise may be deceiving him, he becomes mad with jealousy. A cruel game develops, in which lies are uttered in order to try to discover the truth: the protagonist even dreams of 'hiding himself in a room (he remembered doing this for fun when he was younger) so as to be able to see everything'.[85] Passion has become a disease. This disease leads to death, since the hero, like other characters from *Le Mensuel* and in *Les Plaisirs et les Jours*, is the victim of an accident; it occurs in the Bois de Boulogne, which is shown in a new light: no longer is it the 'women's garden', but a garden of death. Honoré's death throes, described at length, were probably based on Tolstoy's short stories, which Proust may have read in a collection put together by the translator Halpérine under the title of *La Mort*,[86] and they lend a tragic note to the conclusion of a collection of pieces which also begins with a death, that of Baldassare Silvande: it would be some time before Proust understood that it is not necessary to kill off one's hero, as Marcel Prévost does, in order to end a book. This gloomy tone is in contrast to the frivolous title, just like lost time and like Bourget's *Mensonges*.

BOURGET'S INFLUENCE

Proust had very little to say about Bourget, and what he did say was uttered with some disdain, as, for example, when he criticized the middle classes who read Bourget's novels and not those of Anna de Noailles. The reality was more complex; one only has to read *Mensonges* to see this. '*Mensonges*,' Proust wrote to Halévy in 1921, 'which I leafed through as a child one New Year's Eve'; for him this conferred a charm on it that was independent of the book itself.[87] In this 1887 novel, we come across a number of themes taken up by Marcel. Firstly, social experience: 'You go out in society . . . you will never be a part of it . . . no more than any artist would, even if he were a genius, because, quite simply, you are not born into it, and your family does not belong to it. They will entertain you, they will make a fuss of you. But just try to marry into it, and you will see . . .

these delicate women you dream about, so exquisite, so aristocratic, good Lord! If you only knew them! Creatures of vanity, dressed by Worth . . . But there are not ten of them who are capable of a genuine emotion.' These are the society ladies of *Les Plaisirs et les Jours* before they become those of *Le Côté de Guermantes*. And then one of the heroes, Claude Larcher, is devastated by his love for an actress who is not unlike Odette, 'with sad, dreaming eyes and with the melancholy sensuality about the mouth that Botticelli gives to his madonnas and his angels'. There is also a Vicomte de Brèves, a chambermaid by the name of Françoise, a mansion that belongs to the Saint-Euverte family, trips to Florence in the springtime, 'where the sharp breeze is interspersed with the caresses of a burning sun',[88] where one gazes at paintings by Botticelli, Ghirlandaio and Fra Angelico. The protagonist of the story is struck by 'an inner impotence of his own will', intensified by 'the habit of morally divided personality' that Marcel referred to in a letter to Darlu. Marie Kahn, whom Marcel knew and Maupassant had loved, was the inspiration for the heroine, as she was for Maupassant's *Notre cœur*.

In 1890 Bourget published his *Physiologie de l'amour moderne* which also deserves to be linked to Proust's work. Love, according to Nysten's *Dictionnaire de médecine*,[89] was actually considered a disease. The modern lover is analysed in endless detail; he closely observes every movement, expression and kiss in pursuit of certain treachery: he loves with one part of his being and mistrusts with another. The modern mistress, for her part, is described in terms of the 'great neurosis' and hysteria. When these two people meet one another, jealousy results; the *Physiologie* devotes forty pages to this and distinguishes between jealousy of the senses, of the heart and of the mind. These definitions are explained by 'cases' that are rather similar to Proust's short stories. 'La fin de la jalousie' would not have been worthy of this book; in Bourget's work, too, people die gently with a bullet near their heart; here, too, they meditate on art or on the sorrow of breaking up: 'One only really gets over a woman once one is no longer even curious to know who it is she has forgotten you for.' Bourget's hero plans a story about sadism, another about Lesbos: 'To investigate the impotent rage that this unveils, which is so distinctive and is unlike any other type of jealousy, because of its different nature'; and yet it was Proust who wrote 'Avant la nuit'. Furthermore, it is best not to have anything to do with writers: 'The more his inner self is rich and powerful, productive and expansive, the harder he finds it to express himself truthfully in his social behaviour.'[90] When the final chapter of the *Physiologie* refers to *The*

Imitation of Christ, Barrès, Taine, Sainte-Beuve, Ribot, Baudelaire, Pascal, Stendhal (since Bourget had wanted to rewrite *De l'amour*), we catch a glimpse of the intellectual world in which the young Marcel moved.

PROUST IN LOVE

On 1 January 1896 Reynaldo wrote to Suzette Lemaire: 'Marcel is still asleep and it is I who am writing to send you a thousand affectionate greetings.' It is useful to recapitulate on the evolution of Proust's and Reynaldo Hahn's love for one another, which, nevertheless, at the beginning of 1896 was starting to dwindle, slowly but inexorably, as it does in the stories in *Les Plaisirs et les Jours*, as in *Jean Santeuil* and 'Un amour de Swann'. On 16 April 1895 Marcel wrote to Reynaldo: 'Wait for the dear boy, lose him, find him again, love him twice as much on learning that he had come back to Flavie's* house to get me, wait for him for two minutes or make him wait for five, that for me is the real, thrilling, profound tragedy, which one day I may write and which meantime I am living.'[91] Seventeen years later, in a letter to a young man who failed to turn up at a rendezvous on the esplanade at Cabourg, Proust wrote: 'One day I shall depict those characters who, even from a vulgar point of view, will never understand what elegance is, what it is to be ready for a ball and to forgo it in order to keep a friend company. They think they are behaving in a sophisticated way, but it is quite the opposite.'[92] Proust in love: the letters to Reynaldo Hahn from 1894–6 provide the pattern, constantly recopied, from *Les Plaisirs et les Jours* to *Jean Santeuil* and in the draft notebooks of *À la recherche du temps perdu*. The two young men met in the spring of 1894. There were the first rendezvous and the concerts; one concludes *Les Plaisirs et les Jours*, the other *L'Île du rêve*. This 'Polynesian idyll' in three acts, adapted from a libretto by Alexandre and Harmann recommended by Massenet,† was based on *Le Mariage de Loti*, a novel which Marcel, we may recall, had read with voluptuous pleasure at Auteuil.[93] The female role was inspired by Cléo de Mérode, for whom Hahn harboured a platonic passion (like Proust's for Laure Hayman). The score for piano and voice was composed between 1891 and August 1893. Hahn

---

* The Marquise de Casa-Fuerte.

† Massenet observed in *Mes souvenirs*: 'He had dedicated that exquisite score to me. How acute is the music written by this veritable master! How it has the gift of enveloping you in its warm caresses!' (See note 93.) The cover of the score was illustrated with a branch of mimosa by Madeleine Lemaire.

played and sang the score to Loti ('who seemed moved')* at Daudet's house.† Proust had followed the work's final stages:[94] this can be seen from the annotations on the score, which date from the first visit to Réveillon: 'Proust sitting in front of me. Vague but profound sadness'; 'Réveillon. Wind, rain. Discussion with Proust. Sad.'[95] Reynaldo's perpetually melancholy air may well pass over the countenance of Odette Swann, just as his music is steeped in it.[96]

Hahn introduced Proust at several salons: those of Mme Stern, the Princesse de Polignac, Mme de Saint-Marceaux, the Marquise de Saint-Paul and, as we have seen, the Daudets.[97] Next came the phase of pet names – 'Marcel the pony'[98] – the plans for the seaside holiday; then Marcel burst forth with his great declaration: 'I accept everything since I give it back to you, and as for that portion of my inner life which I give to you – and which before giving to you I *owed* to you – were I able to believe that it were worth something, I would be doubly delighted. I should like to be master of everything that you might desire on earth in order to be able to bring it to you – the author of everything that you admire in art so that I might dedicate it to you.'‡ Proust then used the familiar '*tu*' form when addressing Hahn, called him 'my child', 'dear child', and called to mind some passages from *Les Plaisirs et les Jours* in which he muses to his friend about the Catholic dogma of the real presence which 'means precisely the ideal presence'.[99] The drama of a missed rendezvous would be the inspiration for the episode in which Swann pursues Odette along the boulevards and to the Maison Dorée.[100] In the spring of 1895 Proust's love reaches another characteristic stage: 'Should we not, in order to practise for the storms ahead, sometimes not see each other for a week and then a fortnight? – Yes, but please let's not bring that up again.'[101] The test of being apart, the deception that they should stop seeing one another, the trap that is set and then closed, all this can be seen again in Swann, in *À l'ombre des jeunes filles en fleurs* and in *La Prisonnière*. The roles

---

* Daudet, Loti and Hahn even sang Breton choruses together. This love of music which was inspired by Brittany permeates Hahn's song 'Paysage', which was based on a poem by Theuriet, and his visit to Beg-Meil.

† In *Alphonse Daudet*, Fasquelle, 1898, p. 60, Léon Daudet wrote about his father: 'The songs of his "little Reynaldo", which he asked him to play to him three times in succession, were of such precocious genius so wise and delicate, so perceptive and so softly sensual, they put him into a state of positive ecstasy.' Cf. *CSB*, p. 554.

‡ A reference to the dedication of 'Baldassare Silvande' in *La Revue hebdomadaire* of 29 October 1895; 'To Reynaldo Hahn, poet, singer and composer', *Corr.*, vol. I, p. 442, late October 1895.

were shared, for sometimes Marcel was obliged to reassure Reynaldo and to soothe his jealousy: 'You know everything that I do, only this morning I gave you a proof to reassure you, and had I wanted to see this person this afternoon you would also have known about it.'[102] The idyllic sojourn at Beg-Meil brought the two friends closer together. That autumn, they formed a plan to write a life of Chopin, 'a meticulous book in which the psychology of the artist would be revealed in the tiniest detail'.[103]

And then everything went sour and love took shelter in the past: 'My one consolation during this walk which, without any self-pity, I forced myself to take through the leafy paths of my memory and also along the paths rendered leafless in advance by my cruel clairvoyance of my future – was *you*.'[104] Proust no longer found Hahn at home: 'I knocked and even – just once – rang the bell. I heard not a sound, saw no light, no one opened the door to me and I returned feeling very sad.'[105] In *Jean Santeuil*, certainly, Reynaldo would be 'like a god in disguise whom no mortal recognized'.[106] But very soon, the pact whereby Proust required his closest friends to tell him everything, which became his obsession and was motivated by a longing to know everything so as to possess everything, was violated: 'It's an impossible task, alas, and when you in your kindness try to satisfy my curiosity by revealing a little of your past, you are undertaking a labour of the Danaïds. But if my fantasies are absurd, they are the fantasies of a sick man, and for that reason should not be thwarted.'[107] Thus would Swann torture Odette, and Honoré would torture Françoise in 'La Fin de la jalousie'. At this point Hahn, like Odette, refused to come back with his friend, which provoked a brutal letter: 'Do you not realize what an appalling period this has been recently when I have begun to sense how little I have come to mean to you, not out of revenge, or bitterness, you can't think so, can you . . . I simply think that just as I love you far less, you no longer love me at all.'[108] There were periods of remission that intervened in the development of jealousy and the death throes of love: 'So I feel no distress, just a deep tenderness for my darling one, whom I think about, as I used to say of my nanny when I was a child, not merely with my whole heart, but with the whole of me.' Then they decided not to spend the summer of 1896 together,[109] they would write less to one another, they would declare that they were no longer jealous. Proust's last love letter marks the transition from passion to friendship: 'My dearest little one, you would be very wrong to think that my silence is of the sort that is preparing for oblivion. It is of the kind that is like a loyal cinder that keeps tenderness intact and burning. My affection for you remains the same and I can more easily see that it is a fixed star when I see it in the same position after so many fires have taken place.'[110] In any case, Marcel asserted, at our age it would not be sensible to live as Tolstoy demands.[111] Eight years' worth of letters are missing following this alienation, as are all Reynaldo's replies, with a single exception which alludes rather sourly to Lucien Daudet. In the extracts from his diary which he published, Hahn expurgated all intimate passages, except this apparently confessional maxim: 'The pleasure that love brings is not really worth the happiness it destroys.'[112] The friendship which then replaces passion and Hahn's almost daily visits to Proust have something almost conjugal about them that is reminiscent of the relationship between M. and Mme Swann. Finally, the appearances of the two friends at the salons of Mme Daudet or Mme Lemaire* were preparing the way for Swann's appearance at the Verdurins'. In the novel, the reader encounters a relationship for which art is also the pretext.

LUCIEN DAUDET

When did Marcel meet Lucien Daudet for the first time? In February 1895 he was delighted to go to the Daudets' home to listen to Lucien and Léon, who had just returned from Sweden, recounting their adventures, and he copied out two pages of Lamartine's *Confidences* 'to illustrate Monsieur Lucien's memories of skating'.[113] He must surely have noticed him previously, sitting at the end of the table at his parents' house; from the age of sixteen, Lucien's 'only concern was reassuring himself in the mirror that his dinner jacket suited him'. Shy and quiet, his presence would have gone unnoticed,[114] except, no doubt, by someone who was on the look-out for adolescents. On 21 October 1895 Marcel turned to Lucien in order to ask Léon to intervene on his behalf at *La Nouvelle Revue*;† by 28 October he had progressed from 'Dear Sir' to 'Dear Friend', and he proposed to go and see Lucien at work at the Académie Julian, where the young man was taking painting lessons. A few days later, Marcel wrote that he was 'extremely nice' and 'very likeable'.[115] In December they were

---

* In the light of a letter from Proust to Hahn of 18 August 1895 (*Corr.* vol. II, p. 105), one wonders whether Suzette Lemaire may have been in love with Marcel (or Reynaldo).

† 'I have discovered from something said by Mme Adam (who rejected them and returned them to me) that it was your brother who was kind enough to consider my poems . . . I should be very glad to see you shortly' (*Corr.*, vol. XXI, p. 563, 28 October 1895).

in fits of laughter together as they gave imitations of Montesquiou; Proust provided the count with rather unconvincing excuses for their behaviour: 'Well, because of the fact that the body follows where the heart leads, my voice and accent may have taken on the rhythm of this borrowed thought. If anyone should have said anything else, and if anyone mentioned caricature, I would refer to your own axiom: "A word that is repeated is never true".'[116] From the end of that year onwards, it seems that Marcel was beginning to be if not attracted to Lucien, then at least interested in him; so was Reynaldo no longer enough for him? It was better to enjoy himself with little Lucien than get depressed with the melancholy Reynaldo. Their sense of humour, something not very common in France, brought them together: what was the use of cracking jokes, having a sense of the ridiculous, making fun of clichés, of fashionable or superfluous expressions (which the two young men would refer to as '*louchonneries*' – the sort of expression that leaves one goggle-eyed), all by oneself? This was what caused the lunatic laughter that so irritated Montesquiou, a man capable of making fun of others, but not of himself.

Lucien Daudet was born in Paris in 1878;* he was thus seven years younger than Marcel: the age of a little brother. Extremely good-looking, very elegant, slender and fragile, with a gentle, slightly effeminate face and large brown eyes (like Proust's own, which appealed to Marcel in those to whom he was attracted), as can be seen in the portrait that Albert Besnard painted of him in 1894,[117] he was the aristocrat of the family[†] according to his brother Léon.[‡] Drawn to high society, he was to become the devoted escort of the Empress Eugénie, whom he met in 1896 and to whom he would devote three books.[118] A novelist (*Le Chemin mort*, 1908, *La Fourmilière*, 1909, *Le Prince de cravates*, 1910),[119] he also wrote a biography of his father[120] and a book about Proust, *Autour de soixante lettres de Marcel Proust* (1928). He came from a family in which everyone wrote, and he would publish fifteen books. In the boy of seventeen Marcel would

---

* He died in 1946.

† The Daudets lived at 31 rue de Bellechasse (where their 'Thursdays', attended by the entire literary world, from the naturalists to the Symbolists, took place) before moving to 41 rue de l'Université; in 1909 Lucien, who lived with his mother until her death in 1940, returned to rue de Bellechasse. They lived, therefore, in a neighbourhood that was more aristocratic than literary, or, as in the case of the Prousts, simply bourgeois.

‡ Léon was ten years older. Their sister Edmée, eight years younger than Lucien, would be briefly married to André Germain, who would vow a fierce hatred of the family (and of Proust), as his works testify.

soon recognize something of himself, as well as being fascinated by the
hereditary likenesses: the father's face, or that of the mother, present in
the features of the son; Proust also knew Lucien's grandmother, Mme
Allard, who once said, 'That little Monsieur Proust is the most polite
person I've ever met', Alphonse Daudet, Mme Daudet, a writer herself,
as well as Léon, the elder brother, who was a prolific writer. Lucien was
one of those nervous, sensitive children who throughout their lives, in
spite of their talent, beneath the pained but impotent gaze of their father,[121]
bore the burden of having been overprotected by their mother.* Highly
cultivated, his family had nicknamed him 'Mr Know-all'. He was certainly
a snob, as is shown by some of his remarks: 'When I dine in town, I like
to be placed at the end of the table. It proves that I am at the home of
well-bred people.' Or, worse: 'I should have given anything for our name
to be written with a D apostrophe.'[122] Lucien Daudet would become such
a socialite and snob that he maintained, wrongly, that Proust failed 'to be
invited into the true and continuous intimacy of someone such as Mme
de Guermantes'.[123] He was also an artist, and in 1906, at Bernheim-Jeune,
he exhibited a series of *Flowers and Portraits*; Anna de Noailles wrote the
preface for the catalogue.[124] Proust listed a few of these paintings, which
are privately owned or have disappeared: 'I consider that in addition to
all the grounds for admiring you, there is a practical reason – your beautiful
painting, your *Loire blonde*, your *Paradis pas de quatre de Tintoret Degas*, your
Mystérieux Jardin, your *Mère*.'[125] A portrait of Proust has been attributed to
Daudet,[126] and Proust did write to him, on 15 August 1896, on the subject
of a portrait: 'I should very much like you to do mine. Would you like
me to arrange for one of the photographs that are at Otto's to be sent to
you? No, you may prefer to come and choose, there are masses of
ridiculous poses.'[127] Alas! Lucien was too easily discouraged to be able to
pursue anything, even his career as a painter. However, it began under
the auspices of Whistler, and, together with Montesquiou, Daudet may
have helped Proust to know him a little better: 'Whistler, whose only
French pupil I believe I was, gave me a certain taste in painting and made
me understand why a thing is beautiful, but at the same time he gave me
a great disdain for anything that was not first-rate and ... I apply this
same disdain to what I do.'[128] And yet in 1909 Marcel was still speaking
about his 'admirable dual talent', and in 1918 he exclaimed: 'What a painter
you are!' Lucien may have given up painting around 1907, at the time that

* Among Proust's circle, we shall also encounter Gide, Cocteau and Maurice Rostand.

he became a writer; Montesquiou, too, was adept with the paintbrush, and, in their wake, so was Baron de Charlus. Dwarfed on the one hand by Whistler, on the other by Alphonse Daudet, Lucien's tragedy was that of a son who, wishing to follow in his father's footsteps, never finds his own voice: 'I have no ambition,' he wrote to his mother in 1910. 'I am the son of a man whose fame and talent made him respected by several generations, and I am quite content to remain in his shadow.'[129] Here he is in the shadow of Proust.

For Proust, what finer project, be it platonic or socratic, could there be than to shape an adolescent like this, when he was still malleable, rather more so than Reynaldo, and when the age gap of seven years allowed the elder of the two much more freedom! The benefits of his influence probably explain why M. et Mme Daudet allowed their son to go out with Marcel – the numerous literary conversations in which Lucien's precocity played its part, the daily visits to the Louvre, the many precise rendezvous (a quarter past twelve on the Pont de la Concorde!).[130] The pleasure Proust took in his domination was coupled with something else; in the event that he or Reynaldo should grow tired of one another, was it not prudent to have two irons in the fire, or an alternative solution? In the meantime, was it not desirable to provoke jealousy, the guarantee of love?

In Marcel's letters we can thus follow the progress of this affection, to which the salutations at the beginning bear witness: in October 1895 '*Cher Monsieur*' became '*Mon cher ami*' and on 1 January 1896, '*Mon cher Lucien*'[131] was followed on 31 January by '*Mon petit Lucien*'. They trusted each other enough for Proust to rely on Lucien to come up with a title for his book, which, in late March, when he was preparing the page layout with M. Hubert, the production director of Calmann-Lévy, was still called *Le Château de Réveillon*, after Mme Lemaire's property.[132] At Easter 1896 Lucien's departure for Venice with his parents provoked additional affection and sorrow: 'I was especially sad on the evening of your departure, when you waved to me with that little gesture of the hand that usually means: until tomorrow.[133] That little farewell, which would not be followed by another meeting for quite a long time, was very sad.'[134] And it made Marcel want to go to the rue de la Paix, simply because his friend had told him, 'It's so pretty at six in the evening';[135] he was upset if he was not ready in time to 'say good-bye' to Lucien at his parents' 'Thursdays'.[136] In the circumstances, it is pointless to wonder how far the relationship developed, particularly since the letters that provide evidence of the extent of this passion have not been published.* Later, Marcel would reproach Lucien for 'immersing himself' far away from him (after the Dreyfus affair or Proust's friendship with Robert de Flers). He would make this crucial revelation to Antoine Bibesco: as far as Marcel was concerned, an affection did not last more than eighteen months[137] (and he took as an example Illan de Casa-Fuerte, another darling child of a glamorous mother, who was, furthermore, a friend of the Empress Eugénie and of Montes-quiou, who shared the same type of looks, and also represented maternal pleasure promised by a young man's body). As for Lucien, he was not without resentment: 'Marcel is wonderful,' he said to Cocteau. 'But he's a dreadful insect. You'll understand that one day.'[138]

It did not escape Reynaldo Hahn's notice that he was beginning to lose Marcel; he 'scolded' him, reproached him and told him so in Proustian terms that are very close to the letters of the Narrator and Gilberte to one another: 'My little one, life is so short and so boring that it is quite right not to deprive oneself of things (even the most insignificant ones) that amuse or give pleasure, as long as they are not guilty or harmful. So, forgive me, dearest Marcel. Sometimes I really am unbearable; I realize. But we are all so imper-fect.'[139] Yet it was to Reynaldo that Marcel showed, in March, the opening of *Jean Santeuil*, which bore close similarities to their own lives: 'You will help me to correct anything that is too similar. I want you to be there all the time, but like a god in disguise whom no mortal recognizes. Otherwise you will be obliged to write "cut" against the entire novel.'[140] Hahn may have received this affirmation as a proof of love; we know that in his work, as in *Bluebeard's Castle*, Proust buried all his old friends and all his past loves. And, just as he carried on two relationships at the same time, he began one book before having published another – again, he would become interested in Ruskin before he had completed *Jean Santeuil*.

We should consider Proust's article on Jules Lemaître's *La Belle Hélène*, in which Réjane played the leading role,[141] in the light of these love affairs. Jealousy is in fact at the heart of Proust's analysis: 'It is not from dreams, it is not from melancholy, it is not from thought, it is from the body that jealousy comes. She is the dark daughter of pleasure . . . which she resembles in that immense thirst which nothing can quench.' We are jealous of

---

* Robert de Saint-Jean (1901–87) was given a packet of letters by Lucien Daudet: Angelo Rinaldi speaks in these terms of letters 'without periphrasis that were exchanged by the two lovers. Alas! people will have to take my word when I affirm that when they met they were not bored.' 'Lulu et les monstres', *L'Express*, 5 December 1991.

another's pleasure, whether it be given or taken: this, already defined, is Albertine's prison. It is the Proustian division between intelligence and the dark forces of the body and the unconscious: 'Jealousy takes root well before intelligence; but she doesn't know this, and there is nothing that intelligence can say to console her. Confronted with jealousy, the mind is disarmed, as it is when confronted with illness and with death.'[142]

THE DEATH OF LOUIS WEIL

Marcel experienced death for a second time: after having lost his grand-mother, he saw his great-uncle, Louis Weil, die on 10 May 1896 at the age of eighty. He immediately informed Weil's former mistress, the elegant and charming Laure Hayman* (who was then aged forty-five), of the rather sudden death of the 'poor old uncle': 'In his religion, there isn't any service. Everyone gathers at half-past three in the afternoon at his home at 102 Boulevard Haussmann and from there we go on to Père-Lachaise (though I am afraid that this may be tiring for you,' added Marcel delicately, 'and not many women will be going)'; he nevertheless insisted that the presence of Laure Hayman, 'whom one cannot know without admiring and liking her',[143] far from shocking people, would touch their hearts. The burial took place without flowers, according to the wishes of the deceased, but Laure Hayman, who did not know this, arranged for a wreath to be delivered, which Mme Proust had placed on its own in the grave: at the sight of this, Marcel burst into tears, 'less from sorrow than from admiration'.[144] Uncle Louis left 100,000 francs to his great-nephews.[145] So as not to upset his mother, Proust did not go out for a week, but ten days later we find him at the home of Léon Delafosse, who was playing his latest melodies at a soirée at which Marguerite Moreno and Le Bargy recited poems by Montesquiou which were to be published in *Les Hortensias bleus*.[146] On 29 May, Marcel thanked the author for this collection, the best known of Montesquiou's works: he and Lucien Daudet had spent the whole of the preceding day reading it and had been very moved. In it the influence of Gautier, who provided the title,† Baudelaire, Verlaine and Mallarmé is seen to excess, and beautiful poems alternate

---

* Like Odette, she lived at 4 rue Lapérouse.

† As is shown by the epigraph borrowed from the author of *Émaux et camées*: 'We were very struck by these blue hydrangeas, for the blue is the wildest fantasy of horticulturalists, who search in vain for the blue tulip, the blue rose, the blue dahlia . . .'

with platitudes or pretentious expressions that verge on the ridiculous; the collection is split between the concerns of an interior designer, which we also find in the count's memoirs – 'I want these poems to be artistic curios,/ Special, curious, unusual, strange/ . . . The object of rarity that is caressed by the hand and replaced' ('Manières') – and the pathetic search for something new, which he proclaims without giving it substance: 'I want to write poetry that no one else has attempted;/ A poetry that is mysterious and bizarre, and which strikes/ A disconcerting tone' ('Transfusions'). Proust defined his own concept of poetry, a few weeks later, in *La Revue blanche*: it was entitled 'Contre l'obscurité'.

A FOREWORD

Le Figaro and *Le Gaulois* of 9 June 1896 both published Anatole France's foreword to *Les Plaisirs et les Jours*. On 28 November 1892 *L'Étui de nacre* had been published, in which the story 'Mme de Luzy' was dedicated to Proust, who, as we know, had dedicated 'Violante ou la mondanité', in the February 1893 issue of *Le Banquet*, to France. In December 1893 Marcel had asked his help in finding a publisher. Still positioning himself between France and Montesquiou, that is to say, between classicism and a somewhat decadent symbolism, Proust included a few of France's words at the end of a letter he had written to the count, quoting to him a sentence from *Le Lys rouge* (France's 'Un amour de Swann').[147] We know nothing about the circumstances in which France wrote a foreword to *Les Plaisirs et les Jours* (Proust mentioned it as early as 1894 in a letter to Mme de Brantes),[148] at the request or otherwise of Mme de Caillavet, about what was said to Proust's publisher, Calmann-Lévy, or about the publication of the foreword in *Le Figaro* and *Le Gaulois* of 9 June. It has even been implied that Mme Arman wrote a part of France's text[149] – and yet the master's style is easily recognizable. It is rather more interesting to know what image France had formed of the young Proust – who would always remain a young man in France's eyes. The portrait he paints is of a *fin-de-siècle* writer, of a decadent. This old young man does not depict natural suffering (such as that in *Le Lys rouge*), but 'invented' torments and 'artistic sorrows', in 'an atmosphere of a warm greenhouse, among scholarly orchids'.* His characters are 'snobbish souls'; his landscapes have 'the desolate splendour of the setting sun'. The narrator wears 'weary smiles',

---

* They will become the flower of Odette Swann, who had the same sickly beauty.

he has a 'tired bearing' – but he is also vastly cultivated: he belongs with Bernardin de Saint-Pierre, Petronius and Hesiod. 'It is the spring when leaves appear on ancient branches': Proust remained loyal to these images of plants, from the title of *À l'ombre des jeunes filles en fleurs* onwards. At once perverted and naïve, perhaps this is not a bad portrait of Proust at twenty-five (it is certainly far from being merely a conceit), and of the author of *Les Plaisirs et les Jours*. At least one other reading of the book is possible: one which leads us to the disciple of Anatole France, to the man who would thus avoid the trap of decadence. Neither in this context, nor in the character of Bergotte, did the master ever recognize himself.

In 'Contre l'obscurité', his article for *La Revue blanche* (15 July 1896, but submitted six months earlier),[150] Proust again, and for the last time, made himself the mouthpiece for France's aesthetic views. He had read his articles in *Le Temps*, which were then republished in *La Vie littéraire*, and he remembered them six years later.[151] On 19 August 1888 France had responded to Charles Morice: 'I do not forgive the Symbolists their profound obscurity. "You speak in enigmas" is a reproach which the warriors and kings frequently addressed to one another in Sophocles' tragedies. The Greeks were subtle; yet they insisted on the need to express oneself clearly. I think they were quite correct to do so.'[152] The whole of France's article is a polemic 'against obscurity', which ends as follows: 'I shall never believe in the success of a school of literature that expresses difficult thoughts in an obscure language.'[153] And France returned to this subject of the 'young School' in his preface to volume II of *La Vie littéraire*. This school is unintelligible because it is mystical, and it writes in a state of ecstasy. He attacked René Ghil, whose *Traité du verbe* (1886) had a foreword written by Mallarmé, as well as Rimbaud. 'The future lies with symbolism if the neurosis which has produced it becomes widespread.' Poets were becoming 'delightful invalids' who 'argued amongst each other, under the indulgent eye of M. Stéphane Mallarmé'.[154] The protective tone and affectionate adjective disguised the scornful ferocity of the substance of his argument – for disciples tend to shield their master – about what was really to blame. Proust took up this tone, these themes, this stance. 'Contre l'obscurité' is France's doctrine; it is a rejection of symbolism, as well as of the decadent spirit and of the 1890 avant-garde. The following month Mallarmé responded in *La Revue blanche*. His disciples, Valéry, Gide, Claudel, even Régnier, would never again take Proust's side.

Here, we can see the crucial role played by France (as by Darlu) in Proust's intellectual development. Normally, he would have been expected to belong to the avant-garde of his generation, like the majority of young writers from *La Revue blanche*, who also had much in common with symbolism. But it is only too easy to see that he would have come to an impasse. What was left of the Symbolists that was not Mallarmé?[155] The doctrine, the poems, the novels without action, in the manner of *À rebours*, continued to be regarded as 'Art nouveau' curiosities, yet none of them outlasted the turn of the century. The limp, listless, vegetal sentences, the rarefied vocabulary and bizarre syntax became outdated just as they had once been fashionable: Gide and Valéry also abandoned the style of the *Cahiers d'André Walter* and of the *Album de vers anciens*. Because Proust admired France, his style, his books, his philosophy and the aesthetic principles set out in *La Vie littéraire*, he used them as an antidote against the avant-garde, and he developed a sentence structure to oppose the symbolist sentence, a clear thought process and a repertory of classical themes: those of *Livre de mon ami* and *Le Lys rouge*. In Anatole France, he discovered a paternal figure, just as the Narrator does in Bergotte.

But Proustian passions did not last, whether love affairs or aesthetic enthusiasms, probably because they were borne along on the same secret tempo. *Jean Santeuil* provides the evidence for this, between 1895 and 1899. Here we encounter M. de Traves, a 'brilliant novelist', whose presence, conversation and life 'in no way extended the strange enchantment, the unique world into which he transported you from the very first pages of one of his books'. What is more, we can sense the cause of Proust's estrangement, the germ of which manifested itself as early as the *philosophie* class, when Marcel wrote his first admiring letter to France, almost as if decline set in at the very height of his love: M. de Traves was 'an avid follower of the materialist and sceptical school of philosophy', while Jean, under the influence of M. Beulier,* was spiritual and idealistic: 'He could not admit that a materialist could be a man of intelligence.'[156] In another fragment Proust again contrasts his two masters, France and Darlu, when he summarizes the writer's conversation: 'Jean secretly took pity on all those who believed in Science, those who did not believe in the absolute of the Self and in the existence of God.† And this was the case with M. de Traves. Furthermore, whatever the subject under discussion, M. de Traves seemed to be interested in topics that left Jean feeling so indifferent

---

* In other words, Darlu. There are traces of the conversations, and the disagreements, with Darlu in *La Vie littéraire*.

† This would seem to suggest that in the *philosophie* class, Marcel still believed in God.

that he soon stopped listening. There was never a general idea, such as those M. Beulier developed, never any oracular opinions about the nature of the soul, or about intelligence. But about factual matters, the original meaning of a word, the usage from which the word derived, the factual reasons for which it was not possible to believe that a particular writer had intended such and such a meaning, the period to which an object could be attributed on the basis of its style, the connection between other, similar objects – on all of this he was inexhaustible. Tidying his bookcases, searching for trinkets, these were his greatest pleasures, occupations that were entirely inimical to Jean and bored him to death. As to literature, he cared only for the eighteenth century, a period which meant nothing to Jean.'[157] If we add to this the fact that Traves believed beauty to be something real, that lay within the object and not in the mind, we come to realize how Proust grew progressively detached from Anatole France: from the way he thought first of all, possibly while Marcel was in the *philosophie* class; then from his personality and his conversation; and finally from his work, when the discovery of Ruskin – whom France did not like – came as the final blow. But this estrangement did not occur before the young man had taken everything that the older man could give him: his esteem, his character and his language.

We know that France gave the impression of being the godfather of *Les Plaisirs et les Jours*, because M. Hubert, of the publisher Calmann-Lévy, wrote to France asking him to check the text of the book, even though 'the delightful boy', the author, 'would not hear of it', and that Messrs. Calmann-Lévy 'accepted the book with their eyes shut'.[158] We do not know what the reply was of 'the man of genius who is our master', as Proust wrote to Maurras, who mentioned France's foreword in his article on *Les Plaisirs et les Jours*.[159] The young man observed his future character sometimes at the home of Mme de Caillavet, where he ironically recorded one of her conversations with France,[160] or sometimes at his own home, when he invited him to dinner.*

* On 24 May 1896, for example, together with painters (J. Béraud), writers (Porto-Riche, Rod), R. Hahn, and, in particular, Montesquiou. Proust never stopped interposing himself between the two men, as if to draw closer to or to confront his two sources of inspiration in a sort of laboratory experiment (cf. *Corr.*, pp. 85–6). On 24 April 1899 Cora Laparcerie read France's poems at Proust's home.

PROUST AND MALLARMÉ

In order to draw closer to France, Proust severed links with Mallarmé, even though, as we shall see, he understood the latter rather better than he appeared to do. In 'Contre l'obscurité' he took issue with the young symbolist generation, to whom *Les Plaisirs et les Jours* owed nothing. He criticized simultaneously the obscurity of their ideas, their imagery and their grammar. In the same issue of *La Revue blanche*, Lucien Mühlfeld responded sharply to Proust in an article entitled 'Sur la clarté': 'he has summarized in a graceful hand the objections of the literary salons'; Mühlfeld implicated 'M. Anatole France, his eminent master', and concluded, 'Oh, Clarity, Clarity, what obscure and foolish utterances are spouted in your name.' Proust conceded that poetry is a mystery which is addressed to the elect, but he considered that the mystery of the Symbolists was false; they constructed a theorem or a puzzle out of poetry. Words should be comprehensible so as to retain the poetry of their history and etymology: 'The poet relinquishes that irresistible power to awaken so many Sleeping Beauties in us if he speaks a language that we do not know.' Nature teaches us clarity, 'the shape of everything is individual and clear': 'She enables every man, during his passage on earth, to explain the most profound mysteries of life and of death clearly.' Proust's aesthetic views, vigorously propounded here, would not alter again; this is therefore a crucial landmark in the genealogy of his ideas. Yet Mallarmé's poetry broke away from the romanticism of nature and of the past, and even with Wagner.

Mallarmé, in turn, took up his pen, and his article, 'Le Mystère dans les lettres' appeared six weeks later; in his reply, he attacked Proust's very title 'Contre l'obscurité': 'I prefer, in the face of the attack, to retort that some of our contemporaries do not know how to read.' The poet then distinguished between the superficial level of the text, 'the surface that is conceded to the retina', 'the dreary level that suffices for intelligibility', and a deeper level, a 'treasure': all writing conveys a primary meaning, the language of the crowd, the vulgar, as well as a secondary meaning, 'that of an object that is other'; the 'idle' person ignores this secondary meaning, 'delighted that nothing in it, at first sight, concerns him'. The reader has an initial perception of this treasure, through a 'shimmering that lies beneath it, not easily separable from the outward appearance'. But there is an obscureness 'in the depths of everyone', the poet included, the essential mystery of man, 'that signifies what is closed and hidden'. The poet reveals this signifier; the reader should not ask for an intelligibility that possesses only minor interest, because it exhibits 'things at an imperturbable first level, like a hawker's wares' and displays merely banality. If what is immediate is vulgar, poetry offers a precious cloud that floats over the intimate depths of every thought. Music had opened the way, because it does not encounter the barrier of representation and touches directly upon the human mystery, 'face to face with the Unutterable or the Pure, the poetry that is without words!'[161] Music does not awaken our feelings, but rather an imaginary archetype, a contrast of light and of shadow. Mallarmé did not accept that obscurity should be attributed to music and clarity to literature: 'Writing has claims on Mystery.' There is a primitive logic, that of the human imagination, that is divided between night* and day, between nothingness and eternity, anxiety and dream. Proust compared clarity and obscurity, Mallarmé compared black and white, virginity and mystery. The whiteness of the page purifies the reader, who then attains access to the Idea present in the text: 'Nothing would be elucidated beyond that.' Just as there is nothing beyond this life ('The radiant eternal genius has no shadow'), in the same way there is nothing beyond the page; everything is within the writing and the reading. This dialogue from *La Revue blanche*, which gave rise to one of Mallarmé's finest commentaries, contrasted two aesthetic viewpoints and revealed Proust to be closer to Mallarmé than either of them believed. The younger man conclusively rejected all allegiances and believed that everything could be said clearly; yet he also loved music, sought the essence that lay beneath the appearance and explored the night beyond the day: was not this entire generation imbued with the great duet from Act II of *Tristan and Isolde*?

Marcel had an opportunity for a reconciliation with Mallarmé a few weeks after publishing 'Contre l'obscurité'; at the end of August, he commented on an unpublished quatrain by the poet, 'Méry, l'an pareil sur sa course', the text of which had been sent to him by Reynaldo.[162] Proust noted its circumstantial nature: the birthday of Méry Laurent, Mallarmé's mistress (though she would have many other lovers, among them the wealthy Doctor Evans: another Odette!) and a friend of Reynaldo, who would be the executor of her will and also her beneficiary.† Considering

---

* In *Le Temps retrouvé*, Proust would speak of 'the great impenetrable night of our soul'.

† Hahn evidently had a talent for attracting courtesans. After Cléo de Mérode, Liane de Pougy wrote him impassioned letters, which recall those of Proust and of Louisa de Morand, a little-known actress and the mistress of Louis d'Albufera: 'You are the only man to whom I want to give myself and who will not take me . . . No, my Reynaldo, we shall not pick the fruit of love: we shall remain

it pedantic to explain the literary and, especially, the poetic charm of this 'fugitive' piece, he immediately generalized and noted that the 'obscure and brilliant' images were still the images of objects, but were 'reflected . . . in a sombre, polished black marble mirror', 'springtime in a catafalque'. The charm of the quatrain itself consisted in adopting a classic form, 'pure and inflexible', and sinking in it 'in the guise of archaism' the wildest preciosity. Proust's broad culture thus enabled him to identify a type of poetry and a style which, in its subject matter ('the mythology of time') and in its language, that of 'the end of the sixteenth and beginning of the seventeenth centuries', was very unfashionable at the time. This preciosity, however, was decked in modern colours and, in its imagery, with sincerity and an exquisite nature. The organic, plant-like quality of the female body that Proust observed in Mallarmé would be bestowed upon the sleeping Albertine in *La Prisonnière*. 'This *thirsting* foot which will drink like a plant gives us a wonderful notion of those obscure creatures that are our organs and which in fact appear to be alive with an obscure but private life of their own.' Mallarmé achieved a feat by incorporating within a celebratory quatrain the archaic turn of language. The grandeur of his tone, the mythology of his themes, his feeling for nature, his taste: 'It is here "in the final analysis" that the charm lies', just as the role of the poet is to 'solemnize life'.[163] In this remarkable critical analysis, certainly intended for a friend of Mallarmé's, Proust thus recorded, as in 'Contre l'obscurité', certain reservations (neither the archaism nor the preciosity convince him), but equally his respect and his understanding. Marcel would always be closer to Baudelaire than to the author of the 'Le Cygne' sonnet. Yet it is this sonnet* that the Narrator would have engraved on Albertine's yacht, and Marcel on Alfred Agostinelli's aeroplane.[164] The theme of funereal gloom lying beneath the whiteness then recurred in tragic circumstances; in order that Alfred should appreciate this sonnet, which he found obscure, it was first necessary for Marcel, who may have been keen to illustrate the dream of flight, but at the same time the hope that his friend would not fly away, to read it to him and comment upon it, as he did, twenty years beforehand, to his other friend, Reynaldo.

---

platonic, we shall always desire one another' (quoted by B. Gavoty, *Reynaldo Hahn*, Buchet–Chartel, 1976, p. 121).

*'*Un cygne d'autrefois se souvient que c'est lui/ Magnifique mais qui sans espoir se délivre/ Pour n'avoir pas chanté la région où vivre/ Quand du stérile a resplendi l'ennui.*' [A swan of olden times recalls that he,/ Splendid yet void of hope to free himself,/ Had left unsung the realm of life itself/ When sterility glittered with ennui.]

LES PLAISIRS ET LES JOURS: AN APPRAISAL

At the point at which Proust embarked upon an important novel which he would not complete, let us draw up an assessment of his first book, *Les Plaisirs et les Jours*. It can teach us a great deal about the author's technique and about his themes. Even though this book cannot compare in any way with *À la recherche*, or even *Jean Santeuil*, it contains almost everything in a state of germination. The first aspect to stress is that we are dealing with a collection of over fifty diverse texts. In his youth the author discovered the technique which he would never alter and which would make him both so happy and so miserable: writing fragments and pieces that differed greatly in length, style and content. Some of them had been published in magazine form (similarly, extracts from *À la recherche* would appear in *Le Figaro* and in *La Nouvelle Revue Française*). It had taken Proust a long time to write these pieces: he maintained that he had begun them while at school, at 'the age of fourteen';[165] if we are to believe him, it therefore took him ten years. *Jean Santeuil* would take him four years, but would remain unfinished; his work on Ruskin would occupy six years, and *À la recherche*, ultimately, fourteen. The second feature that strikes one upon reading *Les Plaisirs et les Jours* is the variety of techniques that are used, for the book comprises seven short stories, prose poems and verse, pastiches, portraits in the style of La Bruyère, and moral reflections in the manner of La Rochefoucauld, the occasional descriptive piece, and transpositions from art and painting. Fiction, social criticism and poetry are divided according to the literary forms that are used.

In this youthful work a number of subjects, situations and characters, which Proust would not relinquish and which the reader will be surprised to come across in *À la recherche*, appear for the first time: there may well be nothing which the author has allowed to be lost; even the pieces that were not included in *Les Plaisirs et les Jours* would, as we shall see, be reread, replaced, rewritten, passed over, certainly, but also preserved. This explains why Proust, from 1913 onwards, was able simultaneously to extol and denigrate his first book, and why certain readers, such as André Gide, should have discovered and admired it: 'When I now reread *Les Plaisirs et les Jours*, the virtues of this gentle book, which was published in 1896, seem to me so startling that I am astonished that we were not dazzled in the first place. But today our eye has been alerted and everything which, subsequently, we may have been able to admire in Marcel Proust's recent books, we can now recognize here in a place where at first we had not known to look.'[166]

The five stories in the collection describe the progress of a hero, or of a heroine; Proust always remained loyal to this structure. In 'La mort de Baldassare Silvande', the protagonist learns how to die; but, unequal to his vocation, he is overcome with the memories which might have sustained him. We see the same lack of will-power in 'Violante ou la mondanité'; social life cuts the heroine off from 'the natural source of true joy', and, like the Duchesse de Guermantes subsequently, she loses, in old age, the regal society which 'virtually a child still, she had conquered'.[167] 'Mélancolique villégiature de Mme de Breyves' tells of an 'inexplicable love' which punctuates the whole of this woman's life 'with a form of anguish';[168] the beloved is here associated with a phrase from *Die Meistersinger*, which the person she loved used to like to play on the piano. Unrequited love, guilty love – in effect, homosexual love – is the supreme test, the one initiation that is kept in check in a book that is suffused with desire: this is the subject of 'La confession d'une jeune fille' and 'La fin de la jalousie'. Forbidden love, the deed performed under the eyes of the mother who dies as a result of it, followed by the girl's suicide, or indeed Honoré's jealousy, which foreshadows that of Swann, culminating in a death brought about by a horse, like that of Albertine, shows that if we superimpose these stories, adding to them 'Avant la nuit', which Proust did not include,[169] we discover these same stages: a childhood whose purity remains present in the memory, a disgrace, an affronted mother, a death. Love would also be responsible for the deaths of Albertine, the grandmother and the Princesse de Guermantes.

Art, at this period, is an important theme, but a subordinate one. The portraits of painters and musicians, the association of Wagner and of Botticelli with the beloved (as the latter was linked to Odette later on) – these are not enough to reverse the hierarchy where love is the crucial event and the sole source of happiness. *Les Plaisirs et les Jours* is not a book about art, nor one in which art is the subject. Neither is it a book about memory, despite the fact that it contains numerous recollections and that Proust may sometimes combine art and memory, as when he recalls, in a sentence that foreshadows life at Doncières in *Le Côté de Guermantes*, 'the Dutch painting of our memories'.[170] On the other hand, the heroes already possess many of the same characteristics, and share the same actions and feelings as the Narrator of *À la recherche*: the relationship with the mother, the drama of going to bed, the lack of will-power, the illusion of love, the usefulness of sorrow, the women whose eyes 'promise a love that their hearts will not retain',[171] the favourite landscapes, whether wooded or by the sea, the anguish of the hotel room, the attacks of 'nervous asthma';[172] the lesbians are harbingers of Gomorrah, whereas there are no male homosexuals in these stories; and Hippolyta heralds Mme de Guermantes; sadomasochism, which will later be allocated to Charlus, can be found from 'La Confession d'une jeune fille' onwards.

RECEPTION OF *LES PLAISIRS ET LES JOURS*

The book was published on 12 June 1896 (preceded, as we have seen, by Anatole France's foreword, which appeared in *Le Figaro* and *Le Gaulois* on 9 June). It was produced in a large octavo format, with a pale-green, glossy cover, illustrated on both front and back. France's foreword took up two pages, the dedication to Willie Heath, three. The volume consisted of 273 pages. The main print-run was 1,500 copies; most of these waited in vain at the publisher's for library orders.[173] The de-luxe print-run consisted of thirty copies on rice paper[174] and twenty on Japanese paper that included an original watercolour by Madeleine Lemaire.[175] She had also embellished the book with frontispiece drawings, end papers and numerous illustrations in the realist style then in vogue, including her Château de Réveillon, featured on the title-page and the last page, the principal settings for the stories, and a portrait of Marcel surrounded by card players. The vignettes and the end papers contain as many flowers as a vase by Gallé. Furthermore, the work included the score of Reynaldo Hahn's 'Portraits de peintres', which had already been published by Heugel. 'Cuyp' and 'Potter' were marked as *andante*, 'Watteau' as *andantino quasi allegretto* with a 'soft and gentle sound' and a '*ritenuto* like a memory'; 'Van Dyck' was to be played with 'elegance and melancholy'. The typographical layout was important: each piece was separate from the others and started at the top of a new page, whereas in modern editions the pieces are run on.[176] This edition is also therefore a fine *objet d'art* in the style of the time; later on, Proust would be totally indifferent to the actual production, de luxe or otherwise, of his books. The price, at 13 francs 50 centimes,* was high: Marcel's friends would make fun of the fact in a satirical review: 'Proust. – A foreword by M. France, four francs ... Paintings by Mme Lemaire, four francs ... Music by Reynaldo Hahn, four francs ... Prose by myself, one franc ... A few of my poems, fifty centimes ... Total thirteen francs fifty, was this not excessive?'[177]

* About 330 francs by 1999 standards.

The reception accorded to this de-luxe edition was hardly resounding. What is more, Proust's relationship with the press and the general public was launched in an atmosphere of incomprehension: there were no buyers – 329 copies were sent out by the publisher in twenty-two years, many of them given away by the author – and no important article to launch it, yet, on Proust's part, there were no complaints to his friends, no bitter letter to his publisher (with whom he did not even have a written contract): it was the dignified silence of someone who is turning to other projects. Five reviews deserve to be mentioned. The first to appear, in *La Liberté* of 26 June, was by Paul Perret, who stressed at length the originality, variety and modernity of the work. In *Le Gaulois* the Swiss novelist Édouard Rod devoted a few lines to it, in a postscript to an article on Schwob: 'How can there be so many qualities of observation in a mind so young?'[178] More noteworthy was the article by Léon Blum, an acquaintance if not a friend, in *La Revue blanche*, which was certainly obliged to review a book by one of its staff writers, from which it had published lengthy extracts: 'Society tales, gentle stories, melodic poems . . . fragments in which the detail of a feature subsides into the soft charm of his phrases, M. Proust has assembled all the genres and all his assets. And so, the fine ladies and young men will read such a beautiful book with pleasure and emotion.' Charles Maurras, who at the age of twenty-eight had only published the tales in *Chemin du Paradis*, showed a great understanding of the book in *La Revue encyclopédique* of 22 August 1896: its variety and poetry, its clear-sightedness and sensibility, passion and intelligence, its feeling and sense of irony, the transparency of the language, nothing escaped him: 'The new generation will have to get used to relying on this young writer.' His article was illustrated with a photograph by Otto, who for a long time was Proust's 'authorized' photographer. Marcel, who was very touched, declared modestly: 'One day your captivated reader will believe that it is due to some injustice that my book has not endured and that perhaps I had some talent.'[179] But even if the fairies are few, there must always be a wicked one; Jean Lorrain fulfilled this role in *Le Journal* of 1 July, in which he criticized France for writing indulgent forewords for 'nice young men in society who are yearning for literary success in the salons'. Since 'all snobs have wanted to be authors', 'the salon of Mme Arman de Caillavou* has recently overcome any resistance from the author of *Thaïs*, and it is to M. Anatole France, that successor to M. de Fezensac, who

* A witty joke, making the name rhyme with Montesquiou.

until now was unique of his kind, that we owe the young and charming Marcel Proust.' It was certainly not this article that led its victim to like criticism in the manner of Sainte-Beuve; nor did it prompt a duel which we shall discuss later on.[180] Very few letters mentioning the reactions of those to whom copies of the book were sent survive: Montesquiou was delighted to be able to embrace the author's talent comprehensively. Alphonse Daudet thanked his 'dear Little Marcel' 'for the beautiful basket of flowers in which [he sends him] all [his] youth — dreams, music and ripples of emotion — magically adorned with ribbons by a fairy-artist'.[181] Mallarmé, bearing no grudge, doubtless expressed his opinion to Reynaldo and 'thought it very good', as wrote Proust in 1920, 'because he was possessed of the demon of indulgence'.[182]

THE DEATH OF THE GRANDFATHER

On 30 June 1896 Nathé Weil, Mme Proust's father, who had been ill for a long time, died at the age of eighty-two, six weeks after his brother Louis. 'Considering that he had not digested anything for two days [he] allowed himself to die of hunger in a week, while he continued to have himself carried into his bathroom three times a day, where a terrified Papa took his pulse the whole time.'[183] Marcel did his best to stay beside him, while he grew weaker and weaker by the hour and all hope of saving him was lost; he then spent his time trying to comfort his mother in her grief.[184] The young man prone to 'fits of black sadness' described thoughts proper to mourning: 'When you see . . . how it all ends, what is the use of grieving over sorrows or dedicating oneself to causes of which nothing will remain. Only the fatalism of the Muslims seems to make sense.'[185] And in July, when Marcel was helping to empty his grandfather's flat and to let it: 'It still seems to me a real injustice not that we should be separated from him, but he from us who so belonged to him, and still belong to him, whom he loved so much, whom he made so welcome and made his own. We are like a house without its master.'[186] Going to Saint-Cloud to see Reynaldo, with whom relations had, however, grown acrimonious, afforded him some consolation. Thus, silently, did the last representative of the generation before his parents' slip away, the charming confidant of his youth, to whom Marcel turned to ask for money as well as political observations, his host during the holidays at Auteuil, who would soon come to spend them at 'Combray' for ever. As with all Jewish families, he was the ruler, endowed with a special authority, like the family of

Abraham.[187] It was from this cheerful financier, who was wise enough not to leave it too late to retire, and who was prepared to back other foreign-exchange dealers or stockbrokers,[188] that Marcel acquired his taste for speculating, and from him that he conceived the character of Charles Swann's father, as well as being able to observe that humorous anti-Semitism that is the preserve of Jews alone.[189] Mme Proust bore her grief with her customary bravery: 'Maman is not too bad. She seems to be bearing up to her immense sorrow more robustly than I had expected.'[190]

THE DEATH OF EDMOND DE GONCOURT

Proust's sense of grief and condolence was also revived by the death of Edmond de Goncourt, in the arms of Alphonse Daudet, whom he loved like a younger brother or the son he never had. For Proust, Goncourt's importance was such that there is no other writer for whom such lengthy pastiches are composed in *À la recherche*. 'The last of the great', the representative of the generation born in the 1820s, the historian of society and of the arts, the realist against whom, and therefore thanks to whom, Proust formed his aesthetic views. He considered that anyone who kept a diary was lost, and yet he was an attentive reader of the Goncourts' masterpiece. Fate decreed that the last written page of the *Journal*, almost as if it were the raw material of *À la recherche*, should be devoted to several of Proust's models: Doctor Robin, Liane de Pougy's lover; the Castellanes, who had just held a grand, late-night party in the Bois de Boulogne; Montesquiou, who was keen to describe in a prose work 'some of the old characters of the Faubourg Saint-Germain' about whom he knew thousands of anecdotes; and even Zola, who was the subject of a phenomenon of involuntary memory: some sweet peas on his bedside table had caused him to have dreams at night in which his entire childhood had passed before him.[191] Marcel described Edmond de Goncourt with sensitivity in a letter to Lucien Daudet: 'He owed your parents the only consolations of his old age and possibly of his life. And whatever the grief it must have afforded you, I find it beautiful that he should have died in the way he did at your home, amongst you all. And so peacefully! For, where death is concerned, sudden means peaceful.' And he added, he who had already attained one half of his lifespan, this wish, which would be fulfilled: 'I, on the other hand, want to die knowing that it is happening, as long as I am not too ill.'[192]

HYGIENE FOR ASTHMATICS

On 17 July Marcel had an appointment with Doctor Brissaud,[193] a professor at the Faculty of Medicine and editor of *La Revue neurologique*. His book, *Hygiène des asthmatiques*, was to be published in August, with a preface by Adrien Proust. A cultured man, ready to offer advice on artistic matters or local sites of interest,[194] and a Dreyfusard, Brissaud would be the inspiration for Du Boulbon in *Le Côté de Guermantes*, the theorist of that 'neurosis', a plagiarist of genius, who modified the symptoms of every illness. Marcel consulted him and described him on various occasions. He possessed, said Léon Daudet,[195] a wonderful intelligence, he was kind-hearted, he had a sense of irony that bordered on the farcical, and his manner was warm and sympathetic; he was 'a sentimentalist, a romantic'. In his *Traité de médecine*, Brissaud defined asthma as 'a neurosis[196] characterized by attacks of spasmodic dyspnoea'. This disease would strike at certain professions: lawyers, teachers, preachers; 'the poor, at any rate, are spared by comparison with the rich'. As to the remedy, Brissaud pointed out, the patients are better judges of this than doctors, and they know what is good or bad for them. Proust, similarly, wrote that just as 'there are some asthmatics who can only soothe their attacks by opening windows and breathing in the high wind, the pure air of heights, so there are others who shelter in the centre of town, in a smoke-filled room'.[197] Like his colleagues, Brissaud sometimes experimented on his (suitably named) patients with eccentric treatments such as mercury washes, which Marcel, understandably, was hesitant to undergo.[198] Brissaud also recommended that he should keep his sleeping pills on his bedside table, without touching them: the essential thing was the feeling of being able to take them; advice that Marcel, in turn, gave to Louis de Robert.

THE BREAK-UP

Reynaldo, whose presence in *Les Plaisirs et les Jours* is evident in his scores and a few allusions, is above all present in three of the characters in *Jean Santeuil*: Henri de Réveillon, the Marquis de Poitiers and Françoise. And yet it was at the very period that the novel was being written that the two friends inflicted an irreparable wound upon one another. Even now, in my view, insufficient attention has been paid to this fact: deprived of this invisible and omnipresent god whom Marcel had promised would live on in his novel, the book itself would never recover from the hurt endured and, unfulfilled, like passion, it would fade away and die a few years later.

Meeting Lucien Daudet had been a first sign. Already probably keen to divide his time between Saint-Germain-en-Laye and Paris, if not to break off relations, Marcel made a final desperate effort at the beginning of that summer of 1896. Either Reynaldo should consent to become a sort of slave, a 'prisoner', or else it would all be over. What was essential for Proust was the establishing of an ascendancy over the other person and knowing him, which meant possessing every instant of that separate, distinct life, and assuring himself that he was the only one that mattered. That was why he assumed the role of confessor (and of the good apostle) to whom one tells absolutely everything. Concerns of the flesh came second, or were of minor importance; they did however, exist at this period. This is why he declared to Hahn: 'It might be wonderful, but it would not be natural at our age to live as Tolstoy asks us to do.'[199]

At the beginning of July Marcel was still contemplating a journey that they might make together, to Réveillon, for example, in October, so as to revive the memory of happy visits there:[200] the trouble was that Reynaldo happened to be in Germany and Proust was obliged to spend a month with his mother; Reynaldo was still, 'along with Maman', the person whom Marcel 'loved best in all the world'. On 20 June the two friends drew up a pact, which would not be observed and which would bring about the break-up: it entailed Reynaldo 'telling everything' to Marcel, to quell what Marcel termed his 'sick person's fantasies'.* But Hahn refused to give him no cause to be anxious, and took to not 'coming back' to him, which gave Marcel the impression that he 'meant little' to his friend, and Reynaldo raised obstacles which were contrary to Proust's other wishes, even though he was 'full of remorse for so many bad thoughts, so many bad and cowardly plans'. The blackmail is mingled with realism where 'little Marcel' was concerned, 'who, in spite of everything, is astonished at this stage to see – *How little time it takes to change everything* and that this happens more and more quickly'.[201] In mid-August Marcel released Reynaldo from his 'vow', confessed his own weaknesses and pretended not to be any more upset by Hahn than he was by the hero of *La Dame de Monsoreau*,† which he was reading at the time. And, since the break-up was slow and difficult, he thought once more about making a journey together to Switzerland

---

* Hence the instructions on 3 July: 'Just tell me from time to time, in your letters, no mosch, have seen no mosch', which is probably an allusion to homosexual encounters.

† Novel by Dumas *père* (1846). *Tr.*

'or somewhere else', or a visit to Versailles, and he maintained he was no longer jealous. At the end of the month, Proust composed a fine portrait of his friend, which reverberates like a farewell to love: 'I assure you that to me, your sadness is not just the sombre beauty of your character, it plumbs your moral and also your intellectual depths, the genius (I use it in its ancient sense, so that for once your modesty need not reveal itself . . .) of your music . . . It is the high point to which you have risen and from which you will undoubtedly fall if you abjure it, like those who might have been great men if . . .'[202] In early September, despite a vague invitation to Villers, Marcel scarcely mentioned anything apart from his novel, his reading of Dumas and Balzac, and, almost as if to tease the memories they both shared, a visit to the Louvre where he admired a picture by Quentin Metsys, and one to the Jardin des Plantes with their mutual hostess, Mme Arman.[203] It was all over, apart from friendship. The melancholy songs of the one, such as *La Dernière Valse*, and the novels of the other have perpetuated the memories of the passion, so great and so brief, of two exceptional human beings.

AT MONT-DORE

On 8 August Marcel left with his mother for Mont-Dore in the Auvergne. He thought that the pure air would help her recover from her grief. She believed that at this resort, dedicated to the cure of respiratory illnesses, he would nurse his asthma, which had not been improved by the painful emotional circumstances he had been experiencing. 'Marcel leaves this evening with his mother. Let us hope to God that Mont-Dore does him some good. I would so like to see him looking well!' wrote Reynaldo.

Jean Santeuil had already accompanied his mother 'to a watering place situated in a valley surrounded by high mountains. He loathed this scenery and found it frightful, and he felt oppressed by the ring of mountains encircling them.'[204] Mme Proust had always liked thermal spas, as did her husband, who used to go to Vichy (without her) every year. In any case, the treatment tired Marcel* and that 'lovely thing that was bad for [him]', the hay, that provided an opportunity to mention Mme de Sévigné's

---

* We know what it consisted of thanks to a note in *Le Bottin mondain* (1903): 'Arsenical bicarbonate waters, siliceous and ferruginous, are efficacious in the treatment of catarrh and chronic rheumatic pains; they are used in drinks, baths, showers, steam-baths, inhalations, etc.' The journey took twelve and a half hours.

famous letter, gave him a cold. 'Mont-Dore meant little to him; perhaps he would have found it agreeable had he not caught cold,' Hahn confirmed. He would return home prematurely on about 25 August (he was meant to stay for a month), feeling 'unwell', as he always did when anyone tried to cure him. But he had read *La Dame de Monsoreau* (it is not known whether it was this book that inspired him to fight a duel), as well as, 'more slowly', Rousseau's *Confessions*, and, in particular, he had worked on his novel.[205]

CHAPTER VIII

From Jean Santeuil *to Dreyfus*

AUTUMN 1896

After his abortive stay at the resort of Mont-Dore, from which he returned complaining that the only friend he had found was 'a very nice hairdresser', Marcel did not accompany his mother when she set off to Dieppe on 1 September for some beneficial sea bathing. Why? Was it because of the anxiety provoked by a summons to carry out a four-week period of military training, from which he succeeded – and this would become a habit – in having himself exempted? Was it because he hoped, in spite of everything, to go to see Reynaldo at Saint-Cloud? Hahn wrote to Mme Proust that he saw Marcel there every day; the latter vehemently denied this:[1] either the composer must have felt ashamed of the break-up, or else he wanted to conceal it from Mme Proust. Was it so that Marcel could work in Paris? Or so that he could visit his friend Lavallée at the Château de Segrez – although he never managed to reach agreement with him over the dates? Was it in order to go to Champrosay to see Lucien Daudet, to whom he had written at the time of Goncourt's death, telling him that the appreciation which Alphonse Daudet had written for *La Revue de Paris* of 15 August was 'sublime'?[2] And yet he asserted that he was not in a fit state to go, while at the same time adopting a strange tone, one which foreshadows that of Charlus: 'My little one, I should love to be able to see the little scowl you speak to me of and to cure you of it by giving you sharp little smacks,' which, he added, would be both lascivious and vulgar.*

While Mme Proust was in Dieppe – Marcel intended to join her there in October, although she did not wish to stay until then, nor to be alone there with Mme Lemaire – her son attempted to reform his life, by returning home early in the evening and by going to bed at about midnight,

---

* *Corr.*, vol. XXI, p. 577. '*Mauvais genre*' refers to anything concerning inversion.

which did not stop him waking up feeling suffocated, and needing to smoke some Legras or Escouflaire powder, or Espic cigarettes, which were the classic remedies for asthma (Legras powder was on sale until 1992). He even did his best to do without sleeping pills (trional, amyl or valerian), wisely taking herbal tea or bicarbonate instead. Getting down to *Jean Santeuil* once more, he had written ninety pages by 3 September and 110 by the 16th; he then informed his mother of a notebook of 110 pages, which did not represent all that he had done, since he had written previously on loose-leaf pages, and he envisaged working on it for four hours each morning, which would enable him to finish 'for 1 February'. It thus seems likely that Proust had then written a much more substantial portion of *Jean Santeuil* than is generally thought, whereas his pace slowed down greatly between 1897 and 1899. In particular, we may assume that that autumn, when his love for Reynaldo came to an end, he turned it into the story of Jean and Françoise: he would do the same, much later, after the death of Agostinelli. When in shock, Marcel was capable of writing at an extraordinary speed; he belonged to that tradition of writers which goes back as far as Aristotle or St Thomas Aquinas, which makes one wonder how and when they found the time to write all they did. Nevertheless, his anxieties, which would later lead to his abandoning the book, increased and he complained of not being able 'to conceive of it as a whole':[3] 'But as to what it will be like – I can't "see a thing" and I feel it will be dreadful.'[4]

At the same time, he read a great deal. He extended his summer reading by continuing with the novels of Dumas,* so dear to Reynaldo: 'I prefer those,' he wrote to him, 'in which there is no love, nor dark passions [an allusion to what they had just experienced], and I particularly like those with sword fights, policemen like Chicot, royalty, good humour and victorious Innocents.'[5] Proust also rediscovered romanticism during this period in the last novel that Balzac completed – the summit of his art after which he declined – *La Cousine Bette*. Baron Hulot, a man obsessed with the sexual life and who resorts to love affairs with servants, is the elder brother of Charlus, another baron who is eventually brought low. Valérie Marneffe shares certain characteristics with Rachel, or with Morel. The dramatic twists, which stem from Dumas and Balzac, can be seen in

---

* The writer and diplomat Paul Morand (1888–1976) relates that Proust and Lucien Daudet, when recalling times gone by and growing older, were in the habit of saying to one another: 'That's *Vingt ans après*. – No, it's *Le Vicomte de Bragelonne*.'

Jupien's sleazy hotel and in the matinée at the Guermantes', in M. Vinteuil's house or in the brothel at Maineville; and, in *Jean Santeuil*, in the Marie scandal and the story of the nun from Antwerp.

When Proust borrowed Flaubert's *Par les champs et par les grèves* from a reading room, it was in order to search for additional details or even some inspiration about Brittany; he would not find them there since Flaubert only gave a few spare details about the region in which the novel is set. Another loan, from among the 'treasures' which did not actually belong to this library, was more significant still: the correspondence between Goethe and Schiller. Proust, who studied German at the lycée, was doubtless keen to deepen his knowledge of Goethe's novels.* The structure of the formative or apprentice novel is seen to perfection in *Wilhelm Meister*. With a hero who, having emerged from adolescence, must distance himself from his family and face the world, which is to say choose a vocation and discover love, it is very much the theme of *Jean Santeuil*. From his reading of Goethe, Proust learnt primarily that his books do not allow us to reconstruct his existence, but, like an intimate diary, they bear 'the strong mark of the thoughts in which he took pleasure'; he also observed the important role occupied by the arts, by the actor, the architect and the musician. As to his main themes, 'each of us [is] shaped by the facts through which the spirit of truth and inspiration communicated themselves. For some it may be the smells which recall the past and cause them to live for poetry [and here, Marcel was speaking of himself], for others something else.'[6] At the same time, Proust looked back on the whole range of his childhood reading and his picture books, recalling that he would ask to be given any book that had to do with the moon, even a grammar in which, accompanying the word moon, 'there was actually a picture depicting the moon with an eye in the middle and a vague nose', and that he enjoyed showing to the 'fine ladies in the drawing-room' 'the disparate and magical spell of his obscure and sedentary science which was that of an old astrologer and a small child'.[7] This fine passage presages those in *À la recherche* that he would devote to the moon, right up to *Le Temps retrouvé* which conceal a very long-standing fascination. For him, the stars bore the faces of childhood.

---

* In fact, he left *Wilhelm Meister* in Paris when he went to Fontainebleau, and Mme Proust picked it up: 'Looking at my poor exile's books, I started *Wilhelm Meister* and I should be glad if you would tell me whether Wilhelm Meister's ideas are supposed to represent those of Goethe' (*Corr.*, pp. 135–6, 20 October 1896). Proust replied to this question in the note published in *CSB*.

AN IMPERIAL VISIT

Between 6 and 8 October, Nicholas II and the Empress Alexandra paid an official visit to Paris. France was seeking an ally to the east of Germany; Russia was hoping for money from the West.[8] Professor Proust was invited to the ceremonies. The visit is described in 'Le salon de la princesse Mathilde', and also in *À l'ombre des jeunes filles en fleurs*,[9] one of the rare historical events to feature in the novel, where it appears as the visit of King Théodose II and is described by M. de Norpois.[10] Proust no doubt put into his mouth the words of an article by Francis Charmes in *La Revue des deux mondes*,* as well as the account that may have been related by Ambassador Nisard and the Minister for Foreign Affairs, Gabriel Hanotaux, who, like the President, Félix Faure, were known to the Prousts. The visit is depicted here as a great success, at least in the eyes of M. de Norpois, who was particularly delighted by the expression 'affinities' (the Tsar had spoken of the 'so precious bonds' which bound his country and France. Hence at the time that *Jean Santeuil* was being written certain events that Proust experienced – through the medium of reading or conversation, and therefore already in language form – do not feature in the book and reappear a long time afterwards, in *À la recherche*. The character of Norpois is none the less foreshadowed by Duroc, the secretary of state to Hanotaux.[11] Furthermore, it is fascinating to compare this visit of Nicholas II, which is described favourably by Norpois, and expresses the views of the Proust family, whose friendship with the 'sunshine President' Félix Faure† and with several ministers and important ambassadors brought them close to the seat of power, with the opposite view, expressed by Maurice Barrès in his *Cahiers*: the emperor was reticent, there were numerous 'official gaffes', that the protocol was 'dreadful', the Tsar 'neurotic' and the Tsarina 'glacial'.[12] In Republican circles, everyone was satisfied that France had been delivered from the isolation

---

* 15 October 1896; see *RTP*, vol. 1, p. 454, n. 2. Francis Charmes (1848–1916) was Director of Political Affairs at the Ministry of Foreign Affairs (1885–9). Plenipotentiary Minister and an editor at *La Revue des deux mondes* from 1893: he wrote the political column there, became editor of the magazine in 1907, and was elected to the Académie française in 1908. He is one of the principal models for Norpois. The Quai d'Orsay style, however, like the Meilhac and Halévy wit, had something collective about it, and some of the expressions attributed to Norpois date from the war years, after Charmes' death.

† He had hoped to wear a suit of blue satin embroidered in gold, and a hat with white feathers; the Cabinet obliged him to wear a dark suit (J. Chastenet, *Histoire de la Troisième République*, vol. I, Hachette, 1955, p. 101).

it faced vis-à-vis Germany, and the Republican régime was no longer isolated among the monarchies which at that time made up the whole of Europe.

FONTAINEBLEAU

Just as he had experienced abortive holidays and journeys from which he had returned home, Marcel also suffered from 'unfulfilled departures'. He eventually decided to set off, on 19 October, for the Hôtel de France et d'Angleterre* at Fontainebleau, which he described in *Jean Santeuil* and in *Le Côté de Guermantes*, at Doncières.[13] And, since one Daudet may disguise another, he stayed with Léon, who, as he was leaving for Fontainebleau to finish a novel, had suggested to Marcel, who did not know the forest, that he should come and join him.[14] Daudet was to describe these 'ten or so days': 'By moonlight, and well wrapped up, we went for long walks through the forest, during which Marcel told me about his literary projects, which were surpassed by their realization.[†] He was hypersensitive, this dear Marcel, but despite his scars, he was already creating a meticulous tapestry, of admirable brilliance and originality.'[15] Léon Daudet was twenty-nine years old. Having abandoned medicine (which he caricatured in 1894 in a *roman-à-clef* of unusual savagery, *Les Morticoles*, in which one comes across several people whom Proust knew) for journalism and literature, he had published a poetic account of the great Elizabethan in *Le Voyage de Shakespeare*, in 1895, and he completed a novel, *Suzanne*, at the hotel. Goncourt has left us with a colourful sketch of the young man: 'At Léon Daudet's, such is the feverish ferment of copy, conversation, jokes, caricature and *agrichage*,[‡] that I sometimes fear for the future of his brain. On top of that a huge amount of fodder followed by congesting naps.'[16]

Marcel was not as happy as his robust accomplice, who was the complete opposite to the frail and gentle Lucien (who came only once to Fontainebleau, and the visit went badly). No sooner had Proust arrived than he wanted to leave again, even though his mother wisely

---

* 'Grand Hôtel de France et d'Angleterre, opposite the Palace, proprietor A. Dumaine. First-class accommodation. Most important in town. Huge terrace with *à la carte* restaurant. Large and beautiful garden,' reads the advertisement in *Le Bottin mondain*, which adds the important facility: 'Telephone'.

[†] It is most likely that Proust talked to him about *Jean Santeuil*, not about *À la recherche*.

[‡] An invented word, used to convey Daudet's frenzied creative activity. *Tr.*

advised him to see whether he would 'become acclimatized' and his respiratory condition improve: 'You really do need some good air, my darling, to restore the harm caused by the summer.'[17] Just as some people explore the virgin forest, there are others who, unable to negotiate that of Fontainebleau, explore the forests of the soul: they are not the same.

On 20 October an incident occurred that was almost as significant as the evening kiss; the telephone conversation with his mother is a scene which is described on three occasions in the course of his work[18] and several more times in his correspondence. Marcel talked to her that morning; he then immediately rewrote the passages which he entitled 'Jean at Beg-Meil. I. He Telephones his Mother', and sent them to her. Mme Proust, who was in mourning for her father, had had a different, troubled tone to her voice; in 1902 Marcel would describe to Antoine Bibesco the sadness he had felt at that time: 'And then, suddenly, over the telephone, I heard her poor broken, hurt voice, changed for ever from the one I had always known, full of cracks and fissures; and it was on hearing those broken, bleeding fragments down the receiver that for the first time I had the terrible sense of what it was that had shattered for ever within her.'[19] The passage that was destined for *Jean Santeuil*, out of consideration for his mother, did not provide any of these explanations, or rather it broadened them to include others, all the sorrows of these past years. It is an act of love: 'In that tiny fragment of broken voice could be heard the life that she had given to him alone, the only affection that was entirely his own.'[20] When she received these beautiful passages, 'very sweet but very sad', Mme Proust immediately replied that she had been worried thinking of the sadness her son had endured; quoting *Le Misanthrope*, she urged him to develop a heart that was 'less vulnerable and less tender' and nevertheless extolled the virtues of the telephone, something Marcel loathed: 'How many apologies you owe it for all the blasphemies uttered. What remorse you must feel for having despised and alienated such a benefactor! Hearing the poor darling's voice – the poor darling hearing mine!'[21] Proust returned to these themes in an article for *Le Figaro*, in March 1907. In *Le Côté de Guermantes* the telephone rings at Doncières and it is the grandmother who calls; the episode is based on earlier versions, but it is given the lyrical power of an opera: in the final version, what was sensed has come true; the voice on the telephone is that of death itself: 'What presence more real than that voice which seemed so near – in its effective separation! But there was also a premonition of an eternal separation! Very often, listening in this way, without seeing her who spoke to me from so far away, it seemed to me that this voice was crying to me from those depths from which one does not ascend again, and I experienced the anxiety that would seize me one day, when a voice would return in this way (alone, and separated from a body I would never see again) to murmur in my ear words I yearned to kiss as they issued from lips for ever returned to dust.'[22] Proust, who in the course of his life was always at his most profound when dealing with sorrow and the power of language, here returns to his two implicit models, the *De Profundis* and the scene from Book XI of the *Odyssey*, in which Ulysses, in Hades, meets his mother, without being able to grasp her.

When Mme Proust noted with her usual sense of humour that the 'tale of a deportee's arrival on the Île du Salut could not be more distressing', it was because Marcel's first letter had drawn in outline the unfriendly rooms he would depict in his work, and particularly in *Jean Santeuil*. What is more, it was raining, the trees were green and not russet, as they ought to be, 'the town has no character': 'I cannot tell you what a terrible time I spent yesterday between four and six o'clock (a period which I switched to before the telephone call in the little story I sent you).' Never had any of his various anxiety attacks reached this level; Marcel did not even try to describe it. None of the guests wanted to speak to him, and the lights in the lounge were put out in the evening. He even mentions the exorbitant price of the hotel, in the hope that his mother may see some reason to summon him back to Paris. Finally, he had nothing to read.[23] Few episodes in poor Marcel's life show him so unhappy and ill-equipped to deal with life, when faced with what for anyone else would have been a commonplace event – a short journey and a brief separation. He would draw from it some unforgettable passages. Here, we come to realize – and it is the biographer's task to remind us of this – the price that he paid to write them.

On 22 October he declared that he had not enjoyed a single moment of gaiety or reverie, even of well-being. And although he was capable of walking for two hours a day, and going out for drives, he complained that Léon Daudet made him talk a lot while eating, which he loathed (this is why, when Proust entertained, later on, he never ate himself). Were he to return home, he would not go anywhere else, except to the Hôtel des Réservoirs at Versailles, where he would go and work every day. We know that that is where he withdrew to after his mother's death; he thought of it, therefore, as a refuge of his own choosing. Since the only book he had was the Goncourts' *La Du Barry*,* he asked his mother for several Balzacs, including *La Rabouilleuse*, *La Vieille Fille* and *Les Chouans*, certain volumes of his edition of Shakespeare (*Julius Caesar* and *Antony and Cleopatra*), *Wilhelm Meister*† and *Middlemarch*. Thus, we can begin to imagine the composition of his library: George Eliot's novel, which he would refer to on several occasions and would make use of immediately in *Jean Santeuil*, fascinated him in its portrayal of Mr Casaubon, 'who had devoted his entire life to an insignificant and absurd study'.[24] That same day, a further letter to his mother, which revealed the extent of his despair, tells us that Marcel, like those heroes of the burlesque to whom all manner of misfortunes happen, lost his money, thus making it impossible for him to return to Paris, and, perhaps because of this, he had stomach pains: 'I can understand people who kill one another for the slightest thing ... Running after my money like old father Grandet, I am worn out with remorse, harried by guilt, crushed by melancholy.' If he did not return, it was through fear that this capitulation might develop (like the evening kiss) into something permanent. The very next day his mother sent him a hundred francs, asked him whether he would like Robert de Flers to come down for a couple of days, and even suggested that he should return, since 'The only respect in which Fontainebleau is superior to Paris is the cost.'[25] Marcel's untidiness increased his suffering and his exhaustion, what his mother called his '*timoserie*', by which she meant his timorous temperament. He did not persevere for very long, and this visit, so cheerfully described in his novels, came to an end on 25 or 26 October.

On his return Marcel renewed ties with Fernand Gregh. In *La Revue blanche* of September 1896 the latter had published a piece entitled 'Mysteries'.[26] In it, an extremely highly strung young man is subject to psychological disorders, to 'a surge of unconscious memories', when confronted by whatever it may be, 'a book or a flower'. This phenomenon, the author pointed out in 1901, had been investigated by a young writer, Bernard-Leroy, in *L'Illusion de fausse reconnaissance* (1898). In the interval

---

* As Proust never allowed anything to be lost, and since his memory was astonishing, he would mention this book in his pastiche of the Goncourts in *Le Temps retrouvé* (p. 127, and *RTP*, vol. IV, p. 290): 'An entire service of silverware decorated with those myrtles of Luciennes that la du Barry would have recognized.'

† One realizes why Proust confided in Léon Daudet, who, moreover, had already written a biography of Shakespeare, that he felt he needed to have experienced life in order to understand 'the characters of Balzac, Shakespeare and Goethe properly': he was rereading them in his company (*Corr.*, vol. II, p. 278).

between a minute that has gone by and the present moment, the whole of the past is wiped out. But Gregh's hero, unlike Proust's, does not identify the memory precisely and does not experience any real joy: he returns to the theme dear to Nerval and Baudelaire of paramnesia, of our having a former life. Like Proust, on the other hand, Gregh contrasted the superficial self with a deeper self, solitary and unsuspected. He also thought that feeling, like memory, was unlimited, and only the past seemed attractive to him (which was a theme of the master they both shared, Anatole France). In *Les Plaisirs et les Jours*, which had already been published when Gregh's article appeared, Proust had contrasted the two selves, spoken of the 'incurable imperfection' of the present and had made use of involuntary memory in 'La mort de Baldassare Silvande' and in 'La Confession d'une jeune fille'. Like the younger writers of their time, Gregh and Proust were affected by the climate of symbolism which favoured the inner life and memory. They read Anatole France, who celebrated the past. Like them, Bergson, in his *Essai sur les données immédiates de la conscience* (1889), contrasted the two selves; this book is not so much a source for Proust, as a testimony, a partial expression (because it was theoretical) of the mental universe of a generation. Proust, nevertheless, remained more intellectual in his attitude* – in this he opposed Barrès, whose scepticism he disapproved of,† just as he condemned that of France and Renan.[27] Gregh, who sent Marcel his latest book, a collection of poems entitled *La Maison de l'enfance*, in early November, was less than lukewarm in his brief review of *Les Plaisirs et les Jours*,‡ and we have to wait until 1901 when, thanks to a dedication to Proust in one of Gregh's books, their intermittent friendship is renewed.

---

* In a remark that is little known but crucial to an understanding of the relationship between the two men, Bergson wrote to H. Massis (who quotes it in *Le Drame de Marcel Proust*, Grasset, 1937, n. 80): 'Essentially, his way of thinking was very much inclined to turn its back on duration and the life force', in other words, on the philosopher's two great themes.

† He even preferred Desjardins' Christian faith, 'the light of reason', to Barrès' 'scepticism' (*Corr.*, vol. I, p. 172, 1 July 1892, to Robert Dreyfus).

‡ *La Revue de Paris*, 15 December 1896: 'Here is a book that will make an extremely pretty New Year's Day present . . . M. Marcel Proust relates his soul's adventures or those of a few congeneric

BEING A WRITER IN 1896

What were the literary horizons within which a writer might frame a career for himself in 1896? On the one hand, there were those works that had recently become classics, and almost historical monuments: writers such as Balzac (rather more than Stendhal, who had only just been introduced to the literary pantheon through Bourget's *Essais de psychologie contemporaine*) with his taste for the social panorama, his cyclical construction and his portrayal of shady milieux (such as the brothel, as in Maupassant or the Goncourts). Rather more like Balzac than Flaubert, who was seen, quite wrongly, as the master of naturalism, were Hugo and Leconte de Lisle. On the other hand, there were the two main movements or schools, naturalism and symbolism. The differences between them were not as great as they appeared, as can be seen from the friendship of Mallarmé and Zola, the latter's taste for the bohemian style, the Goncourts' aestheticism, and the place of impressionism between the two tendencies: the reactions of Montesquiou and of Breton would confirm that impressionism was a form of realism. It was not Monet who was against what was natural, but Gustave Moreau. Since Loti's impressionism rendered him incapable of depicting a social milieu, his subjectivity was brought to the aid of reality, which appeared to be different because it was seen in the context of a traveller's tale.

Among the generation born around 1870 (and who were therefore aged about twenty-five in 1896), Gide, Valéry and Claudel were drawn directly to Mallarmé and symbolism,[28] whereas Proust, even though he learned many lessons from him, and admired Baudelaire and read Mallarmé's poetry, attacked the latter, as we know, in 'Contre l'obscurité'.[29] What is more, he grew closer to Zola (who would not have been the writer he was without *La Comédie humaine*) in his desire to compose a cyclical work, and to depict society, while reviving the subject of heredity that was dear to the creator of the Rougons.

A third tendency linked Anatole France and his admirers, Bourget, Maurras, Barrès, Lemaître, Schwob and Pierre Louÿs. Proust, an admirer of France's work, was unable to appreciate Mallarmé entirely. France's work was more complex than is generally thought: the account of his childhood, to which, like Loti and Daudet, he returned on several occasions,

---

heroes, melancholy and pensive heroes for whom reality is too brutal and who flee it in an eternal dream of surprised sadness.'

and which played its part as a model for *Jean Santeuil*, the literature of ideas, the philosophical *conte*, the political novel from after the period of the Dreyfus affair, his literary criticism, and also the analytical novel, such as *Le Lys rouge* – a genre which triumphs over the naturalist monograph. To this same genre belong Maupassant's *Notre cœur* (which was partly inspired by Mme Straus and the Comtesse Potocka, both models for Proust), the early novels of Bourget, many a forgotten book, from Rod to Hervieu, and even Maurice Barrès' *Le Culte du Moi*.

We have valuable information about how contemporaries felt about this period, thanks to Jules Huret's *Enquête sur l'évolution littéraire.** This journalist established certain categories: the psychologists (France, Lemaître, Rod, Barrès, Hervieu), the 'magi' (Péladan), the symbolists and decadents, the naturalists (Goncourt, Zola, Huysmans, Maupassant), the neo-realists (Mirbeau, Rosny, Hermant), the Parnassians, the independents (from Claretie to Richepin, none has survived) and the theoreticians and philosophers (Renan). Several of those who were interviewed (France, Lemaître, Rod, Barrès, Leconte de Lisle, even Goncourt) considered naturalism to be dead. Its defeat, Barrès asserted, was beneficial to the psychologists, of whom Bourget[30] was one. The naturalists 'had written meticulous and colourful descriptions of external aspects as well as human gestures, passions and yearnings, whereas the psychologists, such as Bourget, wanted to scrutinize these yearnings much as a scientist would a plant' . . . The naturalists had taken refuge in 'vulgarity'; the psychologists 'had sought milieux other than the mediocre and people who were different to the common souls'. At the same time Lemaître wittily asserted that a psychologist was a writer who studied other people's souls; Barrès, for his part, only contemplated his own. On the question of psychology Mallarmé declared: 'It seems to me that after the great works of Flaubert, the Goncourts and Zola, which are kinds of poems, we have come back to the old French fashion of the last century, much more humble and modest, which consisted not so much in borrowing from painting the means of depicting the exterior forms of things, but in dissecting the motives of the human heart.' He shared the opinion of Moréas, however, who stated: 'I very much like our psychologists; but they must stay in their place, that is to say beneath the poets.' Goncourt predicted 'a

---

* Published in *L'Écho de Paris* from 3 May 1891, then in book form by Charpentier in 1892. Republished by Thot, 1984.

predominance of psychology* over physiology in the movement that is brewing', while at the same time he regarded the novel as 'an overused and worn out genre, that has said everything it had to say'. As if every generation had the sense that after it had disappeared there would be nothing left to say!

So it seems that the young Proust became integrated into the dominant trend of the day, which was the social and psychological novel. To this were added the novel of childhood, such as *Le Livre de mon ami* (1885) and *Le Roman d'un enfant* (1890), the *Bildungsroman* and some Goethe, but also a taste for poetic prose, akin to symbolism. The product of this eclectic mixture, which was none the less unencumbered with clichés, was *Jean Santeuil* – the story of a child, an adolescent, a young man,[31] of his family life as well as his emotional and social life, the tale of a character who did not live beyond the age of twenty-five, like a 'child of the high seas' on his island.

And then there was Stendhal.

AGAINST STENDHAL?

There is no mention of Stendhal in *Les Plaisirs et les Jours*,† but in the introduction to *Jean Santeuil*, written in 1895, the hero reads *La Chartreuse de Parme* 'with the enthusiasm that any fine new work arouses'.[32] *Le Rouge et le Noir* was the poet and novelist Henri de Régnier's favourite book.[33] If you came across it in a bedroom in a provincial inn, the narrator wonders, 'would you not feel as if you were in the presence of a friend who was just like yourself, with whom you wanted to talk?'[34] Later on in the story appreciation gives way to criticism: the passages devoted to love give way to the 'pangs of jealousy'.[35] For Stendhal, everything resides within things: love lies in another, an individual, in his or her beauty: 'There is no real or profound connection', Proust claimed, 'between a particular profile, that delights us momentarily, and our inner life.' Jean, in love with Mme S., as is Swann later with Odette, had first experienced, 'through Julien Sorel, through Fabrice Del Dongo, and in the pages of *De l'amour*', the pleasure which this woman now afforded him, of having

---

* 'Have I not written *Madame Gervaisais*, a novel about a psychologist who is just as psychological as the foremost psychologists of the present time!'

† Stendhal was, however, mentioned in an 1893 article about the composer Saussine, who 'comments on and interprets the characters' in the novel *Le Nez de Cléopatre*, as Stendhal does (*CSB*, p. 358).

her face constantly in his thoughts: but, unlike Stendhal's characters, he takes more enjoyment from being in love than he does in the woman he loves, as if this love were detached from its object.[36] Stendhalian pleasures are to be found in life; Proustian pleasures in the mind. The love scenes in the novel put this doctrine, which Proust would never stop developing, into practice. For him, Stendhalian love did not exist, all he knew about was jealousy, the impossibility of knowing another's secret, of escaping from oneself, perhaps even the absence of all physical union, which was in any case secondary. For Stendhal, crystallization was brought about by love; for his successor, it was through jealousy.

This did not preclude Proust, from 'Sur la lecture' (1905) onwards, from presenting Beyle as the principal victim of 'Sainte-Beuve's cecity' as far as his generation was concerned,[37] or from reverting to the same theme, in January 1908, in his pastiche of the critic,[38] and later in the character of Mme de Villeparisis.[39] It was in *Contre Sainte-Beuve* that he formulated his twofold theory most precisely: on the one hand, he knew and loved Stendhal's work,[40] and defended him against the author of *Les Lundis*. On the other, fighting as it were on two fronts, he refuted his aesthetic principles: a great writer without realizing it, Beyle 'made literature not merely subordinate to life, when on the contrary it was what it led to, but one of its most pointless distractions'.[41] At that time Proust annotated a copy of *La Chartreuse de Parme*,* and he developed these remarks with *Contre Sainte-Beuve* in mind.[42] There was initially no criticism, rather a summary of themes: old age, the exclusive fondness for the 'stirrings of the soul', the 'revival of the past' and the laying aside of ambitions, either due to the proximity of death (Julien in prison) or because of a detachment brought about by love (Fabrice in prison), or owing to the very simple emotions people experienced in the eighteenth century towards nature and lofty, noble scenery. Remorse is a 'sad form of love'. 'A maxim of Stendhal's: never regret'; remorse results in 'extreme passion, sensual abandonment'. Finally, Proust observed that 'the finest books add a slice of the soul of coincidence to events. In *Le Rouge et le Noir*, each action is followed by a phrase that points out what is happening subconsciously in the soul; this is the novel of motive.' The lesson would not be lost.

---

* Catalogue of the 1971 Jacquemart-André exhibition, no. 264; e.g. p. 2: 'Thus literature is nothing more than the equivalent of a pleasant evening in which the zambajon was delicious', which dates his rereading to 1910, based on a letter to Lauris in which Proust said that he had reread the *Chartreuse*.

THE WRITING OF *JEAN SANTEUIL*[43]

Proust had now been working on his novel for a year, and from this period we have a number of documents that relate to the genesis of the text; thereafter, there is silence until he abandoned it in 1899. It is an appropriate moment, therefore, to summarize the genesis, or the biography, of this work, in so far as we can reconstruct it from the manuscript in the Bibliothèque Nationale.[44] To begin with, it is worth noting that Proust never gave a title to his book: he always chose his titles once he had finished. As to the protagonist's surname, which we use to refer to the novel, according to *Le Bottin mondain*, there is a seventeenth-century poet, who wrote in Latin, known by the name of Jean Santeuil. Did Marcel amuse himself by using his name, as if to suggest that he was going to relate the life of a poet, and one who expressed himself in a dead language? Was it not more likely that he borrowed it from a locality to be found between Pontoise and Gisors, on the road to Dieppe, or from another Santeuil, nearer to Chartres and Illiers, between Dourdan and Châteaudun?

It all started at Beg-Meil in September–October 1895. On a loose-leaf pad of school exercise paper (the only paper he may have been able to find at Beg-Meil, almost as if he had not foreseen when he left Paris that he would need any writing material), the sheets numbered from 1 to 105, Proust wrote the first five chapters of the first part, entitled by the editors 'Childhood and Adolescence'. The fragment about Mme Lepic was composed at the same period, as were those concerning the Lycée Henri IV and the portrait of Henri de Réveillon. The chapter devoted to Beg-Meil, like these other passages, dates from October 1895.[45] On 14 December Marcel attended the opening of *Frédégonde* by Guiraud and Saint-Saëns, and published an article in *Le Gaulois* about the latter without mentioning the former, who was a friend of Bizet's; having fallen out temporarily with the Strauses,* he transferred the whole incident to his novel.[46]

The 'introduction' to the novel, which Proust called his 'first chapter', dates from March 1896,[47] which means that the device whereby the story is related to the Narrator by the writer C. was conceived afterwards. This introduction, in which the friend of the hero is none other than Reynaldo, who also features under the names of Henri de Réveillon and the Marquis de Poitiers, relates the circumstances in which the two companions meet

---

* There were no more letters to Mme Straus until the end of March 1897 (*Carr.*, vol. II, p. 183).

the writer C., the author of the manuscript, and provides some invaluable information as to the way in which Proust wrote at this time: 'The drops of rain that began to fall and the reappearance of a sunbeam[48] were enough to remind him of rain-drenched autumns and sunlit summers, of whole periods of his life and of the soul's darker moments, which now grew bright once more, intoxicating him with memory and poetry. Many were the times, hidden with my friend, that we watched him. He seemed to be gazing at something in front of him that he did not comprehend very clearly. And the whole of his body, in a series of firm and delicate movements, particularly those of his hands, which he clenched each time he raised his head, appeared to imitate the pattern of his thoughts. Then, all of a sudden, he seemed to be filled with happiness, and he was ready to proceed with his writing.'[49] Memory and reflection bring the story to life, as do the little *madeleine* and the reverie among the hawthorns in *Du côté de chez Swann*; but whereas in the latter work they are integrated into the hero's experience and their hidden significance is not fully clarified until the dénouement, here the meaning is clear from the outset and the entire aesthetics of *Jean Santeuil* can be found in these first pages. For instance, the writer C. interrupts his narrative 'in the manner of certain English novelists of whom he had once been very fond'; he also affirms, as would Proust much later, that he lacked 'all gift of invention' and could only write about 'what he himself had experienced'.[50] The questions he was concerned with in *Jean Santeuil* and which, he believed, would require a lifetime to resolve, would be those of *Contre Sainte-Beuve* and *Le Temps retrouvé*. 'What are the secret relationships, the necessary metamorphoses, which exist between a writer's life and his work, between reality and art, or rather, as we thought at the time, between the appearances of life and reality itself, which underlay everything and which could be released only by art?'[51] These remarks would give birth to Bergotte, Elstir and Vinteuil, among whom Proust drew a distinction between their lives and their work, and their aesthetic principles, which always consisted in trying to identify the essence that lay beneath appearances.

Marcel must have written the Breton chapter at Beg-Meil. At Réveillon he wrote the passages which now carry this title, as is proved by his use of drawing paper belonging to Mme Lemaire: the period he spent writing closely followed fictional time. This would not be true of *À la recherche*, except for the episodes concerning Albertine and Paris during the war.

From the summer of 1896, Marcel entered into negotiations with Calmann-Lévy with a view to publishing his novel. He had available at the time his 'loose pages' and an exercise book of '110 large pages', containing the passages we have mentioned.[52] He thought he would be able to deliver his novel to the publisher in February 1897; it is a consistent feature of his attitude towards his writing that he underestimated, by a long way, the time he would take to complete a book. A section to do with children's picture books (about which he questioned his mother), in which the moon is depicted with a nose,[53] dates from September 1896 and is matched by a letter to his mother. Possibly the entire 'Illiers' chapter may have been completed at this time, certainly the part devoted to evening walks in summer, in any case. In October 1896, at Fontainebleau, having experienced the scene of the telephone call to his mother, he wrote about it, and he sent her a copy.[54] As for the portrait of Lieutenant de Brucourt,[55] who is based upon the Comte de Cholet, a reference to Manchuria enables us to date it to the end of 1895 or the beginning of 1896. Should we thus conclude that everything concerning the garrison town dates from this period? Or just the part that was written at Fontainebleau, which was grafted on to his memories of Orléans?

It was in the hotel at Fontainebleau that Proust began to tell the story of Charlotte Clissette.[56] Until then, Jean Santeuil had been in love with a certain Françoise, whom he deserted, after outbursts of jealousy that bring to mind the letters to Hahn, for Charlotte. We can assume that Françoise was based upon Reynaldo, particularly since she is associated with the 'little phrase' from Saint-Saëns' sonata which she plays on the piano. Who is Charlotte, if not Lucien Daudet? A revealing indication lies in the fact that she has a brother who is head of a clinic at the Necker Hospital; Léon Daudet, too, had studied medicine.* What is more, Charlotte's manner of waving when she says goodbye resembles Lucien's,[57] as does the way in which the lovers address one another. Certain loosely constructed lines from the novel seem to have been written under the impact of this painful transition: 'While he was dreaming of Charlotte and said: "Let me work as in the past," Françoise replied sadly: "Everything has changed a great deal since then." '[58] Equally, one can imagine that the scene of the interrupted kiss, which would later be given to Albertine, was based upon Lucien, who had come to the hotel and left hurriedly during the evening: 'At first he had been very pleasant but the evening ended badly.'[59] But the love for Françoise emerges as the greater one, the most beautiful, the only true

* 'Un nouvel amour', *JS*, p. 822. Moreover, Jean makes Françoise confess that she had slept with Charlotte; Hahn had in fact known Lucien before Marcel.

love, for Proust deliberately took as his models Frédéric Moreau and Mme Arnoux in *L'Éducation sentimentale*.[60] In fact, the novelist was blending actual models with literary ones. The Flaubertian novel is also a *Bildungsroman* – or an ironical version of one – as was the English novel from Fielding to Stevenson[61] or George Eliot, which Jean was reading.

Jaurès was the inspiration for the 'Couzon in the Chamber' section, which concerns the Armenian Massacres, when he spoke on 3 November 1896 in the Chambre des Députés: 'The debate on the Armenian Massacres has just been concluded: it has been agreed that France shall take no action.' All of a sudden, Couzon, 'the one great orator of the day, who was the equal of the great debaters of the past',[62] rose to his feet, 'driven to speak by that sense of Justice which sometimes took over his entire being'. The Assemblée was in uproar and voted in favour of the government motion; Couzon-Jaurès cried: 'You have just pronounced the death sentence on two hundred thousand Christians.' And the president of the council said, 'It is a disgrace,' for, as Proust commented, 'men whose political opinions "exclude feeling" and who "do not care for generalizations" have always been ready to indulge copiously in generalizations and to exploit the sentiment of "dignity"'.[63] This fine description of a political debate, worthy of Péguy, in which we see the young Proust defend the cause of justice, is enshrined in one of the most mysterious passages of *Jean Santeuil*: that devoted to the Marie scandal. In the character of this corrupt minister of finance, we must distinguish between the historical aspect and, curiously enough, the psychological and moral aspects, which reflect upon Marcel himself. He took as his model Rouvier (1842–1911);[64] minister of finance on seven occasions, president of the council in 1887, in 1892, he became compromised in the Panama scandal. Combes restored him to office as minister of finance in 1902 and Rouvier succeeded him as head of government in January 1905. In this outline for a political novel Proust must have been influenced by the Balzac of *Député d'Arcis* and of *Une ténébreuse affaire*, but also by Barrès' *Les Déracinés*,* which mingled actual characters with fictional ones (Ferry, Jacques Reinach and his nephew Joseph); before Barrès' *Leurs figures*, it made references to the Panama affair. The trial of Zola would soon give Proust another opportunity to develop this aspect of his art. As to Marie's psychology, what is most interesting is his attitude towards his wife and towards religion, in which we can discern Marcel's own views with regard to his mother and

---

* He discussed this with Alphonse Daudet in October 1897 (*Corr.*, vol. II, p. 19).

to Catholicism: Mme Marie is an 'exquisite creature, a wonderful wife and mother' and she is Jewish: 'Even the most bigoted peasant woman must have felt that the soul of such a Jewess was more pleasing to Our Lord than all the souls of Christians, priests and saints.'[65] Marie has a sense of sin and guilt which brings him closer to the common herd: if we substitute homosexuality for corruption, we may deduce that in the Christian sense of guilt, Marcel was able to find a means of drawing closer to his fellow man.[66]

Productive though the previous year had been, very little was written in 1897. Three principal reasons for this have been suggested:[67] the impossibility of finding a plot and a structure; a possible rejection (for which we have no documentation) by Calmann-Lévy; and the lack of success of *Les Plaisirs et les Jours*, which sold poorly, gave rise to very little press coverage and was to provoke a duel with Jean Lorrain. We should remind ourselves of a further reason that was at least as important: the break-up with Reynaldo Hahn, who was the chief inspiration for a book whose conception he had witnessed; it is a fact that Lucien Daudet only appears in *Jean Santeuil* in the guise of Charlotte Clissette. Moreover, when Marcel read Robert de La Sizeranne's article in the *Revue des deux mondes* of 1 March 1897, 'Ruskin et la religion de beauté', he first discovered the English aesthete: there can be no doubt about the impact it made on him, for the shockwaves persisted for eight years; gradually his attention switched from his novel and settled on aesthetics and the history of art. As it is, *Jean Santeuil* contains several important references to Ruskin,[68] almost as if ideas for new books were bursting through the old one. At the end of March a sharp quarrel with his parents is related in *Jean Santeuil*.[69] In August 1897, during his second visit to Kreuznach, Proust composed the portrait of the Duc de Réveillon, basing it on the Duc de Doudeauville,[70] and Mme de Réveillon's salon. The story of the Réveillons, who represent the Guermantes aspect of this book, was written at various times, and includes passages about the Monets belonging to the Marquis de Réveillon, which recall those owned by Mme Straus.[71] The scene in which Jean is insulted must have been suggested by the duel with Lorrain. The passages about the pianist Loisel, who was based on Delafosse, must have been written after the quarrel between Montesquiou and the pianist which occurred in mid-June.[72]

The essential points of Zola's trial are recounted in the pages of the novel devoted to the Dreyfus affair.[73] The section on Picquart dates from the end of the year ('people said that Colonel Picquart might face five years in a fortress'). We also come across a visit by Jean to the Opéra-Comique: Hahn's *L'Île du rêve* is to be performed there (Reynaldo appears under the name of Daltozzi). This section must date from April or May; the continuation of the story of the love affair with Charlotte Clissette[74] and the scene of the rejected kiss, which would be attributed to Albertine, from September;* they had been started, however, the previous year. The journey to Holland[75] was based upon the trip Marcel made there in October 1898, during which he visited the Rembrandt exhibition in Amsterdam, which he mentions in an article on Gustave Moreau written at the same period.[76]

In May 1899 Marcel borrowed from Robert de Billy a copy of Émile Mâle's *L'Art religieux du XIIe siècle en France*, which shows that studying history of art was appealing to him more and more. Nevertheless, his visit to Thonon, near Évian, may have been responsible for the pages in the novel about the Lake of Geneva.[77] The allusion to the Jesuits who may have been seeking to 'hire Jean' harks back to some articles that appeared in *L'Aurore* in June 1899.[78] The portrait of Jacques Bonami, known as Talondebois, who foreshadows Legrandin,[79] appeared in the issue of *La Presse* of 19 September.

In September 1899 Proust was still working on the episode of Jean's love for Charlotte Clissette, which he had begun at Fontainebleau in 1896.† From his visit to the Brancovans, he derived a chapter about the Comtesse de Noailles, who is seen in the guise of the Vicomtesse Gaspard de Réveillon. Furthermore, Jean has an experience of involuntary memory by the shores of Lac Léman, which reminds him of Brittany.

Certain passages incorporated into *Jean Santeuil*, or in the appendices, are so mysterious that we may wonder whether Proust did not consider them as alternative endings, or as short stories in the manner of *Les Plaisirs et les Jours*. This is true of 'Lettres de Perse et d'ailleurs', which appeared in *La Presse*, and which also contains a portrait taken from the novel as well as a conversation between Henri and Françoise.[80]

Towards mid-November, if we are to believe Proust's confidential remarks to Marie Nordlinger,[81] he abandoned his 'very-long-drawn-out book' to get on with 'a little task that is totally different from what [he does] generally, about Ruskin and certain cathedrals': on this occasion, it was modesty that made Marcel err in his forecast: he would take six years

---

* The manuscript contained an invitation for 21 September.
† On the back of an invitation dating from September 1899.

to bring this 'little task' to a successful conclusion, six years at the end of which he would have lost all those he loved and would find himself alone and without anything to do.

By 1901–2 *La Bible d'Amiens* had ceased to inspire him; Proust then wrote a few further passages: the portrait of Mme Jacques de Réveillon, based on the Baronne Deslandes,[82] that of Mme Martial, inspired by Mme Ernest Hébert,* who would become Mme Elstir,[83] and that of Bertrand de Réveillon, based upon Bertrand de Fénelon,[84] composed in 1902, at the time when his feelings for the latter were at their height. Although he had abandoned *Jean Santeuil* in 1899, Proust, not knowing what to do with these handwritten pages, kept them with the manuscript of the novel.

The portrait of Mme Martial, which was written after that of Mme Jacques de Réveillon, also dates from the summer of 1902 (according to the writing paper). It was based on the wife of the painter Hébert (whom he had met at the home of Madeleine Lemaire and at the Princesse Mathilde's); Proust would also use her to create Mme Elstir, the 'beautiful Gabrielle',[85] a fine study of the relationship between the painter, love and his model. Marcel always had a feeling for the portrait, for the 'character study': but this was very different to a fictional scene, and he was unable to provide a fresh impetus for the discarded novel.

Because of a lack of any material clues or comments in letters, however, the greater part of the novel cannot be dated precisely, particularly those passages to do with Jean's social life, or Proust's attempts to recount the passing of time, or his parent's aging. The laying aside of the novel did not entail any lengthy outpouring. Mme Proust was nevertheless involved in the imperceptible transition from one book to another, from the novel to the translation of Ruskin, since it was she who would translate it, just as she had read *Jean Santeuil*. The aesthetic relationship of mother and son was thus reinforced: she supervised his writing just as she had watched over the sleeping child.

WHAT IS *JEAN SANTEUIL*?

In this narrative Proust succeeded in making the transition from the shorter form of portraits and character studies in the manner of La Bruyère, prose poems and short stories, to the novel form, and to a manuscript of considerable length: 724 printed pages. He had wanted to

---

* The portrait of Mme Hébert, *née* Gabrielle d'Uckermann (1892), is at the Musée Hébert in Paris.

write an important classic novel that would link Goethe and Balzac. He had wanted to relate the journey through life of a central character, in which the author could disguise himself, since the story is told in the third person, and in so doing to disclose much of himself, since Jean leads exactly the same life as Marcel. In an early draft preface he wrote: 'Can I call this book a novel? It is something less, perhaps, and yet much more, recounting the very essence of my life, with nothing extraneous added, as it unfolded through long periods of unhappiness.'[86] The following sentence contains the main reason for its ultimate failure: 'This book was never composed, it was assembled.' The collection juxtaposed a large number of disparate pieces, some written on loose pages, some in exercise books, on official notepaper borrowed from his father, on the backs of invitations and in sketchpads,* all of which still had to be assembled, arranged and bound together. Proust numbered whole wads of pages which did not follow on. Like the book's title, most of the chapter titles are not the author's, and we shall see that the titles of *À la recherche du temps perdu*, which now seem so well established, would be the object of a long and faltering search. These fragments have been assembled by the publishers in accordance with two principles: Jean Santeuil's age and the themes that are addressed. This is why his childhood, the places visited – Illiers, Beg-Meil, Réveillon, the garrison town (Proust wavers between Orléans, Fontainebleau or Provins) – and then the political events, the Marie scandal, the Dreyfus affair, social life, love affairs, and, finally, the parents in their old age, group together pages of manuscript that were only a rough draft, in which passages overlap one other and are repeated, and in which details contradict themselves and the names of characters and places keep changing, just as they would later, in the draft manuscripts of *À la recherche*.

In fact Proust took up *Jean Santeuil* once again in 1908–9 and reread and even recopied parts of it. There is therefore no reason for us to be surprised that themes, characters and entire scenes should be encountered again in *À la recherche*. A detailed list of them has been compiled.[87] What the author himself called 'the first chapter' is the prologue of a classical novel, which relates the circumstances that allowed the two friends to meet the writer C., the author of the manuscript. In this way Marcel can distance himself twofold; the story is written in the third person, and it is also told by a third person. The biography of *Jean Santeuil*, as Proust related

---

* From Mme Lemaire's house, at Réveillon, which enables us to date the pages.

it through the device of the writer C., heralds that of the Narrator. The scene of the evening kiss, the love play in the Champs-Élysées, the holidays at Illiers, the reading, the magic lantern, the walks, the Sunday – this is already *Du côté de chez Swann*; the visit to Beg-Meil is a precursor to the Balbec of *À l'ombre des jeunes filles en fleurs*, its little train that of *Sodome et Gomorrhe II*. The seeds of the future *Le Côté de Guermantes* lie in the section devoted to the Réveillons, in the passages about the garrison towns, the Dreyfus affair and Jean's social life. In this book, which is richer in characterization than it is in plot and more static than romantic, the outlines of characters who reappear in *À la recherche* abound: the diplomat Duroc is a forerunner of Norpois, as is Bertrand de Réveillon of Robert de Saint-Loup,[88] the 'brilliant novelist Traves' prefigures Bergotte, as does Rustinlor Legrandin. Jean happens to write: 'Once he had his paper laid out in front of him, he wrote about what he did not yet know, about what enticed him on account of the image beneath which it lay hidden (and which was not, by any means, a symbol) and not what his reason told him was clever and beautiful.' The secret of art lies in the impression which sums up an image, not in the power of reasoning, nor in intelligence: this is already *Contre Sainte-Beuve*, and we see Proust torn between feeling and thought, between poetry and abstraction. The section which groups together the passages on love is a draft for 'Un amour de Swann', particularly the episode of the 'little phrase', in this case from Saint-Saëns, the jealous quest, and the heroine's homosexual relationships. The passing of time is seen in the pages describing Jean Santeuil's parents' old age, twenty years after the beginning of the novel;[89] it is as if here Proust were trying to ward off the deaths of his family and friends rather than writing a '*bal de têtes*',* as he did in the notebooks that pave the way for *Le Temps retrouvé*. The rapture of memories, one of the positive aspects of time regained, is present, in particular, when a storm at Réveillon recalls Brittany, and reveals a new reality, 'a reality that is something we are not aware of in the moment that we experience it, because we connect it to some selfish end. But it is something which, in the sudden flashes of disinterested memory, sets us afloat between the present and the past in an element that is common to both of them, which in the present has recalled the past to us, an essence that arouses us deeply in so far as it is ourself.'[90]

Certain passages, on the other hand, would not find their way into *À la recherche du temps perdu*. These were the scenes depicting Jean at the Lycée

---

* A masked ball at which only the head of the guest is disguised. *Tr.*

Henri IV and at the École des Sciences Politiques; the violent quarrel between Jean and his parents; the straightforward account of the Dreyfus affair and the trial of Zola, which are portrayed in *Le Côté de Guermantes* only through allusions, reflections and remarks made by characters; and also certain places that Proust had visited, such as Beg-Meil and the shores of Lac Léman. One notices that these are all autobiographical scenes, that have not yet been subjected to the characters' points of view, or to the requirements of plot and imagination in fiction. This was one of the reasons for Proust abandoning this vast pile of pages: he was quite able to describe his life and his feelings between the ages of twenty-five and thirty; but he was not capable of giving them an overall structure or any organizational basis. *Jean Santeuil* is neither the story of a life resurrected through memory, nor is it that of a vocational calling: memory and literature are not singled out here, they are merely themes like any others. Finally, the sentence structure is tentative and does not have the fine classical style, reminiscent of Saint-Simon, which it would acquire in *À la recherche*; this is why a number of sentences are incomplete.

WINTER 1896–7

There is little to record as the year of 1896 drew to its end. There was one encounter, however, which would have far-reaching consequences for Marcel: his meeting with Marie Nordlinger, a young Englishwoman and a sculptress, whom he met at the home of her cousin, Reynaldo Hahn. She would be of the greatest help to him in understanding, annotating and translating Ruskin's work. This meeting would be the first milestone on the path towards the inception of this work, the second being the article he read by Robert de La Sizeranne, 'Ruskin et la religion de beauté'. On 24 December Anatole France was elected to the Académie française; from the time of the Dreyfus affair onwards, he would not set foot there again, the Académie being largely anti-Dreyfusard. Bergotte would not be an academician, but Marcel, who did dream of becoming one, followed in the footsteps of Alphonse Daudet* and described an *immortel* tottering about in the courtyard of the Institut Français.

---

* Daudet's novel *L'Immortel*, based on the Vrain-Lucas affair, must surely have cost him a seat in the Académie. Valéry, who was elected to Anatole France's chair, was to deliver a speech that would be long remembered, since, in order to avenge Mallarmé, who was initially unappreciated by France in *La Vie littéraire*, the author of *La Jeune Parque* did not mention the name of his predecessor.

On 1 January he took the opportunity to renew ties with those who were already his friends. To Laure Hayman, who never had much time for impassioned outbursts, Marcel sent a flower arrangement of the blooms that Odette would like, and, in memory of his Uncle Louis, his tie-pin, to be used as a hat pin.[91] Robert de Montesquiou had given him the cold shoulder since the summer, but Proust tried to bring about a reconciliation by paying tribute to a 'mind that was so eminently and magnificently unusual' that he would go so far as to term it unique.[92] Montesquiou has given us an interesting snapshot of Marcel: he reckoned him to be honest, considerate, congenial, too inclined to listen to gossip, and 'somewhat evasive'; as to his defects, he noted observantly, they became the virtues of his books; and he quoted from *Les Plaisirs et les Jours*.[93] Proust replied in a letter that was half-ironic, but which none the less revealed his desire to 'consult the oracle' about the books he had just read: as usual, he imagined that he needed an intermediary in order to understand, in this instance, *Le Curé de village*, *Mémoires d'outre-tombe* and *L'Éducation sentimentale*. We have seen that a familiarity with these books played a part in the writing of *Jean Santeuil*, just as a more substantial knowledge of them would in *À la recherche*. Marcel kept certain important works by him, much as he did his anti-asthma powders. As for Montesquiou, in a ploy worthy of Charlus, he awarded 'fifteen minus' to this 'little epistolary exercise'. The 'teacher of beauty' verged on sadism, and the relationship between the two writers would always continue to display this alternating mixture of flattery, kindness, helpful advice, bitter words and outpourings of muted revenge: Charlus and the Narrator. However, if Montesquiou helped Proust to broaden his mind, as well as his knowledge of the aristocracy, if not of inversion, he certainly did not know how to re-create any of this in his memoirs; he may, like Wilde, have wanted to fashion a masterpiece out of his life, but he was unable to metamorphose it in his work and to become the Saint-Simon of his age.

From letters and a chapter of *Jean Santeuil*[94] we learn of a rather more serious and strange quarrel that broke out between Marcel and his parents. This is the most striking example of disputes that must have been to do with the fact that their son was growing older and hung around at home like a grown-up child, yet expected to be provided with money and total freedom in his habits and movements. Marcel had slammed a glass door, and a pane of glass had shattered; like Jean Santeuil, he also broke a Venetian glass which his mother had just given him as a present; Mme Proust advised him not to walk on the dining-room floor with bare feet, and she saw in this broken glass 'what it represents at the temple', 'a symbol of indissoluble union': this allusion to the Orthodox Jewish marriage ceremony has been interpreted by certain commentators as a Freudian slip. The subject of dispute was a photograph taken by Otto, in which Lucien Daudet* is seen gazing lovingly at Marcel. Daudet's posture and his way of life disturbed Proust's parents, who insisted, before even seeing them, that any other photographs be destroyed. Marcel, who posed for seven photographs, giggling uncontrollably, and who only took notice of what Robert de Flers (who is also seen in the photograph) asked him to do, promised to keep only three copies, and to give the others to his mother, who was under no illusions about her son's tendencies.

More serious still in its potential consequences, our Dumas enthusiast fought a duel. In fact, Jean Lorrain, who had greeted *Les Plaisirs et les Jours* so ironically, and whose relentless pursuit is hard to comprehend in a writer who was both homosexual and a socialite, attacked Proust once more, after a gap of seven months, in *Le Journal* of 3 February. Alphonse Daudet, he asserted, would write the preface for Proust's next book, 'because he can refuse nothing to his son Lucien': this was to make an insinuation about the relationship between the two young men that Proust felt bound to resist. One might have thought that for a man as highly strung as Marcel, a duel would not have been an easy thing to contemplate. Yet he did not waver and, on the three preceding days, he displayed 'a composure and resolution which appeared incompatible with his nerves', though this did not surprise Reynaldo Hahn in the least.† The duel took place in the Meudon woods at the Ermitage de Villebon; Marcel took as his seconds[95] not his close friends, but Jean Béraud, the painter of Parisian life, and the fencing master Gustave de Borda.[96] Two shots were fired without either party being injured. On 7 February Mme de Caillavet wrote: 'I embrace you for having been so brave and for returning to us safe and sound from this experience. I rather wished that some harm had come to the monster, but it is already a fine thing to have attacked him, considering the general cowardice which until now has allowed the ruffian to escape with impunity.'[97] Proust was both extremely sensitive about any gossip-mongering arising from his way of life, and anxious to prove his

---

* See illustration no. 6 in the plate section.

† *Notes*, p. 54. R. de Flers, for his part, wrote to France: 'The day before yesterday, Marcel Proust took the most delightfully heroic revenge upon the wretch whom you know' (M. Maurois, *Les Cendres brûlantes*, Flammarion, 1986, p. 109).

virility (he would, moreover, assert forcibly that inversion did not exclude courage, as the death of Saint-Loup shows); his fondness for duelling is borne out in *Jean Santeuil* and in *À la recherche*, but also in the course of his own life: he had already fought a duel at Mont-Dore in 1896,[98] he did so later, with Paul Hervieu, in 1901, with Henry de Vogüé and the Marquis de Medici, and he fought again, at the end of his life, with Jean de Pierrefeu in 1920, and with Jacques Delgado,[99] at Le Bœuf sur le Toit.[100]

During this month of February* Proust also intervened in a quarrel between Mme de Caillavet and her daughter-in-law on the one side, and Colette and her husband, Willy, on the other. Naturally, like a character in a burlesque, he succeeded in making the situation more acrimonious: 'Mme Arman claimed that Willy, whom she had invited to her home as a friend, had tried to woo her daughter-in-law. And, being outraged, all she could think of doing was to inform Colette Willy and to stop inviting them to her house. As a result of this, Willy maintained that the distress had almost caused his wife to lose her sight. Since they have always been very kind to me and because I felt they had been badly treated, I went to call on them just once (something I did not in the least hide from Mme Arman, who has never forgiven me for doing so) and offered to help them by recommending an optician.'[101] In fact, Willy did pursue Jeanne Pouquet; Colette had tried in vain to put an end to the cooling of relations and had heard Mme de Caillavet say that Willy was the author of a malicious article about her and her salon that had appeared in two newspapers. Marcel's attempt at mediation having failed, Willy poked fun at M. Arman ('keeper of the *collage* de France'†), Mme de Caillavet ('her hair done up like an owl with its wings outspread, lovely above, lovely below'),‡ and their daughter ('The Cabbage-Rose, that chubby girl whose cheeks are like the buttocks of little cherubs') in his novels, in *Un vilain monsieur*, and, with Colette, in *Claudine à Paris, Claudine en ménage* and *Claudine s'en va*.[102] We may wonder whether Proust was not flying to his friends' aid in a curious little satirical article, 'Silhouette d'artiste', that appeared in January 1897 in *La Revue d'art dramatique*,[103] in which he took stock of the clichés that theatre critics use to review actors' performances, and went so far as to mention his private life: 'We learn that, dining in

---

* When he went to hear Alfred Bruneau's *Messidor*, the last act of which he enjoyed.

† '*Conservateur du collage de France*': a pun on Collège de France; 'collage' is also an old-fashioned term for a liaison. *Tr.*

‡ Pun on the double meaning of '*chouette*'. *Tr.*

town on the evening of a first night, he [the critic] left before coffee so
as to arrive in time, and that the curtain only went up a long time later.'

At the end of March the Weil family sold the property at 96 rue La
Fontaine, which had been left vacant following the death of the two
brothers, to a civil engineer, M. Daval, who demolished the house in order
to build flats; it was these, and not the villa, which would be pulled down
when the avenue Mozart was cut through.[104] In 'Combray' all we know
is that 'the staircase wall' where the scene of the evening kiss took place
has not existed for a long time and, from a draft, that: 'The house in
which this took place no longer exists. And the image of it in my memory
is perhaps the only proof of it that still remains and which will shortly be
destroyed.'[105] In the summer of 1897 M. and Mme Proust were still
sufficiently fond of this peculiar village to rent a chalet there at the
Parc-des-Princes; Marcel would catch the train at the Saint-Lazare station
whenever he went to visit his parents.[106] In *Jean Santeuil* these details are
transposed with a strength of feeling that Marcel was not able to express
in his letters: M. and Mme Santeuil rented 'a small property close to the
Château de Madrid and which overlooked the lake in the Bois de Boulogne.
Jean would go to dine with them every evening, but because of Françoise,
he would return to sleep in Paris. M. and Mme Santeuil had changed a
great deal since the day when we saw them for the first time in the little
garden in Auteuil, on the ruins of which there rose three or four six-storey
houses, several of which had already been let', and, whenever the Santeuils'
motor car passed by their former house, 'by what for her was the saddest
of tombs', M. Santeuil said to his wife: 'Close your eyes.'[107] Marcel himself,
who never owned anything except his own mind, would henceforth grow
accustomed to the town houses which he had at first so feared; there
would no longer be a familiar room waiting for him on fine days, either
at Illiers or at Auteuil. But the chestnut and lilac trees of Auteuil and the
Bois de Boulogne would bloom eternally in *Du côté de chez Swann*.

Social life picked up again in the spring: Marcel frequently listened to
works by Reynaldo Hahn, among them his 'Portraits de peintres' recited
by Marguerite Moreno, and he attended musical evenings given by Mme
Aubernon, by Madeleine Lemaire, who also took him to the Opéra in
July,* and by Mme Bartholoni; he went to see la Duse in *La Dame aux
camélias* at the Renaissance and, at Boldini's house, he saw the portrait,
soon to become famous, which the artist had painted of Montesquiou

---

* To hear *Faust* or *Les Huguenots* (*Corr.*, vol. II, p. 207).

and in which, according to Jean Lorrain, he seemed 'to be hypnotized in adoration of his walking-stick'[108] (the same walking-stick which would be the cause of a duel with Henri de Régnier on 9 June). On 24 May Marcel gave a dinner party at his parents' home: *Le Gaulois*, which was more generous in its social chronicle than it had been in its literary pages, observed: 'One of the most literary and most elegant of dinner parties was held yesterday at the home of M. Marcel Proust, who, for the first time, brought his numerous friends together.' Among the guests were Anatole France, Comte Louis de Turenne, Comte Robert de Montesquiou-Fezensac, de La Gandara,* Jean Béraud, G. de Borda, Reynaldo Hahn, the Marquis de Castellane, the writers Porto-Riche and Édouard Rod (who had devoted a few lines to *Plaisirs*, and to whom Proust, on reading his novel *Là-haut*, had written an enthusiastic letter which dwelt on his depiction of time),† and Gaston de Caillavet. There were no women present, according to a British custom, which was less painful to Marcel than to others. Montesquiou and Proust were reconciled: the former finally praised *Les Plaisirs et les Jours* publicly in his book *Roseaux pensants* (1897): 'And in passing I want to pay tribute with eulogistic memory to the fine first book by our young friend Marcel Proust, who moreover has twice been commended to the public through distinguished and charming patronage,‡ and to search its silken pages for an elegant new reappearance of this personality.'[109] 'Now I'm immortal!' exclaimed Marcel gratefully.§

---

* This society painter, to whom Proust attributed the portrait of Jean Santeuil (in reality it was Blanche's portrait of Proust), was a protégé of Montesquiou, who would fall out with him as he did with Delafosse and would write a satirical account of the two artists in *Gil Blas* (20 October 1910), reprinted in 1912 in *Têtes d'expression*. Proust would take Montesquiou's side in the quarrel with Delafosse (*Corr.*, vol. II, pp. 194–5, 16 June 1897) and would remember it when he portrayed the relationship between Charlus and Morel.

† Ibid., pp. 179–80, March 1897: 'You show individuals within their generations like the ebb and flow of a tide which is slower than they are, but just as sure, more vast and fundamentally identical. It is this panoramic painting not merely of places, but of events, that I so loved in a novel like *Middlemarch*.' Here we find ourselves at the root of the Proustian aesthetic: individuals within generations; 'the changing times'; these 'little events of hotel life' which interest Proust more than 'exceptional circumstances'; the influence of George Eliot. Proust's correspondence is often criticized for its frivolousness; yet it is important to read it because it enables us to establish the genealogy of his ideas and their progress throughout the fictional framework. In this context, ideology comes before fiction.

‡ Mme Lemaire and Anatole France.

§ 'The object of research by future scholars who will wonder who this stranger whom you called your friend could be.' Proust's first joke about the comments made by academics, or by posterity, about him. It was also in a letter to the count at this same period that he first formulated one of the laws of *À la recherche*: 'Everything that was once a desire becomes a fact. But when one no

SUMMER 1897

When Reynaldo Hahn lost his father, who died at Saint-Germain on 15 July, Marcel, who was unwell, did not go to see him, but declared that distance meant nothing, and that he was with his friend all the time. Death, or the wish to console his old friend, who was probably a believer, caused him to remark, in one of his rare surges of feeling for a faith he did not share: 'I pray that the Good God, in His mercy, may also be with you.'

Shortly before mid-August Marcel accompanied his mother to Kreuznach to take the waters for a second time;[110] she would stay there for four weeks. Reynaldo meanwhile was recovering at Aix-la-Chapelle, where he read Sainte-Beuve, whom he greatly admired, as his diary attests, as well as Séailles' book on Leonardo da Vinci.[111] As for Marcel, he was extremely bored, for, as he confessed to Mme de Brantes, apart from Marthe de Béhague, the Comtesse de Béarn, who was there for the first few days, he knew nobody. He took advantage of this to work at his novel,* probably the section dealing with the aristocracy and the Duc de Réveillon, since he was delighted to have discovered portraits of the old nobility in Balzac's *Gobseck*, from which he picked up sayings and traits of character 'in the manner of Aimery de La Rochefoucauld',† 'not of course to copy them but as inspiration';‡ he consulted Mme de Béarn about them, and he reproached Mme de Brantes for not wanting to tell him anything: 'In five

---

longer desires it' (*Corr.*, vol. II, p. 197, end of June 1897). Finally, we should note that Proust was reading *La Chartreuse de Parme* at this time, for he leaves it in a cab (ibid.). A copy exists that was annotated by him (exhibited at the Musée Jacquemart-Andrée in 1971); he made use of these notes in the posthumously published article that is included in *Contre Sainte-Beuve* and for *La Prisonnière*.

* Certain pages of the manuscript were written on hotel notepaper.

† Proust would give certain mannerisms displayed by this character (who figured in several memoirs of the period) to the Prince de Guermantes, and would put certain sayings of his, which were well known among *Le Tout-Paris* of the time, into the mouth of the Duc de Guermantes; he would also become friendly with his son Gabriel (who was to portray Marcel in his novel *L'Amant et le médecin*). M. de La Rochefoucauld, whose wife hosted aristocratic salons, was interested above all in rank and etiquette: 'One day when Mme de Chabrillan was paying a visit to the countess, she asked M. de La Rochefoucauld who the subject represented in a certain miniature was: "That's Henri IV, madame." "Really? I would never have recognized him!" "I refer to Henri IV de La Rochefoucauld, naturally," replied the count. It was he, too, who on not being placed on the right of the mistress of the house, exclaimed: "Is one served with all the courses at the place at which I am sitting?"' (A. de Fouquières, *Cinquante ans de panache*, P. Horay, 1951, pp. 79–80).

‡ *Corr.*, vol. II, p. 214, to Mme de Brantes: 'I shall also show you my Duc de Réveillon (I won't keep the name) and you can tell me whether the tics, prejudices and habits I attribute to him are over-exaggerated.' How would this duke have behaved towards M. Haas, he asks her, and this is the first appearance of the model for Swann in Proust's hand.

minutes a woman of wit or a man of taste can sum up the experiences of many years.' As we have seen, Proust never stopped asking questions and investigating, either because he still lacked experience of the world (though he would behave similarly where inversion was concerned), or because he wished to substantiate certain things: hence the importance of his relationships, entirely literary ones, with these glittering society ladies; he blended their stories or character sketches with those he obtained through his reading: everything was put to use.

PROUST AS READER OF BALZAC

Marcel asked Lucien Daudet's advice about what he should read (and from this we know that he had not yet read *The Brothers Karamazov* – about which he would later write some splendid lines – Dickens, or the *Life of Samuel Johnson*), and then plunged back into Balzac. In Proust's correspondence Balzac's name first appears in a letter from Mme Proust.[112] He was a writer who was already part of the family, for *La Muse du département*, which was the book in question, had belonged to Georges Weil and she assumed Marcel knew it. The books that Proust reread – at least those mentioned in his letters and personal writings – indicate that there was not a single moment of literary crisis in Marcel's life in which Balzac did not feature, whether he was quoted, explained, reproduced or imitated. *Splendeurs et misères des courtisanes* is mentioned in 1895,[113] at the time that coincided with the end of *Les Plaisirs et les Jours*. From the start, however, Marcel enjoyed Balzac's lesser-known works, the 'miniatures', which, in 1917, he placed alongside his 'immense frescoes'. If, as a result, he neglected the academic canon, from *Eugénie Grandet* to *Le Père Goriot*, it was because he was influenced by one of the great art lovers of his age, Robert de Montesquiou.[114] In 1896, when Marcel had begun *Jean Santeuil*, his mother had pointed out to him that 'Rubempré's death had affected [her] less than Esther's'.[115] To read Balzac was to speak the family language: in October 1896 Mme Proust read the *Lettres à l'Étrangère*, which was published in *La Revue de Paris*.[116] From Fontainebleau, where he stayed that same month, Marcel ordered, as we have seen, *Le Curé de village, Un ménage de garçon* (*La Rabouilleuse*), *La Vieille Fille* and *Les Chouans* – while losing his money and running after it 'like old father Grandet'. In January 1897 he was keen to question Montesquiou about the first of these novels.[117] During his holidays at Kreuznach (August 1897), he asked Lucien Daudet to recommend him some good Balzac 'of the *Vieille Fille* and *Cabinet des antiques* kind – or like *Goriot* or *Bette'*, while he was reading *La Muse du département*.[118] He also read *La Duchesse de Langeais, Une ténébreuse affaire* and *Gobseck*. Thus we can appreciate how Proust complemented his own descriptions of the aristocracy with those of Balzac. He also read *La Recherche de l'absolu*,[119] the title of which may have inspired him in 1913, and he admitted to Léon Daudet in 1899 that it had been necessary for him to progress in life, 'to mature', in order to understand certain books and 'many of Balzac's, Shakespeare's and Goethe's characters', as well as the 'mortal sadness' of poisoned happiness, which is the 'philosophy of all life'.[120]

Although Balzac's name is closely associated with the writing of *Jean Santeuil*, when Proust abandoned this novel in order to translate Ruskin's *The Bible of Amiens*, he seemed to lose interest in Balzac, all of whose books he had probably read; his name became no more than a familiar reference, mentioned occasionally, as when he compared Anatole France's conversations to Balzac's.[121] Whenever he practised pastiche, however, Balzac was one of his first targets.[122] Furthermore, Proust knew the *Répertoire de la Comédie humaine* by Cerfberr and Christophe, thanks most likely to Anatole France, who mentioned it in *La Vie littéraire*;[123] he bought a copy, and then gave it to his friend Gabriel de La Rochefoucauld. Albert Sorel played an important role as intercessor, through his articles,[124] and during the time that he was one of Marcel's teachers at the École des Sciences Politiques. Marcel acclaimed him as 'the great Balzacien, who in his own way is also a Balzac himself', 'about whose slightest literary predilections, stimulated by his essay *Une ténébreuse affaire* and *L'Envers de l'histoire contemporaine* [he] had made so many enquiries and tried to verify so many anecdotes'.[125] One may conclude that it was Sorel who had helped Marcel to understand Balzac's historical and political novels. Proust was thus suitably mature to be able to distinguish between the theories of *La Comédie humaine* and its beauty: 'The theories of Rousseau, Flaubert, Balzac and so many others, are no doubt false. And even if absolute monarchy and clericalism are not the preserve of France alone, that does not make Balzac's *Le Médecin de campagne* any less fine a work.'[126]

He then went on to identify stylistic details. Concerning Mme Bovary's extreme unction, for example, he asserted that Balzac had made 'twice' 'Flaubert's progress'.[127] Or again, when Antoine Bibesco asked him for 'names used in Saint-Simon that have died out', Marcel began by omitting those that Balzac had used (and which, in any case, had not died out during his lifetime!)'.[128] It was at about this time that he found himself astonished at the errors Sainte-Beuve had made about Balzac,[129] and that he offered his services as a guide to reading: 'The most enjoyable thing of all would be to get down to reading Balzac . . . or at least one cycle of Balzac's, for a single novel cannot be read in isolation; it's difficult to get away with reading less than a tetralogy, and sometimes a decalogy. A few of the short stories, which are truly divine, can be read on their own, this great painter of frescoes having been an incomparable miniaturist. If you would like some advice about Balzac, I shall write to you but it would be a long letter.'[130]

The period of assimilation was therefore over, to be followed by one of imitation, in his pastiches, and one of re-creation, begun already in *Jean Santeuil*, and continued in *À la recherche*. At the same time, his correspondence is strewn with profound comments. On several occasions Proust as we know, reminds us of 'Oscar Wilde saying that the greatest sorrow he had ever known was the death of Lucien de Rubempré in Balzac, and learning shortly afterwards, through his trial, that there are sorrows that are more real still'.[131] He relaxed by portraying George Sand as Mlle de Touches in *Béatrix*. 'In Pornic Balzac placed/ Between flowers of basil/ The illustrious Aurore, a poetess.'[132] Or else he cemented his knowledge by borrowing Balzac's essay on *La Chartreuse de Parme*,[133] or Cerfberr and Christophe's *Répertoire* which he had generously given away ten years earlier.[134]

Balzac thus permeated the whole of Proust's life, or rather he lived within him, and he made jokes because of him, as when he told a friend in 1911 that 'involved as [they] both were in so many Balzacien lives, it made them pleased (thank God!) to be more Flaubertiste',[135] and he was prepared to talk of '*balzacisme*' when referring to his purchase of stock-market shares. He even came to expect the same erudition in those with whom he communicated: 'Remember,' he wrote to Jacques Copeau in 1913, 'how in Balzac's *Les Illusions perdues*, the bishop is thus brought round to the idea of childbirth'.[136] There is that which is 'Balzac' and that which is not,[137] as if life only offered him events which Balzac had described (something which Proust would later say of himself), and when he gave his 'last party' at the Ritz, it was 'like Mme de Beauséant'.[138]

In 1915 one particular event stirred many a memory and furnished a chapter of *Albertine disparue*. It was the '*lettre de faire-part*' [the funeral announcement] of the Comtesse Mniszech, *née* Anna Hanska (1828–1915), Balzac's daughter-in-law. Proust could visualize the Polish aristocracy filing past, and they included people he may have known (his brother's godmother was a Comtesse Puslowska): 'This led to long conversations at rue de Courcelles with papa.' In *À la recherche* Proust employed a similar form of announcement to inform people of the marriage of Jupien's niece to young Cambremer.[139] A posthumous Balzacien reality had become a Proustian one.

From 1918 onwards the author of *La Comédie humaine* is only mentioned passively: this is because critics compared Proust to him. Marcel seemed to accept this relationship: 'This was the way Balzac, who is considered a great illustrator of society, painted the world from his room, but the following generation, who knew and loved his books, suddenly abounded with the Rastignacs and Rubemprés whom he had invented but who once existed.'[140] Neither the one nor the other should be considered 'realists'. Referring to the Guermantes' motto, Proust declared, 'I made up some rather charming ones', yet he added: 'But the finest were those that Balzac discovered. You must know these marvels (for Beaumont, *pulchre sedens melius agens*, and Mortsauf, etc.). It was a Gramont (who I don't think was Gramont at all) who found that one for him.'[141] Marcel could not but be delighted when it was suggested that 'a Balzacien dictionary' of his work should be compiled: '(I blush before this comparison which dwarfs me). I don't believe it should be based exactly on the dictionary of Balzac's work, but should be a little less literal and give a certain amount of room to the history of feelings'.[142] Proust had always mocked the satisfaction with which his illustrious predecessor spoke of his own novels. He nevertheless adopted this tone himself when writing to Gaston Gallimard: 'Once again I recommend that you take a little trouble with the launch of my new book, upon which I would willingly heap all the eulogies which Balzac, with as much naïvety as ingenuity, endowed his own work in his letters.'[143] Now that he had reached the end of his life, he no longer needed his model, whom he had assimilated so perfectly.

Yet it was in his books that Proust really introduced us to Balzac. His influence can be felt from as early as *Les Plaisirs et les Jours*: 'Mélancolique villégiature de Mme de Breyves' imitates *La Femme abandonnée*, as do other passages the 'Études de femmes'. Mention is made of *Le Curé de village* in *Jean Santeuil* through the writer B., who resembles Anatole France, and who declares that it is necessary to read the whole of Balzac, because 'the quality is not found in one book alone, but in the whole body'.[144] A theme emerges, which will be taken up again in *Contre Sainte-Beuve*: the people who must be made to talk about Balzac are not writers, but his readers: 'Old prefects, financiers with a taste for reading . . . intelligent military types . . . there's an almost earthy power about him: he appeals to so many people, though he'll never appeal much to artists . . . it's not by art that he affects us. It's a pleasure which is not really very refined. He tries to win us over, like life itself, through a whole mass of evil things and that's just like him.'[145]

In spite of this verdict, a view that is much harsher than those voiced in his letters, *Jean Santeuil* derives its inspiration from *La Comédie humaine* primarily in its descriptions of surroundings. 'A Balzac could study a dwelling almost as if he were deciphering it and, according to the shapes of its contents, he could bring generations of men and women to life,'[146] Proust observed, describing the home of Mme Desroches. Above all, the author of *Jean Santeuil* dreams of creating the 'modern Rubempré', the writer who yearns to live his life: 'How interesting for the psychologist is the psychological flora that is to be found in that isolated area of life and the world which goes by the name of *society*, and whose most poisonous flower, which is nevertheless one of the most common in this rotten land, is that of snobbery!' And so this 'novelist who is also a snob becomes the chosen novelist of snobs'.[147] In society, the modern Rubempré loses the powers of resistance which a solitary life bestows. Confronted with this character, another one emerges: the modern Rastignac,[148] a man who pretends to despise society, who plays his part in it with reluctance; cold and blunt, he loathes snobs. One can sense Marcel being equally attracted to both these heroes, for they form the double head of the same Janus which so fascinated him.

At the beginning of the twentieth century Proust the chronicler scattered his 'salons' with quotations from Balzac; the very style of the 'salon' is drawn from the great social gatherings in *La Comédie humaine*, and we can sense Proust, following Montesquiou's example, dreaming of seeing a new Princess de Cadignan appear.[149] In 1903 'Madame Madeleine Lemaire's salon' opened with a pastiche of Balzac describing the house of the painter on the rue de Monceau,[150] and one of the Comtesse Potocka, so often quoted,[151] recalling the Princesse de Cadignan. At that moment we sense that her 'inner voice . . . had been trained throughout the entire reading to follow the tempo of Balzac'.[152] He wanted to continue speaking in the way that he did. In the introduction to his two Ruskin translations, Proust defined his critical creed: Balzac's work, 'impure in some ways, is mingled with a wit and a reality that rarely alter'.[153] In 1908 his experience of writing a long pastiche of Balzac and starting the first version of *À la recherche du temps perdu* led Proust to the formulation, at once concrete in the pastiche and abstract in its criticism, of his theory; by fighting on two fronts, he attacked Balzac while at the same time defending him against Sainte-Beuve.[154] The essential question was 'the transforming effect that the writer's ideas have on reality', due to his style. Balzac's 'does not suggest, does not reflect: it explains'.[155] Proust nevertheless conceded that 'the portrayal of the language of characters' concealed 'the most profound intentions'. The beauty of these effects was accentuated, and no doubt originally made possible, by the reappearance of characters from one novel to the next: 'And so a ray of light, emerging from the depths of the work and reflecting an entire lifetime, can come to cast its melancholy gleam over the little Dordogne manor house and the two travellers who are staying there.'[156] And so in this outline we are reading the original version of one of the aesthetic high points of *À la recherche*. 'It is Balzac's touch of genius that Sainte-Beuve failed to appreciate here. It could be said, no doubt, that he did not arrive at this view immediately. Some parts of his great cycles did not come to be linked together until afterwards. Why should this matter? Wagner had composed his *Good Friday Spell* before he thought of composing *Parsifal*, and he incorporated it into the opera at a later date. But the additions that Balzac made, these lovely things that are introduced, the new relationships which his genius suddenly perceives between different parts of his work, which are brought together, come to life and can never be separated again – are these not his finest creative intuitions?'[157] The fine qualities of imagination and observation which a reader such as M. de Guermantes appreciates in Balzac's work are inferior to the joy that pure literature gives us: the vision of *La Comédie humaine* as a unique and all-enveloping work provides an aesthetic enjoyment *par excellence*.

These reflections reappear almost unaltered in *La Prisonnière* and *Le Temps retrouvé*, the books in which the notion of the Balzacien cycle is most successful, those in which Proust really 'redid' Balzac. The criticism that he made of his style, or of the historical and realistic interpretations that may be made of *La Comédie humaine*, enabled him to improve his own style and to distance himself by comparison with the social novel. Yet Proust's correspondence (which also owed something to Balzac) reveals a constant devotion, a profound knowledge and a loyal memory of his work. The more Proust wrote, the more he quoted Balzac. The genesis of his own books led to a revival of his recollections, right up to the day, which he had begun to enjoy without ever expecting it, when people began referring to Balzac's name in the same breath as his own.

AUTUMN 1897

A year later, the sales figures for *Les Plaisirs et les Jours* were not good: Marcel
had hoped that in addition to the de-luxe edition, which had a print-run of
1,500 copies and sold at a price of 13.50 francs, a cheaper edition, selling at
3 francs 50, could be published, from which he might obtain a few royalties.
The publishers preferred to wait until the first printing had sold out, and, in
the absence of any written contract, they would only pay him royalties once
the original printing costs had been covered.[158] Reynaldo Hahn had scarcely
any better luck with Concerts Colonne, who were putting on at the Châtelet
his *Nuit d'amour bergamasque*, about which Willy wrote: 'M. Marcel Proust
and a few society ladies, following his example, applauded energetically . . .
the majority of the audience were left unaffected.'[159] To Marcel, who heard
it on successive evenings, it seemed 'gorgeous'.[160]

That summer a new friend, Douglas Ainslie, had appeared on the scene.
He was to help soothe the pain of the gradual break-up with Lucien.
Grant Duff, born in 1865 at the rue La Pérouse (the home of Odette),
was the son of a British diplomat, who, owing to the subtleties of his
heredity, acquired the name of Douglas Ainslie; in 1893 he was attaché at
the British embassy in Paris, he published some poems,[161] then tendered
his resignation and travelled around Europe for ten years, becoming
friendly with Wilde, Rostand, James and Sarah Bernhardt. Robert de Billy
introduced him to Proust in 1897. In his memoirs, Ainslie would recall
the long, pale face, those dark shadows under the eyes which drew attention
to the illness which Proust gave as his reason for not going out during
the day, and the conversation of a man who made you share in a pleasant
dream. He would declare that it was between three and four o'clock in
the morning that Marcel revealed the secrets of his heart, having first
dragged you back to his home after an evening out in order to paint a
rather uncharitable picture of the people you had just met, and indeed of
le Tout-Paris. In his rather more formal tribute in *La Nouvelle Revue Française*
after Proust's death, Ainslie recalled their meetings at his home or at
Weber's* and their discussions about Ruskin and Pater: 'When I told him

---

* 'I shall always see Proust, the velvet collar of his overcoat drawn up over his ears, arriving late
at the Café Weber. He hastened to say immediately that he intended staying only a moment, but
that moment stretched out indefinitely, and he would stay until everyone had left, so that the
evening seemed to go on longer and longer.' The conversation did not stop there: 'Proust needed
to feel that he had an impatient cab driver beside him in order to give of his best' (*Hommage à M.
Proust*, p. 260).

that Pater had said to me one day: "I don't believe that Ruskin can have discovered more things in St Mark's than I did," he shrugged his shoulders and said: "What more can one say, we shall never agree about English literature."' When he came to translate *The Bible of Amiens*, Proust would consult his Scots friend,* to whom he wrote some extremely affectionate letters praising his charm, the strength of his friendship and the happiness he afforded him. They exchanged their views on painting† and contemplated making a trip to Florence and Venice.‡ A plaque in the cemetery of Proustian friendships reads: 'Douglas Ainslie, 1897–1899'.

THE DEATH OF DAUDET

On 16 December 1897 an event occurred which profoundly upset Marcel and some of his closest friends: Alphonse Daudet died at his home in the rue de l'Université, struck down in the middle of a sentence, during dinner. This sudden death put an end to the terrible suffering he had endured from tabes, a form of syphilis, which he described in *La Doulou*, his moving posthumous diary, in which he recorded the progress of his disease, the treatments using bromide and morphine, and the other unnecessary drugs that were prescribed, the wretched ataxics whom their doctor suspended from the ceiling, the inevitable Charcot, who told him: 'I'm keeping you to the last', his predecessors, whose suffering made them 'his doubles from the past' – Baudelaire and Jules de Goncourt, Leopardi and Flaubert[162] – his isolation in his pain, and those around him who grew so used to his situation that their pity was deadened.

Marcel and Reynaldo hurried over that same evening, 'fraternal and despairing', and they did not leave their friends for three days.[163] In *La Presse* of 19 December (which had published his article[164] 'La personne d'Alphonse Daudet, œuvre d'art' in August), Proust paid tribute to the great novelist who had died. He described this secular Christ-figure, surrounded by a 'saintly family', to whom the most renowned literary figures came to pay their respects, as he who had suffered so much lay on the bed, at rest at last;[165] of his books, there was no mention. Daudet was not Bergotte.

---

* In December 1899.

† Marcel recommended the paintings by Monet, La Tour and Nattier owned by Mme Straus.

‡ Proust wrote to Ainslie saying that he would be happy to see with him 'those masterpieces that related to [his] sensitivity in which he seemed to appreciate intimations of beauty'.

These cruel events brought the two friends together again momentarily. Ever since the spring of 1897, the relationship between Marcel and Lucien had cooled. In March the former had reproached the latter for not letting him know the results of his examinations: 'I suppose that that is one of your ways of giving me the "cold-shoulder" which is why I have not seen you for a long time.'[166] Proust once made this important confession to Bibesco: whenever he grew very fond of someone, it lasted for a year or a year and a half, 'a period after which such affections, in medical terms, always recede and die away. Take, for example, Lucien, Flers, etc., etc., etc., etc.'[167] Letters remained unanswered, their rendezvous were not kept, and the 'vows' that had bound them were no longer respected. During the summer Marcel tried once more to resuscitate the flame, under the pretext of seeing M. et Mme Daudet: 'As for your parents and your brother, I cannot tell you how much I miss them',[168] and he requested a photograph of Mme Daudet: the Narrator would do the same with Swann's parents. Similarly, in 1898, on the anniversary of Alphonse's death, Marcel wrote to his friend: 'Perhaps our friendship is not destined to be revived,'* as if his hero were speaking to Gilberte. And so Lucien distanced himself,† weary perhaps of his older friend's possessive nature; but this alienation, which took place, significantly, at the time of the Dreyfus affair,‡ was also characteristic of how Marcel behaved whenever he was in love; for him, falling in love was always a prelude to the end of the affair. In any case, in 1901, Proust stopped calling Lucien *'Mon cher petit'*, or *'mon rat'*,[169] and told him: 'It's strange to think that we loved one another! And then that's that!'[170]

HOW PROUST BECAME A DREYFUSARD

One evening in August 1897, at the Clos des Muriers in Trouville, Joseph Reinach, a close friend of Émile Straus and his wife, informed the latter that Dreyfus was innocent. In October, she assembled the regulars that

---

* It should be remembered that we have not had access to fifty very important letters from Proust to Lucien (A. Rinaldi, 'Lulu et les monstres', *L'Express*, 5 December 1991). See above, p. 243.

† This is the opinion of M. Bonduelle (*Mon cher petit*, Gallimard, 1991, p. 138).

‡ As Proust was to reproach Lucien later, reminding him of his strange disappearances: 'your unbelievable plunge away from me, just like the one that followed the Dreyfus affair and then the Casa-Fuerte friendship' (*Corr.*, vol. VI, pp. 100–1, June 1906). On the love of the 'very highly-strung', among whom Proust had to be numbered, see the crucial pages in *RTP*, vol. IV, pp. 397–8, which are even more important for the passions that remain platonic (Bibesco, Albufera).

attended her salon; Reinach explained to them what he knew: the *bordereau**
was a fake; Dreyfus was innocent. These revelations caused a split among
the group which consisted of: Gustave Schlumberger, the Byzantine
historian, Arthur Meyer, the editor of *Le Gaulois*, Forain, Degas, Jules
Lemaître, Debussy and Détaille.[171] It would seem likely, therefore, that
Marcel Proust, who was close to the Strauses, learnt from Joseph Reinach
– who, in any case, was one of his regular correspondents – about the
conspiracy against Dreyfus. Marcel would later maintain that he had been
'the first of the Dreyfusards', because in December 1898 he had obtained
the signature of Anatole France in favour of Zola.† The excitement
aroused in him is reflected in his letters: 'There has been no important
news, or rather there has been, but it differs according to different people.
For some, it is that M. and Mme Aimery de La Rochefoucauld . . . were
placed behind the Wagrams twice in succession . . . For others, including
myself, the events are more likely to be those which are venomously
distorted, when they are not passed over in silence, by your reactionary
newspapers. As if the defenders of the Altar should not, any more than
anyone else, have been the apostles of truth, mercy and justice. Here, you
will recognize the ideological sophisms of the irrepressible Dreyfusard.'[172]

Should we conclude that Proust was obliged to take up this position?
It is clear that he belonged to a number of social circles or groups, in
which his role was sometimes modest, sometimes important, that were
Dreyfusard at the same period. First of all, there was his own family: his
mother, his brother Robert, his cousin Michel Bréal[173] – though not his
father: Adrien Proust did not speak to his two sons for a week after
their signatures had appeared in *L'Aurore*; in truth, he belonged to the
'establishment' of the Republic, for he was a close friend of the president,
Félix Faure, and he shared the 'negative, conventional, conservative feelings' of the members of the government. On the other hand, it would be
a mistake to attribute the reaction of Marcel, the son of Jeanne Weil and

---

* The name by which the vital and incriminating slip of paper that triggered the Dreyfus case was
known. *Tr.*

† *L'Aurore*, 14 January 1898. Gregh and Halévy also prided themselves on having obtained this
signature. The publication of Daniel Halévy's *Regards sur l'affaire Dreyfus* cast light on details which
until then had remained unclear: from the end of November 1897, until the appearance of Zola's
first article, Halévy, Bizet and Gregh had planned to petition Zola. On about 12 December Proust
obtained France's agreement; but that was all. The acquittal of Esterhazy revived their proposal:
the petition, which had been prepared at the beginning of January 1898, and which was known as
the 'Intellectuals' manifesto', appeared on 14 January, the day after 'J'Accuse' was printed. Between
14 January and 4 February, *L'Aurore* collected 1,500 names.

great-nephew of Crémieux, to his Jewish roots. Léon Blum showed the error of this facile and woolly explanation:[174] it was in spite of his background that a Jewish intellectual took the side of Dreyfus (to which Péguy added that, 'among intellectual and academic cliques' the affair was taken up by 'a few fanatics opposed to the resistance, opposed to the party's disapproval'). Marcel made no mention of his roots in *Jean Santeuil*.

Another group comprised Proust's friends, the former pupils of the Lycée Condorcet, the children of the secular, Republican middle classes (though not yet 'well-off ' like their parents, and thus more generous), who differed from the former pupils of schools that offered a Catholic education (Proust made fun of the pupils of the Collège Fénelon, who never tipped their servants but imposed their presence every Sunday upon poor families who had no wish to see them): Daniel Halévy, Jacques Bizet, Robert Dreyfus, Fernand Gregh, Gabriel Trarieux, Léon Yeatman, Léon Blum, Robert de Flers, Gaston de Caillavet, Pierre Lavallée and Louis de La Salle.

A third group, which overlapped with the second, had founded the magazine *Le Banquet* (1892–3); 'everyone in the old *Banquet* group was Dreyfusard',[175] and Marcel had been its moving spirit before it merged with *La Revue blanche*. As we have seen, a number of the pieces that were printed in *Les Plaisirs et les Jours* (1896) were first published here. In issue no. 112, of 1 February 1898, *La Revue blanche* printed a remarkable 'protest'. It condemned the 'occult power', the 'military bureaucracy' and the court-martial judges in 1894, the public opinion that had been 'tricked and wound up to a frenzy', and in particular the 'fanatical and anti-Jewish outcry' in lay circles, young people at universities who distorted ideas, the Radical party (apart from Clemenceau) and the Socialist party ('it is a scandal that it should abandon a point in its manifesto just because it might put a few parliamentary seats at risk'). The article ends with a stirring tribute to Zola, which was reprinted in the March 1898 issue. Furthermore, in publishing circles, Calmann-Lévy had published *Les Plaisirs et les Jours* and Charpentier organized gatherings in support of Zola. At one of these, Louis de Robert introduced Proust to Colonel Picquart (before 13 January 1898),[176] for whom, as we can see from *Jean Santeuil* and his correspondence, Marcel professed an intense, if unreciprocated admiration. Among the literary and social salons, we have seen the part played by that of Mme Straus. After Anatole France rallied to the cause, Mme de Caillavet's salon, which was equally dear to Marcel, exerted the same influence. In aristocratic circles, and among Proust's connections, the Noailles clan, one of whom was Anna de Noailles, was Dreyfusard.

Everything therefore would conspire to make Proust support Dreyfus; he did, however, have much to lose, not least, his father's censure apart, his career as a social climber, which was bringing him into contact with the upper levels of the aristocracy. Blum observed shrewdly: 'The most fallible of the workings of the human mind is how to calculate in advance a man's, or a woman's, reaction when faced with a problem that is genuinely unforeseen. We err almost unfailingly when we attempt to resolve our calculation through the application of psychological skills that have previously been acquired, through a sort of logical extension of the known character of past experience. Every problem is new and every problem throws up a new man.'[177] As for Proust, he would reflect on the matter later on, in 1914, in a little-known and rarely mentioned portrait of Joseph Reinach: 'M. Reinach manipulated through their feelings people who had never set eyes on him, while for him the Dreyfus affair only presented itself to his reason as an irrefutable theorem, one which he "actually demonstrated", through the most extraordinary victory of rational politics . . . ever witnessed. In two years he replaced a Billot administration with a Clemenceau administration, he reversed public opinion from top to bottom, and he released Picquart from prison to appoint him, ungrateful as he was, to the Ministry for War. Perhaps this rationalist manipulator of crowds had been manipulated himself by his ancestry.'[178] This analysis, when applied to Proust himself, would indicate that he became a Dreyfusard unhesitatingly, as soon as he learned about the case, emotionally and rationally, but also out of an awakening sense of solidarity with a community brought together by what amounted to mental persecution at the very least.* It demonstrates the role played by Reinach in the revelation and in the fertilization of ideas and feelings; if Proust exaggerated it – at the time that he reread *Histoire de l'affaire Dreyfus* – he did not exaggerate it in his own mind. And, as a result, the overlapping circles we have described were permeated, enlivened and transformed by a current and an energy that concealed the sympathy for the weak, the persecuted and for minorities which the little boy at Combray experienced on behalf of the kitchen-maid who was bullied by Françoise, or the grandmother persecuted by her family: 'These were the kind of things which one grew accustomed to seeing, later on, to the point of being able to laugh as one contemplated them and take the side of the persecutor so resolutely

---

* The character of Bloch embodies this solidarity in *Le Côté de Guermantes*; it is he who then becomes Proust's mouthpiece, and not the Narrator.

and cheerfully that one is able to persuade oneself that it is not really persecution.'[179]

THE NOVEL OF THE DREYFUS AFFAIR: PROUST AND FRANCE

The Dreyfus affair demonstrates once more the bonds that existed between Anatole France and Proust. In September 1898 the young man was sent off, at the other's request, to collect signatures on behalf of Picquart – who was on the point of being arrested (and would be on 22 September) – in particular that of an influential figure in academic and social circles, the Comte d'Haussonville (whose salon Proust would later describe); d'Haussonville's name actually appeared on the lists of the Patrie française, the anti-Dreyfus movement. This explains why Proust, in a letter of seasonal greetings at the end of 1898, extolled France's courage during the year that had just ended: 'You have involved yourself in public life in a manner unknown this century . . . not to make a name for yourself when you already had one, but so that it should weigh in the balance of justice.'[180] France, for his part, referred to himself as Proust's 'friend' by dedicating L'Anneau d'améthyste to him in February 1899.[181] This was why Marcel was able to recall the genesis of Le Lys rouge, which was known as 'the Novel' (in 1893), whereas L'Orme du Mail was spoken of as 'the piece in L'Écho'. Proust had seen L'Histoire contemporaine, the overall title given to the four novels of which M. Bergeret is the hero, take shape, and he would invoke it in 1913 to justify dividing À la recherche du temps perdu into separate volumes, each with its own titles. 'Mme Arman's study',[182] in which France shut himself away, would become that of M. de Norpois at the home of Mme de Villeparisis.* The similarities between Jean Santeuil and L'Anneau d'améthyste are easier to understand.

Strange though it may appear, there were only two novels written during the Dreyfus affair that had to do with the scandal itself.: Jean Santeuil, and the final two parts of L'Histoire contemporaine: L'Anneau d'améthyste† and M. Bergeret à Paris.

---

* This liaison was also inspired by one between the Comtesse de Boigne and Chancellor Pasquier.

† Some may be curious to read what Proust wrote to France upon reading L'Anneau d'améthyste. 'The "pieces in L'Écho" and the "Bergerets" have turned out to be the most vast Comédie humaine, the most complete Encyclopédie des moeurs du temps, the Mémoires of an equitable and good-natured Saint-Simon . . . Your gaiety, like that of Molière and Cervantes, is enjoyed by simple folk. And the sophisticated lose nothing' (Corr., vol. II, pp. 275–6, February 1899).

In *Jean Santeuil*, which deals with exactly the same period, the approach is very different to that of France. Sympathy replaces irony, and almost all the characters are historical figures. The plot consists of an account of some scenes in the trial of Zola and a comparison of two of the central characters, Général de Boisdeffre and Colonel Picquart, though not Esterhazy. Total power is opposed to total innocence. The episode as a whole comprises ten passages[183] which do not amount to a complete account of the affair. Dreyfus himself appears under the pseudonym Daltozzi, but only once: 'Daltozzi was arrested on the charge of having released documents relating to the security of the State, he is sentenced in camera because of evidence that was not displayed, and he is sent to Cayenne.'[184] The main narrative is devoted to three audiences at the trial of Zola (which opened on 7 February 1899). For a month Jean Santeuil goes each morning to the Cour d'assises, 'taking with him but a few sandwiches and a little coffee in a flask, and remaining there, hungry, excited and totally immersed, until five o'clock', on his feet, listening, applauding, rushing to see the witnesses go past, leading a 'feverish existence', which he had lacked up till then, almost as if he had undergone a conversion.[185]

The first important scene sees the appearance of Général de Boisdeffre (on 9 February; Proust gave no date), preceded by a thousand rumours and the belief that the fate of Dreyfus depended upon his testimony. Strangely enough, Proust portrays him wearing civilian clothes, whereas in reality he gave evidence in uniform; was this a novelist's whim? In the space of three pages, using impressionistic touches, an outline of the general's appearance, though not of what he is about to say, is sketched before our eyes: 'He seemed very calm and moved slowly, even though he was clearly quite worried, and the impression given was that the nervous tic that caused his eyes to blink and his hands to pull at his moustache, as well as the red embroidery of his cheeks, the poor condition of his overcoat, and the stiffness of his leg, frequently broken, no doubt, through falls from his horse, were all special characteristics belonging to that august creature known as "Général de Boisdeffre".'[186]

With the appearance of Colonel Picquart, everything changes. Jean is not content to muse about his name, he worships him,* and he is the

---

* M. Paléologue depicts Picquart as follows: 'Forty-two years old, cited for feats of bravery in the Tonkin campaigns, a former professor at the École de Guerre, and highly thought of by Général de Galliffet, Picquart is tall, slim, elegant, witty, shrewd and caustic, but a man who normally hides behind an exterior manner that is stiff and reserved' (*Journal de l'affaire Dreyfus*, Plon, 1955, pp. 53–4, July 1896).

equal of Proustian artists: 'He was a friend of his professor M. D . . . ,*
and like him a philosopher, a man whose entire life had been spent in
seeking and extracting the truth, with the aid of reason, of everything
which might urgently require a degree of self-examination. He was also a
cavalry officer who had just returned from Africa, who knew nothing,
apart from the spiteful things he read in the newspapers, of this world of
journalists, adversaries and judges who packed the courtroom.'[187] Proust
went on to describe the rapid movements and bowed head of the spahi.
He observed the contrast between his appearance and what must be going
on in his mind: 'There was nothing to indicate either his indignation at a
crime perpetrated by the General Staff [in this paralipsis we can read
Proust's own indignation], or his firm resolution to perform his duty to
the end.'[188] The hunt for the truth that lies beneath the character's
appearance takes up a sentence that is two pages long.

It is the psychological and poetic analysis that prevents *Jean Santeuil*, as
later *À la recherche*, from being a novel of ideas. Each of Picquart's answers
is buried in the commentary. And yet for Proust, Picquart, rather more
than Jean Santeuil, plays the role that Bergeret does for France. The two
heroes' beliefs are the same: to seek the truth, to do good for others rather
than to pursue riches and glory: 'We were thinking of a colonel and we
find a brother.'[189] The inclusion of real people brings *Jean Santeuil* closer
to the historical novel than *L'Anneau d'améthyste*, and yet this is not entirely
so, because what interests Proust is the reasoning, the intellectual and
moral attitude, of the witness Picquart or of the experts at the bar. In his
pursuit of the inner life, he seeks to discover the man, whereas France
produces puppets, or, according to the traditions of farce, characters
reduced to a single dimension. The scene in which the handwriting experts
Meyer, Giry and Molinier appear, and are compared to the doctor, a
character whom Proust knew well, juxtaposes opinion based upon the
emotions and that based on well-rehearsed rational arguments, similar to
those of France: 'The truth is something that truly exists within ourselves
. . . Science is something that is quite different from all other human and
political matters.'[190]

As to Jean himself, he makes a strange admission, which clearly reveals
Proust's own qualms and confusion, which arose from his mother's origins
and from his anxiety to understand the enemy rather than fight him, as
if he were the possessor of some incredible truth: 'In our constant efforts

* Probably Darlu. We know that Picquart mixed in intellectual and artistic circles.

to be sincere, we do not dare trust our own opinion and we align our views with those whose opinion is least favourable to us. If we are Jews, we try to understand anti-Semitism, if we are supporters of Dreyfus, we do our best to understand why the jury sentenced Zola and the civil authorities for denouncing the Scheurer-Kestners. Conversely, we are filled with joy when we read a letter from M. Boutroux "in which he states that anti-Semitism is abominable".'[191] This partial description of a few scenes from the affair concludes with a curious conversation, in the course of which a general hints at the possible existence of another guilty party behind Esterhazy; we know that this was the opinion of Paléologue (who implicated three who were guilty, Esterhazy, an 'officer of very high rank', whom he did not name,* and Maurice Weil, a close friend of Général Saussier, the military governor of Paris), which Proust may have heard.[192] More recent theories, which tend to resemble certain remarks made by characters in *Jean Santeuil*, suggest a conspiracy among the branches of the French secret service, whereby Esterhazy may have been ordered by Colonel Sandherr, the head of the Deuxième Bureau, to fabricate the *bordereau* in order to help to conceal the construction of the 75 mm gun from the Germans.[193] The novel does not, therefore, give a complete picture of an affair which, while the book was being written, was not yet over. Proust and France, bound as they were through friendship, and involved in the same struggle, remained loyal to their own aesthetic beliefs and to their artistic leanings at that time. For France, these were the literature of ideas and intellectual comedy in which the opposition was gently ridiculed; for Proust, who was more of a novelist and therefore less ironic and less abstract, they were the scenes from real life, the art of drawing portraits and the complexity of people's minds beneath appearances of simplicity. Two ways of resolving the same problem: how to introduce history and the struggle for justice into the novel without destroying it.

---

* Général Rau; this theory has now been refuted. Paléologue, who was given the task of following the affair on behalf of the Ministry for Foreign Affairs, knew the Strauses well, dined at Mme Aubernon's home and mixed with the 'intellectuals'. Being very reserved, and convinced initially of Dreyfus's guilt, he soon came to believe in his innocence. He probably only allowed his views to become known belatedly. See Paléologue, *Journal de l'affaire*, 3 January 1899, p. 156; M. Thomas, *L'Affaire sans Dreyfus*, Fayard, 1961 and J.-D. Bredin, *L'Affaire*, Presses-Pocket, 1983, pp. 639–51.

ROBERT DE FLERS

As we know, when Marcel was at Fontainebleau, feeling gloomy, his mother had suggested that Robert de Flers should come and stay with him. It was he who, in September 1897, had made enquiries at Calmann-Lévy about the royalties and sales of *Les Plaisirs et les Jours*.[194] He can also be seen in the photograph (together with Lucien Daudet) that led to the scene with Proust's parents. Furthermore, his name was mentioned, after that of Lucien, in Marcel's letter to Bibesco on the subject of 'affections' that last for eighteen months;[195] all the facts leave little doubt about the person who replaced Lucien in Marcel's heart. An article, unsigned, but by Proust, in *La Revue d'art dramatique* of 20 January 1898, confirms this,[196] as do the 'Lettres de Perse', which were written by both writers and appeared in *La Presse* in 1899, and the posthumous dialogue, dedicated by Marcel to Flers, between 'Françoise' and 'Henri'.[197] In the article of 20 January, entitled 'Robert de Flers', Proust enthusiastically attributed all the talents to his friend: a poet, he had also published a travel book and some 'exquisite' short stories. Literary critic and theatre reviewer for a number of newspapers, and an avid fan of the *café-concert*, he was capable of all those enthusiasms 'which wise old men at the end of their lives sometimes regret not having enjoyed, for fear that they might have taken a wrong step'.* He was a theatre director, and he was still planning to make a political career for himself in the Lozère, where 'the peasants [are] witness to the magnanimity of his character'. He bridged the gap between art and life, and thus, Proust proclaimed, in a statement that already reveals what it was that linked him to Flaubert (and which also showed what alarmed him about the single-minded career that he had chosen against his parents' advice): 'M. Robert de Flers is perhaps the only person who need not say to himself: "I may be nothing but a failure. Perhaps it is for the sake of an illusion that I have let slip the prey. My vocation as a writer – which, moreover, all other men of letters deny, even though they are the only ones in a position to know – expresses itself above all in my lack of a vocation for anything else, in the total absence of those qualities which lead to success in life. I may well be a Gustave Flaubert, yet I may only be the Frédéric Moreau in *L'Éducation sentimentale*."'

Born in 1872, a former pupil of the Lycée Condorcet and a contributor

---

* This would be the dying Bergotte's fear.

to *Le Banquet*, a friend of Jeanne Pouquet* and of Gaston de Caillavet (with whom he would write his plays),† 'the young and charming and intelligent and good and affectionate' Flers[198] was a Dreyfusard, a man who was both elegant and handsome, who belonged to the physical type that always appealed to Marcel, podgy, with brown hair and a moustache. Like him, he had degrees in law and literature, and he was drawn to politics (he was to become departmental councillor in the Lozère where (his grandmother owned a property; she was married to a senator who was a member of the Institut de France, and Proust would write her obituary)[199] as he was to women and literature. He would also write novels (*Entre cœur et chair*), travel books (*Vers l'Orient*), and above all plays (*Le Cœur a ses raisons, Miquette et sa mère, Le Roi, L'Habit vert*), libretti for operettas or opéra-comique (*Les Travaux d'Hercule,*[200] *Le Sire de Vergy,*[201] and *Fortunio,* for which Messager wrote the music). In 1901, almost as if the theatre propagated itself through matrimony, he would marry the daughter of Victorien Sardou,[202] he would employ the young Gaston Gallimard as his secretary (who wrote articles and columns for him), and later became editor of *Le Figaro* and a member of the Académie française. In particular, Gaston de Caillavet and Flers were the successors of Meilhac and Halévy, whose wit – shared by Mme Straus, the Duchesse de Guermantes and Swann – is so often evoked in *À la recherche*, consisting as it does of satire, parody, subtle irony, and the final glimmers and last charms of salon conversation. In Proust's work, this wit is only the raw material, which gains in depth from being reprocessed through analysis.

SUMMER 1898

The spring of 1898 was notable for the excitement with which Marcel lived through, and did his best to retrace, the main events of the Dreyfus affair. Of his reading at the time, we know little. A letter from Reynaldo to his cousin indicates how much he admired *La Princesse de Clèves*, '"the most passionate novel that exists", as Marcel says'.[203] Marie Nordlinger thought that one scene, at least, may have inspired an episode in *Jean Santeuil*, as well as one in *Le Côté de Guermantes*; this is the scene in which M. de Nemours, chosen as a dancing partner for Mme de Clèves by the

---

* Jeanne observed in her diary, in June 1898: 'Robert is definitely trying to pursue me.'

† Proust alluded to 'the succession of triumphs which have distinguished this collaboration' (*CSB*, p. 546).

king, walks 'over some chairs to reach the dance floor'. Similarly, Bertrand de Réveillon strides across some tables in a restaurant to be with his friend;[204] certainly, Proust let it be known that Bertrand de Fénelon had been the model for Saint-Loup,* who behaves in the same way in *Le Côté de Guermantes*; though who can say whether this literary model had not lived on in his semi-unconscious memory? Proust's creations often developed in this way: his need for a go-between meant that a literary model would be combined with actual experience. The former provided the latter with a ready-made artistic guarantee. If this meant adapting life to art, the book that was alluded to, if not imitated, ensured that the transition was possible.

At the beginning of July Marcel suffered the most distressing experience of his life so far. Mme Proust was operated on for a uterine fibroid at the clinic in the rue Georges-Bizet, by Professor Terrier,[205] a specialist in this type of surgery. Proust would later give an account of it to his friend Georges de Lauris: 'I remember my poor mother in a very serious condition, deciding whether to be operated upon by Terrier, in a precise, detailed way, and when the operation was under way, if I can put it like that, her condition suddenly became so serious that it would never have been attempted had they suspected this (fortunately, there was no such suspicion, for this operation saved her), and it lasted a terribly long time with all sorts of complications, with Mama lingering between life and death and, for two days, often closer to death, after which there was a complete recovery and her health was restored ... The illness from which she died had no connection with the dreadful operation she had undergone previously.'[206] The operation lasted 'three hours' and her family wondered how the patient had been able to endure it.[207] Mme Proust carried an enormous weight about with her, Marcel confided to Mme Catusse,[208] his mother's closest friend, a few days later. The mood of the patient remained excellent. 'She uttered a few words [on the day after the operation] which, as her son and being biased, I found very witty.' A month later, however, 'a minor complication' that involved a further operation but was 'far less serious'[209] again prevented Marcel from leaving her,[210] and he found he could not predict the state of his mother's health. At the end of the month, while Professor Proust, who was apparently reassured, left for Vichy, and Robert set off for military training, Marcel, who was looking after her on his own, still did not know when he would be able to leave his mother. She was unaware of the gravity of her recent surgery and did not like to

* He told Robert de Montesquiou.

think about it. In this way a tragic period, which Proust did not mention in any of his books, moved towards its conclusion. Fate was to grant him a further seven years to complete his preparation, now just begun, for the death of the person whom he loved best in all the world.

Since the time when Marcel, alone, had set out to obtain the equally solitary signature of Anatole France, to which he added a few words,* for the petition in support of Zola,† there had been some remarkable developments in the Dreyfus affair. Zola, having been sentenced, was in exile in London; Major Henry had committed suicide; Cavaignac, the Minister for War, had resigned, as had his successor. Picquart was held in solitary confinement, something that plunged Marcel into a deep gloom and prompted him to solicit signatures for a petition on his behalf. Zola's lawyer reckoned that such a step could influence the judges. 'The affair', wrote Marcel to Mme Straus, that was 'so Balzacian (Bertulus, the examining magistrate in *Splendeurs et misères des courtisanes*, Christian Esterhazy, the provincial nephew in *Les Illusions perdues*, Du Paty de Clam, Rastignac arranging a meeting with Vautrin in some distant suburb) has become so Shakespearean with its accumulation of hurried denouements.'[211] Once again, his literary education helped him to interpret reality and, later on, conversely, to use what was fiction in reality in the novel. Furthermore, he noted with satisfaction that his society contacts had rallied to the cause of the Dreyfusards, in particular Constantin de Brancovan, the brother of Anna de Noailles and Hélène de Caraman-Chimay, a man who was a great connoisseur of literature, the moving spirit behind the magazine *La Renaissance latine* and friend of the society novelist Abel Hermant;[212] Proust had got to know him that spring.‡

---

* 'Here, my dear Marcel, is my signature on a sheet of white paper so that it can be transferred to the petition for Zola. With good wishes.' 'The piece remains here in my file,' added Proust (*Corr.*, vol. XXI, pp. 584–5).

† Ibid., vol. XXI, p. 584, 13 December 1898, to D. Halévy: 'Madame Straus has had France's signature which I had delivered to her . . . I will try to obtain as many signatures as I can for you.' But, in fact, the lack of other signatures meant this first attempt failed.

‡ They had gone to the Chambre des Députés together to take part in a debate about Crete. Marcel had invited him to dinner in May with France and Montesquiou. On 1 October they both went to a talk given by Jaurès on the Dreyfus affair (*Corr.*, vol. II, pp. 181, 189, 257, 259).

PROUST AS ART CRITIC: REMBRANDT AND MOREAU

In September Marcel accompanied his mother to Trouville, where he looked after her while she was convalescing there for a month. His father took over from him at the end of September. Proust got ready to travel to Holland, where he was keen to see the exhibition of 120 Rembrandt paintings in Amsterdam. From his trip, which was 'made in a hurry, his heart attentive but closed',[213] he brought back material intended for an article about the artist, which was not published in any magazine during his lifetime. And yet this essay, a fine example of art criticism – which vies with Fromentin in his own field, and with *Les Maîtres d'autrefois*, though not with Ruskin, who was not interested in Dutch painting – clarifies the fundamental principles of the Proustian aesthetic. Having drawn up a list of the subjects of the paintings, reducing them to a single impression, an instant flash, such as those we come across in lighted windows at Doncières and in Paris, Proust discerned, deep down, Rembrandt's real predilections, that is to say his ideas: 'Initially, a man's paintings may resemble nature more closely than they do himself. But later, this essence of himself, which each brilliant brush with nature has deepened even more, impregnates them more completely. And ultimately, it can be seen that reality is no more for him than this, and that he struggles increasingly to give of it in its entirety.'[214] The golden light that bathes these paintings is 'the actual daylight of his thoughts'; something seen by this light generates 'other observations full of depth' and causes the artist to experience the joy 'that is the sign that we are in touch with something higher, that we are going to procreate', a joy that is then transmitted to the spectator. We recognize the joy that the Narrator experiences when he sees the steeples at Martinville or contemplates the hawthorns. Proust had discovered something important here; the truth of art lies not in the object but in the mind; yet it is only certain things, the privileged subjects, that compel the mind to create, and which inspire a spiritual joy. Outer reality and beauty itself are subjected to this inner light for which the artist must provide – and the word appears for the first time – the *translation*. This is why the realization of a work of art is 'liberating': it liberates things while providing food for thought. A few premonitory lines foretell Proust's entire destiny: 'All these paintings, therefore, are objects of great gravity, capable of preoccupying the greatest among us throughout their existence – not beyond it, because that would be a material impossibility not of their making, but they do so just as vividly towards the end of their existence, as objects that are undiminished by the passing years and which, during the last years or weeks remaining to one, still seem real and important.'[215]

It was at this point, in order to illustrate these remarks, at the end of his essay on Rembrandt, and perhaps on another occasion, after the death of Ruskin, that Proust conceived a scene for a novel: Ruskin, close to death, goes to see the Rembrandt exhibition in Amsterdam. Here we find a number of sketches for well-known passages: Bergotte's death while looking at a painting by Vermeer; the tottering figures in *Le Temps retrouvé*, like the Duc de Guermantes on stilts ('Through the distant and thickening mist of years that had spread over his dark face, over his eyes, in the depths of which, now so far away, there was no longer any trace of the spirit of Ruskin, or of life, one felt that, though he was just as he always was, albeit indiscernibly so, he had arrived, from beyond the depths of the years, upon his broken legs . . .');[216] the difference between the outer image we have of an artist and the inner reality: 'It was he, Ruskin, two so very different things, this unknown, tottering old man, and the notion we have of Ruskin . . .'

On his return from Holland, Marcel learned of the death of Gustave Moreau, one of his favourite artists, who was also admired by both Huysmans and Mallarmé. True to his practice at this time, he jotted down some notes, which he never published. Strange thought it may seem, the subjects represented in Moreau's paintings are unimportant. So is the intention, 'since saying what we want to do is, after all, nothing'. Assessing the figures and landscapes typical of the artist – including a courtesan 'with a sad and beautiful face', who 'watches as she weaves her hair among her flowers' and who looks like Odette, and pictures in which poets have female faces – only leads us back to the same mystery: 'A painting is a kind of apparition of a mysterious corner of some world of which we know a few other fragments, which are the canvases of a similar artist.' The colour of the world is thus the colour of the canvas. For the first time Proust introduces the theme which he would employ in connection with Vinteuil's sonata, that of the true domain of the poet, which he only inhabits at infrequent moments: 'Inspiration is that moment when the poet can penetrate the innermost places of the heart. The work consists in the effort required to remain there absolutely.'[217] Thus, the poet does not die entirely: Moreau's thought-process can be seen in the 'beautiful blind eyes' of Orpheus, which are 'the thought colours', the artist's vision which 'continues to be seen', as it does in his house, now a museum, where it no longer exists for itself but for others. For the artist, the individual self is blotted out, his physical being is nothing but 'the place where a painting is realized'. When we penetrate this inner spirit, we become aware 'through a secret joy' that the only moments that are truly lived are those we spend there, and that the rest of life is but an exile. Artists are informed by a 'sort of instinct' that is combined with 'a secret premonition of the grandeur of their mission and the brevity of their lives. And thus they neglect all other work in order to create the abode where their posterity shall reside.' Proust himself, in his function as art critic, felt that he was informed 'word by word, of exactly [what he ought] to say', and by the same instinct, the same mysterious domain that he shared with the artist, 'where allegory is the rule of existence'.[218] Critical technique lay in discovering the mysterious similarity, the essence, of a creative artist's entire output. How? In a moment of ecstasy, confessed in this article: 'I, who experience a sensation such as that but once in a year, I envy people whose lives are so well organized that they can devote some time each day to the delights of art. At times, too, especially when I see how much less interesting they are in other respects than I am, I wonder whether the reason they say that they experience these sensations so frequently is because they never have them.'[219] This is a precise definition of one part of the aesthetic of *Le Temps retrouvé*: the contrast between the true creators and the dilettantes or 'art's childless ones', whose enthusiasm is sterile because it does not deepen the feelings. And so, life, career, success and fame have no literary reality: this is what bothers Proust about Chateaubriand, 'who has the satisfied air of having been a great person. Even a great literary figure – what difference does it make? It is a materialist aspect of literary greatness.' As to biographical circumstances: 'For me, circumstances matter. But circumstances are one tenth luck and nine tenths my own ability.'[220] These passages of art criticism, like those on Monet,[221] dating from about the same period,[222] which deal with the relationship between the artist and the place that he allows us to discover, show Marcel, who had indeed included some remarks about Moreau in *Jean Santeuil* (asserting that a detailed knowledge of Moreau's life and character does not enable us to understand the mystery of the provenance and significance of his paintings),[223] distancing himself from fiction so as to identify himself more closely with aesthetic considerations: he was ready to translate Ruskin. On the other hand, Elstir would go through a Moreau stage, and later a Monet stage. These were also the two contemporary painters whose work Marcel would draw to the attention of his friend, Douglas Ainslie.

THE CAFÉ WEBER

Marcel's evenings, at this time when his health was better than it ever would be, were not spent purely at dinner parties in town or at the salons. One of his favourite meeting-places was situated very near his home on the Boulevard Malesherbes: Weber's, the café-cum-restaurant at 21 rue Royale.* Léon Daudet recalled that, in about 1900, artists and literary folk were happy to gather here;[224] people 'did away with the brilliance of the ante-chamber and the salons'. 'At about half past seven, there arrived at Weber's a pale young man, with doe eyes, sucking or twiddling with his floppy brown moustache, and swathed in woollens like some Chinese trinket. He ordered a bunch of grapes and a glass of water, declared that he had just got up, that he had flu and was returning to bed, and that the noise upset him, then he cast a few anxious, mocking glances about him, before finally bursting out in a fit of delighted laughter and staying put.'[225] In *Aimienne*, Jean de Tinan, another regular at the same restaurant, has left us a little known and less flattering picture of Marcel: 'Maurice Sainties is beginning his mysterious peregrination around Weber's that he performs every evening . . . Sainties enters the café . . . then he goes out . . . then he returns . . . then he goes out again . . . then he comes back . . . then leaves once more.' Another character attributes to him the refrain: 'Please forgive me for deserting you, but over there I've just seen . . .'[226] And thus we gain a mental picture of Marcel always on the look-out, always seeking someone more interesting, more important or more disturbing than the person to whom he is speaking at the time. He would subsequently endow Charlus with this questing glance.

The café, the brasserie† and the restaurant thus feature among the meccas of Proustian life. They were places that were accessible at all hours, where one could observe social life, friends as well as strangers, and those precious purveyors of information, people's servants or staff; they were

---

* Baedeker lists it along with the de-luxe restaurants, such as Larue's, 3 place de la Madeleine. It was established in 1865; Weber sold it in 1878 to François, who in turn sold it to Gros in 1891. It was he who transformed it into a fashionable restaurant. Sold once more in 1895, to Millon, it disappeared in 1961. From 1884 to 1941 it had the same manager (J. Hillairet, *Dictionnaire historique des rues de Paris*, vol. II, p. 369).

† 'Weber's is in the rue Royale, it's not a restaurant, it's a brasserie. I don't know whether what they give you to eat there is served properly. I don't believe they even have tablecloths, they just put it down in front of you on the table, any old how,' says Françoise (*RTP*, vol. I, p. 476). Françoise also has comments to make about Henry's, in the Place Gaillon, and Ciro's, in the rue Daunou.

centres of socializing and observation that contrasted with the seclusion of the bedroom, and with the circumscribed coteries of the salon or the club. More unusual venues, but not entirely absent, were the music-hall, the brothel and the nightclub, such as Le Boeuf sur le Toit (after the war). Finally, there were the big hotels, a synthesis of the café, restaurant, salon and bedroom. In 1898 Marcel had already visited the hotels of Dieppe, Trouville, Salies-de-Béarn, Kreuznach; the Splendide at Évian, the Hôtel de l'Europe in Amsterdam, the Hôtel de l'Europe in Venice, the Réservoirs at Versailles, the Grand Hôtel de Cabourg and the Ritz were still to come. Proust scarcely altered any of these authentic locations in his books: the cafés and restaurants, the Paris hotels, from the Maison Dorée to the Chalet in the Bois de Boulogne, appear under their actual names. In the fictitious town of Balbec, based on Cabourg, the Grand Hôtel has an all-purpose name, while the Rive-belle restaurant is derived from Riva-Bella. The brothels are anonymous. Only the private houses have had their names altered, mirroring the fate of their occupants: Les Frémonts at Trouville, which was rented by the Finalys, became La Raspelière, which the Verdurins rented in Balbec. Yet perhaps the most astonishing metamorphosis is that which inspired the Guermantes' town house. The idea for it originated, according to a remark made by Proust to one of his former neighbours, from his parents' home in the Boulevard Malesherbes, and from the arrangement of two buildings around a courtyard; it also derived from the Greffulhes' *hôtel particulier* on the rue d'Astorg.

COMTESSE GREFFULHE OR UNAVAILING BEAUTY

Ever since Marcel had set eyes on her at Mme de Wagram's home on 1 July 1893, her hair adorned, with 'Polynesian charm', with mauve orchids tumbling down to the nape of her neck, her eyes sparkling and enigmatic,[227] there was one woman who fascinated him and who would play an important role in his work: the Comtesse Greffulhe.[228] He used to come across her at grand society soirées, as well as at the regular poetry readings given by her cousin, Robert de Montesquiou, and he let it be known that he admired her. Had she not herself observed: 'Always look at a person saying to yourself: I want them to take away with them a memory of unmatched glamour'?[229]

Born in 1860 to a great European family that was now virtually impoverished, a woman of great beauty who in 1878 had married someone only recently ennobled (whom Goncourt considered to be 'so common') but who was immensely rich and brought with him a fabulous dowry of eight million francs,[230] the Comtesse Élisabeth de Caraman-Chimay,* Comtesse Greffulhe, reigned over high society. Thanks to the photographs, her Worth and Fortuny dresses, the portraits of her by Laszlo, Helleu[†] and La Gandara, and the memorialists, something of her radiance has been passed down to us. She was the daughter of Prince Joseph de Chimay (1836–92) and of his first wife, Marie de Montesquiou-Fezensac (1834–84). Her relationship with Robert de Montesquiou is reminiscent of that of Elizabeth of Austria with Ludwig II of Bavaria. And like the empress, she had her secrets. She was also deeply narcissistic, in love with her own image and her personality. The author of *Le Côté de Guermantes* would remember this. Moreover, she was an unhappy wife, whose husband deceived and maltreated her; her marital relationship would be faithfully transferred to *À la recherche*, in which she would be the Duchesse de Guermantes, so derided by her husband.[‡]

There is a trace of her in Edmond de Goncourt's *Journal*. Initially, he thought of her as 'a female version of the dotty creature known as Montesquiou-Fezensac'.[231] In June 1894 the Comtesse Greffulhe, at Montesquiou's instigation, submitted a project for a book to Goncourt that

---

* The male children bore the title of prince; the females that of countess (*Almanac du Gotha*, 1906, p. 434). The Prince de Chimay was a Spanish grandee of the first rank. The family was related to the Borghesis, the Czartoriskys, and the Bibescos. Joseph, the fourth prince of Chimay and Élisabeth's brother, married Clara Ward, an American who deserted him for a Hungarian gypsy violinist named Janesi Rigó, which scandalized Parisian society. Charlus alludes to the incident (*RTP*, vol. II, p. 123) when speaking of his Chimay cousin, thereby revealing the 'key'. Similarly, Mme de Guermantes says to the Prince de Chimay: 'Your sister is the most beautiful woman anywhere' (ibid., vol. III, p. 73): the person referred to is the Comtesse Greffulhe. In a 'private joke', Proust mingled fictional characters with their models, amusing himself by having them appear simultaneously.

[†] Both of these are mentioned by Proust (*RTP*, vol. IV, p. 761), who continued to ask for a photograph throughout his life: 'May I be allowed to remind you of my request for a photograph (even if it is of the portrait by Laszlo). When you refused me before, you offered a very poor excuse, to the effect that a photograph immobilizes and reduces a woman's beauty. Yet is it not a wonderful thing to immobilize, that is to say perpetuate, a radiant moment? It is the effigy of a youth that is eternal; I may add that a photograph I once saw at Robert de Montesquiou's seemed to me to be more beautiful than the portrait by Laszlo. As for Helleu's portrait, I have it in my copy of Montesquiou's book, but it doesn't look like you' (*Corr.*, vol. XIX, p. 82, 19 January 1920). In the same way, the Narrator requests a photograph of the Duchesse. Neither the Comtesse nor Proust was being quite truthful: he wanted to be able to describe it; she believed that it was 'not done' to give someone your photograph.

[‡] Up to *Le Temps retrouvé*, where the Duc, who is in love with Odette, is modelled on the Comte Greffulhe, who was much taken with Mme de La Béraudière.

would be about 'the states of mind of a woman in high society, about her feelings, her impressions, about the triumphs of beauty and elegance'.[232] It was to be a prose poem which 'celebrated the wild and supernatural joy that sweeps over you when you know yourself to be beautiful', and it reflected all the major themes of *fin-de-siècle* narcissism (as in Valéry or Wilde): 'What fine hymns are sung by those eyes reflected in a mirror, loving themselves vicariously! . . . The unforgettable sensation of *me, me . . .*'[233] The countess never shrank from any praise of herself: 'Her laughter was thoroughbred, her movements infinitely graceful and delightful, the voice was *her voice*, and there was something choice and exquisite about her entire being.' Exposed to the crowd at the opera, she experienced a feeling akin to a blood transfusion, and exclaimed: 'How can one live when one is unable to arouse this great anonymous caress? These insignificant creatures encountered by chance . . . resemble a multitude of ardent lovers, in the midst of whom one passes impulsively.' By an extraordinary coincidence, which must be attributed to intuition and to the careful attention paid by the artist, Proust would describe no differently the attractions of the Duchesse de Guermantes at the opera, and her eyes which 'directed themselves forcefully towards whatever they saw or else gazed into the distance'.[234] Goncourt, who was shocked by this worship of her own beauty and by the intimate confessions about her unrequited, 'murdered' love for her husband, advised against the publication of these notebooks. The 'novel of a woman in high society' for which he had been hoping, would therefore be written neither by him nor by her, but by a fervent observer, the little-known and disdained Marcel Proust.* We know when he encountered her, in Paris and in Versailles, but not – and he had to wait a long time for this – when he was introduced to her. Ten years later she would invite him to her parties and concerts, and would ask him to join her in her box at the theatre. A few years later still, and it would be he who would turn down her invitations: the model's sitting was ended;

---

* In the opera scene in *Le Côté de Guermantes* (*RTP*, vol. II, p. 353), the Duchesse and the Princesse de Guermantes were based upon the Comtesse Greffulhe and Mme Standish, on 24 May 1912: 'I would prefer that neither of them should know of my interest in this . . . because the two women whom I shall dress in their clothes – like two mannequins – have no connection with them, my novel has no key' (*Corr.*, vol. XI, p. 154, July 1912, to Jeanne de Caillavet; cf. p. 157; these letters provide us with the date for the writing of this passage). Neither can there be any doubt that the name Caraman-Chimay, if not Greffulhe, seemed just as 'magical' to Proust as did that of Guermantes-Bavière to the Narrator. Belgium took the place of Bavaria, but it was still 'European' nobility, as Wilhelm II would say after the visit of the Comtesse Greffulhe.

the artist was interested in Princesse Soutzo and the Beaumonts. In the Duchesse de Guermantes he was to combine the physical features, particularly the bird-like nose, of the Comtesse de Chevigné; the elegance, looks and demeanour of the Comtesse Greffulhe; and the 'Meilhac and Halévy wit' of Mme Straus, who was herself a Halévy.

Who would remember the Comte Henri Greffulhe,* whose château of Bois-Boudran has now been converted into a hotel, had he not given (very much in spite of himself, since writers' models do not pose of their own volition as artists' models do) something of himself to the Duc de Guermantes? Born in 1848† into a family of financiers and landowners (his great-grandfather, who was at first an employee and subsequently owner of a firm in Amsterdam, opened a bank in Paris in 1789 and grew rich by speculating on exotic foodstuffs; in 1793 he moved to London), he made a Balzacian marriage at the age of twenty-nine; the wealth of a good-looking man with a blond beard and numerous conquests behind him, in exchange for charm, sophistication and high birth; a love of the arts for a passion for hunting: from September to January the Comtesse Greffulhe was obliged to go to the Château de Bois-Boudran which, the young wife noted in her diary, 'looked like a barracks'.[235] In Paris the couple moved into the Greffulhe property on the rue d'Astorg, which comprised, apart from some flats, two town houses: Élisabeth lived at number 8; her mother-in-law at number 10. A daughter, Élaine, who was to remain an only child, was born in 1882; she married the Duc de Guiche, and later the Duc de Gramont, the physicist and friend of Proust. Henri did not wait for his child to be born before being unfaithful to his wife. He terrified his household and insisted on his wife always being home before midnight; Proust would remember that his nickname was 'Jove the thunderer'. Cocteau depicted him as a monster in his behaviour towards his wife and her sister, Mme de Tinan: 'He lunched at midday. If the two women came back late, he shouted at the servants: "Don't serve anything to these sluts! Let them starve!" They were obliged to heat up left-overs on a stove in their rooms. "My wife", Greffulhe told me, "is the Venus de Mélo." '‡ At the end of his life, the count was deceived and

---

* Originally Vicomte Greffulhe; he took the title of count on the death of his father in 1888. In the same way, the Prince de Laumes becomes the Duc de Guermantes.

† Of this birth, Proust confided to Reynaldo that 'his father's sperm was introduced drop by drop by a lifeless instrument into the maternal cavities' (*Corr.*, vol. VII, p. 42).

‡ J. Cocteau, *Le Passé défini*, vol. I, Gallimard, 1983, p. 301. [The pun is on *mélo*, or melodrama. *Tr.*]

humiliated by his mistress, Mme de La Béraudière, just as the Duc de Guermantes was by Odette. She nevertheless did her best to have his money bequeathed to her.

The countess, who was gifted in all the arts, attended classes in both drawing and photography, with Paul Nadar, the Parisian society photographer; she played the piano and organized chamber-music concerts, and she put on plays;[236] she knew Liszt, Fauré and Gustave Moreau, several of whose paintings she owned. The Société des Grandes Auditions Musicales owed its existence to her and helped put on the first Paris production of *Tristan and Isolde* in October 1899.[237] Montesquiou introduced her to contemporary literature; a subscriber to *La Revue blanche*, in a milieu in which men tended to read *La Revue des deux mondes*, a frustrated writer, who found consolation in her private diary in the way that Mme de Villeparisis (who was the niece of Cordelia Greffulhe, Chateaubriand's mistress and the countess's great aunt) did in her *Memoirs*, she thus displayed a paradoxical attitude among a class whose womenfolk, when they were not entertaining, were busy doing charitable works and bemoaning the fate of the monarchy. In contrast Élisabeth Greffulhe sympathized with the Republicans and she was a friend of Delcassé,* who sent her notes on foreign policy each week. Her husband, who was a Unionist candidate, was elected to parliament in 1889, but, being too lazy, he did not stand in 1893. The Duc de Guermantes inherited this experience of politics: Greffulhe, Blanche relates,[238] would go about distributing friendly handshakes, 'flattering the hoi-polloi', and reckoning, by this familiarity, that he could command the trust of the electorate. The countess also enjoyed involving herself in politics. In fact, she became friends with Waldeck-Rousseau and Galliffet, the two central figures in the government who were in favour of exonerating Dreyfus, and she was blamed for 'having shaped the ministry'. A strange story is told[239] in which the Comtesse Greffulhe, having been received in Berlin by Wilhelm II in 1899, was accused by the right-wing press of having tried to sway the Kaiser in favour of Dreyfus. As she wrote proudly to her more pusillanimous husband: 'We do not depend on anyone; and we should have the courage of our convictions. It is a luxury, the most important one of all.'[240] This was how Proust would portray the gradual conversion to Dreyfusism on the part of the Guermantes. On several occasions, he would hark back

---

* Théophile Delcassé (1852–1923). Politician who was Foreign Minister at the time of the Entente Cordiale. *Tr.*

to the impression made upon him by the countess, whom he defended against Reynaldo, for example, recognizing in her 'an intelligence, charm, kindness and a mind that were unrivalled'.[241]

A number of characters in *À la recherche*, mentioned under their real name or not, were part of the Greffulhe set, among them the Prince of Wales, Grand-Duke Vladimir, the brother of Alexander III,* and his wife, Marie Pavlovna, the Prince de Sagan, Comte Boni de Castellane, the Marquis de Lau, the Marquis de Breteuil, the Prince de Polignac,[242] and a hundred others who are more or less summed up in the character of Hannibal, Marquis de Bréauté-Consalvi. They would be the friends of the Guermantes, having already been, though in rather smaller numbers since Marcel knew fewer people, those of the Réveillons in *Jean Santeuil*. In that novel,[243] the Duchesse was largely based on Madeleine Lemaire, the owner of the château. The Duc was modelled on the Comte d'Haussonville, whose salon Proust had described; the Marquise de Valtognes, who would become Mme de Villeparisis, mistress of M. de Norpois, on Mme de Beaulaincourt, the mistress of Comte Fleury. Perrotin,[244] the future Swann, was Charles Haas.

CHARLES HAAS

It is surprising to discover that one of Proust's main characters was based upon a man whom he did not know very well. He first met him at the home of Mme Straus, with whom he was photographed in the company of Degas, and he recalled him, as it were, from beyond the grave: 'And yet, dear Charles Swann, whom I scarcely knew when I was still so young and you were nearing the grave, it is because he whom you must have considered a young fool has made you the hero of one of his novels, that people are beginning to talk about you again and that perhaps you will live on. If, in the painting by Tissot depicting the balcony of the Cercle de la Rue Royale, in which you can be seen between Galliffet, Edmond de Polignac and Saint-Maurice, people are discussing you so much, it is because they see that there are some of your traits in the character of Swann.'[245] 'Haas', he wrote in 1913, 'is the only person who was not someone I intended portraying, but who (given a very different nature by me, incidentally) was present at the conception of my Swann.'[246] In *Jean Santeuil* the Vicomte Perrotin,[247] a friend of the Duchesse de Réveillon,

---

* He laughed at seeing Mme d'Arpajon drenched by a fountain (*RTP*, vol. III, pp. 34, 57).

has, like Haas, a Spanish mistress who bears him a daughter. He dresses with audacious elegance, 'a case of a work of art being recognized through the prestige of the artist', he has a large nose and is considered in society to be a man of exceptional wit who shares 'the philosophy of a man of the world'. In an amusing way he foreshadows the criticism of writers that is still made about the author of *Le Côté de Guermantes*: 'These gentlemen may have a great deal of wit and imagination, but they talk about matters of which they know nothing. Just such a fellow has the nerve to introduce us into the home of a duchess, when he has never been there himself.'[248] And Jean Santeuil has the nerve to imitate the mannerisms of a dandy; as for Marcel, being unable to imitate Haas in life, he imitates him in his book. The case is a curious one and it provides a clue to a kind of law of biography: someone who plays a walk-on part in real life may become an important character in a book, because an image, which coincides with one's secret expectations, may resound in the imagination for a long time; in contrast, old friends, brothers, even lovers, may disappear without trace: whatever leaves an imprint on a work is a matter for literary biography; the rest, everything else being equal, only demonstrates the negative work of the imagination.

Charles Haas[249] was born in about 1833.[*] He was an *habitué* of literary salons, auction sales and artists' studios, a friend of Montesquiou and of Degas, whom he had met at the home of Mme Hortense Howland,[†] and he regularly attended the parties held at the palace of Compiègne and the revues put on by the Marquis de Massa.[‡] Thanks to Mérimée, he had been appointed inspector-general of historical monuments in 1868. According to his friend Boni de Castellane, who was very like him, he was 'wonderfully intuitive, sensitive and intelligent', a woman's man, and 'he belonged to that breed of witty and useless idlers who were like a luxury among the society of that period and whose principal merit consisted of gossiping, before dinner, at the Jockey Club[§] or at the house of the

---

[*] He died in July 1902. H. Raczymow in *Le Cygne de Proust* (Gallimard, 1989) published his obituary in *Le Figaro* (15 July), which is extraordinarily similar to the one Proust wrote for Swann in *La Prisonnière*, so much so that the latter seems to be a pastiche of the former.

[†] In the Goncourts' *Journal* in *Le Temps retrouvé*, Mme Verdurin is Eugène Fromentin's 'Madeleine'. Mme Howland had in fact been involved with Fromentin. Had Proust, in this enigmatic reference, wanted to transfer the dual relationship of this well-known hostess to one of the two artists?

[‡] These revived his interest in a watercolour by Eugène Lami and the photograph of Réjane with a monocle that Proust liked so much.

[§] Of which Haas was a member from 21 January 1871, elected, so Daniel Halévy wickedly remarks, by taking advantage of the siege of Paris (*Pays parisiens*, Grasset, 1932). He was also a member of

Duchesse de La Trémoille'.[250] Around this time, he had been the lover of Sarah Bernhardt, who wrote passionate letters to him, whereas he treated her like a loose woman and was unfaithful to her up until the break-up of their relationship: 'All this is heavy drama for someone as light-hearted as you. You'll probably laugh a great deal!' wrote Sarah at the time. 'Fine! As for me, I shall take a long time getting over it! Farewell, my dear Charles, I have an indefinable affection for you. I adore you.'[251] They nevertheless remained friends until Haas's death. Proust may have learnt about this liaison through Hahn, who was a close friend of Sarah, to whom he dedicated a section of his diary, published in 1930, under the title *La Grande Sarah*.

Charles Haas's father, Antoine, who originally came from Frankfurt, settled in Paris, at 9 rue d'Artois, in 1816. Eight years later, then a cashier, or rather a senior clerk, at the Rothschild brothers' bank, he married Sophie Lan, the daughter of a businessman. In 1828 he was mentioned as one of the 'fifty best-known Jews in Paris' in the archives of the Consistoire;[252] in 1837 he became a naturalized Frenchman and resided in the rue Laffitte (where the Banque Rothschild is situated). He died in 1833, leaving his widow, who married a doctor seven years later, and a son of six years old. Here we have another example of the path taken by Jews who were immigrants from Central Europe and who, having become French, came to belong to the ruling or leisured classes, as did the Straus or Weil families: Nathé Weil's grandson could recognize himself in Charles Haas. At about the age of fifty, as a result of his liaison with a Spanish aristocrat,* Adélaïde de Arellano, the Marquise d'Audiffret, he had a daughter, Luisita, born, like Gilberte Swann, in 1881. He died in 1902, after a series of strokes, at his home in the Avenue de Villiers – not on the Île Saint-Louis or in the Swanns' flat. Proust invented just as much as he imitated. Such was the end – and for us the beginning – of this 'attractive, fine-featured man, with golden wavy hair and a thick moustache', to whom all doors, under the influence of his charm, were miraculously opened without him having to force them, including, thanks to Proust, those of literature. André de Fouquières has left us with a last image of him, dining at La Grand'Pinte, in the Avenue Trudaine, with a

---

the Cercle de la Rue Royale, where in 1868 he appeared on the balcony, in Tissot's painting, in the company of the Marquis de Lau, the Comtes de Gamay, de Saint-Maurice, de Galliffet, de Polignac and the Baron Hottinguer, who would win the painting by drawing lots.

* Like Perrotin in *Jean Santeuil*, this is no doubt why, in the drafts of the manuscript, Odette's original first name is Carmen.

rather jovial traveller, the future Edward VII,[253] whose insubstantial shadow flits through *Du côté de chez Swann*.

In contrast, it makes no sense to regard Charles Ephrussi (1849–1905) as a model for Swann, as biographers, following Montesquiou,[254] have done. Proust knew him far better than he knew Haas.[255] A keen connoisseur of modern art, he bought paintings from Degas, Manet, Monet[256] and Puvis de Chavannes while they were still working on them, which he intended for his family mansion at 11 Avenue d'Iéna. But his expertise also extended to classical painting; his *Albrecht Dürer* was the definitive study. He was the owner of *La Gazette des Beaux-Arts*, to which Taine, Geffroy, Bourget, Laforgue and the young Berenson were contributors. However, he was not a handsome man, nor was he a dandy. Swann's taste for Vermeer derives from Proust, as does his love for Odette and even his unfinished essay on the Dutch master; Marcel projected on to him his own fear about not finishing his book, his Casaubon complex, his dread of being merely a '*célibataire de l'art*', and his dream of writing about Vermeer. It was thanks to Ephrussi, however, the half-brother of his friend Mme Léon Fould, that he was able to write for *La Gazette des Beaux-Arts* and its supplement, *La Chronique des arts et de la curiosité*. On his friend's death, in 1905, he recalled 'a life that was so harmonious, so filled with images of beauty'[257] and he remembered him in his letters until the end of his life. These two art magazines were a crucial source of information for Proust.

SPRING 1899

At the beginning of 1899, prompted by the latest somersaults in the Dreyfus affair, Proust signed some further petitions. Félix Faure, a family friend, died suddenly in the arms of Mme Steinheil.* On 27 February Marcel attended a performance of *Le Lys rouge*, the play which Gaston de Caillavet helped Anatole France adapt from the love story inspired and commissioned by Mme Arman de Caillavet, in which Réjane played the leading role; on Proust's death, the son of the famous actress would place the ring from *Le Lys rouge* on Marcel's finger. Proust, who borrowed a number of ingredients from this novel-cum-play (Mme Marmet in *Jean Santeuil*, for example), thought the play 'delightful'.[258] The principal event in his social life was the dinner party he organized, after exchanging a quantity of letters with Montesquiou, on 24 April, which was to be followed

---

* A few years later, she would be the heroine of a murder case and would write her memoirs.

by a reading, by the actress Cora Laparcerie, of poems by France and the
Comtesse de Noailles, as well as some of the sonnets in the count's
Les Perles rouges. She would recite them, according to *Le Gaulois*, 'with
incomparable skill'. The list of guests for the dinner, which was not
followed by a reception, gives an insight into the extent and nature of Marcel's connections – people who were sufficiently close that they would come
and sit round his table and listen to these readings, which the author of *À la
recherche* would draw upon when he had Rachel read poems. There were
about twenty guests: apart from his old friends Mme Lemaire, Mme de
Caillavet and Mme Straus, they consisted of aristocratic hostesses and
friends or relatives of Montesquiou: the Marquise d'Eyragues, the Comtesse
de Briey, the Comtesse Potocka, Mme de Brantes, the Baronne Deslandes,*
Mme Cahen d'Anvers and Mme Léon Fould; Prince Giovanni Borghese,
another friend of Comte Robert's, the Comte de Gontaut-Biron, the Marquis de Castellane, who would always remain on close terms with Marcel,
Baron Edmond de Rothschild, Anatole France and the Comtesse de
Noailles, Charles Ephrussi, Jean Béraud, Abel Hermant, a friend of Anna
de Noailles and a society novelist, and Albert Flament.† Montesquiou took
over from the actress in order to read some of his poems himself. Marcel
then made sure that *Le Figaro* printed a complete list of his guests. The
column 'Le Monde et la ville' was compiled by François Ferrari, whose
'society notes', the Narrator of *Le Temps retrouvé* would say, 'had so often
amused Saint-Loup and myself that we used to entertain ourselves by
inventing them'.[259] They were all the more amusing, given that Marcel wrote
some of them for Ferrari. If in this way he was preparing himself for the

---

* 'What is the Marquise d'Eyragues talking about, with her incredible wit, that accomplished
literary phraseology which she knows how to impart to the slightest thing?' ('Le salon de la Comtesse
Aimery de La Rochefoucauld', *CSB*, p. 438). It is one of the first drafts for the Duchesse de
Guermantes. Ibid., p. 437: 'The Comtesse de Briey, *née* Ludre, a delightful woman whom fools
consider spiteful because she has a very amusing turn of mind, and laughs as others cry, covering
her eyes with her hands' – which is a characteristic given to Mme Verdurin. One of Proust's 'Salons'
in *Le Figaro* in 1904 is devoted to the Comtesse Potocka. 'The Comtesse de Brantes with her
delightfully rosy face, rendered fresher still by powder, her looks, at once delicate, majestic and
malicious, her regular features refined by French charm, and whose high intelligence holds sway
everywhere' (*CSB*, p. 438). On 27 June 1899 the Baronne Deslandes, who once quarrelled with
Montesquiou, held a soirée at which Mlle Brandès read sonnets taken from *Les Perles rouges*, and at
which music by Fauré, whose relationship with Montesquiou has already been mentioned, was
played.
† A contributor to *La Presse*, Léon Bailby's newspaper, for which Marcel also wrote, he would
record his memories in *Le Bal du Pré-Catelan*, Fayard, 1946. In 1901 Marcel considered him an
'enemy'.

portrayals of the great soirées in his novel, at the first night of Chabrier's *Briséis*,* on 8 May 1899, Proust had one of his first experiences of lost time, of 'masked balls' and of how other people age, when he came across Philippe Crozier, Félix Faure's former head of protocol; he would comment on this in a draft note of *Le Temps retrouvé*: 'Vital about those people who are disguised by old age (Crozier at the first night of *Briséis*). Was it the touch of ice about his moustache that gave this elegant man the look of an old bogey-man?'[260]

When *Les Perles rouges* was published in June, Marcel informed Montesquiou that he was going to write a review, which he intended – to no avail – for *La Presse*[261] (which printed one by Albert Flament). If, from this point, he was dwelling on the piece as much as on the poems which he would quote, he did not write it until he was at Évian.[262] From afar, he then imagined a walk in Versailles, lured by these 'poems which [he] adored, which are superb and which he knew by heart', so possessed were they 'of indestructible foundations, of deep and mysterious roots in this sacred ground, its nature and its history'.[263] So it was that a myth of Versailles gradually began to take shape in Proust's mind, to which literature would contribute as much as his walks. He would take refuge there after his mother's death; the end of *Du côté de chez Swann* would be set there. The fact was that 'nowhere else in the world was so replete with proud, subtle and melancholy thoughts'[264] as these surroundings. Montesquiou, the poet of Versailles, who was also something of an historian, did not shrink from comedy, horror or erudition, and furthermore he related romanticism to 'a seventeenth century now forgotten' – that of the baroque poets.

Does this review mark a decline in Proust's inspiration as a writer of fiction? A posthumous passage, but one dating from this period, would seem to suggest as much.[265] If inspiration is characterized by a spontaneous enthusiasm, 'the only sign of the excellence of the idea that has come to us', which immediately renders the words 'soft and limpid', then the time 'when these moments in which one is transported no longer occur', or when one still has plenty of ideas but no enthusiasm, is a very sad one. The 'gentle, graceful' countenance, the expression, the conversation with its brilliant rapprochements have not altered, but the writing is no longer carried along, a single idea no longer causes a thousand more to burst forth, and the 'strange power' is lost. The enthusiasm which inspired the passages about the hawthorns or the church towers is undoubtedly what disappeared

---

* He would draw on *Briséis* and *Gwendoline* for Vinteuil's work (see the drafts of *La Prisonnière*, *RTP*, vol. III).

when Proust abandoned *Jean Santeuil*. It is possible to give reasons for this withdrawal: insufficient worldly experience, a lack of a fictional plot, too loose a structure, phrasing that was not strong enough. Over and beyond these, simply and mysteriously, his inspiration ran dry. Yet, just as a new love may emerge before an old affair is over, Proust had begun to be interested in a new art form, a new genre and a new hero before he relinquished *Jean Santeuil*. Very gradually, John Ruskin had entered his intellectual life, preceded by two other English-language philosophers, Carlyle and Emerson.

INTERVAL BY THE LAKE SHORE

That summer of 1899 Proust seemed to have abandoned his novel (apart from a few passages to do with a phenomenon of involuntary memory by the shores of Lac Léman, and the end of the love affair with Charlotte Clissette),* without venturing any complaint, nor saying a word to anyone in any of his letters. It was only in mid-August that he thought of going on holiday and to be with his parents, who were staying at the Hôtel Splendide at Évian. He enquired endlessly about where he should stay, not asking his parents, as one might normally, but an intermediary, his friend Constantin de Brancovan, whose family owned the sumptuous Villa Bassaraba at Amphion, near Évian. Proust described the gardens here, setting them at Féterne,† the property belonging to the Cambremers in *Sodome et Gomorrhe*: 'where fig trees, palm trees and rose bushes grew in the open ground, as far as the edge of the sea which was often as calm and blue as the Mediterranean'.‡ The Princesse de Brancovan, *née* Rachel

---

* We know the date of these passages because Proust wrote them on the back of an invitation. What is more, it is astonishing to note that, as we have seen, the hero was not called Jean, but Marcel: 'It's best if I call you Marcel and you call me Charlotte' (*JS*, p. 831).

† There is a village of Féternes (with an s), twenty kilometres to the east of Thonon, which Proust would set by the sea in *Sodome*. It is less certain that, as Painter believes, Rivebelle derives from Bellerive, in the suburbs of Geneva. The most likely source is Rivabella, near Cabourg, which certainly had a casino and a restaurant.

‡ *RTP*, vol. III, p. 164. The Cambremers actually owned two properties at Balbec which should not be confused: Féterne, inspired by the Villa Bassaraba and Lake Geneva, and La Raspelière, based upon Les Frémonts and Trouville. Prince de Brancovan's gardener had begun his plantations in 1876 and had been awarded a Palme d'Or for 'these collections of conifers and evergreens, these *Abies* from the Himalayas, these different types of cedars, these pines, these *Catalpa bengi*, *Crataegus alindi*, these *Acer japonica*, these rowans' and the 'tropical plants that adorn the greenhouses'. This 'slightly artificial' scenery blended 'with the great expanse of blue water and with the luxuriant vegetation of its shores' (Ardouin-Dumazet, *Voyage en France, Les Alpes du Léman à la Durance*, Berger-Levrault, 1903, p. 80).

Musurus,* the mother of Constantin, as well as of Hélène de Caraman-Chimay and Anna de Noailles, was a highly cultured woman, 'the soul of kindness and moral refinement', but, wrote Proust, 'a mixture of nervous impulsion and oriental extravagance'.[266] She was an excellent pianist, the patron of Enesco and Paderewski,[267] and she organized concerts at her various homes.[268] She was also a friend of the philosopher Caro.† In his pastiche of Saint-Simon, Proust would recall that the Musurus were 'of very noble lineage, one of the leading families in Greece, distinguished by a variety of numerous and distinguished ambassadorships and by the friendship of one of these Musurus with the famous Erasmus'.[269] By the shores of Lake Geneva, the princess led a life 'surrounded by her favourite guests', 'enveloped in music and anxious about the visits to be paid to the owners of the fine houses by the lake'. These people would become Proust's friends: 'Some of them were the owners of rough barns that claimed to have once sheltered the dukes of Savoy or St Francis de Sales, the others liked to show off their modest manor houses ... Residences that were quite exquisite.'[270] Prince Grégoire de Brancovan, a descendant of the princes who once ruled in Wallachia, had died in 1886.[271] The great powers had removed the family from the Romanian throne in favour of a Hohenzollern, and they now lived mainly in Paris, where Anna de Noailles was born, at a house on the Boulevard de La Tour-Maubourg: 'It never occurred to me that my parents were foreigners,' she wrote.‡ The Brancovans owned a yacht, the *Romania*, with which Proust would endow the Cambremers at Féterne, in *Sodome et Gomorrhe*: 'The owners' little yacht used to set off, before the party began, to collect the most

---

* Some have seen her as a model for the Marquise de Cambremer. It was she who loved Chopin, even though he was no longer fashionable. Born in Constantinople to an 'ancient family of Cretan humanists' (A. de Noailles, *Le Livre de ma vie*, Hachette, 1932, p. 22), she was the daughter of Musurus Pacha, ambassador of the Sublime Porte to London, and she had been brought up 'on the lap of Queen Victoria', whose children visited her at Amphion.

† *RTP*, vol. III, p. 214: it is Mme Cambremer-Legrandin who attends Caro's courses at the Sorbonne, influenced no doubt by Anna de Noailles (*Le Livre*, p. 150): 'The spiritualistic philosopher, with the unctuous, fatherly face ... Much loved and very loving, M. Caro commanded that respect that the official title of thinker inspires.' He was, nevertheless, the butt of Comtesse Potocka's practical jokes, to which Proust would devote a page or two (*CSB*, p. 493).

‡ *Le Livre*, p. 29; cf. p. 30. Others would remember for her. She would have been offended by G. de Diesbach's remarks (p. 259): 'What is perhaps most shocking about the young Anna de Noailles was her conceit in claiming to be more French than the French', and by those of Giraudoux: 'Dazzling, but not French' (*Le Livre*). Mme de Montebello, squaring up to the two Brancovan sisters' Dreyfusiste opinions, says as much to them: 'You, Frenchwomen! ... By what right? ... Come now, you're two urchins from Byzantium!' (M. Barrès, *Mes cahiers*, Plon, 1994, p. 123, 1899).

important guests from the other side of the bay, and, once everyone had arrived, its awnings set taut against the sunlight, it would be used as a tea-time dining-room, and in the evening it would set sail again to take back those it had brought. A charming luxury . . .'[272]

Like his mother, his uncle and his sisters, Constantin de Brancovan was passionate about literature. He edited the magazine *La Renaissance latine*,[273] whose title was the antithesis of *La Décadence latine*, a great panoramic study by Péladan, which comprised twenty-one volumes. He invited Marcel to the Villa Bassaraba, or, failing that, he recommended the Hôtel d'Amphion, which Proust had asked him about. Mme Proust advised her son to stay at the annexe of the Hôtel Beaurivage at Évian. This was why Proust, who, throughout his life, consulted everybody but never listened to anyone, stayed at the Splendide. He had, however, once again experienced in advance the drama of the unfamiliar bedroom that is described in *À la recherche*, and had begged his friend to intercede on his behalf: 'You'll see me . . . so sad when I arrive at a new place that . . . I would ask you, so as to comfort me a little in the strange and unfamiliar surroundings, to see if you could find some friend whom we know and to renew a friendship which may have fallen into disuse but which has some link with the past. For in those first evenings I am as unhappy, as profoundly, as mysteriously, as physically, as pathologically unhappy . . . as are those animals at dusk mentioned by – Barrès, I believe? How many times do I repeat to myself Madame your Sister's marvellous poem: "Where should we go to feel less sad?"'[274]

Professor and Mme Proust were guests at the Hôtel Splendide, which stood amidst hilly parkland and had about a hundred bedrooms; although they did not own a country house, they always stayed in palatial surroundings. Marcel occupied a 'charming and convenient suite' on the ground floor. He was concerned to know whether his bedroom had been more, or less, damp at Kreuznach, or at Mont-Dore, and whether, in any case, he had been ill in the Rhineland when the weather was dry and well when it was cold and rainy; he also thought of changing floors; but then, how much would he have to tip the ground-floor staff? And the boy who brought the morning coffee? Furthermore, Marcel was not sure whether he had any tie-pins in his suitcase (though he did not think of looking inside it, preferring to send a message to his mother), nor white cravats, which, in the end, he decided he would not need; however, should he buy some sponges? These details may seem irrelevant: but they demonstrate both how Proust destroyed his calm with this constant questioning which, if it contributed to the greatness of his mind, also sapped his nervous system, and how his illness was also fear of illness, his neurosis, fear of neurosis.[275]

The lake, which was steeped in memories of Rousseau, Lord Byron and Mme de Staël, provided excursions in which literature merged with social life: Marcel was particularly drawn to Coppet, the home of the Haussonvilles, who were descendants of Germaine de Staël, even though he had been unable to rally the count to the Dreyfusiste cause. Although the lake did not inspire him with quite the same feelings of enthusiasm (perhaps he preferred the lake in the Bois de Boulogne, which plays a far more important role in *À la recherche*) as it did the author of *La Nouvelle Heloïse*, it nevertheless featured in some of the last passages Proust wrote of *Jean Santeuil*. Describing trips made in the Brancovans' motor car, he compared the lake with his own face: 'In the peace and quiet of the afternoon, when the lines of the wash made by the boats stretched out and criss-crossed endlessly across the water, the full length of the Lake of Geneva appeared, as lovely as the dark shadows encircling the eyes and the tangled mesh of curls';[276] Jean observes the wake of the boats, 'their routes preserved on the surface of the waters, as if human life had taught geography to nature which now made it visible in the lines etched upon it', the human memories transmuted 'in notations of light and subtle shades'. This description was also the most complete piece of writing that Proust had consecrated to involuntary memory: when a sensation of profound happiness envelops the hero, he remembers Beg-Meil; it is the fusion of the two that produces a sense of joy which lies outside time.

By the shores of the lake, at Amphion, the main centre of social life was the Villa Bassaraba whose garden the poet Léon-Paul Fargue* would describe so eloquently. Here, Marcel met the Prince de Polignac, like himself a Dreyfusard, and this may be the moment to recall a witty remark made by the prince: campaigning to be elected as a member of parliament, he replied to a worker who had asked him whether he was a socialist: 'But come now, how could you have doubted it for a moment!'[277] A photographer assembled the guests at the villa: grouped around the Princesse de Brancovan, her daughters Hélène and Anna, and her son Constantin, with Marcel next to him, one can identify the Prince and Princesse de Polignac, Mme de Monteynard, Léon Delafosse and Abel

---

* 'At Amphion, beside waters as calm as the past, as deep as memory, a garden opens its heart at the memory of Anna de Noailles . . .' (*Portraits de famille*, J.-B. Janin, 1947, p. 9).

Hermant.[278] The latter, who was born in 1862, made his reputation by attacking the people and institutions he described in his *romans-à-clef* and his sensationalist books – the university in *Monsieur Rabosson* (1884) and the army (*Le Cavalier Miserey*, 1887) – and he was influenced by Bourget in his analytical novels (*Amour de tête*, 1890); he had recently devoted a series of novels in dialogue form to the diplomatic world (*La Carrière*) and to royal families (*Le Sceptre*), as well as writing plays about high society (*La Meute*, 1896, *Le Faubourg*, 1899). Even though he was the son-in-law of the publisher Charpentier, Marcel, who did his best to please him by sending him a copy of *Les Plaisirs et les Jours*, must have recognized a kindred spirit; later, when Hermant had adopted a young man, Proust would use him as the basis for Morel,[279] and perhaps too for the society novelist whose monocle is his only organ of observation.[280]

At the heart of this villa was Anna de Noailles. It would be some time before Marcel really became friends with her, yet he added a portrait of her to *Jean Santeuil*. It was previously thought that the chapter was devoted to the Vicomtesse Gaspard de Réveillon, *née* Crispinelli, who had just married and had published some poems, dated from the spring of 1898. In fact, Anna de Brancovan married Vicomte Mathieu de Noailles on 18 August 1897, and she published her first poems in *La Revue de Paris* of 1 February 1898: 'she had just published some wonderful poems.'[281] What is more, Marcel became friends with her brother, Constantin de Brancovan, at this time. However, the wealth of detail about her behaviour, and about her poetry, leads us to date this passage to the summer of 1899. As with Bergotte, Proust distinguished between the poetess's physical appearance and her work. Her body, her eyes, her features were enlivened by a ready charm; but 'the true, poetic nature of this great poet was never evident in what she said. On the contrary, from her continual joking and her mocking comments about this or that person who spoke about spring, love, etc., one would have thought that she was actually contemptuous of such matters . . . It was not that her poems lacked sincerity in any way, but, rather, that they expressed something which in her went so deep that she could not even bring herself to think of it, still less speak of it or define it, as something separate from herself.'[282] Proust here conceives poetry as 'the commemoration of our inspired moments', which contains 'the true essence of ourselves': a perfume from times past, a light that frees us momentarily 'from the tyranny of the present', in such a way 'that we feel something that extends beyond the present moment, the essence of our selves'.[283] It is important to emphasize that Proust was thinking of

Anna de Noailles when he outlined the aesthetic of *Le Temps retrouvé*. With her awakened sensibilities, Marcel sensed that this young woman was perpetually sad and that in her melancholy she discovered 'a point of departure for her exalted dreams'.

He also shared the same sense of comedy, which did not consist in recounting funny stories, but in discovering 'something amusing'[284] in all life's circumstances. Comedy was thus related to that poetry which revealed the essence of things. Only the level was different: charm and gaiety were expressed superficially and in conversation, inspiration on a more profound level and in solitude. And was Marcel thinking about Anna, or about himself, when he spoke of these 'superior beings' who had this marvellous gift of inspiration, but 'who the rest of the time no doubt betray their superiority through the difficulties they have in sleeping, through laziness, the squandering of their talents, through unpunctuality, their heated emotions, neuralgias, egoism, their passionate affections and their excessive nervous sensibilities, but also through a surfeit of their intellectual capacities which in conversation is the cause of this constant awareness'? Hence because of her poetry and her sense of the comic, Mme de Réveillon had different ideas to others in her milieu, who were greatly shocked by her[285] and who disapproved of her bad manners, her gossip, her being late at mealtimes and her mad laughter (expressions at a social level of her marvellous gifts, which in physical terms manifested themselves as palpitations and rashes); in much the same way, she sided with Dreyfus and against the army. Anna, in turn,[286] described 'Marcel Proust in his happy, active, listless youth: his beautiful eyes like a Japanese nightingale – a gaze filled with a brown and golden liqueur – are questioning, as if hanging on some delightful and charming piece of advice that he seems to be eagerly expecting from us. Let there be no mistake: Marcel Proust was not asking questions, he did not obtain information through contact with his friends. It was he himself who, in meditative silence, was posing questions to himself, which he later answered in his conversation, in his actions, in his books ... Indeed, even though his manner and the sound of his voice were extremely gentle, his conversation abounded in affirmations and no one could be more spontaneous, or was less doubtful of the truth. He said what he believed, he poked judicious fun at other people's tastes, he made up his mind firmly and resolutely, as we have seen, and did not worry about being judged himself. He would have defended his convictions against the whole world ...'[287] One warms to this penetrating portrait of the young Proust, polite, attentive, but sure of himself, and possessed of a faith that he shared with a friend who was later deserted by the fame that meant so much to her and which she experienced at so early a stage.

The Dreyfus affair shook the protected world of the villa. Dreyfus' sentence having been quashed, the re-trial opened on 7 August before a court-martial at Rennes. On 11 August, Marcel wrote anxiously to Joseph Reinach: 'It is said that things are going badly at Rennes.'[288] When, on 14 August, Labori, Dreyfus' lawyer, was the victim of an assault, the young man sent a telegram in homage 'to the good and invincible giant'.[289] He followed the proceedings of the trial so attentively that not only are his letters steeped in it, but his entire existence was seen through metaphors and allusions to all the personalities involved in the affair.[290] When, at last, on 9 September, 'the shameful verdict' was delivered, declaring that Dreyfus was guilty 'with extenuating circumstances', Proust considered it 'sad for the army, for France, for the judges who have had the cruelty to expect an exhausted Dreyfus to make another effort to be brave'; as for the 'extenuating circumstances', they were a 'clear and heinous admission of their doubts'; he hoped, probably so as to comfort his mother and his brother, that the government would take 'compensatory measures': Dreyfus would be reprieved on 19 September.[291] At the news of the verdict, Anna de Noailles burst into tears; the Brancovans, Dreyfusards all, stayed behind to discuss the events. We know all the more about what Proust's feelings were since his parents left Évian on 9 September and he wrote to his mother every day. His descriptions of the clientèle, the visitors and the staff of the hotel read like a sketch for the hotel at Balbec: the notary, M. Cottin, and his wife; Doctor Cottet, who practised at Évian, 'a man of prodigious culture for a doctor'[292] and whose name is like an echo; the first president of the Besançon appeal court, François Gougeon;[293] and a few models for the Bloch family, whom Marcel refers to as the 'Syndicate.'* As for the Comte d'Eu, a grandson of Louis-Philippe, Proust described his manner of doffing his hat with an exaggerated bow just as he would the Prince de Sagan in *Swann*.[294]

There was no slackening in Marcel's social and emotional life. In the surrounding area, about twenty kilometres away, Mme Bartholoni and her daughter 'Kiki', with whom he exchanged gallantries in his letters, lived at the Château de Coudrée, a former fortress that had belonged to the noble family of d'Allinges, which was surrounded by a fine park and rich farm land. Proust had known these two ladies for two years.[295] Mme

---

* In a letter to his mother and by allusion to the Dreyfus affair.

Bartholoni, the former lady-in-waiting to the Empress Eugénie, had been extremely beautiful and retained her startling red hair. Her house was furnished in Second Empire style and the conversation of this one-time 'Empire beauty' taught the young man a great deal. At her home Marcel met Delafosse and Henry Bordeaux, at that time a lawyer in Thonon, with whom he would correspond throughout his life. Delafosse accompanied him on visits to neighbouring châteaux, to the homes of his young friends, such as Marie de Chevilly, whom Marcel admired and thought 'gorgeous'[296] during an expedition to Coudrée, 'as she drew a portrait for them of the Sylphide or Mme de Beaumont', beloved of Chateaubriand.[297] During a carriage ride, at dusk, he recited poems from Vigny's *La Maison du berger* to this girl, just as the Narrator does to Albertine.[298] Marie de Chevilly has described her memories of this ride and the conversation of Proust and Delafosse, which made the former seem more like a composer, and Marcel's expression, in which the charm of 'those in love' and his almost naïve brightness disguised 'an astounding maturity'.[299]

Another new and dear friend, Clément de Maugny, 'a nice-looking boy and a good one',[300] whom Marcel knew through the Ludres, Clément's Paris cousins, lived at the Château de Maugny, another fortress, which stood on a mountain road about eight kilometres from Thonon. In a letter to Mme de Maugny, an artist and a designer, Proust was to describe the château, the true abode of Capitaine Fracasse, which was wonderful but not particularly cheerful, 'set in the emerald of this wonderful countryside'. He would not forget the little train that ran along the lake: 'How many evenings we spent together in Savoy, watching, as the sun was setting, the Mont-Blanc become a fleeting Mont-Rose, about to be enveloped by night. Then we had to return to the Lake of Geneva and board, before Thonon, a nice little train rather like the one I have described in a book of mine that has not yet come out.'[301] This friend who was so affectionate even came to spend the night at the Hôtel Splendide, in order to keep Marcel company during one of his fits of anxiety.[302] Proust would recall these moments in 1901,[303] when he dedicated a copy of *Les Plaisirs et les Jours* to him: 'You who have seen me in sorrow, without ever causing me to suffer through any lack of tact or unkindness . . . you have seen the onset and disappearance of moments of sadness, from which those that I have tried to describe here will strike you as no different. The things that cause us to weep change, but the tears remain the same.'

It was Maugny who introduced Marcel to Pierre de Chevilly, with whom he dreamt up a Stendhalian journey – books are still the intermediary –

in Italy, a pilgrimage 'to the shores where Fabrice played', which in the end they would not make: 'I often think of the lakes we had planned to see, the promised glaciers, our chimerical Lombardy, and I dream of the journeys I never made, which is a good way of making them.'[304] It is as if one is hearing the Narrator of *Du côté de chez Swann*, particularly since Proust is already talking about 'the law of fulfilment which always results in our youthful projects being performed sooner or later in life'. When Marcel went to call on Chevilly, his father said to him: 'There must be a lot of Jews at the Splendide'; and he recommended that he stay at Thonon next year instead. 'He's an old boy whose wits have been turned by *La Libre Parole*', but whose son 'is sickened by the verdict at Rennes', observed Marcel. Other encounters were less successful. Mme Proust had wanted to drag her son away from the lake when she learnt of the presence of a certain Chefdebien.[305] Marcel would tell his mother that he had only seen him once all told. Appealing more freely to her kind-heartedness and her innocence, he complained at great length about the unhappy fate of Poupetière, a roof-builder's son, 'who had no money, who was far away from his family and whose lowly social position was out of proportion to his worth and his self-esteem', whereas Mme Proust reckoned this young man to be 'odd and maladjusted'.[306] He needed money and medical help. Mme Proust thereupon sent him twenty-five francs, which gave Marcel great pleasure: 'Great joys are silent,' he exclaimed wittily, but in a manner that seems somewhat disproportionate. Similarly, he developed an affection for a lift-attendant (before Balbec) at the hotel, who had done him a number of favours. The light of friendship has its murkier shadows: the day would come when love affairs with servants would take the place of aristocratic affections.

The many-faceted Marcel simply had to go to Coppet. Recollections of Mme de Staël and her friends drew him there: he prepared himself to 'better enjoy' this pilgrimage by reading *Figures de femmes*, by Paul Deschanel,[307] as well as *Les Correspondants de Joubert*.* Above all, the figures of the Comte and Comtesse d'Haussonville embodied the summit of the aristocracy around the lake, and social climbing remained an imperative. In *Le Temps retrouvé* Proust observes: 'If the name of Haussonville should be extinguished with the present representative of this house, it will

---

* A collection of letters published by Paul de Reynal (Calmann-Lévy, 1883). *Corr.*, vol. II, p. 320. At the same time, though unconnected with Coppet, Proust was reading Mignet's book on the abdication of Charles V. He alludes to this historian on the first page of *Du côté de chez Swann*.

perhaps owe its reputation to its descent from Mme de Staël, in spite of the fact that before the Revolution M. d'Haussonville, one of the leading noblemen of the kingdom, found it gratifying to his vanity to tell M. de Broglie that he did not know Mme de Staël's father ... little suspecting that one of their own sons would one day marry the daughter, and the other the grand-daughter, of the author of *Corinne*.'[308] This family would therefore serve as an example of those social upheavals which he would depict in the transformation of the Guermantes' circle at the end of his great novel. When he visited Coppet, on 21 September, accompanied by Constantin de Brancovan and Abel Hermant, the owners were away, escaping on the day the house was open to the public. He took the opportunity, 'preferring Mme de Staël to Mme d'Haussonville', to visit 'each room in great detail'; later, he would describe his outing: 'It is delightful arriving at Coppet on a silent, golden autumn day, when the vines gleam over the blue lake, entering that rather cold eighteenth-century building, which is both historical and alive, and inhabited by descendants who have both "style" and life about them.'[309] On this occasion Proust discovered the joys of motoring, which always seemed to astonish him; his trips to Normandy in 1907 would allow him to enrich and develop this subject in an article, 'Impressions of a Journey by Motor Car'.[310] Contrary to what one might expect, he admired all the inventions of modern life, and he would devote sections of his book to them.

During these final days of September, apart from the last sections of *Jean Santeuil*, Proust was writing 'Lettres de Perse et d'ailleurs'[311] for *La Presse*, which was edited by his friend Léon Bailby. This was a renewed attempt at an epistolary novel, which, like its predecessor, would be short-lived. This time Proust wrote the part of the man, Bernard d'Algouvres, and Robert de Flers that of his wife, Françoise de Breyves, who had already made an appearance in *Les Plaisirs et les Jours*. The first letter is the cross-questioning of a jealous man, whose mistress is in Touraine (that province which, up to the death of Albertine, would always be associated with jealousy); a portrait, borrowed from *Jean Santeuil*, of the dubious charm of a man with a wooden leg; and an erotic story: the noise of flies helps to bring back 'the summer chamber music', but also, 'when they settle upon you', they recall the caresses of the beloved. The second letter is a description of *Jet d'eau** by Hubert Robert[312] – in *Sodome*,

---

* Sold for 13,000 francs in 1885, a painting bearing this name was sold by René Gimpel in 1918, at the Ledoux sale (*Journal d'un collectionneur marchand de tableaux*; Calmann-Lévy, 1963, p. 22).

much later, it would belong to the Prince de Guermantes. Continuing with its references to painting, the letter mentions the Van Dyck exhibition in Antwerp, which Marcel had not seen, endowing it with some images of Amsterdam and its sea-gulls. *Les Correspondants de Joubert* provided him with a lengthy extract from a letter by Pauline de Beaumont about the Mont-Dore, which enabled 'Bernard' to draw parallels with his mistress. From *Chateaubriand et son groupe* Proust took the story of the writer's unfaithfulness to Mme de Beaumont, and he ended with an allusion to Déroulède's monarchist plot. It is not surprising that on this puzzling question the 'Lettres' come to an end. He would, however, revert to them in the form of a 'Dialogue'[313] dedicated to Robert de Flers: his literary technique changed yet again, almost as if Proust were trying to escape by any means possible from the silence and the running dry that he was experiencing with fiction. In his favourite surroundings of the restaurant in the Bois de Boulogne, Henri speaks to Françoise about his sadness over a lost love, about his continuing jealousy, which consists of imagining the pleasures enjoyed by the person we love, the kisses, 'a sensation with which one can associate too many memories', and about the cure which only a new love can bring. It is a brief synthesis of the love themes in *Les Plaisirs et les Jours* and *Jean Santeuil*, and it does not in any way pave the way for a new book. And yet Marcel had wanted to publish these pieces; in the case of the 'Dialogue', he failed to do so.

It was nearing the end of the season and the hotel at Évian was about to close. Marcel, who had exaggerated his bills and increased his requests for money, which were addressed to his mother, wondered where to go next. He thought of returning via the Italian lakes and Venice (which is not the most direct route), or else going to Rome, where Coco de Madrazo* lived (but not Florence, which he was not 'keen' to see at that time); however, indecisive as he was and not having anyone to accompany him, he next considered contenting himself with a trip to a mountain, to Zermatt or the Rochers de Naye, or even Chamonix ('there's no need telling me to avoid risks since I have no desire to climb any mountains!'),[314] or to Lago Maggiore. This was why he asked his mother for Robert de la Sizeranne's book, *Ruskin et la religion de la beauté*,[315] from his bookshelf in Paris, 'in order to see the mountains through the eyes of that great man'.[316] In this way, the transition between the novel and the aesthetic reflection

---

* Artist and son of Raymond de Madrazo, whose second marriage, it should be remembered, was to Maria Hahn, Reynaldo's sister.

that the reading of Ruskin and his interpreters generated, was a gentle one.

At this same period, Marcel was moved and highly amused at the rumour that Anatole France wanted him to marry his daughter Suzanne: 'Since I would never do it, we'll have to be careful,' he wrote to Mme Proust.[317] The shock receded, as did marriage; perhaps it was by way of compensation that in January 1900 he gave his ex-future father-in-law 'a splendid and extremely expensive Rubens drawing': 'And if I embrace you once more, it is because I am very fond of you,' France wrote to thank him. No doubt Marcel still preferred to embrace the father rather than the daughter. After this, the two men barely exchanged anything apart from dedications and letters of thanks. Proust, for instance, wrote of the evenings he looked forward to spending with Crainquebille, Dean Malorey, Général Decuir, Putois and Riquet.* He praised the 'touches of brilliant invention, the unexpected yet disconcerting truthfulness';[318] 'Le Christ de l'Océan', from the collection entitled *Crainquebille, Putois, Riquet*, published in 1892 in *L'Univers illustré*, had moved him most deeply. In *Sésame et les lys*, he quotes from 'the wonderful *Livre de mon ami*: "Man's entire moral wealth resides in the emotions"'.[319]

Just as Marcel was leaving the hotel, he noted that the receptionist had come to tell him that he had 'never known anyone who was so generous to the staff', 'that all the employees were devoted to him',[320] even though he had asked so much from each of them. Certainly, he almost bankrupted his mother (and later on himself) with the amount of tips he distributed. But he was, and always would be, extremely kind to the poorer members of the working classes, such as servants, who were so plentiful at this period. It is a trait that is more unusual than one might think, and it should not be confused with his quest for information or pleasure: Marcel spent more time in conversation with Céleste Albaret than with the Comtesse Greffulhe, and the latter never wrote a *Monsieur Proust*.

In the end, he gave up all the plans to travel that he had been dreaming about, probably because he did not wish to brave 'the sadness of solitude, the fatigue of travelling alone, the melancholy that unfamiliar surroundings induce without a friendly arm to support one'.[321] So ended a visit that had provided a wealth of encounters, events and observations of scenery, all of which Proust would put to good use in his future work. He had

---

* All characters in short stories by France that had just been published in a collection which the novelist had sent to Proust. *Tr.*

learnt to face loneliness, to confront various crises, to battle against medicaments, but also against those who advised him against taking them and, wrongly, saw in this the root of all his ills.*

* 'I have an idea that you'll be getting a visit from Maugny, who will tell you, for he's a simple soul, that if I took less medicine I should be much fitter and that I'm now much better . . . Cottet, on the other hand, cannot understand why I haven't yet ordered any philogyne.'

CHAPTER IX

The Bible of Amiens

THE DISCOVERY OF CARLYLE

In histories of art, the 'portrait of the artist' is a fascinating subject, whether it be a self-portrait or a portrait of another artist: even Frans Hals, who only painted two self-portraits that we know of, painted certain of his colleagues. Faced with this marvellous expression, the paintbrush poised and a canvas that is still white, it is as if we are about to grasp the secret of this most fundamental and most pointless of activities. Yet, if the contemplation of images helps to fashion the art lover, it does not shape the writer. Another portrait of the artist exists, one that is reduced to words, that is to say to concepts, which is the artist as seen in works of literature: art criticism, the history of art, the philosophy of art, the novel about art, there are as many phases or intermediary stages which, while they distance us from that pleasure which is specific to the plastic arts, draw us closer to the logic of the type of mind that can compose a novel.

It was in this way that a young man, at the end of the nineteenth century, who was interested in literature and in all art forms, began to pursue this secret. None of the great French writers born around 1870 – Gide, Valéry, Claudel – was unaware of the fact that culture amounted to more than words, and that no system of education could ignore the inter-relationship between the arts. The example of Proust allows us to evaluate a curious phenomenon of the intermediary: the true source of an aesthetic philosophy as well as the survival of writers who are forgotten or little read, names that have been half-obliterated on the tombs of literary history. We know little of what Proust owed to Emerson and Carlyle. Yet the source of his thoughts about the artist lie, not in German philosophy, as others have unceremoniously attempted to prove, but in the thoughts of writers who wrote in English. It is illuminating to see how one thought, through some form of transubstantiation, may incorporate another: how do we know, after all, that this influence – and not others – existed? How long did it last? What proof do we have? All too frequently, in fact, proof is replaced by the energetic assertions of aesthetic discourse, poetics or literary criticism.

This analysis of ideas would be of no interest to us, were we not demonstrating the genesis of a form in Carlyle's, Emerson's and Proust's artistic concepts, in their theory of the artist. Is the 'portrait of the artist' a literary form that responds to rules, or is it not? Proust was a novelist: that is to say that in his work ideas became characters. Ideas take shape as they cross languages and frontiers. It is the moment to affirm that ideas have no frontier, that there is no customs barrier, and that the teaching of a national literature – French or otherwise – is the teaching of an international literature, inflated with the weight of history and geography.

Now, just as poor, wittering relatives sit unnoticed in a corner, French literary criticism was oblivious to both Carlyle and Emerson. Proust discovered Carlyle in 1895. The book was *On Heroes, Hero-worship and the Heroic in History* (1841), which he read in Izoulet's French translation (1888), under the title *Les Héros, Le Culte des héros et l'héroisme dans l'histoire*. He had just finished *Les Plaisirs et les Jours* and was about to start *Jean Santeuil*. Hence the aesthetic philosophy that Proust discovered in the series of Carlyle's lectures was not that of *Les Plaisirs et les Jours*, but it underlay his novel *Jean Santeuil*. Let us, briefly, recall what this discovery implied.

For Carlyle, the history of the world was but the biography of 'the Great Men', 'the soul of the whole world's history'.[1] 'The Poet is a heroic figure, belonging to all ages.'[2] The poet, like the prophet (Carlyle came across this image of the poet-prophet, fashionable in the romantic period, in the work of Fichte), had penetrated 'the sacred mystery of the Universe'; that which Goethe called the 'open secret', 'that divine mystery, which lies everywhere in all Beings', 'that Divine Idea of the World, that which lies at the bottom of "Appearance" as Fichte styles it.'[3] Appearance is merely the clothing, the embodiment which renders it visible (Martinville, the three trees). The prophet understands this mystery from the moral perspective, the poet from the aesthetic point of view, as that which is Beautiful: 'the essence of the World is Beauty'.[4] A great poet's thought can be seen in its *musicality*, which is to say that it has penetrated to 'the inmost heart of the thing', 'the melody that lies hidden in it' (Vinteuil): 'See deep enough, and you see musically.'[5] In the modern age, the hero becomes 'the man of letters'; he lives within 'the inner sphere of things'.

Here, Carlyle is influenced by Fichte (*The Vocation of the Scholar*).[6] This may be the principal relationship, albeit an indirect one, between German philosophy and Proust (leaving aside Schopenhauer, whom Proust, in fact, mentions several times, and whose obsession for quotations he mocks, while admiring his theory of music – Wagner here being another intermediary): '. . . Reality lies beneath all appearance. For the vast majority of men, nothing comparable to this Divine Idea is discernible in the world, they live purely, Fichte says, amid superficiality, superficial and practical details, and outward appearances, never imagining that there is something divine underlying them. But the man of letters is sent here specially so as to be able to distinguish for himself, and precisely in order to be able to make manifest for us, this Divine Idea.' And Carlyle states again: the man of letters is 'the light of the world'; furthermore, he must sacrifice everything to his vocation, he must live within it, this 'Divine Idea'. Otherwise he is merely 'a bungler, a *Stümper*', a 'Nonentity'.[7] Goethe is the most significant of these men of letters – whom Proust had read, although for him he represented the eighteenth century, an age which he did not like – 'a Prophecy in these most unprophetic times'.* As for the *book*, the work of the hero, Carlyle speaks of it in terms that are echoed in *Le Temps retrouvé*: 'In Books lies the *soul* of the whole Past; the articulate, audible voice of the Past, when the body and material substance of it has altogether vanished like a dream.'[8] Literature reveals the past, and it is an 'apocalypse of Nature', a revelation of the 'open secret'. He even uses the word 'adoration', prefiguring the 'perpetual adoration' of *Le Temps retrouvé* and the comparison with the Church[9] which we do not find in Carlyle: 'For all true singing is of the nature of worship.'

If we read Proust's quotations from Carlyle in his translation of Ruskin and in the notes he made from 1900 onwards (that is to say, while translating *The Bible of Amiens*, which was published in French, by Mercure de France, in 1904), we soon realize that it was his reading of Carlyle (and also of Emerson, as we shall see) that enabled him to appreciate Ruskin. John Ruskin was a hero to Carlyle (before becoming a hero to Proust): 'Very far from being a dilettante or an aesthete, Ruskin was precisely the contrary, one of those men in the mould of Carlyle, whose genius has

---

* Thomas Carlyle, *On Heroes, Hero-worship and the Heroic in History*, Chapman & Hall, London, 1842, p. 247. Carlyle also disliked it: for him it was 'a sceptic age, of spiritual paralysis', not an 'age of faith, an age of heroes' (ibid., p. 268). Scepticism is enshrined in the spirit of Swann, the Guermantes and Du Boulbon: eighteenth-century men.

made them aware of the vanity of all pleasures and, at the same time, of the presence within them of an *eternal reality*, to be perceived intuitively through their inspiration. The talent that is bestowed on them is akin to a power to fix this reality, to whose omnipotence and eternal qualities they devote their transient lives, with enthusiasm, as if they were obeying some commandment of their conscience, in order to give their lives some value. Such men, ever watchful and anxious in the face of a puzzling universe, are made aware of those aspects of reality which the special gifts assigned to them may reveal in a particular light, by a sort of demon that guides them and by voices that they hear, the eternal inspiration of people of genius.'[10] An ephemeral being is confronted with an eternal reality, which speaks in him through inspiration. Eternal reality is established by talent, beneath the appearance of a universe waiting to be decoded or translated. For Ruskin, as for Carlyle, the poet was really 'a sort of scribe to whom nature was dictating a more or less important part of its secret'.[11] The world was divided into two, into appearance and essence, illusion and truth. From Carlyle Ruskin inherited 'a heroic ideal, aristocratic and stoical' – as did Proust. So it was that after paying frequent visits to Carlyle, the moving spirit behind the London Library, in 1864, Ruskin wrote *Sesame and Lilies*, part of which had to do with reading, and it was on the subject of reading that Proust disagreed with Ruskin: reading, he maintained, can lead us towards the spiritual life, but it does not constitute such a life, since it condemns us to passivity. One cannot read and write at the same time. We can therefore understand why Proust, in 1905, should have told Marie Nordlinger, who helped him translate *Sesame and Lilies*: 'In my deliberately *bare* room, there is only one reproduction of a work of art: a wonderful photograph of Whistler's *Carlyle*, wearing a sinuous overcoat that looks like his mother's dress.'[12] (These two paintings, *Portrait of the Artist's Mother* and *Carlyle*, date from 1871 and 1872–3, and they bear the same sub-title: *Arrangement in grey and black*. Proust, moreover, was reconciling the irreconcilable, those two adversaries, Whistler and Ruskin.) He sent Reynaldo Hahn a caricature of the same portrait, since irony relieved the weight of his admiration.[13] The two characters are shown seated, in profile, the coat billowing out. It may not be insignificant that the hint of a mother, even if it is in the form of a 'sinuous overcoat', should haunt the portrait of Carlyle, who has become, through a strange inversion, or an inversion stranger than others, a maternal figure.

READING EMERSON

At the same period, in about 1894, another figure came to obsess the 23-year-old Proust, that of Emerson. His *Representative Men* (1850) had been published in French in 1863 (therefore before Carlyle's *On Heroes*). For Emerson, in contrast to Carlyle, the different art forms were not interchangeable: 'The most highly placed category . . . was that of poets.' They were a caste who gained access to 'the secrets and structure of nature through a method that was superior to experience'. Attracted, like so many of his generation, men such as Balzac and Baudelaire, to the occultist philosopher Swedenborg, Emerson saw him as the translator, albeit a very imperfect one, of the symbols of the universe. Aware of the 'essential similarities', he perceived 'the law, but not the structure of things'. Everything which, for Swedenborg, was in the world, would, in Proust's case, lie within language: the objective connection would become a verbal metaphor; that which was within the object would no longer be confused with what was within the spirit. After discussing the Swedish philosopher, Emerson refers to Montaigne, whom he had admired since his youth, in terms that foreshadow Proust: 'The trick of thinking consists in being able, having been shown one of two sides, to discover the other . . . the infinite and the finite, the relative and the absolute, the apparent and the real.' In unifying these two abstract sides – which the novelist would one day make concrete – the man of genius, such as Montaigne, has 'the perception of the idealist', whereas the man of action lives with Difference. Action, Malraux was to say, was always Manichaean. *Thought unifies.*

Emerson was, in fact, a poor literary critic. He was prone to generalizations about every writer. On Shakespeare: 'Great men are distinguished less by their originality than by the breadth and impact of their minds.' Proust, in turn, would demonstrate that originality, which is a matter of fashion, is nothing by comparison with the breadth of the mind, which is capable of encompassing the world. For Emerson, the poet, who is purely passive, allows the world to intervene, because: 'Nature is the embodiment of thought. The world has fled from the spirit.' 'Objects are eternal, but there is no representation of them.' The same theme is taken up again in connection with Goethe (whom Carlyle had translated, and about whom Proust, in his youth, wrote some posthumously published pieces): 'Nature wishes to be reported. All objects are involved in recounting their own history.' Nature trains the writer to interpret its meaning. Modern life 'encompasses a multitude of facts . . . Goethe was the philosopher of this multiplicity', he brought together 'the separate atoms in accordance with their own law'. Thanks to him, we would learn that 'the disadvantages of an age exist only for the feeble-hearted. Genius, with its brilliance and its harmony, soars over the darkest and dullest ages.' Here we see one of the last manifestations of the theory of genius, which would reach its conclusion in the twentieth century with Claudel, Valéry and Malraux, after passing through Mallarmé ('Genius vanishes in the future tense'). Crushed by the weight of history, our own century no longer believes in these timeless figures.

These theories of genius initially aroused enthusiasm, then criticism, and finally Proustian metamorphosis. There is a considerable amount of evidence of Proust's early admiration. He read Emerson 'drunkenly', in 1895;[14] and, in *Jean Santeuil*: 'If you should find in your inn-keeper's room, in a distant province . . . Emerson's *Essays*. . . would you not feel that you were in the presence of a friend just like yourself, with whom you would have wished to have a conversation?'[15] *Les Plaisirs et les Jours* was peppered with a literary and typographical convention that is no longer in vogue, the epigraph. Many of these were taken from Emerson, particularly from his *Essays in American Philosophy*.[16] Sometimes these were psychological comments, which Proust would adopt as his own later on: 'We can look upon our own vices without anger when we see them in characters who are distant from us.'[17] These observations are imbued with a spirituality that very much belongs to the *fin-de-siècle*, the Pre-Raphaelite or the symbolist mind (which explains Emerson's popularity): 'We should put our trust unceasingly in our souls; for things that are as beautiful and as magnetic as loving relationships can only be supplanted and replaced by those that are more beautiful and higher still.'[18] But let us not be deceived: the converse of this spirituality, of these souls, is a blind or perverse sensuality: 'Each man is a god in disguise who plays the role of a madman.'[19] As for the poet, Proust quotes this angelic sentence: 'The poet's way of life should be so simple that the most ordinary influences gladden him, his gaiety might be the effect of a ray of sunlight, the air should be enough to elate him.'[20] And Proust would in fact publish an extract from *À la recherche du temps perdu* under the title 'Sunbeams on the balcony'. At this early stage, therefore, he admired Emerson so much that he considered there was not enough of him: 'We should be overjoyed if today, in a manuscript or in a newspaper serial, we were to discover some new passages written by George Eliot or by Emerson,'[21] and, a warning to reticent collectors: 'What would one say if a gentleman kept to himself, as if they were autographs, Voltaire's or Emerson's correspondence?'[22]

During the time that Proust translated Ruskin his tone changed, and it is this that enables us to understand the dialectics of the influence, which extends from identification to refutation, and from refutation to assimilation. Emerson, like Carlyle, included creative spirits of very different types among his 'representative men' – Swedenborg, as well as Montaigne – but he did not 'differentiate sufficiently deeply the various forms of translating'[23] reality (whereas Proust, by creating writers, artists and composers, would do so). Furthermore, in an article of 1902, he criticized Emerson's (and Carlyle's) views on Goethe, who represented, for them, 'the whole of nature': it ought to be, at the very most, 'the whole of humanity'. 'Human, too human' was the eighteenth century, 'which deprives the world of its poetic character by populating it and removes its mystery because it anthropomorphizes it. Solitude alone would confer inspiration.'[24] And so the best part of Emerson, which inspired the deep perceptiveness of *À la recherche du temps perdu*, is that quoted by Proust in his article on the Comtesse de Noailles' *Les Éblouissements* in 1907: 'O Poet, true master of water, earth and air, shouldst thou travel the entire universe, you would never manage to find something that is without poetry and without beauty,'[25] adding: 'The universe portrays itself within thought itself.' This was how *À la recherche* would acquire the poetry inherent in its most insignificant moments, in its humblest objects, and why its author should prefer above all other painters the Dutch master Vermeer and Chardin, painters of still life, of ordinary people and quiet landscapes. Yet Emerson's name is only mentioned once in the novel.

THE ARTIST ACCORDING TO RUSKIN

Proust's aesthetic views were well formulated by the time he embarked upon Ruskin, and this was precisely why he was able to accept, understand and admire him, translate him and, ultimately, forget him. Ruskin, too, composed a portrait of the artist, and Proust, who always needed an intermediary, had read a summary of it in Robert de La Sizeranne's study, *Ruskin et la religion de la beauté*.[26] The artist stands between Nature and ourselves. He is its interpreter, its celebrant and its memorialist. He immortalizes that which does not last, he discovers unfathomable laws, the mysteries from on high; he is the giver of joy. Like Emerson, Ruskin observed that the artist discovers Beauty in the ephemeral leaf on a tree, in the tiniest pebble, 'the very simplest of objects, those that are most banal, those most beloved sights that you see every summer evening along thousands of footpaths, the streams of water on the hillsides . . . of your old, familiar countryside'. The artist paints neither the incredible, nor the exceptional, as the classical or romantic painters did, but rather everyday things (which is what Elstir would do): 'He who does not wish to draw anything, no matter what, cannot draw anything well.' Christian art itself cannot escape this rule: 'Everything in Christian art that is truly great is limited rigorously to what is human.'[27] At this same period Proust wrote to Suzette Lemaire about Wagner: 'The more people think of him as legendary, the more human I find him.' Ruskin's artist, vouchsafed a divine gift, 'a genius for seeing and feeling',[28] has no other mission than 'retelling, as Homer did, what he has seen and experienced'; for Proust: 'The task and duty of a great artist are those of a translator', or, in the preface to *La Bible d'Amiens*, 'it is the power of genius to make us love beauty, which we feel is more real than ourselves, in those things that in the eyes of others are just as distinctive and just as transitory as ourselves'.[29] Thus does Elstir, the Ruskinian artist, teach us to see: but he is just as much Carlyle's or Emerson's artist. We know that both Emerson and Ruskin knew Carlyle. What is more, Proust, who considered himself to be lacking in imagination, found great comfort in a precept of Ruskin's, according to which the artist should not possess any,[30] and should only paint what he sees: 'You cannot draw every single hair in an eyebrow, not because it is sublime to generalize them, but because it is impossible to see them.' One should only draw, wrote Ruskin, 'the crucial lines, the inevitable lines'.[31]

We see, therefore, a triangular structure beginning to emerge: appearance, the essence or the idea, and the artist. It would seem to derive from Plato, but in fact Plato did not care for artists. Modified by classical antiquity, it is a structure that dominates arguments about aesthetics even in our own time. Those who uphold appearance remain loyal to imitation. Those who seek a hidden reality behind the appearance argue for a doctrine of inventiveness and creativity. In its most recent incarnations, this doctrine, which is obsessed with language, has relinquished the third corner of the triangle, and no longer believes in the creative artist, who, it maintains, is affected by the great social, subconscious and linguistic structures that control him. We must therefore be aware that Proust was inheriting a legacy that was a thousand years old, and that he would be one of the last to do so. The 'portrait of the artist' had been a literary genre that had permanent characteristics, and, over the span of eighty years of literature, from Carlyle to Proust, we come across aspects that take us back to one that is much more 'long lasting'. Literary history must also, occasionally, try to keep up with the new historical methods – and also with those of art history: our scientific disciplines are enriched by each other. That, at least, is what Tacitus believed: 'The fact that we know a multiplicity of sciences can be useful to us even when we are dealing with other subjects; it can help us clarify and distinguish things just where we might least expect it.'[32] These theories would be embodied in fictional characters, in *À la recherche du temps perdu*. The idea was given a substance and that substance a history, a biography.

On his return from Évian, Proust, who had read Milsand's and La Sizeranne's studies of Ruskin and modern English painting,[33] and who was already keen to see the world through the eyes of his hero, hurried off to the Louvre, a place whose importance in Proust's formative development it would be hard to exaggerate, and to the Bibliothèque Nationale, in the company of François d'Oncieu, one of his friends from Évian, a cousin of the Chevillys, 'faithful and understanding', 'a free and delightful spirit',[34] who came to see how he was getting on every day.[35] Here he read, in the Belgian *Revue générale* for October 1895, a chapter from Ruskin's *The Seven Lamps of Architecture*. He was so enthusiastic about it that he asked his mother to translate a passage that was in English in the text.[36] At the same time, he finished writing an article about Montesquiou's *Les Perles rouges*[37] that he had begun at Évian; in it Proust described a visit to Versailles incorporating some of the poems from the collection: 'This necessity which they impress upon the mind in the presence of reality is no mediocre proof of their beauty.' Poetry enabled him to interpret the world; he would ask nothing else of his own readers.

After the *Seven Lamps*, this fanatical follower of Ruskin moved on to *The Queen of the Air*.[38] On 5 December, in an important letter to Marie Nordlinger, he summarized his itinerary, the point at which he had arrived.[39] Marcel had been introduced to Reynaldo's 'cousin from Manchester' one evening in December 1896, at Mme Hahn's house. Born in 1876 in a cultured milieu, of German-Italian parentage, she had followed courses at the Manchester School of Art.[40] Very soon, this group of young people – Reynaldo, his sisters, his cousin Madrazo (who would paint a portrait of Marie in which her round face, her big, dark eyes and her hair make her look like a Renoir) and Marcel – start playing, just as Swann does, some very sophisticated party games: they would try to recognize one another in well-known portraits. Marie, in all modesty, looked like a

Titian, with hands by Germain Pilon. As for Proust, they deliberated over Pisanello or Whistler. The conversation also covered architecture (Proust had already developed 'a cult of the cathedral' and a passion for Wagner, unlike Hahn, who, invoking Leonardo da Vinci, only liked classicism and Mozart), literature and the sort of subject that appeared in *La Revue blanche*: symbolism, free verse and metaphor. The young Marie, who for an Englishwoman had a very passionate temperament (though it is true that she came from Manchester, not Oxford), visited the museums with her cousins and friends, and then, moving from the classical to the modern schools, she would drop in at Durand-Ruel to look at the Manets, Monets or Lautrecs. In the evenings they would read aloud, and a particular passage would remind Marcel of many others. Then they would listen as Reynaldo, who had already written his pretty 'Chansons grises', sang and played the piano. And where did England come into any of this? Proust, who had never visited the country, knew it in his own way, Marie Nordlinger explained, and had 'a more or less accurate image' of it drawn from novels he had read. Ruskin confirmed the appeal the country had for him, and Marie shared his admiration for the author of *The Bible of Amiens*. She had visited this cathedral 'stone by stone, following Ruskin's instructions' and, on impulse, she translated a few passages from the book for Marcel. For Proust, she became 'the interpreter of Ruskin's thought and language'. There followed their meeting in Venice, in 1990, where they corrected proofs together in the shelter of the baptistery of St Mark's and read *The Stones of Venice* for an hour during a storm: 'He was strangely moved and overcome with a kind of ecstasy' (by the text, not by Marie). Once they were back in Paris, she would come to rue de Courcelles to help with the translation, but Mme Proust, as convention dictated, was always present, almost as if Marie were frightened of anything happening. She gave her friend some delightful presents: a watercolour of some trees, which he hung by his bed and gave to Reynaldo shortly before his death, and a Japanese game, pieces of paper which opened out in water, taking the shape of flowers, dolls and houses, and providing a marvellous image for the episode of the madeleine.*

Marie was an artist, a painter, a sculptress and an engraver, and she

---

* All this information is taken from Marie Nordlinger's preface to *Lettres à une amie* (Éditions du Calame, Manchester 1942), the fine collection of forty-one letters that she received from Marcel. She lost her son, an RAF officer, in 1941, and died in 1961. A book based on her letters, *The Translation of Memories: Recollections of the Young Proust*, by P. F. Prestwich (Peter Owen), was published in 1999.

also worked in enamel, following courses given by the son of the master of art nouveau, Siegfried Bing, at 22 rue de Provence, beneath the sign 'S. Bing. L'Art nouveau', in a former public baths that had been converted into a shop and studio. Bing had begun as an importer of Chinese and Japanese goods,* he had founded *Le Japon artistique*, and then helped launch Gallé, Whistler and Carrière. It was here that Marie worked, in the engravers' workshop run by Marcel Bing (who was interested in Gothic art and suggested the visit to Saint-Loup-de-Naud, which Marie later recommended to Proust).[41] Her life was transformed when she came to know Whistler's great friend and collector, the American by the name of Freer, a millionaire from Detroit, to whose home Bing sent her in 1905 to sell his collection of *ukiyo-e* art.[42] She returned there the following year to catalogue his Whistlers. We find a Maria in the drafts for Albertine (but Proust had also known a Marie de Benardaky, a Marie Finaly and a Maria Hahn), yet this is no reason to see in her, as many did after the publication of Painter's biography, a model for Albertine, nor, indeed, to think that Marcel may have been in love with her: a cousin, a sister, a mother substitute, a colleague, yes; but no more.

Reynaldo Hahn's English cousin already admired Proust's writing, and Marcel confided in her as he might in a sister: he had been working for a very long time, four years in fact, 'on a very long-winded book but without getting anywhere'. In order to free himself from what would always be his greatest dread, amassing what were merely ruins, and in the same miraculous way that one love affair can take the place of another, he had begun, 'a fortnight ago', to occupy himself with a 'small job that was totally different' from what he had been doing beforehand, 'to do with Ruskin and certain cathedrals'. It was because of something he was writing about architecture that Proust had begun to read Ruskin himself; he then planned to publish this article in a magazine, possibly in *La Revue de Paris*, which Ganderax edited. As was frequently the case, at this stage it was no more than an article. Marcel was convinced that he had just failed to write a full-length work. A shorter text offered fewer risks. Marie Nordlinger then sent him her annotated copy of *The Queen of the Air*.[43]

To begin with, Proust thought of writing about Rheims,[44] rather than Amiens, or indeed Chartres, which was so close to Illiers, without even knowing whether Ruskin had discussed this cathedral. He consulted not only Douglas Ainslie, 'for the English', but also Charles Newton Scott,[45]

* Marcel bought a sword-guard for Billy here.

the historian, who was the author of a number of books about antiquity and about Marie-Antoinette, and a friend of Ruskin. All Proust needed to do was verify one word, one title. In December 1899 his mother had started to translate *The Bible of Amiens*[46] for him, the first in a series of ten volumes that Ruskin, already old and in poor health, had planned to devote to cathedrals under the title *Our Fathers Have Told Us*. Marcel himself was writing the article that would appear on 13 February 1900 under the title 'Pèlerinages ruskiniens en France'. He already knew 'by heart' *The Seven Lamps of Architecture, The Bible of Amiens, Lectures on Literature and Painting, The Val d'Arno* and *Praeterita*[47] ('a sort of autobiography', he would write, which corresponded to *Poetry and Truth* in Goethe's work), and he was researching everything that Ruskin had written on the subject of French cathedrals. At the time, he gave the impression that he wanted not so much to translate the English writer's work, as to use him to write an essay on cathedrals. When Ruskin died, he then published an obituary in *La Chronique des arts et de la curiosité* of 27 January 1900,[48] which reveals the extent of his knowledge about Ruskin at that period.

BUT WHO WAS RUSKIN? AND HOW DID PROUST KNOW ABOUT HIM?

Proust's obituary of John Ruskin is a good summary of the position that he held in European society and culture at the time of his death: firstly, he helped shape the consciousness of his age, the equal of Nietzsche, Tolstoy and Ibsen; secondly, he was a teacher of taste and beauty and an author whose bibliography comprises 160 titles, 'veritable breviaries of wisdom and aesthetic judgement'. This was why the whole of England fell under the influence of Ruskin, the English enthusiasm for Turner came to be mirrored across the Channel, and Venice, Pisa and Florence 'were real places of pilgrimage for Ruskinians'. In contemporary studies, opinions and painting, we can easily recognize Ruskin. And yet he is so forgotten in France today that it is difficult to comprehend why Marcel should have worshipped him as he did from the moment he discovered him. However, before La Sizeranne, other authors had written about him, among them Milsand, in *L'Esthétique anglaise* (1864), Taine (*Notes sur l'Angleterre*, 1890), Rod in *Les Préraphaélites anglais* (1894); the Goncourts, on the other hand, never mentioned him in their *Journal*.

In a hundred or so rigorously argued pages, Milsand had reconstructed, with all its contradictions, the unity of what a Ruskinian system might be.* First of all came architecture, whose splendour belonged entirely to the Middle Ages, not so much for the buildings themselves as for the sculpture that was a part of them and which expressed the individuality of the artist. Next came painting, which displayed 'the truths of the poet, the philosopher, the moral and religious man': in his art the painter expressed the laws that governed the nature of things and all that they had to say 'to the heart or the imagination that looked to them for the secret of life'.[49] As for the imagination, it 'brought forth an organic whole, a living unity'; if it became contemplative, it 'transformed things through the manner in which it beheld them, the power it had to see the image of one object in another'; the artist is given the impression of an image, Ruskin wrote, 'a real vision'; 'he is merely a scribe'† in the service of the imagination which perceives the very essence of things. We are therefore rid of the theory of ideal Beauty and of the pre-eminence of pure technique, since what matters is the sincerity with which the artist conveys the emotion he has experienced. This is what the morality of art is based upon: Ruskin, like Carlyle, was also a moralist.‡

In his much more comprehensive book, *Ruskin et la religion de la beauté*,§ La Sizeranne¶ gives firstly an analysis of Ruskin's personality, his frankness, his enthusiasm, his passionate nature and, nurtured by his admirers, the legend that had been created. He then drew attention to the lack of structure in his books (something for which Proust was also criticized): 'Throughout, Ruskin will tell you about everything'[50] — he expounds clear ideas in a muddled whole. It matters little: Ruskin demonstrates what occurs in the soul of the artist and in that of the onlooker, thus connecting psychology to aesthetics. Furthermore, he is an artist, 'a painter who

---

* After *L'Esthétique anglaise*, Joseph-Antoine Milsand (1817–86), a painter before he became a philosopher, published *Le Code civil et la liberté* (1865), *Le Protestantisme et sa mission politique* (1872), and *La Psychologie et le monde du chrétien* (1880).

† *L'Esthétique anglaise*, p. 141; we recognize the Proustian idea of the artist as translator. Milsand remarks that imagination 'is but the figurative language with which our minds register their impressions' (p. 147).

‡ Milsand criticizes him, however, for not having lent his moral beliefs to the service of art (ibid., p. 170) and attempts to distinguish between Ruskin's successes and his failures.

§ Three hundred and sixty pages, including a list of sources and a bibliography.

¶ Robert de La Sizeranne, born in 1866, was art critic for *La Revue des deux mondes*. In addition to *La Peinture anglaise contemporaine* (1895) and *Ruskin et la religion de la beauté* (1897), he published *La Photographie est-elle un art?* (1899), *Le Miroir de la vie* (1902), *Les Questions esthétiques contemporaines* (1904) and several essays in English on the history of English and French painting; it is to him, too, that we owe Ruskin's *Pages choisies* (1908) the compilation of which Proust would abandon in favour of his colleague.

writes', who can make us see through images.* With his fondness for economics and sociology, for travelling – he wrote some actual guidebooks – and with his taste for history, through which, like Michelet, he brought back to life 'faded works of art and towns that have lost their vitality',[51] he was a modern writer: he teaches us to look, and 'spares us the life of ages long gone and peoples that are unknown. His words flow with life.'[52] The last part of this book is given over to Ruskin's 'social and aesthetic philosophy' of Nature, Art and Life, from 1843 to 1888. This was the part upon which Proust meditated, for it tallied with his personal intuitions. He read here that the aesthetic sense, which was an 'instinct', 'stirs us at the most exquisite moments of our life, at the only moments worthy of being lived', and that it establishes between objects and human beings 'that mysterious sense of harmony which science is unable to explain'.[†] Related to those 'happy, inexplicable instincts from the carefree moments of our childhood', it alone enables us to analyse our feelings. In Ruskin, who studied the details of nature and related his impressions with such intensity, Marcel found a father figure. The aesthetic sense even gives us a theory of the laws of the world: 'The aesthetic relationships of species are independent of their origins.'[‡] Confronted by the beauty of the world, the artist becomes its 'decoder, celebrant and memorialist'.[§] He 'immortalizes things that do not endure' and, as far as nature is concerned, he 'is *adoration*', for – and on this point Proust would not agree with Ruskin – nature is superior to art, even in the most humdrum life, without there being any need to choose or idealize. He was talking about nature in its natural, rather than industrial, state, what remained of a lost paradise, the sheltered valleys and unpolluted seas, Combray or Balbec. The painter has only to concentrate, as does Turner, upon 'what he sees, not what he knows'.[¶] The

---

* Lengthy translated extracts of Ruskin's writing had enabled Proust to assess this. Well before Malraux, Ruskin was perhaps the first to make systematic use of reproductions and comparisons of paintings, as well as written images, in his *Modern Painters*.

† La Sizeranne, *Ruskin*, p. 190. 'The moment we start to reason, the impression vanishes.' It would not be hard to demonstrate that some of the vocabulary of *Le Temps retrouvé* can be found in La Sizeranne.

‡ Ibid., pp. 205–7, quoting from *The Queen of the Air*; it was probably on account of these passages that Proust procured this book.

§ Ibid., p. 212. In this passage there appears a draft of the indefinable feelings experienced at Combray: 'Look at this pebble and these veins, look at this blade of grass which is waving at you.'

¶ Ibid., p. 232, quotation from *Eagle's Nest*. Cf., p. 249: 'However little you are able to see, it is only the supreme masters – Carpaccio, Tintoretto, Reynolds or Vélasquez – who take account of

crime of the Renaissance was to have favoured science above love. If Ruskin preferred Gothic architecture to all other art forms, it was because the sculpture of that period reproduced the forms of nature, its leaves and its flowers, most faithfully. The apogee of this art was to be found in Venice, because its sculpture was coloured. Ruskin's theory of colour, which he derived not merely from Turner, would inspire Elstir's theory: tones should be pure, rather than muted, as they appear in the open air (at this time, in 1845, no one yet painted out of doors). On the other hand, Proust would not approve of his dislike of varnishes and therefore of Dutch painting. At the same time, Ruskin expressed a very Proustian mistrust of theories: 'Does a bird draw up theories about building its nest?'[53] Our principal task is to admire: that is why landscape painters always live a happy life: 'Through admiring, one believes'.[54] La Sizeranne, who was anxious to expound Ruskin's ideas faithfully, did not voice any of Milsand's reservations: the clarity, the vigour of his account, his stylistic qualities, the wealth of quotations, all these were sufficient to entice Marcel and convince him that he could now abandon Darlu and France for this new master. It is worth noting that La Sizeranne would forward Proust's articles, 'John Ruskin' and 'Ruskin à Notre-Dame d'Amiens' to a great English friend of Ruskin's, Charles Newton Scott, and would congratulate Marcel, who must have sent him the articles, in a 'marvellous letter'.*

Proust had yet to read him. Paul Desjardins' *Bulletin de l'Union pour l'action morale*, to which Marcel subscribed, published the first translations of Ruskin, from 1893 to 1903:† short extracts taken, in particular, from *Saint Mark's Rest*, from *Sesame and Lilies*, *The Stones of Venice*, *The Seven Lamps of Architecture* and *Unto this Last*.[55] *The Crown of Wild Olive* and *The Seven Lamps of Architecture* were translated in 1899, *Unto this Last* in 1902. When Proust started to translate *The Bible of Amiens*, only two books had been

---

it or know it' (*Elements of Drawing*). Superior men are those who know how to grasp 'the fateful lines', those that have had an influence on a figure's past and will have one on its future (p. 250).

* *Corr.*, vol. XXI, p. 587, April 1900. Scott would take the opportunity to point out a mistranslation to Marcel (ibid.).

† In 1893 an extract from *Saint Mark's Rest* in which Ruskin sets forth his 'one and only doctrine', 'a loathing for everything that was doctrinal'; in September 1895 an extract from *Sesame and Lilies*; in 1895 and 1896 the second chapter of this book; on 1 December 1896 a description of the golden Virgin of Amiens, which would inspire Proust. Proust also read extracts from his favourite English novelists in this magazine: Hardy, George Eliot, and an article on 'The Enchantment of Good Friday'. In 1894 the review published 'Dilecta', a catalogue 'of books useful in the conduct of life', in which one comes across most of the authors Proust was reading at this period, including Emerson, Tolstoy, Dostoevsky and Carlyle.

published in French, and they had not been widely distributed. If in France Ruskin gradually acquired the stature of one of those great writers – such as Hugo, Valéry, Malraux, even Sartre – who combine morality, philosophy, aesthetics and art criticism, it was due to his expository writing. The translations would continue to appear at regular intervals: Proust's *La Bible d'Amiens* was the fourth to appear, and it was followed, in 1906, by *Sésame et les lys*, *Les Pierres de Venise* and *Les Matins à Florence*; in 1907 came *La Nature du gothique*; in 1908 *Le Repos de Saint-Marc*; *Praeterita* in 1910, and *Le Val d'Arno* in 1911; La Sizeranne published his *Pages choisies* in 1908. After this abundance came oblivion. Marcel's two translations went out of print; Ruskin's name was only remembered by specialists in Proust, who may not all have read him.

He met with the same fate on the other side of the Channel. The British art historian Kenneth Clark has retraced Ruskin's celebrity in Great Britain. He originally came to public attention in 1845 with the first volume of *Modern Painters*, and *The Seven Lamps of Architecture* in 1849 helped to establish his reputation. His collections of lectures, such as *Sesame and Lilies* (1865) also attracted a wide public. The influence of his political and economic writing, on the emerging Labour Party for example, was considerable. However, the decline of his reputation in Britain dated from the publication of his complete works in the Library Edition (which Proust owned), from 1903 to 1912. By 1950 his books could no longer be found on sale.[56] What was the reason for this decline? Firstly, because he was a preacher, and because ours is no longer an age of eloquence; secondly, his lack of scientific rigour and ability to concentrate, and his propensity for not sticking to his subject. His art depended more on emotion than reason, on subjectivism rather than scientific discourse. What might have saved him, however, was the fact that he was originally a poet; but he was also an essayist who liked to write about himself, and he was a prodigious name-dropper of works of art: he himself believed that the artist's function consisted in being a creature who sees and feels.[57] Proust would be influenced by these affirmations, and even by their tone, right up to *Le Temps retrouvé*.

In his own country, important historians have recently taken a different approach to Ruskin in the context of the history of taste, he has been reinstated in a position that better allows us to understand the respect in which Proust and his contemporaries held him. According to Francis Haskell, from the age of twenty onwards, Ruskin had conceived the ambitious project of establishing a new hierarchy of taste to the benefit of the Italian 'primitives' and to the detriment of Renaissance painters such as Raphael; later on, he became fond of the Venetians, such as Tintoretto;* his influence would soon make itself felt among collectors. After 1845 he welcomed the invention of daguerreotype: 'It is such a joy to be able to rely on *every* detail.'[58] Drawing on other writers, as Stendhal did, he revealed the figurative arts to the public in his sensitive but fiery descriptions by 'methods that were unknown until then'.[59] Moreover, he defended the little-known Turner and supported the Pre-Raphaelites. He foresaw the theories of Impressionism, a point made clear by Ernst Gombrich, who refers to him frequently in *Art and Illusion* (1960)[60] and quotes him on the whole issue of the relationship between perception and creativity.[†] His own drawings,[61] watercolours and carvings are finally being rediscovered, as, at the same time, is the work of the Pre-Raphaelites whom he influenced and championed: Rossetti, Millais, Hunt and Burne-Jones.[‡] In his youth, he was influenced by Turner, a number of whose works were owned by his family and with whom he became friendly, as well as by Samuel Prout and by David Roberts.

'PÈLERINAGES RUSKINIENS EN FRANCE'

Proust's main concern, in 1900, was to see the cathedrals through Ruskin's eyes. He therefore appealed to the English writer's travelling companions, in the hope that they might have heard from his own mouth what he would have written about Rouen and Chartres had *The Bible of Amiens* had a sequel.[§] This was also why he went to Rouen in January, accompanied

---

* Walter Pater asserted that he had preceded Ruskin along this path by 'two years'. Proust discussed Pater with Ainslie and with Billy. Mallarmé, in *La Musique et les lettres*, considered him to be the greatest living English prose writer.

[†] The cultural sociologist Raymond Williams devotes a historical chapter to him in his *Culture and Society* (Chatto and Windus, 1958).

[‡] *John Ruskin and Victorian Art*, catalogue of an exhibition held in four Japanese museums in 1993, with articles by James Dearden and Professor Kawamura. A centenary exhibition took place at the Royal Academy in London in 1919 but it was not until 1960 that there was an exhibition of his drawings at the Arts Council of London, who also organized the exhibition *Ruskin and his Circle* in 1964.

[§] *CSB*, p. 443: 'If they could have at least told me something of what Ruskin said during these journeys, they would put an end to the questions I endlessly ask myself and which for me remain unanswered by the stones of Chartres and Bourges.' We see that Proust addresses the questions with which he bombards his friends to himself first. We also see his need for an intermediary every time he encounters a new subject for his interest, his admiration or his love: thus, in *À la recherche*, we move on from questions about Elstir or Vinteuil to those about Albertine. He needed to gather

by his friends the Yeatmans, in order to examine a small figure on the Libraires gate that Ruskin described,[62] just as he was preparing his 'Pèlerinages ruskiniens en France',[63] a logical sequel to his obituary in *La Chronique des arts*, which would appear in *Le Figaro* on 13 February. He suggested to his readers, if they wished to engage in 'hero-worship', that they should also go and see the places in France that Ruskin had loved: Rouen, Abbeville, Beauvais, Dijon, Saint-Lô, Chartres and Amiens. The article also announced the series of 'Ruskin studies' that Proust intended to write for various publications,[64] and, in particular, the publication of 'important extracts' from *La Bible d'Amiens*. Finally, employing an image that would feature in *Du côté de chez Swann*, his homage celebrated the Christian, the moralist, the economist and the aesthetician, who 'reminds one of that figure of Charity that Giotto painted at Padua and which Ruskin often mentioned in his books': Proustian criticism often applied its own expressions to the author in question, thus, by a clever twisting of a quotation, putting a face to the mirror.

The real pilgrimage is related in a long article, 'Ruskin à Notre-Dame d'Amiens', which Proust published in *Mercure de France* in April 1900. It is unusual that a translator should wish to see or revisit all the places mentioned by the author (one senses that Marcel was relieved that he did not have to travel far), and that in his translation he should describe them, attributing a religious character to them: his purpose was to send his readers on a pilgrimage. The article is surprising for its personal tone: the author does not hesitate to say 'I' or to involve himself ('It is impossible that there should be anyone who does not derive some pleasure from something that has afforded me so much, for no one is unique'),[65] while at the same time displaying a scholar's erudition and an extraordinary knowledge of Ruskin's work. He was already well versed in the bibliography of English critical works.* For a simple detail, such as the burial place of Shelley's heart, he threw himself into an exposition of all the scholarly hypotheses. Digression, in fact, was already a feature of Proust's writing, especially when dealing with Ruskin: he wanders from St Martin, who never scorned honest pleasures, to a quotation from Ruskin, to a reference

---

all possible information about an individual, an artist or a particular place, before being able to write about it, almost as if the young Proust was at first shrinking from his own mind's work, a mark of what he called his laziness.

* For example, Collingwood's *The Life and Works of John Ruskin*, 2 vols, London, 1893. Additionally, he drew parallels with other English writers; among them George Eliot (*Scenes from Clerical Life, Adam Bede, Middlemarch*); he did not shrink from quoting forty-four lines of hers (*CSB*, p. 73).

to hosts who were inflexible about seating arrangements at table (a discreet allusion to Aimery de La Rochefoucauld), to Emerson's and Carlyle's liking for cheerful subjects, and a long quotation from George Eliot. He thus alluded to all the English writers he knew of who had written in praise of cheerfulness among religious men.

The footnotes, which often occupy more space on the page than the text itself, were an exercise in exhaustiveness, a quest for all-round knowledge. In *À la recherche* Proust developed this preoccupation still further. Apart from the fact that his already considerable erudition embraced numerous authors, he explained the reasons for the quotations from Ruskin in the notes and, for the first time, he revealed a genuine philosophy of criticism and reading. The first part of any criticism consists of equipping the reader with an improvised memory. This goes beyond the time spent reading; it reconstructs the book around two passages, two particular moments, and causes a timeless moment to spring from them. Yet this memory will not have the properties or the poetry of a memory 'which has created itself'.[66] Similarly, there are two categories of book: those which we write by settling down to research that is specific to the present moment and does not draw on any previous memory; and those, in contrast, which arise naturally from former, disinterested studies which we have undertaken without any thought that a book may result.* Yet 'to read only one book by an author, is to have only one meeting with that author'. The particular features can only be recognized as essential characteristics through a variation of circumstances,[67] and they reveal the moral aspects of the artist. Proust thus shows how *The Bible of Amiens* contains 'things which Ruskin had meditated upon all his life, and hence express his way of thinking most profoundly'.[68] He did no more than 'publish his memory and open his heart'. Did Proust remember these other passages? Or did he try to find them? One can only look for a particular text in an immense work if one knows beforehand that it is

* Thus does Proust's theory of two memories gently unfold: in his first books, he provided a fictional illustration of it and here, for the first time, is a theoretical or abstract formulation. How do we re-invent our past? It is the merging of two ways of expressing memory that would produce *À la recherche du temps perdu*, when the requirements of what was actually being written would reawaken sleeping memories, when what had been experienced would come to mind as often as what has been read. The ways thus converge in life as they do in books. This obscure scholarly process of writing notes, so frequently decried by writers and critics, is therefore the harbinger of the great work. In the drafts of the novel, the notes are the additions, the organizational indications that Proust gave himself.

there. Did Marcel instruct his collaborators – his mother, Ainslie, Marie Nordlinger, Robert d'Humières* – to do this research, thus providing himself with auxiliary memories? In early March he was still asking Marie whether Ruskin's *Poetry of Architecture* included anything about cathedrals, and about a lecture he gave on the flamboyant architecture of the valley of the Somme,[69] while at the same time recalling his conversations with the verger of Rouen Cathedral, Julien Édouard, whom he had met in January and who had known Ruskin.

The second task of any criticism is to chart a *spiritual biography* – the importance of this assertion with regard to my own biography of Proust will be appreciated – to reconstruct whatever 'the particular spiritual life of a writer obsessed by such unusual realities' may be. His inspiration matches his vision of these realities, his talent re-creates them in his work and his 'morality' encourages the instinct that drives the artist to sacrifice his own life to this vision and to its reproduction. Life is 'the only way of coming into contact with these realities'; it has no value other than that of an instrument which the physicist uses for his experiments. Here we discern the influence, and it was not purely medical, that the nineteenth-century scientific credo had on Proust's thinking. The body, and therefore life itself, was at once the subject, object and instrument of research.

To return to the visit to Amiens, Marcel described, just as Ruskin did, the itinerary that he followed, how he witnessed the cathedral transfigured by sunshine, 'some gigantic apparitions of gold and of fire', and even mentioning the charity, quoting *L'Éducation sentimentale*,† to which he gave alms. Autobiography interferes with art criticism, because Proust flaunts his feelings not for the universal, which is a proper quality of a work of art, but for the specific, rooted in a time and a place, which would be reincarnated in the church at Combray and at Saint-André-des-Champs: the gilded Virgin has the 'smile of a celestial hostess', 'in her simple and exquisite costume of hawthorns' in blossom,[70] she holds our attention through the same link that 'people and places' do, because she 'belongs

---

* For the first few pages, he admitted using quotations translated by Milsand and La Sizeranne: 'But afterwards, whenever I give if not an idea, then at least an impression of what I think of Ruskin, I have to do my own translation of the passages to which I refer and which have not been translated hitherto.'

† Frédéric Moreau gives to charity, on the boat, something that he associates in his thoughts with Mme Arnoux; Marcel was thinking of Ruskin. In this accurate quotation from Flaubert's novel, we see how knowledgeable Proust already was about this work, which was not one he had studied at the lycée.

for all time to a particular place on earth' and because she resembles some incomparable individual, whereas the Gioconda is 'without a homeland': 'In my bedroom [this is how we discover how Marcel decorated it*] a photograph of the Gioconda retains merely the beauty of a masterpiece. Nearby, there is a photograph of the gilded Virgin that takes on the melancholy of a memory.' Proust spent long hours contemplating the porch at Amiens, concentrating, as did Monet, on the changing effects of light on the cathedral.

When he enters, he shelters behind a long quotation from Ruskin, before expressing his enthusiasm for the blending of genius with the modest domestic function and the evocation of nature in the choir-stalls; but since he always proceeds from nature to art, in a sort of epistemological circle, he also refers to a poem of Verlaine's set to music by Hahn, and to furniture made by Gallé, and he suggests that, in order to inspect the outer enclosure of the choir, one should read Huysmans' *La Cathédrale*.†
When he finally reached the West Door, which Ruskin refers to specifically as the 'Bible of Amiens', Proust asserts that a cathedral is not just a thing of beauty that one feels. 'Even if it is no more for you than an instruction to be followed, it is still at least a book that has to be understood.'[71] What is more, he did not know that Hugo and Michelet had developed the same image. Describing this porch in detail with the help of a good many quotations, he turns to a writer who, after Ruskin, would have a great influence on his thinking and with whom he was to became friendly: Émile Mâle, whose book, *L'Art religieux du XIIIe siècle*[72] is mentioned for the first time. His commentary is strewn with remarks like 'Unfortunately we cannot', 'We do not have the time to', which often contradict the footnotes. They demonstrate how Marcel's critical method was perfected, in the skill with which he discovered the hidden logic beneath Ruskin's disparate thoughts and in the definition of their depths, which could be recognized by their 'particular colour'.[73] Establishing and developing relationships, plumbing the depths, he would never do anything else. The conclusion of the article is a further confession. There can be no doubt that

---

* As we know, he also hung a reproduction of Whistler's *The Mother* there.

† The comment is made in the Mercure de France edition of *La Bible d'Amiens*, pp. 400–1. A little later Proust mentions *Notre-Dame de Paris*, which Ruskin disliked, *La Cathédrale* once more, then Bossuet's *Élévations sur les Mystères*; and he devotes a long footnote to Renan, which foreshadows his 1908 pastiche: in it he condemns the use of irony, which renders sacred or merely classical words in a mundane manner; his *Vie de Jésus* is the *Belle Hélène* of Christianity. Here we see emerge the Meilhac and Halévy wit, which Proust would bestow on the Guermantes and on Swann.

Proust no longer believed in the Bible, which 'is no longer true in men's hearts'. For Ruskin, the soul of the thirteenth-century artists still resided in the statues at Amiens; for Proust, it was Ruskin's own soul: 'The words of a genius can just as much give immortal shape to things as can the chisel. Literature, too, is a "sacrificial lamp" which burns in order to light the way for those who come after.'[74] Marcel therefore saw himself as his author's spiritual heir, responsible for reaffirming all that he said.

Proust wrote another article about Ruskin, published in the *Gazette des Beaux-Arts* as 'John Ruskin (second article)' on 1 August. He would combine the two to form Chapter III of his introduction to *La Bible d'Amiens*. The manuscripts interweave the two texts.[75] The second is nevertheless more theoretical:[76] in discussing Ruskin's aesthetics, he discovered his own in the process. The chief characteristic of any great work is that it should be universal, rather than personal.[77] Ruskin had been seen as a realist, as an intellectual, as a scientist, or as a pure aesthetician, whose only religion was beauty. This latter role is described by La Sizeranne, from whose views Proust distanced himself; if the turn of the century was a period for dilettantes* and aesthetes, Ruskin's approach had been the reverse of this: through his feelings for beauty, he searched for a reality that was more important than life. Marcel, for whom criticism consisted in seeking the one source of an art form and an idea, found it here. This led him to a theory of biography: 'The events of his life were intellectual ones and the important dates were those on which he fathomed a new art form, the year in which he understood Abbeville, the year in which he understood Rouen . . .'[78] The reality which the artist must comprehend is both material and intellectual: 'The overall shape of something is not merely the image of its nature, it is the voice of its destiny and the course of its history.'[79] On the other hand, Ruskin was wrong to state that a painting was beautiful 'in so far as the ideas which it translated into images were independent of the language of imagery'; on the contrary, according to Proust, 'Painting could attain the bare reality of things and thereby compete with it only on the condition that it were not literary': that is why he would create the characters of Bergotte, Elstir and Vinteuil, who embody three different ways of attaining reality in three languages.

The Bible lay at the heart of Ruskin's aesthetics; it was his religious fervour that had guided his aesthetic feelings: Proust would retain the divine without the religion. Beliefs mattered little, in fact, since their

* This word is put into the mouth of M. de Norpois.

strength mattered more than their subject.[80] Ruskin's Christianity was responsible for Proust's love of Christian art: he inherited this love without the faith. The watchword became *unity*; the Christian art of the Middle Ages (which Ruskin extended to Hellenic art, 'classical sacred art') provides unity in *À la recherche*, where everything – including Saint-Loup and Albertine – stems from the porch of Saint-André-des-Champs. Ruskin lived in a fraternal society, among the greatest minds of all time, added Proust (who would do the same), 'and he could talk about Herodotus as he would about a contemporary'.[81] As for the symbols, they were no less important to science and history than they were to art. We may wonder whether Ruskin's drawings were not the inspiration for Elstir's:[82] like Turner, he drew what he saw, not what he knew, and he did not distinguish the beauty of the cathedrals from the land from which they sprang, thus capturing the particular charm of the places that meant so much to Proust. This joy in the particular, which corresponds to the artist's own free, joyful and personal labour, is nowhere better expressed than in a 'small figure a few centimetres high', in the Libraires porch at Rouen Cathedral.[83] Marcel then expounded several truths that would guide his own existence: the work that each of us has to do must be done wholeheartedly, even if no one notices it; enthusiasm alone leads us along the path to truth; the immortality of those things that have survived* because genius has wrested the tiniest detail away from infinity – from death and from the multitude of other details – such as the ideas of the carver revealed by Ruskin's own thought process; the guide that the latter had been for Proust, he would become in turn for others.

Finally, the most important point that Proust discovered in his analysis of Ruskin's ideas – which he was not content merely to reflect, but which he criticized, since respect should prompt us neither into 'believing without examination' nor into 'admiring trustingly'[84] – was the part played by untruthfulness, which can seep into the greatest sincerity under the guise of what he himself calls *idolatry*.† It consists in subordinating truth and

---

* A theme to which Proust would revert in connection with the names of Assurbanipal's dogs; similarly, the theme of Pompeii, so dear to *Le Temps retrouvé*, appears for the first time here. Another theme from this book arises a little later (*CSB*, p. 128), that of the fountain, which gushes higher the more deeply it has been sunk into the ground, and to which Proust compared a work of art. Ruskin behaves as Bergotte would: 'Dead, he continued to light our way, like those extinguished stars whose light still reaches us' (ibid., p. 129).

† See f. 57 recto of the manuscript, *CSB*, p. 765: 'When art is thus conceived as a transcription of a divine reality, sincerity is not merely one of the duties of the artist, it is the only guide that prevents him from failing . . . "One only writes well about what one loves," Renan said. From the work of Ruskin one draws an aesthetic in which feeling plays still more of a part, and in which

moral feeling to aesthetic feeling while at the same time asserting the reverse, in choosing doctrines not because they are true, but because they are beautiful, and not acknowledging this. The paradox is that there is no 'beauty that is totally mendacious, since aesthetic pleasure is precisely that which accompanies the discovery of a truth'.[85] Another idolater is introduced in an autobiographical but unexpected context here (other very recent personal memories are also incorporated into this article: apart from the trip to Rouen, the journey to Venice and St Mark's, which he visited in a storm while reading Ruskin):[86] Robert de Montesquiou, who praises the beauty of a dress because it is portrayed by Moreau or worn by the Princesse de Cadignan. Proust here admits his fondness, acquired from the count, for rare or little-known works by Balzac: this princess, and her clothes, would be the inspiration for the Duchesse de Guermantes. So as to develop his theory of idolatry, he resorted to yet another personal example, his fondness for apple and hawthorn blossom: 'My love for them is infinite and the suffering (hay fever) that their proximity causes me enables me each springtime to give them proofs of this love which are not accessible to everyone.'* But he loved these flowers in reality, not in works of art. In fact, 'the beauty of a painting does not depend upon the things that are depicted in it'.[87] In order to grasp fully this idolatry of Ruskin's, Proust (who in the process defined his method of reading and criticism, and the way he perceived the world) had to 'descend to the depths of himself so as to grasp its meaning': everything that he wrote was experienced beforehand; which is why the writing of this article was a turning point in his life – the account of an experience, of a self-examination that made him different to other people. Marcel had begun to read Ruskin because of the intellectual benefit it would afford him, because of his love of Gothic cathedrals, of English and Italian painting, of the subjects that crystallized Ruskin's thinking and that had to be seen in order to understand it: 'in Pisa, Florence, Venice, the National Gallery, in Rouen, Amiens, among the mountains of Switzerland'.[88] His

---

enthusiasm rather than facts is the criterion of truth.' In *À la recherche* the Narrator gives evidence of this enthusiasm when he contemplates the hawthorns or the three trees at Hudimesnil.

* Love is infinite because it means suffering; here Proust unveils his theory of love, which is akin to Racine's and Baudelaire's (*CSB*, p. 136). He rounds it off a little further on, with the notion that one begins to court a woman in order to attain a goal that she is unaware of, one then loves her for herself by sacrificing this goal; he concludes that love, 'which allows us to discover so many deep psychological truths, does, however, cut us off from poetic feelings of nature' (ibid., p. 139).

journey to Venice was thus a direct result of this influence.[89] Initially, he developed an admiration for Ruskin's actual ideas. Proust then elaborated a shrewd theory about this influence: 'This voluntary subjugation is the beginning of freedom. There is no better way of becoming aware of what one feels oneself than by trying to re-create in oneself that which a master has experienced. In this profound effort that we make, it is our own way of thinking, together with the master's, that we bring to light.'[90] There can be no freedom without a purpose; there is no work of art without a subject that imposes itself on the poet from the outside; there can be no creator without a master: 'And it is by subjugating one's mind so as to convey this vision, so as to draw close to this truth, that the artist becomes truly himself.' The picture that Proust gives of his own education to the readers of the *Gazette des Beaux-Arts* would not be complete if its conclusion were not devoted to memory. Returning to the history of his passion for Ruskin, which was initially rather superficial but later very profound, he stated that he had had to resort to the 'frozen memory we have of things', without being able to reopen the 'closed doors', without returning to the state in which he had previously existed, without once more becoming what he had been, without finding 'the lost paradise' in a memory. There could be no better way of evoking involuntary memory, taking us as far as the threshold, but no further. Hence Ruskin was far removed from his mind when Marcel wrote of him: 'It is when Ruskin is far away from us that we translate his books and try to pin down the characteristics of his thinking in an accurate image.'[91]

THE JOURNEY TO VENICE

As we already know from the article he wrote in August about Ruskin, it was under his influence that Proust travelled to Italy in May 1900. He kept away from Florence for fear of 'hay and pollen fever',[92] believing himself to be very ill, as he did every spring, and, as he confided in the *Gazette des Beaux-Arts*,* he reckoned his days were numbered. Ruskin himself had established the link between Amiens, the 'Venice of France', the 'Queen of Northern Waters' and the Italian city, founded at almost

---

* It is through this article and Marie Nordlinger's memoirs that we know the essential facts about this visit: scarcely any letters about it are known to us. The loss of Marcel's letters to his father and those of Mme Proust to her husband is infinitely regrettable. *Albertine disparue* is a late source and is jumbled up with fiction.

the same time, in the fifth century: 'The Venice of Picardy* owed its name not only to the beauty of its waterways, but to the cargoes they bore. Like the Adriatic princess, she was an artisan producing gold and glass, stone, wood and ivory.'[93]

Marcel left for Venice, with his mother (his father was either away travelling, as in the novel, or else he remained in Paris),[†] 'in order to have been able, before dying, to draw close to, touch and see the embodiment of Ruskin's ideas on domestic architecture in the Middle Ages in palaces that are crumbling, but which are still rose-coloured and are still standing'.[94] Ruskin's central theme, which Proust does not clarify sufficiently and which critics never remember, emerges in *The Stones of Venice*: religious architecture is nothing more than the perfect development of the common architecture of town houses at the period: 'The sculptures that adorn the porches of St Mark's had once their match on the walls of every palace on the Grand Canal . . . Secular history was constantly introduced into church architecture; and sacred history or allusion generally formed at least one half the ornament of the dwelling house.'[95]

Armed with a library of Ruskin's works, which he offered to lend to his friend Yeatman, who was in Milan – *Saint Mark's Rest*,[‡] *The Stones of Venice*,[§] *Modern Painters* and, naturally, *The Bible of Amiens* – Marcel and his mother put up at the Hotel de l'Europe,[¶] which was then at the Palazzo

---

* So called because of its canals, or '*rieux*', which cut through the '*hortillonages*'. [Both words are used in the Picardy dialect to describe the local method of cultivation of marshy terrain. *Tr.*]

† In June Marcel wrote to Lucien: 'Papa who has been on his own for so long and finds himself with a sick son and a wife who is in bed does not have a very jolly life' (*Corr.*, vol. II, p. 398). Mme Proust was suffering from rheumatism. 'Marcel very oppressed, being unable either to breathe or to sleep, although it is not as bad as in Venice', wrote Reynaldo, thereby informing us that Marcel was unwell in Italy.

‡ A particularly important work because its rediscovery would inspire Proust with the episode of involuntary memory that is linked to *François le Champi* in *Le Temps retrouvé*; however, since Venice had already been used for the uneven paving-stones, it was more skilful to transform Ruskin into Sand, who was in any case connected to Combray. In *La Bible d'Amiens* (p. 246, note), Proust, thinking about *St Mark's Rest*, recalled 'the special tint of the past' which the book retains, the charm of the day on which it was read, and which its pages will ineffably preserve.

§ It did not exist in French. Proust had questioned Robert de La Sizeranne on the subject: 'It would be a great comfort to me to read *The Stones of Venice* in French on the spot' (*Corr.*, vol. XXI, p. 587, April 1900); since he was not considering translating this book, he was searching for an unpublished edition, because his correspondent had told him that for certain titles translations could be found.

¶ According to P. Kolb, not at the Danieli, as Painter (p. 330), following Marie Nordlinger, asserts, probably in order to mention Musset and Sand. G. Cattaui has published (*M. Proust. Documents iconographiques*, Geneva, P. Cailler, 1956, no. 53) a photograph of Proust in Venice, wearing a hat

Giustiniani. To begin with, he was feeling so unwell that he was unable to register any impression: 'Yet Venice was none the less etched into me', he would write to Gide, 'and, when I remember her, I still enjoy a deferred pleasure.'[96] So it was that on a radiant May morning, Marie Nordlinger, who was staying at the Palazzo Fortuny Madrazo* with her aunt and her cousin Reynaldo,[97] saw them arrive. Reynaldo had spent the winter in Rome with his mother and, anticipating that he would encounter Marcel in Venice, had written ironically to Marie: 'Watch out, I foresee the telegraph being kept busy.' Proust recalled '[those] blessed days, when, with the other disciples of the master, we went about Venice in gondolas, listening to his preaching beside the waters, and disembarking at each of the temples which seemed to rise out of the sea so as to provide us with the object of his descriptions and the very image of his thought'.[98] For the same reason, they also went across to San Giorgio degli Schiavoni to see the paintings of St Jerome by Carpaccio[99] (whom Ruskin claimed to have discovered).[100] But the principal working sessions took place in the shelter of the baptistery, not only because Marcel, accompanied by Marie Nordlinger or by Mme Proust,† was collating Ruskin's descriptions[101] with the mosaics and the inscriptions, but because he took advantage of this golden, sacred coolness, so conducive to writing and translating.

Everybody at that time, from Regnier to Barrès, was writing about Venice; Marcel, who was unaware of what was fashionable, neither

---

that makes him look like Charlie Chaplin, sitting sideways on a wicker chair, on what could be the balcony or terrace of his hotel, overlooking the Grand Canal (and not on the beach of the Lido, as the book states). The same volume includes a photograph of Adrien Proust in St Mark's Square, dated by the publisher to 1900, perhaps incorrectly, since the professor came to Venice in 1897 to attend an international conference on protecting Europe from the plague and later wrote his book on the subject; Félix Faure thanked him for it (Exhibition catalogue BN 1965, no. 35).

* It should be remembered that Raymond de Madrazo, born in Rome in 1841 and married to Reynaldo's sister, Maria Hahn, was the son of Federico Madrazo and grandson of José de Madrazo, both painters at the Spanish court and directors of the Madrid museum. He was the father of Federico, known as Coco, himself an artist and the painter of the portrait of Marie Nordlinger, as well as of portraits of Reynaldo Hahn (catalogue of the 1971 Jacquemart-André exhibition, no. 226, pl. XXI), and of Louis Gautier-Vignal in about 1920, (Cattaui, *M. Proust*, no. 163, reproduced as the frontispiece to *Lettres à une amie*); Federico was the brother-in-law of Fortuny, whose palazzo has become a museum.

† 'We were setting off towards St Mark's where I was copying the mosaics in the Baptistery, my mother having thrown me a shawl to keep out the chill air, both of us trampling over the marble and glass mosaics and the uneven paving-stones' (Cahier 48, f. 62 recto). Here we find the only mention – it has disappeared from the definitive text – of the uneven paving-stones that anticipate the episode in *Le Temps retrouvé*; it is important to see it in the context of the mother.

distancing himself from nor being influenced by such concerns, had eyes only for his passion of the moment, Ruskin, who alone understood the truth of this city. He observed in 1906: 'Barrès' dying Venice, the post-humous, carnival-like Venice of Régnier, Mme de Noailles' Venice that is insatiable with love, Léon Daudet's Venice . . . exert a unique fascination on all well-bred imaginations. And, now, here is Ruskin who will take us away from this slightly passive contemplation of Venice.'[102] This is why, taking shelter in St Mark's basilica one stormy day with Marie Nordlinger (who, as we know, was already helping him correct the proofs of his article for the *Gazette des Beaux-Arts*), he read some passages from *The Stones of Venice* with her.[103] He himself remembered 'those moments of storm and darkness when the mosaics gleamed only with their own material light, with an ancient, internal, terrestrial gold'. In her memoirs the young woman described Mme Proust, waiting for them on the balcony of the hotel, the ice-creams consumed in the afternoons at Florian's, the pigeons, which Marcel called the 'lilacs of the bird kingdom',[104] the evenings in the gondolas on the lagoon, with Reynaldo singing as they sailed with the current. For over three weeks they visited all the churches, 'those delightful, rose-coloured, semi-erect buildings, that loom out of the waters', they studied every capital drawn by Ruskin and requested a ladder 'in order to identify a bas-relief, the importance of which Ruskin had pointed out to us and which, without him, we should never have noticed'.[105] When Elstir paints La Salute, Proust's inspiration was Turner's *The Dogana and Santa Maria della Salute*, which was reproduced in *Modern Painters*.[106]

A trip to Padua would have a strong influence on his future work: still following in Ruskin's footsteps, Marcel and Reynaldo travelled there to see the Giotto frescoes in the chapel of the Madonna dell'Arena.* They feature in the sojourn in Venice in *Albertine disparue* but are first mentioned, in a sort of premonitory inversion, at Combray, and they eventually cast their disturbing shadow over the whole of *À la recherche*, as the title of the chapter 'Les Vices et les Vertus de Padoue et de Combray' indicates. The trip to Padua is itself the subject of a very romantic sketch concerning the pursuit of the Baronness Putbus's maid:[107] 'When from the carriage

---

* A journey that is repeated in *À la recherche*, vol. IV, p. 226, which harks back to *Du côté de chez Swann*: 'Once, when the weather was particularly fine, in order to see those Vices and Virtues of which M. Swann had given me reproductions, that were probably still hanging in the schoolroom of the house at Combray, we ventured as far as Padua.' We know that the Vices and Virtues in the Arena Chapel were illustrated in the Library Edition of Ruskin, the plates of which were in front of Proust when he wrote *À la recherche*.

I saw Padua spread out before me beneath a blue sky . . . it's hollowed-out towers, red and shiny with age . . . my heart was set on fire at seeing the ancient Donatellos, the Mantegnas at the Eremitani,[108] and particularly those Virtues and Vices of Giotto's in the Arena Chapel which had looked down on me for so many years.' In the final text, Proust no longer describes the Virtues and the Vices, but the angels in the blue sky, which are reminiscent of 'Garros's young pupils who are practising gliding',[109] as if the beloved aviator (dear, moreover, to Cocteau, one of Proust's friends), who was already dead, had become one of those angels.

In *Albertine disparue*, Proust also introduced the subject of domestic architecture. The role of the houses in Combray is played, in Venice, by the palaces of porphyry and jasper. The care with which words are used that enable one to recognize a family house is here 'devolved upon the ogive, still half-Arab, of the façade that is reproduced in all the architectural museums and all the illustrated art books, as one of the masterpieces of the domestic architecture of the Middle Ages'.[110] Although the Venetian episode was largely fictional, Proust introduced into it his memories of his visit in May 1900 – the window[111] is a theme that is constantly developed in the manuscripts: 'At twelve o'clock each day, when my gondola brought me back for lunch, from afar I often noticed Mama's shawl hung over her alabaster balcony with a book to weigh it down against the wind. And above were the circular foils of her window, lit up like a smile, exuding the reassurance and confidence that a friendly look imparts.'[112] On the other hand, when the novel (and also *Contre Sainte-Beuve*) describes a quarrel the Narrator has with his mother, there is nothing that allows us to assume, as biographers have done, without documentary proof, that it occurred in Marcel's own life; he always felt guilty towards Mme Proust and he may have found a partially fictional outlet for his feelings here.

At the end of May Marcel and his mother returned to Paris; the young man had accumulated memories, made his dream coincide with reality, stored away all his documents, his manuscript notes and his passages of translation, and he had discovered a new impetus with which to settle down to work. The novel which contained the essential moments of his stay in Venice would be published twenty-seven years later, five years after Proust's death. On his return, the family was plagued by health problems – Marcel by his asthma, his mother by rheumatic pains, and his father had an operation for the removal of a gall stone.

HOW TO TRANSLATE?

'How do you manage, Marcel, seeing that you don't know any English?'
Constantin de Brancovan asked him one day.[113] Since Proust did not
speak any English, he composed his translation from a first draft written
by his mother. Strangely, no one has ever commented on the fact that his
trip to Venice did not make him change his mind about the text, nor did
it instil in him a desire to translate those of his master's books that deal
with Italian subjects; it is almost as if he wished to remain faithful to the
work he had already accomplished, to the parallel Ruskin drew between
the two cities, the essential factors being the Gothic cathedral and the
linguistic gymnastics. The countless manuscript corrections demonstrate
how he absorbed Ruskin's period, how he came to understand its structure,
how he delineated it and listened to its music. The structure of Ruskin's
sentences, which were long, rich in incident and imagery, supple and
musical, and had been influenced by the Authorized Version of the King
James Bible, which British men and women of that period knew by heart,
impregnated his own style, which, since *Jean Santeuil*, had been groping
around in search of a model. He must gradually have learnt English, or
at least enough to know what he should ask his collaborators. Just as
Baudelaire and Mallarmé had translated Poe, and just as Gide, for his own
generation, would translate Shakespeare, Conrad and Tagore, as Claudel
would adapt Coventry Patmore, Valéry, Virgil, Samuel Butler, and Larbaud,
so Proust, like them, wanted to make his author famous and he also felt
that translation was a marvellous school for style. Furthermore, what was
essential for him were the annotations, notes and introduction (which he
would criticize his cousin, Mathilde Crémieux, for disregarding in her
translation of *The Stones of Venice*). In his annotations he exhibited prodigious
erudition: apart from his knowledge of Ruskin's other books, there was
Viollet-le-Duc's *Dictionnaire*, and, for Chapter IV, 'Interprétations', Émile
Mâle, who is frequently quoted in the notes; but he also referred to the
Bible, Shakespeare, Augustin Thierry, Huysmans, and to the thinkers of
his day: Pater, Brunschvicg, Tarde, as well as to Ruskin specialists, from
Collingwood to Bardoux. In addition to this, there was his knowledge of
cathedrals or churches – as well as painting – which, with the help of
Mâle,[114] enabled him to refer in a flash to a particular door or porch at
Rheims, Bourges, Chartres, Le Mans, Tours, Soissons or Lyons.

     Jeanne Proust prepared a first draft, the manuscript of which is in the
Bibliothèque Nationale,[115] which was copiously altered and annotated by

her son. His close friends who helped him, such as Robert de Billy, saw him working at the dining-room table[116] (in fact, he never used a desk nor a study), and sometimes in the drawing-room,[117] where it was easier to spread out his countless documents. He entrusted 'a little task' to François d'Oncieu. Reynaldo Hahn was constantly consulted, as, no doubt, was Antoine Bibesco. He gave his mother instructions not unlike those given by Dumas to Maquet: 'Would you very kindly translate for me tomorrow on sheets of the larger format paper that you'll find, without writing on the back, without leaving any blank space, tightening up what I showed you from *Seven Lamps*.'[118] 'Do the end of the *Bible* as before and make a clean copy. The prophets and the months of the year, on the other hand, should be in draft.' The first version would then be polished by Marie Nordlinger, who is linked to Ruskin much as Gilberte is to Bergotte or Albertine to Elstir. But that amended draft would also be reworked further by Marcel: 'Thank you, too, for the fine translation, which I shall look at closely, and, if you will allow, alter.'[119] Robert d'Humières (1868–1915), the translator of Kipling, whom Proust would read thanks to him, and later of Conrad, a playwright and future director of the Théâtre des Arts as well as a novelist and essayist (in 1904 Proust would review *L'Île et l'Empire de Grande-Bretagne: Angleterre, Égypte, Inde* and would praise it for 'the absolute clarity of its thought and its style')[120] also helped him,[121] and would do so even more with *Sesame*. His noble ancestry, his haughty, ironical looks, his manners and his tastes,[122] his death during the war in 1915, after he had requested, as liaison officer to the general staff, to rejoin his Zouave regiment[123] – in all this we can see a model for Saint-Loup; Proust would mourn him at the same time as Bertrand de Fénelon.

The work thus advanced at this pace, and in December 1901 Proust would deliver his translation of *The Bible of Amiens* to the publishers Ollendorff.[124]

1 9 0 0 DRAWS TO A CLOSE

The year of the great Exposition Universelle was drawing to a close without it having made much impression on Proust. Before dining at Weber's with Montesquiou, to whom he was still loyal, Proust even managed to avoid accompanying him to see it.[125] Marcel's parents were at Évian on 8 August and were anxiously awaiting news of their son. With her usual blend of humour, Mme Proust gave a description of the residents at the hotel which heralds those that her son would paint of the hotel at

Balbec: political types, including two members of parliament, Silhol and Chauveau; Dupuy, 'a man with a large red nose', the former president of the Council, who had come and 'tapped' Professor Proust 'on the shoulder'; diplomats, such as Ambassador Nisard (at the time appointed to the Holy See), uncle of Marie Benardaky (and the model for Norpois), 'very nice but very deaf'; lawyers, such as Ployer and Devin, both presidents of the Bar; composers, such as Lenepveu; cousins, such as Cruppi and the Mayers; doctors, such as their devoted friends the Duplays* and Doctor Cottet, who lived there permanently and whom Marcel had consulted at length the previous year. The Parisian bourgeoisie, in short, taking the cure. One can see why Mme Proust should have written to her son: 'I think it would be as well for you to wait before coming to Évian. Not that our hotel is not *dazzling*, but it is packed and *noisy* as a result.'[126] She therefore advised Marcel to go on some interesting Ruskinian pilgrimages: 'I hope that when you do not write it is because you are going on excursions that are interesting or enjoyable, or healthy.'[127]

Moreover she intended to return to Paris to oversee the family's moving house. Having briefly considered the Boulevard Haussmann, Proust's parents, who were still attached to the Parc Monceau, a district of well-known doctors and wealthy patients, where friends and clients lived, finally rented the second floor of 45 rue de Courcelles.[128] It was an attractive apartment with a circular lay-out (like those '*rotondes*' that Zola makes fun of in *La Curée*) on the corner of the rue de Monceau. At the front, over-looking both streets, were M. and Mme Proust's bedroom, the drawing-room, the dining-room, Marcel's bedroom, which was therefore some way away from his parents', and then Robert's bedroom; two other rooms came next; the utility rooms gave on to the courtyard; a long corridor led off to the rooms used by the servants, whose noise used to wake Marcel up; the bathroom was opposite Marcel's and Robert's bedrooms.[129] A boiler provided warm air through vents, which was probably bad for an asthmatic. The heavy, dark furniture cluttered the reception rooms, without being in any way collector's pieces: the three layers of curtains and the dark wall-hangings were very much in the Third Republic style, and Marcel, who was indifferent to furnishing as he was to fashion and loath to criticize

---

* The Prousts and the Duplays represented the 'independent Republican party' at this period of great political divisions. Adrien Proust played dominoes enthusiastically with the Duplays; his friends were greatly amused by the delight he showed when he won (*Corr.*, vol. II, p. 405). In the same way, Cottard also played écarté, and Marcel played draughts.

his parents, does not appear to have wanted to suggest any of the more aesthetic solutions that he could admire in the houses or apartments of the aristocracy, who were going back to the lighter colours and furnishings of the eighteenth century: all he did was to contrast Swann's home with that of the Narrator's parents. For the first time the Prousts installed a telephone, although Marcel continued to correspond by telegram (such as those he sent to his parents at Évian) or messages delivered by servants. The staff comprised a cook, two chambermaids (Félicie Fiteau, whose 'affection is simple and charming', and Marie, 'better read', Marcel would remark, but 'less literary in her language'), Arthur, the manservant, and some extra help brought in for important dinner parties.* There was no coachman, it appears, nor a chauffeur (we know that when he lived in Auteuil, Doctor Proust used to catch the Auteuil–Madeleine omnibus or he hired cabs). Marcel maintained the most courteous and solicitous relationships with the servants, and he continued to write to them when they were ill, if they had to go away or were called up during the war, or once they had retired. This kindness, which he must have inherited from his mother, would one day save his life, and his work.

THE SECOND TRIP TO VENICE

Instead of rejoining his parents at Évian,† and in order to escape all the confusion and distress – as well as the dust – caused by the move, Marcel set off a second time for Venice, having done his best to persuade Douglas Ainslie to go with him. Because he felt a renewed affection for him, he would be happy to view with him certain masterpieces that related to his sensitivity, and in which he believed he 'would appreciate the intimations of beauty'.‡ After a first refusal, Marcel took up the challenge again a week later and, in another letter to Ainslie that makes very interesting reading and which has passed largely unnoticed, he set out his projected

---

* In 1899 this meant Eugénie, and Gustave and his wife.

† There is no proof that he made this journey, which other biographers have taken for granted, and which his letter to Ainslie, sent from Paris, seems to belie; whatever the case may be, Marcel did not go directly from Évian to Venice, as has been suggested.

‡ *Corr.*, vol. II, p. 412, between 30 September and 4 October 1900; Proust proposed leaving on Saturday 6 October. No letter referring to this trip survives, and we only know about it because his signature, dated 19 October 1900, was recognized in the register of the convent of San Lazzaro by a French consul (Marie Dujardin, *Le Figaro*, literary supplement, 10 October 1931) and L. Védrines (*BAMP*, no. 4, 1954, pp. 57–60).

journey: 'A thousand vicissitudes have delayed my journey and a thousand other coincidences have set it "afloat" again, as they say. In view of how late in the season it is, it would consist of no more than Venice, Verona and Padua.'[130] Proust wanted to visit Verona, therefore, which he did not know, and to see Padua again, which he had only seen on a quick trip in May; this would explain his very detailed knowledge of Giotto's and Mantegna's frescoes.

We do not know whether or not the young English poet accompanied his friend; it is not impossible: Proust never travelled alone. The drafts of *Albertine disparue* mention a return to Venice which was initially at the planning stage: 'Since she would not be there,' pondered the Narrator, thinking of his mother, 'if I did go she would not want to leave my father and I would be afflicted by that anxiety for which all the beauties of the world are no consolation.'[131] However, without his mother, he would have a few days alone in Venice with the Baroness Putbus' chambermaid.[132] In the same draft, he meets her in Padua, by the highly symbolic Vices and Virtues: 'Then there was the pleasure of feeling that whenever I wanted to go and look at paintings in Venice, or to go to Verona or Torcello, I would have a woman . . .'[133] This erotic scene has disappeared from the final version of *Albertine disparue*. We shall never know what pleasures Marcel sought, or found, in Venice in October 1900; he himself recalled 'the ordinary women', 'the humble working women' whom nothing 'prevented him from loving'.* Along the little streets, the Narrator accosts the 'ordinary girls',[134] and he lets slip the following admission, so characteristic of inverts: 'What I loved, were the young people.'

Another lover of youth, whose aesthetic views Proust disapproved of, but whose fate he would comment upon, died, abandoned, in the Hôtel d'Alsace, rue des Beaux-Arts, on 30 November: Oscar Wilde. Unlike Pierre Louÿs, Paul Fort and Ernest La Jeunesse, Marcel did not attend his funeral. However, on 7 December he did go to the inaugural lecture, given by Henri Bergson, the rising star who, thanks to Ribot, had been elected to the chair of Greek and Latin Philosophy at the Collège de France on 1 April 1900: his course, in 1900–1, was concerned with 'the idea of cause', that is to say, with the 'psychological origins of our belief in the laws of causality'.[135]

---

* Both Painter and Diesbach emphasize this aspect.

CONCLUDING *LA BIBLE D'AMIENS*

At the beginning of 1901 Marcel, who claimed to have been unwell since New Year's Day, worked regularly with his mother on finishing the translation of Chapter IV of Ruskin's book, scrupulously starting where they had left off the previous day.* Perhaps he lacked a friend to whom he could pour out his heart, for he sent a letter to Constantin de Brancovan, who had left for Romania, where he was elected as a member of parliament,† and who had both written and sent telegrams to him. Between the elegant lines, one senses a fervently confessional tone: 'But if you bear in mind that constantly ill, deprived of all pleasures, aims, activities or ambitions, aware that my life is behind me and of the sorrow that I cause my parents, I have very little joy, you will appreciate how important relationships with friends have become for me.'[136] It is not clear whether Marcel was trying to arouse still more pity for himself, or whether this moment of melancholy was due to the approach of 'the shadow line' of his thirtieth birthday.‡ His work, however, gave his life meaning and direction.

Proust would always require an intermediary to put him on the right track, but once he had found it he would venture further than anybody. In re-creating Ruskin's ideas, he would become fully aware of his own, which were beginning to take shape. Hence the introduction of *La Bible d'Amiens*, although made up of articles that had appeared elsewhere (a new form of montage), follows Ruskin closely, but then breaks away in a 'postscript' to denounce the Ruskinian idolatry that confuses truth with beauty. It is possible to see this introduction as a sort of short intellectual novel, for the first chapter, or article, 'Notre-Dame d'Amiens according to Ruskin', relates the trip Proust made to Amiens, and the second, 'John Ruskin', considers the man of genius, and out of this text Proust's personal

---

* *Corr.*, vol. II, 24 January 1901, p. 414: 'I've done no worthwhile work this evening, so I'm left with some tomorrow, which exasperates me.' It is difficult to understand why Painter should have written that only eight letters survive from the year 1901 (p. 350), when volume II of the *Correspondance* contains forty-three.

† It was not until 15 May 1902 that Brancovan launched his review, *La Renaissance latine*, which survived until 1905, and to which Proust would contribute some important pieces – until the two men quarrelled.

‡ A few days later, he had pulled himself together: 'It suits me wonderfully to be on my own!' (*Corr.*, vol. II, p. 418). It is true that this was in order to make Lucien Daudet visit him. On 10 July he declared to Léon Yeatman: 'Today I am thirty years old and I've done nothing!' (ibid., vol. II, p. 32), proof that Ruskin was not enough for him.

aesthetic philosophy, which then took issue with the British aesthetician, gradually emerges: 'No, I would not consider a painting more beautiful just because the artist had painted a hawthorn in the foreground, even though I know of nothing more beautiful than a hawthorn, for I want to be honest and I know that the beauty of a painting does not depend on the things that are represented in it.'[137] And yet Proust, continuing with his account of his spiritual journey, one which he undertook because of Ruskin, showed how the latter had helped him to understand not just Gothic art, but Italy; he then described his trip to Venice, which he would assign to the Narrator in *Albertine disparue*.

The progress made since his first publications is noticeable; between 1900 and 1905, the year he completed his second translation, Proust was equipping himself with an aesthetic viewpoint that would acquire greater depth, but that would not alter in its principles. The artist learns to see the world; if he eschews all influences, he encounters nothing but a vacuum. The critic becomes a writer by submitting himself to art and to ideas that are extraneous to him. 'The novelist's subject, the poet's vision, the philosopher's truth impose themselves in an almost obligatory way, one that is extraneous, as it were, to their thinking. And it is by subjugating his mind in order to execute this vision, to draw close to this truth, that the artist becomes truly himself.'[138] Proust and Ruskin represent the life and death of a passion, which is then resurrected through voluntary memory, the insufficiency of which the introduction to *La Bible d'Amiens* condemns precisely because it is voluntary. In this piece of writing, and in Ruskin as a Proustian character, a prospective critic can thus recognize Elstir, Bergotte, the church at Balbec, which would be completed and revised under the influence of Émile Mâle, and the trip to Venice; the critic would note that the majority of Gothic works of art and Italian paintings mentioned in *À la recherche du temps perdu* were originally commented upon and reproduced by Ruskin, but that erudition stops at the point fictional creation starts: the meaning of these works has been metamorphosed.

ANNA DE NOAILLES' CIRCLE

Because of his own experience, Proust could not have been better placed to understand the illness suffered by Anna de Noailles, Constantin's sister (once again, a woman – in a line that runs from Jeanne Pouquet to the Princesse Soutzo – would take the place of a man for him): 'One must not complain overly about ill health. It is often under the burden of too great a spirit that the body weakens. Conditions of nervousness and enchanting poems may very well be inseparable manifestations of the same tempestuous power.'* Suffering from a type of depression following the birth of her son, she stayed, on Brissaud's advice, at Doctor Sollier's clinic in Boulogne from December 1900 to February 1901 (as Proust would do in 1905). This illness prevented the countess from attending a poetry recital that Marcel had arranged in her honour for 6 May: Cora Laparcerie, of the Odéon, recited two poems from Le Cœur innombrable, 'La conscience' and 'Paroles à la lune', which Anna had sent to Proust before they were published[139] and had rehearsed with the actress. On receiving these poems, he expressed his admiration, as he always would, by picking out a few quotations which led one to think, rightly or wrongly, that he was familiar with the whole work: 'The pigeons that parade past in their whiteness, the sunlit road without shade or bend, the swans that dance in the wind, the unfathomable land of my affections.' Marcel lapsed into the same habit on 19 June,[†] when the same actress recited other poems from the same collection after a grand dinner party. Gradually, Anna replaced Montesquiou in the Proustian world of poetry. When her letters were published and she was no longer fashionable, Proust was criticized for his admiration (shared by France, Loti, Cocteau and many others) for Anna de Noailles. Yet she must have appeared to him as a fine, young prodigy; in that neo-romantic sensitivity, which flows through the verse of Chénier, Lamartine and Musset, he rediscovered the poets that he had been taught to cherish in his childhood, as well as themes that were close to his own,[140] particularly the veneration of feeling and nature.[141] This was why he compared this book to the thing that was dearest to him, 'the scent of hawthorn flowers'. It may be surprising, but given that Proust did not really care for any poet later than Baudelaire and Mallarmé,[142] these neo-romantic poets had the advantage of being

---

* Corr., vol. II, p. 426, May 1901. The same comments are made by Du Boulbon in Le Côté de Guermantes because they stem from the same books and the same experiences. Cf. p. 424, another idea that is found in À la recherche. 'It is wrong to be sad when one doesn't have things. It is true that they generally come when one no longer wants them.'

† On 30 May Sarah Bernhardt, who had been told about Le Cœur innombrable by Hahn and, according to Proust 'had been very enthusiastic' (ibid., vol. II, p. 428), recited some poems from it at Montesquiou's home in Neuilly, and at the Pavillon des Muses, as did Julia Bartet in June, at another salon.

alive and of belonging to the aristocracy, and they encouraged relatives to come along to the Prousts' very middle-class home.

So it was that at the dinner party on 19 June, Marcel invited, along with the Noailles, Anatole France and his daughter, the Prince and Princesse Edmond de Polignac, Hélène de Caraman-Chimay, the Marquis and Marquise d'Eyragues,[143] Brancovan, Mme de Brantes, the Comte de Briey, Clément de Maugny, Gabriel de La Rochefoucauld, Abel Hermant and Lucien and Léon Daudet.[144] He thus skilfully blended Dreyfusards with anti-Dreyfusards, aristocrats with the bourgeoisie, and writers with close friends: 'The waves of understanding and kindliness, which emanated from Marcel, spread in flurries and spirals over the dining-room and the drawing-rooms, and for two hours, among the Atreids, the most genuine warmth prevailed. I do not believe anyone else in Paris could have achieved this tour de force.'*

THE DEATH OF EDMOND DE POLIGNAC

On 8 August Prince Edmond de Polignac died. This delightful old gentleman, the son of Charles X's last minister (responsible for the decrees that would bring about the 1830 revolution) and a man who did not care for women, had, in 1893, married Winnaretta Singer (of the sewing-machine family, whose sister had married the Duc Decazes), a woman who did not care for men, and whose paintings were exhibited at the annual art salons. Marcel would have the opportunity to remark on this alliance of Sodom and Gomorrah. The couple were united in their love of receptions and of music, as they were in their intertwined initials on the cast-iron banisters that adorned the staircase of their town house, first in the rue Cortambert and later in the Avenue Henri-Martin. Owner of a beautiful house at Fontainebleau, the Prince had also acquired the Palazzo Manzoni in Venice, 'the only city', he used to say, 'where it is possible to converse with the window open without raising one's voice'.[145] It was from here that he organized one of the *sgondolate* described by Reynaldo Hahn, with a piano in a gondola and a group of friends: Paderewski played Chopin, Hahn sang Fauré songs.[146] In the portrait he sketched of the prince in *Le*

---

* Léon Daudet, *Salons et journaux*, in *Souvenirs et polémiques*, Laffont, coll. Bouquins, 1992, p. 505. Among those unable to be there were Montesquiou, Mme Arman, who, without Marcel, had organized a similar party, Dreyfus (who was only invited the day before), and Lucien, whose absence upset Proust.

Figaro,[147] Proust saw him above all as a precursor of the Guermantes: 'Nature, which maintains breeding and does not foresee individuals, had endowed him with a slender body and the elegant and forceful demeanour of a warrior and a courtier. Gradually, the spiritual fire that burned within Prince Edmond de Polignac shaped his face to resemble his mind. But his mask retained the features of his lineage, prior to the advent of his own individual spirit. His body and his face resembled a disused dungeon that had been converted into a library. I remember the sorrowful day of his burial in the church, hung with large black draperies on which there stood out in scarlet, beneath the closed circle of the coronet, the letter P. His individuality had been extinguished, he had returned to his family. He was no more than a Polignac.'[148] This scene and these images would feature in *Le Temps retrouvé*, at the burial of Saint-Loup.[149]

Considered by his family to be an 'insufferable maniac',[150] sickly and oversensitive to the cold, like Marcel, and constantly wrapped in rugs, he used to repeat, like Bergotte: 'What can you expect? . . . Anagorus said it, life is a journey!'[151] This 'sweet prince', as Proust wrote, quoting France quoting *Hamlet*,[152] was also 'a great wit and an able musician';[153] a composer of religious music, songs and outdoor music, a man of 'advanced' literary, artistic and political views, he had his moments of relaxation that were 'more or less childlike and mad', at which Marcel would be present; at these soirées that were transformed into 'jolly parties', he would perform burlesques and play *valses comiques* on the piano. In the hall of the house at rue Cortambert, Proust had listened to Brahms dances, the latest songs, as well as one of the models for Vinteuil's sonata, Fauré's First Sonata,* Bach sonatas and Beethoven quartets. On the walls, he admired the Impressionists,† among them 'the finest painting of Monet's' that he knew: 'A Field of Tulips near Haarlem'. This was why Proust, many years later, in 1918, loyal to his old friend whom, in his books, he had quoted, rejuvenated and buried, would compose the following dedication for *À l'ombre des jeunes filles en fleurs*: 'To the dear and venerated memory of the

---

* Since the principal model for the 'little phrase' comes from Saint-Saëns' First Sonata, it is worth noting what the composer wrote in 1877 on the publication of Fauré's sonata: 'It blends a deep musical knowledge with great melodic abundance and a sort of unconscious naïvety which is the most irresistible of forces. In this sonata is found everything that can enchant, delicacy, originality of form, the pursuit of strange tones and modulations and the use of the most unexpected rhythms. Over all this there hovers a charm which envelops the whole work.' Quoted by R. Hahn, *Thèmes variés*, Janin, 1946, p. 141.

† As the Narrator does the Elstirs at the Duc de Guermantes' home.

Prince de Polignac,/ Homage from one to whom he showed so much kindness and who still admires, in his reminiscences, the uniqueness of a delightful mind and spirit.'[154] Since the princess did not give her consent, the dedication was never printed.

ANTOINE BIBESCO

At 69 rue de Courcelles lived the Prince and Princesse Alexandre Bibesco. The princess (*née* Hélène Epourano, daughter of a former prime minister of Romania),[155] who was very musical, hosted a literary salon. Her son Antoine remembered having heard her play duets with Saint-Saëns and Fauré. Paderewski made his début at her home, and she launched the career of Enesco (who Proust would hear performing Franck's sonata). Gounod and Delibes both sang there, accompanying themselves at the piano. Massenet and Debussy used to visit. France, Lemaître, Loti, Renan, Leconte de Lisle, Maeterlinck and Doumic all came regularly to the house. They were joined by artists such as Bonnat, Bonnard, Vuillard and Redon, and by some ambassadors.* At one of these soirées, Antoine noted 'a slightly stooped man, with very dark, very long hair, who was very pale, with eyes that looked like Japanese lacquer. He held out his hand to me . . . He stretched out a soft, limp hand'.† They did not strike up a friendship immediately, and Antoine, who was preparing for the diplomatic corps and would become secretary at the Romanian Legation in Paris,‡ left to do his military service in Romania and did not return to Paris until the autumn of 1901. It was then that he renewed his friendship with Proust. His brother Emmanuel was on good terms with Marcel at this time, for, among other interests, he shared a liking for Ruskin and for Gothic cathedrals.

Prince Alexandre Bibesco (1841–1911), the son of a ruling prince of

---

* Antoine Bibesco prefaced his edition of Proust's letters with some invaluable reminiscences (*Lettres de Marcel Proust à Bibesco*, Lausanne, Clairefontaine, 1949, pp. 29–31, 120).

† Ibid., p. 30. 'There was nothing pleasant about his handshake. I would show him later how to shake hands with a grip. – "If I followed your example," he objected, "people would think I was an invert."'

‡ Mentioned as such by Proust, who drew a Hellenic and lyrical portrait of him worthy of Bloch in 'Le salon de Madeleine Lemaire' (*Le Figaro*, 11 May 1903, and *CSB*, p. 461). Moreover, on the occasion of the performance of Antoine Bibesco's play at the Théâtre Marigny in 1904, he wrote an article-cum-interview (posthumous) for Serge.Basset, paragraphs of which appeared, under the latter's name, in *Le Figaro* of 8 April 1904 (Bibesco, *Lettres de Marcel Proust*, pp. 160–4; *CSB*, pp. 499–500).

Wallachia, was a bizarre, scholarly man, a great bibliophile and former president of the Société Linguistique de France, who was something of an embarrassment to his children, Emmanuel (1877–1917), Antoine (1878–1951) and the Comtesse Odon de Montesquiou.[156] Left a widower in 1902, in 1908 he would make a second marriage to Hélène Reyé, an actress from the Théâtre de l'Ambigu, and as a result fell out with his entire family. The Bibescos were cousins of the Brancovans, and it was at their house that Marcel had met them in 1899. During the summer of 1901, while his parents were in Zermatt, he did not leave Paris (despite a few plans for visits to Gothic sites, in particular Mantes, Caen and Laon with Billy, and for a rather more surprising trip to Illiers,* in the company, he hoped, of Bibesco and Fénelon, possibly to see the churches there once more). He went for walks in the Bois de Boulogne, or went shopping in a hired cab, and made the most of Marie's[†] home cooking: 'Lunch', he would say with an epicureanism that was most unlike him, 'is my high point.'[157] He also went to the Opéra on 21 August to see Rossini's great and final lyric work, *William Tell*, and, in a rather different vein, being a lover of theatrical spectaculars, he went to see Jules Verne's and Dennery's *Around the World in Eighty Days*, which was enjoying a triumphant success at the Châtelet.

On 24 August, on a visit to his Nathan cousins in Versailles, he was laid low by an attack of asthma that was 'so appalling that I did not know where to shelter, or where to hide myself'.[158] These attacks, which came at night, lasted until the end of the month, and Marcel, who was feeling lonely and anxious and feared that he might have worms after consulting Professor Brissaud's book, which attributed certain types of asthma attacks to these parasites, asked his mother to question his brother as to possible cures. Antoine Bibesco offered to visit him at home and bring his 'precious photographs' of cathedrals – photography was a hobby of both Antoine and Emmanuel.[159] However, on 7 September Marcel bravely set off with

---

* *Corr.*, vol. II, p. 452, 8 September 1901: 'In any case Illiers one of these days' (to his mother). And to Bibesco: 'As you know, I am going to Illiers on Sunday. Illiers is an hour away from Chartres and I shall probably stop for a few moments at Chartres' (ibid., vol. II, p. 454, 3 or 10 August 1901). He tried to borrow Mâle's book from Bibesco to quote from it in his notes; it is likely that he borrowed it (again) from Billy – instead of buying a copy!

† Because of this we have a notion of what his diet, which was less sparse than at the end of his life, consisted of: 'Every day I have a beefsteak, which is huge and not a scrap of which is left, platefuls of fried potatoes, some Gruyère cheese, *fromage à la crème*, peaches and beer' (ibid., p. 441, 26 August 1901; cf. p. 444).

Léon Yeatman for Amiens and Abbeville, where he 'did a bit of work in the church', that is to say at Saint-Wulfram, which was an opportunity to complete his notes and his introduction to the *Bible*.[160] He returned exhausted. Among the books he was reading at the time (which he made use of again in his *Carnet de 1908*) were *Le Comte de Sallenauve* and *La Famille Beauvisage*, sequels written by Charles Rabou for *Le Député d'Arcis*, which Balzac left unfinished.[161]

Antoine Bibesco, whom Marcel referred to as 'a formidable and charming titan',[162] would soon occupy his vacant heart.* He reminded him of Achilles or of Theseus, and his words, like the bees of Hymettus, 'distilled a delicious honey and yet, in spite of that, did not lack a certain bite'.[163] This prince, this hero, had, as Marcel would soon discover, 'a deliciously cruel mind', he was 'serious about ideas and sarcastic where people were concerned', witty, but capable of becoming rapidly malicious, a gossip, someone who lacked tact, a tease to the point of spitefulness[†] and a braggart. A pleasure-seeker, he thought that 'there is no delight or happiness apart from immediate pleasure'.[164] However, he believed he had a literary vocation: from the age of twenty he had written several plays; in 1901 he tried to have *La Lutte* staged; *Un jaloux* would be produced by the L'Œuvre company at Marigny in 1904; in 1910 he arranged for *Jacques Abran* to be put on at the Théâtre Réjane (there were eleven performances). Marcel had made a number of suggestions[165] about this play and tried to help him have it performed.

He only liked women ('I never stop hearing new stories about the women you have attempted to violate,' his friend wrote to him in December 1904),[166] but Marcel was sometimes attracted by virile men, for whom he was doomed to profess a platonic affection. Bibesco, for his part, influenced by crime or adventure novels, believed that friendship could be 'something secret and absolute' and he has described how he proposed to Marcel: 'A pact whereby, without anyone knowing, I would keep him informed about other people's opinions of him, while he, on his side, would let me know

---

* This was when he wrote to Lucien Daudet, who was in love with the Comte Clary: 'It's strange to think that we loved one another! And then, that's that!' (*Corr.*, vol. II, p. 448). See above, p. 299.

† *Corr.*, vol. IV, p. 370. Proust added: 'You complain about often encountering hostility, but it is you who are often hostile ... You are excessively touchy, you get angry about things that are unimportant and you are constantly doing to others things which, according to your scale of values, would call for murder at the very least.'

what others said about me.'* Secrets were sealed with the use of the word 'tomb' – *tombeau*; the levels of friendship were described as 'rising' or 'falling'. Later, the pact was broken: 'In spite of that,' Bibesco declared, 'I found in Marcel an incomparable friend.'[167] It is hard to form an opinion about this complex character, 'nonchalant, insolent, indiscreet, charming', who was always eager to try out anything new and to make fun of everything and everybody.† 'Far more than other friends of Proust's whom I used to know, Lacretelle, Morand, Gautier-Vignal, who were evening visitors, if I may put it that way, Antoine was a key to a younger Proust, in the morning of his life, avid to learn, to acquire knowledge and to develop himself, and happy to share in the fantasies, gaiety and wild pranks of Emmanuel and Antoine, brothers who were so dissimilar and yet so united, and who had the wit to recognize him, discover him and worship him, as had Pierre Lavallée, Armand de Guiche or Léon Daudet, at a time when no one understood him; each in their own way, with conviction, enthusiasm and perseverance, they helped gradually to reveal who Marcel Proust was and what he would give to the world.'‡ At the end of his life, Antoine rather grandly telephoned his friend for a last time and said: 'Have you read *The Death of Ivan Illich*? Well, in a month it will be the death of Antoine Bibesco!'§

It was through him that in October Marcel met another signatory to the pact, Bertrand de Fénelon, whom he already referred to as Nonelef; in the secret society that Bibesco had devised, names were replaced by their anagram: 'Ocsebib', 'Lecram'. We cannot be sure whether Marcel was immediately aware that this young diplomat with an illustrious name, who was born in 1878, was an invert, nor, indeed, whether he was one at the time: *Le Carnet de 1908* alludes to 'Bertrand in love with the sister of Louisa' de Mornand. He was described by Paul Morand as 'the delightful young man with fair hair and blue eyes, the darling of the ladies in 1900, who was used as a model for Saint-Loup' and he added that 'he would transfer well and truly to heterodoxy, or, more precisely, to bimetallism.'¶

---

* Bibesco, *Lettres de Marcel Proust*, p. 120. Marcel had already concluded a pact of absolute sincerity with Reynaldo, which, because of jealous cross-questioning, led directly to their breaking off relations.

† As Denise Mayer, who was close to Antoine at the end of his life, has described him to me.

‡ D. Mayer in a letter to the author on 31 January 1983: these lines are printed by way of homage to this accomplished, sensitive and scholarly woman who died in 1994.

§ Ibid.

¶ P. Morand, *Le Visiteur du soir*, Geneva, La Palatine, 1949, p. 26; the text begins as follows: 'Critics have accused Proust of imposing on his heroes, particularly on Saint-Loup, inclinations which were

The Caillavets emphasized his meanness, but, like the Fénelons, they thought of him as a prospective husband for Simone de Caillavet. Their engagement was, in fact, announced at the beginning of the war,* the latter claimed, which puts us in mind of Saint-Loup marrying Gilberte.† Georges de Lauris, who would come to know Proust through Bertrand, has recalled the brilliance of the circles in which he moved, his vivacity, 'the amused and often affectionate irony of his expression', his courageous spirit, his formidably frank opinions.[168] A man of the left,‡ a supporter of Combes and secular education, 'antisocial',[169] with literary tastes that were very different from Marcel's,§ he had the physical features of Saint-Loup, and his mother those of Mme de Marsantes. As early as 30 October, Proust inscribed one of the copies of *Les Plaisirs et les Jours* printed on Japanese paper to Fénelon 'in the hope that he will live up to the great literary name he bears, and in the less certain hope of becoming his friend'.[170] Later on, he made Bibesco his confidant, if not his intermediary, in his 'affection' for Fénelon, whom they nicknamed 'Ses Yeux bleus'[171] [His Blue Eyes], after the title of a play by Bibesco's friend, Henry Bernstein. And so when a disappointed Marcel moved from Antoine to Bertrand, a strange triangular relationship among these three men came to be established.

However, in the autumn of 1901 it was Antoine Bibesco whom Marcel was trying to win over. He employed a tone very similar to that which he had used with Reynaldo: 'I was very sad not to see you this evening. Up until midnight I had retained some hope. But it is half past one and you will not come again!'[172] Suggesting several further rendezvous, he added: 'But perhaps you don't want to see me any more,' and ended with, 'And be nice.' Shortly afterwards, he addressed some lines of verse to him in praise of his oriental ancestry and of his mind: 'For our powerful spirits swift as the storm/ Frequent the universe from its base to its summit/ We are called X and Antoine Bibesco.'[173] In other verses we can make

---

uncharacteristic of the people he was writing about. Yet Proust invented nothing; his information had been pumped from the best springs.'

* Marcel Proust 'sent a whole host of gigantic chrysanthemums' (ibid., p. 538).

† Particularly since Simone also attributed the plan to Proust. The marriage would not take place and, curiously enough, Simone de Caillavet has bequeathed us an imaginary account of this 'engagement' (M. Maurois, *Les Cendres brûlantes*, Flammarion, 1986, p. 537ff.).

‡ Marcel compared him to Robespierre (*Corr.*, vol. III, p. 103).

§ Ibid., p. 146: 'I am sad to feel myself so far removed from everything that Bertrand likes in literature.'

out the acrostic of Bibesco and some almost amorous words, in which Marcel refers to himself as a mortal wounded "neath your enchanted eyes', and he concludes: 'he who at your feet proclaimed your future,/ O preserve a tender memory of him at least'.[174] The inscription which he wrote in a copy of *Les Plaisirs et les Jours* on 30 October repeated the lines from *Hamlet* which he quoted so often:[175] 'To Antoine Bibesco,/ whom I love and admire' – 'Goodnight sweet Prince,/ And flights of angels sing thee to thy rest.' He attached a photograph of himself.* No doubt in an attempt to impress him, Proust invited him to dinner with Bergson – who, 'tired', put off the engagement.[176] However, he did not reveal his innermost feelings to him, which, in their private language, they referred to by the neologism, based on the name of Comte Sala, of 'Salaïsm'.[177] Proust thus gradually developed a theory of friendship, supported by quotations from La Bruyère and Pascal, and therefore above all suspicion, for and on behalf of Bibesco, and we come across it in his work, sometimes in the form of reflections, sometimes in the portrayal of the relationship between the Narrator and Saint-Loup: 'It's all too much to bother about friendship, which is a thing without reality. Renan tells us to shun individual friendships. Emerson says that we should change friends as we go along.'[178] And then how many visits were announced and then cancelled, traps set and lies told in order to discover the truth: 'I really cannot go out this evening and I am worried that I may have explained myself badly to you since you thought I would be coming.'[179] Marcel practised Baron de Charlus' circumlocutions: 'We must have a few minutes' frank explanation together which will simplify, I won't say the future of our existence, but the future of that portion of our existence which will be characterized by . . . what I am perhaps presumptuous enough to call our friendship';† the end of the letter vigorously rejects all suspicion of 'Salaïsm'; if Marcel talks a lot about it, it is because it interests him 'in the same way as the Gothic, although much less'. We are now far removed from the frankness of his declarations to Halévy, Dreyfus and Bizet. Proust has to dissemble in order to steal a little secret pleasure, and to describe what may be love as friendship: only jealousy flaunts itself fearlessly; there are jealous friendships. That was why he was so keen to introduce his new friend to Reynaldo, just as one introduces a fiancée to one's family, and to initiate

---

* As he did for Léon Yeatman.

† *Corr.*, vol. II, p. 469, 11 November 1901. During this period of warm friendship Marcel wrote a letter a day to Antoine.

him into the latter's '*moschant*' jargon. Furthermore, the two friends were counting on Hahn to persuade Sarah Bernhardt (whom they referred to as 'Haras')[180] to agree to perform in Bibesco's play, *La Lutte*. True model for la Berma that she was, she was rehearsing the part of Phèdre for a Thursday matinée at the time, and turned the play down. To console the author, Proust painted a curious portrait of the tragedienne, 'a woman who is able to resolve the difficult problem of being taken for a woman of twenty at the age of sixty by people who, once they have seen her at close quarters, cannot bear to part from her, and who has a sort of genius when she acts – but whose literary judgement is utterly nil and contemptible' ... And then, as was ever the case with Marcel, there was a tiff, an extremely stiff letter in December, accompanied by worries about his health.

That same month Proust delivered the manuscript of *La Bible d'Amiens* to a publisher; hitherto he had only handed in some extracts which gave the best possible impression of Ruskin, 'the one that most accorded with his genius'.[181] The Société d'Édition Artistique, which was run by Paul Ollendorff, and later by Georges Art, and which published a first volume of Ruskin's complete works in 1900, had asked for an unabridged translation of the book; the firm had then gone bankrupt, which prompted Proust to offer it to Mercure de France.[182] He seems to have suffered a painful experience with Ollendorff: 'As a publisher he had had possession of my Ruskin for a year before I managed to have it returned to me. Had he not left the publishing house and thus forced himself or rather his successor into general liquidation, I don't know whether I would ever have seen my Bible, which was both cruelly ignored and jealously guarded.'[183] As he did with every rejection, Proust took the opportunity to enlarge his book, although at the beginning of 1902 the delay in obtaining a response seems to have considerably slowed down his work rate. Nevertheless, it was the Bible itself that kept him busy – he had asked the Noailles for a good translation – since Ruskin's text was crammed with references to the scriptures.* He also took the opportunity, as we have seen, to write a few passages on Mme Jacques de Réveillon (the Baronne Deslandes), Fénelon, and Mme Martial (Mme Hébert, later to be the model for Mme Elstir). Marcel no longer knew what he ought to be writing, particularly since, in the early months of the year, he was suffering from asthma attacks, which meant that he could only go out once a week. Was this the

---

* 'It was the Bible itself that I used,' Proust pointed out (*Bible*, p. 12).

effect of his literary disappointment, or of his emotional torments?

To return to Proust's and Bibesco's relationship, in the early months of 1902 it changed, bit by bit, in its tone, its nature and its intensity. The invalid certainly succeeded in drawing the healthier of the two to his bedside, but not as frequently as he would have wished. He did not refrain from talking to him about inversion: 'I have had some rather profound thoughts about Salaïsm, which will be communicated to you in one of our next metaphysical discussions. There is no need to tell you that they are of extreme severity. Yet as far as people are concerned it remains a philosophical curiosity. Dreyfusard, anti-Dreyfusard, Salaïst, anti-Salaïst, these are virtually the only things worth knowing about an imbecile.'* And then there were Antoine's mysterious absences, the waiting in vain, the secrets imparted to others, which made Proust want to become a Carthusian monk ('Silence Silence Silence'),[184] the fruitless enticements (such as promising him photographs which would divert him),[185] Bibesco's sudden departures for which he made amends with kindnesses such as chocolates at Easter, a present of Maeterlinck's latest book, *Le Temple enseveli*, the title of which would perturb Proust;[186] all these would lead the future author of *Sodome* towards the 'subjective and jealous disposition of a male Andromeda† for ever chained to his rock, who suffers at the sight of Antoine Bibesco disappearing here, there and everywhere and who is unable to follow him'.[187] With Bibesco, he added, he had nothing more to lose, whereas with Fénelon, he was still – and this is an important remark in the Proustian map of affection – 'at the hopeful stage'. But, alas, Fénelon dispersed his affections 'over so many people'! 'I, too, disperse mine, but successively. Each one's share is shorter but larger.'‡ And, adding the inevitable final judgement, already reminiscent of Charlus: 'you have infinitely exceeded the maximum time that I allot to my friendships. Let us quarrel quickly.' Thus did Marcel, in bed – like Joubert

---

* *Corr.*, vol. III, p. 43, in about April 1902. Having spoken in public too openly about the habits of Comte Sala, Bibesco would write him a letter of excuses and denial, dictated by Proust, who told Antoine: 'We must absolutely stop this horrible business of being the public denouncers of Salaïsm' (ibid., p. 75).

† *RTP*, vol. III, p. 28: the lonely invert is compared to 'a strange Andromeda which no Argonaut will come to rescue'. See above, p. 225. Cf. draft I, p. 933: 'A few of them, silent and marvellously handsome, wonderful Andromedas attached to a sexual organ which would doom them to solitude . . . hateful to those whom they look to for love, unable to satisfy he who is aroused by their beauty.'

‡ *Corr.*, vol. III, p. 62. As with Lucien Daudet, it was when a passion came to an end that Proust described its progress and duration – Bibesco: 1901–2; with Fénelon, it would be 1902–3.

in his, as described by Chateaubriand – destroy his spirit while believing he was resting his body.*

The fact is, they were no longer two, but three. Gradually Bibesco took on the role of confidant as Marcel confessed his affection for Bertrand de Fénelon.† It became his duty to provide the invalid with information about his new friend: where did he dine last night? With whom? Why had he not come to Larue's? Significantly, Marcel attached great importance to the three of them going to see *Tristan and Isolde*, on 7 June, at the Château d'Eau, starring Van Dyck and Litvinne, and conducted by Cortot. This opera, which had its Paris première in 1899, is mentioned nine times in *À la recherche*; the love affairs have gone, but the impression left by this masterpiece remains. It was around this time that, dining with Proust at Larue's, Fénelon walked over the tables and the benches in the restaurant to bring him his overcoat. Marcel would never forget this gesture of friendship, this aristocratic indifference to what anyone might say: we are given a description of his friend and of this scene in *Jean Santeuil*[188] and it is described again, as we know, in *Le Côté de Guermantes*, with Robert de Saint-Loup.[189] There is nothing in his correspondence to record that Marcel was aware of the death, on 14 July, of Charles Haas. It was seven years later, retrospectively, that the novelist's memory resuscitated the model for Swann. And yet 'Swann in love' was what Marcel was experiencing with Fénelon. He described all the details of his love to Bibesco (whom he addressed as '*tu*' from now on).

BERTRAND DE FÉNELON

In August 1902 Marcel felt the inklings of a 'strong affection' for Fénelon,‡ following on from what he had felt for Clément de Maugny,§ a fondness which could only lead to unhappiness, even though it lasted for quite a long time: a year, or a year and a half, as had been the case with Lucien or Flers. Absence would have been a useful solution: either for Bertrand

---

* Ibid.; it was Proust who quoted Chateaubriand.

† The relationship between Fénelon and Proust is considerably harder to fathom since it has not been possible to publish, or even read, their correspondence, with the exception of a few very rare letters. A great part of it has been destroyed.

‡ Bertrand's family, and particularly his mother, did not look favourably on this relationship (unpublished and confidential source).

§ *Corr.*, vol. XIV, p. 135, to C. de Maugny: 'Bertrand de Fénelon, who, when you stopped seeing me, became my Clément and has proved to be an incomparable friend to me . . .'

to be appointed to a foreign post, or for Marcel to set off for Biskra or Cairo! But if neither of the two went away? In that case Proust would be doomed to sadness, on account of the sort of person his friend was. Kindness was a part of his character, as his gesture at Larue's showed, and at every fresh encounter: it fired their friendship. Marcel therefore pretended to try to struggle 'against that Siren with the sea-blue eyes, who comes in a direct line of descent from Telemachus, of whom M. Bérard must have found traces near Calypso's island',* but as in a Marivaux play, he was already too late, even if he did try to space out their meetings. He revealed, incidentally, three reasons for his attraction: his friend's illustrious, literary and aristocratic breeding; the colour of his eyes (Saint-Loup too, like his aunt, the Duchesse de Guermantes, would be fair-haired and have blue eyes); and his metamorphosis into a siren, therefore into a woman. The novelist would proceed no differently in *À l'ombre des jeunes filles en fleurs*.

Marcel would have had an excellent means of absenting himself had he accompanied his parents, who left for Évian on 12 August. He was careful not to do this, perhaps imagining that he might go travelling with Bertrand. As soon as his mother had left, however, he felt abandoned, for Fénelon and Bibesco† were away elsewhere and he was not sleeping well, so he telephoned Doctor Bize (his general practitioner, who had been recommended to him by Robert Proust), who was unable to see him, and then, less on account of his asthma, which was not troubling him at that moment, but because of his 'haywire' pulse rate, he consulted Doctor Vaquez,[190] a cardiologist and a qualified professor of the Faculty

---

* *Corr.*, vol. III, p. 88, 10 August 1902. As P. Kolb indicates, V. Bérard had just published *Les Phéniciens de l'Odyssée*, in which he based Homer's geography on the voyages of the Phoenician sailors. Cf. *RTP*, vol. II, p. 301: 'Geographers or archaeologists may conduct us over Calypso's island.' Here we have a further proof of the way in which Proust made use, many years later, of his scholarly reading as much as he did the events in his private life: Bérard, whom he read at the time he was in love with Fénelon, is used again to convey the Narrator's feelings for the girls at Balbec, and, beneath the coats of varnish, we discover Marcel's memories of Fénelon.

† *Corr.*, vol. III, p. 92, 14 August 1902, to his mother: 'I am quite deserted, as Fénelon has taken no notice of your advice . . . and Bibesco has been taken up every evening lately, immersing himself in a combination of ham acting and love affairs.' It is clear that, ever since childhood, it was in the evening that Marcel needed company. Cf. 15 August, to Bibesco: 'I did not see your friend Nonelef yesterday evening. Nor Ocsebib. And Maman has left. Which isolation not even a belated visit from Reynaldo could make up for, and neither could a bit of debauchery beforehand' (ibid., p. 95). One might guess that it was the 'bit of debauchery' that did not satisfy him. And on 16 August to Bibesco, whom he had asked to come and see him: 'It is in the evenings that I feel unhappy' (ibid., p. 100).

of Medicine. Vaquez found his heart to be 'unscathed', advised Marcel to remain in bed, 'even if he feels sad', rather than tire his heart any more or make himself more anxious, and he prescribed not bromide, a powerful sedative, but a gramme of trional each day, with occasional pauses (his patient decided to do without this hypnotic,* a substitute for veronal, for the time being). The doctor advised his patient against taking morphine ('he need have no fear of that!' Marcel commented) and alcohol.† Because Marcel must have mentioned that he was love-sick: 'Vaquez wonders how it is that invalids are not satisfied with their own illness, but insist on creating new ones, thus making themselves wretched over people who are not worth the trouble. I admired this philosopher,'[191] he told his mother. Much later, Proust would reply to the doctor's argument: 'It is rather like being astonished that people deign to suffer from cholera because of something as small as the virgule bacillus.'[192]

No sooner had he left his surgery than, by a twist of irony that was often his fate, not only did Marcel sustain an attack of asthma, but, in the evening, he dined alone at Larue's, because Fénelon and Brancovan had cancelled their booking at eight o'clock and because, in mid-August, there were no other customers. As for Bibesco, believing himself to be a man of the theatre, he went around with actresses, and with writers such as Porto-Riche and Bernstein.‡ Marcel, who was unhappy enough as it was, now had to confront an unexpected adversary in the shape of his mother, who had written to him with some home truths, in particular the fact that some people had just as many worries as he did and 'what is more, have to work to support their families'. His response to this, firm and dignified as ever, would not vary right up to *Le Temps retrouvé*: 'There is work and work. Literary work makes a constant demand on

* As D. Mabin notes (*Le Sommeil de Proust*, PUF, 1992, p. 184), it was in order to soothe him and help him sleep that Vaquez 'unwisely' prescribed trional for Marcel; but it was also for its anti-asthmatic properties, 'for according to the concepts of the time the origins of asthma were primarily "nervous", one might actually say psychosomatic'. At the same time, Proust was doing his best to wear less, to forgo 'the second pair of underpants' and, when in bed, 'the second Pyrenean wool cardigan'. Nevertheless, he begged Brancovan, who invited him out on 17 August, to allow him to dress as he pleased, and 'not to torment him about what he wore' (*Corr.*, vol. III, p. 104). Wool can also be a drug: asthmatics always wrap themselves up too warmly, for fear of catching cold.

† Marcel must have considered that beer was not alcohol, for he drank, and would continue to drink, 'oceans' of it (ibid., p. 110).

‡ *Corr.*, vol. III, p. 129: 'Alas, since you found this infinitely more sought-after friend on the Marché, you have made a sudden Détour away from me' (an allusion to two plays written by Bernstein, who would be one of the models for Bloch).

those feelings that are linked to pain.'* For the time being, and as he did every time anyone suggested he get on with work, he replied that, on the contrary, he needed frivolity and distractions, which was why he dined so frequently in restaurants such as Larue's, Durand's and Weber's: 'They're my substitute for Évian, for going away, for having a holiday.† He nevertheless visited Versailles, where he saw Constantin Ullmann, a friend of Reynaldo and Madrazo (it must strike you as very Salaïst',[193] he remarked to Bibesco), as well as René Peter,‡ who did him 'a lot of good'.[194]

This restless end to the summer, consisting as it did of sentimental trysts that succeeded or failed, jealous questioning of Bibesco§ and the latter's gossip, all of which reduced Marcel to despair, for he dreaded appearing as an invert in the eyes of his family and his friends,¶ did feature a few social activities as well. On 1 September he gave a dinner on his own for the Comtesse de Noailles, her sister and her husband, their devoted escort Abel Hermant, Bibesco and, of course, Fénelon. On 3 September Bertrand gave a tea party at Versailles which Marcel attended. In his 'great longing to see that beautiful lake again', he even thought of

---

* Ibid., p. 109, 18 August 1902. Proust added a quotation from 'Don Paez' (*Premières Poésies*) by Musset, whose concept of the relationship between the pains of love and the work of art he shared: 'When by so many other ties thou art linked with grief'. This line, in fact, comes after the following, which he did not quote: 'Love, curse of the world, abysmal folly,/ Thou who art linked to voluptuous pleasures by so frail a bond.' Marcel would experience far more grief in love than he would sensual pleasure.

† A premonitory remark: from 1914 onwards, he would take no other breaks apart from visits to restaurants. Though he never alluded to them, he was faithful to the strictures of Montaigne and the Roman moralists, and he would derive much more from these places than many a traveller on a world tour.

‡ René Peter (1872–1947), son of a colleague of Adrien Proust, a future playwright, biographer of Debussy and historian of the Académie française; he had homes in Paris and in Versailles, and Proust would be particularly close to him during the period he stayed at the Hôtel des Reservoirs in 1906. He planned to write a play with him which would portray the Montjouvain episode in *À la recherche*.

§ 'My "Fin de la jalousie" is causing me mortal anguish,' he wrote (*Corr.*, vol. III, p. 134). 'An entire hidden aspect of the life of "Ses Yeux bleus" may be discoverable this evening . . . without you I can learn nothing' (ibid., p. 135, to Bibesco). 'If I had need of you for my secret police operation' (ibid., p. 137); and Bibesco: 'Yesterday "Ses Yeux bleus" lunched at Durand's – reunited with Constantin – and turned down an invitation to go to the Folies Bergère' (ibid., p. 141). The Narrator would spy on Albertine in the same way.

¶ Ibid., p. 134: 'Of course, this would not necessarily have made me look like a Salaïst. But removed from the interpretation that your knowledge of my character and the daily course of events may have given you, it would look extremely odd.'

joining his parents at Évian, but then, feeling too tired, he gave up the idea. Yet on 6 September there was a sudden departure for Amboise, accompanied by Bertrand, who, however, did not continue with him to the Daudets. Having caught sight of Fénelon on the train, Lucien told his mother: 'I saw a ridiculous little creature, even smaller than Marcel.' Years later Proust would tell Daudet that, as he never thought of his own physique, this was the first time it had occurred to him that he was small.* The Daudets lived at the Château de Pray, a building in the Renaissance style with turrets at each corner, with a very fine view over the Loire. Marcel spent 'a delightful time' there, 'thanks to the sunshine, which in spite of everything still retained a great power over [him], a power to bind and unloose many things, and to the noblest type of river and flowers'.[195] Similarly, in his letter of thanks to Mme Daudet, he also referred to the Loire and to the flowers, which he had left suddenly in the morning, to set off, with Lucien,† by motor car, for the Château du Fresne, the home of Mme de Brantes, at Authon, returning to Paris that same evening. This 'headlong flight' was due to his longing to see Fénelon again.[196] It was all that Proust would ever see of the Touraine, where he would have Albertine flee to and where she would die.

Marcel also went to Chartres, and came back feeling very tired. Ruskin had planned a book about the cathedral, which was to be entitled 'The Sources of the Eure'; Proust would retain the lesson he learnt, of not separating the beauty of churches, or of characters, from the charms of the landscape from which they had sprung.[197] As he did in Venice, he took the opportunity to make notes of the utmost precision: he did not fail to mention the location and the appearance of every single statue, even if it meant ending on a quotation from Mâle. When Proust went to call on Charles Ephrussi on 16 September, it was with the same concerns in mind, hoping that Ephrussi would put at his contributor's disposal the entire library of the *Gazette des Beaux-Arts*, for which he was responsible.[198] Until now no one has drawn attention to how Proust could have put together the formidably erudite details with which he filled his notes. This is the answer.

Plans to publish *La Bible d'Amiens* were also revived at this time. Proust

---

* Ibid., vol. IX, p. 100, May 1909. He makes clear, what is more, that Fénelon was at least a foot taller than him, and seemed to him to be earthly perfection. We know that, according to his military record, Proust was 1.68 m tall [5 ft 5 ins].

† Who found him in exaggeratedly expansive mood: no doubt Marcel was happy to escape from the Daudets' residence.

had contacted Vallette, the managing director of Mercure de France, and had, at his request, made enquiries about the future plans of the publisher Beauchesne, who had just translated Ruskin's essay on economics, *Unto this Last*; at the beginning of September he called at the Mercure offices and, on the 29th, he demanded a speedy and definite decision from the managing director.[199] The negotiations would, in fact, take a long time to complete. The publisher initially refused, taking the view that publishing the book in isolation would be meaningless, and he asked instead for a collection of selected texts (*Pages choisies*). Proust was then unwise enough to offer, as he would in the case of *Du côté de chez Swann*, to bear the publishing costs, and in a few forceful lines he defined the interest of the work, which was 'beautiful, unknown and original', 'the finest of Ruskin's works', and the only one which was 'to do with France, being simultaneously about French history, a French city and the French Gothic style'. As to the *Pages choisies*: 'Just the book to dull the impression his genius should arouse! Instead of a living cathedral, what a cold museum of disparate passages. People would discover the ways in which he resembles other great writers rather than the ways in which he differs from them.'[200] The publisher then agreed to publish *La Bible d'Amiens** on condition that he should also have the *Pages choisies*. Proust proposed delivering his book by chapters, for he had not yet finished transcribing his notes, nor had he written his introduction, and he promised delivery of the entire work by 1 February 1903; after that he would compile the collection of selected passages. At the same time, he announced that extracts would be appearing in *La Renaissance latine* in February.[201] Marcel suggested to Brancovan, who had edited this magazine since the issue of 15 November 1902 and had asked him for material, that he run instalments from this 'admirable and essentially "Latin" book . . . (because it is the history of Christianity in Gaul and in the Orient as explained by the cathedral of Amiens)'.[202]

---

* The contract would not be signed, however, until 26 February 1904; Mercure de France was to be responsible for the publishing costs, and Proust would receive royalties, which would not be worth very much.

THE TRIP TO BELGIUM AND HOLLAND

Meanwhile, on 3 October, Proust set off on the last artistic journey abroad that he would make during his lifetime.* His earlier trip, linked as it was to Ruskin, had taken him in search of Italian art; now he was going to look at a school of painting which the English critic despised.† Accompanied by Bertrand de Fénelon, the only person with whom he would have agreed to attempt this expedition, he went first to Bruges, which had prompted the entire trip because the big 'Exhibition of Flemish primitives'‡ being held there had just been extended until 5 October. The two friends followed an itinerary planned by Léon Yeatman,[203] who had also recommended various books to read.[204] Marcel had borrowed, and subsequently bought, Fromentin's *Les Maîtres d'autrefois*[205] and he used it as a guide throughout his travels. Later on Proust criticized this book, which dates from 1876, because of 'the unevenness of its production', its 'lack of precision', and the book's inability, in spite of its careful explanations, its profound arguments and its 'technical touches', to 'make us see a painting'.[206] And yet he must have originally read the book's declaration of principles, with which he would have been in agreement: 'I am coming to see Rubens and Rembrandt on their home ground, and, similarly, the Dutch School in its surroundings, which remain the same: agricultural and maritime life, dunes, pastureland, large clouds and distant horizons.'[207] And he would have agreed with this definition: 'The art of painting is merely the art of expressing the invisible through what is visible.'[208] There can be no doubt that he looked at the paintings he mentioned with the book in his hands, as he did with Ruskin in Venice. Moreover, Proust must surely have thought of Fromentin's portrait of Rembrandt when he composed his own, either during his first trip to Holland or on his return, in 1898.[209] And, he asked his mother whether she had any information about Fromentin's life (just as Odette would ask Swann what he knew about the life of Vermeer): 'It's irritating not to have any "tips" about

---

* This was very much what Mme Proust sensed: 'I think that through tiredness he is prolonging the trip, because he feels he will not be able to do it again' (*Corr.*, vol. III, p. 157, 9 October 1902, to Bibesco).

† 'Ruskin has intoxicated me. All this profane art...' wrote Proust from Dordrecht, where he stayed at the Bellevue hotel (a good hotel situated on the banks of the river where the steamboats pass by), to Léon Yeatman (ibid., p. 160).

‡ At the time, 'primitives' was the term given to painting done before the sixteenth century, or, in Italy, before the Renaissance.

someone I've just spent a fortnight with at the hotel.'[210] Before entering and upon leaving each museum, Fénelon read out passages from Taine[211] to Marcel.

They were at Bruges[212] on 4 October, at Antwerp (from here Fénelon travelled directly to Amsterdam), having seen Ghent, on the 9th, and on the 11th Marcel arrived by train at Dordrecht, 'whose ivy-covered church is reflected in the interlacing of sleepy canals and in the golden, glistening waters of the Meuse'.[213] From there he travelled by boat to Rotterdam and visited Delft and 'the innocent waters of the canal which a little pale sunlight causes to glitter between the double rows of trees, leafless since the end of summer, and to shimmer in the mirrors that are hung outside the gabled houses on either bank';[214] on 14 October he rejoined his friend in Amsterdam, setting off alone the next day, in a 'horse-drawn barge', crossing 'the plains moaning in the wind, while on the banks the reeds bend and then rise again in endless swaying movements',[215] for Volendam, 'an extremely strange and little-known place',[216] a village of fishermen with an artist's colony.[217] On the 17th he left for Haarlem 'to see the Hals', and on the 18th he travelled to The Hague, where he met Fénelon again, setting off that same evening to stay at the Hôtel de l'Europe in Amsterdam (one of the best in town, but whose prices appalled him), returning to Paris on 19 or 20 October. Mme Proust confessed her astonishment to Bibesco: 'Ponsard said it: "When the boundary has been crossed there are no further limits" and after Marcel did not return home on the first evening, he is not coming back at all. The truth is that he coped with Bruges, and is coping with Antwerp . . . This little absence is really a great step forward.'[218] From Amsterdam the heroic traveller admitted to his parents that he might not have had the courage to stay away so long if he had had to decide upon the trip all at once; in fact, he prolonged it day by day: 'Countless times I imagined that I would be embracing you the next day. Never did I think that I would go a fortnight without embracing you. This applies equally to my little brother.'[219]

Not everything went smoothly, however. Certainly, he had made this journey 'so conscientiously . . . so intelligently and so completely' that he had not had a minute to spare.[220] But his emotional state which he complained about, and which predated his departure, was 'so disastrous' that he was anxious not to 'poison poor Fénelon's trip with my melancholia', and so he left him to breathe more freely away from his groaning.[221] Why was Marcel groaning? He was certainly unable to tell his mother that he harboured an impossible love for his friend (especially as he did not yet know what the latter's tendencies were). His absence could therefore be explained by his wanting to escape and leave the scenes of jealousy and the inquisitions far behind. Or else did Marcel already know of Fénelon's intention to leave for Constantinople and was he therefore feeling sad as a result? Fénelon, who had been an embassy attaché since 28 April 1902, was appointed to the French embassy in Constantinople on 31 October 1902; he would depart on 8 December. In any case, since Mme Proust was proposing to her son that he should spend some time in the country, at Illiers, for example (which he scarcely wished to see again), he asserted that there was nowhere he could have prolonged his holidays except in Belgium and Holland, and that the only person he could 'go away with' was Fénelon, who 'couldn't be nicer'.*

We come across Proust's journey in *À la recherche*,[222] scattered in references to the towns he visited: Bruges, because Rachel went there 'to spend All Soul's Day every year'; a hotel room in Antwerp; Dordrecht, because the entry to Querqueville (Balbec) is similar; Delft, on account of Vermeer; Haarlem, because the Guermantes (unlike the Narrator) had seen the Frans Hals there; Amsterdam, because Albertine had been there and describes the sea-gulls, the canals whose lights were reflected in her eyes, and the girlfriends who accompanied her on her dubious evenings out.[223] Before creating Albertine, Proust had conceived a character called Maria, who had come from Holland and whose presence revived memories of the landscape, of Amsterdam and the Herengracht, and of two portraits of Rembrandt.[224] This Maria was no doubt not unlike Fénelon. She would merge, though not without leaving a few traces, into the character inspired by Agostinelli and his Norman images. We also come across The Hague, because Swann considers going there for his study on Vermeer, because the Narrator had visited the city, and because its Royal Museum lent its *View of Delft* for the exhibition at which Bergotte dies. Even the special features of Volendam are compared to Les Baux.[225] We should also add the references to the artists themselves, Hals, Rembrandt, De Hooch, Memling, Rubens, Ruysdael, Van Dyck, Van Huysum, Van der Meulen . . . Proust, in short, enjoyed imitating Dutch painting, both in the illuminated interiors in the evening at Doncières, and in Paris where the windows in every courtyard constituted 'an exhibition of a hundred Dutch paintings

* *Corr.*, vol. III, pp. 164–5. He also informed his mother about his heavy hotel expenses, that he had been the victim of a theft, and that the trip itself 'is not expensive', thus preparing himself for the always painful moment of settling the bill.

side by side'.[226] Once again, nothing that has been experienced is wasted or lost; everything has been disseminated throughout the novel. One day in 1906 Marcel would write to Fénelon, in a premonitory manner, warning him that since he never wrote anything himself, the only recourse left to him was 'as a portraitist, a memorialist who has the ability, the devotion, the affection and the application to pin down the physiognomy which might otherwise remain unknown'.[227]

When he returned to Paris, Marcel grieved for his friend Antoine Bibesco, whose mother had died in Bucharest – her son had arrived too late to see her alive.* Thinking of himself initially and of his own mother, so as to see things from another's point of view, and obsessed by death, as are all those who are prone to illness and anxiety, Marcel wrote his friend letters in which we can already detect the great novelist of mourning: 'My affection for Maman, my admiration for your mother, my feelings for you, all these combine to make me feel your suffering to such a degree that I did not think it were possible to feel such sorrow for another's misfortune.'† And he quoted to him some lines taken from *The Bible of Amiens* about the peace and divine light of eternal Love, lines which he said had done him good, and whose soothing power was still effective.‡ More heroically, not having heard from Antoine, he suggested that he should spend the late winter months with him in Romania, or that Antoine should go to Constantinople to see Bertrand: 'Your presence would sweeten the beginnings of his exile and his unaccustomed loneliness.'§ When Bibesco, taking Marcel at his word, suggested he come immediately, Proust broke the news of his brother's wedding, which meant that he was obliged to remain in Paris for the time being. In any case, Proust's grief was not so great that he was not able to dine in town several times in the same week, and visit the Noailles, the Chimays, Mme de Pierrebourg (Paul Hervieu's mistress) and Mme Straus. He also attended

---

* On 3 November 1902 *Le Figaro* printed a long obituary by Ferrari which praised the pianist and her literary and artistic salon which had been 'open to all that was most elegant in Parisian society' (*Corr.*, vol. III, p. 169).

† *Corr.*, p. 168, 3 November 1902. Mme Proust wrote these words to Bibesco which might one day apply to someone else: 'You will continue to be proud of her, you will be aware of yourself being like her, and the sentiment will be sweet to you' (ibid., p. 170).

‡ Ibid., p. 173, 10 November 1902, and *Bible*, p. 340. As when Reynaldo Hahn's mother died, Proust pretended to believe in everlasting life in order to comfort his friend. Proust's letters of condolence belong to the literary and philosophical tradition of *Consolations* that stretches back to Cicero and Seneca (and Montaigne).

§ Ibid., p. 183. Proust would thus kill two birds with one stone.

the dress rehearsal of Bernstein's *Joujou* and made the acquaintance of the actress Simone de Bargy, later Mme Simone, the playwright's leading lady and mistress.[228]

As the year drew to an end, Marcel's private life was dominated by Bertrand de Fénelon's departure for Constantinople. This was preceded by a curious episode, the principal interest of which is that it recurs in *Le Côté de Guermantes*.* Marcel, in a highly nervous state, spent his nights weeping, and, as soon as he had taken his Trional to help him sleep during the day accused his mother of allowing the servants to make a noise: 'Thanks to you, I was in such a state of nerves that when poor Fénelon came with Lauris, because of something he said – extremely unpleasant I have to say – I flew at him with my fists (Fénelon, not Lauris), and not knowing what I was doing, I seized the new hat he had just bought, trampled on it, tore it to pieces and then ripped out the lining. As you probably think I'm exaggerating, I enclose a piece of the lining so that you can see I'm telling the truth.'[229] In fact his mother was trying to punish him (for being too extravagant? or because he did not lead a normal life?) and spare the staff at the same time: they did not come when he rang the bell, they did not wait on him at table, and, on his mother's instructions, his room was not heated; as a result Fénelon and Lauris could not stay, 'even with their overcoats on'. It was not the first time that Proust had flown into a violent temper, as the story of the broken vase shows; later on, he would declare to Céleste: 'I shall drown you in an ocean of shit.' In this way he soothed his raw nerves. So Mme Proust afforded him no moral consolation for the sorrow he felt at the departure of his friend; this leads us to a reproach which we come across again in *À la recherche*: 'The truth is that as soon as I feel well, the life that makes me feel better exasperates you, and you destroy everything until I start feeling ill again. This isn't the first time.'[230] Thinking that, if he fell ill once more, his mother would treat him nicely again, Marcel let fall this complaint, which was more revealing than he knew: 'It is sad not to be able to have affection and health at the same time.'[231]

Despite these incidents, he was not prevented from going to the Gare

---

* *RTP*, vol. II, p. 487, where the Narrator hurls himself upon M. de Charlus' hat: 'He consisted of nothing but pride, to my way of thinking, and all I could feel was fury within me . . . I hurled myself at the Baron's new top hat, I flung it to the floor, I trampled on it, I did my best to pull it completely apart, I snatched out the lining and I tore the crown in two . . .' This episode does not occur in *Jean Santeuil*, where the passages about 'Bertrand de Réveillon' are uniformly complimentary and focus on the dinner at Larue's.

de Lyon with Lauris to see Fénelon, 'who was fairly tired', off on the Orient Express, bound for Constantinople. Proust must have told him, as he always did, how sad he was at the thought that once Bertrand had left, he, Marcel, would be forgotten. But Marcel would not forget him. In January 1903 he made plans for a trip to Constantinople, where he would join Bibesco (but he cancelled the idea when he discovered that Antoine was returning to Paris); in July he saw Bertrand, who happened to be ill, once more, reserving the rare occasions when he went out for him,[232] and submitted his dinner invitations to the other's approval. Meanwhile, he found himself a new friend, Louis d'Albufera, and he became part of a new trio with Louisa de Mornand. This explains why, when in the autumn of 1903 he wrote a review of a German essay by Charlotte Broicher, *John Ruskin und sein Werk* (Leipzig, 1902),[233] he made a confession in somewhat veiled terms: Goethe asserted that the world was an empty place if it is not inhabited by a 'friend who thinks in the way we do'; Ruskin held an opposite view and as a result discovered the inspiration that only solitude can bring. Proust, putting his own feelings in the mouth of a 'friend', had him say: 'In Constantinople I had one of those friends of whom Goethe speaks . . . Constantinople seemed much closer to me, more pleasant, and it took on more of a spiritual dimension and became more human.' Once this friend no longer lived in this city, and stopped being his friend, 'Constantinople gradually took on in [his] imagination the place it had lost in [his] heart.' This man was 'actually dead for [him]. Never had Santa Sophia seemed so beautiful [to him]'. This was the way in which Marcel, almost invisibly, settled his scores, in his novel as well as in his essays and reviews, and gave Bertrand notice of dismissal. There would, however, be 'intermissions of the heart' in their relationship. In 1904 Proust saw Fénelon again while he was on leave from his subsequent posting in St Petersburg. Fénelon wrote to him afterwards: 'I have been told in a letter that you have recently been a devoted and loyal friend in difficult times, and it was particularly soothing for me to hear your praises being sung. I know what a warm and affectionate heart you have!'[234] At the end of that year Bertrand sent him some Vermeer reproductions, which Proust's 'admiration' for this artist and his friendship for the sender 'made doubly precious to him'.* Again, in 1912, he confided to Albert Nahmias:

* *Corr.*, vol. IV, p. 368. In his letter Proust recalled the 'childish behaviour' which Fénelon considered foolish when he had been the object of it. This was probably to do with the romantic anxieties and jealousies which were a feature of Marcel's relationships with those he loved.

'We have not seen or written to each other for over seven or eight years. None the less we were a thousand times closer than you and I shall ever be, and despite the silence and absence our feelings for one another have not altered. When people spoke to him about me, I knew, and when they spoke of him to me, he would know, for we had not changed.'* The final shock occurred in March 1915, when Marcel learned of the death in the war of, as he put it in *Sodome et Gomorrhe*, his 'dearest friend, the best, most intelligent and bravest of men, whom no one who knew him could forget: Bertrand de Fénelon'.[235] Describing the death of his old friend, he wrote some deeply moving letters.[236] It was through duplicating reality in his imagination that he achieved the death of Saint-Loup.

Shortly before Christmas, having told Bibesco that he reckoned on writing an article each week or every fortnight, and that he needed thirty books in order to do his work on Ruskin (because he 'supplied references for everything'), Proust made an important admission: the work that he was embarked upon was 'tedious in many ways'. He did not consider documentation and translation 'real work': 'It's enough to awaken my thirst for achievement, without in any way assuaging it. Now that for the first time since my long torpor[†] I have looked at myself and my thoughts introspectively, I can sense all the insignificance of my life; hundreds of characters for novels, a thousand ideas urging me to give them substance ... My intelligence was enslaved by my need for peace of mind. In throwing off its chains, I thought I was merely freeing a slave, but I was giving myself a master.'[237] Here his vocation as a novelist is clearly asserted: logically, one would expect him to write a novel after translating *The Bible of Amiens*.

1903

As Proust had told Bibesco, the year that was starting would be devoted primarily to journalism. His articles, like his life, would take two different directions: the arts, and therefore Ruskin, and the salons. Fate also provided

---

* Ibid., vol. XI, p. 169. As early as 1907 he had written to Lauris: 'If you see Bertrand, give him my very fondest wishes ... I sometimes wonder whether I have not neglected the only friend I should have had, whose friendship might perhaps have been fruitful to both of us' (ibid., p. 265). Cf. *RTP*, vol. III, pp. 1640–3, note by P. Robert. It is also worth mentioning that in 1913 Proust sent Fénelon two copies of *Du côté de chez Swann*, affectionately inscribed.

† This no doubt goes back to his abandoning *Jean Santeuil*, although he had only recently added some passages about Bertrand de Réveillon.

this solitary man, whom people were occasionally contemptuous of, with four aristocratic friends,* who appeared on the scene almost as if to replace Fénelon. When people claim that Marcel knew nothing about high society and that he did not belong to it, they disregard the fact that he must nevertheless have had some virtues in order for him, in spite of his ill-health, his immobility, the comparative ugliness of his home and the unintentional extravagance of the way he dressed, to have attracted the scions of the most distinguished families. Certainly, and as Proust himself explained with reference to Saint-Loup and the Guermantes, these people were above matters of title, but valued personal qualities: the charm, intelligence, kindness and the drollness of our hero, but also the iron determination to invite people and be invited, stepping from one salon to another, making sure he was introduced to everyone's friends, unpicking and reassembling the tapestry of high society, fully determined to describe it (he had already done so in his first two books) – these were the qualities that mattered.

When he was delivering the proofs of a section of *La Bible d'Amiens* to Brancovan for *La Renaissance latine*, Proust overheard this cruel remark: 'In actual fact, you don't know any English, and this must be full of mistranslations.' Generally, Marcel preferred not to speak about his work. But just as he was always ready to fight a duel, personal criticism obliged him to explain himself, to delve more deeply into a question and respond: in the process, he provided a veritable theory of translation. It was true that he did not know spoken English (he had learnt it when he had asthma and was unable to speak it), for he could neither pronounce words nor recognize them when they were spoken; but he could recognize every written word: 'I don't claim to know English; I claim to know Ruskin.' Over a period of four years he had come to know the text so well by heart that he assimilated it fully and it became entirely transparent to him. He had closely examined 'the sense of each word, the significance of each

---

* This may have been the inspiration for 'the society of four friends' in *Le Côté de Guermantes, RTP*, vol. II, p. 697: 'On the subject of the Prince de Foix, it may be the occasion to mention here that he belonged to a coterie of a dozen or fifteen young men as well as to a rather closer group of four.' Cf. ibid., p. 699: 'A fifth member had joined the four platonic friends, who was more platonic than any of the others.' 'I asked Bibesco to join me and four other friends of Bertrand's' (*Corr.*, vol. III, p. 368, July 1903, to F. de Croisset). Proust gave a dinner party at home on 16 July, in honour of Fénelon, who was on holiday in Paris: Bibesco made an unfair 'quip', which brought about an equally unpleasant riposte from Marcel's father, about his health, his way of life and the excessive tips he gave (ibid., pp. 373–4, to his mother).

expression, the connections between every idea'. In so doing he won the admiration of both his English advisers, who had not foreseen the difficulties, and of Robert d'Humières, who, believing that certain words were untranslatable, advised him to omit them. To work in this way, however, required four years[238] of effort, but it also provided him with an alibi: there was no question of writing a novel.

The artistic journeys which Marcel and his friends undertook during 1903 also helped prolong his work on Ruskin. The first of these art quests allowed him both to enjoy the company of his dearest friends and to prepare his notes. On 10 April,* Good Friday, and on 21 April, he visited Provins, Saint-Loup-de-Naud,† Dammarie-les-Lys, Laon,[239] Coucy, Senlis, Soissons, and Saint-Leu-d'Esserent,‡ accompanied by the Bibesco brothers, François de Pâris, Lucien Henraux, the future curator of the Louvre, and Georges de Lauris.§ Of the places visited, the choice of sites not mentioned by Émile Mâle was probably made by his friends, and by Emmanuel Bibesco in particular, who had a sound knowledge of the religious architecture of the Île-de-France. There is no trace of these journeys in the notes to *La Bible d'Amiens*: this is because they served to prolong his reading of the work of Mâle, who was gradually beginning to replace Ruskin as the interpreter of Gothic art in Proust's mind. Having visited Auxerre, Avallon, Beaune and Dijon in the late summer, Marcel would hark back agreeably to all the trips he had made: 'I have carried across France, from Romanesque vestibules to Gothic chevets, a burning curiosity and an increasingly ailing body. And of the monuments I've seen, only the Hospice at Beaune suited my acute state of illness.'[240]

At the same time, he was managing to concentrate on his manuscript.

---

* According to Lauris (G. de Lauris, *À un ami*, Amiot-Dumont, 1948, p. 19) and Billy (*Marcel Proust: Lettres et conversations*, Les Portiques, 1930, pp. 121–2). There are so many of these sites that we may wonder whether there were not several visits, which the memories of Proust's friends have condensed into a single one.

† He had borrowed a pamphlet by the Abbé Nape about this church from Marie Nordlinger, further proof of the trouble he took in planning his trips.

‡ Here Antoine Bibesco thought it very witty to play 'En revenant de la revue' [a popular singing game of the period], which led to a quarrel with Marcel (Lauris, p. 19).

§ *Corr.*, vol. III, p. 293: on 7 April Marcel originally planned to go to Autun and Vézelay (which he would only visit in August). In his introduction, he would mention the Magdalene flower at Vézelay (*CSB*, p. 295). He would also have liked to borrow his brother's car (*Corr.*, vol. III, p. 295). Lauris thought he remembered that Fénelon had raised Marcel's spirits by singing 'L'enchantement du vendredi saint' [The Enchantment of Good Friday]; and yet Bertrand had not returned to Paris by this time.

In January he corrected the proofs of the pre-publication extracts of *La Bible d'Amiens* that would appear in *La Renaissance latine* on 15 February ('Figures de saints', thirty-one pages) and on 15 March ('Silhouettes d'église', twenty-three pages). Robert d'Humières came to see him in January and dined at his home on 14 February* and then on 19 March, in order to help him with his translation.† They dined alone together, for Marcel always giggled uncontrollably when he was there.‡ In his introduction, Proust warmly thanked 'the marvellous translator of Kipling', who had been helpful to him on a number of occasions. Since he was unable to go through everything with the latter, when he received the proofs from Mercure de France, he also turned to Antoine Bibesco[241] and to Marie Nordlinger, to whom he admitted having lost all the pages on which he had noted her corrections.[242] In June, to complete his introduction, he wrote an important 'post-script' on idolatry, which sacrifices beauty to the model that inspired it and thus deceives itself. At the beginning of December Marcel corrected a final set of proofs[243] and added a moving dedication to his father.

While waiting with his customary patience for the publication of his Ruskin, Marcel was busy with other literary work. There were book reviews connected with his author, the first of which, 'John Ruskin, sa vie et son œuvre, étude critique par Marie de Bunsen', was published in *La Chronique des arts et de la curiosité* on 7 March 1903.[244] In it he drew attention to the books available on the subject – La Sizeranne, 'unsurpassable', Brunhes' *Ruskin et la Bible*, 'invaluable' and Bardoux's *John Ruskin*, almost as if to suggest that Marie de Bunsen did not compare with them: the author had read only twenty-seven of Ruskin's books, whereas he had written over eighty! The principal merit of the book lay in its quotations, and Proust, who so loved to quote, explained what he meant: 'On every page a ray of genius illuminates the critic's narrative.'[245] At the end of the year, reviewing *John Ruskin und sein Werk* by Charlotte Broicher[246] (German was the first living language he had learnt as a schoolboy), Marcel launched into an

* In *Le Figaro* of 19 February, André Beaunier remarked on 'the fine translation Marcel Proust has done of Ruskin's *La Bible d'Amiens*' (*Corr.*, vol. III, p. 271).

† *Corr.*, vol. III, p. 247. 'I am starting to dose myself so I shall be ready to get up for d'Humières' (ibid., p. 276). He was less meticulous than Proust, as we have seen, and suggested skipping over difficulties (ibid., p. 221). Proust would look upon one sentence of d'Humières in *La Renaissance latine* of 15 May as an attack on Ruskin: 'After Ruskin, ulterior motives in aesthetics are intolerable' (ibid., p. 320).

‡ This, at least, was what he explained to his mother (ibid., p. 276, March 1903).

attack on the eighteenth century, an era he did not care for, and he denigrated its literature, which he considered too humanistic, depriving the world of its poetic character; he also used the article to condemn intelligence, even before he had begun *Contre Sainte-Beuve*, which was no replacement for the inspiration that only solitude could provide.[247] Other figures materialized in Ruskin's wake, such as Dante Gabriel Rossetti and Elizabeth Siddal, in *La Chronique des arts et de la curiosité*, on 7 and 14 November 1903[248] (signed M. P.). In his résumé of an article in the *Burlington Magazine*, Proust introduced the Pre-Raphaelite movement (following Ruskin, whom he had not forsaken) to the French public. In *À la recherche* he sometimes refers to 'the inadequate shrubs of the Pre-Raphaelites', to 'a Pre-Raphaelite spectre',[249] and on several occasions, in his drafts, to Burne-Jones.[250] The guiding principle of these artists was to find in real life (and not in the studio) human beings who had some rapport with the idealized personage who was to be portrayed. This was how Elizabeth Siddal, the future wife of Rossetti, came to be discovered. She had (and she must surely have reminded Proust of himself) 'a body weighed down by the spirit', 'a genius paralysed by illness, whereas for so many other people health serves no noble purpose'. It was an occasion to reflect upon the links between the artist and his model (later he would reflect on Elstir and his wife, and on Helleu and his): 'Artists feel an affection for the creature who is suddenly brought to life before their eyes, in exquisite and living form, a dream that has long been dreamt of, and they look upon her with thoughtful gaze, with expressions that are more intuitive and, truth to tell, more full of love than other men are capable of.'[251]

CHARLES EPHRUSSI

La Chronique des arts et de la curiosité was a supplement to the *Gazette des Beaux-Arts*, which had been edited by Charles Ephrussi[252] since 1894 (he had been the proprietor since 1885). Born in Odessa in 1849, to a family of bankers and wheat exporters, the brother of Mme Léon Fould, and at one stage on close terms with the court in Vienna, he was twenty-five when he arrived in Paris and was frequently to be seen at salons and at the opera. He helped compile the Louvre catalogue of drawings and he mounted a successful exhibition of old drawings at the Musée des Arts Décoratifs. He was a collector of Japanese prints and he made the acquaintance of Cernuschi, who was connected to Duret and the Impressionists. He could be seen at the homes of Mme Straus, the Princesse

Mathilde and Mme Lemaire. He began buying paintings in 1875 (Berthe Morisot, Mary Cassatt) and between 1879 and 1882 he acquired some twenty works by the most famous Impressionists: Monet's *La Grenouillère*, *Le Vieillard* by Constantin Guys, *Le Départ du bateau* and *Les Asperges* by Manet,* two Sisleys and a fan by Pissarro. He purchased two other paintings, including *Galatée*, by Moreau, whom he came to know in about 1880, and several Renoirs. The latter depicted him in his *Déjeuner des canotiers*.† Proust attributed this painting to Elstir ('an identical gentleman . . . wearing a top hat at a boating party where he was clearly out of place, which proved that for Elstir he was not only a regular sitter, but a friend, perhaps a patron')[253] and included it in the Duc de Guermantes' collection. Proust has the latter say: 'For M. Elstir, this gentleman has been a sort of sponsor – he launched him and has often helped him out of awkward situations by commissioning pictures from him.' 'Un amateur de peinture',[254] a piece written for *Jean Santeuil* in about 1899[255] and which foreshadows *Le Côté de Guermantes*, mentions several paintings from Ephrussi's collection[256] (which are very similar to the pictures in the Charpentier collection), such as *Débâcle sur la Seine*, which would become Elstir's 'Thaw at Briseville', some Corots and some Sisleys. 'He kept for himself works in progress by Degas, Manet, Claude Monet and Puvis de Chavannes. It was due to him that many paintings, which had been left at a half-way stage, were actually completed.'[257] Proust also visited the Georges-Petit gallery, where Ephrussi was an adviser, which organized exhibitions of the Impressionists (notably the Renoir and Sisley retrospective in 1892 and 1897). Ephrussi arranged for artists such as Puvis de Chavannes or Delaunay to be given public commissions for the Panthéon or the Hôtel de Ville. And it was he who acted as guide to Queen Victoria when she visited Paris. Additionally, Ephrussi had written an essay on Dürer,[258] and another on his friend Paul Baudry. He liked to have a young man as an assistant: Jules Laforgue in 1882, Ary Renan, Marcel Proust and Auguste Marguillier. For Marcel, he was thus someone who helped him make important discoveries, and he paid homage to him in the character of Swann, who also bears his first name. From 1900 Proust was a visitor at his town house in the Avenue d'Iéna and at the editorial offices

* He paid Manet 800 francs, thus prompting Manet to offer him the extra 'asparagus' at the Musée d'Orsay. He introduced Suzette Lemaire to Manet, who twice painted her portrait.

† But this picture, painted in the summer or autumn of 1880 and dated 1881, was bought by the collector Balensi. It was shown at Durand-Ruel's in April 1899. There is also a portrait of Ephrussi by Bonnat (1895) and a pastel of him by Louise Abbema.

on the rue Favart, where the library was extremely useful to him; in particular, it was here that he was able to look through copies of the *Burlington Magazine*.[259] It is worth pointing out that Charles Haas, the main inspiration for Swann, was only interested in the eighteenth century and in genre painting. Ephrussi died on 30 September 1905 and Proust, who had just lost his mother, would claim to be cruelly affected by his death.[260] His nephew, Théodore Reinach, took over from him as editor.

WHISTLER

An enemy of Ruskin, who had opposed him in a celebrated lawsuit,[261] died on 17 July 1903. Marcel had only met Whistler on one occasion, when he had elicited a few favourable words from him on the subject of Ruskin and kept possession of a pair of his grey gloves, which were later lost. Montesquiou and Boldini had both spoken about him a good deal.[262] In his articles and in his letters Proust referred to Whistler's portrait of Montesquiou (painted in 1891, it was exhibited on 25 April 1894 at the Société Nationale des Beaux-Arts, under the title *Noir et Or. Portrait du comte Robert de Montesquiou-Fezensac*; the count is shown carrying a chinchilla cape belonging to the Comtesse Greffulhe over one arm),[263] to his views of Venice, his paintings that showed 'the magical beauty of London', his relationship with Ruskin, his *Ten O'Clock* (a present from Marie Nordlinger)* and to his *Gentle Art of Making Enemies*. He considered him a master (significantly, he was also the master of Lucien Daudet), and he mentioned the passages that Blanche had devoted to him. In *À l'ombre des jeunes filles en fleurs* there are veritable pastiches or evocations of actual paintings:[264] the portraits of Charlus in evening dress that are reminiscent of a 'Harmony in Black and White' by Whistler (an allusion to the portrait of Montesquiou); or a butterfly (the artist's signature) beneath a 'Harmony in Grey and Pink' (elsewhere a 'Harmony in Black and White') in the style of works by Whistler; or the portrait of Odette, which is contemporary with certain portraits of women done by the American; or a gulf of opal with its silvery-blue harmonies. In *Le Côté de Guermantes*, Charlus addresses some remarks made by Whistler to the Narrator.[265] In *Le Temps retrouvé* the reader discovers that M. Verdurin has written a book about him.[266] Whistler's art has been transformed into that of Elstir, whose name –

---

* A sentence from this book is put in the mouth of Charlus (*RTP*, vol. II, p. 852), which is not surprising, since the count and the artist were very close.

apart from two letters – is an anagram of his. (Did Proust know the great English Impressionist, Philip Wilson Steer [1860–1942], who had been trained in France, whose work was exhibited at Goupil's in Paris in 1894, and whose name provided the last syllable of Elstir's name, while that of Helleu provided the first?)[267] In 1905, in a letter to Marie Nordlinger, Proust observed that Whistler's work was becoming less fashionable in France, where he was no longer seen as a great artist: 'If the man who had painted those images of Venice in turquoise, of Amsterdam in topaz, of Brittany in opal, if the portraitist of Miss Alexander[268]. . . is not a great artist, then it makes one wonder if there ever was one.'[269] Ultimately he thought that Whistler's and Ruskin's theories were not irreconcilable: 'Whistler is right to say . . . that art is distinct from morality. And yet Ruskin, too, utters a truth, on a different plane, when he says that all great art is morality.' Or again: 'Ruskin and Whistler held one another in much scorn because their theories were opposed. Yet there was only one truth and they both perceived it.' This was why Proust promised himself that he would provide 'faithful and impassioned copies' of Whistler.[270] They were to be Elstir's paintings and the metaphorical allusions – as though Proust saw the world through his eyes, in his paintings – to Whistler's canvases and to those 'Harmonies' which, according to Gautier,[271] Baudelaire and Mallarmé, were the basis for both painting and music.

SALONS

In another series of articles Marcel worked his apprenticeship as a writer, not of the novel about art, but of the society novel. These were the pieces on 'salons'; the first, 'Le Salon de S.A.I. la princesse Mathilde', appeared in *Le Figaro* on 25 February 1903 (signed Dominique),* followed by 'La Cour des lilas et l'atelier aux roses. Le salon de Mme Madeleine Lemaire' in *Le Figaro* of 11 May 1903 (signed Dominique), and 'Le Salon de la princesse Edmond de Polignac' in *Le Figaro* of 6 September 1903 (signed Horatio). 'Le Salon de la comtesse Greffulhe' was unpublished and has disappeared. Finally, there was 'Le Salon de la comtesse d'Haussonville' in *Le Figaro* of 4 January 1904 (signed Horatio), which was certainly written in 1903. Proust was careful not to sign these columns with his own name,

* Like Stendhal. Hence Proust's amusement when Comte Primoli, Princesse Mathilde's nephew, said in his hearing, at the home of Princesse Brancovan, that this article 'was idiotic' (*Corr.*, vol. III, p. 454).

so as to retain the freedom of his pen, to avoid being accused of snobbery, and because they constituted a lesser literary form.[272] In July an incident occurred involving Calmette, the editor of *Le Figaro*, who had disclosed Marcel's identity to Madeleine Lemaire; he threatened not to write about salons any more, and he complained furthermore that his articles were not appearing at sufficiently regular intervals.[273]

The purpose of a salon was to bring together artists, writers and people from society. Each of them had its own regular attenders, its own rules and its own passionate enthusiasms, and they had been so well portrayed by Balzac that Proust used a pastiche of his style for the opening of his description of the Lemaire salon.[274] 'Le Salon de S.A.I. la princesse Mathilde' depicts the emperor's niece as we shall meet her later in *À la recherche du temps perdu*, in all her simplicity, with her jokes, and among her writer friends – Mérimée, Flaubert, Goncourt, Sainte-Beuve, Musset, Taine (up until their quarrel), Renan and Heredia. An entire episode, the visit of Nicholas II, is retold in *À l'ombre des jeunes filles en fleurs*.[275] The prince's funeral in 'Le salon de la princesse Edmond de Polignac' would be used later for that of Robert de Saint-Loup, as would the Comtesse Greffulhe for the Duchesse de Guermantes; by quoting a verse from *Trophées*, she too, would be compared to a bird.[276] The speciality of Madeleine Lemaire's salon was painting, and the article was a tribute to the woman who had introduced Marcel into society and had illustrated his first book. It also provided, in remembrance of a former love, a fine portrait of Reynaldo Hahn: 'The head tilted slightly backwards, the melancholy, slightly disdainful mouth, from which escaped the rhythmic flow of the most beautiful, the saddest, the warmest voice that ever was, this "instrument of musical genius" known as Reynaldo Hahn gripped the hearts and brought tears to the eyes of all present, in the ripple of admiration which he spread about him, making us quiver with emotion.'* It also included a portrait 'in miniature' of Antoine Bibesco. The Princesse Edmond de Polignac's salon was celebrated for its music, for Rameau, Fauré and Brahms. That of the Comtesse d'Haussonville (who waved like the Duchesse de Réveillon in *Jean Santeuil* and the Guermantes)[277] comprised the *ancien régime* society,

---

* *CSB*, p. 463. Cocteau also described Reynaldo: 'Whether at the home of Madeleine Lemaire or in his room at the very mysterious Hôtel des Réservoirs at Versailles, Reynaldo would sing, a cigarette in one corner of his lips, his exquisite voice issuing from the other, his eyes gazing heavenwards, the little formal garden that made up his bluish cheeks in shadow, and the rest of him freewheeling, at the piano, along a gentle, nocturnal slope' (*Portraits-souvenirs, 1900–1914*, Grasset, 1935, p. 188, and the very fine drawing, p. 189).

the legacy of Coppet, and the world of M. d'Haussonville, who was an academician, an historian and a man of moderate views, opposed to the 'sectarian' spirit.* He would be mentioned twice in *À la recherche*, and his wife would be used, along with others, as a model for the elegance of the Guermantes. All in all, in this year of waiting, Marcel wrote nine published articles and one unpublished.

ROBERT'S WEDDING

Throughout this period, Marcel's private life was far from lacking in incidents, departures or arrivals. One such event was Robert Proust's marriage to Marthe Dubois-Amiot. The civil ceremony was arranged for 31 January 1903 at the town hall of the eighth *arrondissement*, and the wedding was to take place on 2 February at the church of Saint-Augustin; Marcel worried about it for two weeks beforehand, wondering whether he would not be overcome with giggles when passing round the collection plate at Saint-Augustin's, or while listening to the mayor's speech[278] (in the event, he would not attend the civil ceremony, and neither would his mother, but only the church service). On the day of the wedding, at which he was his brother's best man, he had not slept for three nights; Mme Proust was so ill that she arranged to be taken to church by ambulance.[279] Marcel's female cousin, Valentine Thomson, made the collection with him. She would later describe 'his Lazarus-like countenance, with its melancholy moustache pushed up rather comically by his black woollen cerements. He felt he had to explain himself, and at every pew in turn, he announced in a loud voice that he was unable to dress in any other way, that he had been ill for months, that he would be still more ill that evening, and that it was not his fault.'† Robert had wanted to give his brother a fur coat as a present, which he refused, just as he would return the one that Bibesco sent him in March.[280] This was an important aspect of Marcel's character: he gave sumptuous presents, but he would never accept them from others.

After the wedding, since 'having a brother married is almost as

---

* *CSB*, p. 487. Proust describes Renan, the apologist of the seventeenth and eighteenth centuries, and Jaurès at length. This article was signed Horatio: Proust therefore signed his reviews (with one exception) M.P. and his salon articles with pseudonyms.

† Valentine Thomson, 'My Cousin Marcel Proust', *Harpers Magazine*, vol. 164, May 1932, pp. 710–20, quoted by Painter. 'Come to think of it, I shall be dead this evening (I haven't been to bed for three nights now),' wrote Marcel to Brancovan on 1 February (*Corr.*, vol. III, p. 234). Cf. *Corr.*, vol. III, p. 266: 'Although it was almost the death of me, I managed to attend Robert's wedding.'

exhausting as getting married oneself',[281] he announced that he had a
fever and a sore throat, and he was putting himself to bed until 15 February!
An attack of asthma only made his illness worse. It should be said that
the marriage was imposed on his family, and primarily on his son Robert,
by Professor Proust, who was closely involved with the bride's mother,
an extremely attractive woman. Robert, who had always been something
of a Don Juan, would not be faithful to his wife, would get through a
fortune one way or another, and would later use his brother as a go-between,
particularly during the war, to send money to his mistress, Mme Fournier.
Marthe, and her daughter Suzy, would see very little of Marcel. On Robert's
death, his widow, who was probably weary of the Proust brothers, started
burning, and then selling Marcel's papers.[282] Relations between the two
brothers nevertheless remained good: this explains why Marcel should
have experienced 'great emotion', 'great joy' when Robert received his
agrégation, or licence to teach, while at the same time deploring, as he wrote
to his mother, Robert's inability to take any part in their lives.[283]

CASA-FUERTE

Some new friends began to enter Marcel's life, and perhaps his work too.
Firstly, Illan de Casa-Fuerte, whom he had known, but not seen, for some
time.[284] His mother, Flavie, the Marquise de Casa-Fuerte, an Italian of
French descent, *née* Lefebvre de Clunières de Balsorano, and the muse of
D'Annunzio and of Montesquiou (who had dedicated *Les Chauves-souris*
to her),[285] was a woman of great beauty, who had something Japanese
about her eyes.[286] Her future husband, a Spaniard, Pierre Alvarez de
Toledo, the Marquis de Casa-Fuerte (the hereditary title of his mother),
younger son of the Duc de Bivona and first cousin of the Empress
Eugénie,[287] was, at the age of nineteen, honorary attaché at the Spanish
Legation in Naples when the revolution of 1860 broke out. The Queen
of Naples, *née* Sophia-Maria of Bavaria and sister of the Empress of
Austria, withdrew to Gaeta and defended the town from the ramparts
(Proust would mention her when he referred to this heroic episode, which
he may have heard about through Illan, in *Sodome et Gomorrhe II*). Illan's
father, who had subsequently been posted to Paris, then to Peking and,
after his marriage, to St Petersburg, returned to Naples (where one of his
ancestors had been viceroy) in about 1880: his son was born there in 1882
and he grew up in the family mansion, later in Paris, and then in Naples
once more; he, too, was an asthmatic.[288] His father died prematurely in

1890. The boy followed his mother to Saint-Raphaël, where he met Pierre Loti, a naval officer who wore high heels and make-up, who read *Fantôme d'Orient* to them. Illan thus had memories of the King and Queen of Naples, the Empress Eugénie, as well as the Princesse Mathilde, whose voice was like that of 'an old Napoleonic trooper'.[289] Both mother and son moved into 42 rue Cambon; this was why Proust, who began to call on them with Hahn in 1894, referred to the Marquise as 'the queen of the rue Cambon'.[290] Montesquiou introduced her to some eminent artists, among them Fauré, who played his music 'with a charming touch', 'the strange, illustrious and marvellous'[291] Whistler, and Helleu, and helped to make this salon one of the most elegant in Paris. Illan mixed in artistic circles and had a talent for music and poetry. Having read his poem, 'Vierge de pleurs' [Virgin of tears], Proust was delighted to glimpse 'in the magical light of poetry a delightful soul who interests me greatly, "virgin of tears" ("virgin of voluptuousness" too?)'.[292] The question has a touch of Charlus about it.

The young man had originally made the acquaintance of Lucien Daudet, 'slim, intelligent artistic, slightly affected but full of charm, with a good figure that he is not unaware of'.[293] One evening at the Grand-Guignol, the theatre in the rue Chaptal, which was showing two horror plays and a racy piece of vaudeville, the two friends met a man with 'the collar of his overcoat turned up over his rather creased dress shirt', a pale face, a thin, drooping black moustache, enormous dark eyes with dark shadows beneath them: it was Marcel Proust.[294] They went to dine at Larue's, 'and this was the beginning of a long and precious friendship', which for a period would alienate the jealous Lucien.[295] The friendship prompted Marcel to ask Francis de Croisset for 'two seats in his screened box at the Théâtre des Mathurins to see *Le Coin du feu*, a play by Tarride and Vernaire in which Louisa de Mornand was making her début.'[296] What appealed to Marcel about Illan, who, as usual, was ten years younger than him, was his extraordinary beauty, which impressed the whole of Paris, from Catherine Pozzi to Montesquiou, who shrieked: 'I forbid you to be so handsome',[297] his international and aristocratic breeding, his artistic and asthmatic temperament, his resemblance to his mother, an important theme in *À la recherche*,* and even his work as D'Annunzio's translator:[298]

---

* In the context of Gilberte Swann and her father, the early drafts mention Lucien and Illan (*RTP*, vol. I, p. 966, var. *a*, p. 1022, var. *c*). The theme is also developed in relation to Mlle Vinteuil and to Robert de Saint-Loup; in reality, it concerned Jacques Benoist-Méchin and the Plantevignes.

'I have much enjoyed . . . the fine translations of one poet by another.'[299] He tried, in vain, to have these published by Brancovan in *La Renaissance latine*. While visiting Venice – 'Store up some visions', Marcel had told him – Illan sent him telegrams which Marcel tried, often unsuccessfully, to conceal from his parents: 'My parents took no notice of anything in the first one and the second was not important.'[300] The deaths of their equally beloved mothers (Flavie de Casa-Fuerte died on 18 February 1905, aged fifty-one, from uraemia) drew them still closer to one another,[301] in spite of Illan's first marriage that year; in 1906 Marcel wrote from Versailles, where he had withdrawn, to tell him that he still liked him very much and that he desired to know whether this 'persistent affection' met with his correspondent's approval: 'Just a note, Illan, to tell me whether we're still friends.'[302] In 1907 this affection was strengthened further. Marcel wrote to him: 'You're a real dear and it's not just the way you look.' He then considered adding a sentence in honour of his friend to an article he was writing, 'Journées de lecture', on the subject of Christian names: 'When the late Marquis de Casa-Fuerte wanted to give a christening present to his son, he could find no rarer or sweeter jewel in eleventh-century Spain . . . than this first name of Illan, which no one had borne since the capture of Toledo (1085, I think).'[303] When *Du côté de chez Swann* was published, Illan's copy bore the words 'with all my affection'.[304] Marcel's friend would die in 1962.

ALBUFERA AND LOUISA DE MORNAND

There was one particular encounter that enabled Proust to discover more about the *noblesse d'Empire* which he had chosen to write about that year in 'Le Salon de S.A.I. la princesse Mathilde'. Louis, Marquis d'Albufera (he would succeed to the title of Duc on the death of his father, who was born in 1845), was a descendant of Suchet, who became one of Napoleon's marshals in 1811 and Duc d'Albufera in 1812; his mother was a Cambacérès,[305] and he would marry one of Masséna's grand-daughters. He was born in Paris in 1877 and lived at his father's home at 55 rue Saint-Dominique (at the time, children only left the family home when they got married so one should not be surprised that Marcel was still living with his parents . . .). He did not get on with his parents.[306] He was a charming young man whom Proust praised less for his intelligence than for his 'slender nose and his weary, ironic expression';[307] because he had never 'worked', he retained the political views of his milieu – of its newspapers, in other words.[308] At the time Marcel came to know him, towards the end of 1902,[309] Albufera was involved in a passionate affair with a very young actress at the outset of her career, Louisa de Mornand, who can be seen in a portrait by La Gandara and in several photographs, one of which was inscribed to Proust. Ever since his friendship with Gaston de Caillavet, Marcel, as we have seen, enjoyed the company of couples: apart from the fact that he could disguise his homosexual leanings by taking an interest in the woman, and that his own desire was stimulated by the desires of a third party,[310] the future novelist was interested in that form of love which he had had no direct experience of himself: 'The accursed race' in *Contre Sainte-Beuve* and *Sodome et Gomorrahe I* reveals the author's most direct and personal experiences, whereas in 'Un amour de Swann', Saint-Loup's passion for Rachel (inspired, in fact, by Albufera and Louisa de Mornand — Rachel was Louisa's maid's Christian name)[311] was elaborated on the basis of observation of others: 'I understood that your happiness was hers/ And my own has lain in watching yours.'[312] And so, in the private dining-rooms of Larue's restaurant – 'in that Larue's which is dear and melancholy to me because many of my friendships were virtually born in the rather garish purple of its décor (like those emperors who were known for that reason as Porphyrogenites* – many of whom died young)' – he would be the witness to 'distraught kisses'.[313] What is more, if Proust pretended to be in love with the woman – Jeanne Pouquet, Louisa de Mornand, the Princesse Soutzo (at the time of his friendship with Paul Morand)[314] – it was in order to arouse the jealousy of the man: not so as to quarrel with him (sometimes it almost came to that), but he believed so firmly that it was jealousy that gave rise to love, rather than the reverse, that he entertained the illusory hope of fomenting that love for himself. In the meantime, he displayed a 'loyal and sensitive friendship' for a 'noble and gentle heart' who was 'more dear to him every day'.[315]

He composed a portrait in verse of the young actress, who was starting her stage career that year, acting in curtain raisers on the boulevards:[316] 'Louisa seems to all of us to be a pure goddess/ Of her body there can be no doubt that it holds the promise/ Of her two dream-like eyes, so mischievous and gentle';[317] and another one, in prose, describing her beautiful eyes and her exquisite waist. He did his best not merely to go

---

* The name signifies 'born in the purple' and it became an epithet of children born to Byzantine emperors while their father was on the throne. A purple room was used by the empress for her accouchement. *Tr.*

and watch her on stage, but to arrange for her name to be mentioned in articles in the press. Was she a loose woman? No doubt she was; rather like Odette, who also acted in minor roles in plays, including that of Miss Sacripant,[318] and Rachel, otherwise Proust would not have written her poems which are also, beneath the appearance of bawdy jokes, a confession: 'He who cannot win Louisa de Mornand/ Must be content with Onan's sin.'[319] But unlike Rachel, she was not a former prostitute and she was not Jewish. Nor would she enjoy such a glittering career: Rachel would eclipse la Berma, but Louisa would never rival Sarah Bernhardt or Réjane. The novelist preserves his freedom, and literary criticism begins where biography ends. Louisa de Mornand was born Louise Montaud[320] in 1884, and she was eighteen at the time she made her stage début.* The greater part of her correspondence with Proust was written in the year 1904–5, and it was always Louisa who wrote first, less on account of Albufera than in the hope of securing a part or obtaining favourable reviews. From 1903 to 1910 she played minor roles in twenty plays, at theatres such as the Gaité, the Mathurins, the Vaudeville or the Renaissance; after 1910 her career was over.[321] She stopped acting at the height of her affair with Albufera, who, like Saint-Loup, did not like seeing his mistress on stage. As to the notion of an *amitié amoureuse* with Proust,[†] it can only be based on what the actress said when, in 1928, she published and sold Marcel's letters to her:[322] she had every reason to exploit her relationship at the time (though as she herself pointed out, they saw each other less frequently after she broke off with Albufera in the spring of 1906). It appears that the latter eventually provided her with a small pension (and Saint-Loup would provide Rachel with a large one). He was very kind and very generous, though not very intelligent, Louisa would say to Céleste Albaret. And Proust would tell her in confidence: 'The duke's intelligence is on the same level as Mlle de Mornand's talent. Ah, if only they were both as gifted as he is rich!'[‡] The character of Saint-Loup, therefore, owes its wit to Fénelon, and possibly to the Duc de Guiche. However, when Marcel intervened between Louis and Louisa, when he described a quarrel between the 'lovers' at the Théâtre des Mathurins,[323] or when we hear that in July

---

* Her sister, in whom Fénelon had taken an interest, acted under the stage name of Jeanne Moriane, without ever achieving fame.

† Suggested by Painter.

‡ C. Albaret, *Monsieur Proust*, Laffont, 1973, p. 269. Cf. p. 220, about Louisa: 'It is true that she played in a few very nice roles on the boulevards. But let us say that, by spending a lot of money on her, they had managed to make a walk-on actress of her.'

1904 Albufera became engaged to Anna Masséna d'Essling and married her in October 1904, we cannot avoid thinking of the passionate relationship between Saint-Loup and Rachel. The two lovers did not break off their affair until 1906. Marcel was to learn a great deal from them: what could be more different to everything he had gleaned until then than the stormy love affair of an aristocrat of the Napoleonic era and a small-time variety actress? Proust, in any case, treated them with a kindness and a friendship that was 'deep and twofold'.[324] His work would benefit from the friendship, to such a point that Albufera would break off relations with him when he recognized himself in Saint-Loup. In 1906 Louisa took up with Robert Gangnat.* Proust would discover belatedly through Gaston Gallimard that she had made Gangnat very unhappy, that he had 'put up with abominable behaviour' and that there was a 'mad side' to her. Albufera thought she had 'a deranged mind' and she hurt him a great deal. It was at that moment that Proust must have blackened his portrait of Rachel.[325]

THE DUC DE GUICHE

It was probably at the end of December 1902, at a dinner party at the Noailles', that Proust made the acquaintance of Armand de Gramont, who was then twenty-three.† Tall and handsome, slightly shy or distant, highly intelligent and well regarded as a scientist, he was unusual, though not unique (if one thinks of Maurice and Louis de Broglie, whom, incidentally, he did not know) among the upper ranks of the aristocracy. Proust looked upon him as an ancient *objet d'art*, who was the heir to one of the oldest dukedoms in the land (the title of Duc de Gramont was bestowed on the family by Louis XIII in 1643; that of Duc de Guiche in favour of the eldest son by Louis XIV in 1700; they had been Princes of Bidache since 1570, and the family's line of descent had been established since 1381). Proust alluded to them by copying out the entry from the *Almanach de Gotha*[326] in his pastiche of Saint-Simon: 'It was clear that he was a Gramont, whose family name was Aure, of that illustrious house held in high esteem and distinguished through so many marriages and occupations since the time of Sanche-Garcie d'Aure and Antoine d'Aure,

---

* General Secretary of the Société des Auteurs et Compositeurs Dramatiques, he died in 1910.

† *Corr.*, vol. III, p. 199. Proust related in a humorous way how the young duke's entourage kindled Lucien Daudet's snobbish instincts and made him feel ashamed of having the anti-Semitic Léon for a brother.

Vicomte d'Aster, who took the name and coat of arms of Gramont. Armand de Gramont, whom we are discussing here, and who possessed all the gravity that the other lacked, reminded one of that gallant Comte de Guiche, who had been so well received in the early years of Louis XIV's reign. He towered above all the other dukes, if only because of his infinite knowledge and his admirable discoveries. I can say in all truth that I would speak equally highly of him even if I had not received so many tokens of friendship from him. His wife was worthy of him, which is not faint praise.'[327] His father, Agénor, Duc de Gramont, was born in 1851, and had lost his first wife, Isabelle de Beauvau, by whom he had a daughter, Élisabeth, born in 1875 (she was also a friend of Proust[328] and would write two books about him). In 1878 he married again, this time to Marguerite de Rothschild (who died in 1905); Armand was born in 1879.

With his wife's wealth, the duke had had the Château de Vallières built on the 'English-style' estate that had once belonged to Joseph Bonaparte, and later to the last of the Condé family and its heiress, the Baronne de Feuchères (the festivities described by Nerval in *Sylvie* took place there); in the grounds were the Mortefontaine lakes, so dear to Watteau and to Corot. The château was a replica of Chambord, hung with family portraits and with contemporary paintings by Boldini and Laszlo, and furnished with relics from the sack of Peking; there were thirty bedrooms, a chapel and a private theatre, and it was set in 1,500 hectares of land. From the terrace, above the ponds and the foliage, Marcel could see the towers of Senlis cathedral. Invited to a dinner party (thirty guests), on 14 July 1904, to celebrate Guiche's engagement to Elaine Greffulhe, Proust felt extremely awkward because he was the only person to come in evening dress. The duke, asking him to sign the visitors' book, said to him: 'Your name, Monsieur Proust, but *no thoughts*!', a remark which, as Marcel wrote to Fénelon,[329] would have been more appropriate had their situations been reversed. He returned from this dinner party feeling 'very unwell'. After this Proust would only ever refer to Agénor de Gramont as 'Your name but no thoughts'. He was definitely on top form when he described a conversation between Comte Greffulhe, who was extremely proud of his château at Bois-Boudran, and his future son-in-law, Armand de Guiche: 'Vallières is nice enough. It's not at all unattractive. There's a little lake. It's rather sweet. Of course, I don't think your father would presume to compare it to Bois-Boudran, would he – that would be a real joke, etc.'[330] And here is the Comte Greffulhe, introducing his future son-in-law: 'Let me introduce you to the Duc de Guiche, who got both his *baccalauréats* when he was fourteen; the Duc de Guiche is a doctor –' (to Guiche: 'Doctor of what?' Guiche: 'Not doctor;[331] a science graduate') 'a science graduate, doctor, the whole caboodle!' One is reminded of the satirical verve with which Proust introduces the Duc de Guermantes. On 14 November 1904 the Duc de Guiche married Elaine Greffulhe, whom Proust already knew; no doubt it was their engagement that had made him try to publish an article on 'Le Salon de la Comtesse Greffulhe' in *Le Figaro*, which may have been stopped by the Comte, who mistrusted literary types. As a wedding present, Marcel (having taken one of his friend's jokes seriously) gave them a revolver in a casket on which he had asked Madrazo to paint some watercolours illustrating poems written by Elaine when a child: Marcel resorted to such delicacies when he wished to please. When the Duchesse de Gramont, Guiche's mother, died at the age of fifty in 1905, Marcel displayed all his sensitivity by putting himself in the place, not of the son, but of the mother: 'To think that your mother may have felt that she was leaving you, that she may have believed that never, *never*, in *all eternity* would she see you again, you who were her only happiness; that is the thought that so upsets me.'[332]

Many years later the Duc de Guiche, who by then had become the Duc de Gramont, reflecting on his friendship with Proust, would say that he had been struck from their very first meeting by the shrewdness of Marcel's observations, that he found his introduction and footnotes to Ruskin extremely interesting, even though 'Proust was not taken seriously'. He considered it normal that the novelist should have wanted to compare the different social classes with whom he mingled in the Faubourg Saint-Germain, having succeeded in being accepted by them. Like others, the Duc de Guiche used to come and see Marcel after the theatre: 'He was sitting in the dining-room; he would bring out a bottle of cider from the sideboard and we used to chat gaily . . .' In fact there were friends whom Proust received in the dining-room (and not in the drawing-room), and a few confidants whom he allowed into his bedroom: among these were Reynaldo Hahn and Antoine Bibesco.*

After the war, Proust took offence when the scientist refused to take seriously the comparison a critic from the *NRF*, Camille Vettard, had drawn between Einstein and himself. The duke's recollections end with a final telephone call, made three days before Proust's death. Céleste,

---

* Though not his brother Emmanuel: 'I wouldn't want to see him after I had undressed, wearing my filthy jerseys' (*Corr.*, vol. III, p. 289, to Bibesco).

Marcel's housekeeper, asked the duke for the address of a doctor who would give him camphorated oil injections: 'Was he trying to tell me that he was very ill? Did he want a friend to visit him?'[333]

GABRIEL DE LA ROCHEFOUCAULD

Another friend, the scion of a family that was older still – the first known ancestor was Foucauld I, Seigneur de La Roche, in 1019; François de La Roche was godfather to François I; and the earldom became a hereditary duchy in 1622 – was Gabriel de La Rochefoucauld. He was the son of Comte Aimery, who, despite being a younger son, was, in his speech and his haughty manner, and as described by all the memoirs of the period, the model for the Prince de Guermantes in the 'salon' that Proust created. Gabriel, who was born in 1875 (he died in 1942), lived at his parents' home at 93 rue de l'Université. A man of letters, he wrote a column for *Le Figaro*, where his name particularly appealed to readers, who were used to 'finding a sort of philosophical timeliness and some startling applications'[334] in its pages; he belonged to five clubs, and was a sportsman who enjoyed boxing, fencing, yachting and hunting.[335] 'Beneath his brow, like two precious family jewels, this tall young man has the same bright eyes his mother had',[336] Proust observed, attracted as always by eyes, and by the resemblance of children to their mothers. Gabriel also tried his hand at fiction; after a short story 'in the inwardly sorrowful, outwardly impassive style of Guy de Maupassant',[337] he wrote a novel, *L'Amant et le Médecin* – Proust gave him some advice, which the author accepted,[338] and he himself makes an appearance in it.[339] In 1904 the Comtesse des Garets would commit suicide when the young man's engagement to Odile de Richelieu[340] was announced; his 1920 novel, *Le Moi calomnié*, would be based on this episode. From 1903 Marcel began to find him 'very nice', and in January 1904 he 'began to grow very fond of him'.* He had already revealed to Gabriel how much their notions of love differed: the hero of *L'Amant et le Médecin*, on hearing his mistress say to him: 'Let's just be friends', acquiesces; Marcel, for his part, would have interpreted this remark as 'an admission of satiety', 'the beginnings of indifference', 'a sign

---

* *Corr.*, vol. IV, p. 38, to Mme de Noailles. And he added, à propos of Constantin de Brancovan: 'The end of a friendship is a sad thing and obliges us to replace old friends with new ones ... I feel infinitely sad to see how few people are nice deep down, and the sheer pointlessness of opening one's heart.' He would always remain true to this maxim.

of repulsion': 'I shall never forget', he then confessed, 'the day when those words were said to me by the mistress I most loved. If I did acquiesce, after some resistance, it was out of pride. But I considered that from that day on her desire for my body had been replaced by desire for another. It was the beginning of the break-up. For years afterwards, years of affection and chaste kisses, we never once referred to that moment.'[341] This gradual breakdown of an affair, which has been induced through jealousy, is what Proust described in 'Un amour de Swann' and *Albertine disparue*; here, the avowal appears to refer to Reynaldo Hahn.

Paying tribute to his friend in the January 1923 issue of the *Nouvelle Revue Française*, Gabriel de La Rochefoucauld recalled how extraordinarily cultured Proust was, alluding to his knowledge of Stevenson as well as of Flaubert and Balzac, the colourfulness and gaiety of his sharp conversation, with its witticisms, his love of anecdotes that were 'gentle and acute' in their irony, the dinner parties at which he mixed together a variety of guests, with very differing opinions, and how he would take his plate and sit next to each one of them, thus ensuring that everybody was happy. He did not consider that Proust misjudged high society; he had, in any case, surpassed by far the 'impoverished formula' of the *roman-à-clef*: we see human beings from a far closer perspective and in much greater depth than we do in real life.

RADZIWILL

From 1902 onwards, Proust also saw a good deal of Prince Léon Radziwill, whom he met thanks to Francis de Croisset, and who immediately invited him to dine at Maxim's. Along with Fénelon, Lauris, Gabriel de La Rochefoucauld, Guiche and himself, Marcel included Radziwill among those modern, open-minded and intelligent people who escaped from the daily banter of their social class.[342] The Radziwills were a family of Lithuanian boyars, dating back to Wojskund, who died in 1412; they had been part of the Polish nobility since 1418, and became princes of the Holy Roman Empire in 1515.[343] Prince Constantin, who was born in 1850 and had married Louise Blanc, lived at 5 Place d'Iéna and owned the Château d'Ermenonville. 'He was a highly distinguished gentleman, who was exquisitely urbane. Extremely witty, he retained, even privately, a certain manner that imposed respect ... He received me', André de Fouquières relates, 'dressed in soft pink pyjamas. He took great care over his appearance, and everybody agreed to say that his sets of white and pink pearls were marvellous.'[344] He paid the utmost attention to etiquette. It was said that he liked to surround himself with twelve footmen (among them Albert Le Cuziat, who was destined to play a role in Proust's life, and of whom we shall have more to say). He became a homosexual,* and he served as a model for the Prince de Guermantes and for the father of the Prince de Foix, Saint-Loup's friend.† His son Léon, nicknamed 'Loche' rather unflatteringly, was born in 1880 and was 'a young man full of imagination, irony and charm, and loved nothing so much as the company of those who were well-read and artistic'.[345] He would disappoint Marcel, particularly since their similar tastes must have given him grounds for hope: 'As far as Loche is concerned, I feel such a longing for stability that whenever I am with him I feel as flat as a pancake. I wish you could see me. But he treats me so rottenly that it can't last much longer. And I assure you,' he wrote to Armand de Guiche, 'that it is with a melancholy heart that I shall say to myself: "Yet another lemon squeezed" (Barrès), especially since I had such a liking for this one.'[346] It must have been at this time, in the dining-room of the Château d'Ermenonville, in the chill of the middle of the night,[347] that Proust composed a portrait of this other model for Saint-Loup which, in its cruelty and harshness, is worthy of Saint-Simon, and in which one can detect all the bitterness of disappointed love. Léon was built like a block of stone, with inexpressive eyes, yet possessed of charm and delicacy; he was not very well educated and had 'the heart of a whore, attaching himself to the first person to come along, or, rather, incapable of giving himself', yet he was also generous, sensitive, deceitful and lacking in any will-power: 'To love someone, it is not enough for them to be intelligent,' Proust concluded. 'Not for utility's sake, but out of inconsolable moral loneliness and sadness, I need people of a stable nature with whom one is able to maintain a solid pact and to have a lasting relationship.'‡ In February 1905 he would send Léon a letter breaking off their friendship: 'I no longer wish to see you. I

---

* 'To speak of women is uncivil/ At Constantin Radziwill's' (Montesquiou, 'Papillotes mondaines', *Mercure de France*, June 1929, pp. 557–9). The saying: 'Good year or bad, blackmail costs me seventy thousand francs' is attributed to the prince.

† *RTP*, vol. IV, pp. 406–7. 'He was a tall, good-looking man, like his father ... The Prince de Foix had succeeded in preserving his son from the outside influences of bad company, but not from heredity. Moreover the young Prince de Foix remained, like his in this respect, unknown to his social equals, even though he was wilder than anyone in his behaviour with those from a different milieu.' Here, Proust is referring to Léon Radziwill.

‡ *CSB*, p. 477; we are reminded of this yearning to have a pact, something which failed with Hahn and Bibesco, just as it did with Swann and Odette, and with the Narrator and Albertine.

no longer want us to write to one another, or to know each other. When the friendship I felt for you has died, since such friendships never revive, then I shall be delighted to meet you . . .'[348] When Radziwill married Claude de Gramont, he did not invite Proust to the reception to celebrate the marriage 'contract' on 24 June 1905 (although Marcel was expecting to be asked), nor to the actual ceremony, which took place on 27 June. Loche would desert his wife a week after his wedding.* The marriage would be dissolved on 17 May 1906 and annulled by the Vatican. Loche has been regarded as a model, not only for the Prince de Foix's son, but for the Marquis de Cambremer,[349] along with Henry de Vogüé, with whom Marcel almost fought a duel.

FRANCIS DE CROISSET

Another figure who moved in the same circles at this time was Francis de Croisset,† or, to give him his real name, Frantz Wiener (1877–1937) – the future son-in-law of Mme de Chevigné (after becoming engaged to Mlle Dietz-Monin) – an author of light comedies,[350] who would later collaborate with Robert de Flers after Gaston de Caillavet's death. With his dazzling manner, a flower in his buttonhole, a cigarette in his lips and smelling of perfume,[351] he was to be the inspiration for Bloch's metamorphosis into Jacques du Rozier.[352] In July 1902 Marcel asked him to 'come in for a moment to comfort his sorrows',[353] and on a number of occasions he repeated his invitations to dinner or simply to visit him. He also made use of Croisset in order to please Albufera by obtaining theatre tickets for him, and by helping to further Louisa de Mornand's early stage appearances – for example, he would ask Croisset to arrange for favourable notices to be put in the newspapers. Their relationship was sufficiently close for Marcel to consider travelling to Brussels with him for the first night of *Chérubin*[354] (on condition that he was allowed to do so by his parents!), and intimate enough for him to write to him: 'Like me, you suffer from a persecution mania',[355] or to announce his arrival

* *Corr.*, vol. XVII, p. 145. Proust, who had received as a gift from his former friend a tie-pin in the shape of a hunting horn, would return it to him shortly afterwards, writing that tie-pins brought bad luck and quoting Vigny (on the subject of horns). Several attempts were made to marry Loche off again, in 1907 and 1920 (to Gladys Deacon) and Proust himself, ever obliging, would intervene . . . (ibid., vol. XIX). He mentions him as one of the commanding officers in the Polish army after the war. Loche was to die tragically in Monte-Carlo in 1927.

† The pseudonym is taken from the name of Flaubert's home.

'with his throat covered in cotton wool'.[356] He would organize a group outing for his friends in Cabourg to see Feydeau and Croisset's play *Le Circuit*. They would do favours for one another: Proust, for example, tried to obtain a dispensation from the army for a brief period on behalf of the actor Brûlé, who was performing in one of Croisset's plays; Marcel approached him about obtaining better lodgings at Cabourg, where he went to watch a performance of *Arsène Lupin*, a play written by his friend; and, in 1911, he asked him to give Agostinelli's mistress a job as an usherette.[357] To begin with, Croisset's marriage in 1910 to the Comtesse de Chevigné's daughter must have constituted, if not a bond,* then at least a coincidence, or an additional reminiscence for him, although the Duchesse de Guermantes was childless. However, when Mme de Chevigné took umbrage at being portrayed in *À la recherche*, relationships between Proust and her son-in-law were chilly for a long while.[358]

What was upsetting for Proust during these years was that although he certainly made friends, some, though not all, of whom would remain loyal to him, he was unable to find true love or a relationship in which his affection was reciprocated. 'Yet I know that shared loves exist. But, alas, I do not know their secret.'† Furthermore, the friend he liked best, Albufera, was the least intellectual of the group, and, unlike Fénelon, Radziwill, Casa-Fuerte and Croisset, his behaviour left no room for hope. Thus we see Marcel reverting to the solitary state he knew as a grown-up child, dependent on his parents for everything, even for a short trip away, and with only good friends for company. His tragic notion of love was confirmed during these years when his feelings were never reciprocated. We can see why social life should have become an outlet and a consolation for him, providing hope for an encounter that was becoming less and less likely.

His financial situation added to his woes. He was provided with a fairly

---

* Léautaud noted in his *Journal*: 'Maeterlinck cannot become a member of the Académie because he is Belgian, Mme de Noailles because she is a woman, Porto-Riche because he is a Jew, but Croisset is certain to be elected in spite of the fact that he is all three of these' (11 May 1923), quoted by Painter, vol. II, p. 316. And Cocteau: 'He was a first-rate husband. His wife never knew about his countless escapades, which involved all the sexes' (*Le Passé défini*, Gallimard, 1983, p. 290).

† *Corr.*, vol. III, p. 363. Further on in the same letter Proust laid down once again one of the important psychological laws of *À la recherche*: 'Everything comes to us in the end, even what we desire, but only after we no longer desire it' (25 June or 2 July 1903).

modest personal allowance, which he was meant to manage himself* (something which, even when he was rich, he was always incapable of doing). This was why, when his mother reproached him about the cost of the dinner parties he wanted to give at home – 'as valuable to me as Lyon-Caen† is to Papa, or Robert's bosses are to him' – obliging him to go to a restaurant instead, and failed to appreciate his efforts to settle down to work, he laid such unusual emphasis on his state of mind and his material circumstances. For the first time he contemplated living his life in 'a separate house'; but as his parents would no doubt expect him to pay his own rent – they were already forcing him to pay for his anti-asthma powders – he resigned himself to life as it was: the sadness in which he lived 'at least has the advantage of making me very philosophical'.‡ He envisaged that his departure from the family home would occur when his pen earned him enough money not to be dependent on his parents, even though he would come back 'twenty times a day', because of his need to be with his mother.§

As to literature, as usual we know almost nothing about what Marcel was reading. 'Sublime' was his reaction to René Boylesve's novel, which appeared in *La Renaissance latine* and would eventually be published as *L'Enfant à la balustrade*,[359] an autobiographical story, narrated in the first person, about a rather melancholy childhood; in the same issue he enjoyed Barrès' *Les Amitiés françaises*, which deals with the author's childhood and his son's education. This was precisely the type of book that would be eclipsed by *Du côté de chez Swann*. He also reread Augustin Thierry's *Lettres sur l'histoire de France*, which made him appreciate all that 'those poor enthusiastic citizens and peasants suffered at the hands of the clergy and the aristocracy, particularly at Vézelay'. His historical reading (although

---

* *Corr.*, vol. III, p. 274 ('I am now doing my accounts, and as I am not satisfied with them, I am complaining to my family, who are irritated'), and p. 308.

† A member of the Académie des Sciences Morales, whom Adrien Proust hoped would support his own election to this academy, which was what the Narrator hoped for from Norpois (ibid., p. 266).

‡ Ibid., pp. 267–8. Marcel would, however, give a dinner party at his home on 1 April to which he invited the Noailles, the Chimays, Mme de Pierrebourg and Paul Hervieu, the Strauses, Hermant, Antoine Bibesco (who did not come because he was in mourning), and Croisset after dinner. This did not prevent him from asserting, as he did in his book, that conversation was 'the death of wit'. On 2 April he went to the Folies-Bergère with Lauris to see a 'totally inept' show, about which he wrote an article that *Le Figaro* never published and which has not survived (ibid., p. 285).

§ Ibid., p. 308, spring 1903. Cf. 'I'd rather have asthma attacks and please you than displease you and not have any' (ibid., p. 328).

he claimed not to know the first thing about history, he was passionate about the subject), which was preparing the temporal depths of his novel, also included Lenôtre's *Vieilles maisons, vieux papiers* and *Le Baron de Batz.** Lenôtre, whose real name was Théodore Gosselin (1857–1935), originally a columnist on *Le Temps*, was an admirer of Dumas and enjoyed considerable success by concentrating on 'minor history', that is to say on secondary characters, on anecdotes and on the way of life during the revolutionary and imperial periods. It is these obscure characters who most resemble fictional heroes. The Lemoine affair, the subject of pastiches that Proust would write in 1908, is very reminiscent of Lenôtre, as are the anecdotes in *À la recherche* concerning the Queen of Naples, the Princesse Mathilde and the less important aspects of the Dreyfus affair.

It was some time before *La Bible d'Amiens* was published. In June 1903 Marcel was expecting the proofs 'from one day to the next'. Early summer was the time of year, so hard for those inclined to worry, when he felt 'how empty his life was of those pleasures that would be sweetest to him',[360] when he occasionally succumbed to moments of 'unbelievable depression and stupidity'.[361] In mid-July he received the proofs of his introduction, which, together with the presence of Fénelon, made him 'crazy'.[362] On 27 July Professor Proust presided over the prize-giving at the primary school at Illiers and, as has already been mentioned, gave a speech that Marcel had helped to write,[363] full of quotations from Hugo, Baudelaire, Sully-Prudhomme, Leconte de Lisle, Horace and Malherbe; a reference to the painting in the Louvre in which Léopold Robert depicts harvesters returning home is a reminder of how frequently Marcel used to visit the museum. Two days later, following a lively discussion with Albufera, Fénelon and Lauris, he summarized, in a letter to the latter, his political views on the application of the laws governing religious orders[364] and his overall view of the policies of the centre left, under the leadership of Combes, in the aftermath of the Dreyfus affair: 'At that time the pressing need was to review the injustices of the General Staff, whereas today it is to review the injustices of the government . . . At the present moment, the socialists are making the same mistake by being anti-clerical as the clericals did in '97 by being anti-Dreyfusard.' Proust felt, just as Péguy did,† a particular responsibility as far as their present policies were

---

* Ibid., p. 432, 26 October 1903, to Mme de Noailles. Proust had just visited 'the marvellous abbey church at Vézelay' without suspecting 'the cruelty of the Abbé Pons de Montboissier'.

† Péguy describes this period in *Notre jeunesse* (1910).

concerned. He drew careful distinctions between clericalism and religion; among the clericals were grouped the anti-Dreyfusards and the anti-Semites: 'The mainstay of the Catholic faction (Barrès, etc.) does not consist of believers.' There was no point in throwing out the religious orders, for 'with the orders gone and Catholicism dead in France (if it could be extinguished, though it is not through laws that ideas and beliefs are killed, but rather when their truth and social utility are corrupted or diminished), there will be just as many clerics – unbelieving clerics – more violently anti-Semitic, anti-Dreyfusard and anti-liberal than ever, and they will be a hundred times worse'. Proust even took up the defence of the Jesuits: 'There is a Jesuit philosophy, a Jesuit art, a Jesuit system of education.* Will there ever be an anti-clerical art?' The nineteenth century rejected Voltaire's anti-Christian philosophy: 'Baudelaire himself was loyal to the Church, at least through sacrilege.' Proust always stood up against injustice, and he did so all the more intensely here, given that he was not a believer himself. He would say much the same to Gregh: 'I confess that I prefer to find monks in a monastery re-establishing Benedictine music than a liquidator destroying everything (look at Saint-Wandrille).' Ever since he was a young student, his abstract thought was expressed with clarity, vigour and depth, and controversy enriched it. He was one of those, less unusual among minorities, whose ideas were 'against' the prevailing view. It is worth drawing attention, in passing, to his firm condemnation of anti-Semitism – of which he was only too often the victim (and continued to be so after his death) – which, in spite of the Bloch family, precludes him in any way from being considered anti-Semitic.

In mid-August, after spending some time in Switzerland, Marcel's parents arrived at Évian. Their son would not join them until 1 September. His journey there, as he described it to Georges de Lauris, was not without interest. Having set off by train on his own on 31 August, he stopped at Avallon, then, after a three-hour drive in a hired car, he arrived in Vézelay. He gave a literary picture-postcard description of the town: 'A fantastic place, in a sort of Switzerland, all alone on top of a mountain that towers above the others, visible from all sides for miles around and set among the most strikingly harmonious scenery. The church is vast and looks as much like a Turkish bath as it does Notre-Dame, built in alternate blocks

---

* *Corr.*, vol. V, p. 284. He added: 'Basically, politics don't matter to me. I feel rather irritated by all the noble socialists that I see around.' Another characteristic of Saint-Loup.

of black and white stone, a lovely Christian mosque.'* When he returned to Avallon that evening, with a high fever and 'incapable of going to bed', Marcel walked about 'all night long', doubtless to avoid having to brave a strange bedroom; boarding a train at six o'clock in the morning, and having admired Semur from his carriage window, he arrived at ten o'clock at Dijon, which he felt strong enough to visit and where he particularly admired the great tombs of the dukes of Burgundy.† At eleven o'clock that evening, there arrived at Évian a man so exhausted that he no longer recognized himself in the mirror, and people came up to him asking whether they could be of help: in his desire to study masterpieces of art, Marcel found the strength to overcome his illness and his anxieties. In *À l'ombre des jeunes filles en fleurs* he would remember the sunrise seen from the train – 'an inversion, more delightful to my taste, of the sunset'.‡ While on this trip, he admitted to Lauris, who was keen on bawdy tales and erotic books,[365] that he was filled with 'a wild desire to ravish these little sleeping towns (note the word towns [*villes*] and not girls [*filles*]!'. On the basis of a reminiscence and a play of words, the novelist would create a desirable girl, and he would introduce a milkmaid, the incarnation of the dawn.

After spending several days in bed at the Hôtel Splendide, Marcel began to rise once more at two o'clock in the afternoon. He made the acquaintance of Ambassador Nisard (who had been appointed to the Vatican until diplomatic relations were broken off); he was Marie de Benardaky's uncle and one of the models for Norpois. The strangest thing about this visit to Évian was that Louisa de Mornand and Louis d'Albufera should have taken Marcel, on the back of a mule, to 'Chamouni' (using the spelling of Ruskin and Michelet; it was because 'these marvellous mountain excursions were the greatest joy of Ruskin's life'[366] that Proust wished to imitate him), to Montanvert and over the Mer de Glace. On his return, his friends looked after him during the inevitable asthma attack induced by extreme exertion.[367]

---

* Ibid., vol. III, pp. 418–19, September 1903. In *RTP*, vol. II, p. 19, Vézelay would be reduced to the symbol of those towns whose names are designated by their churches: it is therefore by association with the 'mosque' at Vézelay that the Narrator imagines a church and a name, 'Persian in style', at Balbec.

† He had seen the casts at the Trocadéro museum, and he would place some tombstones in the church at Combray (those of the Guermantes) and also in Charlus' church, in Burgundy (*RTP*, vol. II, p. 830).

‡ *Corr.*, vol. III, p. 418: is inversion always delightful?

After leaving Évian on 10 October, Proust stopped at Bourg-en-Bresse, in order to visit the Brou church, and at Beaune to see the hospice. It was less a case of annotating Ruskin, the translation of which was completed, than of feeding an appetite for religious architecture which would survive until *À la recherche*, and perhaps of writing an article for the *Gazette des Beaux-Arts* on the subject ('Marcel is still busy with his cathedrals', his father would say), not so much about history as about his memories of the journey; his proposal, submitted in October, has turned down by Charles Ephrussi. Anything rather than a novel.

THE DEATH OF A FATHER

On 24 November 1903, by a sudden sinister twist of fate, Professor Proust was struck down with a cerebral haemorrhage. He had gone to preside over an examination jury at the Faculty of Medicine. Like the Narrator's grandmother, the professor was taken ill in a water-closet. One should not read into the scene in the Champs-Élysées any intention of defiling the maternal image: no similar accident happened to Mme Proust, nor to her own mother; it was his father whom Proust was remembering in this scene in *Le Côté de Guermantes*, in which he tried to overcome – to control through his writing – the painful memory that pursued him of his father being struck down in a lavatory.* At about four o'clock that afternoon, Marcel, who was in bed, heard a noise in the corridor: 'Through the open door, without my being able to see her, Maman told me not to be cross (if you knew how sweetly she said that to me), but that there had just been a telephone call to say that Papa had been taken ill at the Faculty and that he was being brought home.'† He was unconscious when his son Robert brought him home, and Marcel watched him being brought in on a stretcher; he died on Thursday 26 November at nine o'clock in the morning. His stoutness, overexertion, inattention to diet, and his age, which was already advanced for the time, all contributed to this sudden stroke. His elder son had not expected anything of the kind: 'He was so healthy and so active that I reckoned he could go on like this for some years',[368] and he rejoiced retrospectively that his own illness, which

---

* When Montaigne asserts that we are born in ignominy, like excrement, and die in full glory, a death that is both religious and dramatic, he was describing precisely what was missing in the case of Marcel and his father.

† *Corr.*, vol. XVI, p. 396, end of November 1903. Cf. ibid., vol. XI, p. 71: 'Maman came to say to me: "Forgive me for waking you, but your father has been taken ill at the School." '

restricted him to the house, should have enabled him to 'enjoy the affection and the company' of his father in those years when he had been closest to him.[369]

Le Figaro devoted a front-page article by Maurice de Fleury to Professor Proust and recalled his brilliant career.[370] The physical portrait he drew of the man touched Marcel: 'He was almost seventy years old. With his grey beard and his regular features, still refined despite the coarsening of old age, his pince-nez astride the end of his nose, causing him to tilt his head upwards, his solemn, ever so slightly nasal voice, and his smile, both perspicacious and indulgent, which was that of a philosopher, Professor Proust gave the impression of an exceptionally lively intelligence inside a rather indolent body.' We know scarcely anything about the details of the funeral arrangements. They are recalled, however, in *Le Temps retrouvé*: 'While in the mortuary the undertaker's men are preparing to take the coffin downstairs, the son of a man who has rendered great services to his country is shaking hands with the last of the friends who are filing past; suddenly the silence is broken by a fanfare of trumpets from beneath the windows outside and he feels appalled, believing that this is some sort of mockery intended to insult his grief. But this man, who has contained his feelings until this moment, can no longer hold back his tears; for he has just realized that what he is hearing is the music of a regimental band which has come to share his mourning and pay homage to his father's corpse.'* The funeral service took place on 28 November: 'At Saint-Philippe-du-Roule, there were black lengths of material embroidered with the initial P hanging from the wall, a huge crowd, the entire Academy of Medicine and other official bodies, candles, a countless number of enormous wreaths, and, at the head of all this extraordinary pomp were Marcel, pale and faltering, and Robert, following behind the mortal remains of their father.'[371] Proust grieved for himself, but also for the person most afflicted, his mother: 'She had given him, to a degree that would be unbelievable to anyone who had not witnessed it, every minute of her life.' And he added words that he would later adapt after the death of Albertine:† 'And now, emptied of what had been their pleasure in life and

---

* *RTP*, vol. IV, p. 462. Cf. draft XXIV, 2, p. 812. This passage appears to be a metaphor for the pain the Narrator experiences on finding in the library a copy of *François le Champi*, which soon awakens memories of evenings at Combray, when the father had actually allowed the mother to go to 'the little one'.

† Cf. 'In the present desperate situation, what is perhaps most cruel of all is the unbearable sweetness of the past, which can be reawakened at any moment by the repetition of situations in

their *raison d'être*, the minutes bring back to her, each in a different form and like so many bad fairies set upon torturing her, the sorrow which will never leave her.'[372] In 1912 he would discover a notebook in which Mme Proust had recounted, hour by hour, the last illnesses of her father, her mother and her husband, 'accounts which, though they had not in the least intended to suggest anything of the kind, are so distressing that one can scarcely go on living after reading them'.[373]

Marcel experienced three aspects of grief simultaneously: an idealization of the person departed ('all his kind-heartedness'),* a sense of aggressiveness towards him ('I rebelled against the excessive confidence and certainty of his opinion', and feelings of guilt ('the remorse – so much more painful now – of feeling that I was the only cloud in his happiness'). But it was a healthy and sober period of mourning and a week later – with some difficulty, it is true – he had come to accept a return to normal life and the passing of time: 'Life has begun again. If I had an aim, some ambition, it might help me to bear it. But that's not the case . . . But at least it is life that has begun again and not the sudden, sharp despair that strikes you just once.'[374] Marcel thought of abandoning Ruskin, then he set to work once more, his mother having invoked the wishes of his father, who had looked forward to publication from day to day: hence the book's dedication: 'To the memory/ of/ my father/ struck down as he was working, on 24 November: died on 26 November/ this translation/ is affectionately dedicated'; this is followed by a quotation from Ruskin which sums up Adrien Proust's life: 'There then comes a time for work . . . ; then a time for death, which, when lives are happy, is very short.' Proust would always write in order to please both his mother and his father and so as to atone for the sorrow that he imagined he had caused them; in *À la recherche du temps perdu*, by a miracle of affection and filial piety, the parents do not die, the happiness of family life continues for ever and the word 'end' does not affect it. To suggest that Marcel did not suffer as a result of his

---

which my father can no longer participate. As to the future, I dare not think about it' (*Corr.*, vol. III, p. 159; cf. p. 461).

* E.g. to Laure Hayman: 'I think he was reasonably pleased with me; it was an intimacy that was never interrupted for a single day and I am especially aware of its sweetness now that even the smallest things in life have become so bitter and so hateful. Other people have a sort of ambition to console them. I have none; all I had was this family life and now it is for ever sorrowful' (ibid., vol. III, p. 456, 10 or 11 December 1903). It would be hard to claim, as one biographer does, that Proust derived 'a timorous solace', that he felt no sadness and was happy to be alone with his mother: this type of half-baked psychoanalysis has no place here.

father's death, one could not have read or been moved by what he wrote ten months afterwards: his habit of harking back to the day that his father died and to all the happiness that preceded it meant 'that one has to work out the dates in order to be able to tell oneself that already ten months have gone by, that one has already been unhappy for such a long time, that one would continue to be so for a long time to come, and that for the past ten months [his] poor little Papa had no longer enjoyed anything and no longer knew the sweetness of life'.[375] At the request of Marcel and his mother, Marie Nordlinger would engrave a medallion depicting Professor Proust, which was intended for his tombstone.* Marcel was delighted with it, and thought it 'extremely pretty'.[376]

---

* His descendants would remove it; it is to be found at Illiers.

CHAPTER X

Sesame and Lilies

How did Proust proceed from the translation of a book about the cathedral at Amiens to that of an essay on reading? The postscript to the introduction to the *Bible* helps us understand how this came about. In addition, the shock of his grieving did not allow Marcel to devote himself to a work of creativity that would emanate entirely from himself, that is to say to a novel. He still had need of a master who would guide him along the track he had begun to explore: that of the discovery of beauty. The theory of reading would provide him with precisely what he needed to understand what he was currently living through. Gradually, he would substitute Ruskin's ideas with his own, and, through reading, he would rediscover his own childhood. In this way he set forth on the route to Combray.

TRANSLATION IN 1900

Was Proust a translator like any other? Probably not, especially if one considers that he refused to follow Robert d'Humières' advice of making cuts, using circumlocutions, avoiding any difficulties in the original text; Marcel did not resort to such methods. There was a long tradition, dating back to the Renaissance and the *'belles infidèles'* of the seventeenth century, that allowed French translators to produce a version that was far removed from the original. Thus the translator of *Tom Jones*, de La Place, wrote in 1751: 'Had Mr Fielding written for French readers, he would probably have suppressed a great number of passages, quite excellent in themselves, but which to them would appear inappropriate. Once their interest has been stimulated by a poignant and adroitly constructed plot, they tolerate all types of digressions, dissertations or moral treatises with impatience.' He put forward this as an excuse for having 'accommodated a few passages to the French taste'.[1] In the nineteenth century Chateaubriand, like all great writers, was an exception to this tendency: his translation of *Paradise*

Lost was very close to Milton's text and he tried to find poetic equivalents for the English verse. But Defaucompret *père* (1767–1843) and *fils* (1797–1865), who adapted 600 books, including the works of Walter Scott, in a veritable factory, and Amedée Pichot, the translator of Shakespeare and Thackeray, produced many a free adaptation that incorporated cuts, as well as mistranslations.[2] Even the early twentieth-century translations of Joseph Conrad's novels by Jean-Aubry or Robert d'Humières required important revisions,[3] and it can only be because of his reputation that Gide's rendition of *Typhoon* escaped criticism. This was a writer's version: it was no longer quite the English author speaking in his own tongue. Proust, however, tried to find the precise epithet* and he stuck to the meaning, the rhythm and the music of the sentence: this explains the use of contrast[†] and oxymoron, or the repetition of terms and the use of three adjectives pertaining to different fields in the work of these two writers. What is more, Marcel imitated Ruskin in his pastiche of him.[‡] He even managed to enhance the force and density of the English phrase. 'It is when Ruskin is far removed from us that we translate his books and try to capture the essence of his thought in an equivalent image.'[4] Translation provided the distance necessary to the imagination, since Ruskin was no longer present, and at the same time it taught through imitation – though from an abstract model, an idea and its concrete expression; finding the equivalent image taught him style.

In 1905, Proust told Gabriel Mourey, the editor of *Arts de la vie*, a magazine to which he contributed: 'I'm only translating a little, you know ... I've put as much care into it as I could.'[5] These modest remarks conceal a philosophical concept of the translator, one which Proust confided to the historian Georges Goyau: 'You know what admiration I have for Ruskin. And since I believe that each of us is responsible for those souls that he particularly loves, a responsibility for making them known and appreciated ... you know with what a scrupulous hand

---

* Thus when Ruskin described the Gothic as 'authoritative', Mme Proust suggested *'pleine d'autorité'* and Marcel chose *'exemplaire'* (*Bible*, p. 250). He actually sought to expand adjectives that were untranslatable.

† 'Important and short-lived' corrected to 'current and enduring'; cf. 'abrupt and ancient', 'inoffensive and monstrous'. But, as E. Wada observes, the rhetoric in the introduction to *La Bible d'Amiens* became poetic in the introduction to *Sésame et les lys*: 'the vapid, honeyed scent'.

‡ *CSB*, p. 202: *'notre époque votive, émotive et locomotive'*, which E. Wada likens to such Ruskinian constructions as 'metalliferous, coniferous and Ghostiferous mountain'. Equally, both writers made use of assonance and repetition.

– but a pious one too and as gently as I was able – I approached it.'[6]

At the same time as he delivered his manuscript of the first part of *Sésame* to Mercure de France, Proust signed a contract with the publisher, Alfred Vallette, on 26 February 1904, which proves that on this occasion he abandoned the dangerous notion of paying for publication. On a book selling at a price of 3.50 francs,* the contract provided for a royalty of fifty centimes for every copy sold after the first 500,† which is approximately 15 per cent. This means that a translation, as long as it sold, which was seldom the case, was better remunerated then than is the case today. Although Proust also received payment for his articles, he would nevertheless have to wait until after the war, and for Gallimard to become his publisher, in order to live by his pen.

On the subject of articles, Proust experienced a great disappointment, which led to his quarrelling with Brancovan: in December 1903 the latter reneged on the literary criticism column that he himself had suggested two months beforehand. Writing to Mme de Noailles, to whom he had just given as a present a Gallé vase[7] decorated with ferns, to illustrate a short story, 'L'Exhortation', which the poetess had just published, in which the plant symbolized death (we come across these vases in *À la recherche*) Marcel explained that when people were nice to him, he was in the habit of 'dissolving into tears of gratitude and affection'; therefore when people behaved towards him in the opposite way, he felt he should tell them what he thought[8] – he thereby revealed, incidentally, that he was just as capable of painting his own self-portrait as Montaigne, and just as lucid as he (or Mme de Sévigné) when depicting his own character. Proust then amused himself by alluding to the magazine as '*Inconstance latine*', '*Jactance latine*', '*Inconvenance latine*', '*Indécence latine*', '*Méconnaissance latine*';‡ none the less, he enjoyed the pages from Thoreau's *Walden*, translated by the Princesse de Polignac.[9] At the same time, he had difficulty extricating himself from the final proofs of *La Bible d'Amiens*, tormented as he always was (he could torment himself over intellectual matters just as he did over moral issues) by new qualms: he hesitated over several meanings, which

---

* The equivalent of sixty-six francs in 1999.

† Sixty centimes after 3,000 copies; seventy centimes after 6,000. Details of the contract were kindly passed on to us by Mme Nicole Boyer.

‡ Proust's parodies of the title of Brancovan's magazine, *La Renaissance latine*, translate approximately as: 'Fickleness' (*inconstance*); 'Conceit' (*jactance*); 'Impropriety' (*indécence*); 'Ignorance' (*méconnaissance*): Tr.

were mutually exclusive;* we can see what translation teaches the analyst
of feelings and the stylist: in his own work he could suggest everything,
'either . . . or . . .'

BEGINNING SESAME

Proust, who, like all intelligent people, was able to do several things at
once, not only began to translate *Sesame and Lilies* in January 1904, but
also rewrote Marie Nordlinger's draft of the beginning, 'changing every
word', in such a way as to improve the French and so as not to lose the
'elusive meaning of the English'.[10] In the process he compiled an entire
notebook, correcting, he joked (since humour consisted of making fun
of oneself and not taking oneself seriously) 'fifty or rather three hundred
mistakes'. During early February, he translated the whole of the first part
of the book, 'Of Kings' Treasuries', which was about reading, and he had
begun to write comments on the text, intended for his introduction and
his footnotes (as usual, his progress to start with was rapid; he felt 'all on
fire').[11] Marie Nordlinger advised him and corrected his mistakes at this
period; other friends lent him books: he asked Reynaldo for Maeterlinck's
La Vie des abeilles,[12] which marked the start of the Belgian writer's long
influence over him (*L'Intelligence des fleurs* would provide the most beautiful
image in *Sodome I*) and which he would refer to in his notes.

At the end of February, just after the contract had been signed and *La
Bible d'Amiens* had been published, Marcel, with his customary generosity,
was busy inscribing copies to his friends:† to Mme Daudet, to Léon and
Lucien, to Louisa de Mornand, to his former classmate at the Lycée
Condorcet, the neo-Kantian philosopher Léon Brunschvicg, whose *Introduction à la vie de l'esprit*[13] he had read and quoted from, to Montesquiou,
to Fénelon, to Daniel Halévy, Henry Bordeaux, Louis de Robert, Robert
Dreyfus, Gabriel Mourrey, to Willy, who sent him an ironic and unpleasant
letter, to Francis de Miomandre, Pierre Lavallée, the Abbé Vignot, Georges
Goyau, Mme de Brantes, Barrès, Abel Hermant (who he hoped would
write an article), and to thirty others. Having received the letters of thanks,
he set about replying to them, thanking the sender and discussing their
contents: some important ideas were raised in the process, as, for example,

---

* *Corr.*, vol. IV, p. 45. On 26 February he sent a further list of judicious corrections, too late for
them to be printed (ibid., p. 65).

† Only seven copies were printed on Holland paper.

when he told Bordeaux that 'it is possible to recover possession of the past. It is what one tries to do when one goes back along the path of enchanted memories, or when one writes a fine book';[14] or when he wrote to Barrès, anticipating what he would say in *Contre Sainte-Beuve*: 'I said that the lives of Racine, Pascal, Tolstoy and Maeterlinck[15] divided themselves into two parts. It is an idea that pleases me.'[16] In oblique terms, he outlined his plans to him: 'I still have two Ruskins to do and after that I shall try to translate my own poor soul, if it hasn't died in the meantime.'

THE PRESS RECEPTION FOR *LA BIBLE D'AMIENS*

André Chaumeix reviewed the book in *Le Journal des débats* on 20 March 1904. *Le Figaro* of April 1904 referred on its front page to the translation, which was the work of 'a young writer of talent . . . His book is filled with elegant grace and scrupulous care'.[17] On 22 May Albert Flament reviewed the book on the front page of *L'Écho de Paris*. Henri Bergson brought it to the attention of the Académie des Sciences Morales et Politiques on 28 May,[18] asserting that Ruskin's philosophy was both idealistic and realistic, and that his aesthetic views sprang from religious sentiments; he saw the introduction as 'an important contribution to the psychology of Ruskin' and considered the translation to be written in a language that was lively and unusual. Albert Sorel lavished warm praise on Proust in *Le Temps* of 11 July: 'He writes, whether in reverie or meditation, a French that is flexible and enveloping, containing infinite vistas of colours and shades, and yet which is always translucent'; comparing him to Gallé, he added that his imagery usually derived from Scripture. This praise from his former teacher, the man who had introduced him to the secrets of foreign policy and to the delights of some of Balzac's novels, such as *Une ténébreuse affaire* or *L'Envers de l'histoire contemporaine*, overwhelmed Marcel with pleasure.[19] In the 15 September issue of *La Revue des deux mondes*, Georges Goyau contributed a few eulogistic if banal lines to Ruskin and his translator,[20] and in *Le Gaulois* of 18 December there was a column and a half on the front page that was much more complimentary about the translation, 'a genuinely artistic effort, in which we observe the interpreter of Ruskin shaping his text lovingly, in a sort of caress, and then adorning it with respectful subtleties'.[21] These words went right to Marcel's heart, and ultimately – although he had devoted as much care and attention to the matter as any modern press attaché – he was rather spoilt by the critics. Happier times! Nowadays it has become extremely rare for reviewers to deign to mention the quality of a translation or an introduction.* Nevertheless, Proust would observe with some pique that his 'literary friends', Léon Daudet and Hermant, had done nothing.[22] By April, a fourth impression had been printed, although each printing consisted of only 1,000 copies.

PROUST AND SAINT-SIMON

Montesquiou, meanwhile, had published privately fifty copies of a booklet entitled *Fête chez Montesquiou à Neuilly*, printed on Holland paper, without knowing who the author was. This was a pastiche of Saint-Simon which Proust, writing under the name Horatio, the Shakespearean pseudonym which he used on several occasions, had published in *Le Figaro* of 18 January 1904.[23] Montesquiou was extremely pleased with the portrait Marcel had sketched of himself, his secretary Yturri and his guests.

It is hard to tell when Proust began to read Saint-Simon: the first reference to him appears in 1899, in a letter to France. We know that Marcel used the Chéruel edition,[24] and in his 1904 pastiche he employed six of the volumes[25] in order to track down the genealogical details of the people he mentioned – La Rochefoucauld, Noailles and Chimay. It was another form of idolatry, since it subjugated the work of art to life itself.[†] Early in 1909 Proust asked Montesquiou if he could borrow a copy of his 1904 pastiche, which he wanted to include in 'L'Affaire Lemoine',[26] something he would delay doing until later. When Marcel emulated Saint-Simon's style, it was in order to pay further tribute to Montesquiou by comparing him to the great nobles of Louis XIV's court, in the self-same style employed by its foremost chronicler. Imitating a grandiose style was also a way of tearing himself away from the banality of social reportage. It was a preparation for the novel: Saint-Simon portrayed social gatherings, so does *Le Côté de Guermantes*. Proust thus imitated both style and subject, form and content, in order to deliver a second text: the party given by Montesquiou, who is not yet Charlus, but who, once he does become

---

* Proust was also mentioned in *Les Arts de la vie* and *La Chronique des arts et de la curiosité* in March, and in *La Revue de Paris* on 1 April.

† Proust has been wrongly suspected of using only the index of the Chéruel edition to look for the names of those of Montesquiou's relatives to whom he wished to allude. After this pastiche, Proust would frequently mention Saint-Simon: in 'Sur la lecture' and in the introduction to *Sésame et les lys* (1905); in his letters to Mme de Noailles (1904) and to Georges de Lauris (late December 1908).

him, will be closely linked to Saint-Simon;[27] everything comes full circle, because the poet who wrote *Les Perles rouges* had devoted a sonnet to the author of the *Mémoires*.*

The pastiche begins with a long description of Montesquiou, which reveals the complexity of his character and describes his physique and his voice, followed by a portrait of his secretary Yturri, who put all his own talent into 'making that of the count burst forth'. Proust took the opportunity to pay homage to the Duchesse de Clermont-Tonnerre, to the Comtesse Greffulhe, to Mme de Brantes and to Mme de Noailles, 'who has given new life and, one might say, extended the miracle of the celebrated Sévigné'. Very cleverly, and with erudition, these characters are given their places in Saint-Simon's court system: they become its puppets. When the style changes, they become Proust's puppets. Thus the portrait of Montesquiou is based on that of the Prince de Conti.[28] Saint-Simon described the Prince de Conti; Marcel, a pseudo-Saint-Simon, described Montesquiou in Conti; Proust, the author of *À la recherche*, portrayed Montesquiou in Charlus, but Saint-Simon was no longer more than an exterior reference – explicit, but kept at a distance – because it was by way of him that Marcel discovered his style.[29]

THE STAGES OF THE TRANSLATION

Whether it was because his mother was too affected by grief, or because the competence of an Englishwoman made her feel she should step aside, but Marie Nordlinger[30] took over from Mme Proust as Marcel's assistant. She provided Marcel with a first draft of the translation of *Sésame* (written in notebooks which he lost, then found again),[31] which he subsequently rewrote entirely: 'When you translate English,' he wrote to her, 'all the original characteristics reappear: the words revert to their type, to their affinities, their meanings, their native rules. And whatever charm there may be in this English disguising of French words, or rather in this apparition of English expressions and English faces breaking through their French accoutrements and masks, all this life will have to be cooled down, gallicized, distanced still further from the original, and all originality

* Unpublished note included in J. Milly, *Les Pastiches de Proust*, A. Colin, 1970, p. 247: 'If Comte Robert de Montesquiou had sung the praises of Saint-Simon in his *Les Perles rouges* [in Proust's pastiche], the great seventeenth-century memorialist generously returned the compliment by including him in his famous *Mémoires*.'

extinguished.'[32] Once this version was ready, he prepared a list of questions to put to Marie:* 'It is best that I revise what you have done on my own, and then later we can discuss everything together.' He suggested to the young woman that they should sign the contract together, which she would refuse to do,† and that they share the royalties. Hence we are able to date the different stages of work,‡ which advanced much more quickly than *La Bible d'Amiens*: on this occasion, there was no journey to make and no churches to visit. The subject of the first part, 'Of Kings' Treasuries', as already mentioned, is reading (that of the second part, 'Of Queens' Gardens', is the education of girls; one wonders why Marcel translated it: probably so that the book should not appear too slim); Proust had only to ask questions of himself in order to annotate and write an introduction to such a subject, in order to converse about it with the author and, ultimately, to disagree with him. As for the introduction, he must have written it during the summer and autumn of 1904, since Brancovan accepted it for his *Renaissance latine* at the end of that year.[33]

In January 1905, Marcel received 'the splendid new edition of Ruskin' as a New Year's present; in this Library Edition, which was published six volumes at a time from 1903 to 1912,[34] he would find, in addition to the text itself, a number of engravings which would inspire his thoughts about art and, in *Du côté de chez Swann*, his observations on sculptures and paintings (notably 'Jethro's daughter' by Botticelli,[35] the Vices and Virtues by Giotto at Padua, and Carpaccio's *Legend of St Ursula*).[36] In March, April and May 1905, in *Les Arts de la vie*, 'read by all the truly intelligent artists in France',§ Proust published an extract from 'Trésors des rois', which Gabriel Mourey had accepted in May 1904, when he had completed his translation, but had not yet revised it.¶ Work appears to have been interrupted in the

---

* E.g. in February: 'Underline all the mistranslations yourself with a special pencil, inserting above . . . the correct meaning' (*Corr.*, vol. IV, p. 55).

† Ibid., vol. IV, p. 272, 17 September 1904: 'Why don't you want your name to be linked with mine on the cover of *Sésame*?'

‡ For example, on 26 January 1904: 'I've rewritten the beginning, altering every word, but at the most I've done ten pages', but without losing 'the elusive meaning of the English'. In February he rewrote the first notebook, *ne varietur*.

§ *Corr.*, vol. V, p. 261. He had corrected the proofs in October 1904, at the time Mme Proust was helping him 'unravel' Ruskin's introduction.

¶ In May he wrote to Marie that he had been retranslating it from 'top to bottom'; this was at the time he was commissioning a bust, which would become a 'medallion', on behalf of Mme Proust, for his father's tomb (ibid., vol. IV, pp. 132–3, 203). And in September, writing to Mourey, he said he had finished a long time ago.

autumn of 1904, when Marie went to the United States to deal with Bing's etchings. In February 1905 he began to translate 'Of Queens' Gardens' on his own. Marie Nordlinger stayed rather longer in America, where she appears to have won the heart of Freer (1856–1919), the collector she had gone to see, who would become the owner of two hundred works by Whistler (some of them would be exhibited in Paris in June 1905, and Proust would go to see them),[37] which were bequeathed to the Smithsonian Institution in Washington.* Marcel sought the help of Charles Newton Scott, 'a charming old English scholar'.† In early June, Marie, who had returned from America, went to see Marcel and found him 'bedridden, his eyes ablaze, his pale face framed with a thick black beard'.[38] They worked on *Sésame* 'until dawn'. By way of thanks, he considered a dedication in which he would mention the bronze medallion of Professor Proust, 'the face of [his] father, whose eyes, now closed for ever, are only open within the memory of those who have loved him. But between his eyes and life, our memory holds up the veil of Time, which cannot be drawn aside'. Those eyes see nothing of life as it passes, 'unless they should be re-opened, in a heavenly refuge, able to see the eternal things, of which we know nothing'.[39] Mme Proust must have rejected this dedication, which was too intimate (but which has a ring of *Le Temps retrouvé*); it was never published. On 15 June *La Renaissance latine*, whose editor was now reconciled with Marcel, published 'Sur la lecture' ['On Reading'], the introduction to *Sésame et les lys*. The completed manuscript was delivered to Mercure de France at the end of June 1905. But there was to be no question of further translations: Proust refused an offer from Rosen, a publisher in Venice, to translate *Saint Mark's Rest*, because otherwise, he said, he would die 'without ever having written anything *of his own*'.[40]

OTHER PUBLICATIONS

Unable to finish *Sésame* as quickly as he would have wished, Marcel took the opportunity to dash off a few lesser articles, such as portraits, pieces about salons and some literary criticism. For example, he published an

* 'I've waited months for you to return from America, then weeks to come back from Manchester, to send you my manuscript, since I have a great deal to ask you about the *Lys*' (ibid., p. 261). None the less, he sent her a copy to obtain her comments.

† Ibid., vol. V, p. 42. In the 1906 Mercure de France edition of *Sésame et les lys* Proust acknowledged 'all the precious information that was kindly supplied by M. Charles Newton Scott, the poet of the erudite, to whom we owe *L'Église et la pitié envers les animaux* and *L'Époque de Marie-Antoinette* [*The*

obituary of Madeleine Lemaire's aunt: 'Une miniaturiste du second Empire: Madame Herbelin', in *La Chronique des arts et de la curiosité* on 23 April 1904. This old lady (1818–1904), 'so lively, so gentle and so unaffected', had known the sumptuous lifestyle and been a member of the most glittering society of the *monarchie de Juillet* and the Second Empire. Is she not reminiscent of Mme de Villeparisis? Her miniatures depicted all the prominent personalities of her day as well as the regulars at her salon. When Mme Herbelin spoke of them, 'her conversation became instructive and piquant' (we can visualize Marcel as he listened to her), and it was like reading authentic memoirs. The daughter of an Empire general, she had gathered together stories that 'still had a vivid, epic quality'. Afterwards, she grew old behind her casement windows 'like one of those charming old miniatures to which she put her name'. She continued to live on in her niece, Madeleine Lemaire, and her great-niece, Suzette, just as Gilberte and Odette did in Mlle de Saint-Loup. She became a figure in *Le Temps retrouvé*, one of those portraits of the old which Proust, like Hals and Rembrandt, whose work he knew so well and could translate into words, excelled in depicting.

'Le Salon de la comtesse Potocka', which appeared in *Le Figaro* on 13 May 1904, opens with a tribute to two of Proust's favourite books: Balzac's *Les Secrets de la princesse de Cadignan* and Stendhal's *La Chartreuse de Parme*, for the Comtesse Potocka was like the reincarnation of both of their heroines; as such she resembles the Duchesse de Guermantes, and was, like her, 'queen of the moment';* Saint-Simon soon completed this literary vision. The countess's faithful admirers followed her to her retreat in Auteuil,† where she lived surrounded by her dogs (who would one day devour her): as a columnist, Marcel enjoyed listing the great names of the aristocracy, interspersing them with a portrait, such as that of Gabriel de La Rochefoucauld, another model for the Guermantes. They were followed by the men of letters and artists, such as Maupassant (who had been in love with her as well as with her friend, Mme Kahn),[41] Barrès, Bourget,

---

Age of Marie-Antoinette (1889), but there is no record of the first of these titles in the British Library Catalogue. *Tr.*], two delightful books which ought to be better known in France, that are full of wisdom, sensitivity and wit' (n. 1, p. 7). In June 1904 Proust was sent a copy of Scott's *Foregleams of Christianity, an Essay on the Religious History of Antiquity* (*Corr.*, vol. IV, p. 164).

  * 'She always had the unknown quality of the future moment' (*CSB*, p. 494).

  † 'It's very pretty,' the Comte de La Rochefoucauld said to her the first time he undertook the pilgrimage. 'Is there anything of interest to see in the vicinity?' (*CSB*, p. 492). She had originally lived at the sumptuous Potocki mansion at 27 Avenue de Friedland.

Caro (whom she enjoyed humiliating, and who we shall see mentioned in *À la recherche*), Montesquiou, Forain, Hahn, Widor and Fauré. Like Oriane, she had a court of admirers, but no lover. And Proust ends with a very Balzacien – or very Guermantes – witty remark of the countess's. The article did not please her, although Proust did not understand the reason why:[42] he would never get used to these misunderstandings with his models.

Literary criticism, too, obeyed the laws of friendship. Robert d'Humières had been of invaluable assistance to the translator of Ruskin, so when Mercure de France, the publisher of both Ruskin and Kipling, brought out Humières' book, *L'Île et l'Empire de Grande-Bretagne*, Marcel reviewed it for *La Chronique des arts et de la curiosité* on 13 August 1904. He praised its passages of human observation, the descriptions of landscape and the art criticism, and he commended the translator (in connection with one of Humières' interviews with Kipling), but he did not care for the exoticism, something to which Proust would always remain indifferent. The two friends disagreed on one important point: one took science as a basis for his ambition and his philosophy; the other, 'since science is only concerned with what is general', believed that it did not mix with art, 'which has as its precise mission the task of gathering together all that is particular, that is individual, which the syntheses of science allow to escape'.* In October 1904, in the same series of tokens of friendship, Proust wrote 'Le Prince Antoine Bibesco', an unfinished article prompted by the first performance of Bibesco's play *Jaloux* at the Théâtre de l'Œuvre, directed by Lugné-Poe.[43] Here we encounter the aristocrat but also the playwright, who ranked among all those writers with whom Proust kept company and who are now forgotten: 'the Paul Hervieus, the Georges de Porto-Riches, the Tristan Bernards, the Robert de Flers, the Henry Bernsteins, the Gaston de Caillavets, the Abel Hermants'. Bibesco's play, with its Proustian title,[44] is first and foremost a work based on actual people; secondly, it is an eighteenth-century-style character comedy and the portrait 'of a thoughtful, infinitely sorrowful and human soul, with echoes of yesterday, of today, of every age – echoes of tomorrow above all'.[45] After this analysis Proust the journalist conducted an interview with his friend in which the latter explained that he ranked the theatre above the novel and said that his two favourite writers were Hervieu and Porto-Riche. It was the last article –

* *CSB*, p. 495. There is little need to emphasize that these are already the aesthetics of *Le Temps retrouvé*, which are revealed bit by bit.

published posthumously moreover – that Proust devoted to this literary genre which he had so enjoyed and been tempted to pursue in a few sketches and dialogues, the excitement of which he would communicate to the child Narrator, who is in love with everything, with the posters on the Morris columns, and with la Berma.

During the month of August, on a much more serious subject, and in a rare return to politics following the Dreyfus affair, Proust wrote an article which appeared in *Le Figaro* of 16 August 1904 entitled 'La Mort des cathédrales: une conséquence du projet Briand sur la séparation'. In this article he would expound ideas similar to those he expressed to Georges de Lauris on 29 July 1903.* As Proust reminded him when he reprinted this article in 1919 in *Pastiches et mélanges*, these pages 'had as their aim to fight one of the articles of the law on the separation of Church and State', which, in a summary of the Briand plan† that Marcel had just read, anticipated that the state could, within a period of five years, secularize the cathedrals. The mood of the moment was very solemn. Combes' government, which since 1902 had been intensifying the more moderate action of Waldeck-Rousseau's cabinet,‡ had decided that spring to prohibit all religious orders from teaching, and had recalled Nisard, France's ambassador to the Holy See, on 21 May 1904. The law governing the separation of Church and State was proclaimed on 11 December 1905. In 1910, in *Notre jeunesse*, Péguy would expound a position that was similar to that taken by Proust: the victorious Dreyfusards had been wrong to turn against the Catholics, just because clericalism had been anti-Dreyfusard. Their youthful struggle on behalf of justice and the Republic had been corrupted as a result. In his article Proust, with an icy irony worthy of a Christian Anatole France – for this is the most Christian of Proust's writings – imagined some government of the future, Catholicism having been eradicated for centuries, trying to restore life to the deserted cathedrals. They would subsidize the revival of Catholic ceremonies that

---

* See above, chapter IX, 1903. Since he was about to set off on a cruise, he did not have time to correct the proofs of the article. Calmette, the editor of *Le Figaro*, and Barrès congratulated him (*Corr.*, vol. IV, pp. 218–20). The version printed in 1919 frequently differs from the longer one in *Le Figaro*, which itself is sometimes different to the manuscript. See these variants in *CSB*, pp. 772–83.

† In the newspaper, Proust pointed out that the Briand plan was far less harmful than the others, 'being the work of a sectarian mind, no doubt, but in certain measures much better'.

‡ Rousseau died on 10 August 1904, and, writing to his mother, Proust expressed a sadness that one senses was more hers than her son's. Proust's parents must have been more anti-clerical than he was (*Corr.*, vol. IV, p. 213, 11 August 1904).

were more interesting than those in *Parsifal*. Scholars would rediscover the lost significance of these buildings. 'Caravan-loads of snobs' would arrive in the holy cities of Amiens, Chartres, Bourges, Laon, Rheims, Beauvais, Rouen, and Paris, just as they did in Lavignac's Bayreuth. But all this would not bring back the lost ceremonies: 'That is what would be said if the Catholic religion no longer existed and if scholars succeeded in rediscovering its rites, and if artists tried to revive them for us.'[46] But given that the Catholic religion continues to exist, the cathedrals 'are not merely the most beautiful monuments in our art, they are the only ones to still live their integral life and to have remained in touch with the purpose for which they were built'.[47] The clause in the law which so alarmed Proust would allow them to be transformed into whatever pleased the government: 'museum, conference hall or casino'. Marcel was an agnostic still convinced by the lessons of Ruskin and of Mâle, who retained such a passion for cathedrals that he would claim to have considered giving his book titles borrowed from them, 'porch, stained-glass windows in the apse', and which led him one evening to spend two hours gazing at a portal of Notre-Dame de Paris; and yet, he wrote, 'the liturgy forms a single unity with the architecture and sculpture of our cathedrals, for they all stem from the same symbolism'.* The pamphleteer who doubled as historian then quoted three pages from his master Émile Mâle[48] which interpret the office of the Easter Vigil and the Mass; he rounded them off with a quotation from Baudelaire,[49] with Renan describing evening prayer in Quimper cathedral,[50] and with the sacrament of extreme-unction described by Flaubert,[51] which was also interpreted 'with a modern feeling'. After a fine passage on church stalls borrowed from *La Bible d'Amiens*,[52] the article makes poetic reference to the donors, either sculpted or captured in the stained-glass windows, who were to appear so often in *À la recherche*: 'at the foot of the stained-glass window, in their coats of purple, ultramarine or sky-blue, which imprison the sunlight and are set ablaze by it, which fill its transparent sunbeams with colour and suddenly scatter them, in all their myriad colours, to wander aimlessly about the nave, which, in their lazy, confused splendour, they tint with their palpable

---

* Cf. *CSB*, p. 774: 'We might say to the Churches what Jesus said to his disciples: "Unless you eat the flesh of the son of man and drink his blood, you can have no more life in you" (St John, VI, 55), these rather mysterious but very profound words of the saviour becoming, in this new meaning, an axiom of aesthetics and architecture.' An important acknowledgement: Proust was becoming accustomed to lending religious texts a 'new meaning': perpetual adoration, real presence, blasphemy, etc.

reality'.* If the donors' wishes are no longer respected, Proust maintained, faithful to the history and heritage of the past: 'The dead will stop looking after the living, according to the profound truth. And the living, being forgetful, will cease to fulfil the wishes of the dead.' After appealing to the eloquence of Jaurès, the man he had depicted in *Jean Santeuil* under the name of Couzon, Marcel ended with a general synthesis – yet one which heralded 'Combray' – of all the churches of France: 'Following the route of a French road which leads between the sainfoin fields and the apple orchards that border it on either side and allow it to pass by "so beautifully", at almost every step you will see a spire that soars up above the clear or stormy horizon . . . the church from which it thus rises contains some beautiful and solemn thoughts, either sculpted or painted, and other thoughts too . . . which have remained more vague, in the shape of fine architectural lines . . . and are capable of enticing our imagination to dwell on their soaring flight or of trapping it entirely in the arc of their fall.'[53] If Proust invoked the artistic aspects of churches, it was in order to convince his adversaries that their beauty, contrary to the 1900 aestheticism of Montesquiou, of Des Esseintes, was inseparable from their function.[54]

In late August Marcel responded to a survey carried out by *Arts de la vie* on the subject of fine arts and the state.[55] The journalist, Maurice Le Blond, Zola's son-in-law, considered that the state had no right to suppress people's temperaments and condemned the 'secular tyranny' of the Académie de France in Rome. Proust, however, did not believe the state had the *power* to do so. What could suppress an artist's temperament was, above all, 'the beneficent strength of a disposition that was more powerful than one's own' – for Marcel, Darlu, France and then Ruskin had performed this role. 'Then there was the pernicious power of laziness, of illness and of snobbery,' he wrote, in a veiled confession. The state could never have stifled Monet, nor Vuillard. The artist, like the neuropath, had a need for discipline. As to the teaching of art, it would be enough to entrust it to the genuine masters: Monet, Fantin-Latour, Degas, Rodin; Moreau and Puvis de Chavannes had taught well at the École des Beaux-Arts. Proust returned to an idea which was dear to him (and which Malraux would adopt in his turn): we must first of all obey others in order to become

---

* *CSB*, p. 149. This long metaphor, which scarcely added to his political argument, nevertheless shows that Proust had discovered his poetic style. Further on, he lists the 'great, silent democracy' of artisans and humble donors who are represented in the windows, 'the faithful determined to hear the service' and who are threatened with not hearing it again.

aware of ourselves. The carvers of Chartres and of Rheims had created masterpieces while still being very close to 'the Byzantine precepts and style'. The influence of the Impressionists had been even more tyrannical than that of Rome: 'The great tyrant is love, and when we are not original we slavishly copy what we love. The truth is that there is only one freedom for the artist, and that is originality.'[56] As Proust explained to Gabriel Mourey: the Viberts and the Bouguereaus are only Viberts and Bouguereaus and not repressed Monets or Vuillards.[57] Here we already have the crucial affirmation of Le Temps retrouvé: 'As Elstir had found with Chardin, you can only re-create what you love by renouncing it.'* Thus, from one article to another, he developed his definitive aesthetic viewpoint. An anodyne letter to a stranger expressed it equally well: when he condemned 'those books, which the best of our contemporaries frequently produce, in which the originality of the thinker cannot entirely make up for the absent talent of the novelist, and in which purely intellectual essays are arbitrarily connected by a fictional link',† he defined the very danger that he wished to avoid. Similarly, when he gave a definition of beauty: 'It's a kind of blending, a transparent unity in which all things, having lost their initial aspect as things, have lined up beside each other in a sort of order, are instilled with the same light and are seen within each other . . . I suppose this is what is called the gloss of the old masters.'‡

On 14 December in Gil Blas Marcel published, as a gesture of friendship, a 'brief note' on Fernand Gregh's Étude sur Victor Hugo suivie de pages sur Verlaine, l'humanisme, Schumann, Massenet, Debussy, Maeterlinck, etc.'[58] The poet-turned-critic knew how to treat each verse of Hugo's 'like a priceless stone', and could discover traces of him in contemporary poets. Criticism scarcely entered into the final sentence: 'And in this forceful but neglected book, F. Gregh has employed all his profound intelligence, all his trustworthy sensitivity, his goodheartedness and all his delightful wit.' The article opened with a remark of Mallarmé,§ 'one of those profound yet

---

* RTP, vol. IV, p. 620. The Narrator of Le Temps retrouvé asserts that he would not write new versions of either Saint-Simon's Mémoires or the Arabian Nights.

† Corr., vol. IV, p. 135. Proust is no doubt thinking of Barrès here.

‡ Ibid., p. 156, to Mme de Noailles. Proust remarked (June 1904) that this idea had come to him for the first time and that he did not know how to express it. He also made this strange confession: 'It is unfair only to appreciate gentleness in people who are hardhearted and only to be aware of the affection of those who love no one else but you, but it is an injustice to which I am so prone that I secretly cherish it, I who never have friendships, but rather pacts with thieves.'

§ 'A critic is someone who interferes with what does not concern him.'

frivolous remarks which, in his work, compared with his lines of dark verse, are like light's exquisite revenge'. These dark lines would be inscribed by the Narrator on the yacht that was destined for Albertine.

DAILY LIFE

Throughout this uneventful period, which none the less foreshadowed future grief, since Mme Proust was experiencing the kidney problems that would eventually prove fatal,* Marcel, after a number of asthma attacks, did his best to look after himself. He consulted Doctor Merklen (1852–1906), a lung and heart specialist at the Laennec hospital, who informed him that his asthma had become 'a nervous habit and that the only way of curing it was to go to an anti-asthmatic clinic' in Germany, where they would help him to lose this habit: 'I probably won't go,' Marcel confided to Bibesco.[59]

On 9 August, the day after Marie Nordlinger had brought him the medallion depicting his father, Marcel caught the train for Le Havre:† it was the most unexpected journey of his life, a 'sailor's cruise' worthy of Buster Keaton, so unconventional was this particular passenger's behaviour. He boarded the yacht *Hélène*, which belonged to Paul Mirabaud, a banker and governor, or *'régent'*, of the Banque de France, and the father-in-law of his friend Robert de Billy. He was 'an immensely strong Saxon god with exactly' the same face as his daughter: the Wagner enthusiast was just as satisfied as the devotee of family history. Had Marcel not experienced the charm of these huge yachts, Elstir would have been unable to describe it: 'The greatest charm of a yacht, of the furnishing of a yacht and of yachting outfits, is the simplicity of things of the sea ... What is so lovely about our yachts ... is their smooth, simple, clear, greyness, which in hazy, bluish weather takes on a creamy indistinctness. The room in which one sits should have the atmosphere of a small café. It's the same with women's clothing aboard

---

* Marcel wrote to her in August: 'You might be in pain, or have nephritic colic . . . your illness of the winter' (*Corr.*, vol. IV, p. 213).

† 'Without any asthma attack or congestion, thanks to a continuous draught of fresh air': Marcel described his journey to his mother (ibid., pp. 209–13, 11 August 1904); R. de Billy also mentioned it in *Lettres et conversations*, in which he published three photographs, frequently reprinted, of Marcel wearing a boater and accompanying his conversation with eloquent gestures (a few days earlier such gestures had caused a Tanagra figurine belonging to the Comtesse de Noailles to be broken).

a yacht.'* Scarcely had he climbed aboard than Marcel was overcome with an intense attack of asthma; having withdrawn to his cabin at about one o'clock in the morning, he gave himself some fumigations, took trional and was unable to undress, and at dawn, at about five o'clock, he went up on to the bridge. After the boat had set sail, his asthma abated. Once they had reached Cherbourg, every morning Marcel would decide not to return to Paris, which he planned to do every evening (and often succeeded in doing on other trips, which ended with his sudden departure home), and went to bed at three o'clock in the morning. M. Mirabaud, who was scarcely less stable in his conduct, and who was given advice on matters pertaining to the heart by his valetudinarian passenger, arranged for the boat to drop anchor at Cherbourg (where Marcel disembarked with the vain intention of doing some writing; a trip on a sailing skiff was of no greater appeal to him: 'he was rather frightened'). Proust used to like chatting to the crew, whom he persuaded to talk about their lives. There were other passengers on board: Mme Fortoul, who would marry the future Maréchal Lyautey, the very pretty Mme Jacques Faure, Mlle Ober-kampf and the Billys, Robert, who was 'brotherly', and his wife, who was 'charming'. Marcel was drawn to 'this yachting life', in spite of the fact that every evening he considered leaving the following day. As a result he went to Guernsey, to Saint-Malo and Dinard (the yacht lay at anchor in the bay for two days), from where he visited Dinan. He returned to Paris on the evening of 14 August and, after eight hours in a train and a week at sea during which he had slept very little, he arrived home exhausted to find the apartment empty, damp and without electricity, as his mother was staying in Étretat, but his memory was full of marvellous scenes 'of nature or humanity'.[60] Years later, in his final memory of this cruise, the Narrator wishes to give Albertine a yacht.†

There were no other journeys that summer. Marcel managed to miss the train to Évreux, where he hoped to meet Albufera, but did not escape the inevitable asthma attacks that always accompanied his greatest disappointments.[61] He contemplated other holidays, where he would find peace and quiet, but not too much isolation, fresh air and the opportunity to work. Dinard? Dieppe? Trouville, where he dreaded the onset of

---

* *RTP*, vol. II, p. 252. Proust drew his inspiration both from his own memories and the paintings of (and perhaps conversations with) Helleu.

† M. Mirabaud spent 25,000 francs a month on the maintenance of his yacht, and Albertine's yacht would cost 200,000 francs a year (*Corr.*, vol. IV, p. 212).

feelings of sadness that overcame him in the evenings and of a 'former nervous condition that had disappeared'?* And, in wintertime, why not Brittany? Or Évian and Chamonix? Or Boulogne? Or the Italian lakes (but not the 'true *midi*' [the Côte d'Azur], which Proust never visited)? Or Biskra, which Billy had recommended, but suppose he were to find it stifling there? 'And 45 rue de Courcelles would also have its charms.' Torn between his 'deplorable' health, fear of travelling and the need for fresh air and sunlight, and extremely irritated by all this indecision which had made him rather 'neurotic',[62] he wrote to his mother: 'The more I think about it all, the less clear it becomes';[63] in fact the more resolute and decisive Proust's thinking became in intellectual and artistic spheres, the more hesitant he became over daily concerns; the qualities of synthesis and of dialectics, and the ability to encompass multiple hypotheses, produced catastrophic results in his ordinary life, but triumphed in terms of ideas. And so Mme Proust set off for Dieppe on her own; she was cold there, like the grandmother in 'Combray', she took healthy walks, and she covered herself up, just as her son did, with four blankets and an eiderdown.[64] Marcel confided his anxieties about his health to her (prompted, in any case, by his decision to go and see Doctor Dubois),[65] fully aware that he was being 'boring': 'If I am feeling well in an hour's time, I shall be very annoyed at having complained!' And he added a quotation: 'The consolation of martyrs is that God, for whom they suffer, sees their wounds.'† He took advantage of the situation by trying to redirect the way he spent his time, and he gave up having dinner with the friends whom he liked so much but who prevented him from going to bed early.

Like anyone who was anyone in Paris, he was amused by the marriage of the sixty-year-old editor of *Le Gaulois*, Arthur Meyer, to Marguerite de Turenne, who was eighty: 'Meyer behaves as if intoxicated. He "notifies" his marriage to all the sovereigns or at least the dukes . . . He came across Barrès and said to him: "I'm off to Versailles, would you like me to greet my cousin Louis XV on your behalf?" '[66] Marcel was also anxious about

---

* And which we come across again in *Jeunes Filles*, at Balbec. *Corr.*, vol. IV, p. 266: eventually he caught a cold and travelled in the imagination, just as the child Narrator does, at the end of *Swann*.

† *Corr.*, vol. IV, p. 280. P. Kolb compares these symptoms or habits, such as 'losing body heat' when he got up, to those of a patient of whom Du Boulbon speaks as follows: 'This man who did not dare turn his neck for fear of catching cold is the greatest poet of our time. This wretched fusspot is more intelligent than anyone I know' (*RTP*, vol. II, p. 101). The whole of this marvellous passage about illness and art stems from these anxieties of Marcel.

Louis d'Albufera's wedding; his presents always suited the person for whom they were intended to such an extent that he was planning to give him a lamp in the shape of an Empire pillar (an allusion to Suchet)!* Unfortunately he was ill on the day of the wedding and was unable to attend. He also felt obliged to comfort Louisa de Mornand and to reassure Louis as to the lot of his mistress during the honeymoon. His friend presented him with a walking-stick bearing the initials M. P. Marcel did, however, attend Guiche's wedding on 14 November at the Madeleine, at which Fauré's *Tantum ergo* was performed. In the bridal procession, everyone noticed that, as far as elegance and beauty were concerned, the Comtesse Greffulhe outshone her daughter, whose poems she recited to Marcel. While on his honeymoon at the Château de Thomery, Guiche sent Marcel a post-card of the church at Moret, and received a reply saying: 'What effrontery to claim that I do not know the church at Moret! I know Sisley's painting of it,[67] which is the finest thing he ever did!' He took the opportunity to ask for photographs – a quirk he shared with the Narrator – of the Comtesse de Guiche† and of Mathieu de Noailles. Proust would study his collection of photographs closely when the time came for him to write his novel, and they helped him to adjust his memories, bringing the story and the portrait to life, as well as the gap between desire, dream and reality. As they reached their thirties, his friends, in fact, tended to get married: Eugène Fould became engaged to Marie-Caecilia de Springer, and Marcel sent him his congratu-lations in a letter in which a slight bitterness is masked by irony: 'Irony is sometimes the deceptive sign of a deep-rooted affection.'‡

On 7 December, somewhat unusually, Marcel went to call on 'his doctors'. Throughout this period, he would consult Doctors Dubois, Linossier and Bize. On 14 December he contemplated a visit to Doctor Léon Faisans, a specialist in the respiratory tract, but this was in order to ask him whether he ought to see Professor Déjerine, a specialist in nervous ailments (Marcel having been persuaded that his asthma was of the nervous kind).[68] He knew that Déjerine would advise a month of isolation in 'some clinic for the nerves', but could not make up his mind whether to go

---

* Louis' most celebrated ancestor was Marshal Suchet (1770–1826), the Duc d'Albufera, who fought at Austerlitz and Iéna. *Tr.*

† Which she sent him; it was 'a very good likeness, invaluable for correcting the memories of someone as forgetful as me', Proust wrote, by way of thanking him, on 12 December.

‡ *Corr.*, vol. V, p. 86. Eugène Fould, Baron Fould-Springer (1876–1929); the wedding took place on 12 April 1905 in Vienna. His daughter would marry the son of another of Proust's friends, Robert de Rothschild.

there.* The following year he thought once more about going to Montreux to see Doctor Widmer, who treated Mme Straus. In the notes to *Sésame* he referred to Dubois' theories, which were closer to those of Du Boulbon than to Cottard.[69] Proust appeared to know all the neurologists in Europe, and it took the death of his mother for him to decide to enter a clinic; the theme of a stay at a sanatorium would punctuate *Le Temps retrouvé*. Visibly worried, he reread Brissaud's *L'Hygiène des asthmatiques*, which scarcely reassured him, because in it he read that every attack 'breaks down whatever it is in the organism and hastens the final end'.[70] In spite of these threatening phrases, Marcel liked the charming and handsome Brissaud, who for his part was a '*médecin malgré lui*', 'whom you had to beat to make him talk about medicine'.[71] He would use aspects of him for Du Boulbon as well as his preoccupation with 'those doctors who do not believe in medicine'. Marcel thus spent a miserable Christmas, too ill to reply to an invitation from Fernand Gregh, whose house he imagined surrounded in mist, 'a crib in the darkness'.[72] As was his curious custom every year, he refused all New Year gifts.† Unlike many people who are ill, Marcel did not like receiving presents or possessing objects (or even books), for the very good reason – he who had visited so many museum collections – that he did not like collecting things: everything was either in the mind or else in museums; happiness depended neither on other people, nor on objects. Hence he could already talk about his 'monastic' life.

SOCIAL GATHERINGS

This 'monastic life' would be disrupted by a dinner party, on 5 January 1905, in honour of Fénelon, who was returning to St Petersburg.[73] Proust, in a manner worthy of Balzac, had assembled his old friends: Hahn, Bibesco, Gabriel de La Rochefoucauld,‡ Radziwill, René Peter and Lucien Daudet, who brought along Albert Flament (who was to paint the master

---

* *Corr.*, vol. IV, pp. 401, 403. Cf. p. 404: 'From time to time I go to see doctors who advise me to go away; I don't go away, but each visit I make to them costs me whole weeks in bed,' he told Mme Straus, who suffered from nervous depression herself, on 20 December. In 1914 Déjerine would publish a *Sémiologie des affections du système nerveux*, illustrated with 560 diagrams and three plates. See also E. Gauckler, *Le Professeur J. Déjerine 1849–1917*, Paris, 1922.

† *Corr.*, vol. IV. But in fact, as we know, he had been given the Library Edition of Ruskin by his mother, no doubt because it was useful to his work. He appreciated, and would make use of, its 'magnificent, new illustrations'.

‡ Proust tried to write or elicit reviews for La Rochefoucauld's novel when it was published in January.

of the house, 'his expression as if heavy with sleep', 'one of those men who speak the best French, but who only rarely consent to give written proof of it'). This dream of an all-male society, of Balzac's thirteen, of the dinner parties in Barbey's *Les Diaboliques*, the soldiers at Doncières, the four who meet at the restaurant on the island in the Bois in *Le Côté de Guermantes*, explains the composition, '*à l'anglaise*' (which was, in fact, not unusual in 1900, and fairly common in clubs and among the aristocracy), of the numerous dinner parties given by Marcel. No doubt because he wished to enjoy its fashionable, male atmosphere, he applied to join the Cercle de l'Union, to which, unlike Haas, Swann and the Duc de Guermantes, he would not be elected, probably because of the Dreyfus affair.* On 6 March he gave a tea party for his aristocratic friends, the Guiches, the Clermont-Tonnerres (who would not attend), the Comtesse Aimery de La Rochefoucauld, the Duchesse de Gramont (who was soon to die), Radziwill and Madame d'Haussonville; he also invited several writers: France, Rod and Barrès, but not Montesquiou, who took offence at this. Mme de Guerne and Reynaldo sang. 'That tea party was the death of me,' Marcel would say. He also said he was worn out by a supper party organized by Reynaldo and the *café-concert* singer Fragson,† who was still singing at half-past three in the morning, when Proust, who was choking with asthma, returned home. In early June he received a genuine shock upon reading the latest novel by Anna de Noailles, *La Domination*. This story of a jealous, unhappy couple who are on a trip to Bruges and the Netherlands must have reminded him of his adventure with Fénelon in 1902. He wrote no fewer than five letters to the author expressing his admiration. In July 1904 he had broken a Tanagra figurine‡ of hers, and had hardly dared see her since. Now he was forgiven; he paid her a visit on 10 June and at her house made his peace with Barrès (they had severed links as a result of the Dreyfus affair), while at the same time delivering 'some harsh political and moral truth';[74] Barrès, Marcel informed his

* This is what Jean Béraud told him (*Corr.*, vol. VIII, p. 41). The Duc de Guiche made him a member of the Polo de Bagatelle on 30 April 1908; this was why, when he was awarded the Prix Goncourt, an English newspaper asked for a photograph of him wearing a polo outfit.

† 'I heard some wonderful performers, singers and wits at the *café-concert*, Paulus, Mayol, Fragson' (*RTP*, vol. II, p. 1098; *Le Côté de Guermantes*, draft XI). Cf. vol. III, pp. 1713, 1714, in which the Narrator hums tunes by Mayol and Fragson. Fragson (1869–1913), who had a supple, warm, ironic voice, and who was thought to be either English or Belgian, sang in the best-known *café-concerts* and at the Folies-Bergère, as well as at society salons ('Les souliers de ma voisine', 'L'amour boiteux', 'Si tu veux Marguerite', etc.).

‡ Which the family kept and showed at a Proust exhibition.

mother, had made excuses to him about his conduct over Rouvier, the President of the Council, Picquart and Labori, 'which, furthermore, were worthless'. Whenever he went out, he returned home feeling still more ill, so much so that he assured his friends, with fine black humour, that he could not conceive of going out even to their burials;* seldom happy, he quoted from Chamfort: 'Happiness is not something easy to come by; it is very difficult to find in oneself and impossible to find elsewhere.'[75] All year he had been planning to go to a convalescent home,† and he consulted his doctors: specialists had so perfected the art of referring their patients to one another that on 28 July, for instance, Brissaud had advised him to go and see Doctor Sollier, who would eventually welcome him at his sanatorium in December.

LITERARY WORK

In the spring, from March onwards, we come across traces of Proust at work: he was annotating the text of *Sésame et les lys*, and he borrowed several books from Georges de Lauris 'in order to check quotations' (which were already in his head). He quoted from Maeterlinck's *La Vie des abeilles* and *La Sagesse et la Destinée* – to this writer he devoted not the article that he had once planned, but a four-page footnote,[76] which is a theory of imagery and style: 'One has the strong feeling that the reason the writer has matured has nothing to do with his progress as a thinker. Conclusion: stylistic beauty is basically irrational.' From Anatole France's *Le Livre de mon ami* he quoted his praise of passionate emotions.[77] He quoted, too, from John Stuart Mill's *Autobiography*[78] and from *Adam Bede* by George Eliot, one of his favourite novelists. And he looked up Fromentin's books, *Un été dans le Sahara* and *Une année dans le Sahel*, in order to illustrate Ruskin's praise of 'a few well-chosen words'.[79] He also amused himself by sending Albert Sorel, who was a poet and composer as well as an historian, a letter containing a long pastiche in verse linking Franck, Fauré, Monteverdi and Wagner, the conclusion to which describes the scenery at Balbec.[80] His medical consultations were the inspiration for a footnote which provided a truly brilliant survey of contemporary

---

* *Corr.*, vol. V, p. 331: 'So they prefer that I should go out as late as possible and, as far as burials go, they even prefer that it should be they who have the inconvenience of going to mine.'

† To Montesquiou, in August: 'On ten occasions I was due to set off . . . for a long period in a convalescent home' (ibid., p. 337).

medicine:[81] 'And so it is that contemporary medicine seems to be on the point of telling us . . . that we are "born of the spirit"[82] and that it continues to control our breathing (see Brugelmann's work on asthma), our digestion (see Dubois, de Berne, *Les Psychonévroses* and his other books), the co-ordination of our movements (see *Isolement et psychothérapie* by Doctors Camus and Pagniez, with an introduction by Professor Déjerine) . . . They sense the presence and effect of the soul in every practical disorder, and in order to cure the body it is to the soul that they address themselves.' Similarly, after positivism came psychosomatic medicine (to say nothing of Freud, of whom Proust was totally unaware, and vice versa). What Proust formulated here in an abstract manner, he would express through the characters who were the doctors and patients of *À la recherche*.

On 21 April, he returned to his introduction, 'Sur la lecture', in order to check or complete certain details, and he hunted for a catalogue from the English furniture store, Maple's, and for some works by William Morris, the former having applied the theories of the latter: that which is beautiful must always be useful. 'According to these aesthetic principles, my bedroom was not at all beautiful.'[83] He also required a Joanne or Baedeker guidebook to Holland. He had imagined a learned person making a trip to a Dutch convent in order to seek the truth, not within himself as he should do, but in a folio of a manuscript that was preserved in the library of a convent near Utrecht.* If the details of the journey correspond to the one made by Marcel (as well as to the guidebook), the theme of the scholarly quest was inspired, as he himself pointed out in a footnote, by a journey of Sainte-Beuve's described by Léon Séché.† He must therefore have already concluded that Sainte-Beuve's was worthless. Again, in May, he questioned Croisset about Holland, displaying that care and precision which would always be typical of him: he was not someone whose books are written in a month, or in a year.‡ On 15 May, having read an article by Camille Mauclair in *La Renaissance latine*, he added a footnote on Rodin to the proofs of 'Sur la lecture'.[84] In June he included an important footnote on the structure

---

* It was no longer about a nun, as in *Jean Santeuil*; *Sésame*, pp. 38–40.

† *Sainte-Beuve*, Mercure de France, 1904, vol. I, p. 229. He would relate entire passages from this book, concerning the relationship between Mme Straus and Marceline Desbordes-Valmore, in an ironic tone to Mme Straus (*Corr.*, vol. V, pp. 120–2).

‡ Again, on 27 April, he wrote to Robert de Billy: 'I've been working very hard since I last saw you' (ibid., p. 117). And on 28 April, to Mme Straus: 'I have worked so much in the last two months, in the moments of respite between my attacks, that I have been unable to have any friends visit me at home' (ibid., p. 119).

of the book:[85] apparently obeying his solitary whim, Ruskin imposed 'a retrospective order up until the final apotheosis' at the end. Proust never stopped gathering information, even at night, and reading things that were 'boring and solemn'. In this way he acquired the discipline that he knew was necessary (not just for 'neuropaths', but for artists): 'I lead a very quiet and restful life of reading and very studious intimacy with Maman.'[86] Three months later, that sort of life would be ended for ever.

On 7 May *Le Figaro* published another 'salon' article (which Calmette had been informed about on 28 March),[87] entitled 'La Comtesse de Guerne', under the byline Écho (like the nymph).[88] Proust considered this lady (who had sung at his home with Hahn) to be 'one of the two or three greatest living singers', because her voice, which was not only pure, but 'spiritualized', the voice of a lunar landscape by Monticelli (a painter whom he mentioned several times and whom he claimed to be very fond of),[89] was capable of singing the great duet from *Sémiramis* with a technique worthy of Patti. It was at her home, at 3 Avenue Bosquet, that they rehearsed the choruses from *Esther*, 'which is perhaps the most beautiful piece written so far by M. Reynaldo Hahn, in which all the charms of the biblical story and Racine's tragedy are transformed and somehow ennobled'.[90] On 8 June, at the home of the Comtesse de Béarn, who had an auditorium at her mansion at 22 Avenue Bosquet, Marcel attended the first night of Reynaldo Hahn's *Esther*.[91] *Contre Sainte-Beuve* gives Marcel's moving account of the private recital, at his home, of fragments of this work, in which he recalled his mother humming 'that *Esther* which she prefers to everything, "*Il s'apaise, il pardonne*", those divine choruses Reynaldo Hahn wrote for *Esther*'. 'He sang them for the first time at that little piano by the fireplace, when I was in bed, while in the meantime Papa had arrived silently and had sat down in an armchair, and Maman remained standing, listening to his enchanting voice. Maman timidly ventured a tune from the chorus ... And in the beautiful lines of her Jewish face, which were filled with Christian sweetness and Jansenist resignation, she resembled Esther herself.'* And so, when the day came that Proust the novelist wished to describe a concert at a salon, he would only have to remind himself of the technique acquired whilst writing these pieces for *Le Figaro*, which he dared not sign with his own name, and when he thought of his mother, he would allude to *Esther*.

---

* *CSB*, de Fallois, 1954, pp. 127–8. The constant recurrence of *Esther* in *À la recherche* is thus implicitly impregnated with the memory of Mme Proust.

But even when Proust wished to escape from social life, it caught up with him again, in the person of Montesquiou, who, annoyed that on the pretext of illness Marcel had not come to hear his lectures, informed him that he would come and deliver one at his home. One can imagine the comedy of the situation and the amused dread of Marcel, who took the opportunity to invite a few friends, but from a list that had been carefully discussed with the indiscreet speaker.* This gathering took place on 2 June: the count read out a satirical portrait of Mme Aubernon, a celebrated hostess who had died recently, who was the subject of chapter XIV of Montesquiou's new book, *Professionelles Beautés*. The chapter was entitled 'La sonnette' [The Bell], because the lady in question was accustomed to choosing a topic of conversation for her dinner parties and calling her guests to order by means of this instrument. It was at her home that Marcel had met Professors Pozzi and Brochard, and Baron Doäzan (who, he would inform the anxious Montesquiou, was the model for Charlus); and he also visited her house at Louveciennes, travelling on a 'little train'. One of the principal models for Mme Verdurin was thus brought to life again beneath the ironic gaze of Proust, who would not forget her. After the party was over, and despite a 'thirty-hour' attack of asthma, Marcel wrote an account of it for the gossip columns of both *Le Gaulois* and the *New York Herald*.[92] But he wished to do even better and write an article. This was 'composed in his head' in mid-June.[93]

On 15 August 'Un professeur de beauté' was published in *Les Arts de la vie*. In this long article,[94] which was probably completed at the end of June, we are given not merely a portrait of Montesquiou, but a comparison between him and Ruskin, and a treatise on criticism and the philosophy of art. Apart from 'Sur la lecture', which was written shortly beforehand and was in part re-used here, it is one of the most important essays on aesthetics that Proust wrote before *Contre Sainte-Beuve*. Montesquiou was skilled above all as an etymologist, because he knew the genealogy of every word: we can imagine with what interest the man who would include so many passages on etymology in *À la recherche* would have listened to

---

* 'State the facts', he wrote to Proust on 17 May: 'that I am doing you a kindness, since you don't go out, by coming to your house to read a (short) chapter from my new book; and this chapter being a portrait of Mme Aubernon, the guests have been chosen from among those who knew her' (*Corr.*, vol. V, p. 153, 17 May 1905). See ibid., pp. 175–8, the list of guests suggested by Proust and for the most part rejected by Montesquiou. Painter (pp. 98–104) gives a brilliant portrayal of the hostess of the rue d'Astorg, assembling all the sayings that were attributed to her at the time and the principal recollections of those who knew her.

'his master and his friend' speaking on the subject. The count was also someone who, like Ruskin, knew how to look at everything[95] and to give a name to everything: in Pisanello's portrait of the Princesse d'Este in the Louvre, he knew that the flowers were columbines.[96] Marcel also imagines him at the Académie française, to which Montesquiou would never belong, in the company of Barrès, Régnier and Maeterlinck (who, like Proust, would never be a member either); it was an opportunity to evoke the irony, verve and passion of the person who, one senses, is already set to assume the guise of Charlus.[97] Unlike that of Fromentin, his art criticism, which in fact remains the best part of Montesquiou's work, enabled one to 'see' a painting. Underlying the analysis there is a philosophy.* What made Ruskin superior to the count, however, was that throughout his fifty volumes, there was a 'one, transcending design', 'the unity of the in some ways divine plan of this sort of discourse on universal Beauty'.[98] No one has noticed that herein lies the seed of the passage in *La Prisonnière* on the great nineteenth-century works – by Balzac, Wagner, Michelet – which, like Proust's own work, are characterized by the unity of a cycle. But the count would derive little pleasure from the article: Yturri, his secretary and friend, who had been ill for a long time, died on 6 July. His dying words were: 'As long as I shall live . . . it will be . . . for those beautiful things . . . which . . . have . . . so . . . enchanted . . . me.'[99] Marcel, who was ill, had sent his mother to enquire after him. In his messages of condolence, he showed he understood the 'maternal' aspect of Yturri's affection for the count[†] (like that of Jupien for Charlus), and how much Montesquiou's affection for his companion was purely narcissistic. In fact the count replied by recalling the last evening on which Proust had seen him, at the reading of 'La sonnette': 'My wonderful friend was once again thrilled with joy at seeing me being praised there',[‡] and he considered

---

* There are also some fine images: Montesquiou depicts Ingres chained like Prometheus to his rock, for having stolen, not sparks of fire, but 'the cold'. Charlus in chains would in turn be compared to Prometheus in *Le Temps retrouvé*.

† 'I should be very happy to be able to talk about him one day in such a way as to make him better known.' Yturri had something of Morel and something of Jupien.

‡ *Corr.*, vol. V, p. 292. Proust had recalled this evening, in what amounts to a veritable theory of the literary genre of the *consolatio*: 'A true and material little memory, to do with someone we have lost, is of infinite value; it seems to add another minute to our hours of bygone moments, and it enriches, however inadequately, the only treasure of the past'; as for life, one should not defer it in our grief, but 'get on with it immediately, for the memory will be just as sharp in ten years' time as it is today'. The value of sorrow is that it enables us to discover some 'precious truths' (ibid., pp. 297–8): this is the theory of grief in *Le Temps retrouvé*.

Marcel to have been 'too involved in our joys and our sorrows not to be the desired confidant, receptive and compassionate, of so many rumours, seen to be without foundation, and of memories, full of yearning'.[100] The confidant would not keep these secrets to himself.

THE WHISTLER EXHIBITION

On 15 June, knowing that he would never see them again, Marcel went to visit the exhibition of 440 paintings, engravings and lithographs by Whistler at the École des Beaux-Arts: it filled a staircase, an entrance hall, one larger room and two small ones, and Marcel drew up two maps so as to make his mother's visit easier, since her kidney trouble must have been making her tired. He advised her to look at the engravings of Venice ('streets, courtyards, canals': it is the journey in *Albertine disparue* that Proust would write through Whistler's eyes). Among the paintings, he recommended 'some sailing boats in a port, at evening'; and 'some fireworks next to them'; the '*Portrait of Miss Alexander*', '*Valparaiso*'; the 'paintings of Holland', and, as in Elstir's other genre, 'the things in the style of Japanese prints', 'a room with bright coloured curtains and three people' and 'a woman at the piano'; the '*Frozen Thames*', the '*Portrait of Sarasate*' and 'a large portrait of a woman'.[101] 'Look at the etching downstairs,' he added mercilessly. 'I'm forgetting practically everything', wrote the man whose visual and pictorial memory was astonishing, and who scarcely ever forgot anything.[102] 'Did you draw Mr Freer's attention to an *Opal beach* and an *Opal sea*?' he asked Marie Nordlinger; 'I must admit that I would be curious to know which this blessed beach is and to go and live there.'[103] This expedition, which was followed, of course, by a serious attack of asthma, was the reason why *À la recherche* is embellished with so many allusions to the artist whom Proust metamorphosed into one facet of Elstir, which is probably less well known than that drawn from the French Impressionists. Marcel considered himself to be among those 'by whose eyes this nomadic beauty ready to return to Boston would have liked to be beheld'.[104]

ON READING

On the same day, 15 June 1905, *La Renaissance latine* (in what was to be its last issue) published 'Sur la lecture' ['On reading'], the introduction to Proust's translation of *Sesame and Lilies*. An unpublished notebook provides a better understanding of how this important essay – for it contained the seeds of 'Combray' – came to be written. It contains a first draft describing the day spent reading* and the bedroom, a lengthy transition before introducing Ruskin, a first version of the ending, and Proust's habit of only using the right-hand page and writing additional material on the blank page opposite – the method he would employ in $\grave{A}$ la recherche. The draft opening was very different to the published one: it was more abstract, and led directly to a discussion of reading, the subject of the introduction: 'Doubtless already in childhood it is a delightful pleasure, and more fruitful then than it will become later on when, at the age of selfish passivity, you are far removed from life, when in the old library with its honey-coloured lines of shelves we dispense with the chore of thinking for ourselves by receiving our spiritual nourishment ready-made . . . No, we do not read like this in childhood, we read in an active and personal way, the book is nothing less than the open door to all the paths which stretch out to the end of the world.'[105]

Ruskin's book is concerned with reading. Proust seized on it as an opportunity to recall his childhood reading during the holidays, improving on some of the passages from Jean Santeuil; the themes and the use of the first person provide a foretaste of Du côté de chez Swann. If old books can conjure up the past, which can rise up into the present through the phenomenon of involuntary memory, as through François le Champi in Le Temps retrouvé, reading can lead us to the threshold of spiritual life, although it is not a substitute for it. This introduction, which was printed in volume form in May 1906, was, as we know, republished in Pastiches et mélanges in 1919 under the title 'Journées de lecture'; this shows the importance its author attached to it. It also shows that he was making a clean break with the past, and with Ruskin, to whom he was bidding farewell; the choice had to be made between reading and writing, between other people's books and his own work: 'We can only nurture the power of our sensitivity and our intelligence within ourselves, in the depths of our spiritual life.'[106] Proust turned back into himself, into fictional creation. Escaping into someone else's work had been both a failure and a success, because it had helped shape his mind, broadened his cultural knowledge (annotating Ruskin had required a considerable amount of research) and it had enriched his use of language. The pen that began Jean Santeuil was very different to

---

* 'Journées de lecture' was the title Proust gave to this introduction when he reprinted it in Pastiches et mélanges (Gallimard, 1919).

that which framed the first lines of 'Sur la lecture': 'There are perhaps no other days of our childhood that we lived so fully as those which we believed we had left behind without experiencing them, those which we spent in the company of a favourite book.'[107] Both actively and reactively, Ruskin had thus given Proust the opportunity to clarify the aesthetic philosophy that he lacked, and to nurture the library of books which this least accumulative of men kept, not in his apartment, but in his mind.* The writing provides us with a foretaste of the structure of *À la recherche du temps perdu*; from *Jean Santeuil* came the fictional qualities of the novel based on personal experience, and the two translations provided aspects of the reflections on art that we encounter in *Le Temps retrouvé*. In 1902, Proust had been keenly aware of the need to begin another novel, as he wrote to Antoine Bibesco: 'What I am doing is not real work, but merely research, translation, etc.'[108] At the time that he was completing *La Bible d'Amiens*, he seemed quite ready to return to his novel. But afterwards, he preferred to occupy himself with *Sésame et les lys*, in which, because the first of the two lectures that comprise the book has to do with reading, we pass from Ruskin as a reader to Proust as an adult reader, and thence to a small boy reading: that is to say, to a fictional character. In this introduction we are present at the birth of the novel – more so than we are in *La Bible d'Amiens*, in which the narrator-hero sets off to visit Holland or to see some churches: here, it is not yet the churches of Combray or Balbec, merely a preparation for them, a preliminary sketch. Fate would decree that just as Dante was abandoned by Virgil as they left Purgatory ('Thee o'er thyself I therefore crown and mitre'), Marcel should be deserted by Ruskin and by his mother, at the very moment that he embarked upon the novel which he had told Antoine Bibesco about in 1902. If he was not unhappy to say goodbye to Ruskin,† for he had obtained everything that the latter could offer him, the death of Mme Proust entailed two years of mourning before the next plan for a book emerged.

It was late June 1905 when Proust got ready to deliver the complete manuscript of his translation and his introduction to Mercure de

---

* 'How unfortunate that you should not like things!' Montesquiou wrote to him in 1905 (*Corr.*, vol. V, p. 317).

† In *Le Figaro* of 19 June, André Beaunier wrote a highly complimentary article of some hundred lines, and Mme de Noailles dashed off a short, but very enthusiastic letter (*Corr.*, vol. V, p. 229): 'I thank you for every line of these pages which are like a perfect, gentle joy.' This was followed by a second: 'Everybody has read these unique pages' (ibid., p. 240). By way of thanks, Proust referred to Homer and to his beloved *Arabian Nights*.

France.* The introduction was dedicated to the Princesse Alexandre de Caraman-Chimay (Anna de Noailles' sister), 'Des jardins des rois' to Reynaldo Hahn, 'the author of *Muses pleurant la mort de Ruskin*', and 'Des jardins des reines' to Suzette Lemaire.[109] At the same time, Proust put some further queries to Marie Nordlinger, who replied to them by return.[110] To thank her, Marcel attempted to convey some of the atmosphere of 'Courcelles and Alfred de Vigny',† which consisted of humour, culture and farce. He thought of replying to Jules Lemaître's pastiches, *En marge des vieux livres*[111] (though it was not until 1908 that his plan to write this prevailed), and to this end he reread 'that wonderful old book', the *Iliad*. Proust displayed his knowledge of the Homeric question: contrary to the theories of the classical scholar, Friedrich August Wolf, it was definitely a book that was written, and the work of a single author.[112] In *À la recherche*, as well as the phrases that are credited to Bloch, which derive from the translation of Homer by Leconte de Lisle, itself a rekindled pastiche,‡ Proust concluded that 'art is no more advanced today than in Homer's day',[113] and that his heroes experience feelings similar to ours.[114] Homer, so far removed in time, became Proust's favourite example of his thinking about the presence of history, albeit literary history.

THE DEATH OF MADAME PROUST

The drama would unfold over a short space of time. Mme Proust, who had set off for Évian with Marcel on 6 September, immediately fell victim to bouts of vomiting, vertigo and 'terrible attacks of uraemia' (like her own mother, who died of the same illness). Marcel telephoned their friend, Mme Catusse, by whom Mme Proust both wanted and did not want to be photographed, 'out of a wish to leave [him] a last image, and because she was frightened she would be too sad'.§ Struck down by aphasia, she

---

* *Corr.*, vol. V, p. 261, 24 June 1905. He nevertheless considered sending a copy of his manuscript, 'in which he had put crosses and underlinings' wherever he had doubts, to M. Nordlinger, and was ready to incorporate her comments on the proofs. On 1 July he wrote to her: 'The book has gone off without my being able to see it again.'

† Allusions to the streets in which Marcel and Reynaldo lived.

‡ E.g. *RTP*, vol. II, p. 553: 'the compound and sonorous names like the epithets which Homer gives to his heroes'.

§ *Corr.*, vol. X, p. 215, November 1910, to Mme Catusse. This episode would be given to the grandmother and to Saint-Loup, in *À l'ombre des jeunes filles en fleurs* (*RTP*, vol. II, pp. 144–5) and in *Sodome* (*RTP*, vol. III, p. 156).

tried to conceal this from her son.* She would not allow herself to be treated and she refused to have any tests.[115] Robert Proust brought her back to Paris, 'dragging her into the railway carriage', while Marcel, who was ill himself, remained, at his mother's request, at the Hôtel Splendide. Around 13 September, while waiting for a telegram which would summon him back to Paris, and feeling very unhappy, he was hoping that 'all this will vanish like a bad dream'.[116] Some slight improvement a few days later offered a ray of hope. The patient preserved an air of absolute calm, and her sons were unable to tell 'what she thought or what she was suffering'. She was paralysed and her speech was affected.[117] Marcel was gripped by the fear that would never leave him: 'She knew how incapable I am of living without her, and how ill-equipped to deal with life, so if she felt, as I fear and worry she must have, and she was perhaps about to leave me for ever, she must have experienced atrocious moments of anxiety that I can only imagine were the most horrible torture.'[118] For a fortnight she refused all food and all medication, and could scarcely be persuaded to see her doctor, Doctor Landowski, a former pupil of her husband and 'the one man who would have cured her had she been curable'.[†] Her son would one day behave as she had done. She was watched over by a nun, who told Marcel that, in his mother's eyes, he was always four years old. She was only in pain on the two final days and she died on Tuesday 26 September 1905,[‡] at the age of fifty-six. Death 'had restored the youthful looks she had before her sorrows', without there being a single white hair. Professor Gosset was the first person to call on them after her death, 'together with one of the sisters from the rue Bizet. He was cheerful and kind.'[§] For two days Marcel stayed beside her, 'weeping, and smiling at her corpse through his tears'[119] and believed she was still with him. But he whom his mother used to call her 'little Frédéric',[120] quoting from *L'Éducation sentimentale*, no longer had anyone to protect him.

Since Mme Proust had retained her Jewish religion out of respect for

---

* 'Nothing can surpass in horror those days at Évian' (*Corr.*, vol. XI, p. 204).

† *Corr.*, vol. VI, p. 111, June 1906, to Doctor Landowski. Ladislas Landowski (1867–1956). Marcel and Robert would give him a pair of Mme Proust's ear-rings (ibid., p. 222, 26 September 1906). 'How moved Maman would have been had she realized,' added Marcel, 'to see the wonderful efforts that you made to keep her for us.'

‡ Doctor Proust also died on a Tuesday.

§ *Corr.*, vol. XI, p. 204. He therefore contributed to the character of Dieulafoy (an actual person, none the less), as did the surgeon Tillaux (*Le Carnet de 1908*, pp. 68–9).

her parents, the mourners gathered, without prayers, at the mortuary; the cremation took place at Père-Lachaise.[121] The hearse could scarcely be seen for wreaths, said *Le Figaro*; many well-known members of the aristocracy and the medical and literary worlds, from the Dieulafoys to the Chevignés, from the Noailles to Bergson, as well as Marcel's friends, attended the funeral.

MOURNING (1905–6)

In the large apartment on the rue de Courcelles, now forsaken by those who had originally chosen it, Marcel's brother, his sister-in-law, Uncle Georges (who was soon to die from the same illness as his sister) and his aunt kept him company for a few days.[122] He accomplished that descent into the underworld which no sensitive soul is spared; as in *Albertine disparue*, space took on the shape of suffering: 'I went into certain rooms in the apartment which I had not been back to and I explored unknown regions of my grief which increases endlessly the more it continues. There is a certain floorboard near Maman's bedroom which one cannot walk over without it making a noise, and Maman, the moment she heard it, used to make a little sound with her mouth which meant: come and give me a kiss.'[123] Even at night his sorrows were not allayed: 'I cannot sleep, and if by chance I do doze, a slumber that is less sparing of my grief than is my alert mind overwhelms me with ghastly thoughts which, when I am awake, my reason can at least attempt to deal with, and to refute when I can't bear them any longer.'[124] In *Sodome et Gomorrhe* his superb development of this nightly descent to the underworld makes it into something worthy of Homer, Virgil and Dante: 'As soon as we have embarked, in order to travel along the arteries of the subterranean city, upon the dark tide of our own blood as if upon some inner Lethe with its six-fold recesses, tall solemn figures appear to us, approach and then drift away, leaving us in tears.'*

---

* *RTP*, vol. III, p. 157; cf. *Le Carnet de 1908*, p. 56: 'Maman's face at the time and subsequently in my dreams.' In this notebook Proust jotted down again: 'Dream of Maman, her breathing, she looks back and weeps. – "You who love me, don't allow me to be operated on again, for I think I am going to die, and it's not worth persisting."/ Dream. Papa with us. Robert spoke to him, made him smile and made him reply precisely to everything. Absolute illusion of life. So you see that when one is dead one is almost alive.' Proust places these dreams, not at the moment of the grandmother's death in *À la recherche*, but later on, in that sort of resurrection created by 'the intermittencies of the heart'.

After an initial period of 'the most silent contemplation', Marcel felt that his mother had drifted a little further away from him[125] and he endeavoured to remain in 'constant communion' with her, by combining his idealization of her ('maternal love is untainted by selfishness') with a sense of guilt, which arose from the worries that his poor health had caused her.[126] When this anxiety 'sent him mad', he tried 'to contain it, to diminish it'. He hardly dared go out, however, in order that he should not have to 'come back home', because in former days his mother used to await his return anxiously – 'to check that I was reasonably well when I came home'. In early November he had a few moments of remission, for which, however, he reproached himself, almost out of fear that he would become accustomed to his unhappiness and acquire a taste for living once more. At the same time, when he described what it was that had killed his mother, he said it was the death of Adrien Proust, not his asthma.* He began to contemplate, not without a wrench, leaving the rue de Courcelles, which he believed to be too expensive for him, and he busied himself answering letters of condolence.† In particular, he prepared to enter a nursing home; having decided against Doctor Déjerine's clinic, where they wanted to retain him for three months, and since Doctor Sollier had come to see him and refused to treat him at home ('without isolating me, without making me go to his clinic, nothing apart from altering the times of my meals and my sleep', which Marcel, unhappy as he was, would have preferred, out of fear of isolation and unfamiliar surroundings), Marcel, in deference to his mother's wishes, entered Doctor Sollier's sanatorium at 145 route de Versailles, Boulogne-sur-Seine. He was forbidden to write, as he mentioned in letters to several of his friends, and to have visitors, which was why he explained to Robert de Billy how to come and see him (Lucien also came twice, without ceasing to be disagreeable);[127] he even received a visit from Louisa de Mornand, who had come to ask whether he approved of her going to live with Robert

---

* *Corr.*, vol. 5, p. 359, 8 or 9 November 1905, to Mme Straus. Cf. p. 363: 'She could not live without my father.' Proust reasoned as if Mme Proust had not had an organic kidney disease (which may not have been unconnected with her earlier fibroma). Cf. to Barrès: 'I was especially touched by the delightful intention you had when you told me that one could see immediately that I was Maman's favourite. That's not correct. It was my father, even though she loved me immensely all the same. But when my father died, she wanted – and was unable to do so! – to outlive him in order not to leave me on my own and so as not to leave me in the state of anguish that she knew I suffered when I was not with her.' The same letter refers to episodes which we read about in *Jean Santeuil* and in *À la recherche* (*Corr.*, vol. VI, p. 28).

† 'This mad letter-writing business' (ibid., vol. V, p. 368).

Gangnat.[128] As always, he maintained a friendly relationship with the staff and with the nurses or the porters. From the outset he claimed that his cure 'was doing him the greatest harm' and that he would shortly bring it to a conclusion. It would last until 25 January 1906. Its principal benefit was a literary one – the experience would be developed and used again in *Le Temps retrouvé*: a long gap was required before actual events could be introduced into his work. However, there is no need for the ironical suggestion, implicit in the work of some biographers, that Marcel wished to continue to be ill in order to remain closer to his mother. It is worth repeating that no one chooses to be asthmatic, and the isolation treatment advocated by Camus, Pagniez and Déjerine in *Isolement et psychothérapie*[129] (which may have led Marcel to believe that his illness was purely due to nerves) could not cure him.* It is true that Proust had a rather lower opinion of Sollier, who considered Bergson to be 'muddled and narrow-minded': 'That didn't help the success of the psychotherapeutic treatment!'[130] New Year's Day 1906 must have been a cruel occasion for him, bringing back memories of his mother that he had lost, particularly memories of her voice.[131] He found the strength to read the newspapers and to follow the Algeciras Conference,† which his friend Billy was attending, and upon which the peace between Germany and France depended. On several occasions he congratulated the rather ungrateful Barrès on his election to the Académie française on 25 January and on his books, *Au Service de l'Allemagne*[132] and *Le Voyage de Sparte*.[133] It was an opportunity for him to assert one of his great principles: 'Joyfulness, enthusiasm, for the artist as for the reader, is the criterion of beauty, of genius, of truth.'[134] With a lucidity that cannot have pleased his fellow writer, Proust identified 'a rather deadpan Chateaubriand' quality in Barrès, alluding to his 'haughty manner, his air of disgust, his mocking attitude', to the 'sterile passages' and the 'exquisite melodist'.

On his return to the rue de Courcelles, around 25 January, he was confined to bed and, still unwell, imagined that he would 'rejoin his dear little mother at last'.‡ Gradually, however, dressed in his 'woolly knitwear',

---

* It was not until research had been done on allergies and doctors had started to use vaccinations, which were not always effective, and, above all, cortisone had been discovered, that any progress was made either in providing relief for sufferers or in the treatment of asthma, a disease we are still unable to eliminate.

† January–March 1906. Instigated, at the insistence of Germany, to consider the political future of Morocco. *Tr.*

‡ *Corr.*, vol. VI, p. 49. However, he never contemplated suicide.

he began to see certain of his friends again;* as Albufera informed Billy: 'Marcel is not in the best of health, nevertheless one can at least see him from five o'clock to ten o'clock each day, which is a great advance.'[135] In the spring, in the same letter to Reynaldo in which he wrote of the 'grief over maman that increases every day', he referred to his good mood, and there were more and more jokes.[136] Hahn had been entrusted with directing *Don Giovanni* at the Salzburg Festival that August (he was to be in charge of the Vienna Philharmonic Orchestra along with Lili Lehmann – the founder of the festival and of the Mozarteum and, Hahn observed, creator of the Mozartian tradition, which did not exist before her – and Geraldine Farrar, which proved he was an important conductor); in a long piece in verse Marcel offered him some financial advice: he should move his account to the Banque Rothschild, follow the counsel of Robert de Rothschild ('handsome as a Charité', 'I suspect him!'), and avoid the Russian loan. With regard to his own finances, emotions and health, Marcel made mistakes, but not where his friends were concerned. Certain of these second-rate poems describe events with the wit of a chansonnier, the humour of the music-hall that appealed so much to the two friends: '*Le régime actuel a beau manger du moine/ Alarmer follement nos plus chers intérêts/ Il est encore crois-moi des placements prospères/ On insulte l'armée, on expulse les pères/ Mais la rente remonte aussi quand tu parais/ Poincaré! Donc ô Buncht, spécule, agiote, espère!*'[†] When people laugh, it means they are cured. Around this time Marcel tried going out a little, initially on his own, so that he would not have to speak to anyone, and later to pay a visit to the Duc de Guiche.[‡] Soon laid low with flu, he discovered a new doctor, who would look after him until his death. Doctor Bize 'has prescribed hundreds of medicaments for me. But we've only had the private consultation. The time for obeying him does not come until later.'[§] After causing him to

---

* But not all of them: Mme Catusse, Albufera, Lucien Daudet, Mme Straus, Mme Lemaire, Casa-Fuerte, R. Hahn and Bibesco.

† *Corr.*, vol. VI, p. 65, mid-April 1906: 'However much the present regime devours the monks/ And sows alarm among our dearest interests/ Believe me, there are still some thriving investments to be made/ The army is insulted, the priests are expelled/ But the rent also increases when you appear/ Poincaré! Therefore, O Buncht, speculate, indulge in agiotage and then hope!'

‡ To whom he nostalgically inscribed a copy of *Les Plaisirs et les Jours*: 'To one to whom it could have meant even more than it does . . . I offer this scarcely recognizable portrait of a self whom he did not know' (*Corr.*, vol. VI, p. 67, 15 April 1906). He added a second humorous inscription to this.

§ Ibid., p. 72. Doctor Bize was 'an excellent general practitioner whom Robert Proust, his former fellow student, had recommended to his brother', and who came to see him every Friday (D. Mabin, *Le Sommeil de Proust*, PUF, 1992, p. 184).

feel pessimistic about his health, the physician then put him 'in a good mood with some friendly words',[137] which reveals Marcel's loneliness, how easily influenced he could be over matters other than artistic ones, as well as his rarely satisfied need for encouragement and reassurance.

Proust, who was now considered an authority on the subject, continued to have his opinion asked on Ruskin studies. This was why he admitted that even if *Mornings in Florence*, of which he had an attractively illustrated copy, was not Ruskin's masterpiece, if ever he went to Florence, it would be to follow in Ruskin's footsteps.[138] The latter had drawn attention to everything that the guidebooks had omitted, and 'at least half the painters and architects whom we admire have been discovered by him'.[139] At the same time he felt drawn to his dear Venice – which he did not feel he had the strength to return to since it was too much of a 'graveyard of happiness for him'[140] – because he had obtained a copy of a book about Carpaccio,[141] a painter who greatly appealed to him, about whom Ruskin had written, and who would be linked with Albertine: it was as if all the various characters in the great work were gradually assuming their places without even their creator being aware of it. Most important of all, *La Chronique des arts et de la curiosité* of 5 May published Marcel's review of his cousin Mathilde Crémieux's translation of *The Stones of Venice*. In November 1904[142] Marcel had tried to persuade Mercure to publish this book, but it actually appeared on the Laurens list in December 1905. The review had been commissioned immediately by Auguste Marguillier, the editor of *La Chronique des arts*, and Marcel began mentioning it in early November 1905.[143] Marcel had proposed that he should write the footnotes to the book and that both names should be printed on the cover. The subdued tone of the review is explained by the fact that this offer was not accepted. He also explained to Marguillier why he had not translated the book: his health was too poor for him to spend the time in which he could be working only doing translations. Having described Venetian literary fashions, which have too passive an appeal, he saw Ruskin as someone who makes us active, who, guidebook in hand, leads us to all the churches and residences, who makes us 'request a ladder in order to identify a bas-relief', and who rediscovers the life of the city. This was how Proust, *The Stones of Venice* in his hand, had visited the city. What is more, 'Ruskin would succeed in doing in France what Turner, Barrès, Mme de Noailles, Henri de Régnier and Whistler had begun'.*

---

* *CSB*, p. 522. Proust justly criticized Mathilde Crémieux's translation for having cut Ruskin's

Still fascinated by the arts, and by the artists who appealed to him (he was neither bulimic, nor encyclopaedic; he had his passions), Marcel, who was too unwell to go to the Moreau exhibition,* which took place at the Georges Petit gallery between 9 and 28 May 1906, acquired a copy of the catalogue; he liked Montesquiou's introduction[144] and he sent a caricature of *Jupiter et Léda* to Reynaldo.[145] In it he noted the presence of paintings from the Straus collection, *Le Chanteur persan, Le Soir et la Douleur, Le Poète persan*, and the absence of Edmond de Rothschild's *David dansant devant l'arche*, 'the finest Moreau in existence'.[146] Similarly, carried along on his Ruskinian momentum, though in ironic vein, he drew thirty drawings for Reynaldo that constituted 'a daring critique of the various schools of painting', including, for example, a 'Presentation at the Temple' by a variety of artists from different periods, among them Giotto and Breughel.[147]

Finally, the proofs of *Sésame* must have reached Marcel in the autumn of 1905, 'during his illness', entailing 'a dreadful amount of work for his convalescence'.[148] They piled up during his period of mourning; gradually, during the first half of 1906, he began dealing with them. It was at this point that he excised any mention of his mother, replacing the word with an 'aunt'.[149] There is an element of mystery here: he had dedicated *La Bible d'Amiens* to his father; one might have expected that he would do the same for his mother, and that he would mention their collaboration. There is nothing of this. He did it, he wrote to Lucien Daudet, 'So that there should be no mention of her in anything I write until I've finished something I've begun which is exclusively about her.'[150] What had he 'begun'? No manuscript has come down to us. Was this text, because it was too intimate, among the notebooks that were burned on his orders by Céleste Albaret? Was Marcel thinking ahead to a project† such as the conversation with his mother in *Contre Sainte-Beuve*? Is part of it to be found in his 1907 'Sentiments filiaux d'un parricide'? Or was Marcel, crippled with grief, only able to write about his mother once he had transformed her into a grandmother, and thus into a fictional character?

---

passages about Carpaccio, when it was Ruskin who claimed to have discovered him. Moreover, he compared Ruskin's book with one by Barrès, and regretted that 'the master's wonderful engravings' were not reproduced. He would make use of these when he came to write about Venice, as he would those of Whistler.

* In May he also missed the Fantin-Latour exhibition at the École des Beaux-Arts (*Corr.*, vol. VI, p. 125, 17 June 1906).

† See later on: 'It would be so sweetly pleasing to me before I die to write something that would have pleased Maman.'

This is undoubtedly the most mysterious period in an existence that was rich in secrets.

We can date the publication of *Sésame et les lys* by the fact that the printing was completed on 12 May 1906. The *Bibliographie de la France* of 2 June mentions the book as having just been published. Since he had not been very pleased with Mercure at the time *La Bible d'Amiens* was published, Proust took it upon himself to dispatch copies to his friends: 'For the last few days I've been doing a grocer's job with balls of string, wrapping paper and volumes of *Tout-Paris*.'[151] Endeavouring to secure some press coverage, he wrote firstly to Calmette, the editor of *Le Figaro*, and was rewarded by a twelve-line 'flash' on 5 June, and, on 12 June, an article by André Beaunier – two columns on the front page – which praised the translation as well as the footnotes.[152] Proust's closest friends, among them Albufera, would not see this article,[153] something which would inspire a comic passage in *Albertine disparue*. In *La Gazette de France* of 2 July Jacques Bainville devoted a 'fairly unpleasant'[154] piece to *Sésame*. On 4 July Léon Daudet reviewed the book in *Le Gaulois*, under the pseudonym 'Poivre et Sel'; Proust considered the article to be full of praise for Ruskin, but not for himself, since he found himself criticized for an 'excess of delicacy and elegance'.[155] Gregh devoted a short piece to him in his published letters, *Mon amitié avec Marcel Proust*. Though he attacked Ruskin in it, he rather patronizingly praised 'the delightful author of *Les Plaisirs et les Jours*'.* André Michel merely appended a postscript in *Le Journal des débats*.[156] All in all, there was far less coverage† than there was for *La Bible d'Amiens*, even though Proust's introduction and his footnotes, so reminiscent of 'Combray', were incomparably finer.

Marcel seemed to be recovering his zest for life: he was taking an interest in political life once more – as a liberal, he thought the victory of the Bloc des Gauches in the 20 May elections was regrettable (he poked fun at Reynaldo, 'a unified socialist'), because of its anti-clerical stance. He considered the official announcement by the Chambre des Députés on 13 July that Dreyfus, who had never been guilty, was now innocent, to be pointless.‡ With his charitable intuition, he even went so far as to assert,

---

* *Corr.*, vol. VI, p. 150. 'Furthermore, you don't like Ruskin,' Proust wrote to him. And he took his revenge by depicting him, aided by Dangeau, Saint-Simon and Montesquiou, as a ridiculous person (ibid., p. 140).

† The *Mercure de France* mentioned the book on 15 July and praised the translation.

‡ 'Even though I consider that Dreyfus is foolish and indiscreet to sue for a rehabilitation which the whole world (the world of the Dreyfusards that is, the others will never be persuaded) attests

on behalf of General Mercier, who had been insulted on the floor of the Sénat, that: 'Even in the wickedest man there's a poor innocent horse which toils away, with a heart and a liver, as well as arteries in which there is no malice whatsoever, and which suffer. And the moment of the finest triumph is spoiled because there is always someone who suffers.'[157] In a series of rather more mysterious activities, no doubt designed to rid himself of his emotional isolation, Marcel asked Lucien (these are the sort of favours one can ask among friends of the same persuasion) for the address of a footman from the Swedish legation: he needed to talk to him.*

PROUST AND MONEY

Mme Proust's estate was settled on 11 January 1906, the day upon which the two brothers agreed to the division of the inheritance in the presence of the notary who had come specially to Doctor Sollier's clinic, interrupting the patient's isolation in the process. They divided between them (half each) a sum of 1,743,573 francs, the apartment building at 102 Boulevard Haussmann (valued at 568,119 francs), to which was added the inheritance from their father. Once all the fees had been paid, Proust's inherited wealth, according to Roger Duchene,[†] amounted to 1,204,155 francs in capital and 142,029 francs as his share of the apartments, which generated an annual income of at least 50,000 francs.[‡] A solid inheritance and a very comfortable income did not prevent Marcel from feeling that he was only modestly well off. For example, in June, when he offered to lend some money to his friend Robert Dreyfus, he said that he now had at his own

---

to, I found, having rather forgotten all of that, that it was still moving to read about these things again and reflect that it was possible for this to happen a few years ago in France, and not among the Apaches. The contrast that exists between their culture and their refined intelligence on the one hand, and the sparkle of these people's uniforms and their despicable morality, is frightening' (*Corr.*, vol. VI, p. 127, he wrote, as early as 18 June 1906, to Mme Straus). On 12 July the Court of Appeal had quashed unconditionally the sentence of the Rennes court-martial. Picquart was then promoted to the rank of general. Cf. ibid., p. 159, 21 July 1906, to Mme Straus: 'Blessed are those who are victims of errors, judicial or otherwise! They are the only human beings for whom there is redress and reparation.'

* Ibid., p. 143, 5 July 1906. The subject of love affairs with servants (already touched upon at Évian, in the case of Poupetière) re-emerges. See Painter, vol. 2, p. 66, who draws up a list which, incidentally, is very incomplete.

† Duchene discovered the minutes of the estate at the practice of Maître Georges Dusablon. *L'Impossible Marcel Proust*, Laffont, 1994, p. 530.

‡ Equivalent to capital of 35,175,000 francs in 1999 terms, 11 million francs for the share of the apartments, and an income of 1 million francs a year (88,000 francs per month).

disposal his 'little fortune', which he believed, mistakenly, was not enough to enable him to stay on in rue de Courcelles (although it was true that this vast apartment was hardly suitable for a bachelor confined to his bedroom). Should one attribute this feeling to his thrifty upbringing, in an environment where one was used to living off the interest on one's income? To the fear of being 'hard up' common among those who, like Adrien Proust, were self-made men? To the impression Marcel may have had, now that his parents were dead, that the source of wealth was drying up* and that it was threatened, given that he was convinced that he would never earn any money? To his total, almost pathological inability to 'do his accounts', or grasp the value of money (from which stems the generous tips and the legendary sumptuousness of his presents,† and also the wild speculations and his taste for gambling)? Should we relate this attitude to the general scorn for worldly possessions, and particularly for furniture, for property and for collecting things,[158] displayed by a man for whom the heart and the mind meant everything when set against the emptiness of the world? In any case, this explains why hardly any figures or prices (nor dates, time's own price) should be mentioned in *À la recherche*.[159]

SUMMER AND MOVING HOUSE

Marcel began to think about the holidays. He could go to the manor house at Sarlabot, near Cabourg, with the Albuferas;‡ to Trouville, where he could rent a cottage§ from the Creuniers, Harcourt or la Tour Malakoff, or the Crémieux cottage (from his Thomson cousin), or he could go to the Hôtel des Roches Noires; or else he could hire a little yacht just for him, in which he would visit Normandy (whose misty climate was unhealthy and 'upset him') and Brittany;[160] alternatively he could go to Évian in August, but that would be to undergo 'a calvary' again. Proust always travelled in his mind's eye amid scenery that stimulated his imagination

---

* Money is so bound up with love that emotional loss can sometimes create the impression of financial loss.

† His gifts included flowers for Calmette, painted by Madeleine Lemaire (*Corr.*, vol. VI, p. 166); watches for the d'Alton daughters; an aeroplane for Agostinelli (ordered, but not delivered).

‡ The plan was cancelled due to the death of a member of their family: the Prince Eugène Murat.

§ The ideal house would be outside the town, but not near trees, and modern-style 'so that he could breathe properly', with three bedrooms (two of them for servants; he would bring his old maid, Félicie Fiteau, the model for Françoise), a dining-room, a kitchen, a bathroom was not essential but would be very nice; 'no need for a drawing-room' – and 'as many WCs as possible' (*Corr.*, vol. VI, p. 168, to Mme Straus; cf. p. 172).

and it was always to the same places – the north-west of France, Italy, the Haute-Savoie: 'At this "holiday" time I devour a fearful (and platonic) number of timetables and I bone up on a thousand "circular journeys" which I make between two and six o'clock in the morning on my chaise longue.'* Finally, exhausted by these imaginary journeys, but principally because he was worried about the health of his uncle Georges Weil, he moved into the Hôtel des Réservoirs at Versailles, where he immediately fell ill. This former mansion belonging to Mme de Pompadour[161] looked straight on to the park, which Marcel, being too ill, was unable to enjoy. His rooms were 'vast and splendid, but terribly gloomy, dark and freezing cold, with pictures, wall-hangings and mirrors. It is one of those historical types of apartment, the kind where the guide tells you that Charles IX died there, where you cast a furtive glance about you as you hurry to get out ... But when you are not only unable to get out but have to make the supreme act of acceptance by sleeping there! It's enough to make you want to die.'[162] This witty description would be reproduced more or less exactly in *À l'ombre des jeunes filles en fleurs*† and even at the beginning of *Du côté de chez Swann*.‡ He was then 'pitilessly' made to move to the annexe where the meals arrived cold.[163] As he always did when he was ill, Marcel allowed his beard to grow and became 'depressed about the future', but he nevertheless enjoyed recounting 'amusing little things' to his friends: 'They're always around even when one is alone, even if one is dying.'§ This is why he sent Reynaldo, who had left for Salzburg,[164] some second-rate poems, the last lines of which were a pastiche of Baudelaire: '*Alors ô ma beauté dites à la Litvinne/ Qui vous mangera des baisers/ Que je garde l'essence et la forme divine/ De mes amours germanisés.*¶ Then there were various pastiches

* Ibid., p. 167, 26 July 1906. We know the part played by timetables in *À la recherche*, as well as dreaming about journeys.

† *RTP*, vol. II, p. 27: thus we see that the Grand Hôtel at Cabourg was not the only model for the one at Balbec; there is never just one key in Proust. However, the Hôtel des Réservoirs is certainly named as such in *La Prisonnière* (ibid., vol. III, pp. 638–40), because Albertine says she had lunch there.

‡ Ibid., vol. I, p. 8, in which Proust describes the hostility of the violet curtains, the strange and pitiless rectangular cheval-glass, the gigantic height of the funnelled ceiling. Cf. ibid., draft IV, pp. 656–7.

§ Ibid., p. 183. He was aware of his own humour: 'What is cruel about the thought of our ultimate death ... is the unwillingness of our beautiful eyes to depart, the drollness which has made us so many friends' (*RTP*, vol. I, draft V, p. 662).

¶ 'And so my handsome fellow, tell la Litvinne/ Who will devour you with kisses/ That I retain the essence and divine form/ Of my Germanized love affairs.' *Corr.*, vol. VI, p. 177. He would hear the great singer Félia Litvinne perform at the casino at Cabourg in 1910.

of the Comtesse Greffulhe,[165] a 'song'[166] in which the lines rhymed with
ac, a parody of Kleinzach's ballad in the prologue to Offenbach's *Tales of
Hoffmann*[167] and a pastiche of Mme de Sévigné, in her letter to Coulanges
about Lauzun's marriage,[168] while leaning all too heavily 'on the stirrup
of a shaky memory on the one side, and on the stirrup of reconstructive
inspiration on the other', as he quipped to Reynaldo, defining his technique
as a pasticheur in the process. He asked Reynaldo, who had stayed at the
hotel in the past, for his advice about tipping, informed him that Hector,
the maître d'hôtel, had become an antique dealer, and that the painter
Hans Schlesinger was his neighbour, which meant he could strike up a
relationship with someone other than Constantin Ullmann,* with whom
he appeared to be on good terms again, and René Peter. The latter, the
son of a former colleague of Adrien Proust at the Académie de Médecine
(and an opponent of Pasteur), was a friend of Reynaldo and of Fouquières,
an author of plays (notably the successful *Chiffon*, written in collaboration
with Danceny, and *Je ne trompe pas mon mari*, with Feydeau), and, later, the
biographer of Debussy, whom he had known in his youth, and author of
the history of the Académie française;[169] he saw Marcel every day, which
explains how he was able to relate that Marcel summoned his maid Félicie
by knocking on the dividing wall,[170] as at Balbec. 'Peter is delightful and
endlessly resourceful in a way that I never imagined, and tireless in the
kindness with which he treats me, and for you,' he wrote to Hahn, 'he
has an affection, an admiration and a fondness that I find touching.'[171]
The fact that he was involved with the theatre explains why Marcel should
have thought of writing plays with him – in mid-September he told
Reynaldo about the following scenario (not the kind one would write with
a stranger), which is reminiscent of 'La Confession d'une jeune fille' and
the scene between Mlle Vinteuil and her girlfriend: a man who adores his
wife takes a sadistic pleasure in sullying her name by talking to prostitutes.
Having caught him doing so, the wife leaves him. He kills himself. It was
because Proust had planned to write a play around this time that he could

* Son of Otto Ullmann, and friend of Reynaldo Hahn and Frederico de Madrazo, he was very
wealthy and led a social life that was 'curbed in later life', says Léon Pierre-Quint, 'by a reputation
which would scarcely be considered scandalous today'. Immensely rich, according to S. Bonmariage,
he proposed a white wedding to Lili Lehmann and to Liane de Pougy. He died in penury. See
Europe, November 1947, pp. 67–9 (information kindly communicated by the Kolb-Proust Archive
for Research, University of Illinois at Urbana-Champaign). Ullmann reappears at several periods in
Proust's correspondence. E.g. vol. XVII, p. 526 (when he introduced Guzman Blanco, who enjoyed
a similar reputation, to Proust).

write, in *Du côté de chez Swann*: 'It is behind the footlights of a Paris theatre and not under the homely lamp of an actual country house that one expects to see a girl encouraging a friend to spit upon the portrait of a father who has lived and died for her alone; and when we find in real life a desire for melodramatic effect, it is generally sadism that is responsible for it.'[172]

Ultimately, he would not have the courage to take this 'fairly good idea for a play'* any further. He also sent Reynaldo, while reproaching him for never asking him for a libretto,† a spectacular, the text of which has never been found. Yet perhaps it was nothing more than a joke of a few lines, given that he wrote, 'The spectacular is unutterably lovely, with some horribly vulgar parts, but two of the five acts and the idea for it are mine'[173] (and the rest, Peter's); at this period Marcel was sending Hahn a number of humorous verses, including a pastiche of a critical textbook: 'Why did you not ask for the sweet fruits of my vigils?' Note: 'Figuratively, my books. For, to judge by the small number of works that he has given us, it seems unlikely that M. Proust went to bed late.'[174] René Peter, 'the compassionate spirit of Versailles', was one of the people of whom Proust was fondest; when he returned to Paris, he wrote to Peter as if he were writing a lament: 'You've never come back! Never come back! . . . How unreliable!' But if friendship depended upon places, if 'places sometimes restore to us the spirit with which they imbued us', Marcel maintained he would be prepared to make Versailles his permanent home, and since his friend only spent six months there: 'I would have six months in which to see you, and six months to be forgotten by you, which would be excellent for one's emotional health.'[175]

We have little information about his reading, which, because of his inactivity, must have been substantial: Emily Brontë, whose *Wuthering Heights* had been translated by Wyzewa in 1892 under the title *Un amant*, and a novel that he liked very much, *Jude the Obscure*, by Thomas Hardy. He returned to his dear Dumas, whom he enjoyed reading while staying at the hotel, just as he did at Fontainebleau, and he wrote to Hahn, who had recommended them to him, about *Le Chevalier d'Harmental* ('in which

---

* *Corr.*, vol. VI, p. 312. Since Proust had told Louis de Robert that the Montjouvain episode in *À la recherche* was based upon Doctor Robin's liaison with Liane de Pougy, one supposes that the same applied to this 'melodrama'.

† Cf. ibid., p. 300: '*C'est avec bien chagrin au cœur/ Qu'il délaisse aux autres la joie/ D'être ton collaborateur.*' [It is with much sorrow in his heart/ That he relinquishes to others the joy/ Of being your collaborator.]

the Denis family is worthy both of Balzac and Paul de Kock') and *Une fille du Régent*.[176] If the twists of the plot did not really surprise him, since he guessed what would happen from the outset,[177] his sensitivity was laid bare: 'How tedious to think that d'Harmental has got himself involved in this conspiracy and that he is going to have to endure some painful struggles in a novel where all I wanted was cheerful curiosity, a victory and some greediness.'[178] When he read *Une fille du Régent* afterwards, he observed that the two novels had structures and plots that could be superimposed exactly one upon the other; this was a fine example of modern criticism and it led him to conclude with a paradox: 'Dumas wrote well, but he lacked imagination.'[179] In addition to these, there were the newspapers and magazines which he said 'overwhelmed'[180] him, and from which he derived part of his learning and his information about current affairs: in particular, he followed the progress of the separation of the Church (which he found very 'disinterested' yet 'stupid') and the State, he admired Briand's moderation which 'softened the final blow' and he blamed the stubbornness of 'the poor and insane Pope Pius X'.*

Furthermore, Proust employed as his 'pseudo-secretary', as he himself would put it, Robert Ulrich, who was the first in a succession of accommodating and rather shadowy escorts. He has been seen as a model for Joseph Périgot, the footman in *À la recherche*,[181] as is confirmed by the letter from Ulrich's mistress that Proust quotes to Reynaldo.[182] Marcel

---

* Ibid., p. 298, December 1906. The pope had condemned the Law of Separation and its applications in the encyclical *Vehementer nos* (February 1906). The French government then conducted an inventory of the property of the clergy. The pope rejected the religious associations elected by the congregations, which the law had charged with responsibility for buildings that belonged to religious bodies (the encyclical *Gravissimi officii*, 15 August 1906). Briand, who was Minister for Religious Affairs, had planned to allow the churches to remain open in accordance with the 1901 law, which required a simple declaration from the priest; the pope forbade this (encyclical *Pascendi*). Parliament would adopt Étienne Flandin's bill of March 1907, repealing the obligation to make a prior statement. But the clergy had lost their special exemption. The churches were occupied without legal title. The occupation of presbyteries was dependent on the good will of the municipalities. Other buildings, such as bishops' palaces, were taken over by the State or by the municipalities. The Church, on the other hand, acquired complete independence in terms of political power. Cf. ibid., p. 318, where Proust's reflections rise above politics to history: in former times, neither Louis XIV nor Napoleon would have accepted 'what Briand puts up with from the pope. And in the old days, too, the clergy would never have had the high-mindedness or at least the disinterestedness which has caused them to renounce all their goods in obedience to the pope. Power, nevertheless, is of little consequence, since now that the pope has neither an army nor territory, he is more powerful (even in France, where he is least powerful) than he ever was in the days of his material power.' Not a word need be changed in this penetrating analysis by the hermit of Versailles.

would ask Robert de Billy to find a post for Ulrich in his father-in-law's organization or in his bank, describing him as a young man of twenty-five years of age, 'very distinguished and of pleasing appearance, with good hand-writing . . . very pleasant manners, very serious-minded, but without any further education'.* Marcel was also interested in 'a manservant by the name of Léon'[183] whom he 'could take to the theatre'.[184]

On 23 August Jeanne Proust's brother, Georges Weil, a member of the Paris Court of Appeal, died at his home at 22 Place Malesherbes of the same illness as his mother and his sister, after two months 'of constant martyrdom'. Marcel, who had been to see him, 'without being recognized by him', while he was in his death throes,[185] was too ill to go to the burial. He was particularly saddened by his death because this affectionate companion of his childhood was the last representative of the generation before his own, the person with whom he talked most easily about his mother, and a man who used to come and call on him every evening after her death.[186] In one of the drafts for 'Combray', as a discreet act of homage, he described very movingly that time 'when there were still some uncles'.[187] In September he nevertheless entertained friends such as Billy and Lauris. Armed with estate agents' particulars, he also began to send his friends house-hunting on his behalf: René Peter was sent to the Place Louvois, the rue Margueritte, the rue d'Artois, 102 Boulevard Haussmann, 77 rue de Prony and to 31 rue Lapérouse. When he received further particulars,[188] he spoke to Georges de Lauris about the rue Washington, the rue Chateaubriand and the rue de Berri; Lauris visited a 'frightful' number of apartments in the rue de Prony and Avenue de Messine. But since Marcel was always talking about Boulevard Haussmann,[189] one has the feeling that it was there, for reasons which he would formulate later, that he wished (subconsciously to begin with) to make his home. He followed up his friends' visits with enquiries worthy of the police, and ended up knowing more about the properties than an estate agent: 'I have the exact measurements, provided by the concierges and measured again by messengers, of various rooms in Prony, Boulevard Haussmann, Saussaies, Théodule-Ribot, etc., etc. None of them has rooms as huge as those in Boulevard Haussmann.'[190]

---

* *Corr.*, vol. VII, p. 268. He would also ask for theatre tickets for Ulrich, and he would use him as his secretary, to send out invitations to dinner, etc. He also tried to find a job for a nephew of his maid, Félicie Fiteau, who had been a Republican Guard for twelve years and was about to be discharged. P. Kolb is mistaken here, confusing the young man, who he believes is anonymous and who is in fact Ulrich, with the older nephew who is a Republican Guard (n. 3 and 5).

On 8 October he had made up his mind: it was to be the family block of apartments at 102 Boulevard Haussmann. Despite the trees, the noise of the trams and the dust, he decided he could not bring himself to live in a house which his mother had not known; he had often come to dine with her here, and he had watched his old uncle Louis Weil die in the bedroom which he would later occupy; there would be memories. He began by sub-letting this first-floor flat from a tenant who was no longer living there.[191] There were six rooms to furnish: a large drawing-room, a small one (in which he thought he would spend most of his time, though in fact his poor health would not allow him to do so), a dining-room, a study, into which he moved the furniture from the rue de Courcelles given him by his brother (Robert probably had nowhere to put it, and they had agreed on 'other compensatory arrangements'), his bedroom (two windows overlooking the boulevard), a smaller room giving on to the courtyard, a linen room and a bathroom. He had his bedroom hung with a cream-coloured Empire wallpaper, a colour that was rather brighter than the cherry-red paper he chose for the ante-chamber and the room giving on to the courtyard.[192] He would keep all the furniture that could be found room for in the apartment, which had a smaller floor area than that of the rue de Courcelles, because it would help a little to re-create 'the lost motherland',[193] while the remainder was put into storage.[194] The grand piano went in the drawing-room, and Marcel hoped to have it converted into an Aeolian pianola (like the one on which Albertine would play). For a desk, he used the one that had belonged to his uncle, which he had in the smaller drawing-room, in the same place that it had been when he was alive. According to his principles, there were to be no pictures in his bedroom: bare walls represented the space in which the mind could cut itself off in order to create. Even the portrait of his mother by Mme Beauvais (1880), which was too painful to look at, went in the large drawing-room (and the portrait of his father by Lecomte du Nouy was sent to Robert's home; Marcel would keep the one painted by Brouardel); the portrait of Proust by Blanche went in the small drawing-room. In any case, the portrait of the young Mme Proust did not look like her (she only regained her youthful looks after her death, like the Narrator's grandmother). Marcel preferred a photograph of her, with which he carried on a poignant dialogue: 'In the evening I tell Maman's photograph,' he wrote to Mme Catusse, 'how kind you are to me and it is as if it is upon you that she is bestowing the delicate, kindly smile that I share with you.'[195] Conscious that the furnishings which he had inherited were imbued with memories rather than beauty, he planned to give certain pieces to the servants and to share out others, such as the bronzes, so fashionable at the end of the nineteenth century, 'among people for whom the beauty of an object is less important than its value'.[196] But he kept all the photographs, because he wanted his grandparents, and even their parents, whom he had not known, to be near him, and he would sleep in his brass bed. In 1910 he had his bedroom walls lined with cork, following the example of the Comtesse de Noailles. He would place his fumigations of Legras powder on small plates; when the smoke spread beneath the doors, the neighbours would protest. From Versailles, he set out his recipe for good health: 'Every speck of dust suffocates me. Every piece of furniture gathers dust. And in a house where it's difficult to beat or clean, because of the hours at which I sleep and my fear of noise, because of my sensitivity to the cold and my fear of open windows, an apartment like a hospital would be the ideal. Since that's not possible, I want at least to have as few bits of furniture as possible, while still retaining a lot. So keep only the best, those pieces that are of some quality.'[197] This, therefore, was what this apartment, to which 'a sweet and sad force'[198] had led him back, would look like. The details of the furnishing, in so far as the very precise letters written by this opponent of detailed descriptions[199] enable us to reconstruct them, and the distribution of rugs were of little importance; even the pictures, which he had hung in the drawing-room and in the dining-room (copies of Snyders) and in the ante-chamber (*Esther and Haman* by Franken the Younger, 'in a suitable dark corner'), were of scant interest to him, since those that one had not discovered, coveted and bought oneself 'with pain and love', did not matter.[200] The important principle in furnishing the rooms was to retain the memories of rue de Courcelles, the last apartment where Marcel had lived with his parents and which was, more than Père-Lachaise, 'the place where for him his mother lay'.* Later on, he would come to realize that it was up to him to construct another memorial to his mother, in his work.

While he waited to move house, Proust neither wrote nor worked: 'I've closed the era of translations, which Maman encouraged, for good. And as for translations of myself, I no longer have the heart.'[201] Yet he did

---

* *Corr.*, vol. VI, p. 326. Proust believed that if he should have to leave Boulevard Haussmann, it would at least have served as a transition point between rue de Courcelles and an apartment that his mother had never set eyes on.

consider writing an article that had been promised for some time on *Gainsborough*, by Gabriel Mourey,[202] the former editor of *Arts de la vie*, a magazine which later went bankrupt. He continued to prolong his stay in Versailles, however, until December, owing to problems with the management and the unhelpfulness of the person from whom he had sub-let the apartment, as well as some repair work undertaken by a new tenant, Doctor Gagey, 'who required an incredible amount of work' on the mezzanine floor. Proust arranged for the work on the building to be supervised by the concierge, Antoine, and by his parents' butler, Jean Blanc. For all that, he was unable to take advantage of the park, being too unwell to go out; since he only woke up once night had fallen, he knew nothing of 'the delights of the season or of the time of day'.[203] He never encountered the beautiful Gladys Deacon, future Duchess of Marlborough, who was living in the room above his. He spent four months in Versailles as if 'in a telephone kiosk without being in the least aware of his surroundings'. Nevertheless, he loved 'these incomparable purlieus', which he used to visit endlessly, and which were the inspiration for a number of passages (following those in *Les Plaisirs et les Jours*) in *À la recherche*. He did, however, go to call on the Comtesse d'Arnoux, and there he met Paul Cambon, the French ambassador to London, 'enveloped in old age, silence and with an air of mystery pierced by the charm of his very fine eyes (an old and wrinkled Fénelon)', a figure who already belonged to *Le Temps retrouvé*. And then on 27 December, in one of those spur-of-the-moment decisions that follow a long pause, and which were quite usual for him, Marcel returned to Paris and moved into Boulevard Haussmann without wanting to inform a soul.[204] This return marked the end of his great period of mourning.

CHAPTER XI

The Renaissance of Literature

RETURNING TO LIFE

In spite of the fact that he suffered from asthma and remained bedridden, beset by those terrible 'arrival fits'[1] which he had foreseen, when Proust moved into Boulevard Haussmann, he achieved a crucial turning point in his life. Not only was this the first apartment that he had bravely moved into on his own, and where in his isolation he faced up to his illness and to the attacks that lasted between thirty and fifty hours, but the move marked the end of his long period of mourning, of that terrible year he had endured since the death of his mother. He himself had explained to friends, like Georges de Lauris, who had also lost their mother, that one had simply to try to survive initially, that gradually the cherished image would return to keep one company, even though there would always be 'something broken' within you, that one never got over the loss, and that 'one remembers more and more'.[2] Once he had achieved a sort of tranquillity in his 'solitary' and 'sleeping'[3] soul, he gradually began to go out again, to entertain (though never again would he give dinner parties at home, as he had done during his parents' lifetime), to travel, meeting the person whom he would one day love more than anyone apart from his mother, writing the most important articles he had yet published and, possibly, beginning to write a new book.

GAINSBOROUGH

In January Proust sent Marguillier his review of Gabriel Mourey's *Gainsborough*. Reckoning it to be one of his 'skimpier little pieces', he only wanted it signed 'M. P.'[4] This was how it appeared in *La Chronique des arts et de la curiosité* of 9 March 1907. The book, published in the series 'Les Grands Artistes – leur vie, leur œuvre' by Henri Laurens, whose 'Villes d'Art' series Proust would praise in *À la recherche*, took the form of a 'critical biography'.[5] Proust mentioned Marguillier's *Dürer* and Paul Desjardins' *Poussin*[6] in the same series, and he also read *Carpaccio* by G. and L. Rosenthal,[7] which he would make use of in *Albertine disparue*. The review, too, was exclusively biographical, and was indeed rather skimpy. At no point could the reader acquire the least impression of the English artist, who was of little interest to Proust. However, on the basis of three anecdotes he went on to outline a philosophy of art: 'the rise of the irresistible force', 'the documentary use of the work of art', the morality that is peculiar to the artist, for whom good is that which induces inspiration and evil that which paralyses it, a distrust of people in society, for associating with them can, if snobbery plays a part, 'kill the greatest talents'.[8] But all this was in order to return to his dear Ruskin: to pay tribute to English painting and to honour the man who testified on its behalf; conversely, to pay homage to him was to praise Gainsborough or Turner. (In his *Modern Painters*, incidentally, Ruskin only mentioned the former in order to sing the latter's praises.) According to Proust, this was why, on Ruskin's death, the well-known collector Camille Groult (1832–1908),[9] ('whose collection is the Louvre of English painting', whereas 'the Louvre has so few'), bought a Turner as a way of paying tribute to him. Later on, however, Proust would remember Mourey's book and, in an unexpected and roundabout way that was typical of his scholarly yet light-hearted approach, he would associate Reynaldo with Mozart, and identify himself with a friend of the composer's, telling Hahn that Gainsborough had painted Elizabeth Linley, the sister of a very dear friend of Mozart: 'I've read that he [Mozart] was as kind to one of his friends as you are . . . Gainsborough dashed off a painting of the wife or daughter of this friend whom Mozart idolized.'[10]

'FILIAL FEELINGS OF A PARRICIDE'

A tragic and forbidding event led Proust to resume writing, in January 1907;* this new article, 'Sentiments filiaux d'un parricide', represented a brutal purging of his entire past, a liberation from his private torments and from the feeling that he had brought about his mother's death because of the anxiety he had caused her on account of his illness or the life he led. It was inspired by a news item. On 24 January Henri Van Blarenberghe, whose

---

* 'It is true,' he wrote to Lucien Daudet, 'that since my translation of *Sésame* I haven't written a word, apart from letters and accounts.'

father, the president of the Chemins de fer de l'Est and a relative of the Prousts, had died in May 1906, killed his mother in a fit of insanity and committed suicide. Now, the Blarenberghes used to see the Prousts regularly and Marcel had occasionally dined at the homes of mutual friends of their son, and recently, 'on behalf of a friend', he had asked him for some information about an employee of the Chemins de fer de l'Est.* Calmette, the editor of *Le Figaro*, who knew of Marcel's links with this family, asked him for an article on 30 January, which he composed on the night of the 31st, between three and eight o'clock in the morning; he added an ending, an admirable one, but which was cut by Cardane, the assistant editor, a 'strict moralist'. He gaily told Ulrich, Proust's messenger: 'Does he really think that anyone is going to read his article, apart from himself and a few people who know him!'[11] Calmette, on the other hand, praised the piece, which he thought 'very fine'. The article appeared on 1 February.

For the first time, Proust provided a work with a circular structure, since 'this word parricide, which had opened the article, also closed it. The article was thereby given a sort of unity',[12] he wrote to the editor of *Le Figaro*, who had allowed the final paragraph to be cut. The dynamic of these pages, dashed off in a few hours and all the more revealing as a result, comes from the narrator's memory as he recalls his parents and the family of the parricide, Henri Van Blarenberghe, in a series of 'snapshots' – the technique used to introduce the characters of *À la recherche du temps perdu*. The eyes of someone who remembers are the 'telescopes of the invisible': 'Seeing them drawn together by memory, one senses only too well the expression – wearied by having to adjust to so many different periods, often in the distant past – the listless expression of old men; one senses so well that the trajectory of that look, which crosses "the shadow of days"† one has lived through and which, it seems, is going to land a few feet in front of them, will in reality land fifty or sixty years behind them.' The fact is, this expression, like that of the Princesse Mathilde, which Proust recalled here, 'joined the present to the past, in a form of resurrection'.[13] The movement of memory is followed by a description of an awakening, which is the true Proustian point of departure, if we think of the openings to *Du côté de chez Swann*, *Le Côté de Guermantes* and *La Prisonnière*. The reading of *Le Figaro* that follows is a foretaste of that

---

* *CSB*, p. 152. One wonders whether this 'friend' might not be Proust himself, for he frequently requested information about 'employees', such as electricians, telegraphers and restaurant waiters.

† *L'Ombre des jours* was the title of a book written by the Comtesse de Noailles.

in *Contre Sainte-Beuve* and in *Albertine disparue*, and of the pleasure which Mme Verdurin took, during the war, in reading about catastrophes as she consumed a croissant. When he came across the news item, Proust interpreted it in the light of a Greek tragedy, firstly *Ajax*, then *Oedipus Rex*: when, after his suicide, the murderer was discovered to have torn out his own eye, the writer saw 'this as the most terrible gesture bequeathed us in the history of human suffering, the eye of the wretched Oedipus himself'.[14] In the age of Freud, whose work he did not know, Proust interpreted reality in the light of myth and literature, and also of erudition, since he acquired his knowledge of parricide in antiquity from Saint-Marc Girardin's *Cours de littérature dramatique*:[15] 'I wanted to show in what a pure, in what a religious atmosphere of moral beauty this explosion of lunacy and bloodlust took place that besmirched him without managing to taint him. I wanted to ventilate the scene of the crime with a breath of air from heaven, and show that this news item was precisely one of those Greek dramas the performance of which was akin to a religious ceremony.'[16] Having deciphered the world with the help of Ruskin, and then made sense of tragedy, Proust would still need Sainte-Beuve, Balzac, Baudelaire and Flaubert before being able to read the world, and therefore write about it, on his own. Beyond having recourse to literature as a go-between, which is quite normal, since literature enables us to illuminate the dark night of the world as well as that of the soul, this article contained a further reflection on the subjects of madness and death, which Proust could not believe in 'without difficulty', and, in particular, keeping what was most important to the end, a confession: 'Basically, as we grow older, we kill all those who love us through the worries that we cause them, through the very affection and anxiety that we inspire and keep in a state of constant alarm.'[17] In *Sodome et Gomorrhe*, the vision of the degradation of a 'beloved body', the sense of guilt, the desire for retribution, would all be taken up again in the context of the relationship of the Narrator to his grandmother, for whose death he would blame himself. In 1907 the still literary structure of the stories in *Les Plaisirs et les Jours* discovered its human truth at the cost of an unbearable vision. The dialectics of fault and expiation, explored again in *La Prisonnière* with reference to Dostoevsky, and of redemption through literature were to shape the moral life of the Narrator, and release him finally from the terrible sense that he had killed his grandmother and Albertine.

In January too, Proust, who had been interviewed by the journal *Les Lettres* about Tolstoy's *Shakespeare*, in which the Russian writer dismissed the English dramatist,[18] declared he was too ill to offer further comment. He nevertheless drafted a letter in which, as ever, he broadened the debate: it was not a matter of doubting Tolstoy's power to recognize beauty and aesthetic truth: the foreign language hid these from him, for 'only the beauty of expression can give an idea individuality and can measure the depths to which it has been developed in the poet's soul'. This was why Goethe so admired Béranger, and Ruskin George Sand. Moreover, writers were frequently mistaken about each other; Sainte-Beuve especially (here there emerges a subject, and certain remarks, that Proust would return to a year later), who was too close to the personalities of the writers upon whom he pronounced judgement, and 'was too well aware that in the society in which Mérimée, Jacquemont[19] and d'Ampère moved, Stendhal was far from being pre-eminent'. Conversely, too little information did not make matters any easier: people had been mistaken about Ossian. Tolstoy's view, therefore, was one to be categorized among those misinterpretations that were common among people of great talent.

At the same period, in order to encourage Lucien Daudet, who was suffering from melancholia and self-doubt, Marcel defined a few further principles of his moral and aesthetic philosophy: 'true ideas' and 'things felt' were at the root of everything. We are, and here we recognize the voice of Ruskin, 'an instrument capable of experiencing beauty and truth'. We should not always see ourselves 'in time'. 'That part of us which is worthwhile, when it is doing something worthwhile, lies outside time', which is why it is never too late to settle down to work: 'La Fontaine began to work when he was forty . . . Hals only produced his really fine paintings when he was over eighty, and Corot did his best work after he was sixty.' Thoughts such as these engendered 'a great passion for life and work'.[20] It is as if we are listening to the narrator of *Le Temps retrouvé*. Above all, we hear a man who, at the age of thirty-six, when there was no longer anyone to tell him to do so, was also about to begin his life's work.

In that month of February building works on the mezzanine floor which were deafening Proust were replaced by those from the next-door building, and they bothered him all the more because he had altered his timetable and decided to wake up during the daytime.* Proust, who until

---

* He described the building works humorously in letters to Mme Straus (*Corr.*, vol. VII, pp. 101, 131): 'For months now, twelve workmen, hammering so frenetically during the day, must have constructed something as majestic as Cheops' pyramid, which must astonish passers-by as they walk between Au Printemps and Saint-Augustin.' It was with Mme Straus and Hahn that Proust joked most readily, writing letters that help us understand how funny his conversation must have been.

now had retained Félicie Fiteau, and Jean Blanc, his parents' manservant, now took on Nicolas Cottin,[21] who had also been in the employ of his parents, but, because of his 'propensity for drinking', had left them. He was already accustomed to Marcel's habits and, like the Boulevard Haussmann apartment, Cottin reminded him of the time when his parents were still alive. However, he was not satisfied with him.[22] Around 1 May he hired Céline Cottin, the wife of Nicolas. Félicie Fiteau and Robert Ulrich (who, however, would continue to help out occasionally) would leave Marcel's service on 1 July.[23]

Abnormally early spring weather soon enabled him to take a few steps outside, either on his balcony or on the pavement in front of the house: 'I found the sunshine to be an extremely pretty and most remarkable thing.' This remark might appear precious or banal, had Proust not been sufficiently inspired by this experience of sunshine after so many months of confinement to write an article for *Le Figaro* of 4 June 1912 entitled 'Rayons de soleil sur le balcon'.[24]

DAYS SPENT READING

In spite of his health problems and the irritation caused by his neighbours' building works, Proust worked a great deal. Two articles were to see the light of day almost simultaneously. On 20 March 1907 *Le Figaro* published 'Journées de lecture',[25] a review of a book that had just been published which constituted an important discovery: *Les Récits d'une tante. Mémoires de la comtesse de Boigne, née d'Osmond (1781–1866)*. Apart from the passage about the telephone,[26] which he took up again in *Le Côté de Guermantes*, but which was derived from *Jean Santeuil*, we find a meditation on those names that conjure up an entire past: 'A past that may be immense. I should like to think that these names, only rare examples of which have come down to us, thanks to certain families' regard for tradition, were quite commonly used in former times – the names of villeins as well as noblemen – and that consequently, through the pictures that these names evoke for us, naïvely coloured by the light of a magic lantern, it is not merely the powerful Bluebeard or Sister Anne in her tower that we glimpse, but also the peasant bent over the lush meadows and the men at arms riding along the dusty thirteenth-century roads.'[27] There is a second phase, however, that deprives the names of their poetry, when the conjunction of men and places proves to be unworthy of them. Here Proust had already formulated the theory of names in *Le Carnet de 1908* and in *À la* *recherche.* Memoirs are nevertheless useful, because they provide the present with an historical background, 'a drawbridge thrown across from the present to an already distant past, and which, in order to make history more alive, and life almost historical, connects life to history'.[28] If this type of thinking arouses our reveries only to disappoint them subsequently, and only circumscribes prosaic time, we must understand that Proust was not a memorialist, and that he was happy to borrow from Saint-Simon, from Mme de Boigne, Mme de Rémusat or the Comte d'Haussonville whatever they could provide him with: raw material, an unrefined past. The passages cut by *Le Figaro* extend his reflections on his feelings for this past. In the *Mémoires* no details were superfluous because, whether they concerned Theseus, Sargon or Assurbanipal, it was these details which had survived: 'M. Maspero can even give us the names of the greyhounds which the thieves kept on a leash.'[29] Proust himself would fill his book with these details, customs and aspects of daily life at the expense of the grand sweeps of history – the history of generals, kings and battles – precisely because not one of these humble, fragile, trifling details has been lost. 'In these vast surviving remnants of everything that once appeared on the surface of the earth',[30] society ladies who wrote their memoirs therefore had their place. The passages in *Le Côté de Guermantes* that Proust devotes to the salon and to Mme de Villeparisis' memoirs can be found here word for word, as well as the philosophy of history expounded in this part of the narrative. Mme de Boigne becomes Mme de Villeparisis, both because the accounts of their salons given in their memoirs are misleading, and because they had both had 'a long liaison with an elderly statesman who comes to discuss politics with them every evening'.* Finally, Mme de Boigne would be used as a model for the imaginary Mme de Beausergent, whose *Mémoires* the Narrator's grand-mother reads. Proust quoted Sainte-Beuve and Saint-Simon frequently in this article, but he kept the former to himself.

LES ÉBLOUISSEMENTS BY THE COMTESSE DE NOAILLES

In mid-March Anna de Noailles sent Proust a pre-publication copy of her new collection of poems so that he could review it for *Le Figaro*. He wrote the article in three hours, around 16 March, but then, because Reynaldo had

---

* *Essais et articles*, CSB, p. 929. M. de Norpois played the same role in relation to Mme de Villeparisis that Chancelier Pasquier did with Mme de Boigne.

pointed out to him that it was too long, he spent the whole night rewriting it: 'I counted . . . 16,900 characters', then, having recopied it, '18,000'.* It was the prodigious speed with which he wrote, which would never henceforth desert him, that enabled him to compose a novel that was 3,000 pages long, preceded by some 7,000 pages of rough drafts, with further outlines superimposed over them, plus typewritten sheets and numerous sets of proofs. From 1908 onwards there was none of Mallarmé's anguish when confronted with a blank page, but rather a frenzied surge of the pen, not unlike that of the motor car which he had recently discovered.

Anna de Noailles put her trust in him, certain that only he would share her feelings. What with the rewriting at proof, the piece was not finished until May; Cardanne asked him to cut sixty lines.[31] The article appeared on 15 June in what Proust wittily dubbed 'the foretaste of eternal oblivion',[32] the literary supplement to *Le Figaro*. It has been somewhat underestimated, just because the Comtesse de Noailles' poetry is no longer in vogue.[33] An old-fashioned romantic, a disciple of Lamartine, Hugo and Baudelaire, she had remained untouched by all the contemporary trends in modern poetry. Until the First World War her beauty, her breeding, her youth and charm, and the ease of manner in which she talked about herself, took people in. In the era of Apollinaire, Valéry and Breton, there was no longer any place for her.

Proust began by burying the collection beneath quotations from authors who would always enchant him: Sainte-Beuve,[34] who was never far from his thoughts, Joubert[35] and the Song of Songs. He then reverted to one of his favourite artists, Gustave Moreau,† who often attempted to portray 'that abstraction: the poet'. But one wonders whether the poet is not in fact a woman. Proust recognized Mme de Noailles in all Moreau's

---

* There were more than 30,000, without counting Cardanne's cuts.

† At the time he was writing this article, he received a copy of Montesquiou's *Altesses sérénissimes* (in which the count had included Proust's 'Un professeur de beauté'), the first chapter of which was devoted to Moreau ('I reread the splendid essay on Moreau,' Marcel told Montesquiou), and exclaimed: 'What a marvellous painter Moreau is!' (*Corr.*, vol. VII, p. 147, 7 May 1907). He also leafed through the book by Ary Renan (*Gustave Moreau*, De la Gazette des Beaux-Arts, 1899) again 'in which are reproduced (very poorly, incidentally) a number of paintings, and it is truly sublime'. Proust pointed out to Montesquiou, however, that he could not find a clever way of mentioning the work 'without it looking purely like a visiting card'! Nevertheless, he would make no bones about alluding to it again, even in *À la recherche*. He refused to devote an entire article to *Altesses*, even though he was curious about the keys, and in particular those that concerned the allusions, which he took up in *À la recherche*, to *La Duchesse de Langeais* and to *La Femme abandonnée* (*Corr.*, vol. VII p. 155). In Proust's mind, Montesquiou the writer was gradually giving way to the character he would become. He would see him again, however, and listen to his poems being read by Berthe Bady, at Madeleine Lemaire's home on 28 May.

representations of the poet; hence in a discreet way, before *Sodome et Gomorrhe*, the poet is represented as a man-woman. Perhaps Proust was acknowledging here one of the reasons why this artist appealed to him. But the man-poet cuts himself off from the beauty of the landscape,* whereas feminine grace forms a part of it. This, among other reasons, is why the 'girls' of Balbec may perhaps be boys, though transformed into women, and why they were the cause of a disagreement referred to in Gide's *Journal*. Moreover Mme de Noailles is both 'the poet and the heroine', 'the author and the subject of her poems': in the same way Proust would employ a first-person narrative in order to be both poet and hero, author and subject, of his poetic prose. However, it was not a case of the 'social, contingent self', but of the 'deeper self, who gives a work individuality and makes it last'.[36] Having thus characterized the narrator, Proust decided to discuss the subject matter of the book around the theme of gardens (the title of the third part of the collection), creating a panorama drawn from contemporary literature. Having alluded to Ruskin's garden† by preterition, he mentioned that of Maeterlinck, whose *L'Intelligence des fleurs* he had just read. From it he would borrow the floral images in *Sodome I*, those that deal with the reproduction of orchids[37] and which for Proust symbolized the difficult union of homosexuals. Rather more innocent gardens followed, aristocratic ones in the case of Régnier, natural and 'divine' ones in Francis Jammes' *Roman du lièvre*. And also Monet's 'colourist garden', less a model for a painting than a 'transposition of art', 'a first, living sketch' that would be the inspiration for his description of the 'gardens of water lilies' on the Vivonne, another 'transposition of art'. All these gardens were the forerunners of those at Combray which would one day emerge from a cup of tea that has become the most celebrated object in French fiction. Subjects that Proust did not discuss, such as Barrès and the East, would be removed.

This article also contained an aesthetic philosophy: Anna de Noailles knew that 'ideas are not lost in the universe, but that the universe is present within the idea'.[38] The critic attempted to draw out 'the essence and the spirit' of the book he was describing, but also its 'technique': it is metaphor that 'reconstructs and gives us back the illusion of our first

---

* 'They feel that the charms that surround them stop at their bowler hat, their beard, their pince-nez' (*CSB*, p. 535).

† 'For which he abandoned the Turners, the Della Robbia, his missals and the collection of minerals in his large study', said the manuscript.

impression', a simile that 'substitutes our observations of what exists with a re-arousal of what we once felt (the only reality of interest)'.[39] This was why Proust spoke of 'literary *impressionism*'. We come to realize that this impressionism is his just as much as the countess's. It was writing all these articles that made Marcel think for the first time of gathering them together in a book.* The project would not be realized until 1919, with the publication of *Pastiches et mélanges*; the essential thing was that the idea of a book should dawn upon him gradually. In the meantime, Mme de Noailles thanked him for his 'divine article'.[40]

MUSIC

On 11 April Proust made his first social appearance since the death of his mother. *Le Bal de Béatrice d'Este, duchesse de Milan (XVIe siècle)*, Reynaldo Hahn's ballet in seven parts, which he composed for piano and orchestra in 1905, was being performed at the Princesse Edmond de Polignac's house, on a stage hung with Renaissance damask and tapestries. Hahn conducted and also played the piano part: 'The candles were loose and several times, especially when you were striking chords by dropping your hands from a height of two metres and were conducting the orchestra with the tip of a sword, they almost fell and set fire to the paper roses by the footlights.'[†] What is more, although Marcel liked the work, declaring that he was 'crazy' about it, and praised the orchestration, 'such power in its purity', he criticized Reynaldo's style of conducting: 'You use too many tricks, too many mannerisms, too many grimaces, and that way of bouncing up and down on your bottom, which I don't find at all *joslie*.'[‡] Hahn also conducted his *Fontaine de Bandusie*, a work for female voice, choir and orchestra: Proust, for whom fountains were a favourite theme, was

---

* *Corr.*, vol. VII, p. 142, 12 or 13 April, to M. Nordlinger. Cf. ibid., p. 237: 'In a book of *Mélanges* [miscellaneous pieces], if I ever regain the strength to assemble those that already exist, I shall certainly include the introduction to *Sésame*' (to Mme Guéritte, a translator).

† Ibid., p. 139, 11 April 1907, to Hahn. Since the piece was composed in 1905, Marcel wondered whether 'Maman had heard it' (at Mme Lemaire's in April 1905 or Mme Hochon's in June). Hahn was to conduct the work at the Duchess of Manchester's house in honour of the British king and queen (B. Gavoty, *Reynaldo Hahn*, Buchet-Chastel, 1976, pp. 216–18), who remembered having met him at dinner at the home of Reginald Lister (1865–1912; secretary at the embassy from 1905 to 1908) on 5 February 1907 (*Notes*, p. 206). Marcel had never seen anything 'so beautiful, intelligent, elegant, meditative and sweet as Mr Lister's face. He's a four-square, golden Régnier, delightful.'

‡ Hahn conducted from the piano. As often in his letters to Reynaldo, Marcel used idiosyncratic spellings (e.g. 'joslie' for *jolie*; 'mopchant' for *méchant* etc.). *Tr.*

impressed that his friend should have obliged so many society people 'to stop and listen to a fountain weeping in silence and solitude'.* Due to his long absence from society, he experienced something which he would put to good use in the *'bal de têtes'* in *Le Temps retrouvé*.[41] 'How all the people I used to know have aged . . . And then a few fierce and rudimentary old divinities in their summary delineation haven't managed to change . . . in the barbaric hideousness of their Lombard effigies.'†

On 1 July, and for the first time since the death of his mother, Proust decided to arrange a dinner party and a concert in honour of Calmette.‡ It was to take place not at his home, but at a venue which would become his general headquarters, the Ritz, in a private dining-room. Gabriel Fauré was asked to perform. Inviting twenty people to dinner, and, as was the custom, a further twenty to listen to the music afterwards, Marcel launched himself into endless negotiations over the telephone and by letter with his future guests and with all his friends, new and old, from Dreyfus and the Caillavets to Casa-Fuerte, from Bordeaux to Rod and Barrès. There were thus twenty guests, with a menu and wines chosen by Guiche. The dinner party struck Marcel as being perfect, and all his friends seemed happy to see him again after such a long time. The Comtesse de Noailles accompanied him, each of them 'looking identical, with their strange faces enveloped in fur like a couple of Eskimos'.[42] But Fauré, who was ill, was replaced by Risler. Proust had chosen a programme of music: Risler§

* *Corr.*, vol. VII, p. 138. This letter resembles a sketch for the concert scenes in *À la recherche*. Proust made fun of someone's drunken laugh and the mannish voice of the Princesse Murat, 'who followed up or rather accompanied every phrase of the music with a tart comment: "Ah! Roses d'Ispahan, the essence of the east! But it's exquisite, bravo! One can smell the mint of the seraglio!"'.' The concert also included some of Fauré's songs, sung by Mlle Leclerc.

† Proust mentioned the Comtesse Odon de Montesquiou, *née* Bibesco, the Comtesse Fernand de Montebello (born in 1852) and Mme de Saint-André. Cf. *RTP*, vol. IV, p. 521: 'Only those women who were too beautiful found it hard to put up with these transformations, or those who were too ugly . . . The latter . . . were monsters, and they no more appeared to have "changed" than whales do.' For other similar experiences observed by Proust, see *Corr.*, vol. XI, p. 337, 1912, and vol. XVII, p. 331. Cf. draft XLI, pp. 873–900 and 903.

‡ 'Who is so kind as to take my long articles which do not appeal to the public very much' (*Corr.*, vol. VII, p. 195).

§ Risler demanded a fee of 1,000 francs (approximately 18,000 francs in today's money), payable in advance. The two other musicians, the violinist Hayot and the harpist Haselmans, were content with 600 francs between them; the dinner cost 700 francs. Proust listed those present in a letter to Hahn: 'Mme de Brantes, de Briey, d'Haussonville, de Ludre, de Noailles, M et Mme de Clermont-Tonnerre, d'Albufera, Calmette, Béraud, Beaunier, Guiche, Blanche, Emmanuel Bibesco. After dinner came the Casa-Fuertes, the d'Humières, la Polignac, la Chevigné, Rod, Gabriac, Berckheim, the young Durfort . . . the young Lasteyrie, Neufville, Lister, Gabriel de La Rochefoucauld, Griffon,

refused to play any of Hahn's work because, he claimed, he knew none of it by heart, not even the waltzes, neither did he know Schumann's *Carnaval de Vienne* (the intermezzo from which would inspire a brief passage in Vinteuil's sonata* nor Liszt's *Soirées de Vienne* (after Schubert). With the compulsive appetite of those who have suffered long privation, Proust also requested the *Sonata for piano and violin* (but not Franck's, nor Saint-Saëns'), a nocturne and *Berceuse* by Fauré, a Beethoven *andante*,[43] *In the evening* from Schumann's *Fantasiestucke*, a Chopin *Prelude*, Chabrier's *Idylle*,[44] Couperin's *Barricades mysterieuses*, and, since transcriptions were all the rage, the Overture to *Die Meistersinger* and the death of Isolde.[45] Most of these pieces were to play a crucial part in *À la recherche*. Proust did not know this at the time: it was later that his memory brought back to him the substance of this concert. But very shortly afterwards, once he had begun his great work, he would commission no more programmes at the Ritz and he would only attend concerts or go to the opera if the pieces had something to do with what he wanted to write.

A GRANDMOTHER

When Mme de Rozières, Robert de Flers' grandmother, died, Proust, being unable to attend the funeral in the Lozère, wrote an obituary of her for *Le Figaro* on 21 July, which appeared on the 23rd, the headline of which, as much as its content, is full of resonances for a reader of *À la recherche*. After his mother's death, Proust perfected the art of the obituary. He had in fact wanted to write one in February for *Le Figaro* on the death of the Marquise de Lauris, but, being too ill at the time, he abandoned the idea.[46] Here he appeared to be more overcome by grief than Flers himself, and he shot a strange little barb at his friend's wife, whose affection for her husband may have harmed the relationship between the grandmother and her grandson: as we know, Proust did not like it when

---

Ulrich, Eugène Fould, etc. Mme Straus, the Caillavets, Miss Deacon and Peter were not able to come, neither was Montesquiou.' Hahn was travelling (*Corr.*, vol. VII, pp. 211–12). This list is valuable, because it enables us to know who Proust's main friends were at this period.

* 'The phrase of Schumann's in *Carnaval de Vienne* (the intermezzo, I think), a gentle stranger whom I saw pass and pass again on so many evenings without ever catching sight of her face and without ever being able to examine it except through the mask of the notes . . . For Vinteuil, it was a carnival, but the true mask . . . was as it is in the sonata, that moving layer of little notes' behind which there passed a phrase, unknown, caressing and different from anything the Narrator had known, 'the offer of the only happiness that was worth the bother of possessing' (*RTP*, vol. III, draft XIII, p. 1145; the edition suggests that this phrase may come from the *lento assai* in the *Carnaval*.

his friends got married (he would, for example, sympathize with René Gimpel's mother at her son's wedding, and he quarrelled with Emmanuel Berl* for the same reason). In this article he identifies himself with this grandmother: 'There are some people who live almost as if they did not have the strength to do so ... They are the most interesting.' Like both Proust and Aunt Léonie, 'she did not leave her bed or her bedroom any more than did Joubert, or Descartes, or other people who considered it necessary for their health to spend a lot of time in bed ... Chateaubriand said of Joubert that he was constantly lying down with his eyes shut, but that that was when he was most troubled and got most tired'.[47] And again, like the neurasthenics in *À la recherche*, 'she made herself such a difficult patient that she might have done better simply to take the more complicated wager of being healthy'.† This grandmother is also identified with Mme Proust, and, retrospectively, with her metamorphosis in the future novel, constantly preoccupied as she was with her grandson, his health, his job, and his marriage: 'She never loved anything, to use Malebranche's phrase, except *through* him. He was her god.' Is not the bond which joins these two creatures that which bound Marcel to his mother? 'Two beings who seemed to be the translation‡ one of the other'? And would death imply that these two beings would no longer mean anything to each other? 'Must we really think so?' It was the question which Proust never stopped asking, right up until the death of Bergotte: 'Dead for eternity? Who can say so?' For it was his own grief that he was summarizing at the end of his obituary of Robert de Flers' grandmother: 'We never think of those whom we have most loved, at the times we are most sorrowful, without fervently addressing the most affectionate smile we are capable of in their direction. Do we do this in order to mislead them, to reassure them, to tell them that they need not worry and that we will be brave, to make them believe that we are not unhappy? Or is it, rather, that this smile is the physical expression of the endless kiss that we give them in the

* Berl relates this in *Sylvia*, Gallimard, 1952. One cannot pretend, incidentally, that Proust was any more interested in the spouses of his female friends, such as Noailles, Caraman-Chimay, and even Straus.

† *CSB*, p. 547. Montesquiou was right in his assessment: 'The most agreeable part of your commentary gives you the opportunity to talk about yourself, while discussing these valetudinarians ... Furthermore, the type you describe to us is but the manifestation ... of maternal love in its laudable excess ... And what a fine counterpart to your article could be written by a friend with your ability, speaking of the one you mourn!' (*Corr.*, vol. VII, p. 233).

‡ The use of this word suggests the work they did together on Ruskin. In *À la recherche* it is this bond that will unite mother and grandmother, under the wing of Mme de Sévigné.

Invisible?'* We do not know whether readers of *Le Figaro* were surprised at the moving tone and the very intimate style of this unusual obituary of another's 'grandmother'. Readers of *À la recherche du temps perdu*, should they look at it, will discover in it a portent of the passages about the Narrator's grandmother.

SUMMER 1907 IN CABOURG

Any departure on a journey is preceded by doubts; they form part of our fantasies: 'I continue to hesitate,' wrote Proust to Reynaldo Hahn on 1 August,[48] between Brittany, Cabourg, Touraine, Germany . . . and Paris.†
He left for Cabourg on 4 or 5 August, for a visit which, unbeknown to him, was to be an important one for his book and for his own life. He took with him his manservant, Nicolas Cottin, and on the train he encountered Doctor Doyen, who was to be one of the models for Cottard.‡
At this seaside resort, which *Le Bottin mondain* listed as a rival to Trouville and where Marcel had already stayed,§ first with his grandmother and later with his mother, the Grand Hôtel had just opened on 7 July. *Le Figaro* devoted a long article on 10 July to this 'palace', describing the opening festivities: 150 guests had travelled on a special train to 'the queen of beach resorts'.[49] Proust's decision was made: here he would spend the season, and many another too. In his book this watering place would reflect the light of an eternal summer.

Cabourg, which dated from 1853, adjoined the ancient town of Dives

---

* *CSB*, p. 548. We can understand why, after an article such as this, Proust should have been surprised not to have received a letter of thanks from Robert de Flers (*Corr.*, vol. VII, p. 233).

† *Corr.*, vol. VII, p. 240. Touraine would be used as the setting for Albertine's flight and her death, the belated appeasement of a traveller's dream. Germany was where Marcel went with his mother; Mme Verdurin wants to hear Wagner there and Swann considers renting a château near Bayreuth. Cf. ibid., p. 224: 'I, who haven't read anything for years apart from Joanne guides, geography books, handbooks on châteaux, anything that enables me to plan journeys, to look up towns and . . . not go. This time, however, I think I will go to Brittany.'

‡ He told Proust, speaking of Mme Greffulhe: 'And for all that she has not succeeded in creating a salon as brilliant as Mme de Caillavet's!' (ibid., p. 245, 6 August 1907, to R. Hahn). Léon Daudet has given us a harsh portrait of this brutal society surgeon (ibid., p. 246, n. 8).

§ We should remember that in 1890 he had spent a leave there, when he wore his uniform, and that the Cabourg maids had blown him kisses (letter to his father of 23 September 1890). In 1893 it was to Cabourg beach that he applied the lines of Baudelaire: 'the sun gleaming on the sea' (28 September). And in 1893 his mother had recommended Cabourg, because he had 'once felt so well' there. Thus, it had traces both of his family and of things that were familiar to him. Once before, in 1906, he had almost returned here.

1. Marcel Proust in 1908, by Otto (*Popperfoto*)

2. Mme Adrien Proust,
née Jeanne Weil, by Mme Beauvais
(*Musée Marcel Proust, Illiers-Combray*)

3. Adrien Proust, by Jean
Lecomte du Nouy
(*Musée Marcel Proust, Illiers Combray*)

4. Mme Adrien Proust
with her sons Marcel and Robert

5. Marcel and Robert Proust

6. *(left)* Marcel Proust
with Lucien Daudet and
Robert de Flers, by Otto

7. *(above)* Comte Gabriel
de La Rochefoucauld

8. Willie Heath, by
Paul Nadar (© *SPADEM*)

9. Reynaldo Hahn

10. *(above)* Marcel
Proust with a group
of friends

11. *(right)* Marcel Proust
with Alfred Agostinelli,
1907

12. *(left)* Mme Émile Straus,
née Geneviève Halévy, then Mme
Georges Bizet, by Élie Delaunay,
1878 *(Musée d'Orsay, Paris)*

14. *(below)* Comte Robert de
Montesquiou, by Lucien Doucet, 1879
(Musée National du Château de Versailles)

13. *(above)* Comtesse Greffulhe,
née Élisabeth de
Caraman-Chimay, 1896

15. *Le Cercle de la rue Royale en* 1868, by James Tissot
(*Collection Baron Hottinguer, © Edimedia*)

16. The promenade at Cabourg (*Private collection*)

17. Gaston Gallimard in 1913
(*Archives Gallimard*)

18. Céleste Albaret
(*Archives Gallimard*)

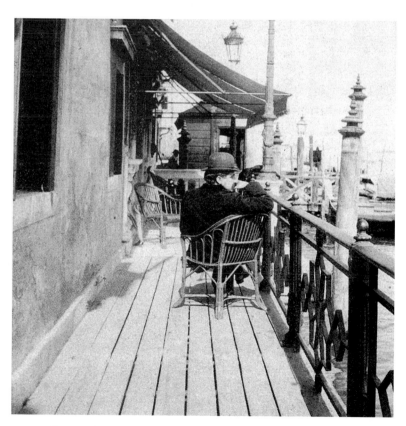

19. Proust in Venice, by Patrick Lorette (*Collection Mante-Proust*)

20. *(left)* *À l'ombre des jeunes filles en fleurs*, 1913, corrected proofs (*Collection Pierre Berès*)

21. *(below)* Marcel Proust on his death bed, by Man Ray (*Musée d'Orsay*)

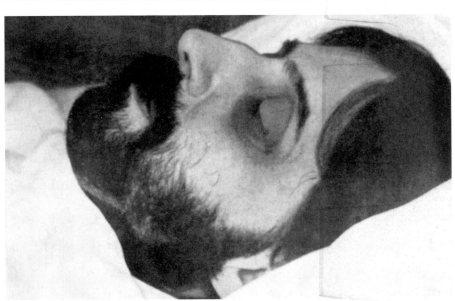

and was built in a semi-circular fan shape centred on the casino; it had had an earlier grand hotel overlooking the sea since 1861. A ring of Anglo-Norman or *art nouveau* villas encircled the centre of the resort and extended the length of the promenade, originally 1,500 metres long, which bordered the magnificent beach. In 1907, on the site of the old hotel and directly on the sea wall, the mayor, Charles Bertrand, had a palace built – 'a veritable Arabian Nights palace', according to *Le Figaro* – by the architect Lucien Viraut.[50] The hotel comprised a large hall, with marble columns, huge chandeliers and Louis XVI furnishings; one entered through a garden, and at the far end of it you could see the sea; a vast dining-room, featuring large bay-windows, which were opened when the weather was fine, gave on to the sea wall; at the front of the hotel there was a bandstand. An Empire-style reading room, an 'American' bar and some smaller lounges completed the reception area.* Each bedroom possessed a large ante-room and a huge bathroom. The manager was Jules Cesari, who came from the Élysée-Palace in Paris.

At this period, Cabourg, which was five hours by train[51] from Paris, was still a family resort, and only received from between 6,000 and 8,000 visitors during the high season,[52] as against 20,000 at Deauville and 60,000 at Trouville. Very slowly, these statistics altered: Trouville lost some of its elegance to Cabourg; Deauville would eclipse both resorts after the First World War. As an additional attraction, Proust, who did not care for solitude, had connections with people all the way along the coast as far as Trouville: Georges de Lauris (with whom he would go for an 'unforgettable walk')† and his father at Houlgate, the Duc and Duchesse de Guiche at the Villa Mon Rêve at Bénerville, where Louisa de Mornand stayed with her lover of the moment, Robert Gangnat, at the Chalet Liouville, and where Gaston Gallimard occupied Le Manoir, a house that belonged to his family; the Strauses, at whose house he met M. d'Arenberg‡ and Paul Hervieu, were at Trouville, as were the artists Helleu and Vuillard,§

---

* These lounges were demolished in the present-day hotel, half of which was sold as flats.

† *Corr.*, vol. VII, p. 264. Lauris, who had just lost his mother, lent a photograph of her to Marcel, who was always fascinated by resemblances between parents and children (ibid., p. 251).

‡ C. Pechenard, *Proust à Cabourg*, Quai Voltaire, 1992, p. 80. Probably the president of the Compagnie du Canal de Suez. Did he give Proust the idea of making M. de Norpois a Controller of the Egyptian Public Debt?

§ A frequent visitor to the Normandy coast, where he painted seascapes, yachts and regattas, and bequeathed a fine etching of Boudin painting the harbour at Honfleur; Helleu, as his daughter has often testified, was one of the principal models for Elstir.

and the caricaturist Sem;[53] the 'amiable Eyragues'[54] were at Falaise. When Marcel was taking Sem from Trouville to Cabourg one evening by taxi, at every bend a loose bullock threw itself at the vehicle: 'You propose an outing to me,' the caricaturist wrote to him, 'and take me to a corrida in the middle of the pampas.'[55] At the hotel at Cabourg, or nearby, he was immediately greeted by the painter Léonce de Joncières, 'a very pleasant juvenile lead',[56] but who, three weeks later, has become 'the most idiotic creature [he] had ever set eyes on',* and also by the father of his friend d'Oncieu and the son of the banker Sigismond Bardac.†

It was then that a miracle occurred, a resurrection of sorts: Proust, who had been ill and bedridden for the past two years, rose from his bed, began going out every day and started making an increasing number of trips. He had originally planned to go to Brittany after Normandy, but he found that he was so comfortable here that he decided to stay where he was – 'thinking that Maman would not have wanted to see me stir from a place where I live tolerably well'. And, since his anxiety to please his mother was always mingled with sorrow, he added: 'But it also makes me sad that Maman did not see me like this. It breaks my heart to wake up after sleeping for a bit and for her not to know this, and to come back from a walk without having had any of the hitherto inevitable asthma attacks that so upset her.'[57] In order to withstand the pace of this new life, Marcel took caffeine, which made him feel dazed and feverish and 'unable to see anything', and he led such 'an artificial (from the health point of view) and busy life' that he didn't know what he thought or felt.‡ But coffee did not explain everything: at other times, he would take even more, without being able to travel. Because he needed to complain as well as entice sympathy – to be loved, in other words – he confided to several friends that 'the sort of people at the hotel are dreadful' and that (though he was joking in this instance) 'the manager of Galeries Lafayette and a former croupier are the two most elegant characters here'. And these people 'are so insolent!'[58] The residents of the hotel at Balbec, mingled

---

* *Corr.*, vol. VII, p. 267. From the day that Marcel went for a walk with Lauris (ibid., p. 265), he was 'totally excluded'.

† His brother Joseph owned the finest Hubert Roberts (R. Gimpel, *Journal d'un collectionneur marchand de tableaux*, Calmann-Lévy, 1963, p. 23).

‡ *Corr.*, vol. VII, p. 261, to R. Hahn. He complained that he was unable either to work or to write a letter – yet this did not prevent him from writing them. As for the 'artificial life', this seems to suggest that for Marcel the only normal life, and the one which he had settled into, was that of an invalid.

with those of the Splendide at Évian, are no longer very far away.

Among his frivolous and unexpected entertainments, Guiche took him to a polo match and introduced him to some charming ladies, the Baronne d'Erlanger and Mlle de Saint-Sauveur. The Grand Hôtel came alive and was transformed into the 'setting for the third act' of a vaudeville.[59] Alfred Edwards,* the founder and former editor of Le Matin, arrived with the wife from whom he was separated, Misia Godebska, who would become one of Paris' fashionable personalities; she would be used as Proust's model for the Princesse Yourbeletieff, and would be the moving spirit behind the Ballets Russes;† she would also write her memoirs. But Edwards also brought along his mistress, the actress Lantelme (who was to die tragically during a cruise on the Rhine with her lover: 'I can see that fateful and beautiful eye'[60] Marcel wrote at the time). She was an important and little-known model for Rachel, mainly because it appears that this actress may have begun her career in a brothel;[61] this detail, which seems rather implausible when one reads the novel, had its basis in reality. The Sapphic tastes which Misia attributed to her have provided a 'key' to the actress Léa: from a single model Proust created two characters, who are linked in another way, since in the Bible Leah and Rachel were the two wives of Jacob. Also staying at the hotel was Thadée Natanson (1868–1951), the founder of La Revue blanche and Misia's first husband, who had sold his wife to Edwards in order to pay his debts (an intrigue related by Edwards in his play Par ricochet; Lantelme played the part of Misia). Also there was the physician (and explorer) Jean-Baptiste Charcot (1867–1936), the brother of one of Edwards' former wives. The painter Vuillard, whom Proust came to know that summer but whom he had met before, through Bibesco, in 1904,‡ was

* A. Edwards (1857–1914) was the son of a French mother whose husband was an English doctor formerly in the service of the Khedive of Egypt. Very rich, and an ardent admirer of both women and yachts (L'Aimée, thirty-five metres in length, with a captain and crew of five), in which he entertained his friends, he was a contributor to various newspapers and wrote plays (Par ricochet, Dans la haute); eye-witnesses depicted him as violent, vulgar and perverted.

† RTP, vol. III, pp. 741–2. Cf. ibid., vol. IV, var., p. 370, in which she serves for a moment as Mme de Cambremer. Misia (1872–1950) would be married, for the third time, to the artist Sert. See A. Gold and R. Fizdale, Misia: The Life of Misia Sert, Macmillan, 1980. Misia then attempted to win Edwards back by imitating Lantelme: 'I got hold of a photograph of Lantelme, which was displayed on my dressing-table and made desperate efforts to look like her, to copy her hairstyle and the way she dressed' (ibid., p. 133), something Proust made use of when Gilberte tries to keep Saint-Loup by imitating Rachel, who had become his mistress.

‡ He had invited them to dinner on 15 December 1904. Vuillard would make a trip to Padua with the Bibescos. He would paint Hahn's portrait in 1930.

a friend of Misia and of her former husband Natanson, and had had a part to play at the time of their break-up. Finally, also staying at the hotel was Francis de Croisset, in whose plays[62] Lantelme had acted. Attracted, no doubt, by the beautiful actress, he eventually fought a duel with Edwards.[63] Proust criticized his way of life, and suggested, to no avail, going on a cruise with him.

At the Grand Hôtel Marcel also became friendly with the famous art dealer René Gimpel: 'It was Vermeer who brought us together', Proust would recall.[64] They used to meet every evening, when everyone in the hotel had gone to bed early, apart from the eccentric Baronne Orosdi, 'the queen of mid-Lent', said Proust. Gimpel never saw Proust in conversation with any other resident, and yet he knew everything about everyone: 'Before he went up to his room at about midnight, he would be playing draughts with some servant or other and he would ask him about everything that was going on beneath this vast roof. He used to give enormous tips.'* Proust, who adored Balzac, urged his companion to reread him; 'his second favourite author was the Duc de Saint-Simon'. According to Gimpel, 'In 1907† Proust had already worked out the complete plan of his book, because he spoke [to him] about the controversy which the delicate subject-matter he was dealing with would provoke.' In order to keep in touch with the world of painting, Marcel called on Vuillard, who wore 'a blue workman's overall' and observed the linguistic traits which he would later give to Elstir: 'He repeats with intensity, "a chap like Giotto, you know, or then again a chap like Titian, didn't he, knew just as much as Monet, didn't he" ... He actually says "chap" once every twenty seconds, but he's an exceptional creature.'[65] Vuillard, in turn, would say of Proust: 'Beneath his social mannerisms which in no way detracted from his charm, one quickly came to believe in the sincerity of his interest in the arts. I think he loved painting, not just from a literary standpoint. It seemed to me that he genuinely appreciated Vermeer and from the few lines he wrote to me I retain a memory of someone who was attentive and much more eager to know than ready to resort to sarcasm, like those in whose society he mixed.'[66] On 30 August, at a charity concert – a

* Gimpel, *Journal d'un collectionneur*, p. 195. Information provided by servants has made a major contribution to Proustian research.

† Or was Gimpel, who was writing this in 1922, confusing the time with 1908, the last year he saw Proust at Cabourg? If his testimony is accurate, it would mean that Proust was composing the book in his mind and was trying it out on a selected audience. Furthermore, it was not until 1908 that Proust saw Bernstein again, on holiday at the house of Réjane.

change from the Marchetti Orchestra 'which is all the rage here'– Proust heard the Comtesse de Maupeou, after singing Schumann and Brahms, sing some songs by Reynaldo Hahn, 'which moved me, even when sung by her', 'pretty things', 'divine things'.[67] Every evening Marcel would set off for the casino, which adjoined the hotel, where he played and lost at baccarat.[68] Gambling, both here and on the stock exchange, played an important part in his life, and contributed to reducing his wealth.

But Proust was not going to spend every day at Cabourg. Taking advantage of the 'automatic taximeters', he planned to 'explore quite far into Normandy', thanks to the Unic taxi company, which was founded by the Rothschilds and managed by Jacques Bizet. The company operated in Cabourg during the summer, and in Monaco and Paris in the winter. Its mechanics (the term chauffeur was not yet in use), Alfred Agostinelli, Odilon Albaret and Jossien,[69] took turns in driving Proust.[70] After a week, he had already visited Caen and was asking Mâle's advice about the old towns and the monuments, though not those which had been restored,* that he should see: yet he already knew about the towns that were recommended to him, through his reading of guidebooks and monographs.[71] He also asked Emmanuel Bibesco for advice about landscapes, monuments and churches.[72] As a result he went to Bayeux,[73] as well as to Balleroy and to Dives. Having dreamed about Bayeux, the town that was 'so lofty in its noble coronet of russet lacework and whose summit was illuminated by the old gold of its second syllable',[74] he was charmed but confused by 'the oriental figures in Bayeux Cathedral (in the Romanesque part of the nave)'. At Balleroy he visited the château built by François Mansart from 1626 to 1636 for Jean de Choisy; in particular he noticed the drawing-room decorated by Mignard (the ceiling of which represented the four seasons), and the tapestries by Boucher, but also the mediocre hunting scenes for which the owner's father, the Marquis de Balleroy, was responsible. Proust's infallible memory would make use of all these details[†]

---

* *RTP*, vol. III, p. 402: ' "I don't like it, it's restored", she said to me, pointing to the church and remembering what Elstir had told her about the priceless, unique beauty of old stone. Albertine could immediately recognize something that had been restored.' And n. 2: in his preparatory notebook, Proust referred to Émile Mâle's, Ruskin's and Monet's critical views of restorations.

† Which are first alluded to, in humorous fashion, in a letter of 27 August, to Lauris (*Corr.*, vol. VII, p. 264). He wrote sarcastically about the errors in the guidebook, which referred to Boucher as Lebroucher, and confused Mignard with Mansart. And in *Le Côté de Guermantes*: 'As for the tapestries, they were by Boucher, bought in the nineteenth century by a Guermantes who was a connoisseur, and were hung, in between some mediocre hunting scenes which he had painted himself' (*RTP*, vol. II, p. 315; see several drafts of this passage on p. 1531).

for the Guermantes' château. In Dives, next door to Cabourg, there was the 'William the Conqueror's hostelry', which he would describe at length, on account of its ancient interior and its meals, which were better and more expensive than those served in palaces, in *La Prisonnière*,* its market buildings from the fifteen and sixteenth centuries and, above all, a church, the oldest part of which dated back to the eleventh century; the apse and choir were fourteenth century, the nave fifteenth; its paving may have been used for the church at Combray.† A miraculous fifteenth-century Christ, found in the sea, which, according to legend, could only be fitted on a cross once fishermen had found one of the correct size at sea. The police station contained the remains of the ancient abbey of Sainte-Marie-du-Hibou, which was built in the twelfth century. In *À l'ombre des jeunes filles en fleurs* Dives becomes Balbec-en-Terre: the sea has receded from both towns; the miraculous Christ can be found in the church.[75] But the town was also drawn from Bayeux, Amiens and Saint-Pol-de-Léon.[76] Proust asked his correspondents where he might find an ancient little town that would prove 'fertile for his imagination': in his great work he discovered, and created, several of them. Thus he visited Pont-Audemer‡ like Mme de Sévigné, and Lisieux,[77] and he saw the abbeys of Jumièges,§ Saint-Wandrille¶ and Saint-Georges-de-Boscherville.[78] At Lisieux Proust, who wanted to see 'some of the foliated tracery which Ruskin speaks of' on the façade of the cathedral by night, saw the porch

---

* *RTP*, vol. III, p. 544. There was an armchair at the inn which was said to have belonged to Mme de Sévigné, several of whose letters were sent from Dives, which is another link with the Narrator's grandmother.

† 'I no longer even remember whether the paving came from Saint-Pierre-sur-Dives or from Lisieux. Some stained-glass windows are certainly the ones at Évreux, the others were from the Sainte-Chapelle and Pont-Audemer' (*Corr.*, vol. XVII, p. 193, 20 April 1918, to Jacques de Lacretelle).

‡ He would tell Jacques de Lacretelle that he had used one of its stained-glass windows for the church at Combray. See *RTP*, vol. II, p. 7.

§ *RTP*, vol. I, p. 732, where Proust relates the story of the 'restless folk of Jumièges', the sons of Clovis II who were buried in this abbey, upon which the novelist, in this draft, makes Guermantes dependent. Ibid., vol. II, p. 1046: 'At Jumièges, these giant cathedral towers in the caretaker's courtyard.' But he also followed Ruskin (*Modern Painters*, George Allen, Orpington, 1843, vol. I, part II, p. 106, which comments on a plate from Turner's *The Rivers of France*).

¶ *RTP*, vol. II, p. 1046: 'At Saint-Wandrille, that rococo binding of a Roman missal.' As with Jumièges, in this sketch Proust wished to illustrate the discrepancies between the place-names in the imagination and what they were in reality. In 1907 Maeterlinck moved into Saint-Wandrille, which the Benedictines must have departed from temporarily; he had *Macbeth*, in his translation, performed there, and also *Pelléas* in 1910. Proust described 'those rooms at Saint-Wandrille over which Maeterlinck cast a spell' (ibid., vol. II, p. 1203).

lit up in the headlamps by 'the ingenious Agostinelli'.[79] In 'the pretty town of Falaise',[80] he called on the Marquis and Marquise d'Eyragues, whose mansion would also be used, according to his notes, for the Guermantes' château, and he would describe the church of Saint-Gervais, whose spire soared up between two eighteenth-century mansions which were 'dear and venerable'[81] to him. At Norray, on the road from Caen to Bayeux, he admired the Gothic church and the decorative friezes of its ambulatory; nearby was Bretteville-l'Orgueilleuse, which would provide the Bricqueville-l'Orgueilleuse in *Sodome* and Marcouville-l'Orgueilleuse (whose restored church Elstir did not care for) in *À l'ombre des jeunes filles en fleurs*.[82]

In addition, Proust asked Hahn for some books.[83] The list is not without interest: he still required Ruskin, but wanted his general books, such as *Modern Painters* and *The Seven Lamps of Architecture*, to which were added Turner's *The Rivers of France*. Furthermore, he compared the view of the church towers at Caen with the spires that dominate Turner's paintings.[84] Was he merely trying to improve his knowledge of the places he was visiting? To reflect on the architecture and painting* which would occupy such an important part in his book? Or was it in order to *write* about these arts in the light of his visits, which were not those of a tourist or of a man on holiday, who would not be quite so determined? The reality is more prosaic: he wished to lend or give all these books to Mme de Clermont-Tonnerre, half-sister to the Duc de Guiche, who had entertained him at the cottage at Glisolles. Yet at the same time he had committed to memory all these books as well as their illustrated plates, which depicted the churches, ports and landscapes that he visited and which in turn he would describe in his writing. This is why his *Le Figaro* article, 'Impressions de route en automobile', is in no way a conclusion or a dead end, but a beginning.

At the end of September, because the hotel was closing for the season, Marcel set off for Évreux, where he spent four or five days while waiting for Reynaldo Hahn to return to Paris. The closer he drew to Paris, the more ill he felt. He visited the bishop's palace (1481–1603), which was 'not very beautiful inside', and saw the 'fine stained-glass windows' of the 'very pretty' church of Saint-Taurin, a former abbey built over the tomb of the first Bishop of Évreux; his legend was depicted in the Renaissance

---

* In a letter to Lauris of 27 August he mentioned the 'hosts of angels who wing their way in Giotto's paintings after the Virgin and Christ', an image that is used in *À la recherche*.

stained-glass windows in the choir, which Marcel admired, as well as those in the cathedral, which were still luminescent despite the 'twilight hour' at which he saw them: 'jewels of light, a purple that sparkled, and sapphires full of fire'. He would draw his inspiration from them for the church at Combray.[85] At Conches he admired the collection of sixteenth-century windows: 'Many of them were by a pupil of Dürer's.[86] It was like a pretty little German Bible from the Renaissance period, with colour illustrations. The windows have captions written underneath in Gothic lettering';[87] the windows from this period did not interest him much, however, 'they're too much like *pictures* on glass'. One evening, on the return journey, after having drunk seventeen cups of coffee, and as a consequence being a bit unsteady on his feet,[88] he stopped at the Clermont-Tonnerres' house at Glisolles. At this 'delightful spot', he liked the 'bright Norwegian wood-panelling' and the 'old French pictures', the 'primitive and refined' charm of the hunting or fishing lodge, 'the studio of two artists'. His hostess would recall that he had his car headlamps directed on the roses in the garden.

'IMPRESSIONS OF THE ROAD IN A MOTOR CAR'

Proust thus spent the summer of 1907 visiting cathedrals, abbeys, churches and ancient towns. This was why, in *Le Figaro* of 19 November 1907, he published an article entitled 'Impressions de route en automobile', an embryo of his future work. When he reprinted it in *Pastiches et mélanges*, referring to the passage about the church steeples at Caen, he pointed out that: 'In *Du côté de chez Swann* it is only mentioned in part anyway, in inverted commas, as an example of what I wrote in my childhood. And in the fourth volume (not yet published) of *À la recherche*, the publication in *Le Figaro* of this redrafted passage is the subject of almost an entire chapter.'[89] Here Proust was alluding to the episode of the steeples of Martinville in 'Combray'[90] and, in *Albertine disparue*, to the reading of the article in *Le Figaro*; in 1919 'the fourth volume' referred to *Sodome et Gomorrhe II* and *Le Temps retrouvé*, which would afterwards be separated, when *Sodome et Gomorrhe II* becomes *La Prisonnière* and *Sodome et Gomorrhe IV* becomes *Albertine disparue*. Thus we see the fate of this passage, which was destined to be republished in *À la recherche du temps perdu*, and the publication of which would itself be transformed into a fictional event. In the meantime *Contre Sainte-Beuve* would also become the story of writing an article. 'Impressions de route en automobile' was, furthermore, already drawn from imagination, since it begins by describing the Narrator's return to his parents' home, when Marcel's parents were in fact already dead; and yet it is still autobiography, because it includes a portrait of Agostinelli, whom Marcel did not know very well at the time: 'My mechanic was clad in a huge rubber mantle and he wore a sort of hood which fitted tightly around his youthful beardless face and which, as we sped faster and faster into the night, made him look like some pilgrim, or rather, a speed-loving nun'; compared to St Cecilia at her clavier, he plays the music of speed and of the engine;* because it also contains the portent of his death: '. . . if only the steering-wheel† held by the young man who is driving me could always remain the symbol of his talent instead of being the premonition of his death throes!'‡ Finally, this article transformed life into art, since the 'mechanic' is compared to the statues in cathedrals, just as, later, Albertine would be compared to the figures in the porch of Saint-André-des Champs, and just as the sound of the car's horn which alerts the parents – whom death has rendered imaginary in the writer's poignant musings – to the return of their son is compared to the shepherd's pipe in *Tristan and Isolde*. This image, which concluded the article, would be used again in *La Prisonnière* and invested with all the weight, not just of Wagner's aesthetic philosophy, but of Proust's too.§

THE RETURN TO PARIS

In late September or early October Marcel, having decided against going to Brittany, which he would never see again, and against visiting Monet's garden at Giverny with the painter Helleu, a new friend from Cabourg, was now back in Paris and was ill as a result.[91] On 7 October 1907 he went on his own to hear Mayol, who had taken over from Fragson, at the

---

* *CSB*, p. 67: note the feminine imagery used to describe the young man.

† Proust compared this 'to any stylization of the wheel in the art of the Middle Ages': the steering-wheel becomes like those works of art he contemplated in Normandy.

‡ *P et M*, p. 67. Albertine at the pianola would also be compared to St Cecilia in *La Prisonnière*. The 1919 edition of *Pastiches et mélanges* which reprinted this article adds the following dry obituary inscription as a footnote: 'I could scarcely have foreseen when I wrote these lines that seven or eight years later this young man would ask to type out one of my books, and would learn to fly under the name of Marcel Swann, thereby sweetly combining my baptismal name and the name of one of my characters, and that he would be killed, at the age of twenty-six, in a flying accident off Antibes' (*CSB*, p. 66).

§ Among the letters of congratulation, the 'prettiest', according to Proust, came from Agostinelli (*Corr.*, vol. VII, p. 315, to Mme Straus).

Scala. Probably in order to please Reynaldo, who was very keen on music-hall and the *café-concert*, he conceded that 'he would like Mayol if he sang real songs', but these were not sufficiently lyrical and 'too mediocre'. What Marcel did enjoy about this artist were his song and dance numbers: his whole body moved to the rhythm of the music and, like Cléo de Mérode, he danced as he walked. On the other hand, his homosexuality, alluded to by Hahn and Madrazo, was not apparent to him.* Proust's jottings bear witness to his enjoyment of the skills of Mayol, Fragson and Paulus, but it was their technique rather than the content of their words that appealed to him.[92]

The apartment block on the Boulevard Haussmann, which belonged jointly to Marcel, Robert Proust and their aunt Mme Georges Weil, was put up for sale at the request of the aunt, who felt she ought to extricate herself from the joint ownership. Marcel, who was always considering moving house and leaving Paris for a climate in which he would no longer suffer from asthma attacks, did not pay sufficient attention to what was going on. He discovered belatedly that the purchaser was his aunt and he did not dare bid a higher price; the sale took place on 8 November 1907. He thus sowed the seeds of his future misfortune, for one day he would be obliged to move house, and never again would he rediscover the precarious equilibrium of a life lived among familiar surroundings, to which, whatever he might say, he was deeply attached.

Another source of anxiety, which seemed rather remote, was the fact that one never knew whether France might react as England had done: twelve years after the trial of Oscar Wilde,[93] there came the Eulenburg affair and the trial of Harden. 'What do you make', Marcel wrote to Billy, having alluded to two of the latter's friends who were lesbians, 'of this homosexuality trial? I think they have struck out rather at random, although it's absolutely true in the case of some of them, particularly the prince, but certain of the details are really comic.'[94] The German journalist Harden had published a series of articles attacking the pacifist and francophile 'camarilla' that surrounded Wilhelm II; Prince von Eulenburg, a favourite of the Kaiser's, and General von Moltke, the military governor of Berlin, were condemned as homosexuals. The prince fell out of favour with the Kaiser; the general initiated libel proceedings against the journalist in October 1907; Harden was acquitted. Eulenburg was obliged to bring

---

* 'I found nothing *"moschant"* about him as you and Coco had told me I would' (ibid., vol. VII, p. 281, 7 October 1907).

civil proceedings because of certain remarks made during the trial. To cut the story short, a second trial took place in Berlin in January 1908 at which Harden was convicted. A third trial, in Munich in April 1908, brought a criminal prosecution against the prince for false testimony: the unfortunate Eulenburg, who was arrested in May 1908 and imprisoned for only five months on account of his health, for he was too ill, was never convicted, but was never able to establish his innocence either.* This affair was to hold an important place in the genesis of Proust's future work: not that he wished to tell the story; he never related any historical event, he extracted the essence. All that he felt now was that when the time was ripe, he ought to speak of the 'cursed race' and enshrine it in some of his characters as a way of facing up, if not to a trial, then at least to the accusation of indecency.

From his trip to Normandy Marcel brought back not just an article, but also a liking for motor cars and the Unic taxis,[95] which had replaced the horse-drawn cabs. There were no aspects of modern life that alarmed Proust; he put all of them into his book, where they play an important role – aeroplane included: the telephone, the motor car, aeroplanes and aerial bombardments would have not only their places, but episodes devoted to them. Since he owned nothing himself, he admired everything with perfect open-mindedness, modern technology as well as Raymond de Madrazo's old masters, which he saw in December at his house at 32 rue Beaujon: 'A truly divine Greco, a little Tiepolo, some Raphael drawings, compositions by Titian, some Goyas, a La Tour.'[96] The El Greco was his *Holy Family*, with its shades of pink, dark blue and ochre, in which Proust praised the 'tones as priceless . . . as those of a Vermeer and of an unspoilt freshness beneath his incomparable glaze'.[97] The artist was unknown in France at this period. Barrès' book, *Greco* (1911), brought him to the public's attention, and it was from him and the reproductions that his book contained that Proust drew his inspiration to write about El Greco in *À la recherche*, both when he compares Charlus to *The Grand Inquisitor* and likens the sky and the ground of bombed Paris to *The Burial of the*

* See *RTP*, vol. II, p. 587; vol. III, p. 955 (it was the Eulenburg trial that introduced the word 'homosexuality', 'too Germanic and pedantic', into France), and note in *Sodome et Gomorrhe*, pp. 1199–201; *Corr.*, vol. VIII, pp. 119, 123, 163. On 10 May 1908 Proust referred to 'poor Eulenburg', while at the same time describing the recollections of Gobineau, which the latter had published (ibid., vol. VIII, p. 119) and, in July 1908, to the sympathy which the ambassador, von Radulin, was showing to Montesquiou on the death of Yturri, and which he should have kept for Eulenburg (ibid., vol. VIII, p. 164).

Count d'Orgaz. In this he showed the scrupulous care he took over his documentation, and how he never neglected anything that might occupy a place in his book.

GUSTAVE DE BORDA

On 26 December 1907 *Le Figaro* published an obituary notice, signed 'D', which Marcel wrote about the man who, together with Jean Béraud, had acted as his 'incomparable' second at his duel with Jean Lorrain in 1897. Was this just an incidental piece? No, for the art of the Proustian portrait is that of paradox, which delves beneath appearances to find a contradictory reality. Beneath the guise of the dueller who had spent his life with his sword in his hand, as in a Dumas novel, was hidden a 'chevalier du Romancero' (a unique literary allusion in Proust's work), 'who was a fearsome opponent of the wicked, but kindly to those who were good and compassionate to those who were unhappy'. Beneath 'the most dangerous of enemies' was the best of men. And he coined the following maxim: 'It is moral standards not opinions that make for virtues.' Borda, a veteran of the Franco-Prussian war of 1870 (compared by Proust to Stendhal, who was a veteran of the Russian campaign and preferred Italian music), liked 'easy' music and he admired the 'great painter' Jean Béraud. Were it not for Proust's loyalty, he would have been forgotten.

TOWARDS SAINTE-BEUVE

In December 1908 Proust mentioned a 'Sainte-Beuve', which had been written in his head 'the previous year already'.[98] Now, *Le Figaro* of 7 July 1907 had published an article by Paul Bourget entitled 'Charles Spoelberch de Lovenjoul', which was a starting point for Marcel's observations about Sainte-Beuve.[99] Marcel had also read Léon Séché's *Sainte-Beuve* on publication in 1904, a vast summary in two volumes.[100] Furthermore, his correspondence, which reveals that he had been musing on the subject of names, leads one to wonder if he had not begun to take notes and write passages on this dual theme: Sainte-Beuve, and names. This would explain why he wrote to Daniel Halévy in the autumn of 1907 saying that he shared with Péguy 'a certain feeling for the geometry of the earth and for villages' . . . 'I have also written some almost identical things about names.'[101] Or did he compose it in his mind, 'construct it in his head', to use his own expression, in one long interior monologue? This may be the key to the irksome question of the book's evolution (though a minor one since it evolved over three months more or less), to which, as with all matters of this kind, one should only respond cautiously. There were further signs of work in October – though this may still only have been the final amendments to his *Figaro* article 'Impressions de route en automobile' (of the writings we know of, this piece is the closest in style to the future 'Combray', to *Contre Sainte-Beuve* and to other passages in *À la recherche* since 'Sur la lecture'); through the intermediary of Robert Dreyfus* Marcel was thinking of hiring as his secretary a grandson of Gobineau by the name of Serpeille. He would ask him to look up information 'in the *Caractéristiques des saints* or in the *Annales de Normandie*', or, when he came around at nine o'clock in the evening to see if Marcel needed anything for the following day, he might even play écarté with him. For the time being, Proust abandoned this dream of having a secretary, propelled by his sensual turmoil and the pathos of his solitude: one of the greatest writers of all time, in search of a partner to play a wretched game of cards with in the evening.[102]

In 1907 we see a structure taking shape, 'a great subconscious skeleton', which consisted of the purging of oedipal feelings, the function of memoirs as a stimulus for a novel about time and social classes, a theory of images, the privileged role played by gardens in childhood – a chorus of pieces which would all reappear, as well as some passages which would be inserted, just as they were, in *À l'ombre des jeunes filles en fleurs*. Above all, we watch the resurrection of a man who is very much alive – animated, brilliant, consumed with curiosity and dreaming only of art (about love, we don't know) – just when we thought him crushed and broken for good. A palatial hotel and its clientele, the sea in summer, the wonders of Gothic art and little Norman towns (would he have gone to see quite so many, unless it was to write about them?) – on these he cast the twentieth century's most captivatingly beautiful gaze.

---

* In as much as he was an expert on Gobineau, and therefore a friend of his descendants.

CHAPTER XII

Contre Sainte-Beuve

The writings of Proust's youth, the translations and the articles all lead us to the year 1908, when everything changed, because Marcel was returning to the novel. From the very first days of January, he was getting ready to write a chapter entitled 'Robert et le chevreau, Maman part en voyage',[1] and was searching for some English engravings, which he would only refer to through paralipsis: wishing to describe his little brother, who was sad at being separated from his pet kid, he would write: 'This scene bore but a scant resemblance to a theme dear to the English painters, that of a child stroking an animal.'

PASTICHES

Almost simultaneously he embarked upon a series of pastiches, all based on the Lemoine affair, news of which broke on 9 January. These pastiches were published, for the most part, by *Le Figaro* between 22 February and 21 March 1908.[2] In the spring of 1909 Proust considered writing a parody of Saint-Simon, a subject he said his head was full of, and asked Montesquiou for a copy of his 'Fête' of 1904; the latter, with an insistence verging on the reckless, asked Marcel to write another pastiche of him; but Montesquiou's time was past and Proust had no wish to write one.[3] However, until 1909 he did dream of collecting his pieces together in volume form, a proposal rejected by the publishers that were approached – Mercure, Calmann-Lévy, Fasquelle.* They were finally published with some additional material in 1919;[4] Proust then provided a summary of the subject in a footnote: 'We may have forgotten, ten years afterwards, that Lemoine had wrongfully claimed to have discovered the secret of

---

* *Corr.*, vol. IX, p. 70, March 1909: 'But that's as it should be,' added Proust, who would always maintain the same balanced attitude when confronted with publishers' rejections.

manufacturing diamonds and having received, as a result of this initiative, more than a million francs from the president of De Beers, Sir Julius Werner, he was then, in an action brought by the latter, sentenced to six years in prison on 6 July 1909. This insignificant petty crime, which nevertheless enthralled public opinion at the time, was chosen by me one evening, entirely fortuitously, as a unique model for writing short pieces, in which I would attempt to imitate the style of a certain number of writers.'[5] Ever since his work on Ruskin, Proust had used reading as a way of tackling the real world. This reading became more and more discerning, both because its passive character was condemned in the introduction to *Sésame et les lys*, and because Ruskin's theories were refuted by his translator. It is in the context of the criticism of reading, and of critical reading, that his 1908 writings should be understood; through them he liberated himself from the writers who obsessed him, but not without having first stolen their secrets.* The pastiche distils and recon-structs what Proust himself felt upon reading the works of his masters; criticism analyses the techniques used by these writers clearly and in such a way that the pastiches and the criticism complement each other.

The Lemoine affair, furthermore, was like a romantic novel, almost a detective novel, but the plot, as presented by Proust, remains incomplete each time, almost as if reality, seen from a variety of viewpoints, only appears in flashes.† The series, the order of which he considered of great

---

* They're 'good imitations', he wrote to the Comtesse de Noailles, who had enjoyed them (*Corr.*, vol. VIII, p. 46), in late February; what is more, he was already talking to her about Sainte-Beuve. Proust also said that he had received 'very flattering' messages from Lemaître, from France, and from Hervieu (ibid., p. 63). Anna de Noailles reiterated her praise on 21 March: 'The Renan seems to me to be marvellous'; it is true that she was mentioned in it (ibid., p. 70). To Maurice de Fleury, the medical correspondent of *Le Figaro*, who had congratulated him, Proust admitted (ibid., p. 75) to having previously written 'some pastiches of medical literature', which he was unable to find. We come across them again in Cottard and Du Boulbon. Furthermore, Lucien Daudet applauded Proust's pastiches in *Le Gaulois* of 30 March 1908, after first mentioning *À la manière de. . .* by Reboux and Muller (December 1907), a book Proust had not cared for. Marcel was also thinking of having the pastiches put together and offering them for publication as a booklet (ibid., pp. 85, 91, 100, 107), firstly to Mercure, then to Fasquelle, and finally to Calmann-Lévy.

† 'The length of a pastiche matters little as long as it contains the generative features which, by enabling the reader to multiply the likenesses *ad infinitum*, spare the author from adding more of them!' (*Corr.*, vol. IX, p. 63, March 1909, to Jules Lemaître). On this occasion, Proust informed the critic of his admiration for what he had written, some time ago, about the voice of the actor Baron, and about Banville, which may have inspired certain of Bloch's remarks as well as part of the Narrator's admiration for Bergotte. Similarly, Marcel remembered 'little family dramas because Pozzi had offered to introduce [him] to him and [his] poor parents considered that he was too young to go out'.

importance,[6] was divided into eight parts and the story recounted by eight separate voices, those of Balzac, Flaubert, Sainte-Beuve, Régnier, Goncourt, Michelet, Faguet and Renan,* each of whom related a brief incident, which are not really consecutive.† In this juxtapositioning, we observe Proust's scorn for the straightforward narrative; what the plot has to say is so unimportant that it remains incomplete. So too does the form taken by the parody, whether play, novel, critical essay or historical account. In 1908, even with the support of writers whose work he reproduced while at the same time poking fun at them, Proust broke off, leaving each of these pieces unfinished: was he satisfied with the impression they produced? Was dialogue a problem that he found insoluble? Should a description of a book be as long as this? These were precisely the questions that would be posed, that same year, in *Contre Sainte-Beuve*.

The 1908 pastiches prefigure *À la recherche du temps perdu* in another way: in his novel Proust would produce many a pastiche, almost as if the novel were written, at times, by another writer. There is the scholarly dissertation in *À l'ombre des jeunes filles en fleurs*, there are the images of the 'new writer' in *Le Côté de Guermantes*, the obituaries, the fashion columns, the newspaper articles, such as those in the Swiss newspapers during the war 'in which one reads, in small print: "The World War, recent fighting, one million losses" — and in huge print, which makes one think that it is a most important event: "Success for Zeiler's of Lausanne at the Grenoble exhibition"'. The most important pastiche is the one devoted to the Goncourts in *Le Temps retrouvé*, which contrasts two moments in time, two worlds, two aesthetic creeds, and, last but not least, two literary genres, setting the private diary, which Proust did not care for, against the novel. Each pastiche offers a view of the world seen by someone other than Proust and thus prepares us for the great résumé of the whole of classical literature that is *À la recherche du temps perdu*.

There is something approaching pastiche in the presentation of the characters in *À la recherche*. Proust incorporated into his work, secretly, rather like the little hidden figure in Rouen cathedral,[7] a number of the heroes of writers who had gone before him, either as a pastiche, or as a

---

* The pastiche of Saint-Simon was not published until 1919, those of Ruskin, Maeterlinck and Chateaubriand were posthumous. That of Régnier was published in March 1909.

† Proust would relate the Dreyfus affair, as well as the 1914–18 war, in precisely this way in *À la recherche du temps perdu*.

tribute. This is the case with Balzac's *La Femme abandonnée* in *Du côté de chez Swann*,[8] the story of which is summarized in a paragraph, and which appears here in a walk-on part. The Guermantes repeat the words of Saint-Simon's Mortemarts because the memorialist praised their wit without explaining it.[9] Similarly, Norpois is reminiscent of Comte Mosca, Nissim Bernard of Nucingen, and the Duchesse de Guermantes and her dresses remind us of the Princesse de Cadignan. The other transformations, such as Anatole France in the character of Bergotte; the inclusion of those close to Proust to whom he wished to pay tribute, such as Bertrand de Fénelon, Anna de Noailles, Céleste Albaret; or the condensing of books that are not mentioned, such as *L'Art religieux du XIIIe siècle en France* by Émile Mâle,[10] put into the mouth of Elstir when discussing the church at Balbec – all these things make us realize that the novel is a summary not just of life, but of literature as well as the other art forms. The vast system of quotations in the definitive text, some of which are ironical, some serious, as well as in the drafts, complete this synthesis, thus making this book the sum of those that have preceded it: an encyclopaedia.

LIVING FOR WRITING

The publication of these pastiches did not prevent Proust from showing an interest in a 'pretty Mlle de Goyon',* whom he would pursue, like the Narrator, through letters and the salons, in photographs and in reality. 'For something that I am writing, and for sentimental reasons, too, I should like to go to a ball,' he wrote to Mme de Caraman-Chimay.† When he finally met her, the fact that he found her 'a thousand times less wonderful' than he had thought gave him, he maintained, a great sense of calm.[11] But she was also a source of inspiration: the girl had the Christian name of the Duchesse de Guermantes; she became 'the girl with red roses' in a draft notebook;[12] and later, one of those pursued women, inaccessible and ultimately disappointing, Mlle d'Orgeville, the Baronne de Putbus' maid, and Mme de Stermaria.

Pulled in both directions, Proust also made enquiries about a 'young

---

* *Corr.*, vol. VIII, p. 63, to Mme L. Fould. Cf. ibid., pp. 93, 112, April and May 1908, to L. d'Albufera. Oriane de Goyon, the Duc de Feltre's niece and related to Albufera, was then aged twenty.

† *Corr.*, vol. VIII, p. 135, 8 June 1908; Mlle de Goyon was in fact at the ball given by Philippe de Chimay at the Washington Palace on 12 June, which Proust also attended (ibid., p. 138): he thanked Mme de Caraman-Chimay for 'that marvellous party at which so many droll faces created a frieze

telegraph operator' whom he needed to get to know 'for something' he was writing. He wished to ask him questions, and see him 'while on duty'.* The telegraph operator is linked to the 'Parisian novel' and the 'essay on homosexuality' that Proust had been contemplating. What with the appeal of the uniform (for want of a soldier, but they would come later), his taste for the telegram that shatters one's seclusion and solitude, there were plenty of obscure reasons for transforming a humble employee into a Hermes. To begin with, it was virtually the only job that did not arouse suspicion: if a young man brought one a telegram, one could hardly suspect the addressee of having peculiar habits. When he was depicting homosexuality, Proust was forced to mask the attraction he felt with denials.† For example, when Abel Hermant adopted a young man, he observed: 'I cannot believe that he wanted to dress up a banal homosexual adventure in the infinitely respectable trappings of incest . . . Adopt! But one does not marry.‡ It is true that homosexuality shows more delicacy, for it still displays the effect of its pure origin, which is friendship, and retains some of its virtues.'[13]

We reach an important turning-point here in this quest for Proust: he lived in order to write and his life now became his laboratory; memories were no longer enough, and so, like a scientist, he induced experiences and invented reality in order to transform it into the language of fiction. From this moment on, whether it was an outing or a meeting, an invitation or a concert, everything had to be written down, but without having recourse to a private diary, or notes: the event that had been brought about would become part of a written text, which was to be frequently rewritten. Sometimes it was something new, at other times it developed

---

of singular grotesques'. We come across these parties, these faces and grotesques in *À la recherche*. François de Paris, the owner of the Château de Guermantes, took offence at a humorous remark made by Proust about the beauty of his face (ibid., p. 136).

* *Corr.*, vol. VIII, p. 76, to L. d'Albufera. This telegraph operator was called Louis Maheux; he would telephone Proust at an inconvenient time, and the latter immediately declared: 'In any case, I'm not sure I won't abandon my Parisian novel' (ibid., p. 112, 5 or 6 May 1908; yet further on, Proust wrote that he was working on 'a Parisian novel').

† Actually, when Albufera had joked about 'this type of relationship', Proust protested, upset that 'so many people should have said it of [him]', and declared: 'I am not so stupid, were I one of that sort of rabble, as to go out of my way to tell the boy my name, enable him to get me put behind bars and tell you all about it, etc.' This declaration is surprising: but was Proust able to tell Albufera the truth without harming their friendship and causing a scandal? He said the same thing in April to Emmanuel Bibesco, complaining to him about his lack of tact in joking on this subject in front of others, thereby risking Proust being compromised (ibid., pp. 108–10).

‡ Proust meant that adoption was the equivalent of marriage in this case.

a story and a study that had already been prepared. In *La Prisonnière*, for example, the episode of the telegraph operator reappears in the mouth of Brichot, quoting Charlus: 'The treatise on ethics, which I had always revered as the most magnificent moral edifice of our age, was inspired in our venerable colleague X by a young telegraph messenger . . . My eminent friend failed to reveal the name of this ephebe in the course of his demonstrations.'[14] When the Byzantine historian Gustave Schlumberger stood for election to the Académie française (in opposition to Raymond Poincaré) it provoked a furious letter from Proust, and then an article (probably rejected by *Le Figaro* on account of its violent tone – it has subsequently disappeared) which is a forerunner of the satirical portrait of 'the famous bogus scientist Humberger'.* A ball at the Murats on 22 June (the very same evening that André de Fouquières introduced Marcel to Mlle de Goyon)† allowed him to imagine a dinner party given by the *noblesse d'Empire*, which can be found among the draft notebooks, but which would not be used in *À la recherche*.

FINANCIAL SPECULATIONS AND VIRTUOUS HABITS

Another theme now began to take shape in Proust's life, one that we come across in his book: speculation on the stock exchange, a pastime that was similar to gambling. One could construct an amusing history of French finance and the stock exchange from Proust's correspondence. He approached Robert de Billy to buy some Pins des Landes.‡ He also took on Louis d'Albufera as his adviser: 'Our poor Rio Tinto is not doing brilliantly. I'd really like to chuck them when they reach the price at which

---

* *Corr.*, vol. VIII, p. 140, 15 June 1908, to Mme Straus; in this letter Proust lists the names of those whom he would prefer to see at the Académie: Boutroux, Bergson, Maspero, Bréal, Alfred Croisset, Mâle, Abbé Huvelin and Abbé Vignot, Porto-Riche, Régnier, Boylesve, Hermant, Jammes, Maeterlinck, Gallifret, Arenberg, Montesquiou. Cf. ibid., pp. 144–5. The portrait of 'Humberger', composed at about this time, can be found in Cahier 36 (*RTP*, vol. IV, pp. 677–8).

† *Corr.*, vol. VIII, p. 148. Proust seems to have been on fairly friendly terms at this period with Fouquières (see p. 151, the 'vulgar' version of the introduction to Mlle de Goyon, sent to Reynaldo Hahn, in which a drunken Fouquières tells Marcel: 'You're looking very smart today, you've trimmed your beard a bit, I rather like the look of you'); Fouquières wanted to take him to Dinard, where Marcel hoped that Albufera would join them (cf. p. 159: 'Fouquières, for whom I have a great deal of affection and to whom I am very grateful, assures me that I could very well work and stay as long as I wish at Dinard, since the weather is very mild', and p. 175).

‡ Or, if they were a better prospect, some 'Harpener' or some 'Gelsenkirchen' (ibid., p. 102). [These were all shares. *Tr.*]

I bought them (1,750). What do you reckon, great financier? Did you see that I wrote about my discomfiture over the De Beers in my *Figaro* parodies?'[15] His affectionate relationship with this friend, his great confidant during 1908, with whom Marcel dreamed once more of forming, even at a distance, an 'indissoluble band of friends',* had become rather less intimate, and the requests for financial or literary advice were an attempt to bring them closer again. Proust actually used the words that the Narrator speaks to Gilberte: 'You on your own would be welcome dear Louis, were we able to meet, but alas fate divides us.'† As his correspondent failed to understand these subtleties, Marcel soon felt obliged to reassure him that his affection had not changed; he took the opportunity to assert that Reynaldo was to him the best, the dearest of friends, a brother: 'Were I to discover,' wrote this reader of Dumas humorously, 'that he had murdered someone, I would hide the body in my bedroom so that people might suspect that I had done the deed.'[16] He also replied to an accusation: there was no more reason for his friends to be accused of homosexuality than Albufera's:[17] through this sort of reply we feel we catch an echo of the rumours that circulated in Paris about Proust's habits and the company he kept. Since he hardly ever went out, being ill and constantly working, he also made use of Albufera to compile notes about dinner parties in town,‡ which he used both to keep himself informed and to excite his curiosity, and which he later forwarded to *Le Figaro*, where they appeared under the byline of the gossip columnist Ferrari.[18]

CONTRE SAINTE-BEUVE

This interlude of writing pastiches, which, Proust said on 17 March 1908, 'sickened'§ him, should not allow us to lose sight of the important task he embarked upon in 1908. Three sets of documents enable us to attempt a reconstruction of this new enterprise.

---

* As at the time of the correspondence novel with the Bibescos and Fénelon. We should remember that Albufera was one of the models for Saint-Loup.

† *Corr.*, vol. VIII, p. 160. Cf. p. 93: 'Since we cannot communicate any more except by letter . . .'; p. 98: 'I felt it was pointless to see you again and thus revive all the strength of my regrets.'

‡ Ibid., p. 120, May 1908; cf. pp. 125, 126 ('There is a d'Avaray whom I am curious to see and identify': these columns gave Marcel ideas for encounters), 128, 132. In the autumn of 1908 Emmanuel Bibesco refused to do the same favour for him.

§ Ibid., p. 61, to R. Dreyfus: 'It was because I was too lazy to write literary criticism, because I found it amusing to write literary criticism "in action". But perhaps after all I may be obliged to do more, to explain them to those who don't understand them.'

Of the first set, all that remains is the testimony of Bernard de Fallois, who in his 1954 edition of *Contre Sainte-Beuve* described the material he had made use of; this collection 'consisted of seventy-five pages, of very large format, and comprised six episodes, which would all be employed in *À la recherche*: these were the description of Venice, the stay at Balbec, the meeting with girls, bedtime at Combray, the poetry of the place names and the two ways'.[19] Of these pages, which have in fact disappeared, Fallois published two extracts, 'Robert et le chevreau' and 'Les hortensias normands'.[20] But Proust had prepared a list of them in a notebook, which its editor Philip Kolb has entitled *Le Carnet de 1908* and which we discuss below; the titles that he mentioned were not used in the Fallois edition. However, this edition did provide an important detail: these lost pages were of the same format and written in the same handwriting as a 'study of twenty or so pages, which was the essay on Sainte-Beuve'.[21] Now, in the Bibliothèque Nationale there are bundles of pages[22] which have been bound together and which contain critical notes and plans for *Contre Sainte-Beuve*. There is reason to think, therefore, that Proust then went on to write the pages that have disappeared and the first passages of literary criticism.* These passages develop the critical notes in the notebook. When did this take place? In April he stated that he was about 'to begin an important piece of work'.†

The second set of documents was filed under the title 'Carnet 1', or, following its publication, *Le Carnet de 1908*,[23] and it comprises some notes from 1908–9, two fragments from 1910 and one from 1912. It does not constitute a consecutive text, but consists of three different sorts of notes: the first concern the work in progress, a novel and a study of Sainte-Beuve; the second are Proust's reading notes, principally on Balzac, Chateaubriand, Barbey d'Aurevilly and Nerval;[24] the third contain actual drafts and written paragraphs. The work done during the first half of 1908 is summarized by the list of 'written pages' he drew up some time in July: 'Robert and the kid, Maman goes away./ The Villebon way and the Méséglise way./ The seal of vice and the revelations of a face. The disappointment of a possession, kissing the face./ My grandmother in the garden, M. de Bretteville's dinner party, I go upstairs, Maman's face at the time and since in my dreams, I am unable to sleep, concessions, etc./ The Castellanes,

---

* Alluding to these pages, Proust wrote to Mme Straus on 2 February 1908: 'I should like to settle down to a fairly long piece of work' (*Corr.*, vol. VIII, p. 39).

† Ibid., p. 99, 21 April, to Albufera. Which means that he had already started this work.

the hydrangeas in Normandy, the lords of the manor, English and German; Louis-Philippe's granddaughter, Fantaisie, the face of the mother in her dissolute grandson./ What the Villebon way and the Méséglise way have taught me.'[25] These 'written pages' correspond to the description that Fallois gives of the seventy-five pages that have now disappeared, with the exception of the Venice and Balbec episodes, which Proust did not mention here. But this summary certainly gives a hint of a novel about childhood, about aristocracy, about sexuality, and thus about 'pederasty' and about sadism,[26] as well as the division into the two ways which would later run through the whole of *À la recherche*. A plan for a 'second part' projected an amorous liaison: 'In the second part of the novel the girl will be ruined, I will look after her without trying to possess her, because of my inability to be happy.'[27] There are a number of notes concerning Cabourg and the desire for several girls: 'The desire to love hovers among people who know one another and who flatter each other for being the friend of the person they each love and vice versa';[28] the subject of bedrooms, and memories of Venice illuminated by a photograph out of Ruskin's *Saint Mark's Rest*: 'We believe the past to be mediocre because that is how we think of it, but the past is not that, it is like the unevenness of the flagstones of St Mark's baptistery (photograph from *Saint Mark's Rest*) which we had forgotten about, bringing back to us the blinding sunlight on the canal.'[29] The mother is omnipresent, since she is one of the two protagonists of the projected book. Equally important, and as if connected to involuntary memory, the theme of the literary vocation appears, along with its crises: 'Perhaps I should bless my ill health, which through the sacrifice of tiredness, immobility and silence, has taught me the possibility of working. The intimations of death. Soon you won't be able to say all this. Laziness, doubt or impotence sheltering uncertainly in the guise of art. Should it be a novel or a philosophical essay, am I a novelist?'[30] 'In order to add to my concept of art in the last part.'[31] We also find the signs of old age observed in his contemporaries, or read about in Chateaubriand.[32] These notes are not meant to be understood in the way that a private diary is, but rather as a stage of fiction. We shall read its development in *Le Temps retrouvé*.

In order to study these documents, and before embarking upon the third group, consisting of notebooks written from 1908 on, we need to cast an eye over the correspondence, which prepares us in advance for the draft material with which we are dealing. So on 5 or 6 May 1908 Proust wrote a letter to Louis d'Albufera, which only partially covers the pages alluded to in July as 'written pages': 'I have in progress:/ a study on the nobility[33]/ a Parisian novel*/ an essay on Sainte-Beuve and Flaubert/ an essay on Women/ an essay on Pederasty[†] (not easy to publish)/ a study on stained-glass windows/ a study on tombstones/ a study on the novel.'[34] This list does not signify that Proust was writing nine books simultaneously, nor even that he had planned them, but rather that, following his usual working pattern, he was writing, or had written, nine fragments, chapters or articles about subjects that were not yet interlinked, but in which readers may retrospectively discover some of the author's important themes, and, already, the project for an essay on Sainte-Beuve. Throughout this same period, as we have seen, it was as if Proust were applying himself as much to living as to writing, to living in order to write, and to making various experiments, whether by getting to know a young telegraph operator,[35] by pursuing a girl he did not know, or by mixing with the young people at Cabourg.

CABOURG, SUMMER 1908

Proust, after hesitating somewhat and even contemplating finding a house overlooking Florence, had just renewed his lease at Boulevard Haussmann; he then departed for the Grand Hôtel at Cabourg on 18 July, where he immediately took to his bed. The hotel had changed its staff as well as its manager, and had become more comfortable. What is more, although Marcel complained about the clientele who frequented the establishment ('No one you could put a name to. A few Jewish "estate agents" are the pompous aristocracy of the place'),[36] he was assured of encountering masses of people he knew in the vicinity. In July, for instance, he gave a dinner party for Louisa de Mornand and her sister, 'Loche' Radziwill and his mistress, and some other young aristocrats.[37] In August he entertained Misia Edwards, Sert and Forain. He met Maggie Teyte, the new Mélisande at the Opéra-Comique, who was giving a recital. He saw the Strauses at the Clos des Mûriers and met their circle of friends there, such as the

---

* It was for this that Proust wanted to meet Mlle de Goyon and Louis Maheux; the latter, who provided Proust with information, seemed to him to be 'much too proper, far too well brought up, not at all representative of his profession. He resembles Bertrand de Fénelon.' Marcel wanted some information about ordinary people, and he had fallen upon a socialite! (*Corr.*, vol. VIII, p. 114, early May 1908).

† Probably the 'forbidden article' referred to in a letter to Robert Dreyfus, which was 'becoming clearer' and 'will be a short story instead' (ibid., p. 123, 16 May 1908).

Hervieus; the Finalys were at Les Frémonts in August, where Marcel came across Billy, and where he met the old Marquis de Castellane, a 'poor but charming Lauzun on wheels'.[38] He was on fairly close terms that summer with Henry Bernstein, to whom he even lent money to pay his gambling debts (the playwright was a '*flambeur*'):* a fashionable figure in the salons on the coast, 'you are a king for all of us', Proust told him.[39] Marcel was no doubt pleased to be able to observe the immense vanity of one of the models for Octave. He found him 'comical', but 'not in his plays', and he thought to himself that he was witty, though 'not when he writes'.[40] Playing the same triangular game as he did with those of his friends who were engaged, he informed Bernstein that he was just a little bit in love with his mistress, the Princesse Murat.[41] Marie de Rohan, the Princesse Lucien Murat, and later the Comtesse Charles de Chambrun, has left us her memories of an impish charm and wit in the best eighteenth-century tradition.[42] On the promenade at Cabourg he was overcome by a powerful poetic feeling when he encountered the actress Lucy Gérard, whom he described in terms of an impressionist painting: 'It was a beautiful evening and the sunset had forgotten only one colour: pink. But her dress was entirely pink and from a distance it added the complementary colour of the twilight to the orange sky. I lingered a long while watching this delicate patch of pink, and I returned to the hotel, having caught a cold, when I saw it merge with the horizon, at the extremity of which she slipped away like an enchanted sail.'† Other girls, whom he would see again each summer, also aroused his interest: the two daughters of the Vicomte d'Alton, a relation of Aimée d'Alton, the love of Alfred de Musset.[43] And there were the young men: André Foucart, Pierre Parent,‡ Max Daireaux,[44] to all of whom Marcel would address affectionate letters,§ and, above all, Marcel Plantevignes, whom he had known since 1907. This young man used to come to see Proust daily until the time when a lady whom he met on the sea front warned him, without him appearing to object, about the habits of his host. Marcel, who was furious, accused the young man of

* A big-time gambler. *Tr.*

† *Corr.*, vol. VIII, pp. 200–1. Cf. *Le Carnet de 1908*, p. 55: 'Lucy Gérard's pink patch' and further on the draft of the meeting with Albertine on the sea front and with the girls at Elstir's.

‡ Parent would become chief engineer at the Deparment of Transport (1883–1964); Proust jotted down his expressions in his notebook, in order to attribute them to Saint-Loup and Albertine (*Le Carnet de 1908*, pp. 57, 65, 77, 99, 101; *Corr.*, vol. VIII, p. 245, n.9).

§ Ibid., p. 234: 'I had written you an affectionate letter . . .' He noted: 'better to love what is local, Plantevignes, Foucart' (*Le Carnet de 1908*, p. 54).

wanting to 'stab him in the back', 'of having ruined a friendship that might have been very beautiful', and he challenged M. Plantevignes *père* to a duel. The misunderstanding would soon blow over, and by the end of the summer Marcel was congratulating himself on having 'discovered the charm of a warm-hearted and profound soul', talking about this mind that was 'still budding', and, referring to the flowers that call to mind the famous title that was to be awarded the Prix Goncourt, he quoted Sully-Prudhomme ('On earth all the lilac trees are dying'), Verlaine, d'Aubigné and Baudelaire.* This group of young people was, as a fragment from *Le Carnet de 1908* confirms, the inspiration for the themes of undivided love and hesitation between a number of 'budding' creatures.

During that summer Proust made some notes about Cabourg. His room reminded him of the one he had had at Évian, with 'the square mirror', the damp and musty smell of a room to which one is not accustomed and which makes one feel unwell, the carpets one walks upon as one dresses, the sunlight on the great expanse of marble, and the curtains that were like those in Venice. He remembered Harrison at Beg-Meil, of whom he had seen nothing, but whom he was glad to have known. At the hotel he noticed that the fashionable people remained enclosed within their own milieu and that the nobility could not bear not being recognized by other people. And he drafted a love story for his novel, an embryo of the discovery of the girls in Elstir's studio. Having attended a performance of *Werther*, this (as well as a gypsy orchestra, incidentally) inspired a description of the 'phrase emerging from a piece of music for the first time, like a walk-on actress whom one had not yet noticed, like a nymph appearing from beneath the sound waves'.[45] Returning to a theme from *Le Mensuel* and *Les Plaisirs et les Jours*, he noted 'the voluptuous and common opportunities offered both collectively and singly by light music'.[46] These passages end with the melancholia of departure and 'the charm of the casino where people used to meet on the last rainy days'.

---

* Inscription of *La Bible d'Amiens*, 'one sad September evening, when the cinematographic show was about to begin', to Marcel Plantevignes (*Corr.*, vol. VIII, p. 222). Plantevignes numbers among the models for Octave.

VERSAILLES IN THE AUTUMN OF 1908

Having learned that his friend Lauris had been involved in a motoring accident, Proust, who was very upset, set off in a taxi, driven by Agostinelli,* for Versailles. Feeling unwell, he moved into the Hôtel des Réservoirs (just as he did when his Uncle Georges was dying). On 28 September, he travelled up to Paris to see his friend, and, in the evening, he went to the Théâtre des Variétés with Plantevignes and four other young men from Cabourg to see the revival of *Roi* by Flers and Caillavet.[47] In early October he sought to prolong the pleasures of the summer by arranging a dinner party at which Plantevignes would meet Albufera, Gabriel de La Rochefoucauld and Radziwill,[48] or by inviting Max Daireaux to dinner in his bedroom.† It was probably the 'very intelligent' Plantevignes who occupied most of his time, either trying to procure a dedication for him from Robert de Flers ('as he's my friend you can put something nice for me which will flatter me and make me happy'),[49] sending him to see Lauris, or recommending him to Antoine Bibesco and Albufera when the young man was about to leave for London. For relaxation, Marcel played dominoes with Nicolas Cottin and Agostinelli. We know that he was always very fond of these simple games. Returning to Paris again, to visit Lauris,‡ and feeling ill each time he did so, he imagined that the change of altitude was the cause! Furthermore, he was restricting himself in the expression of his affections for the same reasons as he had with Albufera: 'Alas, people have been so cruel and always so uncomprehending about me that these are things I scarcely dare say to you, because of the misrepresentations and misunderstandings which would arise in other people's thoughts.'[50] He returned to Paris on 3 or 4 November.

During this stay in Versailles he continued to make notes. He kept a record of 'the days of sunshine and cold when the red of the sun through the bare trees cast, in certain shades of colour, a spell over the houses',

---

* Agostinelli was going to spend some time at Versailles (*Corr.*, vol. VIII, p. 258).

† *Corr.*, vol. VIII, p. 234. He wrote to Lauris: 'I have had some small pleasures with a girl who is new and dear to me, and with a few new young friends too' (7? October, p. 237).

‡ George de Lauris succeeded Albufera among Proust's favoured friends; he would be his main confidant at the time he was writing *Contre Sainte-Beuve*. In the autumn of 1909, however, Proust would blame him for having alienated him from Fénelon: 'Yours is the main friendship in my life and his is secondary. And if he had had as bad an influence on your friendship for me as you have had on his friendship, I would feel the same sort of resentment against him as I have harboured for so long against you, though it has now been entirely dispelled' (*Corr.*, vol. IX, p. 192).

and the whistles of the trains in the countryside, as at Illiers. Of the hotel, he recalled 'the staircase that led to the bathroom at the Réservoirs', the white flowers in the carpet 'matching the gentle white flowers in the wall', 'the smell of seeping damp in the house, and the cinerarias, on arrival'. 'The bars of soap providing continuity with other mornings while travelling by the tempting sea, and the fragrance of the bed and the shape of the room that imprints itself on one's spirit'[51] – these can be found in *À la recherche*.* He would attribute these details to Mme de Montmorency's mansion in *Sodome*.[52] The bedrooms at the Réservoirs reminded Proust of a 'drawing-room of the provincial nobility'; he carefully described the wood panelling, the furniture and even the parquet flooring, as well as the terracotta bust of Marie-Antoinette; he sniffed the cold air of the châteaux, 'where there is the invigorating cold of the park and the country-side',[53] and he thought it interesting to 'redecorate the Chevau-Légers' drawing-room at the Réservoirs'. He also made notes on Chateaubriand, whom he would come to see as one of his masters, one of his brothers, as is indicated by the note 'Chateaubriand and I'. An article in *La Revue de Paris*† had recounted the story of the young English girl Charlotte Ives, whom Chateaubriand had loved during his exile, and who came back to see him when he was ambassador in London and asked him: 'My lord, do you recognize me?' Proust compared this scene to Mme Arnoux's farewell to Frédéric. Perhaps this may have been a source for the last meeting between Gilberte and the Narrator, at the beginning of *Le Temps retrouvé*, the sorrow of irretrievable time and of lost loves.

Fired once more with gambling fever, he told Albufera about an important sale of shares (he was probably bored with owning them), which he wished to reinvest: 'have you . . . any ideas about any dependable and highly remunerative investments 2) any idea about even more remuner-ative and slightly less dependable investments 3) any ideas about specu-lation.'[54] He admitted that he had put the same questions to the banker Lambert (through Hahn), to Léon Fould, to the economist Georges Lévy, and to Gustave and Léon Neuberger, respectively manager and head of department at the Rothschild bank. From Cabourg,[55] he had already consulted Lionel Hauser (1868–1958), the Paris representative of the Warburg bank and the nephew of Léon Neuberger (1840–1932), who had asked him to advise Proust; Marcel thus held accounts at both these

---

* E.g. The bars of soap in the bedroom at the Grand Hôtel at Balbec in *Sodome*.
† A. Le Braz, 'Au pays d'exil de Chateaubriand', 15 September 1908.

banks. Hauser (who was his cousin) was to become involved in a long correspondence with Marcel, in which he sometimes noted his reservations.[56] The proceeds from the building at 102 Boulevard Haussmann had been reinvested in American securities, which Marcel wanted to sell, as well as his shares in Rio Tinto, De Beers and Vichy ('the oldest and most reliable part of our wealth, which derives from my great uncle in Auteuil'). He belonged to that category of small investor who buys on a rising market and sells on the downturn. And what did he buy instead? 'People have mentioned Turkey, Serbia and the Ottoman Bank'; Henri de Rothschild (with good cause) recommended Dutch petroleum to him.[57] With Marcel his investments reflected not incompetence but aspects of his character. He sold out of boredom and above all because he was worried; he bought for fun, because speculating took him away momentarily from the burden of his daily grind: the more he worked, the more the stock exchange (or, in summer, the casino) attracted him. Even the names of the shares exercised a poetic charm over him, from the 'Pines of the Landes' to the 'Mexican Railways' and 'Australian Gold Mines' to the 'Tanganyika Railway':* in his imaginary journeying, he thus travelled to places that he would never see. When he dreamed about these names, stock exchange quotations came to resemble railway timetables.

SAINTE-BEUVE (LATE 1908–9)

On 6 November 1908, in a letter to Mme Straus, Proust set out a theory of language and style which was particularly important given that he rarely discussed this subject in his correspondence.[58] He railed against the clichés (those '*louchonneries*' that left one goggle-eyed which he and Lucien Daudet once made fun of; cf. p. 240) used by Ganderax, the editor of *La Revue de Paris*: 'Why should emotion inevitably be "discreet" and geniality be "smiling", and bereavements be "cruel". He's not defending the French language when he writes like that. The only people who defend the French language (such as the army during the Dreyfus affair) are those who

---

* *Corr.*, vol. VIII, p. 252. Cf. p. 260, where he asked whether M. Straus had any shares in Australian Goldmines, or in Tanganyika, or Rio de Janeiro Tram, Light and Power, or in Harpener or Télégraphes du Nord. Cf. p. 266 ff., his instructions to Lionel Hauser on 1 November as to what to buy and sell and the latter's replies; the upshot of this was that Proust's shares which resulted from the sale of Boulevard Haussmann remained steady (p. 274). Railway shares particularly appealed to him: the railway from Rosario to Puerto Belgrano (in reality, the 'Southern Pacific') and the Buenos Aires Tram, Light and Power (ibid., vol. IX, p. 77).

"attack" it. This idea that there is a French language that exists independently of the writers who use it, and which is protected, is incredible. Every writer is obliged to create his own language, just as every violinist is obliged to create his own "sound". And between the sound of any mediocre violinist, and the sound that Thibaud* makes, playing the same note, there is an infinitesimal difference that is a world apart! . . . the only way to defend the French language is to attack it . . . Because its unity only consists of opposites that cancel each other out, of an apparent immobility which conceals a life that is vertiginous and constant.' We should write differently from writers of the past and write the opposite of classical French. Proust, who had begun to write continuously once more, was aware of the need for inventing a new language, of creating a sentence structure which was unlike any other and a syntax that was different and yet beautiful, 'for only that which carries the stamp of our choice, our taste, our uncertainty, our desire and our weakness can be beautiful'.

In November 1908, a crucial date, Proust began to write *Sainte-Beuve* and thereafter he did not stop. In fact, on 8 November, he wrote very movingly to Georges de Lauris in praise of work: 'You, you have light, and you have it for long years ahead, so work. Then, if life brings setbacks one can console oneself, for the true life is elsewhere, not within life itself, nor afterwards, but outside of it, if a term that refers to space can have any meaning in a world that has broken free of it.'[59] And, in early December: 'Did I ever tell you about a thought taken from St John: Work while you still have the light. Since I no longer have it, I am getting down to work.'[60] In *Le Carnet de 1908* Philip Kolb dates the notes made in preparation for a critical essay on Sainte-Beuve to November, notes that are developed in the bound loose pages in the Bibliothèque Nationale[61] that complement the notebook. But Proust had been rereading the critic for a long time.[62] Finally, in December, he wrote to Lauris: 'May I ask your advice? I am going to write something about Sainte-Beuve. I have more or less two articles in my head (magazine articles). One is an article that takes the classic form, like an essay by Taine, only less good. The other starts with the description of a morning in which Maman would come to my bedside and I would tell her about the article I want to write about Sainte-Beuve. And I would elaborate on it to her. Which do you reckon is best?'[63] At the same period he asked similar advice from the Comtesse de Noailles,

---

* Mentioned in *RTP*, vol. III, pp. 563, 791. Proust had heard him play Fauré and Franck.

referring to a 'study', an 'essay'.[64] Knowing Proust's habits, it seems unlikely that he would pose the question unless he tended towards the more fictional version: everybody wrote articles, including himself; but a novel about Sainte-Beuve would be an original and audacious undertaking, because it would be part autobiography – the presence of his mother – and part theory. So when Lauris replied, in a letter that has not been found, no doubt advising him to proceed with the article, which would seem the sensible thing to do, Proust wrote back: 'Thank you for your advice. It's the right advice. But will I follow it? Perhaps not, and for a reason of which you will no doubt approve. What is annoying is that I have once again begun to forget that Sainte-Beuve which is written in my head and which I cannot put to paper because I am unable to get up. And if I have to begin it again in my head for a fourth time (for I did so already last year), it would be too much.'[65] The mention of the previous year may either refer to the preceding academic year, and therefore to the spring of 1908, or, perhaps, as we have seen, to his reading the article by Paul Bourget in *Le Figaro* of 7 July 1907 entitled 'Charles de Spoelberch de Lovenjoul', which was the starting point for his comments on Sainte-Beuve.[66] On the other hand, Proust may have been admitting that he had written more than he had said originally. Equally, he had 'been buying a lot of books for some time, particularly all the Sainte-Beuves',[67] and he was rereading Saint-Simon, which was his great distraction; if he said that he was mainly occupied with genealogy, it was because he was thinking about the passages about the aristocracy in his novel.[68]

We now come to the third group of documents relating to *Contre Sainte-Beuve*. These are Proust's *cahiers*, or exercise books,[69] a crucial stage in his writing. We do not know exactly when, but one day towards the end of 1908 Proust bought the school exercise books[70] – probably in bulk, since he would need ten of them for *Contre Sainte-Beuve* – ninety-five of which survive in the Bibliothèque Nationale; a further thirty-two Céleste Albaret said she destroyed on her master's instructions. This was a day when the nature of Proust's work was transformed. When he wrote in the pages of these *cahiers*, whether the content was fictional or critical, he was rarely sure whether he would be able to continue, whether he had a lot to say, or how to organize his material; the bulk of the exercise books testify to a project that would be very lengthy or which would take a long time to complete, and there is no sense of any inability to move forward. The scope of the project was linked to a return to childhood: the greatest author of our time had suddenly become a schoolboy, writing in his exercise books, just as his father and mother had once urged him to do. Until August 1909 Proust filled ten exercise books in this way. For a long time it was thought that there were only seven of these books; it is now agreed that there were ten of them.[71] Reckoning that *Contre Sainte-Beuve* constitutes a first version of *À la recherche du temps perdu*, each volume of the Bibliothèque de la Pléiade edition (1987–9) includes a variety of material taken from the *cahiers* under the title of 'Esquisses' [Drafts]. All together there were almost 700 manuscript pages, many of which overlapped and had been revised, but at no point was there anything resembling a linear, continuous and definitive version of the text; everything remained in separate, distinct units. How should we construe this collection of writings, if we set to one side Bernard de Fallois' attractive reconstruction, and if we are dissatisfied with the few critical passages that Pierre Clarac singled out arbitrarily in his 1971 edition of *Contre Sainte-Beuve*? The first approach, which is true to Proust's original project, respects the fusion of fiction and critical analysis, but cuts or interweaves the various texts, without providing all of them; the second, which is fairly scrupulous in the establishing of the text, reduces it to the outline for an essay.

In the absence of a consistent text, it is wise to examine the only semi-official outline of the book by Proust, which was when he put the idea to Alfred Vallette, the head of Mercure de France, in mid-August 1909: 'I am finishing a book which, despite its provisional title: "Contre Sainte-Beuve. Souvenir d'une matinée", is a genuine novel and an extremely indecent one in places. One of the main characters is a homosexual . . . The name of Sainte-Beuve is not there by chance. The book does end with a long conversation about Sainte-Beuve and about aesthetics (just as *Sylvie*, if you like, ends with a study of popular songs) and when one has finished the book, one will see (I hope) that the entire novel is nothing but the implementation of the artistic principles expressed in this final part, a sort of introduction, if you like, inserted at the end . . . It is a book that chronicles events, and the reflection that events have on one another over intervals of years, and it can only appear in large sections. To sum up, therefore, would you be agreeable to giving me, from 1 or 15 October, thirty (or more, which would be even better) pages of the *Mercure* in every issue until January, which would amount to about 250 or 300 pages in book form. The novel part would thus have been published. That would leave the long discussion about Sainte-Beuve and the criticism, etc., which would appear only in the book, which would be about the length of *La*

Double Maitresse (425 pages) and could be published by you if you wish.'[72]
Proust thus suggested juxtaposing the fictional and the critical parts of
the book; the fiction, which would be defined through characters, events
and a blend of purity and indecency, and the essay, which was to be
dedicated to Sainte-Beuve and literary criticism. Two important elements
were stressed as well: the events or episodes are related retrospectively,
because an event in the present recalls an episode in the past, and the
aesthetic conclusion follows on naturally from the narrative, which puts
it into practice. Finally, homosexuality is established as one of the main
themes of the work, as Proust would point out to all its potential publishers:
he was unable to conceive how anybody could reject his book for any
reason other than its indecency. Vallette, who had already turned down
the pastiches and a collection of articles, also rejected *Contre Sainte-Beuve*,
without having read it, a few days later.[73] Despite this Proust would not
alter his ideas about the fictional character of his book, its time structure
which juxtaposed past and present, and the nature of its conclusion, which
was lacking in *Jean Santeuil*, nor would he change his mind about the
presence of Sodom. Having made these discoveries, nothing henceforth
would stop him and this certainty overcame both rejections and illness.
This explains his interest in summarizing the content of the *cahiers* devoted
to *Contre Sainte-Beuve*.

Proust always wrote in snatches of text, which overlapped, repeated one
another, were revised and then completed. None of the ten 'Sainte-Beuve'[74]
exercise books forms a whole; neither the essay nor the story can be found
in its entirety, but fragments of each of them are juxtaposed. By way of
example, let us take 'Cahier 5', which, if we open it at the right place;
contains the following sequence: the pastiche of Régnier, which appeared
in *Le Figaro* on 6 March 1909, a fragment on sleep, a study of *Sylvie*,[75] a
portrait of Françoise, a portrait of the 'Comte' and the 'Comtesse', a
fragment on Gustave Moreau, some passages about the trip to Padua and
the Giotto frescoes, and a portrait of the Guermantes;* turning it upside
down, we find several fragments about sleep and four passages about
Françoise.[76] Although Proust did not edit these various pieces, as one
edits a film, he would have been ready to do so had Vallette accepted his
project, and perhaps he would even have started to write an early version

---

* On 23 May 1909, he asked Lauris whether the name Guermantes belonged to the family of
their friend François de Pâris, or whether 'it was entirely extinct and available to a writer' (*Corr.*,
vol. IX, p. 102; cf. p. 107 and n. 2); the last Comte de Guermantes died in 1800.

of 'Combray', since he told the head of Mercure de France: 'I could have the first hundred pages copied out very legibly, or even typed for you in a few days.'[77] The rest of the letter tells us that the 'immoral' parts, which can be found in 'Cahier 51', could be copied, but that their 'text was not absolutely definitive', which means that at the time when Proust really did begin to write *À la recherche du temps perdu*, he had not yet revised the passages on homosexuality.

Out of these hundreds of pages themes gradually emerge which, when compared with *Le Carnet de 1908*, the correspondence and the detached pages, allow us to understand what the plot of *Contre Sainte-Beuve* would have consisted of. A hero, who speaks in the first person, is unable to sleep and is waiting for the morning, and for his mother.* He then remembers two different places, the countryside and the seaside: Combray, where he grew up and where he had experienced the drama of bedtime and the pleasure of going for walks along two opposite paths, and where he met Swann; and Querqueville, the original name for Balbec, where he stayed at the hotel with his grandmother and Mme de Villeparisis, and made friends with Montargis, the future Saint-Loup. When he wakes up, the Narrator's mother brings him a newspaper in which an article of his has appeared. He also hears the noises from the street and contemplates the rays of sunshine on the balcony. He remembers the journey he made to Venice with his mother. Paris, where he now lives, is also the world of the Guermantes, who are linked to Balzac through their reading of his work, which the Narrator discusses with his mother. The hero is in love with the countess, who lives at the far end of the courtyard. Swann, for his part, loves Sonia. We also see some young girls walk past who arouse the Narrator's desire,† in particular the Baronne de Picpus's maid, Mlle de Quimperlé or de Caudéran, and a peasant woman at Pinsonville. We also see the appearance of the Verdurin clan, which already comprises a pianist, a doctor and a tart. The painter is modelled on Whistler, Vuillard

---

* This subject, a crucial one for him, was emphasized by Proust whenever he encountered it in other writers' books: thus, in a novel by Jaloux, he appreciated 'that last night of the child who is waiting for his mother' (*Corr.*, vol. IX, p. 32, February 1909).

† In March, in a manner that was not fortuitous, Proust praised Porto-Riche's play *Passé*. In this play (Odéon, 1897; Théâtre-Français, 1902) the heroine meets the man who had seduced her, caused her to suffer and abandoned her eight years previously. Physical love is the play's principal theme; there is a painter, a composer and a novelist. Marcel wrote to the author on 20 March 1909: 'The only enviable form of happiness for an artist is to breathe eternal life into that which is most individual and profound within himself' (*Corr.*, vol. IX, p. 67).

and Helleu;[78] his early work is reminiscent of Gustave Moreau. The Marquis de Guercy, the future Charlus, is the 'homosexual' Proust mentioned to Vallette: he allows him to discover the 'accursed race' of homosexuals, one of whom is the florist Borniche, with whom the marquis is in love. The book was to have ended with the conversation with his mother about Sainte-Beuve and other writers, including Balzac, Baudelaire and Nerval; this discussion would also have brought together the various passages on aesthetics that are scattered through the ten exercise books. However, as Sainte-Beuve was not due to feature until the end of the work, we can see that, if Proust resumed writing in the spring or summer of 1909 in order to work continuously on the beginning of what was to be *À la recherche du temps perdu*, there was time for the essay to become dispersed and vanish. Sainte-Beuve was to serve as a foil, as a short-lived intermediary of the kind Proust always needed, and whom he was ready to fight with and then eclipse, just as Ruskin was eclipsed; he was also shared out among several of the characters of *À la recherche*: Mme de Villeparisis, Bloch, M. de Norpois (whose speech to Bloch about the Dreyfus affair uses the same stylistic tricks as the pastiche of Sainte-Beuve), and even the Narrator, when he shows himself to be curious about artists and their lives.

Other remnants, splendid ruins, would feature among the articles or prefaces that Proust published at the end of his life: 'À propos du "style" de Flaubert', 'À propos de Baudelaire',[79] the forewords to Jacques-Émile Blanche's *De David à Degas* and to *Tendres Stocks* by Paul Morand.[80] In all, *À la recherche du temps perdu* contains some fifteen direct allusions to Sainte-Beuve's style, to remarks made by him, and to his depictions of salons, which, unlike Proust, he did not know how to describe any differently one from the other. The longest reference can be found in an episode in *Albertine disparue*, which stems directly from the 1908–9 narrative, since it concerns the scene in which the Narrator reads his article in *Le Figaro*, and the public that read the *Lundis*; the trouble with newspaper articles is that they depend on the reactions of their readers and not just on the author's ideas: readers are not artists. 'Thus Sainte-Beuve, on a Monday, could portray Mme de Boigne in her four-poster bed reading his article in *Le Constitutionnel*, appreciating some pretty sentence or other which he had taken a long time to put together and which might never have emerged from him had he not judged it appropriate to cram into his article so as to make a more far-reaching impression.'[81] If these passages from *Albertine disparue* are based on the original piece of fiction, the reading of an article, we should not forget that it is no longer an article devoted to the author of the *Lundis*. Other passages from *À la recherche*, the various narratives that are associated with bedrooms and the workings of memory, do correspond to the early parts of *Contre Sainte-Beuve*, as we shall see. Finally, there is the aesthetic section, which Proust in any case wished to relinquish before he died, as is proved by the first lines of fragments written on loose-leaf pages that have been put together and edited under the title – not the author's – 'La Méthode de Sainte-Beuve':[82] 'I have reached the moment, or rather, I find myself in circumstances in which one might fear that the things one most wanted to say . . . one may suddenly be prevented from saying.'[83] The aesthetic project is then formulated, which clearly shows that his arguments had already gone beyond Sainte-Beuve: 'It seems to me that I may have things to say about Sainte-Beuve – and presently much more about Sainte-Beuve the writer than about the man himself – which may be of importance; in pointing out where, in my opinion, he has sinned, both as a writer and as a critic, I may perhaps manage to say a few things that I have long had in mind, as to what constitutes criticism and what art is';[84] most of this aesthetic section, developed, examined in greater detail and scarcely recognizable, was placed in *Le Temps retrouvé*; it can be found, too, in the references to Balzac and to Baudelaire that are scattered through *À la recherche*, and in the important passage in the final section, in which the Narrator searches for guarantors and sponsors for his enterprise, and in which he conjoins Chateaubriand, Nerval and Baudelaire in their use of reminiscences.

Throughout the early part of 1909 Proust often used to say he was very ill: he would spend some 6,000 francs a year on medicaments.[85] In March, reading *Jean-Christophe* gave him the idea for a 'Contre Romain Rolland'.[86] His attention was drawn to the large exhibition of Monet's *Nymphéas* at the Durand-Ruel gallery, which opened on 6 May, at the very moment that he was beginning to write about a painter in his exercise books.[87] At the end of June he completed a pastiche of Ruskin, 'La bénédiction du sanglier', and he was having fun writing little pastiches for his friends (*Le Trust*, by Paul Adam, for Dreyfus, in late June).[88] The same letter reveals that Céleste Mogador was a model for Odette (and, in male clothing, of Odette painted by Elstir). Likewise, an allusion by Dreyfus to Charles Haas, who was acting in a show at the Château de Mouchy, 'drew tears' from him. On 29 June he went out with Emmanuel Bibesco to a soirée at Mme Lemaire's (who, he wrote to Hahn, would not like his novel about

Sainte-Beuve), no doubt so as to verify whether Mme Verdurin really did look like her; after that his desire to attend dances in order to describe them in his book led him to that given by Mme Lebaudy.[89] On 12 July he thanked Céline Cottin for her *bœuf aux carottes en gelée*, which would become the dish served by Françoise.*

Marcel, who had been laid low by a fairly high fever, all because of some dental abscesses which he had been unable to have treated, was advised that he should have a change of air.[90] Until now, he had not wanted to go away before he had finished the 'first part' of his book.† As if to avoid any prior anxieties, he left suddenly for Cabourg on 14 August, because it was there 'that he breathed best'. It was at this point that he received the letter of rejection from Vallette, who had not even asked to read his book.‡ He was suffering from the dampness of the bedrooms at the hotel and he changed rooms several times; we come across him on the fourth (and top) floor, overlooking a small yard, with Nicolas Cottin sleeping on the other side.§ He also took with him Ulrich, who acted as his occasional secretary. Marcel rose at about nine o'clock in the evening and set off, via an indoor corridor, for the casino.¶ Here he was surrounded by a group of young men whom he charmed with his conversation and

---

* *Corr.*, vol. IX, p. 139: 'Would that I could bring off as well as you what I am going to do this evening, that my style might be as brilliant, as clear, as firm as your *gelée* – that my ideas might be as succulent as your carrots and as nourishing and fresh as your meat.' When so many famous friends have destroyed Proust's letters, it is rather admirable that his cook should have kept them. From this time on, Marcel's correspondence is dotted with references, which only he was aware of, to his novel: for example 'this Bois that I have loved much without knowing how to portray it' (ibid., p. 151), Talleyrand's saying: 'One should be in imaginary good health' (ibid., p. 172, and *RTP*, vol. II, p. 602), the asparagus, 'a vegetable I admire' (*Corr.*, vol. IX, p. 232), which Françoise puts on the menu at Combray and which Elstir paints, 'Quimperlé, Pont-Aven' (ibid., p. 242, and *RTP*, vol. I).

† *Corr.*, vol. IX, p. 154. However, at the same time he told Vallette he was 'finishing' the book (ibid., p. 155). And, writing to Mme Straus on about 16 August: 'Once the writing is finished, there will be a lot to redraft.'

‡ '. . . which will no doubt remain unpublished', wrote poor Marcel to Lauris, while at the same time already contemplating asking Calmette to help either in finding another publisher, or else in publishing it in serial form in *Le Figaro*.

§ *Corr.*, vol. IX, p. 166. But Proust would change rooms yet again, in order not to be next to the corridor (from room 118 to room 304), and then so as to be able to have, thanks to his friend Croisset, a suite to accommodate his secretary Ulrich and his manservant Cottin (ibid., pp. 178, 179).

¶ Ibid., pp. 162, 167. At the time, the casino comprised a theatre, a gambling room, a 'private' club, a dance hall and a 'grill-room'.

acquainted with the poetry of Anna de Noailles.* On 17 August he read Daniel Halévy's article on Nietzsche in *Le Journal de débats* and quoted from it in his notebook,[91] being struck by the Nietzschean concept of friendship which presupposed intellectual respect (this did not convince Proust at all) and which contradicted the reference to Wagner as 'a genius of untruthfulness'. On 25 August he heard an act from *Werther*, a work that was 'well written, well prepared, well seasoned' and which would 'always whet the appetite', like Voltaire, like France, like Reynaldo.[†] On 26 August it was *Arsène Lupin*, a play by Leblanc and Croisset, with André Brulé. Here Marcel met the publisher Calmann-Lévy, who would not publish him.

At the end of August Calmette agreed to serialize *Sainte-Beuve*, which Mercure and Calmann-Lévy had just turned down, in *Le Figaro*.[92] Though he had hoped to be able to continue living there while it was closed, the hotel would not allow him to stay,[93] and so Proust, deciding not to go to Versailles, returned home at the end of September. In October[‡] and November he then had 'Combray' typed out.[§] In order to relax, make the memories of the holidays live on, and gather together his circle of friends, on 27 November Marcel invited 'some sons of friends from Cabourg, young men who are a little too young',[¶] as well as some older friends, to Feydeau's and Croisset's play *Le Circuit*, at the Variétés. He wanted to introduce his young friends to his older ones, both to enhance himself in the eyes of the former, and to show the latter how they had been replaced. The choice of show was not insignificant. Croisset, a close friend of Marcel, had written two acts, but had been unable to finish the play and had approached Feydeau for help; they completed their work in the spring and it was performed on 29 October at the Variétés,[94] with

---

* Ibid., p. 197, to Mme de Noailles. Displaying little tact and much ignorance, he told her of his deep 'antipathy' for 'Barrès' lack of heart'. Among the 'adolescents', apart from Plantevignes and Parent (Daireaux not being there that year), we must now include Albert Nahmias, whom he advised against cohabiting (ibid., pp. 206, 212, 236). He was also friendly with the d'Altons, the Pontcharras, Mme de Maupeou and Bertrand, the owner of the Grand Hôtel (ibid., p. 236).

† *Corr.*, vol. IX, p. 171, to R. Hahn. He told him that he had cried 'in the large empty dining-room surrounded by twenty dismayed waiters who adopted an appropriate air' while listening to Hahn's 'Rêverie' played by the hotel's tsigane musicians. Another evening he heard Bizet's *Patrie*.

‡ Ibid., p. 192: 'I'm going to have a copy made of the first paragraph from my scraps of notes . . . it's almost a book in itself!'

§ By two brothers, 'brilliant Dioscuri of stenography' (26 November 1909, to R. Hahn).

¶ Ibid., p. 215, to E. Bibesco: 'Nothing Salaïst', he felt bound to add, thus confirming the suspicion. For the Bibescos Sala represented the typical homosexual.

Albert Brasseur in the role of the 'mechanic' Max Dearly, and Lantelme, whom Marcel had met at Cabourg as Edwards' companion, in the role of Phèdre, the mistress of a motor-car manufacturer who is in love with the mechanic. This comedy, the first to make use of a motor car as the focus of the plot, allowed Proust to project on to the features of the racing-car-driver-cum-mechanic,* caught between two women, the face of Alfred Agostinelli, whom he employed each year at Cabourg and who drove him back to Paris. The play also featured a group of characters participating in a couple's amorous exploits (the mistress of one of their witnesses and the husband of another) by means of a two-way mirror. Proust may have remembered this for the scene in which Charlus observes Morel's frolics with the Prince de Guermantes in the brothel at Maineville, in *Sodome*.

Having had 'Combray' typed out, in November he read his novel to Hahn and to Lauris, or had them read it, requesting confidentiality (one of his last and greatest pleasures would be to read his work aloud to his friends: Cocteau described his voice in *Opium*); he then sent it to *Le Figaro* in early December. Each day he expected to see it in print. Calmette, however, was not true to his word, possibly because Marcel, thinking he was doing some good, had set up a complicated intrigue. Aware that André Beaunier, a graduate of the École Normale, a critic for *Le Figaro* and a novelist, was preparing a study of Sainte-Beuve, he sent his manuscript to him (and not to the editor), both out of courtesy and in order to block his path. The latter returned the manuscript to Calmette, but not before he had suggested some corrections to Proust.† The newspaper's editor, annoyed that Marcel should have consulted anyone else beforehand, decided against publishing him and even declared that he did not have time to read him.[95] Marcel waited until 11 July 1910 before he set off, at night, on a melancholy pilgrimage to this newspaper, for which he had stopped writing, in order to retrieve his manuscript. Around 13 December 1909, while still hoping his book would appear in *Le Figaro*, Marcel turned to Lauris (and not Robert Proust), asking him to look after the publication of his novel, were he to die now.[96]

---

* As we have seen, he made references to this profession, and to Agostinelli, from the time of 'Impressions de route en automobile' onwards; he repeated these references in *La Prisonnière*. In *Le Carnet de 1908* he noted 'Croisset's chauffeur' (p. 52).

† 'I have revised the whole of the beginning of my first volume (everything that you read in exercise books) in order to take into account one of your criticisms' (*Corr.*, vol. XII, p. 375, to André Beaunier, 9 or 10 December 1913).

THE METAMORPHOSIS OF *CONTRE SAINTE-BEUVE* (1909–11)

From the spring of 1909 onwards, Proust had been expanding the 'Sainte-Beuve' exercise books, which were now acquiring the aspect, style and proportions of a genuine novel. The ending of the work, a critical conversation, was already written, though in separate segments. Feeling reassured as a consequence, Proust began to revise his opening. It is conceivable that at this period he completed the first series of ten 'Sainte-Beuve' exercise books by adding others to them;[97] he expanded the Combray episode, the holidays by the seaside, as well as Swann's life in Paris, and he increased the amount of aesthetic comments. We should imagine Proust's method, one that would not alter henceforth, as that of a chess player pursuing several offensives simultaneously. He switched subjects, moved from one section to another, from town to town, and from one group of characters to another. The development is never linear, in the sense that a writer tells a story from beginning to end; on the contrary, he would return to some of his original ideas, episodes that had been scaled down, sometimes in order to develop and expand them considerably, at others to remove them. Thus we see a Swann who is in love with girls at the seaside disappear. The theme of the two ways takes on a broader dimension, as do the hawthorns – that is to say, the binary structure of the work, and its contemplative experience. Two other exercise books contain outlines of Swann's love for Odette[98] and that of the Narrator for Gilberte.

At about this time we see the first appearance of the character of the artist,[99] unnamed originally, who had haunted Proust ever since Harrison in *Jean Santeuil*. In *Le Carnet de 1908*, he noted: 'Harrison whom we have seen nothing of and were glad to know, the sense of an important man.' This character is assigned to Querqueville, the future Balbec; the hero visits his studio; then Proust retraces the artist's career,[100] beginning with his study of Gustave Moreau, which represents the painter's early style, before describing a second and a third style. Later on he added the curious name, a Pre-Raphaelite anagram, of Elstir (based on Helleu and Whistler).* His second style is inspired by Japanese art; the third concentrates on seascapes, by which time he paints only landscapes and portraits. This

---

* It was Querqueville bay 'that Whistler painted in the delightful watercolour which he exhibited last year: *The Gulf of Opal*. Monet also worked here' (*RTP*, vol. II, p. 965).

account is later split up among *À l'ombre des jeunes filles en fleurs, Le Côté de Guermantes,* and the end of the narrative. From the beginning, it is established that the artist is 'perhaps the greatest of our age' (the composer and the writer rank at the same level). His early mythological style is influenced by Italy, but already one recognizes his own particular world, which he carries within him: consciousness is naturalized, nature is humanized, 'signs of the mythological event represented, bleeding clouds like a portent of murder ... a bird that knows it signifies death or inspiration ... a courtesan marked by vice ... a hero gentle as young girls'. He constantly seeks 'the same solemn woman's face, with the pureness of ancient features and an almost childlike expression'. When he experiences 'his passion for Japanese art', his floral arrangements, his magots painted on a woman's dress or her fan, the sofa coverings and the screens on which other women stand out, produce an overall effect that resembles 'a very mosaic of Japanese figures and flowers', so much so that one can no longer distinguish 'the women who are flesh from the women made of porcelain'.* This infatuation does not last. Elstir then becomes passionate about landscapes and portraits 'such as those that lay before his eyes'; this is why he settles in Querqueville bay, and paints pure sensation, 'the sensation of whiteness far away across the sea; at first we do not know whether it is a rock, a ship or a reflection of the sun ... He portrayed his first impression'. There follows a sketch of the port of Carquethuit: from that moment, painting is conceived as a metaphor 'expressing the essence of the impression that an object produces, an essence that remains impenetrable to us unless genius reveals it to us'.†
Before Renoir, Monet and Vuillard, Proust here returns to Ruskin's Turner, whose work he had been able to appreciate in Camille Groult's gallery.

The character of the composer, as he appears in the version pieced together from the 'Sainte-Beuve' exercise books of 1910, has not yet been given the name of Vinteuil; the sonata is that of Saint-Saëns.‡ This version tends to favour Bergotte, which allows Proust to develop the theme of reading, which takes him back to George Sand. Reading this author is very important in the first 'Combray'; a portion of it would re-emerge

---

* Here Proust drew his inspiration directly from Whistler's Japanese works.

† *RTP*, vol. II, p. 957. It is interesting to see that after this, in 'Cahier 28', Proust inserted the majority of his old notes on Chardin, just as, by quoting Vermeer, he tried to make use of his trip to Holland and his pieces on Rembrandt (ibid., p. 964).

‡ Ibid., vol. I, draft LXXIV, p. 911: 'It was in the sonata for violin and piano by Saint-Saëns ...' Cf. ibid., p. 941: 'But it's Saint-Saëns' little phrase.'

later in *Le Temps retrouvé*. In fact, Proust rather overdid these first drafts of his aesthetic meditations; he was to realize later, probably in 1910, that it was better to transfer half of them to the end of the book: pose the question first, then the answer can come much later. It was the same with the raptures of memory, the explanation for which is left until the end. With increasing skill, he learned how to delay his effects, how to control the suspense and not say everything straight away. As for Vinteuil, his fate was stranger still, because this character resulted from the belated merging of two different heroes.[101] In 'Combray' there is a naturalist by the name of Vington, whose brilliant work would not become known until later, and which would be edited by the very same friend of Mlle Vington who performs a sadistic scene with her. In 'Un amour de Swann' the author of the sonata, who was originally Saint-Saëns, has become the imaginary Berget. In 1913, after the typing of volume I of *Le Temps perdu*, which was then the title of the first book, Proust had the idea of fusing the two men into one character, and of eliminating the naturalist, though not his biographical appearance, to the benefit of the composer. What better way of refuting Sainte-Beuve's theories than by contrasting, within the same man, the poor and unfortunate piano teacher and the brilliant creative genius? Furthermore Proust was reinforcing his concept of the world, which opposed appearance and reality, illusion and truth. In fact scientists play a virtually non-existent role in his work, and the doctors, from Cottard to Du Boulbon, from Professor C. to Dieulafoy, do not appear to their advantage; there would have been something illogical about having an important naturalist appear on his own. We should not, however, be deceived by this example: Proust sometimes combined characters, but at others he separated them. The *François le Champi* episode is divided between *Du côté de chez Swann* and *Le Temps retrouvé*, having originally been written as a single piece;[102] but it had brought together and come to symbolize a number of George Sand's novels, eclipsing them in the process, for the subject of *François le Champi* touched on the relationship, at Combray, between the child and his mother; it should be pointed out that when it appears again in *Le Temps retrouvé* there is nothing autobiographical about it, since the experience of involuntary memory that it arouses was brought about in real life by Ruskin's *Saint Mark's Rest*.

One of the characters whom Proust invented at this period was Maria, a girl who interested, but later disappointed, the Narrator: given another Christian name, she would become one of the principal characters of the novel: Albertine.[103] This heroine, who features in the exercise books of

1909 and 1910, predates Proust falling in love with his chauffeur, and later his secretary, Agostinelli. A love affair in Paris and one at the seaside – two poles of construction; quite apart from his own experience of such things, Proust felt the need for these encounters because for him, in his novel, to love a woman meant also loving the landscape, scenery and the social milieu that surrounded her. Gilberte is inseparable from Combray and the Champs-Élysées, as is Maria from the sea and Holland, and Mme de Guermantes comes out of the depths of history and from the peaks of society.

By the end of the year, therefore, the book that is sometimes referred to as the novel of 1909, even though no coherent or complete version of it exists, consisted of a great number of fragments, many of which repeated one another, as well as the opening of the final version.[104] A philological examination of the exercise books and the references in the correspondence both confirm this. The letters, apart from those addressed to publishers, should be read with caution, for depending on whom Proust was writing to, they are coloured by humility, optimism that was occasionally excessive, irony, or mystery. In October 1909 he merely told Lucien Daudet that he had 'begun something' and was going to 'live in greenhouse conditions until it's finished', and spoke of his 'wretched mishmash consisting of the word "*que*", and dreary sentences no matter what [he] tries to put into them'[105] – here humility mixed with humour predominates. But when, two weeks later, he led Antoine Bibesco to expect 'the completion of an important piece of work'[106] before the following summer, he was deceiving himself. The extent of the work, which is borne out by the number of exercise books that he had already written, is confirmed in a letter to his friend, the businessman Lionel Hauser, whom he informed of 'a work in 3 volumes (!) begun, promised, not ready'.[107] Proust was foreseeing the schema of the book as it would be in 1913; yet it is also true that at that point, in November 1909, he was hoping to publish his novel in *Le Figaro*, and in Cahiers 8 and 12 he had made a fair copy of the opening; he then recopied it in three exercise books, Cahiers 9, 10 and 63, and had it retyped. He was thus in a position to inform Lauris, at the end of November, that he had read his 200-page beginning to Reynaldo Hahn,[108] and to lend him the first 'Combray' notebooks. One paragraph shows that Proust was nevertheless sufficiently sure of himself and confident of his originality and of what he had discovered to withstand publishers' rejections, if not without sadness, then with self-assurance at least: 'All I ask is that you do not discuss the subject, or the title, nor indeed anything that might suggest what I'm doing (not that anyone would be interested). But, furthermore, I do not want to be hurried, or bothered, or anticipated, or copied, or discussed, or criticized, or denigrated. There will be plenty of time when my thoughts have run their course to give free rein to other people's foolishness.'*

However, Proust was already pointing out the numerous mistakes introduced by the copyists which he had not corrected: worrying about covering the whole of the canvas, about always having to forge ahead, at the cost of literal inaccuracies which he would leave to others to revise, was a constant characteristic of a writer who was pressured by illness and by inspiration, and it was also a torment for his publishers. The more trouble he took to write, unravel and rewrite a sentence, the more he reckoned, when he handed it over to be copied out, typed or printed, that people were incapable of rising to the level of his work: the publishing process had to progress, just like a supply system. He dictated his manu-script to a secretary, who then typed it himself, or, if he was unable to use a typewriter, he recopied it or read it out to a typist. A letter to a young man whom he was seeking to hire gives an account of this method, which was fraught with dangers: 'I am finishing a novel or a book of essays that is a very considerable work, not least for its outrageous length. And I had intended to dictate the parts that have not yet been copied out to someone who takes shorthand. I would read it aloud. The person who is my secretary would take it down in shorthand. And in my absence she would type out the shorthand. Possibly you don't know either how to take shorthand or how to type, and in that case our task would be far simpler. For instead of my dictating and you taking it down in shorthand, I would dictate and you would write it in longhand, which would take much longer ... I would send your copies to a typewriting bureau.'†
Among the secretaries whom Proust employed in this way, we should mention Constantin Ullmann, Albert Nahmias, Alfred Agostinelli, Henri Rochat and Georges Gabory;‡ there may have been others who, to this day, are unknown; servants such as Nicolas Cottin, Forssgren, Vanelli and

---

* *Corr.*, vol. IX, p. 225, early December 1909. Ten years later Proust advised Gaston Gallimard not to allow anyone to read the manuscript of *Sodome et Gomorrhe I*.

† Ibid., vol. X, p. 308, late June or early July 1911. Gaston Gallimard had to insist that *Le Côté de Guermantes* be typed out at the publishing house itself. Proust was ready to send his manuscript directly to the printer, just as he had done with *À l'ombre des jeunes filles en fleurs*.

‡ Gabory was sent by Gaston Gallimard in January 1922, to read the proofs of *Sodome et Gomorrhe II* to Proust.

Céleste Albaret may also have taken notes. The typists, whether male or female, were professionals, not amateurs, and there were many of them: six of them were mentioned for *Le Temps perdu*, the first half of the novel in 1909–12.[109] Up to the second third of 'Un amour de Swann', Proust had certain parts of his text typed out. Typed pages may, in their turn, have been treated like manuscript, that is to say, corrected, moved about and pasted to manuscript pages.

But if we were to sum up the manner in which Proust was working at this period, and even though in his case no rule was ever absolute, we should note that the exercise books that consisted of fragments – the first of the 'Sainte-Beuve' *cahiers* – were followed for the first time, in 1909, by some with continuous text, which gathered together the fragments and assembled them according to a plot, the story of a young man who would one day expound his aesthetic beliefs. At a later date these sequential exercise or notebooks were improved on by other, equally sequential, notebooks, which formed the manuscript used to establish the typewritten version, or versions. But while Proust was writing these sequential notebooks, his ideas were being developed in other notebooks that consisted of fragments to be used in the later parts of the narrative: while it is true that some notebooks containing sketches and others containing the fair copy were written simultaneously, they did not, of course, deal with the same parts of the novel, because the approach was always prospective and looking to the future. Then there were the additions: there was a place prepared for them, in the draft notebooks, for only the right-hand pages were written upon initially, the left-hand pages being blank. Proust made use of the reverse side of the typewritten pages. M. Wada has established that three series of additions were incorporated into the typed version of 'Combray' in 1909, in 1911–12 and in 1913. Between 1917 and 1922, from *Le Côté de Guermantes* on, there would also be four notebooks containing short amendments but no continuous text, which Proust had anticipated using, without always having time to insert them. This was the way the great bulk of typescript was made up. In the Bibliothèque Nationale there are volumes of loose pages, both handwritten and typed, and numerous '*paperoles*' – in Proustian terms, sheets of paper of different format and length, often stuck together, some of which are over two metres long; these provide evidence that the versions which were being written at one moment were later dismantled. The notebooks have numerous pages torn out, which were pasted in elsewhere, and even on to the proofs.

This method of writing, one that was constantly evolving, was not without repercussions for the creation of characters. The places, and even the events, do not retain the same sense of being incomplete as do the characters. Numerous though the characters are – over 500 of them – or perhaps because there are so many and also because of the manner in which they were created, and the way in which they are subjected to the impressions of the Narrator, some of them will always have the unfinished quality, with all its transient beauty, of a draft. In the final text, and especially in the parts published posthumously, the first sign of this is in the incomplete names: thirty-four characters are called X in *À la recherche du temps perdu*; two are called Y; fourteen, A; two, N; one, Z. There are also some uncompleted Christian names, such as that of the mysterious A. J. Moreau.[110] In the notebooks, certain young girls have no name, such as Mlle X in Cahier 12 of 1909, in which the Narrator returns to the seaside to look for her. Of far more importance is Mlle de Stermaria, who is originally referred to as Mlle de Quimperlé, then Mlle de Caudéran, as Quimperlé again, or Penhoët, in six different notebooks.[111] She corresponds to the ghost who is yearned for by a sylph, in the manner of Chateaubriand, to a Breton girl's fantasy, associated with the mist and the moorland, in a castle which was to be a 'Breton Guermantes'.[112] Her first name was to have been Viviane, a name that recalls the wizard Merlin and the forest of Brocéliande. Mlle de Stermaria is linked with Brittany, because Proust always associated a woman with a particular place: both disappear almost completely in the definitive version, and Brittany becomes the island in the Bois de Boulogne in the mist.[113]

The maid of the Baronne de Putbus (originally called Picpus) has much in common with this sensual aristocrat. There are two main sketches of her, one dating from 1908–9, the other from 1911.[114] In the first version, the plot develops as follows: the Narrator is thinking of going to Venice to look for this woman. He walks alone in the Bois, and he finds that the restaurants, which had a Breton atmosphere about them when he was in love with Mlle de Stermaria, now possess a Venetian character. The following year the woman's face is burnt in a fire aboard a liner, and she is 'dreadful to behold'. She confides to the sister-in-law of Théodule, who, in 'Combray', is finally known as Théodore, that she is the same age as the Narrator and they may have slept together: 'Putting her face out of my mind, I threw myself upon her and we indulged in violent caresses that I felt she must have learned from shepherds, and I had the feeling of no longer being myself, of being a young peasant boy whom a rather more bold and worldly wise peasant girl was rolling in the hay.' She loves motor cars; her aunt is the mother of the Verdurins' pianist; M. Verdurin has the following conversation with her, worthy of Christophe:* ' "My name is M. Verdurin – And my name is Mme Maudouillard . . . He was flabbergasted. He didn't utter a word all evening." ' A scene in a restaurant follows, after which the Narrator takes his leave of the maid and her aunt and never again sees the 'poor burnt creature', who writes to him every year.[115] These passages show that Proust, who was certainly attracted by the way characters reappear in Balzac's novels – the maid came from Combray, and she knew other principal characters in the novel – was above all obsessed by the Baudelairean theme of the 'passer-by' and by the poem whose last verse he had quoted in the study of Baudelaire in *Contre Sainte-Beuve*: 'Ô toi que j'eusse aimé, ô toi qui le savais.'† The fact is that the passer-by, if one strives after her, disappoints, just like Mlle de Goyon, the model for the 'girl with the red roses', whom Proust pursued in 1909.[116] In the second draft, which was probably entitled 'Les Vices et les Vertus de Padoue et de Combray' in the summary of *Le Temps retrouvé* printed in *Du côté de chez Swann*, the maid was burnt in a fire. She is reminiscent of Giotto's 'Impurity'. The Narrator has a rendezvous with her in the Giotto chapel in Padua; he presses up against her dress as he inspects the frescoes. The conversation turns to Pinsonville. The hero is then overcome with a furious desire; they go to a hotel room after a delightful walk, 'pleasures that were as solitary as those on leaving the Giottos in the studio, as those [he experienced] when looking at the church tower at Pinsonville, or in the room smelling of oris root'. He comes close to happiness, but discovers that reality had accorded with his dreams. They arrive at the hotel, and they have an affair.

In Cahier 56, on the reverse side of folio 68, Proust decided to divide up different aspects of this character: she becomes Albertine in terms of jealousy, Gilberte in the 'sexual goings-on' with other children in the castle keep at Combray, Cottard and Odette are given the 'foolish love banter', and Albertine acquires the 'carnal gratitude'. This virtually complete character was taken apart and made non-existent, and then restored to the status of a ghost.

Among the unfinished characters, the most fascinating is Albertine. Let

---

* Christophe: pen-name of Georges Colomb, the humorous writer who taught Marcel as a schoolboy; cf. p. 57 *Tr.*

† *CSB*, p. 258. [O you whom I might have loved, O you who was aware of it.]

us look at three unpublished texts: although Albertine appears to have absorbed other characters, she is none the less incomplete. In Cahier 56[117] there is Albertine's false resurrection. The hero is in Venice, in love with a girl who is barely seventeen years old, a 'Titian': there he receives a letter from Mme Bontemps, which becomes a telegram in *Albertine disparue*: 'My dear friend I have to inform you of some news that is scarcely credible and yet perfectly true. You know that the body of my little Albertine was never recovered. She was alive! She had fled because she was in love with someone. She came back yesterday. You can imagine our joy. She is engaged to an extremely rich American. However, I think that if you were prepared to forgive her for the pain she has caused you and were to take up the plans you once had and then abandoned of getting married, she would give up her present intention. But you would have to move quickly. Write to me immediately. In the hope that this letter reaches you, for I am told you are in Italy and I don't know your exact address.' And further on:[118] 'Mme Bontemps, wife of the former under-secretary of state for the post office who for some time had been showing signs of insanity, had been arrested and imprisoned, in the act of firing shots at a person whom she persisted in taking for a niece whom she had not seen for several years, and whom in her madness she had imagined she had found again. Poor Albertine was certainly dead.'

A second draft contains a conversation between the Narrator and Gilberte about Balzac's *La Fille aux yeux d'or*:[119] 'Don't look, what I have just read is very improper. It's called *La Fille aux yeux d'or*.' – 'It's splendid.' – 'Ah! you know it. But I don't believe it can be true. I think that those women are only jealous of other women.' – 'Sometimes, but for others the man is the enemy, he is the one who provides brutal caresses, which is the one thing they cannot give each other. The reverse is true, what's more. I have friends who would be ferocious if their mistress had another lover, but couldn't care if she had a relationship with a woman. For me, it's the other way round. I was very unhappy when I learned that my beloved fiancée loved another man, but it did not cause me as much grief as it would have done if she had loved women.' – 'Did that happen to you?' – 'Yes, with a girl I loved.' In the remainder of the folio, the comparison with Balzac's novel continues: sequestration, surveillance – 'I didn't murder her, but I could have done'. The Narrator then shows Gilberte a photograph of Albertine.

Paradoxically, in the third draft, 'Dernière conversation avec Andrée',[120] the additional material supplies further evidence of its non-completion:

because it is not integrated, because versions are still possible, and also because Proust had the psychology, the aesthetic sense and a technique of putting things into perspective that permitted him to do this: 'Vital. Not to forget in the last conversation with Andrée, I say (but without believing a word, as if I were speaking rather aimlessly): "But did Mme Bontemps have a relationship of this kind with her niece?" Andrée did not appear in the least surprised at such an assumption and replied, as if it were entirely natural, "Since they shared the same bed at Incarville, it is very likely, but in Paris I don't really think they did. No, in Balbec the person who was very much like that was the wife of the first president." And as to what Mme Bontemps may have done with her niece at Incarville, Andrée provided me with some details that were <attenuating?> according to her, because they proved that it amounted to very little, but were of a coarseness that gave me as great a sense of novelty as if I had landed on an island full of cannibals. For, however great or small, it came to the same thing ... In this unpredictability lies the surprise of tomorrow's masterpieces, which, even without building upon the memory of past masterpieces, we are unable to imagine. As far as horror was concerned, the extreme curiosity I felt about the island of cannibals was so different from what I remembered when Mme Bontemps used to say such different things and, at the very most, used to speak of Albertine as if she were an impudent little girl. So I knew nothing about life, and when I wasn't there, Mme Bontemps must have behaved completely differently in front of Andrée for her to have made such assumptions so calmly. People had always been polite and socially effusive in my presence, and at the edge of the strange island I had <only> experienced the smiles and the cannibals' loud shrieks of joy.' On folio 23 there is another addition, intended for the soirée at the Princesse de Guermantes in *Sodome et Gomorrhe*: Saint-Loup insinuates that he could have married Albertine.

This incomplete Albertine took the place of another girl, Maria, traces of whom have been discovered. We come across her at the seaside, with the young girls, or in the bed scene and the abortive kiss[121] that comes from *Jean Santeuil*. She is associated with Holland: the Narrator dreams of going to Maria's home, to her little Dutch house, an idea conjured up by one of the Princesse de Guermantes' Rembrandts that belonged to Proust's friends, the Rothschilds.[122] Now, Albertine would visit the Netherlands on several occasions. Maria was absorbed by Albertine, just as the scientist Vington and the composer Berget were by Vinteuil. In the last image of her in the final portrait we can see many features that have been removed.

She is joined by the girl with the red roses, who can be found in several of the notebooks for *Le Côté de Guermantes* and *Sodome et Gomorrhe*;[123] the Narrator pursues her, in such a way that a love affair might have developed, had the meeting of Gilberte, who was mistaken for a stranger, and Albertine's lesbianism not cast this ghostly presence into the limbo of draft notebooks. One could even go so far as to say that over the years and through the pages of writing and inspiration, Proust gradually built up, from his personal life and his own desires, a stock of characters which he drew upon for his final text, the version that publication or death rendered definitive. The hazards of creating fiction are similar to the laws of psychology: 'As for Albertine I no longer had any doubt, I was sure that it might well not have been her that I loved, that it might have been someone else. It would have been enough that Mlle de Stermaria, on the evening I was due to dine with her at the island in the Bois, had not cancelled the arrangement. There was still time then, and it would have been upon Mlle de Stermaria that I would have directed that activity of the imagination which makes us extract from a woman so special a notion of individuality that she appears to us unique in herself and predestined and necessary to us.'[124]

THE DEATH OF MADAME CAILLAVET

At the time that Marcel was creating the character of Bergotte,[125] his relationship with Anatole France had become strained: in *Sésame et les lys* the most Marcel had done was to mention 'the admirable *Livre de mon ami*'.[126] But on 13 January 1910 he learned of the death of Mme de Caillavet. Shattered by France's infidelity while on a tour of Argentina, a few months previously, she had attempted to take her own life. It was an opportunity for Marcel to relive his youth and to write some sensitive, even distressed letters of condolence. He received a fine letter from France: 'Dear Companion of the good old days, you who disguise your own suffering and show your kind-heartedness, your words, gentle like you, have touched me deeply. I shall be grateful to you throughout the few overlong days that remain to me.'[127] But Proust, through Robert de Flers, learned of certain details, some 'appalling things', concerning France's cruelty towards Mme de Caillavet that profoundly upset him; again, in 1912, he was heartbroken because Mme Scheikévitch told him that 'dear old Mme Arman had come to ask her for information about how to fire a revolver'. 'My only consolation is . . . that she intended to miss.'[128] Proust took refuge from all these deeds by recounting the private life of Bergotte. We know how much this character owed to France:[129] the Sainte-Beuve-like contradiction between his physical appearance and his style of writing, his manner of speaking, his philosophy, certain expressions ('the eternal torrent of forms', the 'mysterious tremors of beauty', the adjective 'mellow'), and then the relationship between his private life and his books, rounded off by the death of Mme Arman. Proust referred to the 'obscenity' of Bergotte's life, which contradicted 'in a shocking way the trend of his latest novels, which were full of such a painfully meticulous concern for what was right and good that the slightest pleasures of their heroes were poisoned by it, and even for the reader himself there emanated from it a sense of anguish in the light of which even the mellowest of lives seemed scarcely, bearable'.[130] The Narrator puts about comments which attest to the harshness of Bergotte, who 'had behaved cruelly to his wife'.* This 'cruelty' in his private life was commented upon even more brutally in a 1910 draft, based upon remarks of Robert de Flers, which allude to four other creative artists, as well as France, whose private lives are discussed: Tolstoy, Bernstein, Debussy and Bataille. But perhaps Proust was also thinking of himself, and he was being spiteful out of over-sensitivity, aware of the sinfulness to which he was condemned.

Nevertheless, Proust had no regrets about dedicating the edition of *Du côté de chez Swann* printed on Japanese paper:† 'To Monsieur Anatole France/ To my first Master, the greatest, the most beloved,/ with the respectful gratitude of/ Marcel Proust/ who still calls him the Nabi and in memory of lost Time',[131] and that same year he spoke of 'the men to whom [he owed] everything, like M. France'.[132] This sense of his past debt and the influence France had over him did not prevent Proust from identifying at least two styles in his writing, and finding the second of these too austere: 'The reflections bore us and the harmonious sentences leave us unaffected the more they attempt to move us (as France and Barrès very often do nowadays).'[133]

---

* France was divorced on 23 April 1893; the person alluded to is his mistress. Cf. *Corr.*, vol. X, p. 44, shortly after 28 January 1910: 'Distressing dream caused by all the awful, irreconcilable things I have learnt about someone who towards me has been . . . full of devotion and sweetness.' He was referring to France.

† This now beats all records at auction sales.

1910

That January, Marcel, who was not at all well, suffering from his asthma attacks and his fumigations, was drugging himself with trional and caffeine[134] and was not entertaining anyone, not even Reynaldo. Yet he wrote numerous letters to people he refused to see, and he worked on his 'long novel'.[135] Initiating a correspondence with Simone de Caillavet, he asked her for her photograph:* he wanted to be able to compare her with her mother, Jeanne Pouquet, with her father, and also her grandmother, who had just died: the entire Swann dynasty.[136] He also studied the young girl's handwriting, which he would borrow for Gilberte, and he recommended one of his favourite novels to her, *The Mill on the Floss*. Engrossed in the English novel, he also read *The Well-Beloved* by Thomas Hardy, which had just been published in translation, and which told the story of a man in love with three women, a grandmother, mother and daughter.[137] From George Eliot to Hardy, from Stevenson to Emerson, he maintained, there was no literature that had a power over him comparable to English and American literature.[138] He joked about the danger he ran of being drowned like the hero of George Eliot's novel: the waters of the Seine, which had flooded that year, had in fact reached the front door and cellars of 102 Boulevard Haussmann. In February, when the building was being dried out and disinfected with phenol, and the rotted floorboards were being replaced, Marcel suffered renewed asthma attacks and was unable to sleep. He did, however, attend 'like a mummy and by some strange miracle' the dress rehearsal of *La Fête chez Thérèse* at the Opéra: the Comtesse Greffulhe was there in a baignoire (reminiscent of the Duchesse de Guermantes' theatre box). Reynaldo Hahn had composed the music for it based upon a libretto by Catulle Mendès, adapted from Victor Hugo: 'His ballet is a delightful affair ... What enchantment ...'† *Le Dieu bleu*, which was written with Cocteau, came

---

* He also contemplated one of Jeanne Pouquet at the tennis club on the Boulevard Bineau (*Corr.*, vol. X, p. 30). She had not 'changed'.

† *Corr.*, vol. X, p. 49, 15 February 1910. Proust regretted on this occasion that his friend should have had 'not much luck with his operas'. He was referring to *L'Île du rêve*, produced on 23 March 1898, and *La Carmélite*, performed on 16 December 1902, both at the Opéra-Comique. The critics praised the latter rather more than the former (B. Gavoty, *Reynaldo Hahn*, Buchet-Chastel, 1976, pp. 58–70). Again, on 18 March Proust heard Reynaldo sing ('never better') at the Strauses. It may have been on this occasion that he encountered Jean Cocteau for the first time, unless, as P. Kolb implies, it was shortly before the publication of *Le Prince frivole* in July 1910, which Proust discussed in *L'Intransigeant* in September. See *Corr.*, vol. X, n. 5, p. 232. In June Proust congratulated Reynaldo

about as a result of this production. Proust took the opportunity to ask Reynaldo to sing 'Les présents', by Villiers de l'Isle-Adam and Fauré* to him. He had probably thought of including this poem, steeped as it is with the emotions of a 'sick heart', with regrets and disappointed hopes, roses and doves, in his novel, but he did not do so: the atmosphere it conveyed must have been sufficient for him. He was also much concerned with painting: having discovered that Bernheim-Jeune were selling copies of old masters 'that he admired', Proust thought of buying some, to satisfy 'his desire for paintings' without having to go to Dresden, or even to the Louvre:† but he did not wish to own paintings so much as to describe them, whether those of Elstir or the numerous old masters which he used in his comparisons, and he would not pursue his plan, particularly since the fall in his American shares meant that he was less well off in July.[139] He would therefore rely on his memory, on art books and on the Library Edition of Ruskin, which had a wealth of illustrative plates. His limitless erudition extended to linguistic preoccupations, which permeate the onomastics of his novel and can be seen to amusing effect in some poems written to Bibesco, in which he mentioned Picot, Bréal, Petit de Julleville, Abel Lefranc and Darmsteter.[140] His reading that spring inspired whole passages on Stendhal (he had reread and annotated *La Chartreuse de Parme*) and Balzac.[141] He also confessed his admiration for Francis Jammes, 'for that sincerity and clear-sightedness which, beyond some vague images that we have learnt and with which we content ourselves, could disentangle and evaluate the exact sensation that had affected him, the precise nuance'.[142] This was exactly what he was striving for himself. On the other hand, his anger on reading some articles about Binet-Valmer's *Lucien* could be explained because it concerned a 'monograph' on homosexuality, and he was frightened at seeing anyone who was a jump ahead of him.[143] Later on he would refer to this book as a foil, in order to explain what his book was not.

All the arts interested him. This was why, at the invitation of Comtesse Greffulhe, he went to the Ballets Russes at the Opéra on 11 June, where

---

on his new *Marche nuptiale*, which the composer had shown him at the same time as he had played the overture to *Die Meistersinger* to him (ibid., p. 124).

* Ibid., vol. X, p. 53; he had just quoted lines from this poem to Simone de Caillavet (ibid., p. 42 and n. 6); he would quote them again to Gide in 1914 (ibid., vol. XIII, p. 131). The music is contemporary with Fauré's *Requiem* and has the same serenity.

† Ibid., vol. X, p. 88, 29 April 1910; cf. p. 98: 'I still don't know whether I am a lover of painting or a buyer of securities . . . with the impressionist or oil-bearing consequence that [his moods] had on some ten thousand francs.'

he saw *Cléopatre* (based on music by Rimsky-Korsakov, Glinka, Glazunov and Moussorgsky, with choreography by Fokine), which he described in a draft that was not used in the definitive text,* *Les Sylphides* (a ballet by Fokine based on orchestral pieces by Chopin) and *Schéhérazade* (Rimsky-Korsakov and Fokine).[144] Nijinsky, Karsavina and Ida Rubinstein were the stars of this show, which was directed by Diaghilev and choreographed mainly by Fokine; the stage sets were by Benois and Bakst. In a draft for *À l'ombre des jeunes filles en fleurs*, Proust immediately described Bakst as 'a painter of genius', with his blue costumes and his fairy-tale garden, and Nijinsky as 'a dancer of genius'. An image in the definitive text draws on his comments, describing the 'genius of a Bakst, according to the blood-red or moonlit lighting into which he plunged his stage sets', that transforms a simple paper shape into a turquoise on a palace wall or a Bengal rose in the middle of a garden.[145] *Sodome et Gomorrhe* describes 'the prodigious flowering of the Ballets Russes which, one after another, revealed Bakst, Nijinsky, Benois and the genius of Stravinsky'.[146] Like his friends, the Comtesse Greffulhe, Misia Sert[147] in her box, Hahn, Vaudoyer, Cocteau and Rivière, Proust admired this explosion of colour and wild rhythm, this fusion of talent in all the art forms, these consummate shows which, with their rhythmical and colourful intensity, were replacing the decadence of the *fin-de-siècle*.

CÉLINE AND NICOLAS COTTIN

We may recall that Proust engaged this couple as servants after his mother's death. Aged about thirty and paid 300 francs, which was twice the normal rate, they did not hesitate to make sarcastic remarks about their strange employer: 'It's your friend Valentin summoning you', said the husband to his wife, 'don't get carried away.' Nicolas, a large man 'of Sancho Panza-like corpulence',[148] with an unintelligent air, who, according to his master, looked like Mayol,[149] occasionally helped Proust assemble and file his papers, and used to take down a few words of dictation. We know something of the way in which Proust lived in his apartment from the confidential details passed on by Céline Cottin, who was employed by him from 1907 to 1914: Marcel, who was a recluse in his bedroom most

---

* *RTP*, vol. I, p. 1002. Note that one of Diaghilev's eccentricities was to give the leading role to a man and not to a woman. This description was eclipsed by that of Sarah Bernhardt who became la Berma (originally called Brema, like the singer) towards the end of 1910 or half-way through 1911 (ibid., p. 1312, note).

of the time, used to wear long-johns, and socks and shawls knitted from Pyrenean wool, 'all of which were singed', because everything had to be put in the oven; at his feet were small jugs full of boiling water, and, to replace a wretched torn blanket, one 'with poppies' had to be brought by Céline from her home village. Sharing the French fear of draughts, he had a sheet nailed to his bedroom door. He asked Antoine, the concierge, to come up to ensure that the windows of the apartment were closed properly. Marcel's sensitivity was extraordinary: one day, from the depths of his bedroom, he informed Céline that she had left the pantry door open. The apartment was cleaned during the visits to Cabourg. Céline has described what her master used to eat for dinner: three croissants, café au lait, boiling hot and steaming, eggs in béchamel sauce, fried potatoes and stewed fruit: 'The same thing for a month.' The man who invented the dishes cooked by Françoise ate very little of them himself. Orders were given courteously: 'Please be so kind as to . . .'[150] When he went out, his grooming preparations had to conform to complicated rules: on coming out of the bath, he must be wrapped in a burning hot towel. The opportunity was to be used to make his bed. At other times, he rested.

Marcel's domestic life was disturbed, if not thrown into confusion, by the birth of Céline and Nicolas Cottin's son. Céline, who was less prepared to sacrifice herself to her master than Céleste Albaret, went away to Champignol, in the Aube, to recuperate. Proust inscribed a copy of *Les Plaisirs et les Jours* to Nicolas 'so as to dispel for us the boredom of the first difficult days of his wife being away in Champignol in spite of us';[151] he sent Céline a charming letter, in which he described how moved he was 'by [her] happiness' and conveyed 'greetings from the patient who is ill in perpetuity to the patient who will soon be liberated'. He made her read *Mémoires d'outre-tombe*, learn some Musset which he first copied out for her, and read Gérard d'Houville (Marie de Régnier) as well as Louis de Robert and his *Roman du malade*. He sent poems to her: '*Puisque vous conservez tous ces papiers divers/ Je suis obligé de vous écrire en vers*',* as well as to Nicolas: '*Si vous ne vous sentez pas las/ Nationaliste Nicolas,/ Cher Nicolas Cottin, ferme soutien du roi/ Dans vingt minutes donnez-moi/ Un bon café au lait qui fume/ J'en prendrai, dit-on, pour mon rhume.*'† With Nicolas, who was

---

* Since you keep all these various papers/ I am obliged to write to you in verse. *Tr.*

† If you don't feel weary/ Nicolas the Nationalist/ Dear Nicolas Cottin, solid supporter of the king/ In twenty minutes' time bring me/ A good steaming *café au lait*/ I will take it, as they say, for my cold. *Tr.*

always a little simple-minded, he would discuss the stock exchange and banking matters: 'When they did not agree, Monsieur used to say: "We are not of the same opinion!"' He gave his chambermaid Zola's *Les Quatre Évangiles* (we know because the first volume was entitled *Fécondité*), with a significant inscription: 'greetings from an infidel'.[152] Ever anxious to educate his staff, Marcel may have thought that Zola would suit Céline perfectly... One of the Narrator's great-aunts would be given her Christian name; and Françoise, whose bellicose nature Marcel had reproached in his maid, is made to cry out: 'I should like to see what it's like, the war!!' Nicolas features in a draft of *Le Temps retrouvé*, in order to illustrate the hereditary qualities of illness: 'At about the age of forty-four his health altered, the large man grew thin and a look of his sickly, cancerous peasant father came over him ... then he returned beneath the ground taking with him his son, who had become a part of him.'[153] He would die in June 1916, from pleurisy contracted at the front line: 'I had to direct my eyes, my pen (and my money) towards his widow,' Proust would write at the time.[154] Yet Céline considered her master to be responsible for the death of her husband: 'Constantly shut up in Monsieur's home, in that hot-house, without air, with that stove heating ... At the front, in the fresh air, my husband caught pleurisy. Monsieur said to me: "You're accusing me of Nicolas' death!" And it was true.'[155]

CABOURG 1910

On 17 July Marcel again left for Cabourg[156] on the spur of the moment, with Nicolas (who 'was starting to honour Dionysius once more'), without even informing Reynaldo. He entrusted Céline with overseeing the redecoration he had arranged to be carried out in his apartment, notably the cork lining of his bedroom, which would become 'like a little bottlestop'.[157] Since his concierges and their sons, who had been put in charge of registering his baggage, had sent his suitcases to an 'unknown destination', and he had found himself with those belonging to a lady, he was at first unable either to go to bed, or undress, or do anything.[158] In fact, he planned to continue with his novel, which he believed would 'be completed shortly', and in no time he wrote to Jean-Louis Vaudoyer, the poet and art critic whose appreciation of Vermeer he already admired, asking him whether he might not publish part of it in *La Grande Revue*.[159] He would have liked to have been able to bring Ulrich to Cabourg as his secretary, but he, like Morel, 'had slipped away as a result of some amorous affair', and as his parents were searching for him, Marcel did not want to appear as if he were hiding him. He saw a good deal of his cousin, Valentine Thomson, of Doctor Gustave Roussy, 'an example of *medical vulgarity*',[160] whom he would make use of for Cottard, and his wife, as well as the Plantevignes. Because he was unwell, he was unable to leave his room except for an hour or two every two or three days.[161] On 8 August he attended a concert given by the great singer Félia Litvinne[162] and the cellist Paul Bazelaire,[163] who used to take aperitifs with Nicolas. Among Proust's friends were the d'Altons; he wanted to give both the d'Alton daughters a watch 'which is worn like a pendant, in blue enamel – periwinkle blue or even a little brighter – and which is fastened around the neck by a thin gold chain'. Initially, he thought of buying them from Cartier, which he subsequently decided was too expensive, and later, from Aux Trois Quartiers.[164] Reynaldo's sister, Maria de Madrazo, ordered the gifts. Why such generosity, and towards women too? Was it because he admired Colette d'Alton's beauty? In order to experiment with the pleasure of giving jewellery to women? The Narrator would give Albertine a vanity-case [a *nécessaire*] from Cartier's 'which was Albertine's pride and joy as well as [his]'.[165] Or was he indirectly thanking Vicomte d'Alton for the amount of genealogical information with which he had provided him, while at the same time pointing out what Léon Séché had written about Aimée d'Alton, and about the social rank of France d'Alton-Shée, 'the creator of the can-can'?* Was he identifying himself with Musset, 'one of his heroes in real life'[166] about whom he wrote a remarkable piece in 1910,[167] in which he recalled the poet's letters to Aimée d'Alton and meditated on the relationship between his life and his work: 'In his life and in his letters, just as in a seam of ore in which they are scarcely recognizable, we glimpse certain lineaments of his work, which was his life's sole raison d'être as well as his feelings of love, which existed only in so far as they were raw material for his work, which were directed towards and had their existence in it alone.' Such were the love affairs of Proust, who based the silhouette of Gurcy, the future Charlus, on that of the Vicomte d'Alton:[168] minor experiences to which only the book itself gives meaning by enclosing them within a structure which overtakes them, but which, without such experience, would remain empty. Thus, when he reminded Marcel Plantevignes of impressions they had shared, 'the mountain with the sun upon

---

* *Corr.*, vol. X, p. 188. *Le Figaro* and later *Mercure de France* had published Musset's love letters to Aimée d'Alton, edited by Léon Séché, in 1910.

it, the tree with the blue-tits, the odalisque',[169] he relocated them in his novel: at Saint-Pierre-des-Ifs 'where, for a moment in the evening, the crest of the cliffs glinted pink like the snow on a mountain at sunset';[170] the Narrator while on a walk near Balbec sees that 'some blue-tits had settled upon the branches';[171] and in Paris Charlus says to the hero: 'What a shame that one of us were not an odalisque!'[172] A biography is also the history of the fleeting impressions that the pen retains.

On 21 September *L'Intransigeant* published an article by Proust, written in June, about *Le Prince des cravates*, a collection of four short stories by Lucien Daudet. He managed to write this, in spite of the amount of work and his poor health, because he said he was 'sickened' by the conspiracy of silence that surrounded the 'delightful talent' of his former friend, whom he hardly saw any more.[173] In this portrait Lucien is presented as the synthesis of both family gifts and the art of the painter, a pupil of Whistler. Whence the human compassion, the subtle nuances, the 'harmonies' and also, beneath the apparent frivolity (*en passant*, Proust praised Cocteau, the author of *Le Prince frivole*, 'a twenty-year-old Banville for whom a higher destiny awaits'), the deep humanity of certain of Balzac's short stories.[174] This was the last article (setting aside the extracts from *Swann* in *Le Figaro*) published by Proust before 1920: which is to say that he had abandoned journalism, and that he only emerged from his silence out of kindness.

AUTUMN 1910

His stay at Cabourg enabled Proust to work, but he was aware of the deterioration of his health compared with earlier years: he only went down to the beach once this time, and he only visited the hotel's public rooms or went to the casino every two or three evenings (it was every evening the previous year).[175] After returning to Paris by taxi, driven, no doubt, by Odilon Albaret, Proust went on a number of occasions to hear Mayol, whom he thought was 'sublime', in his latest show; but he would have liked to have written to him to ask to hear *Viens poupoule* and *Une fleur du pavé* again.*

Lauris announced his marriage to Madeleine de Pierrebourg, 'the girl [he had] gazed at in rapture the first time [he had] seen her'; this 'delightful

* *Corr.*, vol. X, p. 177. Cf. p. 215: 'I still get up once or twice a month and, on those days, I usually go to the Concert Mayol to hear that singer who has the dual advantage of only singing at eleven o'clock and possessing a great deal of talent!'

and damaged creature' (she had previously been married to Louis de La
Salle) had met the man whom Marcel considered the 'most intelligent,
the handsomest, the best';[176] thus did he address his congratulations,
without any of the bitterness which often crept into similar compliments,
and he thought about what he should give as a wedding present (Lauris
had asked for a clock: 'something tells me that he only listed things
that might please me. That complicates the purchase,' Marcel confessed
humorously to Reynaldo).[177] Yet Lauris, this friend who was so dear to
him, the confidant of *Contre Sainte-Beuve*, did not invite Proust to his
wedding: to make matters worse, Fénelon was the best man. Marcel said
he had guessed in advance that he would not be invited because of 'that
alibi silence,* that give-away silence that people adopt when they neither
want to invite you to an occasion, nor tell you they are not inviting you'.
And he was led to suspect that they were ashamed of him: 'Although I
don't think particularly highly of myself, as you know, I do, on the other
hand, consider myself "presentable", knowing quite a few of the people
you know, and thus being one of those persons who, as Mme Aubernon
used to say so marvellously, are convenient to invite because they require
no explanation.'† The theme of the invitation that may or may not have
been received – less superficial than one might think, because it is the
theme of entry to the magic circle, or exclusion from it, that runs through
Le Côté de Guermantes – as well as the philosophy of friendship – shallow
and impossible, as Proust shows it to be in his novel, but not in his letters
– derives from this type of experience.

At this period in his life Marcel received nothing but sad news (in
addition to his losses on the stock exchange, due to the American slump):
the death throes of Robert Dreyfus' brother,‡ as well as the death of
Louisa de Mornand's lover, Robert Gangnat, who had replaced Louis

---

* Legrandin, in the company of the Princesse des Laumes, also looked for a 'mental alibi' for not
recognizing the Narrator's family at Combray.

† *Corr.*, vol. X, pp. 192–4, 1 November 1910. Georges de Lauris did not publish this letter in his
book of correspondence with Proust, *À un ami*, Amiot-Dumont, 1948. One can understand why.
He merely wrote in his introduction: 'My wedding was the occasion for letters which are very
precious to me' (ibid., p. 41). If Lauris did not invite Proust to his wedding because he did not wish
to be seen in his company, this was also the reason why he never asked François de Pâris, as Marcel
had requested him to do insistently, whether he could use the name of Guermantes (*Corr.*, vol. X,
p. 217).

‡ Proust wrote these tender lines to him: 'Don't write to me. But when you are feeling a little
lonely, tell yourself that far away, a Benedictine (I was about to say a Carmelite) is thinking of you
in a friendly way, and praying for you' (*Corr.*, vol. X, p. 212).

d'Albufera in Louisa's affections, though she continued to receive a secret pension from the latter. On 23 March 1911 he heard of the death of Mme Léon Fould, his guardian at Saint-Moritz and the mother of his friend Eugène, to whom he wrote that he had never felt as fond of him as he did now when he was aware that he was so unhappy.[178] In the tone of the *Requiem* in *Le Temps retrouvé* he exclaimed: 'Before leaving this life or rather an existence which so little resembles life, I shall have witnessed the deaths of all those who were good, noble, generous, capable of loving and worthy of living. And those that remain I shall see grieving, wounded and weeping over tombs ever new. I am one of those who are so forgotten that people only write to them when they are unhappy, and therefore I no longer dare open a letter as there seems to be nothing but misfortune.'* He quoted Michelet to his correspondents at this time, as if he were rereading him:[179] in *La Prisonnière* he would rank him among the very great.

JEAN COCTEAU

Where did Proust meet Jean Cocteau for the first time? The latter could not remember.† Could it have been on 18 March 1910, at a dinner party given by Mme Straus, at which Proust experienced 'the refreshing sense of comparing, as in a cathedral, the carved flower with the living flower'?[180] It was in 1910, in any case, that Marcel became friendly with this 'gifted and intelligent young poet', whom he considered 'perfectly nice',[181] but who had 'the look of a siren with his delicate fish-bone nose and his fascinating eyes. And also a look of a seahorse'.[182] Together with François Bernouard, Cocteau had founded the magazine *Schéhérazade*, which was influenced by the Ballets Russes and to which France and Picasso,

---

* Ibid., p. 190, 30 October 1910. Proust had known Gangnat in Trouville in 1907 (ibid., vol. VI, p. 324, n. 4).

† *Opium*, Stock, 1930, p. 160: 'It's impossible for me to recall my first meeting with Marcel Proust. Our group always treated him as a famous person. I can see him, bearded, seated at the red benches at Larue's (1912). I can see him, without a beard, at the home of Mme Alphonse Daudet, being pestered by Jammes, who buzzed around him like a horsefly. I see him again, on his death-bed, with the beginnings of a beard. I see him, both with and without a beard, in that cork-lined bedroom, with its dust and its phials, either in bed, wearing gloves, or standing in a bathroom where something criminal was liable to happen, buttoning a velvet waistcoat over his poor square chest, which appeared to contain his clockwork spring, while he ate noodles on his feet. I see him surrounded by dust sheets. They covered the chandelier and the armchairs ... He was leaning against the mantelpiece in the drawing-room of this Nautilus ...'

Apollinaire and Émilienne d'Alençon contributed. It was there that he met Maurice Rostand, son of Edmond, a poet, and his close friend. Maurice has given us a description of Cocteau at this period: 'A little tapered brown moustache, which no one ever remembered, shaded his face. His sleekly brushed hair did not affect any form of quiff, but he already displayed that fascinating, boisterous intelligence . . .' The two young men both wore gardenias in their buttonholes, bought their shirts at Charvet's and attended the Duchesse de Rohan's salon (which the duke compared to the Gare de Lyon).* Proust and Cocteau very soon quarrelled: Jean returned one of Marcel's letters (which reminded Proust that his mother had done the same thing); Marcel suggested that they start their friendship afresh, despite Jean's 'weaknesses of character' and closed his letter with: '*Tendrement à vous*'. The older man then gave advice to his young friend: that he should isolate himself and wean himself 'from the pleasures of the mind', thereby acquiring in time 'a real hunger' for beautiful books and places, for his marvellous gifts were sterilized. However, he foresaw that Cocteau would not listen to him, since 'diet is less powerful than temperament'. The last lines of his Christmas Day letter in 1910: '*Si je t'aime/ Si tu m'aimes/ Si l'on s'aime*' [If I love you/ If you love me/ If we love one another], a quotation, give the impression of a flirt.†

Their extensive correspondence is evidence of the occasionally narrow-minded friendship that united them; nothing lay beyond this: Cocteau had too many similar tendencies to Proust – in bringing them closer together, they also set them apart – to fall in love with an older man (even if Marcel was attracted by a boy of twenty). They mixed partly in the same circles (described in Cocteau's *Portraits–souvenirs 1900–1914*), those of Lucien Daudet ('Cocteau, whom I have not seen at all, but who writes, seems to me to be "in the clutches" of Lucien Daudet, without having any idea

---

* M. Rostand, *Confession d'un demi-siècle*, La Jeune Parque, 1948, pp. 122, 136. He relates his first meeting with Proust (pp. 169–74) at Larue's in the company of Mme Scheikévitch, followed by a visit to Boulevard Haussmann: 'Everything was left lying around, his aspirins and his dress shoes; books were piled up in pyramids; ties were strewn alongside catalogues, invitation cards to the British embassy lay next to medical prescriptions and, in his extraordinary hoarse voice, Proust began to read the opening of *Du côté de chez Swann* to me!' Maurice Rostand (whom Proust, however, appears to have avoided) said he frequently went back there, neutralizing his Guerlain perfume with some essence of eucalyptus.

† *Corr.*, vol. X, pp. 231–5. From 1910 onwards, Proust, while recognizing 'his extraordinary talent', even though Cocteau had only published two slim collections, reproved him with the criticism that would always be made of him, of taking on too many things at once, of being too social.

that I know who he is'),* of Montesquiou, Anna de Noailles, Misia Edwards, Mme de Chevigné, who was Cocteau's neighbour, and later Mauriac and the Beaumonts; and they shared an enthusiasm for the Ballets Russes, as well as for Stravinsky and Picasso – Proust was introduced to his work to by the younger man, who would also take him along to the Bœuf sur le toit. They also went to the Louvre – Marcel arrived early, driven by Albaret – to see Mantegna's *Saint Sebastian*, homosexuality's favourite martyr, 'one glorious morning when the sun pierced St Sebastian with its arrows'.† They shared the same interest in aviators (Cocteau admired Roland Garros, who is mentioned in *À la recherche* in connection with the Giotto angels at the Arena at Padua).[183] Octave, in *À l'ombre des jeunes filles en fleurs*, at Balbec, was drawn principally from Plantevignes, Finaly and Bernstein. But when he displays his deficiencies of character, and then becomes a great writer, he derives equally from the author of *Le Cap de Bonne Espérance*. In the biographical details given of Octave in *Le Temps retrouvé* we recognize those of Cocteau:[184] the nitwit who was expelled from the lycée, as Cocteau was from the Condorcet, and who runs away,‡ just as he did, is based on information Jean must have confided to Marcel; the society man, so immaculate in the cut of his clothing, was someone Marcel was able to observe. In the young man who puts on little sketches 'with his own stage designs and costumes, which have brought about a revolution in contemporary art comparable at least to that achieved by the Ballets Russes', who 'could be extremely vain, a quality that can go hand in hand with genius', and who 'sought to dazzle in the way he considered appropriate to the world in which he lived', we recognize the author of *Parade* and *Les Mariés de la tour Eiffel*. But although we may do, he did not: Cocteau, who wrote a fascinating, but unfair, account of rereading *À la recherche* in his diary, *Le Passé défini*, in 1952, did not identify himself.

---

* Ibid., p. 249, 21 February 1911 to R. Hahn. And, in early March: '*The utmost* intimacy reigns between Lucien and Cocteau, who went to stay with him in the country' (ibid., p. 262, to R. Hahn).

† Ibid., vol. XI, p. 146, shortly after 20 June 1912; P. Kolb does not explain this obscure passage in the letter; the episode must have taken place at the beginning of the year, since Cocteau recited a poem from *La Danse de Sophocle*, which was not yet published, to Proust; Cocteau, *Opium*, *Le Passé défini* (Gallimard, 1983), p. 305, and *RTP*, vol. III, p. 673, when Albertine comments on this painting, in the background of which the Charterhouse of Pavia is reminiscent of the Trocadéro (a remark worthy of Cocteau), and reveals that the Narrator possesses a reproduction of it.

‡ 'In order to make his parents worried, he had gone to live for two months in the brothel where M. de Charlus planned to surprise Morel.' And if Octave becomes Rachel's lover, it may be because Cocteau had had a liaison with an actress (this information concerning Cocteau has been kindly provided by M. Jean Touzot).

In any case, in June 1912, when Cocteau published his collection of poems, *La Danse de Sophocle*, Proust told him of his own and Reynaldo's enthusiasm for them: 'It's touching to think that out of this solitary flower, as beautiful and as gentle, as innocent and as pensive as you, there could have arisen, without the stem wilting and ceasing to please and remain flexible, the vast, solid and tightly packed pillar of perfume and thought.'[185] But one year later, Proust wrote to him: 'You're an admirable person but you're not a real friend.' And he reproves him for believing that 'a look of disdain can enhance one'.[186]

1911

At the beginning of 1911 Proust's work was interrupted, or nurtured, by a variety of shows. Reynaldo Hahn was in St Petersburg working on his ballet *Le Dieu bleu* with Diaghilev; he gave a recital for two pianos on 28 February, following a banquet to which the entire Russian musical world had been invited; the music was well received, news that caused Proust to weep with emotion.[187] On 5 February, at the Marinski theatre, Nijinsky had danced *Giselle* in a costume designed by Benois which was considered too revealing; as a result, a scandal broke out, and performances were cancelled from the following day. Proust heard of this, probably from *Le Figaro* of 14 February, and wrote to Reynaldo: 'You can relay my sympathy to Vestris and to his friend for what has occurred.'* Proust condemned all forms of censorship. On 9 February Marcel went to the Vaudeville to see the last act of his old friend Hermant's play *Le Cadet de Coutras*, which was 'touching and full of wit', but which had 'a sort of mawkish sentimentality' that made him 'snivel'. He dined after the show with his old friends Flers and Caillavet. Great reader of magazines that he always was, he read Francis Jammes' poems in the *Mercure*, and, unusually, an

---

* The name Vestris, as it does in Diaghilev's correspondence, and no doubt because of Russian censorship, refers to Nijinsky. 'The friend' is Diaghilev (*Corr.*, vol. X, p. 248, 21 February, to Reynaldo Hahn). Proust added on 4 March that 'Vestris' did not interest him except as a 'victim'; Bakst, on the other hand, 'was delightful with him from the first moment', and Proust knew nothing so beautiful as *Schéhérazade* (p. 258). This leads us to think that Marcel had had the opportunity of meeting Bakst and Nijinsky in Paris in 1910, and that the latter was not very pleasant to him. In *Le Côté de Guermantes* (*RTP*, vol. II, pp. 475–9), he introduces a dancer, based on Nijinsky, who makes Saint-Loup jealous, because of Rachel; could it be that Proust had seen Nijinsky behind the scenes and that the dancer was more interested in his companion (Cocteau) than in him? Cf. draft XVII, pp. 1155–7 (Cahier 39): 'It was a celebrated and brilliant dancer from a foreign troupe ...' which contains a remarkable portrait of Nijinsky.

article by Romain Rolland on Tolstoy. Reading Maurice Donnay's lectures on Molière, he criticized the anachronisms that were supposed to be witty (like Brichot's); likewise, he did not find the style of Bernstein's play, *Après moi*, scenes from which had been published in *Le Figaro*, to be especially literary, and he considered it insufficiently influenced by Gide, whom he read in *La Nouvelle Revue Française*,* to which Bibesco had given him a subscription. But when *Après moi* was staged on 18 February at the Comédie-Française, Bernstein was violently attacked by *L'Action française* and by Royalist supporters, who criticized him because he was a Jew, and a deserter too (he had left the army seventeen months before he was due to be discharged, had fled to Brussels, and had then been granted an amnesty and declared unfit for service), so much so that after seeing Monis, the Président du Conseil, who merely made kind remarks to him, Bernstein withdrew his play on 3 March. Proust, on the side of the victim as usual, defended him, condemned 'the dirty tricks that had been played on him' and praised 'the admirable attitude he has been able to maintain'.[188] But the great novelty of the day was the 'theatrophone' – by subscribing to the service, one was able to hear in one's own home performances from the national theatres, the Variétés, the Nouveautés, the Châtelet, the Scala and the Concerts Colonne. This was how Marcel was able to listen to Act III of *Die Meistersinger* on 20 February.† For the Wagner operas, which he knew 'almost by heart' (a rare admission), it 'compensated for the deficiencies of the acoustics'.

---

* Proust considered this magazine to be 'Gide-like', and reckoned Bernstein's *Isabelle*, which was published in January, February and March 1911, to be 'of very little interest'. On the artistic level, the two writers were not made to understand one another.

† In his letter to Reynaldo, Marcel made sarcastic comments about the libretto: the writing of the Prize Song scene struck him as 'inexplicable'. In *RTP*, vol. I, p. 544, in an allusion to the end of Act I, Proust says that it is hard to understand how an artist can compose music by listening to birds warbling. In ibid., vol. III, p. 767, the work is ranked among the greatest operas. In ibid., p. 780, Proust alludes to the end of Act III and to Beckmesser's parody of Walter's song. On 21 February Hahn published a review of this production in *Le Journal*, for which Proust congratulated him (*Corr.*, vol. X, pp. 255–6), while still retaining his own opinion of the libretto. It is intriguing to see Proust, who defended Wagner against Reynaldo at Réveillon, adopt the opposite view (as regards the text, it is true, not the music).

FROM *PELLÉAS* TO *SAINT SÉBASTIEN*

On 21 February 1911 Proust listened to the whole of *Pelléas et Mélisande*, relayed from the Opéra-Comique, and sung by Périer and Maggie Teyte. He confessed to Reynaldo, who he knew did not like Debussy, that it made 'an extremely agreeable impression' and he found it closer to Fauré[189] and to Wagner's *Tristan* than people said. Knowing Debussy's build, he was surprised that he 'could have written it', 'like Goncourt being astonished that the burly Flaubert could have written such a delicate scene in *"L'Éducation sentimentale"* '.[190] He was glad to rediscover the simplicity of old songs, of French eighteenth-century opera and of Gounod's declamation. This belated revelation, for the work was already ten years old, 'rather tyrannized' him.[191] Debussy's musical drama would be mentioned frequently in *Sodome et Gomorrhe*, and it is associated with the musical tastes of Mme de Cambremer and her daughter-in-law. As was his custom, Proust immersed himself in works that he had discovered: 'I'm perpetually asking for *Pelléas* on the theatrophone, just as I used to go to the Concert Mayol. And all the rest of the time there's not a word that does not come back to me. The parts I like best are those in which there is music without words.'* And he quoted the scene 'copied from *Fidelio*' in which Pelléas emerges from the underground vault: 'There are a few lines that are truly permeated with the freshness of the sea and the scent of roses carried to him on the breeze.'† However, if music was to be no more than 'fleeting notation',‡ then he preferred Wagner, who 'expectorates everything he has within him on a subject, be it near or far, easy or difficult', which was what Proust really valued in literature. Almost as if to rid himself of the work that was obsessing him, he wrote a pastiche of it in the form of a duet and sent an extract from it to Reynaldo: Pelléas (Hahn) and Markel (a contraction of Arkel and Marcel) are searching for 'a poor little hat, of the kind that everyone wears!' He presented it as follows: 'If the reader

---

* *Corr.*, vol. X, p. 256, 4 March 1911, to R. Hahn. Cf. p. 273, to Bibesco: having fallen in love with *Pelléas*, he hurls himself upon his theatrophone every evening it is played, and on the days on which it is not performed, he takes over from Périer and sings it to himself.

† A scene described in *RTP*, vol. III, p. 212. He even pretended that the thought of roses gave him allergy attacks.

‡ 'What I hate is the refinement gained by throwing overboard everything one has to express': he would criticize the neo-classicism of France and Gide, on the one hand, and the literary impressionism of Goncourt on the other, the 'literature of notations' that is condemned in *Le Temps retrouvé*.

were to question the speedy and urgent declamation and look for the answer in the melancholy gravity of Debussy's mysterious cantilena, he would appreciate the absolute accuracy of this little pastiche not of Maeterlinck's play, but of Debussy's libretto (there is a distinction).'[192]

In March, Proust was sent *Le Roman du malade* by Louis de Robert (whom he had known since 1897 and who had introduced him to Colonel Picquart), a book which led him to formulate an important aspect of his aesthetic creed: the links between art and suffering. 'Books, like artesian wells, can only ever rise to the heights from which they have descended ... And for those who, like me, believe that literature is the ultimate expression of life, if the illness has helped you to write the book in question, people will think that you must have been only too happy to welcome the inspired collaborator.'*

Marcel went out at least twice during May. At the dance given by *L'Intransigeant*, he made the acquaintance of Princesse Marthe Bibesco. She has described their meeting in *Au bal avec Marcel Proust*: she fled from him, begging each person she danced with not to take her back to 'the place to where Marcel Proust, pallid and bearded, with his coat collar turned up over his white tie, had dragged his chair ever since the beginning of the evening'.† He therefore considered her beautiful and eloquent, but hostile, and he took his revenge a year later when he received a copy of her book, *Alexandre asiatique*, and used the opportunity to indicate where their aesthetic views differed. He did not believe that happiness was to be found in a sensation experienced in the present moment, but rather in the recollection of a sensation, in the link between the present and the past: 'If I don't stop desiring, I can never hope.'[193] This brilliant young woman (1887–1973) would outlive her various publications; she was the author of books of memoirs, including two about Proust, which is a great deal for so few encounters and a recognition that was posthumous, and of novels (*Le Perroquet vert*); she was the cousin of Antoine and Emmanuel, as well as of Anna de Noailles, and a friend of Vuillard, who painted her portrait, and of the Abbé Mugnier, about whom she wrote a book.

On 21 May Proust went to the Théâtre du Châtelet for the dress

---

* *Corr.*, vol. X, p. 271. Cf. *RTP*, vol. IV, p. 487: 'Books, like artesian wells, achieve greater heights the deeper suffering has etched itself into the heart.'

† Gallimard, 1928, p. 8. This book contains very few authentic memories; the princess, who knew Proust only very slightly and had only met him on three or four occasions, bolstered her text with letters from Proust to Antoine Bibesco, which she cut, classified incorrectly and placed in the wrong order; Antoine Bibesco's edition of the book in 1948 was equally unreliable.

rehearsal of D'Annunzio's *Le Martyre de saint Sébastien*, 'a mystery composed in the French tempo', dedicated to Barrès; the music was by Debussy, assisted by André Caplet (who conducted the orchestra). Fokine was responsible for the choreography and the décor was by Bakst. Ida Rubinstein played the leading role. Proust did not express as much enthusiasm as he had for *Pelléas*. Certainly, he admired the perfection of D'Annunzio's French and 'the sublime legs of Mme Rubinstein',[194] but the play, which lasted four hours, bored him, while the music struck him as 'pleasant, but rather sparse, rather inadequate and rather overshadowed by the subject, all the clamour, and an orchestra that was much too large for these few hollow emissions'.[195] Montesquiou, who was sitting beside Proust, was enthusiastic, however, and shook his neighbour with his outbursts to such an extent that it felt as if his seat were an electric chair.[196] The production was not a success; at the dress rehearsal not even the names were called out, and it closed after eleven performances. This evening provided a new experience for Proust, and one which would pave the way for *Le Temps retrouvé*: society people seemed to him to have 'greatly deteriorated'.[197]

In May an obscure character reappeared once more in Proust's life. Alfred Agostinelli, the mechanic who had been depicted in 'Impressions de route en automobile', was trying to obtain a job for his wife, Anna Square (in fact, he was not married, but Marcel probably did not realize this), as an usherette at the Théâtre des Variétés. Proust made enquiries on her behalf through Francis de Croisset,[198] who was now Mme de Chevigné's son-in-law ('All my dreams come back to me', he wrote upon seeing a photograph of her in *La Revue illustrée*). So we see how certain human beings can occupy initially a discreet position in a person's life, before invading it entirely, and prompt the writing of a romantic episode that would extend over three volumes; thus does the path of the model for Albertine cross that of the model for the Duchesse de Guermantes. At the same time, Proust's 'military difficulties' reared up again: he received a visit from a major in the medical corps; however, on 6 September his name would be struck off the army list,[199] although this would not prevent him from experiencing further anxieties when the 1914 war broke out. For the time being, he was relieved no longer to be 'a faulty cog, capable of harming the functioning of a corps'.[200]

CABOURG 1911

As was his wont, Proust, who was on the point of employing a shorthand-typist to whom he could dictate the corrected copy of his novel, left unexpectedly for Cabourg on 11 July. No sooner had he arrived than he sent off some humorous verses to Reynaldo, who was staying at Sarah Bernhardt's house at Belle-Île. He remembered their earlier stay there sufficiently well to be able to draw the fortifications of the Palais, and he referred to himself as *'l'autre Dioscure/ Qui n'aime pas trop les parfums'*.* He was suffering from asthma attacks at Cabourg for the first time, and for a moment he considered leaving in order to go to Doctor Widmer's sanatorium at Valmont. He also followed the course of events in the Agadir crisis,† which would feature in *Le Côté de Guermantes*. At the hotel Marcel discovered a 'highly competent' typist, Cecilia Hayward, who would type out the first 700 pages of *À la recherche*. 'Since she doesn't know French and I don't know English', he wrote wittily, but with a degree of exaggeration, 'my novel turns out to be written in an intermediary language.'[201] In fact, he employed Albert Nahmias as his secretary. He must have been revising 'Combray' at this point, and in particular the passage about involuntary memory, because he asked the art collector Gimpel about the Japanese game (we may recall that Marie Nordlinger had given him one) 'which consists of putting little pieces of paper in the water which then take on the shapes of little men'; he was trying to remember the name of the water-flowers game, and he wanted to know whether it could be done with tea and 'whether there could be *houses, trees,* or *characters'*.‡ On his table he had the catalogue of the Rodolphe Kahn collection, which had been acquired by Duveen and his son-in-law Gimpel

---

* 'The other Dioscuri/ Who does not much care for aromas'. *Tr.* (*Corr.*, vol. X, p. 314.) Hahn had not been awarded the Légion d'honneur because he had not done any military service, and on 29 July Marcel sent him the beginning of a song 'for the final act of *La Vie parisienne*', having also composed the 'pretty music', which he promised to sing to Hahn in Paris: this unexpected talent of Proust's has been unknown until now (ibid., p. 326).

† On 1 July, while French troops were intervening in a revolt in Morocco, a German cruiser appeared in the port of Agadir with the intention of protecting German property. For a time, war seemed likely, but by November the dispute had been resolved by negotiation. *Tr.*

‡ Ibid., p. 321. The passage had been drafted in *Contre Saint-Beuve* (*CSB*, p. 212); at the moment that Proust was writing to Gimpel, he used the same words as he does in the most famous passage from *À la recherche*, which therefore suggests that it had been written already and was being carefully verified. *RTP*, vol. I, p. 47; see var. *a*, p. 1124 and draft XIII, p. 696 (Cahier 8) and var. *a*, which has an earlier version.

for seventeen million francs in 1907, and resold immediately. This collector owned 'twelve Rembrandts, four Hals, possibly the finest Ruysdaël and one of the finest Hobbemas'.[202] Proust liked to back up his pictorial metaphors with precise documentation in this way. His musical enjoyment, however, suffered, for at sunset 'some large women come down to the beach and in the distance they play waltzes with hunting horns and cornets until it gets dark. It's enough to make you want to plunge into the sea with melancholy.'[203] To overcome these feelings of sadness, he amused himself by collecting clichés for Reynaldo that made one want to gnash one's teeth (these references to teeth replaced the '*louchonneries*', that left one goggle-eyed, so dear to Lucien Daudet): '*éternelle cigarette*', '*ce diable d'homme*', '*Ça a l'air bon ce que vous mangez là*', and the Plantevignes* who had '*délaissé Cabourg pour la mer de Glace*'; we come across these clichés in 'Autour de Mme Swann' or in Proust's articles. There were a few juicy anecdotes too: 'Prince Constantin Radziwill caught in the act of having his cock sucked by Lady P . . .'[†] On 16 August Proust attended the Golf Club dance, presided over by the Vicomte d'Alton, at the Grand Hôtel. Here he met Maurice de Rothschild, the Duc de Morny and his daughter, Missy, who had lived with Colette and arrived dressed as a man, the Noailles, the Bauffremonts and Maggie Teyte (who sang regularly with the casino band). Most importantly, he could at last ask François de Pâris (who told him that Lauris had never passed on Proust's pressing enquiries) for permission to use the name of Guermantes.[204] We may wonder what it was that prompted Marcel to attend dances; he provided the reason himself: 'Since I never go out, rather than going to "intimate" gatherings, I prefer the larger "bloodbaths" where among the streaming crowds one sometimes sees a face that makes one want to dream about it for a long time afterwards.'[205]

Among the newspapers and magazines he read were articles by Maeterlinck, 'La Mort',[206] and Barrès, 'Un discours à Metz'.[207] Proust criticized the former – whom he had originally admired and whose book, *L'Intelligence des fleurs*, as we know, was used in *Sodome I* – for referring to the unknowable 'as if he were talking about his bathroom'; the Infinite that he speaks about is like a forty-horse-power motor car with the brand name Mystère,

---

* *Corr.*, vol. XIII, p. 368, late December 1911, to Marcel Plantevignes: 'So, my dearest Marcel, am I totally forgotten? . . . How I missed your dear parents at Cabourg this summer!' With them, he constructed 'an indulgent mirror of the spectacle' of society.

† Ibid., vol. X, pp. 332–4. Was this the inspiration for the scene in which the Prince de Guermantes is caught off his guard in a brothel at Maineville by Charlus?

he asserted, in an image that he would reuse in the context of Wagner.[208] Anxious to establish a prior claim, he also declared that in what he himself had written about death, 'a long time ago', he maintained, contrary to the Belgian writer, that far from being a negation, death 'manifests itself in a terribly positive way'.[209] In the case of Barrès, he observed that the literary genre 'is the only possible way of making use of impressions that are more precious than it, or of truths over which you hesitate about how best to express them'.[210] This is precisely the same twofold question that Proust posed: how to introduce poetic impressions into a genre that is less precious than they are, what consideration should be given to impressions, to truths – that is to say, to psychological and social laws – and to poetry? As to *La Nouvelle Revue Française*, he was disappointed by what he read: 'They call the Tharaud brothers great writers'; the only one he liked was Claudel, 'very remarkable', 'he's a writer';[211] the admiration would not be reciprocated. In December 1911 he went back to the Goncourts' *Journal*, from which he noted down some phrases that were ambiguous ('Loti tends to rub up against all the women and all the men') or ridiculous (Daudet had asked Loti whether there were any sailors in his family: 'Yes, I had an uncle, who was eaten aboard the raft of the *Medusa*').[212] Otherwise, he reread *The Brothers Karamazov* that year, a book he thought was 'admirable';[213] the house where the crime takes place was described in what would become *La Prisonnière*.

AUTUMN 1911

On 1 October, when the hotel closed, Proust returned to Paris; he had now had an important part of his novel typed, which he had developed further in the solitude of his bedroom. And so he declared to Reynaldo, informing him that he had sent off his manuscript: 'I am writing an opuscule/ Which will cause Bourget to fall and make Boylesve recoil.'[214] No sooner had he returned, and in spite of violent asthma attacks, than he arranged for two little vanity-cases to be sent to the d'Alton daughters; he was glad to be away from the gossip-mongering of the casino, which appears to have upset him – he wished to protect himself from 'that terrible and paludal casino, where everything one did was misinterpreted by foolishness, where malice distorted it, where idleness was busy misrepresenting it, and where eternal stagnation dwells on it indefinitely'.[215] Just like the watches from Boin-Taburet that he gave as gifts the previous year, these vanity-cases were the forerunners of the one given to Albertine.

ALBERT NAHMIAS

Proust's relationship with Albert Nahmias had been strengthened at Cabourg; he had known him since 1908;[216] the following year he assured him of his constant friendship[217] and gave him advice about how to treat his mistress.[218] From the summer of 1910, he telephoned him 'on many occasions',[219] did his best to help one of his friends who was a ballerina, and met his sisters on the sea front at Cabourg. This young man, who was born in 1886, was the son of Albert Nahmias, a banker,[220] who lived at 53 Avenue Montaigne and at the Villa Berthe at Cabourg, and had been born in Constantinople in 1854, and of Ana Ballen de Guzman, who was born in Ecuador; short in stature (1 metre 63 cm), so smaller than Marcel, he would later distinguish himself in the First World War and would be awarded the Croix de Guerre; he died in Cannes in 1979. From 1911 he acted as Proust's secretary and passed on his instructions to Miss Hayward, and then later, after she had left, to a second typist: 'You have been divinely kind to me,'[221] Marcel told him at the time. Back in Paris once more, Nahmias clarified the sequence of exercise books for the young Englishwoman,* and so ensured that the 700 pages of typed manuscript which Proust would submit to publishers, and which Grasset would use to print their first galley proofs of the work under the title *Les Intermittences du cœur*, were comprehensible.[222] He was thus a highly intelligent young man, who did not hesitate to insert his own comments in the margins of the notebooks sent him by Proust.† At Cabourg he placed bets on Proust's behalf at the casino.‡ Working at the stock exchange, for a firm of stockbrokers, he carried out the instructions that Marcel preferred to

---

* *Corr.*, vol. XI, p. 25, early January 1911 (this was the description of the Bois de Boulogne). In April Nahmias spoke to Miss Hayward about the 'second consignment' (Criquebec-Balbec, Montargis-Saint-Loup, Fleurus-Charlus). Similarly, in June 1912, from Mourmelon he sent eighty-six pages to Miss Hayward that had been dictated by Proust and which correspond with the ending of the text as it had been finished at the time (that is to say, with the visit to Balbec) (H. Bonnet, 'Nahmias fils', *BAMP*, no. 35, 1985). During the summer of 1912, however, on Grand Hôtel de Cabourg notepaper, he recopied in neat handwriting passages that were so heavily corrected that they had become illegible.

† *Corr.*, vol. XI, pp. 96–8. In April 1912, for example, he noted the change of name from Montfort to Norpois.

‡ Proust also employed the services of the '*tenancier*' at the baccarat table; it was in this connection that he quoted, modifying it somewhat, a remark of Mme de Sévigné which the Narrator's mother repeats to her son in *La Prisonnière*. 'He found a means of losing without participating and of spending without making an appearance' (*Corr.*, vol. XI, p. 32).

conceal from the ultra-sensible Lionel Hauser (with whom he corresponded meanwhile, mentioning 'collapses which acting on his own had brought about').[223] To begin with, everything went smoothly: 'I am receiving crazy sums from you,' Proust wrote to Nahmias, and added '*Tendresses*' [love].[224] Losses were not long in coming, particularly the gold and copper mine shares that he had bought in early December for 400,000 francs: 'This passion for gambling, which had already manifested itself at Cabourg in the form of baccarat and does so now in a more serious way, will not last. Perhaps it is the stagnation of my solitary life which was seeking the opposite extreme.'[225] There remained his affection for Nahmias,* which Proust expressed in November: 'At Cabourg I fell into the sweet and harmful habit of thinking aloud in your presence, of allowing the little things that passed through my mind to be reflected in yours ... If only I were able to change sex, alter my age and the way I look, and take on the aspect of a young and beautiful woman so that I could embrace you with all my heart.'[226] In December he had his '*petit Albert*' call him 'Marcel'; Nahmias' Christian name would turn into Albertine.† By February 1912 Nahmias had become, as Lucien Daudet had previously, '*Mon cher petit*'.[227] He gave presents to Proust, jewels and trinkets, even an electric hot-water-bottle, which the writer refused.[228] Marcel provided a description of him in a letter: 'I seem to see beneath your centre parting the smile in your eyes on your good days, and that distension, that flaring of the nostrils, which in you is a sign of benevolence and also, when it occurs, a great embellishment.'[229] Later on, when he was to send Nahmias in pursuit of Agostinelli, he would allude to the gossip that may have harmed their reputations.

On 5 December Proust accompanied the art historian Lucien Henraux (1877–1926), who was an admirer of Berenson, to the exhibition of Chinese paintings and screens at the Durand-Ruel gallery. There he met an old dandy, 'aged and unrecognizable', with a face like 'a mask': this was Georges Rodier, a friend of Madeleine Lemaire, who told him about the hat worn by Clomesnil, the model for Odette: 'a Rembrandt hat'.[230]

---

* According to Philip Kolb, Henri Mondor, who had examined Albert Nahmias medically, said that he was homosexual (conversation with the author); bisexual would be fairer, since he was twice married. Proust could fall in love with virile men, or at least young married men: Nahmias, Agostinelli. More effeminate types, such as Maurice Rostand, did not appeal to him.

† As I have said elsewhere (*Proust*, Belfond, 1983), when people asked Nahmias whether he was the model for Albertine, he replied: 'There were several of us.'

This is a minor detail, but one which demonstrates the infinite care that Proust took over documentation, and it shows how, in trying to find China, all he found was a hat. Rodier, talking about Cocteau, resembles Legrandin issuing warnings against society life.[231] But Chinese art did not appeal to Proust and only appears in his novel on Mme Verdurin's and Odette's screens, and on the plates in the Goncourt parody, in *Le Temps retrouvé*. It was Japan, not China, that had been fashionable and had had a considerable influence on the art of the Impressionists and the Nabis; the presence of China in literature was restricted to Claudel, Segalen and Saint-John Perse.

THE NOVEL OF 1911

In 1910, a year in which Proust wrote a great deal but revealed little about his work in his correspondence, the exercise books that concern Swann, the young girls and the Guermantes began to take shape. In 1911 he decided to embark upon a further stage in the genesis of the book: if there is a novel of 1909, there is also a novel of 1911, rather like a church, the dimensions of which expand and alter over the years. The manuscript of 'Combray', of 'Un amour de Swann', and of 'Noms de Pays' was complete; Proust also produced a version of *Le Côté de Guermantes* in Cahiers 39–43, and 49. Bergotte and Elstir are in place. In 1911 a number of sketches were written for the final volume, which was to be called *Le Temps retrouvé*: M. de Charlus and the Verdurins, the death of the grandmother – later transposed – in Cahier 47; in Cahier 48, the intermittencies of the heart, the 'Vices et Vertus' of Padua and Combray; in Cahier 50, Mme de Cambremer; Saint-Loup's marriage; the conclusion of *Le Temps perdu*, which ends with the titles included in the 'summary of the third volume' in the 1913 edition of *Du côté de chez Swann*. A version of the novel that might comprise two thick volumes, rather than a single one, as in 1909, was thus ready in 1911. The first of these was almost completely typed. The second was at draft stage.

CHAPTER XIII

Le Temps perdu
(1912–13)

AN OVERVIEW OF THE WRITING PROCESS

At the end of 1911 and early in 1912, Proust arranged to have a novel of 712 pages typed out. It was the first volume, which the author planned to submit to the publisher Fasquelle in 1912. This typescript bore on its cover the words: '*Les intermittences du cœur, le temps perdu, 1ʳᵉ partie*'; in it, there appeared for the first time – it was a late addition, subsequent to the narrative – the actual first sentence of *À la recherche du temps perdu*: 'For a long time I would go to bed early.'

A real revolution in the construction of the book had occurred, which stemmed from the conclusion. In *Contre Sainte-Beuve* the book ended with a conversation with the mother: in this new novel, the grandmother, who in many respects took on the characteristics as well as the place of the mother, died.[1] It has been suggested that, once the grandmother had died, it was no longer possible to end the book in the same way. This is to confuse biography with the novel; in *La Prisonnière* it is still the mother who brings the Narrator his article; and there is nothing that would have prevented a later literary conversation. In fact, Proust had discovered another conclusion for his book. The intended ending in Cahier 51[2] concerns a '*bal de têtes*',* that is to say, the discovery that the characters in all their paint and make up had grown old, the discovery of negative and destructive time. A second version, dating from 1910–11, in Cahier 57, reworks the '*bal de têtes*': 'If I knew almost all the guests, I only recognized them as if in a dream, or at a "masked ball", relying on a simple resemblance to their identity.'[3] The third version would be that used in the manuscript of *Le Temps retrouvé* which was composed during the war.

In Cahier 57 the '*bal de têtes*' is preceded by a first part, entitled

---

* A masked ball, in which the head alone is disguised with a wig and a mask. *Tr.*

'L'adoration perpétuelle', that follows on from Cahier 58. Moreover this first part of the 'last chapter', dealing with time regained, contains the aesthetic philosophy that at the time of *Contre Sainte-Beuve* was intended to be used in a conversation, and which was now, in a far more fictional manner, the result of an experience. The eternal moment, positive Time, Time in its pure state, is thus contrasted to negative Time, just as youth is to ageing, as Parsifal is to Amfortas, for *Parsifal* was played in the salon of the Princesse de Guermantes. In fact, as in *Le Temps retrouvé*, the Narrator, who is back in Paris after a long absence, and prey to doubts about his vocation, has a series of revelations at the Guermantes' house that are induced by involuntary memory: 'No, the past, the real one, no, life was not mediocre. It had to be really beautiful for such humble sensations, assuming that life had allowed us to experience them, for a simple moment from the past to have intoxicated me with a joy that was so confident, with a joy that was so irresistible . . . A simple moment from the past? Much more perhaps; something that was common to both the present [and] the past.'[4] *François le Champi*, partially transferred to 'Combray', also enables him to rediscover his childhood. In the drawing-room, an act from *Parsifal* is being played, and the Narrator hears 'The Good Friday Spell'. Wagner would later be transferred to *La Prisonnière*, and replaced by a piece of anonymous music; Vinteuil, whose quartet was due to be performed, figures in this same section of the novel. Because he then discovers it completely, the Narrator defines his future aesthetic credo, which blends together with his moral philosophy. Some passages on Sainte-Beuve, on Ruskin, and on Bergotte would be cut from *Le Temps retrouvé*, but as a whole this is already close to the published text, whereas the '*bal de têtes*' of 1911 is very different from its final version, and it is shorter. These August 1911 developments coincided with the correcting of *Du côté de chez Swann*, and they bear out what Proust always maintained, namely that the beginning and the end of his work had been written simultaneously. The evolution of the work demonstrates that, through a phenomenon of connecting chambers, correcting the one meant correcting the other: the involuntary memories, the musical scenes, and more generally the responses to the original questions were thus transposed from 'Combray' to *Le Temps retrouvé*, and, later on, when the appendages of *Sodome et Gomorrhe* took shape, from this to *La Prisonnière*. Finally, the exercise books for 'Matinée chez la Princesse de Guermantes' reveal that at the same period, between 1910 and August 1911, the most abstract part, which is to say 'L'adoration perpétuelle', is written in a firm and virtually definitive style: Proust would annotate it with a number of comments on the left-hand pages, as he would Cahier 74, which he called 'Babouche', and which was presented to the Bibliothèque Nationale in 1985, but he would make few corrections. The '*bal de têtes*', on the other hand, which was in its second draft, following the first one in Cahier 51, would be improved still further in the final manuscript of *Le Temps retrouvé*.

The same applied to the style. None of the exercise books of 1909–11 contains the final sentence itself. In 1910, in Cahier 51, we find: 'We have no other time than that which we have experienced and once it disappears we disappear with it'; and, a little further on, after a comment about social life: 'It is true.' Finally, a portion of this exercise book is devoted to the 'Marquis de Guercy (continuation)', to Guercy, the future, fallen, Charlus: 'There was an unpleasant glint in his sad eyes, almost a look that seemed to say I am what I am, something that you know nothing about.'[5] In 1911, in Cahier 57: 'Alas! it was at the moment that a deeper self had flickered to life within me, one which I had only to entrust to a book that would live on after me, that I sensed from one moment to the next what was possible,'[6] a phrase that is replaced in the definitive manuscript by the last sentence. As to Cahier 11, a fragment of which refers to the end of the novel, the text is once more dependent on the Narrator's outburst: 'I left her, I went out.'[7]

The novel of 1911 thus consisted of one part which comprised the future *Du côté de chez Swann* and *À l'ombre des jeunes filles en fleurs*, though without Albertine, which was in the process of being typed; still in manuscript notebooks were a social section, devoted to the Guermantes, and a homosexual section, involving Charlus, who encounters the Narrator initially when he is searching for Mme de Guermantes, and later when he is looking for a girl with red roses; this part was written between April or May and September 1910, together with some additional material written in the first quarter of 1911[8] (the first part of this section, *Le Côté de Guermantes I*, was typed during the first half of 1912);* there was a journey to Italy – to Milan, Padua and Venice; and finally, an ending, which consisted mainly of Saint-Loup's marriage, the moral collapse of the future Charlus, followed by the discovery of time and artistic creation one morning at the Princesse de Guermantes' home. The manuscript was not

---

* *Corr.*, vol. XI, p. 153, 27 June 1912, to A. Nahmias. From the summer of 1912 to the spring of 1913 Proust completed *Le Côté de Guermantes*, with all the episodes we know (*RTP*, vol. II, p. 1504, note).

ready until the trip to Querqueville-Balbec had been written; the rest was in drafts that had already been planned. Now we must examine the fate that Proust hoped lay in store for this entire enterprise, and the evidence for it in his 1912 correspondence.

THE DIVISION INTO VOLUMES AND CHOICE OF TITLE

During the first six months of 1912 Proust was preoccupied mainly with two matters, the completion of the typing of the corrected manuscript, and something that he had never given a thought to since he put aside *Contre Sainte-Beuve*, namely the choice of a title. The writer had begun to realize that a single volume might not be feasible; this raised the questions of the extent of the first volume, of an overall title and one for each of the separate volumes. In March 1912 he therefore wrote to Jean-Louis Vaudoyer: 'My book will be about 800 or 900 pages long. You will have decided whether it should be in two volumes, should have two titles, and a thousand other things!'[9] and to George de Lauris: 'Should one publish a single volume of 800–900 pages? A book in two volumes of 400 pages each? Or two separate books of 400 pages, each with a different title, under the same general title; this appeals to me less, but it's what the publishers prefer.'[10] In the same letter Proust spoke of five parts, four of which were to be in the first volume, but he did not indicate what the divisions were to be in the second one. By April or May, there were to be two volumes of 700 pages each, for which he preferred – and he would not alter his mind on this – one overall title, and separate ones for each volume, as with Anatole France's *L'Histoire contemporaine*.[11] For his overall title, he drew up a very *fin-de-siècle* list, closer to *Les Plaisirs et les Jours* than to *À la recherche du temps perdu*, but all of which manifested an obsession with the past: 'The Stalactites of the Past/ In the presence of some stalactites of the past/ In the presence of some stalactites from days gone by/ Reflections in the patina/ What can be seen in patinas/ Reflections of the past/ Lingered over days. The secular beams (like those of stars)/ The visitor from the Past/ Visit from a past that lingers on/ The Past deferred/ The belated past/ The hope of the Past/ The Traveller from the Past/ Reflections of time/ The Mirrors of Dream.'[12] This deceptive and disparate list of choices shows with what care, how gradually and with what difficulty Proust switched from bad to good titles: they too have their own history and their draft versions, and they come down to us replete with unfulfilled potential.

In October 1912 Proust confided to Mme Straus that he had thought of *'Le Temps perdu'* as a title for the first volume and *'Le Temps retrouvé'* for the third.[13] Hence the last volume was named in opposition to the first, without the second, which Proust did not want, having been given a title: in fact, when he submitted the typescript of the first volume to the publisher Fasquelle, he mentioned the second part, which could be published in two volumes or in one, and which was still 'in exercise books':[14] 'Since I don't think you would allow me to put "I" on the first volume, I am giving it the title *Le Temps perdu*. If I can fit all the rest into a single volume I shall call it *Le Temps retrouvé*. And above these individual titles I shall inscribe the overall title which in the psychological sphere refers to a physical ailment: *Les Intermittences du cœur.'*[15] Here we see the appearance of the title that Proust would retain for a year and which he would eventually insert as the subtitle for a chapter in *Sodome et Gomorrhe*. The first volume consisted of three parts: 'Combray', 'Un amour de Swann', 'Noms de pays'; this final section included the journey to Bricquebec, the former Querqueville and future Balbec, but not the love story by the sea.

In response to a letter from Gaston Gallimard shortly after 5 November 1912, Proust envisaged three volumes: 'For example, overall title *Les Intermittences du cœur*. First volume, sub-title: *Le Temps perdu*. Second volume, sub-title: *L'Adoration perpétuelle* (or perhaps *À l'ombre des jeunes filles en fleurs*). Third volume, sub-title: *Le Temps retrouvé.'*[16]

1912

To return to New Year's Day 1912, it was 'such a sad day for those who are lonely', and Proust's servants arrived very late.[17] Fortunately, he did not lose sight of his one delight, his work. By paying him honoraria,[18] he still employed Albert Nahmias, from whom he demanded 'a religious concentration', in order to supervise the typing,* and also Miss Hayward,

---

* But, according to R. Brydges, there were six typescripts in all for this version of *Le Temps perdu*: 'One done in Paris, before July 1911, two at Cabourg dating from July to September 1911 (Miss Hayward and typescript B) and three, apart from Miss Hayward's, done in Paris, between the autumn of 1911 and the spring of 1912' (R. Brydges, 'Remarques sur le manuscrit et les dactylographies du "Temps perdu"', *Bulletin d'informations proustiennes*, 1984, p. 28). The very complicated instructions which Proust gave to Nahmias make us admire the 'sublime' talent, as Proust put it, with which he applied himself to the task (e.g. *Corr.*, vol. XI, pp. 86 and 87, late March 1912). He then sent Miss Hayward a document that was transcribed and paginated in sequence which she had only to type out (ibid., p. 88, early April 1912). But Proust did occasionally leave out words.

who was now in Paris and who typed out the actual pages. During the first ten days of January he reached page 560, as far as 'Noms de pays'.[19] This was why he made enquiries about spring flowers in Florence, about shopkeepers on the Ponte Vecchio and the frescoes at Santa Maria dei Fiori.* From his work he extracted 'an article on hawthorns', under the title 'Épines blanches, épines roses', which he sent to Calmette on 11 March. It would appear, under the title 'On the Threshold of Spring', a title that 'distressed' the author, in *Le Figaro* of 21 March 1912.[20] It was the first time that a passage had been published from *Le Temps perdu*, which Proust referred to, as he would to other extracts from it published in the same newspaper, as a 'little prose poem', 'an extract, but modified', a montage, with phrases inserted and passages that were not consecutive. His prepublication extracts were all put together in this way. Montesquiou kindly informed him that his article was a 'mixture of litanies and fucking', to which Proust replied with dignity, if crudely, that the most delectable expression of it that he knew occurred in Fauré's *Romances sans parole*: 'I suppose it's the sort of thing a pederast who was raping a choir-boy might sing.'† Charlus was conversing with Charlus.

On 25 March Reynaldo, who was rehearsing *Don Juan* at the Opéra-Comique, lost his mother, who had been very ill for at least a month. Marcel wanted to attend the funeral, which took place on 28 March at Saint-Philippe-du-Roule, of the woman who had 'sown seeds of beauty

---

* *Corr.*, vol. XI, p. 21; *RTP*, vol. I, pp. 379–81; draft LXXVII, p. 955 and quotation from Ruskin reproduced in *La Bible d'Amiens*, p. 70. He also took a close interest in the Agadir crisis, which would feature in *À la recherche* – a comment about the role of public opinion and press coverage of the strength of the German army would be used in the conversations about strategy at Doncières (*Corr.*, vol. XI, p. 36). And, for 'Un amour de Swann', he enquired about the Maison Dorée and Tortoni's (ibid., p. 55). He asked Montesquiou (thinking of Mme de Villeparisis and her friends) why women as well born as Mmes de Blocqueville, de Beaulaincourt, de Chaponay and de Janzé were unable to attract the 'cream' of society (ibid., p. 62). In the same letter we come across the Princesse Gortchakoff *née* Stourdza (1848?–1905), who was probably the model for the Princesse Sherbatoff. A table could be drawn up in this way, one that would be very tedious to read let alone consult, of the concordance between Proust's letters and *À la recherche*, which would show reasonably accurately the genealogy of ideas, characters and images. That is to say, how and at what point the experience had been transformed into literature.

† *Corr.*, vol. XI, p. 79, 25 or 26 March 1912. Proust was therefore making fun of him when he wrote: 'You say hawthorn [*aubépin*], with the same concern for decency as that florist of whom Mme Straus used to say: "She is so respectable that she calls herself Cambron" ' (ibid., p. 103, April 1912). [The allusion here is to the celebrated '*mot de Cambronne*'; at the Battle of Waterloo, the French general Cambronne, when asked to surrender, is supposed to have pronounced the word '*merde*', (shit). *Tr.*]

and kindness around her'. 'And now an awful attack of asthma prevents me from being able to stand up. I am going to try to treat it for I would never *in all my life* get over not coming'; failing that, he hoped to be able to go to the cemetery; but, he wrote to his friend: 'The heart of your Buncht is there beside you all the same, as invisible and present as the souls of the dead.'[21] In the spring he set off on the road to Le Vésinet to visit Montesquiou, but he stopped on the way at Rueil, braving the attack of suffocation which had just begun to afflict him, in order to look at 'the immense white altar of fruit trees in blossom', which he included in *Le Côté de Guermantes*,* and amusingly pretended that some suspicious horticulturists had mistaken him for a member of 'Bonnat's gang', the car thieves who were operating in the Paris area.

Being too ill, Marcel was unable to attend the first night of *Le Dieu bleu* on 13 May; it was based on a sketch by Cocteau and Reynaldo Hahn had composed music similar in style to that of Delibes and Massenet. The choreography was by Fokine and the dancers were Nijinsky and Karsavina. The sets and costumes were by Bakst. The ballet derived from a Hindu legend, conceived as an imitation of *The Firebird*, in which Nijinsky appeared as Krishna.[22] Was Proust present at *L'Après-midi d'un faune*, in which the choreography and Nijinsky's final pose created a scandal? Maurice Rostand in his memoirs confirms that he was. On 24 May he went to the dress rehearsal of *Sumurun*, a mime based on oriental tales written by Freksa and adapted for the stage by Max Reinhardt. He was invited by the Comtesse Greffulhe, together with Mme Standish. The latter, born Hélène des Cars (1848–1933), an 'elegant woman of the *septennat*' (that is to say from the period of Mac-Mahon's presidency), was 'magnificent in her marinated elegance, her artful simplicity'.[23] Proust asked Jeanne de Caillavet about the clothes the two women were wearing, details which he made use of in order to contrast the outfits of the Princesse and the Duchesse de Guermantes at the Opéra, 'two very different, contrasting ways of approaching dress and elegance'.†

---

* *Corr.*, vol. XI, p. 103, April 1912, to Montesquiou; cf. p. 129: 'An even more beautiful impression was gained from going out into the country at six o'clock one evening along a muddy road, and beneath a grey sky, to see some apple trees in blossom with all their frills' (*RTP*, vol. II, p. 453).

† *RTP*, vol. III, p. 61 and n. 1, draft VI, p. 970; var. *b*. p. 1390; vol. II, p. 353; *Corr.*, vol. XI, pp. 154–5. 'Mrs Standish was both one of the most striking as well as one of the most unassuming personalities in Parisian society. Her circle was exclusive. At the Court of St James she had all the right connections. She was often compared to Queen Alexandra, whose height and stature she shared. Around her neck, she wore, as the queen did, a tight-fitting necklace, known as a "choker".' Among Parisian women she exemplified '*le chic anglais*' (A. de Fouquières, *Cinquante ans de panache*, P. Horay, 1951, pp. 97–8). Proust encountered the two ladies again at a musical evening at the

Searching for the precise word to use in his descriptions, he 'thumbed through books on botany, or books on architecture and fashion magazines. But of course they never provide what I want'.[24] In another letter to Jeanne de Caillavet he declared that he was in love, like a Thomas Hardy hero, with her daughter Simone, with her beauty, her pretty smile and with the flowers whose petals reminded him of her cheeks;[25] if Jeanne Pouquet was the model for Gilberte, Mlle de Caillavet would become Mlle de Saint-Loup (and, in real life, as we know, Mme André Maurois).

On 4 June, driven by Odilon Albaret, Marcel went to the Monet exhibition at the Bernheim-Jeune gallery at 15 rue Richepanse: on display were twenty-nine 'admirable' views of Venice,[26] which the artist had visited in 1908 – the Venice that would be the backdrop to the third part of *Albertine disparue*, and which, in painting, fused with the work of Whistler and Turner, and, heavy with memories of Ruskin, would be represented in Elstir's *Salute*[27] and in Proust's 'transpositions of art'.[28] His impressions of these paintings may have helped to improve his vision of Venice, as did some of the articles they prompted. We should note that Venice already featured in his notes for *Contre Sainte-Beuve*, and that Proust took up the subject again in other *cahiers* in 1911. In a letter to Comte Primoli, who was congratulating him on his article, 'L'Église de village', Proust confirmed that he had composed a visit to Venice, in the spirit of Ruskin's attitude to domestic architecture, in which he spoke of 'some architectural masterpieces whose duty is to sum up for us the affectionate language of dear and everyday things'.[29]

On 4 June *Le Figaro* also published 'Rayons de soleil sur le balcon', a montage of some passages from the end of *Du côté de chez Swann* describing the walks in the Champs-Élysées,[30] together with a résumé of some others, and a new preamble: 'I have just drawn the curtains: on the balcony, the sun has spread its soft caresses. I shall not go outside; these sunbeams have no happiness in store for me; why should the sight of them have immediately nurtured an expectation – an expectation of nothing, an expectation unaffected by any one object, and yet, in its pure state, a shy and gentle expectation?' The response comes in the conclusion, which is also absent from the novel and was written especially for the newspaper;

Guiches on 4 July, but was 'no more able to describe them' (*Corr.*, vol. XI, p. 157). On this occasion he quoted a remark that Mme Standish had taken from Mme Récamier, and another which Montesquiou made to Maurice de Rostand, who had sent the count a very small brooch, commending it to him 'because it was a family jewel': 'I was unaware that you had a family, but I did think you had some jewels.' These pleasantries made up for months of solitude.

it is an outline of the Proustian theory of memory: 'Then the day comes when life brings us no more joys. But then the light which has absorbed them gives them back to us ... which for us is nothing more than a recollection of happiness; it allows us to savour them, both at the present moment when it shines and in the past moment it recalls, or rather in between the two, outside of time, and they truly become lifelong joys.'

On 27 June 1912 Albert Nahmias finished correcting the typescript that Miss Hayward had completed: this comprised the 712 pages of *Le Temps perdu*. 'And so, my little Albert,' Marcel wrote to him, 'our collaboration is over for a little while'; and he inscribed a copy of *La Bible d'Amiens* to him: 'To my dear collaborator and great friend as an expression of my deep affection.' But he added that he would have the next part supervised 'by the friend of whom [he had] spoken', or else directly by Miss Hayward.[31] Was it that Nahmias did not have the time to continue this work, or had he grown tired of it? Had there been a falling-out? Their relationship had lasted a long time by Proustian standards; or rather, since they were to see one another at Cabourg, was this one of those reprimands that Proust liked to send to those whom he sensed were getting tired of him? Did he want to be the first to break off the relationship?

Proust, who had most certainly not finished with the Goncourts, wrote a little-known pastiche of them in Mme de Lauris' visitors' book, in which he mocked their 'meticulous inaccuracy', their feeling that they were not appreciated, and the 'crucifixion' they had suffered through injustice.[32] Carrying on with his reading notes, he thought that Boylesve had become very dreary, whereas Barbey d'Aurevilly earned his admiration, on account of 'those particular details that are so profound, but which are so etched, almost medically so, in the flesh of all Barbey d'Aurevilly's main characters'. These comments, which come from *Le Carnet de 1908*, would be transcribed in *La Prisonnière*.[33]

CABOURG 1912

On 7 August, as if to escape the distress indecision caused him, Marcel left by train for Cabourg, together with Albert Nahmias, whom he had asked (in a tone that was chillier than formerly) to collect him and accompany him; as usual, he brought Nicolas Cottin. At the hotel he slept on the top floor, where 'terrible rainstorms' would disturb him. Scarcely had he arrived than he heard of the death of Massenet, one of the favourite composers of his youth, who brought back many memories. The discovery of Wagner and of Debussy had not meant that Proust had grown less fond of Massenet: he delighted in his grace, his originality and his naturalness.[34] Marcel made some new acquaintances: Mme Marie Scheikévitch, the daughter of a Russian lawyer,[35] who was 'perfect' for him, but whom he warned: he had no memory and forgot people he took a liking to extremely quickly![36] She may have been the inspiration for the Saint-Simon-style portrait of Mme Timoléon d'Amoncourt in *Sodome*: 'She was a charming woman, both witty and beautiful, and so entrancing that either of these qualities would have brought her success. But, born outside the milieu in which she now lived, having aspired initially merely to a literary salon, she became the friend – not the lover, her morals were of the purest – successively and exclusively of each great writer . . . chance having introduced her into the Faubourg Saint-Germain, these literary privileges served her well . . . She always had a state secret to disclose to you, a potentate to introduce you to, a watercolour by a master to offer you.'[37] Mme Scheikévitch would devote great efforts on his behalf when *Swann* was published and Proust would write an important dedication to her concerning Albertine. He also met Valentine Gross (who would marry Jean Hugo); a keen admirer of the Ballets Russes, she was to exhibit her pastels of the dancers at the Théâtre des Champs-Élysées. She also became friendly with Cocteau and Gaston Gallimard, and later with Morand and Fargue, and after the war with the Surrealists too (which explains her paintings of members of the group). Guiche, Helleu and Calmette were also staying on the coast. Marcel, who was more active this year, even claimed to 'dance a little every other day in order to loosen [his] joints'.[38]

One evening an incident occurred: Marcel had arranged to meet Nahmias on the promenade, but the latter did not turn up; Proust, who did not know that the reason for this was a motoring accident, wrote him a long, reproachful letter, which resembled those Swann sends to Odette in 'Un amour de Swann': 'You are made of water, commonplace, unfathomable, colourless, fluid, sempiternally shallow water that is constantly flowing away.' And these words ring out like a confession: 'For me, whose affection for you has been very strong, it sometimes makes me want to yawn, sometimes cry, and sometimes want to drown myself.'* This letter, which was prompted by his novel rather than the converse, gives us an idea of

---

* *Corr.*, vol. XI, p. 188, 20 August 1912. Cf. the comparison with 'rotting lilacs'; and, for the delicacy with which an invitation to a dance is foregone in order to keep a friend company, *RTP*, vol. I, p. 285.

the 'scenes' that Marcel could create among those with whom he mixed. That same evening, he none the less went to the Golf Club ball. Once the misunderstanding had passed, Nahmias was to be seen again, attired in frills, with Marcel, and with his sisters[39] on the promenade. Philippe Soupault, who was fifteen years old at the time, also encountered Proust at sunset, on the terrace of the Grand Hôtel, where a deckchair was ritually put out for him. He arrived slowly, with a parasol in one hand; the waiters walked about on tip-toe: 'They knew that the sun and noise really did "hurt" him. He was respected, he was liked.' Later on, he could be seen seated at a large table where he was entertaining: 'He spoke a great deal about himself at that period: all about the charm of coincidences, the sorrows of meeting people, the pleasure of regretting. A smile that was youthful, eyes that were so deep and so distant, movements that were slow and affectionate.'[40] Unable to go to Les Frémonts, he wrote to Mme Finaly (whom he also associated with his dream of Florence, on account of her villa, La Pietra) and showered praise on her son, Horace, the head of the Banque de Paris et des Pays-Bas, whose talents included both literature and philosophy. He would turn to him until the end of his life for financial advice and favours (notably, when he needed to get rid of one of his secretaries). Upset by the accidents caused by his friends who drove motor cars, Proust planned to hire 'the hotel motor coach' in order to visit Mme Straus. Two days before returning to Paris, he went with her to Honfleur by car, which he compared to being taken by fairies to explore the past.[41]

On 3 September *Le Figaro* published a further extract from *Swann* on its front page, 'L'Église de village', which consisted of paragraphs that had been placed in a different sequence, prefaced by a reference to Barrès, 'the admirable author of the true *Génie du christianisme*', who had just published several articles in *L'Écho de Paris* on the conservation of churches. The introduction likened the churches of one's holidays, for it was now the summer, to the churches of one's childhood. Then came a description of the church at Combray (the name is not mentioned). Proust was well aware that one article by him contained the material for ten others, as did the impression made on him by the tombstones;[42] but only he knew this. The logical link between the three articles published in this newspaper – after all, Proust could have chosen many other passages, either comic or tragic; he had chosen poetry in preference to the human comedy – lies in the seasons, the favourite landscapes, the description of family intimacy and then of adolescent love, the philosophy of memory, and the high point, the church which is the book's hidden metaphor. Was it a lucky omen for imminent publication in book form? This was what Proust, who was counting on Calmette to deliver his manuscript to Fasquelle, believed.

AUTUMN: IN SEARCH OF A PUBLISHER

Back in Paris, Proust did not complain about asthma attacks this time. On 1 October he went to hear Massenet's *Hérodiade*, a work he did not know, at the Gaîté-Lyrique. He mentions Herod's dream aria (*'vision fugitive'*) in *Du côté de chez Swann*.[43] Perhaps he intended comparing this work with Strauss' *Salomé*,[44] which, unlike Reynaldo, he admired. He wanted to invite the Vicomte d'Alton, to whose daughters he wished to give fur coats this year. In *La Prisonnière* the Narrator wants to give Albertine a fur coat and he questions the Duchesse de Guermantes on the subject.[45]

As to publishers, both Fasquelle and La Nouvelle Revue Française appealed to him equally. Calmette was his intermediary with the former, Bibesco and Copeau, who had both been Marcel's fellow pupils at the Lycée Condorcet, with the latter. Jacques Copeau, who had originally been a playwright and a literary critic, was a member of the editorial board of *La Nouvelle Revue Française* (together with Jean Schlumberger and André Ruyters, as the managing director) and later the magazine's editor, and he had been reviewing novels there since 1909 (the year when Jacques Rivière became 'secretary'). A 'book publishing branch', linked to the magazine, had been founded, which Gide, Schlumberger and Gaston Gallimard had backed, each contributing 20,000 francs; Gallimard ran the business side of the venture. The sequence of events at both publishing houses, which unfolded at the same time, reveals the inability of publishers of that period to comprehend talent that was beyond their expectations and beyond their readers, one of whom would remain unknown, while the others became famous; Proust, however, did not belong to the same world, and he did not write like them, for he wrote like nobody else.

Around 26 October Proust asked Mme Straus to remind Calmette (to whom the book was dedicated) that he had promised to arrange for *Le Temps perdu* to be published by Fasquelle.* On 28 October Calmette, who

---

* *Corr.*, vol. XI, p. 240, to Mme Straus (in which he incidentally confirms that her red dress and her red shoes, assigned to the Duchesse de Guermantes, would appear in the second volume).

had written to the publisher two days before, assured Mme Straus that Fasquelle 'would be glad to publish it [this volume]; he had his promise', without committing himself to the two following volumes.* Convinced that it had been accepted, Proust therefore submitted his typescript, alerting the publisher to the fact that one of his characters was a 'virile pederast';[46] he hoped the work would be published in March 1913, after he had added a dedication and 'a page of foreword'.[47] He arranged for a recommendation from Louis de Robert, who warmly encouraged him. All these manoeuvres had their purpose: 'I feel so strongly that a book is something which comes from ourselves and yet is nevertheless worth more than ourselves, that I find it quite natural to exert myself on its behalf, as a father would for his child.'[48] Then there was no news, in spite of a fruitless visit to Calmette, who would not see him; no more would Fasquelle, the interventions of Cocteau and of Edmond and Maurice Rostand notwithstanding. In fact the manuscript had been entrusted to a reader, Jacques Madeleine: 'At the end of this 712-page manuscript ... one has no notion – none – of what it is about. What is it all for? What does it all mean? Where is it all leading to? – It's impossible to know! It's impossible to say!'[49] On 24 December Fasquelle returned the manuscript; the book had been rejected.[50] Because Hahn had said that the publisher had enjoyed his articles, Proust wrote to Fasquelle again to suggest a collection of pieces, which would derive their unity from the relationship between the themes they developed; he would add to these his pastiches and his introduction to *Sésame*. Fasquelle would turn this proposal down too.

Meanwhile Proust reckoned that the *NRF*, to which he had already submitted articles via Bibesco, would be a medium that was 'more suitable to the maturation and the dissemination of ideas' contained in his book, and offered to publish at his own expense (which was not something that this publishing house ever considered in any case); he did not consider that the *NRF* was without faults, and he had criticized it in the past, 'but still, it is after all the only review': 'From the literary point of view I think I would not disgrace them.' He was less worried than he would be elsewhere about being criticized for indecency (regardless of the habits

---

* Ibid., p. 253, 28 October 1912. Note that Fasquelle's taste in books (he was the publisher of Flaubert, Zola and the Goncourts, of the naturalists, that is) was paradoxical. Nothing could be further from his taste than Proust, who suspected as much: 'I should like to reach a wider readership, the kind of people who buy a badly printed book before catching the train' (ibid., p. 292).

of Gide and Henri Ghéon, the poet and playwright, the *NRF* had always asserted its hostility to bourgeois morality), and in order that Bibesco could relay his remarks, he expounded his concept of style: 'My deep-down, thought-out, innermost impression I'm careful to conceal among a dozen others in an unemphatic style beneath which, I am confident, discerning eyes will one day discover it.'* As Copeau had informed Proust that the manager of the publishing house was Gaston Gallimard,[51] in early November Marcel tried to contact Gaston (whom he had come to know after meeting him on the Normandy coast in 1908). Shortly after 6 November he sent him the second typescript of *Le Temps perdu*, as well as some extracts from it which he submitted to Copeau,[52] for the *NRF*, which the latter would refuse to publish. Writing to Gaston Gallimard soon after 5 November 1912,[53] Proust originally envisaged two volumes, and he put a number of technical questions to him. The publisher responded in the following terms on 8 November: '1. We can produce books of about 550 pages – of 35 lines – and with 50 characters to each line. Several novels have already appeared on our list that have 33 lines to the page. 2. I think the book could be put on sale in March, or perhaps 15 February – as far as the first part is concerned – and the rest of it in May. 3. It would seem to me truly indiscreet not to acknowledge your right to dedicate your book to whomsoever you wish. Forgive me once again. I should be truly put out if you had not thought of me as a publisher. And, I insist, I should be happy to see you again and to apologize personally, and at the same time collect this typescript even if it means coming myself.'[54] Proust was delighted at this reply, which seemed to suggest an agreement. Yet while he was expecting his book to be brought out by Gallimard, it appears that the publisher yielded to the decision of the reading committee of *La Nouvelle Revue Française*, which was led by Gide and supported by Drouin, Schlumberger, Ruyters and Copeau.† Was the manuscript read? Gide is

---

* *Corr.*, vol. XI, shortly before 25 October 1912, to A. Bibesco. Cf. 'And from impassioned hours, all that remains is a single phrase, sometimes only an epithet, and an overall sense of calm.'

† See A. Anglès, *André Gide et le premier groupe de 'La Nouvelle Revue Française'*, Gallimard, vol. II, 1986, pp. 390–93. Jean Schlumberger, an influential member of the committee, and owner of one third of the capital assets at the time, never disguised his opposition to publication, while at the same time trying to exonerate Gide: 'I maintain that no one, neither Gide, Gaston, Copeau nor I had read the manuscript. At the most, we picked out, here and there, a sentence that looked discouraging. The book was rejected because of its enormous size and because Proust had a reputation as a snob.' (A. Gide–J. Schlumberger, *Correspondance*, Gallimard, 1993, letter from J.S. to J. Lambert). Ruyters' remark is quoted by Anglès, *André Gide*, p. 1080. Cf. J. Schlumberger, *Éveils*, op. cit., p. 216.

said to have been mainly to blame. Schlumberger, like Auguste Anglès, saw it rather more as a collective responsibility: a Right-Bank socialite, who used long and flowery sentences, who had written an interminable book, 'badly composed, badly written' (said Ruyters), did not suit the tastes of these gentlemen, who longed for brevity and concision. On this occasion, there was not even a written report; the deed was done speedily; there was no attempt to justify the unjustifiable. Years later Gaston Gallimard would assure Proust that he had had nothing to do with this decision, because he had not been in charge of the publishing house at the time.[55] Gallimard returned *Le Temps perdu* to Proust around 23 December: the NRF had decided not to publish the book.[56]

This explains why, shortly after 24 December, Proust asked Louis de Robert if he would take his book to Ollendorff, pointing out that he would offer to have it published at his own expense;[57] the choice of this publisher, whose list consisted mainly of books on nature study, was scarcely a fortunate one; his response was to become famous.

Marcel twice accompanied Mme Straus to shows over this period. On 16 November they attended the first night of *L'Habit vert*, written by his friends Flers and Caillavet, at the Variétés; and on 17 November they went to the dress rehearsal of *Kismet*, an 'Arab fairy tale' by Knoblauch, which had been a huge success on the London and New York stage, and which had been adapted by Jules Lemaître and sumptuously produced by Lucien Guitry. Much to his embarrassment and to the despair of his manservant, however, Marcel absent-mindedly wore a dinner-jacket instead of his tails. Their companion, Jacques Bizet, had an altercation with a M. de Pierredon, which provided Proust with the idea for Saint-Loup's quarrel with a journalist at the theatre, and the evening was spent in a commotion, with Marcel seeing nothing of the show.* Escorting Mme Straus backstage, because she wanted to speak to Guitry, he encountered a 'trembling old boy from the *Oresteia* with a charming face': it was Lemaître; this was yet another scene which foreshadowed *Le Temps retrouvé*, particularly since Proust imagined that people he once knew no longer recognized him, 'age and illness having superimposed a mask over [his] features'.[58] However, around 20 November he asked Lauris to take him to see the

---

* *RTP*, vol. II, p. 478. *Corr.*, vol. XI, pp. 316, 318, 336: 'So Guitry', Marcel wrote wittily, 'was fortunate enough to have a clown and a swordsman in this curtain-raiser.' Bizet was to fight a duel with Pierredon on 20 December in which there was no clear outcome.

Henri Rouart collection of art. Born in 1833, Rouart was a painter, an industrialist, a great lover of paintings, like his brother Alexis, and a friend of Degas; he owned a few works by Chardin, Fragonard, El Greco and Goya, but had specialized in French painting of the second half of the nineteenth century: in the 1912 sale there were forty-seven Corots, eight Courbets, four Rousseaus, four Boudins, some *Baigneuses* and two still-lifes by Cézanne, some works by Degas, some Monets (*Les Bords de la Seine à Argenteuil, Effet d'hiver à Argenteuil, Le Champ de foire*) and some Renoirs (*Au bois de Boulogne*).[59] The collector had died on 2 January 1912, and the sale was planned for 9, 10 and 11 December (paintings, old and modern); 16, 17 and 18 December were set aside for drawings and pastels, both old and modern. One can understand why the creator of Elstir should have wanted to see this gallery again before the collection was broken up.* On this occasion Proust reminded René Gimpel that he had been unable to see the Rodolphe Kahn collection; but he may have seen the catalogue. (Gimpel was marrying the daughter of Duveen, the celebrated art dealer; Proust's thoughts were for the sadness of René's mother, Mme Gimpel, who was about to lose her son!) On 3 December, having taken care of himself for a week so that he could go to the Salle Gaveau in order to hear the Capet Quartet play Beethoven[†] – this music and the chamber group would play an important role in his artistic life, in terms of music, and imagining Vinteuil's work – an attack of asthma prevented him from getting out of bed.

BEGINNING AGAIN

After this end-of-year period which was always a sad time for him, particularly on this occasion, overshadowed by the double failure of his dream of being published, Proust would undergo a darker period still, and although 1913 would see the appearance in print of his most famous book, this victory would seem shrouded in melancholy.

On the advice of Louis de Robert, Marcel sent the typescript of his novel to Humblot, the managing director of the Ollendorff publishing

---

* In the end he was unable to go to the sale (*Corr.*, vol. XII, p. 43); but he must have read everything that was written about it.

† Quartets nos 8, 11 and 14. Capet is mentioned in *RTP*, vol. III, p. 791, at the same time as Enesco and Thibaud. See also ibid., vol. I, p. 522, n.1 (the quartets are also mentioned in vol. II, p. 110; vol. III, pp. 39, 346, 398). Proust would not be able to hear the Capet Quartet play Beethoven until February 1913.

house. Never one to bear grudges, on 14 January he went to the offices of *Le Figaro* to give Calmette a cigarette-case he had ordered from Tiffany's: 'I did it for my own sake,'* he said, and indeed Calmette never even thanked him: 'I cast a glance at the box containing my cigarette-case: *Love what you will never see a second time*.'⁶⁰ He also went to call on Emmanuel Bibesco to try to have extracts from *Du côté de chez Swann* published in the May issue of the *NRF*.† Copeau would turn him down:⁶¹ we forget, when the NRF's decision to reject *Swann* is justified on the grounds that the book was too expensive to produce because of its length, that the same argument does not hold for a magazine extract. Proust also suggested to the literary supplement of *Le Figaro* that they publish the cab episode from 'Un amour de Swann', followed by 'A Dinner Party at Mme Verdurin's' and 'Music in Society'; Chevassu, who was responsible for this section of the newspaper, would not agree to anything. Marcel Prévost (to whom letters intended for Proust were sometimes sent accidentally) also turned down an article about Barrès' *La Colline inspirée*, which had just been published, for *La Revue de Paris*.⁶² This explains why Proust eventually began to wonder whether he was right to want to publish his book, since he was 'in such profound disagreement with the less foolish of [his] contemporaries'.⁶³

Around 15 February, he was still thinking of putting together a collection of articles for Fasquelle, while at the same time revealing his sorrow 'at having contemporaries who were so severe and so unaccommodating' and asserting that he no longer had much self-confidence 'since everybody continues to refuse to publish anything' by him.‡ From this stems the following passage in *Le Temps retrouvé*: 'Soon I was able to show a few drafts. Nobody understood any of it.'⁶⁴ It was at this moment that he learned of the rejection of *Swann* by Humblot, the managing director of Ollendorff, which was expressed in insulting terms in a letter to Louis de Robert: 'I may be as thick as two short planks, but I fail to understand why a chap should require thirty pages to describe how he tosses and

---

* *Corr.*, vol. XII, p. 27. This letter is characteristic of Proust's humour, which consisted of making fun of himself and laughing at anything sad: 'I have a thousand sad or comic stories (they're the same one depending on your point of view) to tell you. And one of the ridiculous characters about whom I could tell you some idiotic tales is myself.'

† Ibid., p. 31, 16 January 1913, letter from Emmanuel Bibesco to J. Copeau. Note that *La Revue de Paris* and *Le Journal* also turned down extracts from his book.

‡ *Corr.*, vol. XII, p. 70; he asked Mme de Noailles whether she possessed any of his articles or introductions which he had not kept. She sent them to him immediately. Proust then suggested that he accompany her to Florence, where he had always dreamt of going: 'Sometimes I might get up at nine o'clock in the evening and you could tell me what it was like' (ibid., p. 74).

turns in bed before falling asleep.' At which Proust exclaimed: 'Here is a man . . . who has just had 700 pages to consider in which, as you'll see, a great deal of moral experience, thought and pain have been not diluted but concentrated, and he dismisses it in such terms!'[65]

Straight away, with that marvellous ability to bounce back that was so characteristic of him – 'When we find ourselves circumscribed by life,' he would write, ever hopeful, 'intelligence finds a way out' – he decided to ask René Blum, a close friend of Grasset, the publisher whom he had known in the Quartier Latin, whether the firm would publish his novel at the author's expense; this condition was intended to ensure immediate publication, without any prior discussion.* 'I believe,' he told René, 'that the work . . . will one day do him honour.' Blum discussed the matter with Grasset, who agreed to the proposal.

BERNARD GRASSET

When Grasset[66] arrived on the French publishing scene, it still belonged in the nineteenth century. With the exception of Zola, Maupassant and Daudet, a first-rate novel sold two thousand copies. Grasset was someone whose flair, energy and introduction of modern, creative methods helped to revive the industry, and he put together a list of some of the most important contemporary writers, from Giraudoux and Morand to Mauriac, from Cocteau and Montherlant to Malraux. His father had been a solicitor in Chambéry, had written a book on Joseph de Maistre, and had died when his son was fifteen years old; Bernard would not remember his childhood as a happy one. He studied law at Montpellier, where his uncle, a famous neurologist, lived, took his degree in 1901 and was called to the Bar; he was a follower of Maurras, as well as being an anti-Dreyfusard. After his mother died in 1906, he moved to Paris in 1907 and set up a publishing house, in the rue Gay-Lussac, because his friend Henri Rigal

---

* Ibid. In case this should fail, he had envisaged two other possibilities: to publish in *Vers et prose* or to apply directly to a printer. Proust wrote to Blum around 20 February and told him about his book. René Blum, who was born in 1878, was the younger brother of Léon, assistant editor of *Gil Blas*, and later the artistic director of the Ballets de Monte-Carlo, as well as the author of *Comment parut Du côté de chez Swann* (Kra, 1930). He died a victim of the Germans in Auschwitz in 1944. Proust had known him through Bibesco since 1902: 'Yesterday evening I spotted your friend M. R. Blum, svelte, pink-faced, shy, smiling and curly-haired, like a Hippolytus from the best period of Greek sculpture' (*Corr.*, vol. III, p. 102, 17 August 1903). P. Kolb reckons him to be one of the models for Bloch.

had been unable to find one for his novella *Mounette*. The first titles to appear are totally forgotten today. He employed Louis Brun as his assistant, who would always remain loyal to him, and he published books at the author's expense, which was common practice at this time. He was on friendly terms with two publishers whom he admired: Péguy and Valette. His first important title was a book by Giraudoux, *Provinciales*, in 1909, which was followed, no more successfully, by *L'École des indifférents*, in 1911. In 1910 he acquired premises at 61 rue des Saints-Pères, where he published his first big success, *À la manière de . . .* , a collection of pastiches by Reboux and Muller. Later came *Monsieur des Lourdines* by Alphonse de Châteaubriant, which was awarded the Prix Goncourt in 1911. Grasset launched his books using a strategy that he had refined, which involved publicity, press advertising and approaching influential contacts: Proust would take full advantage of his methods. In 1913 came *L'Enfant chargé*, a first novel by François Mauriac (who would have preferred the NRF). A brilliant publisher whose early fortunes, involving both successes and failures, were mixed; an unstable character afflicted by incurable psychological problems – such was the person with whom the author of *À la recherche* entered into discussions; they were never to become friends. Grasset did not take part in the 1914 war, any more than Gallimard (or Proust) did: in September he collapsed and was to spend the next two years living in nursing homes or hotels. His publishing house remained dormant until 1917, which would provide Proust with an additional reason for changing publishers. The delicate negotiations that took place in 1916 and the compensation that Grasset insisted upon were to earn him a rather unflattering mention in a late addition to *Sodome*: 'A famous Paris publisher who had come to call and who expected to be invited to stay, left abruptly and speedily, realizing that he was not smart enough for the little clan. He was a tall, well-built man, very dark and studious, with a trenchant look about him. He reminded one of an ebony paper-knife.'[67]

On 24 February 1913 Proust wrote to Grasset to ask for a contract, to offer him a percentage on sales while retaining the ownership of the book, and to tell him that he was sending him the manuscript of the 'first volume', *Le Temps perdu, Première partie*; the second, to be published 'ten months later', which only existed in 'illegible drafts', would be entitled *Le Temps perdu, Deuxième partie*,[68] 'since in reality it's a single work'. Then the negotiations took place. Marcel was hoping for a low-priced book (3.50 francs): 'My financial interest is less important to me than the infiltration of my ideas into the greatest possible number of minds susceptible to receiving them.' He very much hoped for a book that was legible (35 lines per page and 45 or 50 characters per line), without exceeding 700 pages (the book would contain 523 pages of 36 to 38 lines per page, and 52 letters per line). Proust was then sent a draft contract, which he returned on 11 March, along with a first payment of 1,750 francs; he would earn 1.50 francs for every book sold at a price of 3.50 francs. In order to preserve his independence, he would later be induced to pay for the additional typesetting costs, incurred by his making corrections at proof stage, as well as the publicity expenses (many of the press releases, paragraphs in newspapers and short articles that appeared at the time were paid for). Having been shown sample copies, he continued to discuss typefaces – he wanted the typesize to be larger (though he was finally obliged to give way) – as well as the size of margins and the paper.

As for Proust's artistic life, which his problems with publishers had not succeeded in stifling, on 31 January 1913 he slipped his fur-lined cloak over his night-shirt and set off to inspect the St Anne portal of Notre-Dame de Paris, 'where for eight centuries there has been a much more charming spectacle of humanity than the one to which we are accustomed'.[69] Émile Mâle had observed that the rows of statues of the kings of France represented the kings of Judah, the blood ancestors of Jesus; Proust transferred these statues to the porch of the church at Balbec, putting Mâle's observations into the mouth of Elstir.[70] He set off to see the apostles and the stained-glass windows of the Sainte-Chapelle again for much the same reason; he also went to look at the house of Nicolas Flamel.* Despite the search for a publisher, therefore, he did not stop writing. Another experience which he made use of in *Le Temps retrouvé* was when he went to call on Comte Clary, who was partially paralysed and blind, just as Charlus would be. And in the evenings, he never forgot music. Listening to *Fervaal* by Vincent d'Indy on the theatrophone around 30 January, he found it very boring, 'of excruciating dryness', apart from 'the delightful entr'acte' and the 'more Mendelssohnian than Schumannesque' prelude to the third act, which had 'a certain musical resemblance to the phrase from Fauré's sonata for violin and piano';[71] we know that this phrase is one of the models for Vinteuil's 'little phrase'. On 26 February, at the Salle Pleyel, he heard the Capet Quartet play Beethoven's Fifteenth, Sixteenth and Seventeenth Quartets (or Great Fugue).[72] Apart from the

---

* 51 rue de Montmorency; tablet inscribed 1407, rebuilt in 1900 (*Corr.*, vol. XII, p. 52).

usual pleasure he derived from the music (for, if he lived for his work, he also enjoyed life), he must have retained elements of it for Vinteuil's work (he had then begun to make notes for what would become the septet – as with Franck, it had first been a quartet, a quintet[73] and then a symphony);[74] in particular it must have helped define his overall aesthetic philosophy: the comments on music in his novel are as plentiful as the actual musical scenes. He was now able to listen to symphonic concerts on the theatrophone: 'I can now be visited in my bed by the birds and the brook from the *Pastoral Symphony*, which poor Beethoven enjoyed no more directly than I do since he was completely deaf.'* On 19 April he went to the Salle Villiers, in rue du Rocher, to hear Franck's sonata 'which he so loved' played by Georges Enesco and Paul Goldschmidt: 'I thought it admirable; the sorrowful twittering of his violin and the wailing calls answered the piano, as if from a tree, from out of some mysterious foliage.'[75]

Since it was springtime, he also dreamt, after a stay at Valmont's clinic, of going to Florence (as in 'Noms de pays') and he read *Quinze jours à Florence* by André Maurel.[76] On 25 March *Le Figaro* had published his article 'Vacances de Pâques',[77] probably at Calmette's insistence, since the newspaper had turned down Proust's earlier offers; the main theme was a reverie on the name of Florence and travelling in Tuscany. In it he interwove condensed passages from *Du côté de chez Swann* with pages from *La Prisonnière*, also abridged – the opening and the street cries of Paris – with *Fervaal*, which he had just heard again,[78] and with his reading matter: books about Florence, *L'Annonce faite à Marie* (*NRF*, December 1911–April 1912) and 'the admirable work of the great poet Francis Jammes', whose impressionism and sense of imagery had always enchanted him;† it was not without malice that he mentioned him, for Jammes was now involved in Copeau's magazine.

That same spring, Proust, always attracted by speculation, made heavy losses on the stock exchange[79] and believed that he was 'ruined'. However, he discussed it all humorously: 'I need only make a financial speculation

* *Corr.*, vol. XII, p. 110; words used again in *Swann*, and he added: 'They are also pastoral symphonies which I make up in my own way by depicting what I can no longer see!' The *Pastoral Symphony* is mentioned in *RTP*, vol. II, p. 850.
† *Corr.*, vol. XII, p. 125, to Mme Daudet, who invited him to a matinée in honour of the poet on 3 April: 'The feeling I have for his work, which expresses itself in readings and daily meditations, is a fact of my existence . . . My manservant returns home with an air of triumph if he has bought me a newspaper or a magazine in which there is something by Francis Jammes.'

in order for the king of Montenegro to choose the day it clears to refuse to give back Scutari.' That was why he refused to put money into the firm of stockbrokers that Albert Nahmias was considering setting up; he would be too worried thinking about the fate of this sum, however modest it was. He took the opportunity to inform his 'dear Albert' that he lacked wisdom and calm: 'Though one can like someone whom one does not think is reasonable very much.'[80]

On 21 May music once again dragged him from his bed, dressed in his fur-lined cloak and with an eight-day growth of beard, to see *Boris Godonov,* produced by Diaghilev* and sung by Chaliapine, at the Théâtre des Champs-Élysées. He would make use of the experience in *La Prisonnière* when depicting the noises of the Paris streets, referring to the 'scarcely lyrical' declamation, the recitatives 'in the music – so very popular – of *Boris,* in which an initial tonality is barely altered by the inflexion of one note leaning upon the next, a music of the crowd that is more language than a piece of music'.[81] On 29 May he attended the first performance of *Le Sacre du printemps,* Nijinsky's extraordinary ballet, in which he danced with Karasavina to a score by Stravinsky that has remained his masterpiece; the stage sets were by Bakst. Marcel dined at Larue's with the composer, Diaghilev, Nijinsky and Cocteau.† Nobody could have taken greater advantage of his rare outings than Proust did: 'The passionate love [that he had] for things, which may in fact have been over-stimulated by privation' was accompanied by a pleasure that he never expected,[82] and which came as an additional reward.

---

* According to P. Kolb, on 17 May Proust saw Nijinsky dance in *L'Après-midi d'un faune,* in the new season of the Ballets Russes. And, if we are to believe Maurice Rostand, the dancer, 'who, once he had had his make-up removed, became . . . a Russian urchin with a dreamy air', came to have supper with Proust and himself at Larue's (*Confession d'un demi-siècle,* La Jeune Parque, 1948, p. 175). Yet this ballet was not performed in 1913 (see R. Buckle, *Diaghilev,* London, Weidenfeld and Nicolson, 1979, p. 249 ff.); that year Nijinsky danced in *Jeux* and *Le Sacre du printemps, Le Spectre de la rose* and *Prince Igor.*

† *Corr.,* vol. XII, p. 12. I have not discovered any further evidence of Proust's presence at this historic dinner party, and it is surprising that it is not mentioned elsewhere. See Buckle, *Diaghilev,* p. 252 ff.; according to Kolb's sequence of events, Proust may also have attended the performance on 15 May, which consisted of *Jeux,* a ballet by Nijinsky danced to music by Debussy.

AGOSTINELLI

For some time Marcel had been complaining in his letters that, emotionally, he had 'a great deal of sorrow',* adding that he did not have sufficient strength to face up to happiness. The fact was that at the beginning of the year his former 'mechanic' from Cabourg, Alfred Agostinelli, who had lost his job, had come to ask Proust to employ him as his chauffeur.† Proust did not want to hurt Odilon Albaret by giving his job to someone else. Probably because he was struck by the physical and mental changes that had come over Agostinelli, he suggested, 'without much confidence', taking him on as his secretary, 'to type out his book'. At the same time he took him under his roof, along with Anna, his wife or companion. 'It was then,' he told Émile Straus, 'that I discovered him, and that he and his wife became an integral part of my existence.'[83]

Who was Alfred Agostinelli? 'An extraordinary person who possessed perhaps the greatest intellectual gifts I have ever known!' said Proust, shocked with grief at his death.‡ 'An unstable boy who had ideas above his station', according to Céleste Albaret.[84] Originally from Monaco, he had worked with Odilon, who considered him 'a nice boy', both there and in Cabourg, in the taxi company run by Jacques Bizet. Having left the firm, he had returned to Monaco, where he had met his girlfriend Anna (whom he called 'Nana'), and soon lost his new job. He was then twenty-five years old. 'Out of kindliness and goodness, M. Proust agreed to take him into his home. He lodged there with Anna.' The couple took their meals outside. In the spring of 1913 the two couples (Odilon Albaret married Céleste Gineste on 27 March 1913) went to spend the day in the forest of Fontainebleau. While the men recounted stories about taxis,

---

* Ibid., p. 70: 'At present I am overwrought by sorrows' (mid-February, to Mme de Noailles); p. 109: 'All my troubles might be a little less cruel if I were to tell you about them' (mid-March, to Mme Straus); p. 212, June 1913. Cf. p. 214: 'some great sorrows I have endured this year and which I still have' (late June); 'life is so cruel for me at the moment' (July, to Cocteau).

† An ironic detail: in July Proust tried to find employment for Ulrich, 'who is dying of hunger', as a chauffeur at Mme Bizet's home (ibid., p. 236).

‡ *Corr.*, vol. XIII, p. 228, 3 June 1914. P. Kolb finds this assertion 'exaggerated' and compares it with *Albertine disparue*. 'I had certainly known people of greater intelligence. But the infinitude of love, in its egoism, means that the people whom we love are those whose intellectual and moral physiognomy is least objectively defined for us; we endlessly alter them according to the whim of our desires and our fears, we do not separate them from ourselves, they are but a vast and vague space in which we exteriorize our affections' (*RTP*, vol. IV, p. 77; *Corr.*, vol. XIII, pp. 229–30, n. 3).

Céleste got 'horribly' bored. Anna was ugly (Odilon called her 'the flying louse') and 'not very pleasant'. According to Odilon, Agostinelli took himself very seriously as a secretary; Proust had bought him a typewriter, which would end up – a sad symbol – next to the till at Larue's. After a while, this job was not sufficient for him: passionate about anything mechanical, he switched from the motor car to aviation. Proust offered him flying lessons at Buc airport, and had Albaret drive him there.

In the rare photographs that survive, Agostinelli appears as a handsome, dark-haired young man, with intelligent, dreamy brown eyes, and a full face. His family 'was not a patch on him':[85] there was Anna, who was ugly and jealous of her friend's adventures; a sister, who was the mistress of the Baron Duquesne, about whom Proust would request information;[86] a brother, Émile, who was a chauffeur; a half-brother, who was a hotel waiter; and a father to whom he would promise money: all people 'with whom one can fairly easily have difficulties'[87] and to whom Alfred may have sent a portion of the money that his employer so generously provided. What was his relationship with Marcel? The sorrows that the latter refers to from the spring of 1913 leave us in no doubt; caught in a trap, he had fallen in love with his secretary, and he would one day say as much to Reynaldo: 'I really loved Alfred. It's not enough to say that I loved him, I adored him.'[88] Rather curiously, just as with Caillavet, Albufera, Bibesco and Nahmias, the female relationships of the beloved were not an obstacle to Proust: he preferred virile men. Since his physical relationships were few, or even non-existent, the presence of Anna was no more of a hindrance than was that of Céline Cottin. Proust, who endured emotional and sexual loneliness and even misery, was thus the victim of one of those phenomena of the crystallization of love that he himself described. Since physical possession, 'in which one possesses nothing anyway', was far less important than mental possession, he quickly wove threads of dependence around the beloved, like a spider in the centre of its web. One can imagine Agostinelli having to undergo long interrogations that were intended to soothe the jealousy that, for Marcel, was inseparable from love, and the blackmail he subjected Proust to in return: money, presents, flying lessons, and finally an aeroplane. At the same time Proust required that confidential letters addressed to Agostinelli should be secured with sealing-wax.

CABOURG 1913

Such was the man whom Proust brought with him to Cabourg, together with Nicolas Cottin and Anna, on 26 July. Like a bad omen, the journey was 'dreadfully disrupted', for they took a wrong turning: it was five o'clock in the morning before they arrived at the Grand Hôtel, to which Marcel was returning for the sixth year running and where he was very comfortable.[89] But shortly afterwards, he thought of returning to Paris for a few days. On 4 August, while he was on a visit to Houlgate with Agostinelli, he suddenly decided to catch the train to Paris with the young man (who, noticing that he looked very sad, had advised this himself),[90] 'without any of his things, without luggage' and without having told the hotel that he was leaving: from a café he sent word to Nicolas, who would rejoin them with Anna a few hours later. To explain this departure, which was the result of a fit of anxiety, we have only a confidential note, probably misconstrued, addressed to the Vicomte d'Alton, who must have been shocked by what he read: 'A propos Agostinelli, I think I told you that he was in a delicate situation as regards someone whom both you and I know . . . But since, in any case, you don't know to whom I was referring, so as to avoid any dangerous gaffes, I should prefer that you tell no one that I have employed Agostinelli as my secretary, in other words not mention his name to anyone.'[91] Proust therefore wanted to hide Agostinelli and distance him from someone's amorous advances. In *La Prisonnière* the Narrator decides to leave Balbec and to return to Paris with Albertine once he discovers that she knows Mlle Vinteuil and especially her lady friend.[92] There was a similar recommendation to Nahmias: 'Avoid speaking about my secretary (the former mechanic). People are so stupid that they may see (as they did with our friendship) something pederastic about it. It would not matter in the least to me, but I should be upset if I caused the boy any harm.'[93] However much Marcel called his correspondent '*mon cher petit Albert*', whom he regretted not seeing at Cabourg and 'embracing tenderly with all [his] heart', the peak of their relationship had passed. Let there be no mistake about this: he did not deny the 'pederastic character' of this friendship, he simply did not want it spoken about; equally we should understand that Proust's reputation was already solidly established, that it reflected on his companions, and that he was aware of this.

In Paris he regained a certain calm: at Cabourg he had 'felt far away and anxious'; here he was on firm ground once more. Having considered setting off again, his health became so bad and he had lost so much weight[94] (thirty kilos, he would say, which, in his case, was impossible; besides, how did he weigh himself? Yet love and jealousy also transformed Swann) that he gave up the idea. However, he did shave off his beard – 'so as to alter my features a little for the person I have met again'.[95] On 11 August he dined alone at Larue's, but he saw the Princesse de Poix's son,* Charles de Noailles, there, accompanied by two young aristocrats, one of whom was the Prince de Chimay: one of Saint-Loup's friends was the Prince de Foix (whose father was an habitué of Jupien's brothel). At the end of the month he sent the proofs of his book to Lucien Daudet, without 'the last-minute improvements'; the latter immediately professed his 'admiration'. In early September Proust informed him of his intention of adding to the ending of *Swann* 'a few pages which come further on', concerning the walk in the Bois, but he asked Lucien whether he would prefer 'Rayon de soleil sur le balcon';[96] Vinteuil, meanwhile, has already been transformed into a single character: 'I thought it more effective to depict Vinteuil as an old beast first without allowing anyone to suspect that he's a genius, and in the second part refer to his sublime sonata.'† He had also envisaged the marriage of Mlle Swann and Robert de Saint-Loup 'in the third volume'. Equally, he took advantage of his new amorous experiences to add 'some very important little incidents that tighten the knots of jealousy around poor Swann';[97] the fact was Proust was once more overcome by 'an immense and unremitting grief'.[98] The demands for money on the part of his secretary prompted him, in order to 'pay him what was due' to sell 'telegraphically' half of a Royal Dutch share,‡ or at least 6,000 francs worth of one.

Reading André Beaunier's *Idées et les hommes* inspired some important reflections, similar to those in the published passages of *Contre Sainte-Beuve*, which herald the articles he wrote in the 1920s. Proust pointed out that, true to the whims of fashion, everybody was 'unfair these days' about

---

* A friend of the Duchesse de Guermantes (*RTP*, vol. II, pp. 493, 498). Proust confused the issue by including the fictional character (Foix) as well as a character with the real name (Poix) (*Corr.*, vol. XII, p. 269).

† *Corr.*, vol. XII, p. 259. He also told him about his scruples concerning flowers and even chickens. Cf. p. 271, to L. de Robert: 'I shall add only five or six pages from the middle of the second volume, which will create a slightly more extended climax'; this passage, as we have seen, was to do with the walk in the Bois.

‡ Ibid., p. 274. Finally, he sold an entire share. In 1906 he had said of these shares that it was the first time that he had made money (ibid., vol. VI, p. 197); in 1912 he asked L. Hauser to buy two more for him (ibid., vol. XI, letter 145). The sum of 6,000 francs would be about 132,000 francs by 1999 standards.

Flaubert. When he writes, combining two of Beaunier's expressions, of the 'emblematic agony' of Baudelaire, we think of the 'emblematic' character of the death of the grandmother and of Bergotte. He also returned to his differences of opinion with Maeterlinck, who consoles us for a death 'which is not the one we dread, a death from before the time of Christ', and then rejects Christianity, but 'only to lapse into spiritualism'.⁹⁹

But his sorrows welled up again, and letters to a diverse assortment of acquaintances are scattered with references to them, almost as if acquainting the world with his unhappiness was a comfort to him. Marcel even thought of becoming an expatriate, and renting a house that was 'quiet and remote, in Italy* – the Farnese palace at Caprarola, for example, which was rented by an American woman at the time – either because he wished to keep Agostinelli there, or because he wanted to run away there on his own, as the hero of *La Prisonnière* does just before Albertine's departure.† What was going on in the flat in the Boulevard Haussmann that autumn? We do not know.

However, in the outside world important events were unfolding. Proust could not keep his secretary a captive at home. Agostinelli had relinquished motor cars for aviation! And he was urging Marcel to go along to the aerodromes with him: the novelist covered his 'Carnet 2' with notes on the subject, and in *La Prisonnière* he gives an account of the Narrator visiting the airfields around Paris with Albertine.‡ At the same time Proust must have suffered, thinking of the hours that Agostinelli would be spending without him. However, he arranged a meeting one November evening, at the Hôtel des Réservoirs at Versailles, through the intermediary of Nicolas Cottin, with Ferdinand Collin. Since 1910 this man had been in charge of the Blériot school of aviation at Buc. Proust signed a contract for flying lessons: 880 francs for the lessons and 1,500 francs as security. But, despite his talent, the pupil would not go to Buc until he was ready to take his pilot's licence: 'Both for him and for me, it was a delight,'

---

* On 5 December, in fact, Proust sent a telegram to Nahmias telling him to make Agostinelli realize 'that the house would no longer work' (ibid., vol. XII, p. 360).

† Ibid., p. 314. Cf. p. 326 (16 November): 'I am very unhappy at the moment . . . and I don't even know whether I shall have the courage to copy out the last two volumes which are nevertheless both completed. And . . . like a lunatic I rent a place so as to get out of Paris, then I stay here, and then I want to leave.' 'Yes, I had to go; the moment had come . . . allow Albertine to go out, not have any good-byes, leave a note for her . . . and leave' (*RTP*, vol. III, p. 1180).

‡ Ibid., pp. 612–13; draft XI, pp. 1133–6. These passages and those in *Le Temps retrouvé* make Proust, who was always curious about every form of modern life, one of the first novelists of aviation.

wrote the director of the school, 'he was really gifted and he understood everything immediately'; but 'just when he was ready to take the Aéro-Club de France licence', he disappeared 'for a reason that is unknown'. After Agostinelli's death, 'overwhelmed by grief', Proust went back to see Ferdinand Collin, and refused the reimbursement of the deposit, 'explaining that he was responsible for the death of the young pilot and he begged [him] to accept this sum in memory of the fatal weakness he had shown in yielding to the entreaties of his secretary, who dreamed of nothing but aviation'.[100]

The solution to the mystery only recedes further: Proust had given Agostinelli everything he wanted in the way of money and pleasures (he may even have assisted him in deceiving Anna, his girlfriend), and yet he ran away . . . Was he homesick? Was his employer too much of a tyrant? The endless questioning from a jealous man? Was it the pressure put on him by Anna, who was no longer prepared to put up with an existence in which she was dependent upon two elusive and authoritarian men and who 'did not enjoy herself in Paris',[101] where she spent her time with the Cottins, who did not like her at all? Was it because, having collected his booty which would enable him to become a pilot, he could do it far away from Proust? A considerable amount of money was found in Agostinelli's clothing, which he must have taken with him because he mistrusted his own family. As with Proust, and with Saint-Simon, all these things are probably true simultaneously: Agostinelli had already revealed his instability by changing jobs frequently. But the last change of direction was to be fatal.

TITLE AND STRUCTURE, 1913

To return to the novel, it was shortly after the middle of May 1913 that the overall title we know today appeared for the first time, in place of *Intermittences du cœur*, which was printed on the first set of galley proofs from Grasset (abbreviated to '*Intermittences*'), which were being corrected. It was appended to the titles of the first two books, which were provisionally divided into three volumes: 'The first volume of the book will be called: *Du côté de chez Swann*. The second will probably be: *Le Côté de Guermantes*. The overall title of the two volumes: *À la recherche du temps perdu*.'[102] In February 1913 Proust had suggested to Grasset that the 1,500 pages of the complete work – an approximate extent since half of it was still in draft notebooks – should be divided into three volumes. Volumes II and

III were the result of dividing up the second book. In fact, volume II would also contain the ending of the first book, which, much to the author's dismay, was considered too long, and it would be printed in proof, though not published, under the title *Le Côté de Guermantes* in 1914. But why did Proust change the overall title? He answered this question in the same letter to Grasset: 'This change is due to the fact that in the meantime I have seen the announcement of a book by M. Binet-Valmer entitled *Le Cœur en désordre*. This must be an allusion to the same morbid state that characterizes the intermittencies of the heart. I shall retain the title *Les Intermittences du cœur* for a short chapter in the second volume.'* We do not know why Proust should have chosen *À la recherche du temps perdu* rather than any other title: did he have Balzac's *La Recherche de l'absolu* in mind? He could have dispensed with the preposition *À*, although it is its rare, but fortunate, usage that gives the book the force and impetus of an important new endeavour.

Du côté de chez Swann, the title of the first volume to appear, thus replaced *Temps perdu*, in spite of the opinions of his friends, who considered it 'inconceivable it's so ordinary'.[103] Proust responded by citing *Le Rouge et le Noir, Connaissance de l'Est, Les Nourritures terrestres* and *L'Annonce faite à Marie*, which were not 'poetic titles'[104] either. The title should reflect the simplicity of the subject and of the writing, not a spurious poetic charm: 'I told you, did I not? that *Du côté de chez Swann* is so named because of the two ways [*côtés*] at Combray. You know how people in the country say: "Are you going by way of M. Rostand's?"'[105] He conceived of it 'as a whole, even though it was a part'.[106]

The problem of length arose. Louis de Robert urged him to cut: 'That would be awful,' Proust replied, 'my book is a tableau';[107] elsewhere he used the image of a tapestry that should not be broken up.[108] When Lauris recommended smaller volumes, he did not want anything less than 520 pages; but he regretted not having 700 pages, which made up a unity and which 'had been proceeding so well'.[109]

Similarly, he refused any cuts of a moral nature, because he was 'obeying a general truth'.[110] The book that finally appeared in November 1913 consisted of 537 pages; Proust must therefore have reinstated what was

* *Corr.*, vol. XII, p. 177, shortly after mid-May 1913. We know that Proust did not care for Binet-Valmer, whom he suspected of pre-empting him in his depiction of homosexuality in his book *Lucien*. There may have been another reason, hinted at in a letter to Copeau: the 'word play' in the name of this malady [it can suggest heart failure, as well as love, *Tr.*], linked to that of '*temps perdu*', could give an 'impression of preciosity' (ibid., p. 245, August 1913).

to have been the ending of *Du côté de chez Swann* at the beginning of the second volume, 'a good dozen galleys',[111] and finished it with the scene in the deserted Bois de Boulogne, which had previously come further on. A press release from Grasset anounced this volume as the first of a 'trilogy'.[112] The original contents page gives some extra information about the structure of the trilogy: 'For publication in 1914: *À la recherche du temps perdu – Le Côté de Guermantes*: Mme Swann at home – Place-names: the place – Preliminary sketches of Baron de Charlus and Robert de Saint-Loup – Names of people, the Duchesse de Guermantes – The salon of Mme de Villeparisis / *À la recherche du temps perdu – Le Temps retrouvé:* / Within a budding grove – The Princesse de Guermantes – M. de Charlus and the Verdurins – Death of my grandmother – The intermittencies of the heart – The vices and virtues of Padua and Combray – Mme de Cambremer – Marriage of Robert de Saint-Loup – Perpetual adoration.'

In this outline, which future events would render null and void, we note that the original *Du côté de chez Swann*, which included the first visit to the seaside and was to serve as the opening to the entire work, because all the characters were introduced in it, had been shorn of 'Chez Mme Swann' and of 'Noms de pays: le pays' as well as the 'premiers crayons de Charlus et Saint-Loup'. What in 1919 would become *À l'ombre des jeunes filles en fleurs* was therefore jumbled up with *Le Côté de Guermantes*.* Paradoxically, the additions and the divisions were to make the structure of the work more solid. Certain chapters from volume III, such as 'Padoue et Combray' and 'Mme de Cambremer' would lose some of their importance. This three-part structure, which, as we can see retained some logic, would, however, be drastically altered by the introduction of two important episodes, the story of Albertine and the 1914–18 war. And the chapter entitled 'À l'ombre des jeunes filles en fleurs', which was envisaged in volume III, would, together with the chapters from the 1912 *Du côté de chez Swann*, become a self-contained volume II; the love story Proust was writing in 1913 was not about Albertine, who had not yet been created, but about Maria. His experiences between June 1913 and the summer of 1914, followed by the suspension of all publishing at Grasset's on account

---

* At the time that *Du côté de chez Swann* was published, and despite this outline, Proust wrote to Robert de Flers that volume II would be called '*Le Côté de Guermantes* or perhaps *À l'ombre des jeunes filles en fleurs* or perhaps *Les intermittences du cœur*. The third: *Le Temps retrouvé* or perhaps *L'Adoration perpétuelle*' (*Corr.*, vol. XII, p. 298); and p. 309: 'The last volume will be called *Le Temps retrouvé*. The second *À l'ombre des jeunes filles en fleurs* (it's not decided). One of the parts is called: *L'Adoration perpétuelle*' (Letters written between 8 and 12 November 1913).

of the war, would alter all existing plans and, in a totally unexpected way, make the work double in size – it would expand from 1,500 to 3,000 pages in eight years. Proust began to have a premonition of this in December 1913, in the midst of his sorrows: '1914 was only put in at the request of the publisher, so as to introduce a sequel. But even supposing that my health allows me to complete all this, it will be three or four years before it could be ready. Everything is written, but everything has to be revised.'[113] Once again, therefore, it was just when he thought that he had reached the end that everything collapsed.

PROOFS AND THE GRASSET EDITION

In early April 1913 Proust received the first proofs, sent in packets, of *Du côté de chez Swann* and started to correct them: 'Not one line in twenty of the original text remains . . . It's crossed out and corrected in every blank space I can find, and I stick in bits of paper above, below, to right and to left.'[114] Sticking in meant not just adding, but transferring text. 'I am changing everything, the printer will no longer recognize it,'[115] he wrote. The proofs took even longer because he frequently made further enquiries, on account of some pointless scruple, about a passage or just a word that he had already written.* On 19 April he offered an additional sum of money to Grasset;[116] the latter had asked him for 595 francs for the first forty-five galleys (there were eight pages to a galley). On 25 April the galley proofs of 'Un amour de Swann' were printed. In order that the printed galley text could be fitted into a single volume, Proust suggested cutting the paragraphing in the dialogue, which in any case he preferred to see 'absorbed into the continuity of the text'.[117] Meanwhile he refused to receive Grasset when he called, offering poor health as an excuse.[118] In late May 1913 he received the opening of 'Noms de pays'. He took the opportunity to cut four passages from 'Combray', which had now been corrected, on the subject of lilac, which he sent to Mme Scheikévitch, at whose home he had dined, and who had sent him a 'marvellous bouquet of lilac'; it was she who had given him the idea for a title he had considered for his book, 'la colombe poignardée'[119] [the stabbed dove], which was

---

* *Corr.*, vol. XII, pp. 201–2, three questions to Colette d'Alton, which show that Proust was interested in the girl partly so that he could obtain information about the aristocracy. This explains the presents he gave to her and her sister every year. Ibid., pp. 204–5, to M. Daireaux (about a passage from *Sodome* and three from *Jeunes Filles*, which were therefore already written in June 1913).

inspired by Anatole France.[120] On 11 June Proust received the final galleys of the first printing, and by 18 June he said that he had exhausted himself finishing his corrections.

Over the course of the summer he resigned himself to cutting a book which would be 800 pages long: 'So it must be a book of 520 pages or one of 680. I shall make it 520. But only if you see a great advantage in this, for the one of 680 pages ends superbly . . . and the one of 520 pages ends extremely poorly.'[121] The second solution would have brought us to the end of 'Autour de Mme Swann'; the first, to just after the games in the Champs-Élysées; Proust would leave the scene of Mme Swann in the Bois until later, in order to provide a better 'ending'. Grasset had written to him: 'A book has to be a book, that is to say something complete, sufficient unto itself. The problem of dividing it up is therefore something that only you yourself can resolve.'[122] At the same time, Grasset reinstated the paragraphing in the dialogue, so that the book should not be 'too compressed'.

The ninety-five galleys of the second set of proofs of the novel were printed between 30 May and 1 September.* There are very few corrections on them. Chartres was amended to Jouy-le-Vicomte, and, in particular, Proust merged the naturalist Vington and the musician Berget into a single character. Some time after this he contemplated a future composition by Vinteuil. Around 15 October he was wondering about the way in which the two final volumes, 'which would appear in 1914', should be announced; Beaunier advised him to talk about a 'trilogy'.[123] The problem would be resolved by printing 'to be published in 1914', on the verso of the half-title page. After the third set of proofs, only typographical corrections could be made: there would be five sets of proofs in all,[124] yet there were still a number of literals, which would be corrected by Proust and by others on a copy of the Grasset edition[125] for the 1919 Gallimard version. The publisher, who had originally thought of printing 1,250 copies of an 800-page book, decided, so as not to have to alter the price, to print 1,750 ('250 gratis copies and 1,500 copies comprising three editions of 500'),[126] he wrote on 25 October, even though he had instructed the printer on 18 October: 'The print-run will be 2,600 copies', plus twelve on Holland paper and five on Japan paper. If Proust was told therefore, and received

---

* Proust sent the forty-five original galleys to his friend L. de Robert for his opinion, saying that he preferred what came after the forty-fifth galley, that is to say the Sainte-Euverte soirée (*Corr.*, vol. XII, p. 211). Louis de Robert wrote to a third party: 'It's admirable.'

a letter to this effect, that the first print-run was 1,750 copies, there was a second and a third printing of 500 copies each. From the sales of the first printing, 285 press copies should be deducted, as well as 207 copies sent to the author for his personal use.[127] In December 1913 a second printing was planned: 1,380 copies representing the fourth and fifth editions would be delivered before 30 April 1914; 2,800 copies must have been sold before the war; all in all, Grasset must have sold about 3,300 copies, that is to say, as many copies as Gallimard would print in 1919. Sales slumped because of the war: in September 1916 there were still 500 copies in the bookshops. In October 1917 Gallimard bought up the remaining 206 copies and rejacketed them. *Du côté de chez Swann*, therefore, was far from a commercial failure for Grasset. If we take into account the small print-runs at the time, these figures imply that, contrary to what we have been led to believe, the book was a success. The same would apply to the press reception.

LAUNCH AND PUBLICATION OF
DU CÔTÉ DE CHEZ SWANN

Grasset, who had always had a genius for publicity, wanted to discuss the 'launch of this fine book'[128] with René Blum, the assistant editor of *Gil Blas*, to whom he owed *Swann*. He came to see Proust on 29 October to talk about this very subject. He promised to send out at least 400 review copies, not counting the advance proofs sent to critics. As the publisher wrote to the author: 'There are three methods of discussing a book journalistically, which are, in chronological order: the "leaks", the "extracts", and the "critical articles".'[129] The novelist paid heed to the lesson and immediately approached his friends for help with the three methods. On 9 November *Gil Blas*, at the request of Proust (who had explained the philosophy of his book to René Blum, and in particular what distinguished him from Bergson),[130] announced the publication of the book, and printed 'Une soirée de musique' as an extract on 18 November. On the 8th Proust received a visit from Élie-Joseph Bois, to whom he dictated an interview* for *Le Temps*, which appeared, 'terribly

---

* *CSB*, pp. 557–9. The wording is similar to that used in the letter to R. Blum: Proust covered much the same ground with all the press: the literary youth of the author, who is not a novice, the composition of the book, which was an initially delicate experience, the role of the two memories, and the reawakening. The end of Bois' interview also included comments on aesthetic matters which would appear in *Le Temps retrouvé*.

mutilated', on 12 November (issue dated the 13th); on the 20th, this newspaper published a fragment about Gilberte. On 16 November a piece by Robert Dreyfus* in *Le Figaro* announced the first part of *À la recherche du temps perdu*. On the 19th Marcel André Arnyvelde† came to see Proust for an hour; the interview appeared in *Le Miroir* on 21 December 1913. On 23 November *Les Annales* devoted some pages to provincial rooms together with a 'sketched photograph' of the 'still unknown'[131] portrait by J.- É. Blanche, and *Excelsior* ran an article by Cocteau (with a portrait of Proust set on a plinth!).‡ *Le Figaro* of 27 November carried a fine piece by Lucien Daudet on its front page, which touched Marcel deeply, and on 8 December there was another article, by Chevassu. Proust and Grasset had both contemplated the Prix Goncourt, but among the jury, Proust did not even obtain the vote of Rosny senior, who had nevertheless sent him a eulogistic letter[132] on 3 December. Marcel had seen it as an occasion to meet someone who thought as he did and who would not otherwise have had the opportunity to read him.[133] On 9 December, just after receiving a letter from Francis Jammes, who compared him 'to Shakespeare and to Balzac and praised his "sentences worthy of Tacitus"',[134] Paul Souday published a long article in *Le Temps* which expressed reservations that hurt Proust§ and resulted in some sharp reactions on his part: 'I glimpsed my book there as if in a mirror that advised suicide', he wrote to Cocteau.¶ Maurice Rostand wrote a frenetic eulogy for *Comœdia*. In the

---

* As Proust had asked at the beginning of the month in letters to R. de Flers (*Corr.*, vol. XII, p. 298), and later to Calmette (ibid., p. 324, n. 2).

† Playwright, journalist, novelist, author of *L'Arche* (1881–1942), who died in a concentration camp. Proust inscribed a copy of *Swann* to him. *Textes retrouvés*, pp. 292–5. Bois and Arnyvelde give a picture of 'the room with the shutters almost closed'; Arnyvelde describes the little electric light whose green lampshade filters the light, the large table by the bed, 'weighed down with books, papers, letters, and also little boxes of medicaments', his 'wonderfully lively and feverish eyes', the sheets of paper, the pen and the inkwell at the foot of the lamp.

‡ 'A gigantic miniature, full of mirages, with superimposed gardens, plays on space and time, and broad, cool brushstrokes in the style of Manet.'

§ Having emphasized the lack of subject matter, the fact that it was 'riddled' with 'printer's errors' and the pointlessness and naïvety of 'Un amour de Swann', Souday nevertheless recognized some talent, 'some precious elements with which the author might have made an exquisite little book'.

¶ *Corr.*, vol. XII, p. 332 (almost as if it were a parody of Cocteau himself). See Proust's reply to Souday (ibid., pp. 380–1, 11 December), in which he counterattacked with irony and drew attention to mistakes in Souday's article. I do not wish to go into further detail about a newspaper review and the public reception of the work, which I have already discussed in my two earlier books (*Lectures de Proust*, A. Colin, 1971, and *Proust*, Belfond, 1983). Proust subscribed to *L'Argus de la presse* and received copies of everything.

NRF Henri Ghéon mingled compliments with acid criticism ('the very opposite of a work of art'). The *Mercure de France* review on 15 January 1914 was no better: Marguerite Rachilde refused to drink this 'soporific'.

Among the dedicatees of the enormous number of personal and review copies that we have tracked down were Lauris, Mme de Pierrebourg, Léon Daudet, Louis de Robert,* Bertrand de Fénelon, A. France (on Japan paper),† E. Hermann, Gabriel de La Rochefoucauld, René Blum (on Holland paper), Robert Proust ('To my little brother, a Souvenir of lost Time, rediscovered for an instant each time we are together'), as well as Copeau, Gide, Gallimard, Claudel, É. de Crauzat,‡ G. Calmette, Lucien Daudet, Anna de Noailles,§ H. Finaly, Hervieu,[135] G. Astruc (the founder of the Théâtre des Champs-Élysées, who, having been declared bankrupt, was rescued from his depression by reading the book, which he had bought before receiving this copy and had suggested some typographical corrections, which Marcel would take note of when it came to the fourth impression),¶ the Comtesse Greffulhe, who forty years later had cut only the first pages of the book,[136] J. Bizet,[137] D. Halévy and Régnier.** These copies were delivered directly to the recipients' homes by a new, part-time employee, Céleste Albaret.

---

* *Corr.*, vol. XII, pp. 303, 306, n. 2, 313, 315. Proust claimed he dedicated a copy almost every day (p. 340)!

† Two copies (Catalogue Drouot, 4 May 1994, Bibliothèque Jean Lanssade): 'One of the human beings whom I love most deeply'; 'To the first Master, the greatest, the most beloved' (*Corr.*, vol. XII, p. 316).

‡ *Corr.*, pp. 317, 318, 318–19, 320, 321. 'If Gide knew the number of stories about Turkish baths, young Arabs, and Calais–Dover ships' captains that are told by another of your contributors, etc., which I've tried to refute among his best friends, perhaps he would be a little more circumspect when talking about me' (p. 322).

§ On 23 August 1917 Proust wrote to the Princesse de Caraman-Chimay telling her that neither she, nor her sister Anna de Noailles, nor her brother Constantin de Brancovan had thanked him (ibid., vol. XVI, p. 212).

¶ Ibid., pp. 383–90. In particular, Astruc recognized Haas and Monet (the *Water-lilies*, seen in 1900 at an exhibition) and Proust suggested that he told him some little-known anecdotes (p. 387).

** Not including the copies we do know about: to Mme Straus, Mme de Chevigné, and to so many others.

THE FUGITIVE

These articles, inscriptions and letters concealed a drama. On the morning of 1 December 1913, while Proust slept, the Agostinellis had fled.* One can imagine the anguish that gripped Marcel, who had always broken off his friendships gradually and gently. He had to put an end, at once, to the intolerable anxiety, which revived in him all the worries of his early childhood and the experience of being the lonely little boy who has been deserted, for ever, by his mother. Feeling entombed, he sought a way out: this was why he wrote to Nahmias immediately. Firstly, in order to ask him for the addresses of detectives capable of 'shadowing someone', and also to ask him to come round. He then dispatched him to Monte-Carlo, to Agostinelli's father, in order to guarantee him a substantial monthly allowance if he could persuade his son to return home until April. Albert was to stress that this was in the son's interest and that he was running serious risks; above all he was not to offer money to Alfred himself, which would ruin everything. 'I'd rather you sent me ten telegrams rather than one,' cabled Marcel, who used coded signatures (Maurice, Max Werth). He must have imagined, therefore, that it was all a question of money, for he suggested haggling and issuing an ultimatum. But Nahmias had heard that 'it was all over': and so, on 7 December, Proust instructed him not to hand over any money and to come back.† Alas! he had not realized that Agostinelli had already extracted enough money from him not to need any more for a while. There was nothing to prevent him from continuing to extort money later on, dangling the prospect of his return before his former employer. They would resume contact by letter, as we shall see, and Marcel would give in to pity or allow himself to be swindled, to the extent of promising Agostinelli an aeroplane and, possibly, a motor car. This correspondence no longer exists, apart from lines quoted by Marcel in his last letter to Alfred (and possibly in *Albertine disparue*), since it was destroyed by the Agostinelli family, but it was what restored a little calm to Proust's life and enabled him to get on with his book. The only

---

* The sentence 'Monsieur Alfred has left!' used by P. Kolb in his chronology (*Corr.*, vol. XII, p. 15) appears to have been borrowed from *Albertine disparue*, even if it is fairly likely that Céline Cottin, who underwent an operation on 14 November, and assuming that she had returned to work afterwards, may have announced the departure in this way. But if she did not return until January, as Céleste believed, then it was the latter who may have announced the news.

† Ibid., pp. 355–66, from 1 to 7 December 1913. We know nothing more, for once Nahmias had returned, he saw Proust and no longer needed to write to him.

surviving letter that Proust wrote to Alfred shows how he kept his friend informed about everything, about Grasset's reaction, the fate of *Du côté de chez Swann* and events in the news: one is reminded of Mme de Sévigné writing to her separated daughter. This was the nature of the intrigue that the novelist would very shortly introduce into his book: Albertine fleeing, Saint-Loup setting off to search for her and then being summoned back to Paris, Albertine refusing to come back straight away while at the same time holding out hope for a future return,[138] and then reappearing immediately, once the Rolls has been ordered. The aeroplane which Proust ordered from Collin was intended to bring about and celebrate the return of someone who had treated him so badly, and whom he loved dearly.

CHAPTER XIV

The Novel of 1914

COMPOSITION

In 1914 the second volume of *À la recherche du temps perdu* was entitled *Le Côté de Guermantes*. The contents list that we referred to previously and the proofs that Grasset printed enable us to know precisely the very different content of the volumes now known under this title. The opening still takes place 'chez Mme Swann',[1] as Proust wrote at the time, and in Paris; the chapters 'Noms de pays: le pays' and 'Premiers crayons du baron de Charlus et de Robert de Saint-Loup' would become the second part of *À l'ombre des jeunes filles en fleurs*. In it, Proust tells of a first visit to Balbec; all the familiar characters are in place, with the exception of the young girls. However, at this point he completely altered the structure of the visit to Balbec in his *cahiers* by introducing both the girls, who had originally been intended for a second visit, and Albertine, who had just been invented. After 1913, in fact, he wrote a 'chapter II/À l'ombre des jeunes filles en fleurs' in Cahier 34, which was intended to follow a chapter I of *Le Côté de Guermantes I*, in which the Narrator visits Mme de Villeparisis and meets the Duchesse de Guermantes. Finally, a third visit to Balbec had been planned for volume III, *Le Temps retrouvé*; a trace of it survives, which many forget to take into account, at the end of *Albertine disparue*: in it the Narrator meets Robert and Gilberte de Saint-Loup, Bloch and Aimé. In 1914 Proust considerably expanded the first two visits to Balbec at the expense of the third, and he would continue to do so until the proof stage of *À l'ombre des jeunes filles en fleurs* and of *Sodome et Gomorrhe*.

To return to this volume II, *Le Côté de Guermantes*: it was typeset by the printer Colin and made up in proof between 6 and 11 June 1914,* but had already been superseded by rough drafts; the section that is really

---

* *RTP*, vol. II, p. 1504, note. Proust was already reading through the typescript in February 1914, without having 'the courage to correct the spelling mistakes' (*Corr.*, vol. XIII, p. 94).

devoted to the Guermantes, which in the listing in *Du côté de chez Swann* was entitled 'Noms de personnes', so as to mirror and contrast with 'Noms de pays', consisted of two chapters, 'La duchesse de Guermantes' and 'Le salon de Mme de Villeparisis'. In 1910–11 Proust had made a fair copy of the five exercise books, Cahiers 39 to 43, which provided the first consecutive version of *Le Côté de Guermantes*;[2] in 1912–13 he drafted the manuscript in Cahiers 34, 35, 44, 45,[3] and in 1914 we arrive at the proofs, which correspond approximately to 300 pages of the Pléiade edition. This version, which encompasses *Le Côté de Guermantes I* and *Le Côté de Guermantes II*, describes, in sequence, the Narrator moving into a new apartment, close to the Guermantes; his reveries on the names; the matinée at the home of Mme de Villeparisis; the efforts made by the hero to know the Duchesse; the evening at the theatre; the time spent in a garrison town; and, from *Le Côté de Guermantes II*, the soirée at the home of Mme de Villeparisis, the dinner party at the Duchesse de Guermantes', the reflections on the Guermantes' salon, the Narrator's visit to the Duc and Duchesse de Guermantes, the incident of the Duchesse's red shoes and, in anticipation of what would become the opening of chapter I of *Sodome et Gomorrhe II*, the soirée at the Princesse de Guermantes' home.

This formed a very coherent entity, but for reasons of space it could not appear in its entirety in the 1914 proofs of volume II, which ended with the matinée at the home of Mme de Villeparisis, when M. de Charlus departs in a cab. Equally, the grandmother's illness, and Albertine, were missing from it. The important point is that this *Le Côté de Guermantes*, whether in its entirety or divided into parts, was an apprentice novel, which related the hero's passage from adolescence to youth and his ascent in society, for he is introduced into the most elevated and exclusive circles of high society, as well as the price he pays for these conquests. This upward mobility is, in fact, punished by a double renunciation, of love and of his artistic vocation. The Narrator cannot be admitted into the realm of the Duchesse unless, like Alberich in *Das Rheingold*, he renounces his love for her; and, in order to mix in society, he no longer writes. But the punishment is more severe still: to have access to the Guermantes is to dispel the poetry conjured up by their name; people's names are just like place-names, and life always refutes dreams: *Le Côté de Guermantes* refers back to Balzac's *Les Illusions perdues*, just as *Sodome et Gomorrhe* alludes to his *Splendeurs et misères des courtisanes*. The titles of books themselves, as the missing draft notes on Walter Scott referred to in Cahier 39 reveal, can disappoint when dreams give way to memory: 'And [it] will probably be better for one of the girls, or for Gilberte later on, or for a book (that was inspired by the title: *Chronicles of the Canongate, St Ronan's Well, Woodstock, Waverley, Peveril of the Peak*).'⁴ A study of the early drafts demonstrates that the additional material confirms the sense of disillusionment, which stems from the moment of the meeting with the Duchesse de Guermantes. Proust found it very hard to know where to place this meeting, and he kept postponing it – the delay had a dual effect, both technical and psychological. Composed of long, straightforward segments which had initially evolved separately in the notebooks, this section of the narrative then had to be pieced together; Proust emphasized this himself: 'It was only logical that after having contrasted the poetic place-name of Balbec with the humdrum Balbec landscape, I needed to proceed in the same way with the family name of Guermantes. It is one of those books said to be weakly organized or not organized at all.'⁵ He wanted to endow the substance of the book with a touch that was reminiscent of Balzac in its social ambition, its quantity of characters and its big banquet and salon scenes, and of Dostoevsky in the adjustment of illusions and beliefs.⁶ This tone of voice is in contrast to the poetic allure of volume I that evokes Nerval, Baudelaire and Ruskin, in the same way that childhood is distinct from adulthood.

The 1913 edition of *Du côté de chez Swann* also announced a third, and final, volume: *Le Temps retrouvé*. The substance of it is contained in several exercise books, sometimes based on earlier material, which have been collected together in the Pléiade edition. We have already mentioned Cahiers 58 and 57, which describe the final morning and the discovery of 'regained time'. Cahiers 47, 48 and 50 contain some sections that would appear in *Le Côté de Guermantes II*, in *Sodome et Gomorrhe* and in *Albertine disparue*.⁷ For Proust a summary was a catalogue of segments that were written, but which had not always been assembled into a continuous narrative, which he set to one side; however, the catalogue was unfinished and incomplete, and it provided no details of the scenes. 'À l'ombre des jeunes filles en fleurs', the first chapter that is listed, returns to the second stay at Balbec. 'La princesse de Guermantes' may correspond to the reception given at the home of the Princesse, who, having been conceived in *Contre Sainte-Beuve*, was developed in Cahier 43 in 1910–11, and made her definitive appearance in the first chapter of *Sodome et Gomorrhe II*. The title 'M. de Charlus et les Verdurins' is based upon a description of the Verdurin salon, which was situated in the Place Malesherbes, and upon the parties which Odette's former friends gave at Ville d'Avray, which one reached by train (as with Mme Aubernon's home at Louveciennes). Gurcy, the future Charlus, the friend of the 'young pianist', is introduced here. However, 'M. de Charlus et les Verdurins' does not reflect the considerable importance already given to homosexuality in the drafts – both in the number of pages devoted to the subject and in the character of Charlus – even though Proust had stressed, ever since his letter to Vallette in 1909, the significance of the character and the subject: 'One of the main characters is a homosexual.'[8] He described just such a character and his adventures at length in a letter to Fasquelle in October 1912, emphasizing his originality,[9] and, a few days later, he wrote to Gallimard: 'The appearances of this character are sufficiently scattered among various completely dissimilar passages for the book not to look in the least like a specialized monograph ... Nevertheless, we do see this old gentleman picking up a concierge and keeping a pianist.'[10] What is not suggested by the summary of 1913, but which is referred to in the correspondence and confirmed by the exercise books that are the basis of *Sodome et Gomorrhe*, is the existence of the Charlus-Jupien-Morel trio.

Another amorous pursuit that sustains the plot but is not mentioned in this summary appears in Cahiers 36, 43 and 49: the Narrator is searching for a girl with red roses as well as for the Baronne Putbus' chambermaid. Ever since 1908, there was, at the heart of the book and in order to sustain the main plot, the quest for a woman and possibly a love affair. Yet if one compares the drafts and the final version, in which Albertine supplants both the girl and the chambermaid, one realizes that the invention of the character of Albertine filled an immense void, for instead of casual, inconsequential love affairs and passing flirtations, we have the grandeur of Racinian passion in all its violence and tragedy. To this would be added a new theme, which was missing from the early outlines, though not from *Les Plaisirs et les Jours*: the subject of female homosexuality – Gomorrah really would match Sodom.

So, to return to the summary made at the end of 1913, it is under the name of M. de Charlus alone, therefore, that we must locate the list of exercise books which, since 1908–9, had been devoted to the subject of Sodom.[11] In the early drafts, it was at the Opéra, during a performance of Wagner's music, that the Narrator discovered Gurcy-Charlus' true nature. This discovery was responsible for the essay on homosexuality which appeared in *Contre Sainte-Beuve* and would pave the way for 'La race des tantes'[12] in *Sodome et Gomorrhe I*. After this would come the encounter with the concierge and the liaison with the pianist; in the original version, this began at the Gare Saint-Lazare. In 1913, however, 'M. de Charlus et les Verdurin' was far less 'indecent' than the important developments Proust used to amplify and extend the character during the 1914 war. The following chapter, 'Mort de ma grand-mère', now opened *Le Côté de Guermantes II*. Planned ever since *Contre Sainte-Beuve* and the *Carnet de 1908*, this part of the text signifies the end of childhood, the hero's solitude confronted with life and death, and the disappearance of Combray, although he does not immediately appreciate the extent of his loss, the revelation of which is dealt with in the next chapter, 'Les intermittences du cœur', which was, as we have seen, so important to Proust that he had wanted to make it the overall title of the book. The hero, in fact, resumes his amorous quests: in pursuit of Mlle de Quimperlé, the future Mme de Stermaria, of a young girl, who will turn out to be Gilberte, and of the chambermaid, whom he follows to Italy.

In the 1912 version 'Les intermittences du cœur' retraced the Narrator's dreams, which brought back memories of his grandmother in the very middle of this journey in Italy. In Cahier 48 the young man dreams of his grandmother in a hotel bedroom in Milan, during a halt on the way to Venice; in Cahier 50 this occurred on the way back from Venice; in the draft versions the Narrator would have six dreams in all, similar to those in the *Carnet de 1908*. But at the point when the hero encounters the Baronne de Putbus' chambermaid in Padua, he is struck by the violence of the contrast between the two heroines, between the conquest of the one and the resurrection of the other. The 'intermittencies of the heart' are the memories of the physical body, the state of forgetting that is followed by the brutal return of the past; the past[13] is made responsive to the heart, but, unlike in 'Combray', where this emanates from a cup of tea, the return is distressing: like Ulysses in the underworld in *The Odyssey*, the hero can see his mother or his grandmother, but is unable to embrace her. At this stage of the book, he finds her again at the very moment that he has lost her for ever.

In this same Cahier 50, in the train on the way back from Venice, the Narrator learns about two letters: the first is the invitation to the marriage of Montargis, the future Saint-Loup, to Mlle de Forcheville, and the second is the wedding announcement of young Cambremer, who is marrying Jupien's daughter; whence the two titles of the synopsis, 'Mariage de Robert de Saint-Loup' and 'Mme de Cambremer'. In a matter of only seven pages,[14] as in a novel by Balzac, Proust started to settle his heroes' scores. Then we come to Cahiers 58 and 57, which make up the conclusion to the novel of 1911. In the final version 'Les intermittences du cœur' takes place at the time of the second visit to Balbec, and the trip to Venice is in *Albertine disparue*, where the Narrator's memories of his grandmother are replaced by him forgetting the dead Albertine. In the genesis of the novel as well as in its structure, in fact, there is a correspondence between these two females: they require one another, they resist one another, but they balance each other: and so, in *Sodome et Gomorrhe II*, 'Les intermittences du cœur' comprises two parts, each of which is devoted to one of the two heroines. By the end, as we have seen, Albertine has supplanted the chambermaid, who was the principal subject of the chapter entitled 'Les Vices et les Vertus de Padoue et de Combray'.

By 1914, we have a novel of which two thirds had been printed, and one third had been written a few years earlier. Suddenly the book was thrown into confusion by the invention of the character of Albertine, whom we have frequently had cause to mention in anticipation. Proust may, in fact, have begun to use her name from May 1913[15] onwards, as a substitute for Maria in the second visit to Balbec. She would be involved in the development of *À l'ombre des jeunes filles en fleurs*, and of *Le Côté de Guermantes*, through allusions, and through alterations and additions, which would be minimal when compared to the eventual size of the four parts of *Sodome et Gomorrhe*, of which *La Prisonnière* and *Albertine disparue* constitute the two final parts. Over the last eight years of Proust's life, the work doubled in size. As we know, the creation of Albertine was not the only cause; another reason was the First World War, which obliged Grasset to suspend publication and also provided the novelist with new subject matter. *Le Temps retrouvé* did not become a novel about the war, but the war did play a part in the book.

Moreover, if a chronology suffices, if the entire life of the author is present in the book, transformed and reinvented through language, it is because no previous event had upset the writing of the novel; Proust's life and his book evolved along parallel lines. All of a sudden, from the day in May 1913 when Proust gave house-room to Alfred Agostinelli and employed him as his secretary, those lines were at right angles, and life began to cut across the book. All we know about that impassioned relationship, about the young man's flight on 1 December 1913 and his death on 30 May 1914, and about the stages that led to him eventually being forgotten, is to be found in a curt news item and in what Proust himself tells us in his correspondence. It is certainly the case that Alfred Agostinelli was not the only model for Albertine, as a note in Cahier 57 confirms: '*Vitally important*: when I say that Albertine, etc., have posed for me, so have others whom I can't remember; a book is a vast cemetery in which one is unable to read the faded names on most of the tombstones. Occasionally, however, it is the name that comes back to me, without being able to remember whether anything of the woman survives in these pages. The girl with the delightful look in her eyes, who speaks so sweetly, is she here? And in which part of it? I no longer know.'[16] For the character of Maria, who had been invented before 1913, Proust may have thought of other friends, such as Bertrand de Fénelon.[17] Above all, the literary structure of the work provided a framework for life itself, which now began to fill it, for, from *Le Carnet de 1908* onwards, a second part of the novel had been projected, in which the hero would take care of a ruined girl 'without enjoying her', 'because of his inability to be loved':[18] to mirror and complement 'Un amour de Swann', it needed 'Un amour du Narrateur', for which Gilberte and the Duchesse de Guermantes had only provided an outline. It is utterly pointless to wonder whether Albertine resembled Agostinelli or whether she was a man in drag, because the tragedy that Proust lived through was later internalized, analysed and reconstructed. The distance which thinking deeply about something lends to reality – and to biography – is the space given over to the imagination. The impact that a real man had on Proust's emotions can later be attributed to an imaginary woman. A woman? *The* woman in *À la recherche du temps perdu*, since the name of Albertine is mentioned in it 2,360 times, mostly in *À l'ombre des jeunes filles en fleurs, Sodome et Gomorrhe, La Prisonnière and Albertine disparue*.[19] No other heroine comes close to matching this figure, nor does any hero; only the Narrator intervenes more frequently, but that is because the entire novel is seen or re-examined through his eyes, and because he is both a character and the person telling the story. Proust described the purpose of Albertine in a letter of dedication to Mme Scheikévitch in November 1915:[20] 'I should prefer to introduce you to characters whom you don't yet know, especially the one who plays the biggest role and brings about the peripeteia, Albertine', before giving a summary of her role in *À l'ombre des jeunes filles en fleurs, La Prisonnière* and *Albertine disparue*, the drafts for which must therefore have been written at the time.

Hence a new series of events came to interfere with the ones that were in place in 1911, and which gave rise to what Proust referred to as the 'episode', that is to say the whole story of Albertine, the framework of which was ready in 1915. Its writing was made possible by another tragic circumstance, the First World War, which led to the temporary closure of the publishing house of Grasset, where only two employees remained.[21] Proust, afflicted as he was with grief, used it as a further reason to alter the proofs of volume II, *Le Côté de Guermantes*, which would never therefore be published in the form they took at the time. What is more, from 1914 the NRF publishing house was keen to publish the book, and in 1916 the novelist, who was very tempted, accepted Gaston Gallimard's offer. One of the justifications for this was the closure of Grasset, as René Blum, who intervened on Proust's behalf with the publisher of *Du côté de chez Swann* on 7 July 1916, pointed out: 'Your firm has been shut down, and the NRF, which hasn't, can publish it fairly quickly. He therefore asks you to allow him to go back – without this annoying or upsetting you – on his promise to publish the other volumes with you and also, consequently, to take back the first book (in which he had retained copyright anyway).'[22] This was merely a pretext, for Proust preferred to be published after the war, while at the same time hoping to make a start on the printing beforehand. And so it transpired: Grasset agreed to waive their contract on 29 August 1916.

The Albertine episode began to be written from 1913 onwards, and it opened with her appearance at the seaside, at Balbec, and later in Paris; these are the visits which would eventually take place in *Le Côté de Guermantes II*. The second visit to Balbec, in *Sodome et Gomorrhe II*, developed the theme, in two draft exercise books to begin with. An early account of *La Prisonnière* and of *La Fugitive* can be found in four other exercise books,[23] which were worked on up until 1915. In Proust's Carnet 2, a dozen pages are filled with the subject of aviation.[24] There are notes in Carnet 3[25] showing that an alternative episode of *La Prisonnière*, the performance of Vinteuil's septet, was being prepared.

To summarize the integration of Albertine into the novel, one could say that, up to *Sodome et Gomorrhe*, Proust added this character – in narrative that may have been read, and which was sometimes typed and printed, without his knowledge – to sections and chapters that had already been written and structured. In *Le Côté de Guermantes II* there are a few passages – devoted to calling on people, a walk in the Bois and a kiss – that modify the image of her already established at Balbec, and the kiss that is bestowed is in contrast to the kiss that is refused at the Grand Hôtel. In *Sodome et Gomorrhe II* a trip to Paris takes place after the evening at the Princesse de Guermantes', which had already been written; it is in chapter II of this book that everything collapses, because a jealous relationship develops between the Narrator and the girl, which is interrupted by the soirée at the Verdurins at La Raspelière. This soirée makes use of elements from 1911, from Cahier 47, in which the Verdurins entertain somewhere near Paris; from Cahier 46, dating from 1914; and from Cahier 72, numbered IV by Proust, which comes after it. Cahier 53, numbered V, contains 'Les Intermittences du cœur II', which mirrors 'Les Intermittences du cœur I', and is devoted to the grandmother: it is in the future chapter IV of *Sodome et Gomorrhe II* that the Narrator learns that Albertine knows Mlle Vinteuil and her girlfriend, a scene which corresponds to the subtitle in the contents list in *Sodome et Gomorrhe*, 'Désolation au lever du soleil'. From *La Prisonnière* on, everything is reversed: the sections that are already written are inserted in Albertine's story, up to the end of *Albertine disparue*. Hence in *La Prisonnière*, for the mornings, and the recurring theme of awakening, which is at the root of the whole of *À la recherche*, Proust returned to some early sketches from *Contre Sainte-Beuve*, and later to some material from Cahier 50 dating from 1910–11; for the essential parts, however, a continuous narrative can be found in the draft exercise books that Proust numbered IV, V, VI, which are Cahiers 72, 53, 73. The performance of the Vinteuil septet, which is central to the soirée at the Verdurins, comes from Cahier 57, and was to take place in *Le Temps retrouvé*, where, in the passages set in 1914, it is referred to as a quartet.[26] All the rest appears to be new. In *Albertine disparue* everything to do with Albertine's flight and death, and her being forgotten, forms part of the main plot, and dates from 1914 at the earliest; but the reading of the article from *Le Figaro* goes back to 'Impressions de route en automobile' in 1907 and to *Contre Sainte-Beuve*. The journey to Venice was anticipated, as we know, in the novel of 1911, and the heroine of it was to have been the Baronne de Putbus' chambermaid. However, the Venetian theme is linked directly to the translations of Ruskin and to *La Bible d'Amiens*: '. . . I left for Venice so that, before dying, I could approach, touch and see embodied, in palaces that are crumbling yet still standing and rose-coloured, Ruskin's ideas about domestic architecture in the Middle Ages.'[27] The weddings made up two chapters of the novel of 1911, and the stay at Tansonville at Mme de Saint-Loup's is anticipated in the first pages of *Du côté de chez Swann*.

CÉLESTE ALBARET

One of the virtues of *À la recherche du temps perdu* is the interest shown in ordinary people, in rural society and in the working classes. This interest was one that Proust himself shared. His long conversations with hotel staff, and with electricians and delivery boys are proof of this. He displayed the same courtesy to and interest in his domestic staff, as can be seen from the letters he wrote to the Cottins and the Antoines, the concierges at Boulevard Haussmann. From old Félicie Fiteau (who, together with a certain Marie, was the inspiration for the portrait of Françoise in *Contre Sainte-Beuve*) he borrowed the coarse features of a Françoise who was an elderly countrywoman; from Céline Cottin he obtained the nervous, authoritarian temperament and the bellicosity.* But nobody played so important a role in his life, or in his book (in which she appears under her maiden name, as does her sister, Gineste, in the guise of the *courrières* at the hotel at Balbec) as Céleste Albaret. There is something unique about the affectionate understanding that united two human beings who were so entirely dissimilar. With his intuition and his habitual kindness, Marcel perceived Céleste's intelligence, her fidelity and her solitude, which was the loneliness of an exile. She herself, a woman who was scarcely literate and who knew only one poem by heart ('Ici-bas tous les lilas meurent', which Proust wrote out for her), was aware that she was living with a man of genius, whose essential distinctive personality had to be protected, served and loved both before and after his death: no biography or critical essay is more moving than *Monsieur Proust*, in which this ordinary woman, who retained the freshness and simplicity that she had always possessed, became the Boswell or the Eckermann for another important man. 'How did "little Marcel" become a genius?' Jean Guitton asked her. 'Little Marcel always knew he would become the great Proust,' she replied.[28] What feelings did they share for one another? Nothing need be added to the affection, admiration and devotion that Céleste felt for him; for Marcel, she was both a maternal and a filial presence, the confidante of tragic heroes, but also, since the social barrier between them was never abolished (unlike some of the young men, from equally modest backgrounds, Céleste was never promoted to the rank of secretary, and she listened to Proust's stories standing at the foot of his bed), a housekeeper ready to carry out all his instructions.

---

* *Corr.*, vol. XIV, p. 174, early July 1915 to Céline Cottin: 'I have always told you that, whatever you may think about the usefulness of wars, this one is a very great misfortune.'

This beautiful, tall young woman of twenty-one, who came from Auxillac, had never left her native village when she married, in a wedding arranged by her family, Odilon Albaret on 27 March 1913. For several years he was a taxi driver; he put himself at the special disposal of Proust, who telephoned him whenever he had need of him. He moved to Levallois-Perret with his wife, who, in her loneliness, became very homesick. Hence, when her husband introduced her to Marcel, who needed someone to deliver parcels containing his new book, and later, when he employed her eight hours a day because Céline Cottin had gone away for reasons of health, a new life became available to her. When Céline returned, the two women would not get on: she nicknamed the newcomer 'the cajoler', and very soon Céleste was left on her own with Nicolas: it was at this point that she started to work nights (which coincided with her husband's work) and the Albarets began to keep the same hours as their strange employer. In mid-November 1914 he spoke of his 'chambermaid (who was also cook, valet, etc.)'.[29]

A REVIEW OF THE PRESS AND OTHER REACTIONS TO *SWANN*

In early 1914 articles on *Du côté de chez Swann* continued to appear. Jacques-Émile Blanche wrote a long study, which Proust, at the beginning of January, tried to have printed, firstly in *Le Journal* and then in *La Revue de Paris*.[30] He was astonished and delighted by this article.[31] Having succeeded in getting it published in *L'Écho de Paris* of 15 April, he worked hard to arrange for extracts or mentions of it to appear in several newspapers or magazines: *Le Figaro, Gil Blas, Le Journal des débats*, some of which he paid for. On 30 April Proust himself received 1,762,60 francs in royalties from Grasset, which corresponded to the first print-run of 1,250 copies (or a sale of 1,175 books): in 1918 Grasset would acknowledge that he still owed him money for the second and third printings.[32]

Proust, wrongly as usual, took the trouble to reply to a rather poisonous and foolish article by Henri Ghéon in the *NRF*, which, despite some complimentary concluding remarks, was full of affectation and invidious comments. In the long plea in his own defence,[33] Proust explained his method of synthesizing: 'By placing end to end the little impressions I experienced during the impassioned and lucid hours that I was able to spend over the course of various years at the Sainte-Chapelle, at Pont-Audemer, at Caen and at Évreux, I have pieced together *the stained-glass* *window.*' He also noted the part played by the imagination: 'If I write about illness in the following volumes, it is an illness that is invented for the psychological needs of the work . . . Because I say "*I*" people think I am subjective.' More important was a letter from Gide of 11 January, which has become famous: 'For several days I have been unable to put your book down. Alas! why should it be so painful for me to like it so much? . . . The rejection of this book will remain the most serious mistake ever made by the NRF and (since I bear the shame of being very much responsible for it) one of the most stinging and remorseful regrets of my life.'* The reasons which he then put forward and the image he had formed of a society dilettante, who wrote for *Le Figaro*, can only have hurt Proust, even though they were immediately mitigated by his 'singular affection, admiration and predilection'.† There are two mysteries here: why did Gide now like Proust? Why did the latter attach such importance to the opinion of the former, who was certainly a great writer, but who had not yet published any of his masterpieces? It is true that a printed book, especially if it is greeted by favourable reviews, will carry more weight than a typescript; furthermore, if it is published elsewhere, the book is seen from another person's viewpoint. Faced with the facts, Proust knew that although Gide was not the titular head of the NRF, he was its strong man, and he also realized that in this desert of literature in which neither Hervieu, nor Bourget, nor Bourdeaux, nor even Barrès really appealed to him, this magazine represented the one hope of revival, that it stood for the highest standards, and that it was the most exclusive of clubs according to the intellectual criteria of the time. Gide's letter foreshadowed another, of 20 March, in which he stated that the NRF was prepared to take over publication of the two other volumes.[34] Meanwhile, Jacques Rivière, the young assistant editor of the magazine and already a brilliant critic, wrote an enthusiastic letter which brought the celebrated response: 'At last I find a reader who has *grasped* that my book is a dogmatic work with a structure!'[35] It was the beginning of a friendship of the kind that Proust did not usually seek, one that was purely 'spiritual'. Later on, by combining his own personal tastes with the interests of the magazine, Rivière would publish many articles defending Proust's work[36] and he

---

* *Corr.*, vol. XIII, pp. 51–3. In a draft letter, Gide supplied an explanation: he had been put off by the vertebrae on Aunt Léonie's forehead, and by a 'cup of camomile' (ibid., p. 50).

† Ibid., p. 53. See Proust's detailed reply, pp. 56–8, 12 or 13 January 1914, in which he wrote of the 'distinguished atmosphere' that his book deserved, and the pleasure of being read by Gide, whose book, *Les Caves du Vatican*, had begun to be serialized in the magazine that January.

would request extracts from it for the *NRF*. He was the best critic of his generation: he combined an intuition which guided him towards the best writers, to whom he would devote some important '*études*', with sensitivity, conscientious analysis and stylistic elegance; what is more, he was interested in and wrote about everything: the Ballets Russes, operas, concerts, exhibitions, as well as literature. Rivière would write only analytical novels (*Aimée, Florence*), and, on the eve of war he launched an appeal on behalf of the adventure novel. His correspondence with Alain-Fournier, whose sister he married, remains an important testimony to intellectual youth in the early years of the century. Such was the man whom Gaston Gallimard would put in charge of the magazine after the war.

FROM ONE PUBLISHER TO ANOTHER: THE RETURN OF FASQUELLE, GIDE AND THE NRF

As in a fairy tale, everything was turned topsy-turvy: the very people who had not wanted *Du côté de chez Swann* now clamoured for its sequel. In March Fasquelle, through the intermediary of Maurice Rostand, asked Proust whether he could publish the last two volumes, but Proust declined the offer, 'not wanting to leave Grasset'.[37] After that, the NRF made the same offer. Proust then consulted the lawyer Émile Straus to find out whether he could leave his first publisher.[38] Grasset, however, wrote to him on 26 March, proposing that volume II be published in May or June.* On 28 March Marcel wrote telling him of the NRF's offer, and asked him, diplomatically and somewhat feebly, to view it favourably.[39] In early April the matter was brought to a head: at first Grasset invoked the contract which bound them,[40] and then, because Proust pointed out that he had retained copyright in his book and 'the right to have other editions done elsewhere', gave him back, 'more as a friend than a tradesman', his freedom.[41] But Proust, true to character, having obtained what he desired, was seized by doubts, and decided 'to surrender the freedom that had been given back to him' and stay with Grasset, while at the same time permitting the *NRF* to run extracts: 'I am defenceless against your kindness.'[42] At the same time, not to leave anyone out, in April he arranged

---

* *Corr.*, vol. XIII, p. 124. 'It seems to me that it would be very difficult for it to appear before October. At the present moment, I have the beginning in galleys, and everything else is still in manuscript, not even completely re-typed,' Proust replied to him on 28 March. This letter gives an idea of the state of volume II at this date.

for a volume of his essays and articles to be submitted to Fasquelle, but he was on holiday. With Grasset's agreement, he then thought of giving it to the NRF.* By 30 April Grasset had received the typescript of volume II, which he sent to the printer the following day,[43] and he offered to publish this new book at his firm's expense, with a first print-run of 3,000 copies. At the beginning of April Marcel, using some proofs from Colin the printer, had given Rivière the passages (not the whole book, as the editor had naïvely hoped) which were to appear in the June issue of his magazine, and which ended with the portrait of Charlus.[44] He would do the same the following month for the July issue; the passages included Françoise, the Guermantes' *hôtel particulier*, the theatre, the hero's love for the Duchesse, Doncières, Saint-Loup and his mistress, and the grandmother's illness[45] – a montage of extracts, therefore, from *Le Côté de Guermantes I*. Up until the end of his life, Proust would always attach great importance to the publication of his work in magazines, and he was not content with giving them selected passages: he worked in scholarly fashion, cutting the text and reassembling it; if it were not understood, the story of *Albertine disparue* would not be understood either. Before July 1914, when he believed that his second volume (out of three) would be published in the autumn, he wanted to give the select readership of the *NRF* a synthesis of the best moments from the forthcoming book, a sort of digest of *Le Côté de Guermantes*.

MUSIC AND PIANOLA

In these first months of 1914 the keen music-lover, who, from the moment he had begun to give more substance to his character, had wanted to increase Vinteuil's output and expand his role, was not idle. Proust's letters are dotted with references to a crucial event that was taking place in Paris: Wagner's music had come out of copyright and was now in the public domain; *Parsifal*, which the composer's family had forbidden to be performed anywhere except at Bayreuth, was staged at the Paris Opéra on 1 January.[46] Proust went to see it at the end of the month, or else he listened to it on the theatrophone. As a result he compared the disenchanted phases of his book and its 'objective and believing' conclusion to the end of the first act, in which Parsifal, who does not understand anything about

---

* Ibid., pp. 175–76. But not to Cocteau, who had suggested publishing the pastiches at the publishing house he had just founded with Iribe.

the ceremony, is sent away by Gurnemanz as events reach their climax. It was probably at this point that he sketched a scene in which Charlus, listening to the Flower Maidens, discloses his homosexuality, or that he began to outline his reflections on 'L'enchantement du vendredi saint'; most of his ideas about Wagner would eventually appear in *La Prisonnière*, and yet the whole of *À la recherche* is influenced by him: the great, unique structure which integrates episodes that were written beforehand, the leitmotif, the religion of art, the sacred that has become profane.

'I rarely get up, and usually it's to go to the Schola or to the Concert Rouge when they're playing Beethoven quartets,' wrote Proust in January.[47] At this period Wagner and Beethoven were two new sources for the second of Vinteuil's works to be heard in *À la recherche*, the septet. If Wagner provided the overall aesthetic concept, so too did Beethoven's quartets, particularly the last ones, and Proust would only stop listening to them once he had succeeded in transmuting their substance into words: he would need another three years (during which time he would arrange for the Capet and Poulet quartets to come to his home). In these quartets, which had long been neglected on account of their originality, he must have sensed the testamentary profundity of Beethoven's message, the perfection of their expression of suffering and of the victory over suffering. In addition, being still loyal to Diaghilev, on 28 May he set off to the Opéra to hear Stravinsky's *Song of the Nightingale* and Rimsky-Korsakov's *The Golden Cockerel*.[48] Finally, he acquired a pianola, which we come across in *À la recherche*, on which he hoped to be able to play Beethoven's last quartets to himself (but no one could provide the music for him).

In contrast, we know little about what he read during this period, although we do discover that he was rereading Michelet's *Le Tableau de la France*, looking for 'the French saying that [he] most admired at the time'.[49] He also commented on *Les Caves du Vatican*, which was being published in extracts in the *NRF*, contrasting his aesthetic ideas with those of Gide: though he liked the adventure, which was as exciting as Stevenson, with its episodes converging 'as in a rose window', he criticized the presence of 'thousands of prosaic details': he was incapable of recording 'anything which hadn't produced [in him] an impression of poetic enchantment, or in which [he had not] felt he had grasped a general truth'.[50]

FINANCIAL DÉBÂCLE

During the previous year Proust had begun to draw on his capital: we should not forget that the income it produced was his only source of funds. In January he asked Lionel Hauser to sell his Royal Dutch shares (five tenths of the stock).* At the same time, on the advice of Albufera, he became involved in speculating in Oural[51] oil shares, which were evidently far less reliable, through the intermediary of Nahmias, who was employed to negotiate risky transactions. In May he did not dare approach M. Neuberger, at the Banque Rothschild, any more, having already sold shares 'for more than 20,000 francs a few days earlier',[52] and he asked Hauser to sell some bonds that were held by Warburg's, up to a limit of 10,000 francs. And on 28 May, at a particularly dramatic moment in his life, he asked Hauser to sell 20,000 francs worth of Suez held by MM. de Rothschild.[53] This was the very day that he went to see the airman Collin, to discuss the purchase or part-exchange of an aeroplane. Because Hauser did not disguise his concern about the enormous extent of these sales, on 29 May Marcel promised him a letter of confession, a request for absolution and for some advice.†

This enormous expenditure was not purely due to a liking for gambling. For some time Marcel had no longer complained about his emotional distress, something he had done constantly the previous year. An important discovery made by Philippe Kolb, the only surviving letter Proust wrote to Agostinelli, holds the explanation and allows us to make guesses about what was not said in it. Proust must have been making regular payments of money to his friend, in the hope that Alfred would return, and for the pleasure of keeping tabs on him. Better still: this letter provides evidence that Proust, unbeknown to Agostinelli, had ordered an aeroplane for 27,000 francs, and had placed another for about the same amount (Kolb supposes that it was for a Rolls, as in the novel). Agostinelli appears to have suggested cancelling this order, having refused the gift; this was why Proust declared that the plane would probably remain in its hangar, and that he would have engraved upon it Mallarmé's sonnet 'Le Cygne': nothing could be more appropriate for an aeroplane which would never

---

* *Corr.*, vol. XIII, p. 77; he had already sold some the previous October. In May he asked Hauser to sell some for him, forgetting that he no longer had any.

† Agostinelli's death must have prevented him from writing it: I have not come across any trace of it.

fly. He faithfully transposed the details of this letter into *Albertine disparue*, substituting a boat for the aeroplane: 'Now that we shall never see one another again, and since I have no hope of persuading you to accept either the boat or the car (to me they would be quite useless), I had therefore thought . . . that by cancelling their purchase yourself you might spare me this yacht and this car which are no longer required,'[54] and he added, in the same terms: 'In any case if I keep it (which I rather doubt) since it will probably remain in the stable, I shall have engraved . . . the lines of Mallarmé.'[55] These presents would not succeed in making the young man come back; was Proust still hoping for a happy outcome when he threatened to cancel these sumptuous gifts?* His letter gives no information about any breaking off of their relationship. Céleste Albaret gave a rather more chilling picture of Agostinelli: 'From Antibes, where he continued with his flying lessons in order to obtain his pilot's licence, he wrote to M. Proust. He was a flatterer. From what I understood later, his idea was to persuade M. Proust to buy a machine for his own use, which he would have christened "Swann" he said . . . He was also impudent and a bit of a dare-devil.'[56]

As Proust explained to Émile Straus: 'I have had to go on with the terrible financial speculations which I told you about and which I intended to stop at the first rise, because the stock market has continued to fall continuously; each month I pay the brokers almost thirty or forty thousand francs, and my capital won't hold up much longer.'[57] It was because of the sums paid to Agostinelli or paid on his behalf that in May Proust declared himself 'more or less ruined', and asked his friend Robert de Flers† to obtain for him in *Le Figaro* 'some column or other such as the weather, or minor news items or the music column, or the theatre column, or the stock exchange, or the society page', to give him time to rebuild his wealth, 'which has not been completely wiped out'.[58] However, when Flers agreed to do so, Proust retracted, and proposed nothing else apart from extracts from his volume II:[59] on 15 July the newspaper would announce 'a long short story: Odette mariée' (imagine if this were the only text to have been found: people would have spoken of a short version

---

* Between them, 1,100,000 francs in 1999 terms.

† He asked Robert de Flers, and not Calmette, who had been assassinated on 16 March by Mme Caillaux, following a campaign against her husband, the minister of finance; the news had very much upset Proust, who lost in Calmette a friend, a loyal supporter and the dedicatee of *Swann*. When Mme Caillaux was acquitted, he signed a letter of protest in *Le Figaro* on 1 August.

of 'Autour de Mme Swann'); it would not be published, probably on account of the war.

However, because Hauser had telephoned him towards the middle of July to remind him about the possibility of a 'European conflagration', Proust began to 'reduce his financial commitments',[60] just when the markets were at their lowest, following the 'thunderbolt of the Austro-Serbian incident'.[61] The July settlements were catastrophic for him, for he had to settle his liabilities with shares that had been bought on credit and which had fallen heavily. On 22 July *Le Figaro* mentioned two dreadful days at the Paris stock exchange, following similar ones in Vienna and Berlin ('the currency collapsed without encountering the least resistance').* Hauser took note of the 'confession' that Proust had sent him 'with much interest' and advised him to check whether the income that remained to him was still enough to live on.[62] This was the moment when rumours of mobilization were circulating in Austria, Serbia and Italy. On 25 July panic caused the markets to close. We come across these speculations, losses and near financial ruin in *À la recherche*.

AGOSTINELLI DISAPPEARS

Agostinelli never came back. Rather touchingly, he had enrolled at the flying school run by the Garbero brothers at Antibes under the name of Marcel Swann. On 30 April, during the course of his second solo flight, he ignored instructions and ventured out over the Mediterranean. His aircraft crashed, the pilot could be seen waving desperately; a boat was rowed over, but it did not arrive in time: the plane, along with its pilot, had sunk.[63] Alfred's companion, Anna, sent Proust a desperate telegram.[64] The drowned man's brother asked Marcel for 5,000 francs to pay for frogmen to bring up the body (Agostinelli had all his savings with him, some 6,000 francs, which shows that he did not trust his own family any more than he did Proust.[65] It was found on 7 June; he had been wearing (like Albertine) a gold signet ring, bearing the initials AA. His funeral took place the following day, attended by the brothers Hector and Joseph Garbero, the pilots Dumas and Nicolas Kastérine, the staff of the flying school and some Antibes notables. Marcel sent a 400-franc wreath, but

---

* *Corr.*, vol. XIII, p. 273, n. 6. Cf. p. 276, end of July 1914: Proust explained his situation to Hauser, his hurried selling and the credit line of 218,000 francs which the Crédit Industriel had agreed against securities.

the family regretted that the flowers were not artificial ones.[66] Proust, who claimed he had done everything to dissuade Agostinelli from flying ('but his wife was convinced he was going to make a million'), had, 'after some far too unpleasant conduct', written to the young man some time previously: 'If ever you should have the misfortune to have an aeroplane accident, you can inform your wife that she will find in me neither a protector nor a friend and she will never have a penny from me';[67] in the face of the misfortune, however, he forgot this, and he asked for help from the Prince of Monaco on behalf of a woman whom he did not realize was not married to Agostinelli, and who, furthermore, had been denounced to the prince by Alfred's family as someone who, because she was not legally married, could not therefore inherit anything. She arrived at Boulevard Haussmann a few days later and stayed there for a short while: Marcel did his best to console 'the poor widow'. After some initial feelings of guilt – if Alfred had not met him, if he had not received so much money from him, he would not have been able to learn to fly – Proust went through the normal stages of mourning: he idealized Alfred's death (although during a third stage, at Cabourg, he was to observe that Agostinelli had behaved very badly with him), and, writing to Straus and to Gide, he extolled his 'delightful intelligence', 'a worthiness that was marvellously incompatible with everything that he was' and which Proust did his best to make him realize, as well as his letters, 'which are those of a great writer'.* He expressed his grief very movingly: 'Anyhow, I who had put up so well with being ill, who never felt sorry for myself, I found myself hoping with all my heart, every time I got into a taxi, that the approaching bus would run me over.'[68] Marcel's letters are not only about his grief, however; he explained the character of Charlus to Gide (who, in an extraordinary about-turn, would have liked to ask him to write an article on *Les Caves du Vatican*[69] in *Le Figaro*, even though Gide claimed it was Proust's collaboration with this newspaper that had prevented him from appreciating *Swann*), he prepared his extracts for Rivière, gave instructions on stock exchange matters to Nahmias and Hauser, and congratulated Abel Bonnard on his latest novel. On the other hand, he did not correct the proofs of his volume II, dated from 6 to 22 June 1914

---

* Ibid., p. 245, 10 or 11 June 1914, p. 257. These letters have disappeared; on the basis of the quotation that Marcel alludes to in his letter of 30 May, and which also appears in *Albertine disparue* ('crepuscular, etc.'), it could be thought that Albertine's letters are those of Agostinelli locked away as if in a tomb.

by Charles Colin, even though the publisher had announced the book for November. And he observed that 'the scope of one's conscience has several dimensions, and that one may think of several things at the same time', for his grief was undiminished.[70]

Posthumous jealousy, and possibly the wish for inspiration for the description he was writing in *Albertine disparue*, prompted him to visit Collin, at Buc, and to question Louis Gautier-Vignal, who was surrounded by pilots from Nice: 'Please remember me to your friend M . . . , if you see him, to MM Kastérine and Semichoff, who were taught by the Garberos and perhaps at Buc beforehand, and to Barraut and Deroy, and even Bidaut.'[71]

WAR

On 2 August it occurred to Proust that 'millions of men are going to be massacred in a war of the worlds comparable to that of Wells'.[72] He went to the Gare de l'Est with his brother, who had been called up and appointed as medical officer at Verdun hospital. He claimed never to have stopped thinking about the war from that moment on. A fortnight later Nicolas Cottin, who had hoped not to have to go to the front on account of his age, was called up, as was Odilon Albaret, whose wife now moved in fully to Proust's home. He was looking for a manservant, and, after a few unsuccessful trials, he responded to an advertisement and took on a very good-looking Swede, blond and 6 foot 6 inches tall, by the name of Ernst Forssgren, who had just been dismissed by Prince Orloff 'and was so infatuated with himself that he must have believed he was at least the King of Sweden, if not God'.[73] The massive German offensive towards Paris did not alarm Marcel: he thought he ought to stay near his sister-in-law and his niece (who left shortly for Pau). It was only when he felt reassured about their future, in late August, that he made plans to leave for Cabourg, on 3 September (the government departed for Bordeaux on 2 September). A few days earlier, he went out for a walk in Paris: 'I know that two or three days before the victory of the Marne, when the siege of Paris was thought to be imminent, I got up one evening and went out in the light of a moon that was clear and brilliant, reproachful, serene, ironic and motherly, and at the sight of that immense Paris that I never knew I loved so much, waiting in her superfluous beauty for the onslaught that nothing seemed to be able to prevent any longer, I could not help weeping.'[74] These ideas would be taken up again in *Le Temps retrouvé*, in which the central section deals with Paris during the war: 'In this Paris, where in 1914 I had seen her almost defenceless beauty awaiting the threat of the approaching enemy, there was certainly, now as there had been then, the ancient unchanging splendour of a moon cruelly and mysteriously serene, which poured out the superfluous beauty of its light over buildings that were still as yet undamaged.'[75] Proust was also anxious about all his friends, or their children; he wept, what is more, for those he did not know, he no longer lived.[76]

Reynaldo was in Albi, but would shortly have himself transferred to the front, to the despair of Marcel who would attempt many manoeuvres to prevent it; Hahn did not want to be taken for a 'shirker', and he would send some deeply moving letters[77] from the front line, in which he revealed the inanity of the official propaganda about the morale of the *poilu* and his sublime commanders: the truth, according to him, was that the troops were badly treated and were devastated by anxiety, and that there were officers who had been discharged by their commanders, who showed no mercy to the soldiers, even those who had heart conditions. It was certainly from him that Marcel derived part of his information, which, furthermore, he did not dare use in its entirety, so contrary was it to received opinion.

CABOURG FOR THE LAST TIME, FORSSGREN

On 3 August Proust, accompanied by Céleste and by Forssgren, left for his 'customary Cabourg'. According to Céleste, he found himself 'too deserted in Paris. The war had emptied the city of almost all his friends',[78] some of whom had been called up, while others were taking refuge in the country. He only arrived there, 'not at all well', on 4 August, after a journey of twenty-two hours, in a train that was so packed there was no room to sit down, and it was with great difficulty that a third-class seat was found for him.[79] So great was the panic that there were some passengers riding on the roof (in the first great exodus they were fleeing Paris for fear of the Germans: the enemy might have reached Paris, but, instead, turned back towards the Marne); the locomotive had scarcely been able to pull such a heavy load; this was why it had taken so long to get to Mézidon, where one changed trains for Cabourg: Proust and Céleste stayed at the hotel there and the trio set off again on the 4.00 p.m. train.

Marcel had brought with him a large and very ancient suitcase, in which he kept all his manuscripts and from which he was never separated, and an enormous wardrobe trunk containing his blankets, his clothes, including two overcoats made from vicuna wool – which he had had specially made for the seaside! – as well as all his medicines. As usual, he and his companions occupied three bedrooms, with bathrooms, on the top floor. To call Céleste, Marcel tapped on the wall, just as the Narrator does with his grandmother at Balbec. He worked during the daytime, drawing back his curtains in the afternoon; he occasionally came downstairs in the evening and would walk on the hotel terrace with Céleste, but he no longer went to the casino, for it was closed. Feeling unwell, he refused to receive the Comte Greffulhe and Montesquiou, who came to visit him. Moreover, the hotel, or at least the two first floors, had been requisitioned to accommodate wounded soldiers: according to Céleste, none arrived;[80] Marcel, however, said that he had spent 'what he had left'* on the wounded of Cabourg, and made a note that he must jot down 'the effect that the wounded of Cabourg who had arrived from the Marne made on him'.[81] He offered to play 'games of draughts' with the Sénégalais and the Moroccans (the colonial troops had already been forced to enlist).† Forssgren sat by his bed, reading to him for an hour each day from newspapers or books, or playing draughts, a game that Marcel 'adored', cards (he did conjuring tricks), or chess.‡ He, too, mentioned his employer's courteousness: 'Whether you were a servant or someone in society, there was no difference, in this respect, as far as he was concerned.' Very soon he was promoted to the rank of 'private secretary and confidant': 'Ernest, you are invigorating,' Proust would say to him, holding out his arms to embrace him.[82] And when Forssgren started singing *La Marseillaise*, Marcel told him, not without humour, that he sounded 'just like Sacha Guitry'. The presence of this Nordic Adonis helped him to detach himself from the image of another secretary, one who had also sat by his bed playing draughts.

Cabourg, which might have been a distressing experience for Proust because of memories of Agostinelli, turned out to mark 'a first stage of detachment' from his grief; for hours on end the dead man disappeared from his thoughts. The fact was that the notion of a duty towards the dead, which unintentionally fixes our grief, did not exist for Marcel. Once

---

* *Corr.*, vol. XIII, p. 354, to Lucien Daudet. Forssgren also referred to Marcel's generosity in this respect; the money would be redistributed to the wounded.

† *Corr.*, vol. XIV, p. 45; it was on this occasion that he heard the saying, 'Me negro, but you swine,' which he put into *Jeunes Filles* (*RTP*, vol. I, p. 526).

‡ 'What he had against chess was that it challenged the brain too much' (*Études proustiennes*, vol. II, p. 131.).

back in Paris, however, his suffering returned intermittently.[83] He thought about his brother, too, who was mentioned in dispatches for having continued to operate while his hospital was being bombarded.[84] The journey back from Cabourg, around 14 or 15 October, took five or six hours, and they travelled first class, but there was a distressing incident: at Mézidon Marcel suffered a bout of asthma (as he did on every trip home: 'Going back . . . the idea that there is still all the journey ahead . . .' he said to Céleste) and his medicaments were in the luggage van, so with great difficulty Céleste went to get them at the next station.[85] The sick man then obtained some relief. He returned to Paris, never to leave the city again, despite the dreams he sometimes had of going to Italy or to Brittany once his book was completed. As for Forssgren, threatened with Swedish military service, he emigrated to the United States. According to him, Marcel told him, as he told others: 'Ernest, throughout my whole life, I have never known anyone whom I have loved as much as I love you.'[86] Was it because of this that Proust complained that people had found the means, 'without anyone being able to imagine on what grounds, however, to spread incredible gossip', which had given him 'a horror for this beach' and left him 'with ulcers'?[87]

MILITARY DISCHARGE, AGAINST CHAUVINISM

Proust's principal concern on his return was having to appear before an army medical board. Doctor Bize, at Reynaldo's request, wrote a certificate testifying to 'the absolute impossibility of [his] doing military service'.[88] Pozzi, 'in a charming way and with the utmost courtesy', refused to write anything.[89] Marcel then approached his former acquaintance from the days of the Dreyfus affair and Mme Straus' salon, Joseph Reinach; Proust had been rereading the sixth volume of his *Histoire de l'affaire Dreyfus*, entitled *La Révision*, for his novel. Reinach assured him that he knew Marcel was anything but a shirker, and that since his name had been struck off the army lists, he was exempted from any military duties.[90]

Proust therefore followed the course of the war from his bed; but he was very soon criticizing the press and its chauvinistic attitudes. For instance, due to 'imbecilic' articles in *Le Figaro*, written by the historian Frédéric Masson and by Saint-Saëns, Wagner soon became the man to attack: 'If, instead of fighting a war with Germany, we were fighting one against Russia, what would they have said about Tolstoy and Dostoevsky?'[91] Reynaldo Hahn, for his part, observed that even the officers were shocked by Saint-Saëns' anti-Wagnerian articles in *L'Écho de Paris*. It was wrong to deprive not just our musicians, but our writers, too, (Proust added, thinking of his own example) 'of the tremendous fertilization that hearing *Tristan* and *The Ring* cycle represents, like Péladan, who doesn't want us to learn German any longer'.[92] He himself remained just as much an admirer of Wagner and Beethoven.[93] Even Péguy's 'admirable' death[*] did not make Proust alter his critical attitude towards his art 'in which something is repeated ten times over'.[94] Literature and life were not of the same order. Finally, among all the newspapers which he read daily, the 'only decent thing' he could stand was 'The Military Situation', written by Henri Bidou, in *Le Journal des Débats*. We should remember that a law of 5 August 1914 prohibited the publication of 'all information or articles concerning military or diplomatic operations likely to favour the enemy and exert a harmful influence over the morale of the enemy and the public'.[95] Newspapers had to be submitted to the Press Office before being printed.

All these matters, as well as some remarks of Bidou's, would be found in *À la recherche*, in an abstract way, enshrined either in anti-patriotic characters like Saint-Loup or Charlus, or in chauvinists, like Cottard, among the Verdurin clan.

DAILY LIFE IN 1915

The same anxieties dominated Marcel's life throughout this year. Firstly, the war: what he could understand of it, from following operations on a General Staff map and from reading seven different newspapers;[96] what he felt about it, seeing certain of his friends ('All my dearest friends are at the front')[†] and his cousins die; what he feared on his own behalf, faced with the army medical board – not because he was frightened of going to war, but because he would feel as useless at the front line as he

---

[*] Charles Péguy was killed in the first days of the Battle of the Marne in September 1914. *Tr.*

[†] *Corr.*, vol. XIV, p. 23, 3 January 1915; and he added: 'I have already had friends and even relations killed': these were Jean Bénac, the son of friends of his parents, who had put him up at Beg-Meil, as well as Jean Cruppi and Victor Ramillon, who were distant cousins. Proust wanted to see a collection of young Bénac's letters published; his family rejected the idea; he criticized this attitude in a letter to Mme Catusse and in *Sodome et Gomorrhe* (*RTP*, vol. III, p. 489), condemning the diffidence of families who prevented 'one from cherishing life and establishing some glory around the poor dead man, who would prefer that his name be spoken on men's lips to all the wreaths, borne extremely piously though they are, on his tomb'.

felt himself to be indispensable, both to and through his book: 'No doubt there is nothing very pleasant about the life I lead and even though I know I can be of no use to the army, I can be useful to myself by allowing myself to be withdrawn. For I very much want to finish the book I've begun and to set down some truths in it which I know will inspire many people and which would otherwise be destroyed with me.'[97]

At the beginning of 1915, in any case, he felt that victory was very far away, and that the press was 'greatly inferior to the great things it speaks about'.[98] The truth was that, anxious though he was to describe the war, for this invalid, this recluse, war was mainly something he read about or listened to through the accounts of witnesses: it was a text. He would only see the consequences: the dead, the wounded, the soldiers on leave and their cruel, ironic destinies, the bombardments. But he was anxious to understand the thinking of those who gave orders, since for him, as for General de Gaulle, the commander was also an artist, one who pursued a great idea. His conversations with Antoine Bibesco on this subject would inspire those of the Narrator and Saint-Loup.[99]

FRIENDS LIVING OR DEAD

There were few friends he could see: Lucien Daudet; Louis Gautier-Vignal was in Nice (he had just lost his brother and his brother-in-law, but, writing to Mme Catusse, who was also living in Nice, Marcel distanced himself from him, claiming that he was better disposed towards his work than to him);* also Jean Cocteau, the Strauses, Lauris, Misia Edwards, whom he called on in late January, occasionally Bibesco, and Mme Scheiké-vitch, who had lost her brother. Hugo Finaly died at the age of seventy, linked in Marcel's mind 'to the dearest memories of the irreparable, the sweet, the heartrending past', that of Ostende and Trouville. The cruellest death in this early part of the year was that of Gaston de Caillavet, from uraemia, on 13 January. He was one of the models for Saint-Loup; Marcel confessed to his widow, Jeanne Pouquet, herself one of the models for Gilberte Swann, who became Gilberte de Saint-Loup: 'To think that I knew him and adored him even before he knew you!'[100] She would go to

---

* Ibid., p. 50: perhaps he was afraid of gossip, adding that he did not mean to 'disown someone who seemed [to him] to be utterly sensitive and pleasant, and who had been so kind ... What I mean to say is that I don't know him well and have not known him long. That does not mean that we do not get on extremely well.'

see him in April in order to carry out one of the deceased's wishes, and to tell him that Gaston had broken off relations with his mistress because of his wife and his daughter.[101] By a tragic stroke of irony, it was also around this time that Proust learned of the disappearance of Bertrand de Fénelon; on 17 February his sister, the Marquise de Montebello, wrote telling him that an officer had seen Bertrand fall, mortally wounded, but Marcel still refused to believe the truth: 'I think about him so much that, having fallen asleep for an instant, I saw him, and I told him that I had thought he was dead. He was very nice.'[102] Bibesco came to see him in early March and removed any hope he had: it was 'while leading his section that he disappeared', as did Saint-Loup. Like him, his courage was not fired by any degree of hatred. A great connoisseur of German literature, he did not hold 'the Kaiser' responsible for the war: 'It is highly likely that this view is erroneous. It shows nevertheless that, even if he was wrong, there was nothing narrow or exclusive about the patriotism of this hero. But he loved France passionately.'[103] And then, in mid-May, came news of the death of Robert d'Humières, a lieutenant in the Fourth Zouaves,* who was killed by a bullet in the heart while leading a charge; 'dearly loved', Proust linked his memories of Fénelon to those of his former colleague, the translator of Kipling, to whom he had written affectionately: 'Dear Mowgli, man cub',† who was 'so eager to learn everything, to experience everything, this incandescent flame'.[104] Finally, on 20 April 1915, Marcel had to inform Céleste Albaret that her mother had died, and urged her to set off immediately for Auxillac, where she arrived after the burial. During her absence, she was replaced by her sister-in-law Léontine Albaret, who proved to be incompetent and a chatterbox. On Céleste's return, Marcel wept and, taking her gently by the hand, told her: 'I have never stopped thinking about you.'‡ At this

---

* Saint-Loup commanded a company of Senegalese troops: 'He derived, chastely no doubt, from spending days and nights in the open with Senegalese soldiers who might at any moment be called upon to sacrifice their lives, a cerebral gratification of desire which was mingled with much contempt for "the little scented gentlemen"' (*RTP*, vol. IV, p. 425).

† *Corr.*, vol. II, p. 333, 2 February 1899. Another trait Robert d'Humières held in common with Saint-Loup was that, although married, he had combined heroism with homosexuality. Cf. ibid., vol. XIV, p. 119: 'There are certain deaths which I admire none the less, but which differ very much from the picture-postcard way in which they are portrayed.' Robert d'Humières had himself posted to a Zouave regiment, it was said, to avert a scandal.

‡ C. Albaret, pp. 142–3. *Corr.*, vol. XIV, p. 109, to Marcelle Larivière: 'We can't do anything to soothe her suffering. All we can do is try to make sure that her poor body tolerates as painlessly as possible the worst blow that could have befallen her.'

same time Jean Albaret, Odilon's brother, was killed at Vauquois, and Proust sent messages of deep sympathy to the family. This constant association with grief and death led him to spell out his ideas about religion to Lionel Hauser: 'Although I have no faith . . . religious preoccupations are nevertheless never absent from my life for a single day. Furthermore, I discussed only recently (by letter naturally) with M. Neuburger the possibility that he might see his son again one day. But the more religious one is, the less one dares assert an affirmation beyond what one believes; now I deny nothing, I believe in the possibility of everything, objections based on the existence of Evil, etc., seem to me absurd, since Suffering alone seems to me to have made, and continues to make, of man something more than a brute. But it's a long way from there to certainty, or even to Hope. I haven't got there yet. Will I ever get there?'[105]

During the course of this year, Marcel developed a special friendship for Henri Bardac, whom he had originally come to know through Reynaldo Hahn and whom he had described in 1906 as 'this guinea pig in pink coral'.[106] Called up as a sergeant in the infantry, Bardac was wounded at the Battle of the Marne. In July 1915 Marcel wrote in praise of him to Lucien Daudet: 'Henri Bardac is remarkably intelligent and excessively pleasant; . . . it has taken me a long time to realize, but he is truly perfect, nothing stunning, but a type of dry, compact mind, rather like the characters in Dumas. And then there is the sense of security, an all too rare asset in relationships.'[107] As a result of his injuries, Bardac was appointed as an attaché at the French embassy in London. 'Within a few months the poor fellow has lost an ear, his facial nerve, a nerve in his leg, his father, and much else besides; it's rather sad' (the scar on his forehead inspired Saint-Loup's), and Marcel sent 'his most affectionate wishes' to this man whom he 'liked immensely'. He also made use of him, as he once had Nahmias, for stock-market transactions. They saw one another frequently over the following years, sometimes in curious circumstances: on 13 March 1916, for instance, Marcel dined at Ciro's with Bardac and Charlie Humphreys, a former valet to Bardac and his legatee: as a result Morel was given the first name of Charlie instead of that of Bobby.[108] Bardac later described a few of his memories of Proust, such as a visit, in 1918, to a palm-reader, who exclaimed: 'What do you expect of me, sir? It's for you, rather, to reveal my character to me.' He saw Proust as a visionary and a mind-reader. He mentioned a gala evening at the Opéra after the end of the war, at which *Antoine et Cléopatre* was being performed. Proust, sitting in a box, never stopped chatting to his neighbours, which did not prevent him from describing the tiniest details of the production a few days later.[109] It was also at Henri Bardac's home, in late August or early September 1916, that Marcel met Paul Morand, who was 'charming' and whom he was 'so pleased' to know.[110] As for Reynaldo Hahn, in spite of Marcel's initiatives, he had himself transferred to the front line from the south-west, where he had been posted. Proust saw him again on 11 or 12 November when, while on leave, he gave the first performance of *Ruban dénoué, valses pour deux pianos*, which he had composed at Vauquois. Marcel considered it to have the purity of Rimsky-Korsakov and the depth of 'the old deaf one'. The last waltz made him want to quote a comment (probably made by Lenz in *Beethoven et les trois styles*, 1909) about the Seventh Quartet. Once again, however, his work would not feature in *À la recherche*, and one can imagine how disappointed Reynaldo must have been when he discovered that so much praise would not be passed down into immortality.

FIGHTING THE ARMY

The anxieties that his summons to appear before an army medical board occasioned were to cause Proust to fall out with Joseph Reinach, on whom he had depended, who had given him a letter which he could not submit as evidence: in it Reinach asserted that he did not know whether Proust was in good health or not.* (Thereafter Marcel would continue to be sarcastic about Reinach, as well as his articles, which were signed Polybe.) On 9 April he received a summons to appear before the medical board on the 13th, at 3.30 a.m. Doctor Bize certified that he was not in a fit state to attend. On 11 April there was a further summons for the 13th for 8.30 a.m.: he sent his medical certificates to the president of the board. On 28 April he was summoned once more; and yet again at the end of June, to appear before the special committee. On 25 August some army doctors came to examine him; they pondered whether to discharge him: 'They don't know that Papa was, and Robert is, a doctor, and each time they asked me: "You're an architect, aren't you?", but I was so ill that my case was never in doubt. It is a recommendation that is likely to become

* *Corr.*, vol. XIV, p. 33; cf. p. 36: 'I always feel very sorry when I see very dear illusions fade away at close hand and when a man whose courage in public life I have admired ... displays such unfriendly wariness in private life.' Proust added that he would find consolation for the human failings of the man in his work as author of the fine history of the Dreyfus affair.

increasingly efficacious up until my death . . .'[111] On 10 September an officer of the military government in Paris wrote telling him to appeal to the general commanding the *département* of the Seine, adding, almost as if he were familiar with the style of the person he was dealing with: 'Do so in concise terms, without going into all the details you have given me.'[112] It should be clearly understood that although Marcel felt himself incapable of going to war, he thought of nothing else: 'Night and day we think about the war, perhaps still more painfully when, like me, one is not taking part.'[113]

PROUST, THE PRESS AND THE WAR

'Each day,' wrote Proust, 'I devour everything the French or Genevan military commentators think about the war.' His reading matter included *Le Mot*, the weekly review founded by Cocteau and the cartoonist Paul Iribe (28 November 1914–1 July 1915), which tried to be at once patriotic and humorous, avant-garde and true to national tradition, with its ironic content confined to the Germans. Marcel, for example, admired one of Iribe's cartoons, 'Lohengrin and the crayfish: the march on Paris', while at the same time observing 'that it would have been even funnier applied to the Grand-Duke Nicholas' (the Russians were meant to have invaded Prussia, but had suffered heavy losses which had thrown them back behind the Niemen). In defending himself for criticizing the 'sublime commanders', his remarks were aimed at the 'foolish journalists who have the capacity to forget they were telling us constantly that the Russians would be in Berlin by the end of October, and who rejoiced over the fact that the Germans had not celebrated Christmas in Warsaw'.* Proust would not cease his criticism of the press, which was chauvinistic, and confused information with propaganda: it was true that it took a long time for the public to discover the extent of the early defeats in 1914. But the newspapers relied upon the information communicated to them by the government and by General Headquarters, or on what had not been suppressed beforehand by the censors (who must have been very active, if one thinks of all the articles which Clemenceau could only print scattered with blank spaces in *L'Homme libre*; this newspaper, which was suspended for a week

---

* *Corr.*, vol. XIV, p. 40, to J. Cocteau. *Le Mot* published drawings by him, signed 'Jim', by Dufy, Bakst and Gleizes. He nevertheless defended the performance of German music in Paris. See K. Silver, *Esprit de corps*, Thames and Hudson, 1989, pp. 43–9.

for having disobeyed the orders of a general, later became *L'Homme enchaîné*). 'Provided that there is no mention in what one writes,' said Alfred Capus, the editor of *Le Figaro*, 'of those in authority, the government, political matters, constituent bodies, money-lending organizations, the wounded, German atrocities, or the postal service, one can print quite freely under the supervision of two or three censors.'[114] Meanwhile there were articles saying that German soldiers were starving, to the extent that they would leave their trenches if they were offered a slice of bread and jam. The attitude of the press and the government, and this disinformation, would be depicted in *Le Temps retrouvé*.

From March 1915 onwards Proust defined his ideas clearly, as Mme de Chevigné and no doubt Cocteau had started some malicious gossip about him: 'It is true that "Boche" does not figure in my vocabulary and that things do not seem as clear-cut as they do to some people.'* Similarly, he believed that 'people generalized German crimes too much', while at the same time condemning the 'vitriolizing' of Rheims Cathedral.[115] 'They indulge a little too freely in terms such as "Kultur", "scrap of paper", "nation of prey" and "kolossal".' And he congratulated Paul Souday for having defended Wagner and Richard Strauss against Saint-Saëns and Zamacoïs. This led him to draft a scholarly study of Strauss's music which he made use of in *Le Côté de Guermantes*, where he condemns a 'certain impotence or laziness in controlling the sources of melodic inspiration'.† Books that ushered in a literature of war, 'really a little too soon', found no more favour in his eyes: Jacques-Émile Blanche's *Lettres, Hors du joug allemand* by Léon Daudet, Montesquiou's *Offrandes blessées*: '188 elegies on the war. He must have started the day after mobilization.'‡ What is more, a writer ought not to devote himself purely to war, according to Proust, because he has a higher vocation.[116]

As to military operations, he displayed a critical mind: 'All in all, it is we who are being manipulated, despite the opposite point of view, which is still in circulation ... I am always rather frightened to see the field of

---

* *Corr.*, vol. XIV, p. 66, to Lucien Daudet. Cf. p. 229, quoting Françoise ('Only those who enjoy it should be made to go'), Proust added: 'A naïve remark (though not overly so since it's the English system), which would have avoided us being invaded, for how many Germans wanted to go to war?'

† Ibid., p. 99, 11 April 1915; cf. 'A victory whose sole result would be to substitute the aesthetic beliefs of M. Zamacoïs for those of Wagner would not be a fruitful one.'

‡ Ibid., p. 151, early June 1915. On p. 167 he congratulates Montesquiou in rather different terms.

operations stretch out indefinitely, when our enemy's principal knack is precisely that of moving troops around.'[117] He told Bibesco, just as Saint-Loup tells the Narrator in *Le Côté de Guermantes*: German manoeuvres were never the result of 'eccentric whims', as Antoine believed: 'With a people who had prepared precisely for what they had not foreseen (munitions for the duration of a war which only they expected to be short and for which they alone were equipped; withdrawing at Lens in order to deprive us of it and make use of it themselves when they didn't expect to have to withdraw; the seizure of the Dardanelles in order to block Russia which they thought was already defeated, etc.), one could hardly believe that they were likely to indulge in disorderly whimsicality . . .'[118] In October he commented to Nicolas Cottin on 'the unbelievable suffering of the Serbs', who were fighting against the Bulgarians and the Austro-Germans. In his novel as well as in his letters, Proust manifested a subtle critical mind on military matters, and he was anxious to raise himself, over and beyond the facts, to the level of general theory, to what it was that made the enemy function, to the laws that governed thought.

AN END TO SPECULATION

Proust had believed himself to be protected from harsh financial reality because of the suspension of activity on the stock exchange. He then discovered that a settlement (deferred since 31 July 1914) was to take place (he had hoped for a moratorium until the end of the war). This was scheduled for 2 October 1915: moratorial interest had to be paid by this date. In contrite mood, he turned therefore to his austere adviser in bad times, Lionel Hauser, and, in letters that are full of wit, he took stock, if not of his ruin, then at least of his insolvency. What complicated matters (as well as his own understanding of them), was that Marcel had several banks (the Crédit Industriel, Rothschild's), three stockbrokers (the Crédit Industriel, Léon, Neustadt), not including the official advisers and the occasional intermediaries (in whom love and money were mixed). Furthermore, his instructions were not expressed with the clarity to which financial institutions are accustomed. M. Ullmann, an employee of the stockbroker David Léon, testified to this seventy years later.[119] 'David Léon and his colleagues used to receive four or five pages in "the Proust style". One never knew whether he wished to transfer or sell off his balance.' As to his financial policy, it consisted in borrowing on the assets he owned, in order to speculate forward on other shares, according to the information or 'tip-offs' he had collected. The war led to disaster, reducing the value of certain shares to nil.[120] Moreover, Proust began to realize that by paying in stages, he had to pay enormous amounts of interest: he never looked at his accounts, he admitted, and he suddenly became aware of the colossal sums of money that were being swallowed up.[121] Hauser therefore immersed himself in an analysis of Marcel's accounts, and asserted that of the people who dabbled in the stock exchange, 'There are those who are born to this profession, and others who are born to burn their fingers. I don't think I exaggerate when I say that you belong to the latter . . .'* As for bankers, their interest was 'in inverse proportion to that of the client'.[122] On 29 October, came the verdict: Proust's debit balance stood at 274,183.04 francs, and it was in his best interests to pay off his debt at the earliest by selling shares, a list of which had been prepared by Hauser. In this way he would only lose 5,387.79 francs in interest† (that is to say in income), whereas if he did not repay the amount, he would have to pay 22,000 francs each year. If he followed Hauser's advice, he would still have 27,390 francs in income. The financier then asked him whether he lived on a footing higher than this figure, to which Proust wittily replied: 'Generally on neither foot, but on my back. In any case, my foot is rarely the sort to be put forward at a moment's notice and I fear that it may soon be feet first in the coffin.'‡ It was not easy to sell the shares; Proust followed Hauser's advice and subscribed to the new 5 per cent national loanstock. He bravely confronted a personal situation which would have caused many people to despair, displaying that humour 'which is the evangelical gift of the sick and the poor'.§

So ended 'the sterile year',[123] in which the balance of the war remained equal between the two sides. Proust found himself surrounded by increasing solitude, his wealth reduced by a third, his work largely unpublished. He did not go away to Cabourg. The hotel was closed and he did not rent a villa; when the Nahmias wanted to lend him their house, he turned the

---

* Corr., vol. XIV, p. 255; cf. p. 257: 'your letters that sparkle with wit and which display an admirably carefree attitude to reality'.

† Multiplying these figures to obtain the approximate value in 1999 terms, Marcel thus owed 3,688,584 francs at the 1999 rate; he would retain an income of 368,500 francs per annum. Note that between 1914 and 1915 the franc dropped by 17 per cent. In 1918 it was only worth 0.48 of its 1914 value. In 1922, the year of Proust's death, it stood at 0.33.

‡ Corr., vol. XIV, p. 266, 29 October 1915. [Proust's puns on the word pied (foot) do not translate easily: he used the idioms 'le pied levé', to be ready at a moment's notice, and 'les pieds devant', i.e. dead, or in the coffin. Tr.]

§ Ibid., p. 298. He was the former and believed himself to be the latter.

offer down, with his customary delicacy. He would never again leave Paris, which he was rediscovering under the constant threat of an enemy that was only seventy kilometres away.

WRITING IN 1915

À l'ombre des jeunes filles en fleurs

By comparing the Grasset proofs of 1914 with the definitive text of *Jeunes Filles*, we can appreciate the extent of the additional material. The title 'Chez Mme Swann' was replaced by 'Autour de Mme Swann': it no longer dealt exclusively with Odette, but with her milieu. The episode was developed in Carnets 3 and 4, in which Proust noted down expressions intended for Norpois or for the Duc de Guermantes; further additional material can be found in Cahier 61, where he wrote: 'to be added to the proofs that Gallimard have (that is to say, in the first part of *À l'ombre des jeunes filles en fleurs*)'. These were the Grasset proofs consigned to Gallimard in 1916. Marcel may have begun this *cahier* in 1915, particularly since that was the year he asked Lucien Daudet to prepare a portrait of the Princesse Mathilde for him: he wished to compare what he had already written about this princess in the Jardin d'Acclimatation with his friend's memories of her.

The addenda are much more important in the second part of *Jeunes Filles*, which takes place at Balbec,[124] than they are in the first. Unfortunately, because the manuscript was broken up when preparing the fifty copies of a de-luxe edition in 1920, we are unable to piece together the process exactly. Cahier 61 contains some important further details that portray the girls, and especially Albertine. The proofs that Gallimard printed in 1918 show these alterations,* carried out from 1914 onwards; it is not possible to establish exactly what was written in 1915. It nevertheless seems likely that Proust completed his portrait of Saint-Loup at the time he learned of the disappearance of Fénelon, in March.

---

* An unpublished letter of Proust's bound into the Gallimard book proof of *Swann* (private collection), indicated how the printer should deal with the Grasset proofs, the *cahiers* and the typescript.

Sodome et Gomorrhe 1915

Assuming that the subject of homosexuality was present from the beginning of the book, the main modification in *Sodome*, from 1914 on, was the invention of the story of Albertine. Cahier 54 contains a first sketch of *Albertine disparue*, written shortly after the death of Agostinelli. Cahier 71, written afterwards, describes the arrival at Balbec for the second visit, the first suspicions, an outline of *La Prisonnière* and the flight. Cahier 46 incorporates 'Les intermittences du cœur' and the stay at Balbec. A series of five exercise books (numbered by Proust IV–VIII: in the manuscript that is numbered I–XX, *Sodome* occupies Cahiers I–VIII) date from 1915.[125] This section of the novel forms an entity from this year on. It was at this time, too, that Albertine took the place of Baronne Putbus' chambermaid once and for all, and that the etymological conversations, based on the book by Hippolyte Cocheris, *Origine et formation des noms de lieu*, were introduced.

La Prisonnière

Cahiers V, VI and VII of the manuscript, from *Sodome* to *Le Temps retrouvé*, which come after the second visit to Balbec, date from 1915. The first of these, having reached the end of *Sodome*, relates the life of the Narrator with Albertine, her lies and the matinée at the Trocadéro. Cahier VI, after the arrival of *Le Figaro*, contains the description of waking up, some conversations ('Well, supposing it is my destiny to die in a riding accident. I've often had a presentiment of it!' One thinks of Agostinelli and the aeroplane) and some walks with Albertine, as well as a description of Wagner's music. It then describes the evening at the Verdurins and the Vinteuil concert (originally a quartet, then a symphony). Cahier VII extends from the return from the evening with Brichot up to Albertine's departure. Some notes from Carnet 2, which mention Albertine and the aeroplanes, are placed next to a reference to *Le Temps* of February 1915. It was in 1916 that Proust prepared his fair copy of the manuscript of *La Prisonnière*.[126]

Albertine disparue

As we have seen, it was in Cahiers 71 and 54 that Proust wrote his first sketch of the flight and death of Albertine, and of the grief and jealousy that resulted.[127] In fact, most of Cahier 54 was written by October 1914, as Proust observed: 'I wrote this at the time I returned from Cabourg, probably at the end of this notebook.'[128] In 1915–16 he organized the various episodes of the story in Cahiers VII, VIII, VIII *bis* and IX, and he introduced Vinteuil's theme into *La Prisonnière*. He also prepared the Albertine episode by making additions to *Jeunes Filles*, *Guermantes* and *Sodome et Gomorrhe II*. Also linked to Albertine, Proust introduced *La Fille aux yeux d'or*.[129] One important passage dealing with general aesthetic views, which is now in *Le Temps retrouvé* but which might have figured in *Albertine disparue*, also dates from 1915, as is proved by the correspondence, which testifies to the fact that Proust was reading the Goncourts' *Journal* once more. Originally Gilberte came across people whom her father had known in the *Journal*, and we were getting close to the chapter about the wedding invitation (inspired in 1915 by the funeral announcement of the Comtesse Mnizech, Balzac's daughter-in-law).* Marcel had also reread the Goncourts' *Journal* in 1911, perhaps in order to read about his own models, the Princesse Mathilde, the Comtesse Greffulhe, Robert de Montesquiou, the Daudets, Hahn and many others; and also to re-experience the customs and fashions of his youth. The Goncourts were to society life what Sainte-Beuve was to literature. But in 1915[130] he was more concerned with freeing himself from this book by composing a pastiche of it, and making use of this pastiche to reveal an unfamiliar aspect of his characters' youth, which Goncourt, who was older than the Narrator, and more narrow-minded, may have known about.

Finally, Proust incorporated the Venetian episode, anticipated for some time, into the narrative. At the beginning of November 1915 he sent Mme Scheikévitch, along with a copy of *Swann* printed on Holland paper, the whole story of Albertine, the grieving and the forgetting; he had begun this summary in the summer, and he took the material from Cahiers 55 and 56.[131]

---

* *Corr.*, vol. XIV, pp. 146–8, shortly after 3 June 1915, to L. Daudet: in the 'third volume of *Swann*', a single unexpected marriage causes all these names to file past; 'but this is towards the end'.

Le Temps retrouvé

Here Proust essentially made piecemeal changes to a structure that had already been worked out beforehand. The death of Gaston de Caillavet, on 14 January 1915, for example, suggested to Proust Bloch's death.[132] His relationship with Jeanne Pouquet was, as we have seen, the basis for the description of the Saint-Loup ménage. The comments about Albertine may have been inserted at the same time as *La Fugitive* was being written. There is no doubt that from this date Proust began making notes about the war in Cahier 74, to which he gave the title 'Babouche' and which he would make use of up until 1920. The death of Saint-Loup was directly inspired, therefore, by those of Bertrand de Fénelon and Robert d'Humières. When, in June, Proust paid a visit to the Comtesse de La Béraudière, the Comte Greffulhe's mistress, it may have been to take some obscure revenge on the Comtesse Greffulhe, who showed not the least interest in his work (as he was well aware), but it was principally in order to portray the mistresses of the Duc de Guermantes. He found her to be 'delightful, from every point of view, and someone who had great vivacity and was very frank in her thinking'.[133] According to Céleste Albaret, Mme de La Béraudière 'was at M. Proust's feet; she didn't know what to do to make him interested in her'; when he, delighted, finally went to call on the lady, the Comte Greffulhe was there, 'fuming in his chair' because Marcel had been allowed in.* Similarly, several visits to see Comte Clary,[134] who was paralysed, almost blind, and looked after by his Japanese manservant, were the inspiration (as was the Prince de Sagan, who was in a wheel-chair towards the end of his life) for Charlus, whose chair was pushed by Jupien.[135]

WRITING IN 1916

It was only in 1916, after having signed a contract with the NRF, that Proust went back to the Grasset proofs of *Guermantes*; the work of rewriting these proofs would last until March 1920. He received the first proofs in June 1919. The date on which the printing of volume I was completed was 17 August 1920. For the second visit to Balbec, in *Sodome et Gomorrhe*, Proust questioned Albert Nahmias as to how girls would have dressed 'to

---

* C. Albaret, p. 194. The acquaintance lasted two or three months; Proust, having satisfied his curiosity, did not see her again.

go out to dinner in town by the seaside during our early years in Cabourg' and about 'the little railway that served the local community' and the nicknames it was given; Nahmias' reply provided him with a development on the theme of the '*tortillard*' [the slow, local train], the '*tacot*' [the old banger], the '*transatlantique*' [the deckchair], the '*decauville*' [the name of the inventor of the narrow gauge track] and the '*funi*' [funicular].[136] In this same year Proust completed the final manuscript version of the Albertine episode. For instance, when he questioned Gautier-Vignal on several occasions about the students of aviation at Buc and Antibes, or about Baron Duquesne, who had lived with Agostinelli's sister, these experiences would pave the way for the posthumous enquiries about whom his heroine had been associating with and the theme of jealousy beyond the grave. On a lighter note, the same care he took over perfecting his novel prompted him to ask Céleste's niece, Marcelle Larivière, for outlines for an essay, the knowledge and subtlety of which he praised: they would become Gisèle's composition in *Jeunes Filles*.[137]

Proust also elaborated on a highly original subject: the dresses designed by the couturier Fortuny.[138] On 11 May 1915, at the Strauses', he had asked Mme Straus about Fortuny's dresses, and she had offered to lend Marcel a coat designed by him.[139] But it was Maria de Madrazo who provided the answer to his principal question: had Fortuny used the coupled birds, 'so recurrent on the Byzantine capitals at St Mark's'[140] as motifs for his dressing-gowns? Reynaldo's sister told Proust that the couturier had drawn his inspiration from Carpaccio. Proust then explained the latest development of his plot to her: at Balbec, in Albertine's presence, Elstir relates how an artist has discovered the secret of the old Venetian fabrics. In 'the third volume', the Narrator, who is engaged to Albertine, gives her these gowns, which evoke Venice and the longing to go there, as a present. After her death, in Venice the hero discovers 'a dress such as [he had] given her' in paintings by Carpaccio: 'In the past this dress evoked Venice for me and made me want to leave Albertine; now the Carpaccio in which I see it evokes Albertine and makes Venice painful to me . . . thus the Fortuny *leitmotiv*, which is not very extensive but is crucial, plays a part that is in turn sensual, poetic and sorrowful . . . Carpaccio happens to be a painter I know very well, I have spent entire days at San Giorgio degli Schiavoni and in front of *St Ursula*, and I've translated everything that Ruskin wrote about each of these paintings.'[141] As usual, Marcel wanted to consult books: Mme de Madrazo lent him Ludwig and Milmenti's study of Carpaccio (but he also knew the one by the Rosenthals);

the painting *The Patriarch of Grado Exorcising a Demoniac*, and its comparison with Whistler, inspired the description of Venice in *La Fugitive*.* At the same period, Proust added Boldini's *Leda* (merged with Moreau's), which Helleu owned, to *Albertine disparue*.[142]

As for *Le Temps retrouvé*: Proust inserted the conversations on military matters in *Le Côté de Guermantes*, as if they dated from before the war, around May 1916; he then wrote to Gallimard: 'The conversations about military strategy have led me to make a connection at the end of the book, to introduce not the war as such but a few of its episodes, and M. de Charlus gets his due, incidentally, in this Paris bedecked with colourful soldiers reminiscent of a town in a Carpaccio painting. There is nothing anti-militarist about any of this, needless to say; quite the reverse. But the newspapers are very foolish (and are treated extremely badly in my book).'[143] That spring, therefore, Proust must have written at least a first draft of the episode devoted to Paris during the war, which is set in 1916, as well as adding a visit to the capital in 1914.[144]

But he also worked on the '*bal de têtes*'. On 4 November he went to the Opéra to see *Briséis* by Chabrier. He met Philippe Crozier, Félix Faure's former head of protocol, which led to some lines about 'people disguised by old age'. 'Was it the touch of ice about his moustache that gave this elegant man the look of an old bogeyman? This inconvenient white moustache on his rigid mouth had the desired effect and gave him the appearance of an elderly Bismarck, but he would have done better to have had it removed, it was embarrassing to see . . .'[145]

DAILY LIFE IN 1916

For France 1916 would for ever be the year of Verdun. For Proust it began overshadowed by war and death; it had carried off Bertrand de Fénelon: 'Alas, 1916 will have its violets and its apple blossom, and before that its flowers flecked with frost, but there will never be a Bertrand again.'[146] And although Marcel was confident of victory, he considered that the arguments of the official propaganda could do with improvement. For example, when it was said that Germany was constricted within a 'fortress', if she conquered the whole world, she would still be in a fortress,

* *RTP*, vol. IV, p. 225: 'Carpaccio almost succeeded in reviving my love for Albertine' and what follows.

but with plenty of room to move: 'At present I find their fortress a bit large for my liking.'[147] He also observed that the gulf that separated 'the pre-war years from this colossal geological convulsion'[148] was profound, an idea that he took up some while later in *Le Temps retrouvé*.* He believed that his solitary existence enabled him never to be wrong about the war, because he had all the time needed to reflect on it. It was this solitude, as well as his vocation as a writer, that caused him to have doubts about friendship: 'It is my fate to be incapable of benefiting from anyone but myself . . . I am myself only when I am alone, and I do not profit from others except in so far as they enable me to make discoveries within myself, either by making me suffer (which is more likely through love than through friendship), or by their ridiculous behaviour . . . which I don't make fun of, but which helps me to understand the human character.'[149] These themes can be found in *Le Temps retrouvé*, even though we cannot say, as we can in many other cases, whether the letter preceded the novel. The role of correspondence is to integrate the idea, or the theory, with the life or the biography, to show it as something experienced and not fictional.

MUSIC

As Proust wrote, 'for some years . . . Beethoven's last quartets and the music of Franck had been [his] principal spiritual nourishment'.[150] To this, one should add Fauré. On 14 April he attended a Fauré festival given at the Odéon by the Poulet Quartet, with the composer at the piano.[151] A few days earlier the Poulet Quartet had come to Proust's home to play Beethoven's Thirteenth Quartet and Franck's quartet.[152] Contemplating a further private concert[153] at which the same players would perform Franck's quartet and Fauré's First Piano Quartet, he hoped that Pétain would play the viola in the latter work, and he asked him whether he was also a pianist, so that he could sight-read certain pieces for him. He was even attracted by the musician's lock of hair, just as Charlus is by Morel's.[154] It seems likely that Marcel's interest in this young musician extended

---

* *RTP*, vol. IV, p. 306: 'One of the ideas most in vogue was that the pre-war days were separated from the war by something as profound, something that appeared to be as long-lasting, as a geological period . . . The truth is that this profound change wrought by the war was in inverse proportion to the quality of the minds which it affected . . . those who have constructed an all-encompassing inner life for themselves have small regard for the importance of events.' There can be no doubt that Proust was thinking not only of Chateaubriand, whom he quotes later, but of himself.

beyond music as does Charlus' in Morel or as did Montesquiou's in Delafosse. Furthermore, from Pétain[155] and Amable Massis Proust gleaned information about the street cries of Paris for *La Prisonnière*. In any event we know how Proust listened to music thanks to the memoirs of two of the musicians in the quartet, Gaston Poulet and Massis.

According to Poulet, one evening in 1916, at about eleven o'clock, a stranger rang the bell: 'I am Marcel Proust. I am tormented by the desire to hear you play César Franck's quartet.' He offered to go and collect the other three musicians by car (Massis last); at one o'clock in the morning they all went back to Boulevard Haussmann by car. Proust stretched out on the divan in his bedroom. When the quartet had finished, he asked them to play the piece again. Four taxis delivered the musicians to their homes. He asked them back on several occasions so that he could hear Mozart, Ravel, Schumann, and above all Fauré and Franck. 'He was familiar with everything. Fauré was the composer most in tune with his sensibilities.' But very often he asked them to play the third movement of Franck's violin sonata for him again, and Beethoven's last quartets. 'For us Marcel Proust was a marvellous listener, straightforward, direct, a man who drank in music without raising any questions . . . And, conversely, we could sense the reverberations of his style, within him.'

According to Massis, during the interval at one of his concerts,[156] a man came to look for him and invited him to come and play at his home one evening in the near future. At twelve o'clock one night, the bell rang, and Proust asked the viola player to gather his friends together. They went downstairs to Odilon Albaret's motor car, which had a vast eiderdown inside; on the folding seat was a soup tureen containing mashed potatoes. Odilon indicated, with a gesture, that 'his employer was a little bizarre but not dangerous'; they went to collect the three others. Back in his bedroom, Marcel lay down in the darkness. Franck's quartet was played; not a sound, not a movement from the writer. He asked them to play it again. He gave each of the musicians 150 francs. A few weeks later, it was Fauré's piano quartet, with an encore. For all that, he did not forget Reynaldo Hahn, whose new opera, *Nausicaa*,[157] he went to hear performed at Versailles in May, in the company of Henri Bardac. But in 1918 Proust would say that his thirst for music was 'quenched somewhat' (which shows that he had finished with the music in *La Prisonnière*), and he complained about the ingratitude of Massis, for whom he had done 'some truly considerable things' and who had never got in touch with him again; on the other hand, he still saw that 'very nice viola player, young Pétain'.[158]

READING

For *La Prisonnière* Proust wanted to borrow Dostoevsky's *The Possessed* from Bibesco (the following year, he borrowed *The Brothers Karamazov* from him)[159] and, for *Le Temps retrouvé*, the *Arabian Nights*.[160] He also enquired of Lucien Daudet whether he ought to read *Sindbad the Sailor* in the Mardrus or the Galland translation. It so happened that when the British had just been captured by the Turks at Kout-el-Amara, in Mesopotamia on 29 April, he wrote the following passage for *Le Temps retrouvé*: 'I must admit that because of the books that I had read at Balbec not far away from Robert, I had been more impressed . . . in the Middle East, à propos the siege of Kout-el-Amara . . . to see, close by the name of Baghdad, that of Basra, which is the Bassorah mentioned so often in the *Arabian Nights*, the town which, whenever Sindbad the Sailor left Baghdad, or before returning to it, was used as his port of embarkation or disembarkation, long before General Townshend or General Gorringe, in the days of the Caliphs.'* He also searched for aristocratic names in Tallemant des Réaux,† observing that Balzac had delved as deeply in Réaux as he had in Saint-Simon.[161] In Montesquiou's *La Castiglione*, he came across Mme Standish, whom he placed at the Opéra in *Sodome*.[162] He also asked Lucien Daudet (who came to see him every Saturday, and with whom he seemed to have rekindled a closer relationship) about what a girl might do with a vanity-case, which we find in *Sodome*.‡ Since he was reading books about Carpaccio, we can assume that his reading, about which we know very little, was still orientated towards his work (setting aside the books sent to him by friends, which in general he was content to leaf through sufficiently to be able to thank them, as with Montesquiou's *Têtes couronnées*;[163] he did, however, read *Poétique* by Pierre Louÿs: the brevity of this treatise by Louÿs, who had not responded to the copy of *Du côté de chez Swann* that he had been sent, struck Proust as a criticism: the length of a book was not 'a proof of its smallness'; neither could he approve of the axiom, 'Never use drafts'.)[164] Out of this casual reading, certain titles

---

* *RTP*, vol. IV, pp. 560–1; cf. vol. II, pp. 257–8, in which a Creil plate illustrates the same subject. Around the same time he wrote a letter to Cocteau about the *Arabian Nights*, which has not been found (*Corr.*, vol. XV, p. 240).

† Seventeenth-century historical writer. *Tr.*

‡ *Corr.*, vol. XV, p. 111. *RTP*, vol. III, p. 424: Albertine looks at herself in a little gold mirror taken from a vanity-case bought at Cartier's, and given to her by the Narrator (a reminder, as we have seen, of the vanity-cases given to the d'Alton sisters).

featured in his own book, such as *Éloges* by Saint-Léger Léger, sent to him by Gaston Gallimard, which he showed to Céleste, just as the Narrator does in *Sodome*: 'It was a volume of the admirable but obscure poems of Saint-Léger Léger. Céleste read a few pages to me and said: "But are you quite sure that these are poems? Aren't they more like riddles?"'[165] Gallimard also sent him *Foi en la France* by Henri Ghéon, but Proust thought it lacked 'the abrupt combination of thought and image, instantaneous and disrupting, that was necessary'; it was the work of a literary scholar 'more ingenious than straightforward'. 'This poet speaks to me but does not transform me.'[166] Writing about Romain Rolland's *Au-dessus de la mêlée*, he intimated that the author was rather more beneath it, 'for heroism probably occupies a higher level'.[167] On the other hand, he did not read *Œuvres* by P. Rapin, given to him by a new friend, Walter Berry, an American, who was president of the US Chamber of Commerce in Paris; it was a book made to be looked at; its binding bore the coat of arms of the Guermantes: 'The *fatum* of this little book,' Proust wrote to Berry, defining the object of his own work in the process, 'decreed that, through you, it should come to the person who has exhumed the Guermantes from their tombs and has sought to revive the lustre of their *extinct name*.'[168]

All this time Lionel Hauser was busy trying to sort out Marcel's financial affairs; Proust was paying 16,000 francs a year in interest to the Crédit Industriel, which could be reduced to 11,000 francs at another bank. However, out of 'family' considerations, Marcel wrote that he did not want to leave this bank; to which Hauser responded by quoting *Le Médecin malgré lui* (one should not intervene between a husband and a wife who has been beaten by him). Proust, touched to the quick, replied by mentioning the gentleness which Albufera or Fénelon had shown him, unlike the sarcastic Hauser. But the businessman remained adamant, and he sketched a cruel portrait of Marcel: 'You live unfortunately in an atmosphere of idealism from which you certainly derive pleasures that are not easily available on earth ... You have grown up since your childhood, but you haven't aged, you have remained the child who does not allow himself to be scolded even when he is disobedient. This is why you have more or less eliminated from your circle all those who, refusing to succumb to your cajoling, have had the courage to scold you when you were being naughty ... I am quite happy to allow you to plunge body and soul into the Absolute, but only when you have paid back all your overdrafts.' To complain that he was ruined, as Marcel did to his entourage, was a great exaggeration.[169] Proust replied by invoking the 'retractile reflexes' which can be provoked in those of a nervous disposition by too much brusque-ness. He added that he lamented the deaths and the sufferings of others, but he would not talk about his financial losses, which were 'caused by [his] stupidity', in an 'elegiac mode', even though he regretted them deeply.[170] It becomes clear that if, despite Hauser's advice, Proust had difficulty stabilizing his financial situation, it was because he could not bring himself to sell certain of his shares without any compensation. The dialogue would continue.

FROM GRASSET TO GALLIMARD

On 24 February 1916, emphasizing the fact that Grasset had been called up, Gide suggested to Proust that the sequel to *Swann* be published by the NRF.* On 29 February Gaston Gallimard wrote to him: 'If ever the opportunity arises of republishing or buying more of your work, you can absolutely depend on me, without any restrictions. If your second book is ready and if you liked the idea of my being your publisher, I should be ready to have it printed tomorrow, and put it on sale within a month. I would accept all your conditions. I like reading a fine book, but I also like it to be well printed. I have a good printer . . . Finally, allow me to press this matter most particularly: I should so much like to make amends for our mistake and for you to join us, and that my friends should have me to thank, in part, for this.' This charming letter, which did not lack intuition, since it was addressed to an author who was still not particularly famous, was followed by the complicated negotiations (Marcel initially raising all the obstacles that stood in the way of what he wanted) that led to Proust moving from Grasset to Gallimard; this went unnoticed at first, since none of his books would be published before 1919. Furthermore, as a result of the move, Proust would see the collection of the Gallimards' family portraits, and, in particular, 'a Monet that is the finest of Manets'.[171]

Proust, believing that he was committed to Grasset, replied with a letter of regretful refusal that was imbued with a desire to accept.[172] In May 1916 Gallimard renewed his proposal, René Blum having offered to act as intermediary with Grasset. Proust then reminded Gallimard, 'to try to

---

* *Corr., avec G. Gallimard*, p. 27: 'Yes, Gide told me, in 1914 and again the other day, that the NRF would willingly publish me.' Gide, *Journal*, Bibliothèque de la Pléiade, p. 543: 'Finished the evening at Marcel Proust's (whom I had not seen since '92). I promised myself I would describe this visit at length; but I'm no longer in the mood to do so this morning.'

discourage him', of 'the duty of scrupulousness that tied him to his original publisher', of the immorality of the volume entitled *Sodome et Gomorrhe*, and of his fear of being abandoned along the way, while at the same time leaving the final decision to him: 'If the reasons I have given do not dishearten you, then I shall do my best to have myself released from Grasset.'[173] On 15 May Gaston replied delicately to all of Marcel's objections: 'The length of your book does not matter. The audacity of your portraits does not deter me . . . The obligations you feel towards your book are ones that I shall feel myself . . . I formally undertake from now on to publish all your books . . . on whatever conditions you wish . . . None of the reasons you give me has put me off, quite the contrary.' He stated finally that he was prepared to give an indemnity to Grasset. Acting as an intermediary, René Blum made repeated approaches to Grasset, who had forbidden that his address should be given out; it was not until 1 August that he replied from a Swiss clinic where, he said, he had spent six months convalescing after an attack of typhoid fever, without making a full recovery. After expressing considerable reluctance, he declared that he had 'too much pride to retain an author who no longer had confidence in him'.[174] Offended, Proust wrote back on 14 August reminding him that his request dated back to 1914, that there was no contract between them, that the Grasset publishing house owed him money, that since their business activities had been suspended he was entirely justified in approaching the NRF, and that an indemnity could be paid to him. On 29 August Grasset agreed to forgo publishing 'the second volume of *À la recherche du temps perdu*'.[175] On 28 September Marcel was thus able to inform Gide, to whom Gallimard had shown Grasset's first letter, and without whom, he knew, nothing got done at the NRF, that he had broken off his agreement with Grasset.[176] That month Gallimard paid Proust a visit, spending virtually the whole night with him, and found him 'just as he appears in his work, his conversation is like his writing style, lively, full of incidents that had happened to him, charming and full of affection'.[177] And on 5 or 6 November Proust sent him the first part ('Autour de Mme Swann') of *À l'ombre des jeunes filles en fleurs*, 'a flowery cushion' upon which 'the two rather fearsome storeys' of *Sodome et Gomorrhe* were built.[178] He informed him that the second part (that is to say 'Noms de pays: le pays') would be much better and would justify the title better.

GASTON GALLIMARD

Gaston Gallimard[179] was born in 1881, the same year as Grasset and ten years after Proust, at 79 rue Saint-Lazare, the son of Paul Gallimard, 'architect', and his wife, Lucie Duché. Paul Gallimard had no need of a job; a dilettante, a great lover of art and a bibliophile, like his father Gustave, he mixed in the world of artists and galleries. Renoir spent two summers on his estate at Bénerville, and the young Gaston used to watch the artist at work.[180] An El Greco, a Goya, seven Delacroix, eight Daumiers, as well as paintings by Manet (*Le Linge*), Monet, Degas, Sisley, Cézanne and Toulouse-Lautrec could be seen in the rue Saint-Lazare. But the art collector was also interested in women, he invested his wealth in theatres, he kept some Odette Swanns, and he set himself up in the rue de Clichy, away from the conjugal home. Gaston would suffer as a result, but he retained some of his father's tastes. Timid as an adolescent, unaffected, charming, indolent and absent-minded, he wanted above all to preserve his independence. After secondary studies at the Lycée Condorcet, he did not continue with higher education. Born in an age when, if one was rich, one could live without working, he led the life of a dandy in a Balzac novel, and he became Robert de Flers' secretary; in this way he assuaged his passion for the theatre and wrote a few reviews. It happened that *La Nouvelle Revue Française*, which had been founded in 1909, was looking for a wealthy and disinterested manager: Gaston, at the age of twenty-five, would take charge of the sales department of the newly launched publishing house, which had its offices at 1 rue Saint-Benoît. In May 1911 he went into partnership with Gide and Schlumberger (each of them contributing 20,000 francs), and he became manager of the new publishing house. Their first three books in 1911 were Claudel's *L'Otage*, Gide's *Isabelle* and Charles-Louis Philippe's *La Mère et l'enfant*; a fine start indeed! In 1912 the firm moved to 35 rue Madame. When Proust submitted *Du côté de chez Swann*, Gaston Gallimard was not therefore the 'boss': it was a self-governing board, in which Gide and Schlumberger took the lead and wanted to stick to short books, that turned down his manuscript. From January 1914 Jacques Rivière, the assistant editor, had drawn Gide's and Gaston's attention to the error that had been made. On 23 October 1913 the magazine also established the Théâtre du Vieux Colombier, run by Copeau and Dullin. And then, after an attempt by Gide to get rid of Gallimard, a reading committee was formed, comprising Gallimard, Tronche, Rivière, as well as the six founder members.[181]

In 1914 Gaston was opposed to the war: 'As you can imagine, I'm no hero!' and he resorted to every means not to have to fight. He had 'deceased' written on the register at the *mairie*, he made himself ill, he lost twenty-six kilos and had himself discharged. Constantly depressed and made ill by this war in which he did not participate, he spent his time in nursing homes in Switzerland, and Berthe Lemarié took responsibility for the running of the magazine, the book publishing and the theatre. In January 1916 he returned from a clinic in Montana, and it was at this point that he renewed contact with Proust. He developed an excellent strategy: those writers whom he had not discovered himself, he would later attract to his firm, through either his own celebrity or his charm. The man who would become the greatest of French publishers would always retain a secret frailty – along with his passion for independence,[182] and beneath a mixture of affability ('lovely, but a bit Lucifer-like', said Max Jacob), generosity tempered by a hard-nosed business sense, attraction and detach-ment. It was this frailty that made him invite André Beucler to share his bedroom in the rue Saint-Lazare, and that prompted Proust to give him medical advice: he was to see a doctor to ensure that there was nothing physiologically wrong with him, before undergoing a 'psychotherapeutic cure'; Cottard, in short, before Du Boulbon.[183]

On 4 July 1916 Proust learned of the death of his manservant, Nicolas Cottin, who left a son. It was impossible to take Céline back into his home, 'because of her hatred for Céleste',[184] and he had no cause to get rid of the latter. He was saddened, too, by the death of the Duc de Rohan (born in 1879), 'a noble anti-aristocrat'[185] and a *député*, 'who went to the front not to keep an eye on the generals but to fight', who had already been wounded twice before; Marcel wrote two long letters (which have not survived) to the duke's mother* and his widow. Doing his best to comfort those who had lost someone dear to them, he made it known that in his forthcoming book there were some passages about death which

---

* On Herminie de Verteillac, Princesse de Léon and later the eleventh Duchesse de Rohan, see É. de Gramont, *Les Marronniers en fleurs, Mémoires II*, Grasset, 1929, vol. II, p. 71 ff. She was the mother of a friend of Proust's, Marie Murat. She entertained a great deal, mingling the aristocracy with poets, she wrote some poetry herself, and during the war she transformed her house into a hospital. Her husband strutted about among the young women saying: 'I am sure you don't know who I am?' He would inspire one characteristic of the Duc de Guermantes in so far as his mistresses were concerned: 'When, after a month, he had had enough of them, he relinquished them to us and we had them for life,' his wife used to say.

'may bring sorrow and do some good ... It may contain the kind of literature that is nothing but the most profound scrutinizing of both life and death, and which as a result can be of use to those who are afflicted.'[186] In addition Marcel complained of eye trouble, but he refused to go and consult a specialist for what was probably nothing more than ordinary long-sightedness. He sent Céleste to an optician, 'with the task of bringing back a whole choice of spectacles' for him to try; she returned with ten pairs, which he tried, retaining those that suited him and not bothering to send back the others.[187]

PAUL MORAND

Born in 1888, Paul Morand had sat the *petit concours des chancelleries* examinations in 1912, and then, in 1913, the *grand concours des ambassades*; he had then been appointed to the French embassy in London, where he mixed in high society. Having been called up, he was transferred on 28 August 1914 to the cipher department of the War Ministry, and later retained by the Army Medical Board in the auxiliary services. He had met Proust around 1 September at the home of Henri Bardac, having first heard of him through Bertrand de Fénelon* in London in 1913. On 31 July 1916 he became an attaché on the staff of Philippe Berthelot, Head of Cabinet at the Ministry for Foreign Affairs. Morand had written a novel, which Giraudoux advised him not to publish, and a short story, 'Clarisse', which *Le Mercure de France* would publish in May 1917. Since 16 August 1916 (the time he became friendly with Hélène Chrisoveloni, the Princesse Soutzo), he kept his *Journal d'un attaché d'ambassade*,[188] which provides some valuable information about this period, and particularly about Proust.

On 16 December 1916, accompanied by Henri Bardac, Morand called on Marcel. He first encountered Céleste: 'What a curious character is Céleste, who copies down all Proust's novels by hand, gives her opinion, reads the books that are sent to him, etc., her eyes lowered, her tone of voice studied, looking too much as if butter wouldn't melt in her mouth.' Then her employer: 'Proust, wrapped up in his pelisse, wearing a jacket and grey suede slippers, with a cane and pearl-grey gloves that are too tight, as in paintings by Manet, which make the hands look as if they are

---

* Of Proust he wrote, 'He has published two books at the author's expense, he told me, and would doubtless remain unknown. He's a Saturnian, and very difficult as a friend' (P. Morand, in *Hommage à M. Proust*, p. 93).

made of wood; a gentle, elegant face, his temples hidden by his black hair, his heavy chin sunk into his collar, prominent cheekbones, contorted ears, looking more ill than ever, yellowish, with a stooped back and sunken thorax.' Proust showed them some faded photographs of the Princesse Mathilde, of Montesquiou when young, of Maupassant, Lucien Daudet, the Prince de Polignac with Charles Haas, of 'Loche' Radziwill, of Mme Straus. 'Proust really does live in the past.'[189]

But who is this Paul Morand, who was destined to play an important role in French literature, adulated one moment, forgotten the next and then fashionable once more? Some writers shut themselves away in their studies, writing in the early hours of the morning. Others roam the world and scribble away in the cabin of a steamship, the sleeping compartment of a train, or in an aircraft seat. Some are invalids and their journeys are the soul-searching ones of inner suffering; others are bursting with health, never get tired and retire to bed so late that one never realizes how early they get up. Some have literature as their only vocation; others sparkle in that most glamorous of careers, diplomacy. Paul Morand was a champion of the world. He travelled it with the ambition, worthy of a Jules Verne (who travelled less than him), of knowing it in its entirety: 'I have swum in every lake in the world,' he said one day. 'The largest bar in the world' is the subject of one of his best passages in *Rien que la terre* (a title which makes one feel the earth is a disappointment). Hence his liking for the short story: the form captures a fleeting moment, a place, a woman. His novels are long short stories, their characters like silhouettes or cartoon strips. Paul Morand enshrines perfectly the literature of 1925, with its taste for English chic (such as French literature imagines it), for speed, for sudden emotions that are fashionable and short-lived, and its return to traditional writing. The terseness, the geometrical precision, the surface decorated with a few golden touches, are, as in the work of Cocteau, Colette and Giraudoux, typical of this period. *Lewis et Irène*, a triumph in the manner of a gaunt and fever-ridden Balzac, is a novel about the stock exchange, about travelling, about love being sacrificed to business. Lewis, who emulates Don Giovanni, has known as many railway stations as he has had mistresses (413). Irène prefers the bank to love. These two new-age financiers meet, fall in love and separate between two trains, two steamers, two telegrams. The speed of the action should not mislead us, however: Morand wrote with difficulty, crossed out everything and only discovered the ellipsis after long hours of work.

It would require the calamity of the Second World War, in which our hero behaved in a somewhat unheroic and not very British way, the arrival of maturity and then of old age, when the habitual dandy, the seducer surrounded by women, began to look like the statues of the buddhas that surrounded him in the Avenue Charles-Floquet, for this precious but rough talent to plumb darker depths than it had previously done. *L'Homme pressé* and *Lewis et Irène* vanished rapidly into the distance, driven out by *Hécate et ses chiens*. This was the man whom Proust would introduce to the literary world by writing a preface to *Tendres Stocks*.

On 27 December 1916 Marcel attended a dinner party given by Mme Daudet in honour of Francis Jammes; they listened to songs by Milhaud based on poems written by Jammes and by Claudel. Among the guests were the younger Daudets, Misia Edwards, Hélène Berthelot, Mme Chausson, the Hinnisdaëls, Claudel and Hélène Vacaresco. Mme Daudet's pink immutability delicately reminded Marcel of the portrait that Lucien had painted of her: 'In the collection of portraits of "Mothers", it was one that, in the meticulousness of its adoration, was the most affecting.'[190] He was no doubt thinking of Whistler, of Blanche and of himself.

At the end of 'this appalling year', which he never at any time referred to as the 'year of Verdun', saddened as he was 'by the universal misery',[191] he observed that it was not easy to be happy nor even to dare hope for happiness as long as 'the Germans are at Noyon'. 'We are like people in mourning for whom there are to be no more celebrations.'[192] This was the year, however, in which he chose to set the longest part of 'M. de Charlus pendant la guerre'.

1917: THE RITZ

During 1917 Proust, at the age of forty-five, rediscovered his youth, and in spite of complaints about his eyesight and his heart, he went out or entertained more frequently than he had done for the past fifteen years. Some new faces began to appear in his life: Jacques Truelle, Jacques Porel, Jacques de Lacretelle, Pierre de Polignac, Emmanuel Berl,* Ramon Fernandez,[193] and above all the Princesse Soutzo and Paul Morand. This

---

* Berl has described his quarrels with Proust in *Silvia* (Gallimard, 1952): in 1917 his admiration led to a series of visits and then to a violent quarrel followed by a break-up; Berl believed in his love for Silvia, whereas Proust maintained that a true union of hearts was impossible. Marcel yelled at him: 'You are more stupid than Léon Blum' (who reckoned himself to be an expert on love), and hurled his slippers at Berl's head.

couple instilled a strange passion in him, and it was as if René Girard's theory of triangular desire applied here: the object of his desire (Morand) was assigned to the man (Marcel) by a third party (in this case the princess), to whom he was bound by feelings of admiration and rivalry.[194] The Ritz and the Crillon became the centres of Proust's life. At the Ritz, in particular, he formed close links with the staff and the maîtres d'hôtel, among them the famous Olivier Dabescat, who showed him many a kindness and supplied him with a great deal of information. Dabescat had been a former maître d'hôtel at the Princess restaurant, and later at the Ritz, in London. He was adept at recognizing and welcoming every guest in a personal manner, and he had come to know the whole of international high society. A waiter in the restaurant has described the first time he served Proust at dinner: entering the deserted room at about half past eleven, Marcel ordered a roast chicken, potatoes and fresh vegetables, followed by salad and a vanilla ice-cream. He then asked for a large pot of coffee to be served in a small room, where he consumed sixteen demitasses of an excellent coffee. Throughout the meal Marcel questioned this waiter about the clientele at the Ritz, which at this period included senior members of the English aristocracy, the Prince of Wales and his brothers, King Alfonso XIII, the King of Portugal and Queen Marie of Romania.[195]

It was from this observation point that Proust contemplated Paris under bombardment. Other more mysterious outings go unmentioned in his letters. They can be traced in a poem by Morand, in notes made by Cocteau, and in the memoirs of Sachs, Faÿ, Germain, Gide and John Agate.

WITH GALLIMARD

In early 1917 Gaston Gallimard, who was not at all well, was convalescing in Switzerland. Proust explained to Berthe Lemarié, who looked after the production of books at the NRF, that he had shown his maid where his manuscript notebooks were kept. Should he die, Gaston Gallimard would know where to find Proust's 'essence, that is to say [his] book' and he could publish it 'drawing attention to the fact that it was only a draft'.[196] He hoped that this eventuality would not come about, for 'the author clings strongly to life'. Nevertheless, certainly from this time onwards, he had a version of the whole book that was always (or never) in a state of readiness, so much so that Gallimard was under the impression that Proust wanted to print and publish the final four volumes simultaneously, and he was relieved to discover that Marcel only required the volumes to be printed 'one at a time'. In wartime the great difficulty for a publisher is to find a printer whose employees have not all been drafted to the front line. Having searched for a firm in Switzerland, Gallimard approached La Semeuse in Étampes. In March 1917 Proust delivered the entire manuscript of *À l'ombre des jeunes filles en fleurs*, which he asked to be printed immediately, along with the first twenty pages of *Le Côté des Guermantes*.[197] In early October he received the proofs ('5,000 pages', he claimed) and foresaw 'a crazy amount of work'.[198] Gallimard seemed reluctant when confronted with a book of 600 pages. Proust pointed out to him that it would come to 570 pages in length, whereas the Grasset edition of *Du côté de chez Swann* ran to 523, so the difference was minimal. During this time, Gallimard had bought back from Grasset the 206 remaining volumes of *Swann*, and he ordered book jackets bearing the NRF imprint from Bellenand, the printers.[199] He informed Proust that he would soon be able to reprint this first volume, with any corrections he wanted made. But in December the printer, because of a shortage of staff, sent no further proofs.[200]

Anxious, once again, to test the lie of the land with a pre-publication piece, on 12 November Proust proposed to Robert de Flers 'a distressing episode in his book (a study of oblivion)', part of which would take place in Venice and 'would contain descriptions that no one has done until now' (Venice, which was now under threat from the Austrians, was back in the headlines again). If Flers were agreeable, Marcel 'would rewrite this part immediately'; otherwise, he would suggest some more amusing passages describing the married Mme Swann's parties.[201] Proust, still behaving as if he were ruined, went on to ask for Flers' help in 'earning a little money' by bringing out his unpublished 'five volumes' beforehand in newspapers and magazines.

A HECTIC LIFE

The tenor of 1917 was struck by Marcel in early January, when he compared himself to an H. G. Wells character, because he had not been to bed 'for fifty hours', and to one of Jules Verne's, because he 'had not sat down either, nor stopped talking'.* Throughout this year, he would go out two or three times a week, a great deal for him. On 1 February he entertained Bibesco and Morand, and while quoting from Saint-Simon and Balzac,

---

* *Corr.*, vol. XVI, p. 29. He was alluding to *The Time Machine* and *Around the World in Eighty Days*.

whose *Les Illusions perdues* and *La Femme abandonnée* he rated 'above every-thing', he told them thousands of anecdotes, including one about Grand-Duke Paul, the brother of Alexander III, applauding the great Comédie-Française actress Bartet and exclaiming, 'Bravo! Old girl!'* On 15 February he paid a visit to Cocteau, who was unwell; Proust had looked forward to seeing this unpredictable poet whom he had not been in touch with for a long time.[202] His friends in the army came to see him, or wrote to him: Albufera, who was a lieutenant in the artillery, Maugny, Foucart, Charles d'Alton, and his brother Robert (who now had four stripes; his mention in dispatches for 9 March 1916 says much about the conditions at the front line: 'He succeeded, working in very makeshift installations where operations were being carried out in proximity to the enemy trenches, in saving a great number of human lives').[203] At Larue's, where Marcel dined on 22 February, he came across Tristan Bernard, who 'blinked his elephant's eyes in a face that manages to combine the style of Darius' archers with the character of Labiche's bourgeois',† and Léon Daudet, whose *Souvenirs* he had not yet read, and to whom he declared: 'I want to have your intellectual esteem.'[204] A few days later, having been sent a copy of this book, Proust was hurt by the adjective 'stupefying' applied to *Du côté de chez Swann*, and he retorted: 'I know what it means to find *Swann* "stupefying", to think that it isn't condensed and ultra-condensed, that I don't know how to control myself, that I allow myself to be guided by fortuitous associations of ideas. I do not share this verdict . . .'[205] Also at Larue's, on 4 March, he met someone who was to be important to him and to this period of his life: the Princesse Soutzo. To Morand, that evening, Proust appeared 'whiter than he looked in his bed, his complexion that of a vegetable grown in a cellar, his eyes shining, like some wonderful oriental pearl'; he ate a tart, drank some coffee, then gulped down a Russian salad, without removing his grey linen gloves. He suggested to Hélène Soutzo that he take her to hear the Poulet Quartet play Franck at the Ritz, where he arrived an hour later, but because the cellist was in hospital, 'everything was ruined'; instead, he spoke for an

---

* Morand, *Journal d'un attaché*, p. 161. Transposed to *Sodome et Gomorrhe*, *RTP*, vol. III, p. 57: Grand-Duke Vladimir (1847–1909), seeing Mme d'Arpajon soaked by a jet of water, uses the same words. Proust also told Morand and Bibesco some stories about the mistaken ownership of top hats with initials inside the brim, which he himself made use of in his book.

† *Corr.*, vol. XVI, p. 60, to P. Morand. Proust must have drawn his inspiration from Tristan Bernard for the portrait of Nissim Bernard, Bloch's uncle (*RTP*, vol. II, p. 132), where a reference is made to Darius.

hour about Flaubert: 'This concert was just as good as the other.'[206] On 16 March Bibesco, Hélène Soutzo, Morand and Proust dined together at Ciro's; Marcel was mortified to discover, upon his return, that Céleste had allowed him to go out with a shirt that had been soaked by the barber's soapy water, and an old waistcoat,[207] so incapable was he – as he had been when his mother was alive – of looking after himself.

HÉLÈNE SOUTZO

She was the estranged wife of Prince Dimitri Soutzo,* the military attaché at the Romanian embassy (they were divorced in 1924 and she would be allowed to keep the name of her first husband), and until the end of her life she would retain the title of princess, which Morand always used when talking about her. Hélène Chrisoveloni was the daughter of a Greek banker, born in Galatz, in Moldavia, in 1879, and legitimized at the age of eleven after the marriage of her parents; she was petite, very pretty,† intelligent, witty and very rich. It was she who commissioned Charles de La Morine to build the town house at 3 Avenue Charles-Floquet, near the Champ-de-Mars, where, after their wedding (3 January 1927), she would live with Morand until her death in 1975; he died in 1976, one of the last witnesses to Proust's life. During the war, however, she moved in permanently at the Ritz, where she gave brilliant dinner parties, the guests partly from society, partly literary.[208] A person of great integrity, kindness was not her chief virtue, as Princesse Bibesco discovered after the war,‡ and it was no doubt she who persuaded Morand to accept the appointment as Vichy's ambassador to Bucharest during the Second World War, mainly in order to get rid of her possessions there. 'What struck me most about this woman,' wrote Ernst Jünger in his *Journal*, 'was her acute political sense, that distinctive strength that fascinated me as much as it horrified me. There was always something magical about her, and above all there was that passionate will-power.'[209]

As for Proust, finding himself back once more in the sort of triangular relationship he so enjoyed, his affection for this couple grew stronger

---

* G. Guitard-Auviste, *Paul Morand*, Hachette, 1981, pp. 76–81, 'a Romanian Minerva'. She was nine years older than Morand.

† Paul Nadar photographed her in 1909. She bears a resemblance to the two women whom she loathed, Anna de Noailles and Marthe Bibesco. Cocteau likened her to 'a Minerva who had swallowed her owl'.

‡ Malicious gossip accused her of having been the mistress of the Kronprinz.

and stronger. He pronounced himself a friend of Morand, who was a low-ranking diplomat and still unknown as a writer, but who, Marcel knew, with his usual intuition, would have a great future; what is more, he was a handsome, virile man, 'who set everyone's heart a-flutter', of the type that appealed to Proust. He declared himself to be in love with the princess, both as a writer whose job it was to describe women, as an aesthete who loved beauty, and as a man of the world who enjoyed the special charm of intelligent women. Within a year or two, Princesse Soutzo became what Mmes Straus, de Noailles, de Chevigné and Greffulhe had once been for him . . . So much so that he offended Mme de Chevigné (Marcel had told her he never went out in the evenings), who encountered him at the Ritz on 22 April in the company of Cocteau, Morand, the Abbé Mugnier and the Marquise de Ludre. Marcel replied to her with a stern letter: 'The harshness – and the partial mediocrity – of someone whom one has loved so much, should, all the same, be of little interest twenty years later . . . You were never more beautiful, however . . .'[210]

All these outings took place in the evening. But Proust declared that, 'in order to obtain details which can only be experienced by day', his book could not appear until he was in a fit state 'to go out once or twice in the daytime'.[211] Did he mean Versailles, where he planned to meet Morand?[212] The Bois de Boulogne?

HEALTH

For some time, and probably ever since 1911, Proust had complained of new health problems: 'some terrible heart seizures that had left him between life and death'.* Asthma and its development into emphysema were having an effect upon his heart, as was his excessive use of medicaments such as adrenaline and caffeine, as well as psychosomatic complaints. 'The problems outlined probably derive from a chronic pulmonary heart condition that results in breathing difficulties and spells of dizziness.'[213] He did not consult an eye specialist and reading became more of a strain for him. Drawing some advantage from his misfortunes as usual, he informed his friends who were writers that the condition of his eyes prevented him

---

* *Corr.*, vol. XVI, p. 70, 6 March 1917. Cf. p. 339: 'I feel that the hours left to me for work are limited, and alas for living too, for I have had a lot of heart trouble lately' (December 1917, to J. Truelle).

from reading their books.[214] It was as if the various instrumentalists were taking their places one by one to play a funereal symphony: with increasing frequency Marcel announced his forthcoming death. He nevertheless offered medical advice to Lucien Daudet: 'Follow my treatment, and for once, as the third of that name, I shall be Doctor Proust.'[215]

NEW FRIENDSHIPS

Throughout this period of the war, because his old friends had been called up or had been appointed to posts abroad (like Billy, who was secretary at the Athens embassy), Proust's circle of friends changed and grew younger: diplomats, writers and socialites, they were generally younger than him, and it was as if he were keen to establish contact with the next generation and with a new circle of friends. Among these was Jacques Truelle, who had lost a leg in the war; after completing his studies at Sciences-Po, he would be appointed as an embassy attaché in 1919; Morand would replace him as ambassador to Bucharest in 1943. Marcel would either invite Truelle home or to a luxury hotel, speak to him about Saint-Simon, Balzac and about Swann, and make him tell him about the various times he stayed in the countryside. Very soon he was discovering in detail how he occupied his time, and he received a 'delightful' letter from him which made him happy.[216] They took part in the dangerous 'series of secrets', of misunderstandings that required clarification.[217] For example, when Truelle lost his father, a stockbroker, Proust regretted having known him, because he suffered with him.[218] And in November: 'You should know this, that I like you more and more, as I've already written to Reynaldo.'[219] During the war, having read that civilians were to be employed in the fields, he said to Truelle: 'Can you see me driving a plough or organizing the grape harvest, when I can't even go near a flower without instantly succumbing to a fit of sneezing?' And in April 1918: 'My eyes are troubling me too much to be able to write. But their weakness has not unfortunately diminished their ability to weep, to weep all day long for the captured villages and the destroyed cathedrals, and even more for the men.'* Jacques Truelle lent him 'Mademoiselle Monk'

---

* J. Truelle, in *Hommage à M. Proust*, pp. 98–9. Cf. *Corr.*, vol. XVI, p. 272, late October 1917, to H. Soutzo: 'I mourn the death of everyone, even people I have never set eyes upon. It's an additional sense the war has given us, with its appalling daily drill of anguish, which makes us suffer on behalf of strangers.'

by Maurras, who appears in *Le Temps retrouvé*,* out of gratitude for Maurras' article on *Les Plaisirs et les Jours*.

Someone else who appeared on the scene was Jacques de Lacretelle, tall and handsome, who came from a family that boasted three members of the Académie française, and whom Proust had attempted to see on several occasions, initially in vain. Lacretelle had written a novel about his youth, but Proust had not yet read anything by him. On 20 April he inscribed a copy of *Swann* to Lacretelle, in which he gave him the *clefs*, or keys, to the novel, while at the same time asserting that 'there are no *clefs* to the characters in this book; or rather there are eight or ten for each one of them'.† And Cocteau appeared once more: Proust must have seen the ballet *Parade*, for which Cocteau had written the story (about a parade in front of the circus and the public who do not go in), on 21 May. The music was by Satie (the orchestra included typewriters, ships' sirens and pistols), the choreography by Massine, and the backdrops, sets and costumes were by Picasso, in his Cubist style. The production caused a scandal, and the show was taken off at the end of the month. Proust mentioned 'the melancholy endlessly provoked in me by the dominical blue with the white tali of the misunderstood acrobat', the little girl in tartan, and the mauve horse: 'What regret, when I still had the legs for it, not to have known the sawdust of circuses.'‡ Marcel also wore himself out in 'fruitless attempts' to see Jacques Porel, Réjane's son, a friend of both Truelle and Morand, whom Céleste liked but whom she considered 'lightweight'. Porel would leave some interesting memoirs, in which he described his meetings with Proust: 'I used to stay at his bedside until four o'clock in the morning. He spoke to me about everybody and everything. About our friends, about his favourite books ... The word culture did not suit Proust. He had an immense knowledge about everything. Impossible to be less didactic, less predictable in one's observations.'[220] With Morand, things sometimes went wrong, and Marcel recalled

---

* *Corr.*, vol. XVI, p. 181; *RTP*, vol. IV, p. 376: 'You once made me read Maurras' admirable *Aimée de Coigny*. I should be extremely surprised if there were not an Aimée de Coigny who is expecting a similar outcome from the war the Republic is waging to the one the original Aimée de Coigny hoped for in 1812 from the war the Empire fought.' This was in connection with Maurras' article on the memoirs of Aimée de Coigny, Chénier's 'young captive', published in 1902; Maurras included the article in *L'Avenir de l'intelligence* (1905; 1917).

† *Corr.*, vol. XVII, p. 189. Together with the dedication to Mme Scheikévitch, this was the most important inscription that Proust wrote, and the richest in explanations.

‡ In contrast, Proust thought the other ballets were 'nothing special': *Soleil de nuit, Petrushka* and *Les femmes de bonne humeur*.

'a certain conversation', 'about fixing a date'.[221] On 15 June he did not go to Morand's home for Cocteau's reading of his *Cap de Bonne-Espérance*, which was, he said, 'something sacred': 'Now if I had Jean's talent, which I should like very much, it seems to me that I would not attach any importance to my book, and even less to whether it is read, and to the ritual of being read.'* Curiously, this did not prevent him from describing to the Princesse Soutzo the distinctive features of Morand (who should be 'an ambassador everywhere'), who 'looks at you with his mouth as well' and in whom 'a certain parting of his lips is the most meaningful of glances'.[222]

Proust found another acquaintance, Pierre de Polignac, with whom he dined at the Ritz on 5 July, 'charming', having previously been of a different opinion. The great-great-grandson of Charles X's last minister and a great-nephew of Prince Edmond, Polignac was a diplomat who was on the point of leaving for Peking; Proust dragged him into a long private conversation.[223] Proust somewhat incongruously betrayed his obsession with these young men who had something feminine about them, when Louisa de Mornand lost her brother in the war: 'I felt a great curiosity to know him, for I have always been curious about the effect of the transposition of a friend's, or a loved one's face from the masculine sex into the feminine, and vice versa. This is why three years ago I was very keen to meet young Benardaky, the brother of a woman who, when she was fifteen, was the great love of my youth.'[224]

From 1916 Marcel was also on friendly terms with Walter Berry, the president of the American Chamber of Commerce, to whom he gave a box of cigars, 'as an ironic souvenir of the smoke rings [which he] had not managed to make rise to the firmament of the Beaumonts' ceiling' (on 21 July). It appears that Marcel expressed great feelings of friendship (nothing more, probably, given the American's age) for him: 'This Walter is worthy of the one who is called Pater, or Scott, or even the Walter who, although a Boche, launched over Nuremberg, more real than the bombs of 1914, a certain *Preislied* which was not at all bad,'† he wrote. And again, in 1918: 'I know of no finer sight for the eyes than your face, nothing

---

* *Corr.*, vol. XVI, p. 202, 4 August 1917. In *Journal d'un attaché*, 12 August 1917, Morand related that Cocteau had invited Proust to a reading of the *Cap* at Valentine Gross's home. 'Proust came at midnight accompanied by W. Berry and by Scheiké(vitch?). Cocteau, furious, threw them out. Letters, visits and fuss ensued. Proust reproaching Cocteau for being, under the guise of a young poet, an old dandy of the Montesquiou variety.'

† *Corr.*, vol. XVI, p. 163, in about June 1917. An allusion to the Walter of *Die Meistersinger*.

more pleasing to the ears than your voice . . . as if you had been painted by Tintoretto and orchestrated by Rimski.'[225] Proust had discovered the beauty of prehistoric wall paintings through a lecture given by Berry. After Proust's death, the American paid tribute to him: 'I see him still, arriving down the long corridor at the Ritz, an hour late for his rendezvous, looking rather haggard and distraught, emerging from a dream, like a pilot stranded in the clouds, uncertain whether or not to land . . . Then, gradually, he would pull himself together. He gazed joyfully around the room where the whirl of society people bustled about. Often he would stop at a table and pick up frivolous comments which he would relate to me with delight – remarks worthy, he would say, of the Duc de Guermantes.'[226] And, as with others, shortly before he died, Marcel wrote to him: 'You, the person I love most in the world.'

In mid-April Jacques-Émile Blanche, whom he had lost touch with for a long time, asked Proust to write a foreword to his *Propos de peintre, De David à Degas*, which Blanche intended to dedicate to him. Marcel could not refuse this old friend who had praised *Swann* so warmly. He asked him for any of his old letters, so that he could glean some ideas from them. One of the themes Proust wished to develop was that Blanche was the Sainte-Beuve of art criticism, and that his essays were the *Causeries du lundi* of painting. The inscription read: 'To Marcel Proust, as a token of my high esteem, these pages which will remind him of the Auteuil of his childhood, of my early days and my long friendship.'[227] And so Marcel would base the beginning of his introduction on memories of Auteuil; so much so that when he was led to believe that the painter intended to dedicate his book to Walter Berry, he said that he would no longer write the introduction after all;[228] the relationship between these two men of obdurate character was not straightforward: for instance, Proust was unable to dissuade the artist from praising Forain, who had in fact behaved very badly towards Blanche (and who quarrelled with Proust, despite their friendly contacts at Cabourg). In his introduction, he mingled praise with reservations: 'The trouble with Jacques Blanche as a critic, as with Sainte-Beuve, is that he takes the opposite path to the one the artist takes in order to fulfil himself, which is to explain the real Manet or Fantin – that part of them which can only be found in their work – with reference to the perishable man, who, like his contemporaries, is steeped in blemishes.'[229]

At the home of Princesse Soutzo, probably on 22 April, Proust also made the acquaintance of Abbé Mugnier. He was originally the curate at

Sainte-Clotilde, then later, after he had been criticized for his connections with a former modernist priest, Père Loison, chaplain to a convent in the rue Méchain and an old friend of Huysmans, whom he had converted; he was never again looked upon favourably by the Church authorities. Witty and highly cultivated, he became a sort of private chaplain to a number of society figures, who delighted in his company and frequently invited him to dine at their tables. Some of them, such as Èlisabeth de Gramont and Princesse Bibesco, paid handsome tributes to him after his death. Was the priest referring to Proust when, quoting Chateaubriand, he spoke of *cicada noctium*, 'the night cicada'?[230] For Marcel maintained that he retained nostalgic memories of the dinner parties at which the priest treated him with 'delightful kindness'.[231]

On 28 July he experienced another event which can be found in his novel. He was dining at the Ritz with the Princesse Soutzo, Morand, the Beaumonts, Monzie, Porel, Cocteau and Joseph Reinach (Proust, who had not forgiven him for the business about the army medical board, now compared him to a monkey with an almost human expression who had left the zoo for the Institut Français). After dinner, there was a session of hypnotism. The air-raid siren sounded at half past eleven, and the end of the alert came at a quarter past one in the morning. French aeroplanes took off. A few bombs fell over the suburbs, but there were no casualties.[232] 'Proust, perfectly calm, continued the conversation.'[233] 'I went out on to the balcony,' wrote Marcel to Mme Straus, 'and stayed there for over an hour watching this wonderful Apocalypse in which the aeroplanes climbing and diving seemed to complement and eclipse the constellations . . . The extraordinary thing was that, as in the painting by El Greco in which there is a celestial scene above and a terrestrial one below, while we were watching this sublime "Open Sky" from the balcony, the Ritz Hotel below us . . . looked as if it had turned into Feydeau's Hôtel du Libre-Échange. Ladies in nightdresses or dressing-gowns roamed around the "vaulted" hall clutching their pearl necklaces to their bosoms.'[234] The scene in *Le Temps retrouvé*, which is based on this, takes on an epic beauty in which El Greco, Wagner and Feydeau, who are enlisted to describe modern-day warfare as seen from a balcony, display the beauty of aeroplanes soaring up into the night for the first time in the history of the novel.

On 20 August Marcel attended a soirée at the Palais-Royal given by Valentine Gross, a talented painter who would marry Jean Hugo on 7 August 1919. The interior decoration was unusual, the walls covered in tarred paper behind a trellis of string, with a table painted in red and rattan chairs with cushions covered in the American flag; inside a large butterfly box was a portrait of Cocteau by Thévenaz. At the soirée, in addition to Cocteau, Proust met Charles Daudet, the son of Léon,[235] Fargue, Morand and Porel: 'The plaintive voice,' Hugo recalled, 'never stopped, and his beautiful bruised eyes sometimes took on a beseeching expression, but very soon there would be a burst of laughter, which he would stifle with a black-gloved hand.'[236]

THE DEATH OF EMMANUEL BIBESCO

On 22 August 1917 Emmanuel Bibesco, who was suffering from an incurable illness,* committed suicide in London by hanging himself in his hotel bedroom. Marcel, who had foreseen this fate 'too soon and too clearly', had seen him for the last time in April, and he described this meeting very movingly. Antoine Bibesco and Morand had come to pick him up; Emmanuel had stayed below in the cab, because he did not want anyone to see him. Out of politeness, he wanted to sit on the folding seat; his brother insisted he stay on the back seat: 'Then Emmanuel said with a laugh: "The cabbie should drive backwards so that Marcel Proust and Paul Morand can think they are facing forwards." It was the only thing he said, but I wept all through the night, the only person to see me being my housekeeper.'[237] The circumstances of his suicide struck Proust as so dreadful that he thought that, had the sick man 'been in possession of his reason and his will', he would not have chosen 'a manner of dying so unnecessarily painful, so atrocious in the memory of others'.[238] The first surviving letter on the subject that he wrote to Antoine Bibesco dates from mid-September;[239] in it he said that life ceases to be comprehensible or bearable when people like Emmanuel die and people like Antoine lose what they most loved.[240] At the same time, he wondered whether mental suffering had not accompanied Emmanuel's physical pain, which had seemed to be diminishing.

On several occasions throughout this year, Proust could be seen at the town house of the Beaumonts, 2 rue Duroc. At their parties, they used

---

* 'In the three years since he had first been struck down by an inexorable illness, one could sense this tragedy hovering . . . He was an intelligent and pleasant person, but already very unbalanced when I knew him in 1908. He was passionately interested in Gothic art and in architecture' (Morand, *Journal d'un attaché*, 27 August 1917).

to mingle members of the aristocracy with artists, whom they favoured with their patronage. Étienne de Beaumont had furthermore established a mobile hospital to which he recruited artists such as Cocteau (who related the experience in *Thomas l'imposteur*), with whom he appeared one evening, on the staircase of an inn, wearing black pyjamas with gold bracelets round his ankles, beneath the astonished gaze of Douglas Haig and his general staff. Beaumont[241] and his wife are the models for the principal characters in Raymond Radiguet's novel *Le Bal du comte d'Orgel*. After the war they would ask the painters Marie Laurencin and Sert to stage their fancy-dress parties. Beaumont appears to have been well disposed to Proust;[242] he reckoned him to be 'one of the men who will mark our century' and he confirmed that 'his friendship was precious to him'. It was at the home of this strange and munificent character that Marcel would spend one of his last soirées.

On 17 September Gide sent Proust a copy of a reprinted limited edition of *Les Nourritures terrestres*. 'It will quickly become quite rare,' he wrote with modesty.[243] Since his first letter of thanks got mislaid, Marcel wrote another. This book had already nourished a generation, he told Gide, paraphrasing the title rather more than he had studied the contents, and many others will be sustained by it: 'A great writer is like the seed that feeds others with what it first fed upon itself.' But the finest thing about this book was not its substance, but its tone. And Marcel confessed to Gide, in praise that must have gone straight to his heart, that Céleste, who never had the patience to read half a page of Proust, having had to read a few pages of *Les Nourritures* aloud to her master, could no longer speak without parodying the book: 'Nathanaël, I will speak to thee of Monsieur's lady-friends. There is she who has made him go out again after many years, taxi to the Ritz, bell-hops, tips, exhaustion.' And he added that *Les Plaisirs et les Jours* had contained a phrase that was analogous:[244] the two books shared something of the aesthetics of symbolism. The two writers, in any case, expressed the strongest desire to see one another again. They both sensed the importance of each other's work; they shared particular tastes which numbered them among the outcasts; they coexisted at the NRF. Proust would tell Gide all about his habits; Gide would be more secretive. And yet there was no deep affection between them, and no real admiration. What Gide wrote was of no interest to Proust. The former noted the existence of *À la recherche* as he would that of Mont Blanc: there was nothing he could do about it, even if he deplored it. But great writers do not like one another: they like their admirers and their court, but otherwise they only converse with the great classical writers. Morand, Cocteau, Lacretelle: they served at Proust's court; Ghéon, Schlumberger, Martin du Gard, at Gide's.

Incidental remarks indicate that Proust was working not only on 'M. de Charlus pendant la guerre', but also on the 'Bal de têtes' from *Le Temps retrouvé*, and that he was enlarging the number of characters: 'I went out on one occasion,' he wrote to Lucien Daudet, from whom he concealed the number of times he had been out so as not to arouse his jealousy, 'and I saw the strangest people, or rather the most insignificant ones, but exhumed from the oblivion of so many years.'[245]

In late October Marcel learned that Morand had been appointed attaché to the French embassy in Rome, and he sent his congratulations, tinged with sadness: 'I cannot be sufficiently stoical to accept that Paul Morand came into my life, and that he is leaving before it is over.'[246] In Morand's *Journal* there are numerous mentions of meetings with Proust: dinner at the Ritz on 10 August, with Marie Murat, Mme Scheikévitch and the Russian General Zankévitch, the commander-in-chief of the Russian troops in France ('You have the face of a sub-lieutenant,' Proust told him). A visit on 5 September: Marcel spoke to him of his illegible notebooks, which no one would be able to decipher, and about the four volumes of his book that were completed, but which he did not want to have published; and he told him stories about the Hugo, Hermann-Paul and Ménard-Dorian families. On 22 September Proust went to dine at the Trianon Palace, at the invitation of Mme Scheikévitch, together with General Zankévitch (who collected him in his car),* Hélène Soutzo, Jean de Gaigneron and Calmann-Lévy.[247] On 25 September Morand came to see Marcel, who went out to lunch for the first time in ten years (at the Ritz): 'He sent Céleste out to look for a cab, and she, never having seen daylight and being blinded by the sun, got lost!' He told him about Céleste reading Gide and declaring: 'I could do just as well. – No, replied, Proust.' On 15 November Proust brought a pile of proofs, which had been pasted on to large sheets of paper, to the Crillon, which, not being situated next door to the Ministry of Justice, could keep its lights on at times when the Ritz could only be dimly lit;[248] Céleste had thrown him out of Boulevard Haussman so that she could clean the flat, and so he corrected the proofs in a corner of this

---

* In April 1918 the general would drive Proust to Versailles in his open-roofed car, and Marcel caught a cold as a result.

hotel.* He felt more comfortable there than at the Ritz where, he said, he felt 'obliged to be excessively polite to Olivier', the celebrated maître d'hôtel Dabescat, and he drank coffee quite late into the night. That evening he read out the portrait of Norpois to his guests, Berry and Soutzo. Another dinner, at the Ritz on 20 November, with Billy and Berry: 'Proust amusing, happy to see Billy again.' On 21 and 23 November Marcel dined again at the Ritz with the Princesse Soutzo, Morand, Truelle and Mme Catusse. He talked to them about a husband who, having nothing to do, always adopted the same type of employment as his wife's lovers: he had done everything; and also about Anatole France, who was living with Mme de Caillavet's second chambermaid, M. de Caillavet having taken the first. On 2 December 'an amusing dinner party at Hélène de Soutzo's': Proust, Mme de Chevigné, Billy, Paléologue and Mme de Polignac. They discussed King Ferdinand of Bulgaria (1861–1948), 'intelligent, perverted, cruel, timorous', whose arm was covered in bracelets up to his shoulder. We come across him in À la recherche.† Proust and Mme de Chevigné were talking quietly in a corner. People thought they were flirting. You drew closer: Proust was making some notes. Then you heard: 'So you think that the Prince de Sagan used white silk handkerchiefs . . .'‡

In late November Marcel tried to sell some of his furniture (four armchairs, a sofa, some leather-covered dining-room chairs, a large carpet, a wardrobe with a mirror, some chandeliers, some bronzes, a piece of Louis XIV furniture, and possibly the family silver, which was 'useless'), by approaching Walter Berry, then Mme Catusse[249] and Émile Straus.[250] He was thinking of offering half of the proceeds of the sale to Mme Scheikévitch, who had been ruined by the Russian revolution.[251]

On the eve of Morand's departure, Marcel told the Princesse Soutzo of his infinite sadness, after a year of friendship 'paralysed by two foolish misunderstandings': 'The thought that he will leave in ten days' time, that tomorrow one will have to tell oneself there are only nine days left, and

---

* Cf. *Corr.*, vol. XVI, p. 287: 'If need be I can correct my proofs there' (8 or 9 November 1917, to J. Truelle).

† *RTP*, vol. II, pp. 540 ('You wouldn't have found the Prince of Bulgaria clasping Major Esterhazy to his bosom.' 'He would have preferred a private soldier,' murmured Mme de Guermantes who had once told the king that she was jealous of his bracelets', those mentioned in Morand's *Journal*), 817; vol. IV, pp. 350, 366, 367.

‡ Proust renewed his affectionate admiration for Mme de Chevigné in a letter that November (*Corr.*, vol. XVI, p. 285).

the next day eight, it makes one want to turn one's face to the wall, or to take such a large dose of veronal that one would only wake up once he is in Rome. I have not told him anything of this but my heart cannot contain it.'252 His sorrow at seeing a solicitous, affectionate friend depart could not be better expressed; neither could his intense feelings for him. We find these sentiments in *Le Côté de Guermantes*.* Through a sort of transference, Marcel worried about an operation for appendicitis which Princesse Soutzo was about to undergo, and he did his best to reassure her in every way possible. She was to be operated upon in her bedroom at the Ritz by Doctor Gosset on 29 December.† On 9 December Morand left for Rome, where he would not be happy, having spent the previous evening at the home of the Princesse de Polignac; Proust would write to him, on 23 December: 'I cannot understand why it is that your face should be so continuously in my mind, or why I remember the slightest relaxation in your smile, the unaffected manner in which you displayed your kindness, so many things that one took for granted.'253 On 16 December Marcel did go to hear an organ concert at the Princesse de Polignac's, and on the 24th he attended a Christmas Eve party given by the Princesse Marie Murat at the Ritz, with an infante of Spain, whose mannerisms and whose 'Charlus' behaviour, he found extremely irritating, especially at times when he felt rather sad.

So it was that a year that had been full of activity – in a literary sense as well, since Proust had improved 'M. de Charlus pendant la guerre' and had added to the conversations at Doncières, in *Guermantes II*, some observations based on events that had taken place during the year and on newspaper reports – ended sadly, with the snow 'and all those things that make you feel sorrowful and for which one cannot find a cause' adding to the melancholy of New Year's Day.

---

* *RTP*, vol. II, p. 418: 'There were evenings when . . . I missed Mme de Guermantes so much that I had difficulty in breathing: it was as if a portion of my chest had been dissected by a skilful anatomist, removed and replaced by an equal portion of ethereal pain, by an equivalent amount of nostalgia and love.'

† Proust sent a telegram to Morand to tell him the operation had been successful (*Corr.*, vol. XVI, p. 374, 29 December 1917).

CHAPTER XV

The Novel of 1918

FROM *SODOME* TO *LA FUGITIVE*

In 1916, as we know from a letter written in May to Gaston Gallimard, Proust decided to assemble a volume which he entitled *Sodome et Gomorrhe*.* A manuscript was compiled by dividing up the material gathered together in the exercise books: *Sodome et Gomorrhe* was written in 1916 in Cahiers I–VII; *La Prisonnière* in Cahiers VIII–XII and *La Fugitive* in Cahiers XIII–XV in 1917.† The same procedure was used as before: writing fragments, putting them together, and then separating them in order to re-assemble them in another way; the matinée which opens *La Prisonnière*, for example, appears in several different versions. The cutting of a text enabled Proust to strengthen the structure of the work, by repeating some themes and progressing by trial and error. The development of a character, such as Morel in *Sodome et Gomorrhe* after 1915, reinforced the symmetry with Albertine. This was why, once a fair copy of the manuscript had been made, Proust did not stop and the additional material increased: in Cahiers 59–62 and 74, and on the typescript pages, as well as on the proofs, at least those which he was able to check before he died. These circumstances explain why the manuscript of *Le Temps retrouvé*, which is contained in Cahiers XV–XX, and was written from 1916 to 1918 or 1919, is the least finished of them all, because the last revisions Proust made were to *La Fugitive*. The chapter on the war had been written as

---

* *Corr. avec G. Gallimard*, p. 35. In this important letter from the Paulhan archives, we find the only version I know of this title, prior to 1918, which Proust said was inspired by Vigny's poem and which he used as an epigraph to *Sodome et Gomorrhe I*.

† Where I am dealing with the genesis of the novel, I have tried to retain the title Proust originally wanted, but in the case of the published text as we read it today, I have used the second title, *Albertine disparue*, which appeared in Cahier 71, f. 37 recto.

early as 1916,* but additional material can be dated to 1917–18 (the parts
that deal with the bombing of Paris), and to 1918 (the newspaper articles
that are referred to from that year). The Goncourt pastiche dates from
1917–18. Much of the additional material appears in Cahier 74, which the
author entitled 'Babouche'.

Céleste Albaret stated that on Proust's instructions she burned thirty-two
exercise books during the war. According to R. Brydges,[1] these burnt
cahiers may have constituted an early manuscript of the second volume,
which followed on from *Le Temps perdu* – the 1912 version, that is to say
the first draft of *Le Temps retrouvé*; at one time the central section, *Le Côté
de Guermantes*, which was typeset by Grasset in 1914, it may have been
replaced by the manuscript notebooks numbered I–XX, from *Sodome* to
Le Temps retrouvé. Proust may have had them burnt in groups of two or
three at a time, as and when he had made use of them, in 1916–17. But
what is unclear in this hypothesis is why he should have kept all his early
draft exercise books, when they, too, had been replaced by a consecutive
text, a typescript, proofs and a finished book. And it is not clear why Céleste
should have lied: one might lie and boast of having saved documents, but
not of having burnt them when one hadn't done so.

We must now deal with the summary of forthcoming titles included in *À
l'ombre des jeunes filles en fleurs*,† which provided a new outline of *À la recherche
du temps perdu* at this point, even though it was virtually completed and
Proust had a finished fair copy of the manuscript available. It was to
consist of five volumes, two of which, *Du côté de chez Swann* and *À l'ombre
des jeunes filles en fleurs*, had been published. Volume III was *Le Côté de
Guermantes*, which, like the following volumes, was listed as 'in production':
'Names of people: the Duchesse de Guermantes. Saint-Loup at Doncières.
Mme de Villeparisis' salon. The death of my grandmother. Albertine
reappears. Dinner at the Duchesse de Guermantes. The wit of the Guermantes. M. de Charlus continues to disconcert me. The Duchesse's red
shoes.'[2] Volume IV was entitled *Sodome et Gomorrhe I* and it goes considerably
beyond the future *Sodome et Gomorrhe*, which would include only the first
chapter: 'Sudden revelation of what M. de Charlus was. Soirée at the

---

* Mentioned in a letter to Gaston Gallimard in 1916 (*Corr., avec G. Gallimard*, p. 37). Of the two
dates given in the narrative of *Le Temps retrouvé*, the first is 1914 and the second is 1916 – the years
the Narrator makes a trip to Paris.

† Gallimard, 1918; the printing was completed on 30 November. Proust wrote the summary in
hand: autograph sheet, Guérin sale, 6 November, Drouot.

Princesse de Guermantes. Second visit to Balbec. The intermittencies of the heart I. I am finally aware that I have lost my grandmother. M. de Charlus at the Verdurins' and in the little railway train. The intermittencies of the heart II. Why I suddenly left Balbec, determined to marry Albertine.' This summary would be considerably expanded in *Guermantes I* (1921) and *Guermantes II* (1922), but here it has the merit of stressing the contrast more strongly between 'The intermittencies of the heart I', which is brought about by the grandmother, and 'The intermittencies of the heart II', induced by Albertine. Furthermore the 1922 summary emphasizes the social character and the human comedy of this section of the novel, by introducing numerous names of secondary characters, and it reflects the importance of the role belatedly taken by the character of Morel: 'First sketch of the curious character of Morel'.

The 1918 summary ended with volume V, *Sodome et Gomorrhe II. – Le Temps retrouvé*: 'Living with Albertine. The Verdurins quarrel with M. de Charlus. Albertine disappears. Sorrow and forgetting. Mlle de Forcheville. Exception to a rule. Visit to Venice. A further aspect of Robert de Saint-Loup. M. de Charlus during the war: his opinions, his pleasures. Matinée at the Princesse de Guermantes. Perpetual adoration. Time regained.'[3] In 1920 the edition of *Le Côté de Guermantes I* announced that volume IV would include *Le Côté de Guermantes II* and *Sodome et Gomorrhe I*; nothing had yet been changed for volume V. What this summary principally confirms is that the 1913 structure retained all its significance: *Sodome et Gomorrhe* stemmed from *Le Côté de Guermantes* through the intermediary of the character of Charlus. And if *À l'ombre des jeunes filles en fleurs* also derived from the volume II of 1914 that was never published, it is because, through Albertine and Andrée, the work introduces Gomorrah. In *Sodome et Gomorrhe I*, in the 1918 summary, the sodomites of Paris mingle with the gomorrheans of Balbec. It is clear, too, that neither the titles nor the volumes of *La Prisonnière*, *La Fugitive* or *Albertine disparue* existed; they were simply chapters of *Sodome et Gomorrhe II*, indicated by the first seven titles up to 'A further aspect of Robert de Saint-Loup'; this is confirmed by the correspondence with the NRF, in which Proust, once he had fully appreciated how long the manuscript with the additions would be, spoke of *Sodome et Gomorrhe III: La Prisonnière* and of *Sodome et Gomorrhe IV: La Fugitive*,[4] and later, so as to link the two-part book more closely, of *Sodome et Gomorrhe III*, 'first and second parts'. There is, after all, no obvious division between these three future parts. *Albertine disparue* would thus follow on legitimately from the last sentence of *La Prisonnière*. The start of *Le Temps retrouvé* was determined not from the manuscript, but from the typescript of *Albertine disparue* in the Bibliothèque Nationale: where it ends is where the last section of the work begins, as Robert Proust clearly saw when preparing the editions of these two texts in 1925 and 1927. In 1954 P. Clarac and A. Ferré would place this cut-off point incorrectly, seven pages too soon.[5] This continuity respects Proust's dearest wish, which was to have written a single book. Can we go so far as to say that '*Le Temps retrouvé* actually begins with *La Prisonnière*, because it is after *La Prisonnière* that the true face of the characters is revealed?[6] Albertine, in any case, is the great goddess of time, and she features in the numerous additional notes in Cahier 57 that prepare the way for *Le Temps retrouvé*; when the Narrator draws lessons from his past, the woman that he has loved, then forgotten, comes to symbolize several aspects of his life story; she was the instrument of an overall knowledge, the equivalent of an artist's model: 'Perhaps the people we know and the feelings we experience because of them are for the psychologist what models are for the painter. They pose for us. They pose for our suffering, for our jealousy, for our happiness.'[7] Like Venice, or social life, Albertine thus represents an element of what he was trying to do,[8] the last temptation, the final lap in the course of the book, time, not timelessness.

WAR IN THE NOVEL

In 1918 this summary of the final volume mentions war only in the title 'M. de Charlus during the war: his opinions, his pleasures'. Like the love for Albertine, this important addition was brought about by outside events. Proust had always been interested in the war, in the generals and in theories about strategy: we see it in *Jean Santeuil*, which harks back to the conversations at the Doncières barracks; in the references to the Russo-Japanese war and the Balkan wars in *Le Côté de Guermantes* and *Le Temps retrouvé*, and to the Boer War in *Le Côté de Guermantes* and *Sodome et Gomorrhe*; in his reading and in the private conversations recalled by his friends.[9] A large part of the episode dealing with the First World War must have been written after 1916, not merely because 1914 and 1916 are the two dates given by Proust, very unusually for him, for the Narrator's two trips back to Paris during the war, but also because Proust, as we know, referred to it in a letter to Gaston Gallimard in the spring of 1916.[10] As ever, additional material was superimposed on the narrative, which is mostly contained in Cahiers 57 and 74, but it consisted of analysis and conversations rather than new events. The 'opinions' of M. de Charlus run counter to the chauvinistic wartime propaganda, and they go beyond Proust's own more moderate views. His 'pleasures' stem from Proust's experiences in Le Cuziat's brothels.

With regard to the war, Proust made his feelings clear in a letter to Princesse Soutzo: 'For me it is less an object (in the philosophical meaning of the word) than a substance placed between myself and the objects. Just as other people are possessed by God, so I lived in the war . . . As for the guns and the Gotha raids, I will admit that I never gave a second's thought to them; I'm frightened of many less dangerous things – of mice for instance – but since I'm not actually afraid of the bombing and still do not know how to get to my cellar (which the other tenants do not forgive me for), it would be affectation for me to pretend to fear them.'[11] In *Le Temps retrouvé* Proust would make use of the bombing raids he described in his letter,[12] and of his walks. In fact, he used his correspondence to try out certain sentences that he had already written, or that he intended using, in his novel on those he corresponded with and on himself; in *Le Carnet de 1908*, he commented on the same characteristic in Musset: 'In his life and in his letters, just as in a seam of ore in which they are scarcely recognizable, we glimpse certain lineaments of his work, which was his life's only *raison d'être*, as well as his feelings of love, which existed only in so far as they were raw material for his work, which were directed towards and had their existence in it alone.'[13]

The war provided the novelist with the poetic and metamorphosed backdrop of Paris in peril. It also changed individuals and their positions in society, and it transformed nations into characters in the novel: if the novelist 'is master of the psychology of individuals, then these colossal masses of conglomerated individuals confronting one another will take on a more powerful beauty in his eyes than does a battle stemming solely from a conflict between two characters'.[14] To understand nations, you have to have understood individual people. However, we find neither accounts of battles nor the full history of the war in *Le Temps retrouvé*. The unfolding of events is, as in the rest of the novel, subject to the characters' points of view: it is Françoise who speaks of the obsession with the front line. The warmongers, such as Brichot and Norpois, are opposed to the pacifists, such as Charlus; Saint-Loup, who reappraises the strategic concepts he had developed at Doncières, is the hero of the war without hatred. What the 1918 summary does tell us is that the central figure of this episode is very much Baron de Charlus: 'his opinions' are expounded in long, frenzied monologues, and 'his pleasures' are no longer restricted to the search for male partners, but achieve a sort of grandeur in the abnormal: the great sado-masochistic scene that takes place in Jupien's brothel occurs during the bombing raids. The arrest for desertion of Morel, who denounces Charlus and Argencourt, the elections won by the Bloc National and a broken off paragraph about Russian émigrés bring the episode to an end. Finally, Proust's daily reading of the newspapers prompted him to strategic reflections which he put into the mouths of his characters, particularly the Narrator and Saint-Loup. Additions to the manuscript indicate that he was responding in particular to Henri Bidou's articles in *Le Journal des débats* up until 1918, and that he employed the same procedure as he did when attributing to Elstir remarks made by Émile Mâle. Proust included in his book all the areas of knowledge he had scoured through, from cookery recipes to horticultural matters, admitting the source whenever he quoted, and disguising it when he failed to mention the true author who had prompted his reflections. Just as aesthetics and the history of art had introduced him to art, so military reportage had acquainted him with war: he had to break through the intellectual canvas of his reading so as to discover the world, 'simply in order to excite himself'.[15] Belatedly, war, not as a science but as an art form, became like painting, music and architecture: Proust was less interested in the mistakes the generals made during the war – as recorded by Jean de Pierrefeu[16] for example – than in seeking for some creative thought behind the vicissitudes of the war: an unpublished text in Cahier 74 reads: 'Saint-Loup will express my praise for Pétain who has created the war of this war'; on the Eastern front, Hindenburg was imitating Napoleon. But there was better yet; the general invented in the same way that Proust wrote: 'A general is like a writer who wants to produce a certain play or a certain book, but the book itself, due to the unexpected possibilities it reveals one moment and the impasses that it presents the next, causes him to pursue it in a very different manner from the one he had planned.'[17] Everything always had to do with literature, everything provided him with material.

In another way war allowed Proust to clarify the relationships between literature, history, politics and society. War had produced a deluge of patriotic books and theories about politically committed art: when Proust was awarded the Prix Goncourt for *À l'ombre des jeunes filles en fleurs* in 1919, a large sector of the press criticized the jury for not having given the prize to Dorgelès' *Croix de bois*. The author of *À la recherche du temps perdu*, who was as reticent about Romain Rolland as he was about Maurice Barrès, explained his thinking in *Le Temps retrouvé*: 'From the beginning of the war M. Barrès had said that the artist (in this case, Titian) must first and foremost serve the glory of his country. But he can only do this by being an artist, that is to say only on condition that, at the moment when he is studying laws, carrying out experiments and making discoveries that are as delicate as those of science, he thinks of nothing – not even his country – other than the truth that is before him.'[18] This also means that if war can drastically change society, shaking it up, according to an image dear to Proust, like a kaleidoscope, it cannot, as something alien to artistic development, affect literature. When Barrès, jointly with D'Annunzio, suggested in *L'Écho de Paris* that literature should confine itself to depicting France 'in its finery' only, Proust considered that such 'madness' would produce nothing but Goethe's epic idyll *Hermann und Dorothea*; if people wanted to 'repudiate the mistakes of the pre-war years', they would be abolishing all that was newest in art, the Ballets Russes for example.[19] Neither the kaleidoscope, nor that other instrument to which Proust alluded, the telescope, allowed one to see everything through rose-tinted spectacles.

M. DE CHARLUS' PLEASURES

Ever since 1911, Proust had known a strange character by the name of Albert Le Cuziat.[20] Born in Tréguier in 1881, he was employed as a footman by Prince Radziwill (Loche's father), later by the Comtesse Greffulhe and Prince Orloff, at whose home Marcel must have made his acquaintance (unless it was at Radziwill's house), and finally by the Duc de Rohan. Le Cuziat had a passion for genealogy and protocol, which Proust exploited by inviting him home. According to Céleste Albaret, Le Cuziat originally bought a public baths, situated initially next to the Bourse, and later in the rue Godot-de-Mauroy (the 'Bains du ballon d'Alsace').[21] Proust may have helped the ex-footman to acquire the Hôtel Marigny, a small town house at 11 rue de l'Arcade (certain guests of the Princesse de Guermantes lived in this street,[22] which did contain some aristocratic houses), and provided him with some furniture.* This gift features in

---

* C. Albaret, p. 236. According to Céleste (p. 237), Proust had given furniture he did not need for Le Cuziat's own room in rue Godot-de-Mauroy, and he was very shocked to find it in rue de l'Arcade: this corresponds with a passage in *Jeunes Filles*: 'Had I violated the dead I would not have suffered so much!' (*RTP*, vol. I, p. 568). The sofa given by the Narrator is the very one upon which he discovered the pleasures of love for the first time; should we refer this back, and think of Marcel

À l'ombre des jeunes filles en fleurs (added during the war). By 1917 Le Cuziat was doomed. The two men had broken off their friendship because of a mutual affection for a certain André, probably the man who, according to Céleste, looked after the brothel while the owner was away.

Maurice Sachs has described this character: 'For those who have known him these past twenty years, he was a man of very great distinction, slim and with an aristocratic and *conservative* face, bald but still retaining a ring of white hair. It was hard to imagine anyone who took so much pleasure in involving himself.'* 'He was a Breton beanpole,' said Céleste rather less kindly, 'fair-haired, coarse-featured, with blue eyes that were as cold as a fish's – the eyes of his soul – and he wore the anxieties of his trade in his expression and on his face. There was a hunted look about him, which was hardly astonishing, for there were constant police raids on his establishment and he frequently spent short spells in prison.'[23] The money that Proust gave him was a reward for the information he provided. One only had to look at Le Cuziat once, Céleste continued, to see that he did nothing for free. Proust thanked Olivier Dabescat, the maître d'hôtel at the Ritz, in the same way, and he provided a great many details: 'Who had dined with whom, and what dress Mme So and So was wearing that evening, or what the protocol had been at this or that table.'[24] Politicians

---

caught unawares with Jacques Bizet, who in the book becomes 'a girl cousin'? Or should we, as some do, think of a boy cousin?

*M. Sachs, 'Historiette', *NRF*, 1 May 1938, pp. 863–4. Le Cuziat had just died at the age of fifty-seven. Cf. M. Sachs, *Le Sabbat*, Corrêa, 1946, pp. 279–80. Walter Benjamin visited Albert Le Cuziat one day in 1930, accompanied by his friend D. He described the atmosphere of the establishment, which was 'very much that of a family guest-house', and the frosted glass windows in Albert's office. Albert was 'a perfect combination of the utmost subservience and the most extreme determination, something that is characteristic of the lackey'. He also owned a second establishment, the Bal des Trois Colonnes. The old chums, who were joined by Maurice Sachs, had dinner at Ouistiti's, with its unbelievably handsome waiters, and a place that probably had close links with the vice squad. The scenes witnessed at Albert's house, which for Proust was a 'pied-à-terre' and a 'laboratory', provided him with information about all variations of homosexuality, and he would make use of certain of them for the episode of Charlus in chains. There were certain pieces of furniture belonging to Proust's family in this house. And it was here that Marcel, whose true identity was not known, was given the nickname 'the rat man'. Le Cuziat also told the story of how Proust was passing a butcher's shop one day and, attracted by the sight of a butcher's boy cutting up meat, stopped his car and stayed for several hours watching him work. Benjamin observed of *RTP*: 'It's a book in which Proust seems to me to exhibit the broad characteristics of sadism, even if they are deeply concealed. I am thinking here of the insatiable character of Proustian analysis of the very smallest incidents' (*Le Promeneur*, no. XXX, June 1984, quoted by R. Kahn, *Temps du langage, Temps de l'histoire: Marcel Proust et Walter Benjamin*, doctoral thesis, Paris III, 1996, pp. 225–6). I am also grateful to P. Mauriès for informing me about this text.

and even ministers came to rue de l'Arcade: 'Albert supplied him with details of their vices.'[25] Proust must have visited this establishment on five or six occasions; what's more he was frightened of police raids. On his return, he spoke to Céleste about it just as he would if he had spent an evening at the Beaumonts or the Greffulhes: he told her, for instance, about how he had seen an industrialist chained to the wall and being flagellated.[26] 'But, Monsieur, how could you have watched that?' 'Precisely because it cannot be invented, Céleste.'[27] Proust always remained loyal to the principle that he could not describe something unless he had seen it: 'One feels sorry for the poet, who is not led by any Virgil, having to cross over the circles of a hell of pitch and sulphur, and hurling himself in the fire which falls from heaven in order to bring back a few inhabitants of Sodom. There is no charm in his work.' And Proust added this searching question: 'Before that, this object, what obscure inclination, what fascinating dread had made him select it?'[28] It was thanks to Le Cuziat and his establishment that Proust was able to describe the important scene with Charlus in chains, in *Le Temps retrouvé*.

Among the grimmer legends that surround Proust – those that feature in the volumes of recollections, from Sachs to Faÿ, from Jouhandeau to Castellane, and are vulgarized by Painter – are those involving the desecrated photographs* (though Céleste denies that they could have left the house; we recall that the Montjouvain episode may have been inspired by Doctor Robin and Liane de Pougy, who mentions it in her memoirs) and the stories about butchers' shops and rats. Albert apparently recounted how he had accompanied Proust to a butcher's shop, where Marcel asked the boy there: 'Show me how you kill a calf'; or else, he would have a live rat brought to him, so that it could be pricked with hat-pins as he looked on.[29] The English writer John Agate, who frequented the *hôtel* Marigny, claimed to have encountered a pale-faced client with large eyes, followed by a man carrying some white mice in a cage.[†] And according to Gide, in a confessional scene worthy of Dostoevsky, Proust confided

---

* 'Laon Cathedral reminds me of some great pleasures (virtuous pleasures, I hasten to say, because my sentence seemed to suggest some sort of profanity),' wrote Proust to Mme Catusse, revealing in the process his awareness of sacrilege, which is confirmed by the use of religious quotations in a sacrilegious context, and by the reference to sons who in their expressions desecrate the face of their mother (something which elicited an article by Georges Bataille, reprinted in *La Littérature et le mal*, Gallimard, 1957).

† J. Harding, *Agate*, Methuen, 1986, p. 52: it is significant that Agate spoke of mice, which Harding, his biographer, steeped in Painter, transformed into rats.

to him that in order to achieve orgasm, he had to 'muster together the most disparate sensations and emotions'. 'This was the justification for the pursuit of rats; Proust, in any case, invited me to see it in that light. I saw it mainly as an admission of a kind of psychological deficiency. How many adjuvants he needed to attain his paroxysm!'* The Narrator admits his fear of mice and rats and relates his dream of his parents being locked in a cage, transformed into white mice and covered with pustules. This fear of rats stemmed from Proust's early childhood (although it did not prevent Marcel from calling Lucien Daudet 'Mon Rat')[30] and was linked to Doctor Proust; it can also be found in France's *Le Lys rouge* ('everyone has their rats'). Had Proust been psychoanalysed, which he never was, the psychoanalysts would no doubt furnish an explanation for it, linking it to anality and masochism. In his '*Rat Man*': *Notes upon a Case of Obsessional Neurosis* (1909) Freud has shown that obsessive neuroses derive from a struggle against the sexual instinct which is particularly intense in early childhood. The most complex and repellent perversions have commonplace origins. Proust cross-questioned certain of his acquaintances (but not all of them), including the now forgotten writer Sylvain Bonmarriage, about them: one night, having met him in the company of René Peter and Constantin Ullmann, Marcel suddenly appeared at Bonmarriage's home on the Boulevard Lannes and proceeded to question him on his views and his scruples about homosexuals and his memories of them; the following day he had him collected in a taxi in order to continue the interrogation, asking to be told the tragic story of an Italian count, in order better to depict Charlus.[31] Proust the novelist studied the pleasures of others, whether seen or heard, in the depths of their perversions, and from them he created those of Mlle Vinteuil and her curiously unnamed friend, and of M. de Charlus. As far as his own gratification went,

---

* A. Gide, *Ainsi soit-il*, in *Journal (1939–49) – Souvenirs*, Bibliothèque de la Pléiade, p. 1223. Cf. A. Germain, *Les Clés de Proust*, Sun, p. 71, which contains the story about the rats as recounted by Bernard Faÿ (who did not publish it himself). Faÿ also described how, after the war, at a dinner party at the Beaumonts, at which the Gramonts, Cocteau, Valentine, Jean Hugo and Proust were present, he had told the story of a sergeant who had thrust his cigar into the mouth of a German major ('Smoke it, you bastard!'), and how Proust then wanted to meet the sergeant: 'His keen desire and the impatience he displayed left me feeling puzzled.' It was then that a lady, passing by Proust's taxi, saw him, 'but he was not alone nor was he unoccupied. She then turned away uttering a little cry.' Faÿ said that he had been careful not to introduce this man to Proust, for fear that Marcel might be beaten up (*Les Précieux*, Perrin, 1966, p. 45). Proust made the same remarks about the pleasures of the flesh and the conjoining of a variety of heterogeneous elements to Faÿ as he did to Gide (ibid., p. 98).

increasingly ill and tired as he was, he resorted, very rarely no doubt (or so he told Mme Straus), to increasingly complicated scenarios; voyeurism and masturbation had always been at the wretched core of this: Proust possessed nothing and no one, despite his attempts at relationships: the power he tried to exercise over other people was of a moral kind, which explains the cross-questioning, the pacts and the fact that his affection took the form of a trial. He never succeeded in these relationships except with his mother, and with Céleste Albaret. We should console ourselves with the thought that no historian has ever classified writers according to their sexual achievements.

DAILY LIFE IN 1918

This year, which was already an important one for the writing of the book, would also provide the public with a triple discovery: a new version of *Du côté de chez Swann*, and the publication of *À l'ombre des jeunes filles en fleurs* and *Pastiches et mélanges* by Gallimard. What is more, Proust completed his fine foreword to Blanche's *De David à Degas* on 20 January, the first of a new series of important introductions; instead of being substitutes for his own work, as were those to Ruskin's books, they contained the 'leftovers' or the rejects. He corrected the proofs of this introduction ('a lot of corrections and not a single alteration')[32] in January 1919, pointing out to the painter that they had very different ways of writing. This did not prevent *Le Figaro* from preferring Abel Hermant, with his sound instinct, to Proust as a literary critic, or from turning down extracts from *Jeunes Filles* in September. The start of a new liaison meant that the year did hold a few pleasures, but also, as usual, sadness and expense.

Reassured as to the health of Princesse Soutzo, Proust felt so happy that he sent an increasing number of telegrams and letters to Morand. Disappointed by the staff at the Crillon, he started to dine on his own once more at the Ritz (although on 6 January he invited Berry) – arriving there at nine o'clock, even though the lights were put out an hour later, and probably hoping to catch sight of the princess – and he put a temporary stop to all social life. All the same, he was happy not to feel ill at ease and to be able to consume his six cups of coffee quietly, at the end of his meal.[33] On 4 February he dined (listening to Mme Lacoste singing Jammes and Ève Francis reading from Claudel) at Mme Daudet's with her sons Léon and Lucien, Francis Jammes (whose work he admired even though he could not get used to his personality),[34] François Mauriac (who struck him as 'charming'), Thérèse d'Hinnisdaël and the Abbé Mugnier. The latter came out with a host of paradoxes, which Proust took pleasure in quoting: Jammes was a 'sacristy faun'; Chateaubriand's *La Vie de Rancé* was written by a sinner who had not repented; by the time he finished his novel, Marcel would be the 'good Samaritan' of literature; 'Hell exists, but there's nobody in it'; and, because Mme de Chabrillan believed it was she who had discovered Mérimée: 'One should not forget that she lives in rue Christophe-Colomb.'[35] On 13 February he dined with the Abbé again ('I like him very much,' he told Lucien Daudet)* at the Ritz, at the invitation of Princesse Soutzo, together with Cocteau, Gautier-Vignal, the Baronne de Brimont and Henry Channon, an American lieutenant whom he considered poorly read. Sitting next to the Abbé, he merely listened,† liking the 'spicy details' and 'flavour' of his conversation.

The Princesse Soutzo left Paris without giving Marcel her address, which was unkind and which hurt him. He none the less dined every other evening at the Ritz, Odilon Albaret having returned home ill. On 9 April Comte Clary, who was an old friend of Marcel and especially of Lucien Daudet, died. In the spring, there were further health problems: Proust believed he was threatened with facial paralysis.[36] He would complain about it until early June and was even frightened of being trepanned; he therefore consulted Doctor Babinski, a neurologist and a disciple of Charcot, who reassured him. Like many people, Babinski did not know who Proust was, and he asked him: 'Do you have a job? What is it?'[37]

On 14 June Marcel learned of the death of Professor Pozzi (a flamboyant character, and one of the models for Cottard), who had been murdered the previous day by one of his patients. Recalling 'his kindness, his intelligence, his talent, his good looks', he remembered having known him *for ever*, that he had seen him at dinner at his parents' home, where the Strauses had met him, and that it was at Pozzi's home at 10 Place Vendôme that he had dined in town for the first time; furthermore, Robert Proust had been his assistant until 1914. As after the equally tragic death of Calmette, Marcel was deeply upset, and he had a strange premonition: the war had followed the first of these deaths; perhaps peace would follow

---

* *Corr.*, vol. XVIII, p. 107; cf. p. 112, 14 February 1918, to Abbé Mugnier; Proust sent him his article on hawthorns and some pastiches.

† Ibid., p. 113; cf. p. 132. Occasionally, when Proust was not talking inexhaustibly, this was the posture he adopted: Donna Maria Ruspoli, the third wife of Agenor, Duc de Gramont, confirmed this: 'What did Proust say to you?' 'Nothing; he listened to me with his big eyes.'

the second.[38] At this period, in his novel as well as his correspondence, he compared Paris to Pompeii: 'Women getting ready to dine in town may find themselves interrupted and delayed for ever, on the point of departure, just as they are applying the last touch of powder to their cheeks, halted by flying Vesuvius lava from the Boches; all those fancy goods, now rendered august and immutable, will be used for the instruction of children in the schools of a better age.'[39] He nevertheless dined on 27 June at the home of the Marquise de Ludre, 'a woman whose great charm is matched by the most acute intelligence', who entertained politicians of both the left and the right,[40] and on 29 June at the Comtesse Robert de Fitz-James', a woman of humble birth, but well known because of her husband (now dead, and unfaithful to her, incidentally), who gave dinner parties at the rue de Constantine for literary people and academicians, 'the leading figures in Europe'.*

At the end of July Céleste caught flu and went away to be looked after by her own family. Her sister-in-law took her place, 'backed up by others'. This was the reason Proust gave for not going to Cabourg, despite having intended to (or else he used as an excuse the asthma attacks that the journey, rather than Cabourg itself, induced). So he made do with dining on his own at the Ritz (Hélène Soutzo was in Biarritz). He did, however, meet socially someone who would serve as a model for the '*bal de têtes*', and in particular for the old Duc de Guermantes; this was the Duc de Gramont, 'huge, venerable and white-haired, with a wife who, in contrast, was younger (it's true that she's not the same one; and it may be the new one's extreme youth that has caused him to age)'.† On 14 August, worried about leaving Odilon Albaret, who was ill and on leave, alone with Céleste, Marcel dined at the Ritz, but he was not very pleased that the manager, Henry Ellis, stood by his table throughout dinner. At nearby tables he spotted Winston Churchill, the American minister Stettinius, and the Duke of Marlborough, who was wearing an enormous and unfashionable white cravat.

In early July, keen to republish his pastiches, he rewrote his Saint-Simon pastiche and had almost completed it by the end of September, but he wanted to obtain some scientific information from his friend, the Duc de Guiche, who was a physicist; since the duke ignored his invitations, Marcel

---

* A. de Fouquières, *Cinquante ans de panache*, P. Horay, 1951, p. 75. A Fitz-James was the great-uncle of the Duchesse de Guermantes.

† *Corr.*, vol. XVII, p. 331, 30 July 1918. The Duc de Gramont, who was born in 1851, was sixty-six at the time, and his third wife, Maria Ruspoli, was thirty. She had children both by the duke, and by Jean Hugo.

took offence and told him he had sent the text to the NRF without the amendments (though he did revise it).[41] He slipped a portrait of Guiche into his parody,[42] however, as well as one of Mme Straus, whom he also consulted on various occasions, informing her each time about some new aspect of the man.* The pretensions of the Murat family, the modern-day equivalent of those of the foreign princes in the age of Saint-Simon, gave shape to his narrative.[43] At the same time he was very worried about his brother, who had been involved in a serious motoring accident; his sister-in-law wrote to him with news every day, and he replied immediately; his letters were not preserved by the lucky recipient. Robert came to see him in early November.

Marcel had felt deeply hurt by Princesse Soutzo's failure to inform him that she was returning from Hendaye and by the fact that he only discovered this through Morand a fortnight later. His reasons for going to the Ritz 'no longer existed'. But he had become so accustomed to the climate of the place and the surroundings there that it had become rather like his own dining-room. Moreover, he had been introduced by Olivier Dabescat to Mme César Ritz, 'whose hair, worn with great charm, was like that of Ophelia'.[44] At one table he sometimes noticed the Comte Sala, elderly and ready for the 'Bal de têtes',[45] whose behaviour had made him an object of mockery to the Bibescos and from whom Proust maintained waiters ran away. To console himself, and in order to see someone who was one of his models and who was a mine of information, Marcel invited Mme de Chevigné to dine with him alone on 8 October, when he looked again into her forget-me-not eyes, the eyes of Oriane de Guermantes.[46] He told her that there were passages in his books in which 'an expression, an attitude, an artifice' were hers, and, before he died, he would like to be able to point them out to her.[47] After a period of coldness, which prompted a pathetic letter from Marcel ('Is it really the end of our seeing one another?'), and with no news of Morand either, whom he 'liked more and more',[48] friendly relations between Proust and Hélène Soutzo were gradually resumed, and on 28 December he attended a dinner party given by her. He went to a Christmas Eve party at Count Zucchini's, the Italian delegate to the Peace Conference: the Princesse Lucien Murat, who was in charge of the guest list had invited Proust, Hahn, Lacretelle, Madrazo, Cocteau, Mme Simone and Blanche. Marcel, who was proud to have been

---

* *Corr.*, vol. XVII, p. 381, 8 October 1918; p. 479, 20 November 1918: 'Blood princesses call on you without you bothering to visit them . . . On a pretext of illness that has become a privilege . . .'

placed on the princess's right, forgot his walking-stick, which Albufera had given him.[49] On 28 December he went to see a 'Charlus', Guzman Blanco, the brother of the Duchesse de Morny and a friend of Constantin Ullmann. On the 29th he dined at the Ritz, and was 'snapped at' by Boni de Castellane.[50] On 30 December, after dinner, he called on Mme Hennessy in the Avenue Henri-Martin. And the following evening he was invited by the Beaumonts to a grand dinner party in honour of Lord Derby, the British ambassador; there he met the First Secretary at the embassy, Reginald Bridgeman, 'whom he liked more and more', and Cocteau; in a lounge at the Ritz, where he went afterwards, he caught a fever and a cough.[51] When he got home, he wrote a strange and belated letter of condolence to Cocteau about the death of the aviator Roland Garros, who had been Cocteau's friend. After expressing his deep sympathy, and pointing out, so as not to annoy Cocteau, that he had never met Garros, Marcel added: 'My consolation is to think that you, who have so loved him, will have that sweet pleasure of having fixed him for ever in your poetry in a sky from which he can never fall and in which human names endure like those of the stars.'[52] Had Garros known Agostinelli? Proust then corrected the passage in *Albertine disparue* about the angels in the Giotto frescoes at Padua: the names of Fonck and of the Wright brothers were replaced, like a flower on a friend's grave, by that of Garros.[53]

HENRI ROCHAT

In mid-July Marcel had become friendly with a good-looking young Swiss boy who believed he had a gift for painting, who earned his living as a waiter at the Ritz. Proust had begun by asking for Henri Rochat to be put in charge of his table. A maître d'hôtel, Camille Wixler, has described how gradually Henri started to wear well-made suits and garments of the finest quality which he could not have afforded on his salary; they had been bought with M. Proust's assistance. 'At that age,' said Wixler, 'my education did not permit me to imagine what was going on, but afterwards I discovered from M. Proust himself what it was all about. He gave me to understand that certain kinds of human beings were not made as others were.'* The young man's financial demands were considerable; Marcel

---

* C. Wixler, 'Proust au Ritz: souvenir d'un maître d'hôtel', *Adam International Review*, no. 394, 1976, p. 19. Proust had promised that his name would be included in his book: a servant of the Swanns is in fact called Camille (*RTP*, vol. I, p. 502).

very soon spoke openly about the situation to Lionel Hauser. 'When one is in love with a person from the working class, more or less, rather than someone in society, these heartaches are generally coupled with considerable financial difficulties.'[54] It was the first and only admission Proust made of having a love affair with a servant. To Jacques Blanche, he spoke of his 'very depressed mood', which would certainly be the death of him and which poisoned every minute of his day,* and to Gallimard, of an 'unforeseeable burden, that was enormous and beloved besides'. He finally confessed to Hauser that he had spent the 20,000 francs he had withdrawn at the time he feared he might have to leave Paris, and a further 10,000 francs, which were meant for his own victuals (scanty) and his pharmacopeia (abundant).† This confession made his business adviser angry: he would willingly give him a piece of judicial advice had he the power to do so, and he suggested he put what he had left into an annuity with a life insurance company: his income would thereby increase, and so would his capital 'shielded from the impulses of his heart'.‡ But Proust refused to remove his capital. On the contrary, in order to procure more money, he tried to hasten the sale of his carpets, furniture, silverware and objets d'art, which Mme Straus was looking after.§ The carpets would be sold at auction in December, and Marcel would earn 3,000 francs.[55]

By a tragic coincidence, Émile Agostinelli, Alfred's brother, died in the war aged twenty, on 11 November, at the very time when Alfred was being replaced in Proust's affections. It was Proust who had introduced Émile to the Rostands, and 'his clothes were what were left from the things' belonging to Professor Proust. Marcel, who claimed he had only come across Émile on four or five occasions, always hoped to see him again so that he could talk to him about Alfred, 'whose life he must have known well';[56] however, he did not imagine that he would find in him, a married man in any case, a substitute for the deceased.

To return to Rochat, he was, according to Céleste, a somewhat sullen

* *Corr.*, vol. XVII, p. 360, 15 September 1918. Cf. p. 482, late November to Mme Straus: 'I have become involved in love affairs that are inextricable, joyless and which constantly create fatigue, suffering and absurd expense.'

† Ibid., p. 405. Equivalent to 220,000 francs in 1999 terms. To apologize to Olivier Dabescat, the Ritz's first maître d'hôtel, for one of 'Henri's' absences, Proust sent him 200 francs! (ibid., p. 514, December 1918).

‡ Ibid., p. 411, 20 October 1918. Proust replied that love, *crudelis amor*, was a passion that paid no heed to life, and *a fortiori* to riches.

§ He spoke to her about it on 11 November, an odd sign of egoism, or anxiety (ibid., pp. 448–9).

and silent young man, with a 'superior' side to him. Once Proust moved into the rue Hamelin, he would occupy a bedroom at one end of the flat, with Marcel's at the other. 'Rochat had only one thing going for him: nice handwriting. Apart from that: "He thinks he can paint", M. Proust told me.' When he was hired as Marcel's secretary, he sometimes took down passages of dictation from his employer at the end of the day. 'After that, he didn't ask him to do anything else. Rochat stayed in his room messing about with his painting, or else he went out. One seldom saw him.'[57] Certain friends, among them François Mauriac, nevertheless dined with him. Proust kept him for two years. That is all that is known about the man whom Proust engaged as a full-time secretary and who stayed with him firstly at Boulevard Haussmann, and later at his two last homes, and to whom Albertine owed her taste for drawing and painting.* Rochat stayed at Marcel's home four times as long as Agostinelli, and without a companion, and he, rather more than Agostinelli, provided the model for *La Prisonnière*. But whereas Rochat did not ask to leave, Agostinelli ran away – it was he who was *Albertine disparue*: one can understand why this text should have been written first. Proust examined the flight, the death, and then the prison. In *Le Carnet de 1908*, certainly, the novelist noted down the idea that first inspired *La Prisonnière*: 'in the second part, a ruined girl is kept, without her being enjoyed . . . because of incapacity of being loved'.[58] And in 1915 Proust summarized the basic plot of this novel for Mme Scheikévitch. A first draft of the manuscript was completed in 1916. But from 1917 to 1921 the additions increased the original material by half, while in the exercise books containing the additional material, Cahiers 60, 62, 59 and 75 (1919–22), the author made a note of the passages that were intended for *La Prisonnière*. Some of them were based upon the situation in which Rochat found himself, even though all this did was to reawaken memories, or old fantasies: a relationship lasting two years – as long as the relationship between Marcel and Reynaldo – provided the author with 'practical work', by increasing the experiences which he then transformed into consciousness. Furthermore, Rochat, as we shall see, was also Morel[59] (for whom there were several models: the pianist Delafosse, the viola player Pétain, Forssgren). The same model provided several characters; a single character stemmed from several models; taking up a line, a page, or an entire episode.

* *RTP*, vol. III, p. 576: 'She was busy working on some drawing'; p. 685: 'And Albertine's paintings, the captive's touching entertainment, moved me so much that I congratulated her.'

HISTORY, WAR, POLITICS

Throughout this year Proust remained fully involved with the great upheavals taking place in Europe. In the aftermath of the Russian Revolution, for instance, he sympathized with his friend Mme Scheikévitch, who had seen one of her two countries break off so completely with the other: 'What is more,' he added tactfully, 'do not be offended by what I say about Russia. Even leaving to one side her present political situation, which takes too long to discuss, you know that I shall always remain loyal to the Russia of Tolstoy, of Dostoevsky and of Borodin'* (just as he remained loyal to the Germany of Beethoven and Wagner). He was painfully affected by the Treaty of Brest-Litovsk,[60] which removed all hope of peace in the west, since the Austro-Germans would be able to take back all their troops.

On 30 January German aircraft bombed Paris: Marcel described the event both in his letters and in his novel: 'I shall try to come one evening when there are no Gothas . . . and despite the fact that I have never gone out except on evenings when there are zeppelins and storms.' That same evening Proust was obliged to wait in the streets because of his taxi breaking down while on his way to hear Borodin's Second Quartet at the home of Gabriel de La Rochefoucauld; a bomb had fallen very nearby, in the rue d'Athènes.† That night, from 11.30 onwards, the planes dropped 256 bombs over the city and its suburbs; there were sixty-five dead and

---

* *Corr.*, p. 76, 21 January 1918. Proust added that he was shortening a list that did not even include his favourite writers and composers (Mussorgsky, no doubt, whose *Boris Godunov* he had admired at the Champs-Élysées on 22 May 1913). On the subject of war loans, on 31 January 1918 the finance minister Klotz declared that the French government would pay interest for February (though it would stop doing so shortly).

† *Corr.*, vol. XVII, p. 104, to Mme Straus; *RTP*, vol. IV, p. 356: 'It was a period when there were continual Gotha raids, and the air droned constantly with the watchful sound and vibration of French aeroplanes. But occasionally the siren rang out like the harrowing cry of the Valkyrie – the only German music that could be heard during the war up until the moment when the fire brigade announced that the alert was over.' The Gothas were twin-engine aircraft laden with 1,000 kg of explosives. E. Hausser, *Paris au jour le jour*, Minuit, 1968, p. 665 ff. There were further bombardments on 8 February (13 dead, 50 wounded); on the 11th (34 dead, 79 wounded); the 23rd, a single shell fired from a long-range gun (15 dead, 36 wounded), as well as on the 24th (11 dead, 34 wounded). These figures were published with the agreement of the censors; they may therefore have been understated. The long-range gun was 'big Bertha', named after Bertha Krupp; on 29 February a shell hit the church of Saint-Gervais during mass: 77 dead and 80 wounded (*Corr.*, vol. XVII, p. 160). Usually, the *métro* served as a shelter, but the entrances to other shelters (cellars or trenches) were barely visible. After 9 April, barrage balloons, known as 'sausages', appeared over Paris.

187 wounded, struck down in the streets or at their windows: it shows how foolhardy Proust was, refusing to go down to the cellar (unlike Céleste, who did not share his lack of concern and spent 'half her time in the cellar'; Marcel began to fear she might never leave it) and going outside during the bombing raids, which earned him the disrespect of the other occupants of the building:[61] he had no fear of the guns and the Gothas.[62] As can be seen in *Le Temps retrouvé*, Paris was bombed almost daily after this, and there were numerous casualties. Proust was deeply affected by the death of his friends, and he was filled with dread at the thought of 'the new land we shall live in, from which so many dear faces will have disappeared'.[63] At the same time he found that unlike 'working-class people, those in society had a great facility for consoling themselves'.[64] He therefore sent 'a certain number of soldiers' 'some tobacco, cakes and chocolate each week'.* Among those back home on leave, he was overjoyed to see his brother, who had returned from Padua at the end of April: Robert had continued to operate in difficult circumstances and had carried out his work with the greatest courage, but he was very tired.

The bombing raids over Paris continued. During the one that occurred on 29 May, the courtyard of Proust's building was struck by 'large amounts of shrapnel and splinters from bombs'; Céleste claimed to have found some in the rim of Marcel's hat after he returned home on foot, brave as ever, 'through a barrage of firing'. 'Now, Monsieur, look at the bits of metal all over you! Didn't you come back by car? Weren't you frightened?' – 'No. Why, Céleste? The spectacle was much too fine for that.' The truth was that Proust needed to see something in order to describe it. In the course of that same night, he was approached by a street lout who did not dare attack him: 'Oh! Not someone like you, sir!' Even street louts were charmed by Proust's exquisite courteousness.[65]

But the German offensive at this period also worried Proust a great deal. On 27 May thirty German divisions were thrown into the attack on the Chemin des Dames sector; on the 29th the enemy was at Soissons, and on the 31st at Château-Thierry, seventy-five kilometres from Paris: 'I have never realized the extent to which I love France,' wrote Proust to Mme Straus on 31 May. 'You, who love the area around Trouville so well, will understand what the countryside around Amiens, around Rheims,

---

* Ibid. The addresses of soldiers to be found in Proust's notebooks may thus denote a charitable purpose.

and around Laon which I visited so often, means to me. Laon I visited with Emmanuel Bibesco ... But we ought to love men more than things, and I mourn and admire the soldiers more than the churches, which were only the result of a heroic gesture, which is repeated today at every moment.'* The resistance began to be organized; reinforcements arrived. And on 4 June the Germans adjourned their offensive; they resumed it on the 9th, in the Compiègne region, where they were thrown back by Mangin. On 5 May Proust, who had turned into a strategist, wrote a letter alluding to the service of Tenebrae: 'It really is like Tenebrae. I have faith in the glimmer of light, but I don't know where it will come from. This battle, alas, is like *Oedipus and the Sphinx*. We risk being devoured if we don't make up our minds about the enigma of Hindenburg, that is to say we are sacrificing our reserves over something which is not the real issue.'[66] Paris had been threatened; sixty kilometres had been conquered; in the Chambre des Députés some members had demanded the dismissal of Foch and Pétain, which Clemenceau rejected. A final enemy offensive took place on the Marne on 15 July, which was halted on the 17th. The Germans then held a line from Soissons to Rheims. Céleste was anxious and wanted to drag her employer away from Paris – for the time being he refused to leave (unlike other people: members of society had, in some cases, left the capital; certain politicians wished to leave, as they had in 1914; Clemenceau and Poincaré would not agree to this). Proust nevertheless equipped himself, in case of a general exodus, with 20,000 francs in cash[67] (which he spent, because of his love 'for the people', in a short time). Soon afterwards came the victorious counter-offensive, and the demand for an armistice before the allied troops crossed into Germany.

In spite of everything, Proust did not bear any hatred towards the Germans: 'like Don Juan', he spoke only 'out of love for mankind'.[68] And on 11 November he was happy enough writing to Mme Straus: 'Together, we have thought about war too much not to be able to exchange an affectionate word with one another on the eve of victory, one that is joyful as a result of it, but that is melancholy because of those whom we loved and who will not experience it.' And, taking in the entire war in a glance and synthesizing it in a single phrase: 'What a marvellous allegro presto in this finale, after the endless slowness of the beginning and its after-math. What finer playwright than Destiny, and man who has been its

---

* *Corr.*, vol. XVII, p. 270, to Mme Straus, 31 May 1918. Cf. p. 274: 'Like everyone else, I have no idea how the present episode of this terrible drama will end.'

instrument!'[69] The next day he pursued his comparison, his artistic vision of history: 'Only in Shakespeare's plays does one see all the events come together in a single scene, and hear in a single scene: Wilhelm II: "I abdicate." The King of Bavaria: "I am the heir to the most ancient race on earth, and I abdicate." The Kronprinz weeps, signs, and his soldiers murder him.'* But from the day after the armistice Proust felt that, 'if they wanted total victory and a solid peace treaty, then it would have been better if it had been more solid still. I prefer to all others those peace treaties that leave no one with any grudge in his heart.† But since this is not one of those peace treaties, it might perhaps have been wise to make it impossible to exercise the desire for vengeance once it arose.' He thought Wilson 'very gentle', and he feared a 'German Austria'.

READING

When Colette sent Proust *Les Heures longues*, he picked out a few quotations from ten or so pages so as to compliment her on them. This was his method for making people believe he had read a book.[70] It was the same with *La Valse ardente*, by his childhood friend Maurice Duplay, with *La Dimension nouvelle* by Lucien Daudet (he had read the typescript), *La Guerre totale* by Léon Daudet, and *L'Incertaine* by Edmond Jaloux.[71] But he admitted the truth elsewhere: 'I am rereading La Bruyère (finding contemporary writers unbearable)',[72] and he quoted two comments from the chapter entitled 'Des femmes'. Once again he revealed himself to be second to none in his knowledge of *L'Almanac de Gotha* (which he copied down with the help of a magnifying glass), proving to Princesse Soutzo that the Empress Eugénie came from the family of the Dukes of Alba.[73] He was also obliged to read an essay on 'social reconstruction' by Lionel Hauser, *Les Trois Leviers du monde nouveau*, which gave him the opportunity to reply with a manifesto on morals, aesthetics and philosophy, a *Le Temps retrouvé* in miniature. Style was not an ornament that was appended, 'it cannot be

---

* Ibid., p. 453. Luitpold, of Wittelsbach stock and the first Duke of Bavaria, ruled in the tenth century. The murder of the Kronprinz was a rumour circulating on 11 November, which was refuted the following day.

† In his draft notes Proust approved of the attempt at mediation (December 1916 and March 1917) made by the Bourbon-Parmes, the brothers of the Empress Zita. *RTP*, vol. IV, pp. 776–7: 'I spoke to him about the noble intervention by the Prince de Parme that had been disclosed' (disclosed by Clemenceau in order to scupper it: it came to light with a letter in which the Emperor Charles proposed ending the war and returning Alsace-Lorraine to France).

separated from the thought or the impression'. A sense of equilibrium and good health sometimes led to sterility, whereas 'the new way with words which discovered an unknown part of the mind or an additional nuance of affection, was bursting with all the drunkenness of a Musset or a Verlaine, with the perversions of a Baudelaire or a Rimbaud, even a Wagner, with the epilepsy of a Flaubert'. 'I believe that, if only for the creative value of pain, physical illness is . . . almost a condition of intellectual strength, and a rather brilliant one.' And the good that artists achieved was done without concerning themselves with other people: 'They have made their honey like bees do, and this honey has then benefited everyone else.' Finally, a confession from Marcel about his social comportment: he tended to the class of well-bred people, and he had put up with 'constant sacrifices on behalf of uncouth types who would never mean anything' to him.* He also read *Histoire de Samuel Bernard* by Élisabeth de Clermont-Tonnerre, which he quoted from discreetly.[74]

PUBLISHERS AND NEW EDITIONS

Correcting the proofs of *Jeunes Filles* progressed.[75] On 9 January 1918 Proust returned to Mme Lemarié the second set of proofs of pages 1–172 (in which one episode was entirely revised and three pages had an enormous amount of additions to the manuscript) as well as the first set of proofs of pages 184–277.[76] In April, shortly before Gaston Gallimard returned from America, Proust requested that a complete proof of *À l'ombre des jeunes filles en fleurs* be run off, 'which would not be amended further' (even though he reserved the right of 'a final revision') and that they should start work immediately on the galleys of *Le Côté de Guermantes*,† the complete manuscript of which he had also delivered.‡

Proust's self-esteem had been wounded by his very first publisher, Calmann-Lévy, who wrote to him on 15 May concerning *Les Plaisirs et les Jours*; out of a print run of 1,500 copies, seventy-one bound copies and 1,100 sets of unbound sheets were left; sales had completely dried up. He therefore proposed to the author either to remainder these copies, or to

---

* *Corr.*, vol. XVII, pp. 212–17. Cf. p. 228: 'All mystics were generally in a physical condition that was found to be pathological.'

† Ibid., pp. 220–1, to Mme Lemarié. Cf. p. 234, 2 May 1918, to Marcelle Jeanniot, of Gallimard's, in which he explained that *Guermantes* was 'in Grasset proofs which, alas, had been very much added to with little bits of paper and even large bits'.

‡ Ibid., p. 435, late October, in which he complained about not having had any proofs of *Guermantes*.

sell them off at three francs a copy. Marcel talked of an 'unspeakable',[77] 'dirty trick', and refused the offer.* The fact remains that the publisher did not revert the rights to Proust until 28 October 1921, when he authorized Gallimard to publish a small-format edition of *Les Plaisirs et les Jours*.[78]

On 14 June Gallimard suggested to Proust that he put together a collection of his pastiches.[79] Although Marcel feared that Gallimard would not include this 'in the aftermath of *Le Temps perdu*', in August he chose the final title, *Pastiches et mélanges*, and decided to include some of his articles, possibly with subtitles, such as 'La mort des cathédrales', or even 'L'affaire Lemoine'.[80] Proust wanted the titles to be simple and direct, but he always found it difficult to reach a decision; he was in a similar state of confusion over Blanche's book, for which he was writing the foreword: 'I weep over not knowing how to find a title',[81] and he suggested 'Les Maîtres d'aujourd'hui', which his friend would not use. Against Marcel's advice, Blanche would choose *Propos de peintre*.[82]

In July, when Proust asked Grasset for the arrears due on royalties from sales of *Du côté de chez Swann*, the publisher in turn requested an indemnity of 300 francs for the withdrawal of *Le Côté de Guermantes*; Marcel was extremely displeased by this, particularly since Gallimard, who had left for America, was not there to advise him. Grasset then instructed his colleague Louis Brun (to whom he had written in 1916: 'We would have been bound to have difficulties with this fellow, and then we had no rights of ownership')[83] to do everything that Proust wanted, by negotiating with Gallimard, and he expressed, though in a pleasant way, 'his bitterness and jealousy' at not publishing Proust.[84]

When *Jeunes Filles* was about to be printed, Proust considered dedicating it to the memory of Prince Edmond de Polignac.[85] In early September he asked his widow for her consent, but with so many qualifications and references to her antipathy for him, even alluding to Baron de Charlus, that she understood the reverse of what he had said, and thought that Marcel must have seen drawbacks to the dedication; in spite of a second attempt made on the advice of Morand, she would not go back on her refusal.

---

* We know of this from a letter in January 1919 to C. de Maugny: 'I naturally refused to buy back a thousand volumes which I would not know where to put, and it is in any case immaterial to me what they do with a book which is so entirely different to what I am doing today' (ibid., vol. XVIII, p. 45).

Financial need prompted Proust to consider a de-luxe edition of *Jeunes Filles*, consisting of a limited number of copies sold at a very high price, into which he would insert proof pages corrected by him.[86] He suggested doing the same for *Pastiches et mélanges*, with a manuscript page and a drawing by Sert. Only the first of these ideas would succeed, to the great misfortune of the scholars who would like to reconstruct the manuscript of the novel, but to the delight of bibliophiles, whom Proust did not understand, 'their minds being fairly closed to him'.[87] In the face of persistent delays by the printer and the justified impatience of the author, Gallimard withdrew *Le Côté de Guermantes* from La Semeuse and entrusted the job to Bellenand. Yet on 7 December Proust said he had received 'four volumes of proofs to correct'.[88]

As for the 'Mélanges', in early December Proust was busy searching or asking his friends and at *Le Figaro*, for copies of the articles that he could not find at home. He 'demolished' two *Bible d'Amiens* and two copies of *Sésame* in order to redraft the sections which were to be included.

THE SAINT-SIMON PASTICHE

In these pages, the only new ones, of the *Pastiches*, Proust brought together all his social connections from this period. It is thus a valuable record of his social life: many of the names from his youth have disappeared; others have appeared; as in *Le Temps retrouvé*, people and times had changed. Although one could still recognize Montesquiou and Yturri, and Mme Straus,* it also included Princesse Soutzo,† Morand, the Beaumonts, Louis de Talleyrand-Périgord, Guiche,‡ the Murats, Albufera, the Comtesse de Chevigné, Antoine Bibesco marrying Elizabeth Asquith,§ Mme de Clermont-Tonnerre, the Comtesse de Noailles, Mme Standish, Aimery de La Rochefoucauld, Boni de Castellane, Olivier Dabescat, 'the king's premier maître d'hôtel', the painter Sert, the Comte de Fels, 'whose name is Frisch', and a Prince of Orléans 'travelling in France under the very

---

* 'It would fill a book if one were to report all the things said by her and which deserve not to be forgotten.' Proust showed his text to Mme Straus in January 1919 (ibid., vol. XVIII, p. 73). She gave him her consent.

† 'She looked like Minerva . . . Her charms had enslaved me and I hardly stirred from my room . . . except to go to see her.'

‡ He 'recalled the charms of that gallant Comte de Guiche, who had been so involved in the early part of the reign of Louis XIV'.

§ 'One of those beautiful faces one sees painted in frescoes in Italy.'

strange name of the Infante of Spain';[89] as for Proust, invisible but ever-present, he was Saint-Simon.

The work had been prepared minutely.[90] The first note dealing with Saint-Simon, subsequent to the 1904 pastiche, is to be found in Carnet 2 and dates from 1915. It may also have been made with the novel in mind. The first event mentioned in the pastiche dates from 17 November 1917, so the real writing must have begun after this date. Proust started with two accounts: the first, like the 1904 version, dealt with the Lemoine affair, the second with the Murat scandal (into which he incorporated his 1904 pastiche, 'Fête chez Montesquiou à Neuilly'). What the parodist poked fun at were the pretensions of the Murat family to titles, forms of address and privileges that were the preserve of members of the royal families. At the same time he showed that from now on 'he couldn't care less' about society.[91] But the essence of the pastiche lay in the verve of his imitation, based as it was on flawless scholarship, and in the amiable or melancholy greeting that Proust addressed to his friends and his models in transferring *Le Temps retrouvé* to the Regency period and writing it in the style of Saint-Simon. He reversed the terms of his aesthetic approach, which consisted in 'writing the Memoirs of Saint-Simon of another age', by amusing himself and producing the novel by Proust of another age. He acquired such a taste for this that he announced a sequel, in which he planned to include a second portrait of Princesse Soutzo, 'given the position she had occupied' in his life over two years, as well as portraits of Mme de Chevigné and Morand.[92]

THE FOREWORD TO *PROPOS DE PEINTRE, DE DAVID À DEGAS*

This introduction to a collection of Blanche's articles had given Proust endless trouble, on account of the artist's extreme touchiness and the two men's deep differences over aesthetic matters. What was more, Proust did not know all the texts he was supposed to write about. This was why he stated that he had a very poor knowledge of Cézanne, Degas and Renoir, 'whose paintings he would have been very keen to have known'. He did, on the other hand, want to discuss Vuillard and Denis: 'Since they are two artists whose paintings – as well as the artists themselves – I happen to know, I should be glad to put in a line on each of them.'[93] As for Picasso ('Another painter whom I have met and whose work I know'),[94] who was not mentioned by Blanche, he described him as 'great' and 'admirable', and he praised his portrait of Cocteau, which had concentrated all the features of the poet in an image of noble rigidity, worthy of Carpaccio.

The book went on sale on 10 March 1919: Proust described it as 'beautiful', with the exception of the introduction, which had been written absentmindedly one evening when he was in a bad mood.[95] In this he behaved with that aristocratic politeness that consists of self-deprecation and which should not be taken literally. Indeed the compliments he received after publication would make him change his mind about the calibre of his pages.

DAILY LIFE IN 1919

Proust began 1919, as he did so many other years, with laryngitis and a temperature of 39°. Some bad news severely disrupted his life. In mid-January he heard that the owner (that is to say, his aunt) had sold the building at 102 Boulevard Haussmann to the banker Varin-Bernier. She told Marcel (who did not dare discuss the matter with Robert, 'who is violent, for fear that he might insult her') that she preferred 'the sweet name of aunt to that of landlady'. He was obliged to move because he had no lease and the building was to be turned into offices. He also dreaded having to pay arrears on the rent (the government had suspended payment of all rents in 1916, until the end of the war), amounting to approximately 25,000 francs,[96] which his former landlady had not collected, and having to search for a new flat. Some tapestries and antique furniture that was no longer used would have to be sold to cover these costs: Marcel asked Walter Berry to accommodate these things in the premises of the American Chamber of Commerce, where an eventual buyer might see them.[97] With Berry's consent, Proust would dedicate *Pastiches et mélanges* to him.* Worst of all was the shock of it: 'An asthmatic never knows whether he will be able to breathe, and he can be virtually sure of suffocating in a new dwelling. Now the (physical) condition of my heart does not allow me to bear the brunt of my attacks, which in themselves are not dangerous. I, who in spite of everything love life so much, can understand that death is our only hope,' he added in an important admission.[98] We should not imagine Proust as a depressive, void of desires and with no

---

* *Corr.*, vol. XVIII, pp. 104, 114. In this way he wished to pay homage to the part played by the Americans in the victory, which allowed the French to make a final offensive: 'If all we achieved were sublime battles such as Verdun, it could not have continued like that for ever.'

wish to live: he was only unhappy when he was ill.* But the trauma of moving house twice in 1919 perhaps marked the moment when, if we are to believe this avowal, like Montaigne, Seneca or Baudelaire,[99] he began to get ready to die.

Towards mid-January, Proust was once more in a fit state to dine at the Ritz,† in spite of his 'physical decline', but he was unable to go to the Beaumonts on 26 January to hear Cocteau read his *Cap de Bonne-Espérance* again. The latter had inscribed Proust's copy: 'Marcel, Je vous aime/ Je vous admire/ Acceptez le *Cap* comme je vous le donne/ de tout cœur/ Jean.'‡ On 2 February an incident occurred that tells us a great deal about the way in which Marcel organized his private life: he had always refused, 'out of the most basic vanity', to receive a woman 'at his sick bed'. Now Bibesco, having succeeded in eluding Céleste's vigilant eye, had smuggled his fiancée in, 'thanks to a diabolical trick', by diving into the bedroom behind Céleste, with Elizabeth Asquith in his arms, where Marcel, 'with his burnt cardigans' was lying in bed: 'I suffered the martyrdom of thus being seen by a girl I didn't know.'[100] He nevertheless attended a dinner party given by Antoine in early March to celebrate his engagement, where he made the acquaintance of Harold Nicolson, a delegate to the Peace Conference, whom he thought 'delightful, and so intelligent!' Nicolson's marriage to Vita Sackville-West became famous because of the homosexuality of the two spouses, their parallel literary activities, and the liaison of Vita, the model for Orlando, with Virginia Woolf;§ he was less indulgent in his judgement of Proust (though both of them could have been mistaken): 'Pale, unshaven and dirty, with a face like papier-mâché' and 'very Hebrew'.[101]

Nor did Marcel go to Misia Edwards' (who would marry Sert in 1920) to listen to Gide playing the narrator in Satie's *Socrate*. The invitation from the writer pleased him, however, because he had not had news of him for a long time: Gide would never number among Marcel's

---

* This is what Paul Morand confided to me: Proust did not strike him in the least as an unhappy person.

† He went back there on 3 February, without being able to visit Princesse Soutzo, who had gone out. On 3 March, as well as on the 18th, he attended dinner parties given by the princess.

‡ *Corr.*, vol. XVIII, p. 67, n. 4. Proust replied to Cocteau on 11 February, mingling praise with veiled criticism of expressions that were too emphatic and of repetitions. Curiously, Proust showed very little reaction to aviation, a subject that may have reminded him of Agostinelli (and he did not talk to Cocteau about the passages from *À la recherche* devoted to this subject).

§ Nigel Nicolson, their son, has described this union of a homosexual with a lesbian in *Portrait of a Marriage*, which bears out certain affirmations made in *Sodome*.

'evening visitors': 'All the same, a little real active friendship would have been pleasant', wrote Proust,* who, in the exchanges between these two *monstres sacrés* would always be the more needful and demanding of the two.

In March Marcel complained about the same problems that had led him to consult Babinski, and in particular about his confused speech and his difficulty articulating words; even though he feared they were 'caused by a serious brain problem', he himself observed that they may have been due – and this is probably a good diagnosis – to 'poisoning through excessive doses of veronal';† he complained of these symptoms until the end of his life, while at the same time expressing his fear of dying an aphasic 'like his poor Maman'.‡ This did not prevent him from recommending veronal (even leaving some on his bedside table, knowing that he was there) to Louis de Robert, who was an insomniac. He invoked Brissaud's advice: 'an admirable man, with enormous intelligence but a bad doctor, who reckoned (I'm barely exaggerating) one should live on trional'.§ We know something of his dietary habit, thanks to a dinner invitation from Mme Hennessy: 'I am not on any sort of diet, I eat anything, I drink anything, I don't think I care for red wine, but I like all the white wines in the world, and I like beer and cider. My only dietary requirement is that you should allow me to bring with me a bottle of Contrexéville or Évian, which I shall drink a little of in another glass.'[102] The fact that he did not follow a diet was probably the reason why he had 'scarcely changed' in appearance, did not have a single grey hair, but had put on some weight.[103] At the end of the Hennessy dinner party, Princesse Soutzo allowed herself to be accompanied home by the Beaumonts rather than by Marcel, and this offended him, just as Swann was offended when Odette was taken home by the Verdurins and not by

---

* *Corr.*, vol. XVIII, p. 108, shortly before 20 February 1919. Proust had a visit from Gide in March (ibid., p. 147); the latter does not mention it in the entry in his published diary for that date.

† Ibid., p. 135, to W. Berry. Proust was very upset that Berry joked about these health problems, and he described to him Ribot's 'law of regression' on the subject of memory. Marcel considered the latter to be 'a philosopher of the twenty-fifth rank' (p. 140). Doctor Bize diagnosed a case of 'poisoning'.

‡ E.g. ibid., p. 188. The illness thus gave him the joy, as well as the sorrow, of identifying himself with his mother.

§ Ibid., p. 214, May 1919. 'I haven't seen Bergson for years,' he disclosed, 'but when I used to see him he had been taking trional for years and felt very well on it.' Louis de Robert replied that he had been taking trional for seventeen years, as well as veronal, but that later 'it was necessary to double the dosage'.

him.[104] She none the less invited him to a dinner in honour of Queen Marie of Romania, which he did not attend. In mid-April Proust made contact for the first time with the English writer Sydney Schiff, who asked him for an extract from his work for the magazine *Arts and Letters* (1917–1920), which he edited together with Frank Rutter and Osbert Sitwell:* the contributors included Katherine Mansfield, T. S. Eliot and Edith Sitwell.[†]

SYDNEY SCHIFF

The author of a clutch of novels in the modernist style, written under the pseudonym of Stephen Hudson (translated for Gallimard in four volumes[105] by Emmanuel Boudot-Lamotte, who was Gaston Gallimard's secretary) and some short stories,[106] one of which is devoted to Céleste, Sydney Schiff (1868–1944), whose second wife[107] was Violet Beddington (1875–1962), is one of the great casualties of English letters. His name no longer appears in any of the textbooks on literary history, nor in any of the Oxford Companions or in the *Dictionary of National Biography*. It was Proust who introduced him to the NRF: 'The early seeds were due to my good friend, Marcel Proust', he wrote at the beginning of one of his translations. And Boudot-Lamotte, his translator, confirmed that the NRF had published him 'on the advice of Marcel Proust, who was a fervent admirer of Stephen Hudson'.[108] Schiff was also to translate *Le Temps retrouvé*, in 1931, after Scott-Moncrieff's death.[‡]

The poet and novelist Valery Larbaud noted in his *Journal*: 'I sensed in him (from reading his book) a writer of the same species as myself, that

---

* Inviting him to his home, Schiff, in his commendable rather than correct French, wrote: 'There will be twenty or so people, homogeneous and homosexual' and he mentioned the Sitwells and Wyndham Lewis.

† *Corr.*, vol. XVIII, pp. 167–8. Cf. ibid., vol. XIX, p. 614: apart from Proust, there were only two people with whom the Schiffs wished to exchange views, Eliot and Wyndham Lewis. On the latter, see ibid., vol. XXI, p. 295. Wyndham Lewis drew a portrait of the Schiffs, and, at Sydney's request, nearly drew Proust too: he was out when Céleste came to look for him (ibid., p. 347): 'And yet to be drawn by you would have been my only chance of becoming famous!'

‡ Schiff started translating Proust in 1919: 'The British public for good literature is very small, especially for good French literature, and this public, or the better educated among them, prefers to read these books in French.' He was the only person, he asserted, able to write a fitting translation (*Corr.*, vol. XIX, p. 451) and he would criticize that done by Scott-Moncrieff. Only 1,300 copies of his translation, *Time Regained* (Chatto & Windus, 1931), were printed.

is to say "a gifted amateur", and one who, like me, never made much of an effort.'[109] Schiff was the brother of Édith Gautier-Vignal, the mother-in-law of Louis, whom they were not very kind about in their discussions.[110] Very much a depressive, his remedy was champagne, which Proust, who stuck to beer, categorically advised him against.[111] In his letters Schiff drew a portrait of his wife, whom he adored, and whom Proust, pretending to feel closer to the wife than to her husband,[112] called 'the angel Violet',[113] or again: 'A retiring, fragrant and miraculous flower, whose peduncle and efflorescence Leonardo da Vinci, in the drawings that you may have seen in the Ambrosian Library in Venice, has sketched so minutely.'* Marcel dedicated *Sodome et Gomorrhe II* to the couple: 'You alone seem to me to be what one is seeking constantly.'†

On 18 May 1922 the Schiffs held a reception at the Majestic following the first production of Stravinsky's *Renard*. They invited Diaghilev, the dancers from the Ballets Russes, Joyce and Picasso.‡ Sydney suggested to Marcel that he should have his portrait done by Picasso: 'Only a drawing – it will take an hour.'[114] Nothing would come of the idea. On the basis of his poor knowledge of French, Schiff also spoke disparagingly to Proust about Scott-Moncrieff's translation of *Swann*, thereby causing him unnecessary anxiety.§ He renewed his criticism in his last letter to Proust, on 14 November 1922,[115] and told him that he would be sending him his latest book, *Prince Hempseed*, which would bear the dedication: 'To the Memory of My Beloved Friend Marcel Proust, November 18 1922'. Eighteen months later the *Criterion*, edited by T. S. Eliot, published Stephen Hudson's *Céleste*,[116] in which Proust appears as Richard Kurt, the hero of Schiff's autobiographical novel. In its pages we come across Louis, the NRF's young courier, Olivier Debascat, Odilon, Ellis, the manager of the Ritz, Reynaldo (under the name of Fernando), Rivière (who is called Rémy, and who always leaves Proust feeling 'restless', whereas Robert leaves him in a 'dreamlike' state), the party in honour of *Renard*, and the memories which Céleste must have related to him: 'Then suddenly, one

---

* *Corr.*, vol. XXI, p. 373. There is no Ambrosian Library in Venice. It is in Milan (Saint Ambrose is the patron saint of the city).

† A modification of the line of Vigny's poem: '*Toi seule me parus ce qu'on cherche toujours*' (*Éloa*). In the same dedication, Proust advised them against living at the Ritz, hoping, no doubt, to be left in peace there.

‡ For a somewhat over-embellished account of this evening, see Painter, pp. 340–42.

§ *Corr.*, vol. XXI, p. 295. Letter to Scott-Moncrieff of 9 or 10 October 1922, to which the translator replied in English, pleading his imperfect knowledge of French!

afternoon, "Look, Céleste," he said, holding up the violet copy-book: FIN [The End].'*

On 30 April there was another dinner party at the Ritz, with Princesse Murat, Gladys Deacon, Harold Nicolson, Jean de Gaigneron (to whom Proust was to explain his book's relationship to a cathedral). On 7 May Marcel entertained Jean-Louis Vaudoyer and Reynaldo Hahn to dinner; Henri Rochat was present, but 'said nothing'.[117] Berenson saw Proust at Mme Hennessy's on 16 May. On the 25th Proust went to Princesse Edmond de Polignac's house to hear a concert which was conducted by Hahn.

RUE LAURENT-PICHAT

That April Proust considered renting a villa in Nice belonging to Mme Catusse, but he also thought of moving into a fifth-floor apartment on the rue de Rivoli, since the noise of the street bothered him less than that of neighbours.[118] At the end of the month, after having seen the managing agent of the Boulevard Haussmann building (whom the Duc de Guise had met first, to discuss the terms of Marcel's departure), he signed an agreement whereby he would move out on condition that he was paid 12,000 francs in compensation and given a reduction of 20,000 francs for the rent that was owing.[119] He had to leave by 31 May. Meanwhile he foresaw, and never stopped saying as much, that moving house would increase his intake of toxic substances, because in any new dwelling he experienced 'constant fits of breathlessness over a period of several months which could not be treated in any other way'.[120] In early May Misia Edwards suggested that he should live, as she did, at the Hôtel Meurice, but he refused, in spite of his desire to 'try out the effect of the Seine on [his] asthma', because he feared the noise.[121] To make matters worse, the preparations for moving 'made Céleste insufferable',[122] and he did not know what to do with his furniture: this was why he arranged for an auction house to sell some of it.[123] Alarmed at the prospect of noise in the future, he enquired of the Comtesse de Noailles about who supplied her with cork, and he asked Mme Simone about wax earplugs, a subject on which he would base a passage in *Le Côté de Guermantes*.[124] On 26 May,

---

* *Céleste*, Blackamore Press, 1930, p. 39. This was probably the first written version of an episode that was related frequently by Céleste.

not knowing where to go, he accepted the furnished apartment that Jacques Porel, the son of Réjane, had suggested to him, which was situated on the fourth floor of his mother's house, at 8 *bis* rue Laurent-Pichat, near the Porte Dauphine.[125] Just as he was leaving, Proust destroyed certain documents – or so he said in a letter to Abel Desjardins: 'Before leaving Boulevard Haussmann, I burnt some valuable signed books, some manuscripts of which no copy exists and some photographs that have become rare.'* He had moved into his new flat his brass bed, his bedside table and a bed for Rochat, 'cured of gonorrhea'; some dresses that had belonged to his mother would go to her closest relatives, and the things that he was unable to move into Réjane's furnished flat would be put into storage. An electrician worked on equipping the new flat for him: this explains the curious comment in *À la recherche* about how these workmen 'count among the ranks of the real chivalry nowadays'.[126]

We can imagine Proust's parting glance, this 'tenant who would die if he was uprooted', upon leaving the apartment in which his old Uncle Louis had died and which was the last place his family had known, to set off towards the Bois de Boulogne, which was far removed from the centre of his life, if not of his book, and which, especially in springtime, exacerbated the suffering of anyone with allergies. In the new building Réjane, who was sixty-two and had a heart condition, lived on the second floor, while the Porels and their baby lived on the third; Proust would occupy the fourth floor, which was intended for the actress's daughter, who was then in America; it was fairly large: but 'the partitions were made of paper, you hear every noise',[127] and the rent was high: it would do for a temporary stay, a month, he thought initially. On the opposite side of the courtyard lived the actor Le Bargy. Proust the novelist was ready to make use of everything: he transferred the flat's wall-paper 'with black and white flowers against a red background' to a bathroom at Doncières.[128] 'The neighbours who are separated from me by a partition make . . . love every day with a frenzy that makes me jealous. When I think that in my case this sensation is weaker than that obtained from drinking a glass of cold beer, I envy those people who can cry out in such a way that the first time I thought a murder was taking place, although very soon the

---

* *Corr.*, vol. XVIII, p. 338, July 1919. Céleste Albaret contradicts what both Painter and Kolb (*Corr.*, vol. XVIII, pp. 21–2), following what Proust wrote, have asserted: 'I don't know who it was who wrote that before leaving Boulevard Haussmann, M. Proust made me destroy quantities of papers, photographs and other things. That's untrue' (C. Albaret, p. 390).

woman's cry, which was repeated an octave lower by the man, made me realize what was going on. I am not responsible for this din, which can surely be heard at distances as great as the cry described by Michelet of whales making love and holding themselves as erect as the two towers of Notre-Dame. Furthermore, the man and the woman appear to have as much a horror of children as they have a liking for caressing one another. For no sooner is the last cry achieved than they rush off to take a hip bath and the murmurs draw to a close with the sound of water. The absolute absence of any transition exhausts me on their behalf, for if there is anything I loathe *afterwards*, or at least *immediately afterwards*, it is having to move. Whatever the selfishness required in preserving the warmth of a mouth that has nothing more to receive.'* This extraordinary confession is the only one to my knowledge that reveals certain habits of Proust's; it is astonishing that he should have confided in Porel in this way. Yet more surprising still is the fact that this letter employs the same words and the same images as the passage in *Sodome I* in which the Narrator listens to the frolics of Charlus and Jupien through a partition wall;† since this page does not appear in the manuscript, Proust must have added the passage in the novel after having heard his neighbours in the rue Laurent-Pichat.

Marcel probably derived some consolation from living close to an actress whom he admired above all others,‡ and to her son, of whom he was very fond: 'He is as pleasant and delightful as a gust of wind on a summer's evening,' he told Céleste; she recalled that Réjane, fearing that her life was in danger, had written to Marcel to entrust her son to him: 'Céleste, it's awful. Yes, M. Porel is a weak-willed fellow; but I'm a sick man; I cannot take on this responsibility.'§ However, he would draw on

---

* *Corr.*, vol. XVIII, p. 331, to J. Porel, a text quoted by Kolb on the basis of a P. Bérès catalogue, which I have reproduced in full. On a copy of the second edition of *Sodome I*, which Proust had corrected in hand, he put aside his own preferences for the benefit of fictional verisimilitude (the Narrator cannot spend half an hour glued to the partition) – 'after half an hour' was deleted (*RTP*, vol. III, p. 11, var. *b*).

† *RTP*, vol. III, p. 11: 'These sounds were so violent that had they not always been repeated an octave higher by a parallel moan, I might have thought that someone was slitting someone else's throat next door to me . . .'

‡ See his inscription to Réjane in a copy of *Jeunes Filles*: 'To one who has lived the most beautiful life, to the creative spirit who has achieved a revolution in the art of the theatre parallel to that which has brought back the novel and painting into the framework of truth . . . respectful homage from an insufferable tenant' (*Corr.*, vol. XVIII, p. 271).

§ C. Albaret, p. 386. Cf. *Corr.*, vol XVIII, p. 317, to Réjane: 'I do not share your opinion about your son. He is one of the only human beings in whom, along with his countless virtues, I can find not a single fault.'

the relationship between Réjane, her son (a victim of gas poisoning in 1917, Porel was unemployed), and her daughter-in-law, and on Le Bargy[129] for his portrait of la Berma in old age, obliged to appear on stage in order to provide money for her daughter and her son-in-law, and giving a tea-party to which nobody comes.

In spite of the shock of moving and the crises that ensued, Proust would shortly enjoy some gratification with the publication of his three books. On 13 June Gallimard was expecting delivery of the new edition of *Swann* at any moment. Proust received his copies a few days later, and managed to find the strength to write numerous dedications* and to ask Robert de Flers for an article in *Le Figaro*; all he would obtain was an article from the devoted Robert Dreyfus on 7 July; since he signed himself 'Barrolo', Proust considered that it was something of a 'comic compliment'.[130] In the meantime he returned on three or four occasions to dine in the one home base he had, the Ritz, at about half past ten.[131]

Towards the end of June Céleste went away for the wedding of a niece, and Marcel found himself 'alone'. He turned to his friend, the diplomat Jacques Truelle: he wished to obtain a safe-conduct so that Rochat could return to Switzerland. Rochat had gone to the Côte d'Azur to await his papers, had spent the money that Marcel had given him, and had come back with a venereal disease, which had obliged Proust to 'hospitalize him' at home once more. Quite clearly, Rochat's employer was growing weary of him, and he could not stand the fact that he was 'lingering' in the South of France, particularly since it had become difficult for foreigners to stay in France: they were being expelled.[132] He mistrusted Rochat to such an extent that he did not want to send him on his own to the *préfecture*. Once Truelle had supplied the necessary papers, Marcel accompanied Rochat to the Gare de Lyon on 9 July.[133] Afterwards, he went to dine at the Ritz with Princesse Soutzo and Morand. But unfortunately, Rochat, who had not found employment in Switzerland, returned at the end of July without alerting Marcel and eventually persuaded him to put him up, which 'poisoned [his] existence'.[134] Marcel tried in vain to send Henri to stay with the grandmother of his fiancée ('lovely, but a concierge's daughter') in Deux-Sèvres: 'But he thought he would be compromising her.' And so Marcel, who said that he was 'very nice' all the same, played draughts with

---

* *Corr.*, vol. XVIII, p. 270 and ff. In his dedication to Mme Catusse, in which he recalls the memory of his mother, he confided: 'In the moments when I support the new – and very old – philosophy which suggests that souls live on, I am drawn towards it' (p. 397).

his 'secretary' and spent his time moving counters around the board instead of correcting his proofs.[135] On 14 August he dined at the Ritz with Princesse Murat (who would be infuriated by the Saint-Simon pastiche),[136] Berry and the Chambruns. He returned home at five o'clock in the morning, 'after having gone off to doze in the Bois de Boulogne, sublime in its silence, its solitude and the moonlight' in order to recover from champagne that was too good, which prevented him accepting an invitation to travel to Cabourg by car. He thus saw his dear Bois de Boulogne once more, which he still wanted to write about, in *Guermantes*, *Sodome* and *Albertine disparue*.

PUBLISHING IN 1919

Around 20 January 1919, Proust received the 'folded sheets' of *À l'ombre des jeunes filles en fleurs* (printing had finished in November 1918). He considered that they had been printed in such faint type that the text was impossible to read, whereas he had asked for a larger typeface than that used for *Swann*. The book was actually a hundred pages smaller, whereas, using the same type, there would have been a hundred more.[137] What is more, there were countless printing errors: Reynaldo Hahn told Mme Lemarié that he was endeavouring to correct them himself;[138] he left for Monte-Carlo, however, without handing over his copy: so Proust marked the mistakes that struck him 'on a fresh copy'.[139] On the other hand, he reckoned that the dust-cover of the book was 'gorgeous'. However, the book was not put on sale until the two other titles, the *Pastiches* and *Du côté de chez Swann*, were ready. *Pastiches et mélanges* came off the presses on 25 March, but at about this time Proust sent in a contents list and some corrections of literals for *Jeunes Filles*,[140] and it was not until 12 April that Gallimard returned the proofs of *Swann* to the printer, Bellenand,[141] informing him that this book would not be corrected by the author and that there would be no textual corrections. This is surprising, since, as I have recently discovered, one of the Grasset copies bore some hand-written corrections made by Proust and by some of the staff of the NRF.[142] He must have changed his mind later.

On 17 April Gallimard asked Bellenand to start typesetting *Le Côté de Guermantes* from a series of galley proofs and three manuscript notebooks (II, III, IV).[143] On 13 May he assured Proust that he was doing everything possible to make his books available as early as possible, but that the printer had told him that there had been 'a strike, delays in dispatching, the impossibility of finding basic materials, and a dearth of typefaces'.[144] Proust was not convinced: *Jeunes Filles* had been 'sabotaged'; even if all the errors were his, 'proof readers were meant to do something'. There were plenty of busy printers, for he never stopped receiving other people's books. As to the additional material, Gaston had been warned about this, and the virtues of Proust's books stemmed from the 'overnourishment that he infused into them. Finally, he no longer had the same energy to make the corrections. This explains the clause in his will: 'As long as everything appears in my lifetime all will be well, and if it should happen otherwise, I have left all my numbered exercise books which you must take, and I depend on you to make the publication complete.'[145]

On 19 April Jacques Rivière asked Proust to launch the first issue of the new series of the *NRF* on 1 June. Under the title listed in the table of contents, 'Légère esquisse du chagrin que cause une séparation, et des progrès irréguliers de l'oubli', Rivière would like to include: the portrait of Gilberte and the disintegration of the hero's love for the girl.[146] Proust feared, with good reason, that this would delay publication of his books, but eventually he agreed so as to please Rivière.[147] The discussion would continue by correspondence over the choice of pages (fifty) in a dizzying whirlwind of skipped and repeated passages, so much so that although Proust cut material, he also added some.[148] On 31 May, as he was leaving Boulevard Haussmann, he finally received the proofs of *Le Côté de Guermantes*, which he started to correct in the rue Laurent-Pichat.

Despite Proust's hopes and entreaties then, his three books (one of which had been in print since November 1918 and another since March) would not go on sale until 21 June. On 23 June he received an advance of 2,430 francs for the first thousand copies of the three titles, and a further 5,490 francs on 26 August for the three titles combined.* In December, *Swann* and *Jeunes Filles*, which until then had been available as single volumes, were each divided into two volumes† and their price was raised when they were reprinted; a three-volume edition of the second title would follow.

But Proust did not want to limit publication in magazines to the *NRF*. This was why in October he gave 'something [he had] written about

* That is, 2,700 francs for 3,000 copies of *Jeunes Filles*, 900 francs for 1,000 copies of *Swann* and 1,890 francs for 3,000 copies of the *Pastiches*. Roughly 66,000 francs in all by 1999 standards.

† On a copy of *Jeunes Filles* belonging to the banker Henri Gans, Proust wrote that he disapproved of this subdivision (*Corr. avec G. Gallimard*, p. 213), but perhaps this was to excuse himself for not having sent the one-volume edition.

Venice' to *Feuillets d'art*; it was the extract from *Albertine disparue* that he had once suggested to Robert de Flers for *Le Figaro*, entitled 'À Venise', illustrated with 'superb studies by Maxime Dethomas';[149] Proust extracted a section of it, which *Le Matin* ran on 11 December under the title 'Mme de Villeparisis à Venise'. Altering the text of his original manuscript for this paper, he removed the references to Albertine and to the grandmother, and, in the conversation between M. de Norpois and Mme de Villeparisis, he replaced the allusions to the Morocco affair with the seizure of Fiume, which D'Annunzio had just captured in September 1919. It was a case of using a less amorous and more political episode than the fictional one. Proust would later make use of the article to revise the text of the novel: this explains the difficulties editors have had in discovering which was the true text of the visit to Venice in *Albertine disparue*.

Conversely, and in order to tie him to his magazine, Jacques Rivière suggested to Proust, 'the current master of the genre', that he provide him with a monthly column, in the form of notes, on the novel, while at the same time asking him for 'as extensive extracts as possible' from *Guermantes* and from *Sodome*.[150] Naturally, Proust replied that it was impossible, reserving his reasons for a subsequent discussion: no doubt he did not wish to speak ill of writers he did not care for (but whom he sometimes complimented in his letters: people like Hermant, whom Rivière, rightly, hoped he would slate), nor did he wish to distract himself from completing his novel with a burdensome and restricting monthly task. Nevertheless, he did suggest to the editor of the *NRF* that he write a letter in response to Thibaudet[151] on 'Flaubert's style'.[152] For this Proust made use of passages from *Contre Sainte-Beuve*, and he also found polemical issues stimulating; the article was written extremely quickly. He submitted it on about 8 December;[153] it appeared on 1 January 1920. The text is one of the foundations of modern literary criticism: as ever, along with a kind of naïvety, Proust brought a freshness and an absolutely new slant to bear on Flaubert, one that was not cluttered with bibliographical details and scholarship: 'A man who through his utterly new and personal use of the preterite and past indefinite tenses, of the present participle, and certain pronouns and prepositions, has renewed our vision of things almost as much as Kant, with his Categories, and his theories of Knowledge and the Reality of the exterior world.'[154]

PRESS RECEPTION OF *À L'OMBRE DES
JEUNES FILLES EN FLEURS*

Before the award of the Prix Goncourt, the press gave a modest initial
welcome to *Jeunes Filles*. Apart from an article by Robert Dreyfus, the
critic Fernand Vandérem (whom Blanche, in a letter to Proust, recognized
as one of the models for Bloch) alluded to 'a soul', 'a sensibility', 'an
intelligence' (but a faulty style and a lack of any fictional technique) in *La
Revue de Paris* of 15 July. In *Le Figaro* Abel Hermant felt that this confession
aroused the 'shiver of the miraculous'.[155] Binet-Valmer saw in Proust a
'great poet of the sorrowful' (*Comœdia*, 5 October),[156] while André Billy,
writing in *L'Œuvre*, criticized his gossiping (26 August).[157] On 1 October
Le Crapouillot published a pastiche in questionable taste: 'À l'ombre d'un
jeune homme en boutons',[158] which Proust, who missed nothing, thanks
to the *Argus de la presse*, considered 'really stupid'. *Pastiches et mélanges* was
praised by *Le Figaro* and *Le Gaulois*, but was considered too serious by *La
Revue mondiale*. Aragon wrote in *Littérature* in October: 'Eventually one
marvels, when Marcel Proust does a pastiche of Marcel Proust, at finding
so little brilliance in someone who displays such talent. To tell the truth,
my digestion cannot cope with miscellanies';[159] very much the same could
be said about him. In the June 1919 issue of *Feuillets d'art*, Giraudoux
devoted an article to the revised edition of *Swann*, entitled 'Du côté de
chez Marcel Proust'. First of all he argued that after the war readers needed
a holiday and a life of ease, happiness and poetry; he then sketched a
portrait of Proust and spoke of his style, about childhood, memory,
'society', and about women: finally, he related the story of 'Un amour de
Swann'. On 15 October Proust told Porel: 'It was beautiful and full of
wit, and it disappointed me up to a point.'[160] And to Morand, whom he
blamed for having prompted his friend Giraudoux to make constant jokes
about 'the Boulevard Haussmann, the exercise books, the closed shutters',
he said, 'But in actual fact there's nothing accurate about me.'[161]

Proust meanwhile continued to prepare the de-luxe edition of *Jeunes Filles*,
which was to be published in May with a print-run of fifty copies, each
selling at 300 francs and comprising two corrected galleys, and he was trying
to find subscribers. He arranged for the portrait of him by Jacques-Émile
Blanche to be reproduced, kept a close watch on the number of lines per
page, and, prompted by the Library Edition of Ruskin, he requested a red
cloth binding.[162]

READING

In March 1919 Proust read *Mitsou* by Colette, and he 'wept' as he read the letter from the heroine at the end of the book, even though she was 'a little too pretty', and 'a touch precious'.[163] Always anxious when he read of things in other writers' books he had written about himself, he made a mental note to compare Mitsou's restaurant with the 'countless inferior restaurants' in his forthcoming books. In early April Jacques Rivière's *L'Allemand, Souvenirs et réflexions d'un prisonnier de guerre* aroused Marcel's pity for what Rivière had endured and his 'admiration' for the man's 'nobility' and the lively turn of mind with which he portrayed positive German qualities, 'such as their strong will and their systematic minds'. He added a word of advice: 'Don't believe too much in words,' which concealed his criticism of preciosity.[164] In May he skimmed through a novel by Vaudoyer, *Les Permissions de Clément Bellin*,[165] and another by Louis de Robert called *Roman d'une comédienne*.[166] In early June, still in the throes of moving house, he thanked Henri Ghéon for *L'Homme né de la guerre, Hommage d'un converti*, but did not refrain from observing that his conversion to Catholicism had caused him to lose his critical judgement, nor from mentioning 'the so disparaging article' that Ghéon had written about *Swann* in the *NRF*. *Le Coq et l'Arlequin*, in which Cocteau ventured into the field of musical aesthetics, induced 'wonderment' in Marcel: he liked the historical background to *Parade*, Cocteau's eulogies of Chardin, Ingres and Manet, as well as the portrait of Nijinsky and the felicitous style. On the other hand, he defended Wagner, Saint-Saëns and Strauss, and he side-stepped the central question of a return to classicism, which Cocteau had advocated.[167] With greater interest still did he read in the *NRF* of 1 July 'Nuit à Chateauroux', by Giraudoux, which was the inspiration for a passage in *Guermantes* about the appearance of a new writer who outshone Bergotte. Giraudoux also sent him a copy of *Elpénor*, 'an excuse for perpetual *enchantment*'.* Similarly, Proust considered *Charles Péguy et les Cahiers de la Quinzaine* by Daniel Halévy 'admirable', but this must have been an expression of pure politeness, given his hostility to the subject. Still loyal to Porto-Riche, Marcel praised his play *Le Marchand d'estampes*, and even more so his introduction, in which the author wrote that

---

* *Corr.*, vol. XVIII, p. 422, shortly after 10 October 1919, to Paul Morand. Giraudoux had inscribed it: 'To Marcel Proust because I like his book, I adore it.' (Catalogue of the BN exhibition in 1965, no. 451 *bis*.)

the enthusiasm of the intellectual young 'assigned him to the plagiarists'.[168]

One of the books that should have brought Proust most pleasure was the very one which would cause him the most distress: Paul Morand's *Ode à Marcel Proust*, which opened his collection of poems *Lampes à arc* (Au Sans-Pareil, 1919). The poems that hurt Proust referred to 'the mysterious terrors which [had] apparently caused him to look pallid for evermore. It obviously raises the supposition that [he had] been caught in a police raid or left for dead by Apaches.' Marcel added with a dignity that is praiseworthy: 'I am not fainthearted, but I really would not have been able to face experiencing or causing such grief', especially to 'a friend who is disarmed by his very affection'. To which was added a stylistic precept, akin to *Le Temps retrouvé*, against 'the literature of straightforward notation'. Morand's remarks struck home, but he had no right to go to the limits of indiscretion, even of defamation. Marcel's stinging letter, to which his indignation lent a superb touch ('the *Ode* in which you cast me into that Hell which Dante reserved for his enemies'), was not included among those that the author of *Ouvert la nuit* published in *Le Visiteur du soir*.*

THE QUARREL OF 'THE INTELLIGENCE PARTY'

On 19 July, on the front page of its literary supplement, *Le Figaro* published a manifesto entitled 'For an intelligence party', signed by Bourget, Bainville, Beaunier, Ghéon, Halévy, Jaloux, Jammes, Maurras, Schlumberger and Vaudoyer, which was largely the work of Henri Massis.† He sought an 'intellectual federation of Europe and the world' under the aegis of France, 'the guardian of all civilization'. Proust vigorously objected to this intellectual chauvinism. According to him, there was no specifically French intelligence: it detracted from the overall worth of a work to seek to 'nationalize' it. And he added this piece of advice: 'Why adopt this sharp tone towards other countries in matters such as literature, in which one can only predominate through persuasion?' Proust disapproved of the very idea of a manifesto, as well as of the contents of this one. Art and

---

* Ibid., pp. 421–4, shortly after 10 October 1919. Paul Morand, however, told me that he knew nothing of Proust's private life, 'because of the homosexuals' rule of silence', and he did not show me this letter. But by the 1960s, he may have forgotten it all.

† He was responding to a 'Manifesto of the Communist Party' that appeared in *L'Internationale* of 7 June 1919, and to an appeal by R. Rolland, published in *L'Humanité* on 26 June, to the writers of Europe to band together to form a spiritual union.

science, he maintained, can have no other end than they themselves, that is to say they could not allow themselves to be used for political ends. Neither was it for France to say that she should 'watch over the literatures of the entire world', which was reminiscent of '*Deutschland über alles*'. The Church, after all, had not always been 'the custodian of man's spiritual progress'; Proust recalled that at the time of the Dreyfus affair, Catholics 'had not provided very much backing for French justice', and neither had Maurras.[169] When Halévy replied that he could not refuse his signature to men whom he felt 'are solicitous of everything that we love', Proust stressed that it was 'extremely dangerous to support ideas that are wrong, just because of the virtues of those who preach them. For between supporting ideas, and giving carte blanche to their actions, is but a short step'.[170] And to Rivière he added that he didn't even think that intelligence was 'the most important thing about us'; above it he placed the unconscious, which was 'intended to clarify – but which also gave a work its reality and its originality'.[171]

Thus we see that the chief characteristic of the causes for which Proust stood in his time was the struggle, similar to that waged by Montaigne and Voltaire, against sectarianism, be it anti-Semitic, militarist, sexist, bellicose or chauvinist. He would then step outside his middle-class comfort and arise from his sick bed, in support not of a social class, but of men and of minorities, not those who were victorious.

RUE HAMELIN

Meanwhile, the search for a permanent home continued. Jacques Porel had actually informed Proust that his mother planned to take back the flat and that he must leave by about 10 September.[172] After considering a flat in Boulevard Malesherbes, which was let very quickly, he consulted an agency in Place Victor-Hugo. As a result, Céleste was told about 44 rue Hamelin, which had just been acquired by an owner who wished to convert it into furnished apartments. 'He quite liked the neighbourhood; he looked to see who lived there; "Go and see it", he told me; "you can tell me all about it." ' He then suggested renting the fifth floor, which was unfurnished, and he signed the lease.* The building had no lift.[173] Moving

---

* Probably around 23 September (*Corr.*, vol. XVIII, p. 401). The rent was 16,000 francs, he wrote to Porel (p. 433) and to Hauser (as against 6,500 francs at Boulevard Haussmann, p. 453). Hauser pointed out that this rent should have provided him with a 'very affluent' flat.

in took place after some work had first been carried out – electricity and carpet-laying to keep out noise – on 1 October. There was a baker's shop on the ground floor, from which Céleste used to telephone. On the top floor lived Aristide Briand's cleaning lady; Proust arranged for Céleste to give her money in order that she should not make any noise. From the kitchen one could see Mme Standish's town house. The flat, which was not as modest as some have stated, was a smaller version of Boulevard Haussmann. It comprised a drawing-room, hung with portraits of Professor and Mme Proust, the picture by Helleu and the portrait by Blanche; a boudoir in which the black bookcase contained the work of Mme de Sévigné, Ruskin and Saint-Simon 'in a fine binding with the initials M. P.'; Marcel's bedroom, which no longer contained a piano and a wardrobe with a mirror, but which still had a piece of Chinese furniture, a screen, a large armchair for visitors and three small tables by the brass bedstead, for his work, the notebooks and the medicaments, and there were books on the mantelpiece; his bathroom, which led on to another bedroom (in which Rochat, whom Proust had not dared get rid of, probably stayed).* Céleste's bedroom was to the right of the entrance hall.[174] Proust told Jacques Porel that he had dismissed Céleste: 'And then, naturally, I took her back.'[175] He also employed her sister, Marie Gineste. No sooner had he moved in than Proust took up his work and his correspondence, despite his asthma attacks, with astonishing bravery. His true home, as he knew now that he expected nothing more from life than to be allowed to live, was his book.

He none the less had to look after his budget; the faithful and strict Hauser (whom Proust had consulted about stock-market 'tips', which had brought about his financial downfall) reminded him that with an annual income of 25,500 francs and a rent of 16,000 francs, once his staff and food had been paid for, all he would have left would be 'enough to buy a packet of eucalyptus cigarettes'.[176] But Marcel hoped to lower the rent by half, by removing the owner's furniture, and he was counting on his royalties.

---

* Ibid., vol. XIX, p. 402: 'Henri's fate is uncertain. I cannot say that it will be *invitus* like Titus. But the *dimittere* would be hard to utter.' [The allusion is to Racine's play *Bérénice. Tr.*]

THE PRIX GONCOURT

In early September Proust knew that Léon Daudet, who was a member of the Académie Goncourt, would be voting for him.* Rosny senior, while at the same time reminding him that he had 'once been hesitant', asked him if he would allow him to speak up and support his cause: he assured him of the intense pleasure afforded him from reading his books: 'You have added something to my human universe; not for a long time have I made such a beautiful journey.'[177] He stressed that the prize could help to stir up the élite, which was 'just as inert as the masses':† thus the Prix Goncourt was not considered a popular prize, even by those who conferred it; this helps us to understand why Proust, who was prepared to do whatever he could,[178] should have wanted to be awarded it. He would never refuse any honour. The Légion d'honneur, the Académie française, the Nobel Prize – none of them aroused his repugnance: for this man who had suffered humiliation and who was one of a minority, they appeared like so many compensations, so many guarantees not of immortality, but of assimilation and of esteem.

Geffroy, Rosny junior, Céard and Élémir Bourges voted with Daudet and Rosny senior on 10 December.[179] *Les Croix de bois* by Roland Dorgelès obtained four votes. Proust explained to Céleste that 'it's the only prize of any value nowadays, because it is awarded by men who know what a novel is and what the point of a novel is'.[180] No one had ever seen Proust display such excitement: Léon Daudet and some of the other members of the Académie came and woke him up to tell him he had been awarded the prize. Then Gallimard, Rivière and Tronche, the publishing house's administrative director, arrived to congratulate him. So tiring were the day and the evening that Marcel had 'a terrible attack of asthma'; he took some medicine to soothe himself and in order to be able to undress.‡ The following day letters of congratulation never stopped arriving: he may have been joking or exaggerating, but he claimed to have received 870.[181] However the press was not unanimous in its acclaim: in *Débats*, Jean de

---

* Ibid., p. 391. In October Proust made approaches to several people: for example, he wrote to Bergerat, who had just been elected to the Académie Goncourt.

† Ibid., p. 455, 3 November 1919; after this date Rosny assured him of 'six votes, of which four were 'unshakeable'. Proust was very much courted that year: Mme Gregh wanted to award him the Prix Femina-Vie heureuse, and Régnier and his wife, the Grand Prix de l'Académie française.

‡ *Corr.*, vol. XVIII, p. 507; he still had enough strength to send Rivière a few amendments to his article on Flaubert.

Pierrefeu was amazed that the prize should have been awarded to '*un talent d'outre-tombe*' [a talent from beyond the grave], 'out of touch with the trends of a new generation that celebrates the beauty of conflict and the properties of daylight'; Proust complained to André Chaumeix,[182] whom he mistakenly thought was the editor of the newspaper. Certain critics were ready to sing the praises of *Les Croix de bois*. In *Le Populaire* of 12 December, Noel Garnier wrote: 'We old soldiers voted for Dorgelès. Marcel Proust owes his prize to the recognition of six men whom he took out to dinner.' Others criticized the age of the author: 'Make way for the old!' exclaimed *L'Humanité* on 11 December; reading *L'Éclair*, or *Le Petit Parisien*, which each day made him out to be a year older, Proust saw himself age 'with the speed of a character in a fairy tale'.[183] Others complained that he had had links with the jury;[184] the left-wing press did not forgive him for having Léon Daudet as a champion. *L'Œuvre* considered the book 'infinitely tiresome'; in *Le Mercure* of 1 January Rachilde reckoned it was 'ill-mannered to submit such a book'. Léon Daudet justified his choice in *L'Action française* on 12 December, as did Rosny senior in *Comœdia* on 23 December, having asked for a great deal of information from Proust, who responded with a veritable autobiography: his illness, where he went when he went out, his religious views ('I have never been to Mass since I made my first communion')* and his political ones (the party that opposed Léon Daudet's during the Dreyfus affair), the background to his book ('all the volumes are written'; during the war, without touching the ending of the book at all, he had added 'something about the war which was very appropriate to the character of M. de Charlus'); he had five volumes to correct, and he hoped they would all be published together 'so that people might understand their structure', to which he had 'sacrificed everything'.[185] For his part, Jacques Rivière answered the overall criticism in an article in the *NRF* of 1 January 1920 entitled 'Le prix Goncourt', emphasizing the work's profoundly original vision and the way it altered all the methods of psychological analysis. On the same date, Paul Souday published a favourable article in *Le Temps*.

There was another incident that cast a shadow over Proust's and his publisher's peace of mind: Albin Michel put bands on copies of Dorgelès' novel suggesting that it had obtained the 'Prix Goncourt' (in large characters) 'four votes out of ten' (in small), in such a way as to cast some doubt over the winner of the prize.[186] On 31 May 1920 the Court of the Seine

---

* A response to *L'Œuvre* which accused him of being 'a friend of the aspersorium and the sacristy' (*Corr.*, vol. XVIII, p. 550).

would order Albin Michel to pay 2,000 francs in damages and to destroy the offending bands.

This explains Proust's somewhat bitter impression of the attitude of the press: 'The journalists, who arrived open-mouthed to ask me questions, and who could not be seen by me because I was asleep, were received in a very ill-mannered way (which I deplore) by my publishers and so they went away feeling furious';* he attributed some of the adverse reaction to this. He requested Gaston Gallimard not to be 'rude to the journalists'; the publisher replied: 'I don't see why you should advise me to be pleasant to the journalists; I've seen a great many of them lately; I did my best to satisfy them.'[187] Marcel also complained that his novel could not be found in bookshops† and he felt sad at the thought that his Goncourt prize had been 'bungled'. Finally, he observed that his early work was very much forgotten: 'At each period of one's life, the forgetfulness of what one once was is so deep-rooted among one's contemporaries, due, it is true, to the young who do not yet know and the elderly who have forgotten, that one is obliged (I, a Prix Goncourt winner), however well-known previously, to cope with the ignorance of the prevailing milieu ... And were we not particularly concerned that they might say crazy things about us that create the need for our speaking out ... we should be obliged to reject our credentials and our good qualities and to say that we belong to another age, our last years being like setting foot in a strange country, where those who live there have never heard our names mentioned.'[188]

As for the book's commercial success, at the beginning of December, just before the prize, 3,000 copies had been sold.‡ After printing 6,600 copies in December, there would be a further two impressions in February and July 1920, that is to say as many as for *Swann*, but no more. The prize brought the book to the attention of an élite, but it was not the popular success that *Les Croix de bois* was. This novel, which had sold 17,000 copies by the autumn of 1919, had a reprint of 11,776 copies in December, and

---

* Ibid., p. 545, to Rosny senior. He had given instructions to Céleste not to let anyone in and not to answer any questions: 'Throw everyone out' (C. Albaret, p. 367).

† Ibid., p. 550. Proust appears to have sent his staff, Marie Gineste and Odilon Albaret, to a number of bookshops, in the Place du Trocadéro, Avenue Mozart, etc. (p. 564). The publisher admitted that the book had sold out on the actual day of the prize (*Corr. avec G. Gallimard*).

‡ Letter from G. Gallimard, 3 December 1919 (*Corr avec G. Gallimard*, p. 208). Proust also received the 5,000 francs prize money, which Painter, relying on what Léon Pierre-Quint has said, claims he spent immediately on dinner parties of gratitude, which Céleste denied (C. Albaret, p. 308). She must have been right, because no trace has been found of invitations to such dinners: on the contrary, Proust hardly went out in December, and he gave one dinner party at the Ritz in January.

a further printing of 45,000 copies in May 1920: in all, three times more than *Jeunes Filles*.[189]

To console himself for a success which had not been without its sadness, weariness or its irritations, and which had not spared him any insults, Proust celebrated New Year's Eve (the only meal that was consumed at an hour that suited him perfectly) at Cécile Sorel's house, with the Infante of Spain, the Duchesse de Gramont, José Maria Sert, Bernstein and Croisset.[190]

DAILY LIFE IN 1920

A biography cannot be partitioned neatly into years, least of all one of Proust, who, rather more than most people, believed neither in keeping time nor in keeping to a timetable. Yet after the award of the Prix Goncourt, Marcel achieved not so much fame, nor even success exactly, as a notoriety among an élite. It would be a few months still before some slight public acknowledgement, the only formal honour he would ever receive, was accorded him. When he contemplated the Académie française, he was soon given to understand by Régnier and Barrès that it was not for him: when he was seventy, perhaps ... This was also the year of *Le Côté de Guermantes*, which appeared at a time when he was in the process of renewing his social connections. Meanwhile, lurking constantly in the background, was his illness, which continued its pitiless course, hardening his lungs, wearing out his heart and obliging him to depend on increasingly toxic medicines. The improvement so long hoped for would never happen.

JACQUES RIVIÈRE

On 1 January 1920 the *NRF* published a piece by Jacques Rivière on the Prix Goncourt, in which, observing that overall the daily press had opposed the choice of the Académie Goncourt, he had two points to make: true youthfulness was to be found in the work of 'the most rejuvenating' of novelists; Proust extended 'all the techniques of the psychological novel'. Assessing the controversy raised by the prize, the following month he provided an article that ranged far wider, 'Marcel Proust et la tradition classique'.[191] Rivière, who had been the magazine's unassuming subeditor before the war, had not been consulted at the time that *Swann* had been rejected. He first made contact with Proust in January 1914, when, as we know, he had written to express his admiration in a letter that deeply touched Marcel, in which he understood that his book was both structured and 'dogmatic': nothing upset him more, in fact, than seeing critics write that Proust had jotted down his childhood memories in a disorderly way and without a conclusion.

On returning from captivity in Germany and internment in Switzerland, Rivière was appointed editor of the *NRF* by Gaston Gallimard, who was keen to get rid of Gide, whom he disliked and whom he never once invited to dinner in his life. In connection with the magazine Rivière resumed his relationship with Proust, one which soon developed into a friendship: by August 1920 they were on first-name terms. Rivière would occasionally call on Proust: shortly before midnight, Marcel would send Odilon and his taxi to pick him up, he would serve him a supper delivered from the Ritz, and he would detain him for three hours.[192] Rivière had returned from captivity suffering from nervous exhaustion. He needed money: so Proust lent him some. He wrote a novel: Proust carefully corrected it and encouraged him to publish it. The one felt a great intellectual sympathy, the other admiration, which were thwarted by the problems that arose between the inflexible magazine editor and the scrupulous author: it is clear that for Rivière the magazine took precedence over everything else. At the end of his life, Marcel reacted to this with a cry of pain.

It was Rivière's character, which tended to be analytical and introspective, that enabled him to speak about Proust more valuably than anyone else at that time; moreover he was a great literary critic. This was primarily because of the breadth of his interests: he would review Claudel's first plays, the Ballets Russes or Fauré's *Pénélope* as easily as he would a Cézanne exhibition. His understanding – for he wrote about what he liked or in order to defend what he liked – was profound; he reconstructed the world of the artists he wrote about with great literary skill, as if it were his own world, without ever losing his sense of value: 'There is much greatness in a little truth.'[193] Hence his criticism was a form of identification: 'I need an existence other than my own',[194] he said, with a humility that sometimes paralysed him. This explains his admiration for Claudel, Gide and Proust. At the same time, the brother-in-law of Alain-Fournier dreamed of being a novelist. But he would write only two novels, *Aimée*, which told of his platonic love for Gaston Gallimard's wife, and the posthumous *Florence*. In spite of the delicacy of their analysis and their elegant, classical style, these books scarcely helped to extend the boundaries of fiction, which was the quality he so admired in Proust, a writer who also had the capacity to be a great critic because he had understood, in abandoning *Contre Sainte-Beuve*, that criticism should not stifle fiction.

Proust, who was grateful for what Rivière wrote in the *NRF*, did what he could to help him. When the latter was exhausted and depressed, Marcel arranged a consultation for him with Professor Roussy.[195] He excelled himself calling on people, writing letters and going out at times that were normally impossible for him in order to obtain for Rivière a grant awarded by Mme Blumenthal.* Had little Rivière caught bronchial pneumonia? Marcel enquired after him daily. He would take the same trouble, later on, in reading the manuscript of *Aimée*, which Rivière, who was always self-deprecating, hesitated to have published.[196] The fact was that once he felt his friends needed help, Proust gave of his all, be it money, literary prizes (for Paulhan, Breton, Lacretelle, Giraudoux)[197] or book reviews. In 1921, for example, he asked a newspaper to commission Montesquiou, who was very much forgotten, to write a column of art criticism; and he made sure that the *NRF* gave a good review to Lucien Daudet's latest book.

LE CÔTÉ DE GUERMANTES I

After it had been agreed that Grasset would not publish *Le Côté de Guermantes*, the text had to be reset from the old proofs that were used as a basis for a manuscript. It was only in June 1919, at a very inopportune time, just as he was moving house, that Proust received a first complete set of proofs. Further proofs would reach him after 8 December: the timing was equally difficult, since they arrived at the moment of the Prix Goncourt.[198] In February 1920, he therefore felt obliged to ask Jacques Rivière to help him, particularly since the first and second proofs had become mixed up, and Proust asked for a third set, which he had read to him: 'I won't make any more changes and they can be passed for press.'[199] It was at this time that André Breton was employed to reread the proofs, something he did extremely badly: 'No care has been taken',† said Proust,

---

* Boylesve, who was thought to have liked Proust, described his appearance before the panel of judges: 'Flesh that was blue, like the colour of high game, the eyes of an almah ... Despite his moustache, he had the look of a sixty-year old Jewish lady who might have been beautiful. His eyes, in profile, were oriental ...' (*Feuilles tombées*, p. 266, quoted by G. de Diesbach, *Proust*, p. 707). Here we find all the clichés of anti-Proustian imagery.

† *Corr.*, vol. XIX, p. 438, 2 September 1920, to G. Gallimard: 'Monsieur ... Breton thought he had read them, Jacques Rivière thought he had read them ... Never have I awaited a book with such impatience or read it with such gloom.' Cf. p. 472, to P. Soupault: 'I could see that my next book, even though it had been reread by Monsieur Breton, contained so many mistakes that if I did not compile an erratum I should be brought into disrepute. It took me over a week, and it amounts to 23 pages. I picked up over two hundred errors.' Yet Rivière wrote the following

who only met Breton once, but whose *Les Champs magnétiques* he thought highly of.[200] In all this confusion, certain galleys that had been corrected by the author himself did not reach the printer.[201] Moreover, Proust was making corrections up to the last moment, either directly on to the proofs, or in a list of addenda prepared in a draft notebook.* In March, at Gaston Gallimard's request, the novel was divided into two volumes. Proust still believed that he would be able to have them published simultaneously, along with the two volumes of *Sodome et Gomorrhe I*, 'and, a few months later, the two volumes of *Sodome et Gomorrhe II*,† *Le Temps retrouvé*'.[202] None of this would actually happen. Just one of the two volumes of *Le Côté de Guermantes* was published initially: Proust returned the corrected proofs in July.[203] This explains why 'La maladie de la grand-mère' was cut in two, and would be published in *Le Côté de Guermantes II*. In June 1920 Proust expected *Le Côté de Guermantes II* to be published in one volume with *Sodome et Gomorrhe I*. 'It will be better separated like this.'‡ It had taken twelve years for *Guermantes I* to evolve; while waiting for it to be published, the author had, right up until the last moment, prepared additional material in a draft exercise book (Cahier 61). Printing was completed on 17 August 1920. In possession of some folded sheets, Proust, who was 'in despair' at the poor quality of the typesetting (they had printed 'Bergson', for example, instead of 'Bergotte'), made about fifteen corrections on his own copy, and he drew up another list of errata twenty-three pages long[204] – it is pitiful to see Proust obliged to spend so much time, and wasting his eyesight, on a task which proof readers at the publishing house should have been able to do. In spite of this, the printed book was not without inconsistencies, mostly due to errors made in deciphering the author's original manuscript. He dedicated it to Léon Daudet, in gratitude for his

---

astonishing remarks to Proust, which are not confirmed by Breton in anything he wrote: 'André Breton, the leader of the Dadaists, who came to help us correct your proofs, told me of his intense admiration for you, based appropriately on the poetic gems he discovered in your book' (29 June 1920).

  * Cahier 60, for example, one of those containing additional material, includes passages that are preceded by the words 'to be added to the proofs of *Guermantes* which Tronche should send back to me': this is the case with the scene in which Saint-Loup punches a homosexual. Similarly, the pastiche of the 'new writer' in *Guermantes II* is an addendum that derives from this same notebook.

  † At this point it comprised what would eventually become *La Prisonnière* and *Albertine disparue* (*Corr.*, vol. XIX, p. 348).

  ‡ *Corr.*, vol. XIX, p. 323, to G. Gallimard. The book was due to appear in November 1920, Proust believed, then in December, and later on 15 February 1921, but it would not actually be published until May 1921.

efforts in obtaining the Prix Goncourt for him, and it went on sale on 22 October 1920. If he told Gaston Gallimard that he felt more loyal to the NRF than he could say, he none the less blamed his publisher for continuing to create obstacles, for not telling him where he was staying, and for not being at the magazine's office much,[205] which made communication difficult. In July, however, Gallimard had put the limited edition of fifty copies of *Jeunes Filles* on sale by subscription, each one accompanied by two corrected galley proofs that had been used by the printers. Marcel supplied a list of possible purchasers (Berry bought five of them).

But Proust would not forgive the delays in printing his book. Feeling increasingly ill and in a hurry to finish, he took against his publisher and his associates, and he had his revenge in a passage in *La Prisonnière*, in which he refers to the 'unfortunate author' who, confronted with the 'impenetrable solidarity of certain companies, bookshops or newspapers', will never get to 'know whether or not he has been rooked'. The newspaper or magazine editor 'lies with a demeanour of sincerity that is all the more solemn-faced because he himself needs often to disguise the fact that he does exactly the same thing and engages in the same mercenary practices as those which he condemns in others . . . when he raises the standard of Sincerity against them. The partner of the "sincere man" lies in a different and more ingenuous way. He deceives his author just as he deceives his wife, with vaudeville stunts. The assistant editor, an honest, uncouth man, lies quite simply, like an architect who promises you that your house will be ready at a time when it will not have been begun. The editorial director, an angelic soul, flutters about among the three others, and, without knowing what is at issue, with his fraternal punctiliousness and his affectionate solidarity, he brings to them the precious support of a word of honour that is above suspicion. These four people live in a state of perpetual disagreement, that is brought to a halt by the author's arrival'.* One can recognize André Gide in the guise of the sincere man, Gaston Gallimard as his partner, Tronche (in actual fact the manager) or Paulhan as the assistant editor, and Rivière as the 'angelic soul'.

---

* *RTP*, vol. III, pp. 684–5. This was an addition to the third typescript of *La Prisonnière*, dating therefore from 1922. It was at this same period that Proust inserted the comment about Grasset in *Sodome II*.

RECEPTION OF *LE CÔTÉ DE GUERMANTES I*

When this book, which deals with the hero's social advancement and his love for the Duchesse de Guermantes, and to which the grandmother's illness supplies a tragic ending, was published, Marcel's friends, Mme Straus, Lucien Daudet, Blanche and Cocteau,[206] wrote enthusiastically to him; the Beaumonts were 'among his most loyal admirers'. But the models were shocked: Albufera recognized himself in Saint-Loup, the lover of Rachel, and the Comtesse de Chevigné, even though she appreciated her portrait as the Duchesse de Guermantes, would gradually fall out with the author and would burn his letters: 'You are asking the "nude model" to understand the painting,' wrote Cocteau to Proust. 'All the model sees is the artist making a few incomprehensible movements and the reverse side of the canvas.'[207] But Paul Souday, with whom Marcel was on friendly terms, accused him of snobbery: 'You are probably aware,' replied Proust, 'that I have known duchesses of Guermantes all my life, so how could you fail to understand the effort it took to put myself in the place of someone who had not met one and wished to know one?' And he explained that he had created the Guermantes wit because Saint-Simon spoke of the Mortemart wit without ever describing what it consisted of, but basing it upon 'a woman who was not well-born', Mme Straus.[208] Neither did Proust like the fact that Souday should have found him 'feminine': 'From being feminine to effeminate is but a short step. Those who have served me in duels will tell you whether I share the spinelessness of the effeminate'; he was all the more upset that *Le Figaro* reprinted extracts from Souday's article.[209] All in all, Souday, like many others, 'does not enter into the transfiguration desired by the author'.[210] Worse still, Jean de Pierrefeu, in *Le Journal des débats*, considered that Proust's 'only guiding principle is one of those diaries in which socialites jot down their rendezvous and which they occasionally grace with hurried notes: "Saw so and so, spoke about Z"'.[211] This critic had written to Marcel: 'Didn't you know that I am entitled to call myself the Comte de Pierrefeu?' On the other hand, Henri Bidou in *Les Annales politiques et littéraires* was more favourably disposed and dwelt on the book's structure.[212] In *L'Opinion* of 4 December, Jacques Boulenger hailed a true creator and artist who was 'full of originality'. In the *NRF*, the young Martin-Chauffier wrote about the book on 1 February 1921[213] in terms that filled the author with enthusiasm. Montesquiou remarked to Marcel, quite aptly in the circumstances, that he took exception to these last-minute admirers: 'It is as if they have *become aware* [that he might] do something very good.'[214]

In December Proust, in common with many a novelist, had to prove that he had used the name of a real person unwittingly: a certain Harry Swann had written to him, seven years after publication, to protest against the use of his family name; Proust replied that his character was based upon Charles Haas. The name, he said, had been invented because it looked English, and because of the purity of its *a* sound; there were two *n*s so as to avoid the notion of a swan (the bird is associated with the Duchesse de Guermantes): in Britain, the Princess Royal actually said that the novel was 'the story of Leda seen from the swan's point of view'.[215] These comments help us to understand Proustian onomastics, even if they underestimate the part played by instinct. We do not know the response of the real (or bogus) Swann.

SOCIAL LIFE

It would be tedious to list all the dinner parties that Marcel organized at the Ritz, where it had become fashionable to invite people, or those to which he was asked. He kept to the same pattern as he had the previous year, going out two or three times a week.* There was one new aspect to the parties: he slipped in among his other guests literary critics whom he was trying to win over, such as Jacques Boulenger (who refused), Paul Souday and Jean de Pierrefeu. Proust thus carried out, on behalf of his publisher, the role, which in any case did not exist at the time, of press officer. His three aims in doing this were to make his work known, to make it understood and to make it sell: quite suddenly, and unlike Mallarmé, or his dear Saint-Simon in former times, he considered that it was pointless to write if one was not read, and he maintained that his work was so original and so difficult that it was worth his while to explain it. The critics failed to understand it because in the spring of 1920 it had been necessary

---

* 'People would cancel an invitation rather than apologize for not being able to come. I think that most of them would have fought one another in order to please him' (C. Albaret, p. 298). Among the dinner parties: 8 January (Polignac, Castellane, Louis de Beauvau, Pierrefeu, Souday); 28 April (Jaloux, Guiche, Morand); in October Proust was invited by Prince Firouz, the Persian Minister of Foreign Affairs. On 3 November he went to Boni de Castellane's. On 27 November he invited Mme de Noailles, Berry and Souday to the Ritz: it was 'a long monologue, a fine Noailles recital' (*Corr.*, vol. XX, p. 218). There were not many shows: *Schéhérazade* at the Opéra on 4 May. The stage sets were by Bakst, who was suffering from general paralysis, which saddened Proust. He thought the ballet was distorted. He was struck by the sight of old Haussonville, whose head had taken on a majestic bearing over the years: another figure for *Le Temps retrouvé* (*Corr.*, vol. XIX, p. 257, 4 May 1920).

to abandon the dream he had cherished until then of publishing all the recent volumes simultaneously: without *Le Temps retrouvé*, the true meaning was not revealed. Marcel's sole purpose as press officer was to suggest methods of reading his work, and to avoid misinterpretation. He would no longer accept dying misunderstood, it was as though posterity was happening today, as though he were confronting a dozen Sainte-Beuves.

Social life served the interests of his book: if Proust wished to go to the Opéra at the end of January, it was in order to see 'the way in which people age . . . The auditorium of an opera house would make a marvellous observation centre'.[216] On 21 February he went to the Comédie des Champs-Élysées to see *Le Bœuf sur le toit*, a farce by Cocteau, with stage sets by Dufy and music by Milhaud. On 14 June he was at the Opéra for the dress rehearsal of *Antony and Cleopatra*, translated by Gide (who had invited him, but he preferred the Princesse de Soutzo's box) and starring Ida Rubinstein, when he was informed during the interval that Réjane had just died. He set off immediately for the rue Laurent-Pichat, to be at the bedside of the woman who was also la Berma (and who was to be his inspiration again in *Le Temps retrouvé*, when he describes her going back on stage when unwell, in order to raise money for her son), and to be with Jacques Porel. The pang he endured was 'so physical [that he] stood transfixed, like animals who are so motionless it is as if they are paralysed'.[217] 'I saw her,' wrote Proust to her son, 'at moments when she really did live, suffer and die for you.'[218]

When he went out, Proust was less interested, for example in meeting the Queen of Romania, who was staying at the Ritz, and with whom Princesse Soutzo wished to invite him to dinner, than the Grand-Duke Dimitri, 'because of the drama he had been involved in'.* 'Naturally I shall not say a word about it to him. But faces do speak.'[219] Other adventures were rather more curious: on 17 August, having gone to a Montmartre hotel to collect some antiquarian books which a 'friend' had asked him to have valued, in order to take them to Tronche, who was 'very knowledgeable', the landlady refused to open the door to him. Overcome with 'a mad fury', he started to beat on the door with his walking-stick, and as a result his friend heard him and brought the books down to him. He was worried in case the landlady registered a complaint against him for disturbance of the peace at night, and he asked Morand whether he knew anyone at the Montmartre police station, or

---

* The Russian Revolution, presumably. *Tr.*

even the superintendent, adding, in a denial tantamount to an affirmation: 'nothing of Charlus'.[220] Everything about this story related by Proust seems odd: that he should have a friend at a hotel in Montmartre (and not at the Ritz!), that this person should possess some antiquarian books, that in Marcel's state of health he should put himself out rather than having them delivered to him, or that a landlady who did not know his name should be able to register a complaint about him. In *Albertine disparue* the Narrator is summoned by the head of the Sûreté, but it was for the abduction of a minor.[221] This adventure does reveal that Marcel had not given up the somewhat sleazy escapades and his romantic war-time outings at night: we glimpse in them an unknown aspect of his existence.

In September, as already mentioned, Proust attended the meeting of the committee of the Blumenthal prize to ensure that it was given to Rivière. There he encountered Bergson, with whom he had a discussion about narcotics and insomnia (from which the philosopher suffered), the way in which one's attention was stimulated, the mental work thus engendered, and its psychological use. 'I shall always see them,' Edmond Jaloux recalled, 'Proust and Bergson, standing by a window, the one stout, despite his unhealthy condition, with his bulging chest, his head thrown back, his overcoat too tight for him, the other, thin, slender, almost ethereal ... Both of them looked like great birds of night.'[222] This was the period when Proust made a number of remarks in his notebooks about sleep, and when he expressed his disagreement with what Bergson had written about 'the dream' (*Le Rêve*, 1901, reprinted in 1919 in *L'Énergie spirituelle*).[223] He would continue to make use of the notes later in *Guermantes II* or in *La Prisonnière*,[224] up until 1922.

At home, he only entertained his friends one at a time, and occasionally his publishers too. He was still trying to sell, through the intermediary of the faithful Mme Catusse, what remained of the furniture that was in storage at the antique dealer Imbert.

PIERRE DE POLIGNAC, BONI DE CASTELLANE AND OTHERS

New acquaintances included Pierre de Polignac and Boni de Castellane, both of whom are mentioned in the novel. Proust had met the former in 1917 and, as we know, thought him 'charming'. Originally a diplomat, who had been sent to China in 1917, he would give up his diplomatic career when he married. He was interested in art and literature, and he frequently attended Princesse Edmond de Polignac's salon. Elegant and of robust appearance, with blue eyes (like Bertrand de Fénelon) and a dreamy expression, he was also dissatisfied and 'as a rule retiring, if not distant, particularly where the "fair sex" was concerned'.[225] His story casts a curious light over the chapter dealing with marriages in *Albertine disparue*: Mlle d'Oloron, Jupien's daughter or niece, is adopted by Charlus, and then marries young Cambremer. This passage was written in 1919, but reality caught up with fiction. Charlus conferring noble rank on a person who was not of aristocratic birth* corresponds to Prince Louis de Monaco adopting Charlotte, the daughter born to him in 1898 by a laundry-maid, who was legitimized in 1900 and whose adoption was legally recognized in 1919 by Prince Albert I (contrary to what has sometimes been stated, Louis II was not yet a ruling prince): the titles of Duchesse de Valentinois and Hereditary Princess of Monaco were bestowed on Charlotte. Pierre de Polignac married her on 19 March 1920,† thanks to the intervention of Poincaré.[226] In February 1920, as soon as he learned of Polignac's engagement, Proust wrote to his friend: 'With that prescience that makes life so dull for me (because things happen after they occur in my books) I had written (in one of my forthcoming volumes) of your marriage (without your name, of course, nor anything about you) a year ago . . . I had called the girl Mlle de Vermandois, which sounded too much like Valentinois; people might have thought that I was talking about you and the Duchesse de Valentinois in a manner that might have displeased you.'[227] Marcel was deeply upset by this engagement: 'This time, just when we had a great friendship, you're leaving for ever.'[228] But they did not fall out with each other yet,[229] and when Proust saw Pierre again at home on 8 June, he was 'even nicer than when he was a Polignac'[230] (his full title was now 'Son Altesse Sérénissime Monsieur le Duc de Valentinois'). In July Polignac sent off his address‡ in order to subscribe to one of the de-luxe copies of *Jeunes Filles*. Their friendship came to an end in October

---

* *RTP*, vol. IV, p. 540: very few people knew that young Mme de Cambremer was not 'a Valentinois'. Cf. p. 236 and n. 2: after Charlus adopted Jupien's daughter, 'she took the name of Mlle d'Oloron (avoid Vermandois on account of Pierre de Polignac)' (Cahier 60, 1920). Probably out of vengeance, Proust made Mlle d'Oloron die from typhoid (ibid., p. 250).

† According to Céleste, Proust would not forgive him for this (p. 156): he must have forgotten that he himself was the grandson of a village grocer-woman. But perhaps he had more profound reasons for being hurt by this marriage.

‡ Hôtel de Monaco, 10 Avenue du Président-Wilson. *Corr.*, vol. XIX, p. 355, 10 or 11 July 1920.

with a four-line note signed 'Pierre Grimaldi duc de Valentinois': 'Don't worry yourself, my dear friend, I have received all your recent letters, and I very much regret them. Please accept this as an assurance of the loyal memory I shall retain of you.'[231] Marcel had planned to meet his friend in the South of France and was obliged to give up the idea. As regards their quarrel, we know what the Abbé Mugnier had to say: Marcel must have sent the young bridegroom some 'sealed envelopes' during his honeymoon, addressed to the Villa d'Este,* where he was staying. For his part, Proust confessed that he had broken up with Pierre de Valentinois out of 'ill temper': '. . . while at the same time retaining great respect for his intelligence and being very grateful for his kindnesses. Everything that is said about him (that he thinks he's become a little king, etc.) is idiotic, and unfortunately everybody says it and invents the most absurd stories. I had not yet become angry with him in the period just after his wedding and I can vouch for the fact that he had never been so pleasant. But I'm angry all the same.'[232] It was precisely these 'absurd stories' that he related in *Le Côté de Guermantes II*, when Pierre de Valentinois becomes the adoptive Grand Duke of Luxembourg, Comte de Nassau.[233] Having complacently recounted them, Proust added that they were 'untrue': 'for a more intelligent, more decent, more refined, in a word more exquisite man than this Luxembourg-Nassau, I have never met'.[234] Such was the way he took his revenge on a man whom he nevertheless missed, and who was probably the last aristocrat he loved.

If the bonds that linked Polignac and Proust had been very strong, those between him and the Marquis de Castellane were of an entirely different kind. The grandson of Mme de Beaulaincourt, the model for Mme de Villeparisis, he allowed Proust to study once more how the features of ancestors are passed down to their descendants and to mention him in his introduction to *Tendres Stocks* as his friend, a relation of Mme de Sévigné.[235] Nicknamed 'Boni', he also served as a mine of information to Proust: he knew everything about social life and its fluctuations, and, being a former *député*, a great deal about foreign and domestic politics. He justified what Proust wrote in *Sodome* about the psychological value of the 'gossip', who can turn reality inside out.[236] This unusually elegant and

---

* Abbé Mugnier, *Journal*, Mercure de France, 1985, pp. 509–10. But the letter from the prince breaking off their friendship, if correctly dated, was written seven months after this trip: it is clear from his note, however, that Proust must have asked him whether his letters had reached him safely.

handsome man used to give sumptuous parties* in the Palais Rose, which he had had built with the wealth of his wife, Anna Gould. When she left him to marry his cousin, Hélie de Talleyrand, he found himself ruined from one day to the next. He withstood his misfortune bravely, became a journalist, and then an antique dealer and interior designer, 'the only properties he had being the cemeteries of [his] forebears': 'I could have owned magnificent houses,' he wrote, 'built palaces, restored châteaux, made many people jealous and tried to live according to the traditions of my ancestors; but nothing would have lasted for me.'[237] He displayed his admiration for Proust in his correspondence.[238]

Another friend also provided Marcel with social information: André de Fouquières, who, for his part, would mention Proust frequently in *Cinquante ans de panache*. They had first met at Madeleine Lemaire's house[239] and continued to see each other at infrequent intervals until the end: 'So we shall become friends again, good friends, like we were before,' wrote the man who was known as the 'arbiter of elegance' to Proust in 1920.[240]

As for Henri Rochat, he was still around. On 12 May 1920 Morand was invited home by Proust. Their conversation was interrupted by Henri, 'who had just got up and made his appearance dressed in very dazzling pyjamas'. As soon as Henri had left, Marcel complained that every time he went out he ran up 'ten thousand francs of debts'. The previous day he had bought 3,000 francs' worth of new clothes; furthermore, Rochat made financial investments, and asked Morand for advice about the stock exchange.[241] In January Marcel told Mme Edwards that he would take her to the Opéra by taxi with Lucien Daudet and 'this Swiss boy', whose arm he was very happy to lean on to get upstairs should an asthma attack affect him: 'In the darkness of the taxi, I cannot think you would be in the least bothered by someone who is not "of your circle" and whom all my friends know in any case.'[242] In December Proust believed (incorrectly) that he had found Henri a post in Japan.[243] Marcel also remained on friendly terms with other messenger boys from the Ritz, such as Émile and Henri Burnet.[244]

To Misia Godebska, who had married her lover, the painter José Maria Sert, he wrote wittily that 'this marriage has the august beauty of things

* B. de Castellane (*Mémoires*, Perrin, 1986, pp. 123–5) also relates how he rented Le Tir aux Pigeons for his wife's twenty-first birthday, complete with a 300-foot-long stage, an orchestra of 200 musicians, eighty dancers, a flock of twenty-five white swans, and fireworks. Note that Boni de Castellane does not mention Proust's name in his memoirs, even though they sent each other extremely friendly letters.

that are marvellously useless'.[245] In such a way did he show her the gratitude an artist has for his models, and he mentioned Sert twice in his novel.[246] Similarly, he marked his affection for the Daudet family by informing Léon's wife, who wrote cookery books under the name of Pampille, that he had mentioned her in *Guermantes II*.[247] He also told her how, in a church in Normandy, he had seen a wild rose flowering all over the porch, on the foundations of which eglantines were carved. Sending off this literary flourish, he added, thinking of his Prix Goncourt without naming it: 'Some very French writers had discovered the *Guirlande de Julie* before arranging the spray of *Le Lys dans la vallée*.'*

LITERARY FRIENDS

Proust was on friendly terms with Edmond Jaloux, the future academician, who would dedicate a book to him. He was particularly intrigued by a passage in his novel *Les Sangsues*, which was set in the Saint-Louis-de-Gonzague school, where 'the ferocity of an older boy had caused the death of his younger friend'. 'And at a moment that is always identical in my sleep I wonder how the proportions of pity and sadism are determined (assuming that there is a blend) in this appalling and gripping passage.'†
Albert Thibaudet, one of the greatest writers and historians of our century, sent Proust admiring letters, in spite of their disagreements over Flaubert.[248] And when the Duchesse de Clermont-Tonnerre published an *Almanach des bonnes choses de France*, Marcel used her description of asparagus in *Guermantes II*.[249] In July 1920 François Mauriac sent Proust his *Petits Essais de psychologie religieuse*, on Lacordaire, Amiel, Baudelaire and Beyle, and Lucien Daudet sent his *Évidences*, which Marcel believed to be 'probably a masterpiece'.[250] He told Cocteau, having looked at his *Poésies* and *Carte blanche*, that he had never shown such talent.[251] And to Porto-Riche, he declared that the title of his *Anatomie sentimentale* was 'a glorious title'.[252] He also sustained a sort of literary flirtation with the 'amazon' Nathalie Clifford-Barney, to whom, uniquely, he also suggested having dinner together, probably because he wanted to finish *Gomorrhe*.[253] We see him

---

* Ibid., p. 679. [A series of French literary bouquets: the *Guirlande de Julie* was written by Charles de Montausier (1610–90) in honour of his wife Julie d'Angennes; *Le Lys dans la vallée* is a novel by Balzac; and now, with *À l'ombre des jeunes filles en fleurs*, Proust was sending these flowers to Mme Daudet. *Tr.*]

† *Corr.*, vol. XIX, p. 276. This novel dates from 1904; it is therefore a memory which stayed with Proust.

obliged to come to terms with *Le Félin géant*, the novel by Rosny senior which described those immemorial times and that mysterious life 'in which there already flourished, at a vast distance from our own lives, all that is best about the olden days'.[254] And when Mme de Noailles wrote him a eulogistic letter to accompany a copy of her latest collection of poems, *Les Forces éternelles*, Marcel, who knew from Bibesco that she spoke maliciously of him, replied: 'There are two Madame de Noailles in you, the one who writes these books . . . – and another about whom I should be lying to you if I pretended not to know her.'[255]

NEWSPAPER SURVEYS

In his youth, Proust had completed questionnaires in miscellany albums; now he replied to newspaper surveys, but he did so in writing. On 24 January *L'Opinion* published a questionnaire set by Vaudoyer about the Louvre (which eight French paintings should be included in a special exhibition, as there had recently been for Italian paintings?), and its responses, including one submitted by Proust: although he did not approve of the public's mind being made up for it in this way, he listed 'the self-portrait by Chardin', the 'portrait of Mme Chardin', 'Chardin's *Nature morte*', *Le Printemps* by Millet, Manet's *L'Olympia*, Monet's *Falaises d'Étretat*, 'a Renoir' or Corot's *Barque de Dante* or his *Cathédrale de Chartres*, *L'Indifférent* by Watteau, or his *Embarquement*.[256] In a questionnaire published by *L'Intransigeant* he refused to draw a distinction between intellectual and manual work:[257] he knew better than anyone the physical effort that his job demanded – in its combination of the material and the spiritual, he compared it to the effort required in making love. This humorous image would be cut by the newspaper, which was either too solemn or too prudish. On another occasion, he declared himself to be in favour of reading rooms, because there were two types of people who did not buy books: those who had no money and were prevented from doing so because of poverty, and the rich, out of avarice. When Émile Henriot questioned him about the links between classicism and romanticism, Proust replied that 'all true art is classical', but was not initially recognized as such; the great innovators, such as Baudelaire, were the only true classical artists; they obeyed a strict inner discipline and were builders first and foremost; since their architecture was new, it took a long time for people to appreciate it.[258]

INTRODUCTIONS AND ARTICLES

To all appearances, Proust no longer bore any grudge against Morand for his disastrous *Ode*, and he agreed to write an introduction to his first work of fiction, *Tendres Stocks* (a title he considered 'frightful'),[259] which consisted of three short stories. Gallimard sent him the proofs on 9 September; Marcel completed his text in early October, which he then published, having offered it himself to André Chaumeix,* in *La Revue de Paris* of 15 November under the title 'Pour un ami; remarques sur le style'. His praise was mingled with reservations, which is explained as much by the past as by the stories (he showed the same reserve with the collection of poems *Feuilles de température*).† We come across part of the introduction in *Guermantes II*,‡ where Giraudoux's 'La Nuit à Chateauroux',§ which it also mentions, eclipses Morand. At the heart of Proust's argument was the theory of the 'new writer', who 'brings things together by establishing new visions': 'We adore Renoir's women, and those of Morand or Giraudoux, in whom, before treatment from the oculist, we refused to see women . . . Such is the new and perishable universe that the artist creates and which will endure until a new one appears.'[260] Morand's mistake was occasionally to use images which were 'approximate': 'Better, then, not to have images.'

---

* *Corr.*, vol. XIX, p. 517, early October 1920; p. 518. He would earn twenty francs for this article, which he reckoned was very little, considering that was what *Le Figaro* paid him before the war (ibid., p. 609).

† Ibid., p. 380: Morand created a reality that was the opposite of reality, one that seemed to Proust 'ugly and not very poetic'.

‡ *RTP*, vol. II, p. 622; see my 'Proust et le "nouvel écrivain"', in *Revue d'histoire littéraire de la France* January–March 1967, pp. 79–81. Giraudoux, who had come to call on Proust at rue Laurent-Pichat in 1919, brought along by Morand (as the latter relates), never wanted to go back to see him (for fear of the sick, or of homosexuals, or because of some less defined antipathy). Proust took his revenge by writing in *Guermantes II* that 'the new writer', who was primarily Giraudoux or Morand, was not unlike Bloch: 'This image thenceforth loomed over the printed pages and I no longer felt myself compelled to understand them.' As a way of showing his gratitude for Proust's introduction, Morand published an article about him in *The American* (July 1920), see *Corr.*, vol. XIX, pp. 129–30.

§ *Corr.*, vol. XIX, pp. 129–30, late August 1920: Proust told Morand of his admiration for 'La Nuit à Chateauroux', in particular, and for *Adorable Clio*, the book in which the story appears.

PROUST AND ANATOLE FRANCE (CONCLUSION)

In 1920 France, in *La Revue de Paris*, had replied to the question 'Did Beyle write well?' Proust's rejoinder* brought him into conflict with him: 'Anatole France . . . maintains that all idiosyncracies of style should be rejected . . . Had I the pleasure of seeing M. France, whose many kindnesses to me are still very much alive, face to face again, I would ask him how he can believe in the unity of style when our sensibilities are unique . . . In [his novel] *Le Crime de Sylvestre Bonnard*, do we not find that the dual sense of wildness and sweetness which the cats emanate is encapsulated within one of his admirable sentences . . . But M. France would not agree with me that this passage is admirable, because we have been writing badly ever since the end of the eighteenth century (according to him).' Proust therefore relinquished Guizot, Thiers, Villemain, Cousin and Taine to France, but not Renan. Against France, he championed Baudelaire and Stendhal. He went so far as to assert that the opposite of France's view was equally true: talent was identified more and more with the object that was being described, as with Flaubert, for example. 'But M. France denies this. What is our canon? he asks us in this article', proposing Racine's '*lettres imaginaires*'. 'Nothing so dry, so poor, so brief,' replied Marcel: 'It is not difficult for a form that contains so little thought to be light and graceful. Yet *Lettres imaginaires* is not.' Proust himself rejected any 'canon'. The truth was that from time to time a 'new, original writer' comes along, who gives a unity to everything by establishing new connections, and who shows us a world that has been re-created – until the next one comes along. Style did not attain perfection in Racine's time and then stop; it never ceases to evolve, to perfect itself, and to make improvements as a result of differences. These are not artificial, since they depend on a new vision of the world. And so it was that the old master lost his disciple for good. This was what France himself felt, according to one of his secretaries who reported his final conversations:[261] 'Then we spoke about M. Proust./ M. France: "I knew him and I believe I wrote an introduction to one of his early books. He is the son of a doctor who's a hygiene specialist at the Ministry of the Interior. Unfortunately, he has apparently become neurasthenic to a degree; he never leaves his bed. His shutters are closed all day and the electric lamps are always lit. I don't understand his work

---

* *CSB*, pp. 607 and 951. France's article was published on 1 September; Proust responded to it, in the same magazine, on 15 November.

at all. He was pleasant and very witty, and he had a sharp sense of observation. But I stopped associating with him very quickly, and I haven't seen him for twenty years."/ Mme Daudet says that she likes him./ M. France: "I've tried to understand him, and I haven't succeeded. It's not his fault, it's mine."'

France's sentences also hover watchfully at the very heart of Proust's work, and are so numerous that they cannot be listed here. In one page of *Du côté de chez Swann* there are enough to provide Bergotte with an anthology.* The disenchanted tone of voice (which also owes something to Pierre Loti) marks the Narrator's earliest experiences; he discovered it in *La Vie littéraire*: 'At each step we break one of the invisible links that attach us to people and to things.'[262] The New Year's Day in *À l'ombre des jeunes filles en fleurs*, which brings nothing new, is a day typical of France: 'We know that life never brings anything new, and that it is we, on the contrary, who give it something new when we are young. The universe is as old as each one of us.'[263] This leads us to the lesson about solipsism: 'We are locked within our selves as in a perpetual prison',[264] which foreshadows the Proustian assertion that man is unable to escape from himself and, stating the contrary, he lies.

That love should be bound up with destructive jealousy was something that the author of *Le Lys rouge* experienced in the flesh: 'Jealousy has the effect of salt on ice in us: it precipitates the dissolution of our entire being with a terrifying speed. And like ice, when we are jealous, we melt into the mud. It is a torture and a shame. We are condemned to the anguish of knowing and seeing everything . . . for to imagine is to see . . . without even having the means to turn away or close our eyes.'[265] This confession in a piece of literary criticism was not forgotten either in 'Un amour de Swann' or in *La Prisonnière*. The Albertine episode, like the 1893 correspondence novel and *Le Côté de Guermantes*, conjures up the image of a man who believed he held the princess of China shut up in a bottle.[266] Proust had read it in an article by France on Mérimée, and the image hit him like an anterior archetype of the situation he would experience and relate. Agostinelli in his life, and Albertine in his book, would be this princess, who would escape from the bottle, rescuing Marcel, or the Narrator, from madness, but leaving him, as in the passage from Mérimée used by France, in a daze.

---

* *RTP*, vol. I, p. 93: 'The vain dream of life' (*Sylvestre Bonnard*); the 'sterile and exquisite moment that beauty gives to those that desire to understand it' (*Livre de mon ami*); the 'venerable and charming' works of art (*Pierre Nozières*).

France had taken one further step into the recesses of the soul, that would also ring out in Proust's heart. In his article on 'Les criminels',[267] he observed: 'All that anthropology sees in the criminal is an incurable invalid; it looks upon the scoundrel with gentle pity; it tells the murderer what Jocasta says to Oedipus, after having pierced the mystery of the destiny of this blind man: "Miserable wretch! . . . This is the only name I can call you and I shall never give you any other."' Proust, in turn, in his 1907 article 'Sentiments filiaux d'un parricide', alludes to the tragedy of Œdipus in order to exonerate Henri Van Blarenberghe, who had killed his mother before committing suicide.[268] And when Marcel mentioned the *Imitation of Christ*, or *Hamlet*, he repeated the words his former master had used: 'Good night, sweet prince . . .'[269] One of his remarks on Balzac is reproduced in *Le Côté de Guermantes*: 'Thus it is that the man who dominates the century, Napoleon, is only mentioned six times in the whole of *La Comédie humaine*, and at a distance, and in circumstances that are completely incidental.'[270]

The importance of literary work also brought Proust and France together when the latter asserted that literary truth was called poetry,[271] that the only moral purpose of art lay in art itself (genius, 'like fire, purifies everything'),[272] or that the literary critic had an eminent role to play: 'Without revealing anything about himself, he writes the cultural history of mankind. Criticism is the most recent of all literary forms; eventually it may absorb them all.'[273] The man who wrote the introductions to Ruskin, the author of *Contre Sainte-Beuve* and the critic of the *NRF* may have seen this remark as giving encouragement to the novelist to be a critic at the same time. For Proust may have read *Le Lys rouge* as an invitation to go beyond the rules of the society novel,[274] with its descriptions of furniture and clothing, its portraits, its evaluations and its obligatory opera or dinner-party scenes; he may have read it as the story of a passion that was longed for but never requited, of impenetrable lovers and jealousy and relationships breaking down. And who knows whether lines such as the following may not have stirred his most hidden and most terrifying obsessions? 'The house was small, poorly equipped and infested with rats. She acknowledged that there was nowhere one could feel comfortable and that there were rats, either real or symbolic, everywhere, armies of little creatures that tormented us.'[275] Here, in a few words, is a summary of the obsessive described, rightly or wrongly, by Maurice Sachs in *Le Sabbat*.

Such was the story of the friendship between these two men, France's somewhat condescending, while Proust's, to begin with at least, was intensely admiring. Proust was the more loyal of the two, and remained in his debt even when he stopped believing that France was the absolute master. Childhood, the sense of the past, passion, irony, the Dreyfus affair, *La Vie littéraire* – all this can be found, invisible but present none the less, in *À la recherche du temps perdu*; we do not see it because the philosophies of the two writers differ, as does their turn of phrase. France's style, melodious, classical and succinct, looks to the past, to the eighteenth century he so loved. That of Proust, which is focused on an unknown future and a synthesis that his master no longer believed in, gave new hope to syntax and to the way we think.

The painter and illustrator Rita de Maugny, who was Polish by birth, pursued Marcel, via her husband, to write an introduction to an album of her First World War drawings, entitled *Au royaume du bistouri*. Eventually he complied by producing one in the form of a letter, a device he favoured (for his 'Flaubert' was principally a letter to Rivière). In it, he recalled his evenings spent in Savoy twenty years beforehand, the sunsets on the Mont-Rosc, the little train that was the basis for the one at Balbec in *Sodome*, the Maugnys' country house, 'set in the emerald of that wonderful countryside', but which was sad like that of Capitaine Fracasse. With his encyclopaedic knowledge, Proust was aware that this novel was to end sadly, with the return of the lonely hero to his home, and that it was the publisher who had insisted on a happy ending, in which the captain returns with Isabelle, who enlivens the house; this was the role Mme de Maugny played in her own home.[276] There were only a few lines about the drawings, describing the 'fat penitent ladies' who had become nurses, those 'few *grandes dames* who only became saintly late in life'. A few months later Proust would do everything he could to find a job for Clément de Maugny, who was in financial straits.

In April, ever grateful to Léon Daudet, who had brought out his fifth volume of memoirs, *Au temps de Judas*, Proust wrote an article[277] about him which he was unable to get published anywhere (as was the case when he had wanted to praise Montesquiou). After comparing Daudet to Saint-Simon and his portraits, as someone who wrote in a state of dreaming, Marcel then distinguished him from the polemicist, who did so purely for effect. Proust only approved of the former category, but this eulogizing of the far-right-wing journalist must have seemed excessive to the newspapers to which he submitted the article, and even to *La Revue universelle*, which Jacques Bainville edited.[278] On the other hand Proust turned down

Rivière's request for an article on Sainte-Beuve: the subject probably meant too much to him for him to be able to deal with it hurriedly, and he did not wish to use his 1909 notes.

HEALTH PROBLEMS

If we take Marcel's complaints seriously, then his health was deteriorating, he was growing increasingly tired and it was becoming ever more difficult for him to work. Particular problems badly disrupted his way of life. Occasionally his beloved Quiès earplugs would give him otitis, for which he consulted Wicart, 'charming but too intelligent for [him]': the doctor's crime was actually wanting to cure Marcel of his asthma: 'Ah! how soothing are doctors like the good Bize, who hasn't examined my chest for ten years.'[279] Sometimes he poisoned himself by mixing a packet of veronal with dial and opium:* he was so intoxicated that he could not sleep, but he was in terrible pain. Or else, having expended all his energy on behalf of Rivière and the Blumenthal scholarship, he would again experience difficulties in forming words.[280] In October his asthma attacks became so bad that for the first time Doctor Bize had to give him morphine injections, the only effect of which was to 'daze him totally':[281] Marcel was delighted that he did not become addicted to them. But what was most serious of all, and an important turning point, was the fact that whereas he had previously stated that he was ill, he was now convinced that he was soon going to die: 'a strange woman has chosen to make her home in my brain', he wrote openly in his introduction to Morand's *Tendres Stocks*[282] before taking up the theme again with the death of Bergotte and in *Le Temps retrouvé*.

'*CURSUS HONORUM*'

Aware of the scale and importance of his book, and being respectful of institutions, Marcel considered that the Prix Goncourt was a step on the way to the Académie française. His election would be revenge for the obscurity and the sneering he had suffered. There were three vacancies. This was why he somewhat naïvely approached two men whom he had

---

* *Corr.*, vol. XIX, p. 618, 23 November 1920. He gave up trional, extolled by Cottard in a passage in *Sodome*, *RTP*, vol. III, p. 351. Cf. p. 373, hypnotic drugs and memory, remarks credited to Bergson (cf. Cahier 59). Proust also complained that veronal caused him memory loss (*Corr.*, vol. XIV, p. 78).

known for a long time, but who did not care for him.[283] Henri de Régnier, after offering to vote for him,* pointed out that there were other candidates who should precede him: 'Wait for the next vacancy,' he said; and when Marcel paid a belated visit to Barrès, the latter, as the Tharaud brothers have told us,[284] considered it perfectly ridiculous that he had approached him: Proust had 'an exaggerated sense of his own importance'; *Swann* was a book in which everything repelled him. And so, on 3 June, the Académie elected Robert de Flers,† Joseph Bédier and André Chevrillon. Rivière had warned Proust: 'On the whole they're unable to understand you: their slumber is too deep.'[285]

As for the Légion d'honneur, although Proust did not ask to be nominated, he was sufficiently concerned about it to ask his brother to write to General Mangin, who would intercede with General Manoury's brother.[286] He remembered that the Comtesse de Noailles had not received the award originally, because her work was considered scandalous.[287] Should his homosexuality, and the fact that he had not fought the war and been decorated be mentioned? He was awarded the rank of 'chevalier' on 27 September, and he received more letters of congratulation than he had done for his books; René Gimpel gave him a diamond cross from Cartier's, which Robert Proust, who had been promoted to the rank of officer of the Légion himself, presented to him on 7 November. Marcel confided to him: 'I wonder whether you recall a fine passage from Saint-Simon on Fénelon's death, in which his lips closed just as he was about to drink from the cup ... Everything that has been refused me all my life is now offered to me in the most insistent way.'‡ He then had to reply to all those who had congratulated him, while at the same time inscribing copies of his last book with his customary generosity.§ The publication of *Le Côté de Guermantes I*, which was the turning point in *À la recherche* and the volume that would give rise to the greatest misunderstandings – to the myth that he was a novelist fit for duchesses, to magazine articles and notoriety – might have been useful to Proust at last, except

---

* *Corr.*, vol. XIX, p. 213, 14 April 1920: 'A priceless vote,' wrote Proust to him, 'which, because of its unique quality, can practically make up the required amount'.

† Marcel congratulated him, adding: 'I shall be a candidate when one of your colleagues dies.'

‡ *Corr.*, vol. XIX. Cf. p. 430, to P. Morand: 'How terrible death is. For a week they have been offering me all the positions I should have loved to have had, a year ago. But now it's death.'

§ To Valéry, for instance: 'To Monsieur Paul Valéry who, in *Le Cimetière Marin*, has set abstraction in a fluid concrete, as no one else had done until then. Admiring homage' (ibid., p. 552). It was only during his final illness, in 1945, that Valéry began to read and love Proust.

that publication of his work was fatally delayed, because his publisher was unwilling and unable to publish so many books and so many pages simultaneously (and Proust was unable to correct them, having so little strength: though we have seen that he was in a sufficient hurry to accept outside help); it was at this juncture that he realized (and he alone, so used were others to his complaints) that he was fatally ill.

CHAPTER XVI

Between Life and Death

HEALTH

The year 1921 was marked by deteriorating health as Proust was worn down by illness, by the ever-increasing doses of medicaments used to combat it,* and by the intimation of approaching death: 'Lamartine was quite right to say that it's tiresome to die more than once,' said Proust (confusing him with Musset in 'Lettre à M. de Lamartine').[1] Various incidents complicated his life still further: he scalded himself with milk;[2] on another occasion the chemist mistakenly increased his dosage and he poisoned himself;† he fell in his room, which 'damaged' him a bit;[3] and another time he suffered rheumatic attacks. He asked his brother for the name of one of his pupils who might be prepared to come out at night. He consulted Babinski about his difficulties in speaking and was made to pronounce '*constantinopolitain*' and '*artilleur de l'artillerie*': 'One knows only too well what it means if he himself thinks one doesn't know.'[4] The medicaments resulted in oversights and forgetfulness: he would leave a letter unfinished and cause a character in his novel to die twice. What is more, he lost his ability to feel temperature: during a heat-wave when it was so hot that the 14 July parade was cancelled, Marcel was writing 'beneath seven layers of wool, a fur coat, three hot-water-bottles and a fire'.[5] Nevertheless, he was hopeful that 'this will change': 'For fifteen years I have lived from day to day.'[6] Yet with his end-of-year depression

---

* 'My excellent doctor is wearing out my body with morphine, aspirin, adrenalin, evalpine, spartéine, in short, all the medicaments you can – or, I hope, cannot – imagine. The results are scant so far, apart from a great weariness of the mind' (*Corr.*, vol. XX, p. 163, about 7 April, to L. Hauser).

† Ibid., p. 491, 14 October 1921. The mistake did not involve sleeping tablets, which would have killed him, but rather caffeine, as Professor Mabin has pointed out (*Le Sommeil de Proust*, PUF, 1992 p. 149). According to Céleste Albaret, there must have been an accident in 1917 that was due to an overdose of sleeping pills and which caused Proust to be comatose for two days, but there is no mention of this in the correspondence (ibid., pp. 144–8).

and 'the appalling state of [his] health', he told Gallimard that he regretted not possessing any cyanide.[7]

For us these health problems are as important as his work correcting and making frenzied additions, including some of his most brilliant innovations, such as the death of Bergotte.

MAGAZINES AND CORRESPONDENCE

Proust was no less concerned about the publication of magazine extracts, a custom established ever since he had offered extracts to *Le Figaro*, or if we go back to *Les Plaisirs et les Jours*, ever since *Le Banquet* and *La Revue blanche*. For him it was a means of making his work known, and it allowed him to read a part of his work that had not yet been published in book form. The care with which he discussed the extracts for *La Nouvelle Revue Française* with Jacques Rivière, and the passages that he agreed or refused to have published may surprise us: eight issues of this magazine carried extracts of *À la recherche du temps perdu* during the lifetime of its author. In addition extracts appeared in *La Revue hebdomadaire, Les Œuvres libres, Intentions, Les Feuilles libres, Feuillets d'art*, two articles in *La Nouvelle Revue Française* and one in *La Revue de Paris*. In general, the texts published by Proust were never afterwards used in the unpublished manuscripts, but they consisted of a montage of selected passages. Here, for instance, is how he informed Rivière what should be published from *Sodome et Gomorrhe II* under the title 'En tram jusqu'à La Raspelière':[8] 'Get rid of the Cambremer visit; from it take the Norwegian philosopher . . . ; take, too, the Le Sidaner enthusiast; it's very easy to put them in the little tram. Finally, take the old Cambremer woman's salivation. Don't put that in the little tram, but at the moment when the faithful discuss in the tram the fact that the young couple are going to dine that same evening at La Raspelière . . . In this way, you will have a coherent whole, which is not diffused, one that makes me want to read the book, and which will not exceed the forty-six pages you have allowed me.' Occasionally, however, when pressured by the magazine's editor, Proust, who was very ill, exploded: 'Dear Jacques, forgive me. But it fills one with hatred, when I see that other people's lives, other people's souls do not exist for you, but only ten lines, even though they may be so bad that they could destroy everything.'[9] The principal lesson we can draw from all this cutting and re-pasting is the extreme importance that Proust attached to the composition of these texts in terms of their length, the public for them, and what people already knew of his work. Because they had sometimes been written in fragments, as they were in the exercise books containing additional material, and were very short, these montages served to emphasize the 'suppleness'[10] and flexibility of the material available. The drafts and the variants in the Pléiade edition of *À la recherche* reveal a mind that was constantly expanding, constantly more aware, constantly more complex, confronted with an immense jigsaw puzzle, in which the position of the pieces is not clear at first; with a game of chess in which an infinite number of combinations are possible; or with the inside of a large frame in which everything has been decided on beforehand.

Whether it was a sign or a portent, on 1 January 1921 the *NRF* published 'Une agonie', the account of the illness and death of the grandmother taken from *Le Côté de Guermantes II*.* According to Rivière, these passages aroused the enthusiasm of Gide, Schlumberger, Du Bos, Gaston, and others. The same magazine ran 'Un baiser' on 1 February, 'Les intermittences du cœur', taken from *Sodome II*, on 1 October, and 'En tram jusqu'à La Raspelière' on 1 December. The printing errors continued to upset Proust. When Rivière told him about the *NRF*'s proof correction department, he replied ironically: 'But, you wretch, you concealed the existence of this department from me! Its existence is revealed to me at the moment that I am unable to make use of it. A wonderful organism that is still pagan, it does not know the name of Jesus Christ, which it persists in spelling Desus, etc.'[11] *La Revue hebdomadaire*, on 26 February, ran 'Une soirée de brouillard',[12] with an introduction by François Mauriac, and in November *Les Œuvres libres* published 'Jalousie', which incorporated over a hundred pages from the first chapter of *Sodome II*.[13] This magazine was edited by Henri Duvernois and contained several short novels in each instalment; Fayard, the publisher, offered Proust a fee of two francs per line.[14] To Gallimard's great fury, Marcel allowed himself to be tempted. His publisher criticized him for wanting to appear in a 'station kiosk anthology'; besides, there was a chance that the reader might be satisfied with the extract and not buy the book. Marcel promised that he would have nothing further to do with this publication (which was untrue), but that since the NRF owed him 60,000 francs and his monthly payments were not made regularly, he was justified in earning money elsewhere.[15] And thus we see how Proust

---

* The same issue published 'Au platane' by Valéry, which Proust thought was 'admirably written', and 'L'ermite' by Jammes, which disappointed him. 'Une agonie' differs from the text of the novel, as Proust pointed out, notably because of the absence of Bergotte's illness.

used subtle financial and literary tactics to unveil his forthcoming work.

Not content with the *NRF* publishing extracts from his novel, Proust wrote his last important article, 'À propos de Baudelaire' for its centenary issue. On 23 October 1920 Tronche had sent him a copy of an edition of *Les Fleurs du mal* that Proust had asked for (probably in connection with his introduction to *Tendres Stocks*). In April 1921 he asked Gallimard for 'a scholarly edition for literature graduates', as well as for *Phèdre* and Stevenson's *Catriona*.[16] Since Rivière did not know which edition to choose, Marcel ordered the best one, that by Crépet. On 21 April he had finished this 'enormous and exhausting article on Baudelaire',[17] having 'used quotations from memory'. Proust identified himself with the author of *Les Fleurs du mal*: 'Perhaps, alas! we have to suppress the death within us and be threatened with aphasia, in order to acquire that lucidity in true suffering, that religious flavour in the satanic pieces.'[18] He also recognized in Baudelaire (wrongly, no doubt) a fellow homosexual, because of his interest in lesbians. But, as ever, it is in his analyses of forms that he showed himself to be without equal: the variations of tone, the pauses, the vigour of the poetry, which he compared to Beethoven's last quartets, Baudelaire's knowledge of Antiquity, his similarities to Racine. Proust then turned to the subject of love according to Baudelaire, and the 'accursed women' who are reminiscent of Vigny's poem 'La Femme aura Gomorrhe et l'Homme aura Sodome' and of Morel, who, like Baudelaire, made the link between the two 'ways'. The article ends with a cavalier view of all poetry published since (though he did not mention Rimbaud or Mallarmé), in which Proust saw no one who was the match of his subject.

When Joseph Reinach died on 18 April, Proust, rather oddly, thought of creating 'a comic Reinach': we find elements attributed to Norpois or to Brichot. Finally, for *Les Annales politiques et littéraires*, he replied to André Lang, who had asked him whether literary schools still existed, and whether there was a difference between the novel of adventure and the analytical novel. Proust suggested the term novel of introspection instead of the analytical novel, and he stressed that the adventure story also enabled one to point up the important rules of life: 'yet an adventure story of this kind is, under another name, introspective too. What appears to us to be exterior, we discover within ourselves'. As for the 'schools', Proust provided a profound definition: 'They are but a material symbol of the time required for a great artist to be understood and placed amongst his peers, for the despised *Olympia* to lie beside works by Ingres . . . As soon as the innovator is understood, the school, for which there is no longer any need, becomes redundant.'[19]

In early 1921 Proust made a disconcerting request: that his letters should be destroyed. 'I insist absolutely (I shall give my grounds for doing so at the beginning of *Swann*) that none of my correspondence should be kept, and *a fortiori* published.'[20] On this matter, he consulted Bernstein, Finaly and Émile Straus, who left him with little hope: recipients hold the copyright in correspondence. Proust cannot have understood that he retained the moral right to forbid its publication: in any case, as his editor Philip Kolb has pointed out, he could have made no provision for this in his will, for it was his own brother who began publishing the *Correspondance générale* with Plon in 1930.[21] And Marcel himself had made use of letters written by Balzac, Baudelaire and Flaubert; as with his drafts, he both wanted and did not want them to be used. What is more, he did not realize that his letters revealed nothing about his private life; his most intimate notes or messages – those to Reynaldo Hahn (at least five years of their correspondence is missing), to Lucien Daudet, Fénelon and Agostinelli (whose family burned Marcel's letters) – were to disappear for a long time, perhaps for ever. But why destroy them? Proust revealed far more about himself and the world in which he lived in his work than he did in his letters, and one looks in vain for anything scandalous in them.*

PREPARATION FOR *LE CÔTÉ DE GUERMANTES II— SODOME I*

After January 1920 Proust thought of publishing *Le Côté de Guermantes* and *Sodome et Gomorrhe I* simultaneously.[22] We should remember that this latter title included all of the actual *Sodome et Gomorrhe II*. In early September he was still demanding the proofs of *Guermantes II*, which he was 'in a great hurry' for. On the other hand, he considered that *Sodome I* was corrected and complete.[23] But, in order that the book should not be too long, he finally delivered only the first chapter of *Sodome*, that is to say the discovery and theory of homosexuality, under the title of *Sodome et*

---

* Philip Kolb told me that he had never found anything in the least shocking among the thousands of letters he had seen. As for casual encounters, they only feature in messages making appointments (it is said that Léon-Pierre Quint and Doctor Le Masle collected these kinds of messages; none of them is to be found in the Bibliothèque Nationale collection). Numerous letters to Mme de Chevigné, and to Madeleine and Suzette Lemaire, have also disappeared.

Gomorrhe I. On 11 January 1921 Proust told Gallimard of his plan for the volumes of the remaining parts of his book that were still unpublished: *Le Côté de Guermantes II* would fill one and a half volumes; *Sodome et Gomorrhe I* half of the second.* Proust then realized that the extent of his corrections made it impossible for *Guermantes II* to be published in February; he suggested a date of 1 May; the book would come out on the 2nd. After that would follow '*Sodome II, Sodome III, Sodome IV* and *Le Temps retrouvé*, four long books which would follow on from each other at fairly well-spaced intervals (if God granted [him] life)'.

At the same time he reported to Gaston that there were rumours to the effect that Gallimard had financed his own bookshop, which had just opened on Boulevard Raspail, with his authors' money, and even that he had been seen going around Normandy during the war wearing a false beard! Proust himself was the victim of a barb in *Aux écoutes*, which claimed that he had decorated the 'Théâtre libertin' in Montmartre.[24] He took the opportunity to ask for his royalties, which he reckoned were late: Gallimard sent him 7,500 francs and suggested making him payments of 2,500 francs per month from 15 February, while alluding to the very serious crisis that bookshops were going through; he added: 'I know that your friendship is on its guard against the treachery of friends who are ill-disposed towards us, most of them probably for personal reasons: rejected manuscripts, refusal to help, criticism in the magazine, etc.'[25] Whereupon, Proust, much moved, suggested he lend Gaston money, which the latter refused.

On 20 January 1921, Marcel sent him the last batch of corrected proofs of *Le Côté de Guermantes II* and the typescript of *Sodome et Gomorrhe I*, which 'must not be mentioned to anyone', and he passed the proofs for press on 6 March.† Gaston, Rivière and Paulhan checked the final proofs, which were delivered to the printer every evening.[26] *Le Côté de Guermantes – Sodome I*, 'dedicated to no one', was published on 2 May; the book was 284 pages long, and was wrapped in a band which the author disliked, and which the publisher would have removed.

---

* In actual fact, there would be only one volume, in May 1921: what it includes of *Sodome* is even shorter.

† *Corr.*, vol. XX, p. 119, 6 March 1921. There were four sets of proofs in all. But on 8 April Proust made still more stylistic amendments.

In early January, in spite of his annual bout of bronchitis, Proust was searching for mottoes for Baron de Charlus' books: 'I found some rather pretty ones in the last book (not yet published). But those that Balzac found were the most beautiful.'[27] As he did with his etymological research, which would also keep him busy this year, Proust took advantage of his publisher's delays to enhance the precision of detail and the wealth of historical and literary layers in his novel: hence nothing that Balzac did should be forgotten, he had to match him. Further proof that everything was grist to his mill: when Souday sent him chocolates from Boissier's, Marcel amused himself by making Morel confuse the confectioner with Gaston Boissier, the author of *Cicéron et ses amis*.[28] On 22 March, after passing the proofs for press, he sent in a two-page manuscript addendum about the Princesse de Parme's lady-in-waiting (based upon Princesse Mathilde's).[29] Similarly Italian political events were added to Norpois' and Mme de Villeparisis' dinner in Venice, in *Albertine disparue*.

FRANÇOIS MAURIAC

Mauriac had met Proust on 3 February 1918 at Mme Daudet's house, at a party in honour of Jammes: 'He struck me as rather short, squeezed into a very close-fitting suit, his thick black hair casting a shadow over the pupils of his eyes, dilated, it appeared, by drugs . . . He fixed a nocturnal eye on me, the intensity of which intimidated me.'[30] Invited to dinner at rue Hamelin on 22 February 1921, together with Henri Rochat, Mauriac wrote delicately to Proust the following day: 'You are the only person I admire effortlessly and without any ulterior motive . . . I enter the enchantment of your books just as I did as a child those of Jules Verne and Féval.' He hoped to see Proust again, but he had little more than this long private discussion with him: 'The tiresome thing about people as kind and as pleasant as you is that one risks boring them without them showing any sign that one is doing so.'[31] But in Mauriac's *Journal d'un homme de trente ans*, the tone is shocking: 'A curious supper last month at ten o'clock at night at Proust's bedside: sheets none too clean, the stench of the furnished flat, his Jewish features, with his ten-day growth of beard, sinking back into ancestral filth. A subject resumed in his books.'[32] Proust responded to Mauriac's letter in moving terms, when one takes into account his state of health: 'We ought to see ourselves as two jolly men who love life (even the one who appears to be half-dead) . . . who react honestly to all the distractions of the good people who are not artists and will not admire one another.'* When *Guermantes II* was published, Mauriac expressed his admiration for the important scenes in the book, the grandmother's death and the visit to Charlus. *Sodome I* filled him with contradictory feelings, 'admiration, repulsion, terror, disgust', at 'this tremendous fruit of his labours' in which he feared the scandalous effect on young people 'on the brink of the accursed frontier' and who might be driven back towards *Sodome*. For many of them, 'it's a terrible choice, a sentence of purity', added the author of *Souffrances du chrétien* in a partial confession. In June Proust read *Préséances*, which he praised, without being sure that he understood the 'inner life': 'Nothing I like more, or in which I recognize myself less. We must be strangely different to one another.' And suddenly Marcel began thinking about his own death, which he knew was close, asking that Jammes, through Mauriac's intercession, recommend him to his favourite saint, that he might grant him a gentle death, even though he felt brave enough to face up to a very cruel one.[33] Mauriac, for his part, admitted to Proust that, because of his family, he had to be careful in expressing his feelings openly in his books: 'I have chosen not to be free.' And yet his inclination was 'for a life that would be neither calm nor simple', while at the same time loving his family and friends: 'Yet so many different beings dwell within us!'[34] Mauriac's secret was much the same as Proust's, and the man whose life was filled with earthly joys, and later with honours, was no more at peace, nor perhaps any happier, than the great solitary invalid. Proust would not influence Mauriac's novels, but for the author of *Un adolescent d'autrefois* right up to the superb pages of *Mémoires* and *Nouveaux Mémoires intérieurs*, he would continue to be a constant reference point, rather like a guardian angel, its finger raised to its lips.

THE LAUNCH OF *GUERMANTES II*

As usual, Proust gathered his strength to inscribe copies of his book and send de-luxe editions of it to those who were close to him. To Céleste, he wrote: 'To my faithful friend of eight years, but who is so close to my thoughts that it would be truer to call her my lifelong friend, being unable to imagine any longer that I have not always known her . . .'[35] He also

---

* *Corr.*, vol. XX, second fortnight of March 1921. Same style of joking, to Paul Morand: 'Your very affectionate friend but who will remain a bachelor for fear that if he married a "pretty woman" you might instantly make him a cuckold' (*Corr.*, vol. XX, pp. 115–16).

wrote to Gaston Gallimard '[whom he] loved with all [his] heart';* to Gide: 'To André Gide, homage of an affection and an admiration that cannot be condensed into a few words like this, written while people were addressing me. And with infinite gratitude for the adorable Billet à Angèle.'[36] He referred to Reynaldo as '[he] whom he loved most in the world'.[37] To the Strauses, he alluded to the scene of the red slippers, which had been inspired by them, and which he would 'come to collect one evening'.†

RECEPTION OF *LE CÔTÉ DE GUERMANTES II* AND *SODOME ET GOMORRHE I*

In *Le Temps* of 12 May, Paul Souday, while finding the book 'less substantial' than its predecessors, hailed Proust as 'a Bergson or an Einstein in the psychology of fiction'. Marcel criticized him for mentioning neither *Sodome* nor Charlus;[38] Jaloux praised the book in *La Revue hebdomadaire* (21 May), as did Allard in the September issue of the *NRF*. André Germain, on the other hand, wrote a savage review in *Les Écrits nouveaux* (July 1921). In *Comœdia* (22 May) Binet-Valmer condemned 'the depravities in which M. Marcel Proust wallows'; 'these sordid books', he added, did not reflect the 'French soul'; but the same man would write a favourable article on 'Jalousie' in November.[39] Furthermore, Proust's notoriety encouraged foolish articles in humorous newspapers: 'New Swan pen, manufacturer Marcel Proust' or 'We have received a letter from Marcel Proust requesting us to state that he is not related to the Capitaine Proust accused of theft and espionage.'[40]

The author's friends were divided: Albufera was furious at recognizing himself in Saint-Loup. Mme de Chevigné refused to read the book.‡ '[As if she had guessed that the Duchesse de Guermantes] slightly resembles

---

* He even wrote two dedications to him; the second has never been published: 'Dear friend, may I inscribe this book to you like this in your presence. Modesty prevents me from expressing in front of you the profound affection I feel for you' (private collection).

† *Corr.*, vol. XX, p. 285; *RTP*, vol. II, pp. 883–4. Mme Straus wrote to Marcel: 'I am not in the least shocked by the subject. Besides, we discussed it together when you used to come in the evening' (*Corr.*, vol. XX, p. 286).

‡ Was this the book that caused her to say to her neighbour, Cocteau: '*Mon petit Jean*, Marcel has just sent me a book. It would be kind if you were to mark all the passages in which he mentions me.' It was also she who, on seeing that a letter had arrived from Marcel and feeling the weight of it, said: 'Here's a letter from poor Marcel. Who's going to read it?' (A. David, *Soixante-quinze années de jeunesse*, A. Bonne, 1974, pp. 11, 12).

the tough old hen whom I once mistook for a bird of paradise, and who, like a parrot, could only repeat "Fitz-James is expecting me" when I tried to capture her beneath the trees in the Avenue Gabriel. By making a powerful vulture of her, at least I prevent her being taken for an old magpie.'[41] And Proust wrote to Mme de Chevigné 'that to be misjudged at a distance of twenty years by the same person, in the same incomprehensible way . . . is one of the few sorrows that can affect a man who, at the end of his life, has renounced everything'.[42] At the same time Marcel assured the Comtesse Greffulhe's son-in-law that she was the Princesse de Guermantes. Colette, who knew what she was talking about, was delighted by *Sodome et Gomorrhe*.[43] But the most interesting reactions were those of Gide and Montesquiou.

DISCUSSIONS WITH GIDE

Thanks to Gide's *Journal*, the discussions that took place between these two men who would never be friends – even though they must have been drawn to each other by their middle-class upbringing, their passion for literature and the *NRF*, and their homosexuality – are well known.[44] At the *NRF* Proust sided with Rivière: in April 1921 Gide published one of his 'Billet à Angèle' pieces that was hostile to the magazine, which he considered boring; Marcel then intervened in the hope that Gide would remove the 'more unpleasant insinuations' about the editor.[45] However, on 23 April, when he received the proofs of another 'Billet à Angèle', which Gide had devoted to Proust, every sentence 'made him marvel': his style, wrote the 'apostle of sincerity', had all the virtues, his books were an enchanted forest, 'he had a treasure chest of analogies, metaphors and similes at his disposal'.[46]

Gide spent an hour at Proust's home on 13 May, and he lent him a copy of *Corydon*, probably so as to let him know his own views about pederasty. He found Marcel looking 'plump, or rather, bloated'. Proust asked Gide to talk to him about the Gospel, in which he hoped to find 'some support and solace for his wicked deeds'. 'Far from denying or concealing his uranism, he paraded it, and I would almost say that he prided himself on it. He said that he had never loved women other than spiritually and had never experienced love except with men . . . He told me of his conviction that Baudelaire was a uranist.'[47] Gide came back on 17 May and spent the entire evening with him. Proust pretended to blame himself – though it was really so as to please Gide – for 'this "indecision" that had caused him, in order to sustain the heterosexual part of his novel, to transpose to "within a budding grove" everything that had been graceful, tender and charming in his homosexual memories, in such a way that all that was left of Sodom for him was what was grotesque and abject'.[48] The subjects they discussed had been hinted at in the letter Gide wrote thanking Marcel for *Sodome*:[49] Proust stigmatized 'the vice', and the invert draws from these passages 'the sense of his own disapproval'; uranism was presented 'in its most revolting aspect'. 'A pederast (in the Greek sense of the word) would never consent to recognizing himself in the portrait you paint of inverts.'[50] Yet Proust defended himself against having wished to 'stigmatize uranism', and he appeared very upset by this criticism from the author of *Corydon* (who, incidentally, did not consider himself a uranist; rather, he preferred to count himself among the admirers of classical beauty, in the flower of their adolescence and youth). Proust clarified his views to Maurras, who had named Gide as the lover of Phidias, in August 1922: 'In those times, these propensities, which were very often a reflection of fashion, of the desire to be like others, were natural. So many centuries of disapproval have meant that they are only allowed to survive among the sick who are powerless to cure them. And that is why in my books I appear to be blaming something I do not condemn, as I continue joylessly through the valleys with their stench of pitch and sulphur.'[51]

Another man who might be perturbed by this portrait of Charlus was Montesquiou.

FAREWELL TO MONTESQUIOU

When Montesquiou questioned Proust about the 'keys' of his book, while pointing out those that he had discovered himself,* Marcel indicated some of them: Mme de Villeparisis was inspired by Mme de Beaulaincourt, who made flowers out of paper and cloth. Charlus was a portrait of Baron Doazan, the habitué of the Aubernon salon; and, as if this were not enough to reassure Montesquiou: 'My character was created beforehand and is purely invented (although you may say he is Vautrin), and I believe that he is much larger and possesses a much more varied humanity than he would if I had limited him to resembling M. de Doazan.'[52] Did Montesquiou have any doubts? He did not reveal any ('I have never more than glimpsed the baron, with his waxed moustaches and his waxed hair;

---

* For instance, he saw not only Albufera in Saint-Loup, but above all, Guiche.

he lacked all the breeding you have conferred on him'),[53] yet he wrote to a friend: 'I am in bed, sickened by the publication of three books that have deeply upset me.'[54] To Proust he confessed: 'solitude thickens around my work and around my life', and he declared that he was moved to be called 'the only superior man in our circle'.* In June, and then again in July, Proust, who considered the count to be 'an art critic and a marvellous essayist, who can portray in prose as no one else can the work of a painter or a sculptor he likes',† tried to obtain a column for him in *L'Opinion*: 'I should so much like his name to appear again.' The count left Paris for the Hôtel des Îles-Britanniques at Menton. Suffering from uraemia, and refusing to allow himself to be treated, he died there on 11 December 1921. The last lines that Proust received from him, at the end of September, were written on a copy of *Élus et appelés*: 'To Marcel Proust/ Author whom I believe I judge correctly/ Friend whom I know I love truly.'[55] There is thus nothing to justify the notion that Montesquiou died as a result of reading *Sodome I*; Charlus owes as much to Marcel Proust as he does to Robert de Montesquiou.[56]

Proust wrote a letter of condolence to the Duchesse de Guiche, Élaine Greffulhe, the daughter of the 'immutable Muse of the dead poet', whom Montesquiou adored. He said that he was capable of writing volumes about the deceased, 'so inexhaustible was the subject', and that he had always been astonished never to have fallen out with him: 'At least his memoirs will set me straight about this.' He also mentioned the unfairness of the fact that his books had fallen into obscurity, and he predicted: 'He will nevertheless come back. Injustices have their time. And, in spirit and in truth, at least, he will return once more.'[57] The count's funeral took place on 21 December 1921, in the church of Sainte-Élisabeth de Versailles: he had quarrelled with so many of his relatives and members of the aristocracy that only the Duchesse de Clermont-Tonnerre and the Comtesse de Noailles were present; *Le Figaro* also listed the Strauses, M. and Mme Helleu and Léon Bailby; Henri Pinard, the deceased's secretary

---

* *Corr.*, vol. XX, pp. 321, 327; *RTP*, vol. II, p. 844. 'What talent, what drollness, what justified bitterness, what noble melancholy there is in this dazzling letter-writer,' Proust wrote to Guiche on 17 June 1921 (*Corr.*, vol. XX, p. 350).

† Ibid., p. 371, late June 1921, to J. Boulenger. He added: 'He's a nasty man, who out of sheer folly caused his parents to suffer a great deal. But his sad old age, deprived not just of the glory to which he imagined he had a right, but of absolute fairness, melts my heart.' But Boulenger replied with an 'icy' letter (ibid., p. 379, to Montesquiou), and Montesquiou, in turn, with a note that was 'insane'.

and executor of his will; Doctor Couchoud, the publisher of *Les Pas effacés*, gave an address; Lucie Delarue-Mardrus read a poem. The creator of Charlus, being unwell, did not attend.

PREPARATION FOR *SODOME ET GOMORRHE II*

In March Marcel considered that *Sodome II* 'needed real reshaping'; he had just added some amusing 'bits about doctors',[58] where Professor E— hears about the grandmother's death, and about Cottard and Du Boulbon. Cottard had become a specialist in intoxicants; several remarks here were prompted by Marcel's own complaints: 'Intoxicants are also used to reassure the patient who discovers with joy that his paralysis is merely a toxic malaise.'[59] He also portrayed 'a well-known specialist in nervous diseases', possibly Babinski, whom he had consulted since 1918[60] and whom he saw again that spring.

Proust began sending in the typescript, typed by an employee of the publisher, 'extremely ineptly, incidentally', to Gallimard from 8 April 1921.[61] Because of mistakes that had crept in, he now requested proofs, which he would work on. He also announced that *Sodome III* (which would become *La Prisonnière*) was 'all ready'. For *Sodome II* Proust hesitated between a publication date of October 1921 (a bit soon) and May 1922 (a bit far away). Gallimard said he was ready to have it sent off for setting, once the text was 'correct and definitive'; but when Proust did not receive any proofs, he began to wonder whether he had not been 'for some years the dupe of the *NRF*'.[62] By the end of April, in any case, he 'was working as best he could', and hoped to have finished in October. On 10 May, very concerned about his health, he informed Gaston that he would like to leave the whole of the rest of his book to him.[63] And on 1 or 2 June he complained of waiting for several months for the proofs of *Sodome II*: 'Lacking any material to work on, I have spent some productive weeks.'[64] 'I await the proofs impatiently,' replied Gaston, poker-faced, the very next day. At the end of June he arranged to have the famous proofs delivered to Proust as and when they reached him.[65] In September Marcel said that he was working on *Sodome II* all the time and on nothing else,[66] and he reckoned the book would be published in May 1922. On the other hand, despite Gaston's offer, he did not want *Les Plaisirs et les Jours* to be reprinted before he had finished *À la recherche*.[67] It was on 20 October that he spoke in any detail of *Sodome III* for the first time. Discussing the ending, he said that he had done nothing better: 'the death of Albertine, the forgetting'.[68]

On 30 November he explained to Gaston[69] that his additional material should be printed separately from the typescript, and that 'Jalousie' should be printed at the beginning. He would add half a page about 'the *courrières* of Balbec',[70] as a homage to Céleste and her sister, and a visit to Mme de Cambremer.[71] At that time, he believed that *Sodome III* would be short and dramatic in its action, and that it could therefore be published fairly quickly, in October 1922:[72] this must mean that the pangs of jealousy suffered while Albertine stayed at the hero's home were not written in full, nor were certain passages of dialogue. He even suggested, given the hurry he was in, printing from a corrected typescript, which could be used as the final text for the final proofs, and engaging a typist himself (which he would do in 1922).

AN EXHIBITION

On 21 April an exhibition of Dutch paintings opened at the Jeu de Paume, the profits of which were to go to areas of Flanders that had been laid waste by the war. Proust had already read an article about it by Léon Daudet[73] when he received a letter from Morand claiming that he had insisted the Dutch organizers send Vermeer's *View of Delft*, so that Marcel could see it.[74] The previous day Proust had read an article by Jean-Louis Vaudoyer which affected him more than any other, and he wrote to him: 'Ever since I saw the *View of Delft* at the museum in The Hague, I knew that I had seen the most beautiful painting in the world.'* But it was some time before Marcel decided to go to see the exhibition:† Vaudoyer's second article, on 7 May, must have prompted him to do so, for it is quoted in *La Prisonnière*: 'You see that stretch of golden sand again, which constitutes the painting's first outline', as is the article on 14 May: 'There is a Chinese patience in Vermeer's craft', a reference to the lacquers of the Far East.[75] It was therefore Vaudoyer whom he asked to accompany him, some time between 18 and 24 May: 'In order to be able to go and see the Ver Meers and Ingres this morning, I did not go to bed. Dead as

---

* *Corr.*, vol. XX, p. 226, 1 May 1921. The article, 'Le mystérieux Vermeer I', appeared in *L'Opinion* on 30 April 1921. Proust told Vaudoyer that he had once sent a letter to Vuillard so that he could go and see the copy of the Vermeer belonging to Paul Bagnières.

† He spoke about it to Vandérem on 3 May: 'Alas, if only I could get up this once and drag myself off to see the Dutch exhibition' (*Corr.*, vol. XX, p. 245). He reminded him, as he had Vaudoyer, that he had made Swann write a paper on the artist; and he blamed Fromentin once again for having mentioned him without any praise.

I am, would you be so kind as to take me there and allow me to lean on your arm.'[76] Étienne de Beaumont had in fact invited Proust to accompany him to the Ingres exhibition[77] which had opened at the Hôtel des Antiquaires et des Beaux-Arts in the rue de la Ville-l'Évêque; on 9 May Marcel had told him of his wish to see both exhibitions at the same time, and he employed the same words he would use in the account of the death of Bergotte: 'the "brief news item" of your exhibition'.* Although it may have been inevitable that a sick man, who never went out, and expecially not during the daytime, should suffer spells of dizziness, Proust had in fact described some of Bergotte's symptoms before he went to the Jeu de Paume: Bergotte's illness was 'quite new', he had written to Gallimard on 8 April. The fact that Marcel was able to see two exhibitions and lunch with Vaudoyer at the Ritz, then recount his day to Céleste at length, as well as go out on the two following days, leads one to question the theory, put forward by Robert Proust,† that he was taken ill at the Vermeer exhibition. Jean-Louis Vaudoyer described this visit to the Jeu de Paume in a letter to Jacques Rivière, dated 9 January 1923, after having read the passages on Bergotte's death in the special 'homage to Proust' issue of the *NRF*: 'Proust knew Vermeer's work perfectly; he loved him with the most loyal passion. I can tell you . . . the way in which, for the *Mort de Bergotte*, he made use (if one can put it like this) of a visit we made together one morning in May (or June) in 1921 to the Dutch exhibition at the Jeu de Paume, which included the *View of Delft*. Proust was occasionally kind enough to let me know when he wanted me to go with him to either a museum or a gallery. With much kindliness and friendly indulgence, he had read a study on Vermeer that I had submitted to *L'Opinion*; and he was struck by the passage about the "little patch of yellow wall" . . . That morning, at the Jeu de Paume, Proust was not at all well: you can imagine the effort he must have made to be at the Tuileries gardens at eleven o'clock in the morning! Several times he came back to sit down on that "circular settee" which Bergotte rolls off to die. I can still hear him excusing himself in that gentle voice that left you not knowing what to say. Eventually he asked to leave so that he could go home. But later, in the

---

* *Corr.*, vol. XX, p. 251, to É. de Beaumont. Cf. p. 329: 'I went out . . . in a state that would make one believe that my death would be a brief news item the following day, among all the dogs that had been run over.'

† *Corr. gén.*, introduction to vol. IV. See P. Kolb, *Corr.*, vol. XX, pp. xi–xii. Philip Kolb obtained Céleste's testimony in 1948. Cf. C. Albaret, p. 404: 'It was a young man I was seeing and listening to.'

car (where, in a pâtisserie box, there were some excellent strawberry tarts), he felt a little better and wanted to go and see the Ingres, which were being displayed, not far from there, in the rue de la Ville-l'Évêque. I must say, he was not very enthusiastic about this Ingres exhibition. It was no doubt only out of courtesy and kindness, and so as to please me, that he agreed to say anything nice about the marvellous portrait of Granet, lent by the museum at Aix. Then Proust noticed a few faces he knew in the room; and he was quite adamant that he wished to leave. Paul Morand told me recently that after that spring of 1921, Marcel Proust never went back to see any paintings again.'[78]

Proust had foreseen and imagined Bergotte's death before the exhibition, and he expanded it afterwards; but he did not die in front of the *View of Delft*.* For all that, the comparison between the life of the writer and that of the painting loses none of its grandeur, nor are the repeated words, 'Little patch of yellow wall . . .' any less moving.

ROCHAT LEAVES

Back in January 1921, in a letter which he dictated to Rochat, Proust wrote, 'I feel that we would come to blows were I to lead him to believe that I love him as I do myself.'[79] But on 1 June he informed Gallimard that Rochat had gone away the previous day, for several years. Horace Finaly, who was director of the Banque de Paris et des Pays-Bas, had found Rochat a post in a branch office in Buenos Aires. His one regret was not to have seen Princesse Soutzo.[80] According to Reynaldo, he had become 'untruthful and nasty'[81] (which was what made him a model for Morel). When he left, he would desert his fiancée, just as Morel abandons Jupien's daughter (or niece): 'M. Proust,' relates Céleste, 'went to console her after his departure. He never had any regrets about Rochat himself. His only comment was: 'At last, Céleste, here we are quietly on our own.'† He was the last 'captive'.

In June Proust began to go out a little once more. He dined at the Ritz

---

* This is not true of the fragments which date from the eve of his death, and which do not, in any case, occur in the definitive text.

† C. Albaret, p. 231. Céleste did not care for the young man at all. The searches made by my friend Professor Berretta Anguissola to find traces of Proust's secretary have been inconclusive: neither the bank, nor the French consulate have kept any details. But perhaps he very soon went somewhere else?

again at the beginning of the month. On 15 June he was a guest at the dinner given by Mme Hennessy to mark the Duke of Marlborough's engagement to Gladys Deacon. The duke invited him to Blenheim, and promised to put him up at the Gare du Nord, on the boat, and at his stately home. He explained to him that from the moment you believed you were well, you were.[82] On 24 June Marcel even attended their civil wedding at the British Consulate.

THE NORWEGIAN PHILOSOPHER

In February 1921 Bergson had asked his 'dear cousin' to see Algot Ruhe, a Swedish philosopher who had been writing about *Swann* since 1917.[83] We come across him in *Sodome et Gomorrhe*.[84] The translator of Bergson, as well as his biographer, Ruhe (1867–1944) has described his meetings with Proust in two articles and in a novel. Their first meeting probably took place in the spring of 1921. It all began with the Bergsons, who looked upon Marcel as a socialite: 'My attempts to evaluate his qualities as a writer met with polite astonishment . . . But if I should go to rue Hamelin and were I to meet their dear cousin, I had, without fail, to bring him best wishes from the family at rue Vital.' When Ruhe was shown in by Céleste, according to the usual ritual, 'eyes of oceanic depths' gazed at him; Proust, with 'a wide, almost voracious smile' held out 'a huge, far too flabby hand' to him; the Swedish philosopher found himself being served supper at the writer's bedside; Marcel did not eat anything and 'did not even utter the international word: Skåll!' Proust then began to cross-examine Ruhe about his books: 'a sort of Socratic method, the subtlety of which was worthy of admiration'. He suggested arranging for the *NRF* to publish Ruhe's short stories and poems, which he did submit, unsuccessfully, to Rivière in November.* In *Sodome et Gomorrhe* Ruhe, in the guise of the Norwegian philosopher, is introduced initially in a comical light, because of his slow manner of speaking, which gave the impression that he was searching for words in an 'internal dictionary', and which was in contrast to the speed with which he slipped away. He also informs the Narrator, thus reflecting his conversations with Proust, about Bergson's

---

* Algot Ruhe, 'Some who have not been forgotten', *BMF* (Journal of Swedish assistant librarians), May 1939; 'A nocturnal visit to Marcel Proust', *BMF*, June and September 1939. Kindly communicated and translated from the Swedish by C. G. Bjurström. *Corr.*, vol. XX, pp. 534, 540 (Proust suggested that Bergson or he himself should check the Swede's French).

theories on 'the peculiar effects on the memory of soporific drugs' (which destroy the recall of memorized quotations); the Narrator's own experience differs: 'The lofty thought remains in place; what the soporific has put out of action is the power to act in little things.'*

On the night of 17 or 18 November Marcel had a visit, at his own request, from Bernard Faÿ, who was leaving for the United States, where he was to give a lecture tour on contemporary writers; his students at Columbia wanted to do some 'research and theses' on Proust, and he wanted to obtain the writer's opinion. The future professor at the Collège de France (1893–1979, appointed in 1932, but revoked at the time of the Liberation) has recalled his memories in *Les Précieux*,[85] in a tone of voice reminiscent of Maurice Sachs, André Germain and Maurice Martin du Gard. Faÿ had told Proust the story of a young sergeant who was keen on torture, and whom Marcel had wanted to meet (in order to add him to staff at Jupien's brothel, no doubt).† Marcel explained to Faÿ that each of his characters corresponded to a tendency within himself and to a need that he had to express; his work on the proofs reinforced the inner logic of each of them, but took into account the changes that occurred during his life. Faÿ understood, on leaving, that Proust's book 'exhausted him, but was also his reason for living and the sole cure for his ailments'.

On 8 December Marcel returned to dine at the Ritz, at midnight. He drank a bottle of 345 Port, which he later assigned to M. de Cambremer in the guise of a sleeping draught,[86] and he told Walter Berry that an American woman, who had been reading his work for three years, had not understood any of it and had written to him: ' "Dear Marcel Proust . . . Tell me in two lines what you meant to say" . . . I reckoned there was no point in replying to her.'[87] At this period he also had the impression that the Duc de Guiche was avoiding him and detaching himself; he threatened him with a pastiche which would begin like this: 'The Duc de Guiche . . . cultivates the sciences; they do not cultivate him.' He nevertheless wished to question him about Einstein and the relativity of time (but the duke did not believe in reconciling literature and science) and to invite him to the Ritz ball on 25 December (but the duke would be on his

* *RTP*, vol. III, p. 374. See also the discussion with the 'Norwegian philosopher' on the immortality of the soul.

† 'What became of the soldier on the road to anthropophagy?' Proust asked Faÿ on 12 August 1922 (*Corr.*, vol. XXI, p. 413).

travels).[88] After Proust's death, the duke was to regret not making himself sufficiently available to Marcel.

NEW YEAR'S EVE 1921

Proust accepted the Comte de Beaumont's invitation to his end-of-year party, which he was determined to attend: 'I have taken such an excessive amount of drugs that it will be a man who is semi-aphasic and, in particular, unsteady on his legs because of dizziness, whom you will have.' And he asked Beaumont not to introduce him to too many intellectual and tiresome ladies.[89] Jean Hugo remembered the ball given by the Comte and Comtesse de Beaumont: they applauded the exotic dances performed by the beautiful dancer Djemil Anik, the friend of Caryathis, the future Élise Jouhandeau. 'Proust was expected, and Étienne de Beaumont announced: "Céleste has just telephoned for the tenth time; she was checking that there were no draughts and that the herbal tea for which she has provided the recipe had been prepared." Finally, at midnight there was a sort of stir among the crowd and we knew that Proust was there.' Jean Hugo, who had not seen Marcel since 1917, thought his face looked pale and bloated: 'He only spoke to dukes. "Look at him," Picasso said to me, "he's keeping his eye out for models."'[90]

1922

In early January 1922 Proust spoke of his 'infinite depression coming on top of the physical pains'. 'However ingenious the doctors are, my terrible clairvoyance sees right through their contradictions and removes all my hope. How unfortunate that doctors should be "conscientious" and that one can't say to them "kill me" instead of "look after me", since they are unable to cure you. But let's not bother about doctors, except when we come across them in À la recherche du temps perdu.'[91] Marcel did, however, have some evenings of remission* when, after dosing himself with adrenalin, he took the opportunity to go out. On 19 January, for instance, he was able to attend a musical evening at Jacques Porel's house: he arrived there at two o'clock in the morning, his hair too long, his clothes too big for his emaciated body, his fingers rigid and his voice emerging as a whisper;[92] there he met Fargue, who extolled Cocteau's poems, which had been

---

* 'I still (once again) have certain good evenings' (to L. de Mornand).

published in *Aventure*, and spread the rumour, just as Morand did, that the NRF was collapsing.[93] On 28 January he went to his brother's house – an extremely rare occurrence – for an eighteenth-birthday dance for his niece, Suzy; it struck him as 'medical, military and social'. 'All told, my presence did not cast the chill of the resurrection of Lazarus too much. It is true that I'm going back to the tomb.' He must have seemed tired, for the Comtesse Treilhard, and then Doctor Bouffe de Saint-Blaize in turn forced him to take their chairs.* What was someone who had seen so much still searching for at these parties? He told Guiche in September: 'What I enjoy are those soirées with masses of people mingling together like a fireworks display. The Ritz provided me with that up to a point but it was always the same thing.'† On 5 February, 'an agoraphobic and wobbly accomplice', he went to a party at Princesse Soutzo's. Thérèse d'Hinnisdaël danced a few 'numbers' with him; he was surprised and delighted 'to see that with all the naturalness in the world, even when indulging in the most 1922 of dances, she could still look like a unicorn on a coat of arms'.[94] And on 7 February he went to another party given by Morand's lady friend: he even made some suggestions for the guest list: young Boisgelin, whom he had met five years ago and who seemed 'extremely pleasant' – a cousin of Beaumont (who would also be there, and who was to bring him a photograph of his great-aunt, Jeanne de Beaumont, *née* Castries, whom Montesquiou had portrayed 'in a silver sheath, like a woman sculpted by Germain Pilon'),‡ Marcel had been interested in him for some time – and Maurice Martin du Gard.[95] Morand, who was dancing with a woman in mauve, aroused his satirical wit: 'For all his glamour, Morand has the physical elegance that is peculiar to certain rather plump young men. He can reduce his volume at will. Although he looks chaste and gallant when he dances, his eyes make his nose look thinner and his nose makes him look slender . . .'[96]

Proust sometimes returned to the Ritz on his own. There he met a new recruit, a very young man by the name of Vanelli, whom he asked, through the intermediary of the maître d'hôtel Camille Wixler, to come and see him: 'When he had finished his meal, he made me promise to sound out

---

* *Corr.*, vol. XXI, p. 50, 28 January 1922, to P. Morand. Bouffe de Saint-Blaize is mentioned as an 'authority' by M. de Cambremer (*RTP*, vol. III, pp. 349–50).

† *Corr.*, vol. XXI, pp. 460–1, early September 1922. Proust had just learnt that Mme Hennessy had invited him to a soirée '*pas select*' [not smart], but that was all the same to him.

‡ *Corr.*, vol. XX, p. 590, to É. de Beaumont. It was always the desire to discover the key to a literary portrait: Proust cross-questioned Montesquiou as much as Montesquiou did Proust.

young Vanelli . . . Vanelli himself had asked me whether I could introduce him to M. Proust . . . M. Proust then said to me: . . . You will serve me as usual but you will leave the task of serving me coffee to Vanelli. I discovered afterwards that not only had Vanelli served him his coffee, but that he had also been taken home by him. From that day on, Vanelli became his favourite, and he found a post for Rochat in America.' Proust liked to converse with Wixler: 'One evening at the Ritz, a few months later, M. Olivier said to me: "Camille, M. Proust has just died, you know." I wept in front of everyone. Oh! If only I could remember everything that M. Proust said to me!'*

Proust's most pressing work was to put the finishing touches to *Sodome et Gomorrhe II* and make it ready for the printers; Gallimard now wanted to publish it in three volumes, given the typesize the author wanted. For the sequel, which he had provisionally entitled *Sodome III*, and which Gaston had suggested tidying up himself, Proust announced his intention of hiring a typist: she was 'a pretty girl from the Lozère', Yvonne Albaret, Odilon's niece, who started work at the beginning of February and moved into rue Hamelin around the 20th. She would type out *La Prisonnière* and *La Fugitive*, or *Albertine disparue*. What with Céleste, her sister Marie, and Odilon, one can understand Marcel remarking that the Albaret family 'seemed to be expanding' around him; in this way he felt 'safe'.[97]

Among the additions to *Sodome II*, some were inspired by the deaths of Montesquiou and Cardinal de Cabrières,[98] and were incorporated in order to 'diversify' Charlus and lend him characteristics which would add to the 'complexity of the character'; an additional page and a half. Events – not historical events (for the Russian Revolution is never mentioned), but rather that which happened to Proust and to the models for his heroes – enabled him to enrich his book. Nevertheless, he was not indifferent to what was happening in the outside world: he wrote, for instance, to Philippe Berthelot, the secretary-general at the Ministry for Foreign Affairs,

---

* C. Wixler, 'Proust au Ritz: souvenirs d'un maître d'hôtel', *Adam International Review*, no. 394, 1976, pp. 19–21. Wixler was one of the people whom Proust asked to note down the Paris street cries (*RTP*, vol. III, pp. 623–7) to be heard in the year-round markets. He remembered '*J'ai du veau, du foie de veau*', for example. Marcel also asked him to jot down the patter of the street hawkers. Other employees of the Ritz also make brief appearances, such as the 'blond page-boy from Godberry's' (*Corr.*, vol. XXI, pp. 162–3, 1 May 1922). It was at the Ritz hotel that he found the models for the tomato-faced twins dear to M. Nissim Bernard (*RTP*, vol. III, p. 248, and *Corr.*, vol. XXI, p. 266, 14 June 1922: 'One of the two twins . . .').

and the patron of Giraudoux, Morand, Claudel and Léger, who had just been relieved of his duties for ten years: 'Your judges are very naïve, what is more, if they believe that they have got rid of you for ten years. At a time when everything is called into question every three months, do they reckon that their ruling alone will endure?'* In *Le Temps retrouvé* we read of the rehabilitation of a former Président du Conseil, 'once the subject of criminal proceedings and abhorred by society and by the people. But due to their changing composition, and the fact that the passions, and indeed the memories of the surviving individuals change, no one knew this any longer and he was honoured.'[99] This historical precept, which could be applied to so many current and future examples, may have struck Proust as a result of the cases of Freycinet, Rouvier and Clemenceau. He may also have foreseen that Caillaux, who in 1920 was sentenced to three years in prison, would become Minister of Finance once again in 1925. Similarly, on 28 April 1922 there occurred the death of Paul Deschanel, the former President of the Republic, whom Proust had known ever since the time they both used to attend Mme Lemaire's salon, and with whom he had corresponded; Proust described him, having said that he was prepared to write an article about him and his mental illness, in a little-known passage in *Le Temps retrouvé*: 'During those days, no one could ask anything of the President of the Republic any more, for he forgot everything. Then, if he was allowed to rest for a few days, his memory of public affairs returned to him, by chance, as if in a dream.'[100]

In March, and in the very different sphere of music, Proust required some urgent information, probably needed for *La Prisonnière*, from the Princesse de Polignac.[101] He was also able to send Mme de Clermont-Tonnerre the 'old books of mottoes' by Guiguard that she had lent him, and with which he filled *Sodome II*.[102] To Gide, he continued to express ambiguous feelings, in which admiration (feigned, no doubt, in terms of his work, but not as regards the man) was mingled with criticism of some pieces he had written about Oscar Wilde: 'I felt that you were addressing Wilde very contemptuously. I have little admiration for him. But I do not understand your reservations and your severe tone when speaking about a poor wretch.'[103]

With all the additions he was making to *Sodome II*, Proust was frightened

---

* Berthelot, who was blamed for having provided diplomatic assistance to the Banque Industrielle de Chine, which was presided over by his brother (the model for Ferral in *La Condition humaine*) and was in difficulties, was actually reinstated three years later.

of repeating himself and he asked for the help (which Gaston had offered him) of Georges Gabory (who would write an essay on Proust) to reread the book in two or three days and point out any repetitions; he would not be pleased with Gabory's work, incidentally.[104] Furthermore, the proofs were late and Proust, who took medicaments every time in order to have the strength to correct them, suffered as a result.[105] He therefore made very few alterations: when he thought of selling the proofs, repeating the commercial deal he had made with *Jeunes Filles*, to the collector Jacques Doucet, Gaston pointed out to him that they contained relatively few hand-written bits.[106] Doucet then asked for the proofs, as well as the original manuscript, for which he offered a sum of 7,000 francs. What caused Proust to hesitate was not so much the price, which was fairly low, but the thought that his papers would end up in a public library: 'It isn't very agreeable to think that anyone (if anyone still cares about my books) will be able to study my manuscripts, compare them with the definitive text, and infer suppositions which will always be incorrect about my manner of working and the evolution of my thought, etc. All that rather bothers me . . . but I have not yet been able to make up my mind clearly about the matter.'[107] Proust had foreseen everything.

On 30 March Proust had a visit from Gallimard and Rivière. Two days later, Gaston suggested replacing the percentage Proust received with a fixed royalty per copy, which was to the publisher's advantage rather than to that of the author. Proust replied immediately that he was not 'in favour of changes' and put forward a more expensive solution. The financial discussions between the two men always had their comical side: was the one, who seemed so far removed from material considerations yet who worried about every new proposal, attracted by the ruses of the other? In this instance it was Gallimard who retreated gracefully.

Because the daughter of his concierge was ill, Marcel, who was obsessed that his health might become worse than it was, had his post dipped in a formalin steam bath;[108] he often received his visitors wearing gloves. This did not prevent him writing, without the least humour intended: 'In general, I don't like talking about my health.'[109] With increasing frequency he communicated with Céleste by writing her little notes, since his asthma attacks prevented him from talking: 'There's a lot of draught. Have a little Vichy water warmed up for me, this has lost its sparkle. I was unable to ask you for my potatoes, the horrible tart having made me feel sick. I am freezing. Is it warmer in the kitchen than here? . . . Sorry to ring so much.'[110]

As he had done with the previous volumes, Proust placed extracts from *Sodome II* in the newspapers and he asked his publisher to submit news items, gossip pieces and other publicity. On 29 April *Le Figaro*, whose literary editor was Robert de Flers (its political editor was Alfred Capus, whose articles, particularly the one on the Genoa Conference between Great Britain and France, Proust did not always care for), published the portrait of Princesse d'Orvillers, 'the natural daughter of the Duke of Parma', who was inspired, Marcel explained to Robert de Flers, by Mme Jacques de Waru and by 'Cloton' Legrand (who was also the model for Mme Leroi).[111] In its April–May issue, *Les Feuilles libres* published 'Une soirée chez les Verdurin', and *Intentions*, a new magazine edited by Pierre-André May, ran 'Étrange et douloureuse raison d'un projet de mariage'. The book was put on sale on 29 April, with an 'absurd' band wrapped round it: 'One million two hundred and thirty-five thousand one hundred and sixty-eight letters', and Marcel, feeling like a risen Lazarus,[112] found the strength to write a number of dedications.* What was more, Gallimard had sent him a list of possible people to send copies to, and had brought a hundred copies of the first impression, of which twenty were printed on special paper. Proust did not send his work to Francis Jammes for fear of shocking him, but once again he addressed these disturbing but moving words to him: 'In your prayers to St Joseph ask him to grant me a death sweeter than my life has been.'†

REACTIONS TO *SODOME II*

Robert Kemp wrote a mocking article in *La Liberté* on 8 May, in which he admitted (this would not always be true of his successors) not having read the book he was writing about.[113] In the *NRF* on 1 June Roger Allard published an article that Proust thought was 'very fine'. He clarified his ideas about homosexuality to its author: it was 'an entirely nervous perversion with compensating superior aspects', which did not affect

---

* Among those that have been published: to Léon Daudet, to Jaloux, to Mme de Noailles, to Souday, to Vandérem, to Ajalbert, to P.-A. May, to Mauriac, to Bergson ('to the first great metaphysicist since Leibnitz (and greater yet). His creative system may evolve, but it will always retain the name of Bergson') (*Corr.*, vol. XXI, p. 163), to Middleton Murry, to Louis Brun, to Louis de Robert ('I have been almost unable to send out any books'), to René Gimpel, to Mme Straus, to Henri Gans, to Marie de Régnier (in which he recalls the poor Nijinsky 'of *Le Spectre de la rose* and the lunatic asylum', ibid., p. 233), and to Jean Béraud.

† Ibid., p. 199, May 1922; in 1921 Jammes had published a book entitled *Livre de saint Joseph*.

morality. He distinguished it from inversion, because it was 'the illusory, aesthetic, theoretical aspect, beneath which inversion appears and likes to consider itself'.[114] Paul Souday wrote about the book in *Le Temps* on 12 May, 'an indictment that is allegedly grammatical', to which Marcel responded with a pastiche of the critic, which he sent to him.[115] Henri de Régnier, being 'rather tired', had to limit himself 'to moderate readings'.[116] But the great German scholar, Ernst-Robert Curtius, devoted the first in a series of remarkable essays to Proust.[117] *Le Gaulois* of 1 July published a laudatory article by André Chaumeix,* and *Le Figaro* one by Jean Schlumberger on 16 July. An Italian maître d'hôtel at the Ritz informed Marcel that 'the day before yesterday the *Corriere della sera* said that Monsieur Proust's books were very tiring, that one had to climb and climb all the time but that afterwards you were rewarded because you could see very far'.[118] Henry Bridoux praised the book in *La Revue de Paris* on 1 June, as did Jaloux in *L'Éclair* of 7 September. Finally, *L'Écho de Paris* asserted that Marcel Proust was being talked about for the Nobel Prize.[119] In short, there was no reaction of outrage: Charlus and Nissim Bernard frightened nobody. 'I am amazed not to have caused more of a scandal!' exclaimed Proust, seeing himself praised as if he possessed 'the innocence of the Comtesse de Ségur'. And he added: 'People are devouring *Sodome et Gomorrhe* as they would a religious trinket.'[120] Right up to the last, he never stopped concerning himself with press reactions, arranging for favourable articles to be mentioned in gossip pieces in other papers, and doing so with surprising energy, as if the future of the book depended on it: concerned solely with his books, which he fingered because he was unable to read them, all he now wanted to do was 'supply intellectual minds all over the world with the expansiveness that had been denied [him]'.[121]

Among his friends, Sydney Schiff expressed his enthusiasm, as did Mme Straus: she was unable to put the book down, and she read it day and night. Cocteau sent a light-hearted note, saying that he thought it was brilliant, which did not touch upon the subject matter. Mauriac regretted that in all this hell there were not ten just men at least, or a character who was saintly. Morand, who was more pragmatic, pointed out that the book

---

* Proust thanked him with his customary courtesy on 4 or 5 July (*Corr.*, vol. XXI, pp. 338–40). He also thanked Schlumberger on 16 July, while at the same time refuting the allusion to 'transpositions of sex'. Proust did not like people saying that his 'young girls' were 'men in disguise' (ibid., pp. 355–7).

was on display in every bookshop window and that everybody was talking about it. Laure Hayman, who was furious at recognizing herself in Odette, wrote to Proust saying he 'was a monster'.[122] Proust refuted this and did his best to prove that she was the opposite of Odette.[123] Camille Barrère, who had been France's ambassador to Rome for over twenty years, believed that he recognized himself in Norpois – 'simply because when I was a child,' wrote Proust, 'he dined once a week at our house'.[124] In such cases Marcel only acknowledged minor similarities: the Duc de Guermantes resembled the Marquis du Lau (who appears in *À la recherche*), but only in the way he shaved; Mme Straus' salon was like Odette's, because of the guelder roses.[125]

SODOME ET GOMORRHE II, III, IV

In January 1922 Proust had begun to envisage splitting *Sodome III* into two parts, even though he expected it to be a short book of the size of *Guermantes I*. But the length of *La Prisonnière* and of *Albertine* show how much Proust wrote in 1922.[126] The first of these two titles began to emerge around 15 May 1922.[127] In order to complete his comments on Vermeer in Bergotte's death scene, Marcel was not satisfied with his own memories and with Vaudoyer's articles, so he procured a book by Gustave Vanzype, *Jan Vermeer de Delft*, 'whose numerous reproductions' enabled him 'to recognize identical incidental details in different paintings'.[128] On 2 July, Proust told Gallimard that neither of the two parts was 'what is called ready', that 'there was still more to do', and he anticipated publication in 1923, torn as he was between the desire to let the public 'have a break', and the fear that readers might forget the ending of *Sodome II* – in which 'I go off to live with Albertine'. He had found two symmetrical titles: *La Prisonnière* and *La Fugitive*. The publication of *The Fugitive* by Tagore, as we know, led him to abandon this solution.[129] In early August he changed his mind about his original intention to send '*Sodome III – La Prisonnière*' to Gallimard, and to 'revise extensively' on the proofs; he had just re-engaged Yvonne Albaret, who had left in June, and there were to be three successive typescripts of *La Prisonnière*.[130] At first Proust did not know whether this novel would be sufficiently short to be published at the same time as its sequel, *La Fugitive*: 'In order to have a book that is not so long, one should not have people saying: "It's not nearly as long."'[131] Whether or not to make a book short or long was a dilemma that dogged Marcel to the end of his life, and it explains his deliberations over *Albertine disparue.* On 3 October, he went back to the title of *La Fugitive*, which, when it was discarded, upset the symmetry.[132]

When Proust died he had reached page 136 of the third typescript of *La Prisonnière.* These concrete stages enable us to appreciate the considerable amount of work that was done once he had written the manuscript, on the typescripts and the different sets of proofs, not just because he made corrections as he read them, according to his inspiration, but also because he wrote additional material to be inserted, in exercise books or on loose sheets of paper. The most famous example of this is the death of Bergotte, a fragment that was rewritten after his visit to the exhibition of Dutch paintings at the Jeu de Paume in May 1921, which was inserted into the third typescript of *La Prisonnière*[133] after having been written in the form of notes in Cahier 62. It gives us an idea of the importance of these additions, and, knowing that they were never completed, it may fill us with regret. On the other hand, we should not make the mistake of believing that Proust had wanted to write a book that was impossible to finish, that was aleatory and composed of several combinations, like Mallarmé's 'Book'. Unlike Roger Martin du Gard with *Maumort*, Proust accepted that the books should appear in his lifetime. This meant that the possibilities for transferring passages and for making alterations and additions became fewer as the various volumes were published, so in 1922 only *La Prisonnière, Albertine disparue* and *Le Temps retrouvé* were still in a state to be altered. Hence it was Proust's premature death that left the draft passages, though not all of them, open to being moved around. This is why I would not agree that 'in this perpetual reorganization, we see one of the underlying reasons why the writer should have continued writing up to the moment of his death, and consequently the proof that *À la recherche* remains unfinished and unachievable'.[134] If this were the case, Proust would never have published anything, and *À la recherche du temps perdu* would be another *Jean Santeuil*. Yet in early November 1922, in one of his last letters, he mentioned to Gaston Gallimard '*La Prisonnière* (ready but needs to be reread)',* as if he knew that he would never be able to reread anything himself, but that his book, which, ever since the spring of 1922, had displayed the word *end* on the last line of the manuscript of *Le Temps retrouvé*, would nevertheless be ready.

---

* *Corr., avec G. Gallimard,* p. 636; the last line reads: 'Letter follows when I am able.' This letter informed Gallimard that Proust had despatched a typescript of *La Prisonnière*, from which proofs were to be made, which the author would correct. Gaston Gallimard replied as follows on

ADDITIONS

During the period following the completion of the main manuscript, Proust spent a great deal of his time making additions. For example, although the manuscript of *Sodome et Gomorrhe* appeared to be complete and the title had been found in 1916,[135] the beginning of *Sodome et Gomorrhe I* was redrafted and the ending added. The first part of the evening at the Princesse de Guermantes' was completely revised, notably when the section was published under the title 'Jalousie' in *Les Œuvres libres*, in November 1921. In the second visit to Balbec, Proust added the adventures of Nissim Bernard to the manuscript. The reflections on sleep in chapter III replace a dream concerning the grandmother in the typescript. Only traces remain of the comparison between Brichot and Swann. In chapter IV the description of the sunrise comes from the first visit to Balbec, and it is an example of the way in which Proust endlessly continued to transfer passages from one place to another. These additions seem to represent an evolution in terms of the characters which only serves to emphasize the Balzacian comedy. This is true of the introduction of new characters, such as Mme de Citri, the Turkish ambassadress and the 'three charming ladies', who come from the two exercise books containing additions, Cahiers 62 and 60, written between 1919 and 1921. The language of the characters, their peculiarities and their tics are developed on the typescript. There are a great many variations on the theme of inversion, by way of quotations from Racine, which are used to describe Vaugoubert, Nissim Bernard and Charlus. The liaison between the Prince de Guermantes and Morel was written on a scrap of paper. The Norwegian philosopher encountered at the Verdurins, was, as we have seen, a late invention.* Morel became a leading character, whose function was made clear in the article Proust wrote entitled 'À propos de Baudelaire' in *La Nouvelle Revue Française* in June 1921: 'It appears that Baudelaire allowed himself to be "affected" in a most privileged way by this "liaison" between Sodom and Gomorrah, which in the latter sections of my book I have entrusted to a brute of a man, Charles Morel (it is to brutes, moreover, that this role is usually assigned). How interesting it would have been to know why

---

7 November 1922: 'I have received your manuscript. I am sending it for setting straight away. I shall send you the proofs as soon as I have them' (ibid., p. 637).

* See *Corr. avec J. Rivière*, p. 213; in fact this was the Swede Algot Ruhe: 'I hope that this eminent Swede will not in any way recognize himself in the Norwegian philosopher in *Sodome II*, though I shudder at the thought' (letter of 29 or 30 November 1921).

Baudelaire chose this role, and how he filled it. What is comprehensible in Charles Morel remains profoundly mysterious in the author of *Les Fleurs du mal*.'[136] Just as Mme de Villeparisis is the reincarnation of Sainte-Beuve and Mme de Boigne, it is as if Morel, an artist himself, had come to resemble Baudelaire in the way that Proust had imagined him, that is to say as an invert, but one fascinated by female homosexuality,[137] like the author of *Les Plaisirs et les Jours*. Studying these late additions as a whole, it is possible to extract the principal dramatic, comic, intellectual and sensory themes, and to show that they are not purely concerned with facets of character and society, but also with poetic images.[138] Some veritable prose poems, a term that Proust employs in his correspondence to designate the extracts he was giving to *La Nouvelle Revue Française*, thus appear belatedly, such as the scene of Albertine sleeping in *La Prisonnière*, or the passage in *Albertine disparue* that follows the girl's death. '*Que le jour est lent à mourir par ces soirs démesurés de l'été!*' [How slow the day is in dying on these unending summer evenings!] Right up to the end, intelligence, humour and poetry go hand in hand; up to the end, the additions, through their effects of anticipation and repetition, of turning backwards, reinforce the structure of the whole work. The interest and the importance of the exercise books containing the additions also lie in the fact that they contain some notes which Proust did not wish, but was also unable, to insert; one such was this passage on pity, reminiscent of Dostoevsky, which Morel's cruel treatment of Charlus inspires in the Narrator: 'It sometimes happens that it is not the Morels who are without pity, but honest and just men, who punish evil and are indifferent to the suffering they cause a person whom they deem to be lacking in probity or honour. But pity no longer cares about what a man may have done that is evil, as soon as he suffers morally. She loathes the judge who knows, without being disconcerted, that he has exacerbated heart attacks, and she kneels, weeping, before the anxious pallor of the corrupt official.'[139]

Among the additions from this period, there was Tissot's painting, *Le Balcon du Cercle de la rue Royale en 1867*, which depicts Charles Haas, the Marquis de Lau, Prince Edmond de Polignac, the Marquis de Galliffet and Saint-Maurice on the terrace of the club; a reproduction of it from *L'Illustration* had been sent to Proust by Paul Brach, which delighted him and which he looked at constantly.[140] He also thought of revising his lines about Dostoevsky by borrowing *The Possessed* from Morand.[141] In early August he finished his piece on the 'street cries of Paris', claiming that he himself had reaped a 'reasonably abundant harvest of sound, that is often pretty'.[142]

In *La Prisonnière* the Narrator, playing Vinteuil, and later Wagner, to himself at the piano, comments on the 'always incomplete' character of 'all the great works of the nineteenth century'. The greatest writers of this century 'had bungled their books', but they still had the great merit of having imposed a retroactive unity on their work, which made it beautiful and original. This belated unity had formed Balzac's *La Comédie humaine*, Hugo's *La Légende des siècles*, Michelet's *La Bible de l'humanité* and *The Ring of the Nibelung*; it should not be confused with 'all the other systematizations of mediocre writers who with copious titles and subtitles give themselves the appearance of having pursued one single and transcendent design,'* because it was something that had come about naturally, through a process of development which was life itself. Thus the writer could 'integrate with the rest' a 'fragment composed separately', because it was not the 'artificial development of a thesis'. In these important passages Proust defined his poetic art, just as much as he did in *Le Temps retrouvé*. He did manage to preserve that unique beauty of a cycle which has been built up naturally and over the course of years, under the triple effect of real-life experience, culture and meditation: a single book, which bore the title *Les Plaisirs et les Jours*, or *Jean Santeuil*, or *Contre Sainte-Beuve*, or *Les Intermittences du cœur*, or *À la recherche du temps perdu*. From *Contre Sainte-Beuve* onwards the book was meant to come full circle, as it were, from the reading of an article to the final conversation about criticism and literature. But this was neither arbitrary nor systematic, because the book never stopped growing, appending to itself the 'contemplation of nature', action, and 'individuals who are not merely the names of characters'.[143] Since, from the start, Proust imagined that he would co-ordinate the first and last chapters, he avoided the incompleteness that he criticized in the great works of the nineteenth century; but, committed to that form of inspiration which, for him, was an endless descent into the night of interiority, into the uniqueness of a vision, into the distinctions of a language, he escaped from the rigidity and systematic mind of Zola or Romain Rolland. This circular structure thus made it possible, without affecting the nature of the work, to swap round the final conversation in *Contre Sainte-Beuve* with the matinée at the Princesse de Guermantes'. It could be applied to the account of a vocation, to a principal character who is destined to become a writer; it was not

---

* Proust has Romain Rolland's *Jean-Christophe* in mind here.

compromised by any external event, neither the meeting with Agostinelli, nor the First World War. The unity of Proust's creative ideas was similar to that he observed in Ruskin in 1905: 'He moves from one idea to another without any apparent order. But in fact the imagination which drives him follows its own deep affinities which, whether he wishes it or not, impose a superior logic on him.'[144] The ending of his introduction to *Sésame et les lys* foreshadows that of *Le Temps retrouvé*: 'So at the end he finds that he has followed some kind of secret plan which, when it is finally revealed, imposes a sort of retrospective order on the whole work and makes it appear to lead, in a series of magnificent steps, to that final apotheosis.'* The whole story of Proust's successive projects, the layered versions, and the drafts that were completed and then surpassed, had no other purpose than to draw attention to this order and these layers, up to the 'final apotheosis', aspired to in 1905 by an unknown translator, and realized in 1911 in a school exercise book by a novelist without a publisher.

But Proust had taken his precautions, by scattering through his narrative signs, warnings and discreet confessions which define his manner of writing in a way that is just as effective as a foreword: he wrote an introduction to Ruskin, and not to *À la recherche du temps perdu*, no doubt because a preface to his novel would have destroyed what was most original about it, which was gradually to unveil his philosophical and aesthetic views, and to transform the discovery of meaning, art and the past, into experiences. And were it necessary to emphasize this, the fact is that these remarks of Proust formulate exactly how his book should be published. Above all, his fondness for unpublished work, in this passage from *Jean Santeuil*: 'We should be overjoyed if today, in a manuscript or in a newspaper serial, we were to discover some new passages written by George Eliot or Emerson';[145] for the enthusiast, nothing that has slipped from Proust's pen, especially if it is to do with the novel, is without interest. What do the unpublished fragments provide us with? We learn of the death of Bergotte in an allegorical way. The attention of the dying writer as he contemplates the painting by Vermeer is transfixed by 'the precious substance of the tiny patch of yellow wall'.[146] This word 'substance' [*matière*] is used by Proust when, in *À l'ombre des jeunes filles en fleurs*,

---

* *Sésame et les lys*, Mercure de France, 1906 p. 62. The last sentence of this book, Proust also observed, took up the themes of the first by recalling 'the tone of the beginning in the harmony of the ending'. The last sentence of *Le Temps retrouvé* ends with the word '*temps*', which, within the word '*longtemps*', is the first word of *Du côté de chez Swann*. See P. Kolb, 'Proust et Ruskin', *Cahiers de l'Association internationale des études françaises*, Les Belles Lettres, 1960, pp. 267–73.

he refers to painting the evenings at Rivebelle. The secret of the 'substance' lies in the superimposition of 'several layers of colour'. This is something that cannot be overstated: the precious character of *À la recherche* derives from the superimposition of these successive stages. From one version to another, from one correction to another, the page acquires a depth, a transparency and a gloss that are not present in the first draft. A great artist therefore subjects himself to obligations ignored by the mediocre, the writers who are in vogue and are interchangeable; he believes he is 'obliged to rewrite a passage a score of times, even though the admiration it arouses will matter little to his worm-eaten body, like the patch of yellow wall painted with so much skill and refinement by an artist destined to be for ever unknown and barely identified by the name of Vermeer'.[147]

Vinteuil, like Bergotte, is one of Proust's allegorical figures. In *La Prisonnière*, in which he eclipses Bergotte, the Narrator listens to his septet, a masterpiece which surpasses his sonata. This piece would not have become known had it not been for the work of his editor, Mlle Vinteuil's friend. On his death Vinteuil had left nothing but 'indecipherable scribblings' and the young woman spent 'years unravelling the scrawl . . . in establishing the correct reading of those strange hieroglyphs', in disentangling 'papers more illegible than strips of papyrus dotted with cuneiform writing, the formula, eternally true and for ever fertile, of this unknown joy, the mystic hope of the scarlet Angel of Dawn'.[148] And thus, 'what she had enabled us to know of Vinteuil, thanks to her labour, was in fact the whole of Vinteuil's work'.[149] In a sort of subtle plea, as Proust approached the end of his book, and, still more swiftly, the end of his life, he introduced into his pages an allegory, not just of the way in which he wrote and of his manuscripts which were doomed to remain posthumous, but also of the work that awaited their editor. This person was invited to decipher the unpublished writings and to present these successive layers which, once unfolded, allow us to understand the composition of the work and the depths of its substance. What penetrated it very gradually, in every word, in every sentence, was the life of the artist himself, which he slowly 'infused' into it.[150]

THE END OF *LE TEMPS RETROUVÉ*

According to Céleste, it was in the spring of 1922 that Proust, smiling and looking weary, summoned her: 'I have important news. Tonight, I wrote the word "end" . . . Now, I can die.'[151]

The final sentence

In Cahier XX, the last of the exercise books containing the definitive manuscript, a considerable amount of stylistic work has been carried out on the final sentence. If we examine this, only the end of the sentence can be considered finished: a symbolic situation? The beginning has been deleted. The final, closing words, words that are so important because they refer back to the first word in the book, '*Longtemps*', and summarize the work, had initially been set out as: '*Dans le temps*'. We can see how these words were gradually pushed back as the beginning and the middle of the sentence were developed. In the first version:

Du moins ne manquerais-je pas d'abord avant tout d'y décrire les hommes et/ cela dût-il leur donner la forme d'êtres monstrueux et indéfiniment prolongés comme occupant une place infiniment plus considérable que celle si restreinte qui leur est réservée dans l'espace, une place dans le temps.*

In the second version:

Cela dût-il les faire ressembler à des êtres monstrueux/ une place indéfiniment prolongée d'êtres hideux, comme occupant une place prolongée sans mesure/ dans le temps.†

In the third version:

Une place si considérable à côté de celle si restreinte qui leur est réservée dans l'espace une place au contraire prolongée sans mesure/ dans le temps.‡

In the fourth version:

Puisqu'ils touchent simultanément comme des géants plongés dans les années à des époques vécues par eux, si distantes, entre lesquelles tant de jours sont venus se placer – dans le temps.§

---

* At least I should not fail to describe men first and foremost and/ even if the effect were to give them the form of monstrous and indefinitely prolonged creatures, occupying an infinitely more considerable place than the restricted one which is reserved for them in space, a place in time.

† Even if the effect were to make them resemble monsters/ an infinitely prolonged place of hideous creatures, as occupying a place prolonged past measure/ in time.

‡ A place so considerable compared to the very restricted one that is reserved for them in space, a place on the contrary prolonged past measure/ in time.

§ For simultaneously, like giants plunged into the years, they touch epochs through which they have lived that are so distant, between which so many days have ranged themselves – in time.

To which may be added a further question: in which version was the word *Fin* placed at the end? Certainly before the fourth; but after the third. It was when Proust had succeeded in inserting the image of giants, which may have taken the place of the '*êtres monstrueux*', that he stopped; it was both because he had achieved a rhythmical fullness, and also because of the effect, not dissimilar to silence in musical tempo, of the single dash (not a pair, as in the Clarac-Ferré edition) which precedes '*dans le temps*'.[152]

It so happened that Proust revealed some of the ideas that were to feature in *Le Temps retrouvé*. He said, for instance, that his book was entirely the result of a 'special sense' – a 'telescope fixed upon time', which 'allows unconscious phenomena to appear in the consciousness', with style expressing only the 'profound and authentic impressions' that obeyed the 'natural progress of his thoughts'.[153] And there was a further instance, when he wrote to Curtius: 'Bad literature diminishes us. But real literature helps to reveal the still unknown part of the soul.'[154]

DAILY LIFE IN 1922

On 1 May Marcel burned his stomach by taking neat adrenalin and was in agony for three hours; he was unable to eat anything and said that his digestive tract ought to be 'put in plaster'. He stopped writing to anybody.[155] As a result of these burns, he claimed to live on nothing but ice-cream, which he arranged to have collected from the Ritz[156] day and night, and, on one occasion, on asparagus. He did go out, however, on 18 May to attend the first production of *Renard*, a ballet by Nijinska (music by Stravinsky and sets by Larionov),[157] and afterwards he went to the reception given by the Schiffs at the Majestic Hotel. They had invited Diaghilev and several members of his company, as well as Stravinsky, Picasso and Joyce. Proust spoke to Stravinsky, who immediately took him for a snob, about Beethoven's last quartets. As to whether any discussion took place between Joyce and Proust, the accounts differ: in any case, the two greatest novelists of the century failed to understand one another. The Irishman, who complained about his health as much as the Frenchman did, attempted to open the window and smoke in Odilon Albaret's taxi. Joyce would observe in his notebook: 'Proust shows life as analytical and immobile. The reader finishes his sentences before he does;' and, in a letter to Sylvia Beach, he said he had read 'À la recherche des Ombrelles perdues by several Jeunes Filles en Fleurs du côté de chez Swann and Gomorhée et

Cie, by Marcelle Proyst and James Joust.'* A week after Proust's death, Joyce wrote: 'His name has often been linked with mine. In Paris people did not appear to be surprised about his death, but when I saw him last May he did not look ill. In fact, he seemed to be ten years younger than his age.'[158] Nothing survives of this glittering evening, either in Proust's letters or in his novel: as he often said, meeting his peers, his colleagues, artists or intellectuals, mattered little to him.

In May a comical incident took place. Proust had struck up a relationship with young Jacques Benoist-Méchin, who would later write two books about him. Marcel believed he remembered his mother, who was 'superb and very tall', and he asked Jacques for a photograph of himself: 'I am always very interested by these reincarnations of an admired physical type, in another sex.'† When Benoist-Méchin pointed out that he must be thinking of his father's first wife, rather than his mother, Proust was not in the least put out: 'Your photograph bears out the validity of my ideas about love ... I actually think that men do not love any particular, individual woman, but a certain type of woman from which they never deviate ... If your father's second wife was the lady who is your mother, it was because she enshrined that special type that he loved above all others. She must, in some aspect, have resembled his first wife. It is not surprising therefore that in your photograph I should find certain characteristics of a woman who was not your mother and whom you probably never set eyes on.'[159]

On 24 May Proust, after having spent the night working on it, sent *Le Gaulois* a reply to the survey on 'the Goncourts as seen by a younger generation'.[160] He recalled his memories of meeting them at the Daudets and how Princesse Mathilde had become wary of Edmond because he took notes. But writing a diary 'is not what a great artist, or a creative writer does'. In *Le Temps retrouvé*, which Proust was foreshadowing here, he says the same thing, and he ends with his pastiche, 'a pseudo-unpublished text of the Goncourts in which the different characters of [his] novel are appraised'. One sentence sums up everything: 'This noble artist, this historian of the highest and most original worth, this genuinely impression-istic novelist who was so unappreciated, was also a man possessed of

---

* R. Ellmann (*James Joyce*, Penguin 1960) has assembled most of the accounts; Painter, p. 828, gives an indiscriminate montage of differing memories. I prefer to retain what Joyce himself wrote, where his misgivings are mingled with irony and praise.

† *Corr.*, vol. XXI, p. 203. He is harking back to his study of the similarities between Gilberte Swann, her father and her mother.

naïvety, credulity and a charming and restless geniality.' He would also respond to two further surveys, on 22 July and 14 August. In the first of these, for *La Renaissance politique et littéraire*, he answered two questions about style: 'One should be concerned purely with the impression or the idea that has to be reflected . . . It requires all one's strength to submit to reality, to succeed in giving the most apparently simple impression of the invisible world in the so different concrete world in which the inexpressible resolves itself in clear formulae.'[161]

In June it seems that Proust began to frequent Le Bœuf sur le Toit – 'Pastoral in its name, but no more than an inn', as he described it in the poem he sent to Serge André, the editor of *L'Opinion*, 'In memory of an evening alone.' This mecca of Parisian night life, whose name derived from a pantomime written by Cocteau and Darius Milhaud,[162] was first opened by Moysès in the rue Duphot, under the name of the Gaya Bar; Gide and Allegret could be seen there, as could Diaghilev, Picasso, Misia Sert and Mistinguett; having become too small, it moved to the rue Boissy d'Anglas, where it opened on 10 January 1922 under this new name: 'The main room, which was square, was much larger than that of the Gaya and was extended at the rear by a recess containing the bar and the piano. On the wall there hung *L'Œil cacodylate*, a large picture which Picabia had painted with the help of his friends. Each of them was made to stand in front of the canvas with a paint brush and a tin of Ripolin, and had to write down whatever went through their minds. The words "*Couronne de mélancolie*" crowned Jean Cocteau's signature. Paint brush in hand, Valentine had said: "My heart is beating!" "Write that!" said Picabia.'[163]

Proust was pleased to become acquainted with this fashionable spot, where Weiner and Doucet played jazz tunes or parodies of Chopin on two pianos, where Cocteau occasionally took over on the drums, and which was frequented by avant-garde artists; but he did not include it in his great work, almost as if the Maison Dorée, the Ritz, the restaurants of the past, had taken up all the space.

For the Prix Blumenthal that year, Proust supported Jean Paulhan, who would be judged too old, and, as second choice, another critic from the *NRF*, Benjamin Crémieux,[164] to whom it would be awarded; for another award, he favoured Gabory, 'an exquisite creature, full of intelligence and curiosity',[165] who would fail to obtain the grant. On 12 June Marcel attended a large reception given by Mme Hennessy in her town house at 85 rue de la Faisanderie, 'the most beautiful residence in Paris'. There he met Guiche (who informed him that he had been invited to a '*journée*' [a gathering] that was not very chic, something Proust had worked out for himself as he entered),[166] the Comtesse de Durfort, the great-niece of Chateaubriand, the Marquise de Ganay, the Princesse de Polignac, who was looking just like Dante, the United States ambassador, Thérèse Murat and Gustave Schlumberger, and Boni de Castellane. They listened to a lady singing Gounod. Proust portrayed himself in a 'little piece of buffoonery' – a conversation overheard between two guests – which he sent to the lady of the house: 'A dark man, with dishevelled hair, who looked very ill. "By his look I immediately sensed that he was not one of our circle." "Be quiet, he's a genius. He's got hay-fever . . . It's the famous Marcel Prévost, the author of *Les Don Juanes*." '[167]

On 16 June Marcel dressed before noon and went to his brother's home, as well as to the Ritz, in spite a bout of rheumatic fever which would cause him pain for several weeks. He was also in contact with another English friend, Sir Philip Sassoon, whose mother, Lady Sassoon (1865–1909), the wife of Sir Edward, was born Aline de Rothschild and was the sister of Robert de Rothschild (1880–1946). Sir Philip (1888–1939), who was an acquaintance the Bibescos and Proust had in common,[168] was a Member of Parliament at the age of twenty-two, secretary to Sir Douglas Haig during the war and to Lloyd George at the time of the Peace Conference, and Under-Secretary of State for Aviation in Baldwin's cabinet.[169] At the Air Ministry he was very well disposed towards T. E. Lawrence, who, in the wake of the 1929 elections, would regret only Sassoon's departure and that of Churchill.[170] Schiff has left us a portrait of this 'intelligent and very highly strung' character: 'I don't know whether he's ambitious, but, being colossally rich, if he's talented too (which I think likely on account of his blood and his parents), he could attain a considerable position, apart from his social one, for he is very close to Lloyd George and other politicians . . . I can well imagine that Sassoon discerned your unique virtues and that he would like to add some sparkle and personality to the socially distinguished and I suppose boring circle that must make him stagger with exhaustion.'[171] In 1921 Proust appears to have devoted a pastiche, which he then tore up,[172] to this man, and then advised him against coming to see him again, recalling the disastrous example of Fénelon at Constantinople: do not love me, because 'of the sadness of so many farewells'.[173] None the less he found it amusing to describe their proximity at the Ritz: 'I have not heard anything of you for a long time apart from an aquatic murmur . . . Menacing noises could be heard beside me, I thought there would be a veritable deluge, I felt certain that to punish [me] . . . Jupiter would hurl his bolt of lightning. But no, they told me it was only Sir Philip Sassoon taking a bath.'[174]

In July, thanks to an astonishing remission, Marcel dined 'every evening or almost' at the Ritz, always on his own;[175] he knew every nook and cranny there, from the kitchens to the freezer room, he knew how to get rid of cockroaches, he could operate the showers.[176] Feeling the 'need for fresh air', he even contemplated taking a holiday.[177] But, because he caught another cold on 7 July, he missed the opportunity to have his portrait drawn by the great English artist and novelist Wyndham Lewis.[178] Nevertheless, he came close to fighting a duel with a drunkard who had insulted him, but who later apologized, Jacques Delgado: on 15 July Jaloux and Paul Brach (a young poet and novelist, who was one of the 'evening visitors' that year, and who died prematurely in 1939, after having edited the *Correspondance générale* with Robert Proust)[179] took him to the cabaret. 'Everybody had been drinking (not me),' Marcel related, and from this sprang a brawl with some pimps who were 'unbelievable', especially since 'the manager and the staff had taken the side of the pimps and the poofs': 'I believed that the charming age of duels was beginning once more for me, but it appears that the assailants were not the sort of people with whom one can fight.'[180] And he came close to having a 'very hot chicken', followed by an ice-bucket, thrown at his head.

Shortly before 20 July *L'Intransigeant* asked Proust: 'And if the world were coming to an end . . . what would you do?' He replied that 'life would suddenly seem delightful, if we were threatened with death as you suggest . . . Ah! if only the cataclysm does not happen this time, we should not fail to visit the new galleries at the Louvre, to throw ourselves at the feet of Mlle X . . . to visit India. The cataclysm does not take place, we do none of these things, for we find ourselves back in the swing of normal life again, where negligence dulls desire.'[181] He was less than four months away from his own death. He taught this lesson, too, to Gaston Gallimard, who thought his own life was 'inane': happiness 'flows freely among those who do not seek satisfaction and who live outside of themselves for an idea'.[182]

In early August Marcel read *Lucienne*, by Jules Romains, and imagined, wrongly, that it bore similarities to his own work, something he detested: 'I came across sentences in *Lucienne* that were mine almost word for word,' he wrote to the author (while at the same time expressing reservations about his style) – which gave him the melancholy impression that Romains had read nothing by him, as well as the 'reassuring feeling of a sort of endorsement of the truthfulness' of his ideas and images.[183] Romains replied that he had read him; firstly *Guermantes II*, which Proust had sent him, and then, slowly, *Swann*, which Adrienne Monnier had given him, and he denied any influence: 'In my eyes you are a splendid heretic.'[184] At the same period Proust made a curious admission to Paul Brach: 'I am beginning to say a little less frequently: "I shall drown you in an ocean of shit",[185] proof of a reversion to a very infantile, anal stage, which also characterizes his sexuality.

On 20 August he was asphyxiated by a fire in the chimney, which made him go outside, even though it was three o'clock in the morning.[186] Around this time, following Paul Morand's example, he decided he wanted to give *Les Œuvres libres* a further extract from *La Prisonnière*, and he admitted to Gallimard and to Duvernois that it was 'for the simple reason that *Les Œuvres libres* pays better than the other magazines';[187] it would appear in 1923 under the title 'Précaution inutile', because Gallimard preferred another title to 'La Prisonnière'.[188] Jacques Rivière even mentioned a plan to publish 'La Fugitive' in Duvernois' magazine [*Les Œuvres libres*],[189] and he requested 'Le Sommeil d'Albertine' for the *NRF* (for the November issue: Proust proposed a new title, 'La regarder dormir')[190] as well as the Paris street cries. His dealings with *Les Œuvres libres* gave rise to a lively dispute with Gallimard, who eventually gave way. Proust wanted to give 'six thousand lines' to this magazine, but Gallimard told him to 'try to shorten it'.[191]

A few worrying signs now became apparent, rather like blows of fate: on 4 September Marcel fell down five times 'through dizziness'.[192] On the 8th he complained of fainting fits: 'As soon as I get out of bed, I lose my balance and I fall . . . Living is not always easy.'[193] Schiff made him anxious by talking to him about the Scott-Moncrieff translation into English with the overall title of *Remembrance of Things Past*, and *Swann's Way* for the first volume, which his English friend considered a mistranslation: 'It destroys the title,' wrote Proust to Gallimard,* and he pointed out to the translator that 'the intended amphibology of *Temps perdu*, which corresponds to the *Temps retrouvé* at the end of the book, disappears'.[194] On 18 September he went to a hotel where his former valet, Forssgren, had arranged to meet him, but they did not find one another.[195] Over the following days he was seized with violent attacks of asthma. Doctor Bize, who gave him an

---

* *Corr.*, vol. XXI, 14 September 1922. The title was taken from a Shakespeare sonnet, as were the majority of the titles of the different volumes.

injection of evatmine and cola to revive him, reckoned he was in the process of 'killing himself' over the extracts for the *NRF*, and reproved him for working 'in such a state'.[196] He returned on 28 September and left a very weary Marcel, in no state to see Rivière. At the beginning of October, he may have gone, according to Céleste (though the correspondence does not mention it), to a soirée at the Beaumonts for the last time. It was there, already ill with flu, that he must have caught another chill.[197]

After that, it was a slow chronicle of pathological symptoms. On 11 October Marcel noted that his temperature had 'risen appreciably'. There was a succession of pathetic notes to Céleste: 'I have just coughed more than three thousand times'; 'I am feeling impossibly tense'.[198] Mingled with his complaints was his exquisite kindness: 'I have so much fever . . . I have written some gentle, pretty poems about you.'[199] On 21 October he received a note from his brother, who had already come to talk to him, though 'too much as a doctor and he had upset him', having spoken of a clinic and a nurse:[200] Bize had done some tests which showed that Marcel had pneumococci, and Robert advised him to summon his doctor back.[201] Proust wanted to ask for some medical information from Jacques Rivière's brother, who was a doctor: in actual fact, he wanted to check the meaning of the word pneumococcus, which he meant to discuss in his novel, and on 25 October he obtained a sensible scientific definition.[202] Shortly afterwards Reynaldo, on Robert's behalf, wrote him a very affectionate letter begging him to allow himself to be looked after: his brother would not leave him and would play the role of nurse; Hahn observed, however, that Céleste (on Marcel's instructions, no doubt) would not allow Robert into the room again, and Proust would eat nothing further, not even a little purée.[203] It was a last attempt to reason with the invalid.

On 25 October Proust wrote to Rivière, who thought only of the *NRF*, and who was unaware of the state of Marcel's health, informing him that the previous day he had put the finishing touches to *La Prisonnière*: 'And then, Jacques, imagine a miserable wretch who is at his last gasp and who, feeling better yesterday, corrected a whole book for Gaston.'[204] On 30 October or 1 November, Proust wrote to Gaston: 'At this moment I think that the most urgent thing is to hand over all of my books to you. The sort of relentless fury that has gone into *La Prisonnière* (ready but needs to be reread) . . . this determination, especially in the state I've been in these past few days, means that I've had to put aside the volumes that come afterwards. But three days of rest may be enough, I'm stopping dear Gaston/ Letter will follow when able.'[205] These heartbreaking words, in which the punctuation and the syntax are beginning to disappear, would be the last he wrote to his publisher and friend. Gaston acknowledged receipt of the manuscript of *La Prisonnière* on 7 November.

ALBERTINE DISPARUE

The first 'public' appearance of this title occurred in an advertisement in the *NRF* of 1 December 1922[206] (printed before Proust's death): the editors of the magazine and the publishing house therefore knew about this new title by Proust.

After arranging for just the manuscript of *La Prisonnière* (which would be revised after his death by Robert Proust and Jacques Rivière, given the publication date of 1923), not all his manuscripts, as he had first indicated, to be delivered to Gallimard, Proust returned to the typescript (which was duplicated;* he only worked on the top copy and kept the carbon copy intact) of his manuscript at page 527. At the top of the page, in hand, he wrote: 'N.B. Here begins Albertine disparue, sequel to the preceding novel la prisonnière.' He deleted the first lines up until '*il fallait la faire cesser immédiatement*' ['I must put an end to it at once'] and adding '*ma souffrance*' ['my anguish'], and he inserted in the margin: 'ALBERTINE Disparue chapter I. So what I had believed to be nothing to me was simply my entire life! How ignorant one is of oneself.'[207] There was nothing exceptional in any of this up until now, apart from the confirmation of a title: for fear of being accused of plagiarism, Proust had abandoned 'La Fugitive', but retained *La Prisonnière*, and he proposed a breakdown into chapters. We must now jump to page 648 of the typescript.[208] At the bottom of the first paragraph, Proust had written: 'End', which he crossed out and replaced with 'end of first chapter of Albertine disparue' (repeated at the foot of the page). And, in the margin, there is a first annotation: 'NB Definitely not. La Prisonnière will make up a whole and Albertine', which

---

* Proust wrote to Gallimard in June 1922 on the subject of 'Sodome III': 'The work of redoing this typescript, to which I am making additions everywhere and changing everything has scarcely begun. It is true that a duplicate copy has been made' (*Corr.*, vol. XXI, pp. 544–5). Let us be clear: the alterations could always be called into question thanks to the duplicate copy. This duplicate can be found in the Bibliothèque Nationale, in its entirety, though annotated by Robert Proust and the 1925 editors. The top copy was discovered by M. Claude Mauriac, who saw fit to show it to me, and to allude to my communications with Nathalie Mauriac, in *L'Oncle Marcel* (Grasset, 1988), pp. 330–85). She did some considerable work editing and interpreting this document, and two editions were printed (the second in Livre de Poche, Hachette).

he crossed out (we are to understand: and Albertine as well); then a second: 'End of Albertine disparue, or if M. Gallimard prefers to have a longer book: End of the first part of Albertine disparue', which was also deleted. At the top of the page, he then wrote: 'N.B. At the foot of this page ends the first chapter of "Albertine disparue". From 648 to 898 nothing I've removed everything. So we skip from 648 to chapter II of Albertine disparue. We must jump without a break to chapter two 898.'* Finally, on page 936, after the word 'premise', there is a mark which accompanies the marginal addition: 'End of Albertine disparue.'[209] Most important is the reference to Gallimard: Proust, hounded by death, may have wished for a complete and (relatively) short volume, such as the one which he had already spoken to his publisher about: *La Prisonnière*, and a chapter of *Albertine disparue*, which would end provisionally there: 'End of Albertine disparue'; but this book could always be increased in size, 'if M. Gallimard prefers to have a longer book', which leads us to: 'End of the first part of Albertine disparue.' And then a qualm: 'Definitely not. La Prisonnière will make up a whole and Albertine' ('as well', I believe). Thus Proust abandoned the idea of an Albertine that was an appendage to the preceding novel, and then he made a further deletion: we certainly have the ending for a first chapter. As for the pages that were 'removed', they have never been found, and are only known through the duplicate typescript, which Proust must have used as a spare copy or for reference. So what is the solution to the enigma posed by this last-minute removal of material, and by an important textual addition: Albertine dies, not in Touraine any longer, but at Montjouvain?† As far as I am concerned, this was an experimental version, an experiment that was tragically interrupted, the creator of which was already semi-conscious in those early days of November. Just as some people on their death-bed disinherit their family so as to leave everything to their nurse, Proust removed some of the finest passages from Albertine in order to bestow them on a hypothetical 'Sodome IV or V'.

Another hypothesis has been put forward by Giovanni Macchia:

---

* Cf. *Corr.*, vol. XXI, to C. Albaret: 'You see that my coughing fits have begun again because I spoke to you. Cross out everything (except what we left in *Albertine disparue* – up to my arrival in Venice with my mother' (facsimile in *BAMP*, no. 40, 1990, pp. 100–1). Kolb has inserted a parenthesis after 'disparue', which has a bearing on the meaning.

† The reader of the short version understands immediately that Albertine has come to meet Mlle Vinteuil or her friend at Montjouvain. It is worth remembering that the Daudets' property was all that Proust knew of Touraine.

supposing that Proust had shortened his book not for Gallimard, but for *Les Œuvres libres?* Since he had extracted a summary from *Sodome* to provide 'Jalousie', as well as a second extract from *La Prisonnière* that became 'Précaution inutile' (published in February 1923), he may have had a triptych in mind, and may have retained a shorter version of 'Albertine disparue' for Duvernois. The general public would then have had a short novel about Albertine, about love, death and forgetting.* All that is lacking to support this thesis is a letter (which Proust would, in any case, have been incapable of writing at the time); what is more, the mention of 'M. Gallimard' seems to point to the shorter version being intended for the NRF.†

In short, given the present state of the documents and their interpretation, I believe that the spirit should prevail over the letter, and the complete duplicate copy of the typescript of *Albertine disparue* over the one that has been shorn of over 250 typed pages. Even if he had wished to do so, Proust did not have time to put together this sequel in which he would have inserted the pages that had been removed. And the most uncompromising editors do not consider that these passages could have been suppressed definitively by an artist who was always making additions and who never deleted material. It would not have been long before Proust realized that, by inserting the second part of chapter I and chapter II after the trip to Venice, the reader, who already knows everything, would find it hard to be interested in these majestic shreds, which correspond to a stage that is already surpassed at the time of the trip to Italy. He must have abandoned a working hypothesis that was dictated not by beauty – it should be stressed that the removed passages are aesthetically perfect,

---

* *Corriere della Sera*, 13 and 14 October 1991; *L'Ange de la nuit*, Gallimard, 1993, pp. 237–58. See also the edition of *Albertine disparue* by Jean Milly, Champion, 1992, which gives both versions and dates the shorter one to a period between 7 and 17 November (the very period when Céleste, thanking Rivière for sending a copy of *Aimée*, wrote to him that 'Monsieur is not aware of anything') and the Italian edition, edited by A. Beretta Anguissola, *Alla ricerca del tempo perduto*, Milan, Mondadori; 4 vols., 1983–93, pp. 782–97, 816–19, 882–3 (in which he shows that the visit to Venice was pruned dramatically in the shorter version), which in my view is the most thorough and far-reaching examination of the question. Note that A. Beretta Anguissola reckons that a volume entitled 'Sodome IV' could have begun after the visit to Venice and ended with the part entitled 'M. de Charlus pendant la guerre' in *Le Temps retrouvé*, which would then have begun with the Narrator's final return to Paris, for the Guermantes' reception (p. 919). This is only a hypothesis. This Italian edition of *À la recherche* is furthermore admirable for the quality of its translation, its presentation and its notes.

† Unless it meant: if M. Gallimard prefers that *Les Œuvres libres* should have only this chapter.

and 'among the most beautiful and most profound that Proust wrote'* –
but by the pathetic desire to have the episode which he considered to be
the most beautiful in his book, 'the death of Albertine, the forgetting',[210]
published quickly – the shorter it was, the easier it would be to print and
to correct, and so the quicker it would appear.

DEATH

But while Proust was grappling with the pages of *Albertine*, he was
withstanding a very different sort of struggle, which seems to have escaped
the discussions of insensitive philologists. First of all there was a viral
infection, a pneumonia which Marcel made no attempt to treat, since he
refused the injections of camphorated oil which Doctor Bize wanted him
to have, and though he had the prescribed medicaments bought for him,
he would not take any of them. Secondary infections developed. An
abscess formed on the lung, which led to septicaemia. The drama was
played out over several weeks, during which Marcel exhausted his remaining strength in correcting his manuscripts – that of *La Prisonnière* up until
the end of October, that of *Albertine disparue* in November – although he
was in a semi-comatose state at the time. The question arises: could Proust
have cured himself had he looked after himself? If we consider that before
the discovery of antibiotics, pneumonia (a disease that has never stopped
inflicting casualties) was treated with digitalin and cupping-glasses,† that
Proust's organism was completely wasted, his lungs progressively ravaged
by asthma (which can also be fatal) and his heart worn out, then the
answer must be no.‡ For a year he had felt himself decline, and he no
longer spoke of his illness, but of his death: he had sufficient medical
knowledge to understand that his illness left him with little hope. On the
other hand, we must admire the fact that he battled for such a long time,

* Beretta Anguissola, *Alla ricerca*, pp. 785–6. This critic compares this descent into the underworld
of feelings of guilt, followed by a return to life (the involuntary memory of the baptistery of St Mark's
where the baptism of Christ is depicted), to Freud's most lucid analyses of the roots and the cure
of neurosis.

† This was the treatment that was attempted on the final day, camphorated oil, intended to
stimulate the heart, replacing digitalin.

‡ He confided in Céleste: 'Ever since childhood, the asthma attacks have absolutely ruined my
health . . . My bronchial tubes are nothing but cooked rubber, my heart itself no longer breathes,
used up as it is by the effort of so many years trying to obtain the air I lacked. I am a very old man,
Céleste, old like my aged lungs and my ancient heart. I shall not live for much longer' (C. Albaret,
p. 401).

up to the age of fifty-one, like Balzac, sustained by his fierce determination to complete his book.

From now on we must rely on the few facts, related on numerous occasions by the one and only Céleste – alone before history, just as she was alone with Proust – assisted by Odilon, who were the only people to be privy to the tragedy. In a copy of *Jeunes Filles* Proust had inscribed these undiscovered lines to them: 'To the young woman in flowers (no flowers without thorns, alas!) but, over the top of our blood-stained clothes, there smiles peacefully with her mirror-of-heaven eyes, a Joan of Arc-Récamier-Botticelli, who does seem to be smiling at us, but what an error! Her husband, dear Odilon, leans forward like the Titian in Laura Dianti's painting. But, a mirror reflected by a mirror, it is not at Odilon nor at me that she smiles, but at herself.'* Together, the Albarets guarded the closed door. Reynaldo came every day, wrote down his questions on a piece of paper, and Céleste transcribed the sick man's replies on to it. Around 15 November, Doctor Bize, frantic at the state of health of his patient, who was refusing to eat – Marcel had said he would do this, just as his grandfather Nathé Weil had done, and he drank only iced beer, herbal tea or milky coffee – went to look for Robert Proust. It was then that the latter made one final attempt to have his brother moved to the Piccini clinic; Marcel sent him away. On 17 November he declared to Céleste: 'Tomorrow will be the ninth day of my attack. If I get over it, I shall show the doctors what I'm made of. Ah! Céleste, I knew you were kind, but I would never have thought that you could be to such an extent.'

And, during the night, he dictated some sentences to do with Bergotte's death: a partially incoherent passage, into which he put himself, and he described the activity of the doctors dancing attendance on the dying man: 'They stood out among themselves, giving each other an imposing position in the background, but a gloomy one . . . they approached the patient, held endless conferences among one another, but as to talking to him about his condition . . . no, medicine was not something for the sick. How incredibly rude, said Bergotte. He wanted to know how much time . . .' Another fragment: 'And then one day it all changed. Everything that had been detestable to us, that had always been forbidden, was allowed. "But for example, I couldn't have some champagne?" "But

---

* 'Céleste, the good-hearted servant, describes Proust's last days for us', *Les Nouvelles littéraires*, no. 1316, 20 November 1952. Céleste claimed to have given this copy of *Jeunes Filles* to Reynaldo Hahn as a present (p. 435).

absolutely, if that gives you pleasure." It was scarcely credible. Brands were ordered which had been those that were most forbidden, and it was this that lent something rather despicable to this unbelievable frivolity of the dying.'* This expression, which Proust jotted down on the night he died, had been unearthed a very long time ago, when he was translating *The Bible of Amiens*. ' "There's nothing so frivolous as dying," said Emerson.'[211] Marcel quoted it, without mentioning that the words were not his, to Montesquiou in 1912: 'It's the frivolity that ensues after an appalling attack of the kind that I had this afternoon (There's nothing so frivolous as death) that is responsible for a remark of this kind.'[212] It arose again finally, as if to bring some comfort to the dying man dreaming of champagne. At about three o'clock in the morning, Proust, who had been dictating or writing and was exhausted, let his head fall back on the pillow. He asked that his lamp with the green shade should be left alight. It was at dawn on Saturday 18 November that he thought he saw a large woman dressed in black appear, whom no one could touch, and whom poor Céleste promised to make go away. That afternoon Doctor Bize came to give him an injection of camphorated oil; Marcel pinched Céleste, whom he had asked to ensure that none was given him, for having disobeyed him. Robert Proust then arrived, and applied useless cupping-glasses: 'I'm tiring you, my dearest Marcel . . .' 'Oh, yes, my dear Robert.' Then the professor had oxygen tanks brought. Babinski came and observed that there was nothing more to be done. Robert and Céleste returned to the bedroom: 'M. Proust's eyes never left us. It was dreadful.'† Five minutes later, between five and six o'clock in the evening, it was all over. Reynaldo Hahn took on the responsibility of alerting Proust's friends and he spent the night watching over him. Abbé Mugnier came the following day to recite prayers, as Marcel, it appears, had wished. Helleu and Dunoyer de Segonzac sketched him, and Man Ray photographed him, on his death-bed. The funeral took place on Wednesday 22 November at the Père-Lachaise cemetery. The Albarets stayed at rue Hamelin until April 1923 to put everything in order and to file the papers with Robert Proust. But Céleste did not leave Marcel: 'He has never forsaken me. Every time that I have

---

* *RTP*, vol. III, p. 1667, n. 4. In *RTP*, vol. IV, p. 203, Proust speaks of 'these forbidden foodstuffs which are no longer refused to the dying, when it is certain that they can no longer be cured'.

† C. Albaret, p. 430. On the morning of 18 November, according to Céleste, he must have referred to some shares that he had sold, the revenue from which he wanted to bequeath to her, and to write her a cheque, but he feared that the signature of a dying man would not be recognized: 'My God, Céleste, how sorry I am . . . how sorry!'

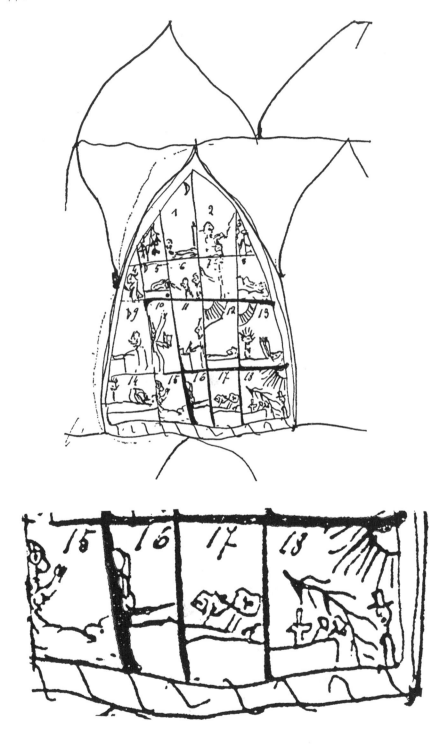

had to take a step in my life, I have found an admirer of M. Proust's who has smoothed over the difficulties for me, and it was as if, in death, he continued to protect me.'[213]

Thus arrived the day, so frequently forecast, 'when the fading brightness merges and effaces every last shimmer, in which the reflecting water has become the water of Lethe'.[214] Marcel Proust had alluded humorously to his own death, one day in July 1910, as he sketched stained-glass windows for Reynaldo (in the caption, Marcel is called Buncht, and Hahn Bunchtnibuls): 'Doktor-medic with spectacles tells Buncht that he going to die', 'Death of Buncht (this window has suffered much)', 'Bouquets have been placed on the bed where Buncht lies dead', 'Tomb of Buncht upon which lie flowers, with trees and hawthorns above, and sun now that it causes him no harmch. And his Bunchtnibuls, wearing a top hat, comes to the little Kemetery to pay his last respects to Buncht.'[215] And we too address our respects to a man who suffered so much in order that his work should shine like the sun, now that it causes him no more harm.

List of Abbreviations

C. Albaret   *Monsieur Proust*, Laffont, 1973

G. de Diesbach   *Proust*, Perrin, 1991

G. Painter   *Marcel Proust: A Biography*, revised and enlarged edition, Pimlico, 1996

BN   Bibiothèque Nationale

Notes

PREFACE

1. M. Schwob, *Vies Imaginaires*, Gallimard, 1957, p. 22.
2. G. de Diesbach, *Proust*. (See Bibliography, p. 932.)
3. *CSB*, p. 556, article about Reynaldo Hahn. (See List of Abbreviations, p. 781.)
4. Ibid., p. 674.
5. J. Risset, *Le Monde*, 5 March 1993.

CHAPTER 1: *Roots*

1. On the Auteuil of Proust's time, see Denise Mayer's study, 'Le jardin de Marcel Proust', published in my *Études proustiennes*, vol. V, Gallimard, 1984, pp. 9–51. A somewhat fanciful account is given by G. de Diesbach, *Proust*.
2. J.-É. Blanche, *Propos de Peintre, De David à Degas*, Émile-Paul, 1919, Foreword by Marcel Proust. This is referred to again in *CSB*, pp. 570–86.
3. Ibid., p. 573.
4. Valentine Thomson, 'My Cousin Marcel Proust', *Harpers Magazine*, vol. 164, May 1932, pp. 710–20, quoted by G. Painter, *Marcel Proust*, p. 423.
5. *CSB*, p. 570.
6. *JS*, p. 278. Exactly sixty hawthorn trees.
7. *RTP*, vol. I, draft LXII, p. 852.
8. *JS*, p. 310. An urban tree, as Mayer points out in 'Le jardin', p. 21; they are not found at Illiers.
9. 'The chestnut trees', *P et J*, p. 142.
10. A. Dumas, *Le Comte de Monte-Cristo*, Garnier, 1962, vol. I, ch. XLIV, 'La maison d'Auteuil', p. 642.
11. *Les Environs de Paris*, ed. P. Boizard, Paris, 1855, p. 362, quoted by Mayer, 'Le jardin', pp. 9–10.
12. *CSB*, p. 575: 'Returning to Paris in the evening, he passed by the railway viaduct, and the sight of the wagons that were able to transport those insane

seekers after the unknown beyond the "break of day" or "Boulogne", made him feel, deep within his compartment, an intense feeling of *Suave mari magno*. "And to think", he cried, as he looked at the train with a mixture of astonishment, pity and fear, "to think that there are people who like travelling!"'

13. Ibid., p. 572.

14. *Journal, 1870–1871*, ed. Charpentier, p. 22, 1 March 1871.

15. Ibid., p. 317.

16. *RTP*, vol. I, p. 14; vol. IV, p. 623. *JS*, p. 868.

17. P. Vidal de La Blanche, *Tableau de la géographie de la France*, 1903, repub. Tallandier, 1979, p. 146.

18. See *RTP*, vol. I, draft XXIII, XXV.

19. On this point, Painter corrected his first edition of *Marcel Proust* (p. 514).

20. For instance, Querqueville and Bricquebec, the original names for Balbec (which itself derives from Bolbec).

21. On Illiers, see Canon Marquis, *Illiers*, historical archives of the diocese of Chartres, 1904, 2nd ed., 1907; A. Ferré, *Géographie de Marcel Proust*, Sagittaire, 1939.

22. *Textes retrouvés*, pp. 178–9. Perhaps he is thinking of Renoir's wheat fields.

23. *JS*, p. 281; the other names for Illiers are Éteuilles, Étheuilles, Sargeau: see *JS*, p. 277, n. 2. Éteuilles could have derived from Auteuil.

24. *RTP*, vol. I, p. 103 and n. 3 (Hilarius). The etymology is taken from J. Quicherat, *De la formation française des anciens noms de lieu*, Paris, 1867, pp. 65–6.

25. *RTP*, vol. I, draft XV, p. 702. Cf. drafts XVI, pp. 703–4, XVII, pp. 712–14, XXIV, p. 730 ff., XXV, p. 734, XXVI, pp. 734–6, XXVIII, pp. 738–43.

26. Reprinted in *Chroniques*, pp. 114–22.

27. *RTP*, vol. I, draft XXVII, p. 737.

28. *JS*, p. 281.

29. As noted by Ferré, *Géographie*, p. 93.

30. *RTP*, vol. I, drafts LVIII–LX, pp. 842–51; already in *JS*, pp. 284–6, 295–7, 305–9, 322–5. In this garden, Marcel met his Amiot cousins, which he mentions in this unfinished novel.

31. 'Impressions de route en automobile', *CSB*, pp. 63–9.

32. From the name of the Arrachepels, as Canon Marquis points out in *Illiers*, *RTP*, vol. III, pp. 204–53.

33. *JS*, p. 314. The Introduction to *Sésame et les lys* provides a fuller description of the room: copper bedstead with white curtains and laden with quilts, counterpanes, cambric pillowcases; hem-stitched stoles on the armchairs; clocks in glass cases, sea-shells, a chest of drawers on which stood two vases, a guipure lace cloth, a picture of the Saviour and some palms that had been blessed, and a prie-dieu; three layers of curtains over the window,

making it difficult and comical to open it; on the wall, an etching of the Prince Eugène (*CSB*, pp. 164–7).

34. *CSB*, p. 161.

35. *JS*, p. 304.

36. Ibid., pp. 281, 320. The cook in question is Félicie Fiteau (*CSB*, p. 161).

37. *CSB*, p. 161.

38. *JS*, p. 322. Cf. *CSB*, p. 168.

39. *JS*, p. 286.

40. Ibid., p. 293. P.-L. Larcher, in 'La ferme des Aigneux', *BAMP* no. 16, 1966, has identified the farm belonging to the Aigneux, the destination of Sunday walks (*JS*, p. 349), as the place known as 'le Galerne', the farm where Mme Prévert, Mme Laudet in *Jean Santeuil*, served cider.

41. *JS*, p. 300.

42. *Corr.*, vol. XXI, p. 605.

43. Marquis, *Illiers*.

44. *RTP*, vol. III, p. 204.

45. See the death of the grandmother and Jupien's brothel.

46. *Textes retrouvés*, pp. 173–80.

47. *Corr.*, vol. III, 29 July 1903, p. 383. Cf. 'L'église de village' (*Le Figaro*, 3 September 1912, *Chroniques*, pp. 114–22). Canon Marquis was then in his seventies.

48. P. Bourdrel, *Histoire des juifs de France*, Albin Michel, 1974, pp. 138, 562.

49. Ibid., p. 143.

50. This information, and that which follows, comes from D. Cohen, *La Promotion des Juifs en France à l'époque du second Empire (1852–1870)*, University of Provence, 1980, pp. 56–599; Cohen excludes 'those whom one may call *half-Jews*, born to a Jewish mother or father', as was Marcel Proust. See also J. Ruffie, *De la biologie à la culture*, Flammarion, 1976, p. 454: 'Every investigation carried out hitherto proves that there is no biological characteristic that enables one to distinguish between a Jew and a non-Jew.'

51. Cohen, *La Promotion*, p. 332. It is worth noting that in the Bas-Rhin, for example, the number of indigent Jews was twice that of other religions in 1871.

52. Ibid., pp. 429–31.

53. Ibid., p. 796: 'Do Christian families seek to marry into wealthy Jewish families?'

54. D. Mayer, unpublished memoirs and conversations with the author.

55. C. Francis and F. Gontier, *Marcel Proust et les siens*, and *Souvenirs de S. Mante-Proust*, Plon, 1981, p. 35.

56. Ibid., p. 17.

57. At the family tomb, at Père-Lachaise, the inscription reads: 'Baruch Weil died in 1828/ member of the Schools committee/ chief administrator of the

Temple/ vice-president of the Comité israélite in Paris.' A. Fournier, 'Du côté de chez Proust', *Europe*, August–September 1970, p. 247. B. Weil had lived at 55 rue du Temple, and later at 23 rue Boucherat (now rue de Turenne).

58. R. Soupault, *Marcel Proust, du côté de la médecine*, Plon, 1967, p. 34.

59. D. Mayer, 'Nathé Weil and Léon Levot', unpublished memoirs. On this trade, see E. Feydeau, *Mémoires d'un coulissier*, Calmann-Lévy, 1882. The Narrator refers to his stockbroker in *Albertine disparue* (at this time it was probably Lionel Hauser).

60. Confidential information from D. Mayer.

61. *Corr.*, vol. XXI, letters 393, 395, 400.

62. Ibid., letter 402, p. 556. Ten francs on 30 January 1889, to pay off some debts, and for 'a little pleasure, of a light-hearted nature'.

63. Ibid., p. 555.

64. Fournier, 'Du côté de chez Proust'; *Le Bottin mondain*, 1830–51; *Corr.*, vol. II, p. 62, announcement of death. Maurice Duplay recalled 'this Weil uncle, the wealthy bachelor who was a friend of whores and Laure Hayman's protector, with his cloth skullcap, his vague manner and mysterious behaviour', who 'was more like an alchemist than an old boy trying not to look his age' (*Mon ami Marcel Proust*, Gallimard, 1972, p. 18).

65. Did Proust know that this house had belonged to the sister of Punkett, the close friend of Pierre Loti and the protagonist of Loti's *Aziyadé*? Thus the shades of Loti, of Dumas *fils*, and, through Monte-Cristo, of Dumas *père*, inhabit this part of Auteuil.

66. Catalogue of the 1971 Jacquemart-André exhibition, no. 32, a signed letter from Marie Van Zandt to Louis Weil.

67. Catalogue of the 1965 Bibliothèque Nationale exhibition, no. 317. In *RTP*, Morel gives back to the Narrator the photographs belonging to this Uncle Adolphe. One wonders whether the photograph of Louise Théo triggered the wrath of Marcel's parents.

68. *RTP*, vol. III, pp. 91, 94. Schiller's play, *Der neffe als onkel*, was translated with the title *Oncle ou neveu?* in 1892. The word 'uncle' appears six times more frequently in *RTP* than it does in the average contemporary text.

69. *RTP*, vol. I, p. 71, and Fournier, 'Du côté de chez Proust', p. 249.

70. *Corr.*, vol. II, p. 62.

71. Ibid., vol. V, p. 180, 29 May 1905: '*La Libre Parole* had said that a certain number of young Jews, among them M. Marcel Proust, etc., despised Barrès. To correct this impression one would have had to say that I was not a Jew and that I did not dislike him.'

72. A. de Fouquières, *Mon Paris et ses Parisiens*, P. Horay, 1953, pp. 139–41. It is from him that Painter obtained his information. Cf. R. Dreyfus, *Souvenirs sur Marcel Proust*, pp. 44–8 (Grasset, 1926, pp. 129–30). Just as Odette calls on Cottard, so Laure Hayman visited Adrien Proust.

73. Duplay, *Mon ami Marcel Proust*, pp. 10–11.

74. *RTP*, vol. IV, draft LXIX, p. 976.

75. *Corr.*, vol. III, p. 455.

76. Ibid., vol. VI, p. 206, September 1906. The suggestion was made at the time Marcel had just lost his mother and his uncle. He did not want it for the tomb, but accepted it for somewhere else. We do not know whether this bust was ever finished.

77. Ibid., vol. I, pp. 102–3.

78. Ibid., p. 152.

79. *JS*, pp. 243, 245.

80. *Corr.*, vol. I, p. 138. Cf. ibid., quotation from Loti's *Roman d'un enfant*.

81. D. Mayer, unpublished memoirs.

82. *Corr.*, vol. III, p. 356; in 1900 Gregh had gone to stay for six weeks at Doctor Dubois's clinic in Berne. In 1903, Proust sent Gregh Dubois's book *De l'influence de l'esprit sur le corps*, Berne, 1901.

83. Ibid., p. 438.

84. Ibid., vol. XXI, p. 542. Cf. ibid., the desire for 'a long (healthy) walk'. In the same letter, Marcel compares his grandmother to Greece: 'the finest tribute I can pay her'.

85. Ibid., p. 545.

86. *Corr. avec sa mère*, p. 14, 12 September 1889 (*Corr.*, vol. I, p. 133): 'Une lettre très drôle de ton oncle G.'

87. Ibid., 7 September 1889 (*Corr.*, vol. I, p. 129).

88. Ibid., p. 39.

89. *Corr.*, vol. XVII, p. 349. Louise Crémieux also performed in Banville's *Les Fourberies de Nérine*, which Léa performed in at the Trocadéro, in *RTP*, vol. III, p. 651.

90. *Corr.*, vol. I, p. 421, 20 August 1895. According to P. Kolb, *Ferdinand le Noceur* is the title of a successful play by Gandillot, put on at the Déjazet theatre.

91. *Corr.*, vol. I, p. 156.

92. Ibid., vol. I, p. 153, 14 August 1890.

93. Ibid., vol. II, p. 406, 17 August 1900.

94. Ibid., vol. IV, p. 301, 26 September 1904.

95. Ibid., vol. I, p. 155, 18 August 1890.

96. In 1883 Marcel wished Mme Nathé Weil, 'long and happy hours at the piano (keeping time!)' (Ibid., vol. XXI, p. 542).

97. 'Someone I know occasionally says to her son: "I wouldn't mind in the least if you married a woman who didn't know who Ruskin was, but I couldn't bear you to marry a woman who said 'tramvay' (instead of pronouncing it tramouay"' (*Sésame et les lys*, p. 89. n.2).

98. *Corr.*, vol. I, pp. 138–9.

99. Ibid., p. 141: 'Ah! How impatient this waiting makes me!' (*Esther*, II, 1).

100. Ibid., p. 147, 1 August 1890. Cf. the questionnaires which Marcel filled in as a boy.

101. 1896.

102. *Corr.*, vol. I, pp. 140–1, 1890.

103. Ibid., p. 138.

104. Ibid., vol. III, p. 393, 12 August 1903. La Fontaine, 'Les Deux Amis' (*Fables*, VIII, 11).

105. *Corr.*, vol. IV, p. 277.

106. Ibid., vol. III, p. 414.

107. Ibid., vol. II, p. 150, 23 October 1896.

108. Ibid., vol. III, p. 399, 18 August 1903. Cf. ibid., vol. IV, p. 299, 25 September 1904: 'Be sure to check your appearance. If you have to dress up during the day, are you sure that your suit is immaculate? But above all no more hair in the style of a Frankish king, your hair obstructs my view whenever I think of you.' Last complete letter to have been kept.

109. Ibid., vol. II, p. 122.

110. Ibid., p. 122, September 1896.

111. Ibid., pp. 340–1, 22 September 1899. So it is clear that Mme Proust was concerned about her son's male relationships.

112. Ibid., pp. 312, 324, 325, 327, 332, 333, 336, 341.

113. Ibid., vol. IV, p. 410, 1904? Proust met Weisweiller, like himself an asthmatic, at Évian in 1899.

114. Francis and Gontier, *Marcel Proust*, h.t., pp. 96–7.

115. Letter of 24 May 1903, Francis and Gontier, *Marcel Proust*, p. 227.

116. *Corr.*, vol. V, p. 354.

117. We have a photograph of him at the time of his doctorate; and another, when he was elected to the Académie de Médecine; the portrait of him in a toga was painted by his cousin, Lecomte de Nouy; there is a photograph of him on the balcony at the rue de Courcelles, with Robert (but not with Marcel).

118. The archives of the Paris prefecture of police.

119. Ibid., Adrien Proust file.

120. Though it is not unlikely, I have found no trace of Adrien Proust having been a Freemason.

121. R. Soupault, *Marcel Proust*, p. 44.

122. R. Le Masle, *Le Professeur Adrien Proust*, Lipschutz, 1935.

123. C. Vanderpooten, *Samuel Pozzi*, In Fine, V & O editions, 1992, p. 31.

124. There were 1,600 doctors in Paris in 1863, 1,962 in 1893, 3,342 in 1903. The eighth *arrondissement* breaks all the records (fifty-seven doctors per 10,000 inhabitants; one for every 175 people; the Paris average was one per 850). At the time that Adrien Proust became a professor (the salary in about 1900

was 15,000 francs per annum), there were nineteen chairs. See P. Darmon, *La vie quotidienne du médecin parisien en 1900*, Hachette, 1987.

125. Le Masle, *Adrien Proust*, pp. 33–4. A few dates: Pravaz introduced his hypodermic syringe in 1853; in 1857, Pasteur published his observations on lactic fermentation; in 1867, Lister treated antisepsis with phenol spray (continued by Pozzi); Koch discovered the tuberculosis bacilli in 1882; in 1884, the causes of tetanus, cholera and diphtheria were isolated.

126. Ibid., p. 35.

127. There are photographs of Professor Proust at Luxor, in agreeable company.

128. Le Masle, *Adrien Proust*, pp. 43–4.

129. *RTP*, vol. II, p. 750.

130. Ibid.

131. Aphasia, which Proust feared would afflict him at the end of his life.

132. In the same collection there is *L'Hygiène des asthmatiques* [Hygiene and Asthmatics], by E. Brissaud, 1896. See M. Miguet, 'La neurasthénie entre science et fiction', *BAMP*, no. 40, 1990.

133. *Textes retrouvés*, pp. 175–9. See J. Léonard, *Archives du corps. La santé au XIXe siècle*, ch. II, 'L'air respiré'; ch. V, 4, 'Alcool': 'The obsession with dust was to be applied very strictly to household chores' (p. 58).

134. *Textes retrouvés*, p. 171. Speech given at Chartres by Adrien Proust to mark the unveiling of the statue to Pasteur on 7 June 1903. The art historian Émile Mâle's knowledge was conveyed by the son to the father.

135. *Le Progrès*, a Republican newspaper in the Eure-et-Loir, 4 August 1903.

136. Doctor Le Masle recalls two, 'meteorological' in style, and confirms that Adrien Proust wrote few letters.

137. Duplay, *Mon ami Marcel Proust*, p. 15: 'Marcel, who was curious about everything, questioned my father on the subject of his profession.' His name also appears in the paper about Cottard and Odette (*RTP*, vol. IV).

138. Exhibited at the Bibliothèque Nationale in 1965; see *Corr.*, vol. I, p. 237.

139. Vanderpooten, *Samuel Pozzi*, p. 123. Robert Proust became Pozzi's assistant.

140. Marie Van Zandt (1861–1920), a singer at the Opéra-Comique, and the star of *Lakmé* in 1883, appears in *Jean Santeuil* (p. 686); *Corr.*, vol. I, p. 47. Another photograph, inscribed on 10 March 1881 by the singer Juliette Bilbault-Vauchelet, who was also a friend of Louis Weil. Bibliothèque Nationale, 1965 exhibition catalogue, no. 318.

141. Bibliothèque Nationale, 1965 exhibition catalogue, no. 319; *Corr.*, vol. VII, p. 242, n. 14. He may also have been influenced by the comic opera *Sacripant*, which was staged at the end of the Second Empire.

142. Soupault, *Marcel Proust*, pp. 122–3.

143. *RTP*, vol. IV, draft LXIX of *Le Temps retrouvé*, p. 978.

144. A. Germain, *Les Clés de Proust*, Sun, 1953, p. 146. Cf. *JS*, p. 866: 'M. Santeuil saw a great likelihood of unhappiness in his son's nature, owing to his health,

his gloomy character, his extravagance, his laziness, his absent mindedness, and the waste of his intelligence.'

145. *Corr.*, vol. IV, p. 31, 8 January 1904.

146. Ibid., vol. VII, p. 235.

147. *Corr. avec G. Gallimard*, p. 70, 6 November 1916, to Gaston Gallimard.

148. *JS*, p. 732, about the famous Doctor M.: 'He knows that a man who wrote fine books was someone who did not sleep, who believed he was ill, who had attacks of asthma which could not be cured . . .'

149. These include affection: 'All I will send you today is this brief token of my constant and tender thoughts for you. Until tomorrow, my dearest little Papa . . .' (*Corr.*, vol. I, p. 161, 23 September 1890).

150. *JS*, p. 859, and Jean cannot 'disguise his secret longing to hit his father, as he often did in his office when he drummed out a quick march against the table top'. A good analysis of the deeper causes of insignificant gestures.

151. Ibid., p. 865. Among several other mutually incompatible duties, M. Santeuil enjoys the friendship of the President of the Republic, which is a reference to the friendship between the Faure and the Proust families (p. 212).

152. Ibid., p. 866.

153. Ibid., p. 877.

154. Ibid., p. 213.

155. *Corr.*, vol. III, p. 443, obituary of Adrien Proust by Doctor Maurice de Fleury, himself the author of *Introduction à la médecine de l'esprit* (1897), *Grands Symptômes neurasthéniques* (1901), and *Manuel pour l'étude des maladies du système nerveux* (1904).

156. *RTP*, vol. III, pp. 586, 598, 616–17.

157. Ibid., vol. I, draft XII, p. 692. Cf. p. 673.

158. Ibid., vol. IV, p. 230. Cf. *JS*, p. 857: 'His imprisoned childhood, and whose only knowledge of the family was slavery.'

159. *RTP*, vol. I, pp. 488–90; vol. II, pp. 425–6, 594–600, 618.

160. A. Camus, *Théâtre, récits, nouvelles*, Bibliothèque de la Pléiade, pp. 1934–5.

161. Interview with Professor Proust about plague, *Le Matin*, 23 March 1899 (or 1900?), on the subject of a new epidemic.

162. The dream about parents changed into white mice comes into the episode at Doncières.

163. Duchêne, *L'Impossible Marcel Proust*, p. 464.

164. The transfer fees, according to the same source, amount to 21,238 francs and lawyer's fees to 16,000 francs, which shows the weakness of the inheritance laws at that time, added to which is the absence of any tax on revenue to balance the growth or disparity of the inheritance.

165. Darmon, *La vie quotidienne du médecin*, p. 146.

CHAPTER II: *Childhood*

1. *Corr.*, vol. XV, p. 241, to L. Daudet.
2. In particular L. Jones, *BAMP*, no. 12, 1962; M. L. Miller, *Psychanalyse de Proust*, Fayard, 1977, and G. D. Painter's *Marcel Proust: A Biography*. On the other hand, R. Soupault clarifies the matter excellently, *Marcel Proust, du côté de la médicine*, Plon, 1967, pp. 161–9. Soupault, who, like Doctor Pierre Mauriac, Doctor Giraudoux, and Doctor William James, was the brother of a writer, confirms the frequency of these fraternal couples: doctors and writers can discern the secrets of both body and soul.
3. *CSB*, de Fallois edition, p. 347. Proust entitled this passage 'Robert et le chevreau' in his *Carnet de 1908*.
4. Ibid., p. 349.
5. Ibid., p. 352.
6. *Corr.*, vol. I, p. 96, 2 January 1883, letter from Robert Proust concerning *Voyages involontaires* by Lucien Bart, the third volume of which they had just received.
7. Ibid., p. 113, 6 September 1888. Robert is riding.
8. Ibid., pp. 143, 146, 148.
9. M. Duplay, *Mon ami Marcel Proust*, Gallimard, 1972, pp. 18–19.
10. For a full sketch of Robert Proust, see R. Soupault, 'Robert Proust, frère de Marcel', *BAMP*, no. 17, 1967, pp. 553–68.
11. *Corr.*, vol. II, p. 450, 8 September 1901.
12. The quotation from *Rodogune* (V, 4, v. 1653) reads, 'Ô frère plus aimé que la clarté du jour'; Marcel replaced the word *'aimé'* with *'chéri'*, which is more affectionate (*Corr.*, vol. IV, p. 422, 12 June 1896).
13. *Corr.*, vol. I, p. 421, 20 August 1895. Cf. p. 423 (23 August 1895): 'Life there does not mean a thing to me!' Robert Proust had written to his mother asking for money. She replied humorously: 'My reply is filled only with my displeasure.' (The 'filled letter' contained banknotes.)
14. *Hommage à M. Proust*, p. 24.
15. His great-granddaughter, Nathalie Mauriac, strongly criticized him for this; nevertheless, it is Robert Proust who, by keeping the novel intact and publishing the complete text, has enabled us to appreciate its full depth and its beauty, which would disappear in an abridged version. Similarly, he supervised the publication of *La Prisonnière* (1923), *Le Temps retrouvé* (1927) and the *Correspondance générale* (after 1930).
16. T. Volckmann-Delabusse, 'Première crise d'asthme: 1880. Pourquoi?', *BAMP*, no. 17, 1967, p. 551.
17. *JS*, pp. 693–9.
18. *RTP*, vol. I, p. 4.

19. Ibid., draft II and variants, pp. 640, 641, 642. In draft III, p. 645, the cutting of the curls is compared to 'the fall of Cronus, the finding of Prometheus, the birth of Christ'.

20. Opera quoted by Proust.

21. *RTP*, vol. I, draft III, p. 645.

22. *JS*, pp. 202–11.

23. As a later letter from Proust to his mother testifies.

24. *JS*, p. 211.

25. This visit was described in *Jean Santeuil* (*Corr.*, vol. II, pp. 134–51).

26. *Corr.*, vol. VI, p. 28.

27. Ibid., vol. II, p. 444, 31 August 1901.

28. *L'Âge d'or. Souvenirs d'enfance et de jeunesse*, Grasset, 1947, p. 156.

29. R. Dreyfus, 'M. Proust in the Champs-Élysées', *Hommage à M. Proust*, pp. 27–30. *JS*, p. 218.

30. J.-É. Blanche, *Mes modèles*, Stock, 1928, repub. 1984, p. 100.

31. *JS*, p. 216.

32. *Qui êtes-vous?*, 1909, p. 38. *Jean Santeuil* (p. 123) attributes 'loose manners' to Mme Kossichef; similarly, Odette Swann, in the early drafts, is likened to 'a fat Russian woman'.

33. A. de Fouquières, *Mon Paris et ses Parisiens*, P. Horay, 1953, p. 113. On the French ambassador Nisard, the possible model for Norpois, ibid., p. 60; on Vera de Talleyrand, ibid., pp. 81–2.

34. Letter written in 1918 to Princesse Soutzo, *Corr.*, vol. XVII, p. 175.

35. *Corr.*, vol. I, p. 99. Cf. catalogues of the 1965 Bibliothèque Nationale exhibition, nos 59–65.

36. R. Dreyfus, *Hommage à M. Proust*, pp. 22–3, and *Souvenirs sur Marcel Proust*, Grasset, 1926, pp. 14–18.

37. *Corr.*, vol. XV, p. 75.

38. A. Ferré, *Les Années de collège de Marcel Proust*, Gallimard, 1959, pp. 66–67. Text in *CSB*, pp. 336–8.

39. *Corr.*, vol. I, p. 112, n. 6.

40. Ibid., note in *RTP*, vol. I, p. 1320.

41. *JS*, p. 326.

42. *RTP*, vol. I, draft II, 3, p. 643.

43. Here we see the first appearance of the famous words 'à la recherche'.

44. *RTP*, vol. I, draft III, p. 646. Hubert Robert's fountain appears elsewhere (*RTP*, vol. I, p. 40; vol. III, pp. 34, 56, 58), without this sexual context.

45. Tissot, repub. Le Sycomore, 1980, p. 31. Note by M. Delon, Louvet, *Faublas*, Folio classique. Cf. G. Ballet and A. Proust, *L'Hygiène du neurasthénique*, Masson, p. 154: 'At the time of puberty, those who by reason of hereditary abnormalities are prone to morbid impulses of any kind shall be subject to particularly careful supervision. The awakening of sexual instincts and desires can pro-

foundly affect the balance of the nervous system among adolescents. The majority of them resort to the practice of masturbation in an abusive way, and, as we have seen with the causes of neurasthenia in students, this can often be a powerful factor in nervous exhaustion.'

46. *RTP*, vol. I, p. 12.

47. *Corr.*, vol. XX, p. 403, July 1921.

48. Ibid., vol. XXI, pp. 550–1, 17 May 1888, to Nathé Weil.

49. Letter from M. Proust to J. Bizet, recopied by D. Halévy in his diary, dated 14 June 1888; *Corr. avec D. Halévy*, p. 43.

50. Four versions: *JS*, pp. 305–6; *RTP*, vol. IV, p. 232 and its variant *b*, p. 1128; vol. IV, p. 738: 'And so this basin of the Arsenal . . . filled me with the same mixture of disgust and fear that I experienced for the first time as a small child when I accompanied my mother to the Deligny baths.' And the father's swimming pool, *JS*, p. 307, 'square and mysterious'. The swimming pool becomes, p. 738, 'the free polar sea', an expression that terrified the child.

51. *JS*, p. 306.

52. *RTP*, vol. IV, p. 127.

53. *JS*, p. 307.

54. 'Marcel Proust intime', *Hommage à M. Proust*, p. 24.

55. 'L'indifférent', *La Vie contemporaine*, March 1896, and in book form, Gallimard, 1978, pp. 42–3.

56. *Corr.*, vol. XX, letter 223.

57. Quoted by R. Soupault, *Marcel Proust*, p. 222.

58. Ibid., p. 283. Cf. E. Brissaud, *L'Hygiène des asthmatiques*, Masson, 1896.

59. Duplay, *Mon ami Marcel Proust*, p. 10.

60. *RTP.*, vol. I, p. 582, and n. 2, n. 3.

61. Ibid., p. 583.

62. Ibid., vol. III, p. 413.

63. *Corr.*, vol. XIX, p. 609.

64. Ibid., vol. XX, p. 92, 29 January 1921. Jules Verne wrote a sequel to *The Narrative of Arthur Gordon Pym* entitled *The Sphinx of the Ice-fields*.

65. Ibid., vol. XII, p. 142, 1913, to H. Bordeaux. On Musset and Proust, J. Pommier, *BAMP*, no. 2, pp. 59–77; G. de Lauris, *À un ami*, Amiot-Dumont, 1948, p. 253; *Lettres à R. Hahn*, p. 176; M. Plantevignes, *Avec Marcel Proust*, Nizet, 1966, p. 47 (Proust compares himself with Fantasio), p. 56 (quoting Musset's poems). *JS*, pp. 130, 762.

66. *JS*, pp. 313–15. Cf. *CSB*, p. 239, against Faguet, who only likes the first volume of *Le Capitaine Fracasse*; *Sésame et les lys*, preface, pp. 20–31. Proust read *Le Capitaine Fracasse* aged fifteen, at Salies-de-Béarn, and read long excerpts from it to his grandmother (*Corr.*, vol. XXI, letter 388, August 1886).

67. In 1843 Saintine (1795–1865) had sent *Picciola* to Louis-Napoléon Bonaparte,

then in prison in the fort of Ham, who wrote to him: 'Your book reminds me of my kind-hearted grandmother, it reminds me of the precariousness of human things, of the unhappiness that exists in all regimes; it comforts me by its affirmation that the philosophical minded man has hidden treasures in his heart, which may occasionally allow him to experience happiness' (preface to the 1872 edition, p. xviii). The novel is quoted several times by Proust: *JS*, pp. 307–8, 332; *RTP*, vol. I, p. 144 (associated with the moon, with the theme of the faded flower and with 'those works that were naïvely unformed as were [his] own impressions'), and draft LV, p. 832.

68. *RTP*, vol. I, p. 832.
69. On Galland and Mardrus, the translator of *The Arabian Nights*, see *RTP*, vol. III, pp. 230–1.
70. *Corr.*, vol. IV, p. 113.

CHAPTER III: *The Schoolboy*

1. The lycée, founded in 1803 in a Capuchin monastery built by Brongniart (1790) had successively been known by the names Bonaparte, Bourbon, Condorcet in 1870, and Fontanes from 1874 to 1883.
2. Bibl. J. Guérin, Catalogue Ader-Tajan, 20 May 1992, no. 54. *Corr.*, vol. XXI, p. 540.
3. Ibid., vol. I, p. 95.
4. *JS*, p. 367: 'Our mother smiled as she watched us leave for the beach, always taking a book of Stevenson's with us.' Not a spade, or a ball or a boat. Just as they did when younger, on trips to the park. 'Furthermore, even then, when we were young, there was a certain book which we tucked under our arms to go to the park and which we read lovingly.'
5. R. Dreyfus, *Souvenirs sur Marcel Proust*, Grasset, 1926, pp. 19–20.
6. 'La classe de cinquième au lycée Condorcet', J.-É. Blanche, *La Pêche aux souvenirs*, Flammarion, 1949, pp. 114–17.
7. Ibid., p. 115.
8. Ibid., p. 117.
9. V. Chauvin, *Histoire des lycées et des collèges de Paris*, Hachette, 1866; quoted by A. Ferré, *Les Années de collège de Marcel Proust*, Gallimard 1959, p. 55. Among former pupils were Banville, Labiche, the Goncourts, Sully Prudhomme, Sadi Carnot, Casimir-Perier, the publisher Ollendorff, Ampère, Becquerel, C. Richet, Taine, Bergson and Sainte-Beuve. From 1834, the pupils at the lycée had founded a magazine, *La Presse des écoles*.
10. C. Rim, *Mémoires d'une vieille vague*, Ramsay, 1990.
11. Ferré, *Les Années de collège*, p. 90. This valuable work has provided us with all the details of Marcel Proust's school reports.

12. Ibid., p. 92.

13. *CSB*, pp. 315–18.

14. Ibid., pp. 318–21.

15. Ibid., pp. 321–2 and n. 1, p. 871.

16. Ibid., pp. 322–5.

17. BN, n.a.fr. 16611.

18. Ibid., f. 29. Cf. f. 31, corrected from the Latin version, 'Incendie du Capitole par les soldats de Vitellius' (Tacitus, *Historiae*, III, ch. LXX). Note the use of the word 'neurosis'.

19. *JS*, pp. 224, 225 (every day 'from two till four').

20. Ferré, *Les Années de collège*, p. 111. *Corr.*, vol. I, pp. 105, 107, 146. Dreyfus, *Souvenirs*, p. 24. Cf. J. Schlumberger, *Éveils*, Gallimard, 1950, p. 92: 'How brilliant the classes of the historian Jallifier were.'

21. Dreyfus, *Souvenirs*, p. 135.

22. *CSB*, pp. 325–7.

23. Ibid., pp. 327–9.

24. *Corr.*, vol. I, p. 108 and n. 6. The historian's name is mentioned twice in Marcel's replies to Antoinette Faure's questionnaire, which Philip Kolb dates to the same year. Cf. *JS*, p. 329; RTP, vol. I, p. 152 (by name, vol. III, p. 230) and draft XXV, vol. I, p. 734.

25. *Corr.*, vol. I, p. 61.

26. Ferré, *Les Années de collège*, p. 148.

27. *Corr.*, vol. I, p. 97: 'the two first places in all the divisions of all the lycées'.

28. Ibid., 15 July 1887.

29. Illiers Museum. Ader-Tajan catalogue, no. 63.

30. *Corr.*, vol. I, p. 108.

31. Ibid., p. 59.

32. A. de Cossé-Brissac, *La Comtesse Greffulhe*, Perrin, 1991, p. 77 and photograph, p. 152.

33. Blanche, *La Pêche aux souvenirs*, ch. II, Dieppe, pp. 50–6.

34. Née Laffitte, and the cousin of Mme Baignères, she was one of the 'belles of the Empire period', according to Proust (RTP, vol. II, p. 695; vol. III, p. 389), who mentions her at Trouville in 1894 (where she was staying at the manoir des Roches, with her friend, Princesse de Sagan; G. Painter, p. 84). Prince de Sagan liked to tease General de Galliffet about the fact that they were both deceived husbands (A. de Fouquières, *Mon Paris et ses Parisiens*, P. Horay, 1953, p. 152.

35. De Cossé-Brissac, *La Comtesse Greffulhe*, p. 152.

36. *Corr.*, vol. I, pp. 95–6, to Mme Nathé Weil.

37. Ibid., p. 111. *Le Bottin mondain* (1903, p. 781) reads: 'The waters . . . highly recommended for those who are lymphatic or scrofulous and for children

suffering from rickets . . . Very popular resort, but fairly expensive, during the season, and not very lively, due to the number of sick . . . Grand Hôtel de France et d'Angleterre, recommended to the nobility.'

38. *Corr.*, vol. XXI, letter 388.

39. *CSB*, p. 466.

40. *Corr.*, vol. I, p. 104, 28 August 1888, to Robert Dreyfus.

41. Ibid., p. 105. M. Gaucher may have been the model for Rustinlor in *Jean Santeuil*.

42. Quoted by Ferré, *Les Années de collège*, p. 181.

43. *Corr.*, vol. I, p. 105.

44. Ferré, *Les Années de collège*, pp. 182–8.

45. *RTP*, vol. III, p. 324–7. Gaucher's and his colleagues' style of teaching confirms what another Condorcet pupil, Jean Schlumberger, has written: 'At that period the better-known lycées prided themselves on training an élite. The teachers focused their attention on the best pupils, and it was for them that the courses were given. The "Monsieur" with which they scarcely ever failed to preface our names indicated that they felt they were talking to the future top brains of the land' (*Éveils*, pp. 89–90).

46. BN, n.a.fr., 16611.

47. *À la recherche de Marcel Proust*, Hachette, 1949, pp. 33–49. *CSB*, pp. 329–32.

48. *CSB*, p. 332.

49. *Corr.*, vol. I, p. 105. Cf. P. Lavallée, who recalled Marcel 'reading his work aloud, and the excellent and delightful M. Gaucher commenting, praising, criticizing, then suddenly collapsing into wild laughter at the audacity of a style which deep down enchanted him' (*Corr. gén.*, vol. IV, p. 3).

50. *Corr.*, vol. I, p. 104, 28 August 1888, to Robert Dreyfus.

51. Ibid., pp. 103–6.

52. Ibid., p. 106. Marcel wrote in similar terms in a letter to Bibesco in 1902, and to Lauris in 1908, to denote the return of his inspiration.

53. Raoul Versini, of whom we shall have more to say, won the prize for the older students. Marcel was presented with the works of La Bruyère, Hachette, 1882 (BN exhibition catalogue 1965, no. 69).

54. *Corr.*, vol, XXI, letter 396, 3 August 1888, to Nathé Weil.

55. Dreyfus, *Souvenirs*, pp. 68–72. *Écrits de jeunesse*, pp. 91–109: apart from some important details about the *Lundi*, they contain three pieces of criticism by Proust (pp. 101–7). The five issues of *Lundi* that have been consulted are in a private collection. Among the staff were D. Halévy and Abel Desjardins (Paul's younger brother). I have taken my information and my quotations from this source.

56. Issue of 5 December 1887; classical matinée at the Odéon in October 1887: *Horace*, *L'Avare*, lecture given by F. Sarcey. Proust drew his inspiration not only from a review by J. Lemaître, but from *Cours de littérature* by Saint-Marc

Girardin (which he would also refer to in 1907 in 'Sentiments filiaux d'un parricide').

57. *JS*, pp. 313–16; *CSB*, p. 175 ('Sur la lecture', preface to *Sésame et les lys*).

58. This is the first mention of Anatole France in Proust's hand: 'Just like him, he has no ideas, like him, all he has is charm.'

59. *Écrits de jeunesse*, p. 106.

60. J.-P. Halévy, Introduction to *Corr. avec D. Halévy*.

61. Ibid., p. 14: 'Marcel Proust was fascinated by Ludovic Halévy' (letters of 1888, 1907, 1908, 1910, 1921). He quoted *La Belle Hélène, L'Abbé Constantin;* he knew *Carmen*. The Meilhac and Halévy type of wit described in *Le Côté de Guermantes* was also his.

62. The disappearance of the correspondence between G. Bizet and his wife means that we have very little information about their relationship, or Jacques' childhood. See C. Bischoff, *Geneviève Straus (1849–1926)*, Balland, 1992, pp. 87–90.

63. Ibid., pp. 96–105.

64. Ibid, pp. 101–4.

65. A. de Fouquières has given an excellent portrait of J. Bizet in *Mon Paris*, vol. II, *Le Quartier Monceau*, pp. 120–1. See Bizet's photograph in *Écrits de jeunesse*, *album* no. 6.

66. *JS*, pp. 234–6.

67. *Écrits de jeunesse*, p. 41. He ends his letter with a declaration: 'I embrace you and love you with all my heart.'

68. Ibid., pp. 50–1, and Halévy's remarks, pp. 52–3: 'This was written without a single deletion. This mad creature is very talented, and I know NOTHING that is sadder and so marvellously well written as these two pages.' Cf. *JS*, p. 253.

69. *Corr.*, I, pp. 101–2. Letter dated by P. Kolb 'Towards the spring (?) of 1888'. It is more likely to have been June 1888, in view of the date in the diary kept by Halévy, who must have been sent a letter from Proust by Bizet.

70. *Écrits de jeunesse*, p. 70: 'I have somewhat over-amplified here that I loved Jacques (whom I still love very much) less. I did not in any way mean to suggest by this that he was stupid, but that the ideal which I had formed for myself had slightly faded, rather as when one falls out of love a little.'

71. *Corr.*, vol. I, p. 105. Cf. Dreyfus, *Souvenirs*, pp. 33–43, 52.

72. *Corr.*, vol. I, p. 105.

73. Ibid., pp. 112–13, 7 September 1888. Followed by a long observation on Halévy's attitude.

74. Head of clinic at the Faculty of Medicine in 1909, he married in 1908.

75. *Corr.*, vol. XVIII, p. 324.

76. Ibid., p. 338, July 1919.

77. Ibid., vol. I, p. 117.

78. Ibid., pp. 108–9.

79. *P et J*, p. 58; see n. 1. Loti did not reject the copy of *Les Plaisirs et les Jours* that Proust had sent to him (L. de Robert, *De Loti à Proust*, Flammarion, 1928, p. 152). At the age of twenty, Loti, along with France, was still Proust's favourite author (Questionnaire, *CSB*, p. 337). In 1890, Mme Proust, after the death of her mother, as we have seen, was 'permeated with Loti' (*Corr.*, vol. I, p. 136), and with his *Roman d'un enfant*, which was then being published in *La Nouvelle Revue*.

80. *CSB*, p. 240.

81. *JS*, pp. 258–9: 'It was a small group of the most intelligent boys in the class.'

82. *Corr.*, vol. I, p. 116, completed in *Écrits de jeunesse*, pp. 65–6.

83. Ibid., p. 118, 25 September 1888.

84. Ibid., p. 117.

85. Ibid., p. 116.

86. Bischoff, *Geneviève Straus*. Her portrait appears in most of the memoirs of the 1900 period, and, naturally, in all those that concern Proust. See, in particular, D. Halévy, 'Two portraits of Mme Straus', *Corr. avec D. Halévy*, pp. 173–80; Dreyfus, *Souvenirs*, pp. 53–5.

87. Bischoff, *Geneviève Straus*, p. 39.

88. Bizet completed Halévy's opera *Noé*. Proust remembered Sainte-Beuve's interpretation, which revealed to him what an all-round mind F. Halévy possessed (*Corr.*, vol. VIII, p. 116).

89. Proust wrote to Mme Straus in 1907: 'And then that jolly Carmen, is it really you? Is there not something of Perdita, of Imogen, in you too?'

90. Musée d'Orsay.

91. D. Halévy, *Corr. avec D. Halévy*, p. 179.

92. Bischoff, *Geneviève Straus*, pp. 115–17.

93. *Journal*, 12 August 1886, Laffont, Bouquins, 1989, vol. II, p. 1262.

94. Ibid., 12 January 1887, vol. III, p. 6.

95. Ibid., 21 April 1890, p. 417. He is referring to the Rodrigues.

96. Ibid., 28 March 1887, p. 25.

97. Ibid.: 'It is extremely unusual that two lovers should love one another equally and this inequality on the part of one or the other can lead to shaky harnessing and an uneven pace . . . There is even a moment in which she celebrates the joy of being alone in life, which is quite a revelation.'

98. Ibid., 5 July 1890, p. 443.

99. Ibid., 18 February 1895, p. 1094. Goncourt compares her conversation to that of Mme Baignères, who had the charm of an eighteenth-century woman.

100. Ibid., 21 January 1886. *Journal*, ed., Charpentier, vol. VII, 1894, p. 103; it was in this edition that Proust may have read this quip, which he incorporates into his portrait of Mme Straus in his Saint-Simon pastiche (*CSB*, p. 53),

pointing out that 'her wonderful replies were remembered by all'. An early reference to Mme Straus can be found in a passage from *Les Plaisirs et les Jours*, first published in *Le Banquet* (April 1892; *P et J*, p. 38).

101. 18 October 1920, *Corr.*, vol. XIX, p. 530.

102. *Corr. avec D. Halévy*, pp. 173–80.

103. *Corr.*, vol. I, p. 163, Germinie with Réjane; p. 164, 'these bunches of lilac'; p. 166, in which Marcel, writing to Mme Straus, paints a portrait of her that is reminiscent of the Goncourts' *'allumeuse'* [a flirtatious, alluring woman *Tr.*]: 'I thought afterwards that you liked people and I can see that you don't care about them. I believe that there is only one kind of life that appeals to you, one that brings out not so much your intelligence as your wit, not so much your wit as your delicacy, not so much your delicacy as the way you dress. Someone who likes this way of life above all – and who can enchant' (March 1891).

104. *Hommage à M. Proust*, p. 146. It was with Desjardins that Proust studied 'those great philosopher-poets, Heraclitus and Lucretius' at home (ibid., p. 150).

105. Ferré, *Les Années de collège*, pp. 215–52. H. Bonnet, *Alphonse Darlu, maître de M. Proust*, Nizet, 1961.

106. 'La morale chrétienne et la conscience contemporaine', 1900.

107. 'Après une visite au Vatican de M. Brunetière', 1895. And, under the heading 'Questions pratiques', 'Après le procès'.

108. F. Gregh, *L'Âge d'or*, Grasset, 1947, p. 142, quotes these verses: 'Forgive me, sir, but did he please?/ Look upon the poetic flora/ Which has just bloomed/ In the heart of the Lycée Condorcet … It's one of Darlu's classes.' Among the philosophers who emerged from his class were Élie Halévy, Xavier Léon and Léon Brunschvicg.

109. A. Ferré, *Les Années de collège*, p. 240. Lachelier was the author of *Fondement de l'induction* and the dedicatee of Bergson's *Essai sur les données immédiates de la conscience* (1888). He was then inspector-general. Lagneau was Barrès' teacher, after Burdeau, at the lycée in Nancy (1880); after his death, his *Célèbres Leçons et Fragments* was published.

110. M. Barrès, *Les Déracinés*, ed. J. Borie, Folio, 1988, 'Le lycée de Nancy', pp. 69–101.

111. *JS*, pp. 259–64. Perhaps it is from here that Marcel derived his hostility to 'decadence' and to the poets and artists of the decadent movement, who were nevertheless fashionable among young people in those years, and among certain of his friends.

112. Ibid., p. 267. It is worth noting that M. Beulier introduced Jean to Michelet's *La Bible de l'humanité*, which Proust, in *La Prisonnière*, placed among the great syntheses of the nineteenth century.

113. Ferré, *Les Années de collège*, pp. 224–9.

114. On 16 January 1889 (*Corr.*, vol. I, p. 54); the following day Marcel asked for several of the author's books to be inscribed to him.

115. *JS*, p. 269. At the time he wrote *Contre Sainte-Beuve*, Proust returned to Joubert (*CSB*, pp. 650–51), and to his inner genius in his relationship with his social self. Proust's course notes also deal with La Rochefoucauld (Ferré, *Les Années de collège*, p. 243).

116. Darlu quotes Tolstoy in an article in 1900, 'La morale chrétienne at la conscience contemporaine', when he asserts that 'love is really the answer to a large part of the problem of morality'. The Tolstoyan voice can be heard in the stories in *Les Plaisirs et les Jours*.

117. Ferré, *Les Années de collège*, p. 234. Furthermore, Proust had as a textbook Rabier's *Leçons de philosophie*, Hachette, 1888. (A copy that had belonged to him can be found in the BN, ms.)

118. *Le Carnet de 1908*, f. 40 verso, p. 101. Note that A. Henry did not believe in this influence (*Marcel Proust. Théories pour une esthétique*, Klincksieck, 1981, pp. 76–9), on account of the brevity of this work, and the fact that his manner of thinking was exactly that of his contemporaries. This is to ignore the importance of the personal relationship between the teacher and the pupil. Besides, in his preface to *Les Plaisirs et les Jours* (1896) Proust still recalled 'his inspired words, more certain of lasting than if they had been written', which, in him 'as in so many others, induced thought'.

119. Testimony of Louis Weulersse, Darlu's grandson, in Ferré, *Les Années de collège*, p. 249.

120. *Corr.*, vol. I, pp. 121–2.

121. *Corr. avec D. Halévy*, p. 49.

122. Ibid., pp. 50–1; *Corr.*, vol. I, pp. 123–4.

123. *Écrits de jeunesse*, p. 123.

124. Exhibition catalogue, Jacquemart-André, 1971, no. 58.

125. Letters sold at Drouot, no. 56 in the Boisgirard catalogue, in June 1988. The letters were dated '26 October 1888' in hand. Raoul Versini entered the École Normale Supérieure and made his career in the administration of public education; he died in 1940. (Information given, as is that in main text, by his grandson, Laurent Versini, a professor at the Sorbonne.) R. Versini had destroyed the letters he had received in his youth. These ones no longer belonged to the family.

126. See de Fouquières, *Mon Paris*, pp. 138–41. In 1893 Proust dedicated a paper, published in *La Revue blanche*, 'to Gladys Harvey' (*JS*, p. 112 and n. 4).

127. A. Gide, *Journal*, 14 May 1921, Gallimard, 1939, Bibliothèque de la Pléiade, p. 692.

128. February 1888, reprinted in *Pastels*: 'Her most envious rivals acknowledged the accomplished elegance of her way of dressing . . . The expression in her eyes, by turn surprised and sad, shrewd and romantic, the faint trembling

of her nostrils, her rippling smile, lent her face a mobility of physiognomy that revealed a woman of imagination and passion' (quoted by Dreyfus, *Souvenirs*, pp. 45–6). Bourget's letter dates from December 1888 (*Corr. avec D. Halévy*, pp. 63–4).

129. Dreyfus, *Souvenirs*, p. 46. Cf. D. Halévy, diary, 5 December 1888: 'Summer with Proust, Jacques and myself, walking. We passed Laure Hayman's house, and naturally Proust could not resist the temptation to go in. He stayed there for a quarter of an hour . . .' (*Corr. avec D. Halévy*, p. 63).

130. Exhibition catalogue, BN, no. 119.

131. M. Proust, 'Poems for Laure Hayman', copied down by Daniel Halévy in his diary (*Écrits de jeunesse*, p. 152).

132. Ibid., pp. 112–13. If it did exist in anything other than draft form, I have been unable to trace the only copy of this magazine. What survives is a list of the editorial staff, the address of the magazine, that of Jacques Bizet, and therefore of the Strauses (134 Bd Haussmann), and a verbal account of a meeting (ibid., p. 114).

133. Ibid., p. 118.

134. Dreyfus, *Souvenirs*, p. 56.

135. Full text in *Écrits de jeunesse*, pp. 121–7.

136. Ibid., p. 124.

137. Ibid., p. 126–7, shortly after 29 October 1888.

CHAPTER IV: *Summer Holidays*

1. *Corr.*, vol. I, p. 131, September 1889.

2. *Le Bottin mondain*, 1903, p. 768.

3. F. Gregh, *L'Âge d'or, Souvenirs d'enfance et de jeunesse*, Grasset, 1947, p. 164; Horace Finaly (1871–1945).

4. See the note by Brett Dawson, J. Giraudoux, *Œuvres romanesques*, Bibliothèque de la Pléiade, vol. I, p. 1794; he refers back to D. Desanti (*La Banquière des années folles*, Folio, 1980), H. Coston and E. Beau de Loménie for biographical information about Finaly; they all drew upon R. Mennevée, 'Notices biographiques, personelles et familiales', *Les Documents politiques, diplomatiques et financiers*, September 1937, pp. 401–19. Giraudoux gave Moses Finaly's ugliness and corpulence, as well as his political and social connections, 'his secret political and financial influence'. Proust would make greater use of these qualities than he would of the man in his novel. Bloch is Finaly less Moses.

5. F. Gregh adds in a rather more Proustian way than he may have realized: 'One could imagine his son Hamlet-Horace in fencing costume, shouting out: "A rat, a rat!" and stabbing it through the arras' (*L'Âge d'or*, p. 164).

6. *Corr.*, vol. I, p. 197. We will discuss the Finalys again when Marcel stays with them, at Trouville, in 1892.

7. This was how Jeanne de Caillavet, *née* Pouquet, described the Finalys at Trouville: 'Everyone avoided them because they were garish, loud and common' (M. Maurois, *Les Cendres brûlantes*, Flammarion, 1986, p. 477).

8. Gregh, *L'Âge d'or*. In this he was the model for Nissim Bernard.

9. *RTP*, vol. II, pp. 756–8.

10. *Corr.*, vol. I, p. 258, 24 May 1894. Again, this is a physical portrait of Nissim Bernard.

11. *JS*, p. 392.

12. Ibid., p. 397.

13. *Corr.*, vol. I, p. 129.

14. *JS*, p. 396.

15. 'La mer', *P et J*, pp. 142–3, September 1892. Published in *Le Banquet*, November 1892.

16. Ibid., p. 143.

17. See M.-C. Bancquart, *Anatole France, un excentrique passioné*, Calmann-Lévy, 1984, pp. 143–54, 164–6, 179–93, 202–6, 214, 283–323; Gregh, *L'Âge d'or*, pp. 173–83. A. France and Mme de Caillavet, *Lettres intimes*, Nizet, 1984; M. Maurois, *Les Cendres brûlantes*, pp. 51–64 and *passim*.

18. As did Mallarmé in the rue de Rome; as did Valéry later, before he, too, took his place in the bed of the mistress of the house.

19. Gregh, *L'Âge d'or*, p. 180.

20. Bancquart, *Anatole France*, p. 145.

21. *Corr.*, vol. I, pp. 125–6, 15 May 1889, letter signed 'A *philosophie* student'.

22. Gregh, *L'Âge d'or*, p. 174 ff.

23. Ibid., p. 173.

24. Ibid., p. 182.

25. *Corr.*, vol. XXI, p. 137, 19 April 1922. The letter also refers to Gaston's friendship for Marcel and to Marcel's affection for Gaston, which immunized him 'against the too painful suffering occasioned by [his] love for Mlle Pouquet' (p. 138).

26. *La Revue blanche*, April 1896.

27. P. Valéry, *Lettres à quelques-uns*, Gallimard, 1952, p. 11, December 1889.

28. Mentioned in *RTP*, vol. II, pp. 404–531.

29. First battalion, second company (*Corr.*, vol. I, p. 136, n. 4). The volunteers from the department of the Seine were recruited at Blois, Orléans or Montargis: eighty 'volunteers' were sent to Orléans, to the Coligny barracks, 131 faubourg Bannier; the conditional volunteers were mixed in with the other recruits, on the orders of the minister, Freycinet; on these matters, see Clovis Duveau's remarkable article 'Proust à Orléans' and the photographs that illustrate it, *BAMP*, no. 33, 1983, pp. 9–68.

30. *CSB*, p. 337.

31. *Corr.*, vol. XVIII, p. 412, October 1919, to Binet-Valmer.

32. Ibid., p. 56. Cf. *JS*, p. 569: 'They walked down the faubourg Bannier and arrived at the little house where they had their room. They pushed open the door, took their post and went up to their room. Fortunately, it was warm in there, and Jean asked Mme Renvoyzé to bring up some punch which he could offer to the others.' The Renvoyzés, 'restaurateurs who ran a boarding-house', had six rooms they rented out, five minutes away from the barracks. Marcel spoke to his mother about 'pleasant comforts in the Renvoyzé manner' (*Corr.*, vol. II, p. 138).

33. *RTP*, vol. II, p. 623.

34. *JS*, p. 568, and G. Cattaui, *M. Proust. Documents iconographiques*, Geneva, P. Cailler, 1956, nos. 30 (without shako), 31, 32, 33 (open book in hand).

35. R. de Billy, *Marcel Proust. Lettres et conversations*, Les Portiques, 1930, p. 22. 'We used to like remembering that evening, added Billy, borrowing Flaubert's language when he brings Bouvard and Pécuchet face to face.'

36. 14 December 1889, after a cancellation of leave and a visit to Orléans by Horace Finaly (*Corr.*, vol. I, p. 136). On 16 December Marcel joined the training unit.

37. Letter of 28 December 1893 to Pierre Lavallée, who was doing his national service at Chartres, *BAMP*, no. 11, p. 339.

38. P. Robert, 'Le paradis militaire de Marcel Proust', *BAMP*, no. 33, 1983; *Corr.*, vol. V, p. 183, May 1905, to M. Duplay: 'Curious . . . that you should have seen the regiment as a prison, and I as a paradise.'

39. Ibid., vol. I, p. 161.

40. *RTP*, vol. I, p. 634. Cf. pp. 634, 635, 638. The memory of the morning coffee would reappear in *Le Côté de Guermantes*, as would that of the siesta (referred to firstly in *JS*, p. 551) on the barrack-room beds in the afternoons (vol. II, p. 393), and a great many other details for which we do not have the source.

41. *RTP*, vol. IV, p. 387.

42. *JS*, pp. 130–1.

43. Gallimard, 1937; 1989 edition, pp. 99–107.

44. See M. Miguet, 'La neurasthénie entre science et fiction', *BAMP*, no. 40, 1990, pp. 28–42. The author compares *L'Hygiène du neurasthénique*, by G. Ballet and A. Proust (Masson), with the solutions outlined in *RTP*.

45. *Corr.*, vol. XIV, p. 336, letter of 30 November 1899 to Pierre d'Orléans. Proust was writing to one of his former lieutenants and took care to refer to his support of Dreyfus in very precise terms. Similar memories of his officers, in a letter of 1916 to Charles d'Alton (*Corr.*, vol. XV, p. 53), included M. d'Orléans and M. de Cholet.

46. Ibid., vol. I, pp. 138, 147, 239, 293, 448.

47. *JS*, pp. 576–8.
48. Ibid., p. 578: 'Once, at a social gathering, however, Jean reintroduced himself to M. de Brucourt who said "Delighted" in a distracted manner and moved on.'
49. M. Proust, *Alla ricerca del tempo perduto*, ed. A. Beretta Anguissola, Mondadori, 1986, vol. II, p. 153.
50. *RTP*, vol. II, p. 429.
51. *JS*, p. 543, Cf. *RTP*, vol. II, pp. 406, 426–7, where this theme is taken up and developed.
52. E.g. letter from Mme Proust, 26 June 1890: 'As soon as you have fixed your double leave teleg. Paris and Auteuil' (*Corr.*, vol. I, p. 145). On 10 August 1890: 'Since you made no mention of Sunday I flattered myself that you were coming.' Mme Proust sometimes went to Orléans too (ibid., p. 149). The correspondence between them was, in principal, daily (which enables us to measure the amount of lost letters), hence the 'Nothing from you today'; 'Buy, I beg you, ten blocks of large, cross-ruled writing paper (which makes sixty double pages). Two packets of white envelopes will fit them exactly (fifty envelopes in total), and you will keep them specially to write these sixty letters to me – that will be very nice for me' (28 August 1850, ibid., p. 159). On fencing: 'I've begun fencing,' wrote Marcel to his father (on 23 September 1890), who advised him against riding and swimming (23 April, ibid., p. 162). Marcel's final report includes the comment: 'does not know how to swim'.
53. *L'Encre dans le sang*, Flammarion, 1982. These letters also testify to Marcel's friendly relationship with Lieutenant de Cholet.
54. Ibid., p. 76.
55. A group photograph was sent to me.
56. J. Pouquet, *Quelques lettres de Marcel Proust*, Hachette, 1928. Jeanne Pouquet destroyed most of Marcel's letters.
57. *Corr.*, vol. XIV, p. 29.
58. Ibid., vol. X, p. 40, January 1910, to Simone de Caillavet, to ask her for a photograph. The Pouquets had a house in the Périgord. Cf. *RTP*, vol. I, p. 494 (where the 1910 remark was added in 1917, see var. *b* and n. 4, p. 1365). Similarly, Marcel confessed to one of the Pouquets' servants, 'I don't know whether I love the mother or the daughter more!' (Marie or Jeanne), like the Narrator torn between Odette and Gilberte.
59. Letters from J. Pouquet to G. de Caillavet, in Maurois, *L'Encre dans le sang*, p. 153.
60. Ibid., pp. 179–80.
61. Ibid., pp. 223–4.
62. Quoted by Maurois, ibid., p. 225.
63. *Corr.*, vol. I, p. 138, 23 April 1890.

64. Ibid., p. 144, 26 June 1890 (or 17 July).

65. See P. Kolb, 'M. Proust et les dames Lemaire', *BAMP*, no. 14, 1964, p. 116.

66. *Corr.*, vol. I, p. 161. 'And I have been punished,' adds Marcel, 'if M. Cazalis will permit me to quote one of his finest poems, *Pour avoir dédaigné les fleurs de leurs seins nus* [For having scorned the flowers of their naked breasts].' Cazalis, a poet (under the pseudonym of Jean Lahor), a friend of Mallarmé's and the author of *Salomé* (1875), was a doctor and a friend of Adrien Proust's.

67. Duveau, 'Proust at Orléans', *BAMP*, no. 33, 1983, pp. 40–3.

68. *Corr.*, vol. I, p. 163.

69. *JS*, pp. 272–6, 'L'École des Sciences Politiques'.

70. Ibid., p. 272–3.

71. Ibid., p. 273.

72. *RTP*, vol. I, p. 439; II, p. 525; III, pp. 73 and 566.

73. Ibid., vol. I, p. 15.

74. A. Siegfried in *Hommage à Émile Boutmy et Albert Sorel*, Fondation Nationale des Sciences Politiques, 1956, p. 17.

75. See J. Chastenet and A. Siegfried, *Hommage*; J. Bariéty, 'A. Sorel: L'Europe et la Révolution française', in *1889: Centenaire de la Révolution française*, Berne, Lang, 1992; P. Favre, *Naissances de la science politique en France*, Fayard, 1989.

76. *JS*, p. 273.

77. Siegfried, *Hommage*, p. 23.

78. Comte de Saint-Aulaire, *Confession d'un vieux diplomate*, Flammarion, 1953, pp. 8–9.

79. *JS*, p. 275. However, the author of *L'Histoire de l'unité allemande*, attributed to a certain Boisset (p. 274), could also point to Lucien Lévy-Bruhl, who gave a course on this subject.

80. *RTP*, vol. I, pp. 250–1, in the artist's mouth.

81. G. Painter in *Marcel Proust* mentions courses given by Bergson and Paul Desjardins: I have been unable to trace their names among the teachers at this period.

82. R. de Billy, *Marcel Proust*, p. 24. I have been unable to trace the notebook in which Marcel wrote the quatrain that is often reproduced: '*Vandal, exquis, répand son sel/mais qui s'en fout, c'est Gabriel/Robert, Jean, et même Marcel/Pourtant si grave d'habitude*' [The exquisite Vandal sprinkles his salt/ but who cares, it's Gabriel/ Robert, Jean, and even Marcel/ Normally so serious].

83. P. Rain, *L'École libre des sciences politiques (1871–1945)*, Fondation Nationale des Sciences Politiques, 1963, p. 42. Proust's course notes.

84. *JS*, p. 274; *RTP*, vol. I, p. 445.

85. P. Rain, *L'École libre*.

86. *Corr.*, vol. V, p. 284, n. 15. In *Le Côté de Guermantes*, it is Paul Leroy-Beaulieu, an economist, who is mentioned. Cf. ibid., vol. I, p. 172, n. 2.

87. *Corr.*, vol. I, p. 188, November 1892.

88. *RTP*, vol. I, p. 218.

89. *Journal*, vol. III, p. 194, when it was first performed, in December 1888. The critics panned the play, but the young seemed to like it, as a letter from a pupil of the École Normale Supérieure, Romain Rolland, to Edmond de Goncourt, testifies: 'Your play gripped us, moved us and filled us with enthusiasm' (ibid., p. 203). Cf. 21 March 1891, vol. III, p. 565.

90. *Comœdia*, 20 January 1920; *CSB*, p. 600.

91. *Corr.*, vol. XVII, p. 120, 19 February 1918.

92. Inscription to Réjane, *Corr.*, vol. XVIII, p. 271, June 1919. She, too, inscribed a photograph of herself as Prince de Sagan, signing herself, 'Réjane, who performed Goncourt' (10 December 1919); cf. 'those perfectly awful evenings at Germinie's', ibid., vol. XIX, p. 312, 1920.

93. *CSB*, p. 643, *Le Gaulois*, 27 May 1922. Marcel cried even more at *L'Arlésienne*.

94. Ibid., p. 642.

95. Ibid.

96. *Le Mensuel*, February 1891.

97. *Corr.*, vol. I, p. 165, 27 March.

98. *Écrits de jeunesse*, p. 171.

99. He appears in a draft of *Le Temps retrouvé* under the name of 'M. de Raymond' (vol. IV, p. 878); cf. var. *a*, p. 877, which identifies the character: 'Don't forget Koechlin', whom Proust describes as a 'Levite with a light-coloured beard'. Born in 1860, Raymond Koechlin became a well-known lover of art and an art historian, and was General Secretary of the Société des Amis du Louvre in 1913. His article in *Le Mensuel* was about Goncourt's *Outamaro* (July 1891).

100. *Corr.*, vol. I, p. 1895.

101. 'Galerie Georges Petit. International exhibition of painting', *Le Mensuel*, no. 3, December 1890, pp. 4–6.

102. This was *Valparaiso*, which Proust would point out to his mother at the 1905 Exhibition (Catalogue Orsay 1995, no. 44).

103. *Le Mensuel*, no. 5, February 1891, pp. 4–5.

104. Yvette Guilbert called her 'the diva with the velvet eyes' (*La Chanson de ma vie*, Grasset, 1927, p. 172).

105. *Écrits de jeunesse*, p. 127: 'Saw Jules Lemaître for the first time. Fine head like a young bull, his face that of a dreaming faun with two eyes of a very pure blue, blue as the reflection of a periwinkle in a clear pool' (autumn 1888).

106. *Le Mensuel*, no. 10, pp. 7–9.

107. In 1906 Proust, cloistered away in Versailles, was indignant at the protective tone ('cruel, unjust and shameful') of the appeal for the farewell matinée for Paulus, who had fallen upon hard times, which should have reflected 'the great artist he had been and would always remain even though his voice had given up'. Hahn, who was also a great admirer of Paulus, had wanted

to sign a letter of complaint with Proust (*Corr.*, vol. VI, p. 311, 8 December 1906). Cf. R. Hahn, *L'Oreille au guet*, Gallimard, 1937, pp. 231–4). Hahn often alluded to the subject of French diction, which begins with song and ends with opera. Whence the two friends' liking for these people 'who knew how to sing, knew how to enunciate, knew how to discern the slightest hidden meaning in a text, knew how to pace and carry off "the effect", knew how to emphasize or suggest an allusion . . . they knew their job, they had talent!' (ibid., p. 246).

108. *CSB*, p. 303.

109. *RTP*, vol. I, p. 607, and n. 1, p. 608.

110. For Gustave Laurens de Waru (1871–1941), see *Écrits de jeunesse*, pp. 193–4. He is mentioned in *Corr.*, vol. I, pp. 202, 210; vol. II, p. 312. Cf. *RTP*, vol. II, p. 379, and *P et J*, pp. 42–3, where he appears as one of 'Hippolyta's nephews (Gustave had a brother). Cf. *Corr.*, vol. XII, p. 118, in which Proust links his love for the Comtesse de Chevigné to the memory of her nephew, Waru: how fortunate to find the aunt's looks in those of her nephew, and what light is thrown on the creation of Saint-Loup, Oriane de Guermantes' nephew, as well as on the Baron de Charlus! If the Narrator had not been in love with Oriane, he could have been with Robert – had he shared Proust's tastes.

111. See the volume published by the Institut Français d'Architecture, *Trouville*, Mardaga, 1989, pp. 86–7.

112. Ibid., p. 158.

113. *RTP*, vol. III, p. 204.

114. Ibid., p. 296.

115. The note in *Écrits de jeunesse* refers to this quotation in *RTP*, vol. II, pp. 34, 67, and draft XXXIV, p. 906; also in a letter from Cabourg to Mme Scheikévitch (*Corr.*, vol. XI, p. 210, 7 September 1912). 'Le port' is mentioned in *RTP*, vol. II, p. 34.

116. All these quotations are taken from 'Choses normandes', *Le Mensuel*, no. 12. 'Souvenir', in the same issue, takes place in the grounds of a house with 'two red-brick turrets', from which the heroine contemplates the sea, the waves and the beach. Cf. 'Avant la nuit' (*La Revue blanche*, December 1893; *P et J*, p. 167), in which the sea can be seen from the terrace through the apple trees; 'Sonate clair de lune' (ibid., pp. 116–18); 'Sous-bois' (ibid., p. 141, dated from Dieppe, August 1895), 'La mer' (ibid., p. 142) and 'Marine' (p. 144) repeat the images from *Le Mensuel*, which explains why Proust did not rework his first text: he started afresh, developed and transformed it. At Beg-Meil, too, the apple trees overlook the sea (*JS*, pp. 362, 381); cf. *RTP*, vol. III: 'the rural sea', p. 180; La Raspelière, pp. 289–90, 297, 387–8.

117. Connection suggested by M. Troulay, who believes that it is enough to insert

'Avant la nuit' in the middle of 'Souvenir' in order to have a complete story.

118. *P et J*, p. 168.

119. *RTP*, vol. III, p. 881.

120. *CSB*, pp. 644–5.

121. G. Cattaui, *M. Proust. Documents iconographiques*, Geneva, P. Cailler, 1956. This drawing, given to Hahn, was bequeathed to M. Nordlinger.

122. *CSB*, p. 571.

123. J.-É. Blanche, *Mes modèles*, Stock, 1928, p. 116.

CHAPTER V: *From* Le Banquet *to* La Revue blanche

1. *Corr.* vol. I, p. 409, 1895; vol. XXI, 4 August 1922.

2. Ibid., vol. I, pp. 166, 199.

3. For Wilde's period in Paris, see R. Ellmann, *Oscar Wilde*, Hamish Hamilton, London, 1987. ch. XIII, and for his links with Proust, p. 347 (which relies solely, as do biographies of Proust, on the remarks made by Mme Baignères' grandson reported by P. Jullian, *Oscar Wilde*, Perrin, 1967, p. 246).

4. Ellmann, *Oscar Wilde*, p. 338.

5. 17 December 1891, ibid., p. 351. We are not far from the aesthetics of *Contre Sainte-Beuve*. Léon Daudet provided a Jekyll and Hyde, dual portrait of Wilde in 'L'Entre-deux-guerres', in *Souvenirs et polémiques*, Laffont, Bouquins, 1992, pp. 278–9.

6. *RTP*, vol. III, p. 888.

7. Ibid., p. 17.

8. Bibliothèque Nationale, MS. See C. Bischoff, *Geneviève Straus (1849–1926)*, Balland, 1992, pp. 128–31.

9. L. Daudet, 'Fantômes et vivants', in *Souvenirs*, pp. 115–26. The flavour of Daudet's remarks is reiterated by G. de Diesbach, pp. 115–20.

10. 25 February 1903; Princesse Mathilde died in 1904.

11. *RTP*, vol. III, pp. 532–4; cf. vol. II, pp. 754–60.

12. G. Flaubert, *Correspondance*, Bibliothèque de la Pléiade, vol. III, pp. 691–2.

13. Ibid., p. 523 and n. 7.

14. 'Le Salon de la princesse Mathilde', *CSB*, p. 450.

15. Ibid., p. 452.

16. *RTP*, vol. I, pp. 532–3.

17. *CSB*, p. 451.

18. J. Guitton, *La Vocation de Bergson*, Gallimard, 1960.

19. He told J. Guitton: 'You shouldn't exhaust yourself giving your lectures . . . Keep as much time as possible for your inner life, your reading, your private reflections. Your pupils will benefit from this, and from everything that emanates from you, without your saying anything to them' (ibid., p. 67).

20. His additional thesis, which was in Latin according to custom, bore the title: *Quid Aristoteles de loco senserit* (Alcan, 1889).

21. Guitton, *La Vocation*, p. 122.

22. In the spring of 1910, *Le Carnet de 1908*, p. 113.

23. *CSB*, p. 558, 1913.

24. G. Maire, *Bergson mon maître*, Grasset, 1935, p. 157. Swann took the same attitude at the beginning of the affair.

25. The anecdote about the Quiès ear-plugs is related by Jacques Chevalier, *Entretiens avec Bergson*, Plon, 1954, p. 109.

26. *Corr.*, vol. XIX, 30 September 1920, p. 492. After making this comment, Bergson spoke about Jacques Rivière (a fuller text than that of P. Kolb, given by Guitton, *La Vocation*, pp. 40–41). Cf. *La Pensée et le Mouvant*, p. 20, in which Bergson observed that, when he published his first book, 'no [novelist] had yet thought of proceeding methodically "in search of lost time"'. One must 'furthermore' assume that Bergson feared homosexuality: 'Proust, furthermore, posed me an even more incomprehensible problem than Gide' (Chevalier, *Entretiens*).

27. *CSB*, p. 558.

28. On the circumstances surrounding the launch of *Le Banquet*, see F. Gregh, *L'Âge d'or*, Grasset, 1947, p. 148 ff. and R. Dreyfus, *Souvenirs sur Marcel Proust*, Grasset, 1926, pp. 67, 78, 163.

29. Only 200 copies of issue no. 2 were printed.

30. J. Bizet's minutes, quoted by Dreyfus, *Souvenirs*, p. 81.

31. But not Schopenhauer: the *Entretiens* in issue no. 5 are apocryphal (Gregh, *L'Âge d'or*, p. 151).

32. 'This article could be written by Barrès' lackey', Proust wrote to Gregh, criticizing 'the *fin-de-siècle chromo* [colour lithography of poor quality], which was the most repulsive of all' (*Corr.*, vol. I, p. 170, June 1892).

33. Dreyfus, *Souvenirs*, p. 108.

34. *Corr.*, vol. I, p. 174, 1 July 1892. Cf. *RTP*, vol. II, p. 762, on Mme de Guermantes' changing literary tastes.

35. In *Les Plaisirs et les Jours*, they appear in a different sequence, the first two under the title 'Cires perdues' (p. 42 with variants), the fourth is untitled and the fifth under the title 'L'Inconstant' (pp. 40–1).

36. 'Hippolyta', in *P et J*, p. 42.

37. Ibid., p. 41.

38. Ibid., pp. 110–11.

39. Ibid., p. 125.

40. Ibid., p. 142, and not reprinted in volume form before the Pléiade edition, p. 166.

41. *Le Banquet*, Slatkine reprints, p. 171, and *P et J*, p. 143.

42. As Dreyfus thought, *Souvenirs*, p. 96.

43. This person has been identified by Philip Kolb (*Textes retrouvés*, Gallimard, 1971, p. 92). See also G. de Diesbach, pp. 133–4, who confirms that the portrait did not resemble the model.

44. As Y. Sandre, the editor of the Bibliothèque de la Pléiade edition of *P et J*, has observed (p. 916).

45. *CSB*, p. 343. 'Un conte de Noël. Les Petits Souliers par M. Louis Ganderax' (*La Revue des deux mondes*, 1 January 1892). *Le Banquet*, no. 1, March 1892.

46. *Le Banquet*, p. 17. *CSB*, p. 345.

47. This remained unpublished until 1954. *CSB*, p. 342.

48. *Le Banquet*, p. 59. *CSB*, p. 347.

49. Dreyfus, *Souvenirs*, pp. 95–6. The article opens with a reference to Bourset's *Le Disciple*. *CSB*, pp. 348–9.

50. *CSB*, p. 141.

51. *Croisière autour de mes souvenirs*, preface by Colette, Émile-Paul, 1933. Henri de Rothschild was a friend of Fernand Gregh and of Jacques Bizet (p. 109) and must have known Proust through them.

52. *CSB*, p. 351.

53. Ibid.

54. Ibid.

55. P. Citti, *Contre la Décadence*, PUF, 1987, pp. 81–2.

56. *Corr.*, vol. I, p. 147, July 1892.

57. *Le Banquet*, no. 6, November 1892.

58. *CSB*, p. 354.

59. *Le Banquet*, no. 7, February 1893.

60. *CSB*, pp. 355–7, and Dreyfus, *Souvenirs*, pp. 97–103.

61. *Corr.*, vol. I, p. 210.

62. Ibid., p. 236.

63. Ibid. See R. de Billy, *Marcel Proust. Lettres et conversations*, Les Portiques, 1930, p. 25.

64. *BAMP*, no. 27, 1977, p. 375, mentioned by G. de Diesbach, p. 136.

65. De Billy, *Marcel Proust*, pp. 24–30.

66. *Corr.*, vol. I, p. 186.

67. Ibid., pp. 187–8.

68. Ibid., p. 201.

69. *RTP*, vol. III, p. 68. Cf. vol. III, p. 299, the portrait of the 'pious relation' who is a Protestant, paying a social visit.

70. From issue no. 6, 1892: 'À Phyllis', a long poem on the memory of love; 'Aube'; in one of the last issues, 'La comtesse de Tripoli'; and 'Légende', dedicated to Marcel Proust, which ends with a 'to be continued' – like the magazine, in what was to be the final issue.

71. *Corr.*, vol. I, p. 199.

72. Ibid., vol. VI, p. 312.

73. *CSB*, preface to J.-É. Blanche, *Propos de peintre, De David à Degas*, Émile-Paul, 1919, p. 572.

74. Aged twenty-five, 'his hair dull and in poor condition, his skin olive-coloured, looking thin, and wearing a grey coat, with a yellow carnation in his buttonhole and his arms crossed over his chest', wrote Blanche, *Mes modèles*, Stock, 1928, p. 11 (he mentions Barrès' gratitude).

75. S. Monneret, *L'Impressionisme et son époque*, Laffont, Bouquins, 1987, vol. I, pp. 56–7. Blanche bequeathed a hundred of his pictures as well as his diary, which is mostly unpublished, to the museum in Rouen. Art critic, novelist (*Aymeris*), he was also a remarkable memorialist (*La Pêche aux souvenirs*. Flammarion, 1949). The portrait of Gide was completed at the same time as that of Proust (A. Gide and P. Valéry, *Correspondance (1890–1942)*, Gallimard, 1955, p. 165, mentioned by P. Kolb, *Corr.*, vol. I, p. 176).

76. 'Salons et journaux', in *Souvenirs*, p. 476. Apollinaire spoke of the 'dry authority of M. Blanche', of his anglomania 'as regrettable in his painting as in his language . . . Notwithstanding, his paintings are very useful for what they tell us about the refined taste of our age. What a subject for a thesis by some scholar from Boston in the year 2000' ('Jacques Blanche et la littérature élégante de son temps', 1910, *Œuvres en prose*, Bibliothèque de la Pléiade, vol. II, p. 177–8). F. Gregh also thought the portrait of Marcel 'a little dry' (*L'Âge d'or*, p. 556).

77. *CSB*, p. 571.

78. *Hommage à M. Proust*, p. 57.

79. See Monneret, *L'Impressionisme*, p. 410.

80. *JS*, p. 675.

81. *Corr.*, vol. I, p. 62. He had an opportunity to contrast Sorel's lectures with reality, when on 7 August he met Comte Benedetti, ambassador to Berlin 1870, at Princesse Mathilde's home at Saint-Gratien.

82. Ibid., p. 178.

83. Paul Baignères, who had become an experienced painter, is mentioned favourably on several occasions by Apollinaire, on the occasion of the Salons des Indépendants or d'Automne (*Œuvres en prose*, vol. II, pp. 83, 150, 227, 375, 412, 482, 613). In January 1893, he painted a portrait of Proust which we have not been able to trace (*Corr.*, vol. I, p. 198, 10 January 1893).

84. *Corr.*, vol. I, p. 185.

85. Ibid., p. 183, 19 August 1892.

86. Gregh, *L'Âge d'or*, p. 168.

87. *Corr.*, vol. I, p. 167. Marie Finaly would marry Thomas de Barbarin, had three children, and died of the Spanish flu after the First World War.

88. As F. Gregh, *L'Âge d'airain, 1905–25* (Grasset, p. 256), and G. Painter. Contrary to what the latter says, 'Sous le clair de lune' (*P et J*, p. 116) does not date from this summer of 1892, but from 1894, as the letter to R. Hahn of 16 September 1894 suggests.

89. Like the church at Carqueville, *RTP*, vol. II, p. 75.

90. *Corr.*, vol. V, p. 301: 'all bunched together beneath its ivy'.

91. Marcel would go to see his plays and would correspond with him. He is buried at the Varengeville cemetery; on his grave is the inscription: 'Perhaps I shall have a name in the history of love.' Perhaps ...

92. Proust evokes all this scenery, which he also describes in *Les Plaisirs et les Jours* (p. 118) and *Jean Santeuil* (p. 507), in a fine letter to Louisa de Mornand (*Corr.*, vol. V, p. 300) in 1905.

93. *Corr.*, vol. I, p. 185, 29 August 1892, and *RTP*, vol. II, p. 126. Charlus to the Narrator: 'Eh! You little rascal!' Proust was fond of the word *'canaille'* [scoundrel or rabble], which he uses seventeen times in *À la recherche*.

94. *Corr.*, vol. I, p. 186.

95. Gregh, *L'Âge d'or*, p. 161.

96. P. Kolb dates this essay to after the article by G. Larroumet (*La Revue des deux mondes*, 1 July 1892, p. 155) which Proust attacked (*Corr.*, vol. I, p. 63). *CSB*, pp. 338–41.

97. Gregh, *L'Âge d'or*, Appendix A, pp. 326–7.

98. *RTP*, vol. I, p. 93.

99. *P et M*, pp. 31–8. E.g. p. 36: 'For me, the only precious stones which would still be capable of making me leave the Collège de France ... [9 lines].'

100. *CSB*, p. 608.

101. *Corr.*, vol. I, pp. 190–1.

102. *Le Banquet*, no. 2, April 1892, 'Les maîtresses de Fabrice'; no. 3, May 1892, Etudes, I: 'A woman does not conceal her love of dancing, shopping, even gambling'; no. 5, July 1892, Études, III: 'her huge, dark eyes as well as some sorrows'.

103. *Corr.*, vol. I, pp. 195–6. As early as September 1888 Marcel had spoken of a 'platonic passion for a famous courtesan', in respect of Laure Hayman (ibid., p. 119).

104. Billy, *Marcel Proust*, p. 79.

105. A. de Fouquières, *Mon Paris et ses Parisiens*, P. Horay, 1953, vol. II, pp. 244–5, has provided the best description. Cf. A. Germain, *Les Clés de Proust*, Sun, 1953, pp. 30–2.

106. *Corr.*, vol. XIX, p. 510, 1920. Cf. *RTP*, vol. II, p. 205: 'Mme de Guermantes wore a boater bedecked with cornflowers', and vol. III, p. 42: 'Your cornflower hat that I liked so much!'

107. *Corr.*, vol. I, p. 384.

108. Germain, *Les Clés*, p. 30.

109. *Corr.*, vol. XIX, p. 527; cf. *RTP*, vol. I, p. 296.

110. No. 3, May 1892, Études, III, 'Esquisse d'après Mme *** '.

111. Gide, *Journal*, Gallimard, 1939, Bibliothèque de la Pléiade, p. 692.

112. *Corr.*, vol. I, p. 197, 1 January 1893.

113. Ibid., p. 201, 26 January 1893.

114. Ibid.

115. Ibid., p. 202.

116. Abbé Vignot, *La Vie pour les autres*, Poussielgue, 1895. Cf. *Corr. gén.*, vol. IV, p. 29, n. 1 and 2. According to P. Kolb (*Corr.*, vol. I, p. 204), Proust had written a review of a sermon by the Abbé Vignot, possibly intended for *Le Banquet* (which ceased publication at the same time). In 1908 he would say to Mme Straus that the Abbé Vignot ought to belong to the Académie française.

117. *Corr.*, vol. I, p. 234: 'I will bring back your *Imitation* which I have used and enjoyed a great deal' (September 1893). See 'La confession d'une jeune fille', 'Violante ou la mondanité' (*P et J*).

118. P. Lavallée, *Souvenirs inédits*, by courtesy of Monique Lavallée and Mme Lavallée-Pessard.

119. P. Lavallée's principal books were to do with the history of French drawing. He died in 1946.

120. 'Quarante-deux lettres à P. Lavallée', introduced by B. C. Freeman, *BAMP*, no. 11, 1961, pp. 323–64. It was also the Lavallée family that Marcel portrayed in 'Famille écoutant la musique' (*P et J*, p. 108).

121. Billy, *Marcel Proust*, pp. 63–4.

122. The Heath family lived in a town house in Neuilly at 54 rue Charles-Laffitte (*Le Bottin mondain*, 1903). See also *BAMP*, no. 11, 1961, p. 328.

123. W. Howard Adams, *A Proust Souvenir*, London, Weidenfeld and Nicolson, 1984, p. 46.

124. G. Painter merely transforms this dedication into his narrative (vol. I, pp. 137–8), as does G. de Diesbach, pp. 138–9). Proust's letters to Heath and to Aubert were destroyed by their family, so one of its members has told us, who also confirmed that Heath and Aubert were first cousins (through their mothers).

125. *P et J*, p. 6.

126. *Corr.*, vol. I, p. 210: those present were R. de Flers, F. de Carbonnel, F. Gregh, W. Heath, Gustave de Waru, Jacques Baignères, Aymar de Martel (Cuyp's son), L. de La Salle, François Picot (a future diplomat), the Vicomte de Léautaud, Robert Proust and Charles de Grancey.

127. 'The courtyard with lilacs and the studio with roses. Mme Madeleine Lemaire's salon', *CSB*, p. 457. In his description of the salon, G. Painter uses Proust's account.

128. Ibid., p. 458. Bénézit's dictionary confirms this information. Proust mentioned the portraits of Mme Kinen and M. de la Chevrelière; cf. Goncourt, *Journal*, vol. III, p. 412: 'This portrait by Madeleine Lemaire is frightening, what with the eyes that look as if they had been punched and that dazed female face.'

129. *CSB*, pp. 487–9.
130. Ibid., p. 458.
131. Ibid., p. 463. A draft of *Le Temps retrouvé* describes 'this laughing mask' of the mother migrating to her daughter's home (*RTP*, vol. IV, p. 970).
132. *Journal*, 15 January 1883, vol. II, p. 981. Cf. ibid., vol. III, p. 823 (Mme Lemaire throwing out J.-É. Blanche). However, Goncourt must have appreciated her rather more when she cried at *Manette Salomon* (ibid., vol. III, p. 1245).
133. Daudet, *Souvenirs*, p. 1018.
134. See H. Bardac, 'M. Lemaire and M. Proust', *La Revue de Paris*, August 1949, pp. 137–42; P. Kolb, 'Marcel Proust et les dames Lemaire', *BAMP*, no. 14, 1964, pp. 114–22: Fouquières, *Mon Paris*, vol. II, p. 206. P. Kolb points out that the letters from Proust to Madeleine Lemaire have disappeared.
135. *BAMP*, no. 14, 1964, p. 151.
136. The key source for an understanding of Robert de Montesquiou is Antoine Bertrand's doctorate thesis, *Les Curiosités esthétiques de Robert de Montesquiou* (Paris-Sorbonne, 1992, 2-vol. typescript). See also E. de Clermont-Tonnerre, *Robert de Montesquiou et Marcel Proust*, Flammarion, 1925; R. de Montesquiou, *Les Pas effacés, Mémoires*, 3 vols., Émile-Paul, 1923, and P. Jullian, *Robert de Montesquiou, un prince 1900*, Librairie académique Perrin, 1965.
137. Montesquiou, *Les Pas effacés*, vol. I. p. 249. He dedicates 'Ancilla', the poem from *Les Hortensias bleus*, to her.
138. R. de Montesquiou, *Têtes couronnées*, Sansot, 1916, p. 211.
139. Described by Clermont-Tonnerre, *Robert de Montesquiou*, p. 23.
140. Ibid., p. 33.
141. *Les Pas effacés*. Quoted by M. Fumaroli in his edition of *À rebours* (Folio, Gallimard, 1977, p. 364). Montesquiou devotes a fine passage to Mallarmé: 'La Porte ouverte au Jardin fermé du Roi' in *Diptyque de Flandre/ Triptyque de France*. He had met him at the home of the Duc de Chaulnes, the friend of Charles Cros (whom Proust would come to know, and quote, through Montesquiou), shortly before 1877. In his book, he includes personal letters from Mallarmé and unpublished texts (some of which will remain so), as well as memoirs and some fine turns of phrase: writers such as Mallarmé are like 'sanctuaries of language, rather like those banks of eternal snow, which Michelet [an author whom Montesquiou probably discussed with Proust] claims remain there like sources ready to irrigate mankind after seasons of deadly drought'.
142. *Journal*, 13 February 1890, vol. III, p. 389; 7 July 1891, vol. II, pp. 604–6.
143. *Corr.*, vol. XVII, p. 156, to J.-É. Blanche.
144. Ibid., vol. I, p. 220, 3 July 1893.
145. Ibid., p. 206, April 1893. Edmond de Goncourt wrote in his diary: 'It's absolutely mad, but not unintelligent, not without talent' (*Journal*, 11 July 1892, vol. III, p. 730).

146. Clermont-Tonnerre, *Robert de Montesquiou*, p. 58.

147. Ibid., p. 59.

148. Ibid., p. 88.

149. *Corr.*, vol. I, p. 204, April 1893.

150. Ibid., p. 206.

151. Ibid., p. 214, 28 June. The two women had poems dedicated to them in *Chef des odeurs suaves*.

152. Ibid., p. 215: 'The other evening, you advised me to admire the great poets "like a brute".' In the same letter, Marcel refers to Emerson, who was making a considerable impact on him at this time.

153. Ibid., p. 217.

154. Ibid., p. 219, 3 July 1893.

155. Ibid., p. 220, July 1893. It was Marcel who had compared himself to Brutus (ibid., p. 215).

156. Edmond de Goncourt, *Journal*, 7 July 1891, vol. III, pp. 604–6: the description of the interior at rue Franklin, and Montesquiou talking about Whistler ('very interesting').

157. *Corr.*, vol. I, pp. 210–11. See 'Un Amour de Proust. Textes inédits à Germaine Giraudeau', introduced by Bryant C. Freeman, *BAMP*, no. 13, 1963, pp. 9–15.

158. *BAMP*, no. 13, 1963, p. 13.

159. *Corr.*, vol. I, p. 211, 25 June 1893.

160. *P et J*, p. 51.

161. *Textes retrouvés*, pp. 61–2 and 236–8.

162. Ibid., p. 61; cf., in the original version of the article, p. 236: 'Art is an instinct, and those that think about it are somewhat impotent.'

163. Ibid., p. 62.

164. *La Revue blanche*, 15 September 1893; *Die Walküre*, Act I, Scene 5.

CHAPTER VI: *The Genesis of* Les Plaisirs et les Jours

1. 'In the social circles in which we moved, tea was taken at 1,800 metres, in just the same way as it was in Paris' (É. de Clermont-Tonnerre, *Robert de Montesquiou et Marcel Proust*, Flammarion, 1925, p. 22, describing his walks with Montesquiou).

2. *Écrits de jeunesse*, p. 265. The castle described by the heroine is probably Griefenstein, in Silesia.

3. It is not Alpgrun, as in the Bibliothèque de la Pléiade edition of *Les Plaisirs et les Jours* and in G. de Diesbach (p. 157). It is hard to understand how this biographer, in the wake of Painter, whom he follows very closely here, could have made Marcel travel up to Righi by funicular ('traditional way up'),

when Righi overlooks the Lac des Quatre-Cantons, and is accessible by train, from Vitznau, a long way from Saint-Moritz! He was even less likely to have followed in the steps of Tartarin over the Alps, as Diesbach suggests, or to have made a pilgrimage to the home of Nietzsche, still very much alive at the time!

4. *P et J*, p. 137. 'Juliers' refers to Mt Julier, on the road from Coire to Saint-Moritz.

5. *RTP*, vol. IV, p. 603; cf. *Corr.*, vol. VI, p. 225. Meredith's sister-in-law was Hortense Howland, a neighbour of Gustave Moreau, who introduced Montesquiou to the painter, with whom the count corresponded before writing about him.

6. One of them was named Geneviève, in homage to Mme Straus.

7. *P et J*, pp. 66–75.

8. *Écrits de jeunesse*, authors' correspondence, pp. 227–43; letters for the novel, pp. 247–71.

9. Grade de Saint-Loup in *Le Côté de Guermantes*.

10. Lemerre, 1893. In it, ten characters exchange forty-two letters. Proust refers to this novel, and to *Flirt*, by the same author (1890). *Écrits de jeunesse*, p. 241.

11. A connection kindly drawn to my attention by Mr Brian Rogers.

12. Barbey d'Aurevilly, *Œuvres romanesques complètes*, Bibliothèque de la Pléiade, vol. II, p. 371.

13. *Écrits de jeunesse*, p. 251. Notice the reversal of the sexes.

14. This is where there are similarities with Barbey. See *Écrits de jeunesse*, p. 265.

15. Ibid. p. 254. This type of work is reminiscent of works like D'Annunzio's *L'Intrus*, in which a husband abandons his wife on several occasions, and, when he finally returns, discovers that she has had a child by another man; he lets the child die (it will be the subject of Visconti's *The Innocent*).

16. Ibid., p. 264.

17. *P et J*, pp. 46–53, 57–62, 112–14, 114–15, 119–20, 120–1.

18. Ibid., p. 119. Cf. below: 'We know that one day she, the thought of whom we live for, will matter as little to us as all others apart from her do now.'

19. Ibid., p. 121; Proust actually writes: 'After [seeing] *L'Invitée* by M. de Curel', a play which had been running since January 1893.

20. See above, p. 50.

21. *Corr.*, vol. I, p. 233.

22. F. Passy (1822–1912), economist, labour historian, militant pacifist and winner of the Nobel Peace Prize in 1901.

23. The diploma for his law degree is dated 10 October 1893.

24. *Corr.*, vol. I, p. 234.

25. According to P. Kolb, he did, however, work for a fortnight for Maître Brunet, a solicitor, 95 rue des Petits-Champs, in October 1893 (*BAMP*, no. 25, 1975, p. 9), that is to say before he consulted Charles Grandjean. Maître

Brunet helped Proust at the time that Mme Georges Weil sold 102 Boulevard Haussmann, and again in 1914 when he was trying to cash a cheque from a German bank. In 1919 he congratulated Proust on the Prix Goncourt; Proust sent him 'all the compliments of his dreadful former clerk' (ibid., p. 11).

26. *Corr.*, vol. I, p. 236.

27. *La Revue blanche*, December 1893; not reprinted in *Les Plaisirs et les Jours*. Not to be confused with 'Souvenir' in *Le Mensuel*.

28. *P et J*, p. 171.

29. Ibid., p. 106.

30. *Corr.*, vol. I, p. 237.

31. Ibid., p. 239, October 1893. The article is also found in *CSB*, pp. 405–9, but not under its actual title.

32. *Corr.*, vol. I, p. 406.

33. Ibid., p. 262, December 1893.

34. Ibid., p. 245, 5 November 1893, to Robert de Billy, who acted as intermediary between Marcel and the Aubert and Heath families over the dedication of *Les Plaisirs et les Jours*: 'Because, I believe,' wrote Billy, 'of certain scruples in the Aubert family, the book appeared with the single dedication to Willie Heath' (*Hommage à Marcel Proust*, p. 28).

35. Proust would make the same comment about *Du côté de chez Swann*.

36. *Corr.*, vol. I, p. 245.

37. Madeleine Lemaire had already illustrated *Flirt*, by Paul Hervieu.

38. *Corr.* vol. I, p. 244. *BAMP*, no. 6, 1956. Grandjean, born in 1857, a friend of Anatole France and Frédéric Masson, ended his career as chief inspector of historical monuments. Marcel must have met him at Princesse Mathilde's home.

39. Ibid., p. 249.

40. For example *Corr.*, vol. I, p. 96, 22 October 1896.

41. *Corr. avec sa mère*, p. 92, 22 October 1896, letter from Mme Proust.

42. On 15 February 1902; he qualified in surgery in June 1904.

43. See A. B. Jackson, *La Revue blanche (1889–1903)*, Minard, 1960, and O. Barrot and P. Ory, *La Revue blanche, histoire, anthologie, portraits*, 10–18, UGE, 1989.

44. Jackson, *La Revue blanche*, p. 13, on one of its founders, Paul Leclercq.

45. *P et J*, pp. 44–5, 127–30, 134–7, 167–73. The two last stories would not be included in the original edition of *Les Plaisirs et les Jours*.

46. Ibid., n. 3, p. 128.

47. Ibid., pp. 169–70.

48. Rodin did like to depict female couples; had Proust seen any in Rodin's studio, or heard tell of a visit the sculptor had made? *Femmes Damnées* (1885), at present in the Musée Rodin, is one example. (Information kindly provided by Mme Nicole Barbin, Keeper of the Musée Rodin.)

49. *Corr.*, vol. I, pp. 262, 264, December 1893. Cf. p. 283.

50. By M. Mossot, Professor of Rhetoric at the Lycée Condorcet (ibid., p. 265; F. Gregh, *L'Âge d'or*, Grasset, 1947, p. 136, n. 1).

51. *Corr.*, vol. I, p. 297, 28 May 1894.

52. Hachette, 1884. Cut-out pages were found among Proust's student notes (Bibliothèque Nationale, MS).

53. Ibid., vol. I, pp. 649–52.

54. Ibid., p. 195.

55. R. de Montesquiou, *Les Pas effacés, Mémoires*, Émile-Paul, 1923, vol. III, p. 25. Montesquiou endeavoured to restore this poet's popularity.

56. *Corr.*, vol. III, p. 271.

57. Like d'Indy, Bizet and Albeniz, Delafosse had been a pupil of Marmontel (1816–98).

58. *Corr.*, vol. I, p. 276.

59. In 1895, Delafosse published *Six Mélodies*, Le Ménestrel: one of them was based upon a poem of Proust's, 'Mensonges' (*CSB*, p. 367 and more complete text in n. 3).

60. *Corr.*, vol. I, p. 285.

61. Ibid., pp. 301–2, n. 3.

62. *RTP*, vol. III, pp. 434–5 and J. M. Nectoux, 'Proust et Fauré', *BAMP*, no. 21, 1971, pp. 1113–14.

63. *Corr.*, vol. I, pp. 310–11, 18 July 1894.

64. I. de Casa-Fuerte, *Le Dernier de Guermantes. Mémoires*, Julliard, 1994, p. 148.

65. *Corr.* vol. I, p. 278, 11 March 1894.

66. Ibid., pp. 279–80.

67. Ibid., p. 281. Bonsais will be found in *RTP*.

68. Ibid., p. 283.

69. Ibid., p. 271: 'These flower-girls which another master has made so dear to me' (in two poems from *Chef des odeurs suaves*: 'Simples' and 'Blumenmädchen', as P. Kolb points out).

70. *CSB*, pp. 360–5.

71. *Corr.*, vol. I, pp. 76, 294.

72. Ibid., p. 305.

73. Ibid., p. 310.

74. Ibid., p. 312, 30 July 1894.

75. Ibid., p. 310, 15 July 1894.

76. Ibid., p. 313, 2 August 1894.

77. As T. Laget points out in his edition of *Les Plaisirs et les Jours* (Gallimard, Folio classique, 1993, p. 336), Barrès wrote about Versailles in 'Notes de Versailles', *Le Journal*, 3 November 1893, reprinted in 'Sur la décomposition', *Du sang, de la volupté et de la mort*, 1894; Régnier, in *Apaisement* (1886). *La Cité des eaux* was not published until 1902.

78. *P et J*, pp. 105–6.

79. *CSB*, p. 411.

80. *RTP*, vol. II, p. 679, vol. III, pp. 56, 906, draft II, pp. 1202–3.

81. 'Le Réveil de Flore', 'Le Banc songeur', 'Adieux au soir tombant', 'Le Pèlerinage inutile'; and *Notes*, p. 83 ff.

82. *P et J*, pp. 6, 81–2. See above, p. 152.

83. Ibid., pp. 6–7.

84. Ibid., p. 7.

85. *CSB*, pp. 365–6.

86. Situated to the east of Paris, between La Ferté-Gaucher and Sézanne, built at the beginning of the eighteenth century and refurbished by J. R. de Cotte, the château consists of a central building and two wings flanked by towers at each corner; it is surrounded by woods and a park. From it, and from the Château de Segrez, Proust drew his inspiration for the Château de Réveillon in *Jean Santeuil*. Madeleine Lemaire illustrated it twice in *Les Plaisirs et les Jours*, Calmann-Lévy, 1896 (*Album Proust*, Gallimard, 1965, p. 148). Later, Proust tells Céleste Albaret that he spent 'two delightful months, among the happiest days of his youth' at Réveillon.

87. *JS*, pp. 457–539.

88. *Hommage à M. Proust*.

89. Mme Verdurin also had a dog (*JS*, p. 472; *RTP*, vol. III, p. 756). Animals are extremely rare in *RTP*.

90. 'The dove [after the dedication], the flowers on the grave (that have disappeared), the pansies (in "Confession d'une jeune fille"), the château' (on the frontispiece and the contents page) (*Corr.* vol. I, p. 329, 17 September 1894).

91. *Corr.*, vol. I, p. 349.

92. Ibid., pp. 320–1. Marcel quotes to Reynaldo the phrase of Shakespeare's that he uses so often: 'Good night, sweet prince . . .'

93. This principle, which he does not entirely adopt: 'French music will be light or it will be nothing', is one to which Hahn subscribed.

94. R. Delage, 'Reynaldo Hahn et Marcel Proust', *BAMP*, no. 26, 1976, p. 231 (who is mistaken about Verlaine's title), interprets this as 'a full admission'.

95. *M. Proust en son temps*, catalogue of the Jacquemart-André exhibition, 1971, no. 228. In the same catalogue, no. 233 proves that Proust knew how to read a score – that of *Dieu-bleu*: 'I wanted to decipher the score before leaving' he wrote (1912). Cf. the stained-glass window reproduced in *Lettres à R. Hahn*. In another letter, Hahn adds: 'Marcel Proust, who is here, has a poet's soul and a heart of gold: he feels the music in the way that an aeolian harp quavers in the wind! I have promised him that I will let him hear you; he no longer sleeps' ('Douze lettres de Reynaldo Hahn', *BAMP*, no. 43, 1993, p. 40).

96. S. Mallarmé, *Œuvres complètes*, Bibliothèque de la Pléiade, p. 860 (the date given is incorrect). The 'Portraits de peintres', written to accompany the poems in *Les Plaisirs et les Jours*, were certainly performed at this concert. Cf. *P et J*, p. 155: 'The tears that sing in the language/ Of the poet, Reynaldo/ Hahn gently release him/ Like gushing water on a pathway' (Mallarmé, *Correspondance*, Gallimard, 1983, vol. IX, pp. 133–4). Mallarmé wrote Hahn a warm letter of introduction to Catulle Mendès in 1897; he entrusted him with the libretto of *La Carmélite* (ibid., vol. X, p. 58; the editors were unaware of this collaboration).

97. On Reynaldo Hahn, see the study by Bernard Gavoty (*Reynaldo Hahn*, Buchet-Chastel, 1976). The musician's own books, which show him to be a writer as well, can also be referred to: *Du chant* (Gallimard, 1957), *Thèmes et variations* (Janin, 1946), *L'Oreille au guet* (Gallimard, 1937), and particularly *Notes*. The complete manuscript of his diary is deposited at the Bibliothèque Nationale; no one allowed to consult it.

98. These biographical details are taken from Gavoty, *Reynaldo Hahn*.

99. In *BAMP*, no. 43, 1993, see the letters from R. Hahn to Risler.

100. See *La Revue de musicologie*, no. 1, 1993.

101. G. de Diesbach, p. 198.

102. *BAMP*, no. 43, 1993, p. 49.

103. Unpublished letters from R. Hahn to M. and S. Lemaire.

104. G. Condé, *R. Hahn, Mélodies*, EMI, 1989.

105. Letter to Marie Nordlinger, in Gavoty, *Reynaldo Hahn*, p. 89.

106. M. X., president of Hermès, recounted by B. Raffali.

107. Catalogue of the London exhibition, no. 354.

108. *Corr.*, vol. I, pp. 388–9, 1895.

109. Ibid., p. 97, 1885 or 1886.

110. Ibid., pp. 340–1. Bréville (1861–1949) was a pupil of Franck.

111. Ibid., vol. IV, pp. 66–7; this is why Proust dedicates the first part of *Sésame et les lys* to Hahn by alluding to this musical work.

112. Ibid., vol. XIV, 1915, to Mme Catusse; cf. ibid., vol. I, p. 321, letter from Mme Proust, 11 September 1894.

113. *Corr.*, p. 324.

114. *P et J*, pp. 116, 138.

115. *Notes*, p. 44; cf. pp. 57, 93.

116. *P et J*, p. 27.

117. A. Henry, *Marcel Proust. Théories pour une esthétique*, Klincksieck, 1981, pp. 34–5. *The Death of Ivan Illich* was published in France in 1886, in an anthology of extracts (Charpentier, trans. Halpérine), as A. Henry points out; it also includes the death of Prince André from *War and Peace*. See below, ch. VII, n. 2, p. 824.

118. See *BAMP*, no. 43, 1993, p. 44. The musical project does not appear to

have been taken further, and Reynaldo confined himself to 'Portraits de peintres'.

119. *Corr.*, vol. I, p. 324, 16 September 1894.

120. Ibid., p. 331, 22 September 1894.

121. Ibid., pp. 332–3, 24 September 1894.

122. Ibid., p. 325. 'The role of the herald and the whole of the king's part, Elsa's dream, the arrival of the swan, the choir passing judgement, the scene between the two women, the *refalado* [a four-note theme], the prelude, is it not all beautiful?' It is worth noting that Proust is speaking of the music here, rather than the libretto (otherwise he would have summarized the plot).

123. Ibid., p. 332, 24 September 1894.

124. Ibid., p. 339, 1 October 1894.

125. 'To M. le comte Robert de Montesquiou-Fezensac.' Cf. ibid., p. 358, 3 January 1895.

126. *P et J*, p. 86.

127. Christian name of Jacques Bizet.

128. *P et J*, p. 89.

129. A. de Fouquières, *Mon Paris et ses Parisiens*, P. Horay, 1953, vol. IV, 'Le Faubourg Saint-Honoré', pp. 50–2.

130. J. Richardson, *Judith Gautier*, Seghers, 1989, p. 172.

131. He describes these extravaganzas in *À la recherche* in a way that has often gone unnoticed: *RTP*, vol. I, p. 119; vol. II, pp. 227, 377, 431, 828, 830; vol. III, pp. 142, 777, 780; vol. IV, pp. 499, 504, 515.

132. September–October 1888. Let us also mention *Madame Sans-Gêne* (1 November 1893); *Leurs gigolettes*, by Meilhac and Saint-Albin (8 November 1893), *Gigolette* at the Ambigu (16 December 1893), Loïe Fuller and Otero at the Folies-Bergère (April 1894).

133. Unpublished letter to S. Lemaire.

134. 'Un dimanche au Conservatoire', *CSB*, p. 370.

135. V. Egger, notebook preserved at the Victor Cousin Library, quoted in H. Bonnet, *Alphonse Darlu, maître de M. Proust*, Nizet, 1961, p. 77.

136. See *Lettres à R. Hahn*, p. 37 (note by P. Kolb).

137. Quoted by Bonnet, *Alphonse Darlu*, p. 181.

138. Darlu considered Emerson one of 'the thinkers who without having a doctrine as such have nevertheless mulled over the most ideas', along with Chateaubriand, Michelet and Renan: one recognizes the Proustian sources (ibid., p. 23) for religious thought without a proper religion. 'We felt ourselves obliged to declare, in the magazine [*La Revue de métaphysique et de morale*] in 1900, that even to our profane point of view, Christ's words were not at all acceptable'; above love, he placed 'the faith of the new age, the rule of justice, based upon the rights of the person' (ibid., p. 32).

139. *La Revue de métaphysique et de morale* (*RMM*), March 1895, in response to Brunetière's article, 'After a visit to the Vatican' (*La Revue des deux mondes*, January 1895). In another article by Darlu, in the *RMM*, May 1898, against Brunetière's article 'After the Trial' (Zola) in *La Revue des deux mondes* of 15 May 1898, he asserts that man is 'an element of a Whole which conceives of the Whole and acts upon the Whole, which is why he rejects pure individualism and pure socialism'.

140. Ibid., May 1898, p. 397. E. Halévy, a former classmate of Proust's, inferred that one 'can be an idealist without being a Christian' (Bonnet, *Alphonse Darlu*, p. 53).

141. *JS*, p. 269.

142. *CSB*, p. 337. See A. Contini, *La Biblioteca di Proust*, Bologna, Nuova Alfa Editoriale, 1988, pp. 54–66, 'La licenza in filosofia: Proust studente alla Sorbonne'.

143. A. Ferré, *Les Années de collège de Marcel Proust*, Gallimard, 1959, pp. 224–5.

144. *Corr.*, vol. IV, p. 139: 'You write some really fine things, and so true! about Ravaisson's physiognomy' (Bergson to Proust, 2 June 1904). Proust had seen Ravaisson at one of Charles Secrétan's meetings, organized by Desjardins at the Societés Savantes building in January 1893, at which he spoke, as did Séailles and Brochard (*Corr.*, vol. I, p. 200).

145. E. Boutroux, *De la contingence des lois de la nature* (1874), quoted by Contini, *La Biblioteca*, p. 60.

146. In Ferré, *Les Années de collège*, p. 227.

147. See the contents lists in the centenary issue (1993).

148. Uncle of Pierre Janet (1859–1947), with whom he should not be confused, Paul Janet was the author of *Morale* (1874), a work of both Aristotelian and Kantian leanings. In 1887, with his colleague Séailles, he published *Histoire de la Philosophie. Les problèmes et les écoles*, and fought against the materialism that relies upon the sciences (*Les Causes finales*, 1877). Bergson devoted an article to him in 1897, and a critical reference in *L'Évolution créatrice*.

149. *CSB*, p. 420.

150. *Corr.*, vol. I, p. 369.

151. Ibid., pp. 443–4, 15 November 1895; the dinner took place on 14 November.

152. Ibid., p. 446.

153. *CSB*, p. 400, clarification of an article that appeared in *La Presse* (11 August 1897), four months before Daudet's death. The latter recorded the thoughts inspired by his suffering in *La Doulou*.

154. Ibid., p. 399.

155. Ibid., p. 402.

156. *Corr.*, vol. XVII, p. 356, September 1918, to Lucien Daudet.

157. Ibid., vol. I, p. 375. Cf. p. 448, where Proust had ordered another score from Fauré's publisher.

158. Ibid., vol. II, p. 162.

159. Ibid., vol. X, p. 395.

160. 'One heard ... sometimes original and enthusiastic performances of all Fauré's latest pieces, of Fauré's sonata . . .' ('Le salon de la princesse Edmond de Polignac', *CSB*, p. 468).

161. *Corr.*, vol. II, p. 283.

162. Ibid., p. 424. Although Marcel's passions may have been short-lived, he still heard Fauré's *Pavane* at Madeleine Lemaire's home on 17 June 1902 (ibid., vol. III, p. 55).

163. Ibid., vol. VII, p. 187.

164. Ibid., p. 197. On 1 July 1907 Fauré, who was ill, was replaced by Risler, who played Wagner, Beethoven and Schumann; Marguerite Hasselmans and Maurice Hayot played Fauré's Sonata for Piano and Violin, one of the models for Vinteuil's sonata, which was beginning to replace that by Saint-Saëns in Proust's imagination (ibid., vol. VII, p. 230), and which was mentioned again in 1913 in connection with *Fervaal*, less restless and more voluptuous. In 1909 Proust, contrasting the city of reality with the 'ideal and true city', deplored the fact that Fauré should have taken so long to be elected to the Institut (ibid., vol. IX, p. 67).

165. Ibid., vol. XI, p. 79.

166. Ibid., vol. XIV, p. 234.

167. *RTP*, vol. III, p. 991. See G. Fauré, *Correspondance*, ed. J.-M. Nectoux, Flammarion, 1980, pp. 203–19.

168. *Corr.*, vol. XV, p. 77.

169. Ibid., p. 84.

170. See especially Hahn's *Thèmes et Variations*.

171. Willy, *Entre deux airs*, Flammarion, 1895, p. 198, quoted by R. Delage, *BAMP*, no. 26, 1976, p. 233.

172. *Claudine en ménage*, in Colette, *Œuvres*, Bibliothèque de la Pléiade, vol. I, pp. 427–8. Instead of '*garçon*' [boy], Colette had at first written '*youpin*' [yid], which Willy changed.

173. *Trait pour trait*, in ibid., p. 1350.

174. *P et J*, pp. 97–103.

175. *Corr.*, vol. I, pp. 390, 392.

176. Ibid., p. 393, 27 May 1895.

177. *BAMP*, no. 43, 1993, p. 44.

178. Around this time, but not necessarily before the recital, Collete wrote to Proust that Willy and she had thought his 'glosses on painters' 'perceptive and beautiful': 'You mustn't spoil them as you do by reading them badly, it's a great shame to do that.' *Corr.*, vol. I, p. 385.

179. *Poèmes*, Gallimard, 1982, pp. 29–33.

180. *Corr.*, vol. II, p. 491.

181. R. Hahn, *Portraits de peintres. Pièces pour piano d'après les poésies de Marcel Proust*, folio, in sheets in original folder.

182. *P et J*, p. 946.

183. *Corr.*, vol. I, p. 382. Proust wrote these passages to Hahn as a warning; it was in April that he waited in vain and followed his friend, and had the feeling that he was experiencing a tragedy before writing to him (ibid., p. 380).

184. *P et J*, p. 140.

185. The decree, signed by Poincaré, was published on 24 June, and the secondment on 3 July.

186. *Corr.*, vol. I, p. 85. This information is taken from Germain Calmette, 'Proust à la Mazarine', *Cahiers Marcel Proust*, no. 6, 1932, p. 277 ff.

187. *Corr.*, vol. I, p. 407, 5 July 1895.

188. Ibid., p. 431; cf. p. 439.

CHAPTER VII: *The Pleasures of* Jean Santeuil

1. *RTP*, vol. II, pp. 553–4 and draft XXI, *Le Côté de Guermantes*, pp. 1172–4; cf. draft XXXII, p. 1247.

2. They would make a second visit in 1897.

3. *RTP*, vol. II, p. 1173.

4. *Corr.*, vol. IV, p. 266, 16 September 1904.

5. *BAMP*, no. 43, 1993, p. 44. B. Gavoty (*Reynaldo Hahn*, Buchet-Chastel, 1976, p. 103) portrays the visit as a reunion of the two friends and Maria Hahn at Clarita Seminario's home, at the Pavillon Louis XIV. This is not what emerges from the letter to Risler that I quote, nor from those of Proust to Maria Hahn.

6. *Corr.*, vol. I, p. 410, 16 July 1895.

7. Ibid., p. 415, 2 August 1895.

8. Ibid., p. 418.

9. Ibid., p. 416, letter of 4 August to P. Lavallée, shortly after Reynaldo's gloomy remarks to Risler.

10. Ibid., p. 88.

11. *P et J*, Folio, p. 207. Dated: 'Petit-Abbeville, Dieppe, August 1895'.

12. *Corr.*, vol. XXI, p. 201, shortly after 16 May 1922, to Mme de Saint-Marceaux.

13. Gavoty, *Reynaldo Hahn*, p. 103. This little-known letter seems to indicate that Brittany is associated with Reynaldo, and thus with *Jean Santeuil*. This is why it disappears from *À la recherche* to make way for Normandy, where Agostinelli, among others, held sway.

14. *Corr.*, vol. I, p. 426. Hahn and Proust stayed in the best hotel on Belle-Île: 'It's the Adrets' inn. If Marcel had not had colic, we should have left already for Beg-Meil' (Gavoty, *Reynaldo Hahn*, p. 106).

15. R. Hahn, *La Grande Sarah: souvenirs*, Hachette, 1930, p. 135.

16. *Le Bottin mondain* (1903), p. 737, which adds: 'Facilities for an inexpensive budget'. It is true that Marcel was not yet seeking palatial surroundings: rather cheapness and calm, far away from prying people.

17. *Corr.*, vol. II, pp. 492–3.

18. One of the Bénacs' family customs.

19. *Corr.*, vol. I, p. 427.

20. Letter to F. de Madrazo (Gavoty, *Reynaldo Hahn*, p. 104).

21. *BAMP*, no. 43, p. 51, letter to Édouard Risler. Proust added a few affectionate words intended for the pianist to this vindictive letter: 'I hope that you will be just as nice to me as you were when you left for your regiment', and he was looking forward to seeing him often the following year.

22. Letter from R. Hahn to É. Risler; cf. *JS*, p. 183.

23. *JS*, pp. 183–201, 354–402.

24. 'Mozart', verse 9. In 1925 Hahn had written the music for Sacha Guitry's *Mozart* and wrote numerous articles about Mozart. His suite, 'Le rossignol éperdu', included a 'Chérubin tragique'. In 1912 Proust was searching for an autographed manuscript by Mozart or Chopin to give to Reynaldo (*Corr*, vol. XI, p. 329).

25. *P et J*, Folio, pp. 330–1, notes by T. Laget. See *Corr.*, vol. XX, p. 612, n. 5.

26. P. Kolb went there in 1954 and saw the apple trees which run down to the beach ('Historique du premier roman de Proust', *Saggi e ricerche di letteratura francese*, vol. IV, 1963, p. 227).

27. *JS*, p. 183.

28. S. Monneret, *Dictionnaire de l'impressionisme*, vol. I, p. 334; she points out that later on Proust would go, with Marie Nordlinger, to Harrison's Paris studio, where there were a number of paintings of Beg-Meil: 'I never imagined that I was taking tea with Elstir', Marie Nordlinger wrote.

29. Painted by Elstir's brush, this became 'a sunrise over the sea' (*RTP*, vol. II, p. 183). At the Hôtel de la Plage P. Kolb saw 'a sunset by Harrison'. André Benac's daughter remembered Harrison; he was wearing 'a strange suit, with baggy trousers', and he set off towards the dunes every evening, at a gallop, to watch the sunset (Kolb, 'Historique du premier roman', pp. 215–27).

30. *JS*, p. 374.

31. *Corr.*, vol. III, p. 408.

32. *RTP*, vol. II, p. 210. Cf. draft LV, pp. 965, 966 (which refers to the relationship with Whistler's 'Opal Gulf').

33. *Corr.*, vol. III, p. 408. Cf. ibid., vol. IV, p. 227, in which the same expressions are used.

34. *JS*, p. 186.
35. Ibid., p. 354. Proust added a comparison which applied to himself: 'They liked to feel that they were pre-eminent in some way . . . like the man of letters who is not recognized, but whose work expresses and retains something of his own personality, however much he may try, like everyone else, to establish his place in the hierarchy.' The Bénacs' name recurs in all Proust's correspondence; a copy of *Les Plaisirs et les Jours* that belonged to them was sold at Clermont-Ferrand on 23 October 1993, as well as a letter from Proust describing Brittany. Their son was killed in the First World War.
36. Ibid., p. 365. In *La Prisonnière* Proust would have less to say about the physical relationship between the Narrator and Albertine. It is true that he did not revise the passage that I quote before its publication. Reading what he wrote at this period – the passages from *Les Plaisirs et les Jours* and the burgeoning *Jean Santeuil* – we find a sensuality that is more violent, fresher and more naïve than in *À la recherche*, that of youth itself.
37. Ibid., pp. 362–4, 365–6.
38. See the article by R. Bales in *Revue d'histoire littéraire de la France*, December 1974.
39. *JS*, pp. 370–6.
40. Ibid., p. 391.
41. Ibid., pp. 382–3.
42. Another image which Proust associated with homosexuality (from 'Avant la nuit', *P et J*, Folio, p. 251, onwards). *Corr.*, vol. IV, p. 227. Cf. ibid., vol. III, p. 408, in which he gives the same advice to Georges de Lauris, in August 1903.
43. *Corr.*, vol. I, pp. 430, 431, 436.
44. *P et J*, Folio, p. 195.
45. Bibliothèque Nationale, n. a. fr., 16611 f. 38; see M. Miguet, 'Sur quelques vers de Théocrite', *BAMP*, no. 43, 1993, pp. 92–102.
46. *RTP*, vol. III, p. 710.
47. Ibid.
48. Ibid., vol. I, pp. 414–15.
49. For Réveillon, see C. Fregnac, *Merveilles des châteaux d'Île-de-France*, Réalités-Hachette, 1963, pp. 280–3, and the two illustrations provided by Madeleine Lemaire for the Calmann-Lévy edition of *Les Plaisirs et les Jours*.
50. Proust rediscovered the chestnut trees from the garden at Auteuil, which he would re-create at Combray.
51. *P et J*, Folio, p. 208.
52. *JS*, pp. 457–539.
53. Ibid., p. 458.
54. Ibid., p. 471.
55. *RTP*, vol. III, p. 1194 (note by A. Compagnon). In the margin of draft II

of *Sodome*, at the point where Guercy (Charlus) and Borniche (Jupien) meet, Proust had written: 'The foxglove in the valley' (p. 938).

56. Ibid., vol. I, pp. 645–51, drafts I to IV.

57. R. Hahn, unpublished letter to Mme Lemaire.

58. *Corr.*, vol. I, p. 446, November 1895, to Pierre Mainguet. The magazine would not publish either this article or another, 'Contre l'obscurité des jeunes poètes', which Proust submitted at the same time; we shall discuss this piece when it is published in *La Revue blanche*.

59. *Notes*, p. 19. For his portrait of Chardin, Proust borrowed from the Goncourts. For Rembrandt, he consulted Émile Michel's articles in the *Gazette des Beaux-Arts*.

60. *CSB*, pp. 373–4.

61. *RTP*, vol. II, p. 713; vol. IV, p. 620.

62. *CSB*, p. 380.

63. *RTP*, vol. IV, pp. 474, 485. A number of Proustian interiors evoke Rembrandt's paintings in their imagery.

64. R. de Billy, *Marcel Proust. Lettres et conversations*, Les Portiques, 1930, pp. 75–6.

65. *Corr.*, vol. I, p. 449.

66. Ibid., vol. I, p. 243. Proust exchanged publications with Louÿs, and thanked him for sending his translation of Meleager. E.g. ibid., vol. XX, p. 618, 5 August 1899: Louÿs had sent him Jean de Tinan's posthumous book and Marcel recognized himself in the rather unflattering portrait of Sainties.

67. Ibid., p. 616.

68. Ibid., p. 619.

69. Ibid., p. 611.

70. *CSB*, pp. 382–4. The chorus from *Samson*, 'Israel, break thy chains', is quoted in *Du côté de chez Swann*.

71. *CSB*, p. 386.

72. *Notes*, p. 10. Proust sent his article to Saint-Saëns with 'the homage of a respectful and fervent admirer, still under the spell of a certain visit made to Dieppe ... to Madame Lemaire' (*Corr.*, vol. II, p. 493, 14 December 1895).

73. *JS*, pp. 679–82.

74. Ibid., pp. 816–19.

75. *RTP*, vol. I, p. 911: 'It was in the Sonata for Violin and Piano by Saint-Saëns'; cf. pp. 935, 941.

76. *JS*, p. 818.

77. Ibid., p. 843.

78. *Corr.*, vol. IX, p. 240. On the other hand, we discover that Marcel had no idea of what the financial arrangements were to be.

79. Ibid., vol. I, p. 453.

80. In the end, there would be no colour at all. Ibid., pp. 454–5.
81. Ibid., p. 457.
82. Ibid., vol. XII, p. 251. Cf. ibid., vol. IV, pp. 104, 1904.
83. In the margins of the manuscript of *À la recherche* there is a note concerning another kiss on the neck, made by Nahmias, Proust's secretary (who may have thought he was reading a different word): 'Oh! Dear Marcel!'. In *Les Plaisirs et les Jours* there is an admission of sensuality: 'Between your neck and my mouth, between your ears and my moustache, between your hands and my hands, there is a special little friendship' (*P et J*, Folio, pp. 213–14).
84. Honoré also suffers an attack of nervous asthma (ibid., p. 230), then his asthma worsens: 'He could not draw breath, his entire chest made a painful attempt to breathe' (ibid., p. 231).
85. Ibid., p. 222: 'The motif of the voyeur, present in all the short stories, can be found in "Combray", in *Sodome et Gomorrhe* and in *Le Temps retrouvé*'.
86. 'The Death of Ivan Ilich', 'Three Deaths', 'The Death of Prince Andrei', 'The Death of Nicolas Levine'. See A. Henry, *Marcel Proust. Théories pour une esthétique*, Klincksieck, 1981, pp. 34–7, and *P et J*, Folio, p. 307.
87. *Corr.*, vol. XXI, p. 678.
88. P. Bourget, *Œuvres complètes*, Plon, 1901, vol. II, pp. 31, 41 (like Odette, Colette is 'too thin'), 48, 74 (at the society soirées, one comes across the snobs from *Les Plaisirs et les Jours*), 540.
89. Bourget quotes: 'Love. Among the majority of mammals and sometimes even among men, the destructive instinct intervenes at the same time as the sexual instinct.' Bourget's hero is 'a doctor who detects strange symptoms in his illness and studies them' (*Œuvres*, p. 327).
90. Ibid., pp. 368, 397, 499, 527, 549, 571.
91. *Corr.*, vol. I, p. 380.
92. Ibid., vol. XI, p. 189, 20 August 1912. Cf. *RTP*, vol. I, pp. 284–5.
93. P. Blay, H. Lacombe, 'In the shadow of Massenet, Proust and Loti; the manuscript of R. Hahn's *L'Île de rêve* in his own hand', *La Revue de musicologie*, 1993, no. 1, pp. 83–107. This article is a model of erudition.
94. The heroine of *L'Indifférent* is reminiscent of Loti's and Hahn's 'in the Polynesian charm of her hairstyle'.
95. Blay and Lacombe, 'In the shadow', p. 107.
96. R. Hahn, *L'Oreille au guet*, Gallimard, 1937, p. 110: '[Melancholia] set in none the less! It settled one day among the ruins and spilled out like some subtly penetrating and revealing emanation . . . the poignant sweetness of regrets, the sense of things vanishing, the bitter and agreeable certainty of the fragility of happiness.'
97. Blay and Lacombe, 'In the shadow', p. 93.
98. *Corr.*, vol. I, p. 327, 16 September 1894.
99. Ibid., p. 363.

100. Ibid., p. 380, 26 April 1895.

101. Ibid., p. 381, April–May 1895.

102. Ibid., p. 394.

103. R. Hahn, Journal, *Candide*, 29 August 1935.

104. *Corr.*, vol. I, p. 438.

105. Ibid., vol. II, p. 52, March 1896.

106. Ibid.

107. Ibid., p. 97, July–August 1896.

108. Ibid., p. 101.

109. Ibid., p. 89: 'And then if we cannot see each other at all we can think about one another.'

110. *Lettres à R. Hahn*, p. 69.

111. *Corr.*, vol. II, p. 105.

112. *Notes*, p. 18.

113. *Corr.*, vol. I, p. 369. See M. Proust, *Mon cher petit*, ed. M. Bonduelle, Gallimard, 1991, p. 78. In this book Doctor Bonduelle, who knew Lucien at the end of his life, has gathered together, in addition to the letters that he possessed, some valuable biographical information about Proust's friend. Note, however, that the term 'Mon cher petit' [My dear little one] was certainly not confined to Lucien.

114. Lucien Daudet, *Vie d'Alphonse Daudet*, Gallimard, 1941, p. 246, quoted by Bonduelle in Proust, *Mon cher petit*, p. 25.

115. *Corr.*, vol. XXI, p. 564.

116. Ibid., vol. I, p. 452; the axiom is repeated by Charlus in *Le Côté de Guermantes*. See L. Daudet, *Autour de soixante lettres de Marcel Proust*, Gallimard, 1929, pp. 30–2, and A. Flament, *Le bal du Pré-Catelan*, Fayard, 1946, pp. 39–42.

117. Proust, *Mon cher petit*, p. 16.

118. *L'Impératrice Eugénie*, Fayard, 1911; *L'Inconnue (L'Impératrice Eugénie)*, Flammarion, 1923; *Dans l'ombre de l'impératrice Eugénie, Lettres intimes adressées à Mme Alphonse Daudet*, Gallimard, 1935.

119. Lucien also wrote a novel about the Parisian homosexual world, *La Planète*, the manuscript of which must have disappeared on his death (A. Rinaldi, 'Lulu et les monstres', *L'Express*, 5 December 1991).

120. *Vie d'Alphonse Daudet*.

121. In 1894 A. Daudet wrote that 'Lucien has become a tall, handsome boy, a little too "chic" but very affectionate'. Lucien added that he looked as if he were twenty years old (Proust, *Mon cher petit*, p. 26). On 1 March 1895, at the Goncourt banquet, Jules Renard described 'a handsome young boy, curly-haired, well spruced, pomaded, made up and powdered . . . He speaks in a little waistcoat pocket voice' (Goncourt, *Journal*, Bibliothèque de la Pléiade, p. 266).

122. J. Cocteau, *Le Passé défini*, vol. I, Gallimard, 1983, p. 274.

123. Daudet, *Soixante lettres*, p. 22. This is the thesis of some of the 'Guermantes' and of G. de Diesbach in his *Proust*.

124. *Corr.*, vol. VI, pp. 119–25.

125. Ibid., p. 72, 29 February 1904.

126. A. Borrel, 'On an alleged portrait of Proust by Jacques-Émile Blanche', *BAMP*, no. 42, 1992: a portrait attributed to Blanche at an auction sale which may have been by Lucien Daudet.

127. *Corr.*, vol. XXI, p. 576.

128. Letter to his mother, in 1905 or 1906, quoted by Bonduelle in Proust, *Mon cher petit*, p. 32. It is not known where Lucien's paintings are. Some 'portraits of women' which he painted, however, remain at the Château de La Roche-Chargé, near Amboise, a former property belonging to the Daudets (see P. Lechantre, 'Chez la veuve Daudet, princesse de lettres', *La Nouvelle République du Centre-Ouest*, 21 July 1944).

129. Proust, *Mon cher petit*, p. 38. Cf. 'I am the dunce of the family, the one who does not matter': it is true that Léon Daudet would help to eclipse his brother, if not stifle him: in 1915 Lucien wrote to his mother that, had he been an only son, he would now be 'someone famous' (ibid., p. 43).

130. *Corr.*, vol. XXI, p. 569: Proust waited for him there from 6.10 to 6.20 p.m.

131. A quarrel had alienated the two friends and Marcel wrote, 'I should be very happy were I to return home this evening and find a note from you telling me, if not that you love me still . . . that you have forgiven me' (ibid., p. 565). And the same day, at a quarter past one in the morning: 'I have seen my feelings for you very well and kindly understood . . . by M. de Goncourt at the princess's home' (ibid., p. 566).

132. The 'book to which you have not yet given a title' (ibid., p. 569).

133. So they saw one another every day. Proust gives this little gesture to Charlotte Clissette in *Jean Santeuil*.

134. *Corr.*, vol. XXI, p. 561.

135. Cf. *RTP*, vol. II, p. 503: 'It was the smell and dust of twilight, just as it had been earlier, when Mme de Guermantes had encountered them on the rue de la Paix.' Thus everything was of use to the writer, who, twenty years later, was unwilling to allow any trace of a subject and an emotion that was transient, yet bathed in the light of a vanished passion, to be lost.

136. *Corr.*, vol. XXI, p. 572.

137. Cf. A. Rinaldi, 'Lulu et les monstres', who quotes a letter from L. Daudet to R. de Saint-Jean: 'One evening, after a tiff, he threw me out: "When human beings drift away, I should like to be able to make them disappear"' (ibid.).

138. Cocteau, *Le Passé défini*, p. 308.

139. *Corr.*, vol. II, p. 68, 21 March 1896.

140. Ibid., p. 53. In the last sentence Proust changes to the familiar '*tu*' form. By

March 1896 Proust had therefore written the first chapter, or preface (*JS*, 183–91), the account of the meeting with the writer C., who on his death-bed bequeaths the manuscript of his novel *Jean Santeuil* (Kolb, 'Historique', p. 235, and *Corr.*, vol. II, p. 53, n. 3).

141. At the Vaudeville, from 31 January. In this unpublished article Proust supplies proof of his erudition by quoting, in the manner of Plato's *Phaedrus*, the anecdote about the poet Stesichorus, who lost his sight for having maligned Helen, and recovered it for having retracted.

142. *CSB*, p. 388.

143. *Corr.*, vol. II, pp. 62–4, 11–12 May 1896.

144. Ibid., p. 64. The inscription of *Les Plaisirs et les Jours* to Laure Hayman, in June, employs the same terms: 'in admiring homage to Madame Laure Hayman for her infinite delicacy of heart, her beauty and her incomparable wit' (ibid., vol. XXI, p. 573). Her personality, that of the noble courtesan, was the complement and opposite to that of Mme Proust.

145. R. Duchêne, *L'Impossible Marcel Proust*, Laffont, 1994, p. 308.

146. *Corr.*, vol. II, p. 69.

147. Ibid., vol. I, p. 331, 18 September 1894.

148. Ibid., vol. II, p. 491.

149. G. de Diesbach, p. 201. G. Painter also refers to a rumour which attributed the entire preface to her. The origin of this rumour is to be found in J.-J. Brousson's *Itinéraire de Paris à Buenos Aires* (1927). See *P et J*, p. 911. Brousson claimed that France had protested against the need for writing a foreword for an author 'whose sentences were so interminable that they wore out your lungs': but Proust was not writing these yet, and the accusation is anachronistic.

150. Letter from Proust to his mother, 16 July 1896.

151. See the article on Maupassant's *Notre cœur* in *La Vie littéraire*.

152. *La Vie littéraire*, vol. II, Calmann-Lévy, 1890, in *Œuvres complètes*, vol. VI, p. 519.

153. Ibid., p. 525.

154. Ibid., p. 323. See 'Anatole France et l'esprit fin de siècle', by M.-C. Bancquart, *Europe*, November–December 1991, in which it is established that the question is not so simple: France suffered the temptations of his age, but upheld freedom of thought.

155. Proust quotes 'Soupir' to Mme Straus (*Corr.*, vol. IV, p. 411, July 1893), a poem that France had published in *Le Temps* of 15 January 1893, in his review of Mallarmé's *Vers et prose*, published three weeks previously.

156. *JS*, p. 479.

157. Ibid., pp. 479–80.

158. *Corr.*, vol. II, pp. 50–1, 29 February 1896.

159. Ibid., p. 109, 28 August 1896.

160. Ibid., p. 119, 1 September 1896.

161. S. Mallarmé, *Œuvres complètes*, Bibliothèque de la Pléiade, 1945, p. 389.

162. Mallarmé, *Œuvres*, p. 155.

163. *Corr.*, vol. II, pp. 111–12.

164. Ibid., vol. XIII, pp. 217–21. Cf. *RTP*, vol. IV, p. 39 and n. 1.

165. Letter of 28 May 1921 to Capitaine Bugnet, *BAMP*, no. 3, 1953, p. 16.

166. André Gide, 'En relisant *Les Plaisirs et les Jours*', *Hommage à Marcel Proust*, p. 110.

167. *P et J*, p. 37.

168. Ibid., p. 78.

169. Ibid., pp. 167–71; 'Avant la nuit' was published in *La Revue blanche* in December 1893.

170. Ibid., p. 130.

171. Ibid., p. 125.

172. Ibid., p. 160.

173. *Corr.*, vol. XVII, p. 290: on 25 June 1918 Gaston Calmann-Lévy wrote to Proust: 'I must confess to you that, out of a print-run of 1,500 copies, there remain in all 1,100 copies in sheets and 71 bound, making a total of 1,171 copies.'

174. Among these, Pierre Lavallée's copy contains a particularly moving inscription (ibid., vol. II, p. 76). Other published inscriptions: to Mme de Brantes (ibid., p. 74); to Robert Proust, 'O brother dearer than the brightness of day (Corneille)' (ibid., vol. IV, p. 422); and to Laure Hayman (ibid., vol. XXI, p. 573). Others are in private collections: Proust distributed review copies generously.

175. See G. da Silva Ramos, 'Bibliothèque proustienne', in *Cahiers M. Proust*, no. 6, 1932, p. 31.

176. See B. Gicquel, 'La composition de *Les Plaisirs et les Jours*', *BAMP*, no. 10, 1960, pp. 249–61, and P. Daum, *Les Plaisirs et les Jours de Marcel Proust*, Nizet, 1993, pp. 175–8.

177. *P et J*, Folio, p. 298.

178. Proust replied to him on 28 June (*Corr.*, vol. II, p. 80).

179. Ibid., p. 108, 28 August 1896.

180. The reviews of *Les Plaisirs et les Jours* are published in the Folio edition, pp. 288–99.

181. *Corr.*, vol. II, p. 79.

182. Ibid., vol. XX, p. 153. The 'demon' is an allusion to Mallarmé's prose poem, 'Le démon de l'analogie'.

183. Ibid., vol. XXI, p. 288, 16 June 1922, to P. Morand: Marcel, who was no longer eating anything, feared that he might have reached the same stage as his grandfather.

184. Ibid., vol. II, p. 80. She inherited 500,000 francs (the equivalent of 9.9 million

francs in 1999 terms) from her father (Duchêne, *L'Impossible Marcel Proust*, p. 308).

185. *Corr.*, vol. II, p. 92. Neither the Jewish nor the Christian faith was mentioned.

186. Ibid., p. 93.

187. 'Ask Papa!' the already elderly sons of James de Rothschild used to say (E. Feydeau, *Mémoires d'un coulissier*, Calmann-Lévy, 1882).

188. Ernest Feydeau, who was at the Bourse [the Paris stock exchange] at the same time as Nathé Weil, explained that no foreign-exchange dealer was able to take responsibility for the funds in his care on his own; which was why backers were needed (ibid., p. 221).

189. E. Feydeau relates that James de Rothschild used to say: '*Ah! fous foilà; sacré foleur de juif allemand!*' (ibid., p. 139). ['Ah! there you are; you wretched German Jewish thief!'; by substituting the sound 'f' for 'v', Rothschild was mimicking the supposed Jewish accent in French. *Tr.*] Chapter XIX of Feydeau's book is devoted to 'Jews at the Stock Exchange'.

190. *Corr.*, vol. II, p. 91, 3 July, to R. Hahn.

191. Goncourt, *Journal*, 3 July 1896, vol. III, p. 1303. Germinie Lacerteux was the Goncourts' Françoise, and Manette Salomon their Rachel or their Odette; Elstir surpassed any of their artist characters.

192. *Corr.*, vol. II, p. 96, 16 or 17 July 1896.

193. Édouard Brissaud (1852–1909), a member of the Académie de Médecine, and, after Babinski, the most brilliant of Charcot's pupils, had published, with Charcot and Bouchard, a *Traité de médecine*; asthma was the subject of volume IV (Masson, 1893). See the remarkable article by Doctor Nicolas Postel-Vinay, 'Notes sur le décor médical de l'univers proustien', *La Gazette du CHU*, vol. 4, no. 8, Colloque 'Proust et la médecine', Tenons, 28 November 1992. It is to him that I owe details about Brissaud.

194. *Corr.*, vol. II, p. 138.

195. *Souvenirs*, Laffont, coll. Bouquins, pp. 159–60.

196. That is to say, in the vocabulary of our own time, symptoms explained by nervous stimulation, in this case the pneumogastric nerve.

197. *RTP*, vol. III, p. 539.

198. *Corr.*, vol. II, p. 451.

199. Ibid., p. 105, 18–20 August 1896.

200. Ibid., p. 89, 3 July 1896.

201. *Corr.*, vol. II, p. 101.

202. Ibid., p. 110, 28 August 1896. Here we recognize a suggestion of the image of the artesian well compared to pain, which we come across in *Le Temps retrouvé*.

203. Ibid., p. 119, 3 or 4 September 1896. Proust mentions *Le Banquier et sa femme*, and he was particularly struck by the 'little domed mirror which reflected

what was happening in the street' and by the technique of perspective and reflection; he himself would become a virtuoso of this technique.

204. *JS*, pp. 286–8. This description applies equally to Kreuznach.

205. *Corr.*, vol. II, pp. 106, 118, 113.

CHAPTER VIII: *From* Jean Santeuil *to Dreyfus*

1. *Corr.*, vol. II, p. 124, 16 September 1896. Hahn had been at Villers while Proust was staying at Mont-Dore; he had returned to Saint-Cloud around 3 September.

2. Ibid., vol. XXI, p. 576. Proust compared this story with the one Edmond de Goncourt had written about the death of his brother Jules, who 'was not, as Flaubert said, just an illusion for him to describe', an expression which Marcel would use in his 1920 article on Flaubert, which demonstrates the growth and persistence of his aesthetic and critical ideas.

3. Ibid., vol. II, p. 124, 16 September 1896.

4. Ibid., p. 130, September 1896, to his mother.

5. Ibid., p. 118.

6. *CSB*, p. 649. Cf. *Corr.*, vol. II, p. 277, in which Proust, revealing his knowledge of Goethe, observed that it is 'a small fact' that served as a core to *Elected Affinities*.

7. *JS*, pp. 306–7, and *Corr.*, vol. II, p. 130.

8. Six and a half million gold francs were already in circulation in France. 'For the banks and the press, the successive issues constituted a mine of commissions and subsidies. The public's enthusiasm, which was cleverly maintained, was undiminished. The mood was ripe for further loans.' (J. Chastenet, *Histoire de la Troisième République*, vol. I, Hachette, 1955, p. 102, and, on the imperial visit, pp. 100–2.) It is worth noting that Proust would later portray the financial investments counselled by Norpois as disastrous.

9. *RTP*, vol. I, p. 533; cf. *CSB*, p. 446, on Princesse Mathilde's salon. *Corr.*, vol. II, p. 130: 'Papa would be much freer here without you during the Russian celebrations.'

10. *RTP*, vol. I, pp. 451–5. It was originally Vaugoubert (based on the Marquis de Montebello, the ambassador to St Petersburg, who master-minded the visit) to whom these remarks were attributed: 'The use of all these linguistic subtleties enabled him to write articles for *La Revue des deux mondes*' (ibid., p. 1340).

11. *JS*, pp. 439–42. The conversation here concerns Jean's future career.

12. M. Barrès, *Mes cahiers*, Plon, 1963, 1994, pp. 61–2.

13. *JS*, pp. 549–53, 554–6. *RTP*, vol. II, p. 381 ff. and 1125, 1127–9.

14. Lucien Daudet, *Autour de soixante lettres de Marcel Proust*, Gallimard, 1927, p. 22.

15. Léon Daudet, *Souvenirs*, Laffont, Bouquins, p. 998. And again: 'We spent a delightful week together, walking in the forest and spending the evenings by the fireside in the quiet, deserted sitting-room.'

16. *Journal*, 30 July 1893, vol. III, p. 856.

17. *Corr.*, vol. II, p. 135, 20 October 1896.

18. *JS*, pp. 360–1, 'Journées de lecture' (*CSB*, pp. 528–31); *RTP*, vol. II, pp. 431–5, and n. 4, p. 432: during the summer of 1919 Proust completed a passage that, with admirable tenacity, he had taken twenty-three years to write. Cf. A. France, *La Vie littéraire*, Calmann-Lévy, 1890, in *Œuvres complètes*, vol. XI, p. 632 ('Roman et magie', 13 January, 1889).

19. *Corr.*, vol. III, p. 182, 4 December 1902.

20. *JS*, p. 361.

21. *Corr.*, vol. II, p. 1472.

22. *RTP*, vol. II, p. 432.

23. *Corr.*, vol. II, p. 138.

24. *JS*, p. 489: Proust was surely thinking of himself when he added that sentences of genuine beauty had been a consolation to 'someone whom [he] regarded as ineffectual and who, beneath his pride may have concealed as much melancholy mistrust and as many feelings of regret and outrage at his helplessness as did Mr Casaubon'. Cf. *RTP*, vol. II, p. 899 and, for Goethe, p. 900.

25. *Corr.*, vol. II, p. 149.

26. See R. de Mesières, 'Un document sur Proust', *The Romantic Review*, New York, 1942, vol. XXXIII; H. Bonnet, 'Proust en 1896', *Europe*, August–September 1970, pp. 120–9.

27. *Corr.*, vol. I, p. 193, December 1892, to Paul Desjardins. Proust poked fun at Barrès in 1894, on the publication in *Le Figaro* of an extract from *Du sang, de la volupté et de la mort*: 'You will see,' he wrote to Reynaldo Hahn, 'that the mule's lust is the start of a love of cliché' (ibid., p. 344, letter of the same date).

28. See Brichot's satirical remark (*RTP*, vol. III, p. 346) and my own *Roman au XXᵉ siècle*, Belfond, 1990, p. 132.

29. He mentions him in *P et J*, p. 15 (in the epigraph) and p. 58 ('a brilliant conversationalist', say Bouvard and Pécuchet).

30. For Zola, Bourget 'had gone to the opposite extreme to naturalism, by deliberately concerning himself purely with the inner human impulses'. Huysmans criticized Bourget and 'his teapot psychology', and Barrès with 'his anaemic toys'.

31. Very different to the one described by Barrès in the 'dedication' to *Un homme libre* (1890): 'Our strong sense of life's problems is due to our perpetual

anxiety. We don't know which foot to put forward first . . . Let us be both passionate and sceptical. It's very easy to be so given the pleasant dispositions we all have these days.' Barrès' anxiety has metaphysical pretentions; Jean Santeuil's are domestic and emotional.

32. *JS*, p. 197. Cf. Saraydar, *Proust disciple de Stendhal; les avant-textes d'"Un amour de Swann' dans 'Jean Santeuil'*, Minard, 1980.

33. *JS*, p. 453.

34. Ibid., p. 556.

35. Ibid., p. 744.

36. Cf. 'It is said that beauty is the promise of happiness. Conversely, the promise of pleasure may be a beginning of beauty' (*RTP*, vol. III, p. 647). But M. Crouzet contends that Stendhal would have approved of Proust's objection ('Le "contre Stendhal" de Proust', *Stendhal Club*, no. 140, 15 July 1993, p. 316).

37. 'Having belittled the novelist in Stendhal unbelievably, by way of compensation, he extols his modesty and the man's gentle behaviour, as if there were nothing else to be said in his favour!' (*CSB*, p. 190).

38. Ibid., p. 19; he is parodying the *Causeries du lundi*, ed. Garnier, vol. IX, p. 272.

39. *RTP*, vol. II, p. 70.

40. He even knew Stendhal's correspondence: the narrator of *CSB* tells his mother that these letters contain 'some cruel things for her family' (*CSB*, p. 259). In his 'Le Salon de la Comtesse Potocka', in 1904, Proust sees in her a reincarnation of the Comtesse Pietranera, in chapter VI of *La Chartreuse de Parme*. He knew that Stendhal looked down on the gothic (ibid, p. 524) and he deplored this. But he also knew that, taking the style of the *Code civil* as his model, Stendhal could not care less about fashionable clichés and romantic lyricism: yet, today, 'we rank him on a level with the greatest romantics' (ibid., p. 555). Although he tended towards vagueness ('these enchanting surroundings', 'these beautiful places', 'this adorable woman'), his style was no less characterized by 'this great subconscious framework that underpins the desired structure of his ideas' (*CSB*, pp. 611, 654, and *RTP*, vol. III, p. 879).

41. *CSB*, p. 612.

42. Ibid., pp. 653–6.

43. P. Kolb, 'Historique du premier roman de Proust', *Saggi e ricerche di letteratura francese*, vol. IV, 1963, pp. 215–77. M. Marc-Lipiansky, *La Naissance de monde proustien dans 'Jean Santeuil'*, Nizet, 1974.

44. As well as a few documents conserved by the University of Urbana and published by P. Kolb.

45. *JS*, pp. 202–42; 226–8; 236–42; 252–8; 361–2, 362–4, 364–5, written on the same sheet of paper.

46. Ibid., p. 677: 'Jean's growing aversion to Madame Marmet'; p. 679: 'War

declared between Jean and the Marmets. The first night of *Frédégonde.*'

47. *Corr.*, vol. II, p. 52, March 1896, to R. Hahn.

48. The appearance of a 'beam of sunlight on the balcony', developed in *Le Figaro* in June 1912 and used again in *Du côté de chez Swann.*

49. *JS*, p. 186.

50. Ibid., p. 190.

51. Ibid.

52. *Corr.*, vol. II, p. 124, 16 September 1896.

53. Ibid., p. 130 and *JS*, pp. 307–8.

54. *JS*, pp. 356–61.

55. Ibid., pp. 576–8.

56. P. Kolb has identified the paper for *JS*, pp. 835–7, with that of a letter written in October 1896 (*Corr.*, vol. II, p. 149).

57. *JS*, p. 825: 'with a very hurried movement of her hand, with which she gave a series of little waves', and, further on: 'Story of the paper on which is written: "My dear little one"'. This was how Marcel addressed Lucien. Charlotte calls the hero 'Marcel', p. 831.

58. Ibid, p. 830.

59. Ibid., p. 840; Lucien came to Fontainebleau on 22 October. See above, p. 266.

60. Ibid., p. 830: 'But the brevity of his first love did not discourage him from others . . . His love affairs multiplied. In none of them was he any longer as confident as he had been the first time, though he still felt its influence.'

61. Ibid., p. 572. Apparently, Proust had not yet read Dickens, about whom he would make further enquiries in the summer of 1897.

62. Ibid., p. 601.

63. Ibid., p. 604.

64. As a note in *Le Carnet de 1908* confirms, in which Proust mentions Rouvier in conjunction with Eulenbourg and Balzac (for *Splendeurs et misères des courtisanes*).

65. *JS*, p. 581.

66. See Marc-Lipiansky, *La Naissance*, pp. 138–9, which emphasizes that Marie only felt guilty in the presence of his wife, as did Proust with his mother.

67. Kolb, 'Historique', p. 240.

68. *JS*, pp. 556, 572, 887. Ruskin's sentences quoted in *Jean Santeuil* come from this article; cf. *Textes retrouvés*, p. 49, note by P. Kolb.

69. Ibid., pp. 411–23. Pages numbered by Proust from 1 to 27, under the title 'The novel' and, below, 'Jean's quarrel with his parents about dinner at the Réveillons'.

70. Ibid., pp. 708–11. He is mentioned several times in letters; it is true that there was no lack of *'panamistes'*. Painter mentions Floquet, Freycinet and Clemenceau.

71. She owned paintings by Daumier, Forain, Fragonard, Greuze, La Tour, Millet, Moreau, Pissarro, Renoir and, by Monet, *Bras de Seine, près de Giverny, à l'aurore,* which Jean Santeuil comments on, *L'Inondation* and *Nature morte.* See *Catalogue de la collection Émile Straus,* Petit, 1929, 64 pages, 21 plates (sales on 3 and 4 June, 1929). *JS,* pp. 895–7.

72. *JS,* p. 806. *CSB,* pp. 662, 674.

73. *JS,* pp. 619–59.

74. Ibid., pp. 830–7.

75. Ibid., p. 392.

76. *CSB,* p. 667.

77. *JS,* pp. 399–402.

78. Ibid., p. 573 and Kolb, 'Historique', p. 258.

79. *JS,* p. 93.

80. Fragment of manuscript, Catalogue Tajan, Drouot, 25 April 1994, no. 44. *CSB,* pp. 431–5. *Textes retrouvés,* pp. 104–9. Marcel complained to Bibesco and La Rochefoucauld, in September 1904 and March 1905 respectively, that *Gil Blas* had not published this conversation. He then wrote a sequel (unpublished until the Pléiade edition of *La Prisonnière*: P. Robert has transcribed this sequel in his preface).

81. Letter of 5 December 1899, *Corr.,* vol. II, p. 377.

82. *Textes retrouvés,* p. 55. *JS,* p. 741 ff.

83. See *Le Carnet de 1908,* n. 28.

84. *JS,* p. 477 ff. *Textes retrouvés,* p. 60.

85. *Textes retrouvés,* p. 12. *RTP,* vol. II, p. 206. The first name is the same: Gabrielle Hébert, Gabrielle Elstir. Hébert painted the portrait of the Comtesse de Guerne (which Proust mentions in his 'salon').

86. Variant of the manuscript, crossed out: 'as it could be felt flowing by'. *JS,* p. 181.

87. Marc-Lipiansky, *La Naissance.*

88. *JS,* pp. 437–46; 447–55.

89. Ibid., pp. 703; 745–853; 842–4; 864–79.

90. Ibid., p. 537.

91. *Corr.,* vol. II, p. 163.

92. Ibid., p. 164.

93. Ibid., p. 165.

94. Ibid., pp. 160–1. Unpublished letter by Proust, Catalogue Tajan, Drouot, 15 November 1996, no. 272: 'I think there's nothing wrong in being photographed with Robert de Flers, and if Lucien Daudet does have rather garish cravats and a somewhat pale skin, it is a drawback that disappears in photography which does not register colours' (4 November in the evening, 1896).

95. Proust first thought of Heredia. Lorrain's seconds were Paul Adam, 'who

was so emotional he had a fit of hysterics', Marcel recalled in 1922 (*Corr.*, vol. XXI, p. 161), and Octave Uzanne, a painter of nineteenth-century women (*Corr.*, vol. II, p. 208).

96. Ibid., pp. vii–viii. When Borda died in 1907, Proust wrote an article about him in *Le Figaro* of 26 December (signed D. for Dominique), *CSB*, pp. 549–50: 'Not only was M. de Borda a wonderful duellist, a man of unrivalled skills, and a person of unusual sensitivity and kindness, he was an incomparable second . . . If memory serves, the last person whom he supported as a second was our contributor, M. Marcel Proust, who always worshipped him.' Proust took the opportunity to pay tribute to his other second, the 'great painter' Béraud, 'that marvellous artist', Borda's closest friend.

97. Ibid., p. 174. Lorrain's articles were in fact often defamatory (but the laws governing the press were much less strict then).

98. E. Jaloux described this scene in his book on Proust (*Avec Marcel Proust*, Geneva, La Palatine, 1953); *Corr.*, vol. II, p. 113. On these various duels, see also the testimony of Léon Daudet, *Souvenirs*, and Georges de Lauris, *À un ami*, Amiot-Dumont, 1948.

99. *Corr.*, vol. XIX, p. 75; vol. XXI, pp. 352–3; different account in Fargue, *Le Piéton de Paris*, Folio, pp. 49–50.

100. M. Maurois, *Les Cendres brûlantes*, Flammarion, 1986, p. 101.

101. *Corr.*, vol. II, p. 178, to L. de Robert. Maurois, *Les Cendres brûlantes*, pp. 100–5.

102. Colette, *Œuvres*, vol. I, Bibliothèque de la Pléiade, pp. 267, 287, 427, 542, 560, and Willy, *Indiscrétions et commentaires*. In these *romans-à-clef*, we also meet France (Gréveuille), Anna de Noailles ('Candeur', p. 542), Madeleine Lemaire and her guests (Mme Lalcade, p. 563), the Comtesse Greffulhe and Fauré (pp. 564–5).

103. *CSB*, pp. 397–9. It is here, in fact, that he denies attacking M. Henri Gauthier-Villars (Willy).

104. *RTP*, vol. I, p. 36. See D. Mayer, 'Le Jardin de Marcel Proust', *Études proustiennes*, vol. V, p. 40.

105. *RTP*, vol. I, p. 675.

106. Mayer, 'Le Jardin', p. 40. See *Corr.*, vol. XXI, p. 581: 'I am going to dine at Parc-des-Princes', or 'for once I shall not be dining at Parc-des-Princes' (July 1897). P. Kolb did not understand that Marcel was going to dine at his parents' house and that this was an obligation he never failed to fulfil, even for Lucien Daudet, except when they were away (ibid., p. 582).

107. *JS*, p. 864. This passage was therefore written after March 1897, while the block of flats was being built.

108. *Corr.*, vol. II, p. 185; J. Lorrain, *La Ville empoisonnée*, pp. 147–9.

109. *Roseaux pensants*, pp. 355–6.

110. 'For Maman's health', 'because it does Maman good, but although it was a

bit of a nuisance for me. I worked so hard there that I wrote no more letters' (*Corr.*, vol. II, pp. 213, 215).

111. *Léonard de Vinci, l'artiste et le savant, 1452–1519, essai de biographie psychologique*, Perrin, 1892. R. Hahn, *Notes*, pp. 58, 62, 63 and *Corr.*, vol. II, p. 211. A. Henry has endeavoured to show the influence of Séailles' book on Proust (*Marcel Proust. Théories pour une esthétique*, Klincksieck, 1981). It is intriguing to see Hahn reading books that one would expect to be read by the author of *Contre Sainte-Beuve*.

112. *Corr.*, vol. I, p. 143, June 1890.

113. Ibid., p. 428.

114. It was also Montesquiou who compared the 'Études de femmes' with the studies of the painter Helleu, in an article to which Proust referred (*Corr.*, vol. II, p. 364, October 1899). Montesquiou wrote about Balzac in *Professionnelles Beautés* and *Roseaux pensants* in particular, which are mentioned by Proust in his article on him, 'Un professeur de beauté', 15 August 1905 (*CSB*, p. 514).

115. *Corr.*, vol. II, p. 133.

116. Ibid., p. 135.

117. Ibid., p. 170 (and about *Mémoires d'outre-tombe* and *L'Éducation sentimentale* at the same time).

118. Ibid., p. 211.

119. Ibid., p. 278.

120. Ibid.

121. About *Crainquebille, Putois, Riquet*, letter to France, May 1904 (*Corr.*, vol. IV, p. 119).

122. 'Le salon de Mme Madeleine Lemaire', *Le Figaro*, 11 May 1903 (*CSB*, pp. 457–8).

123. *Corr.*, vol. IV, p. 144, May–June 1904.

124. Particularly in *La Renaissance latine* (15 January 1904) and in *Le Temps* (1 October 1901). See A. Sorel, *Lectures historiques* (Plon, 1894), *Pages normandes* (Plon, 1907), *Vieux habits, vieux galons* (1913).

125. *Corr.*, vol. IV, p. 176, 10 July 1904, to A. Sorel, to thank him for his article on *La Bible d'Amiens* in *Le Temps*, dated 11 July 1904.

126. Ibid., vol. V, p. 182, 1905.

127. Ibid., p. 283.

128. Ibid., vol. V, p. 324. In 1916 Proust noticed that Balzac had taken as many names from Tallemant as he had from Saint-Simon (ibid., vol. XV, p. 150).

129. Ibid., vol. VI, p. 353. Letter to Montesquiou, 'powerful and delightful Balzac' (ibid., vol. VII, p. 105, March 1907). Montesquiou is identified with Balzac, as is Charlus in *À la recherche* (see ibid., p. 155, where Proust discusses, in order to find the 'keys', Montesquiou's recollections of *La Duchesse de Langeais* and *La Femme abandonnée*, which he would use in 'Combray').

130. Ibid., vol. VII, p. 226, 20 July 1907, to Mme de Caraman-Chimay.

131. Ibid., vol. VIII, p. 123, 16 May 1908. See O. Wilde, 'The Decay of Lying', in *Intentions*, and *RTP*, vol. III, p. 438 and n. 1; *CSB*, pp. 273–4.

132. *Corr.*, vol. IX, p. 246, 29 March 1908.

133. Ibid., vol. X, p. 119.

134. Ibid., p. 153, 1901. See *Le Côté de Guermantes*, *RTP*, vol. II, p. 826, n. 5.

135. *Corr.*, vol. X, to Robert de Billy. Quite unaffectedly, in a letter to Gide, he compared Lafcadio to Rubempré (ibid., vol. XIII, p. 107, 1914).

136. Ibid., vol. XII, p. 65. See ibid., p. 180, in which Proust informed Copeau that he had picked up from Balzac some 'profound aspects' of his 'instinct' (an allusion to the passages that would eventually appear in *La Prisonnière*).

137. Ibid., vol. XIII, p. 353, 1914. See ibid., vol. XIV, p. 146 ('a past perfect that was very Balzac'), or vol. XV, p. 241 (the use of '*intelligentiel*').

138. Ibid., vol. XIV, p. 359, 1915, and vol. XVI, p. 50, 1917. See ibid., p. 129.

139. Ibid., vol. XIV, pp. 146–7, June 1915, to Lucien Daudet; see ibid., vol. XVI, p. 266. And ch. 4 of *Albertine disparue*.

140. Ibid., vol. XIX, p. 224, 20 April 1920, to L. Hauser. See ibid., p. 660: 'I simply made use, as Balzac did, of real names belonging to actual people.' See also Proust's enthusiasm, when Francis Jammes compares him to Balzac (ibid., vol. XIII, p. 26).

141. Ibid., vol. XX, p. 36 (and n. 11, p. 37, which refers in particular to a letter from Ferdinand de Grammont [*sic*] to Balzac, in which he suggests some mottoes, late March 1843, and to his coat of arms which he offered to M. de Balzac, in June 1839). See ibid., p. 282.

142. Ibid., p. 264, May 1921.

143. Ibid., p. 465, 19 September 1921.

144. *JS*, p. 199.

145. Ibid., pp. 199–200.

146. Ibid., p. 435.

147. Ibid., pp. 427–8.

148. Ibid., pp. 429–30.

149. *CSB*, p. 136.

150. Ibid., p. 457.

151. Ibid., p. 489.

152. Ibid., p. 594.

153. Ibid., p. 171.

154. Ibid., pp. 263–98.

155. Ibid., p. 269.

156. Here, Proust develops the theme of the 'Olympian sadness of homosexuality' that he puts into the mouth of Charlus in *Sodome et Gomorrhe*, and returns to the tragic case of Wilde (*CSB*, pp. 273–4).

157. Ibid., p. 274.

158. *Corr.*, vol. II, p. 218, letter to Robert de Flers of 20 September 1897.

159. *L'Écho de Paris*, 26 October 1897.

160. *Corr.*, vol. II, p. 220.

161. *Esclarmonde and Other Poems*, followed by a translation of Barbey's *Brummell* in 1897, an epic poem, *John of Damascus*, in 1901, and other poetry anthologies up until 1942; he translated Croce into English, and he died in 1948. In 1922 he published a memoir, *Adventures, Social and Literary* (Fischer Unwin). See the article by Bryant C. Freeman, *BAMP*, no. 10, 1960, pp. 161–7, from which this information is taken.

162. *La Doulou*, Fasquelle, 1931. In his notebooks that were published subsequently, Daudet refers to the Queen of Naples and her courage at the siege of Gaeta, also mentioned in *À la recherche*.

163. *Corr.*, vol. II, pp. 222–3; Daudet, *Autour de soixante lettres*, p. 34.

164. See p. 208.

165. *CSB*, pp. 402–3.

166. *Corr.*, vol. XXII, p. 580.

167. Ibid., vol. III, p. 87, 10 August 1902. Here we find confirmation of Proust's and Flers' friendship. The cascade of 'etc.' disguises other affections. This period would be that of his 'affection' for Agostinelli, or Rochat. The shorter the period to which it applies, the greater is the jealousy. *À la recherche* simplifies these psychological tempi by parading the Narrator's love for Gilberte, Oriane, Mme de Stermaria and Albertine.

168. Ibid., p. 582.

169. Ibid., vol. II, p. 328; around 1922 B. Faÿ would hear him again speaking about 'little Lucien' while at the same time displaying his friendship for Léon.

170. Ibid., p. 448, September 1901.

171. G. Painter, pp. 227–8. See J.-É. Blanche, *Mes modèles*, Stock, 1928, p. 119. G. Schlumberger (*Mes souvenirs, 1844–1928*, Plon, 1934, pp. 305–8) relates how, on that October evening in 1897, he left Mme Straus's salon, accompanied by Lemaître and Forain; F. Gregh, *L'Âge d'or*, Grasset, 1947, pp. 286–95; Maurois, *Les Cendres brûlantes*, pp. 124–32; J. Reinach, *Histoire de l'affaire Dreyfus*, Fasquelle, 1903, vol. 2, p. 546 (during the summer of 1897, J. Reinach told a number of his friends, including Albert Sorel, A. Leroy-Beaulieu, some members of parliament, and Darlan, the Minister for Justice, of what he had been told by Scheurer-Kestner), and vol. 3, pp. 244–50.

172. *Corr.*, vol. II, p. 243, summer 1898, to Mlle Bartholoni. 'Truth, pity, justice'; we can sense the influence of Tolstoy, and of *Les Plaisirs et les Jours*.

173. L. Blum, *Souvenirs sur l'Affaire*, Gallimard, 1935, p. 38. The attitude of Proust's other cousin, Bergson, was less glorious.

174. Ibid., pp. 42–3. Péguy, *Notre jeunesse, Œuvres en prose*, vol. II, Bibliothèque de la Pléiade, 1988, p. 870: '[the anti-Dreyfusards] explained that people

were pro-Dreyfus because they came from Jewish backgrounds'. Proust, having qualms, returned to this question later, in respect of Joseph Reinach, Bloch, and thus himself; Daniel Halévy also recalls, among his Dreyfusard friends, the 'Jews trembling over their race' ('Apologie pour notre passé', *Cahiers de la Quinzaine*, 5 April 1910, reprinted in *Luttes et problèmes*, M. Rivière, 1911; mentioned by R. Gauthier, *Dreyfusards!*, Archives, Gallimard/Julliard, 1965). See also C. Charle, *Naissance des 'intellectuels'*, Minuit, 1990, p. 215.

175. Blum, *Souvenirs*, p. 91; he made the same remark in *La Revue blanche*.

176. *Corr.*, vol. XI, p. 270, n. 13, 1912.

177. Blum, *Souvenirs*, pp. 75–6. Blum writes favourably about Proust, p. 83, and particularly p. 118, where he considers the chapter of *Le Côté de Guermantes* which deals with the Dreyfus affair to be one of the masterpieces of Dreyfusiste literature; cf. p. 153.

178. *RTP*, vol. II, pp. 592–3. On J. Reinach, see also Péguy, *Notre jeunesse*, pp. 633–4.

179. *RTP*, vol. I, p. 12: 'Our indifference to the sufferings that we cause on earth is a brutal and permanent form of cruelty.' The theme of the oppressed person being defended appears in *Jean Santeuil*: it is when the politician Marie is defended by General Couzon (based on Jaurès, whose speech condemning the massacre of the Armenians, Proust, as we have seen, went to hear).

180. *Corr.*, vol. II, p. 272; cf. p. 251, 2 January 1899.

181. Ibid., p. 276, n. 2.

182. Ibid., p. 275.

183. *JS*, pp. 619–59.

184. Ibid., p. 619.

185. Ibid., p. 620.

186. Ibid., p. 625.

187. Ibid., p. 632.

188. Ibid., p. 635. See J.-D. Bredin, *L'Affaire*, Presses-Pocket, 1983, p. 331. Cf. Reinach, *Histoire de l'affaire*, p. 375.

189. *JS.*, p. 643.

190. Ibid., p. 650. All three of these experts came from the École des Chartes; they did not recognize Dreyfus's handwriting: 'Thus a man whose profession it is to seek the truth that lies hidden in handwriting or in the intestines is somewhat ruthless . . .'

191. Ibid., p. 651.

192. Also discussed by Bredin, *L'Affaire*, and by H. Guillemin, *L'Énigme Esterhazy* (Gallimard, 1962), who directly implicates, though without any proof, General Saussier. On Paléologue, see *Corr.*, vol. V, p. 235, n. 1, and *RTP*, vol. III, p. 46.

193. J. Doise, *Un secret bien gardé, Histoire militaire de l'affaire Dreyfus*, Seuil, 1993.

194. *Corr.*, vol. II, p. 218. Flers ends his letter with the turn of phrase that indicates

he belongs to the circle of Proust's most intimate friends: 'I embrace you very affectionately, my dearest.'

195. Ibid., vol. III, p. 87; already mentioned in connection with Lucien, whose name came *before* that of Flers.

196. *CSB*, pp. 403–5.

197. Ibid., pp. 431–5. The subjects of this dialogue, which uses some of the first names in *Jean Santeuil*, are love, jealousy, forgetting and the restaurant in the Bois. See also the continuation of this dialogue, reproduced in *RTP*, vol. III, introduction to *La Prisonnière*.

198. *Corr.*, vol. I, p. 198, early in 1892, to Billy.

199. 'Une grand-mère', *Le Figaro*, 23 July 1907, *CSB*, pp. 545–9.

200. Together with the composer Claude Terrasse (1901). Proust wrote, ' "I should tell you that in our circle I am one of a small group who could not care less about personal achievement," says one of the characters in the astonishing *Travaux d'Hercule*. . . in which in the middle of the most delightful operetta, there are some superb comic scenes' ('Le salon de la Comtesse d'Haussonville', 1904, *CSB*, p. 486).

201. 'The brilliant authors of the triumphant *Vergy*,' wrote Proust in 1903 ('Le salon de Madeleine Lemaire', *CSB*, p. 459). The play was performed at the Variétés by Ève Lavallière. Marcel was less enthusiastic at the idea of going to see this show (*Corr.*, vol. III, p. 301, to Bibesco).

202. 'He found her pleasant and had no thought of marrying her. She rushed things, and that was that!' wrote J. Pouquet; and Gaston de Caillavet: 'He continued to be happy, very happy, without displaying much emotion. In actual fact it was I who had the better deal, for he's a real battering ram when it comes to forcing open theatre doors' (Maurois, *Les Cendres brûlantes*, pp. 46–7). Sardou's support would actually be very useful to the two young writers. Proust responded to this marriage with polite enthusiasm (*CSB*, p. 546).

203. M. Riefstahl-Nordlinger, 'Et voici les clefs du *Jean Santeuil* de Marcel Proust', *Le Figaro littéraire*, 14 June 1952.

204. *JS*, pp. 451–2.

205. Félix-Louis Terrier (1837–1908), professor at the Faculté de Médecine in Paris, hospital surgeon, an instigator of liver surgery (*Corr.*, vol. VI, p. 244 and n. 6).

206. Ibid., vol. VI, pp. 320–1, December 1906.

207. Ibid., vol. II, p. 236, to Mme Catusse; cf. p. 237, to Montesquiou.

208. Ibid., p. 238.

209. Ibid., vol. II, p. 248, 30 August 1898, to Lucien Daudet: 'Maman is now very well but she is still at rue Bizet and she does not get up.'

210. Ibid., p. 241.

211. Ibid., vol. II, p. 252, September 1898.

212. 'I know you get on well with him,' Proust wrote to him (ibid., vol. II, p. 290). Hermant would depict this milieu in his two *romans-à-clef*, *Le Faubourg* and *La Discorde*. See G. de Diesbach, p. 254 ff.

213. *CSB*, p. 674.

214. Ibid., p. 660.

215. Ibid., p. 662.

216. Ibid., p. 663. Proust may have drawn his inspiration for this scene from a passage in R. de La Sizeranne, 'Ruskin et la religion de Beauté', *Revue des deux mondes*, 1 March 1897.

217. *CSB*, p. 670.

218. Ibid., p. 673.

219. Ibid., p. 674.

220. Ibid.

221. Cf. *JS*, pp. 890–7. He discusses the paintings seen at the home of Charles Ephrussi, who would be one of the models for Swann the art lover, or in the Charpentier collection.

222. *CSB*, pp. 675–7.

223. *JS*, p. 478. The passages in the novel were probably written at the same time as the article.

224. *Souvenirs*, pp. 502–6: the portrait Léon Daudet drew of Proust is marvellously accurate, subtle and elegant.

225. Ibid., p. 506.

226. J. de Tinan, *Œuvres*, Mercure de France, 1923, vol. II, pp. 29, 173.

227. *Corr.*, vol. I, p. 219: 'I have never seen a more beautiful woman.'

228. A biography of her was written by her great-granddaughter, A. de Cossé-Brissac, *La Comtesse Greffulhe*, Perrin, 1991.

229. Ibid., p. 103.

230. Ibid., p. 21; his wife's dowry was a mere 100,000 francs.

231. *Journal*, vol. III, 17 February 1890, p. 388.

232. Ibid., p. 979. Comtesse Greffulhe also kept a diary, or at least she did so from the age of seventeen. It is kept in private archives, and her biography quotes extracts.

233. Quoted by Goncourt, ibid., p. 990.

234. Ibid.

235. Cossé-Brissac, *La Comtesse*, p. 27. Most of the biographical information has been taken from this book.

236. *Béatrice et Bénédict* at the Odéon in 1890.

237. At the Nouveau Théâtre, with Litvinne and Brema (a name which Proust would remember), directed by Lamoureux.

238. J.-É Blanche, *La Pêche aux souvenirs*, Flammarion, 1949, p. 202. The count's brother-in-law, the Prince d'Arenberg, for his part, kept 'his distance': a model for the Prince de Guermantes?

239. Cossé-Brissac, *La Comtesse*, p. 166 ff.

240. Ibid., p. 168.

241. *Corr.*, vol. VII, p. 42, January 1907, to R. Hahn.

242. Comte Boni de Castellane: *RTP*, vol. II, pp. 1051, 1255, 1266; vol. III, p. 1332; he wrote a memoir. The Marquis de Lau: vol. III, pp. 142, 546; vol. IV, pp. 167–8. The Marquis de Breteuil: vol. IV, p. 167. The Prince de Polignac: vol. II, p. 826; vol. III, p. 705.

243. On the 'keys' to *Jean Santeuil*, see Marc-Lipiansky, *La Naissance*, pp. 88–120.

244. *JS*, pp. 465–8.

245. *RTP*, vol. III, p. 705; in June 1922 *L'Illustration* reproduced the painting by Tissot, which enables us to date these lines to the last months of Proust's life.

246. *Corr.*, vol. XII, p. 387. Haas entered into correspondence with Proust in 1897 (vol. II, p. 215). In 1920 Marcel replied to a Harry Swann, who was belatedly rather surprised to see his name appear in a novel: 'The prototype for Swann was M. Charles Haas. Haas, the friend of princes, the Jockey Club Jew. But he was only a starting point. My character developed very differently' (ibid., vol. XIX, p. 660; see below, p. 715, for the invention of Swann's name, its sonorities and the theme of the swan).

247. *JS*, pp. 465–8.

248. Ibid., p. 468. However, the character is endowed with other characteristics that do not belong to Haas and, like many of the other characters in this first novel, he is depicted superficially: in the manner of Balzac and the English novelists, Proust tells us immediately what we ought to think of the hero. In *À la recherche*, his technique would acquire a greater sympathy and sense of mystery.

249. See H. Raczymow, *Le Cygne de Proust*, Gallimard, 1989. Some first-hand biographical information is combined with a more personal monologue and a meditation on Swann.

250. B. de Castellane, *Mémoires*, Perrin, 1986, p. 56.

251. Quoted by A. Gold and R. Fizdale, *Sarah Bernhardt*, HarperCollins, 1992 (French translation, Gallimard, 1994, p. 89).

252. Raczymow, *Le Cygne*, p. 72.

253. *Mon Paris et ses Parisiens*, P. Horay, 1953 p. 48. Fouquières had come to know Haas through the Comtesse de Fitz-James, at whose house Proust may also have met her, having been introduced to the salon by the Marquise de Brantes.

254. *Corr.*, vol. XX, p. 337: 'Charles Ephrussi as Swann' doesn't fit as well as Haas does (14 June 1921).

255. Ibid., vol. II, p. 286, 25 April 1899. Ephrussi was then fifty; it is therefore a little exaggerated to refer to him, as one biographer does, as 'old Ephrussi'. Note that, like Haas, he was a Dreyfusard.

256. The Marquis de Réveillon's Monets (*JS*, p. 893) derive partially from him, particularly *Dégel* ['The Thaw'].

257. *Corr.*, vol. XII, p. 402; cf. vol. XVII, p. 540.

258. Ibid., vol. II, p. 280, 2 March 1899, to Gaston de Caillavet.

259. *RTP*, vol. IV, p. 338; Ferrari died in 1909 at the age of seventy-two.

260. Ibid., p. 903. For Crozier, see André de Fouquières, *Cinquante ans de panache*, P. Horay, 1951, p. 21. A friend of the minister Hanotaux, he introduced André's brother, Pierre de Fouquières, who would be head of protocol for twenty years, to the diplomatic service.

261. *Corr.*, vol. II, p. 289: so as 'not to miss the bus as I did with the Autels privilégiés', he wrote to the author.

262. Ibid., p. 374.

263. *CSB*, p. 411.

264. Ibid.

265. Ibid., pp. 422–3.

266. *Corr.*, vol. II, p. 311, 12 September 1899.

267. As an adolescent, A. de Noailles was dazzled by him: 'I would see a sort of red-haired archangel, whose blue eyes, pure, hard, scrutinizing and defiant, were turned towards his soul' (*Le Livre*, p. 211). Once she was widowed, the archangel would come and console the princess every evening.

268. In Paris, at first 'in a sombre mansion on the Avenue Hoche', with a hall, wrote Anna, 'full of portraits of paternal ancestors who had ruled over the Danube and the Carpathians', then at 81 Avenue Victor-Hugo.

269. Anna de Noailles, *Le Livre*, p. 51. Prince Paul Musurus, the brother of the princess, was originally a diplomat, then a poet.

270. Ibid., p. 137. These were the Menthons, the Maugnys, the Chevillys, the Bartholonis and the Rothschilds.

271. The *Almanac de Gotha* (1906, p. 297) makes it clear that the dynasty was well known from about 1300, through Jugomir Bassaraba, Prince of Wallachia; the family had acquired the principality of Brancoveni in about 1600 and the title of Prince of Brancovan and the Holy Roman Empire had been conferred in 1695. Grégoire's father, Georges Demeter Bibesco (1804–73), Hospodar of Wallachia (1842–48), had married the adopted daughter of the last Prince of Brancovan and taken the royal name of Brancovan. A. de Noailles has portrayed her father (*Le Livre de ma vie*, Hachette, 1932, pp. 17–20), who inspired 'great love and extreme fear' in her, and her mother, 'perfectly beautiful', with a 'brilliant talent as a musician'. The family had backed the Republic, but maintained links with the Prince of Wales, and with Prince Napoléon at Prangins (ibid., p. 35).

272. *RTP*, vol. III, p. 164.

273. This had originally been the title for two articles (15 December 1894 and 1 January 1895) by Lemaître and Vogüé in *La Revue des deux mondes*, which

Brunetière edited. D'Annunzio is hailed as the principal architect of this renaissance. See P. Citti, *Contre la Décadence*, PUF, 1987, p. 183 ff., which alludes to many books whose authors are identified with the Latin movement. It is easy to see why French-speaking Romanians should be associated with it.

274. Last verse of 'Soir d'été', published in *La Revue de Paris*, 1 February 1899, and reprinted in *Le Cœur innombrable* (1901). *Corr.*, vol. II, pp. 301–2, 24 or 25 August 1899.

275. *Corr.*, vol. II, p. 307, 11 September 1899, to his mother.

276. *JS*, p. 398. It is here that we recognize Proust's face.

277. *Corr.*, vol. II, p. 311, 12 September 1899, to his mother.

278. G. Brée, *The World of Marcel Proust*, London, Chatto & Windus, 1967, pp. 116–17. See the plate section, illustration 20.

279. *RTP*, vol. III, p. 1877, n. 1; vol. IV, p. 973; and *Corr.*, vol. VIII, pp. 72–3, on Hermant and adoption by homosexuals, to Mme de Noailles. Furthermore, Proust criticizes Hermant's affected purist style (*RTP*, vol. II, p. 1697).

280. *RTP*, vol. I, pp. 321 and 938.

281. *JS*, p. 520; cf. *Corr.*, vol. II, p. 270 and n. 3.

282. *JS*, p. 520.

283. Ibid., p. 521.

284. Ibid., p. 522.

285. Ibid., pp. 523–4.

286. *Corr. gén.* vol. II, p. 20. Cf. *Hommage à M. Proust*.

287. *Corr. gén.*, vol. II, pp. 20–1.

288. *Corr.*, vol. II, p. 294.

289. Ibid., p. 295.

290. E.g. ibid., pp. 307–8.

291. Ibid., p. 340: 'The first news I heard of Dreyfus' pardon was your letter,' he wrote to his mother on 22 September.

292. Ibid., p. 327: the remark is comical if one thinks of Marcel's father and his brother. But Du Boulbon is also a cultured man.

293. Ibid., p. 347.

294. Ibid., p. 319. 'A bow', Proust adds naïvely, 'such as I have never had from any of the people to whom I, similarly, step aside, who are simple bourgeois folk who walk past stiffly like princes.' Proust, therefore, had still to discover these laws of etiquette which he would take so much care and pleasure in describing in *Le Côté de Guermantes*.

295. *Corr.*, vol. II, p. 200, 7 July 1897, to Kiki Bartholoni.

296. Ibid., p. 326.

297. H. Bordeaux, *La Douceur de vivre menacée*, Plon, 1956, p. 75.

298. *Corr.*, vol. II, p. 367, and M. de Chevilly, 'Proust en Savoie', *BAMP*, nos 23 and 24, 1973 and 1974.

299. 'Proust en Savoie'. Marie de Chevilly was mistaken in asserting that it was only in 1900 that Proust would be entertained by the Chevillys at Montjoux, because of the anti-Semitism of his friends' father. The young woman, who seems to have been almost in love with Proust, described this visit at length, as well as another visit to the Maugnys' home (which must have been later, since Maugny was not yet married in 1899), at which the latter's young wife tried, through the intermediary of her husband, to obtain the petrified Marcel's help in publishing her drawings. After the war Proust would write a preface for a book by Rita de Maugny. As for the prevailing anti-Semitism, Marcel was given further proof of it when a certain M. Galard said to him: ' "You are M. Weil's nephew" with a look that suggested he had exposed me, which annoyed me greatly' (*Corr.*, vol. II, p. 341).

300. *Corr.*, vol. II, p. 354, end of September 1899, to his mother. Proust was hoping to marry off his friend at the time.

301. Ibid., vol. XIX, pp. 538–9. Here Proust points to a source for the little train in *Sodome et Gomorrhe*, *RTP*, vol. III, p. 784. One notes the time and patience needed, far removed from what he terms the literature of reportage, to make use of a memory.

302. *Corr.*, vol. II, p. 315: 'Maugny came to dinner yesterday and slept at the hotel last night. He had room no. 2 and so slept in Papa's bed.'

303. The date suggested by Kolb (ibid., p. 291) seems improbable, since this letter is also a declaration of a break-up: 'God knows whether our paths will cross again.'

304. Ibid., p. 367, 13 October 1899.

305. Ibid., p. 321. Jacques Dubois de Chefdebien, the son of a former member of parliament.

306. Ibid., p. 332, 18 or 19 September 1899.

307. Ibid., p. 326.

308. *RTP*, vol. IV, p. 546; cf. ibid., vol. II, p. 859, n. 1.

309. *CSB*, 'Le salon de la comtesse d'Haussonville', p. 485.

310. *Le Figaro*, 19 November 1907; cf. *RTP*, vol. III, p. 385 ff.

311. *Corr.*, vol. II, p. 344, 24 September: 'On the day the hotel closes, I shall probably feel full of health for the first time, and full of ideas! I haven't anything I need for this stupid contribution to *La Presse*. I'm reduced to doing a sort of article on Mme de Beaumont.' These pieces appeared on 19 September and 12 October 1899. They are reprinted in *CSB*, pp. 427–30.

312. *RTP*, vol. III, pp. 56–7 and n. 1. This passage underwent a number of early drafts.

313. *CSB*, pp. 431–5. A manuscript containing variants of this passage was put up for sale at Drouot's on 25 April 1994 (Catalogue Ader-Tajan, no. 44).

314. *Corr.*, vol. II, p. 360.

315. Hachette, 1897.

316. *Corr.*, vol. II, p. 357, 2 October 1899.

317. Ibid.

318. Ibid., vol. IV, pp. 118–19, May 1904.

319. Mercure de France, 1906, p. 116. Cf. *Corr.*, vol. V, pp. 72–3: 'I know of nothing quite so beautiful as *Sur la pierre blanche*.'

320. *Corr.*, vol. II, p. 358, 2 October 1899.

321. Ibid., p. 361.

CHAPTER IX: The Bible of Amiens

1. Thomas Carlyle, *On Heroes, Hero-worship and the Heroic in History*, Chapman & Hall, London, 1842, pp. 1–2.

2. Ibid., p. 122.

3. Ibid., p. 125.

4. Ibid., p. 128.

5. Ibid., pp. 130, 131.

6. Trans. W. Smith, 1845.

7. Ibid., pp. 246–7.

8. Ibid., p. 251.

9. Ibid., pp. 257.

10. *CSB*, pp. 110–11.

11. Ibid.

12. *Corr.*, vol. V, p. 43, 9 or 10 February 1905.

13. *Lettres à Reynaldo Hahn*, Gallimard, 1956, p. 163.

14. *Corr.*, vol. I, p. 363.

15. *JS*, p. 556.

16. *Essais de philosophie américaine*, 1841–4; French translation by Montégut, Paris, 1851.

17. Ibid., p. 57 (*P et J*, p. 38).

18. Ibid., p. 102 (*P et J*, p. 156).

19. Ibid., p. 78 (*P et J*, pp. 8–9).

20. Ibid. (*P et J*, p. 104).

21. *JS*, p. 368.

22. *Corr.*, vol. XVIII, p. 320, 10 July 1919. We know a few gentlemen who behave in this way.

23. Introduction to *La Bible d'Amiens*, *CSB*, p. 112.

24. Ibid., p. 480.

25. Ibid., p. 540.

26. 1897; 10th edition, Hachette, 1920, which gives an idea of the influence and popularity that this book, but above all Ruskin, enjoyed in France at this time.

27. Ibid., pp. 212–13; 214–15 (and *RTP*, vol. I, p. 43: 'The Celtic Beliefs'); 217; 221; 226.

28. *La Bible d'Amiens*, Mercure de France, 1904, p. 92.

29. Ibid.

30. La Sizeranne, *Ruskin*, p. 230 (J. Ruskin, *Modern Painters*, III, George Allen, Orpington, Kent, 1888, ch. XIV, sections 13, 16, 17).

31. Ibid., pp. 219–50 (quotation from *Elements of Drawing*, II, paragraph 104).

32. *Dialogues des Orateurs*, XXXII, 1, Tacitus, *Œuvres complètes*, Bibliothèque de la Pléiade, 1990, p. 94.

33. Milsand, *L'Esthétique anglaise* (1864); La Sizeranne, *Ruskin*; first published in *La Revue des deux mondes*, in October and November 1894 and in January 1895.

34. *Corr.*, vol. II, p. 367.

35. Ibid., p. 373, October 1899.

36. Ibid., p. 365. The French translation of the complete book, by George Elwall, was published in May 1900.

37. *CSB*, pp. 409–11.

38. *Corr.*, vol. II, p. 375, 30 November 1899.

39. Ibid., p. 377, 5 December 1899.

40. See L. Fearn, 'M. Riefstahl-Nordlinger (1876–1961)', *BAMP*, no. 12, 1962, pp. 485–90.

41. See M. Nordlinger, 'Fragments de journal', *BAMP*, no. 8, 1958, pp. 521–7.

42. Gabriel P. Abrams, *Art nouveau: Bing*, Smithsonian Institution, Washington, DC, 1986, pp. 41–2, 247.

43. *Corr.*, vol. II, p. 384, January 1900.

44. Ibid., p. 378: 'I have something to do on Rheims which is very urgent' (December 1899, to Ainslie).

45. Ibid., p. 402, no. 3.

46. Ibid., p. 28: chapter IV.

47. Ibid., p. 387, 7 or 8 February 1900; cf. p. 391.

48. *CSB*, pp. 439–41.

49. *L'Esthétique anglaise*, p. 112.

50. La Sizeranne, *Ruskin*, p. 96.

51. Ibid., p. 161.

52. Ibid., p. 167.

53. Ibid., p. 276.

54. Ibid., p. 329.

55. Translated in its entirety in 1899, together with *The Crown of Wild Olive*, by George Elwall, Société d'édition artistique. *Lilies: Gardens of Queen's*, sixty-seven pages extracted from *Sesame and Lilies*, was published by l'Union

pour l'action morale in 1896. See J. Autret, *L'Influence de Ruskin sur la vie, les idées et l'œuvre de Marcel Proust*, Geneva, Droz, 1955, pp. 9–15.

56. See K. Clark, *Ruskin Today*, Penguin, 1964, pp. xi–xiii.

57. *The Stones of Venice*, in ibid., p. 142.

58. F. Haskell, *La Norme et le Caprice*, Flammarion, 1986, p. 197. Ruskin is quoted very frequently in this book by our leading historian of artistic taste.

59. Ibid., p. 205.

60. Phaidon, London, 1960; see pp. 324–6 for impressionism.

61. Cf. Ruskin, *Elements of Drawing*.

62. *CSB*, p. 125.

63. Ibid., pp. 441–4.

64. That is to say, his articles of 1 April and 1 August 1900.

65. *CSB*, p. 71.

66. Ibid., p. 76.

67. This is the theory of concomitant variations expounded by Claude Bernard in *Introduction à la médecine expérimentale*.

68. *CSB*, p. 83.

69. *Corr.*, vol. II, p. 391.

70. *CSB*, p. 84.

71. Ibid., p. 89.

72. Ibid., p. 96.

73. Ibid., p. 103.

74. Ibid., p. 104.

75. Ibid., p. 756.

76. It begins on p. 115, l. 7, of *CSB*.

77. 'He searched for the truth, he discovered beauty even in the chronological tables and the social legislation' (ibid., p. 106).

78. Ibid., p. 111.

79. Ibid., p. 112.

80. Ibid., p. 113.

81. Ibid., p. 119.

82. Ibid., pp. 120–2.

83. Ibid., pp. 124–6.

84. Ibid., p. 135.

85. Ibid., p. 132.

86. Ibid., p. 133.

87. Ibid., p. 137.

88. Ibid., p. 138.

89. Ibid., p. 139.

90. Ibid., p. 140.

91. Ibid., p. 141.

92. *Corr.*, vol. II, p. 396, late April 1894, to M. Nordlinger.

93. *Bible*, p. 107; E. Bizub, *La Venise intérieure, Proust et la poétique de la traduction*, Neuchâtel, À la Baconnière, 1991, p. 98.

94. *CSB*, p. 139. No mention here of St Mark's, which was destined eventually to play such a major role.

95. J. Ruskin, *The Stones of Venice*, George Allen, Orpington, Kent, 1884, ch. IV, §LIII, pp. 154–5. Proust's term '*architecture domestique*' is a translation of 'dwelling-house architecture' (p. 153). Clearly, it embraces the palaces on the Grand Canal.

96. *Corr.*, vol. XX, p. 208, 23 April 1921.

97. M. Nordlinger, *Lettres à une amie*, Éditions du Calame, Manchester, 1942, p. ix, 'Eight unpublished letters to Maria de Madrazo introduced by Marie Riefstahl-Nordlinger', *BAMP*, no. 3, 1953, p. 36.

98. *Bible*, p. 245, note.

99. Ibid., p. 219: 'You take a gondola and in a quiet canal, shortly before reaching the simmering, glistening infinity of the lagoon, you come to this "Altar of the Slaves" where you can see (when the sunshine illuminates them) Carpaccio's paintings of St Jerome' (note by Proust).

100. *CSB*, p. 522.

101. In *Saint Mark's Rest*, ch. VIII and IX, which Proust followed closely in Cahier 48 (See J. Yoshida, 'L'après-midi à Venise', *Études proustiennes*, vol. VI, pp. 179–80); the baptistery is the Ruskinian 'holy of holies', said Proust (*Bible*, p. 306, note).

102. 'John Ruskin: *Les Pierres de Venise*, trans. Mme Mathilde P. Crémieux', *La Chronique des arts et de la curiosité*, March 1906; *CSB*, p. 521. The lines that follow draw on the recollections contained in this little-known article. Proust was irritated that his cousin should have cut the passage devoted to San Giorgio and to Carpaccio.

103. Nordlinger, *Lettres*, p. ix. These passages on the decay of Venice are mentioned and discussed in *CSB*, pp. 131–2.

104. *CSB*, p. 133.

105. Ibid., p. 521. Further on, Venice is described as a 'complete and intact museum of domestic architecture during the Middle Ages and the Renaissance'.

106. Vol. I (III); Autret, *L'Influence de Ruskin*, pp. 134–5.

107. *RTP*, vol. IV, pp. 723–5.

108. Cf. *Corr.*, vol. VII, p. 174: Proust noted that at the home of Mme André (the present Musée Jacquemart-André) there was a replica of the Mantegna fresco of the Eremitani, 'one of the paintings I like best in the whole world, which I glimpsed one day at Padua'. (Cf. ibid., vol. II, p. 30.)

109. *RTP*, vol. IV, p. 227.

110. Ibid., p. 204 and n. 1. They are the exact words of Ruskin. Cf. draft XV.4, p. 696.

111. Ruskin illustrated chapter VII, 'Gothic Palaces', of *The Stones of Venice* with

drawings of a number of windows (pp. 232–45). The window in *Albertine disparue* is the quintessence of them.

112. *RTP*, vol. IV, draft XV. 2, p. 694; cf. p. 695, about the same window: 'And if I cried the day I saw it again, it was simply because it said to me: "I remember your mother well."'

113. G. de Lauris, *À un ami*, Amist-Dumont, 1948, introduction, p. 22, quoted by Bizub, *La Venise intérieure*, p. 17. Lauris' response was that Proust only knew Ruskin's English.

114. *Bible*, p. 319.

115. BN, n.a.fr. 16617–18: *La Bible d'Amiens*, 2 vols, 214 and 207 pages, 40 ff from ch. II (n.a.fr. 16623). *Sésame et les lys*, p. 130 ff. in three notebooks, n.a.fr. 16624–6. Translations of *Mornings in Florence* and of *Deucalion* by Mme Proust, and proofs of the translation of *The Crown of Wild Olive* and *Seven Lamps of Architecture* by G. Elwall are evidence of the preparatory work.

116. R. de Billy, *Marcel Proust. Lettres et conversations*, Les Portiques, 1930, p. 120; L. Daudet, *Autour de soixante lettres de Marcel Proust*, Gallimard, 1929, p. 35.

117. *Corr.*, vol. II, p. 414, to his mother: 'I am leaving everything in the drawing-room apart from my copied manuscript which I am taking with me so that the pages can no longer get lost' (24 January 1901).

118. Ibid., p. 365.

119. Ibid., vol. IV, 1904; Lauris, *À une amie*, p. 45. This is about *Sésame et les lys*, on which the young woman collaborated much more, as we shall see.

120. *CSB*, p. 494.

121. E.g. *Bible*, p. 184, n. 1: 'An allusion, Robert d'Humières tells me . . .'; p. 215: 'Robert d'Humières tells me . . .'

122. 'If you leave your son with Robert d'Humières/ Make sure you leave the light on,' wrote Montesquiou. See Painter, vol. II, p. 227.

123. 'Following a serious misunderstanding which deeply wounded his honour,' wrote J. Porel who served under him (*Fils de Réjane*, Plon, 1951, vol. I, p. 283).

124. *Corr.*, vol. II, p. 35.

125. Ibid., p. 401, 30 June 1900.

126. Ibid., p. 409, 21 August 1900.

127. Ibid., p. 408.

128. At this period, people bought buildings, but they rented their apartments or flats.

129. R. Soupault, *Marcel Proust, du côté de la médecine*, Plon, 1967, pp. 59–67.

130. *Corr.*, vol. XII, p. 398, mid-October 1900.

131. *RTP*, vol. IV, p. 691.

132. Ibid., p. 722.

133. Ibid., p. 733.

134. Ibid., vol. IV, p. 207.

135. See H. Bergson, *Mélanges*, PUF, 1972, p. 438 ff.

136. *Corr.*, vol. II, p. 416, 31 January 1901.

137. *P et M*, p. 137. This edition reprints the text of Proust's introduction to *La Bible d'Amiens*.

138. Ibid., pp. 140–1.

139. *Corr.*, vol. II, p. 423: 'I have just put them in an envelope for Mlle Laparcerie' (1 May 1901).

140. C. Mignot-Ogliastri, *Anna de Noailles*, p. 128, clearly reveals that Anna, rather like the author of 'Contre l'obscurité', scarcely read the Symbolists and became steeped in the pessimism of Schopenhauer, whom she read very early; she liked Laforgue, Marceline Desbordes-Valmore, Verlaine and Samain ('*Le Jardin de l'Infante* dazzled me when I was very young'). Moreover, she remained loyal to the Hellenism of the Parnassians and Anatole France, and she read Leconte de Lisle. Her tastes were thus similar to those of *Les Plaisirs et les Jours* and of *Jean Santeuil*: 'I do not only believe in love that is sad and sweet.'

141. 'Nature binds me to her in a most unusual way . . . These hours spent in contemplation are precious to me,' she wrote in August 1899 to Mme Bulteau (quoted by Mignot-Ogliastri, *Anna de Noailles*, p. 134). And in *Le Cœur innombrable*, she exclaims: 'Nature gives us back the mornings of our childhood.'

142. Mallarmé's mistress, Méry Laurent, with whom he conversed about Marcel, had just died on 26 November, bequeathing her house on the Boulevard Lannes to Reynaldo Hahn (see Painter, vol. I, pp. 217–19).

143. Marcel would go to see them at Falaise and would refer to them in *CSB*, ed. Fallois, 1954, pp. 274–5, the chapter known as 'Normandy Hydrangeas' (*Carnet de 1908*): their Provençal name had become Norman 'like those beautiful pink hydrangeas'. The Marquise was a cousin of Montesquiou's.

144. *Corr.*, vol. II, p. 435, n. 3. The guests must also have included someone whom Marcel would later become fond of, Illan de Casa-Fuerte (*Le Dernier des Guermantes. Mémoires*, Julliard, 1994, pp. 187–8); Lucien had introduced him to Marcel, and he would be the cause of a quarrel owing to the jealousy that existed between Daudet and Proust.

145. *CSB*, p. 467, Cf. *RTP*, vol. II, p. 826, in which Proust refers to him as a 'delightful "fantasist"', and vol. III, p. 705, in which he recalls that the prince appeared in Tissot's painting, with Charles Haas, Swann and Galliflet.

146. R. Hahn, *Thèmes variés*, p. 137. The same festivities take place on the grand canal in Versailles in 1910, in honour of Fauré (ibid., p. 138). It was in this important book that Hahn sang the praises of the musical salons (pp. 180–1).

147. 6 September 1903, 'Le salon de la princesse Edmond de Polignac'.

148. *CSB*, p. 465.

149. *RTP*, vol. IV, p. 429.

150. *Corr.*, vol. II, p. 445.

151. *CSB*, p. 467.

152. *Pet J*, p. 25, spoken by Horatio, whose name was used by Proust in 'Baldassare Silvande', whose career as a composer may have been inspired by the prince. A. France, *La Vie littéraire*, Calmann-Lévy, 1890, vol. I, pp. 1 and 8.

153. *CSB*, p. 464.

154. *Corr.*, vol. XVII, p. 359, September 1918.

155. It is not clear why G. Painter, vol. I, p. 295, should describe her as a widow, when she died in 1902, nine years before her husband. There is a genealogy of the Brancovan-Bibesco family, from the seventeenth century onwards, in Mignot-Ogliastri, *Anna de Noailles*, p. 33. G. de Diesbach, the biographer of Antoine's cousin Marthe Bibesco, provides numerous details about the family (see pp. 250–2 and 285–8).

156. *Corr.*, vol. X, p. 330, letter about the death of Prince Alexandre and n. 2 and n. 3.

157. Ibid., vol. II, p. 450.

158. Ibid.

159. Ibid., p. 439, August or early September 1901, and pp. 440–1.

160. Ibid., p. 450, 8 September 1901. Cf. *La Bible d'Amiens*, p. 61: 'The gilded lacework of the porch at Abbeville'.

161. Ibid., p. 459, to Lucien Daudet. Kolb does not explain the reference to these two books, nor to whom they belonged (nor is there any mention in *Le Carnet de 1908*).

162. Ibid.

163. *CSB*, p. 461.

164. Ibid., p. 501.

165. *Corr.*, vol. VI, pp. 52–5.

166. Ibid., vol. IV, p. 369.

167. A. Bibesco, *Lettres de Marcel Proust à Bibesco*, Lausanne, Clairefontane, 1949.

168. Lauris, *À un ami*, p. 10.

169. *Corr.*, vol. III, p. 111.

170. Ibid., vol. IV, p. 423.

171. Hardy's novel, *A Pair of Blue Eyes*, was published in 1873, but had not yet been translated; it is erroneous to see it (as P. Kolb does in particular) as the source for the Bibescos' nickname for Fénelon.

172. *Corr.*, vol. II, p. 455.

173. Ibid., p. 458.

174. Ibid., p. 460.

175. In particular, when he described the burial of the Prince of Polignac.

176. *Corr.*, vol. II, p. 462.

177. Ibid., pp. 463, 470; vol. III, p. 42 and especially p. 74.

178. Ibid., p. 464, 8 November 1901.

179. Ibid., p. 468.
180. Ibid., p. 470.
181. Ibid., vol. IV, p. 79.
182. Ibid., vol. III, p. 180.
183. Ibid., vol. IV, p. 243; in 1904 Ollendorff, in his role as editor of *Gil Blas*, had in his possession a copy of 'Dialogue' (*CSB*, pp. 431–5), which he did not publish either. He would reject *Du côté de chez Swann* too.
184. *Corr.*, vol. III, p. 47.
185. Ibid., p. 49.
186. As would the last part, 'L'avenir'. As P. Kolb observes (*Corr.*, vol. III, p. 60), Proust used to read the beginning of a book and then turn to the ending. This was probably the first book by Maeterlinck that he read. He would make extensive use of *L'Intelligence des fleurs* to write *Sodome et Gomorrhe I*.
187. *Corr.*, vol. III, p. 61, June 1902.
188. 'Bertrand de Réveillon'.
189. *RTP*, vol. II, p. 705.
190. Doctor Henri Vaquez (1860–1936), a hospital doctor and later professor of clinical therapeutics at the faculty, was a specialist in cardiac pathology and published a number of studies, notably on hypertension and cardiac arrhythmia.
191. *Corr.*, vol. III, pp. 99–100, 15 August 1902.
192. *RTP*, vol. I, p. 337.
193. *Corr.*, vol. III, p. 117.
194. Ibid., p. 119, 25 August 1902.
195. Ibid., p. 132, 8 September 1902, to Bibesco.
196. *Corr.*, vol. IX, p. 100.
197. *Bible*, p. 68. For Chartres, see Proust's notes, pp. 113, 175 ('There are ... many other things besides that in these statues at Chartres'), 260–2, 298, 299, 320, 321, 322, 325. It is worth pointing out, too, that in a draft he described the sources of the Loir at Illiers, as if to make the church at Combray correspond to Chartres.
198. Ibid., Foreword, p. 14.
199. *Corr.*, vol. III, p. 153.
200. Ibid., pp. 179–80, 27 November 1902. Here Proust is suggesting a theory of the book as a totality, as a cathedral, and rejects in advance any fragmentary reading of it.
201. Ibid., pp. 187–8, 6 December 1902.
202. Ibid., p. 175, shortly before 24 November. *La Renaissance latine* would publish these extracts on 15 February and 15 March 1903.
203. *Corr.*, vol. III, p. 158.
204. The *Gazette des Beaux-Arts* frequently published articles on Dutch and Flemish painting. Thoré-Burger, who revealed new information about Vermeer

(and about Hals) in this very journal, had published in 1858 and 1869 *Musées de la Hollande* (2 vols). Taine had devoted a section of his *Philosophie de l'art* to the Netherlands, which he had visited on two occasions (and Proust mentions this: *RTP*, vol. II, p. 423, var. *c*, as well as Rodenbach's novel, *Bruges-la-Morte*).

205. In the Goncourt pastiche in *Le Temps retrouvé*, M. Verdurin would speak of 'those pitiful *Maîtres d'autrefois* which are deemed a masterpiece in my wife's family' (*RTP*, vol. IV, p. 287 and n. 15). Mme Verdurin is also presented, wrongly, by the bogus Goncourt as the model for Madeleine in Fromentin's novel *Dominique*. Was this because Fromentin had been in love with Mme Howland, who, as a society hostess, would be a key to Mme Verdurin? Such a subtle game is entirely typical of the 'private jokes' Proust used to play. What is more, in his introduction to *Sésame*, Proust affects to despise Fromentin, who painted an 'extremely mediocre' painting of himself and whose talent had something rather shallow and insubstantial about it (*CSB*, pp. 188–9). Cf. ibid., p. 518 (1905) and the preface to *Propos de peintre* (ibid., p. 580), in which Proust criticizes Fromentin for not having 'even mentioned' Vermeer (in actual fact, he spelt his name Van der Meer and he is the subject of brief mentions: e.g. *Œuvres complètes*, Bibliothèque de la Pléiade, p. 1140, his marginal note in the catalogue: '*View of Delft*, very charming, totally modern').

206. Fromentin, *Œuvres*, p. 518 (1905). This criticism seems undeserved: in fact Fromentin's originality lay in 'the accuracy of the look and the expression' (Sagnes, review of *Les Maîtres d'autrefois*, ed. quoted, p. 1524).

207. Fromentin, *Œuvres*, p. 567. See the introduction by Guy Sagnes, who emphasized that *Les Maîtres d'autrefois* was meant to be a lesson addressed to the Impressionists, whom Fromentin disliked and never helped (which may be one of the reasons for Proust's hostility).

208. Ibid.

209. Ibid., pp. 732–83 (and particularly p. 753 ff. on chiaroscuro), and *CSB*, pp. 659–64.

210. *Corr.*, vol. III, p. 165, Amsterdam, 17 October.

211. *La Philosophie de l'art dans les Pays-Bas* (1868).

212. From here he sent Bibesco a view of the city from the Quai du Rosaire; similarly, he sent Georges de Lauris a view of Ghent town hall, and a panorama of Antwerp, and later a view of Amsterdam to Bibesco (*Corr.*, vol. III, pp. 155–63). He also sent postcards (unpublished) to Hélène de Caraman-Chimay.

213. *CSB*, p. 181; this quotation and those that follow are taken from the introduction to *Sésame et les lys*. Proust sent a humorous poem about Dordrecht to Reynaldo Hahn, a pastiche of Baudelaire, Verlaine and Musset (*Corr.*, vol. III, p. 160): 'Dordrecht, so beautiful a spot/ Grave/ of my cherished

illusions . . .' In *Lettres à Reynaldo Hahn*, p. 70, P. Kolb has published, above these verses, a drawing by Proust (Bradley Martin collection) entitled 'Church at Dordrecht'. Further on, another sketch shows the reflections of boats in the water, rather like the port of Carquethuit by Elstir (reprinted in *Corr.*, vol. III).

214. *CSB*, p. 182; Proust situated this canal in Utrecht, while making clear in his note that it was in Delft.

215. Ibid., p. 181.

216. *Corr.*, vol. III, p. 163.

217. Baedeker, *Belgique et Hollande*, p. 437. It should be mentioned that this guide book, which Marcel, like all travellers at this period, would certainly have used, contained a remarkable history of classical painting (including ten highly complimentary lines on Vermeer and his work, 'pearls of Dutch art', p. xxvii); on the subject of the Mauritshuis in The Hague, it stated that: 'Rembrandt and Vermeer are the heroes of this gallery' (p. 347). Furthermore, the guide quotes Thoré-Burger at length, especially on the *View of Delft*: 'Among the many Vermeer landscapes, one should mention in particular the celebrated view of Delft, which had a considerable influence on the landscape artists of the XIXth century . . . At the centre of the background, dominating all else, is the town with its red and blue roofs, partially bathed in golden sunlight. Nowhere else will one encounter so perfect a rendering of air and light, or the power and sparkling brightness of the shades of colour that we admire in this canvas' (p. 353). If Fromentin makes only brief references to Vermeer, the artist had been mentioned before him by Viardot (1852), Du Camp (1857), Gautier (1858), Goncourt (1861), and after him by Estaunié (*Petits Maîtres*, 1893), Verlaine (*Quinze jours en Hollande*, 1893) and Léon Daudet (*Souvenirs et Polémiques*, 1915).

218. *Corr.*, vol. III, p. 156.

219. Ibid., p. 164, 17 October.

220. Ibid., p. 163, 17 October 1902, to his mother.

221. Ibid.

222. *RTP*, vol. II, p. 813: 'I said that I had once been to Amsterdam and The Hague . . .'

223. Bruges: ibid., p. 423 and var. *c*, where Rachel plans to spend New Year's Day in Bruges, 'with its church towers overlooking the canals and its nuns', to give performances there with 'photographic projections of the main primitives'; Antwerp: ibid., vol. I, p. 635, var. *a*, replaced by Ostende; Dordrecht: ibid., vol. II, p. 899, draft XXXII; Delft: in *Le Temps retrouvé* the sky at sunset is reminiscent of a field of tulips at Delft or Haarlem (ibid., vol. IV, p. 229), and the same image in ibid., vol. II, p. 860; Haarlem: ibid., p. 813; Amsterdam: ibid., vol. III, p. 209, and ibid., pp. 887, 894 – a fine variant in *À l'ombre des jeunes filles en fleurs* describes 'sunset on the Amsterdam

canals' and the Herengracht, where there is a portrait of a woman by Rembrandt and a glass of Schiedam (ibid., vol. II, p. 1421).

224. Ibid., vol. IV, pp. 894, 896. H. Bonnet (*BAMP*, no. 28, 1978) has identified these paintings as being those which were taken from Amsterdam to become part of the collection of Robert de Rothschild, a friend of Proust (who describes them as being exiled at the home of the Princesse de Guermantes).

225. *RTP*, vol. II, p. 1281.

226. Ibid., p. 860. Cf. vol. IV, p. 229, same image.

227. *Corr.*, vol. VI, p. 267.

228. See Claude Mauriac, *Une amitié contrariée*, Grasset, 1970; Simone, *Sous des nouveaux soleils*, Gallimard, 1957, pp. 117–22, in which she draws a portrait of Bernstein; nicknamed Bichtin ('foolish like Bichtin'), he reminds us of Octave 'in a mess'.

229. *Corr.*, vol. III, p. 190, 6 December 1902, to his mother.

230. Ibid. Cf. ibid., p. 265; *RTP*, vol. II, pp. 569–70 and vol. III, p. 407, in which the Narrator alludes to the many suggestions for reform put to him by his mother and grandmother, which come to nothing.

231. *Corr.*, vol. III, p. 191.

232. Ibid., p. 379; cf. p. 378: 'What with Fénelon and my proofs I feel as if I am going mad' (21 or 28 July).

233. Published in *La Chronique des arts et de la curiosité*, 2 January 1904 (*CSB*, pp. 478–81).

234. *Corr.*, vol. IV, p. 200, July 1904. The news came from Albufera.

235. *RTP*, vol. III, p. 168.

236. Unpublished and confidential source.

237. *Corr.*, vol. III, p. 196, 20 December 1902.

238. Ibid., pp. 220–1, late January 1903, to Constantin de Brancovan.

239. Proust mentions the statue of the oxen at Laon in *La Bible d'Amiens* and in 'The Death of the Cathedrals', *CSB*, p. 148.

240. *Corr.*, vol. III, p. 427. Proust mentions Viollet-le-Duc, who said that it was 'so beautiful that it made one want to fall ill at Beaune' – further evidence that Marcel consulted the *Dictionnaire raisonné de l'architecture française* assiduously.

241. *Corr.*, vol. III, p. 340, 8 June 1903.

242. Ibid., p. 391, early August 1903. It must have been in July that Proust showed his proofs to her, for they had already been sent off to the publisher when he made this admission.

243. Ibid., p. 448.

244. Under the byline Marcel Proust.

245. *CSB*, pp. 456.

246. She was also the translator of *Modern Painters*, which was the subject of another article.

247. *CSB*, pp. 480–1.

248. But written shortly after May 1903 (ibid., p. 470).

249. *RTP*, vol. I, p. 623, and vol. II, p. 586.

250. Ibid., vol. II, pp. 1043, 1275, 1278 (the Duchesse de Guermantes is compared to one of this artist's princesses), and vol. III, p. 1476.

251. *CSB*, p. 73; cf. *RTP*, vol. II, p. 206, for Mme Elstir; and already in *Jean Santeuil*, Mme Martial (pp. 455–6; cf. p. 788).

252. J. Adhémar and P. Kolb, 'Ch. Ephrussi', *Gazette des Beaux-Arts*, January 1984, pp. 29–39, provided the bulk of my information. See also S. Monneret, *Dictionnaire de l'impressionisme*, vol. I, p. 224, and J.-É. Blanche, *La Pêche aux souvenirs*, Flammarion, 1949, pp. 174–5.

253. *RTP*, vol. II, p. 713.

254. *JS*, pp. 890–5.

255. See in *Études proustiennes*, vol. I, T. Johnson, '*Debâcle sur la Seine* de Claude Monet'.

256. However, when Proust described a river landscape in the mist in 'Les Monet du marquis de Réveillon', he was referring to *Bras de Seine, près de Giverny, à l'aurore* (1897), exhibited at the Georges-Petit gallery in 1898 and bought by the Strauses.

257. Blanche, *La Pêche*, p. 174.

258. Proust mentions this artist in *À la recherche*, and parodies him, too, in drawings sent to Reynaldo: *Melancholia* and *Adam and Eve* (Prado Museum, Madrid) (see *Corr.*, vol. VI, p. 152).

259. As a manuscript in the Urbana (Illinois) collection attests; according to Blanche (*La Pêche*, p. 175), it is 'an illustrated dictionary which all historians should consult' – as Marcel did when describing Dürer. Proust also made use of articles in the *Gazette* when writing his own: one by Émile Michel for Rembrandt (November and December 1898); for his Monet, he drew on Geffroy, Mirbeau and Rodenbach (according to Mme Borowitz: 'The Watteaus, the Chardins, the Monets of Marcel Proust', *Cleveland Museum Bulletin*, January 1982 and February 1983).

260. *Corr.*, vol. XII, p. 402, to Auguste Marguillier, assistant editor of *La Gazette des Beaux-Arts* and editor of *La Chronique des arts et de la curiosité*, late October 1905. Vigoureux painted his portrait in 1897. In 1904 Proust thanked Marguillier for his monograph on Dürer (Laurens): 'one of the geniuses who most appeals to me and whom I know the least'. In *RTP*, vol. I, p. 318, a servant is compared to one of Dürer's soldiers. Proust was thus able to recall one of the plates from this book.

261. Goncourt, *Journal*, 5 April 1893.

262. *Corr.*, vol. V, p. 42, February 1905, to M. Nordlinger; cf. ibid., vol. IV, p. 54: 'Thanks to Reynaldo, I saw Whistler one evening. And he told me that Ruskin knew absolutely nothing about painting.'

263. E. Munhall, *Whistler and Montesquiou*, French translation, Flammarion, 1995,

p. 150. The countess would accuse Yturri, who was entrusted with returning the cape, of having wanted to steal it. When Montesquiou sold this portrait in 1902, the artist was deeply upset.

264. *RTP*, vol. II, pp. 10, 114, 163, 218, 328, 852; Saint-Loup exclaimed: 'It's as beautiful as a Whistler!' and Charlus admires him just as Montesquiou did. The baron's tailcoat is compared to a 'Harmony in Black and White' by Whistler (ibid., vol. III, p. 52). Elstir paints the portrait of a 'man in tails'.

265. Ibid., vol. II, p. 852: 'It is the moment when, as Whistler says, the bourgeois return home . . . and when it is befitting to begin to look at things.'

266. Ibid., vol. IV, p. 287. At this period the only Frenchman to have written a book about Whistler was Théodore Duret (*Histoire de J. McN. Whistler et de son œuvre*, 1904; repub. 1914); in 1878 he had published a history of the Impressionists (*Histoire des impressionistes*), of whom he was a friend. A collector and a specialist in Japanese art, both Manet and Whistler painted his portrait (*Catalogue Whistler*, RMN, 1995, pp. 205–7).

267. In Camille Mauclair's novel *Le Soleil des morts* (1897), there is an artist by the name of Ellstiern.

268. *Harmony in Grey and Green. Miss Cecily Alexander.*

269. *Corr.*, vol. V, pp. 260–1, 24 June 1905. Proust had in fact noticed a decline in Whistler's popularity in France: he was regarded by many, including Blanche in *La Renaissance latine* (same issue as 'Sur la lecture'), as a man of exquisite taste, but not as a great artist.

270. Ibid., vol. IV, pp. 53–4. Proust quotes Whistler's famous remark in his legal battle with Ruskin: 'You say I painted this picture in a few hours. But the truth is that I painted it with the knowledge acquired over a lifetime,' which he compared with what Ruskin wrote to Rossetti: 'What you draw in any one instant is the result of many years of dreams, love and experience.'

271. 'Symphonie en blanc majeur' (*Émaux et camées*).

272. *Corr.*, vol. III, p. 259, to Antoine Bibesco: 'Isn't it the case that *no one* can guess from the articles, nor indeed does anyone think of guessing, alas.' Cf. p. 317: *Le Figaro* of 14 May published an 'echo': 'In every nook and cranny, everyone is talking about the *Figaro* article on society salons. Who is this "Dominique"? Someone else replies: "It's a novel by Fromentin". Curiosity is running very high.'

273. *Corr.*, vol. III, p. 367, 11 July 1903.

274. *CSB*, p. 457.

275. *RTP*, vol. I, p. 533.

276. 'A large golden bird which observes its prey from afar', *CSB*, p. 468, and *RTP*, vol. II, p. 361.

277. *CSB*, p. 486.

278. *Corr.*, vol. III, p. 214, 19 January 1903, to Bibesco.

279. Ibid., p. 233, 1 February 1903.

280. Ibid., p. 274.

281. Ibid., p. 235, 3 February 1903, to Mme A. Daudet.

282. On this point, see the evidence of Jacques Guérin, Catalogue Ader Tajan, 20 May 1992.

283. *Corr.*, vol. IV, p. 167, 22 June 1904.

284. Ibid., vol. III, p. 238, 4 February 1903.

285. 'To / L.T.B.F.A.F.B.B.C.: A sidereal person/ I offer this ZAIMPH/R.M.F.' (I. de Casa-Fuerte, *Le Dernier des Guermantes. Mémoires*, Julliard, 1994, p. 108, n. 2, for the translation . . .). In this collection the poet attacks Eugénie violently: 'Whom we could not find more loathsome.' He scarcely liked Princesse Mathilde any better, and he called her 'the Widow of Saint-Gratien', because she refused to receive him, as others did, on account of his relationship with Yturri.

286. Ibid., p. 24.

287. Eugénie would entertain Illan at Farnborough (ibid., pp. 73–86).

288. 'Basically, asthma is not an illness, but rather a nervous condition. Those who are afflicted have a mutual understanding; I realized this later, when I made the acquaintance of Marcel Proust . . . and if we became friends so quickly, on the very first day we met, it was because there was an affinity between us created by the same anxieties, the same inability to breathe: all in all, a kinship in suffering' (ibid., p. 52).

289. Ibid., p. 91.

290. *Corr.*, vol. I, p. 356, and Casa-Fuerte, *Le Dernier des Guermantes*, p. 108, n. 1.

291. Letter from Montesquiou to the Marquise de Casa-Fuerte (Casa-Fuerte, *Le Dernier des Guermantes*, p. 147).

292. *Corr.*, vol. X, p. 395, 12 February 1903.

293. Casa-Fuerte, *Le Dernier des Guermantes*, p. 185. It was his mother who introduced Lucien to the empress and, as we know, he became her devoted escort and her biographer.

294. Ibid., p. 187.

295. *Corr.*, vol. VI, p. 100, June 1906.

296. Ibid., vol. III, pp. 303–4. Proust had seen Francis de Croisset's *Les Deux Courtisans* there shortly beforehand, with a musical score by R. Hahn. He would return there on 23 May to see this actress in *On n'a pas le temps*.

297. P. Jullian, *Robert de Montesquiou, un prince 1900*, Perrin, 1965, p. 275. See the excellent introduction to Casa-Fuerte's *Mémoires* by P. Michel-Thiriet, who was such an acute connoisseur of society at this period, and who died too young.

298. Illan appears in D'Annunzio's novel, *Forse che si, Forse che no*, in the guise of Aldo.

299. *Corr.*, vol. III, p. 395, 12 February 1903, and vol. III, p. 329, late May 1903, to Brancovan.

300. Ibid., p. 332, 30 May 1903.

301. Casa-Fuerte, *Le Dernier des Guermantes*, pp. 239–42.

302. *Corr.*, vol. VI, p. 301.

303. Ibid., vol. VII, pp. 66–7. It was from Billy that Proust took his information on these precise and erudite details (some of which I have omitted). Marcel also made Illan repeat countless times 'very simple Italian or Spanish words which pleased him because of their sonority' (Casa-Fuerte, *Le Dernier des Guermantes*, p. 384).

304. Casa-Fuerte, *Le Dernier des Guermantes*, p. 282. After making fruitless attempts at writing plays, Casa-Fuerte published *Le Problème de l'espace* in 1920 (Alcan).

305. *CSB*, p. 47; cf. p. 469, in which Proust mentions that the Marquis d'Albufera was preparing, apart from a volume of his memories of a trip to Tunisia, a résumé of 'Unpublished memoirs of a famous marshal of the First Empire'.

306. *Corr.*, vol. IV, p. 189: 'I very much fear that they may be completely heartless and that Louis, whose heart is so big, suffers a good deal.' P. Kolb compares them to Mme de Marsantes, Saint-Loup's mother, 'who did not have the strength to miss her father and mother for very long'.

307. Ibid., vol. III, p. 350.

308. Ibid., p. 385.

309. An early letter to Louisa de Mornand, which is dated 4 February 1903, already mentions a meeting between the three of them (ibid., p. 237).

310. As René Girard has shown in *Mensonge romantique et vérité romanesque*, Grasset, 1961.

311. *Corr.*, vol. IV, p. 372.

312. Lines addressed to Louis d'Albufera, which constitute a disguised confession (ibid., vol. III, p. 351, 18 June 1903). Albufera, upset at having to return these verses because he had promised to do so, wrote to Marcel: 'Send them back to me – Your Albu. I've read them at least ten times over.'

313. Ibid., p. 351.

314. One of the reasons why he extols Giraudoux to her, notably in the preface to *Tendres Stocks*, was so as to arouse Morand's literary jealousy.

315. *Corr.*, vol. III, pp. 351, 366, July 1903.

316. E.g. ibid., p. 334 and n. 3. See notes 4 and 5 for the reviews. Similarly, 'Rachel played what was almost a simple walk-on part in the little play' (*RTP*, vol. II, p. 472).

317. *Corr.*, vol. III, p. 350.

318. This type of nickname was in fashion: R. Veisseyre has noted sixteen such names preceded by 'Miss' between 1897 and 1908: Miss Cocktail, Miss Flirt, Miss Poustouflette, Miss Lively, etc. ('À la recherche de Louisa de Mornand', *BAMP*, no. 19, 1969, p. 869). Note that Odette, like Louisa, performed in Nice.

319. *Corr.*, vol. IV, p. 73.

320. See Veisseyre, 'À la recherche de Louisa', pp. 864–78.

321. Apart from a few cinema roles, between 1932 and 1935. Ibid., p. 868.

322. 'My friendship with Marcel Proust', *Candide*, 1 November 1928.

323. *Corr.*, vol. IV, p. 169.

324. Ibid., to Louisa.

325. *Corr. avec G. Gallimard*, p. 31.

326. 1906 edition, pp. 349–50.

327. *CSB*, p. 56.

328. *Corr.*, vol. III, p. 343: 'Dined with . . . a Mme de Clermont-Tonnerre, whom I had not met before' (11 June 1903).

329. Ibid., vol. IV, p. 198. In fact, no one had written any 'thoughts' that day. Similarly, when Proust asserted that he had appended his signature 'beneath a tiny Gutman followed by an enormous Fitz-James, and an immense Cholet followed by a tiny Chevreau', it is a clear case of comic distortion; the people concerned were all of the same height. I am indebted to the Duc de Gramont for his extreme kindness in allowing me to visit the château, which was then his property, and to examine the visitors' book as well as some letters that were then unpublished. He told me that Proust had been invited not so much on account of his books, but because the Comtesse de Noailles and Marcel were the two funniest people in Paris. Finally, passing the site of the Ratodrome at the Porte Champerret (where, in the 1960s, there was still a 'Bar du Ratodrome'), he told me: 'That's where Proust got his kicks.' But that is another story . . . See below, pp. 672–3.

330. Ibid., p. 199.

331. In fact, he would defend his doctoral thesis, *Essai d'aérodynamique du plan*, in 1911.

332. *Corr.*, vol. V. p. 313, 28 July 1905.

333. Duc de Gramont, 'Souvenirs sur Marcel Proust', *BAMP*, no. 6, 1956, pp. 171–80.

334. *CSB*, p. 492.

335. *Qui êtes-vous?*, 1909, p. 289.

336. Henriette de Mailly-Nesle. *CSB*, p. 492.

337. Ibid., p. 438.

338. *Corr.*, vol. IV, pp. 332–4. The novel was published in early 1905.

339. Under the name of Larti, a hypochondriac, who does not feel attracted to women, who travels to Holland with his great friend Hermois, quotes Schopenhauer and does not believe that love can lead to happiness (pointed out by Painter, vol. I, p. 30, n. 2). In the letters we have seen, Proust does not reproach him at all for this portrayal.

340. *Corr.*, vol. IV, p. 280 and n. 11. He would marry her on 9 February 1905, 'on the hoof, without inviting anybody' (ibid., p. 396).

341. Ibid., p. 333.

342. Ibid., vol. III, p. 385.

343. Marie de Benardaky married Prince Michael Radziwill.

344. A. de Fouquières, *Cinquante ans de panache*, P. Horay, 1951, pp. 444–5.

345. Ibid., p. 445.

346. *Corr.*, vol. IV, p. 383, December 1904.

347. *CSB*, p. 476.

348. *Corr.*, vol. V, p. 49.

349. P. Kolb, ibid., vol. IV, p. xxi.

350. *Le 'je ne sais quoi'* (1900); *Par politesse*; *Qui trop embrasse*; *Les Toiles d'araignée*; *Tout est bien* (1901); *Chérubin* (1902), which would be the basis for Massenet's opéra-comique in 1905; *La Passerelle*; *Par vertu* (1902); *Les Deux Courtisanes*, *Le Paon* (1904), etc. Proust mentioned this latter play (*Corr.*, vol. IV, p. 207).

351. *Corr.*, vol. VII, p. 160.

352. *RTP*, vol. IV, pp. 530–1.

353. *Corr.*, vol. III, p. 76.

354. Ibid., pp. 415–16.

355. Ibid., vol. IV, p. 171.

356. Ibid., p. 423.

357. From 1912 onwards, very few letters exist. Proust nevertheless sent his wishes for a speedy recovery to his friend during the war and, again in 1917, he asked for news of him from Mme de Chevigné.

358. Sylvain Bonmariage, however, said he had met them at the Bœuf sur le Toit, therefore after the war.

359. *Corr.*, vol. III, p. 318, May 1903.

360. Ibid., p. 358, 24 June or 1 July 1903.

361. Ibid., p. 381.

362. Ibid., p. 379, 21 or 28 July 1903.

363. *Textes retrouvés*, pp. 173–80.

364. *Corr.*, vol. III, pp. 381–7.

365. Proust would give him some later, by Verlaine in particular.

366. *Corr.*, vol. VI, p. 188, August 1906, to Robert de Billy. Ruskin devoted Volume IV of his *Modern Painters* to 'Mountain Beauty'.

367. *Corr.*, vol. III, p. 426.

368. Ibid., p. 452.

369. Ibid., p. 450.

370. 27 November 1903. Maurice de Fleury (1860–1903), who signed himself Horace Bianchon, doctor of medicine, was the author of *Introduction à la médecine de l'esprit* (1897) and of *Grands Symptômes neurasthéniques* (1901). At the Ministry of the Interior, he sat on the same committee for protection against tuberculosis as Professor Proust.

371. M. Nordlinger, *BAMP*, no. 8, 1958, p. 527.

372. *Corr.*, vol. III, p. 447.

373. Ibid., vol. XI, p. 138.

374. Ibid., vol. III, p. 447.

375. Ibid., vol. IV, p. 293.

376. Ibid., p. 314, October 1904, to his mother: 'I have you there, both reunited.'

CHAPTER X: Sesame and Lilies

1. *The History of Tom Jones*; French trans. by M. de La Place, Paris, Rollin, 1751, pp. viii–ix.

2. See S. Monod's introduction to Thackeray's *Vanity Fair*; French trans. by A. Pichot, Folio classique, Gallimard, 1994.

3. J. Conrad, *Œuvres*, Bibliothèque de la Pléiade, vol. I, 1982, introduction by S. Monod, p. xxxii.

4. *Bible*, p. 95.

5. *Corr.*, vol. V, p. 30; cf. J. Autret, *L'Influence de Ruskin sur la vie, les idées et l'œuvre de Marcel Proust*, Geneva, Droz, 1955, p. 62: Proust wrote to Mourey on 9 February 1905 to say that he wanted his translation to be vivid and 'faithful like love and like pity'. Autret none the less pointed out several misinterpretations made by Proust.

6. *Corr.*, vol. IV, p. 399, to thank Goyau for his article in *Le Gaulois*.

7. At the same time, he gave her sister, the Princesse de Caraman-Chimay, a cast of one of the 'months' from Notre-Dame de Paris that he liked (*Corr.*, vol. IV, p. 34).

8. Ibid., p. 32, 8 January 1904.

9. Ibid., p. 38, 15 January 1904.

10. Ibid., p. 50, 30 January 1904.

11. Ibid., p. 57.

12. As well as *Gustave Moreau* by Ary Renan, Gazette des Beaux-Arts, 1899.

13. *Bible*, p. 254, n. 1.

14. *Corr.*, vol. IV, p. 99.

15. Concerning this writer, Proust added that he considered him 'a very great thinker' and that he was reading more of him. Moreover, he compared himself to Bouteiller, the professor of philosophy in *Les Déracinés*, whom Barrès condemns. Barrès' antipathy towards Proust, despite the latter's growing reputation, never ceased, right up to his final, ridiculous comment at Proust's funeral: 'He was our young man.'

16. *Corr.*, vol. IV, p. 93.

17. In the 'Échos' column (twenty-three lines); *Corr.*, vol. IV, p. 105.

18. The review was published in *Séances et travaux de l'Académie . . .* , 1904, pp. 491–2 and reprinted in H. Bergson, *Mélanges*, PUF. The correspondence between

the philosopher and Proust on this occasion reveals that in a letter that is lost Proust had struck home when he described 'the features of Ravaison', to whom Bergson admitted he owed the enthusiastic tone of his review.

19. Ibid., vol. IV, p. 177.

20. Ibid., pp. 276–7.

21. Ibid., p. 400.

22. *Corr.*, vol. V, p. 183, May 1905.

23. Published in *CSB*, pp. 710–13.

24. *Mémoires du duc de Saint-Simon*, 22 volumes, 1873–86, published by Chéruel et Régnier *fils*, together with the index compiled by the author, which Proust made much use of, as, for example, when he pointed out to Bibesco which of Saint-Simon's names were not used by Balzac. One reference also proves that he knew of the additions the duke had made in Dangeau's *Journal* (M. Plantevignes, *Avec Marcel Proust*, Nizet, 1966, p. 238: 'over-scented', Coirault de Saint-Simon (ed.), vol. II, p. 1113, no. 598). See also H. de Ley, 'M. Proust et le duc de Saint-Simon, University of Illinois Press, 1966; J. Milly, *Les Pastiches de Proust*, A. Colin, 1970. Proust quotes the Chéruel edition in 'Le salon de la comtesse Potocka' (13 May 1904). He may have read Sainte-Beuve (*Causeries du lundi*) and Gaston Boissier (1888), and he may have heard Albert Sorel speak on the subject of Saint-Simon at the École Libre des Sciences Politiques.

25. Vols. X–XIV and XVIII of the Chéruel edition.

26. *Corr.*, vol. IX, 1909.

27. *RTP*, vol. IV, p. 409.

28. Milly, *Les Pastiches*, p. 226; Saint-Simon, *Mémoires*, ed. Truc, vol. III, ch. IV, pp. 51–3.

29. At the same period A. Albalat, in his *Formation du style*, stressed the beneficial role of the pastiche.

30. At the same time, since she worked for Bing, she introduced Marcel to Japanese art and told him about these 'dwarf trees', 'trees for the imagination' and 'trees with a past', that he would mention in his article on the *Éblouissements* and in *Le Temps retrouvé* (*RTP*, vol. IV, p. 504), where Montesquiou's initiation is completed: 'I've got the feeling that this Japan is wonderful . . . And I thank you for having shown me . . . some true images in advance' (*Corr.*, vol. IV, p. 50, 30 January 1904). She also sent him the catalogue of the Gillot sale. In particular, as we know, she gave him the 'Japanese game' which would provide one of the loveliest images in 'Combray' (ibid., p. 111, April 1904: 'Thank you for the marvellous hidden flowers which have enabled me this evening to "make a springtime" as Mme de Sévigné says, an inoffensive and fluviatile spring'). Marcel, for his part, gave her a pamphlet by Whistler, *The Gentle Art of Making Enemies* (February 1904), while she would send him, at the beginning of 1905, a copy of *Mr Whistler's Ten O'Clock*

(*Corr.*, vol. V, p. 41); he would write thirty or so poems as a tribute to her skill as a sculptor and a translator (ibid., pp. 60–1). In April 1905, he also accompanied her to the Louvre, to the exhibition of 'Primitifs français (1350–1589)' which 'half killed' him (ibid., p. 111).

31. In May 1904 he found 'the six *Sésame* notebooks' that he had lost at the beginning of the year.

32. *Corr.*, vol. IV, p. 111, April 1904.

33. Ibid., p. 384.

34. Thirty-nine volumes, London, G. Allen.

35. Reproduced in Autret, *L'Influence de Ruskin*, p. 119; cf. p. 120.

36. Ibid., p. 137.

37. *Corr.*, vol. V, p. 260.

38. *Lettres à une amie: 41 lettres de Marcel Proust à Marie Nordlinger* (Éditions du Calame, Manchester, 1942), p. x.

39. *Corr.*, vol. V, p. 193, early June 1905, to his mother.

40. Ibid., vol. IV, p. 272, 17 September 1904, to M. Nordlinger.

41. Both of them models for the heroine of Maupassant's *Notre cœur* (ed. M.-C. Bancquart, Folio, Gallimard, 1993, p. 20). Marie Kahn was also Bourget's mistress. They were both painted by Bonnat (Bayonne museum), and the countess by Boldini; they may have had a relationship (and with their friend Mme Straus, ibid., p. 22). Cf. p. 47: in Maupassant's novel Mme de Burnes had a slang term for male genitals as her patronymic.

42. *Corr.*, vol. IV, p. 121.

43. The dress rehearsal took place on 6 October 1904. Whole sections of Proust's article were reproduced in an article by Serge Basset in *Le Figaro* (8 October 1904); see *Textes retrouvés*, pp. 205–7 (Basset's article) and pp. 351–4 (Proust's manuscript), and *CSB*, pp. 499–501. Basset completed Proust's unfinished notes ('Mot sur les interprètes/Mot sur les autres pièces'). As with Ferrari, Proust never refused to attribute his social writing to others or to practise the art of the gossip columnist and press attaché.

44. Bibesco would publish 'Jalousie' himself in *Les Œuvres libres*.

45. *CSB*, p. 500.

46. Ibid., p. 773, text of *Le Figaro* article.

47. Ibid., p. 143.

48. *L'Art religieux du XIIIe siècle en France* (1899), chapter I of the Introduction. Cf. below, the idea was borrowed from Mâle and marvellously summarized; the same applies to *À la recherche*: 'Never was such a comparable sight, such a vast mirror of science, art and history held up to the eyes and minds of mankind.'

49. 'A forest of symbols, which regard him with familiar looks' (*CSB*, p. 147).

50. 'La double prière', in *Feuilles détachées* (1892).

51. *Madame Bovary*, part III, chapter VIII.

52. The foliage is compared to that of Gallé, further proof of Proust's liking for this artist.

53. *CSB*, p. 782.

54. Cf. *Corr.*, vol. V, p. 284.

55. *CSB*, pp. 495–8. Proust never did send his response to the magazine, for fear of displeasing the editor, Le Blond (*Corr.*, vol. IV, p. 257).

56. *CSB*, p. 498. Notice that Proust mentions neither the Post-Impressionists, nor the Nabis, whose work he did not know.

57. *Corr.*, vol. IV, p. 257.

58. *CSB*, pp. 501–2. Proust has more to say about this in a letter to the author, dated 27 November 1904 (*Corr.*, vol. IV, pp. 356–8). Concerning Maeterlinck, he would return to the idea he expressed here: 'I know these people who have a need to talk about miracles and mystery. In my introduction to *La Bible d'Amiens*, I've already tried to puncture a few rather different sacred cows.' Proust said that he was thinking of writing an article about Maeterlinck, which has not survived (if he did write it).

59. *Corr.*, vol. IV, p. 196, July 1904. He met Doctor Vaschide socially; he was a Romanian who was the author of *Psychologie du rêve au point de vue médical* (1901), which put forward some 'absurd medical theories' and who replied '*C'est nelveux*' to whatever subject was raised. [Presumably he could not pronounce his r's. *Tr.*]

60. Cf. *Corr.*, vol. IV, p. 225: 'I gave myself the impression of having had the imagination of a character in Verlaine *(Beams): Il voulut aller sur les flots de la mer/ Et comme un vent léger soufflait une embellie . . .'* [He wanted to float upon the waves of the sea/ And like a gentle wind blowing during a lull . . .]

61. Ibid., p. 240, 4 September 1904.

62. Ibid., p. 270.

63. Ibid., p. 265, 16 September 1904.

64. Ibid., p. 278.

65. A neurologist who had treated Fernand Gregh. Author of *Psychonévroses et leur traitement moral*, preface by Professor Déjerine, Masson, 1904.

66. *Corr.*, vol. IV, p. 246, 9 September 1904, to R. Hahn; same anecdote, p. 315, to Lucien Daudet, mid-October. On A. Meyer, see his memoirs, and also Barrès, *Mes cahiers*, Plon, 1994, pp. 214–16.

67. Now in the Petit Palais. Exhibition catalogue BN 1965, no. 287.

68. *Corr.*, vol. IV, p. 389.

69. *Sésame*, p. 106: 'These days Dr Dubois states in every letter he writes that a man with a stomach ache is a pessimist.'

70. *Corr.*, vol. IV, p. 395 and n. 8, p. 397. In 1895 Brissaud published *Leçons sur les maladies nerveuses (Salpêtrière 1893–1894)*, in which we can see the influence of Charcot.

71. *Corr.*, vol. V, p. 318, August 1905, to Mme de Noailles, written after a visit to Brissaud.

72. Probably a misquotation of Mallarmé's 'une rose dans les ténèbres' [a rose in darkness] (ibid., vol. IV, p. 407).

73. It was P. Kolb who first drew attention to this dinner party, referred to by Diesbach and Duchêne, who reprints part of Albert Flament's account of it in *L'Écho de Paris*, quoted by Kolb (*Corr.*, vol. V, p. vi).

74. Ibid., p. 213.

75. Ibid., p. 330, 5 August 1905.

76. *Sésame et les lys*, Mercure de France, 1906, pp. 79–82. Proust started with an image of Ruskin's that is to do with 'kings and queens', with false grandeur, and, basing his argument on a passage in Maeterlinck's *Le Temple enseveli*, a book that he had just read, suggested that we renounce this false grandeur and these misleading images that are supposed to illustrate great thoughts. He preferred a strange image, which expressed 'the ordinary notion that there is sometimes an accidental justice': 'Just as an arrow, fired by a blind man into a crowd, might by chance result in parricide.' In this quotation Proust was alluding to Bouts or Breughel, but also, unconsciously, to the Oedipus complex and the feeling of guilt, which he was to develop in 1907 ('Sentiments filiaux d'un parricide'), and at the end of *Le Temps retrouvé*, in which the Narrator blames himself for causing the deaths of those he loved and condemns himself to suffering. In his pastiche of Maeterlinck, in a more revelatory manner still, if we superimpose the two complements of the object, the arrow strikes a 'Hermaphrodite' (*Textes retrouvés*, p. 78; *CSB*, p. 199).

77. *Sésame*, p. 116; notably: 'We should not speak ill of the passions. Everything that is great in this world is created by them . . . The passions constitute all man's moral wealth', which Proust likens to Ruskin: 'Our dignity is in exact proportion to our Passion.' He even compared the word 'dignity' to the famous stanza from 'Phares': '*Et c'est encore Seigneur le meilleur témoignage/ Que nous puissions donner de notre dignité/ Que cet ardent sanglot qui roule d'âge en âge . . .*' [And, Lord, there is no better token/ We can give of our dignity/ Than this fervent lament that rolls on from age to age . . .]

78. *Sésame*, n. 2, p. 78. Ruskin asserted that what people do not read today they will not read tomorrow, because life is short; in his support Proust quotes Mill, who had learnt Greek at the age of three and read the great Greek authors aged eight, but immediately counters this with Taine's essay 'in which he shows that it is the times when one wanders idly that are the most fruitful for the mind', as well as old Loisir's oration in George Eliot's *Adam Bede* (end of chapter LII).

79. *Sésame*, p. 90. Proust, who did not care for Fromentin, probably because he was frightened of being like him, recognized in the introduction to *Le Sahara*

the same praise for very simple words, while observing that, in the case of this author, all they provided was a sparse, dry style.

80. *Corr.*, vol. V, p. 98: 'The smell of the Normandy countryside . . . the shade of the Gothic towers . . . those orchards that I can readily imagine along the road from Caen to Honfleur' (9 April 1905).

81. *Sésame*, p. 106.

82. St John, 3: 8 and 9, quoted by Ruskin, *Sésame*, p. 105.

83. *Corr.*, vol. V, p. 102; *Sésame*, p. 14.

84. *Sésame*, p. 52, n. 1: 'M. Rodin, the true commentator on Greek sculpture'. Only the romantics, or the moderns, know how to read the classics. Proust had just stated that Vuillard, whom he frequently mentions in the early years of the century, and Maurice Denis went to the Louvre. Malraux would take up this idea.

85. Ibid., pp. 61–3.

86. *Corr.*, vol. V, p. 147, mid-May 1905.

87. Ibid., p. 95.

88. *CSB*, pp. 503–6.

89. Cf. ibid., p. 444; *Corr.*, vol. VIII, 1908, at the time when the Grand Palais put on an exhibition of 180 paintings by Monticelli.

90. *CSB*, p. 506. See *Corr.*, vol. V, p. 150: 'I was unable to go to a single performance of his *Esther* at Mme de Guerne's home.' Ibid., p. 174, to Reynaldo Hahn.

91. According to a letter from R. Hahn to Marie Nordlinger, mentioned by P. Kolb, *Corr.*, vol. V, p. 14.

92. *Corr.*, vol. V, p. 208, thirteen lines. Montesquiou kindly dedicated his book 'to Marcel Proust/ to our dear/ "Cathedralizer", this little chapel'. Another account in *L'Écho de Paris*.

93. *Corr.*, vol. V, p. 227.

94. *CSB*, pp. 506–20.

95. 'Such an extraordinarily minute vision of precise and characteristic detail' (ibid., p. 517). Proust would retain this lesson in precision, but would reject the technical vocabulary, which irritated him equally in Gautier's *Le Capitaine Fracasse*: 'We are carried along in this whirlwind to places we might not have been willing to venture except with one's dictionary.' Similarly, he criticizes the Goncourts for the pictorial quality of the vocabulary they use in their descriptions (*'glacis', 'empâtements'*).

96. Cf. *RTP*, vol. II, p. 511.

97. A saying of Montesquiou's quoting Molière is put in the mouth of Charlus (*CSB*, p. 514, and *RTP*, vol. III, p. 399).

98. *CSB*, p. 512. So it did not matter that Ruskin should have been mistaken about his contemporaries (and particularly about Whistler); although Proust invokes Sainte-Beuve's assertion, which he turns against him ('Everyone is

good at giving their views on Racine and on Bossuet. But the wisdom of the judge and the critic's perspicacity are demonstrated mainly by new books, that have not been sampled by the public'), he forgave Ruskin, while at the same time extolling the soundness of Montesquiou's verdict on his contemporaries.

99. R. de Montesquiou, *Le Chevalier de fleurs*, 1908, p. 209.

100. *Corr.*, vol. V, p. 296.

101. *Nocturne in Blue and Gold: Southampton Water* (1905 exhibition, no. 67); *Nocturne in Black and Gold: The Wheel of Fire* (1905, no. 65); *Nocturne in Black and Gold: The Falling Rocket* (1905, no. 66); *Harmony in Grey and Green: Miss Cecily Alexander* (1905, no. 18); probably *Twilight Coloured Flesh and Green: Valparaiso* (1905, no. 59); Whistler made a dozen engravings in Amsterdam in 1889, which are considered the finest of his engravings; in 1880 he had painted nocturnes in watercolour of Amsterdam; *At the Piano* (1905, no. 2a); *Arrangement in Black: Portrait of Señor Pablo de Sarasate* (Whistler wrote to his model: 'If my portrait can capture your wonderfully artistic look, I shall be very proud of my work'); perhaps *Pearl and Silver: The Andalusian Woman* (1905, no. 25) or *Symphony in White no. 1: The White Girl* (1905, no. 4). However, Marcel did not suggest *The Artist's Mother*, either out of modesty, or because it was unnecessary, since the painting was already at the Musée du Luxembourg.

102. *Corr.*, vol. V, pp. 219–21. Proust made two drawings, a larger and a smaller one. Only the smaller one is printed with the letters.

103. Ibid., p. 282. Cf. a painting in the 1995 Orsay catalogue (not included in 1905), *Twilight in Opal: Trouville*. Proust thus rediscovered these Normandy beaches he loved, and where, from 1907 to 1914, he used to spend his holidays.

104. Ibid., p. 260, 24 June 1905. In fact, it was in Detroit that Freer, 'to whom all the finest Whistlers belong', had his collection (ibid., n. 4). In the same letter to M. Nordlinger, Proust noted the critical reservations expressed by Jacques-Émile Blanche in *La Renaissance latine* of 15 June, an article reprinted and amended in *De David à Degas* (March 1919), with a preface by Proust, which referred to the palette and to the black curtain in front of which Whistler's model posed (*CSB*, p. 580).

105. Laurin-Guilloux-Buffetaud-Tailleur catalogue, Drouot, 23 April 1993, no. 180.

106. *CSB*, p. 189.

107. *P et M*, p. 160.

108. Letter to Bibesco, 1902.

109. *Corr.*, vol. V, p. 255, end of June 1905. Hahn had dedicated his *Muses* to Proust.

110. Ibid., p. 327.

111. In a posthumously published article, which was probably written in 1896, he had already mentioned Lemaître's play on Homeric themes, *La Bonne Hélène* (*CSB*, pp. 387–90). Réjane played the principal role. The article included a theory of jealousy and an erudite description, in the manner of Plato, of the poet Stesichorus, 'the Jules Lemaître of Antiquity'. We know, too, the importance that Proust attached to this critic's *Racine*.

112. Proust relied on an article by his cousin through marriage, Michel Bréal (*La Revue de Paris*, 15 June 1905). *Corr.*, vol. V, p. 329.

113. *RTP*, vol. II, p. 553.

114. Ibid., p. 710.

115. *Corr.*, vol. V, pp. 342–3.

116. Ibid., p. 338, 13 September 1905.

117. Ibid., vol. VI, pp. 200–1, to Mme Catusse.

118. Ibid., p. 341, to Montesquiou. Similar letter to Mme Straus, ibid., p. 343.

119. *Notes*, p. 99.

120. *Corr.*, vol. V, p. 320.

121. Ibid., p. 345, 27 September 1905, to Anna de Noailles.

122. Ibid., p. 350.

123. Ibid., p. 346.

124. Ibid., pp. 348–9. 'Then I am subjected, without any defence, to the most appalling thoughts.'

125. Ibid., p. 354, 26 October 1905, to Mme Alphonse Daudet.

126. Ibid., p. 355.

127. Ibid., vol. VI, p. 49.

128. *Corr. avec G. Gallimard*, p. 30.

129. Referred to in a footnote in *Sésame*, p. 106.

130. *Corr.*, vol. VII, p. 107, April 1908, to Georges de Lauris.

131. Ibid., vol. VI, February 1906, to Mme de Noailles: the first hint of the theme of the 'intermittencies of the heart'.

132. Published in 1905 as the first volume of *Bastions de l'Est*, it is a novel about a young man in occupied Alsace. Proust studied the book closely, and wished to know who Mme d'Aoury was, 'a noble little creature whose luminous face was not in the least bothered by the sound of swordplay' (no doubt in order to reassure himself – he was not mistaken – that she was based upon Mme de Noailles, who appears under the guise of a 'young Gasmule' in *Le Voyage de Sparte*, and to whom the book is dedicated at length, a point on which Proust congratulated Anna).

133. *Corr.*, vol. VI, pp. 38–9, February 1906.

134. Ibid., p. 38.

135. Ibid., p. 43.

136. Ibid., pp. 71–2, April 1906.

137. Ibid., p. 72.

138. İbid., p. 75, May 1906, to Mme Catusse. Proust's copy was the Library Edition, in which the volume on Florence had just been published.

139. Ibid., p. 148.

140. Ibid.

141. *Carpaccio* by Molmenti was published in French in Venice in 1893. Proust also consulted a work by L. Rosenthal (1906).

142. *Corr.*, vol. IV, p. 326, n. 4. Cf. ibid., pp. 364, 365.

143. Ibid., vol. XII, p. 403.

144. Included in *Altesses sérénissimes* (1907).

145. *Lettres à R. Hahn*, p. 85.

146. *Corr.*, vol. XIV, p. 344, May 1906, to Mme Straus. Montesquiou noted the presence of a *Sapho*, 'an elder sister to the one that belonged to Mme Émile Straus'. Cf. ibid., vol. VI, p. 88.

147. Ibid., vol. VI, p. 87, 21 or 22 May 1906.

148. Ibid., vol. XII, p. 403.

149. Ibid., vol. VI, p. 100, and *Sésame*, pp. 12, 15, 17.

150. Ibid., early June 1906. Cf. to Barrès, concerning his introduction: 'Nothing can indicate my distress' (ibid., p. 113, June 1906).

151. Ibid., p. 101. Among the published inscriptions are those to Calmette, Suzette Lemaire, Louisa de Mornand, Georges de Lauris, Edmond Jaloux, Emmanuel Bibesco, Lucien Daudet, Stéphane Brossard, Paul Desjardins, Lucien Fontaine, Jean Sardou, Fernand Gregh, Mme Catusse, Doctor Landowski, Maurice Barrès, Robert Dreyfus, Mme Straus and André Chevrillon. Not all of them have been found: Proust may therefore have thought of sending copies to Vuillard and Maurice Denis.

152. Ibid., p. 118.

153. Ibid., p. 132.

154. Ibid., p. 141.

155. Ibid., p. 142.

156. Ibid., p. 130, 19 June 1905. It is also worth drawing attention to an article by Marcel Cruppi, Proust's cousin, in the monthly review *Le Mouvement*. Proust let him know of his disagreement with him on a number of points (ibid., p. 145, July 1906).

157. Ibid., pp. 155–6, 16 July 1906, to the Comtesse de Noailles.

158. E.g. ibid., p. 163: 'the idolatry of the bibliophile'.

159. In fact, in *Le Temps retrouvé* books which contain theories are compared to objects on which the price has been left.

160. He consulted Émile Mâle (*Corr.*, vol. XVII, pp. 540–4), who, while he extolled the poetry of Brittany, its unspoilt villages and its granite churches covered in lichen with their *calvaires*, recommended Normandy, with its fifteenth-century churches and its ruined monasteries, for a person who was ill (ibid., vol. VI, p. 192, 18 August 1906).

161. She had it built on land given her by the king in 1752; a corridor led directly into the château (Goncourt, *Madame de Pompadour*, Didot, 1888, p. 90). The hotel building still exists in the rue des Réservoirs at Versailles. Mme de Pompadour also owned the Château de Crécy, which calls to mind Odette's surname.

162. *Corr.*, vol. VI, p. 179, 8 August 1906. There were even two pianos, so the Marquise de Saint-Paul, 'the sonata snake', could come there to practise.

163. Ibid., pp. 181, 183.

164. Ibid., p. 177: Proust also made fun of Lili Lehmann. See above, p. 463. She sang the role of Donna Anna, and Geraldine Farrar (the memory of whom would haunt Reynaldo), that of Zerlina. See R. Hahn, *L'Oreille au guet*, Gallimard, 1937, p. 53, in which he protests against the destruction of these recordings by the record company, when she was 'the most illustrious vocal technician of the past fifty years' (*Corr.*, vol. VI, p. 179).

165. *Lettres à R. Hahn*, pp. 88–92. These passages, like others in this correspondence, are not included in the Plon edition, and neither are the drawings that accompany them.

166. Ibid., p. 93: '*Plus grosse que la baleine/Et le narval/Est la bedaine, la bedaine/De Bréval.*' [Larger than the whale/And the narwhal/ Is the paunch, the paunch/ Of Bréval.] It was the sort of music-hall ditty the two friends loved.

167. *Corr.*, vol. VI, pp. 294–5; a parody hitherto unnoticed by critics. Note the allusion to a future friend of Proust: '*Tu vas retrouver ton cornac/d'Oxford, le jeune Bardac.*' [You'll meet your mahout from Oxford again, young Bardac.] It was for him that in 1915 Hahn composed 'Pour bercer un convalescent', for two pianos. Cf. 'Air du pont des Soupirs', *Corr.*, vol. VI, p. 316.

168. Ibid., pp. 180–2, 9 August 1906, to R. Hahn; letter to Coulanges dated 15 December 1670, quoted in reference to young Cambremer's wedding (*RTP*, vol. IV, p. 236) by the Narrator's mother, who, however, adds: 'I shan't say ... We don't deign to collect such hackneyed Sévigné', and also quotes the letter parodied by Proust in his letter to Hahn: 'What a pretty thing haymaking is' (22 July 1671) (Mme de Sévigné, *Correspondances*, Bibliothèque de la Pléiade, vol. I, pp. 139, 304).

169. *Vie secrète de l'Académie française*, 4 vols, 1938. In it he relates a few memories of Proust.

170. See G. Macchia, *L'Ange de la nuit*, Gallimard, p. 214.

171. *Corr.*, vol. VI, p. 197.

172. *RTP*, vol. I, p. 161.

173. *Corr.*, vol. VI, p. 282, mid-November 1906. And further on: 'I won't never do spectaculars for you again coz cwoss.'

174. Ibid., pp. 282–3, 15 or 16 November 1906.

175. Ibid., vol. VII, p. 35, 14 January 1907.

176. Ibid., vol. VI, pp. 330, 340.

177. 'With the exception of the death of Captain Roquefinette, which is too idiotic to be foreseen by a sane person' (ibid., p. 340).

178. Ibid., p. 331. This is why he prefers *Bragelonne*.

179. Ibid., p. 342, 19 December 1906.

180. Ibid., p. 287, when taking out a subscription to *La Chronique des arts et de la curiosité*.

181. Ibid., p. 192.

182. Ibid., vol. VII, pp. 284–5.

183. Cf. ibid., p. 214, to R. Hahn: '*Si Léon n'intercède, je subirai le sort/ Hélas d'Orphée . . .*' [If Léon does not intercede, I shall suffer the fate/Of Orpheus alas . . .]

184. Ibid., p. 197.

185. Ibid., p. 200.

186. Ibid., p. 196, 26 August 1906. Cf. p. 232.

187. *RTP*, vol. I, p. 655, draft IV.

188. From the estate agents Paris-Office and John Arthur.

189. Annual rent, 7,400 francs, *Corr.*, vol. VI, p. 226.

190. Ibid., p. 228, to Lauris.

191. Ibid., pp. 230–1, to Mme Straus.

192. Ibid., p. 238. Eventually he would put in some wooden panelling which came from the ante-room at rue de Courcelles and which Marcel, because of the pleasure it gave his mother, was delighted to have back here.

193. Ibid., p. 302.

194. Ibid., p. 262.

195. Ibid., p. 273.

196. Ibid., p. 279.

197. Ibid., p. 317, to Mme Catusse.

198. Ibid., p. 326.

199. 'I haven't the *foggiest notion*, and don't want to have too many because I think it's bad for a writer' (ibid., p. 336).

200. 'One day I dream of buying . . . a Venetian primitive on the one hand, and a Tuscan, Sienese or Roman primitive on the other.' Proust thought of 'Vivarini, for example, a relic of whose would be a subject for infinite reveries, or some Sienese or Roman painter' (ibid., p. 337). He was influenced here either by Ruskin, who did not know the precise attributions of these works (*Mornings in Florence*, §IV, 77, 78), or by Berenson, about whom he was seeking information and whose books he was searching for at this time (*Corr.*, vol. VI, p. 247). It is worth pointing out that this great 'connoisseur' had followed history of art courses in Boston given by Charles Eliot Norton, through whom he discovered Ruskin, and that he had known Whistler and, in particular, Montesquiou (to whom he denied ever practising sodomy, saying that he, who caused all inverts to 'salivate', would have known). See

E. Samuels, *B. Berenson*, Harvard University Press, 1979. Besides, collecting paintings did not interest Proust except through an association of ideas (as with *François le Champi* in *Le Temps retrouvé*), if they 'retain the scent of a town or the dampness of a church and which, like trinkets, contain as much dream through association of ideas as they do within themselves' (*Corr.*, vol. VI, p. 337). As regards Berenson, who had probably criticized Ruskin's attributions, Marcel responded by quoting a passage by the latter, which formulated an important theory: 'There is a method of knowing about painting that is attributable to the artists, and another that is attributable to antique dealers and art dealers. This second method is dependent on a precise knowledge of the painting and on the way people behave and does not imply any competence relative to its actual aesthetic qualities . . . All this does not alter the fact that I should very much like to know Berenson' (ibid., pp. 241–2). Proust would make Berenson's acquaintance in 1918, thanks to Walter Berry.

201. Ibid., p. 308, to Marie Nordlinger. She had just returned to Marcel a book by Maspero about the Eastern races, which he mentioned in his article on Mme de Boigne's *Mémoires* (*CSB*, p. 925) and in *Jeunes Filles* (*RTP*, vol. I, p. 469).

202. *Corr.*, vol. VI, p. 287. He even suggested to Marguillier, the editor of *La Chronique des arts*, that he review Ruskin's *Mornings in Florence*, which had just been published in French translation; the plan came to nothing.

203. Ibid., p. 326. He also referred to Barrès' work 'Automne à Versailles'.

204. Ibid., p. 345.

CHAPTER XI: *The Renaissance of Literature*

1. *Corr.*, vol. VII, p. 63.

2. Ibid., p. 86. Cf. Letter to Robert de Flers on the death of his father, ibid., p. 93, 27 February 1907.

3. Ibid., p. 98.

4. Ibid., p. 26, to Auguste Marguillier.

5. 'Illustrated with twenty-four plates', 128 pages.

6. *CSB*, p. 525.

7. Published in 1906. *Corr.*, vol. VI, p. 40.

8. *CSB*, p. 525.

9. He had first met Groult, probably through Montesquiou, in 1894 (*Corr.*, vol. I, p. 316), but not one of his paintings is mentioned by Mourey in his book, any more than he pays tribute to Ruskin! Proust thus criticizes the author discreetly on two counts. Proust was a great expert on eighteenth-century, as well as English, art: 'Groult's Turners always provoked great

merriment in Paris because as many as three out of four of them were fakes. Did he realize this? Perfectly. He paid two hundred thousand francs for the real Turner, and barely three hundred francs for the fake. But he enjoyed watching the true connoisseurs admiring these botched jobs for fear of displeasing him' (R. Gimpel, *Journal d'un collectionneur marchand de tableaux*, Calmann-Lévy, 1963, p. 39). Groult owned twenty Turners. From him, Proust drew his inspiration for Elstir's paintings (and, in particular, for the *Salute* at Venice, described by Goncourt, and the *Vallée de la Seine*, a painting now in the Louvre). Groult had wanted to found a museum of English painting at Bagatelle. He was refused permission by the authorities. See *CSB*, pp. 440, 526. Moreover, he 'had transformed his garden at 116 Avenue de Malakoff into a landscape in the style of Hubert Robert, with a fountain, columns and ruins' (Gimpel, *Journal d'un collectionneur*, pp. 39–40): unrecognized until now, it was the model for the Princesse de Guermantes' *hôtel particulier*. It was also from Groult that Proust borrowed the anecdote in *Le Côté de Guermantes*, according to which the owner of 'an immense fortune made from flour and pasta', having invited M. de Luxembourg to lunch and received a refusal from the latter addressed to M.—, Miller, replied to the nobleman: 'There would only have been the miller, his son, and you at the meal' (*RTP*, vol. II, p. 827 and n. 1, which quotes Painter, who makes the Marquis de Breteuil, who was anxious to invite Edward VII, the source of the incident). The anecdote is also to be found in Gimpel, who attributes it to the King of Greece (*Journal d'un collectionneur*, p. 40). On Groult, see the article by A. Flament in *L'Illustration*, 18 January 1908.

10. Unpublished letter to R. Hahn. Laurin catalogue, Drouot, T. Bodin valuer, sale of 18 April 1991, no. 99. On Mozart's relationship with Linley, see J. and B. Massin, *W. A. Mozart*, Club français du livre, 1959, p. 96, and W. Hildesheim, trans., Farrar Straus & Giroux, New York, 1982, p. 30, which refers to a short and intense liaison in Florence in the spring of 1770; Mozart and Linley were both fourteen years old. In fact it was Linley's older sister, Elizabeth Sheridan, whom Gainsborough had painted (Dulwich College, London), and her portrait that was reproduced by Mourey, *Gainsborough*, p. 48. On Linley and Mozart, see T. Laget, *Florentiana*, p. 98.

11. *Corr.*, vol. VII, pp. ix and 52.

12. Ibid., p. 53, 1 February 1907, to Gaston Calmette. Proust here provides the ending of the article, which we also find, out of place, in *CSB*, p. 786, n. 7. It ought to have been reinserted at the end of the article, as P. Kolb points out.

13. 'Sentiments filiaux d'un parricide', *P et M*, p. 152.

14. Ibid., p. 156; compare this with the description at the end of *King Lear* and *The Brothers Karamazov*, ibid., p. 157. Oedipus will not be mentioned in *À la recherche* again except when linked with Baron de Charlus.

15. *Corr.*, vol. VII, p. 56, and n. 3; *Cours de littérature dramatique*, new ed. 1899, vol. I, pp. 189–90.

16. *Corr.*, vol. VII, p. 157.

17. 'Sentiments filiaux d'un parricide', *P et M*, pp. 158–9.

18. *Corr.*, vol. VII, p. 23. *CSB*, pp. 523–4 and n. 1. On 15 August he also read an article by Wyzewa in *La Revue des deux mondes* on the subject of Tolstoy's attack on Shakespeare.

19. An example often quoted by Proust; cf. *Corr.*, vol. VII, p. 23, 21 October 1907.

20. Ibid., pp. 58–60.

21. Ibid., p. 78. N. Cottin (1873–1916).

22. Ibid., p. 135.

23. Ibid., p. 213.

24. Cf. *RTP*, vol. I, pp. 389, 397.

25. *Essais et articles*, *CSB*, pp. 527–33, and, for the section cut by *Le Figaro*, pp. 924–9, and *RTP*, vol. II, p. 481, n. 1 (pp. 1610–14). This newspaper, wrote Proust to R. Hahn on 18 March 1907, 'cut the whole of the long section for which the article was written, the only bit I liked' (*Corr.*, vol. VII, p. 110). Curiously, I have not come across a single letter in which Proust mentions reading the Comtesse de Boigne. It is true, as I have frequently pointed out, that he says very little about the books he is reading in his correspondence, either out of politeness (towards those who read less than he did), modesty, or his love of secrecy.

26. *Essais et articles*, *CSB*, pp. 528–9.

27. Ibid., p. 531.

28. Ibid., p. 532.

29. Ibid., p. 925. See also *RTP*, vol. II, p. 469.

30. *Essais et articles*, *CSB*, p. 926.

31. *CSB*, pp. 931–2; they would be used again, in part, in *À l'ombre des jeunes filles en fleurs*.

32. *Corr.*, vol. VII, p. 107, 17 March 1907, to Mme de Noailles.

33. Her book, published by Calmann-Lévy on 24 April 1907, ran to 416 pages. It had great success in the press (fifty or so articles in France and abroad) and in the bookshops: the publishers announced a fifth impression on 10 May: see C. Mignot-Ogliastri, *Anna de Noailles*, pp. 218–19.

34. This was why, in October 1907, Proust discussed with Dreyfus a story about money spent by Sainte-Beuve when he was Keeper at the Mazarine library, which caused him to be suspected of having laid his hands on secret funds, a story that is related in the first introduction to *Chateaubriand et son groupe littéraire* (*Corr.*, vol. VII, pp. 301–3, to R. Dreyfus).

35. Cf. *JS*, pp. 269, 488; *CSB*, pp. 650–1, inspired by his reading of his letters.

36. *CSB*, p. 534; cf. pp. 105, 255, 667–74, 'the hero with the gentle manner of

a virgin', 'this poet with a woman's figure', p. 669; 'the *Chanteur persan*', p. 670; 'the *Chanteur indien*', p. 673: 'the singer who is within me is also gentle as a woman'; *RTP*, vol. II, pp. 714–15, in which Moreau's paintings are attributed to Elstir.

37. *RTP*, vol. III, pp. 3–6 and var.

38. *CSB*, p. 540.

39. Ibid., p. 542. In this context Proust referred to the fountains at Damascus; we know that Hubert Robert's *Jet d'eau* is mentioned throughout *À la recherche*.

40. *Corr.*, vol. VII, p. 183, 15 June 1907.

41. He made a note of it in his very first draft notebooks for *Le Temps retrouvé*, in about 1909.

42. According to the testimony of É. de Clermont-Tonnerre, *Robert de Montesquiou et Marcel Proust*, Flammarion, 1925.

43. In Beethoven's Sonata no. 8 (the *Pathétique*), the second movement is an adagio; it could also be the andante from the *Appassionnata*, no. 23. See *RTP*, vol. I, p. 203, where it is a matter of playing the piano arrangement of the andante from Vinteuil's sonata: 'It was as if . . . he had said that we were to hear only the overture from *Die Meistersinger*', and var. *a*: 'or only the andante in the *Pathétique*'. It could also be the andante in F major.

44. Ibid., vol. III, p. 1149: 'I thought especially of Chabrier: for anyone who has heard a work played on the piano knows only the photography of the piece' . . . *Idylle*, a piece for the piano (*Dix pièces pittoresques*, 1881) then becomes the first bit of the *Suite pastorale*, an arrangement for orchestra. César Franck, after hearing these pieces for piano, declared: 'We have just listened to something quite extraordinary. This music links our age to that of Couperin and Rameau.' One should not be surprised therefore to see Proust, confident about his tastes and his erudition, choosing Couperin and Chabrier for the same concert.

45. On *Tristan and Isolde*, see particularly *RTP*, vol. III, pp. 664–5.

46. *Corr.*, vol. VII, p. 84.

47. *Mémoires d'outre-tombe*, Bibliothèque de la Pléiade, vol. I, p. 450; proof that Proust knew this book well. Earlier, Chateaubriand also referred to Pascal and to Mme de Sévigné (letter of 24 January 1689).

48. The day of the Duc de Gramont's third marriage, to Maria Ruspoli, who was only nineteen years old. The duchess has described to us how, upon arriving at Vallières with her husband (who was thirty-six years older than her) for their honeymoon, and being greeted by the household with hunting horns in these remote and stately surroundings, she collapsed in tears. Tactfully, Proust did not congratulate the Duc de Guiche on his father's remarriage, which he did not attend.

49. See A. Ferré, *Géographie de Marcel Proust*, Sagittaire, 1939; G. Désert, *La*

Vie quotidienne sur les plages normandes du second Empire aux années folles, Hachette, 1983; C. Pechenard, *Proust à Cabourg*, Quai Voltaire, 1992; B. Coulon, *Promenades en Normandie avec un guide appelé Marcel Proust*, Charles Corlet, 1986.

50. Viraut worked on the Hôtel Terminus in Paris and built a number of hospitals, town houses and villas.

51. In July 1910 the new manager of the hotel, Henri Dubal, arranged for an 'express' train via Mézidon, which made the journey in three hours and forty-five minutes.

52. At the casino, in 1908, a sum of 400,000 francs was the amount being played for, far less than at Trouville.

53. Sem (1863–1934) often drew caricatures of Montesquiou and his friends; the count mentions this in *Professionelles Beautés*, ch. XV, p. 236 ff.

54. In 'Le salon de la comtesse d'Eyragues', published posthumously but written in about 1900, the Marquise d'Eyragues speaks 'with that unbelievable mind, that accomplished literary breadth that she is able to confer on the slightest thing' (*CSB*, p. 438). Cf. *CSB*, Fallois, pp. 274–5, and *Le Carnet de 1908*, 'the Normandy hydrangeas'.

55. *Corr.*, vol. XXI, p. 358, shortly after 16 July 1922.

56. Léonce de Joncières (1871–1952). We can conjecture what Marcel means by 'very pleasant', writing to Reynaldo. 'A rather overdone Léandre or Octave', Proust added, referring to *Les Fourberies de Scapin*; in *À la recherche* he would recall this first name when he created the character of the 'juvenile lead', a sportsman who became an artist of genius, and who also had something of Plantevignes, as well as Cocteau.

57. Unpublished letter to Hélène de Caraman-Chimay, included in Pechenard, *Proust à Cabourg*, pp. 79–80.

58. *Corr.*, vol. VII, p. 79.

59. In *RTP*, vol. IV, p. 339, Proust alludes to *L'Hôtel du Libre-Échange* by Feydeau and Desvallières (1894).

60. *RTP*, vol. IV, pp. 152–3. *Corr.*, vol. X, p. 324.

61. G. Bernstein Gruber and G. Maurin, *Bernstein le magnifique*, Lattès, 1988, p. 74.

62. In particular, *Paris-New York* at the Théâtre Réjane from March 1907. *Corr.*, vol. VII, p. 265, n. 8; *Le Figaro* mentions that on 12 August Croisset, Proust, Tristan Bernard and Lantelme were seen together at tea time. Vuillard stayed with the 'charming' Tristan Bernard (*Corr.*, vol. VII, p. 267) at Château Rouge, and with the Hessels (whom he painted) at Amfreville. Proust knew the painter. He may have seen his paintings of the Normandy coast and drawn his inspiration from them for Elstir's; Vuillard's paintings from those years were exhibited at Bernheim's (thirty-eight canvases in February 1908).

63. *Corr.*, vol. VII, p. 292.

64. Gimpel, *Journal d'un collectionneur*, pp. 194–8. At that period Gimpel owned *Le Géographe* (now in the Stadelsches Kunstinstitut, Frankfurt; see A. Malraux, *Tout Vermeer de Delft*, Gallimard, 1952, pl. xx and commentary).

65. *Corr.*, vol. VII, p. 267.

66. M. E. Chernowitz, *Proust and Painting*, New York, International University Press, 1945, letter from Vuillard to the author, 6 December 1936, p. 200.

67. *Corr.*, vol. VII, p. 267.

68. Ibid., p. 276.

69. In ibid., p. 290, n. 8, P. Kolb notes that Jupien was originally called Joliot; he suggests that Proust used his name for that of Jupien (since he is a tailor, the first syllable would stem from the word '*jupe*' [a skirt]).

70. Ibid., pp. 287, 288 and n. 8, 9, 10. C. Albaret, *Monsieur Proust*, Laffont, 1973, p. 131.

71. *Corr.*, vol. VII, pp. 249–50.

72. Ibid., p. 252: 'You'd be amazed to see me on the road every day. But it won't last.'

73. Reading *Seven Lamps of Architecture* had prepared Proust for some of these visits: in it Ruskin writes about Bayeux, Caudebec, Falaise and Lisieux.

74. *RTP*, vol. I, p. 381.

75. Ibid., vol. II, p. 19.

76. Ibid., p. 1349; quotation from Cahier XII, ff. 125 and 126 verso.

77. *CSB*, p. 66.

78. *Corr.*, vol. VII, p. 256.

79. *CSB*, p. 66.

80. *RTP*, vol. III, p. 329.

81. Ibid., vol. I, p. 735.

82. *Corr.*, vol. VII, p. 296.

83. Ibid., p. 260.

84. *CSB*, p. 64.

85. *Corr.*, vol. VII, p. 287, 8 October 1907, to Mme Straus; the 'key' to the stained-glass windows was given to Jacques de Lacretelle. The windows at Évreux represent, in particular, Louis XI kneeling before the Virgin Mary, the heavenly court, and the apostles (right cross bar); in the choir are Peter of Navarre, the son of Charles the Bad (1322–87), the King of Navarre, who seized the earldom of Évreux (Baedeker, *Nord-Ouest de la France*, p. 170) after the Battle of Cocherel (Charles the Bad became Gilbert the Bad, lord of Guermantes, in a window at Combray). Proust returned there after his visit to Mme de Clermont-Tonnerre's house at Glisolles (*Corr.*, vol. VII, p. 275).

86. The seven stained-glass windows in the choir are by Aldgrever (Baedeker, *Nord-Ouest de la France*, p. 172).

87. Ibid.

88. *Corr.*, vol. VII, p. 295.

89. *P et M*, p. 64.

90. *RTP*, vol. I, pp. 179–80.

91. *Corr.*, vol. VIII, p. 50: 'From my bed I could all the time see before me Rouen, Helleu and Monet, and I was very upset not to be able to be with you.' Proust promises to visit Helleu and expresses his friendship in the following terms: 'I am thinking much about you, about Madame Helleu, about your daughter, and about that beautiful faded and golden moment in the harbour which was like a kind of pearly ante-room to the Infinite.' During this visit Proust admired Helleu's painting *Automne à Versailles*; the artist generously sent it to him; Marcel, who was embarrassed, was torn between wanting to refuse the present, wanting to buy it, and gratitude (ibid., pp. 51–2, late February 1908).

92. *RTP*, vol. II, pp. 1098–9, 1899, and vol. III, p. 1713.

93. Ibid., vol. III, p. 17.

94. *Corr.*, vol. VII, p. 309, 9 November 1907.

95. Ibid., p. 315.

96. Ibid., p. 319.

97. Madrazo kept the painting until 1909, the year he left for New York (Hispanic Society). See K. Yoshikawa's remarkable article 'Proust et le Greco', *BAMP*, no. 44, 1994, pp. 29–41: Proust rarely mentioned Spanish painting: 'the *Lances*' (*RTP*, vol. II, p. 844) and *Las Meniñas* (ibid., vol. III, p. 874) by Velázquez; Goya is only referred to once (ibid., p. 320). El Greco is mentioned three times: firstly in *À l'ombre des jeunes filles en fleurs* (vol. II, p. 61): the Narrator's father, an admirer of this artist, is going to spend a day in Toledo, imitating the journey made by Barrès. In *La Prisonnière* (vol. III, pp. 711–12) Charlus is compared to 'a grand inquisitor painted by El Greco', that is to say, to the Cardinal Fernando Niño de Guevara (Metropolitan, New York). In *Le Temps retrouvé*, describing how the sky and the earth are parallel, the Narrator refers to *The Burial of Count d'Orgaz* (vol. IV, p. 338; a passage written in 1918, according to a letter to Mme Straus in 1917, *Corr.*, vol. XVI, pp. 196–7, and Barrès' 1911 book, pp. 15–17). On 26 September 1908, in the literary supplement to *Le Figaro*, Proust read Montesquiou's article, 'Autour de Greco' (*Le Carnet de 1908*, p. 58), which describes this painting as 'the most extraordinary one in the world', and anticipates Barrès' book, which would not be published until 1911 (bound together, under the title *Greco*, with an essay by Paul Lafond, curator of the Pau museum, 91 plates, and dedicated to Montesquiou). The latter sent a copy to Marcel (*Corr.*, vol. XI, p. 52, a letter wrongly dated by Kolb, who is a year out, because in 1912 Barrès republished his *Greco ou le secret de Tolède* on his own).

98. *Corr.*, vol. VIII, p. 320.

99. *CSB*, pp. 218–20.

100. *Sainte-Beuve*, Mercure de France, 1904. Proust refers to Séché's work in his introduction to *Sésame et les lys* (*CSB*, p. 182).

101. *Corr. avec D. Halévy*, p. 97. This is vol. I of series IX, 6 October 1907, 'De la situation faite au parti intellectuel dans le monde moderne'. Anne Borrel, who edited this correspondence together with J.-P. Halévy, compares certain phrases of Péguy's which struck Proust, particularly those to do with place-names and his reveries about the names of towns and of people, and which he jotted down in Cahier 4, and later in Cahier 8. She sees here proof that Proust had 'rewritten some of his notes and fragments of text on the subject of his reverie on names from 1907 onwards'; he then read Péguy (*BAMP*, no. 44, 1994, p. 132). It should be pointed out that this 'reverie' appeared originally among the seventy-five lost pages which B. de Fallois has described in his edition of *Contre Sainte-Beuve* (and of which Proust gave a summary in *Le Carnet de 1908*, under the title 'Pages écrites'). Daniel Halévy tried very hard to make Proust read Péguy, without being able to make him like him, however; Halévy took out a subscription to *Cahiers de la Quinzaine* on Proust's behalf on 1 February 1908, and Proust received series IX, including the volume I to which Halévy's letter referred (*Corr.*, vol. VIII, p. 39).

102. *Corr.*, vol. VII, p. 304.

CHAPTER XII: Contre Sainte-Beuve

1. See *Corr.*, vol. VIII, pp. 24–7, between 1 and 8 January 1908, to Auguste Marguillier (Proust was looking for engravings 'in which an animal is depicted beside the person or people who are the subject of the painting'); P. Kolb, 'Le mystère des gravures anglaises recherchées par Proust', *Mercure de France*, no. 327, 1 August 1956, pp. 750–5, and this chapter in *CSB*, ed. Fallois, pp. 293 ff.; *Le Carnet de 1908*, pp. 11–13, 56, 141 (n. 60). Marcel also asked Vallette for two books published by Mercure, the *Lettres de Carlyle à sa mère* (from which he quotes on the first page of *Le Carnet de 1908*: 'I do not suffer as much as I tell you I do') and Walter Pater's *Imaginary Portraits*.

2. They appeared on the front page of the Saturday literary supplement, edited by Francis Chevassu. Proust had planned to send him a letter about pastiches, which was never published (*Corr.*, vol. VIII, p. 43). Balzac, Faguet, Michelet and Goncourt appeared on 22 February; Flaubert and Sainte-Beuve on 14 March, Renan (which had come to Proust 'in a flood', ibid., p. 67) on 21 March. Proust attached great importance to the balance and to the 'measure' of the publication (ibid., p. 58). As to their composition, he had adjusted his 'inner metronome' to the rhythm of each of them, and he could have written 'ten volumes like that'.

3. Ibid., vol. IX, p. 34.

4. With the exception of Ruskin, 'La bénédiction du sanglier', which was left unfinished, as well as parodies of Chateaubriand and of Maeterlinck, which in March 1909 (ibid., vol. IX, p. 61) Proust said he was unable to publish (*Textes retrouvés*, pp. 72, 76, 257; in this volume, on p. 74, P. Kolb published a second parody of Sainte-Beuve, which Proust mentioned in the same letter of March 1909). On 7 July 1909 he also amused himself by writing a 'Commentary by H. Taine on the reasons why you bore me by talking about Pastiches'.

5. *P et M*, p. 7, note by Proust.

6. See *Corr.*, vol. VIII, p. 58, letter of 11 March 1908 to F. Chevassu.

7. Introduction to *La Bible d'Amiens*, *P et M*, p. 125.

8. *RTP*, vol. I, p. 168. See also Balzac's *Ferragus*. A summary of the end of *Colonel Chabert* is given in *RTP*, vol. II, p. 474.

9. *Corr.*, vol. XIX, p. 574, November 1920, to Paul Souday.

10. Quoted extensively in the introduction to *La Bible d'Amiens*, Mâle's name is not mentioned again in *À l'ombre des jeunes filles en fleurs*.

11. Ibid., p. 175, 8 or 9 July 1908.

12. Cahier 43, *RTP*, vol. III, drafts VI and VII (see note, pp. 1213–14).

13. *Corr.*, vol. VIII, p. 72, to Mme de Noailles.

14. *RTP*, vol. III, p. 832.

15. *Corr.*, vol. VIII, p. 76, 26 March 1908; *CSB*, p. 27; the Rio Tinto shares had fallen by 45 per cent in one year. Cf. *Corr.*, vol. VIII, p. 130: 'I have to sell some Vichy' (29 May 1908).

16. Ibid., p. 111.

17. Ibid., p. 112.

18. *RTP*, vol. IV, p. 338.

19. *CSB*, ed. Fallois, p. 14. This edition contains a montage of a section of the drafts written by Proust in 1908–9, but it is not a critical edition. The Pléiade edition, compiled by P. Clarac, reproduces the section on literary criticism, together with additional pages which do not all form part of the *Contre Sainte-Beuve* project and come from a folder which can now be found in the Bibliothèque Nationale, often referred to by specialists as 'Proust 45'. This is also the name given to it by P. Clarac in *CSB*, Pléiade.

20. *CSB*, ed. Fallois, pp. 291–7 and pp. 273–5. The first extract was dated to January 1908 by P. Kolb, thanks to the English engravings requested in early January, and mentioned in this fragment.

21. Ibid., p. 14.

22. 'Proust 45' (BN, n.a.fr., 16 636), ff. 1 recto to 31 verso, published in *CSB*, ed. Clarac, pp. 211–32. For a structured classification of these pages, see Claudine Quémar, 'En marge du travail de Proust sur Sainte-Beuve: tableau des correspondances entre les notes du carnet 1 et les fragments du volume

45 du fonds Proust', *Bulletin d'informations proustiennes*, no. 6, autumn 1977, pp. 29–37.

23. M. Proust, *Le Carnet de 1908*, edited and introduced by Philip Kolb, Gallimard, 1976. It was on 2 February that Proust thanked Mme Straus for the gift of five little notebooks from Kirby Beard's. There are four of them in the Bibliothèque Nationale. The fifth, unused, was at the home of Céleste Albaret.

24. Maurice Bardèche, *Marcel Proust romancier*, Les Sept Couleurs, vol. I, 1971, pp. 168–76, made it very clear, following Fallois, that this notebook was a 'ship's log' of *Contre Sainte-Beuve*.

25. *Le Carnet de 1908*, p. 56.

26. f. 2 verso: Vautrin et Rubempré, 'Tristesse d'Olympio de la pédérastie' (repeated in *CSB*, p. 274, 'Sainte-Beuve et Balzac', and *RTP*, vol. III, p. 437), f. 12, 12 verso, and Gurcy (the future Charlus, f. 43, 49 verso). Proust is probably referring to himself here: 'He wanted to find, and believed he had found, some non-effeminates, for, filling his strange desire with all its natural desire, he believed he had a natural desire which could be reciprocated outside of homosexuality.'

27. *Le Carnet de 1908*, p. 49.

28. Ibid., p. 58.

29. Ibid., p. 60.

30. Ibid., pp. 60–1.

31. Ibid., p. 101.

32. 'Vieillesse, Laroze, Louise Baignères, Borghèse, Sala, Neufville' (f. 3, p. 49). 'Mylord me reconnaissez-vous? (vieillesse, vicillesse de Plantevignes, Scène de l'*Éducation*)' (f. 10, p. 59).

33. At the same time, Proust provided Henry Bernstein with some names and titles of the nobility for his play *Israël*, which would be put on at the Théâtre Réjane in October (*Corr.*, vol. VIII, p. 174).

34. Ibid., pp. 112–13.

35. Ibid., pp. 98 and 114, and *La Prisonnière, RTP*, vol. III, p. 832. He finds the theme of homosexuality again in Lucien Daudet's novel *Le Chemin mort*, which he hoped to review (*Corr.*, vol. VIII, p. 176) for *Le Figaro*, which did not accept his article; it eventually appeared in *L'Intransigeant* of 8 September 1908 (*CSB*, pp. 550–2).

36. *Corr.*, vol. VIII, p. 193.

37. Ibid., p. 191.

38. Ibid., p. 210; it is Antoine de Castellane (1844–1917) who salutes Mme Swann in the Bois de Boulogne.

39. Ibid., p. 209. See *RTP*, vol. IV, p. 1105.

40. *Le Carnet de 1908*, p. 51.

41. *Corr.*, vol. VIII, p. 185.

42. A. de Fouquières, *Cinquante ans de panache*, P. Horay, 1951, pp. 66, 255.

Cf. G. de Diesbach, p. 430, which gives a portrait based on the unpublished memoirs of Ferdinand Bac, 'an air of panache, an easy gait and generous to a degree'. G. Bernstein Gruber and G. Maurin believe it was more a case 'of complicity than of passion' (*Bernstein le magnifique*, Lattès, 1988, p. 82).

43. *Le Carnet de 1908*, pp. 108–10, 'Musset', based on an article by Léon Séché, 'Un amour d'Alfred de Musset', *Le Figaro*, 12 January 1910, which preceded the publication of the poet's letters to the girl.

44. Ingénieur des Mines (1884–1954); his family rented the Villa Suzanne at Cabourg.

45. *Le Carnet de 1908*, p. 58 (cf. p. 57: 'We hope that the same musical phrase will return, it does return, and it has less effect on us than it did the first time' . . .); Cahier 27, ff. 48–50.

46. Ibid., pp. 53–6, 58.

47. *Corr.*, vol. VIII, p. 241, to R. de Flers: 'For me it was a marvellous delight.' M. Plantevignes, *Avec Marcel Proust*, Nizet, 1966.

48. *Corr.*, vol. VIII, p. 227.

49. Ibid., p. 240.

50. Ibid., p. 239.

51. *Le Carnet de 1908*, p. 60.

52. *RTP*, vol. III, p. 147.

53. *Le Carnet de 1908*, p. 64, f. 13; p. 62, f. 12.

54. *Corr.*, vol. VIII, p. 243, October 1908.

55. Ibid., pp. 213–17, about 10 September 1908.

56. Regarding the Bank of the River Plate: 'I beg you not to involve me with your investments in these kinds of stocks and shares' (2 December 1908).

57. They were probably Royal Dutch shares.

58. *Corr.*, vol. VIII, pp. 276–8.

59. Ibid., p. 286. St John 12: 35. See 'Proust 45', f. 15 recto, *CSB*, p. 219, where the same idea occurs.

60. Ibid., p. 316.

61. 'Proust 45' (n. a. fr. 16 636). This was how a reference in November 1908 to stock-exchange shares came to be in the middle of notes about Sainte-Beuve (f. 15, p. 67).

62. In May 1908, for instance, he referred to the article from *Les Nouveaux Lundis* on Fromental Halévy, Mme Straus' father (17 April 1862, vol. II, pp. 227–46). And he had also reread it, from the beginning of the year, for his pastiche (*Le Carnet de 1908*, pp. 128–31).

63. *Corr.*, vol. VIII, p. 320.

64. Ibid., pp. 320–1.

65. Ibid., p. 323, letter dated mid-December 1908.

66. *CSB*, pp. 218–19. Nevertheless, I know of no paper that can be dated from

1907; of course, there was nothing to prevent Proust from thinking about his project without noting it down immediately, as the letter to Halévy discussed at the end of the previous chapter suggests.

67. *Corr.*, vol. VIII, p. 324; cf. p. 326: 'and, similarly, the Chateaubriands', which enabled him to write a pastiche, originally noted in *Le Carnet de 1908*, pp. 127–8.

68. *Corr.*, vol. VIII, p. 331.

69. To these should be added some loose pages, 'bundles of papers' ['*paperoles*' was Céleste's word for them *Tr.*], typewritten sheets and proofs. In this account of the genesis of Proust's novel I have quoted these documents, but most of them are published in the Pléiade edition of *RTP*; where these are numbered, I have supplied the reference. See also, in *RTP*, vol. I, Florence Callu's note on the Proust collection in the Bibliothèque Nationale, p. cxlv.

70. 'The notebooks in which Proust wrote were the exercise books that were used at the Lycée Condorcet', Suzy Mante-Proust points out (Claude Francis and Fernande Gonthier, *Marcel Proust et les siens* together with *Souvenirs de S. Mante-Proust*, Plon, 1981, p. 207).

71. Following the work done by Henri Bonnet and Maurice Bardèche, Claudine Quémar's research is responsible for the remarkable progress in classifying the 'Sainte-Beuve' notebooks. See C. Quémar, 'Autour de trois "avant-textes" de l'"Ouverture" de la *Recherche*: nouvelles approches des problèmes du *Contre Sainte-Beuve*', *Bulletin d'informations proustiennes*, no. 3, 1976, and no. 9 in *Bulletin*, 1979, which presents a detailed list of the ten exercise books.

72. Letter from M. Proust to A. Vallette, published by F. Callu, *Bulletin de la Bibliothèque Nationale*, March 1980, pp. 12–14; *Corr.*, vol. IX, pp. 155–7. Proust alluded to Régnier's novel because his correspondent had published it.

73. See *Corr.*, vol. IX, p. 161.

74. Following the numbering system used by the Bibliothèque Nationale, Cahiers 1–7, 31, 36 and 51; following the classification proposed by C. Quémar (*Bulletin d'informations proustiennes*, n. 3, 1976), 3, 2, 5, 1, 4, 31, 6, 7, 36 and 51; following J. Yoshida (ed. *RTP*, Bibliothèque de la Pléiade, 1987–9), 3, 2, 5, 1, 4, 31, 36, 7, 6 and 51.

75. Written from the notes in *Le Carnet de 1908*, pp. 64–6.

76. Readers anxious to understand the entire archaeology of the text should refer to Florence Callu's note on 'The Proust Collection at the Bibliothèque Nationale', and to the notes and footnotes on the text which accompany each section of *À la recherche du temps perdu* in the Bibliothèque de la Pléiade edition (1987–9).

77. Letter quoted in *Bulletin de la Bibliothèque nationale*, pp. 12–13.

78. 'Even physically he is charming', wrote Proust of Helleu, before going on

to praise his 'Paris lodgings', 'the exquisite taste of the décor': 'He has the very simple nature of the true artist' (*Corr.*, vol. IX, p. 163, to Mme Straus). About the painter, see J. Bersani and C. Quémar, 'M. Proust le peintre', *Cahiers critiques de la littérature*, summer 1977, pp. 7–19 (edition of a fragment from Cahier 28).

79. Here we also come across some verses from 'Booz endormi'; Proust was trying to find a reference for it in February 1909 (*Corr.*, vol. IX, p. 41 and *CSB*, p. 619).

80. These articles are collected in *Essais et articles*, *CSB*, pp. 570–639.

81. *Albertine disparue*, *RTP*, vol. IV. In *CSB*, p. 227, we find a first version of this paragraph that is close to the final text.

82. The title is used by L. Séché in his *Sainte-Beuve*. Proust had read the same critic's *Alfred de Musset* (Mercure de France, 1907, 2 vols), which he mentioned (*Corr.*, vol. IX, p. 172). There is no doubt that for his own Sainte-Beuve, he informed himself fully about nineteenth-century literature, including scholarly works on the subject.

83. *CSB*, p. 219.

84. Ibid.

85. Or 132,000 francs in 1999 terms. *Corr.*, vol. IX, p. 50, letter from Lionel Hauser.

86. Ibid., p. 10 and *CSB*, pp. 306–8.

87. According to the footnote on Harrison in *Le Carnet de 1908*.

88. *Corr.*, vol. IX, p. 118.

89. Ibid., p. 122.

90. Ibid., p. 150.

91. f. 38 verso.

92. *Corr.*, vol. IX, p. 179.

93. Ibid., p. 192.

94. See Feydeau, *Théâtre complet*, vol. IV, Classiques Garnier, Bordas, 1989, note by Henry Gidel, pp. 53–6. The play only ran for forty-one performances, until 13 December, and has never been put on again.

95. The account of these events appears in a letter to Lauris of 27 April 1910 (*Corr.*, vol. X, pp. 81–4).

96. Ibid., vol. IX, p. 226.

97. C. Quémar, 'Hypothèses sur le classement des premiers cahiers Swann', *Bulletin d'informations proustiennes*, no. 13, 1982. See especially, in *RTP*, vol. I, the notes on 'Combray' and on 'Autour de Mme Swann' (pp. 1058–68 and 1308–15) and, in vol. II, the note on 'Noms de pays: le pays.'

98. On 3 November 1910 Proust asked Robert de Flers which issue of *La Vie contemporaine* (1 March 1896) had published 'L'indifférent', which included a draft version of 'Un amour de Swann' (*Corr.*, vol. X, p. 197).

99. In Cahiers 7, 6 and 31. See 'Marcel Proust, Le Peintre', edited and introduced

by J. Bersani and C. Quémar, *Cahiers critiques de la littérature*, nos 3–4, summer 1977, pp. 8–18.

100. Cahier 28: *RTP*, vol. II, draft LV and LVI, p. 963. Cf. for Moreau, *CSB*, p. 667.

101. See K. Yoshikawa, 'Vinteuil ou la genèse du septuor', *Études proustiennes*, vol. III, Gallimard, 1979, pp. 289–347.

102. In Cahier 10, in the autumn of 1909. See V. Roloff, '*François le Champi* et le texte retrouvé', ibid.

103. Bardèche, *Marcel Proust romancier*, vol. II, 1971, pp. 31–2, is probably the first to have demonstrated this.

104. Proust had three copies of this typed, as M. Wada has established, in November 1909. M. Wada, *L'Évolution de 'Combray' depuis l'automne 1909*, post-graduate thesis, Paris-Sorbonne, 1986.

105. *Corr.*, vol. IX, p. 200, 16 October 1909.

106. Ibid., p. 203, 2 November 1909.

107. Ibid., p. 208, November 1909.

108. Ibid., p. 218.

109. See Robert Brydges, 'Remarques sur le manuscrit et les dactylographies du *Temps perdu*', *Bulletin d'informations proustiennes*, no. 15, 1984, and 'Analyse matérielle du manuscrit du *Temps perdu*', ibid., no. 16, 1985.

110. *Le Côté de Guermantes I, RTP*, vol. II, p. 336.

111. See *À l'ombre des jeunes filles en fleurs*, 'Noms de pays: le pays', *RTP*, vol. II, draft XXXV, pp. 906–10.

112. Ibid., p. 907.

113. *Le Côté de Guermantes II, RTP*, vol. II, p. 678.

114. Published respectively in *La Nouvelle Revue Française* of 1 February 1953, and in Bardèche, vol. II, pp. 393–5; extracts from Cahier 36 and Cahier 50.

115. Cahier 36, f. 1 recto and 9 verso.

116. See, in *Sodome et Gomorrhe, RTP*, vol. III, the note and the drafts.

117. Cahier 56, ff. 102–5 recto. See *Albertine disparue, RTP*, vol. IV, draft VI.

118. Ibid., f. 105.

119. Cahier 55, ff. 91–3 recto. See *RTP*, vol. IV, draft XXIII.

120. Cahier 60, ff. 20–2. See *Albertine disparue, RTP*, vol. IV, draft VI.

121. Cahier 25.

122. Cahier 57. See *RTP*, vol. IV, p. 894 and n. 2. See H. Bonnet, in *BAMP*, no. 28, 1978, p. 610. This would have been a portrait of Marten Soolmans and his wife, Oopjen Coppit, in the Van Loon mansion in Amsterdam.

123. See the note and drafts in *Sodome et Gomorrhe, RTP*, vol. III.

124. *Albertine disparue, RTP*, vol. IV, p. 83.

125. *RTP*, vol. I, drafts XX–XXIII, pp. 1027–34. The name, which was that of a painter in *Jean Santeuil*, first appears in late 1909 or early 1910 (ibid., p. 1311, note in *À l'ombre des jeunes filles en fleurs*). Bergotte's immoral life was elaborated

by Proust from the time when, after Mme de Caillavet's death, he discovered how immoral France had been.

126. Mercure de France, 1906, p. 116.

127. *Corr.*, vol. X, p. 28.

128. Ibid., vol. XI, p. 193, August 1912.

129. J. Levaillant, 'Note sur le personnage de Bergotte', *La Revue des sciences humaines*, January–March 1952.

130. The adjective 'mellow' is a signature. *RTP*, vol. I, p. 548. See draft XXIII, p. 1034.

131. *Corr.*, vol. XII, pp. 316, 1913.

132. Ibid., p. 415.

133. *CSB*, p. 568.

134. *Corr.*, vol. X, p. 30.

135. Ibid., p. 31. Nor did he forget the stock exchange, and he set about acquiring some 5 per cent US bonds, which Lionel Hauser had half-heartedly recommended to him, in order to prevent him buying riskier shares (ibid., pp. 34–9).

136. Ibid., p. 40.

137. 'Something very beautiful which unfortunately very slightly resembles (though a thousand times better) what I'm doing' (ibid., p. 54, to R. de Billy). And he wanted to know what sort of men Hardy and Barrie were, 'society people, keen on women, etc.' In this way he revealed his Sainte-Beuve side, or, in any case, his interest in biography, which was an excuse for writing one. However, in November 1910 he would say he did not like *A Pair of Blue Eyes* so much (which was published by *Le Journal des débats*; the subject is the same, but the situation is reversed: 'here it is the woman who loves three people', *Le Carnet de 1908*, p. 114); he nevertheless wrote a page of notes about this novel in *Le Carnet*, f. 48: the admirable geometric parallels, the obsession with stone whether it was sculpted or not, 'tomb, church, quarry', particularly appealed to him, and he made them his own. Finally, he said he did not care at all for *Barbara (Far from the Madding Crowd)*, Mercure de France, 1901, which he read in early 1911 (*Corr.*, vol. X, p. 240).

138. *Corr.*, vol. X, p. 55, March 1910, to Billy. 'Two pages from *Moulin sur la Floss* [*The Mill on the Floss*] are enough to make me cry' (ibid.) His appreciation of English and American literature is all the more significant since he confessed to Lauris in April to 'liking so little in literature' (ibid., p. 84). In late April he also read Poe's poems, and 'The Philosophy of Composition' in Gabriel Mourey's translation, which the latter had just sent him, along with 'biographical and bibliographical notes' (ibid., p. 91). The grandmother would fear that the suffering and disrepute of a Baudelaire, a Poe, a Verlaine or a Rimbaud might be the lot of her grandson (*RTP*, vol. II, p. 86).

139. *Corr.*, vol. X, p. 131.

140. Ibid., p. 110, June 1910.

141. This annotated copy of *La Chartreuse* was included in the exhibition held at the Musée Jacquemart-André in 1971. See ibid., p. 119, to Lauris (Proust asked him for Mérimée's *H. B.* in June). See *CSB*, pp. 611–12 and *La Prisonnière*, RTP, vol. III, p. 879.

142. *Corr.*, vol. X, p. 121.

143. Ibid., pp. 138, 145–6.

144. Ibid., p. 113; according to P. Kolb (ibid., vol. X, pp. 12 and 114), he had already gone to the Opéra on 4 June, with Hahn and Vaudoyer, for the first night; the programme began with *Le Festin* (a pot-pourri of Russian music choreographed by Fokine) and some 'Danses polovtsiennes' from *Prince Igor*, followed by *Carnaval* (Schumann and Fokine), and *Schéhérazade*, with Nijinsky in the role of the slave and Ida Rubinstein as Zobéide (R. Buckle, *Diaghilev*, Weidenfeld and Nicolson, 1979, pp. 169–70). In his correspondence Proust remarks on an article by R. Hahn (which he made use of in a draft for *À l'ombre des jeunes filles en fleurs, RTP*, vol. I, p. 1002) and by J.-L. Vaudoyer (*Corr.*, vol. X, pp. 114, 142).

145. *RTP*, vol. II, p. 298.

146. Ibid., vol. III, p. 140.

147. She wore an 'immense egret' which a Cocteau drawing has enabled us to identify. Proust referred to Nijinsky in a poem addressed to Cocteau.

148. *Corr.*, vol. X, p. 151.

149. Ibid., p. 176.

150. 'À l'ombre de Marcel Proust', edited by Paul Guth, *Le Figaro littéraire*, 25 September 1954.

151. Ibid. *Champignol malgré lui* was the title of a play by Feydeau.

152. *Corr.*, vol. X, pp. 138–9 and n. 3.

153. 'Nicolas', *RTP*, vol. IV, p. 971.

154. *Corr.*, vol. XV, p. 205, 4 July 1916.

155. Like the rest of Céline's remarks, these are taken from the interview with Paul Guth, 'À l'ombre de Marcel Proust'.

156. Around 3 July he went, for an hour, between trains, to Fontainebleau (*Corr.*, vol. X, p. 12 and n. 2, p. 162), as if to check and complete the passages in *Jean Santeuil*, which, in his new novel, were intended for a small garrison town: 'I returned there alone one Sunday between trains and I roamed around the Hôtel de France et d'Angleterre, without daring to go inside for fear of too poignant a contrast between my life at the time and that of today' (to Léon Daudet, 1912).

157. *Corr.*, vol. X, p. 169.

158. Ibid., pp. 144–5.

159. Ibid., p. 163. *La Grande Revue*, founded in 1895, was edited by Jacques Rouché, the future director of the Opéra.

160. *Corr.*, vol. X, p. 159.

161. Ibid., p. 167.

162. Born in 1863, a pupil of Pauline Viardot and of Victor Maurel, sister-in-law of Édouard de Reszké, she was a naturalized Frenchwoman, and having made her début in Verdi, she specialized in Wagner and was the first Isolde (1899) and the first Brunnhilde (1911) in Paris. She retired in 1917. She published *Ma vie et mon art* (1933). See A. Paris, *Dictionnaire des interprètes*, Laffont, Bouquins, 1995, p. 626. R. Hahn frequently referred to her; Proust joked about her with his friend.

163. A brilliant virtuoso (1886–1958) and composer.

164. *Corr.*, vol. X, p. 169.

165. *RTP*, vol. III, p. 424 and n. 1.

166. Antoinette Faure's questionnaire, *CSB*, p. 336.

167. *Le Carnet de 1908*, pp. 108–10, and *RTP*, vol. I, pp. 1026–7. On 1 October he sent Hahn some poems which were a parody on the twelfth stanza of 'La nuit d'octobre'.

168. *RTP*, vol. III, p. 947.

169. *Corr.*, vol. X, p. 175, 27 September 1910. P. Kolb was unable to trace these passages.

170. *RTP*, vol. III, p. 493; Saint-Pierre-des-Ifs is on the line from Balbec to Douville.

171. Ibid., p. 177.

172. Ibid., vol. IV, p. 388. Proust told d'Alton that he had not got up 'in order to take Plantevignes to the Faubourg Saint-Germain' (*Corr.*, vol. X, p. 188), as Charlus does in the case of the Narrator.

173. *Corr.*, vol. XX, pp. 630–1, 1 September 1910, to Léon Bailby, the paper's editor.

174. *CSB*, pp. 552–4. On 7 November Proust also thanked and praised Lucien Daudet for his book *Lettres après la lettre* (*Corr.*, vol. X, p. 201).

175. *Corr.*, vol. X, p. 215, to Mme Catusse.

176. Ibid., p. 165.

177. Ibid., p. 171.

178. Ibid., p. 264.

179. *L'Insecte* and *Tableau de la France* to Lauris, *La Montagne* to R. Dreyfus. Cf. *Le Carnet de 1908*, f. 10 and f. 39 verso.

180. *Corr.*, vol. X, p. 232.

181. Ibid., p. 278.

182. Ibid. vol. XXI, p. 29.

183. *RTP*, vol. IV, p. 227.

184. Ibid., pp. 184–5.

185 *Corr.*, vol. XI, p. 148.

186. Ibid., vol. XII, p. 222, July 1913.

187. Buckle, *Diaghilev*, who gives the date as 28 February; *Le Figaro* gives it as 3 March; *Corr.*, vol. X, p. 257. At the end of the evening Hahn sang some songs, and Glazounov, the director of the Conservatoire, played some pieces on the piano.

188. *Corr.*, vol. X, p. 258. See G. Bernstein Gruber and G. Maurin, *Bernstein le magnifique*, Lattès, 1988, pp. 17, 29, 106–21.

189. Fauré had composed incidental music (1898, based on several passages which he reworked) dedicated to the Princesse Edmond de Polignac, for Maeterlinck's *Pelléas* (explained by R. Hahn, *Thèmes variés*, Janin, 1946, pp. 139–48), at the request of the actress Mrs Patrick Campbell, for the performances of Maeterlinck's work which she gave in London in 1898 or 1899; two or three years later she performed in the play again, with Sarah Bernhardt in the role of Pelléas.

190. *Corr.*, vol. X, p. 250. The reference to Goncourt can be found in *Le Carnet de 1908*, p. 76 and n. 3.

191. *Corr.*, vol. X, p. 254, to Lauris.

192. *CSB*, pp. 206–7; the complete text remained unpublished until 1971. The extract is in *Corr.*, vol. X, pp. 261–2.

193. *Corr.*, vol. XI, p. 108, 24 April 1912.

194. Ida Rubinstein (1880–1960) had danced in *Schéhérazade*. After the war she would form her own company and commission works from some of the greatest artists of the time. Proust thought she was 'half like Clomesnil, half like Maurice de Rothschild'; her androgynous looks are evident in the nude portrait of her by Romaine Brooks.

195. *Corr.*, vol. X, p. 289, 23 May 1911, to R. Hahn. The version of the text that is performed today is greatly abridged. In 1956 Charles Munch recorded the full score and an abridged edition of the libretto (RCA Victor).

196. Ibid., p. 300. Montesquiou wrote about the work in an article in the June issue of *Le Théâtre* (reprinted in *Têtes couronnées*, Sansot, 1916), for which Proust congratulated him; he praised the count's list of Sebastians in the history of painting and his tribute to Bakst (*Corr.*, vol. X, p. 301).

197. *Corr.*, vol. X, p. 293.

198. Ibid., pp. 294, 298.

199. Thanks to the intervention of Calmette's brother, who was head of the medical corps of the Paris military government, ibid., pp. 344–5, 347–8.

200. Ibid., p. 348, to Gaston Calmette.

201. Ibid., p. 321.

202. Ibid., p. 320; R. Gimpel, *Journal d'un collectionneur marchand de tableaux*, Calmann-Lévy, 1963, p. 306.

203. *Corr.*, vol. X, p. 323.

204. Ibid., p. 338.

205. Ibid., vol. XI, p. 69.

206. *Le Figaro*, 1–6 August 1911.

207. *Le Figaro*, 16 August 1911. Introduction to Mrs Oliphant, *La Ville enchantée*, Émile-Paul, 1911.

208. *RTP*, vol. III, p. 668. Cf. *Corr.*, vol. X, p. 353.

209. *Corr.*, vol. X, pp. 337–8, 23 or 24 August 1911, to Lauris.

210. Ibid., p. 342, late August 1911.

211. Ibid., vol. X, p. 384.

212. Ibid., p. 389.

213. Ibid., vol. XI, p. 19.

214. Ibid., vol. X, p. 374.

215. Ibid., p. 358. I interpret the word as *'ressasse'* [dwells] and not *'rassasie'* [fills], as P. Kolb does.

216. Ibid., vol. XIX, p. 714: at the time he signed his letters simply *'votre dévoué'*.

217. Ibid., vol. IX, p. 206.

218. Ibid., p. 212.

219. Ibid., vol. X, p. 161.

220. It so happened that at a sale at Drouot's in 1995 a catalogue described a copy of *Les Plaisirs et les Jours*, inscribed in an entirely polite manner to the father, as being the son's copy. The name of Albert Nahmias *père* appeared in *Le Bottin mondain* and in *Le Tout-Paris*. See H. Bonnet, 'Nahmias fils', *BAMP*, no. 35, 1985, p. 381.

221. *Corr.*, vol. X, p. 376.

222. *RTP*, vol. I, note for *À l'ombre des jeunes filles en fleurs*, p. 1285.

223. *Corr.*, vol. X, p. 379.

224. Ibid., p. 375, about November 1911. Ibid., vol. XI, p. 41, early February 1912: Proust was questioning Billy about whether he should delay settling his account (he bought forward) until the following month.

225. For the losses, ibid., vol. X, p. 388, 24 December or shortly afterwards, to R. Hahn, and n. 26.

226. *Corr.*, vol. XIII, p. 367, about November 1911.

227. Ibid., vol. XI, p. 46.

228. Ibid., p. 95.

229. Ibid., April 1912.

230. *RTP*, vol. I, p. 237.

231. *Corr.*, vol. X, p. 388: 'If he goes out in society he's lost.'

CHAPTER XIII: *'Le Temps perdu' (1912–13)*

1. The scene was worked on in several of the exercise books.

2. See *Matinée chez la princesse de Guermantes, Cahiers du Temps retrouvé*, ed. H. Bonnet and B. Brun, Gallimard, 1982; the editors date the first version of

'*bal de têtes*' from 1909, but other researchers maintain it is from 1910.

3. Ibid., p. 189. Cahier 57, f. 41.

4. Ibid., p. 149. Cahier 57; compare with *Le Temps retrouvé*, *RTP*, vol. IV.

5. *Matinée*, pp. 37, 46, 66.

6. Ibid., p. 234.

7. Ibid., p. 240.

8. *RTP*, vol. II, p. 1494, note to *Le Côté de Guermantes*.

9. *Corr.*, vol. XI, p. 68.

10. Ibid., p. 76.

11. Ibid., pp. 118–19.

12. Ibid., vol. XI, p. 151, first half of 1912, to R. Hahn.

13. Ibid., p. 241.

14. Ibid., p. 255, 28 October 1912.

15. Ibid., p. 257. The title also appeared on the folder of the typescript. See M. Bardèche, *Marcel Proust romancier*, Les Sept Couleurs, vol. I, 1971, pp. 238–40.

16. *Corr.*, vol. XI. p. 17.

17. Ibid., p. 19.

18. Ibid., p. 43: 300 francs in February, 1,700 francs on 29 March, on top of which he had to pay the typist.

19. Ibid., pp. 25–6. In this letter, Marcel spoke of typing out the 'red exercise book' and the 'blue exercise book' which contain this section (Kolb's notes are incorrect here). The exercise books in question are Cahiers 65 and 70. See the note by F. Callu, *RTP*, vol. I.

20. Reprinted in *Chroniques*, pp. 92–9. See *Corr.*, vol. XI, p. 63. The montage was taken from pages 111, 113, 136–8, 143 of 'Combray', *RTP*, vol. I. On 4 June 1912 'Rayon de soleil sur le balcon' was published (*Chroniques*, p. 100) and on 3 September, 'L'Église de village' (ibid., p. 114).

21. Unpublished letter. Catalogue for the sale on 10 May 1995, MM Laurin-Guilloux-Buffetaud-Tailleur, Drouot, no. 100 and no. 101. Part of the correspondence with Hahn from this period seems to have disappeared.

22. See the description of this ballet, which was a success, in R. Buckle, *Diaghilev*, London, Weidenfeld and Nicolson, 1979, p. 222.

23. *Corr.*, vol. XI, p. 128.

24. Ibid., p. 157.

25. Ibid., p. 136. Cf. *RTP*, vol. I, p. 939: 'Don't forget: Statue of my youth: (Simone).'

26. Six views of the Grand Canal, seven of the Doges' palace (*RTP*, vol. I, pp. 319, 380; vol. II, p. 750; vol. IV, p. 208), five of San Giorgio (vol. IV, pp. 204, 233, 466), three of the Palazzo Dario (vol. IV, p. 696), three of the Rio de la Salute (vol. II, p. 660; vol. IV, pp. 288, 552), two of the Palazzo da Mula, two of the Palazzo Contarini (vol. IV, pp. 696–7) and one 'Dusk'.

One album reproduced nine canvases, preceded by a study of 'Monet et Venise' by Mirbeau. See G. Geffroy, *Monet, sa vie, son œuvre*, Crès, 1924, new ed. Macula, 1980, pp. 421–5.

27. *RTP*, vol. II, p. 1585.

28. Ibid., vol. IV, p. 690.

29. *Corr.*, vol. XI, p. 208.

30. *Chroniques*, pp. 100–5; *RTP*, vol. I, pp. 389–90, 391, 405, 408.

31. *Corr.*, vol. XI, p. 153. We don't know the identity of this 'friend' who replaced Nahmias. Proust, furthermore, sent another 1,700 francs.

32. Ibid., p. 161, n. 5.

33. Ibid., p. 166, 25 July 1912, to J.-L. Vaudoyer; *Le Carnet de 1908*, p. 94 ff. Vaudoyer would stay at Cabourg, at the Villa Hélène, which allowed Proust to invite him: 'We shall go and chat in the baccarat room at the casino where we shall be undisturbed' (*Corr.*, vol. XI, p. 180).

34. *Corr.*, vol. XI, p. 182, to R. Hahn.

35. Ibid., p. 182 and n. 9, p. 193.

36. Ibid., p. 211, 7 September 1912.

37. *RTP*, vol. III, p. 67. Marie Scheikévitch was to publish her *Souvenirs d'un temps disparu*, Plon, 1935.

38. *Corr.*, vol. XI, p. 185.

39. Estie Nahmias sent André Maurois a poem, in 1949, which vouches for the fact that she was one of the *jeunes filles en fleurs*: 'La jeune fille en fleurs du tome dont je sors/ Est une vieille dame en feuille jaune morte' (quoted by G. de Diesbach, p. 453). [The girl from the budding grove in the book from which I come/ Is an old lady dressed in fallen yellow leaves.]

40. 'Marcel Proust à Cabourg', *NRF*, January 1923, p. 67.

41. *Corr.*, vol. XI, p. 222.

42. Ibid., p. 236, late October 1912, to Bibesco.

43. *RTP*, vol. I, p. 191.

44. Ibid., vol. II, p. 741; *Corr.*, vol. XI, p. 191, in which Proust said he liked works that Hahn did not care for, '*Pelléas, Salomé*'.

45. *Corr.*, vol. XII, p. 202.

46. Ibid., p. 255 ff., 28 October 1912, to E. Fasquelle.

47. Ibid., p. 265, the only mention of a plan that would come to nothing.

48. Ibid., p. 294.

49. Report published by H. Bonnet, *Le Figaro littéraire*, 8 December 1966, and later in my own *Lectures de Proust*, A. Colin, 1971, p. 10 ff.

50. *Corr.*, vol. XI, p. 331.

51. Ibid., p. 246, 25 October 1912.

52. Ibid., p. 289.

53. *Corr. avec G. Gallimard*, pp. 10–14.

54. Ibid., p. 14.

55. Ibid., p. 397, 22 September 1921.

56. *Corr.*, vol. XI, p. 331.

57. Ibid., p. 334.

58. Ibid., p. 337.

59. S. Monneret, *Dictionnaire de l'impressionisme*, p. 791. Helleu did at least two fine etchings of Henri Rouart, and Degas painted several pictures of him. In January 1913 Proust would also learn of two articles by J.-É. Blanche in *La Revue de Paris*. 'Notes sur la peinture moderne (à propos de la collection Rouart)' (*Corr.*, vol. XII, p. 36).

60. *Corr.*, vol. XII, pp. 48–9.

61. Ibid., p. 54 ff. This did not prevent Copeau from asking Proust to subscribe to shares in the Théâtre du Vieux-Colombier, which he was trying to establish, on 17 April 1913 (ibid., p. 138). Harbouring no grudges, Proust did his best to help find subscribers and, in spite of his own financial difficulties, would himself subscribe to 3,000 francs worth of shares (ibid., p. 181, n. 9), which was accepted without any compunction.

62. Ibid., p. 285; in his letter to Barrès Proust gives an idea of the content of the article that is now lost. *Le Temps* also rejected it.

63. Ibid., p. 38, 25 January 1913, to L. de Robert.

64. *RTP*, vol. IV, p. 618.

65. *Corr.*, vol. XII, p. 77.

66. J. Bothorel, *Bernard Grasset*, Grasset, 1989.

67. *RTP*, vol. III, p. 296.

68. *Corr.*, vol. XII, pp. 95–7.

69. Ibid., p. 45, 31 January 1913.

70. Firstly in Cahier 34, which dates from this time, then in *RTP*, vol. II, p. 198 and n. 1, which gives all the sources. J. Autret (*L'Influence de Ruskin sur la vie, les idées et l'œuvre de Marcel Proust*, Geneva, Droz, 1955, pp. 144–51) first pointed out that Proust had copied Mâle in order to describe the porch of the church at Balbec.

71. *Corr.*, vol. XII, p. 44; Proust had been interested in d'Indy as early as 1902. *L'Intransigeant* observed that Fauré and Debussy had both chosen the same heroine, Mélisande; Proust commented ironically: 'Sigismond Bardac may think that they should have been satisfied with that'; Emma Bardac had a daughter, Dolly, by Fauré and later married Debussy.

72. We are beginning to be aware of the greatness of Beethoven's late masterpieces, for which Romain Rolland and André Suarès also made a case. Lucien Capet, who had taught at the Conservatoire de Paris since 1907, had written a book on Beethoven's seventeen quartets.

73. In November 1913 Proust inscribed a copy of *Swann* to Édouard Hermann which bore the initial theme from Franck's piano quintet (*Corr.*, vol. XII, p. 318).

74. *La Prisonnière*, draft XIII, *RTP*, vol. III, pp. 1143–53. *Le Temps retrouvé*, draft XL, pp. 870–2 (Carnet 2); Cahier 57 contains a quartet by Vinteuil. See K. Yoshikawa, 'Vinteuil ou la genèse du septuor', *Études proustiennes*, vol. III, 1979, pp. 289–347. Also to be found in Carnet 3 are some preparatory notes from 1913 for the septet.

75. *RTP*, vol. I, p. 346 and n. 1.

76. *Chroniques*, p. 113. Cf. p. 74.

77. Ibid., pp. 106–13. *RTP*, vol. I, pp. 379–86; vol. III, pp. 623, 1098.

78. The melodic motif of spring 'had the fragrant, delightful and fragile delicacy of the theme of convalescence and roses in M. d'Indy's *Fervaal*' (*Chroniques*, p. 112).

79. *Corr.*, vol. XII, p. 133, to L. Hauser.

80. Ibid., p. 192, 2 or 3 June 1913.

81. *RTP*, vol. III, p. 624.

82. *Corr.*, vol. XII, p. 180.

83. Ibid., vol. XIII, p. 228, 3 June 1914.

84. C. Albaret, *Monsieur Proust*, Laffont, 1973, pp. 231–4.

85. Letter quoted to É. Straus.

86. From Gautier-Vignal, in particular.

87. *Corr.*, vol. XV, p. 321.

88. Ibid., vol. XIII, p. 311, late October 1914.

89. Ibid., vol. XII, p. 237.

90. Ibid., p. 250, to Lauris.

91. Ibid., p. 243, shortly after 4 August 1913.

92. *RTP*, vol. III, pp. 499–509.

93. *Corr.*, vol. XII, p. 249, 11 August 1913.

94. Ibid., pp. 250–1, to Lauris. Cf. p. 255.

95. Ibid., p. 269, to C. d'Alton.

96. Ibid., p. 286.

97. Ibid., p. 265, early September 1913. Cf. D. Alden, *Marcel Proust's Grasset Proofs, Commentary and Variants*, Chapel Mill, University of North Carolina Press, 1978, pp. 31–7, 269–313.

98. *Corr.*, vol. XII, p. 271, early September, to L. de Robert.

99. Ibid., vol. XII, pp. 280–1. Proust also defended this notion in his article, now lost, on *La Colline inspirée*.

100. F. Collin, *Parmi les précurseurs du ciel*, Peyronnet, 1947, pp. 254–7; *RTP*, p. 1635, note by P. Robert. *Albertine disparue*, Folio classique, p. 349 (n. 1 to p. 280).

101. C. Albaret, p. 233: 'I think that there was a great deal of his wife's influence there.'

102. *Corr.*, vol. XII, p. 176, to Bernard Grasset.

103. Ibid., p. 220, July 1913, letter from L. de Robert; see also p. 222. Louis de Robert preferred 'Charles Swann'.

104. Ibid., p. 218.
105. Ibid., p. 232, July 1913, to L. de Robert. In this same letter there are suggestions for three other titles for the three volumes: *L'Âge des noms, L'Âge des mots, L'Âge des choses.*
106. Ibid., p. 278.
107. Ibid., p. 222. Those who endorse the short version of *Albertine disparue*, please note!
108. Ibid., p. 224.
109. Ibid., p. 228.
110. Ibid., p. 230.
111. Ibid., p. 233, July 1913, to B. Grasset.
112. Ibid., p. 281. Announcement in *La Bibliographie de la France* of 14 November 1913.
113. Ibid., p. 367, 8 December 1913, to André Beaunier.
114. Ibid., p. 132, 12 April 1912.
115. Ibid., p. 182.
116. Ibid., p. 145.
117. Ibid., p. 185.
118. Ibid., pp. 161–2, early May 1913.
119. See ibid., p. 295, 5 or 7 November 1913, for the second volume; but Proust must have discovered that it was the title of a novel by Maurice Magre.
120. Ibid., p. 174.
121. Ibid., p. 239.
122. G. Boillat, *La Librairie Grasset et les lettres françaises*, Champion, 1974, p. 78.
123. *Corr.*, vol. XII, p. 280.
124. See note to *Du côté de chez Swann* in *RTP*, vol. I.
125. Private collection.
126. Boillat, *La Librairie Grasset*, p. 178.
127. Ibid., p. 279, n. 47.
128. Ibid., p. 290.
129. Ibid., p. 278, n. 40, letter of 30 October 1913.
130. *Corr.*, vol. XII, p. 295; text of the 'leak', ibid., p. 300.
131. Ibid., p. 309.
132. See Proust's letter of thanks, ibid., pp. 392–3.
133. Ibid., p. 352.
134. Ibid., pp. 372–3.
135. Ibid., pp. 325, n. 4, 328, 336, 340, 347.
136. Anecdote related by G. de Diesbach, according to M. de Lasteyrie.
137. *Corr.*, vol. XII, p. 395.
138. *RTP*, vol. IV, p. 36.

CHAPTER XIV: *The Novel of 1914*

1. This was the original title for 'Autour de Mme Swann', which Proust offered to *Le Figaro* for extracts that spring.
2. See note in *Le Côté de Guermantes I, RTP*, vol. II.
3. The manuscript is folioed up to page 244.
4. Cahier 39, f. 10 verso. Further new light on Proust's reading: he read Scott, as well as Balzac.
5. *Corr. gén.*, vol. III, pp. 305–6, December 1920, to L. Martin-Chauffier.
6. *Corr. avec G. Gallimard*, p. 297: '. . . *Le Côté de Guermantes* constructed in a way – forgive the term – more like Dostoevsky', and 'If *Le Côté de Guermantes* were better and worthy of such an epigraph, I should apply a line of Baudelaire's to it: "*Mais où la vie afflue et s'agite sans cesse*"' [But where life surges and swells unceasingly] (November 1920, to Gaston Gallimard).
7. See K. Yoshikawa, *Études sur la genèse de 'La Prisonnière' d'après des brouillons inédits*, post-graduate doctoral thesis, Université de Paris-Sorbonne, 1976, vol. I, pp. 20–34 (typescript copy).
8. *Corr.*, vol. IX, p. 155.
9. Ibid., vol. XI, p. 256.
10. *Corr. avec G. Gallimard*, p. 18, shortly after 8 November 1912.
11. See the note to *Sodome et Gomorrhe, RTP*, vol. III.
12. Ibid., draft I.
13. In March 1913 Proust asked Vaudoyer whether he liked the title *Les Intermittences du passé* (*Corr.*, vol. XII, p. 114).
14. Cahier 50, ff. 34–40. These pages would pave the way for the fourth and final chapter of *Albertine disparue*; one may wonder whether this did not already belong to *Le Temps retrouvé*, at least in terms of the themes it deals with. Other factual indications also support this hypothesis. See *RTP*, vol. IV.
15. Cahier 13, f. 28 recto; in *À l'ombre des jeunes filles en fleurs, RTP*, vol. II, see the note in 'Nom de pays: le pays' and draft XVII.
16. *Matinée chez la princesse de Guermantes, Cahiers du Temps retrouvé*, ed. H. Bonnet and B. Brun, Gallimard, 1982, p. 326.
17. See the note to *La Prisonnière, RTP*, vol. III.
18. *Le Carnet de 1908*, p. 50. Gradually, the structure that links a beloved woman to a place, to an artist, to inspiration, to an influence that is accepted or rejected, was being finalized.
19. Her name appears 270, 444, 751 and 731 times respectively; there are seventy-one mentions of it in *Le Côté de Guermantes* and ninety-three in *Le Temps retrouvé*. See E. Brunet, *Le Vocabulaire de Proust*, Slatkine-Champion,

1983, vol. III, p. 1528. The mother and the grandmother between them only appear 1,404 times.

20. *Corr.*, vol. XIV, p. 281.

21. G. Boillat, *La Librairie Grasset et les lettres françaises*, Champion, 1974, p. 192.

22. Ibid., p. 283.

23. Exercise books that were numbered by Proust as V (Cahier 53 in the Bibliothèque Nationale), VI (73), VII (55), VIII (56, for *La Fugitive*) and which run parallel to Cahiers 54 and 'Dux' (71). It was after the publication of *The Fugitive* by Tagore in 1921 (which appeared as *La Fugitive* in France in 1922) that Proust changed his title to *Albertine disparue*.

24. *La Prisonnière, RTP*, vol. III, draft XI, p. 1133 ff.

25. Ibid., draft XIII, p. 1143 ff.

26. *Matinée*, pp. 292–8. Among the composers that Proust would have known, only Beethoven, Ravel and Saint-Saëns had written a septet.

27. 'John Ruskin', *P et M*, p. 139; the text was published in 1904 in *La Bible d'Amiens*.

28. J. Guitton, 'Lettre ouverte à M. Proust', in *Lettres ouvertes*, 1995.

29. *Corr.*, vol. XIII, p. 335.

30. Ibid., pp. 34, 67, 75. (In the case of *La Revue de Paris*, Proust relied on Reynaldo, who was a friend of Mme de La Béraudière, the mistress of the Comte Greffulhe, and himself a friend of Marcel Prevost. The manoeuvre came to nothing.)

31. Ibid., p. 85.

32. Ibid., p. 167 and n. 2; p. 180.

33. Ibid., pp. 22–7, 2 January 1914.

34. Ibid., p. 114.

35. Ibid., p. 98, 6 February 1914.

36. Collected in *Quelques progrès dans l'étude du cœur humain*, ed. T. Laget, Gallimard, 1985. Other articles by Rivière were printed in *Études*, Gallimard, 1912, and *Nouvelles Études*, Gallimard. See also the excellent biography of him by J. Lacouture, *Une adolescence du siècle*, Seuil, 1994.

37. *Corr.*, vol. XIII, p. 115, 21 March 1914, to Gide.

38. Ibid., p. 121, 24 March 1914.

39. Ibid., p. 125.

40. Ibid., p. 129 and n. 3. His letter is missing, but we know what Grasset's terms were from a letter written by Louis Brun and from Proust's reply (ibid., p. 132).

41. Ibid., p. 134.

42. Ibid., p. 140.

43. Ibid., p. 167.

44. Ibid., pp. 169, 182; *Textes retrouvés*, p. 388. Forty-eight pages of the *Nouvelle Revue Française*, containing extracts from the future *Jeunes Filles*.

45. *Corr.*, vol. XIII, p. 171, n. 6. Fifty-two magazine pages.

46. Ibid., pp. 38, 87 and n. 6 (*Parsifal* was performed on eleven occasions in January), 99, 183 (of interest for Rivière's article).

47. Ibid., p. 49.

48. Ibid., p. 217. See J. Rivière's article on this show.

49. Ibid., p. 101, to R. Hahn.

50. Ibid., p. 108, 6 March 1914, to Gide.

51. North Caucasian and Oural Kaspien (25,000 francs worth of each, and 25,000 francs of Hauts Fourneaux de Caen). Proust would try to resell them in October 1915 (ibid., n. 3).

52. Ibid., p. 187 and n. 5, 7 May 1914. Carnet 4 refers to 16,000 francs 'earned for his kitty' (f. 8 recto), and to 12,400 francs of assets.

53. *Corr.*, vol. XIII, p. 213.

54. *RTP*, vol. IV, p. 38.

55. *Corr.*, vol. XIII, p. xv.

56. C. Albaret, p. 233.

57. *Corr.*, vol. XIII, p. 229, 3 June 1914.

58. Ibid., pp. 195–6.

59. Ibid., p. 260, early July 1914.

60. Ibid., p. 271, 26 July 1914.

61. Ibid., p. 271.

62. Ibid., p. 280.

63. These details were originally put together by Robert Vigneron, who taught Philip Kolb (*Revue de l'histoire de la philosophie*, 15 January 1937).

64. *Corr.*, vol. XIII, p. 228.

65. Ibid., p. 224, 2 June 1914.

66. Ibid., p. 137, 27 May 1915. Proust asked Mme Catusse to arrange for a wreath or a sheaf of flowers to be laid on Agostinelli's tomb on the anniversary of his death.

67. Ibid., p. 228.

68. To Lucien Daudet, *Autour de soixante lettres de Marcel Proust*, Gallimard, 1929, p. 109; *Corr.*, vol. XIII, p. 354, shortly after 21 November 1914.

69. *Corr.*, vol. XIII, p. 250.

70. Ibid., p. 276.

71. Ibid., vol. XV, p. 31, 14 January 1916. See Carnet 3, f. 9 verso.

72. *Corr.*, vol. XIII, p. 283, 2 August 1914. Cf. letter to Lucien Daudet of 14 March 1915.

73. C. Albaret, p. 46. Forssgren's memoirs were published by J. Bersani and Michel Raimond, *Études proustiennes*, vol. II, pp. 119–42; his photograph is on p. 128.

74. *Corr.*, vol. XIV, p. 71 and n. 6, March 1915 to Albufera.

75. *RTP*, vol. IV, p. 380. Kolb dates the writing of this passage to March 1915

(*Corr.*, vol. XIV, p. 16), but Proust could have written it straight after his walk.

76. *Corr.*, vol. XIII, p. 297.

77. To Madeleine Lemaire, in particular.

78. C. Albaret, p. 46.

79. Ibid., p. 302. Proust's account is extremely short, Forssgren's is full of detail; it is his I have followed.

80. Painter and Forssgren say the reverse.

81. *RTP*, vol. IV, draft X of *Le Temps retrouvé*, p. 775.

82. *Études proustiennes*, vol. II, p. 134.

83. *Corr.*, vol. XIII, p. 311, to R. Hahn.

84. Ibid., p. 305, to Marthe Proust.

85. Ibid., p. 306; C. Albaret, pp. 47–54.

86. *Études proustiennes*, vol. II, p. 122.

87. *Corr.*, vol. XIV, p. 130, to Vicomte d'Alton.

88. Ibid., vol. XIII, p. 310, 23 October 1914.

89. Ibid., p. 311.

90. Ibid., p. 351 and n. 2.

91. Ibid., p. 333, 16 November 1914.

92. Ibid., p. 334.

93. Ibid., p. 351.

94. Ibid., p. 353.

95. Quoted by G. Weill, *Le Journal*, Albin Michel, 1934, p. 311.

96. *Corr.*, vol. XIV, p. 76.

97. Ibid., p. 213, 27 August 1915, to L. Hauser.

98. Ibid.

99. Ibid., p. 221.

100. Ibid., p. 29, 14 January 1915.

101. C. Albaret, pp. 223–4.

102. *Corr.*, vol. XIV, p. 56, early March 1915, to A. Bibesco.

103. Ibid., p. 71, to Albufera. Cf. *RTP*, vol. II, p. 92; vol. IV, p. 425.

104. *Corr.*, vol. XIV, p. 132.

105. Ibid., p. 218, early September 1915.

106. Ibid., vol. VI, p. 136, to R. Hahn.

107. Ibid., vol. XIV, pp. 176, 220, n. 3 (incorrect), 221, 296.

108. Ibid., vol. XVI, p. 329, letter to Paul Goldschmidt, a wealthy collector and a friend of Charlie Humphreys (C. Albaret, pp. 229, 286); n. 3, information and comments by P. Kolb.

109. 'Marcel Proust devin', *NRF*, January 1923, pp. 103–5.

110. *Corr.*, vol. XIV, p. 221.

111. Ibid., p. 228, September 1915, to Lucien Daudet.

112. Ibid., p. 226, 10 September 1915, letter from Commandant de Sachs.

113. Ibid., p. 130, May 1915, to Charles d'Alton.

114. 27 September 1914. Quoted by J. Chastenet, *Histoire de la Troisième République*, Hachette, 1955, vol. IV, p. 225. *Le Temps* itself wrote: 'The censorship has put itself beyond the law' (8 October 1915). Joffre, for his part, complained of the feebleness of the censorship (*Mémoires*, vol. II, p. 384), whereas Lavisse wrote: 'The determination to maintain a mood of optimism in the country is certain, and such determination is dangerous' (*La Revue de Paris*, 1 July 1916). See Weill, *Le Journal*, pp. 311–15.

115. *Corr.*, vol. XIV, p. 71.

116. Ibid., p. 158, to Blanche.

117. Ibid., p. 144, early June 1915.

118. Ibid., p. 221, about 9 September 1915.

119. Writing to Bernard Frank (*Le Monde*, 6 July 1986).

120. By way of example, shares in the Crédit Lyonnais bank fell by 50 per cent as a result of the war (*Corr.*, vol. XIV, p. 288, 10 November 1915).

121. Ibid., p. 231, mid-September 1915, to L. Hauser.

122. Ibid., p. 277.

123. Chastenet, *Histoire*.

124. Which was called Bricquebec (after being Querqueville in 1909) in the typescript that was delivered to Grasset in 1913. See R. Bales' edition of this, *Bricquebec*. Brichot takes Balbec to be a distortion of Dalbec.

125. See *RTP*, vol. III, pp. 1234–47, note by A. Compagnon.

126. See ibid., pp. 1657–58, note by P. Robert.

127. Ibid., vol. IV, p. 1007.

128. Ibid., p. 1008.

129. Ibid., draft I of *Le Temps retrouvé*.

130. *Corr.*, vol. XIV, p. 78: the year 1885 in the Goncourt *Journal*.

131. Ibid., pp. 273, 280–5; Yoshikawa, *La genèse de 'La Prisonnière'*.

132. Cahier 57, f. 14 verso.

133. *Corr.*, vol. XIV, p. 165.

134. Ibid., p. 250.

135. *RTP*, vol. IV, p. 438, and, for the Duc de Talleyrand, former Prince de Sagan (1832–1910), B. de Castellane, *Mémoires*, Perrin, 1986, p. 283.

136. *Corr.*, vol. XV, p. 257, about August 1916. Transposed in *RTP*, vol. III, p. 180.

137. *Corr.*, vol. XV, p. 43, 31 January 1916. *RTP*, vol. II, pp. 264–5 and n. 1, n. 3; p. 268, n. 2.

138. *RTP*, vol. IV, p. 1012; *Corr.*, vol. XV, p. 49. In Cahier 55 the 'blue and gold' dress by Fortuny is an addition.

139. *Corr.*, vol. XV, p. 57.

140. Ibid., p. 49, 6 February 1916.

141. Ibid., pp. 57–8, 17 February 1916. *RTP*, vol. II, p. 252; vol. III, pp. 43, 552, 663, 687, 715, 871, 872; vol. IV, p. 226.

142. *RTP*, vol. IV, p. 108, and *Corr.*, vol. XV, p. 58.

143. *Corr.*, vol. XV, p. 132; *RTP*, vol. IV, pp. 301–432; and, for the newspapers, pp. 355, 357, 360, 365, in particular.

144. *RTP*, vol. IV, pp. 315–34. Note, p. 1167.

145. Ibid., p. 903, draft XLIII. *Briséis* was first produced in 1899, the year of F. Faure's death; this must have been the revival, because Crozier would not have seemed so old on the first night.

146. *Corr.*, vol. XV, p. 23, 1 January 1916, to A. Bibesco.

147. Ibid.

148. Ibid., p. 54, to C. d'Alton.

149. Ibid., p. 27, to E. Berl.

150. Ibid., p. 61, around 7 March 1916, to Mme Albert Hecht.

151. C. Albaret, p. 126.

152. *Corr.*, vol. XV, p. 77, to R. Pétain; cf. p. 80, where he suggests a meeting. Céleste Albaret attributed this to the viola player Amable Massis.

153. Ibid., pp. 81–2, 5 May 1916, to Gaston Poulet. The date of the concert was not mentioned. See the 'Souvenirs de Gaston Poulet et Amable Massis' *BAMP*, no. 11, 1961, pp. 424–8. Céleste Albaret gave a third version of what happened and was sure that there was only one concert, and that it was at rue Hamelin. On this last point, she was surely mistaken.

154. *RTP*, vol. III, p. 790. *Corr.*, vol. XV, p. vi, introduction by P. Kolb.

155. I. de Casa-Fuerte, *Le Dernier des Guermantes. Mémoires*, Julliard, 1994, p. 361.

156. The Fauré concert at the Odéon.

157. *Corr.*, vol. XV, p. 106, May 1916.

158. Ibid., vol. XVII, p. 393, mid-October 1918, to J.-É. Blanche.

159. Ibid., vol. XVI, p. 144.

160. Ibid., p. 108.

161. Ibid., vol. XV, p. 150, May or June 1916. Proust was also looking for the *Mémoires de la comtesse de La Ferronays*, Olendorff, 1899.

162. *Corr.*, vol. XV, p. 180, and *RTP*, vol. III, p. 61.

163. Here Proust came across the Turners belonging to Camille Groult, the friend of the 'sunshine thief', Rostand, and the Baron and the Baronne Adolphe de Rothschild and their estate at Prégny, near Geneva (*Corr.*, vol. XV, pp. 176–7).

164. Ibid., pp. 81–2, 26 April 1916. Other reading: the *Contes du matin* by Charles-Louis Philippe, sent by Gallimard (*Corr. avec G. Gallimard*, pp. 32–3).

165. *RTP*, vol. III, p. 243; *Corr. avec G. Gallimard*, pp. 25, 31, February 1916.

166. *Corr. avec G. Gallimard*, pp. 46–7. Among the books read, *La Vermine du monde, roman de l'espionnage allemand*, by Léon Daudet (*Corr.*, vol. XV, p. 185).

167. Ibid., p. 290, September 1916, to W. Berry.

168. Ibid., p. 201.

169. Ibid., pp. 136–7, 29 May 1916.

170. Ibid., p. 159, 4 June 1916.

171. *CSB*, p. 584.

172. *Corr. avec G. Gallimard*, pp. 27–32, shortly before 15 May 1916.

173. Ibid., p. 35 ff.

174. *Corr.*, vol. XV, p. 246.

175. Ibid., p. 279. *Corr. avec G. Gallimard*, pp. 61–3.

176. *Corr.*, vol. XV, p. 309.

177. *Corr. avec G. Gallimard*, p. 60, letter from Gallimard to Tronche.

178. Ibid., p. 72; these were the proofs printed by Grasset in 1914, with manuscript corrections.

179. See the essential work by P. Assouline, *Gaston Gallimard*, Balland, 1984; A. Beucler, 'Ma jeunesse avec Gaston Gallimard', in *De Saint-Pétersbourg à Saint-Germain-des-Prés*, Gallimard, 1980, pp. 91–105; J. Rivière, *Aimée*, Gallimard, 1923 (in it Gaston appears under the guise of Georges Bourguignon); A. Anglès, *André Gide et le premier groupe de la NRF*, Gallimard, 3 vols., 1978–86.

180. His talent as an art critic was remarked upon by Proust (in connection with Bonnard), yet he published a severe article on Renoir, and he attended the sale of his father's Renoirs in 1912 without any apparent sadness.

181. Gide, Schlumberger, Copeau, Ruyters, Ghéon and Arnauld. A. Anglès has retraced the details of this struggle.

182. 'He could not bear any emotional behaviour, or irritations, or social obligations' and he hated providing explanations. Three years after his father's death, he replied, to anyone who asked for news of him: 'He's very well, thank you' (Beucler, *De Saint-Pétersbourg*, p. 98).

183. *Corr. avec G. Gallimard*, 5 or 6 November 1916, p. 71.

184. *Corr.*, vol. XV, pp. 205, 257.

185. Ibid., p. 284; like Fénelon, or Saint-Loup.

186. Ibid., p. 320, early November 1916, to Mme de Pierrebourg.

187. C. Albaret, p. 322.

188. Published in part in 1948. See P. Morand, *Nouvelles complètes*, Bibliothèque de la Pléiade, chronology (ed. M. Collomb).

189. P. Morand, *Journal d'un attaché d'ambassade*, La Table ronde, 1949, pp. 111–12.

190. *Corr.*, vol. XVI, p. 30, n. 10 (which mentions Mme Daudet's *Journal de famille et de guerre*).

191. *Corr.*, vol. XV, p. 346, to L. Hauser.

192. Ibid., p. 344, about 27 December 1916, to Mme Straus. Quotation from Clemenceau.

193. Fernandez wrote a novel about inversion, *Philippe Sauveur*, and read extracts from it on 4 and 10 November at the Castries' (Abbé Mugnier, *Journal*, Mercure de France, 1985, *Corr.*, vol. XVII, p. 244).

194. R. Girard, *Mensonge romantique et vérité romanesque*, Grasset, 1961.

195. C. Wixler, 'Proust au Ritz: souvenirs d'un maître d'hôtel', *Adam International Review*, no. 394, 1976, pp. 17–18.

196. *Corr. avec G. Gallimard*, p. 76, January 1917.

197. Ibid., pp. 78–9, according to the résumé in the sales catalogue of a missing letter.

198. *Corr.*, vol. XVI, p. 257.

199. *Corr. avec G. Gallimard*, pp. 83–90.

200. *Corr.*, vol. XVI, p. 365, 21 December 1917, to André Gide.

201. Ibid., p. 292. Nothing appeared in *Le Figaro*.

202. *Corr.*, vol. XVI, p. 51, to L. Daudet.

203. Ibid., p. 53, February 1917, to C. d'Alton, and n. 5.

204. Ibid., p. 64.

205. Ibid.

206. Morand, *Journal d'un attaché*, p. 185.

207. *Corr.*, vol. XVI, p. 74; Morand, *Journal d'un attaché*, p. 199.

208. See G. de Diesbach, pp. 615–16.

209. Quoted by G. Guitard-Auviste, *Paul Morand*, Hachette, 1981, p. 225.

210. *Corr.*, vol. XVI, p. 104, 22 April 1917.

211. Ibid., p. 118.

212. Ibid., p. 159, May or June.

213. D. Mabin, *Le Sommeil de Proust*, PUF, 1992, p. 48.

214. E.g. *Corr.*, vol. XVI, p. 265, to Boylesve.

215. Ibid., p. 280, 3 November 1917.

216. Ibid., p. 80.

217. Ibid., p. 128, 8 or 9 May 1917.

218. Ibid., p. 136, 15 May 1917.

219. Ibid., p. 288.

220. *Fils de Réjane*, Plon, 1951–2, vol. I, p. 321.

221. *Corr.*, vol. XVI, p. 159, May or June 1917.

222. Ibid., p. 165.

223. Ibid., p. 181. Morand, *Journal d'un attaché*, p. 306.

224. *Corr.*, vol. XVI, p. 163, about June 1917.

225. Ibid., p. 115, 16 February 1918.

226. *NRF*, January 1923, p. 79.

227. *Corr.*, vol. XVI, p. 123. In the published book, the dedication was very slightly different.

228. Ibid., vol. XVII, p. 63.

229. *Propos de peintre, De David à Degas*, Émile-Paul, 1919, pp. xvi–xvii.

230. *Corr.*, vol. XVI, p. 236, 2 October 1917.

231. Ibid.

232. E. Hausser, *Paris au jour le jour*, Minuit, 1968, p. 644. On 29 January 1916 bombing from a zeppelin had resulted in twenty-six deaths and thirty-two wounded in the nineteenth *arrondissement*, without any action being taken by the French air defence force. Measures must have been taken subsequently, for some planes did take off on 27 July 1917.

233. Morand, *Journal d'un attaché*, p. 325.

234. *Corr.*, vol. XVI, p. 196, late July 1917. *RTP*, vol. IV, pp. 337, 338.

235. Later, he would publish a *Répertoire des personnages* in the *Cahiers Marcel Proust*.

236. Jean Hugo, *Le Regard de la mémoire*, Actes Sud, 1983, p. 122.

237. *Corr.*, vol. XVI, p. 212, 23 August 1917, to the Princesse de Caraman-Chimay.

238. Ibid., p. 216, to the Princesse de Caraman-Chimay.

239. Ibid., p. 225.

240. Ibid., p. 216.

241. On Beaumont, see especially B. Faÿ, *Les Précieux*, Perrin, pp. 44–5; A. Gold and R. Fizdale, *Misia: The Life of Misia Sert*, London, Macmillan, 1980, p. 288 ff.; A. de Fouquières, *Cinquante ans de panache*, P. Horay, 1951, pp. 180–1. É. de Beaumont founded 'les Soirées de Paris', which were shows organized on behalf of Russian refugees and war widows; Milhaud's *Salade* was one of their productions.

242. *Corr.*, vol. XVII, p. 183, April 1918, E. de Beaumont to M. Proust.

243. Ibid., vol. XVI, p. 226.

244. Ibid., pp. 239–40, and n. 8, n. 9.

245. Ibid., p. 263, mid-October–November 1917.

246. Ibid., p. 274, to P. Morand.

247. Ibid., pp. 227–8 (Kolb was incorrect in denying, on the strength of a lie told to Montesquiou, that this visit actually occurred; it is also attested to by Mme Scheikévitch's *Souvenirs*, p. 156). Morand, *Journal d'un attaché*, 23 September 1917.

248. *Corr.*, vol. XVI, p. 339.

249. Ibid., pp. 313–14, 23 November 1917, to Mme Catusse.

250. Ibid., p. 324. He would make 14,000 francs from it (ibid., p. 368).

251. Ibid., p. 317, 23 November 1917, to Mme Scheikévitch. She turned down this offer.

252. Ibid., p. 331, 1 December 1917, to the Princesse Soutzo.

253. Ibid., p. 370. Cf. ibid., p. 143, mid-March 1918: 'Marble of Phidias, young successor of Mosca, sometime Enfant de Marie . . .' [Count Mosca is a character in Stendhal's *La Chartreuse de Parme*; the Enfants de Marie was a Catholic children's guild devoted to the Virgin Mary. *Tr.*]

CHAPTER XV: *The Novel of 1918*

1. *Bulletin d'informations proustiennes*, no. 15, p. 28. C. Albaret, p. 325.

2. The summary of forthcoming titles in *Le Côté de Guermantes*, published in 1921, differs slightly. 'Chapter I' develops 'Death of my grandmother': 'My grandmother's illness. Bergotte's illness. The Duke and the Doctor. My grandmother's decline. Her death.' In chapter II, 'Albertine reappears' is altered to 'Albertine's visit' and 'Dinner at the Duchesse de Guermantes' to 'Prospect of a wealthy marriage for some of Saint-Loup's friends' and 'The wit of the Guermantes in the presence of the Princesse de Parme'. The ending is virtually identical.

3. *La Prisonnière, Albertine disparue* and *Le Temps retrouvé*, published posthumously, contained no list of forthcoming titles; Proust died too soon to write them.

4. *Corr. avec G. Gallimard*, p. 545, 25 June 1922. Titles confirmed by the typescript of the manuscript.

5. For more on the title, finalizing the text, and the divisions of *La Fugitive–Albertine disparue*, see the note for this book in *RTP*, vol. IV.

6. M. Bardèche, *Marcel Proust Romancier*, Les Sept Couleurs, 1971, vol. II, p. 258.

7. Addition to Cahier 57, *Matinée chez la princesse de Guermantes, Cahiers du Temps retrouvé*, ed. H. Bonnet and B. Brun, Gallimard, 1976, p. 371.

8. Ibid., p. 391.

9. R. de Billy, *Marcel Proust. Lettres et conversations*, Les Portiques, 1930; P. Morand, *Journal d'un attaché d'ambassade (1916–17)*, La Table ronde, 1949.

10. *Corr., avec G. Gallimard*, p. 37.

11. P. Morand, *Le Visiteur du soir*, Geneva, La Palatine, 1949, p. 82. This may be compared with *Le Temps retrouvé*, vol. IV: 'It is wrong to think that the scale of fears corresponds to that of the dangers that inspire them. One may be frightened of not being able to sleep, but not in the least about a serious duel; of a rat, but not of a lion.'

12. *Choix de lettres*, Plon, 1965, p. 231, early August 1917, and *Corr. gén.*, vol. VI, p. 197, March 1918.

13. *Le Carnet de 1908*, p. 45; see also p. 59: 'Letters of Chateaubriand to Charlotte used for *Les Natchez* and the words of Mme Michelet spoken by Michelet in his lecture.'

14. *Le Temps retrouvé*, *RTP*, vol. IV.

15. *Le Carnet de 1908*, p. 63. See also p. 99.

16. J. de Pierrefeu, *Plutarque a menti*, Grasset, 1923.

17. *Le Temps retrouvé*, *RTP*, vol. IV.

18. Ibid., p. 467. Compare with *Matinée*, pp. 299–300, 307–8, in which Proust refers in particular to *L'Écho de Paris* of June 1916; these additions to Cahier 57 are longer than the manuscript text.

19. Notes in Cahier 74.

20. As R. Duchêne has clearly shown (*L'Impossible Marcel Proust*, Laffont, 1994, pp. 733 and 826), at the source of all the gossip that abounded on this subject was a story dating from 1929 (summarized by L. Guichard, *Introduction à la lecture de M. Proust*, Nizet, 1956, pp. 167–71) that appeared in the German magazine *Querschnitt*. The police archives contain nothing on Le Cuziat.

21. According to Cocteau, in *Le Passé défini* (Gallimard, 1983), who was writing much later and must have been confused, there were apparently two brothels: 'Gabriel's' in the rue de l'Arcade, and 'Le Cuziat's' in rue de Madrid.

22. *RTP*, vol. IV, p. 529.

23. C. Albaret, p. 235.

24. Ibid., p. 237.

25. Odilon Albaret even mentioned a *maréchal de France* and a *président de Conseil*.

26. From the eighteenth century, flagellation was considered an erotic adjuvant: 'There is no public establishment at which there cannot be found handfuls of rods ready to provide unstimulated debauchees with the ritual' (E. M. Benabou, *La Prostitution et la Police des moeurs au XVIIIe siècle*, Perrin, 1987, p. 394). Even Brantôme (1537–1614) tells the story of a gentleman who had himself whipped by women. And in *Le Grand Larousse* (1930) flagellation was still considered to be a remedy for impotence.

27. C. Albaret, p. 240.

28. *RTP*, vol. III, p. 711.

29. M. Sachs, *Le Sabbat*, Corrêa, 1946, p. 285.

30. E.g., *Corr.*, vol. IV, p. 291.

31. S. Bonmariage, 'Document sur la personalité de M. de Charlus', *Défense de M. Proust*, Le Rouge et le Noir, Paris, 1930.

32. *Corr.*, vol. XVIII, p. 61, to Blanche.

33. Ibid., vol. XVII, p. 501.

34. Ibid., p. 107.

35. Ibid., p. 215.

36. Ibid., pp. 147, 152.

37. Ibid., p. 279.

38. Ibid., p. 285, 15 June 1918, to Mme Straus; cf. ibid., p. 286, to Jean Pozzi.

39. Ibid., p. 289, 24 June 1918, to Étienne de Beaumont.

40. A. de Fouquières, *Mon Paris et ses Parisiens*, P. Horay, 1953–9, p. 254. The Marquise de Ludre lived at 4 Square du Bois-de-Boulogne.

41. *Corr.*, vol. XVII, shortly before 2 October 1918, to the Duc de Guiche.

42. *CSB*, pp. 43–4, 50, 55–7.

43. *Corr.*, vol. XVII, p. 403, 18 October 1918. Proust planned to devote a passage in this pastiche to Luis Ferdinand, the Infante of Spain (1888–1945), and son of Eulalie, Duchesse de Galliera (1864–1958); was this why Lacretelle told Marcel how Antonio de Vasconcellos, the favourite of both the son

and the mother had been taken ill at the Ritz? (ibid., p. 463). Cf. M. Rostand, *Confession d'un demi-siècle*, La Jeune Parque, 1948, pp. 167–8, who compared Ferdinand to a Velázquez dwarf, took pity upon him and alluded to his debauched habits. He had been very much in demand in fashionable Paris circles, before being forsaken and forgotten. *CSB*, pp. 57–9.

44. *Corr.*, vol. XVII, p. 386, shortly after 8 October.

45. *Le Carnet de 1908*, p. 49: 'Old age, Laroze, Louise Baignères, Borghèse, Sala, Neufville.'

46. *Corr.*, vol. XVII, p. 380.

47. Ibid., p. 456, 12 November 1918, to Mme de Chevigné.

48. Ibid., p. 415, about 20 October 1918.

49. Ibid., vol. XVIII, pp. 34–5, to Comte Zucchini.

50. Ibid., vol. XVII, p. 526, to Princesse Soutzo.

51. Ibid., p. 531. The resumption of social life at the Beaumonts did not escape Radiguet: 'It was the Orgels, who, so to speak, opened the ball immediately after the war' (*Le Bal du comte d'Orgel*, Les Lettres modernes, ed. Silver et Odouard, p. 13; a sentence that was suppressed by Cocteau in the original edition).

52. *Corr.*, vol. XVII, p. 531.

53. *RTP*, vol. IV, p. 227 and var. *e*.

54. *Corr.*, vol. XVII, p. 360, 15 September 1918; p. 367.

55. Ibid., p. 524.

56. Ibid., p. 457, to Mme Vittoré, half-sister of the Agostinelli brothers.

57. C. Albaret, p. 231.

58. *Le Carnet de 1908*, f. 3 verso.

59. See A. Beretta Anguissola, 'Morel: un segno dei tempi', in *Personnages proustiennes*, Università di Parma, March 1995.

60. *Corr.*, vol. XVII, p. 145.

61. Ibid., p. 159, 3 April 1918.

62. Ibid., p. 167.

63. Ibid., p. 123, to L. Hauser.

64. Ibid., p. 178, to C. de Maugny.

65. Ibid., p. 281 and n. 8; C. Albaret, pp. 122–3.

66. *Corr.*, vol. XVII, p. 281.

67. Ibid., p. 401, n. 4; p. 405.

68. Ibid., p. 299, 6 July 1918, to W. Berry. Cf. p. 491, to L. Hauser: W. Berry was driven to outbursts of anti-German hatred 'which suit neither [his] temperament nor [his] inclinations'.

69. Ibid., p. 448.

70. Ibid., pp. 33–4, late December 1917 to early January 1918.

71. Ibid., pp. 94; 116, 19 February 1918; 312, 20 July 1918; 321–2, early May 1918.

72. Ibid., p. 39, to Mme Straus.
73. Ibid., p. 100.
74. Ibid., p. 294; *RTP*, vol. II, pp. 107, 559.
75. The typing had been done by Mlle Marchesseau at the publishing house.
76. *Corr.*, vol. XVII, p. 49, 9 January 1918.
77. Ibid., pp. 262, 264, 290.
78. *Corr. avec G. Gallimard*, pp. 406, 420 n. 2.
79. The contract was drawn up on 23 June 1918 (ibid., p. 113).
80. *Corr.*, vol. XVII, p. 343, 14 August 1918, to Lucien Daudet.
81. Ibid., p. 390.
82. Ibid., p. 413, October 1918. This was when Proust was correcting the proofs of his introduction.
83. Quoted by J. Bothorel, *Bernard Grasset*, Grasset, 1989, p. 102.
84. *Corr.*, vol. XVII, p. 315, 22 July 1918. Cf. pp. 350, 358.
85. Ibid., p. 341, 12 August 1918, to B. Lemarié. See ch. X above.
86. Ibid., pp. 440, 443, 7 November 1918.
87. Ibid., p. 444.
88. Ibid., p. 502.
89. This passage was such a successful imitation that neither of the Proust scholars J. Milly or P. Clairac noticed that it concerned a contemporary story.
90. See J. Milly, *Les Pastiches de Proust*, A. Colin, 1970, pp. 225–318. The drafts come from Cahiers 52 (where, as Milly notes, the pastiche comes next to the soirée at the Princesse de Guermantes in *Sodome*) and 56 (where there are passages from *Albertine disparue*). The manuscript is composed of pages torn from an exercise book. There are numerous additions on the proofs and they allude to Proust's contemporaries.
91. *Corr.*, vol. XVIII, p. 440, to Mme Lemaire, late October 1919. This pastiche alienated him from the Murats, it appears, as well as from Louis d'Albufera.
92. Ibid., pp. 82, 85.
93. Ibid., p. 78.
94. Ibid., p. 79.
95. Ibid., p. 137, to Princesse Soutzo. Cf. p. 138, to Blanche.
96. Ibid., pp. 45, 47 (in which he quotes Luke, 9: 58, quoted by Ruskin in *Sesame*: 'Foxes have holes . . .').
97. They were still there in June 1919, when Proust resorted to the antique dealer Imbert, in the rue de Rivoli, who must have taken them.
98. *Corr.*, vol. XVIII, p. 109, to A. Gide.
99. He quoted Baudelaire's 'La mort des pauvres' just afterwards.
100. *Corr.*, vol. XVIII, p. 90.
101. Ibid., p. 122 and n. 4.
102. Ibid., p. 143, March 1919.

103. Ibid., p. 228.
104. Ibid., pp. 148–9; *RTP*, vol. I, p. 280 ff. The incident had already taken place the year before.
105. *Une histoire vraie* (1935), *Richard Kurt* (1936), *Myrte* (1938), *L'Autre Côté* (1950).
106. Cf. *Wartime Silhouettes*, London, Allen & Unwin, 1916.
107. 'When I got divorced, I gave my first wife the entire contents of my villa on Lake Como where I kept the furniture, paintings and other antiques that I had collected for over twenty years' (*Corr.*, vol. XIX, p. 613).
108. Proust had also recommended some of his friend's short stories to Rivière, who would not publish them.
109. V. Larbaud, *Œuvres complètes*, Gallimard, 1950, vol. X, p. 301, 29 January 1935.
110. *Corr.*, vol. XIX, p. 424. Schiff portrayed his sister in his novel *Richard Kurt*, which was dedicated to Proust, using his initials, M. P.
111. *Corr.*, vol. XXI, p. 266. Schiff took his advice (p. 294).
112. Ibid., vol. XIX, p. 451.
113. Ibid., vol. XXI, p. 239.
114. Ibid., p. 295.
115. Ibid., p. 535.
116. Reprinted in volume form, The Blackamore Press, 1930.
117. *Corr.*, vol. XVIII, p. 205, to J.-L. Vaudoyer.
118. Ibid., p. 178, to Mme Catusse.
119. Ibid., p. 481, to L. Hauser.
120. Ibid., p. 182.
121. Ibid., p. 202.
122. Ibid., p. 231.
123. He was upset at the outcome: his father's settee sold for 40 francs and a chandelier for 38 francs (ibid., p. 278).
124. Ibid., p. 238; *RTP*, vol. II, pp. 374–6.
125. J. Porel, *Fils de Réjane*, Plon, 1951–2, vol. I, p. 330.
126. *RTP*, vol. II, p. 139. *Corr.*, vol. XVIII, p. 243.
127. *Corr.*, vol. XVIII, p. 279, to Mme Catusse. C. Albaret, pp. 385–7.
128. *RTP*, vol. II, p. 388; *Corr.*, vol. XVIII, p. 330, to J. Porel.
129. *RTP*, vol. IV, p. 576 and var. *a*, n. 1: 'Réjane's old age, and Le Bargy's for Cahier XX.'
130. *Corr.*, vol. XVIII, pp. 310–12.
131. Ibid., p. 263, to W. Berry.
132. Ibid., p. 286.
133. Ibid., p. 313.
134. Ibid., p. 355, late July 1919, to J. Truelle.
135. Ibid., p. 373, 15 August 1919, to J. Porel.
136. Ibid., p. 422.

137. Ibid., pp. 48–9. By way of comparison, in the present Pléiade edition, *Swann* comprises 420 pages; *Jeunes Filles*, 515.

138. Ibid., p. 145, second fortnight of March 1919.

139. Ibid., p. 154, late March 1919, to G. Gallimard.

140. *Corr. avec G. Gallimard*, pp. 156–8.

141. Ibid., p. 159. Pascal Fouché's edition of this correspondence points out that there were no corrections and that the 1919 Gallimard edition was set from the original Grasset edition. This assertion is incorrect (see *RTP*, vol. I, p. 1052, introduction to *Swann*). The two most important corrections concern the appearance of Doncières (p. 9) and the departure of Mme Swann and Gilberte for the neighbouring city of Rheims and not Chartres (since Combray, based here upon Réveillon, was on the firing line). Clarac and Ferré have drawn attention in their edition to the variants between the Grasset and Gallimard 1919 editions (*RTP*, ed., Clarac-Ferré, Bibliothèque de la Pléiade, 1954, vol. I, p. 959).

142. Private collection.

143. *Corr. avec G. Gallimard*, p. 161.

144. Ibid., p. 163.

145. Ibid., pp. 165–6, around 22 May 1919.

146. *Corr.*, vol. XVIII, p. 169.

147. Ibid., p. 174, 21 April 1919.

148. Ibid., pp. 194, 208. He would earn 200 francs for his extract.

149. *RTP*, vol. IV, p. 205. On this publication, see ibid., pp. 1023–5.

150. *Corr.*, vol. XVIII, p. 438.

151. A. Thibaudet, 'Une querelle littéraire sur le style de Flaubert', *NRF*, November 1919.

152. *Corr.*, vol. XVIII, p. 471, shortly after 13 November 1919.

153. Ibid., p. 501, to J. Rivière.

154. *CSB*, p. 586. Cf. pp. 299–302, 'À ajouter à Flaubert', passage from *Contre Sainte-Beuve* (1909), which follows on from a text in a private collection.

155. However, annoyed that Hermant should have misunderstood the structure of the novel, believing that Proust was following the thread of his memories, Marcel told him so, on 24 October, the day the article appeared (*Corr.*, vol. XVIII, p. 383).

156. Proust thanked him at once (ibid., p. 411), while at the same time observing that he had been upset.

157. Proust would reply to him in early September (ibid., p. 389), as did Blanche in *Le Figaro* of 22 September (ibid., pp. 406–7). Proust thanked Blanche for his article 'which avenged him for a good many insults' (p. 406).

158. J.-Y. Tadié, *Lectures de Proust*, A. Colin, 1971, p. 19. Note that *The Times Literary Supplement* of 14 August devoted an article to *Jeunes Filles* which Gallimard, though not Proust, thought was 'very good' (*Corr.*, vol. XVIII, p. 379).

159. *Littérature*, October 1919, pp. 24–5.

160. *Corr.*, vol. XVIII, p. 427. The article is reprinted in Tadié, *Lectures de Proust*, pp. 47–53.

161. *Corr.*, vol. XVIII, p. 423, shortly after 10 October 1919, to Morand.

162. Unpublished letter of 18 March 1920, quoted in *RTP*, vol. II, p. 1296, n. 1.

163. *Corr.*, vol. XVIII, p. 119, March 1919, but posted six weeks later, to Colette. In August 1922, moved by a 'delightful' article that Paul Léautaud wrote about his cats, Proust thought about getting some: 'Céleste shuddered at the very idea that, in a bedroom which cannot be cleaned because I never get up, I could have thought of having animals that pee etc . . . She is right, it was a moment of madness . . . To console myself for not having live cats, I shall get myself a copy of Colette's *Dialogues*, which I don't know' (unpublished letter to Tronche, Catalogue Hôtel Drouot, Paris, sale of 24 November 1999, no. 230, p. 106).

164. Ibid., p. 171, 20 April 1919, to J. Rivière.

165. Ibid., p. 204.

166. Ibid., pp. 227–8.

167. Ibid., pp. 267–8.

168. Ibid., p. 431.

169. Ibid., pp. 334–5, 19 July 1919, to D. Halévy. Cf. ibid., p. 352, to R. Dreyfus. See D. Halévy's diary in *Corr. avec D. Halévy*, pp. 136–8. For the attitudes of the *NRF* and J. Rivière, see J. Lacouture, *Une adolescence du siècle*, Seuil, 1994, pp. 397–400: Gaston Gallimard and J. Rivière were very hostile towards the 'intelligence party', and Rivière replied to the manifesto in three articles during the autumn of 1919: 'The decadence of liberty', 'The intelligence party' and 'Catholicism and nationalism'.

170. *Corr. avec D. Halévy*, p. 142.

171. *Corr.*, vol. XVIII, p. 388.

172. Ibid., p. 372, 15 August 1919, to J. Porel.

173. Ibid., vol. XIX, p. 105, n.5. Céleste situated this flat on the fourth floor, 'above the mezzanine' no doubt.

174. C. Albaret, pp. 387–92, who contradicts many of the details supplied by Painter (some of which have disappeared in the most recent edition of his biography).

175. *Corr.*, vol. XVIII, p. 427, 14 or 15 October 1919.

176. Ibid., pp. 457–8, 3 November 1919. See n. 101.

177. Ibid., 29 October 1919. In 1913 the prize had been given to *Le Peuple de la mer* by Marc Elder. See T. Laget, 'L'attribution du prix Goncourt à Marcel Proust', *Bulletin d'informations proustiennes*, no. 14, 1983, pp. 63–71.

178. E.g. *Corr.*, vol. XVIII, pp. 466–7, to Rosny senior, concerning the president of the academy's vote.

179. Ibid., p. 505, 10 December 1919, letter from the Académie Goncourt.
180. C. Albaret, p. 367.
181. *Corr.*, vol. XVIII, p. 574; 800 letters: pp. 547, 554.
182. Ibid., pp. 517–18.
183. Dedication to E.-J. Bois, then editor of this newspaper. It will be recalled that he had published an interview with Proust in 1913. Cf. ibid., p. 570: 'My age rises as fast as the Seine.'
184. Billy in *L'Œuvre*.
185. *Corr.*, vol. XVIII, pp. 544–7, shortly before 23 December.
186. Ibid., p. 542. Cf. p. 550 to Gallimard.
187. *Corr. avec G. Gallimard*, p. 218.
188. Cahier 61, f. 112; *RTP*, vol. IV, p. 925. In order to alleviate the annoyance that a hostile press would cause him, Proust himself wrote an article, entitled 'M. Marcel Proust, prix de l'Académie Goncourt', which has remained unpublished, in which he refutes those who are opposed to him: 'The superiority of talent struck the Académie as so spectacular that the question of age could be put to one side.' He explains that *À l'ombre des jeunes filles en fleurs* is merely the second part of 'an immense fresco', the last parts of which have been written. 'We should add that the powerful novelist who wrote *À la recherche du temps perdu* (a book which is in no way an autobiography as has been mistakenly asserted, and which writers such as Henry James and Francis Jammes . . . have compared to Balzac and Cervantes) is scarcely a novice' (Catalogue Hôtel Drouot, Paris, sale of 24 November 1999, no. 225, p. 100).
189. Figures provided by the publishers to Laget, 'L'attribution du prix Goncourt', p. 70.
190. *Corr.*, vol. XVIII, p. 30.
191. Reprinted in *Nouvelles Études*, Gallimard, pp. 149–56, and presented as a fragment of a more extensive work, begun several months previously.
192. *Corr. avec J. Rivière*, introduction by P. Kolb, p. 8 (recollections of Isabelle Rivière).
193. Rivière, *Nouvelles Études*, p. 321. See G. Poulet, *La Conscience critique*, Corti, 1971, ch. V, 'Les critiques de la *NRF*', pp. 60–4.
194. Quoted by Poulet, *La Conscience critique*, p. 60.
195. *Corr.*, vol. XIX, p. 172. 'I am convinced that he is going to pull me out of this appalling languor which I drag around with me,' Rivière wrote to Proust (1 April 1920); and on 6 April: 'I was delighted with Roussy's methods'; out of friendship for Marcel, Roussy charged no fee.
196. Ibid., vol. XX, pp. 100–7, 7–12 February 1921.
197. E.g. ibid., p. 606.
198. Ibid., vol. XIX, p. 125, 18 February 1920.
199. Ibid., p. 154, 12 or 13 March 1920.
200. Ibid., pp. 446, 474, to P. Soupault.

201. *RTP*, vol. II, p. 1521; out of a set of twenty-four galleys, the confusion applied to three of them.

202. *Corr.*, vol. XIX, p. 164, to G. Gallimard.

203. Ibid., p. 376.

204. Ibid., p. 439. Sent on 21 September.

205. Ibid., p. 324.

206. Ibid., vol. XX, p. 48.

207. Ibid.

208. Ibid., vol. XIX, p. 574.

209. Ibid., p. 594 and n. 7. It also published a few favourable lines by Régnier, on 28 November, for which Proust thanked him (ibid., p. 630, 28 November 1920).

210. Ibid., p. 594.

211. 24 November 1920.

212. 21 November 1920. Another complimentary article by Émile Henriot appeared in *La Vie des peuples* (25 September 1920), for which Proust thanked him; he responded to the questions it raised in *La Renaissance politique, littéraire, artistique* (*Corr.*, vol. XIX, p. 641 ff.). Cf. *L'Action française*, 20 November 1920, an article that was mostly complimentary, signed Orion.

213. *Corr.*, vol. XIX pp. 646–7: Marcel explained to him what he had wanted to do. For his reaction, see ibid., vol. XX, pp. 96–7.

214. Ibid., vol. XIX, p. 636, 29 November 1920.

215. Ibid., p. 661, 10 or 11 December 1920; letter discovered and published by M. Raimond in *Un amour de Swann*, Imprimerie nationale, 1987, pp. 360–1.

216. *Corr.*, vol. XIX, p. 104.

217. Ibid., p. 311, 16 June 1920, to J. Porel.

218. Ibid., p. 312. In January 1920 *Comœdia* had published some of Proust's remarks about Réjane, in which he referred to the photograph of the actress dressed up as the Prince de Sagan in order to take part in a show at the home of the Marquis de Massa (both of them died in 1910). It should be remembered that this photograph, which was given to Marcel at rue Laurent-Pichat, bore these words: 'A prince's homage. An actress's admiration. A friend's friendship. Réjane, the interpreter of the Goncourts, 10 December' (1919).

219. *Corr.*, vol. XIX, p. 321, 23 June 1920, to Princesse Soutzo.

220. Ibid., p. 402, 18 August 1920, to P. Morand.

221. *RTP*, vol. IV, p. 27.

222. E. Jaloux, *Avec Marcel Proust*, Geneva, La Palatine, 1953.

223. *RTP*, vol. III, n. 1, p. 370 (p. 1557); Cahier 60, ff. 6, 13, 80–3; Cahier 59, ff. 4–16, 21–3, 51–4.

224. Ibid., vol. II, pp. 384–91; vol. III, pp. 121–6.

225. J. Gallois, *Les Polignac, mécènes du XXe siècle*, du Rocher, 1995, p. 223. Concerning the marriage, Gallois adds: 'The couple's relationship soon fell

apart, due to incompatibility of temperament and possibly more importantly, of taste.'

226. Ibid., p. 217.

227. *Corr.*, vol. XIX, pp. 105–6, early February 1920, draft of a letter dictated to Rochat in Cahier 60, ff. 61–2 recto.

228. Ibid., p. 105, early February 1920.

229. E.g. ibid., p. 159, shortly after 15 March: 'A charming creature'.

230. Ibid., pp. 297, 301.

231. Ibid., p. 542, 21 October 1920.

232. Ibid., p. 602, 18 or 19 November 1920.

233. *RTP*, vol. II, p. 704: 'the absurd calumnies'; pp. 822–3; 826–8.

234. Ibid., p. 828.

235. Cf. *Corr.*, vol. XIX, p. 565. Proust also mentions him in the drafts of *Guermantes*, *RTP*, vol. II, pp. 1255, 1266.

236. *RTP*, vol. III, p. 435.

237. B. de Castellane, *Mémoires*, Perrin, p. 400. B. de Castellane died in 1932. In 1918 he rented an *hôtel particulier* at 71 rue de Lille, which he left in 1921, having become afflicted with lethargic encephalitis, and moved to Avenue Victor-Emmanuel III (now Avenue du Président Wilson).

238. *Corr.*, vol. XIX, p. 522. See C. Albaret, p. 297.

239. A. de Fouquières, *Cinquante ans de panache*, P. Horay, 1951, p. 71. See also the five volumes of *Mon Paris et ses Parisiens*, P. Horay, 1953–9, an unmatched source of information about Parisian high society over half a century.

240. *Corr.*, vol. XIX, pp. 512–13, 6 October 1920.

241. *Paul Morand écrivain*, texts collected by Michel Collomb, Université Paul-Valéry, Montpellier, 1993, p. 292.

242. *Corr.*, vol. XIX, p. 104.

243. Ibid., p. 673, to R. de Billy.

244. Ibid., pp. 204, 616.

245. Ibid., p. 433, 1 September 1920.

246. *RTP*, vol, III, p. 871, mentioned along with Bakst and Benois, in connection with the Ballets Russes season; vol. IV, p. 225, in connection with the designs for the 'dazzling' *Legend of Joseph*, a ballet by Strauss and Kessler, produced by Diaghilev.

247. *RTP*, vol. II, p. 171. *Corr.*, vol. XIX, p. 678.

248. Ibid., pp. 328–32.

249. *RTP*, vol. II, p. 793.

250. *Corr.*, vol. XIX, p. 386. This was a 76-page booklet published by La Sirène.

251. Ibid., p. 398.

252. Ibid., p. 454.

253. Ibid., p. 618.

254. Ibid., pp. 627–8, late November 1920.

255. Ibid., p. 670.

256. Ibid., to Vaudoyer.

257. Ibid., p. 290, June 1920.

258. *CSB*, pp. 617–18. Proust thanked Henriot at length for his novel, *Les Temps innocents*, and gave him advice about style (*Corr.*, vol. XIX, pp. 697–9, 30 December 1920).

259. *Corr.*, vol. XIX, p. 519.

260. *CSB*, p. 615.

261. M. Le Goff, *Anatole France à la Béchellerie*, Albin Michel, pp. 331–2.

262. A. France, *La Vie littéraire, Œuvres complètes*, Bibliothèque de la Pléiade, vol. VI, p. 312.

263. Ibid., p. 251. *Le Temps*, 10 October 1886.

264. France, *La Vie littéraire*, p. 6.

265. Article of 13 November 1887 on *Mensonges* by P. Bourget, France, *La Vie littéraire*, vol. I, p. 312.

266. *RTP*, p. xiv; vol. II, p. 587; vol. III, p. 888 and n. 1, p. 1788; and France's article on Mérimée, *Le Temps*, 19 February 1888.

267. *Œuvres complètes*, vol. VII, p. 404.

268. *CSB*, pp. 156–7. Cf. France, *La Vie littéraire*, vol. VI, p. 41: 'There are dark forces within man that precede him, and which act independently of his will, over which he does not always have control' (*Le Temps*, 16 January 1887).

269. 'Hamlet à la Comédie-Française', *Le Temps*, 3 October 1886, and *CSB*, p. 469 ('Le salon de la princesse de Polignac').

270. Article of 29 May 1887, *La Vie littéraire*, vol. VI, p. 141, and *RTP*, vol II, p. 826 and n. 5.

271. *La Vie littéraire*, pp. 78–9. This article attacking Hermant and Zola would correspond to the Goncourt pastiche in *Le Temps retrouvé*.

272. *La Vie littéraire*, p. 86.

273. Ibid., p. 5.

274. See M.-C. Bancquart, Introduction, France, *Œuvres complètes*, vol. II, pp. 1213–18.

275. France, *Le Lys rouge, Œuvres complètes*, vol. II, p. 394, and *Le Côté de Guermantes*, *RTP*, vol. II, p. 386. Proust also borrowed the name of Mme Marmet from *Le Lys rouge* for *Jean Santeuil*.

276. *Corr.*, vol. XIX, p. 535, about 20 October 1920, pp. 537–9, shortly after 20 October 1920.

277. *CSB*, pp. 601–4. Cf his manuscript dedication in *Guermantes I, Corr.*, vol. XIX, p. 532.

278. *Corr.*, vol. XIX, p. 262. It is true that because Proust praised Bainville, his response was quite modest.

279. Ibid., pp. 467–8, to R. Proust.

280. Ibid., p. 513, 8 October 1920, to P. Souday.

281. Ibid., p. 518, 10 October 1920.

282. *CSB*, p. 606.

283. *Corr.*, vol. XIX, pp. 220, 228, 232.

284. *Mes années chez Barrès*, and *Corr.*, vol. XIX, p. 288.

285. *Corr.*, vol. XIX, p. 284.

286. Ibid., p. 501.

287. Ibid., p. 384. Cf. p. 466.

CHAPTER XVI: *Between Life and Death*

1. '*Et qu'il faille ici-bas mourir plus d'une fois.*' *Corr.*, vol. XIX, p. 117, 5 March 1921 (note 8 is incorrect); pp. 127, 130, 131, 152. A poem often quoted in March by Proust, who added that others kept grumbling: 'Dying? Yet again? Well, die, then, for once and for all and let nothing more be said about it.'

2. Ibid., vol. XX, p. 178, 11 or 12 April 1921.

3. Ibid., p. 462, 19 September 1921; p. 466.

4. Ibid., p. 431, 2 or 3 September 1921.

5. Ibid., p. 413.

6. Ibid., p. 502, 21 October, to Sydney Schiff.

7. Ibid., p. 598.

8. *Corr. avec G. Gallimard*, p. 205, *NRF*, December 1921.

9. *Corr. avec G. Gallimard*, p. 259, letter of 25 October 1922.

10. J. Bersani, 'Un découpage inédit de Proust', ibid., p. 323.

11. *Corr.*, vol. XX, p. 49, 6 January 1921.

12. See ibid., pp. 108, 112, letters from François Le Grix.

13. *RTP*, vol. III, pp. 34–136, 185–98.

14. He paid him 10,000 francs on 12 September.

15. *Corr.*, vol. XX, p. 441, 10 September, to Gaston Gallimard.

16. Ibid., p. 162. In March Proust was already letting it be known that he wished to reply to Valéry's remarks about '*les actes éclairés*' [the enlightened acts] in *Eupalinos* (published in the *NRF* on 1 March 1921 and *CSB*, p. 622). Proust took the opportunity to praise artists who were ill.

17. *Corr.*, vol. XX, p. 197, to J. Rivière.

18. *CSB*, p. 621.

19. *Corr.*, vol. XX, p. 497, October 1921, to André Lang; the text would appear on 26 February 1922.

20. Ibid., p. 35, 1 or 2 January 1922, to the Duchesse de Clermont-Tonnerre. No indication of this would appear at the beginning of *Swann*, which was already published in any case.

21. Ibid., pp. 1, 36, n. 5; C. Albaret, pp. 245–6.

22. *Corr.*, vol. XX, p. 91.

23. Ibid., p. 506, early October 1921, to G. Gallimard.

24. *Corr.*, vol. XX, pp. 54–6. Was this to do with Maurice Proust, the fresco painter from Montmartre?

25. *Corr. avec G. Gallimard*, pp. 311–12, 14 January 1921. As to the slanders, Gaston added: 'They say that I keep women . . . they say I live a life of luxury whereas I can't manage to make ends meet . . .'

26. *Corr.*, vol. XX, p. 346.

27. Ibid., p. 36, to the Duchesse de Clermont-Tonnerre. *RTP*, vol III, pp. 427, 453, 456, 472; vol. IV, p. 384.

28. *Corr.*, vol. XX, p. 38 and n. 7; *RTP*, vol. III, p. 444; vol. IV, p. 405.

29. *Corr.*, vol. XX, p. 147. *RTP*, vol. II, pp. 787–9.

30. F. Mauriac, *Du côté de chez Proust*, in *Œuvres autobiographiques*, Bibliothèque de la Pléiade, 1990, p. 276.

31. *Corr.*, vol. XX, p. 114, 1 March 1921.

32. Mauriac, *Œuvres autobiographiques*, p. 263.

33. *Corr.*, vol. XX, pp. 366–7, about 25 June 1921.

34. Ibid., pp. 391–2, 10 July 1921.

35. Ibid., p. 228.

36. Unpublished dedication in *CG II–SG* (holland paper H.C.), May 1921, Mᶜ de Cagny catalogue, Drouot, 11 March 1995. Dedication to Rivière, *Corr.*, vol. XX, p. 234, n. 2: 'I merely say to you again how much I admire and how much I like you.'

37. *Corr.*, vol. XX, p. 236.

38. Ibid., pp. 258–60 and notes.

39. Ibid., pp. 527–30.

40. *Le Merle blanc*, 19 November 1921; *Corr.*, vol. XX, pp. 537–8, to R. Proust.

41. *Corr.*, vol. XX, p. 349, 17 June 1921, to Guiche.

42. Ibid., p. 474, about September 1921.

43. Ibid., pp. 381–2.

44. A. Gide, *Journal*, Gallimard, 1939, pp. 692–4: on Proust's illness and their discussion of inversion. Cf. Morand suggesting Proust consult the German specialist Magnus Hirschfield and Marcel rejecting this in disgust: the fact was he had nothing to learn and Morand had made a gaffe (Morand, *Discours du 15 décembre 1971 pour le prix Montyon*, in H. Bonnet, *Les Amours et la sexualité de Marcel Proust*, Nizet, 1985, p. 95, and G. de Diesbach, p. 714).

45. *Corr. avec G. Gallimard*, p. 315 and n. 1., *Corr.* vol. XX, p. 79, 20 January 1921, Rivière to Proust.

46. *Corr. avec G. Gallimard*, pp. 208–9, 23 April 1921.

47. Gide, *Journal*, p. 692, 14 May 1921.

48. Ibid., p. 694.

49. *Corr.*, vol. XX, pp. 239–41, 3 May 1921.

50. Ibid., pp. 240–1, 3 May 1921.

51. Ibid., p. 444, 28 August 1922.

52. Ibid., pp. 280–2.

53. Ibid., p. 320, 7 June 1921.

54. P. Jullian, *Robert de Montesquiou, un prince 1900*, Perrin, 1965, p. 289; G. de Diesbach, pp. 719–20.

55. *Corr.*, vol. XX, p. 476. See Proust's eulogy, quoted by Kolb, n. 2, p. 476.

56. 'Montesquiou knew that he would be destroyed by this poison' (G. de Diesbach, p. 719). The poison from which he died was urea.

57. *Corr.*, vol. XX, pp. 586–8, 18 December 1921.

58. *RTP*, vol. III, pp. 40–2, 192–3.

59. 'My brother says "intoxication"; it's a good panacea with which to reassure the sick' (*Corr.*, vol. XX, p. 195, 18 or 19 April 1921).

60. Ibid., vol. XVII, p. 280.

61. Ibid., vol. XX, p. 164.

62. Ibid., p. 200, 21 April 1921, to Gaston Gallimard. Rivière replied to him that Gaston was 'perturbed', to which Proust responded: 'the most perturbed is me' (ibid., p. 204, 22 April, 1921).

63. Ibid., p. 254.

64. Ibid., p. 300, to Gaston Gallimard.

65. *Corr. avec G. Gallimard*, p. 377.

66. On 14 October, he was on page 450 (*Corr.*, vol. XX, p. 491).

67. *Corr.*, vol. XX, p. 478.

68. Ibid., p. 500, 20 October 1921.

69. Ibid., pp. 547–9.

70. *RTP*, vol. III, pp. 240–4.

71. Ibid., pp. 200–18.

72. Which may explain the attempt at a short version of *Albertine disparue* (though not of *La Prisonnière*).

73. *L'Action française*, 23 April 1921; *Corr.*, vol. XX, p. 209.

74. *Corr.*, vol. XX, p. 222.

75. Cf. ibid., vol. XXI, p. 292; Cahier 62, f. 57 recto. *RTP*, vol. III, pp. 687–93; n. 5, p. 691 (p. 1739: sentence dictated by Proust the night before he died). The writing of the passage is described by P. Robert, pp. 137–8.

76. *Corr.*, vol. XX, p. 289, to J.-L. Vaudoyer.

77. An allusion to the Orient of Ingres and the Duchess de Guermantes' change of heart; she had thought him 'the most boring and commonplace of artists, then suddenly the most delectable of the masters revered by *art nouveau*'; this was what Proust took from it for *Le Temps retrouvé* (*RTP*, vol. IV, pp. 388, 602).

78. T. Laget, 'L'Hommage à Marcel Proust de la *Nouvelle Revue Française*' in 'Jacques Rivière, témoin de Marcel Proust', *Bulletin des Amis de Jacques Rivière*

et d'Alain-Fournier, no. 37, 2nd trimester 1985, pp. 23–81. Vaudoyer's letter can be found on pp. 78–80.

79. *Corr.*, vol. XX, p. 85, 23 January, to L. Gautier-Vignal.

80. Ibid., p. 357, to Princesse Soutzo.

81. Ibid., p. 405.

82. Ibid., pp. 343–4.

83. Ibid., p. 109, 16 February 1921.

84. *RTP*, vol. III, pp. 321–2, 326, 365; 373–4.

85. B. Faÿ, *Les Précieux*, Perrin, p. 100 ff.

86. *RTP*, vol. III, p. 351.

87. *Corr.*, vol. XX, p. 571, December 1921.

88. Ibid., p. 578; reply from the duke, p. 580.

89. Ibid., pp. 601–2.

90. J. Hugo, *Le Regard de la mémoire*, Actes Sud, 1983, p. 201.

91. *Corr.*, vol. XXI, p. 27.

92. H. Ellis, *From Rousseau to Proust*, pp. 363–4.

93. *Corr.*, vol. XXI, p. 42, to J. Cocteau; p. 49, n. 8, to Gaston Gallimard. This gossiping would result in Gallimard curtly setting matters straight with him.

94. Ibid., p. 58, 5 February 1922, to Princesse Soutzo.

95. Who would write about Proust in his *Mémorables*.

96. *Corr.*, vol. XXI, p. 69, to Princesse Soutzo.

97. C. Albaret, p. 230.

98. *RTP*, vol. III, p. 472 (because of the etymology of his name). *Corr.*, vol. XXI, n. 13: Doctor Logre treated Deschanel for Elpénor's syndrome.

99. *RTP*, vol. IV, p. 527 and n. 1.

100. Ibid., pp. 551–2.

101. He would do so in a letter which has not been made available.

102. Mottoes which were originally copied down in Cahier 60.

103. *Corr.*, vol. XXI, p. 126, 11 April 1922, to A. Gide. Proust had probably reread Oscar Wilde. *In Memoriam*, Mercure de France, 1910.

104. *Corr.*, vol. XXI, pp. 48, 310.

105. Ibid., p. 56.

106. *Corr. avec G. Gallimard*, pp. 534–5, 10 and 12 June 1922. Cf. *Corr.*, vol. XXI, p. 243: 'I have been unable to correct the proofs of my book.'

107. *Corr.*, vol. XXI, p. 243, around 21 July, to S. Schiff.

108. Ibid., p. 117.

109. Ibid., p. 118, to S. Schiff.

110. Ibid., p. 146, about 27 April 1922, to Céleste Albaret. Cf. pp. 228, 504, 505, 509, 530, 534. Ader-Tajan catalogue, 20 May 1992, no. 92, message dated 20 April, catalogued incorrectly as 'the last words': 'I have neither my little biscuits nor my watch.' The Carlton Lake Foundation at the Harry Ransom University Center, University of Texas, Austin, possesses seventy-nine

messages written by Proust to Céleste Albaret during the final months of his life, on the backs of envelopes or on papers used for his fumigations (A. Borrel, 'Inédits', *BAMP*, no. 40, 1990, pp. 7–8, published three of them). See also Carlton Lake, *Chers papiers*, Seghers, 1991.

111. *RTP*, vol. III, pp. 118–19; *Corr.*, vol. XXI, p. 146, 29 April 1922.

112. *Corr.*, vol. XXI, p. 159.

113. Ibid., p. 169 and n. 11.

114. Ibid., p. 174, to R. Allard.

115. Ibid., p. 206, to G. Gallimard, and pp. 188–9, to Souday.

116. Ibid., p. 228.

117. 'Marcel Proust', *Der Neue Merkur*, February 1922, pp. 745–61.

118. *Corr.*, vol. XXI, p. 344, 5 July 1922.

119. Ibid., p. 298, and n. 16.

120. Ibid., p. 353, 16 July 1922, to R. de Flers; p. 356, to J. Schlumberger.

121. Ibid., p. 494, 3 October 1922.

122. Ibid., p. 206, to G. Gallimard.

123. Ibid., pp. 208–9, 18 May 1922.

124. Ibid., p. 402, 5 or 6 August 1922, to B. Crémieux.

125. Ibid., pp. 210–11.

126. Ibid., pp. 38–9, 18 January 1922, to G. Gallimard.

127. Ibid., p. 197, to J. Boulenger.

128. Ibid., p. 292, shortly after 17 June, to J.-L. Vaudoyer.

129. Ibid., pp. 331–2, 2 or 3 July 1922.

130. Ibid., pp. 379, 401 (shortly before 5 August 1922). He said that he was beginning again for the third time, in early September.

131. Ibid., p. 380.

132. Ibid., p. 492, to G. Gallimard.

133. *La Prisonnière*, ed. J. Milly, Flammarion, 1984, p. 40.

134. K. Yoshikawa, *Études sur la genèse de 'La Prisonnière' d'après des brouillons inédits*, post-graduate doctoral thesis, Université de Paris-Sorbonne, 1976, vol. III, p. 312.

135. See note in *Sodome et Gomorrhe*, *RTP*, vol. III, and A. Winton, *Proust's Additions*, Cambridge University Press, 1977.

136. *Essais et articles*, p. 633.

137. Comments reported by Gide, *Journal*, 14 May 1921, Gallimard, 1939, p. 692.

138. Winton, *Proust's Additions*, pp. 67–123.

139. Cahier 59, ff. 92–4 recto; see letter to J. Rivière in April 1919, *Corr. avec J. Rivière*, p. 43.

140. Lucien Daudet spoke to him about it on 3 July (*Corr.*, vol. XXI, p. 335); it was reproduced in *L'Illustration* of 10 June 1922 and exhibited at the Pavillon de Marsan. *RTP*, vol. III, p. 705. *Corr.*, vol. XXI, p. 409, 9 August 1922, to P. Brach.

141. *Corr.*, vol. XXI, p. 360, 17 July 1922. *RTP*, vol. III, pp. 879–82.

142. *Corr.*, vol. XXI, p. 404, 5 or 6 August 1922. In *BAMP*, no. 44, N. Mauriac has published a first version (private collection) of these 'street cries', about which Léo Spitzer has written a superb study (*Études de style*, Tel, Gallimard, pp. 474–81).

143. *La Prisonnière*, *RTP*, vol. III.

144. *Sésame et les lys*, Mercure de France, 1906, pp. 62–3.

145. *JS*, p. 368. See also, 'What would people say if a person kept to himself the correspondence of Voltaire or that of Emerson, as if they were autographs? A private collection should be kept in a museum, otherwise public interest will be thwarted,' *Corr.*, vol. XVIII, p. 320, 10 July 1919.

146. *La Prisonnière*, *RTP*, vol. III, p. 692.

147. Ibid. This text, dating from 1921, is the last in Cahier 62; Proust transposed it, without making any important changes, to the third typescript of *La Prisonnière*.

148. *La Prisonnière*, *RTP*, vol. III.

149. Ibid.

150. *Sodome et Gomorrhe II*, vol. III, draft V, 'Reception at the Princesse de Guermantes'.

151. C. Albaret, p. 402.

152. See J.-Y. Tadié, 'Proust et l'inachèvement', *Le Manuscrit inachevé*, Éditions du CNRS, 1986.

153. *Corr.*, vol. XXI, p. 77, about March 1922, to Camille Vettard. Vettard would publish an article entitled 'Proust and Einstein' in the August 1922 issue of the *NRF*.

154. *Corr.*, vol. XXI, p. 479, mid-September 1922.

155. Ibid., p. 177, to R. Boylesve.

156. Ibid., p. 221, shortly after 23 May 1922; p. 229, 27 May 1922.

157. Also being performed were *Le Mariage de la belle au bois dormant* by Petitpas, and the 'Polovtsian Dances' from *Prince Igor*.

158. Letter of 25 November to H. Shaw Weaver.

159. *Corr.*, vol. XXI, p. 239, last days of May 1922.

160. *Textes retrouvés*, pp. 332–5. This type of feature, so common until recent years, has disappeared from newspapers.

161. Ibid., p. 336.

162. Performed at the Comédie des Champs-Élysées on 21 February 1920. But the title, which is that of a popular Brazilian song, appears to have been provided by Claudel, who had just returned from Brazil with Milhaud.

163. Hugo, *Le Regard*, p. 203. Cf. J. Wiener, *Allegro Appassionato* (Belfond): 'I invented Le Bœuf sur le Toit; with my friends Milhaud, Cocteau and a few others; one day we wanted to have our own bar, that's to say a place where artists would gather, and which everyone would enjoy coming to.' See

'Wiener et Doucet à l'époque du Bœuf sur le toit', Adès records, COF–7088.

164. *Corr.*, vol. XXI, pp. 257, 271–4.

165. Ibid., p. 265, letter from Gide to Proust, 14 June 1922.

166. Ibid., p. 460.

167. Ibid., p. 262, to Mme Hennessy.

168. Ibid., p. 599.

169. Princesse Bibesco, *Au bal avec Marcel Proust*, Gallimard, 1928, p. 173.

170. *The Letters of T. E. Lawrence*, J. Cape, 1938, pp. 661, 667, 668.

171. *Corr.*, vol. XXI, p. 449.

172. Ibid., p. 323.

173. Ibid., p. 326.

174. Ibid., p. 323. In 1929 Philip Sassoon published *The Third Route*, Heinemann.

175. *Corr.*, vol. XXI, p. 329.

176. Ibid., p. 409.

177. Ibid., p. 346, 7 July 1922, and again at the end of the month.

178. Ibid., p. 347.

179. He was born in 1893; in October 1922 the NRF would publish his novel *Gérard et son témoin*, after Proust had recommended it (*Corr.*, vol. XXI, letter 344 to Gallimard).

180. Ibid., p. 351, 15 July 1922, to E. Jaloux, who had left before the end of the evening. Ibid., pp. 358–9, to P. Brach, who had invited him.

181. *Textes retrouvés*, pp. 337–8.

182. *Corr.*, vol. XXI, p. 369, 20 July 1922.

183. Ibid., pp. 393, 401.

184. Ibid., p. 416, 16 August 1922.

185. Ibid., p. 409, 9 August 1922.

186. Ibid., p. 427, 20 August 1922, to Princesse Soutzo.

187. Ibid., p. 430, shortly after 21 August 1922, to H. Duvernois.

188. Ibid., p. 457; similarly 'Jalousie' would be the title of the extract from *Sodome*; whence *Albertine disparue* instead of *La Fugitive*. Cf. ibid., p. 466.

189. *Corr.*, vol. XXI, p. 439, 26 August 1922. Favourable response from Proust on 29, 30 or 31 August, p. 445.

190. Ibid., p. 464; this was the version that would be used.

191. Ibid., shortly after 6 September 1922.

192. Ibid., p. 460.

193. Ibid., p. 466, to G. Gallimard.

194. Ibid., p. 499, 9 or 10 October 1922, to Charles Scott-Moncrieff.

195. Ibid., p. 480.

196. Ibid., p. 485, 23 September 1922, to J. Rivière.

197. C. Albaret, p. 409.

198. *Corr.*, vol. XXI, p. 503, shortly after 10 October; p. 504.

199. Ibid., p. 505; the poems are at the top.

200. Ibid., p. 513.
201. Ibid., p. 511.
202. Ibid., p. 521.
203. Ibid., p. 514.
204. Ibid., p. 519.
205. Ibid., p. 529.
206. It announced the forthcoming publication of *Sodome et Gomorrhe III: La Prisonnière, Albertine disparue*. Pointed out by A. Beretta Anguissola, *Alla ricerca del tempo perduto*, vol. IV, Mondadori, 1993, p. 784, who then goes on to review the different editions, and put forward his own theory.
207. Facsimile of this page in M. Proust, *Albertine disparue*, ed. N. Mauriac and E. Wolff, Grasset, 1987, pp. 32–3.
208. Ibid., pp. 128–9. Page 648 of the typescript corresponds to page 67, the end of the first paragraph, of *RTP*, vol. IV (see var. *b*). Page 898 corresponds to page 202 of the Pléaide edition. See note, p. 1026 ff., and the comparative table of the two versions, p. 1031.
209. *RTP*, vol. IV, p. 325, and var. *b, c, d.*
210. *Corr.*, vol. XX, p. 500.
211. *CSB*, p. 91.
212. *Corr.*, vol. XI, p. 63.
213. C. Albaret, p. 437.
214. *Corr.*, vol. X, p. 270, 25 March 1911.
215. Ibid., pp. 122–4.

Select Bibliography

All titles are published in France, unless otherwise indicated.

WORKS BY PROUST

John Ruskin, *La Bible d'Amiens*, translated with notes and introduction by M. Proust, Mercure de France, 1904

– *Sésame et les lys*, translated with notes and introduction by M. Proust, Mercure de France, 1906

Chroniques, Gallimard, 1927

Jean Santeuil, together with *Les Plaisirs et les Jours*, ed. P. Clarac et Y. Sandre, Bibliothèque de la Pléiade, 1971

Contre Sainte-Beuve, ed. B. de Fallois, Gallimard, 1954

Contre Sainte-Beuve, together with *Pastiches et mélanges* and *Essais et articles*, ed. P. Clarac and Y. Sandre, Bibliothèque de la Pléiade, 1971

À la recherche du temps perdu, ed. P. Clarac and A. Ferré, Bibliothèque de la Pléiade, 3 vols, 1954

À la recherche du temps perdu, ed. J.-Y. Tadié, Bibliothèque de la Pléiade, 4 vols, 1987–9

Alla ricerca del tempo perduto, ed. A. Beretta Anguissola, Milan, Mondadori, 4 vols, 1983–93

Textes retrouvés, ed. P. Kolb, Gallimard, 1971

Le Carnet de 1908, ed. P. Kolb, Gallimard, 1976

L'Indifférent, ed. P. Kolb, Gallimard, 1978

Matinée chez la princesse de Guermantes, Cahiers du Temps retrouvé, ed. H. Bonnet and B. Brun, Gallimard, 1982

Albertine disparue, ed. N. Mauriac and E. Wolff, Grasset, 1987

Écrits de jeunesse 1887–1895, ed. A. Borrel, Institut Marcel Proust International, 1991

Correspondance avec sa mère, Plon, 1953

Lettres à Reynaldo Hahn, ed. P. Kolb, Gallimard, 1956

M. Proust and J. Rivière, *Correspondance (1914–1922)*, ed. P. Kolb, Gallimard, 1976

M. Proust and G. Gallimard, *Correspondance (1912–1922)*, ed. P. Fouché, Gallimard, 1989

Mon cher petit, letters to Lucien Daudet, Gallimard, 1991

M. Proust and D. Halévy, *Correspondance*, Fallois, 1992

Correspondance générale, ed. R. Proust, P. Brach and S. Mante-Proust, 6 vols, Plon, 1930–6

Correspondance, ed. P. Kolb, 21 vols, Plon, 1970–93

Books by Proust in English

By Way of Sainte-Beuve, tr. Sylvia Townsend Warner, London, Chatto & Windus, 1958

In Search of Lost Time, translated by C. K. Scott-Moncrieff and Terence Kilmartin; and by Andreas Mayor, revised by D. J. Enright, 6 vols, London, Chatto & Windus, 1992

Jean Santeuil, translated by Gerard Hopkins, London, Weidenfeld & Nicolson, 1955

Marcel Proust: Letters to his Mother, translated and edited by George D. Painter, London, Rider & Co., 1956

On Reading, translated and edited by Jean Autret and William Burford, London, Souvenir Press, 1972

Remembrance of Things Past, translated by C. K. Scott-Moncrieff and Terence Kilmartin; and by Andreas Mayor, London, Chatto & Windus, 1981

BIOGRAPHIES AND CRITICAL STUDIES

Samuel Beckett, *Proust*, London, Chatto & Windus, 1931

L. Pierre-Quint, *Marcel Proust, sa vie, son œuvre*, final version, Le Sagittaire, 1935

A. Maurois, *À la recherche de Marcel Proust*, Hachette, 1949

G. Cattaui, *Marcel Proust. Documents iconographiques*, Geneva, P. Cailler, 1956

A. Ferré, *Les Années de collège de Marcel Proust*, Gallimard, 1959

Roger Shattuck, *Proust's Binoculars: A Study of Memory, Time and Recognition in À la recherche du temps perdu*, London, Chatto & Windus, 1964

P. Clarac and A. Ferré, *Album Proust*, Albums de la Pléiade, 1965

H. Bonnet, *Marcel Proust de 1907 à 1914*, Nizet, 1971

William Sansom, *Proust and his World*, London, Thames & Hudson, 1973

Roger Shattuck, *Proust*, London, Fontana, 1974

C. Albaret, *Monsieur Proust*, tr. Barbara Bray, Harvill, 1976

M. L. Miller, *Psychanalyse de Proust*, Fayard, 1977

C. Francis and F. Gontier, *Marcel Proust et les siens*, together with *Souvenirs* by S. Mante-Proust, Plon, 1981

J. M. Cocking (ed.), *Proust: Collected Essays on the Writer and his Art*, Cambridge, Cambridge University Press, 1982

Terence Kilmartin, *A Guide to Proust*, London, Chatto & Windus, 1983

Derwent May, *Proust*, Oxford, Oxford University Press, 1983

H. Bonnet, *Les Amours et la sexualité de Proust*, Nizet, 1985

George D. Painter, *Marcel Proust: A Biography*, revised and enlarged edition, London, Chatto & Windus, 1989, Pimlico (2 vols), 1996

Ronald Hayman, *Proust: A Biography*, London, Heinemann, 1990

G. de Diesbach, *Proust*, Perrin, 1991

D. Mabin, *Le Sommeil de Proust*, PUF, 1992

C. Pechenard, *Proust à Cabourg*, Quai Voltaire, 1992

– *Proust et son père*, Quai Voltaire, 1993

R. Duchêne, *L'Impossible Marcel Proust*, Laffont, 1994

Malcolm Bowie, *Proust Among the Stars*, London, HarperCollins, 1998

P. F. Prestwich, *The Translation of Memories: Recollections of the Young Proust from the letters of Marie Nordlinger*, Peter Owen, 1999

Edmund White, *Proust*, London, Weidenfeld & Nicolson, 1999

Marcel Proust, l'écriture et les arts, catalogue to the Bibliothèque Nationale exhibition, Gallimard/BNF, 1999

MEMOIRS

Barrès, M., *Mes cahiers*, Plon, 1994

Benoist-Méchin, J., *Avec Marcel Proust*, Albin Michel, 1977

– *À l'épreuve du temps (1905–1940)*, Julliard, 1989

Bernard, S., *À l'ombre de Marcel Proust*, Nizet, 1979

Bibesco, Princess, *Marcel Proust at the Ball*, tr. Anthony Rhodes, London, Weidenfeld & Nicolson, 1956

Billy, R. de, *Marcel Proust. Lettres et conversations*, Les Portiques, 1930

Blanche, J.-É., *Mes modèles*, Stock, 1928, rev. ed. 1984

– *La Pêche aux souvenirs*, Flammarion, 1949

Casa-Fuerte, I. de, *Le Dernier des Guermantes. Mémoires*, Julliard, 1994

Castellane B. de, *Mémoires*, Perrin, 1986

Clermont-Tonnerre, E. de, *Robert de Montesquiou et Marcel Proust*, Flammarion, 1925

Cocteau, J., *Portraits-souvenirs 1900–1914*, Grasset, 1935

– *Opium*, Stock, 1930

– *Le Passé défini*, Gallimard, 1983

Daudet, Léon, *Souvenirs et polémiques*, Laffont, Bouquins, 1992

Daudet, Lucien, *Autour de soixante lettres de Marcel Proust*, Gallimard, 1929

David, A., *Soixante-quinze années de jeunesse*, A. Bonne, 1974

Dreyfus, R., *Souvenirs sur Marcel Proust*, Grasset, 1926

Duplay, M., *Mon ami Marcel Proust*, Gallimard, 1972

Faÿ, B., *Les Précieux*, Perrin, 1966

Fouquières, A. de, *Cinquante ans de panache*, P. Horay, 1951

– *Mon Paris et ses Parisiens*, 5 vols, P. Horay, 1953–9

Gautier-Vignal, L., *Proust connu et inconnu*, Laffont, 1976

Germain, A., *Les Clés de Proust*, Sun, 1953

– *Les Fous de 1900*, Geneva, La Palatine, 1954

– *La Bourgeoisie qui brûle, 1890–1940*, Sun, 1951

Gimpel, R., *Journal d'un collectionneur marchand de tableaux*, Calmann-Lévy, 1963

Goncourt, E. and J. de, *Journal*, 3 vols, Laffont, Bouquins, 1989

Gramont, E. de, *Les Marronniers en fleur, Mémoires II*, Grasset, 1929

Gregh, F., *Mon amitié avec Marcel Proust, Souvenirs et lettres inédits*, Grasset, 1958

– *L'Âge d'or, Souvenirs d'enfance et de jeunesse*, Grasset, 1947

Guilbert, Y., *La Chanson de ma vie*, Grasset, 1927

Hahn, R., *Notes. Journal d'un musicien*, Plon, 1933

– *L'Oreille au guet*, Gallimard, 1937

Halévy, D., *Pays parisiens*, Grasset, 1932

Hugo, J., *Le Regard de la mémoire*, Actes Sud, 1983

Jaloux, E., *Avec Marcel Proust*, Geneva, La Palatine, 1953

Mauriac, F., *Du côté de chez Proust*, La Table ronde, 1947

Maurois, M., *L'Encre dans le sang*, Flammarion, 1982

– *Les Cendres brûlantes*, Flammarion, 1986

Montesquiou, R. de, *Les Pas effacés*, 3 vols, Émile-Paul, 1923

Morand, P., *Le Visiteur du soir*, Geneva, La Palatine, 1949

– *Journal d'un attaché d'ambassade (1916–1917)*, La Table ronde, 1949; Gallimard, 1963

Mugnier, Abbé, *Journal*, Mercure de France, 1985

Pascal, A. (Henri de Rothschild), *Croisière autour de mes souvenirs*, Émile-Paul, 1933

Plantevignes, M., *Avec Marcel Proust*, Nizet, 1966

Porel, J., *Fils de Réjane*, 2 vols, Plon, 1951–2

Pougy, L. de, *Mes cahiers bleus*, Plon, 1977

Robert, L. de, *Comment débuta Marcel Proust*, Gallimard, 1925

– *De Loti à Proust*, Flammarion, 1928

Rostand, M., *Confession d'un demi-siècle*, La Jeune Parque, 1948

Sachs, M., *Le Sabbat*, Corrêa, 1946

Saint-Aulaire, Comte de, *Confession d'un vieux diplomate*, Flammarion, 1953

Scheikévitch, Mme, *Souvenirs d'un temps disparu*, Plon, 1935

CONTEMPORARIES

Assouline, P., *Gaston Gallimard*, Balland, 1984
Bancquart, M.-C., *Anatole France, un sceptique passioné*, Calmann-Lévy, 1984
Bernstein Gruber, G. and Maurin, G., *Bernstein le magnifique*, Lattès, 1988
Bibesco, Princesse, *La Duchesse de Guermantes – Laure de Sade, comtesse de Chevigné*, Plon, 1950
Boillat, G., *La Librairie Bernard Grasset et les lettres françaises*, Champion, 1974
Bischoff, C., *Geneviève Straus (1849–1926)*, Balland, 1992
Bothorel, J., *Bernard Grasset*, Grasset, 1989
Buckle, R., *Diaghilev*, London, Weidenfeld & Nicolson, 1979
Cossé-Brissac, A. de, *La Comtesse Greffulhe*, Perrin, 1991
Gallois, J., *Les Polignac, mécènes du XXᵉ siècle*, Le Rocher, 1995
Gavoty, B., *Reynaldo Hahn*, Buchet-Chastel, 1976
Gold, A. and Fizdale, R., *Misia: The Life of Misia Sert*, London, Macmillan, 1980
Gitard-Auviste, G., *Paul Morand*, Hachette, 1981
Jullian, P., *Robert de Montesquiou, un prince 1900*, Perrin, 1965
Vanderpooten, C., *Samuel Pozzi, chirurgien et ami des femmes*, In Fine, V & O éditions, 1992

JOURNALS

Bulletin de la Société des amis de Marcel Proust, 1950–95
Bulletin d'informations proustiennes, 1971–87
Cahiers Marcel Proust, Gallimard, new series, 18 vols – comprising *Études proustiennes*, vols I–VI
Nouvelle Revue Française, January 1923, *Hommage à Marcel Proust* (reprinted in *Cahiers Marcel Proust*, no. 1, 1927)

N.B. Other works consulted are mentioned in the notes, as are articles or manuscripts.

Index